The Family Guide to Movies and Videos

Edited by Henry Herx

Office for Film and Broadcasting
Department of Communications
United States Catholic Conference

In accordance with its mandate to foster wholesome family values in and through its Office for Film and Broadcasting, the Department of Communications of the United States Catholic Conference produces on a regular basis capsule reviews of motion pictures currently available on television and videotape. Edited by Henry Herx, *The Family Guide to Movies and Videos* provides a comprehensive collection of these reviews. Designed to be used by those wishing to know the moral and entertainment values of motion pictures prior to viewing, this book is authorized for publication by the undersigned.

Monsignor Robert N. Lynch
General Secretary
NCCB/USCC

ISBN 1-55586-635-2

Introduction

Old movies never die; most do not even fade away. Their screen afterlife lingers on and, for many, actually increases through the electronic media of television, cable, and videocassette. Hollywood movies today make more money in these forms of home video than they do in movie theaters. Even more important is the fact that they are seen by considerably larger numbers of viewers at home than by the patrons of movie theaters.

This has created something of a consumer problem for the home viewer, because the information and publicity that surround the theatrical release of a movie is no longer available by the time it appears on the home screen. The usual television listings in newspapers are simply inadequate for making an informed decision about whether or not the movie is worth several hours of anyone's time. Yet, most viewers have to make up their minds based on the title, year of release, a hint of the plot situation, the names of a couple of actors, and perhaps a few words or a symbol indicating the fact that it is anything from a classic to a clunker. This is not much better than reading tea leaves.

There are some books that provide plot summaries and observations on many of the theatrical features in circulation, but they are mainly written for those who take movies seriously as a form of popular culture and want to know where a particular movie fits within the history of the motion picture medium.

Parents, of course, have other concerns in searching out the value and appropriateness of a movie for members of their family. It is the intention of this guide to provide concerned parents with sufficient information about the moral dimension of story and treatment, age suitability, and the artistic and entertainment quality of each of the movies listed in the following pages.

How to Use This Guide

Contained within are descriptions and evaluations of virtually all motion pictures in national release to American theaters from 1966 through the fall of 1993. A number of films released prior to 1966 are also included, especially those that have particular relevance—good, bad, and indifferent—for family viewing. Each movie capsule consists usually of two sentences, the first of which summaries the plot or theme of the film, and the second provides an evaluation of its relative merits as entertainment or enrichment and its suitability for various age groups.

Following each entry are the symbols used by three rating groups: the United States Catholic Conference's Department of Communications (= USCC), followed within parentheses by those of the Motion Picture Association of America (= MPAA) and then those of the British Film Board (= BBFC) where available. The USCC classifications indicate moral suitability as well as appropriateness for children, adolescents, and adults. The MPAA ratings and BBFC certificates are divided according to age suitability.

USCC Classifications

* **A-I**—general patronage.
* **A-II**—adults and adolescents.
* **A-III**—adults.
* **A-IV**—adults, with reservations (This refers to certain movies that are not morally offensive in and of themselves but do require some analysis and explanation to avoid mistaken interpretations and false conclusions.).
* **O**—morally offensive.

MPAA Ratings

* **G**—general audiences; all ages admitted.
* **PG**—parental guidance suggested; some material may not be suitable for children.
* **PG-13**—parents are strongly cautioned to give special guidance for attendance of children under 13; some material may be inappropriate for young children.
* **R**—restricted; under 17 requires accompanying parent or adult guardian.
* **X**—no one under 17 admitted; age limit may vary in certain areas.
* **NC-17**—no one under 17 admitted; this rating replaced the **X** rating in 1990.

BBFC Certificates

* **U**—univeral; suitable for all.
* **PG**—parental guidance; some scenes may be unsuitable for young children.
* **12**—suitable only for persons of twelve years and over (introduced on video July 1, 1994).
* **15**—suitable only for persons of fifteeen years and over.
* **18**—suitable only for persons of eighteen years and over.

* **R18**—for restricted distribution only, through specially licensed cinemas or sex shops to which no one under eighteen is admitted.

Abbreviations

* **nr**—not rated (movies that have been released without applying for a rating from the MPAA).
* **br**—before ratings (movies released before the MPAA classification system began in October 1968).

Some Changes Over the Years

In addition to the above, the MPAA in its first years used the symbol **GP** and later **M** for what today has become the **PG** category. However, the MPAA does not allow the automatic substitution of the present **PG** rating for these two former symbols unless it has officially changed these original designations. Consequently, though perhaps confusing, **GP** and **M** are used where appropriate.

Because MPAA ratings are changed occasionally, it was thought advisable to indicate such changes by a slash mark, with the rating following the slash being the present rating. For example **(R/PG)** indicates that a movie was originally rated as restricted but has since been changed to the parental guidance category. Such changes may indicate that the distributor has cut the scenes responsible for the **R** rating or that scenes that had previously been thought inappropriate for young viewers have subsequently been thought to be a decision that parents should make. Since such ratings apply only to the version being shown in theaters, it is important for parents to realize that the video version may contain material that once had been removed. In fact, some videos even state that they have scenes not in the original theatrical version.

Finally, the rating system has an appeal process by which a group of industry representatives can overrule the rating administration. Though this happens rarely, it was thought worth indicating those instances when the appeal process changed the rating. This is indicated by the word *appeal,* for example **(R/PG appeal)**.

The BBFC certificates have also undergone some historical changes. In 1913, when the system was established, the symbol **A** was used to denote "a film more suitable for adults, without the least implication that it might not be shown to children." That definition was changed in 1924 to state that "no 'A' film be shown when a child of under 16 years is present, unless said child is accompanied by an adult." By 1951, the symbols grew to include **X**, which specifically limited the audience to those of 16 years or over. In 1970, the **A** symbol became "advisory," permitting children of 5 years of age, whether accompanied by an adult or not, but warned parents that a film may contain material unsuitable for children under 14 years. Also in that same year, **AA** was added, which allowed the admission of children of 14 years or over, whether accompanied or not. The **X** remained the same as before, except the age limit for admission was raised from 16 to 18 years of age.

The Reason for Ratings

Many people like good movies but do not like taking chances on seeing bad ones. This book tries to take the chance out of selecting movie fare, especially for those concerned about the quality of the screen experience for themselves and, even more, for those who depend upon their guidance. Youngsters are the most vulnerable to current screen fare and need some assistance in selecting movies that help them grow without false values and wrong ideas. This was not always a problem.

The American movie industry was born in the last part of the nineteenth century as a mass medium of entertainment. During World War I, it grew to international stature, with Hollywood dominating the screens of the world until World War II. Hollywood became synonymous with the movies. The genius of American movies was their appeal to the entire family. For the most part, they were simple stories told well. They were relatively inexpensive fare, easily affordable for most, and they became a regular habit.

The post-World War II world changed that by making the home television screen the easiest way for people to see popular entertainment, including movies. In the 1950s, Hollywood tried to fight back by introducing 3-D devices and the wide screen. Neither effort brought back the family audience. In the 1960s, movie producers and exhibitors turned to adult material that television (their chief competitor) would not allow on the home screen. In order to do this, however, the MPAA realized that it would have to advise viewers, especially parents, that certain movies were not for youngsters. This resulted in the MPAA Rating Administration, replacing the MPAA Production Code, which had carefully regulated the content of Hollywood movies. The MPAA ratings are determined by officials of the Rating Administration in Los Angeles and were initiated in October 1968.

USCC Movie Classifications

The USCC Department of Communications classification system is an outgrowth of a program that began in 1934 with the founding of the National Legion of Decency and its initiation of moral ratings in 1936. Over the years, various modifications have been implemented in trying to reflect the development of movies from primarily escapist entertainment to their gradual emergence as also a medium of serious artistic expression.

The classifications are the result of a consensus process involving the staff of the department and a group of outside consultants who contribute their recommendations as to the moral considerations and values—or lack thereof—to be found in the movies that they screen. This volunteer group is today an ecumenical one, representative of the general moviegoing community, which is both Catholic and non-Catholic.

Though the classifications serve busy parents as an instant means of identifying the age suitability and moral quality of a particular movie, they are only labels to be applied in terms of the level of maturity of their own youngsters. The capsule comments attempt to provide enough information to enable parents to decide for themselves what is suitable for their family's screen fare.

In 1964, the department's staff began writing reviews of the best of the new releases, and since 1969, all movies have been reviewed as well as classified. This volume represents the work of many individuals, both staff and consultants, who contributed their moral judgments, aesthetic sensibilities, and considerable writing talents to the task of movie evaluation. The present format makes their work accessible to any seeking guidance about movies.

Henry Herx, Director
Office for Film and Broadcasting
Department of Communications
United States Catholic Conference

adventure
comedy
horror
suspense
war

A

Aaron Loves Angela (1976) The story of a teenage romance between a black youth (Kevin Hooks) and a Puerto Rican girl (Irene Cara) is told in a lifeless movie that tries to get too much mileage out of the charm of its two young principals. Director Gordon Parks Jr.'s absurdly melodramatic conclusion involves violence between a brutal but softhearted heroin pusher (Robert Hooks) and some syndicate types. O (R)

Abandon Ship! (1957) Taut moral exercise in life and death decisions face an officer (Tyrone Power) of a sunken ocean liner who must choose which of 27 survivors should have a place in a lifeboat designed to hold 14 people. Writer-director Richard Sale develops the hazards of the open sea realistically while providing a human dimension for each survivor with harrowing consequences for all. Much menace and stylized violence. A-II (br)

Abbott and Costello in Hollywood (1945) Bud Abbott and Lou Costello play Los Angeles barbers who turn talent agents when they try to help a young singer (Robert Stanton) get a job. Director S. Sylvan Simon sets up a comic situation that goes nowhere as the boys clown their way through Metro-Goldwyn-Mayer's shooting stages and backlot with largely unamusing results. Slapstick humor. A-I (br) U

Abbott and Costello in the Foreign Legion (1950) One of the pair's lesser efforts as directed by Charles Lamont follows the boys from Brooklyn to the Sahara Desert where they get caught in the middle of shady dealings between a greedy legionnaire (Walter Slezak) and a bellicose sheik (Douglass Dumbrille). Comic violence. A-I (br) U

Abbott and Costello Lost in Alaska (see: "Lost in Alaska").

Abbott and Costello Meet Captain Kidd (1952) Tired costume comedy directed by Charles Lamont has the boys find a treasure map, then get shanghaied by the title pirate (Charles Laughton mugging outrageously) who's after the loot. Comic violence. A-I (br) U

Abbott and Costello Meet Dr. Jekyll and Mr. Hyde (1953) Enterprising comedy directed by Charles Lamont casts the two boobies as vintage London bobbies on the trail of the Victorian monster (Boris Karloff). Comic menace. A-I (br) U

Abbott and Costello Meet Frankenstein (1948) The comics deliver some crates to a spooky mansion where they run into the title monster (Glenn Strange) along with Dracula (Bela Lugosi) and the Wolfman (Lon Chaney, Jr.). Directed by Charles Barton, the boys go through their usual routines spiced with some ghoulish nonsense about a brain exchange. Comic violence. A-II (br) U

Abbott and Costello Meet the Ghosts (see: "Abbott and Costello Meet Frankenstein").

Abbott and Costello Meet the Invisible Man (1951) This time around the boys play private detectives hired by a prizefighter (Arthur Franz) who's used an invisibility serum to escape the police after being framed for murder by a gangster (Sheldon Leonard). Directed by Charles Lamont, the formula comedy's highlight is a boxing match in which the inept Costello gets some help in the ring from his unseen client. Comic violence. A-II (br) U

Abbott and Costello Meet the Killer (1949) Comic murder mystery with the boys finding, then trying to lose a couple of corpses in a hotel whose guests include the usual likely suspects, including a sinister swami (Boris Karloff). Directed by Charles Barton, it's mildly amusing fare for the comedy team's fans. Comic violence. A-I (br) U

Abbott and Costello Meet the Mummy (1955) Tired formula comedy directed by Charles Lamont has the boys helping an adventuress (Marie Windsor) search for a lost Egyptian tomb whose treasures are guarded by an unfriendly mummy. Comic menace. A-I (br) U

Abby (1975) Low-budget, black version of "The Exorcist" in which God and the Devil clash, this time in the form of a young woman (Carol Speed) possessed by a demon unleashed by her archaeologist father-in-law (William Marshall) who, fortunately, also happens to be a clergyman. Directed by William Girdler, it has all the defects and excesses of the original plus a few of its own. Exploitative sex and violence. O (R)

Abdication, The (1974) Having relinquished the Swedish throne for various religious reasons, Queen Christina (Liv Ullmann) arrives in Rome to prostrate herself before Pope Alexander VII. Suspecting a Protestant plot to discredit the church, a cardinal (Peter Finch) is appointed to examine the ex-queen and his interrogation forms the bulk of the movie. It is a test the movie thoroughly fails, despite director Anthony Harvey's efforts to breathe fire into a tired historical drama with little historicity and less drama. A-III (PG) AA

Abductors, The (1972) Using local New Jersey talent and a story line that Mickey Spillane would have thrown in the wastebasket, writer-director Don Schain pits sexy, sadistic private-eye Ginger (Cheri Caffaro) against a seedy gang who abducts young women, instructs them in the finer points of depravity and then sells them to needy executives around the country. Trash with violence and nudity. O (R) A

Abe Lincoln in Illinois (1940) Raymond Massey stars as the future president with Ruth Gordon playing Mary Todd in this well-acted drama based on Robert Sherwood's Pulitzer Prize-winning play. Directed by John Cromwell, the movie's emphasis is upon the development of Lincoln's character and his compassionate confrontation with adversity. A-I (br) U

Abominable Dr. Phibes, The (1971) Horror movie featuring superb Art Deco sets and the campy good humor of Vincent Price as the gruesome doctor (of both medicine and theology), but an unnecessarily ugly story about Phibes' taking revenge for his wife's death by following the pattern of the ten plagues found in Exodus. Despite a certain whacky unreality running through the whole exercise, director Robert Fuest uses some full close-ups that seem a little strong for anyone but the devoted horror fan. A-III (PG) 15

Abominable Snowman, The (1957) Mild thriller follows British scientist Peter Cushing and crass American adventurer Forrest Tucker as they face the terrors of the unknown on the trail of the Yeti in the high Himalayas. Director Val Guest's low-budget effort is effective enough in building suspense from the off-screen presence of the legendary creatures, with a provocative glimpse of one just before the ending. Some menace and a minimum of stylized violence. A-I (br) A

About Last Night (1986) Romance set against the vulgar background of the singles scene where the immaturity and insecurities of two young professionals (Demi Moore and Rob Lowe) doom to failure their struggle to form a lasting bond. Played for comedy by director Edward Zwick, the movie is socially, emotionally and morally uninformed about the nature of a truly loving relationship. Rough language and nudity in a sexual context. O (R) 18

Above the Law (1988) Silly convoluted detective yarn featuring a Chicago cop (Steven Seagal) whose martial arts expertise and former involvement with the CIA make him a target for every macho crook and dirty dealing CIA agent in town. Directed by Andrew Davis, it's a disappointing, politically confused story focusing mainly on the martial arts for which Seagal is noted. Excessive violence, much grisly gore and a liberal dose of profanity. O (R) 18

Absence of Malice (1981) Ambitious Miami reporter (Sally Field) is duped into reporting false information on the son of an organized crime figure (Paul Newman). Though director Sydney Pollack slickly stacks the deck against the news media, the movie does succeed in raising serious issues about media responsibility and public opinion. Incidental details include suicide, abortion and an illicit sexual relationship. A-II (PG)

Absent-Minded Professor, The (1961) Mildly amusing Disney comedy with Fred MacMurray as a daffy science professor who discovers a potion that lets people and objects defy the laws of gravity. The resulting silliness might best be appreciated by the very young. A-I (G) U

Absolute Beginners (1986) Youth-oriented musical drama starring David Bowie as an ad man selling materialism to adolescents, represented by a teenage song-and-dance team (Eddie O'Connell and Patsy Kensit). British production directed by Julien Temple links the euphoria of young people in the late 1960s with the birth of a youth subculture and consumer market. Mainly, however, it celebrates lack of conscience and good judgment as the substance of adolescence. An intense scene of violence and a confused perspective on adolescent sexuality. A-III (PG-13) 15

Absolution (1988) A priest (Richard Burton) at a British Catholic boys school is driven to commit a grisly murder after his teenage protege (Dominic Guard) torments the priest in confession with lies about sexual trysts and murder. Director Anthony Page invests the scenario with a promise of menace never fulfilled by screenwriter Anthony Shaffer. Remorseless, gruesome murders and some profanity. O (R) 18

Abyss, The (1989) Derivative sea adventure tracking the attempt to rescue a U.S. nuclear submarine that has sunk in waters inhabited by mysterious, benign alien creatures. Writer-director James Cameron drowns the fantasy in a sea of dopey interpersonal distractions and technological razzle-dazzle. Intense underwater action with drownings, resuscitations and locker-room language. A-III (PG-13) 15

Accident (1967) Cryptic Harold Pinter script begins with an auto crash killing the young man engaged to an Oxford coed, after which the events and forces contributing to the "accident" are presented in flashback, including the rivalry of two dons for the woman student's affection. Director Joseph Losey and an excellent cast use the sparse dialogue and strained situations to give clues to the violence developing beneath the tranquil surface of academic life. Adult situation and treatment. A-III (br) PG

Accidental Tourist, The (1988) Poignant, whimsical adaptation of Anne Tyler's novel about an emotionally shut-down travel writer (William Hurt) struggling to cope with the death of his son and the disintegration of his marriage. Director Lawrence Kasdan depicts the gradual unfolding of this withered, weary man in relation to the two women in his life (Kathleen Turner and Geena Davis) in a sensitively told story of death and rebirth. A discreetly filmed bedroom scene and implied cohabitation without benefit of marriage. A-III (PG)

Accompanist, The (1993) After being hired as piano accompanist for an acclaimed classical singer (Elena Safonova) during the German occupation, a meek young Parisienne (Romane Bohringer) comes to resent her employer's rich life with an adoring husband (Richard Bohringer) and secret lover (Samuel Labarthe) while she remains in the background with no personal life of her own. Director Claude Miller's melancholy tale of love and loss skillfully uses the music track to reflect the characters' tortured emotions. Subtitles. An implied affair and an off-screen suicide. A-III (PG)

Accused, The (1988) In a powerful story of violence and justice, a loose-living young woman (Jodie Foster) is brutally gang-raped in a bar and, after the rapists are sentenced to prison, the district attorney (Kelly McGillis) brings charges against the barflies who cheered them on. Though the rape is explicitly shown in flashback during the trial proceedings, director Jonathan Kaplan clearly portrays it as a crime of violence. Lengthy, graphic gang-rape sequence is excessively detailed and there is much profanity. O (R) 18

Ace Eli and Rodger of the Skies (1973) Cliff Robertson and Eric Shea play a father-son team of Kansas barnstormers in the early 1920s who are flying away from the tragic death of the woman in their life. For Eli, his wife's death triggers a streak of womanizing while for his 11-year-old son, the loss of a mother brings out a raunchy maturity and wisdom far surpassing that of his father but also the search for a new mother-figure. Director Bill Sampson's failed drama is a confusing and confused, largely unmotivated, concoction of scenes alternately nostalgic, crude, cruel, near-perverse and sappy. A-III (PG) AA

Ace High (1969) Revenge with a humorous twist is the theme of this low-budget Italian western starring Eli Wallach as a bug-ridden, baby-sitting Greek bandit. Director Giuseppe Colizzi's action is slapdash but unflagging enough to compensate for rough dubbing, poor color and ragged editing. Stylized violence. A-II (M) 15

Ace in the Hole (1951) Cynical reporter (Kirk Douglas) parlays the local story of a man trapped in a New Mexico cave into a national news event by getting a corrupt sheriff to delay the weakening victim's rescue for a week. Director Billy Wilder's dark study of media manipulation and the public's appetite for sensationalism has few characters with any integrity, save the reporter's editor (Porter Hall), the tragic victim and his devoted parents. Continuing menace and unsavory characters. A-II (br)

Aces: Iron Eagle III (1992) Action-packed sequel follows former World War II fighter pilots (Louis Gossett, Jr., Horst Buchholz, Sonny Chiba and Christopher Cazenove) to Peru where they intend to blow up a cocaine factory with souped-up vintage aircraft. John Glen directs a predictable shoot-'em-up whose comic overtones make the violent outbursts and characters seem cartoonish. Recurring violence. A-III (R)

Across 110th Street (1972) Anthony Quinn plays a tough old-time cop compelled for political reasons to work with a black new-breed policeman (Yaphet Kotto) in tracking down the three blacks who ripped off a syndicate-controlled, black-managed Harlem numbers bank. Unfortunately, director Barry Shear develops neither the broader implications of the story's social conflicts nor the potentially interesting personality clash of his principals, apparently too involved with the mechanics of all the violence that is so grossly in evidence. O (R) 18

Across the Great Divide (1977) Two orphans on the pioneer trail to Oregon in 1876 are guided through the perils of frontier America by a charming gambler (Robert Logan). Directed by Robert Raffill, it provides a familiar mixture of attractive characters, photogenic animals and gorgeous scenery. The slick use of these wholesome elements at the expense of any realism may strike some viewers as rather calculated but that does not lessen its value as fantasy entertainment for family audiences. A-I (G) U

Act of Aggression (1975) French vigilante movie about a man (Jean-Louis Trintignant) whose wife and daughter have been brutally raped and murdered, apparently by vicious bikers, and his lust both for revenge and for his wife's sister (Catherine Deneuve). Director Gerard Pires never grapples seriously with the vendetta theme but concentrates instead on the romance, employing some nudity and kinky sexuality. O (R)

Act of the Heart, The (1970) Sensitive but flawed Canadian drama about a young woman (Genevieve Bujold) whose love for a priest (Donald Sutherland) results in his leaving the ministry, but his subsequent disillusionment with the world leads her to burn herself to death. Until this grisly conclusion, the movie had been a perceptive study of character and feeling in which director Paul Almond explored issues of loneliness, the search for self and meaning in the contemporary world. Inadequately motivated, the violent act of self-immolation is a major miscalculation in what otherwise is a gentle story of idealism and love. A-IV (GP)

Act of Vengeance (1974) Exploitation melodrama about rape and the efforts of five victims, led by Joann Harris, to entrap their assailant, a sadist with a penchant for singing "Jingle Bells." Director Robert Kelljan seems less concerned about showing the degradation and humiliation of rape as an act of violence against women than as using an anti-rape theme as an excuse for displaying naked bodies as sex objects. O (R)

Action Jackson (1988) The ultraviolent exploits of a Detroit police detective (Carl Weathers) are detailed in a contrived series of bloody killings, car chases, crashes and explosions perpetrated by an exotic collection of villains in the hire of a power-mad businessman (Craig T. Nelson). Director Craig R. Baxley laces the special-effects pyrotechnics with some sexual titillation and drug scenes. Excessive violence, some nudity and much rough language. O (R) 18

Activist, The (1969) Amateurish semi-documentary account of several months in the life of a Berkeley student who is a dedicated militant in the protest movement. Directed by Art and Jo Napoleon, the best thing about this fictional reconstruction is some actual newsreel footage of campus demonstrations. Lengthy and explicit love-making scene lacks any dramatic purpose or justification. O (X)

Adalen '31 (1969) Swedish production re-creates a 1931 labor strike by focusing on the lives of individual workers involved in the struggle for subsistence. The political conflict and social commentary are crystal clear, but remarkably unobtrusive amid the vignettes of daily life in a small town during hard times. When scab workers arrive, a peaceful demonstration ends in violence and death. Using a mixture of romantic fiction and economic realities, director Bo Widerburg successfully combines social awareness with lyric beauty. Brief nudity and casual acceptance of abortion. A-IV (X)

Adam at 6 A.M. (1970) West Coast college professor (Michael Douglas), searching for the values of heartland America, spends a summer doing construction work in Mis-souri, decides to settle down and marry a local belle (Lee Purcell) but then realizes that life in the Midwest will be no less conformist than that of the world from which he has fled. Director Robert Scheerer employs a number of easy stereotypes to characterize America's geographic and cultural polarities, but beneath the movie's slick surface is a profoundly cynical commentary upon the country's heritage and the values of its people. A-IV (GP) 15

Adam's Rib (1950) Sly romantic comedy about married attorneys (Spencer Tracy and Katharine Hepburn) battling over the issue of women's rights when she defends a wife (Judy Holliday) on trial for shooting her philandering husband (Tom Weall) while he represents the wounded man. Director George Cukor injects the witty dialogue and visual comedy with screwball overtones and the Tracy-Hepburn exchanges are prime but the feminist humor seems less pointed today. Comic view of the battle of the sexes. A-II (br)

Adam's Rib (1992) Living in a cramped Soviet apartment, a twice-divorced working mother (Inna Churikova) tries to juggle taking care of her own aged mother, two troubled unmarried daughters and a new man in her life. Ukrainian director Vyacheslav Krishtofovich has nothing particularly new to say about mother-daughter relations or the travails of single women, though the cultural context may make them seem a little more interesting than our own domestic melodramas. Subtitles. Some discussion of sexual matters, a comically interrupted bedroom tryst and minimal rough language. A-III (nr) A

Addams Family, The (1991) Based on the tongue-in-cheek clan of grotesques created by cartoonist Charles Addams, the movie version revolves around a scheme to steal the family fortune from Gomez Addams (Raul Julia) and wife Morticia (Anjelica Huston) by a man (Christopher Lloyd) claiming to be their long-lost relative, Fester. Directed by Barry Sonnenfeld, the anemic plot only gets in the way of the eccentric sets, outlandish make-up, sinister special effects and intermittent bits of macabre humor. Much dark comedy, some bizarre comic violence and mild sexual innuendo. A-II (PG-13) PG

Addams Family Values (1993) Macabre comedy sequel has the Addams children (Christina Ricci; Jimmy Workman) attempting to eliminate their mustachioed baby brother while their lovestruck uncle (Christopher Lloyd) marries a murderous fortune hunter (Joan Cusack). Director Barry Sonnenfeld injects some outrageous black humor into a broad, predictable slapstick comedy that is more concerned about style than content. Frequent comic menace to a baby, violence played for laughs, and occasional sexual innuendo. A-II (PG-13) PG

Adding Machine, The (1969) An office worker (Milo O'Shea), saddled with a nagging wife (Phyllis Diller), has fantasies of an affair with his pretty assistant (Billie Whitelaw). When he kills his boss and a sentence of death is carried out, he ultimately winds up in a hell of adding machines. Adapted by producer-director Jerome Epstein from a 1930s' Elmer Rice play, the stagey result speaks less about the contemporary onslaught of automation and economic disparity than it does of a very dated kind of ideological indignation. A-III (PG) A

Adelaide (1969) Director Jean-Daniel Simon has been unable to elevate this pulp story of a widow whose new husband continues to carry on an affair with her teenage daughter. Static and introverted atmosphere, incomprehensible plot development and determined underplaying by Ingrid Thulin and Jean Sorel supply no motivation for the senseless actions of the story's characters. O (R)

Adieu Philippine (1973) French production about a young man awaiting his army call-up who begins a flirtation with two girls who are intimate friends, a situation left unresolved by the boy's departure but with the sense of embarking on a new, more mature phase of life. Directed by Jacques Rozier, this 1961 movie is a mosaic of scenes, beautifully photographed and evocative of the carefree romanticism of youth, carefully knit together by the jukebox music of the period. Without a traditional narrative, however, its appeal is mainly to those who enjoy watching a well-crafted film. A-III (nr) A

Adios, Sabata (1971) Routine Italian western with bounty hunter Yul Brynner polishing off great gobs of humanity in his relentless pursuit of a Mexican revolutionary and a share of Maximillian's gold. Taken seriously, all this violence would be alarming, but played tongue-in-cheek under Frank Kramer's direction, it's a comic fantasy for those who enjoy such action programmers. A-II (GP)

Adjuster, The (1992) Bleak and boring look at the sexual perversions of an insurance adjuster (Elias Koteas), his wife (Arsinee Khanjian) who collects porno films and a phony filmmaker (Maury Chaykin) who uses their home for his own murderous ends. Writer-director Atom Egoyan offers a sick view of characters who deliberately doom themselves and those around them. Frequent sexual references, a shadowy sexual encounter, some nudity and intermittent rough language. O (R) 18

Adrift (1971) Czechoslovakian production about a fisherman who rescues a beautiful woman from drowning and his gradual disintegration (told in flashbacks mixing reality with fantasy) driven by desire for the girl (Paula Pritchett) who has become a member of his household. Although not entirely successful in its fancy time sequences, director Jan Kadar's leisurely pace builds steadily toward his powerful conclusion concerning man's vulnerability to temptation. The erotic element of the film is a necessary one counterbalanced by the very human portrayals of the fisherman and his wife (Rade Markovic and Milena Dravic). A-IV (R)

Adventure of Sherlock Holmes' Smarter Brother, The (1975) Gene Wilder directs as well as stars in a fairly conventional romantic comedy except for his eclectic choice of comedy styles, including some heavy-handed vulgarities. Instead of satirizing mystery movies, the plot is a disconnected series of complications about a stolen document that is at last recovered by chance rather than by ratiocination. The movie's intermittent amusement is marred by some spectacularly tasteless visuals, double entendres and a love scene that goes beyond comic intentions. O (PG)

Adventurers, The (1970) One man's experiences from childhood to early middle age in a revolutionary South American country are the focus of this long, sprawling soap opera based on Harold Robbins' novel and directed by Lewis Gilbert. Motivation is frequently sacrificed for plot elements featuring brutality, pillage, rape, sadism, voyeurism, nudity, lesbianism and adultery. O (R) 18

Adventures in Babysitting (1987) Teenage baby-sitter (Elizabeth Shue) and her wards suffer through an evening of harrowing escapades while trying to rescue their runaway friend stranded in a downtown Chicago bus station. Flawed seriocomic tale deals with real urban dangers in a treatment made irresponsibly light and mundane by writer-director Chris Columbus. Some violence, sexual innuendo and profanity mar this trite diversion aimed at youngsters. A-III (PG-13) 15

Adventures of Baron Munchausen, The (1989) The fantasy exploits of an 18th-century adventurer notorious for his exaggerated stories are recreated in a tongue-in-cheek tale about the wacky adventures of the Baron (John Neville) and his 10-year-old traveling companion (Sarah Polley) in a city besieged by Turks, a trip to the moon and brushes with a volcano and a whale. Director Terry Gilliam's elaborate special effects will entrance all ages, but the plot is so bloated that few will find it interesting and children may be more confused than entertained. Minimal sexual innuendo, a flash of nudity and much comic-book violence. A-II (PG)

Adventures of Buckaroo Banzai, The (1984) Director W.D. Richter's sci-fi spoof is about a punk-rock, space-age neurosurgeon (Peter Weller) who stumbles into the eighth dimension where he learns of an alien plot to destroy the world. How all this happens or, indeed, what happens is not very clear. It's comic book fantasy for people who are content to watch a lot of action and strange characters without asking too many questions. Very stylized violence. A-II (PG) 15

Adventures of Bullwhip Griffin, The (1967) Roddy McDowall deadpans for gold in the Wild West with Suzanne Pleshette along for romantic interest. The plot broadly spoofs Gold Rush days with director James Neilson getting the most from its collection of jokes and sight gags. Karl Malden, Arthur Haydn and Mike Mazurki help make this pleasant comedy one of the better efforts by the Disney studios. A-I (br) U

Adventures of Ford Fairlane, The (1990) Blue stand-up comic Andrew Dice Clay plays the title's repulsive macho detective in search of a dim-witted blonde who holds the key to the murder of a heavy-metal rock star. Supposedly a comic thriller, director Renny Harlin's limp, mirthless vehicle serves only to showcase Clay's sewer mouth, sexist attitudes and penchant for nasty, gratuitous violence. Constant rough language, excessive violence and numerous demeaning sexual situations. O (R) 18

Adventures of Huck Finn, The (1993) Spirited rendition of Mark Twain's tale of an irrepressibly mischievous lad (Elijah Wood) rafting down the Mississippi with a runaway slave (Courtney B. Vance) until a brush with disaster when they become involved with a pair of colorful con men (Robbie Coltrane and Jason Robards). Adapted and directed by Stephen Sommers, the zestful performance of the young Wood brightens the fast-moving, handsomely mounted production that makes abundantly clear its anti-slavery stance. Some menace and stylized violence. A-II (PG)

Adventures of Huckleberry Finn, The (1960) Good production of the Mark Twain classic, though Eddie Hodges is a mite sweet as Huck and former boxing champ Archie Moore a bit stiff as the runaway slave, Jim. Director Michael Curtiz conveys much of the spirit of the original and gets amusing support from the colorful cast of characters, especially Tony Randall and Mickey Shaughnessy as the Mississippi con artists. Enjoyable family fare. A-I (br)

Adventures of Huckleberry Finn, The (for the 1931, 1939 and 1974 versions, see "Huckleberry Finn").

Adventures of Ichabod and Mr. Toad, The (1949) Disney animated double feature begins with Basil Rathbone narrating a lovely, fanciful adaptation of Kenneth Grahame's "Wind in the Willows," followed by Bing Crosby singing as well as telling Washington Irving's "Legend of Sleepy Hollow" with its spooky Headless Horseman. Directed by Jack Kinney, Clyde Geronimi and James Algar, the slight but enjoyable American tale pales alongside the bouncy, whimsical British children's classic. Quality family fare. A-I (br) A

Adventures of Marco Polo, The (1938) Gary Cooper plays the curious 13th-century Venetian on his travels through China where he discovers spaghetti, coal and gunpowder while saving the throne of Kublai Khan (George Barbier) from a villainous court official (Basil Rathbone). Directed by Archie Mayo, the stylish spectacle is undercut by lackluster comedy and halting action. Stylized violence and romantic situations. A-II (br) U

Adventures of Mark Twain, The (1944) Interesting piece of Americana follows Twain's life as Mississippi riverboat pilot, Western prospector, newspaper reporter, popular humorist and acclaimed author. Irving Rapper directs Fredric March in a quite winning performance as the irascible humbug of the title, with Alexis Smith as his cherished wife whose early death devastates the man and darkens his writing. Idealized view of Twain's life provides satisfying, meaningful entertainment. A-I (br) U

Adventures of Mark Twain, The (1986) Combining elements of the author's life and times with excerpts from his writings, this animated fantasy will engage youngsters while providing older viewers with some insights into Twain's complex character. Will Vinton's use of clay animation, with fully modeled characters in imaginative sets, is a visual treat. Several scenes may be frightening for the very young, but otherwise unusually fine family entertainment. A-I (G) U

Adventures of Milo and Otis, The (1989) Fine Japanese live-action movie about a mischievous kitten named Milo and his puppy pal, Otis, who get lost in the autumn wilderness but eventually return home in the spring with their own mates and families. Zestfully narrated by actor Dudley Moore, director Masanori Hata's imaginative photography reveals the wonder of nature and the cycle of life, including brief shots of the birth of a kitten and puppy. Some mild tension in a few scenes involving wild animals, but otherwise it is a welcome, gentle experience for the young and adults who enjoy the beauty of nature. A-I (G) U

Adventures of Robin Hood, The (1938) Rousing costume adventure tale pitting the good Robin (Errol Flynn), Little John (Alan Hale), Friar Tuck (Eugene Pallette) and the rest of the Merry Men of Sherwood Forest against the nasty Prince John (Claude Rains) and the Sheriff of Nottingham (Basil Rathbone), with the lovely Maid Marian (Olivia de Havilland) serving as pawn. Directed by Michael Curtiz and William Keighley, the story's fight against injustice is treated with sincerity but told playfully, the color photography adds zest to the action scenes and the Warner Brothers' cast of supporting players seems to be having as good a time as the leads. Vintage but still sparkling. A-I (br) U

Adventures of Sherlock Holmes, The (1939) Mysterious doings in fog-bound London keep Holmes (Basil Rathbone) and Watson (Nigel Bruce) busy safeguarding a client (Ida Lupino) while Professor Moriarty (George Zucco) prepares to snatch a priceless jewel from the Tower of London. Director Alfred Werker wraps the suspense in a sinister Victorian atmosphere that helps sustain the convoluted narrative to its satisfactory conclusion. Brief violence and some menace. A-I (br) A

Adventures of the Great Mouse Detective, The (see: "The Great Mouse Detective").

Adventures of the Wilderness Family, The (1975) Los Angeles family, fed up with the problems of urban life, leave it all behind to set up housekeeping in a remote section of the Rocky Mountains. What follows is predictable, but director Stewart Raffill tells it with a disarming combination of artlessness and professional competence. Good wild life adventure. A-I (G) U

Adversary, The (1973) Indian production directed by Satyajit Ray tells the story of a former student who has high hopes of achieving more than a dead-end job but, when he falls in love, becomes a rural drug salesman, resigned to becoming part of the faceless Indian masses. Set in Calcutta, a city drowning in its mass of humanity, Ray's protagonist is society itself and the failure of the present system to humanize the process of industrialized urbanization. Ray's blending of human sensibility with a passion for social justice makes this an unusually important work. A-III (nr)

Affair to Remember, An (1957) Lush sentimental melodrama begins as light comedy with a shipboard romance between a wealthy bachelor (Cary Grant) and a former night-club singer (Deborah Kerr), then plunges into heavyweight soap opera when their rendezvous in New York is prevented by an accident. Director Leo McCarey manages to keep the lumbering romance afloat with an old-fashioned mix of smiles and tears, a charming cast and plush settings. Starry-eyed romance. A-II (br) U

Afraid of the Dark (1992) Bizarre, disjointed thriller about a disturbed child (Ben Keyworth), his endangered baby sister, his mother (Fanny Ardant) who may or may not be blind and a neighborhood slasher (Paul McGann). Director Mark Peploe's twisted tale of deadly menace and mayhem is badly structured and largely unintelligible. Exploitative violence, especially that involving two children, a lingering nude shot and frequent nasty menace. O (R) 18

Africa Addio (1967) Cruelty, violence, blood, gore and human indignity are highlighted in director Gualtiero Jacopetti's Italian documentary that claims that its aim is to enlighten viewers concerning the "birth pangs" of emerging African nations. Exploitation of serious subject. O (R)

Africa Blood and Guts (see: "Africa Addio").

Africa Screams (1949) The usual comedy of errors begins with Manhattan book clerks (Bud Abbott and Lou Costello) joining a crook (Hillary Brooke) on an African safari through cannibal-infested jungles in quest of diamonds. Director Charles Barton garners few laughs from the boys' tired routines while encountering domestic thugs, wild animals, puzzled natives and real jungle veterans Clyde Beatty and Frank Buck. Slapstick violence and African stereotypes. A-I (br) U

Africa—Texas Style (1967) Texas cowboys are hired to herd wild animals on the plains of Kenya because domestic cattle are turning the land into a dust bowl. The idea of switching from cattle ranching to game ranching is an intriguing one that director Andrew Marton keeps moving with old-fashioned western action in exotic African settings. Good family entertainment. A-I (nr) U

African Elephant, The (1971) Simon Trevor, a former African guide and game warden turned wildlife filmmaker, has made an in-depth birth-to-death documentary on the world's largest and strongest land mammal. Achieving its aims with beauty, sensitivity and intelligence, the movie conveys an experience of the land, the surrounding wildlife and the environment in which the elephant exists. Unlike many such movies, the violence that is so much a part of the wild is given a rationale and thoroughly integrated into the whole. Parents in search of suitable movies for children will find it a healthy, broadening experience for even their youngest. A-I (G)

African Queen, The (1951) Director John Huston's tale of high romantic adventure set in Africa during World War I features Katharine Hepburn as a prim missionary who enlists the aid of rough riverboat captain Humphrey Bogart in escaping capture by German forces. Sharing a harrowing voyage down a wild jungle river, they gradually develop a relationship that changes both their lives—for the better. Wartime violence. A-II (br) U

African Safari (1969) Interesting and exciting documentary excursion into Central and East Africa with beautiful photography of the area's wild life and native customs. Directed and photographed by Ron E. Shanin, it is a rewarding experience both for young people and sophisticated moviegoers. A few graphically violent animal sequences. A-II (G)

After Dark, My Sweet (1990) Manipulative ex-cop (Bruce Dern) involves a lonely widow (Rachel Ward) and an escaped mental patient (Jason Patric) in a deadly kidnapping plot. Intense performances prop up director James Foley's unsavory tale of three losers mired in mutual mistrust until an unexpectedly moral ending provides a positive note. Brief violence and menace to a child, an extended sexual encounter and minimal rough language. A-III (R) 18

After Hours (1985) A bored yuppie (Griffin Dunne) from Manhattan's fashionable East Side ventures into a dangerous part of town to meet an eccentric date (Rosanna Arquette) only to encounter a series of life-threatening misadventures before escaping back to the safety of his own turf in the dawn's early light. Director Martin Scorsese's black comedy lacks satiric bite, preferring instead to wring laughs out of mental instability and bizarre sexual practices. Sophomoric nihilism and some brief nudity. A-IV (R) 15

After the Fox (1966) Scriptwriter Neil Simon and director Vittorio de Sica collaborated on this surprisingly flat and frequently overdone comedy revolving around a bungling ex-convict (Peter Sellers) who hatches a preposterous scheme to steal the fortune in gold that he has been hired to smuggle into Italy. There are some mildly vulgar jokes, but they offend only one's sense of humor. A-II (br) U

After the Thin Man (1936) The first of five sequels to 1934's "The Thin Man" brings private eye Nick Charles (William Powell) and wife Nora (Myrna Loy) on a visit to her rich family in San Francisco where Nick helps a local flatfoot (Sam Levene) solve a murder case. Though the mystery is not as perplexing as the original, director W.S. Van Dyke II makes it seem almost as much fun, thanks to the breezy byplay between the sleuthing couple and an odd gallery of suspects (notably James Stewart, Joseph Calleia and George Zucco). Murder mystery menace. A-II (br) A

Against All Odds (1984) Los Angeles bookie and entrepreneur (James Wood) sends his buddy, an aging pro football star (Jeff Bridges), to find his runaway mistress (Rachel Ward). Director Taylor Hackford tries to build up a suspenseful and sinister mood but spends too much time developing the improbable romance that develops between fugitive and tracker. Hair-raising Sunset Boulevard chase scene, violence, graphic sex scenes and rough language. O (R) 18

Agatha (1979) Agatha Christie's never-explained 11-day disappearance in December 1926 provides the basis for director Michael Apted's romantic mystery starring Vanessa Redgrave as the shy and retiring writer who strikes up a fragile and tender relationship with dapper journalist Dustin Hoffman. Rich in period atmosphere, but muddled conclusion and mature theme and treatment. A-III (PG) A

Agatha Christie's The Mirror Crack'd (see: "The Mirror Crack'd").

Age of Consent (1970) Australian production about an artist (James Mason) who retreats to an island to be alone but discovers it is already inhabited by a local child of nature (Helen Mirren) who has trouble keeping her shift on. When her gin-soaked grandmother obligingly falls off a cliff, the artist and his new model are free to romp artistically and amourously. Michael Powell directs a sorry little diversion that bogs down somewhere between Lolita and Paul Gauguin. O (R) 15

Age of Innocence, The (1993) Screen version of the Edith Wharton novel about a wealthy young lawyer (Daniel Day-Lewis) torn between his sweet, socially acceptable fiancee (Winona Ryder) and his love for her independent-minded cousin (Michelle Pfeiffer) who has left her faithless husband behind in Europe to face the chilly embrace of the disapproving New York elite in the 1870s. Director Martin Scorsese's visually opulent work skewers the shallow pretenses of high society while delicately exploring the emotions simmering behind the fragile facades of the three protagonists. Mild sexual references. A-II (PG) U

Agent for H.A.R.M. (1966) Mediocre spy melodrama about an American secret agent (Mark Richman) assigned to keep a defecting foreign scientist from being grabbed by

Iron Curtain operatives (led by heavy Martin Kosleck). Directed by Gerd Oswald, the formula is marred by heavy-handed violence and sexual suggestiveness. O (br) A

Agent on Ice (1986) Dreary little melodrama about the separate efforts of the C.I.A. and a crime syndicate to kill a double-agent (Tom Ormeny) who knows too much. Director Clark Worswick's effort lacks suspense and drive but offers excessive amounts of bloodshed and stereotyping of Italian Americans. O (R)

Agnes of God (1985) A psychiatrist (Jane Fonda) sent to a cloistered convent to evaluate the mental stability of a novice (Meg Tilly) accused of strangling her newborn baby provokes the determined opposition of the nun's superior (Anne Bancroft). With the psychiatrist looking for a rational explanation and the mother superior hoping for a supernatural one, director Norman Jewison's movie straddles the fence in a dramatically fraudulent conclusion. Although this pretentious and shallow movie is not meant to be anti-religious, some may be offended by its use of a religious setting. A-IV (PG-13) 15

Agony and the Ecstasy, The (1965) Adapted from Irving Stone's historical novel about Michaelangelo and the Renaissance papacy, the lavish production depicts the clash between two strong-willed individuals as the artist (Charlton Heston) struggles to create the Sistine Chapel's frescoed ceilings while being badgered by Pope Julius II (Rex Harrison). Directed by Carol Reed, the movie is not as great as its subject, but it does provide considerable cultural background in an entertaining, though at times, plodding manner beyond the capacity of most youngsters. A-II (br)

Aguirre, the Wrath of God (1977) Ponderous and plodding German production by avant-garde director Werner Herzog about gold-seeking, power-hungry conquistadores in 16th-century Peru. Klaus Kinski in the title role looks so vicious that one grows increasingly impatient with his failure to do anything interesting. Occasional violence, particularly a beheading. A-III (nr) A

Air America (1990) Jaded mercenary pilot (Mel Gibson) and an idealistic recruit (Robert Downey Jr.) fly missions over Laos in 1969 for a covert, CIA-backed airline being investigated by a U.S. Senator (Lane Smith). Director Roger Spottiswoode's blatantly cocky adventure yarn portrays the two mercenaries as incredibly cool daredevils whose grandstanding antics run rings around the grotesque cardboard characters of the Senator and their military superiors. Idealized depiction of mercenaries, frequent foul language and references to sex as a commodity. A-III (R) 15

Air Up There, The (1994) Arriving in Kenya to convince a tribal lad (Charles Gitonga Maina) to accept a basketball scholarship at his midwestern Catholic college, an ambitious assistant coach (Kevin Bacon) finds he must first win the chief (Winston Ntshona) over to the idea as well as coach a crucial game the tribe has staked their land and cattle upon. Director Paul M. Glaser's light, slight movie is contrived and derivative, but its colorful tale of culture clashes is mildly diverting. Tribal bloodletting ceremony and a few instances of profanity. A-II (PG)

Airplane (1980) This aviation-disaster spoof offers a sprinkling of bright and funny gags. If you don't like one, wait a minute and another will be along. Directed by Jim Abrahams, the comedy is moderately entertaining for those who don't mind an excess of silliness and a certain amount of crudity. A-III (PG)

Airplane II: The Sequel (1982) For those who liked the jokes in the original, here they are again, although many fewer and much farther between this time around under Ken Finkleman's direction. What was of questionable taste in the first movie, however, has now crossed the line into the downright offensive, including quite a bit of nudity. O (PG) 15

Airport (1970) Disaster movie based on Arthur Hailey's best-seller in which the fate of passengers and crew of an airborne 707 are in the hands of a mad bomber (Van Heflin). Director George Seaton's lumbering Hollywood blockbuster revels in its all-star cast of stereotyped characters and surface melodrama. Adult situations. A-III (G) PG

Airport 1975 (1974) This time disaster takes the form of a private plane piloted by Dana Andrews who suffers a heart attack and crashes into a 747's cockpit, leaving chief stewardess Karen Black in command and responsible for landing the plane via radio instructions. On board is the usual all-star cast and a ground rescue team led by Charlton Heston and George Kennedy. Directed by Jack Smight, it has some entertaining thrills that will have viewers reaching to fasten their seatbelts. A-II (PG)

Airport 77 (1977) The third edition of the series has to do with a huge 747 crashing into the ocean, trapping a host of major stars in its watertight fuselage. It's all pretty silly but entertaining enough under Jerry Jameson's direction. Restrained violence and some mild profanity. A-II (PG)

Airport '79 (see: "The Concorde—Airport '79").

A.K.A. Cassius Clay (1970) Documentary on the career of Muhammed Ali, also known as (a.k.a.) Cassius Clay, from his first interest in boxing at the age of 12 to involvement with the Black Muslims and the draft controversy. Fight fans may enjoy several of the clips from some now-classic bouts, but William Cayton's direction is amateurish and superficial, leaving many loose ends and unanswered questions. A-II (GP)

Akira Kurosawa's Dreams (1990) Beautiful Japanese production presents eight short fragments from the imagination of 80-year-old director Akira Kursosawa. These lyric, at times surreal, musings on childhood, tradition, toxic pollution, nuclear holocaust, art and death are timeless, open-ended and calculated to expand the mind of the viewer. Sparse subtitled dialogue. Some unsettling themes and a few frightening visuals. A-II (PG)

Aladdin (1992) Vibrant animated Arabian Nights tale of a genie (voice of Robin Williams), a commoner in love with a princess and an evil vizier who connives to capture the genie and marry the princess. As produced and directed by John Musker and Ron Clements, the story is sweet, the animation delightful and Williams' wisecracks wedded to lightning-fast sight gags should hold adult interest. A-I (G) U

Alamo, The (1960) John Wayne stars as Davy Crockett in a sprawling, over-sized blockbuster re-creating the heroic last stand in 1836 of a small band of Texans facing superior Mexican forces under Santa Anna. Also produced and directed by Wayne, the panorama of large-scale battle scenes is undercut by lumpy continuity, clunky dialogue and stock frontier types. Patriotic entertainment but somewhat deficient in historical accuracy and ethnic stereotyping. A-I (br) PG

Alamo Bay (1985) On the Texas Gulf Coast in 1979, Vietnamese refugees working as shrimp fishermen arouse the animosity of local citizens who feel their livelihood is being taken away from them. Director Louis Malle wastes some good material by bogging down in a melodramatic plot involving adultery and shallow characterizations. Violence and some nudity. A-III (R) 15

Alberto Express (1992) Italian comedy about a panic-stricken father-to-be (Sergio Castellitto) trying to raise money aboard a Rome-bound train in order to honor the family tradition of repaying his father (Nino Manfredi) every lire spent on his upbringing before his own first child is born. Director Arthur Joffe's amusing premise gets overworked by the lead character's hammy portrayal and an abundance of contrived situations. Subtitles. Comic treatment of stealing and some sexual innuendo. A-III (nr)

Alex and the Gypsy (1976) Seriocomic story of an autumnal romance between a bail-bondsman (Jack Lemmon) and a gypsy (Genevieve Bujold) has problems of character motivation and a highly improbable ending. Although director John Korty has brought a strong sense of value and human dignity to what could have been sordid situation, there is a rather extended sexual scene that is both graphic and boorish. O (R/PG) AA

Alex in Wonderland (1971) The only character of interest in this movie about the cinematic and familial hang-ups and private fantasies of a youngish, modish director (Donald Sutherland) is his rather ordinary, sweet and appealing wife (Ellen Burstyn) who can't understand what her husband's problem is all about and won't pretend to be awed by its manufactured profundity. Director Paul Mazursky's self-indulgent effort, with themes and images borrowed from Fellini, wastes itself on condemning such easy targets as Hollywood and Los Angeles' pollution while praising sexual liberation and the peoples' revolution. O (R) X

Alexander the Great (1956) Historical dramatization re-creates the life of the Macedonian prince (Richard Burton) who, after the Greek city-states fell to his father, Philip (Fredric March), went on to conquer the mighty Persian Empire in a 10-year campaign ending with his death in 323 B.C. at age 33. Written, produced and directed by Robert Rossen, the result is both good history and fine drama with a solid cast, some well-staged action scenes and a sense of spectacle, though the narrative is at times stilted and occasionally obscure. The stylized violence, sexual references and political complications make it heavy-going for children. A-I (br) U

Alf 'n' Family (1972) Screen version of the popular British television series, which was Americanized as "All in the Family," stars Warren Mitchell as Alf, the simple but ridiculously opinionated bigot. By movie's end, Alf is an isolated, pathetic man barely tolerated by his wife (Dandy Nichols) and married daughter. Though justly deserving his fate, it is to the credit of Norman Cohen's direction of Johnny Speight's script that we feel pity for the old reprobate. Comedy of insult with a bit of rough language. A-III (PG)

Alfie (1966) A modern rake (Michael Caine) who regards women only as sexual objects is brought to the realization that his way of life is empty and sterile. Caine brilliantly interprets the title role with deadpan expression, flip Cockney dialogue and occasionally addresses the audience directly in a film directed by Lewis Gilbert and adapted by Bill Naughton from his own play. Although the treatment includes a series of sexual escapades, this British production largely succeeds as a contemporary morality play. A-IV (PG) X

Alfred the Great (1969) This elaborate British production re-creates 9th-century England when a youthful prince, later king, rallied the feuding, demoralized Saxon tribes against their common enemy, the Vikings. The barbarism of the period, only slightly leavened by an imperfectly realized brand of Christianity, is handled with some human credibility. Clive Donner's direction is marked by striking visual effects and well-controlled, through necessarily bloody, battle scenes. A-III (PG) A

Alfredo, Alfredo (1973) Mildly entertaining, occasionally quite funny Italian sex farce directed by Pietro Germi, about a shy bank clerk (Dustin Hoffman) whose desperate attempts to avoid marriage to a predatory woman (Stefania Sandrelli) fail and his troubles begin. There are enough character bits pointing up the foibles, battles and games that go on between the sexes to entertain those whose tastes do not run deep. A-III (R)

Ali: Fear Eats the Soul (see: "Fear Eats the Soul: Ali").

Alias Nick Beal (1949) Interesting variation on the Faust theme has a sinister stranger (Ray Milland) with diabolic powers of persuasion trying to corrupt an honest district attorney (Thomas Mitchell) by promises of wealth and fame. Director John Farrow sets the tale in a gritty gangster context but with appropriately dark overtones that suggest more is at stake than simply criminal greed. Unsettling situation and menacing characters. A-II (br)

Alice (1990) After 16 years of marriage to a patronizing husband (William Hurt) and a brief guilt-ridden affair with a divorced musician (Joe Mantegna), a wealthy Manhattan housewife (Mia Farrow) seeks new directions in her life. As written and directed by Woody Allen the film has substance as well as many humorous flights of fancy, though it tends to depict Catholics as more motivated by guilt than any true sense of morality. Adulterous relationships, benign treatment of recreational drug use and minimal blasphemy. A-IV (PG-13) 15

Alice Doesn't Live Here Anymore (1975) A widow (Ellen Burstyn) takes her young son (Alfred Lutter) on a sojourn across the Southwest trying to pursue her dream of a singing career but winds up as a waitress in a greasy spoon where she is courted by a local rancher (Kris Kristofferson). Director Martin Scorsese's somewhat ambiguous and ambivalent picture of a single parent in a contemporary American landscape offers some interesting insights on women in a male chauvinistic society. Though some may be distressed by certain tawdry situations and rough language, the movie achieves its purpose of looking at its subject without too much sentimentality or idealization. A-IV (PG) AA

Alice in Wonderland (1951) Disney animated version of the Lewis Carroll classic about a schoolgirl who daydreams her way through a fantasy world of strange creatures and odd personages, such as the White Rabbit, the Madhatter and the Cheshire Cat, is whimsical entertainment for the entire family, especially youngsters unfamiliar with the original. A-I (G) U

Alice of Wonderland in Paris (1966) Animated movie by Gene Deitch on the further adventures of Alice incorporating children's stories written by Ludwig Bemelmans, James Thurber, Eve Titus and Crockett Johnson, and featuring the voices of Carl Reiner, Norma Macmillan and Howard Morris. Youngsters will enjoy the stories and the animation is passable. A-I (br)

Alice's Restaurant (1969) Based on the popular song by Arlo Guthrie, the movie loosely follows various events alluded to in its lyrics, a kind of personal odyssey in which Guthrie plays himself. Although not a very cohesive work, director Arthur Penn succeeds best in satiric bits done in the style and spirit of the song. Despite its stylistic lapses, the result is a balanced film, presenting the life of flower children neither as dismal nor utopian, but as human. Adult themes. A-III (PG) 15

Alien (1979) Science-fiction thriller about a deep-space freighter whose crew is ravaged by a hungry alien intruder that causes havoc on the long voyage home. Director Ridley Scott goes in for lots of noise and flashing lights rather than characterization and the slick enterprise depends more on shock than on suspense. Considerable gore, graphic violence and foul language make this unsuitable for youngsters. A-III (R) 18

Alien 3 (1992) Crash landing on an unarmed penal colony whose criminal inmates have embraced Christian fundamentalism, a space officer (Sigourney Weaver) finds she has brought along a murderous alien monster whose female version is nesting inside her body. Though this sci-fi sequel covers familiar territory and the religious angle is undeveloped, director David Fincher ekes out sufficient suspense to sustain interest in the outcome. Sporadic shadowy violence and much rough language. A-III (R) 18

Alien Nation (1988) Failed science-fiction thriller in which an alien (Mandy Patinkin) joins the Los Angeles police department and is teamed with a human cop (James Caan) out to find the alien who killed his former partner. Director Graham Baker has little talent for suspense and the comical relationship between the mismatched partners falls flat. Excessive violence, much profanity and vulgar sexual references. O (R) 18

Aliens (1986) Sigourney Weaver returns in a sequel as the maternalistic superheroine who single-handedly battles an egg-laden alien to prevent its infesting the galaxy with slimy creatures from hyperspace. Director James Cameron balances his affinity for moody sets and special effects with a satirical reversal of roles in which a woman dominates inept and witless macho males. Stylized violence and excessive sexually derived profanity. A-IV (R) 18

Alive (1993) Long, sometimes gruesome dramatization of the life-and-death struggle of survivors (including Ethan Hawke, Vincent Spano and Josh Hamilton) of a plane crash high in the Andes where, stranded for ten freezing weeks in 1972, some resort to eating the flesh of their dead companions in order to survive. Director Frank Marshall highlights the strength of the human spirit and the survivors' religious faith in both enduring their ordeal and justifying their actions. Violent aircrash with fatalities and restrained shots of cannibalism. A-II (R) 15

All American Boy, The (1973) Jon Voight stars as a boxer with great expectations in this precious, pretentious little exercise in destroying the myth of the small-town-boy-making-good. Directed by Charles Eastman, this reverse Horatio Alger story, with its poorly staged boxing scenes and amorous goings-on, is sprinkled with helpings of gratuitous nudity and truly foul language. O (R)

All Dogs Go to Heaven (1989) Dark, disappointing animated feature, set in 1930s' Louisiana, charts the death and redemption of a rogue German shepherd (voice of Burt Reynolds) who, after being bumped off by a crooked business partner, cons his way from heaven back to earth where he is reformed by his love for an adorable orphan (voice of Judith Barsi). The orphan proves the only shining light in director Don Bluth's predictable, derivative fantasy with forgettable music and unappealing lead characters. Some cartoon menace and intense moments of mortal danger. A-I (G) U

All I Want for Christmas (1991) Harmless formula comedy about a young teen (Ethan Randall) and his little sister (Thora Birch) conspiring to reunite their divorced parents (Harley Jane Kozak and Jamey Sheridan) on Christmas Eve. Director Robert Lieberman's heavily contrived holiday offering is only lightly amusing as the mischievous kids unfold their goofy plot with predictable syrupy results. A-I (G) U

All My Sons (1948) Stodgy adaptation of Arthur Miller's play about a son (Burt Lancaster) learning that his father (Edward G. Robinson) framed his partner (Frank Conroy) to take the fall for shipping defective parts to the military during World War II. Directed by Irving Reis, the subject of business ethics and personal morality is treated earnestly but gets lost in a welter of family melodramatics. Suicide in plot resolution. A-III (br) A

All Neat in Black Stockings (1969) Without too much imagination or subtlety, this British import centers on the amorous adventures of a young, irresponsible window cleaner (Victor Henry) and his buddy (Jack Shepherd) with whom he shares everything, including the woman he marries. While the visuals and dialogue rarely become offensive, the entire situation as developed in this film can hardly be considered wholesome adult entertainment. O (R) X

All Night Long (1981) After being demoted from the executive ranks to manager of an all-night drugstore, a married man (Gene Hackman) finds himself being pursued by a seductive married housewife (Barbara Streisand). Streisand and Hackman are both good, and director Jean-Claude Tramont's movie has its moments, but it is basically shallow and mean-spirited rather than amusing. Casual acceptance of adultery. O (R) 15

All of Me (1984) Steve Martin plays a lawyer who becomes the host for the soul of a recently deceased client, a rich crank played by Lily Tomlin. Martin gives a bravura slapstick performance in trying to liberate himself of the possession, but director Carl Reiner's sense of humor is largely oriented to the sexual, with some needlessly crude dialogue. A-III (PG) 15

All Quiet on the Western Front (1930) Excellent adaptation of Erich Maria Remarque's novel about the lessons in life and death learned by a patriotic German youth (Lew Ayres) after enlisting in the Kaiser's army and serving at the front during the First World War. In showing the conflict's senseless waste of human life, director Lewis Milestone re-creates with vivid authenticity the horrors of trench warfare while underscoring the humanity of those on both sides of no-man's-land. Classic anti-war picture especially appropriate for older teenagers, despite some strong battlefield violence and a brief romantic interlude. A-II (br) PG

All Screwed Up (1976) Italian tragicomedy about the plight of a group of workers from the agrarian South who come to bustling, industrial Milan to seek a better life but wind up worse off than before. Director Lina Wertmuller's vision is pessimistic but pulsates with the vigor of life and a concern and affection for its characters. Earthy treatment of sex and ambiguous view of prostitution and abortion. A-IV (PG)

All That Jazz (1980) The story of an egotistical, womanizing Broadway director-choreographer who drives himself quite literally to death while rehearsing a new musical. Director Bob Fosse's semi-autobiographical movie stars Roy Scheider who gives a fine performance demonstrating the pitfalls of living in the fast lane, obsessed with one's work while using drugs, sex, alcohol and jazz to heal the pain. The nihilistic mood, and some lewd dance parodies, are wholly self-indulgent. O (R) 15

All That Money Can Buy (see: "The Devil and Daniel Webster").

All the Brothers Were Valiant (1953) Middling 19th-century sea yarn about the captain of a whaler (Robert Taylor) who finds his missing brother (Stewart Granger) in the South Seas, then has to keep him from seizing the ship to search for a fortune in pearls. Directed by Richard Thorpe, the adventure combines the themes of greed and sibling rivalry with more talk than action. Stylized violence, some of it quite nasty. A-II (br)

All the King's Men (1949) Strong adaptation of Robert Penn Warren's novel about a poor country lawyer (Broderick Crawford) whose rise to political power during the Depression transforms him from a populist reformer into a ruthless demogogue with national ambitions. Directed by Robert Rossen, the picture is strikingly realistic in showing the corruption of democratic processes by a politician closely resembling Louisiana's Huey Long, though is less convincing in its portrayal of his personal failings and moral transgressions. Mature themes and treatment. A-III (br) A

All the Loving Couples (1969) This extended stag film has its serious moments contemplating the morality and psychological ramifications of wife-swapping. Gross handling of the subject in graphic exploitation terms negates whatever serious intentions it may have had. O (X)

All the Marbles (1981) Peter Falk plays the manager of a tag team of women wrestlers (Vicki Frederick and Laurene Landon) who battle in dinky arenas across the country on the way to the championship match in Reno. Directed by Robert Aldrich, the vulgar, slipshod story wavers between the farcical and the serious. Sadistic violence of the wrestling sequences, exploitative nudity and general air of sleazy amorality. O (R)

All the President's Men (1976) The investigation by two "Washington Post" reporters (Dustin Hoffman and Robert Redford) of the facts behind the 1972 Watergate break-in has been dramatized with restraint and objectivity. Director Alan Pakula's deliberately low-keyed, well-acted and comprehensive account of a political scandal emphasizes the painstaking work involved in investigative journalism. Though it uses a few coarse words in a realistic context, the movie is one that most teenagers would benefit from seeing. A-III (R/PG) 15

All the Right Moves (1983) The hopes of a high school senior (Tom Cruise) to escape the poverty of his blighted factory town by getting a college athletic scholarship seemed doomed by a clash with his football coach (Craig T. Nelson). Although the situation is realistic enough, director Michael Chapman's shallow treatment lacks any moral perspective, especially in its depiction of the youth's relationship with his girlfriend. Graphic bedroom scene and a casual attitude toward abortion. O (R)

All the Right Noises (1971) Dull British production about a theatrical lighting technician (Tom Bell) who succumbs to the charms of a lovely actress (Olivia Hussey) and seems quite content to divide his attentions between her and his pretty wife (Judy Carne) until the predictable complications ensue. Director Gerry O'Hara competently records this story of adultery without weighing any moral issues so that the result is more a clinical report than a thoughtful, moving drama. A-III (GP) AA

All the Way, Boys (1974) Italian action comedy featuring the hi-jinks and misadventures of the "Trinity" boys (Terence Hill and Bud Spencer), this time as bush pilots in the Amazon where they fly in supplies for emerald-mining outposts and their gradual friendship with one particularly touched prospector (Cyril Cusack). Directed by Giuseppe Colizzi, the clumsy dubbing and sloppy editing seem only to enhance the modest fun offered by a chaotic plot, some whimsical mayhem and the cheerful mugging of its principals. A-II (PG)

All the Young Men (1960) Routine Korean War story of a Marine patrol ordered to hold a critical mountain pass against an overwhelming enemy force. Written, produced and directed by Hall Bartlett, the low-budget production is notable mostly for a subplot involving an inexperienced black sergeant (Sidney Poitier) and a veteran subordinate (Alan Ladd) whose conflict ends in a well-intended but mawkish demonstration of racial harmony. Wartime violence, including a battlefield amputation. A-II (br) A

All Things Bright and Beautiful (1979) Genial family film about the work of a dedicated veterinarian (John Alderton) practicing in the Yorkshire countryside prior to the onset of World War II. Director Eric Till concentrates on the details of healing at the expense of characterization. Graphic depiction of the birth of a calf may be too intense for some youngsters. A-I (G)

All This and World War II (1977) Tasteless, misconceived documentary that reduces the newsreel footage of six years of agony that was the Second World War to a mindless light show for rock enthusiasts grooving to Beatles' music. Director Susan Winslow spares viewers a magical, mystery tour of Dachau, but not much else in a production so inane as to be beneath contempt. Wartime actualities. A-III (PG) A

All Together Now (1970) Low-budget peep show narrated by a blonde corpse (Cileste Eslar) recounting how her experimentation with lesbianism and autoeroticism drove her to suicide. Written and directed by William Louis Allan, the monochromic sex scenes photographed on closet-sized sets will stifle viewers more than shock them. O (nr)

Allan Quartermain and the Lost City of Gold (1987) Richard Chamberlain's overacting as the soldier of fortune and Gary Nelson's direction make the action-adventure yarn play with comic-book superficiality. Like "Indiana Jones," this dramatically silly jungle adventure offers youngsters only laughable mock-heroics and exotic sets. Stylized violence. A-II (PG)

Alleghany Uprising (1939) When colonial backwoodsmen (led by John Wayne) use force to stop a trader (Brian Donlevy) from supplying Indians with guns and firewater, they are attacked as rebels by the local British military commander (George Sanders). Director William A. Seiter's wilderness adventure has some colorful action, more than a little patriotism and a rambunctious frontierswoman (Claire Trevor) who can shoot as well as any of the men. Stylized violence. A-I (br)

Alligator (1981) Director Lewis Teague and writer John Sayles have taken the old chestnut about the baby alligator that grows to monstrous proportions after being flushed down into the sewer system and turned it into a moderately entertaining thriller with some tongue-in-cheek asides. Although the creature has a selective appetite, devouring villains for the most part, such violent actions are graphically depicted. A-III (R) 15

Alligator Eyes (1991) Three vacationing pals (Roger Kabler, Mary McLain and Allen McCullough) pick up a blind hitchhiker (Annabelle Larsen) who tricks them into aiding her in committing a revenge murder. Writer-director John Feldman's low-budget psycho thriller is low on thrills, medium on psychological character studies but high on its own sense of luridly bizarre melodrama. Conscienceless murder, sexual exploitation with gratuitous full nudity and intermittent rough language. O (R)

Allnighter, The (1987) Southern California college coed struggles to have a meaningful sexual encounter before graduation and finally succeeds after several failed attempts. Rock star Susanna Hoffs, directed by her mother, Tamar Simon Hoffs, fails to convey anything of significance in this surf-and-brew disaster whose narrow view of life and permissive view of sex is annoyingly vapid. O (PG-13)

Almost an Angel (1990) An ex-convict (Paul Hogan), convinced he is being given a second chance to do good as a angel on probation, comes to the aid of a woman (Linda Kozlowski) and her wheelchair-bound brother (Elias Koteas) who run an impoverished kids center. As written by Hogan and directed by John Cornell, the one-joke comedy runs out of steam long before the three leads affirm their belief in an afterlife. Very minor violence and minimal vulgar expressions. A-II (PG)

Almost Perfect Affair, An (1979) American filmmaker (Keith Caradine) brings his movie to Cannes, is held up by customs officials and has an affair with the helpful wife (Monica Vitti) of a movie producer (Raf Vallone). Toothless satire from director Michael Ritchie gets bogged down in private conceits leaving only industry jokes and a carnival atmosphere in which adultery is condoned. O (PG) 15

Almost Summer (1978) Dull and sophomoric comedy about a class election at a Southern California high school. Director Martin Davidson presents the school's suffocatingly materialistic and amoral environment in uncritical fashion. Gratuitous nudity and offensive jokes at the expense of the disabled. O (PG)

Almost You (1985) Manhattan couple (Brooke Adams and Griffin Dunne) have everything and are so miserable that the husband contemplates running off with his wife's physical therapist (Karen Young). Adam Brooks directs a trivial and boring effort. Rough language and adultery figures in the plot. A-III (R)

Aloha, Bobby and Rose (1975) Director Floyd Mutrux chronicles the tragic love affair between a tousled-haired auto mechanic (Paul Le Mat) and a starry-eyed, unwed mother (Diane Hull) apparently intending an object lesson in the dangers of too much law and order and too little justice. The message is not expressed at all convincingly in the contrived ending of this inept, low-budget melodrama whose chief merit is the acting of the principals in creating characters for whom one feels real concern. A-III (PG) AA

Alpha Beta (1976) Screen version of E.A. Whitehead's two-character play about a couple (Albert Finney and Rachel Roberts) who feel trapped by marriage, a theme developed with wit and compassion. Although superbly acted and quite affecting, as a movie it suffers from being a straightforward recording of the play. Adult themes. A-III (nr)

Alphabet Murders, The (1966) Tony Randall badly mangles the role of Hercule Poirot, Agatha Christie's dapper Belgian detective, who is investigating a case in which a murderer is killing his victims, apparently in alphabetical order. British production directed by Frank Tashlin, the effort to add comedy to the mystery falls flat and badly hurts the rest of the movie. A-II (br) U

Alphaville (1965) A secret agent (Eddie Constantine) in a future science-fiction world accomplishes his mission of destruction. Jean-Luc Godard directs his own script with imaginative visual gusto, ably abetted by Raoul Coutard's camerawork. The French production is enjoyable both as a spy spoof and as a satire on humanity threatened by the machine. Stylized violence and implied sexual affair. A-III (br) A

Altered States (1981) The talents of director Ken Russell and writer Paddy Chayefsky have joined in this story about a scientist (William Hurt) who, in trying to find the essence of being, takes a hallucinogen and regresses into a primeval form. He is rescued from total chromosomal metamorphosis by his wife (Blair Brown) who proves that love conquers all. Rather than exploring the spiritual self-realization the character sought, the emphasis is on the physical and sexual, with instances of nudity. O (R) 18

Alvarez Kelly (1966) This Civil War film involves a cowboy (William Holden) supplying beef for the Union Army being forced by a Confederate officer (Richard Widmark) to steal the herd for the South. There is plenty of violent action in this colorful production, but director Edward Dmytryk has a hard time keeping all the motivations straight. A-III (br) A

Alvin Purple (1974) Australian sex comedy about a young man (Graeme Blundell) who is absolutely irresistible to women, a malady that takes him through a series of predictable paces from high-school lecher, to waterbed salesman extraordinaire, to star therapist in a sex clinic. Tim Burstall directs in cheerfully inept style, apparently unaware that his sophomoric premise is more boring than it is humorous or titillating. O (R)

Always (1989) Forced romantic fantasy about love, death and the human spirit in which a daredevil firefighter pilot (Richard Dreyfuss) loses his life saving a fellow flier (John Goodman) but comes back to earth to help his girlfriend (Holly Hunter) and an inexperienced pilot (Brad Johnson). Directed by Steven Spielberg, the movie seems too studied and portentous to put across either the romance or its inspirational message that the spirit, however defined, outlives the body. Several intense scenes threatening human life and some vulgar language. A-II (PG)

Amadeus (1984) Director Milos Forman's gaudy evocation of the great age of the Baroque features Tom Hulce in the title role of the young, brash, often vulgar Wolfgang Amadeus Mozart. Though somewhat lacking in dramatic development, the result exquisitely details the pain and anguish of Mozart's spiritual and physical assassin, Salieri (F. Murray Abraham), who's driven by an overwhelming sense of divine injustice and abandonment. Too intense for youngsters. A-II (PG)

Amarcord (1974) Director Federico Fellini recalls his youth in the little seaside village of Rimini through a seemingly plotless series of recollections and fantasies, held together by a genially bombastic host-narrator-historian (Luigi Rossi) who provides social and historical commentary on events that typified life during the Fascist 1930s. Fellini is in full control of these various episodes, which have a powerful and warming effect as the artist looks back with mellow affection, compassion and humor on experiences that shaped his creative life. In celebrating the dreams and schemes, petty and grandiose, of the ordinary folk of this little town, Fellini reminds us of our own past and our own humanity. Though there is some bawdy earthiness, it is a thoroughly humane work, seeing everything but judging no one. A-IV (R)

Amateur, The (1982) CIA technician John Savage forces the agency to train him as a field operative so that he can go behind the Iron Curtain to avenge his girlfriend's murder by terrorists. Director Charles Jarrott weaves a complex spy thriller that is not saved from mediocrity by the fine performances of Marthe Keller and Christopher

Plummer in supporting roles. Stylized violence. A-III (R) 15

Amazing Grace (1974) Comedy with fine black performers, notably Moms Mabley as an earth-mother type who sets out, with the help of retired train conductor Slappy White, to bring Baltimore politician Moses Gunn back to the straight and narrow path. Though there are cameo appearances by such old-timers as Stepin' Fetchit and Butterfly McQueen, director Stan Lathan keeps his camera mainly on Moms' rolling of the eyes, toothless grins and ceaseless line of hilarious homespun patter. Entertaining, frequently quite funny and occasionally moving general audience pleaser. A-I (G)

Amazing Grace and Chuck (1987) Little League baseball player (Joshua Zuehlke) and a pro-basketball star (Alex English) join in a protest against nuclear weapons. When the basketball star is suspiciously killed in a mid-air explosion, his death precipitates a U.S.-Soviet accord on disarmament. Director Mike Newell provides a strained example of how the altruistic actions of the individual can make a difference. Given the complexity of the world affairs, the movie may be more confusing than inspiring for youngsters. A-II (PG)

Amazon Women on the Moon (1987) Tasteless compilation of comic skits and parodies of TV fare from five directors and presented by John Landis. Irreverent satire, excessive gratuitous nudity and rough language are low points of this sophomoric joke-fest whose huge cameo cast is its only remarkable feature. O (R) 15

Ambition (1991) A failed writer (Lou Diamond Phillips) gains the trust of a released multiple murderer (Clancy Brown) in order to entice him into another killing. As written by Phillips and directed by Scott D. Goldstein, the skimpy production values, stiff acting and clumsy staging further hamper this marginally suspenseful thriller. A gory murder, live-in relationship, flash of nudity and minimal rough language. A-III (R) 15

Ambush (1949) Familiar Western tale of the growing antagonism between a seasoned scout (Robert Taylor) and a greenhorn cavalry officer (John Hodiak) on a mission to rescue a woman taken captive by the Apaches. Director Sam Wood puts the cast through the plot's well-worn hoops with enough energy to make it all seem to matter. Indian stereotypes and frontier violence. A-I (br) A

Ambush Bay (1966) Slack World War II action movie with a group of Marines (Hugh O'Brien, Mickey Rooney, James Mitchum) battling on a Pacific island under Ron

Winston's direction offers nothing new to the wartime violence formula. A-III (br) A

Ambushers, The (1968) Dean Martin stars as Matt Helm in a mindless spy spoof that has an almost nonexistent plot and is full of devices from other and better movies. Directed by Henry Levin, the effort is little more than a device for spewing out a succession of smutty jokes and sexual encounters reducing women to objects. O (br) A

America at the Movies (1976) The American Film Institute put together a bicentennial mosaic of some 92 excerpts from 83 American movies, but the result fails to convey much of significance about our nation and way of life. Although the overall tone of the compilation is innocuous, it contains a few instances of strong language and a frank depiction of sex. A-III (PG)

American Anthem (1986) Shallow tale about a teenage athlete (Mitch Gaylord) who, demoralized after his arm is broken during a violent argument between his parents, finds romance and renews his competitive spirit. Olympic gold-medalist Gaylord can't overcome the emotional limitations of a script that plays like a gymnastic music video. Acceptance of casual sex. A-III (PG-13)

American Cyborg: Steel Warrior (1994) Ultraviolent action movie set in a post-apocalyptic society in which a young woman (Nicole Hansen) carrying the world's last human fetus is aided by a mysterious stranger (Joe Lara) in trying to escape the unstoppable cyborg (John Ryan) programmed to kill them. The outlandish plot in director Boaz Davidson's tiresome chase movie is simply an excuse for endless scenes of body blows, bloodshed, and butchery as the body count mounts. Excessive violence, crude sexual references and occasional rough language. O (R) 18

American Dream, An (1966) In this generally inept screen adaptation of the Norman Mailer novel, Stuart Whitman plays an ex-war hero who becomes a muckraking TV commentator. When his exposes are not making trouble for others, personal problems with his wife, mistress and a supposedly "accidental" death come to the fore. Directed by Robert Gist, the treatment of some unappealing adult themes is offensive. O (br)

American Dream (1992) Gritty documentary chronicles the bitter and divisive 1985-86 strike by Austin, Minnesota, meat-packers against wage and benefit concessions demanded by Hormel management. Writer-director Barbara Kopple vigorously explores the human cost of corporate profits as union workers, their families and the entire community experience the financial and emotional strains of the long labor dispute. Occasional rough language and shots of meathouse slaughtering. A-II (nr)

American Dreamer (1984) Director Rick Rosenthal's miserably failed comedy about an Ohio housewife (JoBeth Williams) who wins a trip to Paris and, after suffering a blow to the head, carries on like a female James Bond. Because of its ringing endorsement of adultery, the movie languishes in the realm of soap-opera fantasy derisively stereotyping women. O (PG)

American Flyers (1985) Two brothers (Kevin Costner and David Grant), one with a fatal brain disorder, enter a high-speed bicycle race to face the grueling competition together one last time. A well-acted but mundane tearjerker directed by John Badham. Vulgar language and some casual sex. A-III (PG-13) PG

American Friend, The (1977) Murky psychological thriller in which a shadowy American (Dennis Hopper) is asked by a French gangster to murder an American criminal but winds up getting a German to do the job instead. Although German director Wim Wenders is sensitive to the cultural milieu of his characters and there is some tension in certain scenes, the narrative fails to generate suspense and ultimately becomes trite and dull. Stylized violence. A-II (nr) X

American Game, The (1979) Documentary contrasts the life-styles, motivations and family ties of two high school basketball stars, a black from Brooklyn and a white from Hoosier country. Producer Anthony Jones follows the young men through a crucial decision-making period detailing the uncertainties and pressures of winning and losing in sports and in the game of life. Spotted with some rough locker-room language, but still worth the attention of teenagers facing similar problems. A-II (PG)

American Gigolo (1980) Richard Gere plays a man who lives off women and Lauren Hutton is a politician's wife who falls for him, but his world collapses when he's accused of murder. Written and directed by Paul Schrader, this is a silly and pretentious movie with much nudity, graphic sexuality and a quite muddled moral stance. O (R) 18

American Graffiti (1973) It's the last, long night of the summer of 1962 and for two recent California grads (Richard Dreyfuss and Ron Howard) jetting away to college in the morning, it's a last chance to taste the innocent fantasies of a teenage world about to be lost, perhaps forever. The hugely eventful evening is packed with high school nostalgia but, despite the bemused smiles of its star-crossed lovers,

the mood ultimately turns sober. Director George Lucas's delightful comedy not only captures the signs of former times but comments on them with eloquence and incisiveness. A-III (PG) AA

American Guerrilla in the Philippines (1950) Plodding, predictable war story in which a U.S. naval officer (Tyrone Power), caught on Leyte after the Japanese occupation, joins the local resistance (Micheline Prelle among them) and establishes radio contact with American invasion forces. Director Fritz Lang mutes the situation's potential for action by concentrating on the mundane problems of life in the underground. Stylized violence and ethnic stereotypes. A-II (br)

American Heart (1993) Wrenching tale in which a paroled ex-con (Jeff Bridges) painfully learns to care about his long-estranged teen-age son (Edward Furlong) while holding down a menial job and being pressured by his former partner-in-crime (Don Harvey) to pull a new heist. Director Martin Bell's gritty father-son drama captures the tough reality of rebuilding a shattered relationship as well as the frustrations ex-cons face in trying to go straight in an uncaring society. Brief violence, several sexual situations and some rough language. A-III (R)

American Hot Wax (1978) Nostalgic rock 'n' roll musical focusing upon a few days in the life of 1950s' disc jockey Alan Freed (Tim McIntire) before his last big show at the Brooklyn Paramount in 1959. The work, directed by Floyd Mutrux, will appeal to those who like the music and stars of the time. Occasional vulgarities. A-III (PG) A

American in Paris, An (1951) Stylish musical romance set in elegant 1920's Paris where an expatriate American painter (Gene Kelly) pursues a vision of beauty (Leslie Caron) while eluding the clutches of a wealthy patron (Nina Foch). Despite the flimsy plot, director Vincente Minnelli has no trouble delighting the ear with George Gershwin's music and brother Ira's lyrics while charming the eye with stylized production numbers, evocative period sets and a fine cast. Romantic complications. A-II (br) U

American Justice (1986) Corrupt border police enslave illegal Mexican aliens in a movie that begins as an exploration of the problems of illegal aliens and ends in a blood bath between good and bad lawmen. Excessive violence, some nudity and rough language add to the unpleasantries in the desert. O (R)

American Me (1992) Graduating from juvenile delinquent to prison inmate, an Hispanic gangster (Edward James Olmos) uses his cell as the base of a crime network whose tentacles of violence reach deep into the L.A. barrio, only to engulf him after he is reformed by a good woman (Evelina Fernandez). Also directed by Olmos, the movie makes a powerful statement against the drug culture and its consequences for the young. Much graphic violence including executions and gang rapes, restrained bedroom scene, flash of nudity and constant rough language. A-IV (R)

American Pop (1981) Animated feature by Ralph Bakshi presents a history of American popular music through the story of an immigrant family from the turn of the century to the present, with the great-grandson gaining fame as a rock star. Interesting concept, but the story lacks dramatic focus and many of the characters are unappealing, if not repulsive. Depiction of some sleazy environments and the use of drugs. A-III (R)

American Tail, An (1986) A family of Jewish mice emigrate from Russia to America in 1885 seeking a new life free from Cossack cats but become separated during a storm at sea. While searching for his parents in New York City, a young mouse finds adventure and the meaning of the Statue of Liberty. Director Don Bluth uses Disney-style full animation in meticulous, loving detail on a story that may delight youngsters but which some parents might find a bit too saccharine. A-I (G) U

American Tail: Fievel Goes West, An (1991) Unexceptional sequel continues the animated adventures of feisty Fievel Mousekewitz and his family in the Wild West where he must save them from crafty cats conniving to turn them into mouseburgers. Directors Phil Nebbelink and Simon Wells deliver an uneven story whose pace and images range from gentle to chaotic. Some typical cartoon violence. A-I (G)

American Werewolf in London, An (1981) Trashy, sardonically muddled horror show by writer-director John Landis attempts to combine comedy and fright with a dash of steamy sex. The result is a squalid mess. Contains violence and explicit sex. O (R) 18

American Wilderness (1973) Little more than a collection of self-congratulatory home movies taken during the past decade or so by an Oregon sportsman named Art Dubs. Although it has a down-home folksiness, there are many other fine outdoor adventure documentaries that offer family viewers better camerawork and information on wildlife than this narrowly conceived, often poorly photographed movie. A-I (G)

Americanization of Emily, The (1964) Attached to an American military headquarters, a British volunteer (Julie Andrews) learns fast as a megalomaniacal admiral (Melvyn Douglas) tries to make a hero of himself, while his aide (James Garner) tries to take advantage of her and others. The conclusion to director Arthur Hiller's cynical look at life in World War II England is Emily's own compromise of her virtue and previously unimpeachable character. O (br) X

Americathon (1979) With America about to go bankrupt in this dismal comedy directed by Neil Israel, a massive telethon is held to rescue the national finances. Besides being unfunny, the movie employs objectionable language and graphic depictions of misconduct. O (PG)

Amin—The Rise and Fall (1981) Amateurish and exploitative account of the Uganda dictator's bloody career in a Kenyan production directed by Sahrad Patel. Posing as socio-political document, it offers little more than sensationalism through a disreputable mix of violence and sex. O (R)

Amityville Horror, The (1979) The anemic plot of this tepid horror movie about a suburban couple whose house is possessed by some demonic force doesn't allow for much in the way of a satisfactory resolution. Director Stuart Rosenberg's garish special effects are relatively restrained, but his superficial treatment of the story's religious dimension is ludicrous. A-III (R) 15

Amityville II: The Possession (1982) Set in a period previous to that of the original, director Damiano Damiani's sequel features Burt Young in a partly haunted-house story and a partly wretched remake of the "Exorcist," highlighted by a ludicrously inept depiction of the religious rite of exorcism. Excessive violence and nudity. O (R) 18

Amityville 3-D (1983) The third in this dreary series features Tony Roberts as a writer who moves into the demonic house, confident he's gotten a real bargain. This silly mess is probably all the worse for viewers aggravated by the headache from the 3-D glasses. Absurd, spurious violence. A-III (PG) 15

Amongst Friends (1993) Three buddies (Joseph Lindsay, Steve Parlavecchio, Patrick McGaw) who grew up together in an affluent New York suburb take up a life of crime, leading them eventually to betrayal and deadly confrontations with each other. Writer-director Rob Weiss portrays the trio's smug lawbreaking and violent actions with raw energy but no insights into their wasted lives. Some nasty violence and cold-blooded murders, a bedroom scene, recreational drug use, brief nudity and constant rough language. O (R)

Amos & Andrew (1993) Clunky comedy about a prominent African-American (Samuel L. Jackson) mistaken for a thief, then taken hostage by a kooky crook (Nicolas Cage) in cahoots with a boneheaded police chief (Dabney Coleman) trying to turn the fiasco into a publicity stunt. Writer-director E. Max Frye gets off a few acidly funny lines in an otherwise overly broad, overwrought comedy heavily dependent on dopey stereotypes. Brief violence and shots of recreational drug use and minimal rough language. A-III (PG-13)

Amsterdam Kill, The (1978) Robert Mitchum plays a disgraced but incorruptible ex-narcotics agent who finds himself caught in a bloody struggle among rival Chinese drug-dealers in Hong Kong and Amsterdam. Director Robert Clouse's plot seems no more than a string of action sequences, none of which are very exciting, let alone entertaining. Stylized violence and high body count. A-III (R) 15

Amy (1981) This warm and amiable Disney movie, set in the early 1900s, tells the story of a determined young woman (Jenny Agutter) who leaves her wealthy but unloving husband (Chris Robinson) to teach at a school for the deaf. Director Vincent McEveety does well in developing the contrast between personal and social commitment in a film that is ideal for children except for the marital estrangement in the plot. A-II (G) U

Anais Observed (1974) Anais Nin was both participant in and observer of the avant-garde scene between the world wars. Robert Snyder's feature documentary reveals all the paradox implicit in her work of self-absorption bordering on the narcissistic, combined with a warm and encouraging interest in relating to others (as with some awed students who visit her). The viewer will have to judge, however, how valuable are her aesthetic judgments and personal philosophy. A-III (nr)

Anatomy of a Murder (1959) Overlong courtroom drama in which a small-town lawyer (James Stewart) undertakes the defense of an Army officer (Ben Gazzara) charged with murdering the man who raped his wife (Lee Remick). Directed by Otto Preminger, the case is less interesting than Stewart's genial, intelligent performance, backed by a fine cast including Joseph N. Welch, the lawyer who gained fame in the 1954 Army-McCarthy hearings and is convincing here as the trial judge. Controversial at the time for its courtroom descriptions of the rape, it is relatively mild today. A-III (br)

And Hope to Die (1972) In a considerably shortened version of a French production directed by Rene Clement (originally entitled "The Race of the Hare Across the Fields"), the plot itself seems to have gone the way of the Cheshire Cat. What remains is a series of interesting but capricious scenes involving a gang of colorful cutthroats (Robert Ryan, Jean-Louis Trintignant, Lea Massari and Aldo Ray) that finally culminates in a "kidnapping" from police headquarters in the middle of Montreal. If Clement's intention was to liken this kind of adult entertainment to childhood games, something is missing in the translation. A-III (PG) AA

. . . And Justice for All (1979) Al Pacino stars as an honest but abrasive anti-establishment lawyer who is blackmailed into defending a "law and order" judge (John Forsythe) accused of rape. A heavy-handed and muddled potboiler directed by Norman Jewison. Foul language and sexual promiscuity. O (R) PG

And Now for Something Completely Different (1972) This random sampling of skits from "Monty Python's Flying Circus," the BBC zany comedy series, offers some distinctly British humor ranging from social satire and black comedy to broad slapstick and sexual jokes, most notably at the expense of homosexuals. Under director Ian MacNaughton, the young cast comes over as a quite likeable group of performers, which helps when jokes fall flat. Best of all, however, are Terry Gilliam's animated pieces linking the skits but also standing on their own as contemporary graphic humor. However, it is comedy not for all tastes. A-IV (PG) AA

And Now Miguel (1966) An engaging portrayal of a year in the life of a small boy (Pat Cardi) in New Mexico whose only wish is to become a shepherd like his father (Michael Ansara). Produced by Robert B. Radnitz and based on Joseph Krumgold's prize-winning novel, the film emphasizes the strength of Hispanic family life rooted in mutual love and respect. The natural beauty of the terrain and the naturalistic acting of the cast convey a satisfying sense of reality to this story of a pastoral family. A-I (br)

And Now My Love (1975) French production using the history of Europe from World War I to the present as the backdrop to a love story tracing, in almost surrealistic fashion, the heritages and key events in the lives of a young Jewish heiress (Marthe Keller) and an ex-convict turned film director (Charles Denner). Beautifully produced and directed by Claude Lelouch, history is interestingly put at the service of love and there is no denying that the optimism of his romantic fable makes one feel good even though aware that its selective view of the past is being used only to make a romantic trifle seem more consequential than it really is. A-III (PG)

And Now the Screaming Starts (1973) British horror movie directed by Roy Ward Baker offers no more than average example in this 18th-century tale of inherited guilt from a diabolically inspired family curse. Good production values and special effects, and the cast includes horror veterans Peter Cushing, Patrick Magee and Herbert Lom. A number of the plot elements involve rape and other forms of brutality but their treatment is restrained. A-III (R) X

And Soon the Darkness (1971) Two pretty English lasses (Pamela Franklin and Michele Dotrice) on a bicycle tour of France have a row and Dotrice disappears on the site of an unsolved grisly sex-murder leaving Franklin to search for her friend while eluding the crazed killer. British thriller directed by Robert Fuest takes her up and down any number of verdant but blind alleys, establishing everyone she meets as a prime suspect, but even the pretty French countryside cannot compensate for the overall disappointment in the climax. A-III (GP) AA

And the Band Played On (1993) Ambitious but uneven docudrama from Randy Shilts' book about the first years of the AIDS epidemic begins in 1981 with the efforts of medical researchers (notably, Matthew Modine) to identify a mystery disease seemingly limited to homosexuals, then details the indecisive action of government and medical officials in the battle against what was becoming a worldwide crisis. Directed by Roger Spottiswoode, the scenario's attempt to provide a comprehensive account of complex events results in an unwieldy narrative that gathers dramatic impact from its diverse picture of individuals confronting the reality of this deadly disease. Sympathetic treatment of homosexual relationships and a realistic depiction of the human tragedy of AIDS as well as the indifference of some to it. A-III (R) 15

And There Came a Man (1968) Part documentary and part re-enactment, this screen biography of Pope John XXIII features Rod Steiger as narrator and stand-in for the person of the title. The Italian production is best in its unpretentious re-created scenes of Pope John's early boyhood, but director Ermanno Olmi is less successful in depicting his clerical career. A-I (br)

Anderson Platoon, The (1968) French documentary about the Vietnam War centers not on the issues of the war but on a few weeks in the lives of an airmobile unit under Lt. Joseph B. Anderson fighting in the Central Highlands. Directed by Pierre Schoendorffer, its focus on these men helps give a human perspective to the reality of combat, something the screen too often glamorizes. A-II (br)

Anderson Tapes, The (1971) Director Sidney Lumet almost succeeds in splicing together an exciting perfect heist narrative and an ironic statement about electronic eavesdropping, public and private. Sean Connery masterminds the robbery of an entire luxury apartment building, but all those he recruits for the job are already under surveillance by various law agencies, none of whom has a full picture of what is going on. Adult material with occasional violence that some may find excessive. A-IV (PG)

Andromeda Strain, The (1971) When a New Mexico hamlet is wiped out by extraterrestrial microbes, a team of top medical specialists try to find a way to destroy the deadly bacteria before it destroys the human race. Despite some overdone special effects and unnecessary plot complications, director Robert Wise's screen version of Michael Crichton's best-seller is gripping and its impact is sharp. A-II (G) PG

Andy (1965) The aging parents of a grown man (Norman Alden) with the mind of a small child are forced to make the decision to commit him to an institution. Writer-director Richard Sarafian captures the less-than-understanding attitudes of society toward the mentally handicapped but tinges the realism of the New York City locale with poetic images affirming the joys of simple existence. Challenging but worthwhile fare. A-III (br)

Andy Hardy Comes Home (1958) Clunker directed by Howard Koch tries to revive the Hardy series with the original cast except family patriarch Lewis Stone. Best forgotten. A-I (br) U

Andy Hardy Gets Spring Fever (1939) Judge Hardy (Lewis Stone) falls for an aluminum scam while son Andy (Mickey Rooney) develops a crush on the new high school drama teacher. Directed by W.S. Van Dyke II, it offers the usual family sitcom fare, though Andy's involvement with the school play has its moments. A-I (br) U

Andy Hardy Meets a Debutante (1940) In order to rescue the town orphanage trust fund, Judge Hardy (Lewis Stone) journeys to New York City, taking the family along on a trip that threatens to disgrace Andy (Mickey Rooney) back home until he's saved by a wealthy friend (Judy Garland). Directed by George B. Seitz, this edition of the Hardy series provides some period amusement as well as an incidental lesson in democracy. A-I (br) U

Andy Hardy's Blonde Trouble (1944) As a college freshman, Andy (Mickey Rooney) gets off on the wrong foot with the dean (Herbert Marshall), a lovely co-ed (Bonita Granville) and a contrary blonde who turns out to be identical twins (Lee and Lyn Wilde). Directed by George B. Seitz, it's one of the feebler efforts of the series, sorely lacking the interplay of the Hardy family circle. A-I (br) U

Andy Hardy's Double Life (1942) While Judge Hardy (Lewis Stone) is preoccupied with an accident case, flirtatious Andy is perplexed by girlfriend Polly (Ann Rutherford) and her visiting pal (Esther Williams). Directed by George B. Seitz, the usual domestic misunderstandings culminate in a big finish at the train station seeing Andy off to college. A-I (br) U

Andy Hardy's Private Secretary (1941) Disorganized Andy (Mickey Rooney) gets a secretary (Kathryn Grayson) to help him keep up with his busy activities as a Carvel High senior in a typical episode of the Hardy series under George B. Seitz's direction. A-I (br) U

Andy Warhol's Dracula (1975) In this variation on the Dracula theme, the ever-thirsty Count must live on "virgin's blood," as it is rendered in one of the dreadful accents abounding here. Besides the accents, there's no lack of other offensive elements in director Paul Morrissey's campy efforts in trying to make perversion seem hilarious. O (X/R) X

Andy Warhol's Frankenstein (1974) Written and directed by Warhol's alter ego, Paul Morrissey, this version emphasizes the fatal and the perverse aspects of the Mary Shelley original, ever escalating the campy hi-jinks for shock value. If the gross nudity and kinky sex combinations don't offend, perhaps the gory charnel scraps flying all over the place will. O (X/R) X

Angel (1984) Advertised as "High school honor student by day, Hollywood hooker by night" is all one needs to know about this dismal effort by director Robert Vincent O'Neil to tell the story of a young prostitute (Donna Wilkes) who helps a detective catch a psychopathic killer. Nudity, graphic sex and violence. O (R) 18

Angel and the Badman (1947) Enjoyable low-key Western in which a wounded outlaw (John Wayne) is nursed back to health by a Quaker family whose daughter (Gail Russell) tries to get him to hang up his guns rather than square accounts with a bushwacker (Bruce Cabot). Directed by James Edward Grant, the unpretentious yet thoughtful story features a very likeable cast, including Harry Carey as the sage sheriff. Solid social values with some meaningful stylized violence. A-I (br)

Angel, Angel Down We Go (1969) An 18-year-old virgin (Holly Near), desperate to lose that state, is helped out by a rock singer (Jordon Christopher) who also gives sexual aid to her wealthy mother and father and then destroys them all. Blaming a corrupt society for the depicted immoral activity, director Robert Thom's presentation tries to smooth over the guilt feelings of viewers slightly ashamed at their own voyeurism. Promiscuity and several insulting references to religion. O (R) X

Angel Heart (1987) Director Alan Parker's bloody, often disgusting depiction of one man's grappling with the devil and the consequences of his refusal to face the evil within him forms the core of this parable about a private-eye (Mickey Rourke) hired to find a missing person only to discover it is a missing soul. Graphic mix of sex and violence in a demonic setting, nudity and vivid results of dismemberment. O (R) 18

Angel in My Pocket, An (1968) A newly ordained minister (Andy Griffith) comes to serve his first congregation in a small Kansas town where he immediately becomes involved in the feud between two families that has wrecked the ministry of all his predecessors. Directed by Alan Rafkin, the comedy is broad and mindless, the characters stereotypes and the sugary situations enough to give some viewers diabetes. A-I (G)

Angel Levine, The (1970) A devout old Jewish tailor (Zero Mostel) living in poverty in Harlem seems to have his prayers answered when a black man (Harry Belafonte) arrives claiming to be an angel who can help, but only if the tailor has faith in him. Though some viewers may find the tailor's wavering between belief and disbelief growing tiresomely repetitive, others will see it as the point of director Jan Kadar's brilliant allegory asserting people's need for belief and commitment for the sake of human survival. A-III (GP) AA

Angel on My Shoulder (1946) Seriocomic fantasy about a murdered gangster (Paul Muni) whom the Devil (Claude Rains) puts in the body of a lookalike judge to destroy the man's virtuous career but things don't go according to plan. Though it doesn't make a whole lot of sense, director Archie Mayo has some fun creating the sulfuric pits of hell down below as well as with the tough-talking mug's reformation by the judge's fiancee (Anne Baxter). Some stylized violence and devilish goings-on. A-II (br) A

Angel Unchained (1970) Routine motorcycle melodrama about a biker (Don Stroud) who leaves his cycling buddies to join a commune, but when its peaceful members are harassed by the local cowboys he calls on his old friends to help even out the odds in the big showdown. Director Lee Madden's contrived plot provides the opportunity for some hard-hitting brawls, a touch of sex, an abundance of beer and pot and, of course, plenty of daredevil bike riding. A-III (GP)

Angels Die Hard (1970) Unenlightened motorcycle movie about a gang of bikers that invades a small town, brutally torments the locals and lingers nearby to do it again. Underdeveloped conflicts center on the sheriff's blustering threats to shoot them down, especially since his teenage daughter is keen on joining them. Director Richard Compton leans to admiring shots of the gang riding the road, but the coarse customs and cruelty of these outlaw heroes far outweigh any suggestions of their benevolent humanity. O (R)

Angi Vera (1980) A marvelously subtle and complex Hungarian production set in 1948, the early days of the Communist regime, a tragic and confused era full of idealism and opportunism. Veronica Papp gives a flawless performance in the title role as a young woman with a talent for survival who is sent by the Party to a political training center where she has an affair that could threaten her future. Director Pal Gabor shows that human nature has a way of infiltrating the most resistant of ideologies. Adult situations and politically complex themes. A-III (nr)

Angry Harvest (1986) Set in a Polish village during World War II, a simple but devout farmer abuses the trust of a Jewish refugee he is sheltering by his lust for her. In the Polish production, director Agnieszka Holland offers a compelling portrait of a man whose loneliness undermines his basic moral character resulting in betrayal and death. In this context, several brief scenes of partial nudity and simulated sex are anything but titillating. A-IV (nr)

Animal Behavior (1989) Muddled romance between a sincere music teacher (Armande Assante) and a spacy psychology professor (Karen Allen) who's too caught up in her communication research with a chimp to relate in a man-woman context. Directed by H. Anne Riley, the movie's dopey, implausible script and miscast, overwrought characters fail in a humorless attempt at screwball comedy. Minimal rough language and some sexual innuendo. A-III (PG)

Animal Crackers (1930) In this Marx Brothers comedy, Groucho plays Captain Geoffrey T. Spaulding, the inveterate African explorer and improbable guest of honor at a party given by Margaret Dumont to unveil a valuable painting that is stolen

and replaced by not one but two bogus ones. Chico and Harpo are on the scene to provide the music, Lillian Roth sings and Zeppo, the fourth brother, plays Groucho's private secretary. Directed by Victor Heerman, the coarseness and vulgarity of the early Marx Brothers comedies may not appeal to everyone's tastes, but their zany verbal and physical assaults on conventions of every kind continue to be one of the hallmarks of screen comedy. A-II (G)

Animal House (see: "National Lampoon's Animal House").

Animals Are Beautiful People (1975) Wildlife documentary filmed in a vast tract of desert, swamp and mountains in Southwest Africa with an exotic variety of animal species. Director Jamie Uys provides some humorous as well as fascinating moments, marred slightly by a Disney-style anthropomorphic slant and what some might detect as a paternalistic attitude toward blacks. A-I (G)

Ann and Eve (1970) Swedish story of a jaded journalist (Gio Petre) who takes a young innocent (Marie Liljedahl) on a vacation to a Yugoslav resort where she is initiated into a predictable series of sexual adventures around town. Arne Mattsson directs the lurid melodrama with clinical coldness toward the characters who meander through arbitrary situations. Excessive nudity. O (nr)

Anne of Green Gables (1934) Charming dramatization of the Lucy Maud Montgomery novel about a spunky teenaged orphan (Anne Shirley) who overcomes assorted obstacles to win the hearts of a taciturn farmer (O.P. Heggie) and his domineering sister (Helen Westley) on Canada's Prince Edward Island at the turn of the century. Directed by George Nicholls, the story of a lonely waif finding the loving home of her dreams has special appeal for young viewers while reminding older ones of youth's yearning for unconditional love. Fine family fare. A-I (nr) U

Anne of the Thousand Days (1969) Screen version of Maxwell Anderson's play about the romance between Henry VIII (Richard Burton) and Anne Boleyn (Genevieve Bujold). Directed by Charles Jarrott, the story centers on all the dynastic complications that motivated Henry's break with Rome and his six-year pursuit of Anne. Though the action is limited, the acting is impressive, especially that of Anthony Quayle as Cardinal Wolsey. For those who are not history buffs, there is plenty of royal pageantry, colorful costumes and well-preserved castles. In dealing with the period and its characters, there is some blood-letting and sexual candor. A-III (PG)

Annie (1982) Although John Huston's direction of the screen version of the popular stage musical is somewhat cynical and definitely disappointing, it does preserve much of the exotic ambiance of the comic strip about the little orphan (Aileen Quinn) and Daddy Warbucks (Albert Finney). With awkward dance numbers, some coarse dialogue and Carol Burnett's mean-spirited characterization, the movie's appeal is somewhat limited beyond uncritical viewers. A-I (PG) U

Annie Hall (1977) Director Woody Allen's romantic comedy about an on-again, off-again relationship between a Jewish comedian from New York (Allen) and a WASP from the Midwest (Diane Keaton). Although the movie is frequently very funny and has a touch of humanity lacking in Allen's earlier work, it falls far short of its more ambitious intention of making a serious statement about human relationships. Some rough language and much humor derived from sexual matters. A-III (PG) 15

Annie Oakley (1935) Robust story of an Ohio country girl (Barbara Stanwyck) whose prowess with a hunting rifle starts her on the way to fame as the star sharpshooter of Buffalo Bill's Wild West Show. Director George Stevens provides a lively picture of late 19th-century America as well as a gentle story of Annie's love for a boastful trick shooter (Preston Foster). Enjoyable both for its colorful Western action and appealing success story. A-I (br) U

Anniversary, The (1968) Bette Davis overacts dreadfully as a dreadful mother who rules the lives of every member of the family. Director Roy Ward Baker's comedy of the outrageous fails in satirizing the evils of momism because it lacks compassion and its unhealthy humor is frequently tasteless. O (br) X

Anonymous Venetian, The (1971) A young musician (Tony Musante) calls his estranged wife (Florinda Bolkan) to Venice and they spend their day revisiting scenes that once brought them happiness until the wife learns that, like the city, he and their marriage are dying. Italian production directed by Enrico Maria Salerno, it is a tragically lyric travelogue through the canals and streets of a great city that by day's end slowly sinks into the sea, surrounded by the pollution and technology of modern times. With a little less sentimentality, its story of the fragility of human love and man-made beauty might have been more credible. A-III (GP)

Another 48 Hrs. (1990) Eddie Murphy and Nick Nolte reteam as the convict and the cop in this savage sequel centering on their efforts to nail a drug kingpin before his gang ices them. Director Walter Hill revs up the violence to the max, with brutal shoot-ups at close range taking precedence over storyline, characterizations and comic relief. Excessive violence, continuous raw language and brief nudity. O (R) 18

Another Man, Another Chance (1977) French director Claude Lelouch's romantic sagebrush drama about a widowed veterinarian (James Caan) who falls in love with a charming widowed photographer (Genevieve Bujold). Despite the movie's striking photography and excellent acting, Lelouch's calculatedly relaxed style of characterization and glossy romanticism do not lend themselves well to the more austere mood of a western. Brief violence in a scene of rape. A-III (PG) AA

Another Stakeout (1993) Uneven sequel to 1987's "Stakeout" reteams Seattle detectives Richard Dreyfuss and Emilio Estevez with assistant D.A. Rosie O'Donnell posing as a make-believe family who rent a home next door to a couple (Dennis Farina and Marcia Strassman) who are the friends of a government witness (Cathy Moriarty) running for her life. Director John Badham opens and closes with murderous violence totally at odds with the hilarious meat of the movie in which the innocent neighbors are constantly confused by mixed-up versions of the fake family's cover story. A live-in relationship, some intense violence and a few off-color remarks. A-III

Another Woman (1988) On her 50th birthday, a philosophy professor (Gena Rowlands) is forced to face the fact that she is not as loved and respected as she previously assumed, nor is her life the success that it had seemed. In this serious examination of mid-life regrets, writer-director Woody Allen continues to be sensitive to female protagonists. Brief, explicit talk of marital infidelity and a past abortion. A-III (PG)

Another You (1991) When a pathological liar (Gene Wilder) is released from a mental hospital, he is persuaded to pass himself off as a missing millionaire by a con man (Richard Pryor). A needlessly convoluted script makes director Maurice Phillips' garbled comedy misfire badly with hardly a laugh to be had. Recurring rough language and mild sexual innuendo. A-III (R)

Antonia & Jane (1991) Bland comedy about two longtime acquaintances (Imelda Staunton and Saskia Reeves) individually recounting their sex lives, perceived failures and resentments of each other to the same therapist (Brenda Bruce). Only rare moments of wit punctuate director Beeban Kidron's would-be comedy of two unhappy women. Benign attitude toward affairs, brief bedroom scenes with momentary nudity and several sexual references. A-III (R)

Antonio Das Mortes (1970) Brazilian folk epic about a gunman hired by a feudal landlord to eliminate the leaders of a peasant rebellion in the hills and how the hired assassin eventually joins the rebels himself. Using a gaudy color photography that suits his strange story and setting, director Glauber Rocha intermingles black and Indian rituals and ceremonies with Christian saints and symbols to create a world of bizarre superstitions and revolutionary fervor. It is an episodic movie of unusual power and beauty that some tastes may find too exotic. A-III (nr)

Any Number Can Play (1949) Dreary melodrama of a day in the life of a gambling-house owner (Clark Gable) with a bad heart, a loving wife (Alexis Smith), an estranged son (Darryl Hickman), a weak brother-in-law (Wendell Corey) and an exotic clientele, one of whom (Frank Morgan) is on a winning streak. Mervyn Le Roy directs a fine cast in a plodding scenario crowded with contrived incidents, including an attempted robbery and a hokey finish. Lots of anxiety and a bit of stylized violence. A-II (br) A

Any Wednesday (1966) Jaded successful businessman (Jason Robards) is a good husband six days of the week but Wednesday is reserved for a young lady (Jane Fonda) until his wife (Rosemary Murphy) forces a showdown and his lady friend finds the man of her dreams (Dean Jones). Under Robert Ellis Miller's direction, it's a lively, sappy, broad comedy with some serious overtones about the pain of infidelity. A-III (br) A

Any Which Way You Can (1980) An auto repairman and free-lance streetfighter (Clint Eastwood) finds happiness with a skittish prostitute (Sondra Locke). Director Buddy Van Horn's salute to machismo presents an abundance of violence and an atmosphere of sleazy immorality. O (R) 15

Anyone Can Play (1968) Failed Italian sex farce with Ursula Andress, Virna Lisi and Jean-Pierre Cassel tends to condone adultery. Clumsily directed by Luigi Zampa, its emphasis is on sexual titillation. O (R)

Anything Can Happen (1952) Sudsy romantic comedy in which an emigrant (Jose Ferrer) from Georgia, USSR, works hard at becoming a U.S. citizen while falling along the way for one of the natives (Kim Hunter). Director George Seaton gives superficial treatment to the cultural differences facing a group of immigrants in New York City, preferring to portray them as quaint eccentrics with predictable problems in contrived circumstances. Well-intentioned but sugar-coated view of America's ethnic melting pot. A-I (br) U

Anzio (1968) Huge, sprawling World War II epic about the Allied invasion at Anzio in southern Italy with Robert Mitchum, Peter Falk and Robert Ryan in the thick of combat. Directed by Edward Dmytryk, the movie is graphic in its depiction of the grim images of battle, with appropriately harsh action and language. A-III (PG)

Apache (1954) When Geronimo and his band are sent to Florida in chains, one Apache warrior (Burt Lancaster) manages to escape and find his way back to New Mexico where he makes his last stand with wife (Jean Peters) and infant son. Director Robert Aldrich treats the Indians with sympathy while showing the injustices against them, though the movie's clash-of-cultures theme is on the simplistic side, most notably in its corn-grows-in-the-badlands ending. Stylized violence. A-II (br) U

Apache Uprising (1965) Formula Western in which a cowboy (Rory Calhoun) saves the stagecoach to Lordsburg from a badman (John Russell) who's being pursued by Indians for his crimes against them. Directed by R.G. Springsteen, it is noteworthy only for the remarkably bad acting of DeForest Kelley as a crazed gunman. Stylized violence. A-II (br) U

Apartment, The (1960) Director Billy Wilder's comedy satire about the corporate rise and moral near-downfall of a garden variety office manager whose sudden success in climbing the company ladder comes from loaning out his bachelor apartment to philandering executives. His falling in love with one of their girlfriends (Shirley MacLaine) leads to the usual moral comeuppances for all involved, but Wilder and his talented cast devise startling ways of arriving at the obvious, obligatory conclusion. A-III (br) PG

Apartment for Peggy (1948) Heavy-handed comedy about the post-war housing shortage causing a veteran on the G.I. Bill (William Holden) and his pregnant wife (Jeanne Crain) to move into the unused attic of an aging college professor (Edmund Gwenn) who's decided to commit suicide. Directed by George Seaton, the script turns maudlin when the wife's miscarriage makes the prof realize the value of his own life, but the movie's main value is as a treasure trove of the period's social attitudes and ideals. A-II (br) A

Apartment Zero (1989) Unsettling hothouse thriller set in 1968 Buenos Aires delves into the uneasy relationship between a wealthy, repressed movie theater owner (Colin Firth) and his mysterious tenant (Hart Bochner), a professional assassin. Argentinian-born director Martin Donovan's tale of users and victims has an erotically charged atmosphere that culminates in grisly violence. Some profanity and suggestions of sexual promiscuity. O (R) 15

Apocalypse Now (1979) Director Francis Ford Coppola's uneven attempt to transpose Joseph Conrad's "Heart of Darkness" to a Vietnam setting follows an intelligence officer (Martin Sheen) on a mission to kill a renegade Special Forces officer (Marlon Brando) who has set up a private domain deep in the Cambodian interior. Much ambiguous and unresolved soul-searching in between several brilliant battle sequences, but stealing the show is Robert Duvall's turn as a gung-ho helicopter commander. Much graphic violence and some rough language. A-IV (R) 18

Appaloosa, The (1966) Marlon Brando stars as a would-be rancher whose prize horse is stolen by Mexican bandits (led by John Saxon). British director Sidney J. Furie follows the action conventions of the western but pays more attention to colorful camerawork than to developing character motivation. The result is a picture with lots of atmosphere but little human interest. Assorted stylized violence. A-II (br) A

Apple Dumpling Gang, The (1975) Western comedy about three little orphans left with a gold mine who con suave gambler Bill Bixby into a marriage of convenience with stage coach driver Susan Clark to protect them from greedy townspeople and bungling robbers Don Knotts and Tim Conway. Norman Tokar directs a standard Disney family entertainment. A-I (G) U

Apple Dumpling Gang Rides Again, The (1979) Inept outlaws (Don Knotts and Tim Conway) try to go straight with predictably disastrous results in this Disney sequel. Directed by Vincent McEveety, the comedy is not helped much by a bland romantic subplot (Tim Matheson and Elyssa Davalos), but the humor is carried by the manic efforts of a frenzied marshal (Kenneth Mars) to get the zany pair. A-I (G)

Applegates, The (see: "Meet the Applegates"). U

Appointment, The (1968) Romantic melodrama about a successful lawyer (Omar Sharif) who comes to suspect that his wife (Anouk Aimee) was once a prostitute and, when he tries to find out the truth, tragedy results. Directed by Sidney Lumet, the silly tale of a strange jealousy cannot sustain its length and comes to an unsatisfying conclusion. A-III (br) X

Appointment with Danger (1951) Contrived but fairly interesting crime story of a postal inspector (Alan Ladd) getting some help from a nun (Phyllis Calvert) in tracking the killer of a colleague, then foiling a million-dollar mail robbery. Director Lewis Allen handles the action with the hard-bitten crooks (Paul Stewart, Henry Morgan and Jack Webb) better than the idealistic nun's reformation of a tough, cynical postal agent. Stylized violence. A-II (br)

Appointment with Death (1988) Lackluster adaptation of an Agatha Christie whodunit unfolds during a grand tour of Europe and the Middle East with an all-star cast, including Peter Ustinov as Belgian sleuth Hercule Poirot. Though Piper Laurie shines as a tyrannical stepmother, director Michael Winner pretty much wastes the rest of his cast in an effort that may bore diehard mystery fans but please those who enjoy travelogues. A few brief scenes of violence. A-II (PG)

Apprentice to Murder (1988) In rural 1927 Pennsylvania, an itinerant preacher-faith healer (Donald Sutherland) takes a 16-year-old youth (Chad Lowe) under his wing, but their friendship ends when an attempted exorcism causes the death of a local hermit (Knut Husebo), seemingly possessed by the devil. Moody, listless English-language Norwegian production directed by R.L. Thomas wastes Sutherland's considerable acting abilities. Brief graphic violence and several totally gratuitous sexual encounters. O (PG-13)

Apprenticeship of Duddy Kravitz, The (1974) Superior Canadian drama about an ambitious young man (Richard Dryfuss), growing up in a Jewish ghetto in Montreal, who discovers that making money is not all there is to life. Directed by Ted Kotcheff, the moral problems and mistaken goals of youth are convincingly presented in terms of Duddy's relationships with family and those he meets along the way. More than the story of one man's greed, it is also the chronicle of a ghetto, finely evoking a detailed and realistic world whose humanity transcends any ethnic group, making all the more universal its picture of human self-centeredness. Some crude religious and sexual references used within a purposeful context. A-IV (R) X

April Fool's Day (1986) Group of wealthy college students, acting like retarded adolescents, spend a weekend playing deadly tricks on each other at an island estate. Director Fred Walton treats the women involved solely as sexual objects and the dialogue is preoccupied with profanity, sexual innuendos and off-color jokes. Accepts sexual promiscuity as a natural part of youthful behavior. O (R)

April Fools, The (1969) Director Stuart Rosenberg's comedy-drama involves a New York stockbroker (Jack Lemmon) and a jet-set beauty (Catherine Deneuve) who start a 24-hour romance by flying off to Paris and forsaking their own shallow previous marriages. The underlying seriousness of the film's healthy criticism of the "good" life creates definite moral problems and a credibility gap for its glib resolution, especially when set beside the film's slapstick routines and the unlikely liaison between the central characters. O (PG) A

Arabella (1969) Italian comedy set in the 1920s tells the story of a young Roman aristocrat (Virna Lisi) who tries to help her grandmother (Margaret Rutherford) out of financial difficulties by fleecing various victims (all played by Terry Thomas). Whether director Mauro Bolognini means to satirize the Italian tax laws or indict Italian manners and morals, his farcical complications strain frantically and often repulsively for laughs that seldom materialize. A-III (PG) A

Arabesque (1966) Muddled thriller in which an American exchange professor at Oxford (Gregory Peck) gets involved with several sets of Arab spies, one of whom (Sophia Loren) keeps shifting sides. Directed by Stanley Donen, villains and villainy abound, there's eye-catching violence and sexy romance, but it's all surface and no substance. A-III (br) A

Arabian Adventure (1979) British fantasy is a thrilling flying carpet adventure about a prince on a mission to foil the evil ambitions of sinister sorcerer Christopher Lee. Directed by Kevin Connor, the brisk costume and special effects vehicle is devoid of violence or trite romanticism. Pleasant escapist fare for young and old. A-I (G) U

Arachnophobia (1990) A young doctor (Jeff Daniels) with an avid fear of spiders (arachnophobia) is put to the ultimate test when he relocates his family to a small town unaware that a deadly new species is rapidly reproducing in his barn. Despite one glaring inconsistency in the plot, director Frank Marshall has crafted a deliciously menacing thriller whose moody cinematography and precise editing steadily build the suspense. Some graphic shots of dead bodies. A-II (PG-13) PG

Arch, The (1972) Hong Kong production presenting a doomed tale of unrequited passion in which a widow, true to the memory of her dead husband and her social position, refuses the love of a handsome captain, but then allows her daughter to marry him. The movie's deliberate, timeless creation of mood has been broken up with freeze-frames and some heavy-handed montages by its woman director, Shu Shuen. It is an oriental curio that may best be left to the romantically inclined. A-II (nr)

Aristocats, The (1970) Directed by Wolfgang Reitherman, the first animated feature from the Disney studio since Disney's death in 1966 tells the adventures of a family of felines who, after being made the heir of their millionaire mistress, are catnapped and ditched in the country but then rescued by a pair of bumbling hounds, a couple of giggling geese, a rodent named Roquefort and an alley cat named O'Malley. Enhanced by the voices of Eva Gabor, Phil Harris, Hermione Baddeley and Sterling Hollo-way, with five songs thrown in for good measure, the result, while not purr-fect, is plentifully pleasing. A-I (G) U

Arizona (1940) When a Tucson frontierswoman (Jean Arthur) faces loss of her booming freight business to a cheating competitor (Porter Hall) and his Confederate partner (Warren William), she gets some needed help from a smitten cowboy (William Holden). Directed by Wesley Ruggles, the plot is weak but sturdy enough to anchor the action, including Apache raids, North-South rivalries, well-staged shootouts and a fitful courtship that ultimately proves quite charming. Stylized violence and assorted villainies. A-I (br) U

Arizona Bushwackers (1967) Routine western directed by Lesley Selander in which a Confederate agent (Howard Keel) stops a renegade (Scott Brady) from selling a cache of rebel guns to the Indians and the movie concludes happily with the end of the Civil War. A-I (br) U

Armed and Dangerous (1986) Posing as social spoof, this failed slapstick movie concerns security guards (John Candy and Eugene Levy) who fight organized crime by being more aggressive and anti-social than the criminals. Violent and destructive imagery sprinkled with profanity and sexual sight gags that fail as burlesque. A-III (PG-13) 15

Army of Darkness (1993) Mindless sword-and-sorcery movie about a present-day macho guy (Bruce Campbell) zapped back to the Dark Ages where he must rescue a damsel in distress (Embeth Davidtz) and do battle with legions of undead skeletons before he can return to his own time. Director Sam Raimi's inept attempt at comic horror fails miserably save for a few briefly interesting special effects. Frequent comic violence and mild sexual innuendo. A-III (R) 15

Arnold (1973) At least half of this creaky horror-comedy takes place in a fog-bound graveyard, and all of it centers on a well-heeled, well-preserved cadaver (in the title role). The gimmick derives from a condition in the deceased's will that his wife (Stella Stevens), who married him hastily just after his demise, has to keep him near her for the rest of her life, a condition that leads to a number of murders and other preposterous goings-on. All director George Fenady can do with this bizarre material is to play it for laughs and these do come at reasonably close intervals. A-III (PG) AA

Around the World in 80 Days (1956) In Mike Todd's lavish production of the Jules Verne classic, an English armchair adventurer (David Niven) makes a bet that he can encircle the globe within 80 days and sets off with his valet (Cantinflas) to prove it. Michael Anderson's direction makes the most of the cultural splendor of the late Victorian period, visits just about every scenic locale worth a postcard and offers an all-star marathon of cameo appearances. The result is a wonderful romp that is great fun for all. A-I (G) U

Around the World Under the Sea (1965) Producer-director Andrew Marton's underseas adventure with scientists (Lloyd Bridges, David McCallum, Brian Kelly, Shirley Eaton) setting earthquake warning devices on the ocean floor and meeting monsters of the deep should appeal to most youngsters. A-I (G) U

Arrangement, The (1969) Director Elia Kazan's screen version of his own novel suffers less from being ambitious than from its pretentiousness. Kirk Douglas plays a man who attempts suicide because his life has been a sham, a series of "arrangements" in business as well as with mistress (Faye Dunaway) and wife (Deborah Kerr). Among the many flaws in this failed work, the greatest is its reduction of personal crises to predominantly sexual conflicts and involvements. Rough language and some coy nudity. O (R) 15

Arrivederci, Baby! (1966) Dull, tasteless and vulgar vehicle for Tony Curtis clownishly playing a con man who marries and murders a series of wealthy women. Written, produced and directed by Ken Hughes, the attempts at humor fall flat making the proceedings all the more vulgar and pointless. O (br)

Arrowhead (1953) Dark Western in which an Indian-hating Army scout (Charlton Heston) helps the post's new commander (Brian Keith) put down an Apache uprising led by a messianic warrior (Jack Palance). Directed by Charles Marquis Warren, there's plenty of action but most of it is as unconvincing as the vicious hostiles. Nasty Indian stereotypes and stylized violence. A-II (br) U

Arruza (1972) Documentary by Budd Boetticher on the final years of the legendary Mexican bullfighter, Carlos Arruza. Narrated by Anthony Quinn, it fails to explore the make-up of the man, presenting instead a cold, distant portrait of the torero seen totally from the outside. What will impress most viewers, however, is only the foolish, cruel and debasing side of this contest between man and beast. A-II (PG)

Arsenic and Old Lace (1944) Droll adaptation of Joseph Kesselring's madcap stage hit about an irascible theater critic (Cary Grant) whose dotty maiden aunts (Josephine Hull and Jean Adair) serve lonely old men elderberry wine laced with poison. Director Frank Capra's black comedy features a great cast, including Boris Karloff and Peter Lorre as criminal interlopers, but the wacky proceedings are not for all tastes. A-II (br) A

Art of Love, The (1965) Clunky romantic comedy directed by Norman Jewison is set in Paris where a poor artist (Dick Van Dyke) fakes suicide to raise the value of his canvases, then dons various disguises trying to get revenge on his larcenous roommate (James Garner) who's made off with his money and his girl (Elke Sommer). Slapstick conniving and romantic complications. A-II (br) U

Arthur (1981) A rich and spoiled young man named Arthur (Dudley Moore), who spends his days and nights drinking to excess and pursuing all sorts of women, falls in love with a waitress (Liza Minnelli). Director Steve Gordon tries to distill humor from the playboy's sexual weaknesses and from his indecision about meaningful commitment, but most of the humor comes from John Gielgud's performance as the snobbish, harsh-tongued valet. Adult situations. A-III (PG) 15

Arthur Rubenstein—Love of Life (1975) Extraordinary documentary about one of the world's greatest piano virtuosos is concerned not only with music but also with humanity. Directed by Francois Reichenbach, it captures the artist and the man at age 82 and is equally important as a commentary on classical music as it is a testament to a rare human being. Of far greater appeal than the specialized art audience. A-I (nr)

Arthur II: On the Rocks (1988) Comedy sequel about the perpetually drunk millionaire wastrel (Dudley Moore) whose marriage to a perky waitress-shoplifter (Liza Minnelli) is threatened by a tycoon (Stephen Elliott) and his daughter (Cynthia Sikes). Though director Bud Yorkin adds some weight with a subplot about the couple's adoption of a baby, alcoholism is no laughing matter. Some vulgar language. A-III (PG)

Article 99 (1992) Fast-paced drama set in a veterans' hospital where a dedicated doctor (Ray Liotta) and his new intern (Kiefer Sutherland) continually run afoul of the hospital's budget-conscious director

(John Mahoney). Directed by Howard Deutch, the choppy mix of comedy and dramatic exaggeration focuses attention on the plight of sick and disabled veterans at the mercy of government bureaucracy. Brief violence, including several graphic shots of open-heart surgery, an instance of sexual innuendo and recurring rough language. A-III (R)

Artists and Models (1955) Frenetic, fitfully amusing comedy about an artist (Dean Martin) who uses the vivid dreams of his nutty pal (Jerry Lewis) as the basis for a comic strip that attracts the attention of foreign agents. Director Frank Tashlin's outlandish brand of comedy is unusually flat-footed here, wasting Shirley MacLaine and Dorothy Malone as the romantic interests. Comic violence and sexual innuendo. A-III (br) U

Ash Wednesday (1973) Dowdy middle-aged matron (Elizabeth Taylor), on the verge of losing her successful lawyer husband (Henry Fonda) to a younger woman, undergoes body sculpture in a posh European clinic, but it will take Liz a good deal longer than the audience to figure out that no amount of face-lifting will change Henry's mind. Director Larry Peerce elicits solid performances from a good cast, and the plot moves along smoothly through a series of plush settings, but it is no more than a well-made but uninvolving melodrama without any perspective upon the actions and motivations of its characters and their life-style. A-III (R)

Aspen Extreme (1993) Two Detroit buddies (Paul Gross and Peter Berg) become Aspen ski instructors and end up paying a price for succumbing to the seductive dangers of life among the rich and glamorous. Writer-director Patrick Hasburgh fails to mount much of a story around his main focus—daredevil ski footage and impressive mountain scenery. Implied affair, brief nudity, a shot of drug abuse and minimal rough language. A-III (PG-13)

Assassination (1987) Through his experience and cunning, a Secret Service agent (Charles Bronson) protects the wife (Jill Ireland) of the President of the United States from assassination. Directed by Peter Hunt, the movie is relatively restrained in its violence and sexual treatment. A-III (PG-13) 15

Assassination Bureau, The (1969) British tongue-in-cheek comedy set in the early 1900s about an international organization of killers-for-hire that is commissioned by a neophyte reporter (Diana Rigg) to kill their own leader (Oliver Reed). Good cast, marvellous settings, but Basil Dearden's direction is rather uncertain in its mixture of slapstick and satire. Comic violence. A-III (M) A

Assassination of Trotsky, The (1972) The death of the magnetic Russian revolutionary in his Mexican exile in 1924 is portrayed not from the political angle but the human, centering on the two protagonists—the sympathetic victim (Richard Burton) and the shadowy assassin (Alain Delon) who clearly exhibits classic symptoms of psychological disturbance that his infiltration of the closely guarded Trotsky compound is simply not credible. Despite this central dramatic flaw, director Joseph Losey has fashioned a fascinating movie that succeeds in placing its figures into an historical time and place. A-III (R) 15

Assault on a Queen (1966) Navy veterans (Frank Sinatra and Richard Conte) raise a sunken U-boat and use it to hi-jack and rob the Queen Mary in mid-ocean. Directed by Jack Donahue, it's routine escapist entertainment with the bad guys getting their just desserts and the good guys escaping, but without the loot. A-II (br) U

Assignment K (1968) Masquerading as a toy tycoon, a British agent (Stephen Boyd) matches wits with enemy spies and counterspies in rich and exotic European settings. Director Val Guest's weak spy melodrama is cluttered with plot complications whose only purpose is to afford changes of glamorous locales and chic costumes. Moderate violence. A-III (br)

Assignment to Kill (1968) Private detective (Patrick O'Neal) works his way up the ladder in an organization headed by a mobster who sinks his own ships to collect the insurance. Threadbare plot directed by Sheldon Reynolds but with much action and many dead bodies. A-III (br) A

Assisi Underground, The (1984) Fact-based story of a Franciscan friar (Ben Cross) who helps set up a network of hiding places for Jewish refugees in Assisi's monasteries while the local bishop (James Mason) organizes their escape from German-occupied Italy. Directed by Alexander Ramati, the sincere portrayal of the religious setting adds a spiritual dimension to this example of the Christian resistance to Nazi inhumanity. Much menace and some stylized violence. A-II (PG)

Asylum (1971) British production of four psychological horror tales by Robert Bloch that are tied together by being set in an insane asylum run by Patrick Magee and the gimmick of a puzzle to be unraveled by the end of the last episode. Director Roy Ward Baker provides a few mild chills, a handful of ironic chuckles and a couple of nifty twists at the conclusion. A-II (PG) X

At Any Price (1970) Poor Italian caper movie about a retiring curator of the Vatican museums (Walter Pidgeon) who, though blind, gathers a group of willing and unwilling professional accomplices to carry out the intricate heist of Vatican treasures. Directed by Emilio Miraglia, it is little more than a series of highly improbable, unmotivated and badly dubbed escapades. A-II (PG)

At Close Range (1986) In director James Foley's harrowing, fact-based tale of youth corrupted by the seductive powers of evil, a son (Sean Penn) blindly follows his menacing, ruthless father (Christopher Walken) as he steals, murders and betrays without remorse. Some brief nudity, profanity and intense moments of violence. A-IV (R) 15

At Long Last Love (1975) Tedious, boring musical about a New York millionaire (Burt Reynolds) who becomes romantically involved with a musical comedy star (Madeline Kahn) and, then, with a bankrupt society girl (Cybill Shepherd). Director Peter Bogdanovich has mastered the form of the 1930s' Hollywood musicals but not their spirit, drive nor buoyant style. The miscast principals savage some lesser songs by Cole Porter. Permissive attitude toward casual sex. A-III (G) U

At Play in the Fields of the Lord (1991) Ponderous adaptation of Peter Matthiessen's novel about the cultural chasm separating a group of U.S. evangelical missionaries (John Lithgow, Daryl Hannah, Aidan Quinn and Kathy Bates), the Amazonian tribe of aboriginals they hope to convert and a part-Navaho bush pilot (Tom Berenger) who goes native. In laboring to re-create a remote jungle culture with some ethnographic integrity, director Hector Babenco fails to develop much interest in the colorless missionaries and their part in the human drama of a devastating encounter between civilization and a primitive society. Fairly graphic sexual encounter, much nudity, some violence and occasional rough language. A-IV (R) 15

At Sword's Point (1952) Mediocre costumer in which the Four Musketeers' offspring (Cornel Wilde, Dan O'Herlihy, Alan Hale, Jr., and Maureen O'Hara) come to the aid of France's aging queen (Gladys Cooper). Directed by Lewis Allen, the foursome laugh a lot and wield their swords with gusto but the plot is hardly worth the effort. Stylized violence. A-II (br)

At the Earth's Core (1976) Director Kevin Connor's low-budget science-fiction movie about finding a lost world of prehistoric creatures far beneath the earth's surface falls considerably short of its modest entertainment goals. Considerable special effects violence and monsters. A-II (PG) A

At the Max (1991) Concert film of the Rolling Stones rock band performing on tour in Turin, Berlin and London during the summer of 1990 is presented in the IMAX format, which is 10 times larger than the conventional 35mm film frame and uses a six-channel four-way sound system. Location director Julien Temple uses the enormous size of the IMAX screen to record the spectacle of the stage sets and lighting, the mass energy of the fans and the full spectrum of amplified music as the band performs 15 of their hits from "Satisfaction" to "Rock and a Hard Place." Some vulgar words and gestures. A-II (nr)

Atlantic City (1981) Aging, opportunistic con man (Burt Lancaster) living in poverty in Atlantic City, becomes involved with a young woman (Susan Sarandon) and after her husband is killed in a heroin shipment, he is left with the proceeds from the sale. Director Louis Malle powerfully evokes the seedy side of casino life, as well as a portrait of a small-time loser who takes one last shot at the big time and thinks he can succeed. Some violence, scenes of drug-dealing and brief nudity. A-III (R) 15

Atlantis (1993) Nature documentary explores underwater sea life in such diverse locations as the Galapagos Islands, the Arctic Circle, Tahiti and New Caledonia, focusing on endangered or unusual species such as the marine iguana, the striped-sweater sea snake and the whale shark. Filmmaker Luc Besson's soothing, almost wordless record of life in a watery environment is certainly exotic but grows overlong with its repetitive parade of fish. A-I (nr)

Atragon (1964) Standard Japanese science-fiction fantasy about an evil underseas empire whose plans to rule the world are stopped by the underwater battleship of the title. Director Inoshiro Honda manages some nifty special effects in kiddie matinee story. A-I (br)

Attack on the Iron Coast (1968) Routine World War II action movie about the training of an elite British commando force (led by Lloyd Bridges) and their raid on German positions in France. Director Paul Wendkos adds nothing new to the old story of brave men who give their lives for their country. A-I (br) U

Attica (1974) Documentary recounting the tragic events that took place in the 1971 New York prison revolt at Attica (43 dead, 200 wounded) from the point of view of the inmates, using footage shot inside the prison before and during the National Guard's attack, TV coverage of the state's official investigations as well as its own interviews with participants. Directed by

Cinda Firestone, it takes a clear advocacy position toward prison reform to insure no future Atticas. A-III (nr)

Au Hasard, Balthazar (1970) French production centering on a donkey as a device to tie together a series of vignettes of human injustice. In this unusual and challenging work, director Robert Bresson presents a view of selfishness and inhumanity that is unrelenting in its condemnation of evil. As austere and as uncompromising as any film he has made, it will be hard going for those unacquainted with his previous explorations of the human condition. A-III (nr)

Au Revoir les Enfants (1988) When the Gestapo discover that a priest has hidden three Jewish youths in a Catholic boys' school, he and the boys are arrested and deported to concentration camps. French writer-producer-director Louis Malle recreates a painful memory from his own youth in a restrained, humbling, well-acted dramatization of a boy's firsthand experience of the Holocaust. Subtitles. Some rough language. A-II (PG)

Audrey Rose (1977) Slow-moving, low-voltage thriller about an 11-year-old girl who becomes an object of contention between a man (Anthony Hopkins) who claims that she is the reincarnation of his dead daughter and her shocked parents (Marsha Mason and John Beck). Although director Robert Wise's movie concerns the spiritual dimension of human existence, its poorly developed theme of reincarnation is confusing and youngsters may be discomfited by some graphic scenes of the young girl's acute anguish. A-III (PG)

Auntie Mame (1958) Uneven but never uninteresting comedy adapted from Patrick Dennis's play about an orphan's upbringing by an outrageously eccentric aunt (Rosalind Russell) who loses a fortune in the Depression, then gains another when she loses her husband (Forrest Tucker) in the Alps. Directed by Morton DaCosta, the result is stagey and overlong, but nothing distracts from Russell's delightfully exuberant performance as a self-centered extrovert whose loving concern for her nephew overcomes her wacky sense of propriety. Comic treatment of serious subjects, including an unwed pregnancy. A-III (PG) U

Author, Author (1982) Armenian-American playwright (Al Pacino), left by his wife (Tuesday Weld) with five children on his hands, finds another woman (Dyan Cannon) to help him get through it all. While pleasant enough, director Arthur Hiller's romantic comedy is not especially funny and offers an intemperate moral outlook, viewing adultery and divorce as an inevitable part of self-development. A-III (PG) A

Autumn Afternoon, An (1973) Japanese production about the transient joys of family life and the loneliness of parents after children leave home. Its story is of a widower (Chishu Ryu) who realizes that if his daughter devotes any more of her time to him, it will ruin her life. With his encouragement she eventually marries and after the wedding, the father returns home to the form of loneliness he has anticipated throughout the movie. Directed by Yasujiro Ozu, it is a movie rich in the rhythm of life, the warmth of humanity and the web of relationships that sustain any individual. A-I (nr) A

Autumn Sonata (1978) Ingmar Bergman's bleak examination of a middle-aged woman (Liv Ullmann) and her relationship with her mother (Ingrid Bergman). What results is a film long on talk and short on characterization and dramatic action. Fine acting throughout, but the mother-daughter conflict may be too depressing for young people. A-III (PG) AA

Avalanche (1978) Scorning all ecological considerations, an entrepreneur (Rock Hudson) builds a luxurious ski resort on a Colorado mountainside, hoping to impress his estranged wife (Mia Farrow) enough to effect a reconciliation. With ludicrous dialogue and shallow characterizations, director Corey Allen's run-of-the-mill disaster movie deserves to be buried in the avalanche that follows. Nudity and suggestive sexual behavior. O (PG) 15

Avalanche Express (1979) Cold War thriller in which CIA agents (Lee Marvin and Linda Evans) try to spirit a defecting head of Soviet intelligence (Robert Shaw) out of Italy by train. Noisy ambushes, counterspy intrigue and conventional violence lets the steam out of the plot. Director Mark Robson's last film lacks humor and genuine excitement using its climactic avalanche sequence midway derailing most of attempts at tension that follow. A-II (PG)

Avalon (1990) Multi-generational saga about a Russian Jewish immigrant (Armin Mueller-Stahl) who joins his four brothers in 1914 Baltimore, embraces life in his new land and watches their extended family, especially his son (Aidan Quinn), pursue the American Dream. Writer-director Barry Levinson's tribute to family values is well-acted and its positive message is welcome, but its impact is blunted by the heavily nostalgic and sentimental treatment of the characters. A-I (PG) U

Avanti! (1972) American businessman (Jack Lemmon), in attempting to bring his father's remains back to the U.S. after the old man's death in an auto accident at an Italian resort, falls for the woman (Juliet Mills) his father has been meeting there for the last 10 years. Director Billy Wilder bludgeons the situation with some rather unfunny black humor, a good deal of vulgarity, much rough language and a bit of gratuitous nudity. O (R) A

Awakening, The (1980) The mummy of a dead Egyptian queen tries to fulfill an ancient prophecy with devastating consequences for the family of the archeologist (Charlton Heston) who opened her tomb. The best asset of director Mike Newell's plodding horror story is the location photography of the Valley of the Kings. Implications of incest and some gore. A-III (R) 15

Awakenings (1990) Refusing to give up on his chronically catatonic patients, a caring doctor (Robin Williams) experiments with a new drug that brings a man (Robert de Niro) out of a trance-like state after 30 years. Director Penny Marshall's sensitive, fact-based drama brings the viewer on a moving, emotional odyssey made all the more poignant by superior performances all around. Minimal rough language. A-II (PG-13) 12

B

Babar: The Movie (1989) In a delightful, animated version of the children's books by Jean and Laurent de Brunhoff, King Babar recalls for his own kids how as a boy he saved Elephantland from the rhinos and became an unlikely hero. Director Alan Bunce's Canadian production underscores the value of commitment to friends and family, while Babar's fears in an alien jungle will be identifiable to young children just beginning to explore unfamiliar turf. The movie will enjoy a long life as a family video. A-I (G)

Babe, The (1992) Sprawling saga of baseball great George Herman "Babe" Ruth (John Goodman) from his youth in a home for "incorrigibles" through his exploits on and off the field to his final turn at bat in 1935. Directed by Arthur Miller, the emphasis is less on Ruth's record-setting career than on the simple-minded character whose antics and indiscretions made him one of the era's more colorful personalities. Discreet treatment of infidelity, a bedroom scene and some coarse language. A-II (PG)

Babe Ruth Story, The (1948) In his portrayal of baseball's fabled slugger, William Bendix can't do much with the hollow heroics and phony sentimentality of a bogus script. Director Roy Del Ruth makes mincemeat out of big league baseball and applesauce out of the Bambino's exploits on and off the field. For undemanding fans of the national pastime. A-I (br)

Babes in Toyland (1961) Disappointing Disney adaptation of the Victor Herbert operetta in which Mary Quite Contrary (Annette Funicello) is saved from the clutches of the villainous Barnaby (Ray Bolger) by a silly pair of apprentice toymakers (Gene Sheldon and Henry Calvin). Directed by Jack Donohue, the live-action musical works hard to create the fantasy of a fairy tale world but the result lacks the fun and charm of the 1934 Laurel and Hardy version ("March of the Wooden Soldiers"). The nursery rhyme characters and special effects will keep the children entertained but hold only sporadic interest for their elders. A-I (nr)

Babette's Feast (1988) Screen version of a story by Isak Dinesen, set in a rugged Danish fishing village in 1871, shows the impact of a French housekeeper (Stephane Audran) on two pious sisters who carry on their late father's work as pastor of a dwindling religious flock. The conclusion follows the preparation and consumption of an exquisite French meal, with focus on its sensual and religious implications and its healing effect on the austere sect and the Frenchwoman who prepares it. Danish director Gabriel Axel's low-key and understated work is rich with detail and fine, controlled performances. Subtitles. Cerebral treatment. A-II (G) U

Baby Blue Marine (1976) World War II bootcamp washout (Jan-Michael Vincent) pretends to be a Marine Ranger and is received as a hero in a small Colorado town. When a waitress (Glynnis O'Connor) falls for him, he has to prove his courage. Although the story is abundantly sentimental, director John Hancock warmly evokes the people and the period, the acting is good and the result is a fairly entertaining movie. A-II (PG) A

Baby Boom (1987) High-powered businesswoman (Diane Keaton) chooses the transforming love of motherhood and the ego boost of self-employment when she inherits a baby whose parents have died tragically. Director Charles Shyer's wry and insightful situation comedy has the good sense to affirm that new life is more important than new clients. A-II (PG)

Baby, It's You (1983) Bright daughter of a Jewish doctor (Rosanna Arquette) and the son of working-class Catholic parents (Vincent Spano) fall in love when they're high school seniors in Camden, N.J., in the late 1960s. Director John Sayles's perceptive, compassionate, if uneven, movie is made memorable by an absolutely pitch-perfect performance by Arquette and very good acting by Spano. Some needlessly graphic sex scenes and nudity. O (R) 15

Baby Love (1969) Psychotic teenager (Linda Hayden) is taken into a wealthy London home where she proceeds to destroy each member of the family out of resentment against the father who had had an affair with her own mother (Diana Dors). Alistair Reid directs the British production as if it were a manual on sexual pathology ranging from attempted rape to lesbianism, with plenty of nudity and little concern for characterization, consistent motivation or common sense. O (R) 18

Baby Maker, The (1970) Barbara Hershey plays a freethinking hippie who agrees to bear a child for a couple who want a baby at least half theirs (the wife is infertile). Writer-director James Bridges provides an ending in which the wife is now insecure about her husband's affection, the husband has fallen for the girl and she realizes she wants to keep the child after all. Because the basic immorality of the arrangement is never addressed, their various disappoints seem hollow and crass. O (R) 18

Baby: Secret of the Lost Legend (1985) American couple (William Katt and Sean

Young) exploring in Africa discover a cute baby brontosaurus, which they later reunite with mama from whom it had been separated by some villains. Directed by B.W.L. Norton, it's a pleasant enough adventure tale for most age groups. A violent battle scene and some mild vulgarity. A-II (PG)

Baby, Take a Bow (1934) Little Shirley Temple gets her first starring role as a pre-schooler who recovers the jewels her father (James Dunn) is accused of stealing, then helps nab the real thief. Directed by Harry Lachman, the formula melodrama has little interest other than its Depression-era family setting and, of course, the bubbly presence of its precocious star. Brief violence endangering a child. A-I (br) U

Baby the Rain Must Fall (1964) Paroled convict (Steve McQueen) returns to his wife (Lee Remick) but her love and encouragement are not enough to reform his violent ways. Directed by Richard Mulligan, the narrative never quite jells into an understandable situation, though the backcountry locales and characters provide some interest. A-II (br) A

Bachelor Mother (1939) Flimsy romantic comedy revolves around a shopgirl (Ginger Rogers) who finds an abandoned infant, then tries to convince her boss (David Niven) that she's not the baby's mother. Directed by Garson Kanin, the complications arising from this comic premise are broadly farcical yet always related to the inevitable sentimental ending. Veiled references to unwed motherhood. A-II (br) A

Bachelor Party (1984) Prospective bridegroom Tom Hanks has a tasteless time with crude friends in director Neil Israel's sex farce full of gross, unfunny jokes, exploitative nudity and demeaning raps about women. O (R) 18

Back Roads (1981) A prostitute (Sally Field) and a cheerful down-and-outer (Tommy Lee Jones) hit the road for California, and in the course of their misadventure, fall in love. Under Martin Ritt's direction the performances are appealing, but the basic narrative has an air of sentimental romanticism. Its soapy mix of sexuality and occasional violence is disappointingly emphasized. A-III (R) AA

Back to Bataan (1945) World War II melodrama of an American officer (John Wayne) organizing an underground movement against the Japanese occupation of the Philippines, it pays tribute to the contribution of these guerrillas in the liberation of their homeland. Directed by Edward Dmytryk, the patriotic derring-do of the Filipino resistance fighters begins and ends with the freeing of Allied prisoner-of-war camps. Wartime violence and national stereotypes. A-II (br) A

Back to School (1986) Rodney Dangerfield provides his special brand of uncouth humor in this story about a self-made millionaire who returns to college to help his son but finds that there are some things money can't buy. Alan Metter's direction keeps things moving in a somewhat tame sophomoric comedy about higher education. Brief instance of nudity and a bit of foul language. A-III (PG-13) 15

Back to the Beach (1987) Frankie Avalon and Annette Funicello return to the seashore and discover that the chaste relationships of the 1950s have evolved into the sexual alliances of the 1980s. Fanciful nostalgic trip from director Lyndall Hobbs is consistently upbeat, but accepting of the plot's implied premarital sex while offhandedly affirming the virtues of enduring marriage and fidelity. A-III (PG)

Back to the Future (1985) Above-average entertainment about a teenager (Michael J. Fox) who is transported back through time and obliged to serve as matchmaker for his parents or face retroactive nonexistence. A major problem is that his mother-to-be finds him far more attractive than she does his father-to-be. Directed by Robert Zemeckis, it is funny and clever with a bit of genuine sentiment, that unfortunately is marred by casual profanity, the depiction of violence as manly and, though there is no depiction of it, an implicit acceptance of sexual promiscuity as standard teenage behavior. A-III (PG)

Back to the Future Part II (1989) Mediocre sequel with the time-traveling doctor (Christopher Lloyd) takes Marty McFly (Michael J. Fox) and his girlfriend (Elizabeth Shue) to the year 2015 to save Marty's son (also Fox) from the ravages of destiny and then back to 1955 to stop the growing power of archvillain Biff (Thomas F. Wilson). Director Robert Zemeckis makes an empty show of technical wizardry out of a nonsensical script that features a succession of product endorsements, including a trailer for Part III. Minimal rough language laced with incidental sexual innuendos. A-II (PG)

Back to the Future Part III (1990) Tame, tired second sequel finds Marty (Michael J. Fox) transported to the Old West of 1885 where his professor pal (Christopher Lloyd) has fallen in love but is about to take a bullet in the back. With little more to go on than cardboard characters, cartoon situations and special effects that have by now grown stale, the team of writer Bob Gale and director Robert Zemeckis can't quite triplicate the sense of fun and ingenuity that made the original so appealing. Minimal street language and mild, cartoon-like violence. A-II (PG)

Backdraft (1991) Deep-rooted conflicts boil over when a rookie Chicago firefighter (William Baldwin) is placed under the command of his estranged brother (Kurt Russell) during the investigation of a string of arson-related murders. With the terrifying nature of fire emerging as the real star of the movie, director Ron Howard ambitiously tackles a relationship story, a murder mystery and a special effects action movie with modest success. Some grisly shots of charred bodies, very brief nudity, fleeting sexual innuendo, occasional fisticuffs and intermittent rough language. A-III (R) 15

Backtrack (1969) Standard western directed by Earl Bellamy in which a cowboy on his way to Mexico to buy some cattle gets involved with a trio of Texas Rangers in a desperate battle with Mexican bandits. Stylized violence. A-II (G)

Bad Behaviour (1993) Low-key comedy-drama set in London where a long-married Irish couple (Stephen Rea; Sinead Cusack), tired with the daily grind of work and parenting, go through a restless phase in their marriage with good-humored impatience. Working without a script, director Les Blair gets convincing, down-to-earth performances from the actors meandering through droll slice-of-life situations that ring true to the discontents of mid-life malaise and the comforts of marital commitment. An implied sexual encounter, some heavy drinking and occasional rough language. A-III (nr) 15

Bad Boys (1983) Sean Penn stars as a vicious young criminal sent to a reformatory in this brutal exploitation movie trying to pass itself off as socially significant. The uninspired direction of Richard Rosenthal of a cliche-littered script owes little to real life and everything to some five decades of Hollywood prison movies. Bereft of moral or social perspective, it places a heavy emphasis on violence and vengeance within the gruesome context of prison life. O (R) 18

Bad Company (1969) French production composed of two dramatic variations on a single theme: loneliness is only masked by the companionship of equally lonely pals. Director Jean Eustache skillfully communicates the desperate bravado that hides the gnawing uncertainties of the immature youths in these two stories. Viewers may be put off by the movie's drab documentary style and some gross sexual language but none will be unmoved by the pathetic nature of these young lives. A-IV (nr)

Bad Company (1972) Clean-cut Pennsylvanian youth (Barry Brown), fleeing conscription during the Civil War, joins up with a youthful band of Missouri toughs (led by Jeff Bridges) and as they make their way West, he becomes as adept as any of them at robbing banks and killing hombres. Directed by Robert Benton, its morality tale is not very profound but the period piece is beautifully mounted and painstakingly detailed. One wonders, however, if all the cursing and updated sex talk is really credible for teenagers in 1862. A-IV (PG) X

Bad Day at Black Rock (1955) Morality tale in the form of a tense thriller set in a small Western town whose residents are forced to face their guilty past when a one-armed stranger (Spencer Tracy) arrives in 1945 asking for the whereabouts of a Japanese-American farmer. Director John Sturges gets much suspense from the uneven odds against the lone, handicapped outsider confronted by increasingly hostile locals (Robert Ryan, Lee Marvin and Ernest Borgnine). Growing menace and brief but painfully effective violence. A-II (br)

Bad Influence (1990) Stylish, menacing and perverse thriller about a cunning drifter (Rob Lowe) who lures a wimpish yuppie (James Spader) into a decadent life of sex, lies and murder. Director Curtis Hanson chillingly develops the cat-and-mouse relationship between his two doomed protagonists in a story updating the Faust legend to modern-day Los Angeles. Rough language, recreational drug use, some grisly violence and several explicit sexual scenes with nudity. O (R) 18

Bad Lieutenant (1992) Rancid melodrama about the crackup of a New York City police detective (Harvey Keitel) who's over his head in gambling debts, drugs and sex, all of which is compounded by self-pity and a warped sense of moral guilt. Director Abel Ferrara's disjointed exercise in the emotional turbulence of going over the edge lacks credibility and leads nowhere. Excessive violence, graphic sex, substance abuse and rough language. O (NC-17) 18

Bad Man's River (1973) Tame Italian western with Gina Lollobrigida as a shady lady whose hobby is bilking amorous males (among them, Lee Van Cleef and James Mason) of whatever they're worth. Director Gene Martin stages a lot of forgettable action involving a sheriff's posse, a horde of revolutionary banditos and the Mexican Army. Waste of time. A-III (PG)

Bad Medicine (1985) Misfit American students (led by Steve Guttenberg and Julie Hagerty) attend a bogus medical school in Central America. Director Harvey Miller's movie fails both as social satire and as broad comedy, offering little more than some insulting humor pointed at Hispanic stereotypes along with bad jokes about incest and drug abuse. O (PG) 15

Bad News Bears, The (1976) Walter Matthau stars as a former minor leaguer who takes over a hopelessly misdirected and inept Little League baseball team and makes it a winner. Under Michael Ritchie's direction, the children are cute but used to communicate a cynical, albeit humorous, critique of middle-class values. Profanity, especially from the mouths of children, not exemplary image making. O (PG) A

Bad News Bears Go to Japan, The (1978) The third and least accomplished in the series celebrating the exploits of the inept but lovable and cunning Little League team features Tony Curtis as a somewhat unsavory promoter who hopes to exploit the exhibition game he sets up for the Bears in Tokyo. Director John Berry keeps the language pretty much under control, but Curtis's visit to a Geisha house is sexually suggestive. A-III (PG)

Bad News Bears in Breaking Training, The (1977) An estranged father (William Devane) of one of the team's players takes the Bears to the Astrodome for a taste of Big League atmosphere, but the film's language is anything but tasteful. Director Michael Pressman's sequel, like the original, is too cynical in its view of human foibles to provide solid family entertainment. A-III (PG) A

Bad Timing: A Sensual Obsession (1980) Director Nicolas Roeg's coldly somber account of obsessive love in modern Vienna stars Art Garfunkel as a smug, domineering psychiatrist and Theresa Russell (whose performance gives the movie the only life it has) as an unstable American woman. Some very explicit sex scenes. O (X/R) 18

Badge 373 (1973) New York City detective (Robert Duvall), suspended from the force pending an investigation into the death of a Puerto Rican drug pusher, becomes a one-man crime-stopper. Director Howard Koch places his violent action in the slums and dives of the big city, showing in gritty detail racism, graft, greed and venality on every human level. Add constant coarse language and seamy situations, and the result is a cynical view of humanity. O (R) X

Badlands (1974) Fact-based story of a drifter (Martin Sheen) who takes his teenage sweetheart (Sissy Spacek) on a bizarre shooting spree across South Dakota and Montana in the 1950s. Director Terrence Malik presents a panoramic view of American life and myths, looking at the reality and the fiction behind the American Dream from the perspective of two archetypal characters. It is a dark and troubling vision with senseless violence at its core. A-III (PG) 18

Badman's Country (1958) Low-budget Western teams ex-sheriff Pat Garrett (George Montgomery) with Wyatt Earp (Buster Crabbe), Bat Masterson (Gregory Wolcott) and Buffalo Bill Cody (Malcolm Atterbury) in saving Abilene from Butch Cassidy (Neville Brand) and his Wild Bunch. While director Fred F. Sears provides matinee thrills for the small fry, older viewers may find the outlandish collection of characters something of a hoot. Stylized violence. A-I (br) U

Bagdad Cafe (1988) Lovely little fable about the restorative powers of love and friendship set at the Bagdad Cafe, a rundown truckstop, luncheonette and motel in the desert outside Las Vegas. German director Percy Adlon tracks the unlikely friendship between a German tourist (Marianne Sagebrecht) and the Bagdad's proprietor (CCH Pounder), a black single mother. Also in focus are the Cafe's oddball regulars, including an old Hollywood set painter (Jack Palance) who falls for the tourist. Much profanity and some nudity in several brief scenes involving an artist's model. A-III (PG)

Ball of Fire (1942) Uneven romantic comedy about 8 erudite professors (led by Gary Cooper) whose work writing an encyclopedia is disrupted by a burlesque queen (Barbara Stanwyck) hiding from the D.A. seeking an indictment of her gangster boyfriend (Dana Andrews). Directed by Howard Hawks, the fish-out-of-water plot generates some smiles but never quite measures up to the comic potential of the situation which increasingly falters into sentimental melodrama. Romantic complications and comic menace. A-II (br) U

Ballad of a Soldier (1960) A 19-year-old soldier, on a six-day furlough, makes his way home through the war-torn Russian countryside, encountering a variety of people, each with his or her own unique experience of World War II. Director Grigori Chukhrai avoids the blatant Soviet propaganda of previous Russian exports while fashioning a warm and humanistic tribute to the integrity and goodness of ordinary people. A-II (br) U

Ballad of Cable Hogue, The (1970) Going to some absurd extremes is director Robert Altman's offbeat, turn-of-the-century western about a man's last stand against the machine and the alienation that comes with it. Some violence, bawdiness and profanity undercut Jason Robards' warmly credible performance. O (R) AA

Ballad of Gregorio Cortez, The (1983) Fact-based movie tells the story of Gregorio Cortez, an Hispanic-American (Edward James Olmos), who in 1901 in Gonzales, Texas, shoots a sheriff when a mistake made by an interpreter turns a question into a threat. He flees for the Mexican border, pursued by a huge posse led by Texas Rangers, but surrenders when he learns that his wife and children are being held in prison.

Director Robert M. Young's sensitive, restrained, beautifully photographed movie does justice to both sides in this clash of cultures. There is brief, if graphic, violence. A-II (PG)

Ballad of Josie, The (1967) Director Andrew McLaglen's plotless western stars dungareed Doris Day and offers little else. The form of a ballad is simple and episodic whereas the movie, unfortunately, is merely simple-minded and fragmented. A-I (br) U

Ballad of Little Jo, The (1993) Spurned by her proper Bostonian father after bearing an illegitimate child, a woman (Suzy Amis) ends up alone in a mining town in the Old West where she forges a reclusive, hardworking life disguised as a man, eventually finding love with her Chinese cook (David Chung) when he discovers her secret and plays along. Writer-director Maggie Greenwald shatters the Hollywood image of the heroic male Westerner with a heavy-handed but provocative feminine perspective that is sympathetic in its treatment of women and immigrants. Some violence and bedroom scenes, fleeting nudity and occasional opium use. A-III (R) 15

Ballad of Orin, The (1979) Japanese movie, set in the early part of this century, in which a blind girl raised by blind women becomes a social outcast after being raped, until she is befriended by an army deserter, the only person not to take advantage of her. Director Masahiro Shinoda uses the lyric tale as a vehicle of social criticism directed against Japanese militarism and the inferior status of women. Several restrained scenes of sexual activity. A-III (nr)

Ballad of the Sad Cafe, The (1991) Disappointing adaptation of Carson McCullers' twisted love story of a strong, independent woman (Vanessa Redgrave) in a Southern rural community during the Depression whose downfall is engineered by a dwarfed hunchback (Cork Hubbert) she takes into her home and the husband (Keith Carradine) she threw out on their wedding night. Directed by Simon Callow, the narrative is slow and portentous, the characters unappealing and the conclusion heavy-handed and unenlightening. Brutalizing fistfight between the protagonists and minimal rough language. A-III (PG-13) 15

Baltimore Bullet (1980) Moderately funny comedy about a master pool hustler (James Coburn) who takes on a young protege (Bruce Boxleitner) in order to fulfill the veteran's dream of getting revenge on the greatest pool sharpster of them all (Omar Sharif). Sexual scenes played in a leering and demeaning manner make this Robert Ellis Miller directed road show with Ronee Blakley unsuitably vulgar. O (PG) 15

Bambi (1942) Walt Disney's classic animated feature conveys the simplicity, charm and excitement of Felix Salten's novel, especially in its appealing characterization of Thumper, Flower and all the others who inhabit the young deer's forest world. The story has some intense moments, notably the forest fire sequence and the death of Bambi's mother, though in a context not beyond the resources of most young viewers. A-I (G) U

Bambina (1976) Insensitive Italian comedy about a con artist who tries to exploit a retarded teenage girl but who winds up marrying her instead. Vestiges of humanism and serious intent are overridden by distasteful treatment of mental retardation. O (R)

Bamboo Gods and Iron Men (1974) Honeymooning in the Orient, a black American couple (James Iglehart and Shirley Washington) get mixed up with a ruthless gang. The inept Philippine production, clumsily directed by Cesar Gallardo, spices up its dreary martial arts violence with a massage parlor sequence. O (R)

Bamse (1970) Swedish import about a young man who falls in love with his dead father's mistress (Grynet Molvig) but she does not reciprocate his affections. The situation is far from being morally or psychologically healthy, but it is handled with restraint and artistic sensitivity. A-III (GP)

Banana Peel (1964) Enjoyable French crime spoof about a gang of con artists (notably Jeanne Moreau and Jean-Paul Belmondo) trying their best to outswindle each other. Directed by Marcel Ophuls, the plot doesn't add up to much but it's fast-paced and good-natured. Subtitles. Comic violence and sexual references. A-III (br)

Bananas (1971) Woody Allen's patchwork comedy is loosely tied to a Latin American revolution that serves as the excuse for the standard fare of tasteless insult and irreverence, chock full of gratuitous nonsense dragged in seemingly because there was still a little film in the camera. As those familiar with Allen's approach might expect, religious orthodoxy comes in for its share of ecumenical jibes that many will find needlessly offensive. O (GP) 15

Band Wagon, The (1953) Classy backstage musical in which a veteran Hollywood hoofer (Fred Astaire) tries to revive his flagging career by starring in a Broadway musical comedy authored by old pals (Nanette Fabray and Oscar Levant), but the production lays an egg after its pretentious director (Jack Buchanan) adds a serious Faustian theme and a temperamental ballet dancer (Cyd Charisse). Director Vincente Minnelli's loving spoof of show business serves up a delightful mix of Howard Dietz-Arthur

Schwartz songs, including "That's Entertainment," "Dancing in the Dark" and "I Love Louisa," grand production ensembles ranging from ballet to tap and the show-stopping "Triplets" number with Astaire, Fabray and Buchanan as manic toddlers. Mild romantic complications. A-II (br) U

Bandits (1988) Sentimental but stylish French mystery-romance about an aging criminal (Jean Yanne), his daughter (Marie-Sophie L.) and a handsome, daring young crook (Patrick Bruel). Though Claude LeLouch's direction tends to be slick and glossy, there is some substance to the characters and their feelings. Several scenes of violence, brief nudity and implied sexual situations. A-III (nr)

Bandolero (1968) Uneven western starring Jimmy Stewart and Dean Martin as brothers who redeem their shady past but who finally redeem themselves in a battle against Mexican bandits. Directed by Andrew V. McLaglen, the characterizations are interesting, women are treated in a positive fashion and the humor is sly and refreshing. Some vulgar language and violent climax. A-III (G) 15

Bang Bang Gang, The (1972) Relentlessly brutal, sex-obsessed exploitation movie directed by one Van Guylder, which details the rural escapades of two amateur gangster couples in the 1920s. O (X/R)

Bang, Bang, You're Dead (1966) Standard espionage story directed by Don Sharp in which an American (Tony Randall) gets swept away by romance and intrigue in Morocco. Stylized violence and a bedroom scene. A-III (br)

Bang the Drum Slowly (1973) Director John Hancock's humorous and touching portrait of a young baseball player who wants to play one last season before he dies made Robert De Niro a name to remember. Michael Moriarity co-starred as the best friend who shares his hopes and pains. Realistic but sensitive treatment of terminal illness. A-II (PG) AA

Bank Robber (1993) Vapid surrealistic tale written and directed by Nick Mead features a moronic bank robber (Patrick Dempsey) hiding out in a seedy hotel room where he is troubled by real and imaginary visitors. Explicit sex scenes, violence, drug abuse and rough language. O (NC-17)

Bank Shot (1974) George C. Scott plays a safecracker sprung from jail in order to use his unique skills to direct a bank robbery. Director Gower Champion's fast-paced comedy is a satire on the criminal mind, but its theme may give youngsters the wrong impression that crime pays. A-III (PG)

Banning (1967) Director Don Winston's story of corruption among the operators and affluent members of a California golf club overdoes the plot elements of vice and greed. O (br) A

Barabbas (1962) Uneven costume epic follows the tormented path of the criminal (Anthony Quinn) who, after being freed by Pilate instead of Christ, is sentenced to the sulphur mines in Sicily, brought to Rome to be a gladiator (with Jack Palance as grimacing tutor-adversary) and finally crucified as a Christian under Nero. Directed by Richard Fleischer, the movie begins promisingly with a sequence counterpointing Christ and Barabbas but the religious level gets lost in Quinn's one-note performance as the surly, ever questioning survivor until reemerging in the ironic conclusion. Stylized violence. A-II (br) A

Barbarella (1968) French production about the misadventures of a vulnerable earth woman (Jane Fonda) facing various perils in a science-fiction world where evil has the upper hand. In a movie that is part comic strip and part Marquis de Sade, director Roger Vadim concentrates on the kinky and the unwholesome in this French production. Sexist theme and brief nudity. O (PG) 15

Barbarosa (1982) Country-western singer Willie Nelson plays the title role of a grizzled outlaw who is an unwilling participant in a 30-year old feud with the aristocratic Mexican family into which he married. Gilbert Roland is the patriarch who keeps sending out young men to kill him and Gary Busey is the young farmer with whom he teams and who ultimately receives Barbarosa's mantle. Offbeat concept, mediocre script, but Nelson's performance is fine. Australian director Frank Schepsi's American debut contains restrained violence. A-II (PG)

Barefoot Executive, The (1971) The title character in this Disney spoof is a chimpanzee with an uncanny taste for quality TV programs. An ambitious office boy (Kurt Russell) uses the talents of his monkey friend to become the boy wonder of network programming. The movie is really stolen by dead-panning Wally Cox and a building-ledge sequence as well-timed and suspenseful as Harold Lloyd's silent comedies. A-I (G) U

Barefoot in the Park (1967) Young married couple (Jane Fonda and Robert Redford) live in a five-flight walk-up, which leads to a number of amorous mix-ups. Directed by Gene Saks, Neil Simon's adaptation of his own Broadway hit, offers sure-fire broad comedy with strong supporting cast (Mildred Natwick and Charles Boyer). A-III (br)

Baron Blood (1972) Italian horror movie about an evil medieval baron whose American descendent (Elke Sommer) rejuvenates him to continue his evil doings in the form of an invalid millionaire (Joseph Cotton). Director Mario Bava stresses a fine assortment of torture machines, but the story is a perfectly forgettable bit of nonsense. A-III (PG)

Barquero (1970) Uneven western directed by Gordon Douglas about a ferryman (Lee Van Cleef) who takes on a horde of bandits who want to use and then destroy his barge to delay their pursuers. It proceeds as a battle of wits with some caustic dialogue, amusing characterizations and occasional violence and sexual references. A-III (GP) X

Barren Lives (1969) Brazilian production set in an arid area of the interior where in 1940 a poor family looks for a place to settle and live like human beings instead of like migrant laborers the world over. Stark and unrelieved, filled with the accusing silence of the destitute, this work by director Nelson Pereira dos Santos visualizes a powerful sermon on social justice and the dignity of the human person. A-II (nr)

Barry Lyndon (1975) Delicate screen adaptation of William Makepeace Thackeray's novel about the manners and morals of 18th-century Europe is pictorially exquisite and has an appropriately elaborate musical score. Director Stanley Kubrick pays more attention to setting and mood than to the human dimensions that are part of its story of an ambitious young man (Ryan O'Neal) trying to rise to social prominence. Mature themes. A-III (PG)

Bartleby (1972) Adaptation of Herman Melville's short novel about a perplexed accountant (Paul Scofield) who can neither get his pallid clerk (John McEnery) to do the work desired, nor can he bring himself to fire him. Director Anthony Friedmann's austere movie is faithful to the spirit, if not the flavor, of the original and the acting is superb. However, the decision to update the period the present can only be labeled an interesting failure. A-II (nr) A

Barton Fink (1991) Lured to Hollywood by a fast-talking studio boss (Michael Lerner), a promising playwright (John Turturro) suffers writer's block until his beefy next-door neighbor (John Goodman) provides unexpected inspiration. The writing-directing team of Joel and Ethan Coen have produced a dark satire and stylish evocation of Tinseltown in the 1940s that eventually falters with its morbid imagery. Some gory violence, discreet sexual innuendo and minimal rough language. A-III (R) 15

Basic Instinct (1992) Violent and sordid potboiler has a troubled homicide detective (Michael Douglas) willingly ensnared in an affair with a bisexual murder suspect

(Sharon Stone) who throws suspicion on his police psychiatrist girlfriend (Jeanne Tripplehorn). As directed by Paul Verhoeven, this cat-and-mouse thriller is an empty exercise in audience shock value stressing graphic scenes of rough sex and bloody carnage. Exploitative mix of sex and violence, much nudity, grisly killings and frequent rough language. O (R) 18

Basic Training (1986) This totally offensive sex farce posing as political satire has the look and sense of a badly re-edited, X-rated home videocassette. O (R)

Bat, The (1959) Modest thriller from the Mary Roberts Rinehart story of a mystery writer (Agnes Moorehead) vacationing in a spooky old mansion while the police hunt a missing fortune and a killer dressed as a bat. Directed by Crane Wilbur, the melodramatic proceedings creak along with the usual red herrings and obvious suspects (including Vincent Price) but it adds up to considerable fun for those in the mood. Mild menace and stylized violence. A-II (br) A

Bat 21 (1988) Suspenseful, fact-based story of a high-level intelligence officer (Gene Hackman) who is shot down in the jungles of Vietnam and, lacking firsthand experience with combat survival skills, has to rely upon radio contact with a spotter pilot (Danny Glover) who keeps him going until rescued. Compassionate interracial characterizations by Hackman and Glover and crisp direction by Peter Markle make it one of the better films about Vietnam heroics. Intense but nongratuitous firebombings and individual killings. Some locker-room language. A-III (R) 15

Bataan (1943) World War II melodrama about the battle for the Bataan peninsula where a small group of American soldiers (including Robert Taylor, George Murphy, Thomas Mitchell and Lloyd Nolan) die one by one holding a position against overwhelming enemy forces. Directed by Tay Garnett, the doomed squad is a composite of melting-pot America whose patriotic fervor turns defeat into a moral victory badly needed on the homefront then and of some historical interest today. Much wartime violence and anti-Japanese stereotyping. A-II (br) A

Batman (1966) Movie version of the TV series based on the comic book characters of the Masked Marvel (Adam West) and the Boy Wonder (Burt Ward) have them battling a plot against the United Nations. Directed by Leslie H. Martinson, the very young will find the action exciting and those over 12 may be amused by the movie's consciously heavy-handed and seriocomic approach to the story. A-I (br) U

Batman (1989) Dark, haunting vision of the caped crusader (Michael Keaton) who must battle not only the evil Joker (Jack Nicholson) but the demons left over from his own tragic childhood. Director Tim Burton does not make the eternal fight between good and evil an easy one, but virtuoso performances by the leads and Anton Furst's production design of a Gotham City full of shadowy gothic and modernistic spires make the movie noteworthy. Some grisly comic-book violence and a suggested sexual encounter are too intense for preteens and impressionable younger adolescents. A-III (PG-13) 15

Batman: Mask of the Phantasm (1993) Murky animated movie in which Batman tries to revive a failed romance while chasing after whoever is murdering Gotham gangsters dressed in a Batman-like outfit. Directors Eric Radomski and Bruce W. Timm exhibit a sleek visual style throughout, but the storyline is too cluttered, confusing and menacing for young children while not sophisticated enough for parents. Frequent stylized violence. A-II (PG)

Batman Returns (1992) Bigger isn't better in this overproduced sequel in which Batman (Michael Keaton) must save crumbling Gotham City and himself from the fiendish Penguin (Danny DeVito), a schizophrenic Catwoman (Michelle Pfeiffer) and a power-crazed industrialist (Christopher Walken). Director Tim Burton leaves out the human element of the story in his zeal for mind-boggling mayhem that offers much sound and fury but only signifies the shallowness of Hollywood's interpretation of pop culture. Much stylized violence, some of it quite nasty, and occasionally blatant sexual innuendoes. A-III (PG-13) 12

Batteries Not Included (1987) Failed fantasy about a group of tenement dwellers, headed by an old couple (Jessica Tandy and Hume Cronyn), who are being terrorized by thugs in the pay of a greedy real estate developer until two miniature spaceships come to their rescue. Directed by Matthew Robbins, the alien reproducing metalworks are cute and there are some whimsical special effects, but the fantasy level of this urban melodrama never gets very far off the ground. Some scenes of intense menace and realistic violence. A-II (PG)

Battle Beneath the Earth (1968) Low-budget adventure fantasy directed by Montgomery Tully in which maverick Chinese Reds, undermining the United States with a network of tunnels containing atomic bombs, are stopped by a unit of Marines led by Kerwin Mathews. Stylized violence. A-II (br) U

Battle Beyond the Stars (1980) Young volunteer Richard Thomas goes on a hunt to hire mercenaries to defend a planet threatened with conquest by an intergalactic tyrant. Scripted by John Sayles and directed by Jimmy T. Murakami with some style and humor, it is a moderately entertaining science-fiction action fantasy. Many sexually oriented jokes. A-III (PG)

Battle Command (1976) Old-fashioned war movie of uncertain origin—all the soldiers seem to be Italian no matter what their uniforms—done on a limited budget and with an appalling lack of skill. A-II (PG)

Battle for the Planet of the Apes (1973) Final sequel to the series with Roddy McDowell heading up the ape cast and John Huston as a campy sort of simian Moses. Directed by J. Thompson, the most entertaining sequences are excerpts from the previous movies used as the background of the story. A-II (G) A

Battle in Outer Space (1960) Aliens use the moon for an attack on Earth in this Japanese sci-fi clunker directed by Inoshiro Honda. The stoic heroics of the dubbed characters, cheesy model work and cardboard special effects offer little excitement or interest. A-I (br)

Battle of Algiers, The (1967) The 1954-1958 Algerian struggle for independence from French rule is re-created in this French production directed by Gillo Pontecorvo. Sympathetic to the rebels, yet compromising neither the facts nor the personalities involved, the film's documentary-like authenticity is achieved without resort to actual newsreel footage. It is a remarkable look at the process of revolutionary terror and counter-terror that victimizes ordinary citizens on both sides. A-II (br) X

Battle of Britain (1969) With the fall of France in 1940, Great Britain stood alone against the might of the German air force. The movie pays tribute to the smaller number of British fighter pilots who, in the months that followed, downed so many planes that the Luftwaffe was unable to mount its massive raids. Laurence Olivier, Michael Redgrave and Trevor Howard star in this huge and impressive British production directed by Guy Hamilton. Wartime violence. A-I (G) U

Battle of Chile, The (1978) Documentary on the 1973 overthrow of the Allende government, it shows in painstaking detail the growing agony of a society on the verge of civil war and the inevitable brutal usurpation of power by the military. Assembled from footage smuggled out of Chile and edited in Cuba under the direction of Patricio Guzman, it is a partisan account but one does not have to accept its Marxist politics in examining for oneself the visual record of events showing how the elected government of a constitutional democracy was subverted and overthrown. Some violent actualities. A-III (nr)

Battle of El Alamein, The (1971) Italian-French shoot-em-up World War II movie seen from the Axis point-of-view in which Rommel (Robert Hossein) loses to the superior British forces of Field Marshall Montgomery (Michael Rennie). Directed by Calvin Jackson, it's not strong on characterization but it does have a sturdy string of exciting battle sequences. A-II (GP) PG

Battle of Neretva (1971) Yugoslavian production about the 1943 victory of Tito's Partisans over the German Army re-creates the horror of a ferocious battle and is a tribute to their sacrifices enacted by a large international cast. Directed by Veljko Bulajic, the work is developed with little dramatic punctuation and evokes only mild sympathy and audience identification with the events it portrays. A-II (G) PG

Battle of Okinawa (1973) Japanese re-creation of the ferocious, last-ditch defense of the island of Okinawa by its undermanned garrison. Directed by Kihachi Okamoto, it has a semi-documentary objectivity that distances viewers from the considerable amount of special-effects battle gore and mass suicide by part of the civilian population. A-II (nr)

Battle of the Amazons (1973) Extremely low-budget sexploiter, directed by Alfonso Brescia, features scantily attired, man-hating Amazons in an endless round of battles, sadistic rituals, stylized orgies and gruesome torture scenes. O (R)

Battle of the Bulge (1965) Henry Fonda, Robert Shaw and Robert Ryan star in a big-budget re-creation of the last, desperate German offensive against American forces in December 1944. In an ambitious, wide-ranging epic, director Ken Annakin tries to turn one of the most brutal battles of World War II into star-studded entertainment. Wartime violence. A-I (nr) PG

Battle of the Coral Sea (1959) Captured while gathering intelligence on the Japanese fleet, a U.S. submarine captain (Cliff Robertson) escapes with his crew in time to help win the decisive 1942 naval battle of the title. Directed by Paul Wendkos, the main part of the narrative takes place in a P.O.W. camp where the heroics are standard-issue and the acting perfunctory. Some stylized violence and Japanese stereotyping. A-I (br) U

Battleground (1949) Centering on the dogged resistance of an American infantry unit cut off in the Battle of the Bulge—Hitler's last desperate offensive in the West—the movie makes the most of its cross-section of G.I.s (Van Johnson, John Hodiak, Ricardo Montalban, James Whitmore,

George Murphy, et al.) as representative of the nation's ethnic, regional and social diversity. Veteran director William Wellman keeps the action taut and credible, uses the battlefield's snow-filled terrain to add further misery to the unit's plight and tries to keep his grab-bag collection of civilian-soldiers from turning into super-heroes. Wartime violence and mild sexual references. A-I (br) A

Battlestar Galactica (1979) A fleet of survivors of an alien attack travel through deep space in search of a refuge they call Earth. Lorne Greene is at the helm of the flagship avoiding the dreaded Cylons in this compilation of episodes from the television series. As directed by Richard A. Colla, the only peril is its worshipful portrayal of the military in contrast to a foolish civil government. A-I (PG)

Bawdy Adventures of Tom Jones, The (1976) Dull and unimaginative adaptation of a stage musical based on the Henry Fielding novel. More boring than bawdy, director Cliff Owens has made a sexual burlesque of the original with much sexual innuendo and some partial nudity. O (R) X

Baxter! (1973) British story of a London youngster with a speech defect (Scott Jacoby) who is crushed when his parents ignore his limited speech improvement but his speech therapist (Patricia Neal) stands by him. Director Lionel Jefferies treats his sentimental melodrama with crisp dispatch, some gentle humor and fine performances. It's a bit too serious for the young, but others may find it quite rewarding entertainment. A-II (PG) AA

Beach Red (1967) Directed by and starring Cornel Wilde, the movie attempts to explore the inhumanity of war in the story of a World War II assault on a Pacific island, but it fails by its repetitious emphasis on the realistic details of carnage and its degrading treatment of women in flashbacks. O (br) X

Beaches (1988) The ups and downs of the 30-year friendship between a California blueblood (Barbara Hershey) and a Jewish singer-dancer from the Bronx (Bette Midler) are tracked through rites of passage, life crises, petty jealousies and ultimate tragedy. Director Garry Marshall's positive portrait of a committed friendship overcomes the story's weepy moments with many comedic and rousing musical sequences but gets a tad too sudsy during the poignant climax. Some off-color language and vulgar humor, brief fisti-cuffs and a risque musical number. A-III (PG-13) PG

Bear, The (1989) Glorious nature drama set in turn-of-the-century British Columbia tracks the unlikely companionship of a wounded male Kodiak bear and an orphaned cub, as they explore their natural habitat and fend off two relentless human predators. Director Jean-Jacques Annaud dramatizes the story from the bears' point of view, using impressive wildlife photography to connect these majestic animals to humans in astounding and unforgettable ways. Some bloodied dogs and horses, ongoing menace to the bears and a realistically audible mating sequence may be too intense for very young children. A-I (PG)

Bear and the Doll, The (1971) Rather flat French farce about radio cellist (Jean-Pierre Cassel) preoccupied with providing for a young son and four nieces and apparently the only man in France not willing to fall instantly at Brigitte Bardot's adorable feet. Directed by Michele Deville, there are some amusing moments in this adult comedy, but the two principals seem impossibly mismatched. A-III (GP)

Bear Tooth (1978) Settling into a backwoods cabin, a garrulous old codger (Dub Taylor) and a stray dog spend the winter in director Zack Belcher's low-budget production which has little of interest except the Montana scenery. The result is often pretty to look at but lacks any human depth. A-I (G)

Bears and I, The (1974) A Vietnam veteran (Patrick Wayne) trying to find peace on a remote Indian reservation, unknowingly breaks a tribal taboo when he starts raising three bear cubs whose mother has been killed by a poacher. Disney outdoor adventure directed by Vincent McEveety should please the younger set with its wilderness background and the cute antics of the baby cubs. A-I (G) U

Beast, The (1988) Set in 1981 Afghanistan, the story begins with the brutal destruction of a village by a squadron of Soviet tanks and then follows its aftermath in which a lone, lost tank is stalked by Afghan rebels. Directed by Kevin Reynolds, the gruesome opening massacre is eventually counterpointed with philosophical and psychological conflicts, mainly between the heartless tank commander (George Dzundza) and a young tank driver (Jason Patric) who empathizes with the brutalized Afghans. Extremely graphic violence. A-IV (R)

Beast in the Cellar, The (1971) Pair of dotty spinsters (Beryl Reid and Flora Robson) brick up their draft-age brother in the cellar rather than see him sent off to the Western Front. Director James Kelly's horror movie has its scarey moments, but far too much is given over to the doting sisters trying to rationalize their past errors in rearing their now-mad sibling. Sordid seduction-murder scene. A-III (R) X

Beast Must Die, The (1974) British thriller in which a millionaire (Calvin Lockhart) invites some guests (Peter Cushing, Tom Chadbon, Michael Gambon) to spend a weekend at his remote country estate where everything is wired for sight and sound because the host knows that one of them will turn into a beast when the moon is full. Directed by Paul Annett, the updated werewolf tale offers some novelty and a fair amount of trumped up horror and gore for fans of this kind thing. A-III (PG)

Beast of Blood (1970) Philippine horror movie in which a scientist (John Ashley), searching Blood Island for the crazed creature that shipwrecked him, discovers a mad surgeon (Eddie Garcia) experimenting on human head transplants. Directed by Eddie Romero, the spurting blood, slicing blades and a rape scene will upset the squeamish. O (GP)

Beast of Hollow Mountain, The (1956) An American (Guy Madison) ranching in Mexico faces dastardly rustlers and a special-effects dinosaur. Directed by Edward Nassour and Ismael Rodriguez, the routine Western story is of little interest until the proceedings perk up with a prehistoric monster in a fantasy ending. Mild thrills for pre-schoolers. A-I (br) A

Beast of the Yellow Night (1972) Stone-faced John Ashley and toothy Mary Wilcox team up for some terrible acting and a spot of torrid love-making in a preposterous tale of a vicious army deserter who sells his soul to the devil in a Southeast Asian jungle. Director Eddie Romero packages his low-budget Philippine production of soap-opera sex and disgusting gore with plenty of static dialogue. O (R)

Beat, The (1988) Grim, inner-city drama about some drugged-up, aimless teens who take a turn for the better when they befriend a weird new boy (David Jacobson) who slinks around reciting poetry. They all become poets and are drawn into the boy's mystical fantasy world. Director-writer Paul Mones provides no background on these derelict kids, and no explanation for the boy's spacey behavior. Wall-to-wall profanity, much violence and a clear suggestion of teen sexual promiscuity. O (R)

Beat Street (1984) Skimpy plot, involving the aspirations of young blacks and Hispanics in the Bronx, loosely holds together a series of production numbers, many of which involve break dancing. Director Stan Lathan's lavish production fails because of its pretension and high gloss. Some rough language now and again, but the movie is innocuous for the most part. A-II (PG)

Beau Geste (1966) The French Foreign Legion becomes the refuge for two English brothers (Dean Stockwell and Doug McClure) after the apparent theft of a family jewel worth a fortune. Well-done remake of classic adventure story, the movie is restrained in its treatment of military brutality and the violence inherent to a desert uprising. A-I (br) A

Beautiful Swindlers, The (1967) Cheap European production consists of three stories on the theme of foolish older men being taken advantage of by young seductive women. Sexually exploitative. O (br)

Beauty and the Beast (1991) Enchanting animated fairy tale of a young maiden who rescues her father from a ferocious beast only to fall in love with the creature's gentler qualities. Computer graphics enhance classic Disney animation for eye-pleasing visuals enlivened by rousing musical numbers and delightful characterizations from directors Kirk Wise and Gary Trousdale. Brief scary scenes. A-I (G) U

Bebe's Kids (1992) Dull animated tale in which three bratty kids harass their babysitter (voice of Vanessa Bell Calloway), her little boy and, most of all, her boyfriend (voice of Faizon Love) who is forced to take them all to an amusement park. Under Bruce Smith's direction, the African American characters created by Robin Harris have plenty of sass and brass but neither the story's treatment nor the animation shines. Comic violence and mild sexual innuendo. A-II (PG-13)

Becoming Colette (1992) Dull, plodding picture of the French author Colette (Mathilda May) during her formative years in Paris at the turn of the century married to a hedonistic bounder (Klaus Maria Brandauer) who publishes her writings under his name until she leaves him to embark on her own career. Director Danny Huston turns an interesting subject into a lethargic object lesson in women's rights. Several depictions of sexual encounters with brief nudity. O (R)

Bed and Board (1971) Continuing French saga of Antoine Doinel (Jean-Pierre-Leaud) who, still somewhat delinquent and fumbling, marries his sweetheart (Claude Jade) and gets through the first year of marital adjustment: a change of jobs, the coming of their first child and a test of conjugal fidelity. Director Francois Truffaut has etched a sensitive, compassionate, humorous and exquisitely tasteful picture of the maturation of love and marriage. Whether one has seen the previous two films in the trilogy or not, this will delight, amuse and captivate the imagination. A-III (GP)

Bed-Sitting Room, The (1969) Three years after World War III, which took place in less then two-and-a-half minutes, 20-odd survivors wander around the bizarre remains of London, including such grotesques as Sir Ralph Richardson turning, quite liter-

ally, into a bed-sitting room. Director Richard Lester's screen version of playwright Spike Milligan's surrealistic farce is meant to be a commentary on the horrors of war and middle-class morality, but the result is merely a disappointing jumble of British wit and rude humor. A-III (M) AA

Bedazzled (1968) A shy short-order cook (Dudley Moore) in love with a waitress (Eleanor Moore) sells his soul to a satanic figure (Peter Cook) for seven wishes that turn out hilariously different from what was intended. Director Stanley Donen has reshaped the Faust legend to the cut of contemporary man, though the lust sequence gets a bit too sinful and another satirizing the image of nuns may seem more distasteful than funny. A-IV (br) A

Bedford Incident, The (1965) An American destroyer and a nuclear-armed Soviet submarine are on a collision course that, unless one of them yields, will cause an international incident. Director James B. Harris builds the psychological tension on board the destroyer as its cold-warrior captain (Richard Widmark) comes into conflict with an inquisitive journalist (Sidney Poitier) and others on deck (Martin Balsam, Eric Portman and Wally Cox). Heavy seas for youngsters. A-II (br) A

Bedknobs and Broomsticks (1971) In an English seaside village during World War II, a would-be witch (Angela Lansbury) invokes an army of spectral warriors to rout 20th-century German invaders and takes some trips with three children on her big brass bed. Director Robert Stevenson keeps this Disney musical moving merrily and emphasizes the smiling high spirits of the youngsters. A-I (G) U

Bedlam (1946) Dark tale of London's infamous 18th-century insane asylum to which a sane woman (Anna Lee) is committed in order to silence her criticism of its head keeper (Boris Karloff). Produced by Val Lewton and directed by Mark Robson, the asylum's terrors are only suggested but they work powerfully enough in the imagination to make credible the woman's plight and the viewer's fears. Menacing atmosphere and some brutality. A-II (br)

Bedroom Mazurka (1972) Stale Danish pastry serves up coy breast-and-buttocks nudity with some unintentional humor. A mazurka, by the way, is a spirited Danish folk dance that has nothing to do with this total waste of energy. O (X/R)

Bedroom Window, The (1987) Steve Guttenberg plays a young, carefree executive whose affair with his boss's wife (Isabelle Huppert) ends in her death when a killer-rapist they tried to bring to justice is freed. Director Curtis Hanson's treatment of an engaging, convoluted plot includes brief instances of nudity, profanity and violence, but the themes of dishonesty and betrayal are decidedly for mature audiences. A-III (R) 15

Been Down So Long It Looks Like Up to Me (1971) Episodic melodrama directed by Jeff Young about a college drop-out (Barry Primus) who, disenchanted by his odyssey in the real world, returns to college to mock everything it stands for, take drugs and have sex. It's a bad trip. O (R)

Beethoven (1992) Slap-happy comedy about a fussy father (Charles Grodin) forced to accept a stray St. Bernard into the family, then has to rescue it from the snatches of dognappers and a mad doctor (Dean Jones). Director Brian Levant delivers a likeable, though strictly formula family entertainment. Some strong menace and comic violence. A-II (PG)

Beethoven's Nephew (1988) After winning custody of his teenage nephew (Dietmar Prinz), the composer Beethoven (Wolfgang Reichmann) monitors the boy's every move for 11 years. Director Paul Morrissey's fact-based story suggests more a jealous lover's obsession than extreme parental behavior on Beethoven's part, but these implications are never explored. Some nudity in several heterosexual situations, one of an explicit nature, and a graphic suicide attempt. O (R)

Beethoven's 2nd (1993) Highly contrived canine comedy in which the Newton family dog, Beethoven, and a neighboring St. Bernard have four puppies, which the Newton children try to hide from dear old Dad (Charles Grodin) and a wicked dognapper (Debi Mazur). Rod Daniel directs a cartoon-like sequel peopled with cardboard characters cavorting around the movie's chief attraction, a quartet of adorable puppies. Some menace, adolescent beer drinking and violence played for laughs. A-II (PG) U

Beetlejuice (1988) Good special effects overshadow a silly plot in which a couple of dim-witted ghosts (Alec Baldwin and Geena Davis) reluctantly use the services of a ghoulish demon (Michael Keaton) to scare off the eccentric family who have moved into the ghosts' picturesque New England home. Director Tim Burton's comic fantasy is loud and on the dippy side, with only Keaton's manic performance to maintain interest. Some vulgar language and bloody special effects. A-II (PG) 15

Before Winter Comes (1969) A Russian deserter (Topol) becomes the right-hand man of a British officer (David Niven) responsible for the care of refugees in an Austrian outpost after World War II. Director J. Lee Thompson focuses on the officer's dilemma of following orders to the letter or bending a little to help these displaced persons whose problems are convincingly detailed. A decent little film, but one of the problems is a woman (Anna Karina) who can't say no to anyone in uniform. A-III (PG) A

Beginning of the End (1957) Hokey sci-fi tale of an agricultural specialist (Peter Graves) and a news reporter (Peggie Castle) trying to save Chicago from an invasion of giant locusts before the military nukes them and the city. Directed by Bert I. Gordon, the plot is flimsy, the acting phony and the special effects primitive, though the shot of superimposed grasshoppers on the Wrigley Building is a hoot. A-I (br) A

Beguiled, The (1971) Civil War story in which a wounded Union soldier (Clint Eastwood) takes refuge in a Southern school for ladies whom he must keep beguiled or risk being turned over to the Confederates. Directed by Don Siegel, this murky gothic horror story ends with the captive paying dearly for his ingratitude toward his captors' sick brand of Southern hospitality. In addition to the implied sexual situation, there is an explicit seduction followed by a gruesome amputation scene. A-IV (R) 15

Being There (1980) Slender and austere comic tale directed by Hal Ashby from the screenplay by Jerzy Kosinski about a middle-aged, television-addicted gardener (Peter Sellers) who becomes a national celebrity when the rich and powerful mistake his slow-wittedness and ignorance for profound intelligence. This sardonic commentary about values in the television age has a seduction scene with Shirley MacLaine, which places it in the adult category. A-III (PG) AA

Belated Flowers (1972) Russian director Abram Room has taken a very early, uncharacteristically romantic story by Chekhov and made a simple but moving tale of doomed lovers. Room has fashioned a stylish set piece in which every artifice is used to establish and maintain a lyric mood of idealized romance. A-III (nr)

Believe in Me (1971) Michael Sarrazin plays a promising young intern who gets hooked on amphetamines and Jacqueline Bisset is the girl he takes down the primrose path. Directed by Stuart Hagman, the story is one long TV hospital soap opera, but this one features a number of slow-motion love scenes. O (R) X

Believers, The (1987) Martin Sheen is a detective who saves his son from a ritual death at the hands of a New York City cultist group who derive power from human sacrifices. Director John Schlesinger's flawed, superficial treatment of a serious subject is marred further by graphic shots of naked corpses, bloody animal entrails, some killings and a violent suicide. A-III (R) 18

Bell, Book and Candle (1958) Flat-footed romantic comedy from John Van Druten's play about a comely Manhattan witch (Kim Novak) who casts a spell on an engaged publisher (James Stewart), then falls in love with him. Director Richard Quine plays the romance for cloying sentimentality and fails to find much humor in the situation, despite witches Jack Lemmon, Elsa Lanchester and Hermione Gingold, with Ernie Kovacs as a befuddled authority on the occult. Sexual inferences. A-III (br) U

Bell for Adano, A (1945) Sturdy adaptation of John Hersey's World War II novel in which a U.S. Army officer (John Hodiak) in charge of a liberated Italian town promises to find a replacement for a bell prized by the local community. Directed by Henry King, the story demonstrates the virtues of democracy as well as the common bond of humanity, put over by a good supporting cast, including Gene Tierney as an Italian girl pining for the safe return of her soldier boyfriend. A-II (br) U

Bell Jar, The (1979) Dreary, painful adaptation of the Sylvia Plath autobiography detailing a seemingly well-adjusted college girl's mental breakdown after the death of her father and her rude encounters with the realities of the New York publishing world. Director Larry Peerce resorts to extensive use of nudity groping for the muddled sexual basis for the tragic heroine's problems. O (R) X

Belle de Jour (1968) The marital frigidity of a wealthy Parisian housewife (Catherine Deneuve) is traced to a religiously induced sense of guilt over a childhood incident, which she seeks to expiate by working in a brothel. In this coldly elegant French production, director Luis Bunuel has some surrealistic fun with such themes as sexual perversity among the affluent, middle-class conservative values and traditional concepts of religion. Degrading view of sexuality. O (br) X

Belle of New York, The (1952) Thin musical romance features a turn-of-the-century playboy (Fred Astaire) transformed by his love for a crusading social reformer (Vera-Ellen). Director Charles Walters concentrates on the colorful decor and costumes of the period and the staging of several flashy dance numbers but the flat, predictable storyline is uninvolving and the songs are pleasant but unmemorable. Mild romantic misunderstandings. A-I (br) U

Bells of St. Mary's, The (1945) Director Leo McCarey's sequel to "Going My Way" (1944) pulls out all the emotional stops in a sugary confection that takes happy-go-lucky Fr. O'Malley (Bing Crosby) to a poor parish with a crumbling school run by overworked Sr. Benedict (Ingrid Bergman). Though their conflicting views on education have less to do with the plot than the chasm between their personal relations, Bergman's shining performance as the idealistic nun is still worth watching. Sentimental yet warm picture of Catholic life in an age of innocence. A-I (br) U

Ben (1972) Ben (a rat) moves in with a musician-puppeteer (Lee Harcourt Montgomery) who, though he is recuperating from open heart surgery, exhausts himself trying to protect his new friend from unsympathetic adults. Director Phil Karlson passes the cheese to animal trainer Moe Di Sesso to generate some sympathy for the little fur balls who kill just about everyone but their friendly host. Stylized violence. A-II (PG) X

Ben-Gurion Remembers (1973) Israeli documentary on the 25th anniversary of the embattled state of Israel pays tribute to the unique role played by David Ben-Gurion in its founding. Directed by Simon Hesers, it is a warm, personal portrait of a man not usually known for his congeniality, intermingling documentary footage and reminiscences with friends who today comprise the leadership of the country. A-I (nr)

Ben-Hur (1959) Director William Wyler's classic Hollywood epic about a Jewish prince (Charlton Heston in the title role), betrayed by his boyhood Roman friend (Stephen Boyd), but who finally achieves retribution after suffering many miseries. The conventional melodrama of the narrative is transformed by the grand scale of the spectacle whose highlight is the chariot race with stunts rigged by Yakima Canutt. The principals, moreover, manage to stand out as individuals among all the film's myriad cliches and stereotypes. A-I (G) A

Bend of the River (1952) After escorting a wagon train of settlers to Oregon, two Kansas cowboys (James Stewart and Arthur Kennedy) find themselves on opposite sides in the battle between the new farmers and an influx of gold miners to the area. Directed by Anthony Mann, the pioneer setting is colorful and the action plentiful but too many subplots weaken the dramatic focus. Stylized violence and romantic situations. A-I (br)

Beneath the Planet of the Apes (1970) Lame sequel has astronaut (James Franciscus) reaching the bombed-out earth where the ape people are warring with the subterranean remnants of the human race, a skinless colony of people who worship "The

Holy Bomb" and these deformed humans destroy the planet in the final scene. Directed by Ted Post, it lacks the wit, excitement and ingenuity of the original's warning to war-mongering, damage-prone humanity. A-III (G) 15

Benjamin (1968) Though the French production directed by Michel Deville is a handsomely mounted period piece, this movie about the initiation of an innocent young man (Pierre Clementi) into the depraved society of 18th-century aristocrats concentrates on sexual suggestiveness and titillation at the expense of any meaningful comment. O (X)

Benji (1974) Tough little mongrel maintains his independence by begging food only from people who attach no strings and ultimately becomes the hero of his small town by foiling some kidnappers. Directed by Joe Camp, it is light, wholesome entertainment with enough tension and false leads to keep children on the edge of the seats as the little dog toughs it out and wins on his own. A-I (G) U

Benji the Hunted (1987) Stranded in a hostile wilderness after his master's boat capsizes, the courageous canine finds a new home for some orphaned mountain lion cubs. The Disney production directed by Joe Camp creates a sense of wildlife authenticity and tells the story without any need for dialogue or voice-over narration. Charming simple tale for the very young. A-I (G) U

Benny & Joon (1993) Offbeat love story with a mentally ill, homebound young woman (Mary Stuart Masterson) falling for a would-be mime (Johnny Depp) who encourages her independence despite the objections of her fiercely overprotective brother (Aidan Quinn). While director Jermiah Chechik clearly romanticizes the two social outcasts, the movie's charm lies in its intermingling of sweet pathos, whimsical humor and strong sense of family and caring. An implied sexual encounter and an instance of rough language. A-III (PG) 12

Benny Goodman Story, The (1955) Standard Hollywood biography of the popular bandleader (Steve Allen) from his youth in Chicago to his heyday in the 1940s, with Donna Reed as the romantic interest. Directed by Valentine Davies, the treatment is strictly superficial but the nostalgic period music is good and plentiful. Not for fidgety youngsters. A-I (br) U

Bernadette (1987) The story of Bernadette Soubirous and her visions of a beautiful lady in white at a grotto near Lourdes in 1858 is dramatically portrayed in this French production by veteran film director Jean Delannoy. Sidney Penny, a 17-year-old American actress, portrays the 15-year-old Bernadette with charming down-to-earth innocence and the screen adaptation is simple, direct and faithful to the religious drama of the events portrayed. The result is an uncompromising, spiritually moving picture of a young woman's faith, a story that still has meaning for contemporary viewers. Dubbed into English. A-I (PG) U

Berserk (1967) Lurid story of a series of gruesome murders in a circus run by Joan Crawford is directed by Jim O'Connolly. Macabre atmosphere and violence. A-III (br) X

Bert Rigby: You're a Fool! (1989) Clumsy show biz rags-to-riches fable starring British song-and-dance man Robert Lindsay who succeeds best in mimicking such screen greats as Chaplin, Keaton, Kelly and Astaire. However, the family-oriented musical numbers are poorly staged and writer-director Carl Reiner injects too much sexual innuendo and vulgar references, name-dropping and product endorsements in a misguided attempt to be trendy. Some rough language, brief nudity. A-III (R) 15

Best Defense (1984) Supremely unfunny vehicle for the irreverent humor of comedian Eddie Murphy involves the development of a supertank for the military. Director Willard Huyck tries desperately to revive the brain-dead comedy by resorting to graphic sex and tasteless jokes about sex and the Third World. O (R) 18

Best Foot Forward (1943) Flimsy Broadway musical comedy about a fading movie star (Lucille Ball) sneaking into a military prep school's graduation ball as a publicity stunt. Director Edward Buzzell stretches out the meager plot with some good period music by Harry James and orchestra, peppy comic bits from Nancy Walker and a frivolous patriotic ending. Mild sexual innuendo. A-II (br) U

Best Friends (1975) Low-budget road picture about two discharged soldiers making their way home in a camper accompanied by their girlfriends. Whenever the action drags, a bit of violence or sexual exploitation is brought in. O (R) PG

Best Friends (1982) Burt Reynolds and Goldie Hawn play a happy Hollywood couple, a screenwriting team, who seem to have everything going for them until they put it all in jeopardy by deciding to get married. Director Norman Jewison offers a somewhat cynical comedy about the institution of marriage without insight into the values it represents. A-III (PG)

Best House in London, The (1969) A mansion in Victorian London, donated for the worthy purpose of serving as a residence for the rehabilitation of wayward girls, is soon turned into a high class bordello by a notorious profligate (David Hemmings). Directed by Philip Saville, this witless, tasteless satire on the hypocrisy of the Victorian Age is excessive in its use of nudity and sexual references. O (X)

Best Intentions, The (1992) Episodic Swedish family saga set in the early 1900s focuses on the troubled courtship and stormy marriage of a dour, strong-willed Lutheran minister (Samuel Froler) who had grown up in poverty and his bright, willful bride (Pernilla August) whose wealthy family had opposed their wedding. As directed by Bille August, Ingmar Bergman's autobiographical script offers a moody meditation on the emotional affinity of two completely opposite temperaments whose bond of love withstands the resulting clashes of personality and inevitable misunderstandings only because they are willing to forgive one another and go on together. Subtitles. Restrained scene of premarital relations with brief nudity, several scenes of domestic violence, a suicide and a life-threatening scene involving a small child. A-III (nr)

Best Little Whorehouse in Texas, The (1982) Broadway musical about a Texas brothel threatened by a clean-up campaign has been made into a vehicle for Burt Reynolds and Dolly Parton. The characterizations and country music are so lackluster that the virtues of the original must remain a mystery to anyone who has not seen it. Director Colin Higgins resorts to quite a bit of nudity and several fairly graphic bedroom scenes. O (R) 15

Best Man, The (1964) To win presidential nomination at the national convention, an idealistic liberal candidate (Henry Fonda) seeks support from his party's leader (Lee Tracy) but is threatened by the unscrupulous tactics of a conservative rival (Cliff Robertson). Directed by Franklin Schaffner and adapted by Gore Vidal from his own stage play, the political back-room maneuverings seem depressingly familiar, though brightened by some sharply satiric humor. Ambiguous treatment of a candidate's religion. A-IV (br) A

Best of Times, The (1986) Slack comedy about middle-aged out-of-shape losers (Robin Williams and Kurt Russell) who get a second chance to replay the big football game they lost as high school seniors. Starting with some wry, tongue-in-cheek humor, director Roger Spottiswoode lets the comic situation go downhill and the quest of grown men for their lost youth grows ever more tiresome. Much rough language, some sexual innuendo and a passing reference to locker-room drugs. O (PG-13) 15

Best Way, The (1978) From France comes a drab and pale little film devoted to the theme of sexual ambivalence. Director Charles Miller loosely sets the drama in a boys camp in 1960, but provides undeveloped characters in a story about a sexual confrontation between two counselors (Patrick Dewaere and Patrick Bouchitey). Occasional nudity. O (nr)

Best Years of Our Lives, The (1946) Three World War II veterans (sergeant Fredric March, bombardier Dana Andrews and sailor Harold Russell with hooks in place of hands) meet on their way home to resume civilian lives in the same small town where they try to help each other readjust to peacetime. Director William Wyler gives sympathetic treatment to the post-war rehabilitation of returning G.I.s, portraying in fairly realistic detail their career difficulties as well as personal problems with wives and girlfriends (Myrna Loy, Teresa Wright, Virginia Mayo and Cathy O'Donnell). Mature themes, including a broken marriage. A-III (br) U

Betrayal (1983) Screen version of Harold Pinter's play about a love triangle is a pretentious and anemic exercise that hints at profundities that lie too deep for words, but never delivers the goods. The British production under the direction of David Jones squanders a talented cast (Patricia Hodge, Jeremy Irons and Ben Kingsley). Single instance of obscene language. A-III (R) 15

Betrayed (1988) FBI undercover agent (Debra Winger) falls in love with a Nebraska farmer (Tom Berenger) suspected of involvement with a political terrorist group. Director Costa-Gavras achieves some credibility in his fictional portrayal of the shadowy world of American hate groups and there are some tense moments, but the romance is silly and the movie's stance against racism requires a mature perspective. Some intense graphic violence, implied illicit sex, racial slurs and other rough language. A-III (R) 18

Betsy, The (1978) Supremely trashy novel by Harold Robbins, adapted into a supremely trashy movie about the obsession for power, sex and wealth among the upper echelon of the automobile industry (Laurence Olivier, Robert Duvall and Katherine Ross). Director Daniel Petrie's potboiler contains nudity and is lacking completely in moral perspective. O (R) X

Betsy's Wedding (1990) Mildly amusing look at a family's harried preparations for a lavish wedding that the father (Alan Alda) can't afford and the bride-to-be (Molly Ringwald) doesn't want. Written and directed by Alan Alda, the story lacks real dramatic tension, but the characters and situations are believable, even commonplace, resulting in a sweetly bland comedy where everyone compromises so love can endure. Occasional rough language and a brief mob-related shootout. A III (R) 15

Better a Widow (1968) Weak Italian romantic comedy directed by Duccio Tessari about the daughter (Virna Lisi) of a Sicilian Mafia Don and an Englishman (Peter McEnery) who has come to build an oil refinery. Light treatment of murder and sex. A-III (PG)

Better Off Dead (1985) This crass comedy about teenage suicide has the gall to aim itself at teenage audiences and, indeed, proclaims all the verities of the genre, including the portrayal of parents as congenital idiots. Terribly inappropriate theme as well as jocular view of drug abuse. O (PG) 15

Betty (1993) When a concerned widow (Stephane Audran) takes in a drunken, depressed young wife (Marie Trintignant), the unhappy woman's marital crisis spills over into the older woman's life with disastrous results. Director Claude Chabrol's adaptation of a Georges Simenon novel painstakingly burrows into the psyche of two women who base their self-worth on their sexual relationships with men, an attitude that destroys them in different ways. Subtitles. Several discreet bedroom scenes, some brief nudity, an off-screen suicide and an instance of rough language. A-III (nr)

Betty Blue (1986) A French import that tries to visualize the various moods of a love affair that goes from delirious heights of passion to depths of despair. By emphasizing the carnal aspects of the affair with endless amorous interludes and naked embraces, director Jean-Jacques Beinex fails to create a sense of intimacy and compassion for his characters (Beatrice Dalle and Jean-Hugues Anglade). Excessive amounts of nudity and sexual simulations. O (nr) 18

Between Miracles (1980) Nino Manfredi directs and stars in this dull and insipid film about a not-too-bright young man who as a boy was saved from death by an apparent miracle, raised in a monastery, and then has difficulty coping with the problems he finds in the world outside. Some sexual situations. A-III (nr)

Between the Lines (1977) Rather aimless comedy-drama about the youthful staff of a once radical Boston newspaper attempting to come to terms with changing times. Though director Joan Micklin Silver gets some good acting from a young cast (John Heard, Stephen Collins and Jill Eikenberry), the movie comes off as nothing more than a slick, run-of-the mill Hollywood production emphasizing nudity and sexual innuendo. O (R) AA

Beverly Hillbillies, The (1993) Clunky movie version of the 1962–1971 TV series has billionaire Pa (Jim Varney) nearly robbed of his fortune by a scheming golddigger (Lea Thompson) hired to teach refinement to his tomboy daughter (Erika Eleniak). Director Penelope Spheeris adds nothing to the cornpone formula of the original sitcom, nor to the cartoonish characters and situations that barely add up to a plot. Some blatant sexual innuendo, coarse gestures and slapstick violence. A-III (PG)

Beverly Hills Cop (1984) For those who like the comedic crassness of Eddie Murphy, there's plenty of it in his role as a supercool Detroit detective whose quest for justice in the shooting of a friend takes him to Los Angeles where he bears the brunt of prejudice. Murphy's streetwise charm and cunning overcome a script infused with rough language and director Martin Brest's reliance upon violence, some brutality and awkward stereotyping. A-III (R) 15

Beverly Hills Cop II (1987) Tiresome vanity production directed by Tony Scott features Eddie Murphy as the clever Detroit cop who helps his California friends break up a gang of thieves and gunrunners. Violence and brutality vie with extended demolition-derby chase sequence, unamusingly vulgar sight gags, rampant profanity and topless dancers. O (R) 15

Beware My Brethren (1972) Beware indeed of this annoying British movie, which tells of a fanatical evangelist (Patrick Magee) and his merciless influence upon a pathetically devout diabetic (Ann Todd) and her emotionally unstable son (Tony Beckley). Such things as rape, baptizing in blood and crucifying are treated in detail by director Robert Hartford-Davis' disgusting little shocker that is an insult to moral sensibilities. O (R)

Beware, My Lovely (1952) Harrowing tale of a widow (Ida Lupino) held captive in her home by a mild-mannered handyman (Robert Ryan) who proves a terrifying mental case. Directed by Harry Horner, the threatening situation goes on far too long to sustain credibility, though Ryan's performance as the unbalanced menace is chillingly convincing. Not for the young and impressionable. A-II (br) X

Beware! The Blob (see: "Son of Blob").

Beyond and Back (1978) The movie presents itself as a serious, scientific examination of certain alleged happenings that seem to indicate that there is life after death. The result, however, proves to be utterly uncritical in its treatment of data and many of its conclusions are not merely absurd but at variance with some traditional religious beliefs. Its realistic depiction of death experiences may be too strong for the very young. A-III (G)

Beyond Control (1971) German import in which a pair of young men and their girlfriends rob banks during the 1930s supposedly as a form of anti-Nazi protest is not only suffocatingly inept but made thoroughly offensive as well by splicing in some sex exploitation footage (shot entirely from the neck down). O (R)

Beyond Love and Evil (1971) French sex exploitation movie directed by Jacques Scandelari about the woodland villa of an evil count where a seemingly endless parade of perversity and cruelty take place. O (X)

Beyond the Door (1975) Cheap horror movie directed by Oliver Hellman is an inept, tasteless attempt to combine "Rosemary's Baby" and "The Exorcist." O (R) X

Beyond the Fog (see: "Horror on Snape Island").

Beyond the Law (1968) Novelist Norman Mailer's self-indulgent home movie about brutality in a New York City police station is offensive in its almost jocular use of violence and its coarse and obscene language. O (nr)

Beyond the Limit (1983) Director John Mackenzie's screen version of the Graham Greene novel, "The Honorary Consul," is a plodding, uninspired effort given some merit only by Michael Caine's performance as the hapless diplomat in an Argentine backwater, whom an inept band of revolutionaries kidnap by mistake. Another mistake is Richard Gere as Greene's introspective protagonist. Extensive nudity in the context of an adulterous affair. O (R)

Beyond the Poseidon Adventure (1979) Tugboat captain Michael Caine (aided and abetted by Karl Malden and Sally Field) try to salvage the Poseidon, moments after the climactic rescue of the previous disaster film. Producer-director Irwin Allen supplies only vacuous plot, dialogue and resolution in a boring adventure yarn. A-II (PG) A

Beyond the Reef (1981) This is a South Pacific idyll about a Polynesian lad and his pet shark who helps him win the love of a rich man's daughter, despite interference from her greedy brother and unscrupulous land developers. Directed by Frank C. Clark, it's an amateurish little movie, save for some remarkable underwater photography and a school of apparently trained sharks. Some partial nudity and permissive attitude toward the lover's affair. A-III (PG)

Beyond the Valley of the Dolls (1970) Director Russ Meyers' unfunny spoof of Hollywood lacks story, stars and appeal. Boring as it may be, it abounds in unhealthy fantasies of sex, with some nudity, and violence. O (X)

Beyond Therapy (1987) Based on the Christopher Durang play, Robert Altman's emotionally anemic romance tries to find humor in the failures of modern psychoanalysis and in the flaws of a sexually confused cast (Jeff Goldblum, Julie Hagerty, Glenda Jackson, Tom Conti and Christopher Guest). Shallow insights pervade the movie, which relies totally upon sexual innuendo, negative stereotypes and some vulgar language for interest. O (R) 15

Bible, The (1966) Six episodes from Genesis (Creation, Adam and Eve, Cain and Abel, Noah, the Tower of Babel and Abraham) are pictured as literally as they were written, largely leaving their interpretation to the viewer. John Huston directs, narrates and plays the part of Noah in this reverent but entertaining spectacular. George C. Scott as Abraham takes acting honors among a cast including Ava Gardner, Richard Harris, Ulla Bergryd and Michael Parks. A-I (br) U

Big (1988) When a lad of 12 (David Moscow) wakes up in a 30-year-old body (Tom Hanks), he rises to the top in a computer toy firm by beguiling his boss (Robert Loggia) and a female executive (Elizabeth Perkins) with his innocence and childlike exuberance. Under Penny Marshall's direction, the body-switching gimmick affords a sweet-natured look at the longings, dreams and nightmares of children and adults. Some profanity and a brief, discreetly filmed sexual situation. A-II (PG)

Big Bang, The (1990) An astronomer, a gangster, a painter, a model and a nun-philosopher are among the diverse mix of 19 individuals who tell what they think about love, life, death, the origins of the universe and what lies beyond the grave. Director James Toback's documentary interweaves the interviews into a relatively painless talk show, offering an uneven grab-bag of ideas ranging from the provocative to the pretentious and, at times, preposterous. Some rough language and an explicit description of a sexual encounter. A-III (R) 18

Big Bird Cage, The (1972) Poorly made Philippine movie directed by Jack Hill in which a woman (Pam Grier) smuggles her boyfriend into a women's prison camp in order to foment a rebellion. Much nudity, savagery and raw language. O (R)

Big Blue, The (1988) Mysterious young Frenchman (Jean-Marc Barr), who was taught to dive long and deep by his fisherman father, sets the world diving record, but his affinity for dolphins ultimately ruins his chances for a normal life on land. Exquisite seascapes and beautiful underwater cinematography can't make up for a poorly realized script directed by Luc Besson. Two intense drowning sequences and fleeting nudity in a brief but explicit sexual encounter. A-III (PG) 15

Big Bounce, The (1969) Young drifter (Ryan O'Neal) becomes deeply involved with a supposedly lovable psychotic (Leigh Taylor-Young) whose desire for thrills eventually drives him away, but only after she has committed murder. Directed by Alex March, the heavy-handed melodrama is totally unconvincing. Several ludicrous nude scenes and much coarse language used so self-consciously as to emphasize its offensiveness. O (R/PG)

Big Bus, The (1976) A parody of disaster movies, it follows the misadventures of a nuclear-powered bus on its maiden run nonstop from New York to Denver. The gags work about 30 percent of the time, not too bad an average for this type of film, and director James Frawley keeps a light touch on the often heavy-handed proceedings. Innocent, mostly sophomoric humor except for several sexual references. A-III (PG)

Big Business (1988) Two sets of identical twin girls are mismatched at birth—one set ends up at the helm of a New York-based conglomerate, the other set is raised by a poor, rural couple in West Virginia. Director Jim Abrahams keeps the farce fast and funny in showing how the real twins (both sets are played by Bette Midler and Lily Tomlin) are reunited in New York City's Plaza Hotel, but not before confounding husbands, lovers and all manner of co-workers and hotel employees. Much humor with sexual connotations and some rough language. A-III (PG)

Big Carnival, The (see: "Ace in the Hole")

Big Chill, The (1983) Seven old friends (William Hurt, Kevin Kline, Glenn Close among them) from college days in the 1960s are reunited by the suicide of the most brilliant of their number. After the funeral they spend the weekend together soul-searching and, to some degree, mourning their lost innocence. Director Lawrence Kasdan indicates no political awareness on the part of his characters despite their supposed sophistication and the result is an entertaining but shallow and contrived work. Brief nudity, rough language and a benign attitude toward adultery. A-III (R) 15

Big City, The (1967) From India comes this unassuming but dignified story of the problems that occur when a young mother must work in the city to help support her family. Director Satyajit Ray generates considerable human warmth out of a simple situation of ordinary family life. While the conclusion doesn't exactly follow and audience involvement may wear thin at times, Ray has captured the universal qualities of this Bengali family whom many will find worth a visit. A-II (br)

Big Clock, The (1948) Intriguing suspense thriller embroils a crime magazine editor (Ray Milland) as the chief suspect in a murder committed by his megalomaniacal publisher (Charles Laughton). Directed by John Farrow, the tense narrative is nicely keyed to a collection of quirky characters (including Elsa Lanchester, George Macready and Henry Morgan). Mounting menace and some stylized violence. A-II (br)

Big Cube, The (1969) Lana Turner is sent over the psychic edge by George Chakiris who has been spiking her medicine with LSD in order to control her fortune when she is declared incompetent. Director Tito Davison's low-budget melodrama shot in Mexico splices in some scenes of overage hippies cutting up at drug parties. O (PG) X

Big Doll House, The (1971) Low-budget Philippine sex melodrama directed by Jack Hill about a bunch of desperate women prison inmates (Judy Brown, Roberta Collins, Pam Grier) is full of innuendo as heavy as the passionate breathing on the sound track. O (R)

Big Easy, The (1987) Quirky romance about a Cajun detective (Dennis Quaid) and an assistant district attorney (Ellen Barkin) who weather a conflict of interests and the low moral atmosphere of New Orleans to solve a drug-related crime. Director Jim McBride's nervously stylistic movie stays light and often dopey despite some gruesome flashes of murder victims, a shot of topless dancers and an explicit, albeit fumbling, love-making scene. A-III (R) 15

Big Enough and Old Enough (1968) Family of Mexican migrant workers runs afoul of a motorcycle gang in this wretched movie directed by Joseph Prieto. Rape, mental and physical violence, sexually suggestive dialogue and visuals and coarse language. O (br)

Big Fix, The (1978) A Los Angeles private-eye (Richard Dreyfuss), a former 1960s' campus radical, is now cynical, disenchanted and divorced, scraping a living out of minor gumshoe jobs. When an old college friend (Susan Anspach) asks him to investigate a smear campaign against a political reformer, he is drawn back into the idealism of his youth. Director Jeremy Paul Kagan has made an entertaining though convoluted detective thriller that benefits greatly from the vitality of Dreyfuss' performance. Some of its humor and its less than adequate treatment of the political and moral issues it deals with make it mature fare. A-III (PG) A

Big Gundown, The (1968) In this Italian-made western, snickering ex-lawman (Lee Van Cleef) aids in tracking down a shifty Mexican (Tomas Millian) accused of rape and murder but, discovering his quarry's innocence, he then joins with him to punish the real culprits. Director Sergio Sollima's formula plot is simply an excuse to string together chases and places for the hero to exhibit his brutal brand of six-gun justice. Particularly objectionable in this film is sadistic violence and perversion perpetrated by and upon women. O (R) AA

Big Hand for the Little Lady, A (1966) Henry Fonda, Joanne Woodward, Jason Robards, Burgess Meredith, Paul Ford and Kevin McCarthy are among the ensemble playing cards in the Old West's most comical and colorful poker game. Director Fielder Cook places emphasis on the personalities and the plot's ingenious bluffing makes for fascinating entertainment, even without the clever surprise ending. A-II (nr) U

Big Heat, The (1953) Gritty crime thriller in which a homicide detective (Glenn Ford) whose wife is murdered by a bomb intended for him turns in his badge and goes it alone to bring down a powerful crime syndicate, its unsavory boss (Alexander Scourby) and his corrupt City Hall cronies. Directed by Fritz Lang, the melodrama's harsh action, sordid atmosphere and seedy characters are relieved by the idealistic cop and a gangster's abused girlfriend (Gloria Grahame) who dies helping to crack the case. Much menace and stylized violence, some of it quite nasty. A-III (br) 15

Big Jake (1971) John Wayne western in which he and his two grown sons (Patrick Wayne and Christopher Mitchum) trail the gang who kidnapped his grandson, with occasional pauses for bloodshed, to a Mexican village where they take on villain Richard Boone and his band of eight cutthroats. Directed by George Sherman, it's a rather old-fashioned kind of shoot-em-up, except some of the violence is overdone. A-III (GP) 15

Big Jump, The (see: "Paratrooper")

Big Knife, The (1955) Muddled Hollywood version of the conflict between art and commerce from the Clifford Odets play about a movie star (Jack Palance) blackmailed by an unscrupulous producer (Rod Steiger) into signing a contract for a movie he's dead set against doing. Director Robert Aldrich's melodrama has little action, much high-minded dialogue and good character bits by Ida Lupino, Jean Hagen, Shelley Winters and Wendell Corey. Sexual

references and suicide in plot resolution. A-III (br) A

Big Land, The (1957) Routine oater in which a Texas cattleman (Alan Ladd) persuades Kansas farmers (led by John Qualen) to join him in getting a railroad spur to the area in order to end their mutual dependency on a crooked Missouri trader (Anthony Caruso). Director Gordon Douglas seems more comfortable with cattle drives and shootouts than frontier links to Eastern markets and a sappy subplot involving a reformed alcoholic (Edmond O'Brien) and his marriageable sister (Virginia Mayo). Stylized violence. A-I (br) U

Big Lift, The (1950) During the Russian blockade of Berlin, an American (Montgomery Clift) in the massive airlift of supplies to the beleaguered city falls in love with a German resident, despite the advice of his anti-German buddy (Paul Douglas). Filmed on location in semi-documentary style by director George Seaton, this tribute to the airmen who braved the dangers of the Berlin route is convincingly authentic, though marred by the contrived love story and great gobs of patriotic rhetoric. An outburst of vengeful violence and a romance based on deceit. A-II (br)

Big Mo (see: "Maurie").

Big Mouth, The (1967) Working from what seems an almost totally improvised script, director Jerry Lewis takes a bank clerk (Jerry Lewis) who happens to look exactly like a gangster (Jerry Lewis) through a tediously meandering story-line. The lookalike gimmick sets up encounters with a hotel manager, a lunatic who thinks heEs an FBI agent, a group of smugglers, amusement parlor police, cruel Orientals and so on until its frantic conclusion. For Jerry Lewis fans. A-I (br) U

Big Parade, The (1925) Silent World War I epic centers on a small-town Army recruit (John Gilbert) who goes to France, falls in love with a village girl (Renee Adoree), is sent to the front and returns without a leg. Director King Vidor mounts the big sequences of troop movements and the chaos of battle with realistic effect that, combined with small scenes of human tenderness and comic byplay, add up to a convincing picture of men in war and its inhuman cost. Wartime violence and romantic situations. A-II (br) 15

Big Picture, The (1989) Rambling satire of Hollywood focusing on an aspiring young filmmaker (Kevin Bacon) determined not to compromise his values on the way up the ladder of success—but, of course, he does. Director Christopher Guest beats his rags-to-riches-to-rags message into the ground with cornball fantasy sequences and show biz in-jokes that make the result similar to the self-indulgent, high-gloss student films it seeks to lampoon. Sexual innuendos and vulgar references. A-III (PG-13) 15

Big Red (1962) French-Canadian orphan (Gilles Payant) taken in by a wealthy dog breeder (Walter Pidgeon) devotes himself to raising a beautiful Irish setter who later saves his master's life. Director Norman Tokar's rather flat Disney production has plenty of picturesque scenery of the Quebec countryside and youngsters will fancy the boy-dog story. A-I (br) U

Big Red One, The (1980) Director Samuel Fuller's attempt to honor the bravery of the U.S. Army in World War II has sadly resulted in an episodic and tedious work. Lee Marvin seems to be sleepwalking through his pivotal role as the sergeant in charge of a special infantry unit. Instead of conveying the sacrifice and futility of war, it doesn't get much beyond obnoxious characterizations of some of the G.I.s who fought it. Wartime violence and incidental vulgarities. A-III (PG) 15

Big Shots (1987) Two fatherless youngsters—a streetwise inner-city black and a naive suburban white—help each other through a series of dangerous mishaps while trying to locate one boy's father and the other's watch. Director Robert Mandel unnecessarily emphasizes the boys' recklessly anti-social antics, foul street talk and some violence in what disappointingly amounts to no more than a conventional chase picture. A-III (PG-13)

Big Sky, The (1952) Kentucky frontiersmen Kirk Douglas and Dewey Martin join veteran mountain man Arthur Hunnicutt on a fur-trapping expedition up the Missouri River into hostile Indian territory. Long, sprawling Western adventure directed by Howard Hawks, the period details of the journey are more interesting than the slow pace of the narrative and its occasional bursts of action. Frontier violence and some veiled sexual references. A-II (br) A

Big Sleep, The (1946) Classic hard-boiled crime caper with Raymond Chandler's private eye, Philip Marlowe (Humphrey Bogart), taking a routine blackmail case that turns into a convoluted murder mystery involving a millionaire's bewildering daughters (Lauren Bacall and Martha Vickers). Director Howard Hawks keeps the plot complications simmering with plenty of rugged action, colorful tough guys, much sardonic humor, snappy dialogue and the promise of romance. Stylized violence and sexual innuendo. A-III (br) PG

Big Sleep, The (1978) In a remake of the 1946 Howard Hawks-Raymond Chandler private-eye classic, writer-director Michael Winner makes a disastrous mistake by taking the hard-boiled yet soft-edged detective Philip Marlowe out of his era and environment and plunking him down in contemporary London. This cultural dislocation only adds further confusion to the story's flurry of killings, eccentric cast of characters, and incredibly complex plot. Under the circumstances, Robert Mitchum has no chance of competing with Humphrey Bogart's performance as Marlowe in the original. Violence, brutality and some nudity. O (R) AA

Big Steal, The (1949) Nifty chase thriller on Mexican backroads with a U.S. Army officer (Robert Mitchum) fleeing arrest by a fellow officer (William Bendix) for the theft of an Army payroll while he pursues the real culprit (Patric Knowles) with the help of a Spanish-speaking American (Jane Greer). Director Don Siegel's cat-and-mouse tale has plenty of eccentric curves, some deftly paced comic relief and appropriately tough characterizations. Stylized violence, mild romance and mostly positive Mexican stereotypes. A-II (br) A

Big Store, The (1941) Weak Marx Brothers vehicle in which the veteran comics play department store detectives who turn the place into a shambles before unmasking the gang of thieves (headed by Douglas Dumbrille) out to bankrupt the store. Directed by Charles Reisner, the story's a bust and the Brothers' slapstick routines and zany wordplay are only intermittently amusing. Comic violence and double entendres. A-II (br) U

Big T.N.T. Show, The (1966) Concert film directed by Larry Peerce and featuring such performers as Roger Miller, Ray Charles, Joan Baez, Donavan, The Byrds, Petula Clark, Ike & Tina Turner and Bo Diddley. Mixed bag of positive, wholesome songs and tribal chants whose lyrics are understandable only by rock cultists. A-II (br)

Big Time (1988) Theatrical concert film directed in contrived, artsy fashion by Chris Blum. Showcasies the eccentric talents of singer-songwriter-poet Tom Waits. Best for Waits' fans. Some vulgar comic banter. A-III (PG)

Big Top Pee-wee (1988) Zany child-man Pee-wee Herman (Paul Reubens) matures as a gentleman farmer with a talking pig, a hotdog tree, a school teacher fiancee (Penelope Ann Miller) and his first screen kiss with her rival, a trapeze artist (Valeria Golino). Directed by Randal Kleiser, its colorful circus activity and gorgeous production values are marred by hackneyed images implying Pee-wee's sexual blossoming and loss of virginity. A-II (PG) U

Big Town, The (1987) Small-time hustler (Matt Dillon) tries his luck shooting dice for big-time operators (Lee Grant and Bruce Dern) while taking his time deciding between a nice girl (Suzy Amis) and a stripteaser (Diane Lane). He learns some lame lessons in director Ben Bolt's dingy melodrama, which offers sex, violence and nudity instead of anything remotely uplifting. O (R) 15

Big Trees, The (1952) Wooden turn-of-the-century melodrama about a claim-jumping logger (Kirk Douglas) who tries to wheedle a California religious sect into letting him cut down the giant redwoods they revere as symbols of the eternal. Director Felix Feist's contrived plot lumbers along from one complication to another until the logger's unsurprising reformation. Beautiful forest scenery, stylized violence and mild romantic allusions. A-II (br) U

Big Trouble (1986) A zany pair of con artists (Peter Falk and Beverly D'Angelo) force a broker (Alan Arkin) to become their unwilling accomplice in an insurance fraud until a detective (Charles Durning) nails the pair. Director John Cassavetes elicits amiable performances in this witty but slight farce. Some rough language and brief nudity. A-III (R)

Big Trouble in Little China (1986) Kurt Russell reveals a comic flair for mock heroics in an action-fantasy about a 2000-year-old Chinese wizard who is determined to kidnap and marry the green-eyed girlfriend of one of Russell's pals. John Carpenter directs this martial-arts frolic in a movie teeming with special effects. Much profanity and sadistic violence. A-III (PG-13) 15

Big Wednesday (1978) Three young surfer fanatics spend their time boozing, fighting and womanizing in director John Milius' vulgar glorification of the male bond, arrested in the adolescence of the beach-bum culture of the past, offering viewers little save scenes of nature's grandeur. O (PG) A

Biggest Bundle of Them All, The (1967) Comic crime melodrama directed by Ken Annakin about the kidnapping of an American gangster relies excessively on sexual innuendo. O (br) A

Bill & Ted's Bogus Journey (1991) In this moronic sequel to their 1989 clunker, the two young oafs (Keanu Reeves and Alex White) are murdered by robot look-alikes and, after sampling heaven and hell, force the Grim Reaper to return them to Earth to rescue their girlfriends. Peter Hewitt directs a lame fantasy whose lack of intelligence is no laughing matter. Some mock violence and minimal gutter talk. A-II (PG)

Bill & Ted's Excellent Adventure (1989) Two spacey teenagers (Keanu Reeves and Alex Winter) are saved from sure flunk-out with the help of a futuristic genie (George Carlin) whose magical phone booth enables them to nab some historic figures (Napolean, Sigmund Freud, Billy the Kid, etc.) as show 'n' tell for a crucial oral history project. Director Stephen Herek's cheesy putdown of modern adolescent sensibilities includes moronic depictions of education and parenting. Some gratuitous vulgar references laced with sexual innuendo. A-III (PG)

Billion Dollar Brain (1967) Filmed on location in Finland, the third in the British spy-with-horn-rimmed-glasses series starring Michael Caine as Harry Palmer goes gimmicky, humorless and even offensive with some graphic love-making. Almost nothing of the original Palmer character is recognizable but the glasses, as Caine stumbles stolidly through acres of snow on a mission involving bio-warfare and a Texas millionaire's giant computer. Director Ken Russell's elaborate satire on obsessive anti-Communist types is clear enough, but that's about all that is in this brainless film. Violence and sexual scenes. O (br) PG

Billy Bathgate (1991) Sluggish 1930s' gangster movie about a Bronx youth (Loren Dean) learning the ropes under his idol Dutch Schultz (Dustin Hoffman) while juggling a dangerous relationship with the mobster's seductive girlfriend (Nicole Kidman). Director Robert Benton's less-than-compelling guys-and-molls flick has more vapid valleys than high spots. Sporadic violence, a brief bedroom scene, momentary nudity, a homosexual reference and some rough language. A-III (R) 15

Billy Jack (1971) Simple-minded story of the conflict between a redneck town and a school for runaway teenagers located on an Arizona Indian reservation where the title hero (Tom Laughlin who also directed) champions the area's oppressed Indians, Mexicans, blacks and school's youngsters by fighting violence with violence. Besides the violent proceedings are a rape, brief nudity and rough language. O (GP) AA

Billy Rose's Jumbo (1962) Bright but overlong turn-of-the-century musical about a failing circus whose owner (Jimmy Durante) relies on his daughter (Doris Day) to keep things going but she falls for a helpful stranger (Stephen Boyd) who's out to get their prize elephant for a rival circus. Directed by Charles Waters, the soggy Day-Boyd romance is a distinct handicap but the comic byplay between Durante and Martha Raye as his long-suffering fiancee, the Rodgers and Hart musical numbers and the colorful circus acts offer something for everybody. A-I (br)

Billy the Kid vs. Dracula (1966) Director William Beaudine's low-budget attempt to graft the western and horror movie strains results in a silly hybrid that youngsters might possibly sit through but anyone of the age of reason will find beyond endurance. A-I (br)

Billy Two Hats (1974) Two small-time bank robbers (Gregory Peck and Desi Arnaz Jr.) are on the run from a racist, Indian-hating marshal (Jack Warden) and his deputy (David Huddleston). Directed by Ted Kotcheff, the two friends in crime become symbolic reference points for the death of the Old West with the passing of the buffalo and the advent of the railroad. One very violent sequence. A-III (PG) AA

Biloxi Blues (1988) Coming-of-age comedy adapted by Neil Simon from his autobiographical play about a New York would-be writer (Matthew Broderick) in a Mississippi boot camp at the close of World War II who is constantly in hot water with his brain-damaged sergeant (Christopher Walken) and some of his company's more macho men. Tight direction by Mike Nichols enhances Simon's perceptive reflections on the milestones and meatheads one is forced to confront in such close quarters during wartime. Much rough language and a sexual situation involving a prostitute. A-III (PG-13) 15

Bingo (1991) Contrived fantasy has an amazingly clever little mutt saving a half-drowned boy (Robert J. Steinmiller, Jr.) and tailing him cross country to become part of his family. Director Matthew Robbins' scrappy comedy is no more than a series of cutesy dog tricks in search of a movie. Some slapstick violence, menace to a child and frequent toilet humor. A-II (PG)

Bingo Long Traveling All-Stars and Motor Kings, The (1976) Warmly nostalgic comedy about a black baseball team barnstorming through the Midwest during the Depression summer of 1939, an era when black players were barred from the major leagues. Starring Billy Dee Williams, James Earl Jones, and Richard Pryor as top players who start hamming it up in the style of the Harlem Globe Trotters to make their victories against white teams go down easier. Director John Badham's movie looks back at the way it was, good and bad, without finding villains or making excuses. Good entertainment, but coarse language and a brothel vignette unfortunately limit its appeal. A-III (PG) A

Birch Interval (1976) Charming and affecting movie produced by Robert B. Radnitz, about a pre-teen New York City girl (Susan McClung) who in 1947 confronts the emerging complexities of adult life when she is sent to stay with her grandfather (Eddie Albert) and uncle (Rip Torn) in a tranquil Amish community in Pennsylvania. Director Delbert Mann treats the marital problems of the uncle delicately while depicting in close detail Amish country life. Episodic and a little slow-moving, the movie nonetheless is a refreshing view of family matters that parents and their teenagers might benefit from discussing. A-II (PG)

Bird (1988) Biography of troubled jazz saxophonist Charlie "Bird" Parker (Forest Whitaker), who died in 1955 at age 34 after ravaging his body with years of heroin and alcohol addiction, follows his last years on the road and with his common-law wife (Diane Venora). Directed by Clint Eastwood, there's not a false note in this expressionistic, moody look at the jazz subculture of the 1950s. Realistic view of the consequences of Parker's addiction, a graphic suicide attempt, sexual promiscuity and an offhanded acceptance of out-of-wedlock pregnancy. A-IV (R) 15

Bird on a Wire (1990) Classy slam-bang chase thriller in which a former government witness (Mel Gibson) and his one-time sweetheart (Goldie Hawn) are on the run from vengeful drug dealers (David Carradine and Bill Duke) as well as assorted police agencies. Director John Badham maintains an air of romantic comedy throughout the desperate proceedings, mixing the screwball characterizations of the couple with some spectacular action stunts, notably in a jungle zoo. Much menace and demolition-derby violence, a bedroom scene and some sexually suggestive dialogue. A-III (PG-13) 12

Bird with the Crystal Plumage, The (1970) Failed Italian thriller in which a passerby (Tony Musante) saves a woman (Eva Renzi) from the black-cloaked knifer and then finds himself and his sleep-in girlfriend (Suzy Kendall) the target of the ripper. Directed by Dario Argento, the loose ends and false clues are so apparent that the state of terrifying suspense so necessary to such a film is never fully realized. A-III (GP) 18

Birds, The (1963) Classy suspense thriller begins leisurely as a romantic comedy that gradually shifts into high gear as a vehicle of fear when seagulls, crows and other usually harmless birds suddenly turn malignant and band together in murderous attacks on unsuspecting members of a seaside community. In this adaptation of Daphne du Maurier's story of nature in revolt, director Alfred Hitchcock is up to his old tricks in transforming the ordinary into the menacing as he puts his vulnerable principals (Rod Taylor and Tippi Hedren) and others (Jessica Tandy and

Suzanne Pleshette) through an emotional wringer trying to fend off nightmare attacks by the winged avengers. Mounting menace and special effects violence, with a key sequence involving schoolchildren that youngsters may find especially frightening. A-II (PG-13) 15

Birds Do It (1966) Harmless comedy directed by Andrew Marton in which Tab Hunter plays a secret agent trying to get from Soupy Sales, who he mistakes for a scientist, a secret ionizer that enables people to fly. Innocuous story that young children may find amusing. A-I (br) U

Birds Do It, Bees Do It (1974) Documentary focuses on how living things make other living things from the world of microbes to that of human beings. Very graphic in depicting the mating of birds, bees, and just about everything else. For adults and older teens. A-III (R/PG)

Birds in Peru (1968) French melodrama written and directed by Romain Gary in which a nymphomaniac (Jean Seberg) spends the night with four lovers on a Peruvian beach where each year flocks of birds come to die. Graphic treatment of sex scenes. O (X)

Birds, the Bees and the Italians, The (1967) Director Pietro Germi's biting satire on Italian hypocrisy may prove offensive to some viewers because its story concerns adultery and because of coarse language. A-IV (br) X

Birdy (1984) Vietnam vet (Matthew Modine) left virtually catatonic by a battlefield wound dreams about his past and his boyhood desire to be a bird while a friend (Nicolas Cage) tries to bring him back to reality in the grim confines of an Army hospital. Director Alan Parker gets lost in sketchy characterizations and great globs of tedious monologues that seem pointless, especially recollections of youthful sexual encounters with graphic nudity. O (R) 15

Birth of a Nation, The (1915) D.W. Griffith's still controversial, still powerful picture of the Civil War and Reconstruction links the lives of two families, North and South, each sacrificing sons in the fratricidal conflict, then focuses on the Southern family's plight under greedy carpetbaggers and black opportunists until the Ku Klux Klan rides to the rescue in a swirl of racist propaganda. Griffith's mastery of the silent medium succeeds in combining the sweep of historical spectacle with the intimacy of individual lives in a fashion that still engages viewers' emotions. Though it has a place in film history as the first feature to demonstrate fully the dramatic potential of the medium, the work presents an uncritical view of 19th-century myths justifying white supremacy and its irrational legacy of hate. Not for casual entertainment but has a place in film study programs where its racist perspective can be properly addressed. A-IV (br) U

Birthday Party, The (1968) Good adaptation of Harold Pinter's play about two overnight guests (Patrick Magee and Sydney Tafler) who entertain the permanent lodger (Robert Shaw) with disastrous consequences. Director William Friedkin succeeds in conveying the play's never explained mood of fear that pervades the menacing rooms of the house and the acting is superb. Mature themes. A-III (G) X

Biscuit Eater, The (1972) A couple of kids (Johnny Whitaker and George Spell) train a rejected bird dog for the regional championships which, if it wins, will make Johnny's dad (Earl Holliman) look bad in the eyes of his boss (Lew Ayres). Director Vincent McEveety's version of the James Street classic will appeal mainly to the elementary school set since it follows the Disney formula of animals exceeding humans in intelligence. A-I (G)

Bishop's Wife, The (1947) A debonair, smartly tailored angel (Cary Grant) uses his heavenly powers to help the neglected wife (Loretta Young) of a busy Episcopalian bishop (David Niven) renew her husband's ministry to those in need rather than in raising the money for a new cathedral. Director Henry Koster's sentimental Christmas fable has the virtue of a good script, sincere performances and some amusing moments with Grant's angelic powers and Monty Wooley as a softhearted old cynic. Most of the family will find it charming entertainment. A-II (nr) U

Bite the Bullet (1975) Muddled western directed by Richard Brooks dealing with a 700-mile horse race shortly after the turn of the century. Its hero (Gene Hackman) gives a coolly reasoned critique of the cruel stupidity of the race and its win-at-all-costs spirit but not long afterwards, he himself joins in and submits his horse to the brutal ordeal. Stylized violence. A-III (PG)

Bittersweet Love (1977) A couple (Meredith Baxter-Birney and Scott Hylands) fall in love, but only after getting married and her pregnancy is well advanced do they discover that they have the same father (Robert Lansing). Director David Miller takes a glossy soap-opera approach to the theme of incest in a cloying and tedious film that raises issues about abortion and divorce without much insight. A-III (PG)

B.J. Lang Presents (1972) Only Mickey Rooney's hardiest fans may be able to endure a picture in which their idol rants and rages mercilessly as a movie director driven insane by fantasies of former glory. Director Yabo Yablonsky revels in flashy camera tricks, strobe lighting and sound effects in a pointless exercise in horror. A-III (R)

Black and White in Color (1977) Extremely subtle and probing French comedy set in West Africa at the start of World War I, it tells the story of what happens when a small French settlement decides to attack a nearby German post. In looking at the human factors that lead to war, director Jean-Jacques Annaud avoids sentiment entirely, spares no one in this cast of characters and delivers an outrageous challenging and extremely funny anti-war film. Wartime violence and brief, incidental nudity. A-III (PG) A

Black Beauty (1971) British version of the classic tale of a boy (Mark Lester) and his horse comes to the screen under the direction of James Hill. It is lovely to look at, but, unfortunately, it is flawed by stilted scripting and wooden performances which, one hopes, will not spoil it for younger audiences. A-I (G) U

Black Belly of the Tarantula, The (1972) Confusing Italian murder mystery directed by Paolo Cavara in which a sultry female voice sighs on the sound-track while a hooded psychotic stalks inadequately clad women and commits a series of excessively graphic crimes. O (R)

Black Belt Jones (1974) Black kung-fu movie with Jim Kelly and Gloria Hendry fighting to keep their school of self-defense in the Watts area of L.A. from falling into the hands of the Mafia. Director Robert Clouse goes in for a lot of clowning and sight gags leading to a sudsy climax in a car-wash gone berserk, an approach that makes the movie fairly tolerable despite its deep-down mindlessness and brutality. A-III (R)

Black Bird, The (1976) Unfunny spoof of "The Maltese Falcon" private-eye classic with George Segal playing Sam Spade Jr. and Stephane Audran as the femme fatale who has not quite mastered the American idiom. Director David Giler strains hard for laughs, even trying for some religious parody, but nothing works. The language is frequently blasphemous. O (PG) A

Black Caesar (1973) Black crime movie in which Fred Williamson takes over a Harlem-South Bronx crime syndicate by acquiring pay-off ledgers incriminating New York politicians. Written, produced and directed by Larry Cohen, it trades exclusively in ruthless violence, sex and street language. O (R)

Black Cauldron, The (1985) In this delightful fantasy epic, a peasant boy must prevent the evil Horned King from gaining possession of a black cauldron capable of producing an army of supernatural warriors. Along the way he learns about love, loyalty, courage and the importance of friendship over power. A new Disney animated adventure especially suitable for young viewers. A-I (PG) U

Black Christmas (1975) Nasty Canadian horror movie directed by Bob Clark follows the exploits of a maniac who terrorizes a sorority house over the Christmas holidays. The incoherent script attempts to bridge the gap between the gruesome murder of coeds with obscene telephone calls that are disgusting. O (R) X

Black Eye (1974) Black private-eye Fred Williamson is searching Los Angeles for an antique cane stuffed with heroin and for a missing girl who is reportedly being held in a commune of Jesus freaks. Jack Arnold's direction is fast-paced, but muddying the waters is a subplot involving a bisexual relationship between our hero, his girlfriend (Teresa Graves) and her girlfriend (Rosemary Forsyth). Routine violence. A-IV (PG)

Black Girl (1972) Uneven drama of a black American family, portrays the tensions and conflicts, the misplaced love and bitterness, that stem from a kind of collective familial sense of inferiority. Directed by Ossie Davis, the movie seems largely aimed against its own members, particularly those who attempt to break the mold and escape the family's self-imposed cultural limitations. A-III (PG)

Black Godfather, The (1974) Low-budget black exploitation movie with heavy doses of unrelieved brutality and shrill racism. Written, produced and directed by John Evans, it offers a low view of humanity in general and of black life in particular. O (R)

Black Gold (1947) An Indian rancher (Anthony Quinn) and his wife (Katherine DeMille) adopt an orphaned Chinese boy, become millionaires when oil is discovered on their land and enter a horse they've raised from a colt in the Kentucky Derby. Despite a rambling narrative with predictable plot complications, director Phil Karlson holds it together by focusing on the rancher's mare and her colt, abetted by warm performances from the human principals. An animal story with heart and some social consciousness. A-I (br) U

Black Gunn (1973) Black crime movie features Jim Brown as a posh nightclub owner drawn into a confrontation with the mob when they kill his younger brother for knocking off a numbers parlor. Directed by Robert Hartford-Davis, the story provides ample opportunities for violence of every description, some casual sex and coarse language. O (R)

Black Hole, The (1980) Disney science-fiction movie with some fine special effects and a mediocre plot about a maverick scientist (Maximilian Schell) and his mysterious space laboratory. Unfortunately, director Gary Nelson has made the experience no more intriguing than a ride at Disneyland. Incidental violence. A-II (PG)

Black Jesus (1971) Awkward Italian production about a black African revolutionary (Woody Strode) who tries to maintain a peaceful course in the midst of leading an energetic revolution. Director Valerio Zurlini's narrative suffers from interminable, badly dubbed dialogue, an agonizingly slow pace and a mechanical plot devise drawing rather simplistic and superficial parallels to the passion of Jesus. Some brutal violence. A-III (GP)

Black Knight, The (1954) A blacksmith (Alan Ladd) wins knighthood and his lady fair (Patricia Medina) by saving King Arthur (Anthony Bushell), Camelot and Christianity from the treachery of Cornwall's pagan king (Andre Morell) and his Saracen allies (led by Peter Cushing). Directed by Tay Garnett, the ludicrous plot turns the Arthurian legend into a pulp fantasy whose erratic action, including Arthur's sacking of Stonehenge, may bemuse adult viewers while seeming exciting for those too young to know better. Much stylized violence and a ridiculous Druid orgy. A-I (br) U

Black Mama (1976) A black woman raising her child in a Los Angeles ghetto is gradually radicalized by her experiences in just trying to survive. Although director Haile Gerima uses an impressionistic style, alternating between objective reality and subjective fantasy, its message is clear that the dehumanizing conditions of poverty and racism are intolerable. A-III (nr)

Black Mama, White Mama (1973) Philippine story of two women (Pam Grier and Margaret Markhov) who escape from a prison camp handcuffed together. Director Eddie Romero, no stranger to this kind of thing, features lots of whipping, stripping and degradation. O (R)

Black Marble, The (1980) Joseph Wambaugh adapted his own novel for this movie about the romance that develops between two police officers (Paula Prentiss and Robert Foxworth). Director Harold Becker succeeds with some fine characterizations and valid emotions but fails to integrate a major subplot involving a hapless, bungling dognapper (Harry Dean Stanton). The film's decent edge is blunted by some violence and an acceptance of a premarital relationship. A-III (PG)

Black Moon (1975) French surrealistic fantasy in which a young girl (Cathryn Harrison), fleeing a bloody civil war between men and women combatants, finds refuge in an isolated country house in which live a bedridden old woman (Therese Gieshe), a brother and sister (Joe Dallesandro and Alexandra Stewart) and a band of children. While battles rage around the estate, the girl is preoccupied with her bizarre surroundings, which include a talking unicorn, crying flowers, and an enormous rat named Humphrey. Director Louis Malle is less concerned with the theme of innocence than with the modern preoccupation with death and sex. Mature themes. A-IV (R)

Black Moon Rising (1987) Seething raw sexuality and toughness, Tommy Lee Jones slithers through this implausible drama from director Harley Cokliss as a thief hired to obtain some tax court evidence. He hides his findings in a prototype racing car, which is then stolen. The casual sex, brutal beatings and hair-raising stunts he puts up with to retrieve the data are not worth the viewing time. O (R) 18

Black on White (1969) Exploitation movie directed by Tinto Brass about the sex fantasies of a white woman pursued through London by a black man. Much nudity and graphic sex. O (nr)

Black Orchid, The (1959) Slow but feeling drama of the pitfalls facing a happy-go-lucky widower (Anthony Quinn) in courting a proud widow (Sophia Loren) whom his grown daughter (Ina Balin) regards with contempt. Director Martin Ritt gets good performances in a nicely textured story of Italian-American life in New York City but the plot complications with offspring, relatives and friends keep getting in the way until an entirely predictable conclusion. Troubled characters and perplexing situations make it unlikely fare for young children. A-I (br) U

Black Pearl, The (1977) A young lad (Mario Custodio) in a small Mexican village whose livelihood depends upon pearl-diving is taught to respect the power of the sea by an old Indian (Gilbert Roland). Produced in Mexico and directed by Saul Swimmer, the movie's greatest strength lies in its beautiful natural setting and in its depiction of a youngster coming to terms with his religious beliefs and his doubts about himself. The very young may find the scenes with a sea monster quite scarey. A-II (PG)

Black Peter (1971) Czechoslovakian movie of a 17-year-old boy (Ladislav Jakim) growing up with all the anguished diffidence of adolescence in his dealings with parents and friends, his first job and his shy curiosity about girls. The first feature of director Milos Forman, made in 1964, it is a string of small gems crystallizing the final, wonderfully hazy days of uncommitted youth the world over. A-III (nr)

Black Rain (1989) Glossy crime thriller celebrates the hard-edged cynicism of an American cop (Michael Douglas) who bludgeons his way through Japan in pursuit of an escaped criminal but ultimately is taught a lesson in honor by a self-effacing Japanese detective (Ken Takakura). Director Ridley Scott devotes his energies to endless chase scenes in an exotic foreign culture but is unable to work up any sympathy for the foul-mouthed, small-minded anti-hero portrayed by Douglas. Much excessive violence and incessant rough language. O (R) 18

Black Robe (1991) After arriving in 17th-century New France, a Jesuit missionary (Lothaire Bluteau), guided by Algonquins, endures both a dangerous journey through the Canadian wilderness and an Iroquois attack to reach a distant Huron mission. Only towards the end does director Bruce Beresford manage to put the cultural clash between the humorless priest and the unbelieving Native Americans in a moving spiritual context. Some brief but graphic violence and several shadowy sexual encounters with momentary nudity. A-III (R) 15

Black Rodeo (1972) Documentary about a contingent of black cowboys who bring a Wild West show to New York that serves to make people aware of the black contribution to the heritage of the American West. Directed by Jeff Kanew and narrated by Woody Strode, the result has some expert slow-motion photography and a soundtrack full of pop songs commenting ironically on the action in the arena. A-I (G)

Black Samson (1974) Familiar story of black versus white in the struggle over inner-city turf, though the hero this time is a rather whimsical ghetto bar owner (Rockne Tarkington) who wants to keep his Los Angeles neighborhood drug-and-crime-free. Directed by Charles Bail, it wastes its potential by taking the predictable, brutal path leading to the inevitable bloodbath climax. Violence, rough language and numerous glimpses of the casual nudity in a topless bar. O (R)

Black Six, The (1974) Black motorcycle movie with Gene Washington as the leader of a bike pack of Vietnam War veterans who seem to find nothing but trouble wherever they go. Excessive violence and rough language. O (R)

Black Stallion, The (1979) Strikingly visualized tale about the magical relationship between a youngster (Kelly Reno) and the horse he finds shipwrecked on a deserted island becomes a beautiful metaphor for the force of youthful ambition taming the raw power of nature. Directed by Carroll Ballard from the Walter Farley story, the drama is the perfect children's movie—unsentimental, gripping and good stimulation for the young imagination. A-I (G) U

Black Stallion Returns, The (1983) Uninspired sequel directed by Robert Dalva in which the stallion's original owners spirit it back to Morocco while its present master (teenaged Kelly Reno) pursues them, making his way across the desert to reclaim his beloved horse. The climax, of course, is a horse race but perhaps the dullest ever committed to film. Corny, muddled and a bore. A-I (PG) U

Black Starlet (1976) A serious topic, the exploitation of women, is handled ineptly and is not above incorporating a bit of what it pretends to decry. O (R) AA

Black Sunday (1977) Palestinian extremist group plots to commit a terrorist atrocity at the Super Bowl while Israeli agent (Robert Shaw) tries frantically to avert it. Director John Frankenheimer's thriller is exciting enough, but it unfortunately exploits some larger issues for the sake of entertainment. Some intense violence. A-III (R)

Black Thursday (1974) On July 16, 1942, Paris police rounded up 13,000 Jews for deportation to Nazi concentration camps, from which all but 30 failed to return after the war. Director Michael Mitrani has reconstructed in semi-documentary style that terrible Black Thursday, using as his script the account of a young student who attempted to save those he could. A-III (nr)

Black Widow (1987) Debra Winger and Theresa Russell square off in a confrontation of cunning and guile when a Justice Department data analyst (Winger) tries to put an end to the series of seductions and murders of wealthy men by a mysterious and deadly woman (Russell). The double-bluff conclusion is as flawed as the sensually toned melodrama, which has a brief instance of nudity and a decidedly adult treatment by director Bob Rafelson. A-III (R) 15

Black Windmill, The (1974) Above average British thriller about an espionage agent (Michael Caine) whose son has been kidnapped by enemy agents and, in trying to get him back, he is suspected of being a double agent by his superior (Donald Pleasence). Directed by Don Siegel, the highly charged movie's rapid pace and sharp action gloss over the obvious holes and inconsistencies in the plot, but the real interest is in Caine's characterization and a conclusion that for once is not cynical but rather optimistic. A-III (PG) A

Blackbeard's Ghost (1968) A Disney comedy in which some elderly New England ladies are saved from eviction through the invisible machinations of pirate Blackbeard (Peter Ustinov) who helps the inept local school track team win a meet and a big sum of money. Director Robert Stevenson's simple-minded slapstick and special effects provide laughs, but the team's coach (Dean Jones), after being thoroughly ridiculed for objecting to Blackbeard's tactics, gets into the act himself. The impression that uncritical youngsters might get from all this is that cheating is O.K. if you can't win honestly. A-II (G) U

Blackboard Jungle, The (1955) Screen version of Evan Hunter's novel about an idealistic English teacher (Glenn Ford) confronting juvenile delinquents in an inner-city high school to win over a potential drop-out (Sidney Poitier) and the rest of his class. Directed by Richard Brooks, the movie called attention to the growing problems of public education after World War II and, though dated by its melodramatic treatment, its tribute to the teaching profession is as valid today as then. Some nasty violence and much menace, especially that directed at the teacher's pregnant wife. A-III (br) X

Blacula (1972) African prince (William Marshall), seeking Dracula's signature on a petition abolishing slavery is instead bitten by the Transylvanian count, entombed in the cellar and liberated two centuries later by a pair of swishy interior decorators whereupon he begins teething on the town. Director Bill Crain provides a few genuine thrills on the horror side but, for the most part, the movie tries to have some simple fun with its horror premise. A-II (PG) X

Blade Runner (1982) Science-fiction thriller about a private-eye (Harrison Ford) whose job is to hunt down and dispose of out-of-control humanoids. His work gets complicated when he falls in love with an advanced prototype who doesn't know she's not human (Sean Young). Director Ridley Scott's moody atmosphere and futuristic sets evoke an ecologically fouled and spiritually demoralized metropolis, but the disappointing script meanders listlessly. Excessive violence and partial nudity. O (R) 15

Blame It on Rio (1984) Businessman (Michael Caine) yields to the seduction of the daughter of his best friend (Joseph Bologna) who is depending upon him to help trap the daughter's lover. Director Stanley Donen's misguided celebration of male sexual fantasies tries to milk humor from a promiscuous situation and its use of partial nudity. O (R) 15

Blame It on the Bellboy (1992) Screwball complications abound when a bellboy (Bronson Pinchot) in a Venice hotel misde-

livers messages intended for a meek English worker (Dudley Moore), a philandering Mayor (Richard Griffiths) and a hitman (Bryan Brown). Writer-director Mark Herman concocts a lively, fast-paced comedy whose silly antics make for innocuous escapist entertainment. Some stylized violence and ethnic stereotyping played for laughs, a fleeting bedroom scene and many double entendres. A-III (PG-13) PG

Blast Off (see: "Those Fantastic Flying Fools").

Blaze (1989) Failed dramatization of the love affair between a striptease performer (Lolita Davidovitch) and Louisiana Governor Earl Long (Paul Newman). Written and directed by Ron Shelton, the movie offers little insight into the characters or the era of the 1950s. Sympathetic treatment of adultery and several extended sex scenes. O (R) 15

Blazing Saddles (1974) Vulgar and broad satire on westerns has not so much a plot as a series of wacky situations and comic stereotypes, including black sheriff Cleavon Little, rail baron Harvey Korman and bar room singer Madeline Kahn. Directed by Mel Brooks, it offers some funny moments, but the overall tone of its humor runs solidly toward the coarse, the smutty and the scatological. O (R) 15

Bless the Beasts and Children (1971) Failed melodrama about a handful of adolescent misfits wanting to set free a herd of captive buffalo. Directed by Stanley Kramer, the obvious aim was to deal with man's inhumanity to wildlife and youth, but the result is a heavy-handed succession of mini-soap operas that wrench the emotions without any semblance of insight. Some rough language. A-III (GP)

Blind Date (1987) Bruce Willis goes on a blind date with Kim Basinger but forgets to keep her away from alcohol. The consequences are traditional slapstick sequences of reckless abandon and funny sight gags in this romance from director Blake Edwards. Jealous ex-boyfriend John Larroquette supplies most of the genuine humor, but Basinger shows some flare for the zany. Brief nudity, casual treatment of alcoholism and some rough language are adult fare. A-III (PG-13) 15

Blind Dead, The (1973) Spanish-Portuguese horror movie in which three young people, camping amidst the ruins of a medieval monastery, fall prey to the vampire spectres of 12th-century Crusaders. Directed by Amando De Ossorio, the story is silly and the horror is minimal. Some sexual innuendo and spilling of blood. A-III (PG)

Blind Fury (1989) Blind Vietnam vet (Rutger Hauer) uses a samurai sword to skewer a farflung network of gun-happy criminals. Director Philip Noyce's inept rip-off of the Japanese "Zatoichi" series about a blind swordsman in medieval Japan proves a bloody exercise in the ludicrous with blade pitted against bullets in a modern American setting. Excessive violence and occasional rough language. O (R) 15

Blindfold (1966) Complicated espionage story directed by Philip Dunne starts in Central Park where a psychiatrist (Rock Hudson) is approached by a G-man and asked to treat a top government scientist but when he does, enemy agents and the patient's sister (Claudia Cardinale) get on his trail. Moderately entertaining with some mildly romantic interludes. A-II (br) U

Blindman (1972) Italian western in which the hobo hero of the title (Tony Anthony) is robbed of the 50 women he is delivering to a Texas mining camp by two hairy bandits (Ringo Starr and Lloyd Batista) who have other plans for them. Time and again senseless slaughter follows sadistic torture as blindman and badmen match wits under Ferdinando Baldi's routine direction. Most objectionable is its presentation of women as objects to be abused. O (R)

Bliss (1986) An advertising executive (Barry Otto) dreams that he has died and gone to hell but, when shocked out of this nightmare, he tries to change his already hellish and misdirected life. Directed by Ray Lawrence, this Australian import has difficulty finding a balance between social commentary and sex farce. Nudity and some profanity. O (R) 18

Bliss of Mrs. Blossom, The (1968) Shirley MacLaine plays a housewife with a devoted and hard-working husband (Richard Attenborough) while keeping a male admirer (James Booth) hidden in the attic. Whether or not this is the romantic daydream of all housewives, it does have a comic potential that this menage-a-trois fantasy plays with until the situation wears thin and then falls flat because of an overinflated script. Though director Joe McGrath's broadly exaggerated treatment keeps the questionable shenanigans within the bounds of good taste, the basic material will not appeal to everyone. A-III (PG) A

Blob, The (1958) Tongue-in-cheek sci-fi adventure follows a resourceful youth (Steve McQueen) trying to save his small town from annihilation when it's invaded by a lethal gooey substance from outer space. Directed by Irvin S. Yeaworth, Jr., the premise is a hoot with zero credibility, yet it has a goofy charm, thanks to a lot of hard-working extras and low-budget but imaginative special effects. Some menace and stylized violence. A-II (br) X

Blob, The (1988) Technical wizardry highlights this remake of a 1958 horror movie that centers on the efforts of a preppy cheerleader (Shawnee Smith) and a juvenile delinquent (Kevin Dillon) to save their town from being sucked up by an insatiable blob of plasma. Directed by Chuck Russell, there are several grisly, bloody blob encounters, a sense of menace, some profanity and a dumb segment involving a condom. A-III (R) 18

Blood and Lace (1971) Orphanage operator (Gloria Grahame) has runaways killed by a cleaver-wielding lunatic (Len Lesser) and stashed in the freezer, lest she lose the monthly state subsidy for each orphan. That's only the plot premise of director Philip Gilbert's movie, which goes on to add some sexual titillation to its low-budget bloody horror formula. O (GP)

Blood Beach (1981) A nasty-looking creature devours bathers before they can even get their feet wet, sucking them down into the sand, in this mindless, wholly inept little horror movie directed and written by Jeffrey Bloom. Excessive violence. O (R) 15

Blood Feud (1980) Fascist Italy is the setting for director Lina Wertmuller's serio-comic melodrama about a vengeance-crazed widow (Sophia Loren) who enlists the aid of her two lovers (Marcello Mastroianni and Giancarlo Giannini) to avenge the murder of her husband. Considering the talents involved, the result is a disappointing but ambitious failure. Violence, a frank approach to sex and the complex social, religious and political background serve as sources for the movie's satiric drive. A-IV (R) X

Blood from the Mummy's Tomb (1972) Mild British horror tale taken from a Bram Stoker novel about a professor (Andrew Keir) who gives his daughter (Valerie Leon) a ruby ring pilfered from the hand of an ancient Egyptian princess, who returns to take her revenge. Directed by Seth Holt, it plays the game rather well and is worth exploring for a few chuckles, if not chills. A-II (PG) X

Blood Mania (1971) Wealthy surgeon's daughter (Maria De Aragon) administers a heart stimulant to speed up her father's death, which opens the door to other crimes of passion and greed. Between acts of violence, there are some bouts of nude love-making that place this pathetically sensational melodrama directed by Robert O'Neil in the sticky mire of the sex-violence formula. O (R)

Blood of Dracula's Castle (1969) Vampire couple (Paula Raymond and Alex D'Arcy) keep a collection of young women guests manacled in the cellar of a deserted desert castle where they have taken residence until a new owner (Robert Dix) arrives and tries to evict them. Directed by Al Adamson, the only horrifying aspect of this synthetic foolishness is seeing a fine character actor, John Carradine, playing a moonbaying butler. A-II (M)

Blood of Heroes, The (1990) Excruciatingly violent post-Apocalyptic sports adventure that tracks a band of nomadic players who challenge similar teams to brutal competitions resembling football and rugby. Director David Webb Peoples fails to make sense of his desolate landscape, his dazed characters and the degrading sport in which players fend off opponents with chains, poles and bared teeth. Gratuitous, graphic, grisly violence and some implied promiscuous sexual situations. O (R)

Blood of the Condor (1973) Bolivian documentary investigating charges that a Peace Corps medical clinic had been sterilizing Indian women who came for treatment without telling them what they were doing. Director Jorge Sanjines places the report in the context of Indian culture and politics and has made a quite sophisticated film out of a direct and simple story. A-III (nr)

Blood on Satan's Claw, The (1971) Failed British chiller set in bucolic 16th-century England where an unsuspecting plowman unearths the remains of a devil who comes to life and, with the aid of a seductive local recruit (Linda Hayden), manages to terrify the local yokels. Directed by Piers Haggard, the movie has its gory moments, but it is severely undercut by a clumsy emphasis on the sexual side of witchcraft. O (R)

Blood on the Sun (1945) American reporter (James Cagney) in 1930's Tokyo tries to get a document containing Japan's plans for world conquest out of the country with the help of an Oriental double agent (Sylvia Sidney). Director Frank Lloyd's espionage thriller has some dandy action scenes and not a little suspense but too often bogs down in anti-Japanese rhetoric. Racial stereotypes and stylized violence. A-II (br)

Blood Queen (see: "Little Mother").

Blood Simple (1985) A young wife (Frances McDormand) runs away from her Texas saloon owner husband (Dan Hedaya) who hires a seedy private detective (M. Emmet Walsh) to kill both her and her lover. Joel and Ethan Coen's cleverly plotted, well-acted tale of love, hate and vengeance in which nothing works out as the hapless characters intended, proves to be a work of somber, quirky brilliance, with glints of black humor. Some bloody violence subordinated to plot and characterizations. A-IV (R) 18

Blood Thirst (1972) Low-budget Philippine horror import about an American detective (Robert Winston) called to Manila to investigate a series of murdered women found drained of blood. Producer-director Newt Arnold handles the standard nonsense with the fast economy of a black-and-white movie and nary a gown is shed nor a vein slit before the camera pulls away. A-III (GP)

Bloodbrothers (1978) The tension between father (Tony Lo Bianco) and son (Richard Gere) are at the core of this movie about a tightly knit, Italian American working-class family living in the Bronx, which is under siege from other ethnic groups. The father and his brother (Paul Sorvino) bestow all their hopes for the future on the young lad, but he is not sure that he wants to follow in their footsteps. Director Robert Mulligan's work has a certain amount of raw power, but it is far too melodramatic and lacking in ethnic authenticity to be able to deal convincingly with the important moral and social issues it raises. Excessive profanity and an uncritical attitude toward sexual promiscuity. O (R) 18

Bloodhounds of Broadway (1989) Interweaving four Damon Runyon stories about Broadway denizens on New Year's Eve, 1928, this rambling tale of broken hearts and big bucks gambled, won and lost is narrated by a newspaper scribe (Josef Sommer). Standouts are Randy Quaid and Matt Dillon as comical losers whose luck turns bright. Director Howard Brookner's labor of love will be most effective for those familiar with Runyon's work, distinctive language and characters. Some cartoon violence, sexual innuendos and intimations of promiscuous liaisons. A-III (PG)

Bloodline (1979) Audrey Hepburn, surrounded by a host of veteran actors, inherits control of a vast pharmaceutical empire and becomes the target of a killer. Director Terence Young's treatment of the story adapted from Sidney Sheldon's best seller reeks of sexual exploitation, sadistic violence and a sleep-inducing plotline. O (R) X

Bloodsuckers (1972) British horror movie about a vampire cult in the ruins of ancient Greece and an Oxford professor (Patrick Mower) who believes that vampirism is a remedy for impotency. Directed by Robert Hartford-Davis, there is some stunning photography of Greece, but the disjointed plot doesn't hold together. Some graphic shots of body mutilations and nudity. O (R)

Bloodthirsty Butchers (1970) Poor British horror movie about a Fleet Street barber who shaves patrons too closely, his sadistic assistant who separates their components with his cleaver, and a baker's wife who sells assorted anatomic pies. The real victims are the viewers partaking of this low-budget exercise in sex and cruelty. O (R)

Bloody Mama (1970) Sordid crime melodrama about the 1930s' Ma Barker gang with Shelley Winters in the title role. Directed by Roger Corman, the character is presented as a psychopath and the treatment includes excessive violence and the vagaries of sexual appetites. O (R) 18

Blow Out (1981) A movie soundman (John Travolta) records an auto accident, rescues a young woman (Nancy Allen) and then attempts to bring to light an assassination plot. Director Brian De Palma's thriller is short on suspense and long on sadism, employs ludicrously self-conscious techniques and offers a shamelessly confused moral outlook. Mixture of violence and nudity in a sexual context. O (R) 18

Blow-Up (1967) In this British production, director Michaelangelo Antonioni takes on the themes of alienation in modern society and the uncertain relationship between illusion and reality in a story about an egocentric man (David Hemmings) who becomes indirectly involved in a murder. His cold and impersonal film, however, is unconvincing in its pessimistic vision of modern life. Nudity in a sexual context. O (br) X

Blue (1968) A failed western in which Terence Stamp stars as the adopted blue-eyed gringo son of a Mexican bandit chief (Ricardo Montalban). The son sides with the American settlers against his former comrades but is torn between the two cultures for the duration of this muddled movie. Beautiful landscapes, but English director Sylvio Narizzano offers only a superficial development of a complex theme. Winked-at bedroom encounter. A-III (br) A

Blue (1994) After a car crash kills her composer husband and little girl, a Parisian widow (Juliette Binoche) attempts to withdraw from all human contact until her late husband's assistant (Benoit Regent) begins work on the composer's unfinished symphony, prompting her creative collaboration and tentative emotional recovery. Director Krzysztof Kieslowski's mournful story of a woman entrenched in grief blends evocative images and thunderous bursts of music within a slim narrative that remains distant and largely abstract, despite its hopeful ending. Subtitles. Fleeting nudity and implied sexual encounters. A-III (R) 15

Blue Bird, The (1940) Heavy-handed fantasy from the Maurice Maeterlinck story of two children (Shirley Temple and Johnny Russell) searching for the blue bird of happiness in the land of the past, the domain of luxury and the world of the future until finding it at home. Directed by Walter Lang, the allegorical settings are colorful but the fanciful story has little charm or imagination, save the visit to the future's beclouded nursery filled with children waiting to be born. Best for the younger members of the family. A-I (br) U

Blue Bird, The (1976) Filmed in Leningrad, this American-Soviet co-production presents Maurice Maeterlinck's children's classic about two peasant youngsters searching for the blue bird that will bring health and happiness to the sick daughter of a neighboring family. George Cukor directs this intermittently beautiful but ultimately earthbound musical fantasy whose songs thankfully pass almost unnoticed. The child actors (Todd Lookinland and Patsy Kensit) are fine, which cannot be said of the adult cast (Elizabeth Taylor, Jane Fonda, Ava Gardner, Cicely Tyson). Ponderous but innocuous entertainment. A-I (G)

Blue City (1986) A sour and violent story depicting vigilante ambitions on the part of a wayward adolescent (Judd Nelson) who returns home to discover his dad has been murdered. Under Michelle Manning's direction, Nelson and co-star Ally Sheedy give wretched performances as they mix violence, casual sex and sexually derived profanity in this blue movie. O (R)

Blue Collar (1978) Screenwriter Paul Schrader's directing debut looks at the frustrations of three Detroit auto workers (Harvey Keitel, Richard Pryor and Yaphet Kotto), trapped in a grueling environment while being taken advantage of by their union and management. A dim failed work, it exploits such serious issues as factory conditions, union corruption, management oppression, economic distress and marital tensions, rather than explore them in some coherent and intelligent fashion. Crass cynicism and harsh language. O (R) X

Blue Country (1978) The setting for this French comedy is a gorgeous bucolic valley into which comes a little stream of expatriates from the city in search of a more humane existence. What they find is that the natives are themselves longing for the easy life of the city. Unfortunately, writer-director Jean-Charles Tacchella has burdened his delightful cast and comic anecdotal style with the weight of a seriously flawed broadside against the institution of marriage. O (PG)

Blue Lagoon, The (1980) Two marooned children (Brooke Shields and Christopher Atkins) grow through puberty to the discovery of sex and parenthood on a deserted island paradise. Director Randal Kleiser exploits teen sexuality with cute, peek-a-boo nudity and the only innocence on the screen is its unawareness of the realities of life in the tropics. O (R) 15

Blue Max, The (1966) Saga of a German flying ace (George Peppard) toward the end of World War I details his exploits in sky as well as on the ground with the wife (Ursula Andress) of a general (James Mason) who has turned him into a hero. Directed by John Guillermin, the movie soars with the scenes of biplanes in action but falters on the earthbound melodramatic problems of its characters. Two excessively explicit scenes of love-making. O (br) A

Blue Steel (1990) Visually stunning, graphically violent thriller in which a rookie female cop (Jamie Lee Curtis) is stalked by a commodities broker (Ron Silver) who is also a closet psychopath. Director Kathryn Bigelow's artful depiction of a young woman's struggle to be a New York cop deteriorates into a gruesome night-stalker thriller that sees a female victim turn on her male victimizer with horrifying fury. Excessive grisly violence, some profanity and a sexual incident with brief nudity. O (R) 18

Blue Thunder (1983) Tough, dedicated police helicopter pilot (Roy Scheider) and his callow but brainy sidekick (Daniel Stern) thwart the efforts of some sinister government types to use real people in testing a super-helicoper designed to put down urban riots. The unbelievable plot, however, serves only as a pretext for some slam-bang aerial action in a callous and cynical movie directed by John Badham. Much violence and utterly gratuitous nude sequence. O (R) 15

Blue Velvet (1986) Adolescent (Kyle MacLachlan) confronts the lighter but mostly darker sides of sexual desire in a small town when he comes across a severed human ear in a field and is drawn into a web of sadistic sex and eroticism. Director David Lynch's sinister fable of sex and violence in small-town America leaves only a vivid after-image of decadence and brutality. O (R) 18

Blue Water, White Death (1971) Wildlife filmmaker Peter Gimbel sets out to find and photograph the magnificent Great White shark in its natural surroundings of the open sea. Apart from the menacing sharks themselves, Gimbel's documentary dwells on a number of other forms of sea life and offers some ecological observations on the approaching extinction of the whale. Some terrifying moments with attacking sharks. A-II (G) U

Bluebeard (1972) Richard Burton stars as the infamous lady-killer in a dull version of the story set in pre-Nazi Germany. Some of his victims (Raquel Welch, Virna Lisi, Nathalie Delon) play it for snickers while others play it very straight. Directed by Edward Dmytryk, the movie doesn't succeed either as spoof or as melodrama. Restrained violence and much coy nudity. O (R) X

Blues Brothers, The (1980) Two blues singers (John Belushi and Dan Aykroyd) try to raise money for an orphanage by putting a band together and playing some concert dates. The plot is interspersed with scenes of wholesale destruction and frenzied chases that are spectacularly unfunny and uninvolving. Some good musical portions from Cab Calloway and Ray Charles, but not enough depth from director John Landis to save this zany comedy from milking cheap laughs from rough language and crude situations. A-III (R) 15

Blues for Lovers (1966) Well-intentioned but weak melodrama directed by Paul Henreid about how a little blind boy with an overprotective widow gets comfort and help from blind musician Ray Charles (playing himself). The mother's illicit relationship with a boyfriend makes it mature fare. A-III (br)

Blume in Love (1973) Beverly Hills divorce lawyer (George Segal), who loses his wife (Susan Anspach) when he catches him committing adultery, tries desperately to win her back in this uneven, sometimes amusing, romantic comedy directed by Paul Mazursky. Some casual nudity and harsh language. A-III (R) X

Boardwalk (1979) Aging Brighton Beach Jewish couple (Lee Strasberg and Ruth Gordon) suffer through the deterioration of their health and of their neighborhood in this inept and heavy-handed moral tale from director Stephen Verona. Although some serious issues are presented, the conclusion is crude and melodramatic, overbaked with violence and a frank treatment of sex. A-III (nr) AA

Boat, The (see: "Das Boot").

Boat Is Full, The (1981) A desperate party of Jewish refugees arrives in Switzerland vainly seeking asylum from Nazi persecution. An outstanding Swiss production written and directed by Markus Imhoof, it is a convincing and quite moving depiction of the plight of these refugees and the various attitudes of the Swiss toward them. A richly human treatment of a grim but important subject. A-II (PG)

Boatniks, The (1970) Typical Disney romp follows the slapstick misadventures of a bumbling Coast Guard officer (Robert Morse) and a master jewel thief (Phil Silvers) trying to leave the country with the loot. There's a seasoning of innocuous adult humor to interest the parents watching with their youngsters. A-I (G)

Bob & Carol & Ted & Alice (1969) When Bob & Carol (Robert Culp and Natalie Wood) introduce their friends Ted & Alice (Elliott Gould and Dyan Cannon) to the new freedom of being honest about their feelings, it is only a question of time before the two couples go to bed together. Director Paul Mazursky's modern morality tale about the new morality spoofs much that deserves spoofing but ultimately fails because it exploits the many opportunities for comic titillation worked into the obvious script. Excessive nudity and sexual references. O (R) X

Bob Roberts (1992) Bemused parody of contemporary media politics follows a fictional campaign for the U.S. Senate made by a folksy millionaire Pennsylvania candidate (Tim Robbins) as seen from the perspective of a BBC documentary filmmaker (Brian Murray). Also directed by Robbins, the picture of the smarmy, cynical candidate, his protofascist advisors and their manipulation of a complacent news media is provocative but not especially amusing as the campaign drags on to its bogus conclusion. Satiric exaggerations of serious realities, a political assassination attempt and some rough language. A-III (R) 15

Bobbie Jo and the Outlaw (1976) Inane and brutal western from director Mark Lester about a band of robbers whose antics seem designed as an obvious attempt to grind out a cheap Bonnie and Clyde copy, replete with excessive violence and some nudity. O (R)

Bobby Deerfield (1977) Plodding romantic melodrama directed by Sydney Pollack about a famous racing car driver (Al Pacino) and his relationship with an Italian aristocrat (Marthe Keller) who is dying of an incurable disease. Scenic, sentimental and predictable, the film's theme and brief nudity make it mature fare. A-III (PG)

Bobo, The (1967) Penniless clown with two guitars but no voice (Peter Sellers) aims at becoming Spain's first singing matador, but he must first seduce a girl-about-town (Brett Ekland) in three days if he is to get a contract. Director Robert Parrish's dreary comedy is neither moving nor hilarious and it was aiming at both. Sexual innuendo. A-III (br) A

Bodies, Rest & Motion (1993) Static story of four aimless young adults (Bridget Fonda; Phoebe Cates; Tim Roth; Eric Stoltz) who exchange sexual partners as listlessly as they plan their futures. Michael Steinberg directs a pointless story about the young and the restless who are going nowhere and are unconcerned about anything beyond enjoying the moment. Acceptance of casual sex, recreational drug use, white collar crime and much rough language. O (R)

Body, The (1971) With an impressive list of technical advisers, doctors, scientists, and educators, producer Tony Garnett and director Roy Battersby have set about a visual exploration of the fabric and functions, inside and out, of the human body. While their intentions may be pure, the explicit nature of the sexual material has no place in a movie theater and its use either in classroom or home is highly questionable. O (X)

Body Beneath, The (1971) Venerable British family of vampires, threatened by an infusion of bad blood and local harassment, decides to emigrate to America. The movie suffers from an infusion of bad acting, ludicrous scripting and an overgenerous display of sex, gore and psychedelic nonsense. O (nr)

Body Chemistry (1990) A kinky affair between the project director (Marc Singer) of a sex research lab and one of the lab's clients (Lisa Pescia) gets out of control with disastrous results. Directed by Kristine Peterson, the slack tale of a woman's sexual obsession is as predictable as it is pointless. Several scenes of simulated sex with nudity, gory violence and occasional rough language. O (R)

Body Double (1984) Director Brian De Palma's attempt at concocting an imitation Hitchcock thriller once again combines voyeurism and violence directed at women. Hitchcock might have been cruel but he was clever, while De Palma is only cruel and banal. A self-indulgent travesty with an unnecessary detailed depiction of the vicious murder of a woman and excessive use of nudity. O (R) 18

Body Heat (1981) Passing through a small Florida town, a small-time lawyer (William Hurt) tarries to pursue a married woman (Kathleen Turner), who persuades him to rid her of an unwanted and very wealthy husband. Written and directed by Lawrence Kasdan, its a labored imitation of a dark romantic melodrama of the 1940s, with the only modern touch being its extensive and explicit depiction of sex. O (R) 18

Body of Evidence (1993) Trashy thriller in which a conniving sadomasochist (Madonna), accused of murdering her wealthy lover, then seduces her married defense attorney (Willem Dafoe) and manipulates other lovers (Frank Langella and Jurgen Prochnow) in an attempt to win acquittal. Director Uli Edel's tawdry melodrama glamorizes sexual perversity while ignoring human values. Sexually explicit scenes, several drug abuse reference, climactic gory violence and frequent rough language. O (R)

Body Parts (1991) Schlocky horror movie in which the limbs of a man executed for mass murder replace those of accident victims (Jeff Fahey, Brad Dourif and Peter Murnik) who then experience personality changes with deadly consequences. Director Eric Red sinks a potentially interesting psychological thriller in a bucket of blood, blotting out Fahey's credible performance and a tense car chase. Excessive violence and much rough language. O (R)

Body Rock (1984) Middling youth movie directed by Marcelo Epstein about a youngster (Lorenzo Lamas) who turns his back on friendships to pursue a career as a dance club disc jockey. Focus is on the hormonal rather than the moral. A-III (PG-13)

Bodyguard, The (1992) Sluggish would-be romantic thriller about an Oscar-nominated singer-actress (Whitney Houston) and a former Secret Service agent (Kevin Costner) hired to protect her from a very determined and resourceful killer. Directed by Mick Jackson, the slow-moving action and stilted romance are matched by some unintentionally funny dialogue. Brief violence, an implied sexual encounter and frequent rough language. A-III (R) 15

Bofors Gun, The (1968) British adaptation of John McGrath's play about a long night of guard's duty in a munitions depot during which a fanatic Irish rebel-poet (Nicol Williamson) turns his rage on an ineffectual upper-class superior (David Warner) in an increasingly nightmarish situation. Director Jack Gold builds the growing antagonism between the two characters to the busting point. Harrowing tension and barracks' language. A-IV (nr)

Boiling Point (1993) Violent crime story in which a Treasury agent (Wesley Snipes) tracks down the two badmen (Dennis Hopper and Viggo Mortensen) who murdered his partner. Director James B. Harris' formula action movie is little more than a series of nasty shootouts in between which women are showcased as sexual playthings ripe for abuse. Several violent shootouts, implied sexual encounters and much rough language. O (R)

Bolshoi Ballet 67 (1966) Using the framework of a tour through the school of this famous troupe, the documentary affords a privileged view of the discipline and training that develops its leading dancers after years of effort. Much of the movie consists of performances including the spectacular "Paganinini" and the colorful "Bolero." A-I (br)

Bombardier (1943) The tribulations and hijinks of Army Air Force trainees (Randolph Scott, Robert Ryan, Eddie Albert) under a demanding officer (Pat O'Brien) who readies them for the demands of airborne combat. Director Richard Wallace's dated World War II relic is little more than a wooden exercise in patriotic flag-waving. Wartime violence and stereotyped enemies. A-I (br) A

Bombay Talkie (1970) Western pulp author (Jennifer Kendal) visits India, falls in love first with a screenwriter and then with a young film star but, constantly trailing misery in her wake, she completely ruins both their lives. Directed by James Ivory, the plot is low-key and conventional, with interest lying in the psychological development of the relationships and the unique setting. A-III (GP) A

Bon Voyage, Charlie Brown (And Don't Come Back!) (1980) This fourth animated feature starring Charlie Brown and his friends, brings them to France as exchange students where they find themselves quartered in a spooky chateau. Written by Charles Schulz, the comic strip's creator, and directed by Bill Melendez, the movie is pretty thin fare, talky and episodic, but youngster and Peanuts fans will love it. A-I (G) U

Bone (1974) Beverly Hills household of a used car tycoon (Andrew Duggan) and his repressed wife (Joyce Van Patten) is invaded by a black rapist (Yaphet Kotto) in a movie that apparently intended to show the hypocrisies of the affluent and contemporary American racial attitudes. Incoherently written and badly directed by Larry Cohen, all it shows is human ugliness. O (R)

Bonfire of the Vanities, The (1990) When a wealthy Wall Street broker (Tom Hanks) and his mistress (Melanie Griffith) accidentally run over a black youth in the Bronx, a desperate newspaper reporter (Bruce Willis) helps turn the ensuing court case into a political hot potato and media circus. Producer-director Brian De Palma has turned Tom Wolfe's satirical bestseller into a nasty, overblown and very vulgar comedy having little human dimension. Many sexual references, racial epithets and rough language. O (R) 15

Bonjour Amour (1978) Shy, studious high school lad falls in love with a 17-year-old shopgirl and despite objections from his parents, he tries to run away with her. French director Roger Andrieux is handicapped by a script that oversimplifies and romanticizes the serious problem of irresponsible teenage sexuality. O (nr)

Bonnie and Clyde (1967) Warren Beatty's production stars himself and Faye Dunaway, with supporting cast of Gene Hackman, Estelle Parsons and Michael J. Pollard, in a vivid and strikingly real re-creation of the treadmill existence of the Barrow Gang, ill-fated bank robbers of the Depression. Director Arthur Penn brings a human perspective to the gang's wildly distorted legend and their senselessly violent deaths, which leaves viewers to ponder the brutal frontier ethic of American justice. Scenes of strong violence. A-IV (br) 18

Bonnie's Kids (1972) Lurid crime melodrama about deceitful, promiscuous sisters (Tiffany Bolling and Robin Mattson) who flee their shanty town after killing their lecherous stepfather, become models and end as pawns in a big robbery. Writer-director Arthur Marks bases much of the plot on sexual jealousies from which stem this story of murder and suicide. O (R)

Book of Love (1991) Middle-aged man recalls his fumbling adventures as a teen (Chris Young) when, with the aid of a nerdy buddy (Keith Coogan), he juggled the girl he wanted (Josie Bissett) with the girl who wanted him (Tricia Leigh Fisher). Director Robert Shaye's sophomoric comedy pays more attention to the 1950s' soundtrack and pop artifacts than any semblance of a real story. Benign depiction of teenage drinking, mild sexual innuendo, brief partial nudity and an instance of harsh language. A-III (PG-13) 15

Book of Numbers (1973) Pair of fast-talking slickers (Raymond St. Jacques and Philip Michael Thomas) set up a wildly successful numbers game in a small but monumentally venal Tennessee town, much to the chagrin of some local criminals. Also directed by St. Jacques, some bitter lessons in free enterprise and the futility of bucking the system are put over with lots of broad slapstick and sight gags. Some violence, a suggestive sex scene and rough language. A-III (R)

Boom (1968) Screen version of Tennessee Williams' play in which a wealthy woman (Elizabeth Taylor) who is terminally ill is visited by the Angel of Death (Richard Burton) in her posh Mediterranean villa. Director Joseph Losey fails to give life to what is essentially a play of not very profound ideas. Mature themes with excessively crude sexual references. O (br) X

Boomerang (1947) Semi-documentary account of the arrest and trial of a vagrant (Arthur Kennedy) for the murder of a Connecticut clergyman in a town whose local prosecutor (Dana Andrews) is unsatisfied with the circumstantial evidence presented by the police chief (Lee J. Cobb). Director Elia Kazan's low-key treatment of the fact-based events involves viewers in the police investigation and political pressures to solve the case. Tense scenes and legal ambiguities. A-II (br)

Boomerang (1992) Belabored romantic comedy has the tables turned on a cocky playboy (Eddie Murphy) in the glamorous cosmetics industry when his sexy new boss (Robin Givens) rebuffs his advances. Director Reginald Hudlin gets limited comic mileage out of a trite story whose mostly shallow characters grow quickly tiresome. A few bedroom scenes, sexually suggestive references and much rough language. A-III (R) A

Boost, The (1988) Insecure, young Los Angeles tax shelter salesman (James Woods) and his devoted wife (Sean Young) are caught in the downward spiral brought about by financial speculation and drug addiction. Director Harold Becker takes a harrowing, painfully depressing look at a couple who throw away a promising life due to drugs. Graphic cocaine use, some violence, rough language and brief nudity. A-III (R) 18

Boot Hill (1973) Flat Italian western about a pair of adventurers (Terence Hill and Bud Spencer) who help some Colorado miners fight a corrupt boss (Victor Buono). Unfortunately, rather than try to make any sense out of the story, director Giuseppe Colizzi relies mostly on his cast's acrobatic antics and close-ups of their snickering faces. Some violence. A-II (GP)

Bopha! (1993) Fact-based story of a black South African policeman (Danny Glover) torn between the system he has always upheld and his responsibility to wife (Alfre Woodard) and son (Maynard Eziashi) when he learns the youth is being sought for leading a student protest against apartheid in 1980. In dramatizing one family's story, director Morgan Freeman gives a human perspective to the tragedy of institutionalized racism in South Africa. Intermittent violence, fleeting nudity and some rough language. A-II (PG-13) 15

Bora Bora (1970) Sex exploitation movie in which a husband pursues his wife to the South Seas where they engage in various affairs before reuniting for a happy ending that has no redeeming value. Except for the Polynesian setting, the movie is truly boring, boring. O (R)

Border, The (1982) A member of the Border Patrol (Jack Nicholson) is appalled by the corruption of his fellow officers but then begins himself to take small bribes from poor Mexicans because of his spendthrift wife (Valerie Perrine). Thoroughly muddled in both intentions and structure, director Tony Richardson keeps the narrative limping along until the sustained burst of improbable violence that concludes it. Also profanity and some brief nudity. A-III (R) 18

Born Again (1978) Based on Chuck Colson's book about his years in the Nixon White House, his trial, his prison term and conversion to fundamentalist Christianity, director Irving Rapper's well-intentioned but inadequate movie fails to move, much less convince, because it equates religious conviction with sentimentality. The result is both an insult to those who take religion seriously and an occasion for contempt to those who look down on any form of belief as intellectually indefensible. A-III (PG)

Born American (1986) Absurdly implausible action-adventure yarn about three college lads who, while vacationing in the Arctic, cross into the Soviet Union for a lark. Imprisoned and brutalized by Soviet guards, one of these All-American boys turns into a mini-Rambo visiting death and destruction on their tormentors. Profanity, graphic torture sequences, excessive violence and an imbecilic perspective on international relations. O (R)

Born Black (to White Parents) (1972) German-Italian attempt at soft-core titillation whose title refers to a black child born of Caucasian parents, the result of a sperm transfer, not by promiscuity. O (R)

Born Free (1966) Endearing wildlife story of an African game warden (Bill Travers), his wife (Virginia McKenna) and Elsa, their pet lion who, when grown, must be taught teach how to survive in the jungle rather than being confined in a zoo. Director James Hill relishes the natural beauty of the Kenyan game preserve and gets warm performances from the leads but nothing can stop Elsa from stealing the picture. Splendid family fare. A-I (br) U

Born in East L.A. (1987) Cheech Marin writes, directs and stars in this mild social satire about a Mexican-American's accidental deportation and his struggle to get back into the country. The film gives some sense of the immigration problems of illegal aliens but opts for slapstick humor, sexual innuendo and excessive profanity instead of emotional depth. A-III (R) 15

Born on the Fourth of July (1989) Emotionally wrenching story of an idealistic youth (Tom Cruise) who returns from Vietnam a crippled war hero, grows increasingly disillusioned and alienated from family and friends, turns to alcohol and sex but then rediscovers a purpose in life as part of the anti-war movement. Adapted from Ron Kovic's book by Kovic and director Oliver Stone, the movie captures the period in which the nation became polarized by the war and provides some insight into the problems of Vietnam veterans, but Stone's overly graphic depiction of violence and a sequence in a bordello are not for the fainthearted. Disturbing depiction of violence, a scene with nudity in a sexual context and much rough language A-IV (R) 15

Born to Win (1971) Czech director Ivan Passer's first American movie concerns a Times Square junkie (George Segal) who becomes involved with a woman (Karen Black) after stealing her car but, despite her help and his dreams of breaking his habit, he is a born loser. Though occasionally funny, too many scenes are played simply for their sexual content and the sensationalism of the drug counter-culture. O (R)

Born Wild (1968) Sordid melodrama directed by Maury Dexter about the conflict engendered by the bigoted treatment of Mexican-American students in a Southern California high school is excessive in its sensationalized treatment of sex and violence. O (PG)

Born Wild (see: "The Young Animals").

Born Yesterday (1993) Weak updating of the 1950 Judy Holliday comedy in which a shady land developer (John Goodman), wheeling and dealing in Washington, D.C., gets more than his money's worth when he hires a savvy reporter (Don Johnson) to smarten up his embarrassingly dumb girlfriend (Melanie Griffith). Director Luis Mandoki's flat comedy develops the romantic triangle with no subtlety or interesting characterizations to lift it above the level of mindless adult humor. A live-in relationship and momentary violence. A-III (PG)

Borrower, The (1991) Gory sci-fi horror flick about two detectives (Rae Dawn Chong and Don Gordon) chasing an alien monster who borrows human heads to disguise himself. Director John McNaughton uses gross imagery and ugly humor in a violent, repelling horror fantasy. Excessive violence, fleeting nudity and much rough language. O (R)

Borsalino (1970) French gangster story set in 1930 Marseilles (the Chicago of its day) follows the rise of two petty crooks (Jean-Paul Belmondo and Alain Delon) until they control the city's rackets and are targets for other ambitious criminals. Directed by Jacques Deray, the point is not so much the story as it is the relationship between the two men and the evocation of the mood and feeling of life in the 1930s. A-III (GP)

Boss Nigger (1975) Fred Williamson, co-producer and star of this most recent ripoff of Kurosawa's samurai epic, "Yojimbo," surrounds himself here with a set of supposed actors even more inept then he, with a fine disregard for race, creed, color or natural ability. Gratuitous violence and sex limit this to uncritical adults. A-III (PG)

Boston Strangler, The (1968) Fact-based movie about a sex murderer who terrorizes a city and the investigation that resulted in his capture. Director Richard Fleischer treats the case in plodding semi-documentary style, devoting the first half to the women victims and the last to the compulsive killer (Tony Curtis). Though well-intentioned, its graphic detailing of these brutal sex crimes is needless and offensive. O (R) X

Bostonians, The (1984) Interesting adaptation of the Henry James novel about a strong woman (Vanessa Redgrave), a domineering male (Christopher Reeve) and an innocent young woman (Madeleine Potter) whom both are trying to influence. Director James Ivory gets some notable performances, though Potter lacks the magnetism to be the focal point for the ensuing struggle between feminist and chauvinist, but it does succeed in conveying 19th-century American attitudes about sexual roles. A-II (nr) PG

Botany Bay (1953) Transporting convicts to Australia in 1787, a cruel British sea captain (James Mason) makes life miserable for all aboard, notably an unjustly imprisoned American medical student (Alan Ladd) and a comely thief (Patricia Medina). Directed by John Farrow, the ocean voyage is eventful enough but the action flags after reaching the colony and a contrived ending. Stylized violence and romantic complications. A-II (br) A

Bottom of the Bottle, The (1956) Dull tale of shifting psychological conflicts between a prosperous lawyer (Joseph Cotton) and his alcoholic brother (Van Johnson), an escaped convict trying to slip across the Mexican border. Director Henry Hathaway can't work up much interest in a contrived plot about cardboard characters. Stylized violence and excessive drinking. A-II (br) A

Boulevard Nights (1979) Inner-city Hispanic brothers strive for contrasting ideals. One wants a better life, the other wants gang supremacy. Director Michael Pressman's superficial examination of the macho rituals of gang violence and drug dependence in the Mexican-American community generates bogus excitement, relying too heavily upon their graphic depiction. O (R)

Bound for Glory (1977) Screen adaptation of the 1943 autobiography of folk singer Woody Guthrie (David Carradine) follows his odyssey among America's dispossessed from the Oklahoma Dust Bowl to migrant labor camps in California where his songs about these experiences led to a national radio career. The outstanding achievement of director Hal Ashby's dramatization is its faithful re-creation of the Depression era and Guthrie's passion for social justice. Restrained depiction of promiscuity. A-III (PG) A

Bounty, The (1984) Revisionist account of the mutiny aboard the "HMS Bounty" portrays Lt. William Bligh (Anthony Hopkins) as a flawed hero and Fletcher Christian (Mel Gibson) as an unstable young man bewitched by a Tahitian beauty. Roger Donaldson directs with intelligence and visual flare, but despite fine acting, no real sparks ignite the drama because of a weak script. Extensive Polynesian nudity. A-IV (PG) 15

Bounty Killer, The (1965) After barely surviving an ambush that killed his partner, a bounty hunter (Dan Duryea) becomes a crazed avenger, using a sawed-off shotgun to get those responsible. Directed by Spencer G. Bennet, the hokey plot has equally unconvincing action depite a parade of veteran Western actors (Richard Arlen, Johnny Mack Brown, Bob Steele and Buster Crabbe). Stylized violence and a hero who goes over the edge. A-II (br)

Boxcar Bertha (1972) Trashy melodrama about a former labor unionizer turned bank robber (David Carradine), his woman companion of the title (Barbara Hershey) and some drifters (Barry Primus and Bernie Casey) picked up along the way. Directed by Martin Scorsese, the movie rumbles along through a tacky morass of redneck police and hired railroad thugs, pausing only for a shotgun blast in the chest here or a frolic in the buff there. There is a climactic massacre that leaves Carradine nailed cruciform to the side of a boxcar. O (R) X

Boxing Helena (1993) Tawdry horror tale in which an unbalanced surgeon (Julian Sands) amputates the limbs of the woman (Sherilyn Fenn) he loves, but who does not love him. Director Jennifer Chambers Lynch makes this nightmare of sexual obsession even more repulsive by treating it in the slick manner of a sentimental romance. Excessively graphic sex scenes, perverse violence and occasional rough language. O (R) 18

Boy and His Dog, A (1976) A not very bright boy (Don Johnson) and his extremely intelligent dog try to survive in a post-nuclear holocaust world. The two, moreover, can communicate telepathically with one another until the inevitable love traingle is introduced (Susan Benton). The acting, including the dog's is very good, but it is questionable that the violence and sex add to this black comedy from director L.Q. Jones based upon the Harlan Ellison novella. A-IV (R) U

Boy, Did I Get a Wrong Number (1966) Hopeless comedy directed by George Marshall in which a real-estate operator (Bob Hope) lets a movie actress (Elke Sommer) hide out from the studio in an unsold estate causing all kinds of implausible complications with his wife (Marjorie Lord)

and maid (Phyllis Diller). Sexual innuendo. A-III (br)

Boy Friend, The (1972) British spoof of 1930s Hollywood backstage musicals with Twiggy as the understudy who becomes the star. Writer-producer-director Ken Russell turns Sandy Wilson's romantic musical set in the 1920s into an extravaganza of Busby Berkeley-like production numbers done on a lavish scale. Old-fashioned escapist fare, though a bit overlong for the small fry. A-I (G) U

Boy in Blue, The (1986) Based on the life of a legendary Canadian scull racing champion, the movie not only lacks a romantic vision but features a wholly anachronistic portrayal by Nicolas Cage in what becomes a teenage macho study of false pride and determination in 1870s' America. Moronic teen romance and brief nudity. A-III (R)

Boy Named Charlie Brown, A (1969) First animated movie version of the Peanuts comic strip characters created by George Schulz centers on Charlie Brown's obsession with failure as he enters a national spelling bee contest. The animation team under director Bill Melendez has been completely faithful to the stylized world of the comic strip in giving movement and voice to the small fry characters. Refreshing but meaningful amusement for both youngsters and grown-ups. A-I (G)

Boy of Two Worlds (1970) After the death of his parents, a West Indian boy is sent to live with his maiden aunt in a small Danish village. When she dies, he runs away and lives in the forest rather than stay in an orphanage. All ends happily in a very engaging children's movie directed by Astrid and Bjare Henning-Jensen that will also interest adults. A-I (G) U

Boy Ten Feet Tall, A (1965) Orphaned boy journeys alone across the length of Africa to find an aunt and matures considerably during the course of his adventures. Directed by Alexander Mackendrick, the story is slight but very appealing, especially for youngsters. A-I (G)

Boy with Green Hair, The (1948) Runaway war orphan (Dean Stockwell) tells social worker (Robert Ryan) how he was scorned and rejected after his hair suddenly turned green. Producer Dore Schary's earnest but preachy parable about prejudice gets heavy-handed direction from Joseph Losey, though Pat O'Brien's breezy performance as the lad's whimsical guardian adds some life to an otherwise dour story. A-I (br) U

Boy Who Could Fly, The (1986) A teenage girl befriends an autistic boy and tries to help him overcome his muteness in a tender and sensitive fable about the impor-

tance of friendship for those growing up in a socially inflexible environment. Nick Castle directs this unpretentious, life-affirming movie that uses brief but effective special-effects fantasy to provide some good-natured fun for youngsters. A-I (PG)

Boy Who Cried Werewolf, The (1973) Inept semi-horror movie about a youngster (Scott Sealey) whose father (Kerwin Matthews) is bitten by a werewolf near the family's secluded summer cabin, but no one will listen as the locals are decimated in traditional fashion. Lethargically directed by Nathan Juran, it may frighten youngsters insecure in their parental relationships, but lycanthropy lovers can only lament this travesty of a cherished movie myth. A-II (PG) X

Boyfriends and Girlfriends (1988) French director-writer Eric Rohmer tracks the shifting romantic alliances between four young men and women living and working in a Paris suburb. Its sparkling depiction of the warm friendship between the two women (Emmanuelle Chaulet and Sophia Renoir) is marred by the story's implied cohabitation of unmarried couples. Subtitles. A-III (PG)

Boys from Brazil, The (1978) Fanatical Nazi war criminal (Gregory Peck) oversees the care and feeding of some Hitler clones born in Brazil and distributed throughout the world. Laurence Olivier plays his opponent, an aging Jewish Nazi hunter. Some good acting but, for the most part, director Franklin Schaffner achieves only an overwrought melodrama with a large dose of graphic, sadistic violence. A-III (R) 18

Boys in Company C, The (1978) Directed by Sidney J. Furie with a cast of unknown actors, this muddled movie about a company of young Marines in boot camp and subsequent combat in Vietnam focuses on drugs, atrocities, greed and cynicism. Veering from slapstick to supposedly real emotion, the movie uses foul language, bereft of any significant context, while failing to give any moral or political dimension to the drama. O (R)

Boys in the Band, The (1970) Screen version of a stage play about a birthday party attended by eight homosexual and one heterosexual college friends. Directed by William Friedkin, it is a gripping, frighteningly honest view of human relationships and the introverted homosexual psyche with all its anxiety, bitterness, depression and solitude. A-IV (R) X

Boys Next Door, The (1986) Two socially disadvantaged youths, about to graduate from high school and take on dull factory jobs, vent their frustrations and anxieties in a series of brutal encounters with innocent strangers who have the misfortune to cross their path. Director Penelope Spheeri's exploration of the dark side of maladjusted youth exploits only the violent consequences of alienation without a compassionate insight into adolescent behavior. Excessive use of brutality and foul language. O (R)

Boys of Paul Street, The (1969) Hungarian movie in which two bands of schoolboys vie for possession of a vacant lot in 1902 Budapest, but the outcome of their skirmishes proves as disillusioning to them as the battles they will fight a few years later in World War I. Director Zoltan Fabri's nostalgic production re-creates the historical period as well as the innocent earnestness with which the boys regard their secret societies and strange rituals. Good family fare. A-I (G)

Boys Town (1938) Sentimental but emotionally honest story of how Father Flanagan (Spencer Tracy) built his school for homeless and delinquent youths during the Depression. Directed by Norman Taurog, the Hollywood version centers in the conflict between the priest's charismatic powers of persuasion and a street-tough (Mickey Rooney) who only thinks he's hardboiled. Tracy's Oscar-winning performance as a role model for those in need of one was a credible blend of the idealistic and the pragmatic. A-I (br) A

Boyz N the Hood (1991) Drugs, gang warfare and broken homes take their toll on a determined black youth (Cuba Gooding, Jr.) and two brothers (Ice Cube and Morris Chestnut) who are his closest friends in a violent South Central Los Angeles neighborhood. Writer-director John Singleton's first feature is a harrowing and powerful pro-family, anti-drug statement, though frequently undermined by the preachy tone of its heavy-handed dialogue. Excessive rough language and gutter talk, repeated mindless violence, drug and alcohol abuse and brief bedroom shots with flashes of nudity. A-IV (R) 15

Braddock: Missing in Action III (1988) Brutal sequel in which superhero Col. Jim Braddock (Chuck Norris) returns to Vietnam, this time to rescue his Vietnamese wife presumed killed in the fall of Saigon, the son he didn't know he had and a terrorized group of Amerasian youngsters. Ploddingly directed by Aaron Norris, the movie's threadbare plot serves only as a pretext for extravagant mayhem, laced with comic-book heroics and exaggerated Oriental villains. Excessive violence. O (R) 18

Brain, The (1969) French comedy in which a master criminal (David Niven), whose brain is so large he has trouble keeping his head erect, comes up with a million dollar scheme that becomes an international cops-and-robbers chase. Director Gerard Oury has made an old-fashioned romp with a couple of good laughs, but many scenes are overextended and full of cliches. Comic violence. A-II (G) U

Brain Donors (1992) A trio of loonies (John Turturro, Bob Nelson and Mel Smith) persuades a rich widow (Nancy Marchand) to sponsor them in the formation of a ballet company. Director Dennis Dugan's wacky farce repeats all manner of comic cliches from Marx Brothers comedies before it lurches out of control and runs out of genuine laughs. Mild sexual innuendo. A-II (PG)

Brainstorm (1983) Some dedicated scientists invent a device to enable one person to experience another's thoughts and sensations, but some nasty military types try to take it over for their own purposes. Directed by Douglas Trumbull, starring Natalie Wood and Christopher Walken, the movie is more interested in its special effects than in developing the human dimensions of its characters. Brief but graphic sex scene. A-III (PG) A

Bram Stoker's Dracula (1992) Tawdry retelling of the vampire classic as a doomed love story begins in Transylvania where Count Dracula (Gary Oldman) has his handmaidens seduce a young English realtor (Keanu Reeves), then moves to London in order to ravage the realtor's bride (Winona Ryder) before a cunning professor (Anthony Hopkins) orchestrates the vampire's demise. Director Francis Ford Coppola's erotic version of the Gothic tale gets lost in garishly titillating images that fail to evoke the basic simplicity of the struggle between good and evil and undercut the stark horror of the story. Perverse, sexually suggestive scenes with recurring nudity and intermittent gory violence, including several decapitations. O (R) 18

Brand X (1970) Taylor Mead stars in an underground movie satirizing TV programming with a self-conscious grab bag of humorous improvisations. Some of the skits are indeed witty but the majority are crude, tasteless, vulgar and indeed indecent. O (nr)

Brannigan (1975) John Wayne, violating civil rights at home and abroad, plays a police officer sent to England to extradite a hood with whom he has a personal score to settle. British production directed by Douglas Hickox focuses on Wayne's character as contemptuous of all legal restraint, an attitude in which he is joined ultimately by his London counterpart (Richard Attenborough). He-man violence. A-III (PG) 15

Brass Legend, The (1956) Pedestrian Western directed by Gerd Oswald pits steely-eyed sheriff Hugh O'Brien against wanted outlaw Raymond Burr with predictable results. Stylized violence. A-II (br) A

Brass Target (1979) Yarn blurring the border between history and fiction about a failed attempt to assassinate General Patton (George Kennedy) who wants to retrieve the German gold high-ranking American staff officers have hijacked. John Hough's direction smothers suspense but inflates the violence making the movie unsuitable for youngsters. A-III (PG) 15

Bravados, The (1958) Grim, troubling Western follows a revengeful rancher as he seeks the gang (notably Stephen Boyd, Henry Silva and Lee Van Cleef) who killed his wife and child. Directed by Henry King, the trail is long and bloody but by its end the rancher realizes that justice is not achieved at the end of a gun. Strong stylized violence and vigilante theme. A-II (br) A

Brave Little Toaster, The (1987) Animated feature in which five old appliances—Toaster, Radio, Lampy, electric blanket Blanky and vacuum cleaner Kirby—left in a summer cottage and yearning for the boy who used to use them, set off on an arduous, at times dangerous journey to the big city to find their young master. Though the story doesn't bear much adult scrutiny and the Taiwan-Japanese animation is not up to Disney standards, most pre-teen viewers will find the adventures of the unlikely but lively fivesome imaginative fun and be impressed by the loyalty and perseverance exhibited by the appliances. For all, though several menacing scenes may frighten the very young. A-I (nr) U

Brave Warrior (1952) With the aid of Chief Tecumseh (Jay Silverheels), Americans (led by Jon Hall) put down a British-instigated Shawnee uprising at Tippecanoe, Indiana, in 1811. Directed by Spencer G. Bennett, it's a minor Western with grade-school heroics and some stylized violence. A-I (br) U

Brazen Women of Balzac, The (1971) The only thing brazen about this coarse German-made exploitation movie that portrays sexual activities in a villa overlooking the Rhine is the way its importers have edited in several yards of sexually explicit footage to compete with porno product. O (R)

Brazil (1986) This production combines the failed utopian vision of "Blade Runner" with the whimsical outlook of the Monty Python comedy troupe in a playful, expressionistic fantasy of a madcap totalitarian England where nothing works. Director Terry Gilliam's mix of mirth and menace proclaims the futility of the hero's slapstick struggle to combat conformity and complacency with romantic love. A-III (R) 15

Bread and Chocolate (1978) In this tragicomedy from director Franco Brusati, Nino Manfredi plays an Italian immigrant worker desperately trying to make a go of it in Switzerland so that he can bring home some money to his family. Light social satire contrasting unfeeling bourgeoisie with passionate working-class loser, it resorts to some indecent exposure and a gratuitous incident in which a priest is involved in a bizarre murder. O (nr) AA

Breaker, Breaker (1977) An amateurish little movie directed by Don Hulette about a martial arts master and trucker (Chuck Norris) who cleans out a nest of thugs and criminals with the help of a fleet of trucks called in by CB radio. Considerable violence and some rough language. A-III (PG)

Breakfast at Tiffany's (1961) Bright romantic comedy from Truman Capote's tale of Holly Golightly (Audrey Hepburn), a bubble-headed beauty whose kooky behavior wows Manhattan's social set and bowls over an earnest young writer (George Peppard) despite complications (Patricia Neal). Director Blake Edwards lances the bogus glitter of the big city and paces the action with humor (notably Mickey Rooney's broad performance as an irascible Japanese neighbor) but the movie's main attraction is Hepburn's ability to portray the innate innocence of the free-spirited Holly. Mature themes. A-III (br) PG

Breakfast Club, The (1985) Five teenagers spend a Saturday detention in their school library. After much abrasive interchange and a little marijuana, they become downright chummy when they realize they share common attitudes about adult authority figures, drugs and sex. Under John Hughes' direction the movie lacks any critical perspective, seeming to justify anti-social behavior, casual sex and the concept of drugs as a harmless escape, if not a liberating experience. O (R) 15

Breakheart Pass (1976) This Charles Bronson vehicle is an interesting western that is part mystery and part suspense. Although the action takes place mostly on a train, outside is the world of the U.S. cavalry vs. the Indians. The movie's production values and Tom Gries' direction are tops, but there is some brutal violence. A-III (PG)

Breakin' (1984) Director Joel Silberg's quickie movie cashing in on the break-dancing craze is innocuous, light entertainment. A classical dancer, going nowhere as a waitress (Lucinda Dickey), joins up with break dancers Adolfo "Shabba-Doo" Quinones and Michael "Bongaloo Shrimp" Chambers, and the three conquer the prejudice of the dance establishment and make it to Broadway.

There is some charm in its unpretentiousness but little, if any, style. A-II (PG)

Breakin' II: Electric Boogaloo (1985) Break-dancing sequel is this time a case of "putting on a show of our own" in the old Judy Garland-Mickey Rooney tradition. The necessary ingredient is the dancing, with the plot being only the occasion for it. The performers are pleasantly exuberant and the whole exercise is innocuous. A-II (PG)

Breaking Away (1979) Light comedy chronicling a summer in the lives of four teenagers in mid-America who are determined to stay together despite community and hometown college pressures to the contrary. In centering on one youth (Dennis Christopher) and his bemused parents (Barbara Barrie and Paul Dooley), director Peter Yates reveals a depth and feeling for character that gives weight to the movie's exploration of youthful determination culminating in a vivid bicycle race. A-II (PG) A

Breaking Glass (1981) Brian Gibson directs an offbeat movie that takes a hard look at British society and the empire of pop music. It gets a bit too slick and sentimental at the end, but despite its defects it's fairly entertaining and provocative, thanks in large part to the talent of actress-singer-composer Hazel O'Connor. Restrained portrayal of the seamy side of life. A-III (PG) AA

Breaking In (1989) Refreshing, low-key buddy caper with Burt Reynolds as a graying, gimpy professional safecracker who teaches a young, goofy protege (Casey Siemaszko) the tricks of his dying trade. Scottish director Bill Forsyth peoples his Portland landscape with nutty characters and doesn't glamorize his two harmless protagonists and their whimsical, nonmenacing heists. No violence, though some profanity and suggested sexual encounters with prostitutes. A-III (R) 15

Breaking Point, The (1976) Bo Svenson plays the abused, honest citizen tracked by the hoods against whom he testified in this typically brutal and mindless variation on the revenge theme. Canadian director Bob Clark's viewers are subjected to an assault of violence, maiming and a brutal rape. O (R) X

Breaking the Rules (1992) Maudlin male-bonding saga of estranged friends (Jonathan Silverman and C. Thomas Howell) accompanying a leukemia-stricken buddy (Jason Bateman) on the drive from Cleveland to Los Angeles so the dying man can appear on a cherished TV quiz show, but pick up a woman (Annie Potts) along the way instead. Directed by Neil Israel, the trio's journey flounders in over-cute dialogue, sophomoric pranks, artificial tears and pretentious mus-

ings on what it all means. Recurring sexual references, a seduction scene, satiric treatment of religion and occasional profanity. O (PG-13)

Breakout (1975) Down-on-his-luck pilot (Charles Bronson) contracts to fly a wrongly accused American out of a Mexican prison and finds himself involved with a rogue CIA operation. Directed by Tom Gries, it's an old-fashioned adventure yarn with the emphasis on action rather than violence, except for a grisly depiction of a villain being killed by an airplane propeller. A-III (PG) AA

Breathless (1983) Remake of Jean-Luc Godard's 1963 movie about a petty criminal betrayed by love is a self-indulgent exercise in graphic sex and sentimentality. Neither of the two lovers (Richard Gere and Valerie Kaprisky) shows sufficient humanity to stake a claim on our interest but, to be fair, both are constantly upstaged by a blaring rock score and the slick, flashy, altogether shallow technique of director Jim McBride. O (R) 18

Breezy (1973) May-December romance blooms when divorced L.A. realtor (William Holden) finds a 17-year-old flower child (Kay Lenz) on his doorstep, and soon they are off romping together until, of course, he meets her friends and she his. Directed by Clint Eastwood, the romantic twaddle makes frequent use of nudity and pointless profanity. O (R) AA

Brewster McCloud (1971) Failed allegory about a fallen angel (Sally Kellerman) who inspires a boy (Bud Cort) to fly under the power of his own homemade wings. Director Robert Altman manages to wring spirited performances from a fine supporting cast but not from his principals and the result is a confused narrative with only flashes of humor and satire, much of it bawdy but toothless. A-III (R) A

Brewster's Millions (1985) Richard Pryor stars in another remake of the venerable chestnut about a man who inherits a vast fortune on the condition that he squander a modest one. Under Walter Hill's direction, it's funny enough and fairly good entertainment, though the present version introduces too many needless complications. Some vulgar language. A-II (PG)

Bride, The (1985) In this freely adapted remake of "Bride of Frankenstein," the mad doctor (rock star Sting) decides to keep for himself the mate (Jennifer Beals) he has fashioned for his creature (Clancy Brown). Unfortunately, director Franc Roddam is unable to bring this fine-looking but inert movie to life. Innocuous save for a brief sequence involving nudity. A-III (PG-13) 15

Bride Came C.O.D., The (1941) Screwball romantic comedy in which an aviator

(James Cagney) is hired to bring an eloping heiress (Bette Davis) back to her millionaire father (Eugene Pallette) but their plane crash lands in a desert ghost town. Directed by William Keighley, the fun comes mostly from the battling Cagney-Davis combination, but the good supporting cast and some twists on an old formula plot are added dividends. Some comic violence and romantic complications. A-II (br) U

Bride Wore Black, The (1968) Superior murder thriller starring Jeanne Moreau as a revenge-obsessed bride who sets out to kill the five men responsible for her bridegroom's death. Directed by Francois Truffaut, the French production is an exercise in suspense of the Hitchcock variety. Subtitles. Restrained violence. A-III (br) A

Brides of Fu Manchu, The (1966) This time the Oriental master criminal (Christopher Lee) plans to conquer the world by forcing kidnapped scientists to develop a weapon utilizing intensified sound waves to destroy selected targets. Directed by Don Sharp, the action features mild violence and sexual innuendo. A-II (br) U

Bridge at Remagen, The (1969) While the Germans try to destroy the last bridge across the Rhine in World War II, an American unit (led by George Segal) races to capture it. Director John Guillerman does well in building the tension and suspense inherent in the situation, but the human level of the relationships between the soldiers comes across as affected and shallow. Much wartime violence and strong language. A-III (PG) AA

Bridge on the River Kwai, The (1957) Epic World War II adventure based on Pierre Boulle's novel about British POWs in Burma who build a military supply bridge for their Japanese captors while British commandos make their way through the jungle to blow it up. Though the anti-war pay-off is more hollow than ironic, director David Lean excels in depicting the rigors of prison camp life, the military discipline that sustains the prisoners and, at the story's center, the battle of wills between the British commander (Alec Guinness) and his Japanese counterpart (Sessue Hayakawa) over who will command the work details. Some wartime violence and harrowing camp punishments. A-I (br) U

Bridge Too Far, A (1977) Director Richard Attenborough's epic re-creation of the tragic Allied offensive code-named Market Garden details the fate of the massive paratroop force dropped behind German lines in Holland during World War II. The excellent all-star cast includes Dirk Bogarde, Anthony Hopkins, Laurence Olivier, Robert Redford, Ryan O'Neal, Gene Hackman and Elliot Gould. Although the violence is unusually graphic, the movie has value as an historical dramatization that has tried to be faithful to the facts. A-III (PG) A

Brief Encounter (1945) Bittersweet British romance about a suburban housewife (Celia Johnson) and a married doctor (Trevor Howard) whose chance meeting in a train station becomes a weekly event that deepens into an emotional involvement neither had anticipated. Director David Lean shows this mutual attraction to be more spiritual than physical as conveyed in exquisitely understated performances and evocative Rachmaninov piano concerto on the music track. The question of marital infidelity is treated within a moral framework. A-II (br) A

Brief Season (1971) Pia Degermark and Christoper Jones play a pair of Roman dropouts desperately having a go at life by bedding down, joy-riding in the woods and buying expensive gifts before taking their own lives. Director Renato Castel-lani's attempt to make alienation seem glamorous reduces everything to the most boring and inane level. A-III (R/GP)

Brief Vacation, A (1975) Italian portrait of a woman (Florinda Bolkan), her health broken from overworking to support three children and several relatives, who is sent to a sanitarium to regain her strength. There she has a brief affair with a younger man, but he comes from another class and her life remains unchanged. Director Vittorio de Sica contents himself with a realistic portrayal of a complex human being, letting viewers draw their own conclusions about the larger social implications in his story of the plight of the poor. Mature themes. A-III (PG)

Brigadoon (1954) Fanciful but thin Lerner and Loewe musical with vacationing Americans (Gene Kelly and Van Johnson) lost in the Scottish countryside where they stumble upon an 18th-century village that appears only for a day every 100 years. Kelly's love for village lass Cyd Charisse isn't strong enough to keep director Vincente Minnelli's colorful fantasy from falling disappointingly flat, though the songs are lovely and Kelly's choreography worth watching. For the romantics in the family. A-I (G) U

Brigand of Kandahar, The (1965) Turgid British melodrama about troubles on Victorian India's Northwest Frontier when a fanatic rebel leader (Oliver Reed) teams with a half-caste English officer (Ronald Lewis) seeking revenge on his bigoted commander (Duncan Lamont). Writer-director John Gilling's studio-bound production plods through an unconvincing story of adventure, romance and muddled loyalties. Stylized violence, romantic complications and racial stereotypes. A-II (br) U

Bright Angel (1991) An innocent 18-year-old Montana youth (Dermot Mulroney) and a world-weary runaway (Lili Taylor) who hopes to secure her brother's release from prison encounter a series of unsavory, at times deadly, characters. Cynicism and hopelessness pervade director Michael Fields' pathetic tale of easily exploited youngsters and jaded adults who have given up on life or chosen brutality to get what they want. A nihilistic view of life, occasional violence and sexual references, brief nudity and much rough language. O (R)

Bright Lights, Big City (1988) Lurid adaptation of Jay McInerney's best-seller tracing the downward spiral of a young, aspiring novelist (Michael J. Fox) into sordid New York club life, drugs and alcohol. Director James Bridges fails to fully develop the one-dimensional, dissipated lead character, doing a disservice to Fox's fans who may be led to believe that drug and alcohol abuse are not addictive or lethal. Excessive scenes of substance abuse, some profanity and hedonistic sexual activity within the NYC club scene. O (R) 18

Brighton Beach Memoirs (1986) Screen adaptation of Neil Simon's lighthearted play about a Jewish adolescent (Jonathan Silverman) coming of age in 1937 Brooklyn. Director Gene Saks re-creates the look and atmosphere of pre-World War II America and its traditional family values while finding humor in the young lad's struggle with the onset of puberty. Some discussion of masturbation, adolescent sexuality and a sight gag featuring a nude postcard. A-III (PG-13) 15

Brighty of the Grand Canyon (1967) Brighty, a brave burro with a natural instinct for distinguishing between good people and bad, helps track down the killer of an old prospector. Written and directed by Norman Foster, based on a book by Marguerite Henry, the outdoors adventure offers some dandy suspense as well as glorious photography of Arizona's Grand Canyon country. No violent visuals. A-I (br)

Bring Me the Head of Alfredo Garcia (1974) Down-at-the-heels American (Warren Oates) takes the grisly job of tracking down a man in Mexico and delivering his head to a millionaire but in the process has to kill more and more people until he becomes mad with bloodlust. Director Sam Peckinpah turns the story into sordid essay on the pornography of violence. O (R) X

Bringing Up Baby (1938) Classic screwball comedy in which a serious-minded paleontologist (Cary Grant) gets mixed up with a zany socialite heiress (Katherine Hepburn) whose pet leopard, Baby, is mistaken for an escaped killer leopard and confusions multiply until girl gets boy. Howard Hawks directs the hilarious proceedings with flair and style, abetted by a playful plot, madcap performances by Hepburn and Grant and a great supporting cast (including Charlie Ruggles, May Robson, Barry Fitzgerald and Walter Catlett). Absurdly silly and utterly delightful. A-I (br) U

Brink's Job, The (1978) Director William Friedkin focuses on the crooks (Peter Falk, Peter Boyle and Allen Goorwitz) involved in a spectacular 1950 robbery in Boston, providing a fascinating picture of the underside of society in a particular time and place. Laced with wry humor, the movie has almost no violence, the language is relatively restrained, but there is moral ambiguity in its somewhat romanticized view of criminal life. A-III (PG) A

Britannia Hospital (1983) Crude, muddled British satire about a hospital celebrating its 500th anniversary and whose preparations for a visit from the Queen become reduced to chaos as various factions within and without clash. Director Lindsay Anderson obviously intends the clash of special interest groups as a metaphor of the condition of Britain herself and the world in general. Violence, nudity and a general air of cynical amorality. O (R) AA

Broadcast News (1987) News producer (Holly Hunter) in the Washington bureau of a TV network finds herself drawn away from a hard-working reporter whom she admires (Albert Brooks) by an off-again, on-again attraction to a handsome but unprofessional reporter (William Hurt) being groomed as network news anchor. Written, produced and directed by James L. Brooks, the romantic comedy is often quite funny and also worthwhile in its satiric portrait of television news being more concerned with image and packaging than with the news story itself. Permissive attitude toward casual sex, several explicit sexual references and some rough language. A-IV (R) 15

Broadway Danny Rose (1984) Director Woody Allen's nostalgic essay on showbiz self-deception is a droll and almost provincial tribute to the small-time theatrical agents who, like Danny Rose (Allen), labor with scant hope of monetary reward for some fourth-rate talent. The plot, revolving around reviving the career of a has-been singer (Nick Apollo Forte) only to be betrayed at the point of success, is thin and only mildly amusing. Some Italian stereotyping. A-III (PG)

Broken Mirrors (1987) Dutch import directed by feminist Marleen Gorris examines the ruthless and abusive relationships between men and women as viewed by two women who try to free themselves from the spiritual suffocation of working in an Amsterdam brothel. As a lesson for women to escape victimization, the amateurish production resorts too often to extreme and explicit examples of injustice, sadistic brutality and abuse. Foul language and brief nudity are intermittent. O (nr)

Bronco Billy (1980) Offbeat story of a modern-day shoe salesman from New Jersey (Clint Eastwood) who puts together a modest but competent Wild West Show with other dreamers and misfits like himself. Also directed by Eastwood, the comedy is surprisingly amiable and relaxed though marred by the inclusion of a brutal fight sequence. A-III (PG) A

Bronco Bullfrog (1972) British story of a young worker who falls in love with an underage girl, but its principal intent is to describe a deadening environment that has already condemned him to a life without hope. Directed by Barney Platt-Mills, the 1969 semi-documentary is an honest portrayal of young people's alienation from the modern world. There are subtitles for those who can't catch the Cockney dialogue. A-III (nr) AA

Bronx Tale, A (1993) Growing up in the 1960s, an Italian-American youth (Lillo Brancato) is torn between the decent values of his bus-driver father (Robert De Niro) and the easy-money life of the neighborhood crime boss (Chazz Palminteri), who treats him like his own son. Also directed by De Niro, the well-realized drama makes a convincing moral statement in its picture of a youth who comes to recognize the emptiness of ill-gotten money and the deadly violence it spawns. Some violence, racial slurs, sexual references and much rough language. A-III (R) 18

Brood, The (1979) Canadian movie in which a mentally disturbed woman (Samantha Eggar) generates such intense hatred that she gives birth to children of rage who go out and murder the objects of her enmity. Directed by David Cronenberg, some good acting is overwhelmed by blood and gore, building to an even more bloody conclusion. O (R) 18

Brother, Can You Spare a Dime (1975) Slap-dash documentary supposedly dealing with the hard times of the Depression is not so much edited as spliced together. The vulgarity captured belongs not to the 1930s, but to the people who produced it. A-II (PG) U

Brother Carl (1972) Study of four tortured individuals (Gunnel Lindbloom, Genevieve Page, Laurent Terzieff and Keve Hjelm) who for no apparent reason torment themselves and one another. Director Susan Sontag's effort falls flat because, lacking an understandable human context, it is too abstract to evoke an emotional response from viewers. A-IV (nr)

Brother from Another Planet, The (1984) Black extraterrestrial crashes to Earth and finds sanctuary in Harlem from two bounty hunters determined to find and return him to his home planet. Moderately entertaining social satire from writer-director John Sayles has some profanity and a relatively restrained sexual scene. A-III (nr) 15

Brother John (1971) Returning to Alabama for his sister's funeral, a world traveler and keen observer of humanity (Sidney Poitier) arouses the suspicions of some townspeople when he involves himself in the life of the community. Though there is a certain amount of enjoyment to be had in the movie's vague suggestions about the mysterious title character's other-worldly origins, James Goldstone's heavy-handed direction only emphasizes the emptiness of a story concept that has nowhere to go other than its banal conclusion. Some mature themes. A-III (GP) AA

Brother of the Wind (1975) Kindly old mountain dweller raises four cuddly, frisky wolf cubs amid the scenic splendor of the Canadian Rockies. Short on plot but long on shots of nature, the movie introduces the quartet to a variety of wildlife and, alas, a snowmobile, shotgun-wielding hunter. Though younger children might be frightened by a few scenes depicting hunting and killing in the wild, the beauty of the scenery and the intimate glimpses of wildlife make it a pleasant experience for all. A-I (G)

Brother Sun, Sister Moon (1973) Director Franco Zeffirelli's version of the oft-told story of Francis of Assisi (Graham Faulkner) treats him as secular saint and social heretic, emphasizing parallels between his age and our own. The strength of the movie lies in its rich visualization of the natural beauties of the Umbrian hills and the Romanesque architecture of medieval Assisi. While the lush and lavish production has nothing to do with the Franciscan spirit of poverty and simplicity, it is a pictorially beautiful movie that succeeds quite well in celebrating nature and the quest for finding more to life than accumulating material goods. A-II (PG)

Brotherhood, The (1969) When a Mafia member (Kirk Douglas) kills one of the crime bosses (Luther Adler), he flees to Sicily and the mob sends his younger brother (Alex Cord) to kill him. Directed by Martin Ritt, the core of the movie is the contrast between the older brother's reverence for tradition and the younger one's ambitious pragmatism. Some graphic violence. A-III (M) A

Brotherhood of Satan (1971) Coven of devil worshippers (led by Strother Martin) in their quest for eternal youth abduct 13 children while killing their parents in bizarre, bloody fashion that confounds a dim-witted sheriff (L.Q. Jones) as their bodies accumulate in the local ice house. Director Bernard McEveety ladles out his witchcraft murders with remarkable ineptitude. Visual gore and a conclusion in which evil triumphs over good. A-III (GP) X

Brotherly Love (1970) Peter O'Toole gives an outstanding performance as a Scottish lord caught up in a long-standing and unhealthy relationship with his sister (Susannah York), but the story fails to come alive. Directed by J. Lee Thompson, the movie's unexplained motivations, the slow pacing and unpleasant characterizations contribute to a sense of disinterest in what is happening. A-IV (R)

Brother's Keeper (1992) Compelling documentary about the Ward Brothers, four illiterate and elderly dairy farmers in upstate New York, one of whom is put on trial for the 1990 mercy killing of an older brother. Produced and directed by Joe Berlinger and Bruce Sinofsky, the film provides an eloquent portrait of the rural community which regarded the brothers as eccentric but harmless recluses and came to the defense of the accused brother whom they believed incapable of murder. Some complex justice questions and a graphic scene of a pig being slaughtered. A-III (nr)

Brothers (1977) Fictionalized and highly romanticized account of the friendship between imprisoned radical George Jackson (Bernie Casey) and Communist intellectual and philosophy professor Angela Davis (Vonetta McGee). Although the movie directed by Arthur Barron is obviously sympathetic toward its central characters, it offers intelligent and compassionate insights into the agony of prison life. Rough language, violence and borders on justifying political terrorism. A-III (R)

Brubaker (1980) Henry Brubaker (Robert Redford) is a prison warden and reformer who goes inside a prison disguised as a convict to find out what is wrong with the system. Director Stuart Rosenberg's fact-based movie is uncompromising and harrowingly realistic with graphic and implied violence, a brief scene of nudity and much profanity. A-III (R) 15

Brute and the Beast, The (1969) Formula Italian western in which a cowboy (Franco Nero) returns to his home town, finds it dominated by a petty land baron's band of gunfighters and proceeds to right the wrongs done his family and friends. Directed by Lucio Fulci, some four dozen men, women and children are killed as the unimaginative story unfolds. Much stylized violence and brutality. A-III (M)

B.S., I Love You (1971) Young advertising hustler (Peter Kastner) stumbles into high position by making it with both mother and daughter. Director Steven Hillard concentrates upon the sexual aspects of the narrative portrayed in a series of supposedly humorous, but terribly tasteless scenes. O (R) X

Buccaneer, The (1958) The pirate band of Jean Lafitte (Yul Brynner) help the American forces led by Andrew Jackson (Charlton Heston) defeat the British at the Battle of New Orleans in 1815. Produced by Cecil B. DeMille and directed by Anthony Quinn, the production is good looking with colorful characters and action but little sense of credibility. Stylized violence. A-I (br) U

Buck and the Preacher (1972) Sidney Poitier plays guide and wagon master for a group of freed slaves moving West after the Civil War, but they face wild Indians and a gang of outlaws. Also directed by Poitier, it is little more than a standard shoot-em-up, though Harry Belafonte's cunningly exaggerated performance as an opportunist preacher with a six-shooter in his Bible adds some much needed humor. A-III (GP) AA

Buck Privates (1941) The first of many vehicles starring the comedy team of Bud Abbott and Lou Costello has the boys mistakenly enlisting in the Army where they make a shambles of basic training but wind up leading their unit to victory during field maneuvers. Director Arthur Lubin strings together a series of gags involving several of the team's familiar flim-flam routines, little-guy Lou's talent for slapstick and a tame romantic subplot with the Andrew Sisters belting out "The Boogie Woogie Bugle Boy of Company B." It's a dated period piece, but that's part of its pleasure and the gags still draw smiles, especially from youngsters. A-I (br) U

Buck Privates Come Home (1947) Uneven comedy directed by Charles Barton has Bud Abbott and Lou Costello smuggling a war orphan back from Europe, then as civilians trying to find jobs and a suitable home for their young charge. Sentimental but unpretentious fun, especially for youngsters. A-I (br) U

Buck Rogers in the 25th Century (1979) An American astronaut (Gil Gerard) gets caught in a time warp and flashes forward 500 years just in time to save Earth from evil invaders sent by a sensuous but immature princess (Pamela Hensley). Director Daniel Haller's gadget-ridden, lighthearted space adventure has a few mild double entendres, but is reasonably diverting pulp for sci-fi fans. A-II (PG) 15

Buckskin (1968) Formula western directed by A.C. Lyles about a marshal (Barry Sullivan) who thwarts the plans of a crook (Wendell Corey) to force out the homesteaders and sell their land to the railroad. Restrained gunplay. A-I (br) U

Bucktown (1975) Vicious, mindless black exploitation movie, the first half of which offers racism and violence (Fred Williamson and friends wiping out the corrupt white police force of a southern sin city) and the second half dealing solely with violence (black against black). Director Arthur Marks ends it in a bloody, drawn-out fist fight, witnessed by a little boy, who chortles the movie's last line about how happy he is to be a man. Ugh. O (R)

Buddy Buddy (1981) Ill-conceived attempt by director Billy Wilder and writer I.A.L. Diamond to turn a mediocre French farce about the chance meeting of a ruthless hit man and a suicidal cuckold into a vehicle for Walter Matthau and Jack Lemmon. The result is achingly unfunny, vulgarly sentimental and generally tasteless. Profanity and incidental nudity. O (R) 15

Buddy Holly Story, The (1978) Straightforward screen biography of one of the pioneers of rock 'n' roll music, from his initial success in 1956 to his death in a plane crash three years later at the age of 22. The script by Robert Gittler is extremely competent as is Steve Rash's direction. The movie's best feature, however, is the genial singing and acting of Gary Busey in the title role. A-III (PG)

Buddy System, The (1984) Unwed mother (Susan Sarandon) is brought together with a would-be novelist working as a security guard (Richard Dreyfuss) by her 9-year-old son (Wil Wheaton). Although director Glenn Jordan takes a long time to set up a rather obvious situation, the rest is a gentle romantic comedy, with some sensitive and perceptive moments. Vulgar language and a benign view of a premarital relationship. A-III (PG)

Buffalo Bill (1944) Fanciful story of the frontiersman (Joel McCrea) whose exploits were celebrated in dime novels and led to his success touring the world with his own Wild West Show. Directed by William Wellman, the Western action is colorful but hokey, with Maureen O'Hara and Linda Darnell as romantic interests. Frontier vio-

lence and Indian stereotypes. A-I (br) U

Buffalo Bill and the Indians Or Sitting Bull's History Lesson (1976) Starting with the fact that Chief Sitting Bull once toured with Buffalo Bill's Wild West Show, director Robert Altman proceeds to show Buffalo Bill (Paul Newman) as a mere braggart with no real accomplishments in contrast to the unfailingly noble and heroic Indian chief. The movie is entertaining enough, with some flashes of brilliance and humor, but strikes few genuine sparks in its repetitious debunking of the western myth. Coarse language. A-III (PG) A

Buffy the Vampire Slayer (1992) Insipid horror comedy about a high schooler (Kristy Swanson) who's given the mission of ridding Southern California of marauding vampires. Director Fran Rubel Kuzui starts with some amusing satire of the valley girl mentality, but soon relies on constant cartoonish violence to sustain a brainless storyline. Frequent stylized violence and a few off-color references. A-III (PG-13) 12

Bug (1975) Bradford Dillman, playing a variant of that hoary staple of horror movies, the mad scientist, brings to the role hyperbolic histrionics. Director Jeannot Szwarc's unsubtle special effects are much more likely to provoke nausea than terror and the degree to which the film steps over the line in its depiction of brutal, degrading incidents should cause parents serious concern. O (PG) 15

Bugs Bunny's 3rd Movie: 1001 Rabbit Tales (1982) A compilation of vintage theatrical "Merry Melodies" and "Looney Tunes" cartoons bridged by some new material that isn't nearly as good. Stringing together a 90-minute feature of such cartoon shorts may be too much of a good thing for some, especially youngsters. Cartoon violence. A-I (G) U

Bugs Bunny/Road Runner (1979) Feature-length compilation of vintage Warner Brothers' cartoons created by Chuck Jones has some new material featuring a retired Bugs and the typical Road Runner brand of cartoon violence that some parents may find unsuitable for their very young children. A-I (G) U

Bugsy (1991) Bloated soap opera details the volatile relationship between gangster Bugsy Siegel (Warren Beatty) and his Hollywood mistress (Annette Bening) as he recklessly squanders mob money in building a posh casino hotel in Las Vegas during the 1940s. Despite a cast including Ben Kingsley and Joe Mantegna, director Barry Levinson's melodramatic narrative fails to sustain interest in its callous and conscienceless characters. Intermittent violence, an adulterous relationship and frequent rough language. A-III (R) 18

Bugsy Malone (1976) Director Alan Parker's unique musical is a crime melodrama spoof done with a cast whose average age is twelve. Unique, however, does not mean good. Jodie Foster gives the only redeeming performance, the music is at best inoffensive, the humor consistently misfires and some may note a touch of sexual ambivalence in moppets posturing as adults. A-I (G) U

Bull Durham (1988) Romantic comedy about a minor league baseball team features action on and off the field by such quirky folks as a has-been catcher (Kevin Costner), a rookie pitcher (Tim Robbins) and an overage groupie (Susan Sarandon) who tutors rookies in the fine art of baseball and love-making. Writer-director Ron Shelton gets the baseball scene right but turns the Sarandon character into a male fantasy figure. Thematic acceptance of promiscuity, several sexually explicit encounters and much rough language. O (R) 18

Bullet for Pretty Boy, A (1970) Bloody account of the life of 1930s' gangster Pretty Boy Floyd (Fabian Forte) who commits some daring crimes and is eventually gunned down in a violent shoot-out. Directed by Larry Buchanan, it is of minimal interest. A-III (PG)

Bullet for the General, A (1968) Italian western directed by Damiano Damiani consists of a series of wanton killings and excessive brutality. O (br) X

Bulletproof (1988) Comic-book thriller in which the hero, cop-secret agent Gary Busey, manages to wipe out an entire band of communist-trained terrorists stationed in Mexico and recapture a high-powered U.S. Army tank without tarnishing his "bulletproof" reputation. Busey makes a likeable macho hero, but director Steve Carver can't do anything with the ridiculous script. Intense, gruesome violence from start to finish and a scene with nudity. O (R) 15

Bullies (1986) A city family moves to a rural town in British Columbia only to be terrorized by a clan of demented toughs. A nasty little Canadian production, directed by suspense-terror specialist Paul Lynch, the movie ends in a crescendo of vengeance and retribution as the family's teenage son kills all the bullies. Profanity, promiscuity, rape, brutality, murder and other assorted acts of violence. O (R)

Bullitt (1968) When an underworld informer is killed while in the protective custody of a San Francisco police detective (Steve McQueen), he sets up a ruse in order to smoke out those responsible. Under the direction of Peter Yates, the action thriller displays a convincing degree of realism thanks to close attention to police work details, harrowing car chases through city streets and McQueen's tight-lipped performance. Some graphic violence and sexual references. A-III (PG) AA

Bunny Lake Is Missing (1965) Suspenseful thriller about a child who appears to have been abducted but who, in fact, may never have existed. Otto Preminger directs Keir Dullea and Carol Lynley as a properly mysterious couple with Laurence Olivier as a quietly effective London policeman. Mature themes. A-III (br) X

Bunny O'Hare (1971) Disguised as hippies, a pair of mature citizens (Bette Davis and Ernest Borgnine) pull off a series of bank robberies under Gerd Oswald's unimaginative direction. Their antics supply the frame-work for some heavy-handed, pseudo-satiric statements on everything from a migrant worker's savings and police intelligence to psychiatry and youthful protestors. A-III (GP) A

Buona Sera, Mrs. Campbell (1969) American air force unit has a reunion in the Italian village where it had been stationed in World War II and three of the group learn that each has been supporting a local "widow" (Gina Lollobridgida) who told him that he is the father of her daughter (Janet Margolin). The complications that make up this situation comedy are fairly predictable, but writer-director Melvin Frank comes up with a lively mixture of satire and sight-gags making the most of the comic possibilities in an inherently serious plot. Adult humor. A-III (PG) A

'Burbs, The (1989) Burdened with too much free time and vivid imaginations that seem to have frozen in adolescence, three neighbor pals (Tom Hanks, Bruce Dern and Rick Ducommun) create havoc when they investigate their mysterious new neighbors. Director Joe Dante's innocuous boys-will-be-boys comedy will make its biggest success on the home video circuit as a Halloween rental. Incidental vulgar references. A-II (PG)

Burglar (1987) Whoopi Goldberg is a cat burglar implicated in a murder, which she has to solve in order to stay out of jail. The unflattering vanity production directed by Hugh Wilson offers little chance for Goldberg's talent to sparkle. Instead it is buried under false and demeaning stereotyping of women, brief nudity and mild profanity. A-III (R) 15

Burglars, The (1972) French crime caper with Jean-Paul Belmondo stealing a cool million in emeralds and then playing cat-and-mouse games with Omar Sharif, a sadistic cop who uses Dyan Cannon and her striptease club as one way of persuading Belmondo to share the gems with him.

Director Henri Verneuil opts for speed over suspense and the beautiful scenery on the Greek island of Corfu helps him get away with a preposterous script. A-III (PG) AA

Burn! (1970) Complex Italian dramatization of a 19th-century revolution that takes place on a Caribbean island where the conflict centers on a British agent (Marlon Brando) and the black leader (Evaristo Marquez) he creates and then has to destroy. Directed by Gillo Pontecorvo, there are some uncomfortable modern parallels in the movie's vivid statement that violence only begets more violence. A-III (GP)

Burnt Offerings (1976) Inept horror movie about a family living in a haunted house in which the odds are hopelessly stacked against the best efforts of Oliver Reed, Bette Davis and Karen Black to survive the proceedings. In trying to inject some interest in this rather nasty business, director Dan Curtis relies heavily on visual shock. A-III (PG) AA

Bus Is Coming, The (1971) Black Vietnam veteran (Mike Simms) returns home to discover that his brother has been murdered by a racist policeman, gets caught between a black militant group and redneck cops and eventually becomes the moderate spokesman for his people. Directed by Wendell James Franklin, the movie manages to avoid a simplistic approach to its subject matter. A-II (GP)

Bushbabies, The (see: "The Bushbaby").

Bushbaby, The (1970) Young girl (Margaret Brooks) leaves the ship taking her back to England in order to return her pet monkey to an East African jungle and winds up trekking through the hinterland with a faithful black (Lou Gosset) to escape the police who suspect that he has kidnapped her. Though not explicit, the movie's attitude toward the black natives is condescending, making it less suitable as family entertainment. A-I (G)

Buster (1988) Disjointed look at a small-time thief (Phil Collins) who hit the big time as a conspirator in England's 1963 Great Train Robbery. Director David Green focuses more on his relationship with his saintly wife (Julie Walters) while on the lam than on the infamous caper itself. Some violence, fleeting beach nudity, some sexually suggestive behavior and rough language. A-III (R) 15

Buster and Billie (1974) The story of a high school romance in a sleepy Georgia town in 1948 in which the boy (Jan-Michael Vincent) gives up his sweetheart (Pamela Sue Martin) when he falls in love with a girl from the wrong side of the tracks (Joan Goodfellow). Director Daniel Petrie's sappy and predictable movie has a feel for the era,

the locale and the people but indulges in an excess of violence and nudity. O (R) 18

Bustin' Loose (1981) Richard Pryor and Cicely Tyson star in this frumpy comedy about an ex-con forced into taking a group of developmentally disabled youths and their teacher across the country in a decrepit bus. Scripted by Pryor and directed by Oz Scott, the result is outrageously sentimental with a few laughs and some rough language. A-II (R) 15

Busting (1974) Two honest L.A. vice squad cops (Elliott Gould and Robert Blake) attempt to nail a crime boss (Allen Garfield) but eventually accept the inevitability of defeat under a corrupt system of justice. Director Peter Hyams throws in some comedy but too much violence, nudity and profanity. O (R) X

Butch and Sundance: The Early Days (1979) Buddy movie directed by Richard Lester features William Katt and Tom Berenger as the not very dynamic duo stuck in a lifeless series of comedically failed situations involving their bumbling quest for notoriety. Sparse vulgar language and violence is less objectionable than the film's romanticization of the lawless, irresponsible life-style. A-III (PG) A

Butch Cassidy and the Sundance Kid (1969) Stylish seriocomic western set at the end of the 19th century when a pair of outlaws, Butch (Paul Newman) and the Kid (Robert Redford), realize that civilization has overtaken their profession and head for the Bolivian frontier. Director George Roy Hill brings off the action scenes with gusto and the proper amount of humor though, beneath the surface of the laughter and the silly mishaps, there are enough realistic scenes to show that their criminal exploits have serious consequences. Much stylized violence and a sexually suggestive situation. A-III (PG)

Butcher, The (see: "Le Boucher").

Buttercup Chain, The (1971) Four crazy, mixed-up kids (Hywel Bennett, Jane Asher, Sven-Bertil Taube and Leigh Taylor-Young), resort to a thoroughgoing and deliberate demonstration of the various illicit pairings that lead to regret, tragedy and moral awakening. Director Robert Ellis Miller's clumsy treatment lets the movie run amok in pseudo-serious tangles that only emphasize the sexual misadventures. O (R)

Butcher's Wife, The (1991) Glossy romantic comedy about the clairvoyant bride (Demi Moore) of a Greenwich Village butcher (George Dzunzda) whose advice complicates the romantic relationships in the neighborhood, especially those of the local shrink (Jeff Daniels) and a prim choir teacher (Mary Steenburgen). Directed by

Terry Hughes, it's mostly fluffy fantasy that stumbles in a brief subplot that hints a scorned woman might be happier with another woman. Implied lesbian relationship, mild sexual innuendo and an instance of rough language. A-IV (PG-13) 12

Butterflies Are Free (1972) Good screen version of Leonard Gershe's play about a blind youth (Edward Albert), the cheerfully amoral kook in the apartment next door (Goldie Hawn) who becomes emotionally attached to him and his overprotective but ultimately very wise and sensible mother (Eileen Heckart). Director Milton Katselas keeps the romantic melodrama moving along quite nicely, the acting is quite good and the clash between the new morality and the old is treated very gently. A-III (PG) A

Butterfly (1982) This is the story of a scheming and manipulative girl who uses seduction as a weapon, in this frivolous and inept screen version of the grim James M. Cain novel about incest . . . or supposed incest. With Pia Zadora in the lead role and Stacey Keach and Orson Wells who fail to rise above director Matt Cimber's offhanded material. Some nudity and a general air of sleazy amorality. O (R) 18

Butterfly, The (1971) Scandinavian sexploiter about a streetwalker (Anna Kristina) fluttering around various clients sent her way by director Alexis Neve. O (R)

By the Blood of Others (1978) A French production about an escaped maniac who hold a woman and her younger daughter hostage while demanding that he be sent the prettiest girl in town. The melodramatic situation turns into a static problem play as the mayor (Bernard Blier) and other townspeople debate what to do until action is taken by the mayor's daughter (Mariangela Melato). Some fine acting and interesting observations about people under crisis, but not enough to compensate for the flat and predictable script and a brutal rape scene. A-III (nr)

By the Sword (1993) Returning as an instructor in a New York City fencing academy whose owner he had killed 20 years earlier, a regret-filled ex-con (F. Murray Abraham) tries to undo the harm caused by the man's son (Eric Roberts) in teaching the students to use ruthless methods to win at all costs. Though director Jeremy Kagan develops the characters' emotional and competitive antagonisms in strictly routine fashion, the tale ends on a redemptive note in a climactic showdown between the dead man's son and the new instructor. Fleeting bedroom scenes, a violent duel and occasional rough language. A-III (R) 15

Bye Bye Birdie (1963) Clumsy, unlikeable musical comedy about a vapid teenager (Ann-Margaret) who goes gaga when her Elvis Presley-like idol (Jesse Pearson) comes to town for a last concert before being drafted. Directed by George Sidney, the adults in the cast (Janet Leigh, Dick Van Dyke, Paul Lynde and Maureen Stapleton) are even birdier than the teen fans, the extravagant production numbers are flat-footed and the songs unmemorable, save for "Put on a Funny Face." Blatant sexual innuendo. A-III (br) U

Bye Bye Blues (1990) With her husband (Michael Ontkean) missing in action during World War II, a young Canadian mother (Rebecca Jenkins) gradually builds a singing career, falls in love with her marriage-minded bandleader (Luke Reilly) and ultimately faces a painful choice when her husband returns. Sensitively written and directed by Anne Wheeler, the movie's simple but evocative images, spare dialogue and fine acting build understanding for the sacrifices and uncertainties of those who remained on the homefront. A subplot concerning marital infidelity and the question of abortion is treated in a responsible manner. A-II (PG)

Bye Bye Braverman (1968) In a serio-comic drama, four Jewish friends (George Segal, Joseph Wiseman, Jack Warden and Sorrell Booke) spend an afternoon trying to find the funeral of Braverman, their mutual friend. In concentrating on the mourner's attitudes, hopes and fears, director Sidney Lumet misses more than he scores in a flawed film that culminates in a graveyard soliloquy seeking to find some kind of meaning in an alien universe. A-III (br)

C

C'est la Vie (1990) Two young French sisters (Julie Bataille and Candice Lefranc) begin a carefree summer at the shore with their cousins, but the vacation is marred as their parents (Nathalie Baye and Richard Berry) inch closer to divorce. Director Diane Kury's ensemble cast and her well-written screenplay sensitively capture the innocent joys of childhood and the confusion and pain that offspring feel when parents separate. In French with English subtitles. References to an adulterous liaison, restrained domestic violence and a flash of nudity. A-III (nr)

Cabaret (1972) Bouncy Liza Minnelli stars as an exploited and exploiting American showgirl performing in a decadent Berlin cabaret circa 1930. Showing a nation headed toward moral and political bankruptcy in a spirited musical format results in an entertainment with several levels of meaning given sharp ironic bite by director Bob Fosse. Themes of Nazi brutality, twisted sexual relationships and a bizarre nightclub setting provide some challenging fare for grownups. A-III (PG) 15

Cabin Boy (1994) Sophomoric fantasy in which a spoiled rich youth (Chris Elliott) accidentally boards a grungy fishing boat and is forced to serve as cabin boy to four old salts as they navigate past a six-armed seductress, a vengeful giant and a man-shark. The half-witted humor of director Adam Resnick's comedy clunker is stuck at half mast in an insipid vehicle for cult comedian Elliott. Implied sexual encounters, some mock comic violence and occasional profanity and guttertalk. A-III (PG-13)

Cabin in the Cotton (1932) Dated but still interesting melodrama of Southern sharecroppers battling exploitative landowners until a local youth (Richard Barthelmess), who's in love with a farmer's daughter (Dorothy Jordan) but infatuated with a rich girl (Bette Davis), brings the two sides together. Directed by Michael Curtiz, the story of the young man's emotional turmoil pales beside the realistic depiction of oppressed farmworkers and their unequal struggle for a better life. Scenes of social and economic injustice, some stylized violence, including a lynching, and a restrained sexual situation. A-II (br) U

Cabinet of Caligari, The (1962) Belabored psychological clap-trap in which a woman (Glynis Johns) suffering from a mental breakdown is treated in an asylum by a doctor (Dan O'Herlihy) she imagines is keeping her captive. Scripted by Robert Bloch and directed by Roger Kay, the embarrassingly inept movie borrows the premise from its illustrious 1919 German predecessor but, despite a game cast, does nothing with it. Much sexual innuendo, most of it silly. A-III (br) X

Cactus Flower, The (1969) Screen adaptation of the Broadway version of a French comedy about a prosperous Manhattan dentist (Walter Matthau) caught between a dizzy young girlfriend (Goldie Hawn) and his devoted but staid receptionist (Ingrid Bergman) who ultimately blooms like the prickly cactus on her desk. Director Gene Saks adds proper comic timing to the absurd complications of the lightweight romance, but it is the comic vitality of a talented cast that makes it enjoyable. A-III (PG) A

Cactus in the Snow (1972) Movie entirely devoted to the attempts of an Army private (Richard Thomas) to have his first sexual experience with a teenager (Mary Layne) he has met on a weekend pass. Directed by Martin Zweiback, the movie is quite explicit about contraceptive devices and even resorts to having the soldier tutored by a prostitute. With crude sexual references throughout, it is reprehensible to aim this at young audiences. O (R/GP appeal)

Caddie (1981) Australian domestic drama about a young wife (Helen Morse) who walks out on her brutal and adulterous husband and makes a living for herself and her two young children by working as a barmaid in Sydney during the Great Depression. Morse gives a winning performance and director Donald Crombie's period re-creation is finely detailed, but the story is listless and lacks dramatic force. A-III (nr) A

Caddyshack (1980) Bill Murray and Chevy Chase cavort in this buffoonish slapstick comedy about a caddy's summer adventures at a loony country club. Director Harold Ramis counts on an assortment of obnoxious characters, lewd jokes and brief nudity to energize a sophomoric plot. O (R) 15

Caddyshack II (1988) Dim-witted sequel with Jackie Mason causing havoc as a garish construction tycoon who crashes and finally trashes the snooty Bushwood Country Club. Cameos by Chevy Chase, Dan Aykrod and a pesky golf club gopher highlight this humorless effort directed by Alan Arkush. Some profanity and vulgar humor. A-III (PG)

Cadence (1991) An Army private (Charlie Sheen) confined in the post stockade infuriates his racist jailer (Martin Sheen) by bonding with the black prisoners and rejecting favored treatment. Director Martin

Sheen turns out a subtle, understated film about bigotry, mixing humor with drama and fleshing out the characters without resorting to empty stereotypes. Brief violence, some racial epithets and a fleeting sexual reference. A-II (PG-13)

Cadillac Man (1990) Forced, unpleasant comedy in which a fast-talking car salesman (Robin Williams) tries to pacify a crazed gunman (Tim Robbins) who takes everyone hostage after bursting into the car agency in search of his wife's lover. Director Roger Donaldson gets few smiles out of the salesman's two mistresses, ex-wife and runaway daughter and, despite Williams's comic talents, the hostage situation is no laughing matter. A tacked-on happy ending does not compensate for the movie's emphasis on sexual promiscuity, nor its depiction of terrorized hostages and use of rough language. O (R) 15

Cafe Express (1981) Nino Manfredi plays a Sicilian selling coffee on a train contrary to the rules of the railroad with the action taking place in the course of one night's run. Italian comedy directed by Nanni Loy has its moments but is no more than a vignette and the balance between the comic and the tragic falters. Earthy dialogue and a comic sexual incident. A-III (nr)

Caged Men Plus One Woman (1972) The various manifestations of homosexuality in prison provide sensational subject matter for Edward J. Forsyth's movie about an incredibly ignorant victim (Ross Stephanson) who just as incredibly wreaks bloody revenge on his tormentors inside as well as on the girlfriend outside who had betrayed him. O (R)

Cahill, U.S. Marshal (1973) John Wayne stars in a contemporary western about an overworked peace officer whose two neglected sons are involved in a robbery he is investigating. When Wayne decides to make his pursuit of the criminals into an object lesson for his sons, director Andrew V. McLaglen's movie seems to condone the use of guns in the hands of the young. Worse than the violence is what youngsters may make of the story's muddled morality. A-III (PG) AA

Caine Mutiny, The (1954) Involving drama from the Herman Wouk novel in which young Navy officers (Fred MacMurray and Robert Francis) take control of their ship from a veteran captain (Humphrey Bogart) seemingly in a funk during a typhoon, then are defended in a court martial by an officer (Jose Ferrer) who doesn't relish proving the captain's instability. Director Edward Dmytryk gets a powerful performance from Bogart as the shell-shocked Captain Queeg but does less well with the theme of military discipline and questionable commands. Psychological problems. A-I (br) U

Cal (1984) Set against the background of the present conflict in Northern Ireland is the story of a doomed love affair between the widow (Helen Mirren) of a slain policeman and a shy, sensitive young man (John Lynch) who was inadvertently involved in her husband's death. Director Pat O'Connor has fashioned a nuanced morality tale of human beings caught in a divided world, but there is some use of nudity and a fairly graphic love scene. A-IV (R) 15

Calamity Jane (1953) Doris Day plays the legendary Wild West sharpshooter who must change her tomboy attitudes in order to catch the eye of Wild Bill Hickock (Howard Keel) in this uneven but lively musical. Director David Butler tempers an ultimately subservient image of women with Day's charm and singing abilities. A-II (br) U

Calendar Girl (1993) Witless comedy about three 18-year-olds (Jason Priestley; Gabriel Olds; Jerry O'Connell) driving to Hollywood in the summer of 1962, hoping to have a date with movie goddess Marilyn Monroe. Director John Whitesell panders to adolescent male fantasies in a boringly inept, woefully unfunny movie. A sexist view of women, some nudity, fleeting bedroom scene, brief violence and minimal rough language. O (PG-13)

California Split (1974) Magazine writer (George Segal) befriends a small-time hustler (Elliott Gould) whose wild antics intrigue, but this leads him deeper and deeper into the gambling underworld of dumb call girls, tough losers, impatient bookies, sleazy bars, and hole-in-the-wall games. Director Robert Altman's offbeat comedy ends with Segal's realization that he, unlike Gould, doesn't really care about winning, suggesting that with this knowledge, his obsession to gamble has been exorcised. Questionable attitude toward casual sex. A-IV (R) X

California Suite (1978) Screen version of Neil Simon's play integrates the original's four one-acters into a single narrative with a good cast, including Jane Fonda, Alan Alda, Maggie Smith and Michael Caine. Although not a completely successful adaptation from the stage, director Herbert Ross's movie is good fun for the most part and sometimes unexpectedly moving. Mature themes. A-III (PG) AA

Caligula (1981) The R-rated version of the X-rated original is no less a dreary exploitation movie awash with sex and violence. Directed by Tinto Brass, it brings not a trace of insight to the historical figures of the Roman Empire or to this period of history. O (R) X

Call Me (1988) Basically soft porn all fancied up with an inane plot about hoods on the trail of a woman (Patricia Charbonneau) who inadvertently witnesses a murder and who enjoys trading phone turnons with an obscene caller. Director Sollace Mitchell offers an abundance of gory violence, much profanity and rough language of an explicit sexual nature and a total insensitivity to the offensiveness of real obscene phone calls. O (R) 18

Call Me Bwana (1963) Generally funny but mindless Bob Hope comedy about a space scientist (Hope) who is easily distracted by the feminine wiles of a foreign agent (Anita Ekberg) from his mission of retrieving a space capsule that has landed in the African jungle. Directed by Gordon Douglas, it consists of typical Hope one-liners and double-entendres. A-II (br) U

Call Northside 777 (1948) Fact-based story in which a Chicago newspaper reporter (James Stewart) digs into the case of a convicted cop-killer (Richard Conte) and finds evidence of his innocence. Filming on Chicago locations, director Henry Hathaway gets the flavor of the city's ethnic neighborhoods and the reporter's dogged leg work in following leads is interesting enough but the convict's ultimate release leaves only a sense of his lost years in prison and ruined marriage. Sobering justice theme. A-II (br) A

Call of the Wild, The (1935) Romantic melodrama from Jack London's outdoor adventure in the frozen 1900 Yukon where the search for gold leads a woman (Loretta Young), whose husband has been lost in the snowy wastes, to throw in with a rugged adventurer (Clark Gable) whose only assets are a courageous sled dog and a bumbling partner (Jack Oakie), with a formidable foe (Reginald Owen) on their trail. Directed by William Wellman, the result is well-crafted but predictable entertainment leaving viewers with little that sticks in the mind or touches the heart. Some rough frontier humor, occasional menace and a few tender moments. A-II (br)

Camelot (1967) Director Josh Logan's screen version of the Broadway musical on the King Arthur legend offers the charming Lerner and Loewe score and lyrics, luxurious fantasy settings and a grand cast (Richard Harris, Vanessa Redgrave, Franco Nero and David Hemmings). Emphasizing the human implications of the legend rather than its romanticism, the musical shows that power is not strength and that compassion is not weakness. Never has adultery carried so high a price—the downfall of Camelot. A-II (br) U

Cameraman, The (1928) Buster Keaton plays a newsreel cameraman sent to Chinatown where he finds himself in the middle of a chaotic Tong War. Still hilarious today, the mark of his genius in physical comedy is present in almost every frame of the picture. It was his last silent feature and the last movie in which he was in complete control. A-I (br)

Camila (1985) The daughter of a wealthy family in 19th-century Argentina falls in love with a Jesuit priest in this tragic love story with modern political implications. In this Argentinian production, director Maria Luisa Bemberg deals with difficult historical matters as well as the sacrilegious character of the love affair. Powerful but problematic, with one brief but excessively graphic love scene. A-IV (nr) 15

Camille Claudel (1989) Bittersweet story of French sculptress (Isabelle Adjani) whose troubled life (1864-1943) as a trailblazer in a male-dominated field ended in a mental asylum after an emotionally devastating May-December affair with her mentor, sculptor Auguste Rodin (Gerard Depardieu). Directed by Bruno Nuytten, it's powerfully acted but confusing as to chronology and characters. Unmarried sexual liaisons and nude models in studio scenes. A-III (R) PG

Camille 2000 (1969) In updating Dumas' tubercular heroine, director Radley Metzger has changed the flighty and unstable Camille into an amoral jet-setter who fills her days with hip slang, liquor, drugs and sex. The plot is no more than a flimsy structure for scenes replete with nudity, joyless orgies and 20th-century guilt-ridden anxieties. O (R)

Camouflage (1981) Meditative essay on the corruptive nature of any bureaucratic system and the destructive games people play in seeming to conform to what is expected of them. The Polish production's success lies in an intelligent script and perceptive direction by Krzysztof Zanussi. Several sexual situations. A-III (nr)

Can Hieronymus Merkin Ever Forget Mercy Humppe and Find True Happiness? (1969) Writer-director Anthony Newley plays a star entertainer making a movie about his career and using fragmented and surrealistic techniques both for the film and the film-within-the-film. Apparently an attempt to make a statement about the artist's quest for identity, the result is an incoherent failure, floundering in excesses of explicit sexual adventures and moral relativism that leave viewers with little to share other than the character's lack of self-knowledge and the director's lack of ability to control his material. O (X/R) X

Can't Buy Me Love (1987) Suburban nerd (Patrick Dempsey) pays a popular cheerleader (Amanda Peterson) to date him for a month in director Steve Rash's comic exploration of teen mores that condemns in-crowd conformism and self-deception but passively conveys a permissive attitude toward adolescent sex. A-III (PG-13) PG

Can't Stop the Music (1980) This vehicle for The Village People, a disco singing group, is a high-energy, low-IQ, 100-percent synthetic product. Directed by Nancy Walker, the silly comedy about the music publishing and recording business is marked by sexual situations and jokes as well as a homosexual sheen coloring most of the production numbers. A-III (PG) A

Cancel My Reservations (1972) Bob Hope plays the henpecked half of a husband-wife TV talk-show team who falls victim to a gang of murderous Arizona land-grabbers. Wife Eva Marie Saint races to Hope's rescue and ultimately learns that a woman's place is in the home. Director Paul Bogart strikes out with tired gags and dated topical humor. A-II (G) U

Candidate, The (1972) Robert Redford stars in the title role as a California lawyer who finds himself in the middle of a hot race for U.S. Senator. Director Michael Ritchie, working with an excellent cast and a literate script, has constructed a fast-paced, cool and very slick movie about the process of electing a candidate for major office. How power politics and the hard sell work, as seen from the inside, is all laid bare in this realistic and frequently quite funny political satire. A-III (PG) A

Candidate for a Killing (1972) Itinerant sportsman (John Richardson) is used by a businessman (Fernando Rey) in a scheme to extort gold from the Congo and becomes a target for assassins as he races around Europe accompanied by a questionable ally (Anita Ekberg). Director Sidney Pink pads his picture with silly conversations and irrelevant interludes, many of them of a teasing sexual nature. O (R)

Candleshoe (1978) Jodie Foster plays a Los Angeles juvenile delinquent whom confidence man Leo McKern uses to hoodwink wealthy Helen Hayes into thinking is her long-lost granddaughter. Standard Disney fare from director Norman Tokar that tends toward slapstick rather than anything more gentle and satisfying. A-I (G) U

Candy (1969) Screen version of the Southern-Hoffenberg novel about the travail of a threatened virgin (Ewa Aulin) is no more than a gross sex farce that reinforces all the behavioral patterns it supposedly satirizes. Christian Marquand directs a big-name cast with a sensitivity only for the vulgar remark, the suggestive sequence and the explicitly titillating. O (R) X

Candy Tangerine Man, The (1975) Black exploitation movie makes a hero out of a vicious black procurer and serves up the sex and violence that is the standard of the genre. O (R)

Candyman (1992) Idiotic horror story relates the problems of a skeptical graduate student (Virginia Madsen) after she conjures up a 19th-century hook-handed ghoul (Tony Todd) who goes on a murderous rampage. Writer-director Bernard Rose's badly scripted tale of brutal mayhem in a gang-ravaged Chicago ghetto slowly drowns in its own gore. Excessive violence, continuing deadly menace to an infant and occasional nudity. O (R) 18

Cannibal Girls (1973) The title refers to three beauties in a remote Canadian town whose diner serves beefy portions of male travelers whom they have seduced and slaughtered. Director Ivan Reitman's low-budget movie romps in sex and gore to no entertaining end. O (R)

Cannon for Cordoba (1970) George Peppard, leader of a undisciplined platoon in Pershing's Mexican expedition, is responsible for the loss of cannon and supplies and subsequently must re-capture or destroy them. Directed by Paul Wendkos, the far-fetched adventure is seasoned with torture and violence, in ludicrous fashion. A-III (R/GP) AA

Cannonball Run, The (1981) Banal and tedious cross-country car race movie with Burt Reynolds and Farrah Fawcett, directed by ex-stunt coordinator Hal Needham. Some vulgarity and sexual innuendo. A-III (PG) A

Cannonball Run II (1984) Sequel with Burt Reynolds and friends is a sort of cinematic People magazine-on-wheels. Stuntman Hal Needham's direction of this demolition-derby comedy is geared toward dangerous auto stunts and off-color jokes. A-III (PG)

Canterville Ghost, The (1944) Oscar Wilde fantasy updated to World War II finds American G.I.s quartered in an English castle inhabited by its 7-year-old heiress (Margaret O'Brien) and a 17th-century ghost (Charles Laughton) doomed by his cowardice to remain there until a kinsman (Robert Young) performs a brave deed on his behalf. Directed by Jules Dassin, the wartime American presence adds little to the sentimental amusement provided by the serious-minded little girl and the roguish antics of her cowardly ancestor. Mild comic menace and ghostly fun. A-I (br) A

Cape Fear (1962) Stomach-churning suspense thriller in which a vengeful ex-convict (Robert Mitchum) sets out to brutalize the wife (Polly Bergen) of the lawyer (Gregory Peck) he blames for his imprisonment. Director J. Lee Thompson's picture of an ordinary decent citizen pitted against a cunning sadistic criminal builds the tension to the breaking point on a boat in a lonely North Carolina bayou. Well-crafted exercise in terror, not for the nervous or faint-of-heart. A-III (br) X

Cape Fear (1991) Violent remake of the 1962 thriller has a Bible-spouting psychopath (Robert De Niro) imprisoned for viciously violating a woman returning to terrorize his former lawyer (Nick Nolte) and to rape the man's wife and teenage daughter (Jessica Lange and Juliette Lewis). Director Martin Scorsese loses the atmospheric terror of the original in favor of graphic brutality and a relentlessly ugly vision of the law as powerless to protect the innocent. Excessive violence, perverse sexual innuendo, adult endorsement of teen drug abuse and minimal rough language. O (R) 18

Caper of the Golden Bulls, The (1967) Stephen Boyd and Yvette Mimieux star in a hokey caper movie about a jewel robbery. Directed by Russell Rouse and set in Pamplona, Spain, the only point of interest is the bullring and its environs. Some violence. A-III (br) U

Capone (1975) The rise of Al Capone (Ben Gazzara) from Brooklyn street mug to Chicago's top mobster is depicted with excessive resort to violence and sexual displays. Directed by Steve Carver, the movie is a sleazy, slapdash effort. O (R) X

Capricious Summer (1968) In this Czechoslovakian production set in a small country village between the world wars, three aging friends make fools of themselves over a young woman in a traveling circus and, by summer's end, they realize that their courting days are over. Director Jiri Menzel captures the elegaic mood of period and character with a tolerance of human foibles. Adult situations. A-III (br) A

Capricorn One (1978) Three astronauts are persuaded by a NASA official (Hal Holbrook) to fake a landing on Mars to save the threatened space program, but a hotshot reporter (Elliott Gould) eventually saves the day. Director Peter Hyams has come up with a solid if unspectacular entertainment with some clever twists. A-II (PG) A

Captain Apache (1971) Poor western about an Indian scout for the U.S. Cavalry who becomes the unwilling victim of a plot to fake an uprising that will see the Indians cruelly exiled to uninhabitable territory. Director Alexander Singer's message of brotherhood is as subtle as his battle sequences. Stylized violence and sexual innuendo. A-III (GP) AA

Captain Blood, Fugitive (see: "Captain Pirate")

Captain January (1936) Formula sudser with loveable orphan Shirley Temple cared for by lighthouse keeper Guy Kibbee until the loss of his job forces him to seek out the child's rich relatives. Director David Butler covers all bases with occasional song-and-dance numbers, some playful humor and a capable supporting cast (Slim Summerville, Buddy Ebsen and Jane Darwell). Easygoing, unpretentious family fare. A-I (br) U

Captain John Smith and Pocahontas (1953) Dull low-budget programmer directed by Lew Landers plods through the story of how Smith (Anthony Dexter) and Jamestown are saved by the daughter (Jody Lawrance) of Algonquian Chief Powhatan (Douglass Dumbrille). Stylized violence and romantic complications. A-II (br)

Captain Kronos: Vampire Hunter (1974) Classy British horror import in which the itinerant Kronos (Horst Janson) is called to a rid a village of a vampire who has been putting the bite on local maidens, which he accomplishes with his able hunchback assistant (John Cater). Director Brian Clemens maintains the proper chilling atmosphere for hair-raising encounters with the hooded fiend who comes to a grisly end. Stylized violence and sexual implications. A-III (R) AA

Captain Nemo and the Underwater City (1970) Jules Verne's Nemo (Robert Ryan) rescues a group of landlubbers (Nanette Newman, Bill Fraser, Kenneth Connor and Chuck Connors) on condition that they not attempt an escape from his self-sufficient city 20,000 leagues under the sea. Directed by James Hill, the special effects, the underwater city and the dramatic complications are intriguing enough to engross a child's imagination in this generally pleasing utopian, anti-war fantasy. A-I (G) U

Captain Pirate (1952) Mediocre swashbuckler about a reformed pirate (Louis Hayward) who once again hoists the Jolly Roger in order to stop a Caribbean buccaneer using his name. Directed by Ralph Murphy, this sequel to "Captain Blood" (1935) meanders aimlessly in search of compelling adventure but only comes up with some colorful action scenes. Stylized violence. A-II (br) U

Captive (see: "Two").

Captain Ron (1992) Inept comedy about a Chicago family (headed by Martin Short and Mary Kay Place) who take a Caribbean dream cruise on an inherited sailboat whose disreputable captain (Kurt Russell) involves them with guerrillas and pirates. Director Thom Eberhardt's waterlogged plot soon sinks under the weight of its contrived situations and leaden script. Brief shadowy nudity, some sexual innuendo, stylized violence and an instance of rough language. A-III (PG-13)

Captain Sinbad (1963) Silly Arabian Nights fantasy pits the title hero (Guy Williams) against a dastardly magician-ruler (Pedro Armendariz) who's abducted a lovely princess (Heidi Bruhl). Directed by Byron Haskin, the European co-production limps along with a weak storyline but some passable special effects. A few hideous creatures and grisly fight scenes may scare the very young. A-I (br) U

Captains Courageous (1937) Spencer Tracy won an Oscar for his performance as Manuel, the simple Portuguese fisherman in Rudyard Kipling's story of a spoiled rich boy (Freddie Bartholomew) rescued at sea and turned into a good shipmate by the kind-hearted veteran sailor. Director Victor Fleming provides a gruff but appealing picture of life aboard the fishing boat backed by some memorable sea scenes and the unsentimental transformation of the youth's character under Manuel's manly yet compassionate influence. Youngsters may get teary-eyed at Manuel's death but all is emotionally resolved in the lad's homecoming. A-I (br) U

Captains of the Clouds (1942) Happy-go-lucky but bored Yank aviator (James Cagney) joins the Royal Canadian Air Force before U.S. entry in World War II, rebels against military discipline, then comes through in heroic action against the Luftwaffe. Director Michael Curtiz's patriotic melodrama has plenty of human interest with a good cast (Alan Hale, Dennis Morgan, George Tobias as well as RCAF veterans). Stylized violence and a marriage in name only. A-II (br) U

Car, The (1977) In a new and not at all entertaining twist to the possession theme, an evil spirit takes over a huge car and terrorizes a Southwestern town. Directed by Elliot Silverstein, everything about the movie is embarrassingly bad, save for the special effects of Albert Whitlock. Some violence and a lot of stupidity. A-III (PG) AA

Car Wash (1976) Director Michael Schultz's touching, sometimes extremely funny movie follows the course of a day at an inner city car wash where the employees keep a jive rhythm to their work and to their joking. Richard Pryor, Ivan Dixon, the Pointer Sisters and George Carlin supply the wit and energy in this comic tale of streetwise survival. Some rough language, sexual innuendo and casual acceptance of drug use. A-III (PG) A

Caravans (1978) A young State Department official (Michael Sarrazin) in 1948 Iran is ordered to locate a missing American (Jennifer O'Neill) reportedly in the mountainous domain of a nomad chief (Anthony Quinn). Directed by James Faro, the effort is a silly misfire, with rambling and un-focused plot line, atrocious dialogue and leadfooted pacing. A bloody execution as well as a sequence involving a homosexual dancer make it mature fare. A-III (PG) A

Carbon Copy (1981) Successful business man (George Segal) marries the boss' shrewish daughter (Susan St. James), but finds his snug, affluent nest disrupted when a black youth (Denzel Washington) shows up one day claiming to be his illegitimate son. Director Michael Schultz's crude and heavy-handed comedy attempts to get laughs by some cheap shots at religion, not excluding a dose of male chauvinism. Strong language and two rather distasteful bedroom scenes. A-III (PG) AA

Cardinal, The (1963) Otto Preminger directs an adaptation of the Henry M. Robinson novel about an American priest (Tom Tryon) from the time of his ordination to his nomination as a cardinal. As a dramatization of the humanity of the Catholic priesthood, presented amidst a heritage of liturgical splendor and realized with some sensitive performances, the production is absorbing entertainment. Some issues may be confusing for those unfamiliar with Catholic theology and practices. A-III (br) A

Care Bears Adventures in Wonderland, The (1987) Vastly superior sequel to failed original, the Canadian animated feature is a lively, colorful, complexly designed and orchestrated travelogue through Wonderland with the Bears and a little girl named Alice who must save the kingdom from a power-hungry wizard. Director Raymond Jafelice holds even adult interest with his fast cuts and engaging fantasy characters. A-I (G) U

Care Bears Movie, The (1985) The Care Bears are sweet little pastel-colored creatures who inhabit a saccharine world called Care-a-Lot. Unless they teach the earth to care, Care-a-Lot will fall into ruin. Only very young children will care very much about this sentimental, mediocre effort. A-I (G) U

Career Opportunities (1991) Two young people—a novice janitor (Frank Whaley) and a lonely shoplifter (Jennifer Connelly)—locked overnight in a department store, become friends while warding off a pair of dim-witted thieves. Writer John Hughes and director Bryan Gordon bomb out with a terminally dumb comedy of humorless stick figures and glaringly bad plotting. Mock comic violence and very suggestive double entendres. A-III (PG-13) PG

Carefree (1938) Wacky musical comedy about a psychiatrist (Fred Astaire) whose best friend (Ralph Bellamy) asks him to treat his marriage-shy girlfriend (Ginger Rogers) but matters get complicated when the patient falls for the doctor. Directed by

Mark Sandrich, the thin plot takes some very giddy turns, with the added bonus of appealing Irving Berlin tunes, including "I Used to Be Color Blind" danced in slow motion by Rogers and Astaire as well as Astaire's standout syncopated solo on the golf links. Silly romantic complications. A-I (nr) U

Careful He Might Hear You (1984) Sensitive, extremely well-acted Australian movie about a 1930s' custody fight between two sisters over the six-year-old son of a third sister who died in childbirth. Director Carl Schultz has done well with showing the effect of all this upon the boy, partly in a less-than-wholesome attraction of a woman for a young child. A-III (PG)

Carey Treatment, The (1972) Hip California doctor (James Coburn) comes to a conservative Boston hospital where he uncovers the murder of the chief-of-staff's daughter and the disappearance of large amounts of hospital drugs. Director Blake Edward employs a good deal of rather self-conscious vulgarity and profanity, but worse is the casual attitude toward abortion and marital commitments. O (PG) X

Carlito's Way (1964) Planning to leave crime and New York City gangsters behind for a new life in the Bahamas with his girlfriend (Penelope Ann Miller), a newly released convict (Al Pacino) pays a high price for his friendship with the corrupt lawyer (Sean Penn) who got him out of jail on a technicality. Director Brian De Palma overstuffs his bleak crime drama with a profusion of morally bankrupt characters, who glibly rationalize their murderous acts. Much violence, incessant rough language, some drug abuse, ethnic slurs, topless dancers and brief sexual encounters. O (R) 18

Carmen (1983) During the rehearsals for a dance version of Bizet's opera about the gypsy temptress whose infidelities end in murder, the choreographer (Antonio Gades) falls in love with the young woman (Laura del Sol) in the title role and their affair offstage follows the same scenario as that enacted onstage. Carlos Saura directs the Spanish production which is filled with stunning flamenco dance numbers and its story of life imitating art is intriguing at first but gradually bogs down in operatic melodrama. Subtitles. Mature theme and treatment. A-III (nr) PG

Carnal Knowledge (1971) Producer-director Mike Nichols and screenwriter Jules Feiffer collaborate on a movie with three episodes spanning two decades (late 1940s to late 1960s) in the lives of two men (Jack Nicholson and Art Garfunkel), tracing their nonmaturation from sex-starved college students to sex-saturated, middle-aged men in professional life. It is a feeble morality play that preaches once again, with pathetic exploitation, that the wages of sin is impotence. Brief nudity and rough language. A-IV (R) X

Carny (1980) Set against the background of a traveling carnival is a triangle theme involving a teenage runaway (Jody Foster), a clown (Gary Busey) and his best friend (Robbie Robertson). The theme, however, is undeveloped because director Robert Kaylor is more interested in documenting carnival life, especially its seamy side with generous amounts of violence, sex and rough language. O (R) X

Carousel (1956) Rodgers and Hammerstein musical from Ferenc Molnar's tragic romance in which a macho carnival worker (Gordon MacRae) dies in a robbery trying to provide for his pregnant wife (Shirley Jones), then gets a chance to come back in spirit to set things right for his still-grieving widow and teen daughter. Directed by Henry King, the dramatic portions seem stilted and out of place in the lovely 19th-century New England setting, though the production numbers are eye-filling and the songs memorable, notably "If I Loved You" and "You'll Never Walk Alone." Romantic complications. A-II (br) U

Carrie (1952) Elaborate sudser from the Theodore Dreiser novel about a country girl (Jennifer Jones) who gets a job in turn-of-the-century Chicago, is seduced by a salesman (Eddie Albert), then runs off with a married man (Laurence Olivier) to New York where she leaves him flat while finding fame on the stage. Director William Wyler's studied period piece arouses little interest in the characters and their woes, though Olivier's descent into penury gains some sympathy. Mature theme and treatment. A-III (br) A

Carrie (1976) A repressed high school student (Sissy Spacek) discovers that she has telekinetic powers, which she uses at the senior prom to wreak a bloody revenge on taunting classmates and her religious fanatic mother. Director Brian De Palma's horror movie is too ludicrous and overdrawn to scare, but succeeds in the shock value of its callous, unhealthy mix of nudity and violence. O (R) X

Carry It On (1970) Documentary on an anti-Vietnam draft resister, David Harris, sentenced to a three-year term in federal prison focuses on his last meeting with his wife, folk singer Joan Baez, and then on her activities with the anti-war movement. Robert Jones, Christopher Knight and James Coyne have assembled a very moving and effective statement against war. A-III (GP)

Carry On Camping (1972) Rude British send-up of summer campers employs such familiar funsters as Sidney James, Kenneth Williams and Joan Sims. Director Gerald Thomas has assembled a grab-bag of comic skits but too often strains for double entendres and vulgar sexual shenanigans to carry the day. O (R) A

Carry On Doctor (1972) Director Gerald Thomas commits his comic cronies (Sidney James, Frankie Howard, Kenneth Williams, Hattie Jacques, Barbara Windsor and Jim Dale) to hospital, but the operation results in the same old monkey business. There is a generous share of double entendres, but the ribaldry is fairly tame. A-III (PG)

Carry On Henry VIII (1972) The latest offering in this series from director Gerald Thomas concerns two previously undiscovered wives of King Henry and their topsy-turvy effect on the beleaguered monarch and his court. Coarse language and blatant double entendres. O (GP) PG

Casa Assassinada, A (1974) Brazilian story of an eccentric family of shabby aristocrats living on crumbling, neglected plantation into which comes a woman who throws the entire household into turmoil and finally violence. Director Paulo Cesar Saraceni's study of creeping moral and mental deterioration is heavily melodramatic but visually powerful in its images of the simultaneous fecundity and decay of the jungle surroundings. Explicit sex scene in a story that otherwise unfolds through indirection. A-IV (nr)

Casablanca (1942) Classic romantic melodrama set in the refugee crossroads of French North Africa where an American expatriate (Humphrey Bogart) helps the woman who broke his heart (Ingrid Bergman) and her husband (Paul Henreid), an underground leader, escape the Nazi dragnet. Directed by Michael Curtiz, the story is replete with World War II intrigue, sardonic humor, punchy dialogue ("Here's looking at you, kid!") and a great cast, including Claude Rains as a suave Vichy police officer and Dooley Wilson's rendition of "As Time Goes By." Time stands still for this one, though the wartime atmosphere may be too menacing for the children. A-II (br)

Casanova Brown (1944) Disappointing romantic comedy about a college professor (Gary Cooper) whose marriage is over almost before it starts, then learns months later that his ex-wife (Teresa Wright) has become a mother. Except for a hilarious house-burning sequence, director Sam Wood treats the situation with such deadly coyness that all involved appear to be congenital idiots. Sophomoric treatment of marriage and parenthood. A-II (br) A

Casanova's Big Night (1954) Mistaken for the notorious lover Casanova (Vincent Price), a tailor's apprentice (Bob Hope) escapes imprisonment by the doge of Venice (Arnold Moss) to save a woman (Audrey Dalton) from dishonor and win the heart of his true love (Joan Fontaine). Director Norman Z. McLeod's listless comedy wastes a good cast in a leaden 18th-century period piece from which Hope wrings only a few smiles. Mild sexist humor. A-II (br) U

Case of the Naves Brothers, The (1972) Brazilian director Lutz Sergio Person tells the fact-based story of two peasant brothers sentenced in 1938 for an apparent murder, but even when the supposed victim resurfaced several years later, it was not until 1963 that the brothers were released on parole. The story of a miscarriage of justice contains all too graphic depictions of torture. A-III (nr)

Casey's Shadow (1978) An irascible but basically good-hearted Cajun horse trainer (Walter Matthau) has to make an agonizing decision whether or not to run a horse with an injured leg in a race that could mean fame and fortune for him and his three sons. Director Martin Ritt captures the colorful world of quarter-horse racing in the Southwest, but the movie's benign attitude toward the trainer's moral failings and the frequent use of profanity make it mature fare. A-III (PG) A

Cash McCall (1959) Low-powered romantic drama in which a shrewd corporate raider (James Garner) buys a stagnant company in order to woo the daughter (Natalie Wood) of its owner (Dean Jagger) but things get complicated when the deal produces millions in unexpected profits. In tracking the devious turns of the business world, director Joseph Pevney generates little interest in the characters and even less in their personal problems. Romantic situations and sexual innuendo. A-III (br) U

Cassandra Crossing, The (1977) George Pan Cosmatos directs a disaster epic about a train load of international stars (including Sophia Loren, Burt Lancaster, Richard Harris and Ava Gardner), a crowd of extras and a lovable Basset hound who are exposed to a lethal germ, a decaying bridge and a witless, only fitfully exciting storyline. Extremely violent conclusion and some rough language. A-III (R) A

Cast a Giant Shadow (1966) Standard Hollywood biography of David (Mickey) Marcus, New York lawyer and World War II hero, who helped whip the young Israeli army into shape. Written and directed by Melville Shavelson, the dramatization is at times painfully stilted but for the most part human and likeable. Extramarital attachment and wartime violence. A-III (br) A

Castaway Cowboy, The (1974) James Garner plays a shanghaied Texas cowboy who jumps ship in Hawaii and is persuaded by potato-farm widow Vera Miles to stay around long enough to teach her lazy, fun-loving islanders how to round up the wild cattle that are trampling and eating her farm out of business. Disney director Vincent McEveety makes the most of the sunny story, the location scenery and a good cast, but adults may find it less than riveting. A-I (G) U

Castilian, The (1963) Poorly dubbed Spanish production re-creates the rivalry between the royal houses of Castille and Navarre until they join to stop the Moors from conquering all of Spain. Director Javier Seto does best in staging the clash of medieval armies on the Spanish plains but gets nowhere with the personal problems of the characters (notably Cesar Romero, Broderick Crawford, Fernando Rey and Alida Valli), despite occasional commentary by an earnest troubadour (Frankie Avalon). Much stylized violence and several sexual references. A-II (br)

Castle, The (1969) German adaptation of Franz Kafka's unfinished novel about a land surveyor (Maximilian Schell) trying to report for a job assignment but frustrated by an absurdist bureaucracy and a dehumanized populace. Director Rudolf Noelte's production is strangely flat, despite its effective use of photography, settings and peasant faces to convey a mood of grim eeriness. Perhaps in our era, faceless bureaucracy has become too facile and cliched a target. A-III (nr) A

Castle Keep (1969) Screen version of novelist William Eastlake's surrealistic satire on the absurdity of war is set in a Gothic chateau with its priceless art treasures where an American major (Burt Lancaster) and a company of infantrymen prepare to make a stand against the German army's offensive at Bastogne. Regrettably, director Sydney Pollack fails to incorporate a convincing human and moral dimension to counter-balance the senseless heroics and casual sexual relationships that result. O (R) 15

Castle of Fu Manchu, The (1973) With weapons developed by kidnapped scientists, Fu (Christopher Lee) broadcasts his intention to rule the world, but Scotland Yard sleuth Nayland Smith (Richard Greene) manages to come to the rescue. Directed by Jess Franco, this is not accomplished until the screen has been deluged with flimsy skirmishes, unsynchronized voices and stock footage of a sinking ship, a bursting dam and an exploding house. Phooey. A-II (PG)

Casual Sex (1988) Unfunny comedy about two young single women (Lea Thompson and Victoria Jackson) who, in search of a healthy way to meet Mr. Right, sign on for a vacation at a singles health spa. Director Genevieve Robert uses humor to portray contemporary issues of sexuality and the AIDS epidemic in a frank if noncerebral manner. Much blunt sex talk and a nonsexual nude beach sequence. O (R) 18

Casualties of War (1989) Fact-based story of an atrocity committed by an American patrol during the Vietnam War centers on the moral dilemma of a soldier (Michael J. Fox) who tries to prevent his unit (led by Sean Penn) from gang-raping and murdering a Vietnamese woman. Director Brian De-Palma's treatment of the atrocity and the war's violence is extremely graphic. Intense violence and much foul language. A-IV (R) 18

Cat, The (1966) Poorly done outdoor adventure story of a boy who gets lost on a camping trip and who is saved by a mountain lion who befriends him. Directed by Ellis Kadison, it would only be of interest to the very young and the gullible. A-I (br)

Cat and Mouse (1970) German adaptation of the Gunter Grass novel about a young man's groping for maturity under the Nazi regime, and his subjective way of facing reality and his own handicaps. Directed with precision and style by Hans-jurgen Pohland, it is of interest for what it shows of the period but also has some insights for those working with adolescents. A-III (nr)

Cat and Mouse (1978) Unorthodox police inspector (Serge Reggiani) is baffled by what appears to be a millionaire's murder and theft of his art collection, but as the case progresses nothing is quite what it seems and the viewer is never exactly sure where the abundance of clues will lead. Written and directed by Claude Lelouch, the mystery comedy is both intelligent and playful, especially with its offbeat cast of characters acted with style by the likes of Michele Morgan and Philippe Leotard. A-III (nr)

Cat Ballou (1965) Wild romp out West as the daughter (Jane Fonda) of a murdered rancher (John Marley) seeks justice by enlisting the aid of an over-the-hill gunfighter (Lee Marvin), an Indian ranch hand (Tom Nardini) and a pair of con men (Michael Callan and Dwayne Hickman). Director Elliot Silverstein's frontier spoof has comic flair, droll performances (Marvin also doubles as the chief villain) and musical commentary by balladeers Nat King Cole and Stubby Kaye. Comic violence and mild sexual innuendo. A-II (br) A

Cat from Outer Space, The (1978) A stricken spaceship piloted by a very sophisticated cat lands on earth for repairs and is aided by an odd assortment of friendly scientists (Ken Berry; Sandy Duncan; McLean Stevenson) to get airborne again despite interference from the military (Henry Morgan) and the charms of an earth cat named Lulubelle. Surviving Norman Tokar's unsubtle direction, it proves better than average Disney fare. A-I (G) U

Cat O'Nine Tails, The (1971) Italian director Dario Argento's B-grade murder mystery centers on a series of killings in a medical research center that are eventually unraveled by newspaper reporters (James Franciscus and Karl Malden). The assorted graphic murders and death agonies are utterly pointless, as are the sex interludes with Catherine Spaak and a ludicrous encounter in a gay nightclub. O (GP) AA

Cat People (1942) Effectively understated horror movie in which a husband (Kent Smith) tries to help his bride (Simone Simon) conquer her fear of an old Serbian legend about humans who have the power to turn into deadly panthers. In their first effort to wring suspense from low-budget melodramas, producer Val Lewton and director Jacques Tourneur create a sinister atmosphere and some scary scenes—notably in a hotel swimming pool—but are less successful with the weak plot. Much menace and a broken marriage. A-II (br) A

Cat People (1982) Very loosely based on Val Lewton's 1942 horror classic, this one is tediously explicit in showing the tribulations of a brother and sister (Malcolm McDowell and Nastassja Kinski) who turn into black panthers at odd moments and must kill to regain their human form. Paul Schrader's direction offers clumsy, heavy-handed doses of blood and gore, graphic sex and nudity. O (R) X

Cat's Eye (1985) Three episodes that are an unstable blend of suspense, violence and black humor linked together tenuously by the presence of the same cat in each. Directed by Lewis Teague from a screenplay by horror writer Stephen King, these are moderately entertaining with relatively restrained violence. A-II (PG-13) 15

Catch My Soul (1974) Uneven rock opera version of Shakespeare's "Othello" turns the wicked Iago (Lance Le Gault) into the devil incarnate dressed as a hippie and the noble Moor (Richie Havens) is now a pacifist preacher who heads a hippie commune. The score by Havens and Tony Joe White is quite good, but Jack Good's script ranges from the sublime to the ridiculous in its mixture of Shakespearean imagery, Biblical diction and contemporary argot. Directed by Patrick McGoohan and photographed by Conrad Hall, the New Mexico locations are an impressive backdrop for the opera but the contemporary rarely meshes smoothly with the classic. A-III (PG)

Catch 22 (1970) Screen version of Joseph Heller's black comedy about a bomber squadron in Italy during World War II and its troubled airman, Yossarian (Alan Arkin). Although skillfully done under Mike Nichols' direction, it is more pretentious than profound in its statement that war is madness. Brief nudity and some graphic depiction of wartime casualties. A-IV (R) 15

Catherine & Co. (1976) French production about an English prostitute, played with nauseating coyness by Jane Birkin, who decides to incorporate herself as a business enterprise. Thoroughly unfunny and offensive sex comedy directed by Michael Boisrond. O (R)

Catlow (1971) Flip outlaw (Yul Brynner) shoots his way across the Southwest and part of Mexico with a quixotic marshal (Richard Crenna) in hot pursuit. Directed by Sam Wanamaker, action rather than plot is all this meandering, seriocomic western shoot-'em-up has to offer. Stylized violence. A-III (GP) A

Cattle Annie and Little Britches (1981) Two teenage girls (Amanda Plummer and Diane Lane) join a once famous outlaw gang (led by Burt Lancaster) and inspire its aging members to live up to their reputation. Director Lamont Johnson's contrived western does not measure up to its whimsical intentions and takes a benign view of immorality of various sorts, including sexual. A-III (PG) A

Cattle King (1963) Tired formula Western about an 1880's Wyoming range war between a big rancher (Robert Taylor) and the hired guns of a city boss (Robert Middleton). Directed by Tay Garnett, there's nothing new here, though it does touch on the question of government land policy. Stylized shoot-outs and fisticuffs. A-I (br)

Cattle Queen of Montana (1954) Routine Western directed by Allan Dwan has an undercover government agent (Ronald Reagan) give some needed assistance to the title character (Barbara Stanwyck) in the fight to save her ranch from an ambitious landgrabber (Gene Evans) and his Indian allies. Stylized violence. A-I (br) U

Cauldron of Blood (1971) Far-fetched, unscarey would-be chiller about a mad housewife (Viveca Lindfors) who won't tell her blind sculptor-hubby (Boris Karloff) the source of the skeletons she supplies for him to use as models for his lifelike statues. A bubbly vat of acid has the title role. Directed by Edward Mann, it is pure hokum, but innocuous enough for hardy, undemanding adults. A-III (GP)

Cavalcade (1933) Dated family saga from the Noel Coward play contrasts the changing fortunes of an upper-class London couple (Clive Brook and Diana Wynyard) with those of their servants (Herbert Mundin and Una O'Connor) from the turn of the century to the Great Depression. Director Frank Lloyd's stagey portrayal of parents and offspring suffering through wars, personal tragedies and socioeconomic upheavals is so understated that its picture of the times has little historical interest today and even less emotional impact. Some wartime violence and veiled sexual references. A-II (br) U

Caveman (1981) Prehistoric slapstick comedy with Ringo Starr, John Matuszak and Barbara Bach has at least the virtue of being unpretentious yet garners few laughs along the way. Director Carl Gottlieb's sense of humor is only for those whose weakness for buffoonery and vulgarity borders on total insensibility. A-III (PG) A

CB4 (1993) Satiric misfire in which a fictional black rap group (Chris Rock, Allen Payne and Deezer D) zoom to the top of the charts by patterning their anti-social lyrics and behavior on a local hood who escapes prison promising revenge on his phony imitators. Directed by Tamra Davis, the result never gets much beyond glossy exaggerations of rappers who revel in the obscene, the absurd and the vile. Some unfunny violence and simulated sex scenes as well as much rough language. O (R)

C.C. and Company (1970) Ann-Margret acts bored and Joe Namath doesn't act at all in this aimless, trashy motorcycle melodrama directed by Seymour Robbie. Exploitative sex scenes. O (R/PG)

Cease Fire (1985) A Vietnam veteran has difficulty adjusting to civilian life because of the traumatic effect of his war experiences. Good acting by Don Johnson and Lisa Blount, but the film itself is superficial and not very moving. Some rough language and use of narcotics. A-III (R)

Celebration at Big Sur (1971) Lackluster documentary about a rock/folk music festival at California's Big Sur with performances by Joan Baez, Joni Mitchell, Crosby Stills Nash & Young, John B. Sebastian and, best of all, Dorothy Morrison and the Combs Sisters. The inevitable shots of casual nudity and drug-taking are brief, but they are there almost as tokens of the music scene which, in itself, is very sad indeed. A-III (GP)

Cemetery Club, The (1993) Strained comedy about three close-knit Jewish widows (Ellen Burstyn, Olympia Dukakis and Diane Ladd) whose halting readjustment to single life is complicated by a romantically inclined widower (Danny Aiello). Despite crackerjack performances and often witty

dialogue, director Bill Duke ultimately lets the story wallow in maudlin sentimentality. An implied sexual encounter and minimal rough language. A-III (PG-13)

Ceremony, The (1974) With this chronicle of an influential family that spans from 1946 to the present, director Nagisa Oshima has taken the measure of the Japanese upper-class and found it wanting. His picture of the convoluted relationships within this archetypal family stresses the unthinking ritualistic approach to life that was harmful in the past and even more dangerous today. Violence. A-III (nr)

Cesar and Rosalie (1972) French romance about a liberated woman (Romy Schneider) who divides her time between her young daughter, her current lover (Yves Montand) and her first love (Sami Frey) just returned from America but, in the end, she leaves them both. Directed by Claude Sautet, the movie is a fine character study of middle-aged people and their feelings about life, though some may find the implied sexual relationships offensive. A-IV (R) AA

Chain Gang Women (1972) Two convicts (Michael Stearns and Robert Lott) escape from a Georgia prison farm and two women provide them with places of refuge and plenty of sexual satisfaction. Directed by Lee Frost and Wes Bishop, the women's complicity hardly justifies the title but, in any event, its sex and violence is excessive. O (R)

Chaingang Girls (see: "Sweet Sugar").

Chain of Desire (1993) Dreadfully dull tale of the jaded sex lives of assorted Manhattanites (including Malcolm McDowell, Linda Fiorentino and Grace Zabriskie) who patronize a sleazy transvestite nightclub. Writer-director Temistocles Lopez attempts a feeble cautionary tale in the age of AIDS but fails to develop the situations or characters beyond meager sketches without wit or insight. Various sexual perversions and encounters, brief nudity and drug abuse, minimal violence and intermittent rough language. O (nr)

Chairman, The (1969) A scientist (Gregory Peck) goes to Red China to steal a secret formula at the urging of Western military intelligence who implant a pill-sized transmitter in his skull. J. Lee Thompson directs an entertaining secret agent melodrama that is mildly suspenseful yet also raises hypothetical questions about U.S. cold war policies and procedures. Adult situations. A-III (PG) A

Chalk Garden, The (1964) Subdued adaptation of Enid Bagnold's play set in a British seaside manor whose eccentric owner (Edith Evans) entrusts her troubled 16-year-old granddaughter (Hayley Mills) to a governess with a mysterious past (Deborah Kerr). Directed by Ronald Neame, the fine cast manages to overcome a glossy, melodramatic production and give some point to a quirky tale of wounded psyches and love denied. Psychological problems. A-II (br) U

Challenge to Be Free (1976) Mike Mazurki plays a trapper who accidentally shoots a policeman and leads a posse on a two-month chase through the depths of an Alaskan winter. A family film directed by Tay Garnett, the flimsy plot is no more than a pretext for showing the austere, rugged beauty of Alaska and a number of photogenic animals that children will love. A-I (G)

Challenge to Lassie (1949) After an aged sheepherder (Donald Crisp) is killed by robbers in 1860 Edinburgh, the dog he had trained from a pup overcomes all manner of obstacles to keep vigil beside her master's grave each night. Directed by Richard Thorpe, the fact-based story of a dog's steadfast loyalty is prime fare for youngsters, though older viewers may be more interested in the legal conflict between Lassie's defender (Edmund Gwenn) and the town magistrate (Alan Napier). Engaging family fare. A-I (br) U

Challenges, The (1973) Three-part Spanish movie, knit together by using American actor, Dean Selmier, in three separate roles, each as an outsider doomed to disaster in a foreign land, simply doesn't go very far with its basic theme of alienation. The interplay between cultures and people is a fascinating subject, but each segment is treated with disappointing shallowness by its director (Claudio Guerin, Jose Luis Egea and Victor Erice). Violence. A-III (GP)

Chamber of Horrors (1966) Hy Averback directs a weak murder mystery with wax museum setting and a cast including Cornel Wilde, Wildred Hyde-White and Patrice Wymore. Stylized violence and a sequence set in a brothel. A-III (br) X

Chameleon Street (1991) Bored by his blue collar job and pressured to make big bucks by his wife (Angela Leslie), a handsome charmer (Wendell B. Harris, Jr.) passes himself off as a Harvard-trained surgeon, a Time magazine journalist, a Yale student and a human rights attorney. Harris wrote, starred in and directed this fact-based movie, infusing it with lively originality and sardonic humor that generally makes up for the disjointed narrative. Sporadic rough language and some sexual innuendo. A-III (R)

Champ, The (1979) Over-the-hill boxing champ (Jon Voight) tries a comeback for the sake of his adoring son (Ricky Schroder) in director Franco Zeffirelli's romanticized remake of the 1931 classic. Race-

track atmosphere and Voight's performance are more interesting than the melodramatic plot, but the boxing sequences may be too brutally intense for younger teens. A-II (PG) A

Champagne Murders, The (1967) Uneven French murder mystery about a jaded playboy (Maurice Ronet) who is being made to believe that he has murdered several women in drunken blackouts. Director Claude Chabrol is more interested in showing upper-class corruption than working out the details of a rather complicated plot. Scenes of immorality and decadence tend to be excessive for their purpose. O (br) X

Chances Are (1989) Delightful fantasy fluff about a beautiful 40-year-old widow (Cybill Shepherd) who is reunited with her beloved husband when he returns to life 20 years later in the body of a young aspiring journalist (Robert Downey Jr.). Director Emile Ardolino has fashioned a classy comedy romance that makes the most of a good cast and offers a feeble message about the healthy necessity of moving on after the death of a loved one. Some sexual innuendos. A-III (PG)

Chandler (1971) Private-eye (Warren Oates) falls in love with the French woman (Leslie Caron) he's been hired to follow in a ruse concocted by government agents to flush an underworld biggie out of the shadows. Director Paul Magwood's confused, convoluted plot is a poor imitation of a Raymond Chandler mystery. Sylized violence. A-III (GP)

Change of Habit (1969) Three coy nuns don civilian clothes to work in a Spanish Harlem ghetto clinic run by Doctor Elvis Presley who, unaware of the convent's experimental program, naturally falls in love with one of them (Mary Tyler Moore). William Graham directs with plenty of sentimentality, cliches and stereotypes of the 1940s' variety that some modern nuns may not appreciate. A-II (G) AA

Change of Mind (1969) A white district attorney in a Southern town who is dying of cancer survives by means of a medical operation transplanting his brain into the healthy body of a black accident victim (Raymond St. Jacques). Though burdened with stereotypes, cliches and a far-fetched premise, director Robert Stevens achieves an allegory with some insights into how race affects people's perceptions and actions. Some adult situations and dialogue limit it to mature audiences. A-III (R) X

Change of Seasons, A (1980) Shirley MacLaine plays a loving wife who, shocked to learn that her husband (Anthony Hopkins) is having an affair with a woman young enough to be their daughter (Bo Derek), jumps into an affair with a younger man (Michael Brandon). This pretentious, meandering, excruciatingly cute effort, directed by Richard Lang and written by Erich Segal, features extravagant nudity and lack of any positive moral perspective. O (R) AA

Changeling, The (1980) An unusually subtle and intelligent haunted house melodrama starring George C. Scott as the man who rents a huge, isolated old mansion where soon the fun begins with strange noises, eerie manifestations and a seance that reveals the secret of the house. Directed by Peter Medak, its mood of horror and flashes of violence are remarkably restrained, though there is a scene depicting the cruel murder of a child. A-III (R) X

Changes (1969) A college student (Kent Lane) leaves home looking for a more authentic meaning to his life than he has experienced from his parents and passes through a series of relationships in his quest for self-identity. Writer-director Hall Bartlett's restatement of the problems and inner conflicts confronting youth in an affluent American society is well-intentioned but abounds in cliches both in its romantic visuals and probes of adult hypocrisies. A-III (PG)

Chaplin (1992) Respectful, plodding biography of screen great Charles Chaplin (1889–1977) from his impoverished youth in London to his meteoric rise in World War I Hollywood, decades of popular success and critical acclaim, exile as a political undesirable after World War II and triumphal return to Hollywood for a special Academy Award a few years before his death. Directed by Richard Attenborough, the episodic chronicle captures the changing historical context but not, for all Robert Downey Jr.'s evocative performance in the title role, the essence of the man or his genius for visual comedy. Muted sexual references, incidental nudity and occasional rough language. A-III (PG-13) 12

Chaplin Revue, The (1972) Three silent featurettes written, directed and starring Charles Chaplin for First National were originally released as "A Dog's Life" (April 1918), "Shoulder Arms" (October 1918) and "The Pilgrim" (1923). This sampler of films from what may have been Chaplin's most inventive period helps to explain better than anything else why he will endure in the memory of the movie public. A-I (G)

Chappaqua (1967) In an autobiographical semi-documentary featuring himself, Conrad Rooks chronicles his treatment for drug dependence in a private hospital abroad. Disjointed montage of images convey the nightmarish existence of an addict in the physical agony of withdrawal. A-III (br)

Chapter Two (1979) A successful writer (James Caan) marries an actress (Marsha Mason) but the memory of his dead wife threatens their happiness in this adaptation of a Neil Simon play. Under Robert Moore's direction, the one-liners are still funny but the attempt to deal with more serious material is beset with problems, chief of which is the lack of dramatic action. Attempted adultery figures in a subplot, though it is far from being condoned. A-III (PG) A

Charade (1963) Black romantic comedy about a rich widow (Audrey Hepburn) who is hounded by criminals (James Coburn and Walter Matthau) and seeks help from a mysterious, debonair stranger (Cary Grant) whom she must learn to trust. Director Stanley Donen makes exquisite use of the Parisian locales and Henry Mancini's memorable score. A-II (br) A

Charge at Feather River, The (1953) Standard Western starts with a squad of misfit troopers (led by Guy Madison) rescuing two reluctant women (Vera Miles and Helen Westcott) from their Cheyenne captors, then being pursued and forced to make a stand against waves of attackers. Director Gordon Douglas alternates pitched battles against the Indians with dissension within the rescue party but achieves only slack results. Much stylized violence and veiled sexual references. A-II (br)

Charge of the Lancers (1954) Slack war story of a French captain (Pierre Aumont) attached to British forces in the Crimean War who gets help from a gypsy (Paulette Goddard) in rescuing an English officer held by the Russians in Sevastapol. Directed by William Castle, the action is tediously unconvincing, though the preposterous situation has unintended amusing moments. Stylized violence and minor romantic complications. A-II (br) U

Charge of the Light Brigade, The (1968) Heavy-handed account of the 1853-1856 British campaign against the Russian forces in the Crimea, set in the context of the power politics and social inequalities of the Victorian age. Director Tony Richardson fails to keep the scale of the spectacle from reducing the stature of its characters, thereby wasting a large and talented cast. Anti-war violence. A-III (br) A

Chariots of Fire (1981) Two young Englishmen (Ben Cross and Ian Charleson) overcome quite different obstacles to win gold medals at the Paris Olympics of 1924. One is a Jew determined to beat the anti-Semitic establishment at its own game and the other is a devout Scot who runs for the glory of God. Directed by Hugh Hudson, it is a richly entertaining and highly inspiring movie for the whole family. Several coarse words. A-I (PG) A

Chariots of the Gods? (1974) Eric von Daniken's account of the mammoth constructions of prehistory, from the pyramids to Easter Island, relates their creation to spacemen from more highly developed planets than Earth. The mysteries of man's past are many and awesome, but this pseudo-documentary sheds little light on them. A-I (G)

Charles and Lucie (1980) Uneven French sentimental comedy about a middle-aged Parisian couple whom swindlers leave penniless and on the run from the police in the picturesque south of France. What follows is a series of comic misadventures and absurd encounters that director Nelly Kaplan handles somewhat haphazardly in a mixture of farce, satire and whimsey. Holding the film together are the marvellous performances of Ginette Garcin and Daniel Ceccaldi as the struggling couple who steadfastly face adversity with a comic dignity that is in the best tradition of screen comedy. A-III (nr)

Charles—Dead or Alive (1972) Swiss movie in which a successful businessman (Francois Simon) decides one day that he hates his daily routine and goes off to think about his future. His son, frantic about the welfare of the business and afraid of publicity, hires a detective to locate his father and then commits him to an insane asylum. Director Alain Tanner's story about a mid-life crisis is also a criticism of Swiss conformity but done in such a light-hearted and gently human way that it is first-rate entertainment and not just a social lesson. Mature themes. A-III (nr)

Charley and the Angel (1973) After Fred MacMurry is informed by angel Harry Morgan that he has only a short time on earth, he changes his ways and becomes a dedicated family man. Director Vince McEveety handles the Disney Depression Era story with a suitably light touch that allows Harry Morgan a maximum amount of fun while emphasizing the positive messages of the story. A-I (G) U

Charley Varrick (1973) Unusual, action-packed and curiously disturbing film about a seemingly ordinary individual (Walter Matthau) who supplements his income as a crop-duster pilot by robbing small-town banks on his mornings off. When he happens to rob a bank used by gangsters, he winds up being chased by the mob as well as the police. Director Don Siegel's movie is tense and occasionally quite brutal, with an undercurrent of amorality in the dog-eat-dog atmosphere of the underworld. A-III (PG) X

Charley-One-Eye (1973) Fugitive black soldier (Richard Roundtree) makes his way across the Mexican desert in 1866 in the company of a lame, half-breed Indian (Roy Thinnes), occasionally bothered by Mexican bandits and a bounty hunter (Nigel Davenport). Directed by Don Chaffey, the movie is shallow, ponderous and considerably violent. A-III (R)

Charlie Bubbles (1968) Seriocomic think piece about a sensitive, generous, popular writer of romantic novels who discovers that success is more trouble than its worth but can't go back again. Though some may not care for the movie's nonnarrative style and may even find Charlie's boredom contagious, others will find it thoughtful and provocative. Directed by Albert Finney, who also plays the lead, there is a fine supporting cast (Billie Whitelaw, Colin Blakely and Liza Minnelli). Adult situations. A-III (br) AA

Charlie Chan and the Curse of the Dragon Queen (1981) Called out of retirement to help the San Francisco police solve a series of bizarre murders, Charlie Chan (Peter Ustinov) trades leaden aphorisms with a dotty in-law, her daffy servants and a cloddish Number One grandson. Ineptly directed by Clive Donner, this witless farce relies on vulgarity and profanity for laughs. A-III (PG) A

Charlie, the Lonesome Cougar (1967) Disney wildlife documentary featuring an agile cougar named Charlie who has outgrown the northwoods lumber camp where he was raised and finds happiness with a female cougar in a nearby game preserve. Charlie is a very photogenic animal, but his "adventures" are on the cute side and begin to wear thin. A-I (br) U

Charlotte's Web (1973) Charming animated musical version of E.B. White's classic fable about a piglet named Wilbur who develops from runt of the litter into the county fair champ with the help of his friends, most notably the spider of the title. Directed by Charles A. Nichols, the Hanna-Barbera production is a gentle introduction to the natural cycle of life that will entertain youngsters and most others in the family. A-I (G) U

Charly (1968) Mentally retarded adult (Cliff Robertson) becomes a genius during a medical experiment that has only one drawback, and it's a heartbreaker. A somewhat sentimental adaptation of Daniel Keyes' short story, "Flowers for Algernon," the intriguing plot is delicately handled by director Ralph Nelson and given dramatic impact by the range of Robertson's performance in the title role. Mature treatment of romantic subplot. A-III (br) A

Charro! (1969) Elvis Presley sings only one song, and that off-camera, in a silly western vehicle about a gang of outlaws and a golden cannon in Old Mexico. Directed by Charles Marquis Warren, it contains stylized violence, a bit of sadism and some double entendres. A-III (G) U

Charulata (1974) Director Satyajit Ray's story is of a wife neglected by her husband's total commitment to his work. As the film ends with a freeze-frame of the couple reaching for each other, the picture reaches far beyond the boundaries of Ray's native Bengal. A-II (nr) U

Chase, The (1966) When an escaped convict (Robert Redford) makes his way home, the entire community dissolves in outbreaks of hate and violence, putting local sheriff (Marlon Brando) on the spot in trying to uphold the law. An outstanding cast flounders in a murky political allegory directed by Arthur Penn from Lillian Hellman's adaptation of Horton Foote's play. Confused treatment of significant themes, including racism, greed, lust, alcoholism and religious fanaticism. A-III (br) X

Chase for the Golden Needles, The (see: "Golden Needles").

Chastity (1969) Produced by Sonny and starring Cher, the movie intends to be a personal statement about dropping out and searching for identity and true relationships, here depicted in time-honored trial-and-error fashion. Directed by Alessio De Paola, it unfortunately suffers from a lack of sophistication and insight as well as the severe technical limitations that are common in small-budget films. A-IV (R)

Chato's Land (1972) Failed western about a half-breed Indian (Charles Bronson) who is goaded into killing a brutish sheriff and becomes the object of an intense manhunt led by an ex-Confederate officer (Jack Palance) which ends in the parched Indian country of the title. Directed by Michael Winner, the problem is that once the movie gets into the groove of steady killing, it becomes both tedious and glaring in its cumulative brutality. A-III (PG) X

Chattahoochee (1990) Dark, tedious account of an emotionally disturbed Korean War hero (Gary Oldman) who in the mid-1950s is sent to a degrading mental institution from which he, with the aid of his sister, alerts officials to the brutal mistreatment of the inmates, resulting in legislation that improved treatment of the mentally ill across the country. Mick Jackson's unimaginative direction dilutes the power of the young man's gradual transformation into a mature person committed to social justice. Graphic scenes of brutality, shower room nudity, implicit masturbation and locker-room language. A-IV (R) 15

Che! (1969) Dramatization of different points of view on the life and career of Ernesto (Che) Guevara (Omar Sharif), the Argentinian who was the theoretician and moving spirit behind Cuban revolutionary Fidel Castro (Jack Palance). Directed by Richard Fleischer, it's a boring and lifeless illustrated lecture, devoid of the passion, politics, urgency and conflict that might have involved viewers in potentially interesting and significant political realities. A-II (PG) AA

Cheap Detective, The (1978) Overdone parody of the private-eye melodramas of the 1940s with Peter Falk as a Humphrey Bogart-like detective searching for the murderer of his partner, smashing a smuggling ring led by John Houseman doing a Sidney Greenstreet interpretation and helping a Free French agent gain passage to Oakland. Robert Moore directs a Neil Simon script lacking in wit and invention, sporting tired jokes and some sexually derived humor. A-III (PG) A

Cheaper by the Dozen (1950) Warm family comedy about the unusual domestic arrangements in the New Jersey household of a no-nonsense efficiency expert (Clifton Webb), his equally proficient wife (Myrna Loy) and their 12 children (Jeanne Crain is the eldest). Set in the early part of the century, director Walter Lang's episodic, fact-based story has a strong nostalgic appeal along with a genial sense of humor about family life, some of which proves more than funny (e.g., Mildred Natwick as a bemused planned parenthood representative). Still pleases. A-I (br) U

Cheaper to Keep Her (1981) A divorce lawyer (Tovah Feldshuh), concerned about late alimony payments, hires a private investigator (Mac Davis) who is newly divorced himself in a dreadfully acted, determinedly vulgar attempt by director Ken Annakin at romantic comedy. The humor, when not lewd, comes at the expense of homosexuals and Hispanics. O (R)

Checkered Flag or Crash (1977) Joe Don Baker plays a driver in a 1000-mile road race in the Philippines, with Susan Sarandon as an intrepid photographer-journalist. Directed by Alan Gibson, it is mindless even by the modest standards of racing movies and exhibits a disregard for human life. A-III (PG)

Checking Out (1989) Failed, badly written comedy about one man's fear of mortality when an airline executive (Jeff Daniels) flips out after the sudden death of his best friend (Allen Havey). Director David Leland offers little beyond tasteless ethnic jokes, tired coronary gags, numbingly selfish characters and a particularly gross sex scene. O (R) 15

Cheech and Chong's Next Movie (1980) Second movie with the comedy team of Cheech and Chong (Cheech Marin and

Thomas Chong) assaults the audience with drugs, foul language, crude sexual references and a plot that goes nowhere. Directed by Chong. O (R) 15

Cheech and Chong's Nice Dreams (1981) The dopey duo this time out are entrepreneurs dealing marijuana from an ice cream truck, which leads to the usual rambling misadventures with drugs and sex. O (R)

Cheech and Chong's "The Corsican Brothers" (1984) Cheech and Chong take the plot of the venerable old swashbuckler and bedeck it with their usual slapstick gags, though this time they avoid drugs and nudity. Directed by Thomas Chong, however, it's all very unfunny, especially its gross sexual humor. O (R)

Cheetah (1989) Disney live-action adventure of two teenagers who adopt an orphaned Cheetah cub while spending the summer with their parents in Kenya. Directed by Jeff Blyth, the movie may bore parents familiar with the similar, better movie, "Born Free," but children will be content with the movie's nature photography and the warm friendship that develops between the American youngsters and a local Masai lad who shows them the wonders of his world. A-I (G) U

Cher Victor (1976) French black comedy to which director Robin Davis brings a hard-edged sensibility in a story of two old men for whom petty quarrels turn into a vendetta that ends in tragedy. Bernard Blier and Jacques Dufilho, two great character actors, give a performance worth seeing as the geriatric odd couple who are locked in a symbiotic relationship neither can break. The movie is amusing yet underneath lurks the truth that the frailties of old age await each viewer. A-III (nr)

Cherry, Harry and Raquel (1970) Marijuana operation in the Arizona desert is interfered with by a pesky Indian. Sex exploitation job directed by Russ Meyer with extensive nudity and perverse acts. O (X/R)

Chess Players, The (1978) Indian director Satyajit Ray tells a 19th-century story of British encroachments on a small Moslem kingdom in the north of India, using as his focus two idle aristocrats who pass their days in playing chess, oblivious of the danger that threatens their land and its poet-king. Based on an actual incident and told with some humor and much irony, the film suffers from being overly talky and stagy. Its greatest asset for American viewers is its careful re-creation of a vanished era. A-II (nr) A

Cheyenne Autumn (1964) Western epic of Indian courage in the face of the white man's neglect and broken promises in the story of a Cheyenne tribe who leave a squalid reservation for their homeland and an officer (Richard Widmark) who sympathizes with their plight but whose orders are to bring them back. Director John Ford's rugged locales match the grandeur of the trek even though the melodramatic narrative falters at times. A-I (nr) U

Cheyenne Social Club, The (1970) Jimmy Stewart, a cowboy with moral inhibitions, inherits a brothel but his ownership of the building depends on the ladies remaining there. Sidekick Henry Fonda jumps in and out of ladies beds while Stewart stammers his way through an excruciatingly silly seduction scene (complete with maid in transparent blouse). An exercise in off-color humor directed by Gene Kelly, the result lacks wit, taste and interest. O (GP) AA

Chicago Joe and the Showgirl (1990) Stationed in World War II London, a G.I. (Kiefer Sutherland) and an exotic dancer (Emily Lloyd) take their Hollywood-inspired crime fantasies to deadly lengths within days of meeting each other. Directed by Bernard Rose, the fact-based movie restages the pair's murderous rampage without offering any insight into such cold-blooded behavior. Brutal depictions of violent crimes, brief shots of sexual activity and partial nudity. A-III (R) 18

Chicago 70 (1970) Witty anti-establishment satire intertwines the Chicago conspiracy trial of Bobby Seale and Abbie Hoffman with Lewis Carroll's "Alice in Wonderland." Director Kerry Feltham photographed the stage play as performed by the Toronto Workshop, with its bizarre, colorful costumes and a minimum of props in a black limbo setting. Mature themes. A-III (nr)

Chicken Chronicles, The (1977) Obnoxious youth-oriented comedy set in the late 1960s about a self-indulgent Beverly Hills high school senior determined to get his girlfriend into bed. Though avoiding nudity, director Francis Simon's treatment of sex, drugs and alcohol is exploitative. O (PG) X

Childhood II (1973) Group encounter sessions held in the nude because, we are told, without clothes people can be more honest and open with one another. Martin J. Spinelli's documentary indicates that this technique is as inadequate as most other shortcuts to mental health. O (nr)

Children, The (1980) An orange, radioactive cloud turns a group of children into nasty creatures bent upon murder in director Max Kalmanowicz' cheap, amateurish horror movie that overdoes the blood and gore. O (R)

Children of Fate (1993) Compelling documentary focuses on an abused wife and mother in a Sicilian slum plagued by childhood mortality and pervasive unemployment, where boys aspire to join the Mafia. As directed and edited by Andrew Young, and Susan Todd, the documentary combines 30-year-old footage of the mother's sorry situation then with her family's current conditions, resulting in a moving family portrait of poverty's lasting effects upon generations of the disadvantaged. Subtitles. Several references to wifebeating, drugs, sexual situations and criminal lifestyles. A-III (nr)

Children of a Lesser God (1986) A deaf girl (Marlee Matlin) who has resigned herself to a life of solitude and mediocrity painfully comes to accept the love and admiration of a professor (William Hurt) at the school for the deaf where she works as a janitor. A well-acted sentimental love story, its potential insights into the problems of interpersonal communication are undercut by director Randa Haines' concentration on the sexual aspects of the lovers' relationship. Nudity and harsh language. A-III (R) 15

Children of Rage (1975) Set in 1968, after the disastrous Arab losses in the Six Day War, this movie tries to explain why the Palestinians adopted the desperate policy of terrorism in their fight against the state of Israel. An embarrassingly amateurish production directed by Arthur Allan Seidelman, its failure to do so in any coherent fashion can only serve to exacerbate the feelings of both sides. Violence. A-III (PG)

Children of the Corn (1984) Some nasty kids, in the sway of some demonic power, slaughter all the adults in a Midwestern town where a doctor and his wife (Peter Horton and Linda Hamilton) chance to stop on an auto trip. Fritz Kiersch directs this dull, predictable horror movie adapted from a story by Stephen King. Violence. A-III (R) 18

Children of Theatre Street, The (1978) American documentary on the famous ballet school in Leningrad that produced Nijinsky and whose more recent graduates include Nureyev, Makarova and Baryshnikov. Directed by Robert Dornhelm and narrated by Princess Grace of Monaco, it offers some lovely, if fragmented, ballet sequences and some fine views of Peter the Great's city, but the narrative tends to be bland and repetitive, pursuing its subject in rather aimless fashion. A-I (nr)

Child's Play (1972) Failed screen version of Robert Marasco's play about the tragedy of evil that grows from the school rivalry between a paranoid Latin teacher (James Mason) and a jovial paternalistic English teacher (Robert Preston) who has come to hate him. The only mystery is why director Sidney Lumet weakened what was originally a straight chiller by throwing in all kinds of side-long glances, creaky doors, murky corridors and unsubtle theatrical effects. A-III (PG) X

Child's Play (1988) A widow (Catherine Hicks) buys a talking doll for her son's sixth birthday, but the doll is possessed by the soul of a psychopath (Brad Dourif). Although the boy (Alex Vincent) knows the doll is deadly, no one believes him, including the Chicago cop (Chris Sarandon) investigating the doll's murder victims. Director Tom Holland overdoes the doll's brutal rampages in a tasteless horror movie exploiting a child as ghoul bait. O (R) 15

Child's Play II (1990) Chucky, the doll possessed by the spirit of a psychopath, is reassembled and goes on another murderous rampage as he tries to get his hands on the little boy (Alex Vincent) he's determined to inhabit. Director John Lafia's schlocky sequel is as predictable as it is trite and repulsive. Intermittent gory violence and recurring rough language and gestures. O (R) 15

Child's Play 3 (1991) Formula horror sequel has killer doll Chucky (voice of Brad Dourif) at a military academy intent on transferring his soul into an 8-year-old (Jeremy Silvers) unless a previously intended victim (Justin Whalin) can prevent it. Director Jack Bender sets the foulmouthed doll on another killing rampage in a contrived plot centering on murder and mayhem. Excessive violence, continual menace to a child and much rough language. O (R) 18

Chilly Scenes of Winter (see: "Head Over Heels").

China Girl (1987) Interracial teen romance blooms amid a climate of gang warfare in New York's Chinatown and Little Italy. Director Abel Ferrara emphasizes action and setting over characterization and an understanding of ethnic loyalties and traditions of prejudice that rule the lives of two generations of Chinese and Italians. Bloody violence, a love-making scene and profanity abound. O (R) 18

China Is Near (1968) Italian satire on the country's politics and morals centers on a man's campaign for office in a small town where everything revolves around sex, politics and religion. Marco Bellocchio's confusing direction lacks a clear enough viewpoint to support its heavy-handed and at times offensive treatment. A-IV (br)

China Syndrome, The (1979) Director James Bridges' prophetic drama suspensefully deals with nuclear safety issues in a movie featuring Jack Lemmon as an executive and Jane Fonda as a news reporter whose consciences won't let them conceal the imminent danger of a nuclear meltdown at a power plant. Thoughtful entertainment. A-II (PG) A

Chinatown (1974) Jack Nicholson plays a private-eye trying to unravel a murder bound up with a civic scandal in the Los Angeles of the 1930s. Faye Dunaway is the mysterious, frightened woman at the center of the plot along with wealthy tycoon John Huston. Director Roman Polanski plays a sinister heavy. A superior entertainment, altogether adult in its theme of social and personal corruption, especially its implication of incest. A-IV (R) X

Chinese Connection, The (1973) Martial arts movie with Bruce Lee revenging the murder of his beloved teacher. In the end, the hero goes to jail for his murderous deeds, affording him one last snickering kick at the audience as he's led away. Director Lo Wei employs excessive violence and a totally irrelevant striptease by a geisha girl. O (R)

Chipmunk Adventure, The (1987) Animated feature plays like a musical revue of pop tunes as Alvin and his Chipmunk friends sing and race around the world with their female cousins, the Chipettes, in hot-air balloons inadvertently delivering stolen diamonds for their wicked human guardians. Director Janice Karman's charming, lighthearted diversion for the younger set includes a sweet song about motherhood and the critters' comical conversation. A-I (G)

Chisum (1970) Boisterous, good old-fashioned western stars John Wayne as cattle baron John Chisum, who figured prominently in the bloody Lincoln County cattle wars involving the likes of Pat Garrett and Billy the Kid. Directed by Andrew V. McLaglen with the usual oversimplification of moral issues in the taming of the West, the movie will appeal to those who like action at the expense of historical accuracy. A-I (G) U

Chitty Chitty Bang Bang (1968) Widowed inventor (Dick Van Dyke) takes his two children and girlfriend (Sally Ann Howes) on a magical mystery tour of the imagination involving an evil baron (Gert Frobe), a cavernous castle in the air, the rescue of imprisoned children and the strange flying car of the title. Though adults may be disappointed by the indifferent lyrics and lackluster special effects of this musical fantasy directed by Ken Hughes, there is still more than enough good fun for the young and uncritical. A-I (G) U

Chloe in the Afternoon (1972) French drama about a married man (Bernard Verley) with a wonderful wife (Francoise Verley), lovely daughter, secure job and serene life who is drawn into intimacy with a sensuous woman (Zouzou) that takes him to the brink of actual infidelity. The final episode in director Eric Rohmer's series of "Six Moral Tales" is an elegant, sophisticated story of a smug, self-absorbed man

who viewers will have to decide was strong enough to resist temptation or simply not nervy enough to indulge it. Restrained nudity. A-III (R)

Chocolat (1989) Set in the French Cameroons on the eve of independence in the late 1950s, this picture of life in colonial Africa is seen through the eyes of the young daughter (Cecile Ducasse) of a colonial official (Francois Cluzet). Director Claire Denis takes an unsettling look at the inhumanity of master-servant relationships, especially the anger and sexual frustration arising between the lady of the house (Giulia Boschi) and the devoted family manservant (Isaach de Bankole). Subtitles. Fleeting nudity. A-III (PG-13) 15

Chocolate War, The (1989) When a sadistic Brother (John Glover) in a parochial school for boys unreasonably pushes his students to sell huge quotas of candy to boost his administrative aspirations, one student (Ilan Mitchell-Smith) refuses and is subjected to abusive reprisals from the teacher and the school's secret fraternity of sociopathic thugs. Writer-director Keith Gordon makes parallels between teen peer-pressure and fascist repression, but his ponderous, metaphoric script and artsy camerawork do little to raise the heavy-handed effort beyond mindless mediocrity. Warped, unbalanced view of parochial school education, vulgar language laced with sexual innuendos, and intense violence. O (R)

Choirboys, The (1977) Screen adaptation of Joseph Wambaugh's novel seems to imply that Los Angeles would be a relatively peaceful city if it could only get rid of its corrupt, drunken, violent, perverted and vicious police force. Scriptwriter Christopher Knopf has thrown together a pointless series of clumsy, presumably black-comedy sketches of police antics, which director Robert Aldrich treats in cynical, leering fashion. Excessive profanity. O (R) X

Choke Canyon (1986) Cowboy-scientist (Stephen Collins) fights for his rights against big business, foils the flying hit man (Bo Swenson) sent to silence him, exposes the effort to turn his canyon lab into a toxic waste site, saves his horse, gets the girl and manages to complete his experiment turning sound waves into energy. Supposedly about integrity and personal initiative, the story gets derailed by juvenile action scenes, pyrotechnics, romance and a small bit of rough language. A-II (PG)

C.H.O.M.P.S. (1979) Young engineer (Wesley Eure) invents the perfect home protection device—a robot watchdog—and wins the hand of the boss' cute daughter despite the machinations of some inept industrial spies. This weak little comedy from Hanna-

Barbera might be of passing interest to very young children if its producers had not seen fit to add a sizable amount of vulgar language. A-II (PG/G) PG

Choose Me (1984) Smug, irritating little comedy-drama about a man (Keith Carradine) who gets involved with three very talkative women who are supported by their lovers in Los Angeles. He suffers, but viewers suffer more. Directed by Alan Rudolph, it has a benign view of sexual amorality. O (R) 15

Chopper Chicks in Zombietown (1991) The inhabitants of a sleepy desert town are threatened by the arrival of 8 tough motorcycle babes and a host of flesh-eating zombies. Writer-director Dan Hoskins' cheap horror spoof lumbers along, mired in hackneyed characterizations and dripping with gory dismemberments and witless, vulgar humor. Excessive violence played for laughs, intermittent rough language, some sexual innuendo and a flash of nudity. O (R)

Chorus Line, A (1985) Screen version of the hit stage musical provides a close-up view of backstage fears and emotions at a Broadway audition. Directed by Richard Attenborough, the film tries too hard to translate the theatrical experience to the big screen. Discussion of adult sexual themes. A-IV (PG-13) PG

Chorus of Disapproval, A (1989) Uninspired movie adaptation of British playwright Alan Ayckbourn's comedy about a handsome widower (Jeremy Irons) who joins a light opera company for companionship but instead becomes the obsession of two married women (Jenny Seagrove and Prunella Scales). Local gossip provides some comic tension, but director Michael Winner imparts little energy to a well-acted but otherwise lackluster play within a play. Satiric adulterous liaisons and some rough language. A-III (PG)

Chosen Survivors (1974) Group of people (Bradford Dillman, Jackie Cooper, Diana Muldaur, Barbara Babcock, Alex Cord and a handful of others) are thrown together in a self-contained underground environment and told that they are the only survivors of a nuclear holocaust. Their problems begin, however, when vampire bats start invading the ventilating system. Directed by Sutton Rolley, it is a scarey movie psychologically, especially if bats are not quite your dish. A-III (PG) X

Chosen, The (1978) Italian production about an industrial magnate (Kirk Douglas) building a super nuclear power plant in a Third World country who learns that one of the major backers of the project is the devil and that the Antichrist waiting to take over is none other than his own son (Simon Ward).

Director Alberto De Martino's supernatural slash-'em, crunch-'em movie is abysmal drivel exploiting nudity and gory violence. O (R)

Chosen, The (1982) Set in Brooklyn during and immediately after World War II, different views of life and religious faith confront two Jewish teenagers (Robby Benson and Barry Miller), one the son of a revered Hassidic rabbi (Rod Steiger), the other the son of a secular scholar (Maximilian Schell). Directed by Jeremy Paul Kagan, the only shortcoming in the screen adaptation of the Chaim Potok novel is a certain lack of dramatic tension. A-II (PG)

Christa (1971) Swedish story about a woman (Birte Tove) looking for someone with whom she'd be sexually compatible and who would make a nice father for her illegitimate son. Producer-director Jack O'Connell seems interested only in putting as much of his actress on display as the law allows. O (R)

Christian Licorice Store, The (1971) Beau Bridges plays a California tennis pro whose descent into the nether world of casual sex with proper Hollywood strangers and into TV product endorsements affords neither food for thought nor dramatic morsels to chew. When he winds up killing himself, it is simply stupid, not tragic. Director James Frawley's slick, shallow work is all style and no substance. O (GP)

Christian the Lion (1977) George Adamson, whose story was dramatized in "Born Free," again becomes involved with the task of rehabilitating a tame lion cub to survive in the perils of its natural African habitat. Assisting in this real-life adventure are the stars of "Born Free," Virginia McKenna and Bill Travers who co-directed the film with James Hill. Beautifully photographed in Kenyan game preserve, it is an engrossing picture of wildlife and worthwhile family fare. A-I (G)

Christine (1983) Adaptation of Stephen King's novel about a 1959 car that kills people either for the sheer fun of it or because they're rude to its teenage owner (Keith Gordon) who rescued it from a junkyard and restored it to pristine splendor. Director John Carpenter's plodding, mediocre movie has foul language, sex, violence and an unwholesome view of family life. O (R) 18

Christine Jorgensen Story, The (1970) The story of a sex change operation certainly has a place in medical annals, but whether it's a proper subject for a movie, except perhaps in a documentary, is another matter. Directed by Irving Rapper, the result is neither entertaining nor illuminating. A-IV (R)

Christmas Carol, A (1951) This British version of the Dickens' classic has worn well over the years principally because of Alistair Sim's zestful performance as Scrooge, the old humbug whose transformation into a loving human being is a pleasure to behold. Director Brian Desmond Hurst's period piece does well with its 19th-century London setting and the ghostly visitations are done simply but with considerable flair. The result is dandy family viewing. A-I (br) U

Christmas Story, A (1983) Adapted from Jean Shepherd's nostalgic piece of whimsey, "In God We Trust, All Others Pay Cash," the movie re-creates what it was like to be a boy (Peter Billingsley) yearning for a genuine Red Ryder air rifle for Christmas in the Midwest of the 1940s. Director Bob Clark gets some good performances from Darren McGavin and Melinda Dillon as the understanding parents and the period atmosphere is nicely conveyed in what is essentially a warm celebration of a more innocent, less sophisticated America. A few vulgar syllables. A-II (PG)

Christmas Tree, The (1969) Wealthy widower (William Holden), told that his only child is dying of leukemia, lavishes all his attention on the boy during his final months. Director Terence Young treats the subject of death with a good deal of sense and sensibility and by focusing on the son's acceptance of his terminal condition, infuses the film with vitality (and even some humor) instead of the static and fruitless sentiment that is common in such films. A-II (G) U

Christopher Columbus—The Discovery (1992) Disappointing theatrical version of the first voyage of the Genoese navigator (George Corraface) who set off from Spain in 1492 to reach Cathay by sailing West, but found the New World instead. Though director John Glen tries to inject some sense of adventure into the proceedings, the script by Mario Puzo and others settles for comic-book history, bogus thrills and politically correct ambiguities, none of which illuminates either the character of Columbus or the nature of the times. Muddled historical context, assorted violence and partial nudity. A-III (PG-13) PG

Chrome and Hot Leather (1971) When the girlfriend of a Green Beret (Tony Young) is accidentally killed by a motorcycle gang, he and three of his Green Beret comrades set out to avenge her death. Directed by Lee Frost, the routine biker movie contains occasional and relatively restrained sex and violence. A-III (GP)

Chronicle of Anna Magdalena Bach, The (1969) Unusual concert performance film with brief dramatic scenes from the life of the 18th-century composer connecting the musical presentations. Directed by Jean-Marie Straub, the German production is static, with almost no camera movement, but the ornate settings and elaborate costuming contribute to a rare musical experience in this performance of works by Johann Sebastian Bach. A-I (nr)

Chu Chu and the Philly Flash (1981) Alan Arkin and Carol Burnett struggle desperately for laughs in director David Lowell Rich's contrived mishmash of a comedy about a pan-handler and failed show girl who find secret government documents. Some profanity. A-III (PG)

Chubasco (1968) Story of the regeneration of a rebellious young man (Christopher Jones) through hard work with a tuna fisherman (Joe De Santis) and the love of a young woman (Susan Strasberg) who marries him despite her father's (Richard Egan) objections. Writer-director Allen H. Miner has given fresh life to an old plot by selecting San Diego's tuna fleet as its setting and utilizing to the full the excitement and dangers of deep sea tuna fishing. A-II (br) A

C.H.U.D. (1984) Run-of-the-mill horror movie about monsters created by toxic waste. Ineptly directed by Douglas Cheek, it contains violence and gore. A-III (R)

Chuka (1967) Slack western directed by Gordon Douglas about a lone gunfighter (Rod Taylor) who arrives at an Army fort filled with misfit soldiers just before it is attacked by starving Indians. Much violence and some sexual innuendo. A-III (br) A

Chump at Oxford, A (1940) As a reward for upsetting a bank robbery, Stan Laurel and Oliver Hardy are sent to England for a college education at Oxford where they get into all kinds of comic trouble. Directed by Alfred Goulding, the boys try to overcome a hodge-podge script as they get lost in a shrub maze, unwittingly insult the dean and Stan, turned into a mental genius by a window closing on his head, makes Ollie his personal servant. Flagging slapstick comedy with some hilarious bits. A-I (br) U

Ciao! Manhattan (1973) John Palmer and David Weisman have fashioned a semi-documentary about the sorry life of Edie Sedgwick, a New York society girl who in 1965, at age 28, overdosed on pills. The result proves sophomoric and smart-alecky, with not a little exploitation of the girl's debilitated state of mind and scarred, siliconed body. O (R)

Cimarron (1960) Big, sprawling and generally lethargic Western from the Edna Ferber novel stretching from the 1889 Oklahoma land rush to World War I tells the story of a would-be rancher (Glenn Ford) who becomes a crusading newspaper editor but alienates his wife (Maria Schell) by fighting crime and bigotry instead of getting rich. Director Anthony Mann scores on the big action scenes but bores with the domestic soap operatics. Stylized frontier violence and marital rifts. A-I (br) U

Cinderella (1949) Disney animated feature has the traditional elements of pumpkin coach and glass slipper but adds a pair of mice, Jaq and Gus-Gus, a mean old cat, Lucifer, and a daffy fairy godmother. Good visual fun for all the family. A-I (G) U

Cinderella Liberty (1973) A sailor (James Caan) becomes involved with a bar-girl (Marsha Mason) and her young son who understandably acts surly toward his mother's nighttime visitor. Caan and Mason establish a stable arrangement of sorts, but this unusual family unit is brought to the brink of ruin by various sappy plot devices. Director Mark Rydell coats the transparent soap opera with heartbreak, misery, pathos and, of course, a happy ending. Much foul language and some nudity. O (R) X

Cindy and Donna (1971) The title duo are a pair of teeny-bopper sisters who use their Southern California environment to pollute the screen with any number of crude displays. With adulterous sots as parents, it's a picture of family to be avoided at all costs. O (X/R)

Cinema Paradiso (1990) In this Italian production, a film director (Jacques Perrin) returns to his hometown for the funeral of the movie projectionist (Philippe Noiret) who befriended him as a youthful patron of the local movie house, a social mecca where viewers caroused and the parish priest censored every celluloid kiss and embrace. In comic, nostalgic flashbacks, writer-director Giuseppe Tornatore shows how the movies over the years have enriched people's everyday lives. Dubbed or subtitled. Some fleeting sexually suggestive scenes and vulgar antics. A-III (PG)

Circle of Deceit (1982) German production directed by Volker Schlondorff follows the random wanderings of a journalist through the horrors of strife-torn Beirut, Lebanon. Although some of the terrible madness of urban civil warfare is apparent, there is little clear thinking or real drama in a movie marred by an extremely explicit bedroom scene. O (R) X

Circle of Iron (1979) Ambitious but botched recounting of the adventures of a mythic hero (David Carradine) on a Far Eastern journey toward enlightenment. In homage to martial arts king Bruce Lee, director Richard Moore's action adventure relies too heavily on stylized violence and a ri-diculously inappropriate sex scene that reflects the movie's overall inversion of the values its hero seeks. O (R)

Circus, The (1928) Charles Chaplin wrote, directed, produced and starred in this silent feature for which he has written a musical score as well as a song for the sound version. Charlie, on the run from the police, hides in the circus and becomes a prop man but inadvertently proves funnier than the clowns. He falls in love with the bareback rider (Merna Kennedy) but she loves the high-wire artist and the circus goes on leaving Charlie walking off alone. Admittedly not his best, it is nevertheless a real gem of comic invention and sympathetic understanding of human nature and the human condition. A-I (G)

Cisco Pike (1971) Kris Kristofferson plays a faded flower child forced by narcotics detective Gene Hackman to re-enter the drug-dealing world he hoped was all in the past. Directed by Bill Norton, there are some kinky sex scenes and meanderings through the California drug scene. O (R) X

Citizen Kane (1941) When a Hearst-like newspaper tycoon (Orson Welles) dies, a reporter (William Alland) interviews the man's former associates (Joseph Cotten and Everett Sloane, among them) and wives (Ruth Warrick and Dorothy Comingore) hoping to find the key to the millionaire's contradictory life by discovering the meaning of his dying word, "Rosebud." Also co-written (with Herman J. Mankie-wicz), produced and directed by Welles, it remains a landmark in American cinema, both for its superb use of film technique and its intriguing story of a man who came from nothing, acquired fame and fortune but died without the love he sought. Marital infidelity. A-II (nr) U

Citizens Band (see: "Handle with Care").

City Heat (1984) Police detective (Clint Eastwood) and a private-eye (Burt Reynolds) talk rudely to each other whenever their paths cross during the course of a mob war in Depression-era Kansas City. Director Richard Benjamin apparently means these exchanges to be terribly funny, but they're not. Amidst all the shooting, carnage and violence, the in-joke nature of the two macho stars becomes quite wearing. A-III (PG) 15

City Lights (1931) Produced, written and directed by Charles Chaplin, in which he stars as the Little Tramp, the plot involves his love for a blind girl (Virginia Cherrill) with the classic fade out when, sight restored, she sees him for the first time. Continuing Chaplin's cheerful bout with all manner of adversity in the big city, it was the first of his movies to use sound effects, though not spoken dialogue. A-I (G) U

City of Hope (1991) Powerful drama shows how corruption in a fictional New Jersey city affects a wide spectrum of individuals including an easily compromised contractor (Tony Lo Bianco), his estranged son (Vincent Spano), a victimized teacher (Bill Raymond) and an earnest councilman (Joe Morton). Writer-director John Sayles' cynical, realistic movie ties up many divergent, finely-acted stories in a shattering conclusion that resonates with irony. Brief violence, frequent rough language and a marital bedroom scene with a flash of nudity. A-III (R) 15

City of Joy (1992) The poorest section of Calcutta provides the vivid backdrop for a humanistic drama revolving around the family of an impoverished rickshaw puller (Om Puri) and an alienated American doctor (Patrick Swayze) who serves the residents of the area in an endangered clinic. Director Roland Joffe dramatically captures the spiritual and material desperation of his characters in a story that accentuates the resiliency of the human spirit despite its simplistic ending. Brief violence and mild sexual innuendo. A-II (PG-13) 12

City of Women (1981) Italian director Federico Fellini offers a heavy-handed analysis of the male ego threatened by feminist demands for sexual equality in a story about an aging Lothario (Marcello Mastroianni) and his erotic daydreams. There are touches of the old Fellini magic, but his penchant for the grotesque has grown wearisome, his imagery repetitious and his studio artifice annoyingly obvious. O (R) X

City on Fire (1979) One of the most disastrous disaster movies ever made, the title tells the entire plot. The Canadian production directed by Alvin Rakoff is unbelievably dull and pedestrian. Violence involving fire victims. A-III (R) AA

City Slickers (1991) Three New York City pals (Billy Crystal, Bruno Kirby and Daniel Stern) tackle their individual mid-life crises while trying to survive a working vacation on a cattle drive in the Southwest. Director Ron Underwood's insightful buddy comedy takes on issues of commitment, family and fidelity in a generally entertaining story. Occasional sexual references and vulgar expressions. A-II (PG-13) 12

Clair de Femme (1980) A recent widower (Yves Montand) and a woman (Romy Schneider) who has just lost her daughter in an auto accident and her husband to insanity, meet and a love affair ensues, apparently meant to be the salvation of both. The melancholy romance is directed by Costa-Gavras in pretentious and tedious fashion, wasting the talents of those involved in this French production. Treatment of sex makes this adult fare. A-III (PG)

Claire's Knee (1971) Amusing but cerebral French drama in which a middle-aged diplomat (Jean-Claude Brialy) is introduced to a young woman (Laurence de Monaghan) and becomes disconcertingly obsessed with her knee. Director Eric Rohmer's fifth in his series of "Six Moral Tales" is a droll study of a rather pompous man's self-deception in trying to rationalize his fixation in a movie of literate conversations about everything from love to philosophy. A-III (GP) A

Clambake (1967) In order to know whether he is liked more for his money than himself, a tycoon's son (Elvis Presley) switches identities with a penniless water-ski instructor (Will Hutchins). Directed by Arthur Nadel, the results are entirely predictable, with Elvis singing a few subdued ballads and driving in a speed boat race that is the movie's highlight. A-I (br) U

Clan of the Cave Bear, The (1986) Based on Jean Auel's popular novel about prehistoric times, this movie plods along with its band of dull-witted Neanderthals who raise an orphaned Cro-Magnon child Ayla. Except for the scenery, not much happens until Ayla grows intelligent enough to leave the clan to its caves. Several scenes of simulated sex and some violence. O (R) 18

Clara's Heart (1988) Wise Jamaican housekeeper (Whoopi Goldberg) takes her employer's adolescent son (Neil Patrick Harris) under her wing when she sees that he's being ignored by his estranged, shallow parents. Director Robert Mulligan's cliched story of interracial friendship lacks emotional insight into its characters. Extramarital affairs, some rough language and verbal recollections of a mother's rape by her son. A-III (PG-13) 15

Clarence the Cross-eyed Lion (1965) The comic adventures of conservationists (Marshall Thompson and Betsy Drake) in an African wildlife preserve where they fight off a gang of poachers with the help of their friend of the title. Directed by Andrew Marton, the animals are cute, the action mild and the result painless for the younger members of the family. A-I (G) U

Clash of the Titans (1981) Greek mythology plays second fiddle to a whole medley of not especially enthralling special effects in director Desmond Davis' languid and hopelessly episodic reworking of the Perseus-Andromeda legend. The immense talents of Laurence Olivier, Burgess Mere-dith, Claire Bloom, Sian Phillips and Flora Robson are helpless in this mess of a movie. Incidental nudity. A-III (PG)

Class (1983) Jacqueline Bisset plays a woman who has an affair with a teenage boy (Andrew McCarthy), later discovering that he is her son's (Rob Lowe) best friend. Director Lewis John Carlino can't decide whether to play the contrived, ill-considered effort as romantic comedy, slapstick farce or serious drama. The result settles for adolescent vulgarity and the sensationalism of graphic sex. O (R) 15

Class Act (1992) Two teens, one a parolee (Christopher Martin), the other a brilliant scholar (Christopher Reid) whose academic records were accidentally switched in their new high school, decide to continue the charade. Director Randall Miller's aimed-at-teens rap music comedy has the nerd vs. hip types down pat, but sends out all the wrong messages about casual sex. A teenage sexual encounter with parental approval, much double entendre and frequent violence played for laughs. O (PG-13)

Class Action (1991) A lawsuit charging a giant automobile manufacturer with negligence causing deaths and injuries brings an estranged father (Gene Hackman) and daughter (Mary Elizabeth Mastrantonio) together—as opposing counsels. Director Michael Apted's first-rate courtroom drama is craftily portrayed by the leads and trenchant dialogue raises important moral questions about corporate responsibility and personal ethics. Restrained sexual innuendo and minimal rough language. A-III (R) 15

Class of '44 (1973) Director Paul Bogart's quarter-baked sequel to the half-baked "Summer of '42" takes two of the adolescent boys of the earlier movie into college and one into the Marines. When it is not being either sentimental or tasteless (sex on campus), it is something like an old Henry Aldrich comedy. A-III (PG) AA

Class of Miss MacMichael, The (1979) Dedicated, embattled teacher (Glenda Jackson) struggles with a classroom of maladjusted youngsters and an incompetent headmaster (Oliver Reed). Director Silvio Narizzano can't decide on either a serious or farcical mood for this British story whose flow of obscenities and depiction of sexual misbehavior are objectionable. O (R) AA

Class of 1999 (1990) Experimental androids posing as teachers go berserk in this ultraviolent film in which a student just released from prison discovers the teachers are systematically killing troublesome kids. Producer-director Mark L. Lester's darkly atmospheric tale quickly descends into a nonstop bloodbath, overpowering the suspense with gory special effects and a grisly pileup of corpses. Extremely graphic violence, drug use and rough language throughout. O (R)

Class of Nuke 'em High Part II: Subhumanoid Meltdown (1991) Sex-crazed high school students go on a rampage with mutant subhumanoids inside a defective nuclear powerplant. Director Eric Louzil's sick flick is endlessly amateurish and badly acted, with depraved and dehumanizing humor. Gross sexual exploitation, much nudity, mindless cartoonish violence and sporadic rough language. O (R)

Class of '74 (1973) Three aggressive college coeds teach a fourth how to dispel memories of harsh parents and develop into a sexually liberated woman. Directed by Arthur Marks and Mack Bing, the low-budget package grossly exploits its intended young audience. O (R)

Claudine (1974) Diahann Carroll stars as a welfare mother of six, with James Earl Jones as a sanitation man who likes being her lover but who cannot cope with the idea of becoming her husband. Directed by John Berry, it is an interesting and at times dramatically compelling attempt to create a compassionate, realistic picture of black city life tempered with both humor and bitterness. Some raunchy humor with street vocabulary to match. A-III (PG)

Clay Pigeon (1971) Returned Vietnam war hero (Tom Stern) resents a ruthless narcotics agent (Telly Savalas) setting him up in order to nab L.A.'s top dope dealer, especially when it causes the death of some of the vet's playmates. Also produced and directed by Stern, the result is full of pretense and good intentions, but empty of real achievement. Though against hard drugs, it is in favor of soft ones. Some nudity and rough language. O (R)

Clean and Sober (1988) Gutsy drama directed by Glenn Gordon Caron chronicles the toll of alcohol and cocaine addiction on a successful sales executive (Michael Keaton) and his subsequent slow, painful road to recovery. Realistic characterization by Keaton takes him from criminal behavior and denial to fighting his dependency with the help of some recovering addicts (M. Emmet Walsh and Kathy Baker) and a hard-nosed detox counselor (Morgan Freeman). Much locker-room language, some explicit scenes of drug and alcohol abuse and brief nudity. A-III (R) 15

Cleopatra (1972) Japanese cartoon for adults retells the story of the Egyptian queen, but its main interest is in the mangled pronunciations of historical names and observing the color scheme used for the animation. Directed by Osamu Tezula and Eilichi Yamamoto, the movie's sexual appeal centers mostly in topless cartoon characters and a few mildly erotic abstractions. O (nr)

Cleopatra Jones (1973) Black adventuress (towering Tamara Dobson) is used by the U.S. Government to shake up the illegal drug traffic worldwide, but most of the action unfolds in the L.A. Watts neighborhood as Cleo carries out a personal vendetta. Directed by Jack Starrett, the movie goes down pretty easily as light, action-packed adult entertainment. A-III (PG) X

Cleopatra Jones and the Casino of Gold (1975) Tamara Dobson, tall, black and beautiful, is the main ingredient of a plot whose chief villain is the Dragon Lady (Stella Stevens). Directed by Chuck Bail, it features extravagant violence with a bit of sexual exploitation thrown in for bad measure. O (R)

Cliffhanger (1993) A former member of the Rocky Mountain Rescue team (Sylvester Stallone) and his estranged girlfriend (Janine Turner) attempt to save a colleague (Michael Rooker) who's been captured by a murderous bandit gang (led by John Lithgow) stranded on a mountain peak. Director Renny Harlin's relentlessly contrived action fantasy ultimately overdoes the violence with brutal savagery and gruesome humor. Excessive violence and much rough language. O (R) 15

Climax, The (1967) Italian satire about a polygamist (Ugo Tognazzi), happily married to three women and raising three sets of families. Equally devoted to each, he dies of sheer exhaustion. Deftly directed by Pietro Germi, the black comedy pushes a rather silly male sex fantasy to its absurd conclusion. A-III (nr)

Clive of India (1935) Sanitized life of Robert Clive (1725-74) who made his fortune with the East India Company by driving the French from southern India and establishing British rule but leaving him with a reputation besmirched by charges of corruption. Directed by Richard Boleslawski, the sweep of Empire is mostly off camera, as is his devoted wife (Loretta Young), giving Ronald Colman little to do in the role of Clive except brood, posture and declaim. Some stylized violence. A-II (br) A

Cloak and Dagger (1946) Midwestern professor (Gary Cooper) is sent to Switzerland during World War II to spy on German attempts to develop an atomic bomb. With Lilli Palmer as the love interest, director Fritz Lang almost succeeds in making something more than another espionage thriller, though Ring Lardner Jr.'s screenplay offers little more than wartime intrigue. A-II (br) A

Cloak and Dagger (1984) Lonely young boy (Henry Thomas) escapes from reality by playing superspy, but when reality obtrudes and he witnesses a murder, nobody will believe him—except the killers. Directed by Richard Franklin, it's well-acted, fast-paced escapist fare, but its violent situation makes it questionable entertainment for pre-teens. A-II (PG)

Clockmaker, The (1976) A good-hearted, middle-aged clockmaker (Philippe Noiret) is visited one morning by a police inspector (Jean Rochefort) and told that his son is wanted for murder. Though the father has never understood his son, he stands by him at the trial and afterwards. Bertrand Tavernier directs what is essentially a character study of the father without any sentimentality, yet with sufficient quiet charm and convincing performances to earn one's interest. A-II (nr)

Clockwise (1986) British import about a headmaster (John Cleese) whose neurotic obsession with punctuality makes him suffer inordinately through a series of complications impeding his attempt to arrive at a headmasters' convention in time to deliver his presidential address. Dry wit, gentle humor and general silliness pervade a farce illustrating the futility of a rigid approach to life. A-II (PG)

Clockwork Orange (1972) Produced, directed and written by Stanley Kubrick, the urban scene of the 1962 Anthony Burgess novel is ruled by day by the forces of law and order and by punk teenagers like Alex (Malcolm McDowell), the central character, and his pals by night. The Kubrick-Burgess message about the human right to a free will is not very new or startling, and only Burgess' marvelous language and Kubrick's grandiose style have made it seem at all fresh and significant. Excessive violence and nudity in a sexual context. O (X/R) X

Cloportes (1966) Uneven French gangster movie in which a Paris underworld character (Lino Ventura) takes his revenge on those who left him in the lurch during a robbery. Directed by Pierre Granier-Deferre, the acting is superior, but its treatment of the criminal world and its liberal use of nudity are excessive. O (br)

Close Encounters of the Third Kind (1977) Richard Dreyfuss stars in director Steven Spielberg's epic about UFOs and the humanistic, hopeful and, for some, religious theme of mankind's close encounter with an extragalactic lifeform. The scenes involving simple person-to person relationships may be somewhat flat, but the movie boasts some dazzling special effects and is tinged with a feeling of awe rare in science-fiction works. Some effects might frighten the very young. A-II (PG) A

Close to Eden (1992) Dwelling in a one-room hut on the steppes of China's Inner Mongolia, an isolated herding family (Badema and Bayaertu) find that life is not as simple as it was for their ancestors when the outside world intrudes in the form of a stranded Russian truck driver (Vladimir Gostukhin) and the government's population policy. Directed by Nikita Mikhalkov, the French-Russian co-production contrasts the natural rhythm of life on the vast treeless steppes with the inevitable changes brought by the country's growing industrialization whose impact on one Mongol family is shown with charm, good humor and respect for the human spirit and nature's beauty. Subtitles. Some discussion of contraception, graphic shots of a lamb being slaughtered and occasional rough language. A-III (nr) 15

Closely Watched Trains (1968) Czechoslovakian director Jiri Menzel's story about a young man's blundering search for maturity seems to imply that the transition to manhood cannot be made without the experience of sex. A-IV (br) X

Closer, The (1991) Forced into early retirement, a tenacious salesman's (Danny Aiello) strained relationships with his family (Diane Baker, Justine Bateman and Tim Quill) come to a head over Thanksgiving dinner as he interviews two potential successors (Michael Pare and Joe Cortese). Sharp dialogue but unfinished price ambition. Some rough language. A-II (PG-13)

Closet Land (1991) A government interrogator (Alan Rickman) uses psychological terror and physical torture on an author of children's books (Madeleine Stowe) in hopes of obtaining a false confession of subversive activities. Writer-director Radha Bharadwaj dramatizes the violent methods of a repressive regime in an intimate one-room setting that despite fine acting seems better-suited to the confines of a two-character stageplay. Constant menace, a few depictions of torture and some sexual innuendo. A-III (R)

Clouds over Europe (1939) Amusing British spy caper joins eccentric counter-spy Ralph Richardson, newspaper reporter Valerie Hobson and test pilot Laurence Olivier in solving the mystery of military planes disappearing on test flights. Director Tim Whelan's comic-book adventure of villainous agents with a secret ray gun are no match for the sterling trio and their tongue-in-cheek endeavors. Stylized violence. A-I (br)

Clowns, The (1971) Federico Fellini directs a highly imaginative documentary about the disappearance of laughter and fantasy in modern life, but it concentrates on the tradition of the circus and various kinds of clowns, citing them as sources of his own cinematic inspiration. Most viewers will find more than enough to satisfy their curiosity about the subject and will be abundantly entertained as well. A-I (G)

Club Paradise (1986) Robin Williams and numerous other comics try to create some fun and frolic in the Jamaican sun. The mild satire of the Club Med scene features Jimmy Cliff, his music and predictable drug and sex references that do very little for the funny bone. A-III (PG-13) 15

Clue (1985) Parker Brothers' board game comes to life in a mildly entertaining screen version that is being circulated with three different endings. Although for some it will be nostalgic fun, slapstick comedy prevails. A-II (PG)

C'mon, Let's Live a Little (1966) Silly college campus musical about a country yokel (Bobby Vee) and the dean's lovely daughter (Jackie De Shannon). Directed by David Butler, nothing much happens, but there is enough innocent romance to appeal to some teenagers. A-II (br)

Coal Miner's Daughter (1980) Sissy Spacek, who does all her own singing, gives a warm and utterly winning performance as Loretta Lynn. In this semi-biographical story, director Michael Apted depicts her life from poverty and obscurity in the Kentucky hills to undreamed of riches and success. Tommy Lee Jones plays Loretta's husband who escorts her along the rocky road to stardom. Frank language about sex and a wedding night sequence would rule out younger children. A-II (PG) A

Coast to Coast (1980) Mediocre chase comedy with Dyan Cannon and Robert Blake as an odd couple—she's a runaway from a mental institution and he's a hard-luck trucker—who make their way across the country pursued by various characters with hostile intentions. Directed by Joseph Sargent, the slapstick grows tedious and often abrasive. Some rough language. A-III (PG) AA

Cobra (1986) Sylvester Stallone as the ace crime-stopper of the Los Angeles Police Department single-handedly blows away an army of cultist serial murderers in director George Cosmatos' excessively violent treatment to the vigilante spirit. O (R) 18

Cobra, The (1968) Dated adventure melodrama directed by Mario Sequi about an American agent (Dana Andrews) fighting an Oriental drug-smuggling ring. Fairly heavy violence and sexual innuendo. A-III (br)

Coca-Cola Kid, The (1985) American whiz-kid trouble-shooter (Eric Roberts) for Coca-Cola arrives in Australia determined to boost sales but is stymied by one small town that is content with its own local soft drink. In visiting its manufacturer, the American discovers a competitor who is every bit as fanatical as himself. Directed by Dusan Makavejev, the movie begins with some satiric promise but becomes unglued midway and spins off in several different directions. Despite some good acting and clever touches, it's a disappointing failure. Some nudity and a needlessly graphic bedroom scene. O (nr) 15

Cockeyed Cowboys of Calico County, The (1970) Lumbering blacksmith (Dan Blocker) in a small western town is bilked when he sends for a mail-order bride and sympathetic townsfolk (Mickey Rooney, Jim Backus, Wally Cox, Stubby Kaye) enlist the aid of a local dance hall girl (Nanette Fabray) to take her place. Director Tony Leader's silly charade ends in true love. Youngsters may enjoy the western setting and broad acting. A-I (G)

Cockleshell Heroes, The (1956) After rigorous training under an unorthodox commander (Jose Ferrer) and his by-the-book subordinate (Trevor Howard), 10 Royal Marines use canoes to slip past the German defenses guarding Bordeaux's harbor and mine the naval vessels moored there. Also directed by Ferrer, the fact-based World War II story moves haltingly until the unit reaches its objective and a fiery climax. Wartime violence. A-II (br) U

Cocktail (1988) Young New York bartender (Tom Cruise) learns the ropes about life and love from a heavy drinking, womanizing mentor (Bryan Brown) but manages to jump off the fast track before it's too late for honest success and a good woman (Elizabeth Shue). Australian director Roger Donaldson's colossal bore lacks interesting characterizations and dramatic credibility. Sexual promiscuity, unwed pregnancy, excessive alcohol consumption, off-camera suicide and some profanity. A-III (R) 15

Cocoon (1985) Three old Rover Boys, young at heart, become young in body as well when they take a dip in a swimming pool being used as a rejuvenating force by some genial extraterrestrials. Good acting from some veterans, especially Don Ameche, but the plot premise is weakly contrived and the view of rejuvenation banally condescending. Directed by Ron Howard, the movie reinforces the stereotypes of old age as sexless and of women as passive. Some locker-room humor and an emphasis upon the sexual aspect of rejuvenation. A-II (PG-13) PG

Cocoon: The Return (1988) Disappointing sequel sees the temporary return to Earth of the original's aliens and senior citizens (Don Ameche; Wilford Brimley; Hume Cronyn; Gwen Verdon; Maureen Stapleton; Jessica Tandy) who delightfully debunk aging stereotypes. Director Daniel Petrie has trouble pulling various plot threads together and the rescue of an alien cocoon is suspenseless. Some locker-room language and mild sexual innuendos. A-II (PG)

Code of Silence (1985) Chuck Norris stars as a Chicago detective who uses his martial arts skills to combat evil. Directed by Andy Davis, it's fairly standard action fare, though a cut above Norris' earlier efforts. Violence and profanity. A-III (R) 18

Code of the Secret Service (1939) B-budget action programmer follows federal agent Brass Bancroft (Ronald Reagan) and his sidekick Gabby (Eddie Foy, Jr.) south of the border as they smash a counterfeiting ring holed up in an abandoned monastery. Directed by Noel Smith, it's a pallid mix of juvenile theatrics and dated ethnic stereotypes. Stylized violence. A-I (br) A

Coffy (1973) Black exploitation picture of a woman (Pam Grier) who seeks revenge on the drug pushers who turned her little sister into a catatonic hospital patient. Her weapons range from sawed-off shotguns to her full-blown figure, which lets the sex and violence crowds have it both ways. Directed by Jack Hill, it is a low-grade exploitation piece. O (R)

Cold Feet (1989) Quirky black comedy about a cache of stolen emeralds and a trio of eccentric con artists, one of whom (Keith Carradine) runs out and hides on his honest brother's Montana horse ranch until tracked down by his two cohorts (Sally Kirkland and Tom Waits). Throughout the course of the movie's wacky encounters, director Robert Dornhelm shows empathy for his offbeat characters and a feel for the heartland. In the end, family values remain intact, but there is much profanity laced with sexual vulgarities and some grisly violence. A-III (R) 15

Cold Turkey (1971) Led by the local minister (Dick Van Dyke), a small town in Iowa accepts an offer of $25 million from a cigarette adman (Bob Newhart) provided the townspeople stop smoking for 30 days. Director Norman Lear sets out to satirize rural America, Madison Avenue and all points in between, but the movie's slight sense of humor is overworked to the point of tedium. Some vulgar language, tasteless sexual references and snide portrayal of a venal, self-serving clergyman. A-III (GP) A

Collector, The (1965) Glossy adaptation of the John Fowles thriller about a warped butterfly collector (Terence Stamp) who tries to make a young woman (Samantha Egger) fall in love with him while he holds her captive. Directed by William Wyler, the plight of a woman imprisoned by a psychopath capable of destroying what he cannot have is properly unsettling. Though treated with restraint, its study of a disturbed individual is not casual entertainment. A-IV (br) X

Color Me Dead (1969) Australian production about a man (Tom Tryon) who becomes unwittingly involved in an uranium swindle and is then given a dose of slow-working poison, a plot device allowing him to spend the rest of the movie looking for his own murderer. Director Eddie Davis' remake of "D.O.A." (1949) is slow-moving and not very inventive, but at least the unfamiliar Australian locales give it some interest. Permissive attitude toward sex and a nightclub striptease make it mature fare. A-III (R)

Color Purple, The (1985) Steven Spielberg's glossy screen version of Alice Walker's Pulitzer Prize-winning novel about a young black woman (Whoopi Goldberg) growing up in a rural Georgia between the two world wars. The screen adaptation lacks cohesion and unwittingly reinforces damaging racial and sexual stereotypes. O (PG-13) 15

Color of Money, The (1986) An aging poolroom pro (Paul Newman) is obsessed with turning a young pool player (Tom Cruise) into a champion. Directed by Martin Scorsese, this disappointing sequel to "The Hustler" lets its conflict of personal integrity vs. the lure of money get lost in the clash of male egos. Brief nudity and extensive profanity. A-III (R) 15

Colors (1988) Violent crime movie explores the conflict between a volatile rookie cop (Sean Penn) and his laid-back veteran partner (Robert Duvall) as they battle youth gangs in East Los Angeles. Realistically directed by Dennis Hopper, with gritty cinematography by Haskell Wexler, the emphasis is often less on the cops than on the chaotic and complex subculture of the street gangs. Many scenes of extremely intense violence, heavy drug use, a few graphic sexual encounters and brief nudity. O (R)

Colossus: The Forbin Project (see: "The Forbin Project").

Coma (1978) Screen version of Robin Cook's novel about a spunky Boston doctor (Genevieve Bujold) who uncovers a murderous scheme involving trafficking in human organs. Michael Crichton directs a suspenseful, well-acted drama with a relatively sophisticated plot and some rather graphic operating room scenes, incidental nudity and the casual treatment of an affair. A-III (PG) AA

Comancheros, The (1961) Outlandish but colorful Western in which a Texas Ranger (John Wayne) and a fugitive gambler from New Orleans (Stuart Whitman) join forces in the 1840s to take on a highly organized band of white renegades in league with Comanche raiders. Director Michael Curtiz adds some romance (Ina Balin) and a lot of rough humor to the action formula

with only middling results, though Lee Marvin has a memorable bit as a half-scalped gunrunner. Assorted stylized violence and much horseplay. A-I (br) A

Come Back Charleston Blue (1972) Raymond St. Jacques and Godfrey Cambridge repeat their "Cotton Comes to Harlem" roles as two detectives in a caper movie about a black gang's attempt to wrest control of the Harlem drug traffic from white mobsters. Under Mark Warren's direction, there is a good deal of violence and killing but enough authentic references to ghetto life to cloak the escapist action fantasy with a pathos that was probably not intended. A-III (PG) X

Come Back to Me (see: "Doll Face").

Come Have Coffee with Us (1973) Italian black comedy about a middle-aged man (Ugo Tognazzi) who decides to settle down and marries an aging, grotesque heiress. His virile prowess eventually extends to her two equally unattractive sisters but, when the maid catches his eye, nature strikes him down in an ending that is both fitting and hilarious. Directed by Alberto Lattuada, the rise and fall of this figure of smug satisfaction will not please those who object to earthy humor. A-IV (nr)

Come Play with Me (see: "Grazie Zia").

Come See the Paradise (1990) A Japanese American (Tamlyn Tomita) defies her family by marrying a Caucasian (Dennis Quaid) who is drafted at the start of World War II while she and their daughter are forced to live in an internment camp with thousands of other Japanese Americans. Director Alan Parker sheds some light on this shameful episode in American history but gets bogged down in the interracial love story, which is not the movie's real focus. A very restrained sexual encounter, references to suicide, occasional rough language and a flash of nudity. A-III (R)

Come Spy with Me (1967) Failed spy spoof directed by Marshall Stone about an agent (Troy Donahue) in the Caribbean who joins a scuba diving contest as a blind while he investigates several murders. Stylized violence and mild sexual innuendo. A-II (br)

Come to the Stable (1949) Sentimental but amusing picture from Clare Boothe Luce's story of two French nuns (Loretta Young and Celeste Holm) trying to establish a hospital in New England with some help from an eccentric artist (Elsa Lanchester) and a cynical songwriter (Hugh Marlowe). Director Henry Koster gets some smiles from the nuns' adapting to American ways and the bemused reactions of the locals to the newcomers' otherworldly simplicity, with mostly heartwarming results.

Unpretentious, generally high-minded fun. A-I (br) U

Comedians, The (1967) Multi-leveled tragi-comedy about a man (Richard Burton) who finds himself involved in a plot to overthrow a ruthless dictatorship in Haiti. Strong cast (Alec Guinness, Peter Ustinov, Elizabeth Taylor), thoughtful script by Graham Greene from his own novel and assured direction by Peter Glenville result in a powerful movie about personal commitment in the context of political injustice. Some violence and brutality. A-III (br) AA

Comes a Horseman (1978) Somber, slow-moving western set in 1945, when a small rancher (Jane Fonda) stands up to the encroachments of a cattle baron (Jason Robards) by enlisting the help of a discharged serviceman (James Caan). The best parts of director Alan J. Pakula's movie are its Colorado setting and the depiction of the warming relationship between Fonda and Caan, but the film's violence and the nature of their relationship rule out younger viewers. A-III (PG) AA

Cometogether (1971) Made in Italy by Saul Swimmer, the story of an offbeat menage-a-trois is a compendium of bad production techniques that serve only to emphasize the sordid characters and relationships without satisfying those voyeurs who expect the visuals to exploit the potential of the subject matter. O (R)

Command Decision (1948) The sacrifice of American bombing crews in daylight raids over Germany weighs heavily on the general (Clark Gable) responsible for selecting the targets. Directed by Sam Wood, the setting is an air base in England where the necessity of launching a series of risky attacks is questioned by the general's fellow officers (Walter Pidgeon, Brian Donlevy, Ray Collins and John McIntire), a Congressman (Edward Arnold) and a war correspondent (Charles Bickford). Conflicting views of patriotism and its cost. A-I (br) U

Commitments, The (1991) Soul music, 1960s-style, resurfaces in of all places, Dublin, when an unemployed Irish youth (Robert Arkins) fashions a band out of an experienced trumpeter (Johnny Murphy) and 9 cheeky working-class youngsters. Director Alan Parker's vibrant, gritty movie ultimately goes over the top but not before it has energetically celebrated hope amidst poverty, the vitality of youth and the power of music. Much rough language, intermittent sexual innuendo and minimal violence. A-III (R) 15

Comfort and Joy (1984) The melancholy, comic chronicle of the worst Christmas week ever spent by an aging Scottish disc jockey (Bill Peterson) who, deserted by his mistress, throws himself into his work and becomes involved as mediator in a local ice cream war. Directed by Bill Forsyth, there's not much of interest here except for the Glasgow locale. A-II (PG)

Comfort of Strangers, The (1991) While on holiday in Venice, a young English couple (Natasha Richardson and Rupert Everett) are entertained by a mysterious older couple (Christopher Walken and Helen Mirren) who have very sinister designs on the young man. Directed by Paul Schrader from Harold Pinter's screenplay, the belabored pace and morbidly aberrant characterizations in this exasperating, erotic drama greatly detract from its theme of innocence corrupted. Fairly restrained sexual encounters with some nudity, heavy sadomasochistic references, occasional rough language and minimal violence. A-IV (R) 18

Comic, The (1969) Although this Dick Van Dyke movie is about a silent screen comedian, it is not a comedy. Van Dyke's performance as Billy Bright incorporates some unamusing parodies of physical comedy from the slapstick era, but Carl Reiner's direction lacks any sense of nostalgia or even sentimentality in what is essentially a maudlin presentation of Bright's various problems with alcohol and women. A-III (PG) A

Coming Apart (1969) Rip Torn plays a psychiatrist who uses a hidden camera to record his own disintegration through a series of sexual encounters with neurotic women. The characters, however grotesque, are recognizably human rather than sex fantasy objects, but director Milton Moses Ginsberg hopelessly dilutes any potential insights into psychological anguish and need by indulging in sheer sensationalism. O (nr)

Coming Home (1978) When a Marine captain (Bruce Dern) is assigned to Vietnam in 1968, his wife (Jane Fonda) volunteers to work in a veteran's hospital where she falls in love with a paraplegic Vietnam casualty (Jon Voight). Good performances by Fonda and Voight and fine camerawork by Haskell Wexler, but director Hal Ashby's movie lacks the political sophistication to examine the war issue and concentrates instead only on the theme of romantic love. Brief nudity in a sexual context and acceptance of adultery. O (R) X

Coming to America (1988) The pampered heir to an African throne (Eddie Murphy) travels to New York to find a bride he can both love and respect—a fast-food restaurant owner's daughter (Shari Headley)—but his parents (James Earl Jones and Madge Sinclair) have an arranged marriage all set up for him. Director John Landis spices up this Cinderella story with lush African sets and production numbers. Some nudity and much profanity (but not from Murphy). A-III (R) 15

Commando (1985) When the daughter of a retired Army martial arts expert (Arnold Schwarzenegger) is kidnapped by a Latin American strongman to force him to assassinate a political rival, he turns, instead, to assassinating the kidnapper's entire army. Mark Lester's direction has a certain leavening of comic book humor, but it won't seem especially funny unless you happen to think there is something intrinsically amusing about sudden death. Unrelenting celebration of violence. O (R)

Commissar (1988) In a small Ukrainian village after the Bolshevik Revolution, a pregnant commissar (Nonna Mordukova) is given shelter by a poor Jewish family. Russian director Aleksandr Askoldov's 1967 movie shows compassion for the family whose lives are threatened by local anti-Semites and by political enemies of the commissar. Subtitles. Some rough language, an intense childbirth scene and a harrowing anti-Semitic children's game. A-III (nr) PG

Committee, The (1969) Stage revue featuring the antics of eight young West Coast comics was videotaped during a performance and the results were then transferred to color film. Produced and directed by Del Jack, the program consists of 18 sometimes lively skits, often spiked with adult language, that concentrate on exposing the foibles of everyday life, especially of young couples, married and unmarried. Though there are some good laughs, it's for those who appreciate satire even when it misses. A-III (GP)

Companeros (1972) Italian-Spanish-German production shot mostly in English and set in turn-of-the-century Mexico finds Franco Nero running guns during the revolution. Director Sergio Corbucci clutters the story with plenty of loudly staged massacres, a fair share of unusual tortures and a bit of sexual innuendo. A-III (R)

Company of Killers (1970) Van Johnson heads a special police squad trained for unusual assignments, while Ray Milland sets the wheels in motion for a murder to help his financial designs. Routine crime melodrama directed by Jerry Thorpe contains mild doses of violence, sex and some ambiguous religious themes. A-II (G)

Competition, The (1980) Rival concert pianists (Richard Dreyfuss and Amy Irving) fall in love but have problems because of his sense of insecurity in a romantic melodrama written and directed by Joel Oliansky. Despite good performances, it is but mediocre entertainment marred by crude sexual references and a graphic bedroom scene. O (PG)

Compromising Positions (1985) A former journalist (Susan Sarandon), caught up in the investigation into the murder of a womanizing dentist (Joe Mantegna), does some snooping on her own and comes into conflict with the detective in charge (Raul Julia). Director Frank Perry's shallow, contrived and unpleasant comedy-mystery leans heavily on crude, sexually oriented humor. A-III (R) 15

Computer Wore Tennis Shoes, The (1970) Typical Disney comedy in which none-too-bright college student (Kurt Russell) accidentally has his brain computerized and becomes an intellectual phenomenon who by chance threatens the operations of a racketeer (Cesar Romero). Director Robert Butler's movie is a zany, very superficial comedy intended to amuse youngsters. A-I (G) U

Comrade X (1940) Wacky romantic comedy set in Moscow where an American reporter (Clark Gable) woos a patriotic streetcar conductor (Hedy Lamarr) while trying to keep track of Kremlin intrigues. Director King Vidor's dated spoof of life in Stalin's USSR has some very funny moments but not enough to sustain interest in the slapstick plot and belabored East-West romance. Political menace and romantic complications. A-II (br) U

Conan the Barbarian (1982) Based on a pulp hero's violent exploits in savage prehistoric times, the movie's preliterate narrative ponderously details how the slow-witted Conan (Arnold Schwarzenegger) revenges the slaughter of his parents. John Milius directs with heavy emphasis on brutality, violence and some graphic sex. O (R) AA

Conan the Destroyer (1984) Director Richard Fleischer's sequel may be more polished and less gory than the original, but with Arnold Schwarzenegger again in the title role the result is still nothing more than a lead-footed, muscle-bound costume epic with an extremely high violence quotient. O (PG) 15

Concert for Bangladesh (1972) Saul Swimmer's documentary record of a landmark benefit concert in New York's Madison Square Gardens features the performances of Bob Dylan, Billy Preston, Eric Clapton, Leon Russell, Ravi Shankar and Ringo Star to name a few of those who appeared. A-I (G)

Concorde—Airport '79, The (1979) Another in the series of airport movies with the usual multitude of disasters and film stars (Alain Delon, Susan Blakely, Robert Wagner, et al.) who can do nothing with the script's ineptness. Directed by David Lowell Rich, it contains harsh language and casual love affairs. O (PG) A

Concrete Jungle, The (1982) Low-budget women-in-prison melodrama is directed by Tom De Simone as another exploitative sex-and-violence movie. Much nudity. O (R)

Conduct Unbecoming (1975) Set on India's Northwest Frontier in 1878, the honor of the regiment is at stake when a flirtatious widow (Suzannah York) accuses a young subaltern (James Faulkner) of assaulting her. With an idealist (Michael York) appointed to defend him, the movie turns from larger issues of conflicting claims of duty and loyalty and becomes no more than a whodunit of only moderate ingenuity. Directed by Michael Anderson, the movie offers a very talented cast, magnificent locales and exotic costumes but only mediocre drama. A-III (PG) A

Confession, The (1970) Dramatic re-creation of the 1951 Czechoslavakian Purge Trials in which 14 dedicated Party members were convicted of high treason, to which all confessed though none were involved in any kind of political plot. Director Costa-Gavras focuses on one of them (Yves Montand), showing the process by which the man's idealistic faith in the Party was used against him in obtaining his confession. A-III (GP) AA

Confessions of Tom Harris (1972) The story of a tough mob enforcer (Don Murray) whose chance encounter with a woman (Linda Evans) led to his religious conversion at her father's commune for the spiritual and physical rehabilitation of alcoholics. Murray also wrote and produced, but neither he nor co-directors John Derek and David Nelson seem capable of capturing the spiritual malaise or, for that matter, the religious convictions of the characters in their drama. The result is a series of incidents, ranging all the way from a rape to a symbolic re-creation of the Last Supper, that conveys little of human or religious significance. A-III (PG)

Confessions of a Police Captain (1972) Italian story of corruption in high places features a police official Martin Balsam) who will use any method, including assassination, to get rid of crooks, and a young prosecutor (Franco Nero) who is an honest but ineffectual bureaucrat. Directed by Damiano Damiani, the result is little more than a pot boiler with considerable violence. A-III (PG)

Confessions of a Window Cleaner (1974) Infantile sex comedy with a pimply young apprentice window-washer (Robin Askwith) as he makes his predictable rounds of suburban London. Witless sniggering and leering sex. O (R) 18

Conformist, The (1971) Italian movie about a man (Jean-Louis Trintingnant) who joins the Fascist party and is eventually entrusted with a mission to kill one of his former university professors who is now causing trouble for the regime. Director Bernardo Bertolucci's portrait of a man who goes along with those in authority is frighteningly real and much more dangerous than any political fanatic. The central theme of the movie is a cautionary one for any politically threatened society though it has powerful scenes of violence and sexual inferences including that of homosexuality. A-IV (R) 18

Coneheads (1993) Having crash-landed on planet Earth, Mr. and Mrs. Conehead (Dan Aykroyd and Jane Curtin) pursue the American dream in their own weird ways while raising a precocious teenager (Michelle Burke) and avoiding immigration agents anxious to deport them back to the planet Remulak. Director Steve Barron stitches together a pleasantly daffy assemblage of episodic skits inspired by Aykroyd and Curtin's original 1970's Conehead sketches on TV's "Saturday Night Live." Some mild sexual innuendo, fleeting rear nudity and occasional tasteless humor. A-II (PG)

Confrontation (1976) In 1936 a Jewish medical student assassinated the leader of the Nazi Party in Switzerland, an event and an era that this Swiss production has succeeded in re-creating with vivid force. Directed by Rolf Lyssy, the movie does not defend political murder but poses the kind of moral problems individuals must face in a time when injustice is an accepted national policy. A-III (nr)

Connecticut Yankee in King Arthur's Court, A (1949) Uneven musical fantasy derived from Mark Twain's tale of a blacksmith (Bing Crosby) who is hit on the head in turn-of-the-century New England, then is awakened in sixth-century Camelot by a knight (William Bendix) of the Round Table. Directed by Tay Garnett, Crosby's bemused Sir Boss is entirely agreeable and Sir Cedric Hardwicke's Arthur is drolly dense, but the action rarely measures up to its comic potential and the forgettable songs add little to the entertainment. Brief stylized violence. A-I (br) U

Conqueror Worm, The (1968) Inept British horror movie about a 17th-century witch-hunter (Vincent Price) who combines his delight in human suffering with the profits he makes out of his trade. Directed by Michael Reeves, it offers little more than a series of sadistic episodes. O (br)

Conquest of the Planet of the Apes (1972) This fourth attempt at reworking the same material marks the fatal deterioration of a series that had some good moments. This time around all the apes on earth are abject slaves until a new Moses (Roddy McDowell) leads them in revolt against their cruel masters. Under J. Lee Thompson's direction, there is too much violence for youngsters who might otherwise buy this stale stuff, but it won't satisfy anyone else. A-III (PG) AA

Conrack (1974) Jon Voight gives a convincingly exuberant performance as the idealistic white teacher who comes to a remote sea island off the coast of South Carolina to teach the island's black children. The problems he encounters in adjusting to the island's timeless way of life, in reaching his students with useful knowledge and in dealing with suspicious adults and cranky school officials form the core of an unusual and often moving work. Director Martin Ritt does well with a movie that is enjoyable, funny, sad, poignant, full of hope and real feeling for people. A-II (PG) A

Consenting Adults (1992) Sleazy thriller in which a musician (Kevin Kline) is framed for murdering the wife (Rebecca Miller) of his diabolical next-door neighbor (Kevin Spacey) who then takes up with the musician's wife (Mary Elizabeth Mastrantonio). Director Alan J. Pakula glosses over gaping plot implausibilities with a manipulative scenario glamorizing marital infidelity and making insurance fraud seem an easy solution to financial problems. Brief graphic violence, a titillating wife-swapping scene, many sexual references, occasional nudity and minimal rough language. O (R) 15

Contest Girl, The (1966) Superficial British movie debunking beauty contests tells the story of a newspaper editor (Ian Hendry) teaching a nobody (Janette Scott) the tricks of the beauty game. Produced and directed by Val Guest, the movie and its moral are skin deep. Suggestive costuming and some sexual innuendo. A-III (br)

Continental Divide (1981) A hotshot Chicago newspaperman (John Belushi) and an ornithologist who studies eagles in the Rockies (Blair Brown) fall in love, though both are lost outside of their chosen habitat. The attempt to resurrect a 1940s' type of romantic comedy comes to grief because of Lawrence Kasdan's lackluster script and Michael Apted's uncertain direction. Winks at premarital sex and some brief nudity. A-III (PG) A

Conversation, The (1974) Intricate story about the world of electronic eavesdropping in which a colorless professional bugger (Gene Hackman) is hired to spy on a young couple but then finds himself being spied upon. Directed by Francis Ford Coppola, it is beautifully acted, meticulously paced and of interest because it looks at some of the ambiguities and shades of responsibility in the subterranean area of electronic snooping as practiced by anonymous professionals for hire. Some violence. A-III (PG) 15

Convoy (1978) Kris Kristofferson plays a free-spirited trucker who finds himself turned into a folk hero when he leads a group of fellow truckers across state lines in protest against police harassment. Ali MacGraw goes along for the ride. Director Sam Peckinpah lends some visual energy to an otherwise muddled, pretentious and often quite ludicrous movie displaying casual sex and a sophomoric disregard for the law. O (PG) 15

Coogan's Bluff (1968) Arizona deputy (Clint Eastwood) runs amok in Manhattan while tracking down an escaped prisoner. Action director Don Siegel emphasizes sex and sadism in a plot based on the premise that law enforcement should not be bound by constitutional restraints. Excessive violence and sex. O (br) X

Cook, the Thief, His Wife and Her Lover, The (1990) Boring when not repellent British production about a feral mobster (Michael Gambon) and his wife (Helen Mirren) who spend their evenings in a restaurant owned by the husband—he gorging himself on delicacies prepared by a French chef (Richard Bohringer) while she makes love to a bookseller between courses in an affair that has dire, gruesome results. Written and directed by Peter Greenaway, it's a pointless exercise in moral decadence treated in tedious, pretentious fashion. Excessive violence, unremitting brutality, exploitative sex scenes and rough language. O (NC-17) 18

Cookie (1989) Director Susan Seidelman tracks the comic transformation of an 18-year-old alienated adolescent (Emily Lloyd) into a street-smart Mafia princess who saves the life of her mobster father (Peter Falk) and unifies an offbeat family, including the mobster's wife (Brenda Vaccaro) and mistress (Dianne Wiest). Colorful performances, however, cannot make up for a far-fetched ending, a weak attempt at mob satire and an uninsightful look at an offbeat father-daughter relationship. Much profanity and a cavalier attitude toward murder and adultery. A-III (R) 15

Cool Breeze (1972) Black exploitation movie traces the generally downhill course of a gang of thieves (Thalmus Rasulala, Raymond St. Jacques, Jim Watkins and Lincoln Kilpatrick). Written and directed by Barry Pollack, it has atrocious dialogue covering every racial stereotype and gripe in the book, flashy violence, gratuitous nudity and a particularly offensive attitude toward black women. O (R) X

Cool Hand Luke (1967) Nonconformist loner (Paul Newman), sentenced to a brutal Southern prison farm, gains the respect of his fellow inmates for standing up to the guards's degrading treatment and cruel punishments. Director Stuart Rosenberg believes the grim situation with some well-paced humor and Newman's memorable performance in the title role transforms Luke from a pathetic victim of an unjust system into a symbol of the rebellious spirit that refuses to accept the legitimacy of power. A few scenes of brutality that some might consider excessive. A-IV (nr) A

Cool Ones, The (1967) Once-popular singing idol (Gil Peterson) tries to stage a comeback, but his struggles are complicated by a budding romance that his manager (Roddy McDowall) threatens to ruin. Director Gene Nelson contributes much ado about nothing. A-I (br)

Cool Runnings (1993) Coached by a disgraced former Olympian (John Candy), four feisty Jamaicans (Leon; Doug E. Doug; Malik Yoba; Rawle D. Lewis), who have never even seen snow, arrive in Calgary, Canada, in hopes of representing their country in the 1988 Winter Olympics by qualifying as a bobsled team. Jon Turteltaub directs a high-spirited, loosely fact-based underdog story that never loses its sense of good, clean fun as the foursome practice on junkyard parts under a tropical sun, ignoring ridicule and impossible odds. Fleeting violence. A-II (PG) 15

Cooley High (1975) Director Michael Schultz' story of young blacks, graduating seniors, in Chicago in the mid-1960s, has some good acting (Glynn Turman and Lawrence-Hilton Jacobs) and flashes of honesty and insight about ghetto life, but its narrative is by turns clumsy and pretentious. More seriously, sexual promiscuity is either played largely for laughs, despite the hurt looks on the faces of the girls cast aside, or, in the case of its hero, given lyrical treatment hard to condone in a work aimed at a young audience. O (PG)

Cool World (1992) Catapulted into his own two-dimensional comic strip world, a cartoonist (Gabriel Byrne) is seduced into helping one of his vampy creations (Kim Basinger) cross over to the real world where they are pursued by a hard-boiled detective (Brad Pitt) who knows their secret. Director Ralph Bakshi's manic mix of busy animation and live action produces an outlandishly uneven movie more adult in its sexual content than the juvenile story would suggest. Cartoon violence and suggestive sexual situations. A-III (PG-13) 12

Coonskin (1975) Ralph Bakshi's animated feature with some live action tells the story of three southern blacks (a rabbit, bear and fox) who go to Harlem, take over the rackets and vanquish a corrupt white policeman and a gross Mafia don's brood of murderous homosexual sons. Though it has some effective scenes of indignation at the squalor and hopelessness of ghetto life, the satire places heavy emphasis upon violent action, brutal caricature and a heavy-handed use of sex. O (R)

Cop (1988) Exploitative crime thriller with James Woods as an obsessed Los Angeles detective who concocts a profile of a serial killer responsible for 15 years of unsolved murders of a young women. Written and directed by James B. Harris, the unpalatable, implausible cop melodrama features a detective whose blatant sexism and vigilante mentality are totally repugnant. Extreme violence, gratuitous sex, graphic shots of murder victims and profanity. O (R)

Cop, The (1971) In order to avenge the death of a fellow policeman, an honest cop (Michel Bouquet) takes the law into his own hands, becoming as ruthless as the gangsters he hunts. Director Yves Boisset has made a fast-moving action film, hard-edged in violence, but with all elements completely integrated in expressing his theme of moral and social corruption. A-IV (GP)

Cop and a Half (1993) Cantankerous police detective (Burt Reynolds) humors an 8-year-old (Norman D. Golden II) by making him a member of the Tampa police force in order to get details of a murder the child witnessed, all the while having to protect the boy from the killers. Director Henry Winkler's one-joke comedy wears thin fast and may give children the wrong impression about the very real dangers inherent in police work. Menace to a child, frequent violence depicted comically and occasional toilet humor. A-II (PG)

Cop-Out (1968) Failed British murder mystery directed by Pierre Rouve has a generation-gap story of alcoholic lawyer (James Mason) whose neglect of his daughter (Geraldine Chaplin) leads to her joining the wrong crowd. Muddled storyline fails to integrate several sexually suggestive sequences and a near rape. O (br)

Cops and Robbers (1973) Nifty comedy about two New York policemen (Joe Bologna and Cliff Gorman) who hatch the perfect crime in a scheme to steal and sell $10 million in bearer bonds to the Mafia. Director Aram Avakian breaks up the humor by building in some taut sequences showing the risks and demands of day-to-day police work in a big city environment, keeping the viewer from asking the sort of logical questions that might puncture the plot. Stylized violence. A-III (PG) AA

Corky (1973) Amateur hotshot speedster (Robert Blake) wants to make the big-time as a professional driver but from the very first scene, when he beats out another car at a stoplight, endangering wife, children and best friend, it is obvious this is the story of a loser. Directed by Leonard Horn, the track footage has class, the Southern locales and people are evoked quite well and Blake's performance as a man whose delusions lead to inevitable self-destruction is first-rate. A-III (PG)

Cornbread, Earl and Me (1975) When a black youth (Keith Wilkes) is shot accidentally by two policemen, one black and one white, the city administration engages in a cover-up, but a lawyer (Moses Gunn), hired by the parents, clears their son's name. Directed by Joe Manduke, the movie deals well with the complexity of black-white relations and has a fine, convincing cast. Mature treatment. A-III (PG)

Coroner Creek (1948) Taut, no-frills Western about a cowboy (Randolph Scott) seeking to find the man (George Macready) who robbed a stagecoach and killed all its passengers. Directed by Ray Enright, the plot is anything but subtle yet holds sufficient interest until the final shootout. Stylized violence. A-II (br) U

Corpse Grinders, The (1972) Felines feeding on a new brand of cat food made from grain, exhumed corpses and freshly dispatched winos acquire a desire to attack their slovenly mistresses. Producer-director-editor Ted V. Mikels has made his dumb little movie in dim, closet-size settings that render transparent any horror that the disgusting plot and mangy characters might suggest. A-III (R)

Corruption (1968) Routine British thriller directed by Robert Hartford-Davis about a mad doctor (Peter Cushing) who murders women for their pituitary gland in a vain effort to restore the burned flesh of his beloved (Sue Lloyd). Graphic violence. A-III (br) X

Corvette Summer (1978) Innocent California high school senior (Mark Hamill) goes to Las Vegas to track down a car stolen from his shop class but things get very complicated once there. Boy meets aspiring hooker (Annie Potts), boy loses girl and regains his former ideals. Director Matthew Robbins' movie shows a much too benign acceptance of the affair between the two youngsters. O (PG) AA

Cotton Club, The (1985) Big splashy celebration of the famous white-owned, black-talent nightclub that flourished in Harlem in the 1920s and 1930s has some entertaining moments, but it lacks emotional power and fails to mesh its two diverse elements: gangsters and show business. Directed by Francis Coppola with Richard Gere and Gregory Hines heading a good cast, the movie contains some very graphic violence and two restrained bedroom scenes. A-III (R) 15

Cotton Comes to Harlem (1970) In a high-powered action story focusing on a big-time con game up in Harlem, two bumbling-but-uncanny detectives (Godfrey Cambridge and Raymond St. Jacques) unmask the fraud being worked by a back-to-Africa preacher (Calvin Lockhart). Directed by Ossie Davis, the dialogue and visuals are harsh and raunchy, with a lot of black racial humor and much gore to round things out. A-IV (R) X

Cougar Country (1972) Semi-documentary on the life and hard times of a young cougar in the Great American Northwest makes a fine wildlife story, especially the earlier sequences showing the young animal learning to cope with life within its natural habitat. The going gets a little tougher when the grown cougar has to outwit human invaders of its domain. For the young and curious and all who enjoy the world of nature. A-I (G)

Count Five and Die (1958) Fact-based story of a World War II espionage unit (headed by Jeffrey Hunter and Nigel Patrick) whose mission is to convince German intelligence that the Allies plan to invade Holland rather than Normandy. Directed by Victor Vicas, the dramatic tension centers on neutralizing a double agent (Ann-Marie Duringer) within the London unit rather than on the morality of deliberately sacrificing members of the Dutch underground as part of the deception. Challenging fare. A-II (br) A

Count Yorga, Vampire (1970) Fairly old-fashioned kind of horror movie with an involving, almost believable plot, underplayed stereotypes of good and innocent vs. evil and ghoulish, plus a very effective ending. Director Bob Kelljan suggests more than he shows of the story's sex, blood and violence. A-III (G) X

Countdown (1968) Exciting visual exploration of the frantic behind-the-scenes activity surrounding a space launch. James Caan stars as the NASA astronaut whose life as a scientist spaceman is complicated by domestic troubles. Directed by Robert Altman, the location photography in the Houston ground control center and at Cape Kennedy overshadow the otherwise routine drama. A-I (br) U

Countdown at Kusini (1976) Directed by Ossie Davis and filmed in Nigeria, the movie's theme of struggle against neo-colonialism in Africa is never treated seriously and leads to no new insights into the old story of exploitation. Its muddled structure and melodramatic plot, however, wreck havoc with its credibility and do little to further the black image on the screen. A-III (PG)

Counterfeit Constable, The (1966) Droll British comedy directed by Robert Dhery about a Frenchman (Dhery) in England on the run from a publicity-seeking actress (Diana Dors), the police and his fiancee. Mild sexual innuendo. A-II (br)

Counterfeit Killer (1968) Routine story of counterfeiters and treasury agents directed by Josef Leytes and with Jack Lord as the undercover man who infiltrates the gang and Shirley Knight as the waitress who falls in love with him. Fairly graphic violence. A-III (br)

Counterpoint (1968) The fate of an entire symphony orchestra lies in the balance when a German general (Maximilian Shell) insists that they perform a concert and their conductor (Charlton Heston) refuses. Directed by Ralph Nelson, the World War II melodrama's only merit is its classical music soundtrack. Wartime violence. A-II (br) A

Countess Dracula (1972) Aging countess (Ingrid Pitt) discovers quite by accident that her youth is revived by quick dips in virgin's blood. Directed by Peter Sasdy, the horror aspect is lost in a storyline in which almost every relationship turns about the anticipation of a nude sexual encounter. O (R/PG) X

Countess from Hong Kong, A (1967) The last movie directed by Charlie Chaplin is unfortunately an overproduced, heavy-handed romantic comedy about an impoverished countess (Sophia Loren) who tries to get into the U.S. by stowing away in the stateroom of an American diplomat (miscast Marlon Brando). There are some laughs, mainly from Margaret Rutherford and Patrick Cargill. Sexual inferences. A-III (br) A

Country (1984) An Iowa family (Jessica Lange and Sam Shepard) trying to hold on to their farm while burdened with the interest due on massive government loans extended in more prosperous times. Nicely directed by Richard Pearce, it may be a little too predictable and its heroine a bit too courageous and noble, but it's an admirable achievement nevertheless. The only reservation for pre-teens is some humorous by-play occasioned by a contraceptive. A-II (PG)

Country Boy (1966) Randy Boone of TV's "The Virginian" stars in a story of grass roots patriotism. Scenario and catchy country-western songs by Paul Crabtree. A-I (br)

Country Music (1972) Marty Robbins' company put together what is essentially a feature-length commercial for his kind of music. Directed by Robert Hinkle, the best that can be said for it as a movie is that there is a certain fascination in its naive artlessness as well as its unconscious humor. A-I (G)

Country Music Daughter (see: "New Girl in Town").

Coup de Grace (1978) Sober but rather dull German movie about the entangled passions of three German aristocrats set against the chaotic background of post-World War I Latvia. Starring Margarethe von Trotta and Matthias Habich, director Volker Schlondorff's tale of unrequited love and its wasteful consequences is for the patient and mature. A-III (nr)

Coup de Tete (1980) French comedy about a maverick soccer player (Patrick Dewaere) who wins the big match and becomes the hero of his home town, which once scorned him as a feckless ne'er-do-well but which now is ready to believe that his conviction for rape was a miscarriage of justice. Though the acting is good and director Jean-Jacques Annaud's flair for satire occasionally hits home, the rape's central place in the plot makes for heavy going in a comedy. A-IV (nr)

Coupe de Ville (1990) On orders from their father (Alan Arkin), three battling brothers drive a 1954 Cadillac Coupe de Ville from Detroit to Florida as a birthday gift for their mother but wreck the car along the way. This mildly entertaining coming-of-age comedy is directed in predictable fashion by Joe Roth, with appealing performances by Patrick Dempsey, Daniel Stern and Arye Gross as the brothers. Some locker-room language laced with sexual vulgarities and an incident of premarital sex. A-III (PG-13) 12

Courage Mountain (1990) Uninspired but wholesome story of 14-year-old Heidi (Juliette Caton) who is forced from an Italian boarding school into a rat-infested orphanage by the disruptions of World War I. Director Christopher Leitch strains credibility with some far-fetched action as Heidi and her friends escape across the Alps to Switzerland in the dead of winter. Children will enjoy hissing the despicable orphanage owners and young adolescents may be charmed by the hints of a blossoming romance between Heidi and her dashing soldier friend (Charlie Sheen). Some comic-book menace and minimal battlefield carnage. A-I (PG) U

Courage of Lassie (1946) A lost, wounded pup is nursed back to health and raised as a sheepdog by a young girl (Elizabeth Taylor), then winds up as an heroic Army canine, shellshocked and ultimately vicious, until fate brings him back to his loving mistress and rehabilitation as a sweet-tempered companion. Directed by Fred Wilcox, Lassie goes through her appealing paces as Bill, the dog whose incredible adventures most youngsters will find irresistible, though their elders may be more interested in the story's post-war rehabilitation theme and the gorgeous Sierra locales. Brief wartime violence and some fairly intense scenes of menace. A-I (G) U

Courier, The (1989) Irish import with narrow appeal zeroing in on the victims of a notorious Dublin drug dealer (Gabriel Byrne) who'll stop at nothing to protect his criminal operation. Directed by Frank Deasy and Joe Lee, the movie's contrived romance and revenge plot are poorly focused and surprisingly uninvolving given its gritty subject and working-class setting. Some profanity, clumsy violence and implied heterosexual and homosexual promiscuity. A-III (R) 15

Court Jester, The (1955) Delightful costume comedy with Danny Kaye in top form masquerading alternately as a clown and an assassin in order to help a band of rebels overthrow a corrupt king (Cecil Parker) and his treacherous ally (Basil Rathbone) while saving a damsel in distress (Glynis Johns). Written and directed by Norman Panama and Melvin Frank, the silly court intrigues and mistaken identities are clever nonsense, there are some pleasant songs and Kaye delivers the laughs stylishly, especially in his patter routine with Mildred Natwick about "the brew that is true." Enjoyable romp for the family. A-I (br) U

Courtship of Andy Hardy, The (1942) Judge Hardy (Lewis Stone) asks son Andy (Mickey Rooney) to squire the neglected daughter (Donna Reed) of a custody case but he does such a good job, she wants to marry him. George B. Seitz directs an episode whose sub-plots include mechanic Andy's troubles with the FBI and sister Marian (Cecilia Parker) taking up with a playboy. A-I (br)

Courtship of Eddie's Father, The (1963) Treacly romantic comedy about a widower (Glenn Ford) with a precocious six-year-old (Ronny Howard) who nixes his father's wooing of a bubble-headed drummer (Stella Stevens) and a ritzy fashion consultant (Dina Merrill) in favor of a wholesome divorcee (Shirley Jones). Director Vincente Minnelli can do little with the contrived plot's artificial situations and the result is an embarrassment for all concerned. Sticky romantic complications. A-II (br) 15

Cousin Angelica (1977) A middle-aged man (Jose Luis Lopez Vazquez) returns to the village where he had been a boy during the Spanish Civil War and his recollections help explain his alienation as an adult. Carlos Saura directs the Spanish production with controlled intensity, making the individual's story credible but also using it to show the Spanish character and culture at war with itself. A-III (nr)

Cousin Bobby (1992) Affirmative documentary profile of Episcopal Father Robert Castle, the white rector of a mostly black parish in Harlem, chronicling his decades of social activism in championing minority rights despite countless arrests since the 1960s. Director Jonathan Demme's portrait of his activist cousin is in part an easygoing home movie, but the pastor's undiminished idealism and involvement with his parishioners shines through his own laid-back commentary. Minimal street language. A-II (nr)

Cousin, Cousine (1976) A married man and a married woman (Victor Lanoux and Marie-Christine Barrault) meet at their relative's wedding that makes them cousins and are immediately drawn to each other. The story of marital infidelity that results is an amusing, malicious trifle that has more to do with wish fulfillment than reality. Under the good-humored surface of this French production directed by Jean-Charles Tachella is a pervading acceptance of adultery. Some nudity. O (R) AA

Cousins (1989) Remake of the 1976 French satire, "Cousin, Cousine," centers on the adulterous liaisons between the partners of two unhappily married couples related by marriage (Isabella Rossellini, William Petersen, Ted Danson and Sean Young). Director Joel Schumacher features some delightful ethnic family weddings, but the film's romanticization of adultery and premarital sex are morally objectionable. Discreet nudity and rough language laced with sexual vulgarities. O (PG-13) PG

Covenant with Death, A (1966) Suspenseful drama about an innocent man (Earl Holliman), wrongfully convicted of a crime and sentenced to death, whose fight for his life results in the death of another and a dilemma for a small-town judge (George Maharis). Director Lamont Johnson's lackluster production lets an intriguing moral-ethical-legal premise get lost in side issues. Casual love affair condoning seduction. O (br) X

Cover Me Babe (1970) Bad movie about a student filmmaker (Robert Forster) whose wrongheaded ideas about movie-making alienate his co-workers, girlfriend (Sondra Locke) and department instructor (Robert Fields). Directed by Noel Black, the movie suffers many of the faults it seems to be criticizing, including an exploitative emphasis on sex. O (R/PG)

Cowards (1970) Draft-age youth (John Ross), pondering the alternatives to imminent induction, moves in with his girlfriend (Susan Sparling) and takes part in a raid to destroy draft files. Writer-producer-director Simon Nuchtern makes light of the moral issues, preferring instead to anchor his hero in absolute confrontations with an overloaded anti-war tract disseminated by supporting characters. A-IV (nr)

Cowboy (1958) Rawhide coming-of-age story from the Frank Harris novel in which a callow Chicago hotel clerk (Jack Lemmon) learns from a hardened cattle herder (Glenn Ford) that cow-punching is hard work but, as the youth's character toughens on the trail, that of his mentor mellows. Director Delmer Daves get some modest enjoyment out of the tenderfoot's education but it is Ford's performance as the veteran cowman that dominates the picture. Dangers of the trail from snakebite to a brush with Comanches, some mild romance, rough humor and an off-screen suicide. A-I (br) U

Cowboys, The (1972) When the local cowpokes join the Gold Rush to California, a tough old rancher (John Wayne) resorts to hiring some schoolboys (ages 9 to 15) to drive his cattle to the railhead, teaching them the dangerous craft of cow-punching along the trail. In a traditionally violent finale, the young adolescents slaughter a gang of cattle rustlers who have brutally murdered the rancher (one of the rare roles in which Wayne is not invincible). Well directed by Mark Rydell but definitely not for the youngsters or the squeamish. A-III (GP) A

Crackers (1984) Donald Sutherland plays the ringleader of an inept band of San Francisco characters who devise an elaborate plot to break into their local pawnshop and repay its cranky owner (Jack Warden) by cracking open his safe. Director Louis Malle spends more time trying to find some new angles on the old caper formula than on character development, a miscalculation that results in a flat, lackluster comedy with some sexual situations and a benign view of petty crime. A-III (PG) 15

Crack in the World (1965) Doomsday scenario unleashes widening series of earthquakes caused when a scientist (Dana Andrews) explodes a nuclear bomb to tap the energy at the earth's core. Director Andrew Marton gets some frightening moments in an otherwise sluggish script ending with the earth's getting a second moon. Stylized violence and a menacing premise. A-II (br) U

Crack-Up (1946) Intriguing mystery thriller opens with an art specialist (Pat O'Brien) found raving about a train wreck that police establish never occurred but which eventually leads to evidence of forged masterpieces. Director Irving Reis invests the puzzling proceedings with suitably sinister atmosphere, taut suspense and a solid cast of suspicious characters (Claire Trevor, Herbert Marshall, Ray Collins and Wallace Ford). Stylized violence. A-II (br) A

Crazies, The (1973) Backwoods Pennsylvanians go wild when their water supply is contaminated by Army chemicals and they react viciously when troops are sent in to pacify them. Directed by George A. Romero, the title belongs to the moviegoers who would sit through this frantic, inconclusive, blood-spurting exercise in silly mayhem. A-III (R)

Crazy Joe (1974) Peter Boyle plays the late Joe Gallo, a maverick Brooklyn mobster who paid for his crimes with his life, thanks to the mob's rough system of instant justice. Director Carlo Lizzani's movie is grade-A trash in its pretensions on the "noble savage" theme and the dialogue is ridiculous. Worthless, especially in view of its misguided sense of morality. O (R) X

Crazy People (1990) Madison Avenue ad executive (Dudley Moore), fed up with the lies and deception of his profession, writes some bluntly honest ad copy and is quickly shunted off to a sanitarium where he befriends some wacky mental patients. Director Tony Bill blends a predictable satire on the ad game with a heartwarming comic fairy tale about good guys winning out over bad. Includes much overt product advertising and takes a flip, patronizing attitude toward mental illness. Some profanity laced with vulgarities and numerous sexual references. A-III (R) 15

Crazy Quilt (1966) Burgess Meredith narrates this offbeat attempt at spanning the whole life of a married couple who have completely different outlooks on life. Producer-director John Korty's use of realistic images in unpretentious, semi-documentary style greatly enhances the movie's keen perceptions of human relationships. Mature themes. A-III (br)

Crazy World of Julius Vrooder, The (1974) Vietnam veteran (Timothy Bottoms) is a genially demented soul in a California psychiatric hospital who continues to live out war game fantasies until a comely nurse (Barbara Seagull Hershey) solves his problems by applying large doses of affection. Directed by Arthur Hiller, it's all attractively packaged nonsense but glazed with a gooey sweetness that may thrust some viewers into diabetic comas.

Some rough language. A-III (PG)

Crazy World of Laurel and Hardy, The (1969) Compilation of highlights from the comedy team's many shorts and features from 1927 through the 1940s. The boys are still irresistible as their simple-minded logic reduces a seemingly rational universe to complete absurdity. Short on narration, the excerpts emphasize their two-reelers, most notably "The Music Box," their only Academy Award-winner. Though their work still plays on television, they are seen to best advantage on the big screen. A-I (nr) U

Creator (1985) Harry (Peter O'Toole), the hero of this sentimental comedy-drama directed by Ivan Passer, is a Nobel laureate widely believed by his jealous rivals to be a bit over the hill. Constantly talking about God and the Big Picture, Harry is obsessed with, among other things, finding a way to clone his dead wife. Though it deals with ideals, the movie undercuts them by its lack of discipline and its tendency to veer off into excess, especially scenes involving nudity and graphic sexuality. O (R) 15

Creature from the Black Lagoon, The (1954) A scientific expedition (Richard Carlson, Julie Adams and Richard Denning among them) exploring a tributary of the Amazon River find in its murky depths a bizarre humanoid creature with gills (Ricou Browning) that doesn't take kindly to the idea of being captured. Directed by Jack Arnold, the low-budget monster movie is not very scary but has a few tense moments, plenty of atmosphere reflecting humans faced with the unknown and a funny-looking but ultimately sympathetic creature. A-I (br) A

Creature with the Blue Hand (1972) Murky German mystery based on an Edgar Wallace novel in which a man (Klaus Kinski) is unjustly committed to an insane asylum, then allowed to escape so that he might be blamed for a series of murders. Director Alfred Vohrer employs rats and serpents, secret passageways and poisoned potions, stodgy police inspectors and shadowy villains in a fast-paced tale that cares little for clarifying motives amidst all the dark doings. A-III (GP)

Creatures the World Forgot (1971) British story of the struggle between twin brothers for leadership of a prehistoric band of nomads and the love of primitive pin-up girl Julie Ege. It's entirely forgettable entertainment from director Don Chaffey, but there is enough violence and buttock-and-bosom shots for parents to strongly discourage their youngsters from seeing. A-III (GP) X

Creepers (1985) Maniac terrorizes a Swiss girls' school in this inept Italian horror movie written and directed by Dario Argento. Profusion of blood and gore. O (R)

Creeping Flesh, The (1973) Fair British horror movie about Victorian brothers (Peter Cushing and Christopher Lee) who find the bones of a giant human skeleton that grows flesh when they get wet and their trying to cash in on their discovery results in a predictable ending. Directed by Freddie Francis, horror buffs will find this adequate fare for a rainy day. A-III (PG)

Creepshow (1982) Screenwriter Stephen King and director George Romero join forces in this omnibus of five horror stories, each featuring an abundance of disgusting gore. Although an undercurrent of humor runs though each story, there is a nasty edge to the movie, especially in its depiction of graphic violence. O (R) 15

Creepshow II (1987) Producer-writer George Romero resurrects the pulp horror form in this group of three tales based on Stephen King ghost stories. Light on fright and nudity but heavy on sadistic violence, the moral lessons of the gory fables are bogus and not worth the viewing effort. O (R) 18

Crescendo (1972) British melodrama in which a writer (Stefanie Powers) researching the life of a famous composer is invited by his widow (Margaretta Scott) to visit her estate and soon discovers herself in the middle of some very kinky goings-on involving sex and drugs. Unfortunately, director Alan Gibson never manages to work up much interest in the proceedings, let alone the intensity of the title in the disappointing climax. A-III (R/PG) X

Cria! (1977) Fragile 9-year-old (Ana Torrent) lives with her ultraconservative family in a big house in Madrid where she mourns the death of her mother and ponders the actions of the adults around her. In attempting to present a child's view of the world, Spanish director Carlos Saura shows that while childhood is not all oblivious innocence, children do have a resilience enabling them to bounce back from all but the most traumatic experience. Brief nonerotic nudity. A-III (nr)

Cries and Whispers (1973) Director Ingmar Bergman presents an anguished study of four women, each representing a different aspect of woman as victim. Harriet Anderson plays a spinster deprived of love from the time she was a child; Ingrid Thulin has been destroyed by marriage and five children who mean nothing to her; Liv Ullmann is the empty-headed coquette who must attract everyone but who can be faithful to none; and Kari Sylwan is the simple, uneducated maid who is the only one capable of an active, outgoing love. It is filled with emotional insights, but it takes a dark view of human nature in an alienated world. A-IV (R) X

Crime and Passion (1976) A dark and murky murder comedy filmed in Austria about an unscrupulous financier (Omar Sharif) who encourages his assistant (Karen Black) to marry one of the world's richest men so she can bail him out when his speculations go bust. Director Ivan Passer loses control of his plot quite early on and never recovers. Attempted cuteness about sex throughout and some nudity. O (R)

Crimebusters (1979) Terence Hill and Bud Spencer play rough-and-tumble vigilantes who enjoy beating up crooks and so they join the police force and continue on their merry way. Director Enzo Barboni's Italian spoof of American crime melodrama is tediously violent and vulgar in service of heavy-handed social satire. A-III (PG)

Crimes and Misdemeanors (1989) Writer-director Woody Allen once again examines the limits of our moral universe by focusing on an influential ophthalmologist (Martin Landau) who has his mistress Angelica Huston) murdered when she threatens to spill the beans to his wife (Claire Bloom) and reveal his embezzlement of philanthropic funds. Allen uses humor, pathos and melodrama to depict the man's struggles with feelings of guilt and accountability ingrained in him by his devout Jewish father while interweaving a tapestry of other Manhattanites who have moral choices to make as well. Some rough language, explicit sexual innuendos and a ruthless, off-camera murder. A-III (PG-13) 15

Crimes of Passion (1984) Director Ken Russell's sordid and squalid melodrama about a prostitute (Kathleen Turner), a sexually frustrated married man (John Lauglin) and a crazed minister (Anthony Perkins) leads to little but graphic sex and violence. O (R) 18

Crimes of the Heart (1986) Mutual love and acceptance keep three sisters (Sissy Spacek, Diane Keaton and Jessica Lange) together and help them survive their personal problems in this adaptation of Beth Henley's play. Bruce Beresford's direction elicits performances of insight, tenderness and forgiveness. Casual attitude toward infidelity and some crude language. A-III (PG-13) 15

Criminal Law (1989) Cocky defense lawyer (Gary Oldman) wins the acquittal of a wealthy murderer-rapist (Kevin Bacon) and then is conscience-stricken when he realizes the psycho is back on the street brutalizing women. A cat-and-mouse game ensues between the murderer who regards himself as an anti-abortion avenger since he was almost aborted and the lawyer who thinks he can achieve justice outside the judicial system. Director Martin Campbell's muddled crime thriller is not credible on any level—legal, moral or technical. Grisly shots of corpses, some violence, much menace and a rough sex scene. A-III (R) 18

Crimson Blade, The (1963) Dark doings in 1648 England when a troop of Cromwell's Roundheads under a turncoat officer (Lionel Jeffries) occupy the royalist stronghold of a rebel leader (Jack Hedley) whom the turncoat's daughter (June Thorburn) and a double-agent (Oliver Reed) try to protect. Directed by John Gilling, the British production labors through the muddled narrative with meager results. Much menace and stylized violence. A-I (br)

Crimson Cult (1970) Noteworthy only as Boris Karloff's last major screen appearance, the weak British horror movie concerns a local expert in witchcraft (Karloff) who investigates the mysterious disappearance of a young man. Directed by Vernon Sewell, the plot elements involve ancient cults, witch-burning ceremonies, strange dreams and a brief love affair. A-III (PG)

Crisis (1950) Honeymooning in Latin America, a U.S. doctor (Cary Grant) and his wife (Paula Raymond) are forced to remain as the "guests" of a dictator (Jose Ferrer) in need of an operation for a brain tumor while, outside the palace, an opposition leader (Gilbert Roland) readies a revolution. Writer-director Richard Brooks' political melodrama works hard at setting up the contrived situation but is undone by a flabby plot and ideological posturing. Some stylized violence and menace. A-II (br) A

CrissCross (1992) Distraught over the divorce of his parents, a 12-year-old boy (David Arnott) attempts to sell cocaine so his impoverished mom (Goldie Hawn) can afford to quit a humiliating job as a stripper. Director Chris Menges presents a sad perspective on the tragedy of broken homes, but its deadpan tone undercuts the story's dramatic power. Some suggestive dancing with partial nudity, implied sexual encounter, occasional scenes of drug abuse, rough language and minimal violence. A-III (R) A

Critical Condition (1987) Richard Pryor is the failed con man who tries to plead insanity to avoid going to prison where he's sure to be killed by the mobsters with whom he inadvertently got busted when undercover cops caught them making a deal. Director Michael Apted's keen social satire contrasts the insane patients and the insane administrators of the institution. Although the language is vulgar and incessantly harsh, its message about personal and professional integrity is significant. A-III (R) 15

Critters (1986) Small, fuzzy space aliens invade a small farm community and terrorize a captive family of four who fight off the hungry little beasts with the help of two bounty hunters from outer space. The critters might give young children the jitters as they ferociously bite everything in sight. A subtitled profanity in an otherwise mildly amusing sci-fi movie. A-II (PG-13) 15

Crocodile Dundee (1986) Central premise of this Australian comedy is the clash of cultures when a wild and woolly crocodile hunter from Down Under (Paul Hogan) visits New York City accompanied by an attractive journalist (Linda Kozlowski) assigned to do a human interest story on the Crocodile Man. Director Peter Faiman is more concerned about fashioning a vehicle showcasing Hogan's charming mannerisms than about achieving the lighthearted romance the movie pretends to be. Mild satire of some of the seamier sides of urban life. A-II (PG-13) 15

Crocodile Dundee II (1988) Now a savvy New Yorker, the Australian adventurer (Paul Hogan) saves his journalist girlfriend (Linda Kozlowski) from some Colombian drug dealers (Hechter Ubary and Juan Fernandez) and spirits her away to Australia, one step ahead of the heavies. Directed by John Cornell, much of the movie's laid-back humor comes as Dundee confounds the crooks on his own turf. Some rough language and comic-book violence. A-II (PG)

Cromwell (1970) Alec Guinness and Richard Harris star as king and commoner in the British Civil War of 1640-1649. Director Ken Hughes succeeds in telescoping the wide reaches of the action into a manageable sequence of events centering on the two principals. The lavish historical spectacle, the issues it raises and the competence of its performances make interesting viewing, especially for those studying its history in school. A-I (G) PG

Crook, The (see: "Simon the Swiss").

Crooked Hearts (1991) Three grown sons (Vincent D'Onofrio, Noah Wyle and Peter Berg) in a close-knit family are badly affected by a fleeting affair their father (Peter Coyote) had when they were children. Writer-director Michael Boatman's poorly scripted story offers such hollow dialogue and illogical developments as to invite laughter during what is intended to be a tragedy. Several sexual references, some rough language, brief fisticuffs and a flash of nudity. A-III (R)

Cross and the Switchblade, The (1970) Fact-based dramatization about David Wilkerson, a Protestant minister from rural Pennsylvania, who converted two rival Harlem gangs by the power of his personal dedication and forceful preaching. Directed by Don Murray and starring Pat Boone, it is honest and sincere in its message that the cure for drugs, slums and youthful rebellion is to be found in the simple acceptance of religious faith. A-II (GP)

Cross Creek (1983) Screen biography of author Marjorie Kinnan Rawlings ("The Yearling") begins in 1928 when Rawlings (Mary Steenburgen) walks out on an unhappy marriage and drives to the tiny settlement of Cross Creek, Florida, where she finds herself as a writer. Directed by Martin Ritt, the movie vividly evokes the period and place, has solid acting and is centered in a compassionate regard for human values. A-II (PG) U

Cross My Heart (1987) Blatant sex comedy about two young singles (Annette O'Toole and Martin Short) who wind up in bed on their third date. Directed by Armyan Bernstein, there are some comic moments, but the seduction and sex scenes are heavy-handed and sour. Nudity, simulated sex and rough language. O (R) PG

Cross My Heart (1991) When the mother of a fatherless boy (Sylvain Copans) dies, his schoolmates conspire to keep it a secret so he will not be sent away to an orphanage. Writer-director Jacques Fansten captures the innocence and resourcefulness of youngsters in this touchingly funny, bittersweet story of childhood friendship. Subtitles. Some mild sexual references. A-III (nr) PG

Cross of Iron (1977) World War II movie about a hardened yet humane German Army sergeant (James Coburn) who finds himself fighting not only the Russians but his glory-hungry company commander (Maximilian Schell) as well. Though Sam Peckinpah directs the action with convincing authenticity, the movie proves little more than a sophomoric celebration of nihilism and the bond that shared hardship forges between males. Much violence, some nudity and brutality in a sexual context. O (R) X

Crossed Swords (1978) Director Richard Fleischer's version of Mark Twain's "The Prince and the Pauper" wisely exploits its potential for romance and spectacle. Starring Mark Lester in the dual role of the street urchin who trades places with the Prince of Wales, the story provides sound lessons in trust and loyalty. Well-mounted historical production and good performances from a fine cast (George G. Scott, Rex Harrison, Charlton Heston and Oliver Reed), but there is some graphic violence. A-II (PG)

Crossing Delancey (1988) A 33-year-old New York career woman (Amy Irving) is aghast when her meddling grandmother (Reizl Bozyk) and a matchmaker friend (Sylvia Miles) pair her up with a Lower East Side pickle seller (Peter Riegert), but soon finds herself falling for the guy. Director Joan Micklin Silver's wonderful, sweet-natured story of the collision between old-world and modern-day customs features some fine performances and a knowing portrayal of New York life. Some rough language and sexual situations outside marriage. A-III (PG)

Crossing the Bridge (1992) Slow-starting coming-of-age movie in which three aimless youths (Josh Charles, Jason Gedrick and Stephen Baldwin) stumble into a major drug deal, then have to decide what to do. Writer-director Mike Binder's low-key story improves gradually as the trio finally comes to grips with their floundering lives. Brief violence and drug abuse, frequent drinking, much rough language and an implied sexual encounter. A-III (R)

Crossplot (1970) Harried ad agency executive (Roger Moore) is romantically involved with a model (Claudie Lang) who knows too much about a forthcoming assassination planned by her aunt, Martha Hyer. Shallow but diverting intrigue with a lot of fast action, a dash of violence and nudity, some beautiful photography of the English countryside and a few good laughs. A-III (PG) A

Crossroads (1986) This musically inclined teen romance relates the story of an aspiring adolescent music student who frees an old blues musician from confinement in a nursing home and helps him win back his soul from the Devil. Walter Hill's musical allegory about determination and growing up is weakened by rough language and a permissive attitude toward casual adolescent sex. A-III (R) 15

Crowd, The (1928) Extraordinary picture of ordinary American life follows a young man (James Murray) as he comes to New York, gets work as a clerk in a big company, marries (Eleanor Boardman), tries to make good but loses his job and goes on the skids until the tragic death of his little boy shocks him out of self-pity and into trying again. Director King Vidor's silent masterpiece achieves its impact not through plot or story devices but by capturing the human details of everyday life from its simple joys to its humdrum routines that viewers can recognize as not far different from their own. Domestic problems and the intensely felt loss of a child. A-II (br)

Crucible of Horror (1971) Eerie British horror item about a sadistic father (Michael Gough) whose pretty daughter (Sharon Gurney) and long-suffering wife (Yvonne Mitchell) hatch a scheme to be rid of the old man. Director Viktors Ritelis keeps the proceedings taut until the last 20 minutes when it becomes just another routine chiller. A-III (GP)

Cruising (1980) Al Pacino plays an undercover cop assigned to find a killer who preys upon homosexuals in New York City's sado-masochistic underground. Murky, muddled movie from director William Friedkin depicts a series of gory murders, male nudity and bizarre sexual practices without a single redeeming bit of humanity anywhere to be found. O (R) X

Crush, The (1993) Dumb, witless thriller about a precocious teenager (Alicia Silverstone) whose obsession with a handsome journalist (Cary Elwes) living in her parents' guest house results in her attempting to kill the man's girlfriend (Jennifer Rubin). Written and directed by Alan Shapiro, the vampy teen-age character leers and mugs her way through the entirely predictable proceedings. Brief stylized violence, fleeting nudity, an implied sexual encounter and occasional rough language. A-III (R)

Cry-Baby (1990) Musical comedy about the star-crossed romance between a handsome teen gang leader from the wrong side of the tracks (Johnny Depp) and a wealthy good girl (Amy Locane) in 1954 Baltimore. With some rousing production numbers, eccentric casting and much period humor, writer-director John Waters satirizes the innocence of mid-1950s' teenage rebellion and the problems of conformity. Best for Baby Boomers who survived the period. Some Keystone Cops violence, sexually suggestive action and rude language with vulgar sexual innuendos. A-III (PG-13) 12

Cry Blood, Apache (1971) Irate Indian stalks the gold-seeking murderers of his family who also abducted his sister and only Jody McCrea, who protects the girl from the lecherous prospectors, will survive his revenge. Directed by Jack Starrett, it's a terribly tedious little western with failed pretensions of being something more. Some nasty violence. A-III (R)

Cry Freedom (1987) The story of Steve Biko (Denzel Washington), a black South African leader who died in 1977 from police mistreatment, is told by Donald Woods (Kevin Kline), a white editor who had to escape from his native land to reveal the truth of what had occurred. Director Richard Attenborough's large-scale dramatization re-creates an authentic picture of the enormity of South Africa's racist policy of apartheid and effectively conveys the need for racial harmony in effecting social and political changes in that tragic land. A-II (PG)

Crying Game, The (1992) Quirky tale of an IRA gunman (Stephen Rea) who, after the bungled slaying of a British soldier (Forest Whitaker), escapes Belfast for London where his attempt to make amends to the dead soldier's lover (Jaye Davidson) turns his life upside down. Writer-director Neil Jordan starts with the unnatural violence of republican terrorists and ends with the unnatural relationship of two of society's outcasts in a picture filled with ironic contrivances, bizarre situations and human frailties. The plot hinges on transvestitism and contains some scenes of hard-edged violence, a flash of frontal nudity and recurring rough language. A-IV (R) 18

Cry in the Dark, A (1988) Grim fact-based story of an Australian couple (Meryl Streep and Sam Neill) who were unjustly convicted of killing their 9-week-old daughter in 1980 because of media-induced hysteria in reports of religious sacrifice (the husband was a Seventh Day Adventist pastor) and personal gossip. Australian director Fred Schepisi indicts the media's frightening influence on public opinion and provides a stirring reminder of religious intolerance. Graphic scene of a wild dog attacking an infant. A-III (PG-13) 15

Cry in the Wild, A (1990) A teenage boy (Jared Rushton) survives a plane crash but finds the fight for his life has only begun when he realizes he's now alone in the uninhabited Canadian wilderness. The pristine scenery is the most interesting aspect of an adventure movie that ambles along without any sense of urgency to its expected conclusion. Minor menace and flash of rear nudity. A-II (PG)

Cry of the Banshee (1970) Mild-mannered medieval witch hunter (Vincent Price) is cursed by an old hag for having killed some of her young followers and his own children begin to die as the curse runs its course. Directed by Gordon Hessler, the movie relies on graphic shock effects, with blood and gore, torture, promiscuity, nudity and a casual disrespect for life. O (GP) X

Cry of the Owl, The (1991) A melancholy stranger (Christophe Malavoy) disrupts the relationship of an engaged couple (Mathilda May and Jacques Penot) as puzzling deaths seem to follow him everywhere. French director Claude Chabrol's routine suspense drama lags throughout as the irrational behavior of the characters throttles the movie's credibility. Subtitles. Occasional violence, a suicide, implied live-in relationship and minimal sexual references. A-III (nr)

Cry of the Wild (1974) Fascinating documentary study of the elusive Arctic wolf, as well as an interesting chronicle of Bill Mason's adventures in photographing these wild creatures. Spending months alone in the Artic, his perseverance and ingenuity has resulted in some stunning wildlife footage. Its raw picture of hunting and carnage in the wild and also its matter-of-fact presentation of courting and birth in a wolf pack suggest it is not for young children unless they see it with their parents. A-II (PG)

Cry Rape (1975) German movie shot on a low budget with three characters and a single setting in a sensationalized story of sex and brutality. O (R)

Cry Uncle! (1971) Paunchy New York private detective (Allen Garfield) fornicates his way through half the ranks of the city's netherworld of streetwalkers and porno actresses whilst tracking down a murderous, blackmailing filmmaker. Director John Avildsen apparently intended this to be funny though it is anything but amusing. O (R)

Cuba (1980) Sean Connery plays a soldier of fortune who arrives in 1959 to help the Baptista regime in it's struggle against Castro's rebels. Connery meets a former love (Brooke Adams), now happily married, and their rekindled relationship provides some unresolved conflict working against director Richard Lester's remarkable evocation of period and setting. Adventure romance contains violence and a desultory striptease in a half-empty night club. A-III (R)

Cujo (1983) Stephen King's script of his own horror story about a vicious dog that goes on a rampage and eventually threatens a mother (Dee Wallace) and her young son trapped in their car. Lewis Teague directs this mediocre horror movie, which has some considerable blood and gore. A-III (R) 18

Cul-De-Sac (1966) British thugs threaten a man (Donald Pleasance) and his wife (Francoise Dorleac) in a pointless exercise in terror directed by Roman Polanski. Perverse violence and sex. O (br) AA

Culpepper Cattle Co., The (1972) Gary Grimes signs on as the cook's helper for a particularly gritty cattle drive way out in the Old West. Directed by Dick Richards, the movie reaches a climax of sorts when Grimes and a couple of trigger-happy cowhands decide to make their stand protecting some Quaker squatters, but this degenerates into a pointless bloodbath, making Grimes' final renunciation of the gun a hollow act. A-III (PG) X

Curious Female, The (1970) Sex exploitation movie using a frame device of 25th-century voyeurs watching a 20th-century sex exploitation movie. That's as imaginative as it gets. O (R)

Curly Sue (1991) Formula comedy has a hobo (James Belushi) and his 9-year-old orphan pal (Alisan Porter) winning the affections of a yuppie Chicago lawyer (Kelly Lynch) who has no time for tender emotion in her life. Writer-producer-director John Hughes' trite story is loaded with heart-string music that doesn't quite drown out the cloying and insipid dialogue. Several instances of slapstick violence. A-II (PG)

Curly Top (1935) Lesser Shirley Temple vehicle directed by Irving Cummings in which the little charmer leaves the orphanage behind after captivating a millionaire (John Boles), then helping him realize he's in love with her older sister (Rochelle Hudson). Contrived but still fun thanks to Shirley's zestful screen presence and playful way with such numbers as "Animal Crackers in My Soup." A-I (br) U

Curse of the Cat People, The (1944) Sequel to "Cat People" in which a lonely child is befriended by the spirit of her father's first wife (Simone Simon) who met a dire end in the original as a woman unhappily cursed with the power to turn into a panther. Directed by Gunther v. Fritsch and Robert Wise, the fantasy is not one of horror but of fear for the child's safety. Some eerie scenes evoking dread of the unknown. A-II (br) A

Curse of the Mummy's Tomb, The (1964) When an American showman (Fred Clark) transports the mummy of an ancient Egyptian prince to London for a 1900 exhibition, the mummy comes to life seeking revenge on those who unearthed it. In a British thriller directed by Michael Carreras, the archaeological trappings provide some chills in a fizzled plot done in by the mummy's cursed-with-eternal-life brother. Occasional stylized violence and menace. A-II (br) X

Curse of the Vampires (1970) Family honor, religious piety and a romantic love story provide the diverting background of this low-budget Philippine horror movie. Unfortunately, its plot about the father of a noble family who cannot preserve the secret that his mother is a vampire is alternately confusing and unintentionally amusing. A-II (GP)

Custer of the West (1968) Epic-sized western reduces both the legend of the general (Robert Shaw) and the history of the times to postage stamp dimensions. Filmed in Spain and directed by Robert Siodmak, the re-creation rings as hollow as the motivations of the various characters. Stylized violence. A-II (G) U

Cutter and Bone (1981) Bitter, crippled Vietnam veteran (John Heard), despite objections from his neglected wife (Lisa Eichorn), teams up with his best friend (Jeff Bridges), an aging and feckless beach boy, in a quixotic, obsessive attempt to smoke out a fat-cat oil magnate whom they believe to be responsible for the brutal murder of a teenage girl. Director Ivan Passer's uneven thriller contains strong language, violence and a frank depiction of sex. A-III (R)

Cutting Edge, The (1992) Routine love story about a pampered figure skater (Moira Kelly) who must accept a gruff ice hockey player (D.B. Sweeney) as her new skating partner if she wants a shot at winning Olympic gold. The predictable story with its expected spills and comebacks is as thin as ice in director Paul M. Glaser's blandly cheerful romance. Several implied promiscuous encounters and an instance of alcohol abuse. A-III (PG)

Cyborg (1989) Venomous post-apocalypse pirates, led by a blue-eyed sadist (Vincent Klyn), kidnap a cyborg (a robot that is partly human, played by Dayle Haddon) who holds the cure for a killer plague, but they're pursued by a martial arts expert (Jean-Claude Van Damme) who's out to avenge the slaughter of his loved ones. Director Albert Pyun drowns the somber, badly acted, inept sci-fi scenario in too much grisly violence, compounded by dabs of profanity and nudity. O (R) 18

Cyrano de Bergerac (1990) Swashbuckling poet Cyrano (Gerard Depardieu), despairing of romance because of his enormous nose, helps a soldier under him (Vincent Perez) win the heart of Cyrano's cousin and true love Roxane (Anne Brochet) by composing love letters for him. Director Jean-Paul Rappeneau imbues Rostand's 19th-century French play with fresh energy and cinematic beauty, but the centerpiece is Depardieu's towering performance as the tragic, unrequited lover. In French verse with English subtitles. Battlefield violence. A-II (PG) U

D

Da (1988) Literate, poignant adaptation by Hugh Leonard of his own play and novel about a middle-aged playwright (Martin Sheen) who returns to Ireland to bury his dad (Barnard Hughes) and make peace with his ghost. Director Matt Clark gets outstanding performances from the two leads, which helps overcome some confusing flashbacks and jolting sequence featuring the attempted drowning of a pet dog. Some profanity. A-II (PG)

Dad (1989) When a heart attack fells the domineering wife (Olympia Dukakis) of a 78-year-old man (Jack Lemmon), he relearns independence from his adult son (Ted Danson), but then suffers a series of illnesses require new priorities for the family. Though writer-director Gary David Goldberg's sudsy seriocomic effort has various plot lapses and excessive climaxes, it offers some worthwhile insights on the subject of parenting one's parents and coping with their illnesses and death. Mild sexual innuendos and minimal rough language. A-II (PG)

Daddy Nostalgia (1991) Following her father's near-fatal heart attack, a middle-aged daughter (Jane Birkin) tries to form closer ties with her frightened mother (Odette Laure) and vulnerable father (Dirk Bogarde). French director Bertrand Tavernier elicits luminous performances that enable the theme of reconciliation to emerge with emotional honesty from the film's deliberately slow pace and lack of high drama. Subtitles. Serious treatment of mortality. A-II (PG)

Daddy's Gone A-Hunting (1969) Urban thriller in which a wife (Carol White) and her husband (Paul Burke) are terrorized by her manic ex-boyfriend (Scott Hylands) who seeks revenge for the child that years before she had aborted without his consent. Director Mark Robson manages to work up a little tension in a rather thin story of people living in fear which, together with some silly but nonprurient bits of nudity, makes it mature fare. A-III (PG) X

Dagmar's Hot Pants, Inc. (1971) Copenhagen prostitute (Diana Kjaer) retires to marry the doctor she has been working to put through medical school. Vernon Becker directs a crash course in boredom with special emphasis on bare female anatomy. O (X/R)

Daisy Miller (1974) Good adaptation of the Henry James story about a rich American (Cloris Leachman) touring Europe with her spoiled son (James McMurty) and impetuous daughter (Cybill Shepard). Directed by Peter Bogdanovich, the slight story is a gentle probe of the American character, but what makes the movie so charming and absorbing is the director's care in visualizing the mannered style of a past age. A-II (G) U

Dakota (1988) Alienated California teenager (Lou Diamond Phillips), accidentally responsible for his younger brother's death, motorcycles away from his father's wrath, gets a job on a Texas thoroughbred ranch, befriends the owner's disabled 12-year-old son (Jordan Burton) and becomes a love interest for the boy's older sister (DeeDee Norton). Director Fred Holmes makes the story more interesting than its contrivances and ultimately encourages young viewers to face life's difficulties instead of running away from them and to commit to positive values. Chaste kisses, brief fisticuffs and climactic heroics in a raging fire. A-II (PG) U

Damage (1992) Dreary look at the downfall of a British government minister (Jeremy Irons) whose out-of-control passion for the fiancee (Juliette Binoche) of his son (Rupert Graves) destroys several lives. Producer-director Louis Malle's dull, one-dimensional drama offers little more than the raw physical aspects of a sexually obsessive affair whose tragic consequences are emotionally barren. Explicit scenes of adulterous encounters, some nudity and occasional rough language. O (R) 18

Damien—Omen II (1978) Sequel follows Damien the Antichrist (Jonathan Scott-Taylor), now 13 and living with wealthy Chicago aunt and uncle (Lee Grant and William Holden), as the special effects department disposes of everyone who can reveal his secret. Directed with some intelligence by Don Taylor, the horror movie contains some gory violence and a dubious use of scripture. O (R) X

Damn the Defiant! (1962) Handsomely mounted sea yarn of a British man-of-war whose seasoned captain (Alec Guiness) has his hands full dealing with a sadistic chief officer (Dirk Bogarde), a mutinous crew (led by Anthony Quayle) and Napoleon's fleet. Directed by Lewis Gilbert, the shifting conflict between the honorable captain and his villainous officer gets lost in a busy plot that ultimately proves less interesting than its lavishly detailed picture of life at sea, with some dandy naval battles along the way. Stylized violence, some of it quite brutal, especially that directed at a young lad aboard. A-I (br)

Damn Yankees (1958) Uneven screen version of the Broadway musical about a middle-aged real estate agent who sells his soul to the devil (Ray Walston) to become a baseball star (Tab Hunter) with the Washington Senators as they battle the New York Yankees for the pennant. Directed by George Abbott and Stanley Donen, the plot limps fitfully along in between some zesty musical numbers, the most memorable of which feature Gwen Verdon as Lola, the devil's seductive assistant. Comic sexual innuendo and situations. A-III (br) U

Damnation Alley (1977) The survivors of a nuclear holocaust trek across a devastated America in search of a haven in this muddled and unexciting disaster film directed by Jack Smight and starring Jan-Michael Vincent, Dominique Sanda, and George Peppard. Some violence. A-III (PG)

Damned, The (1969) Using the story of a corrupt aristocratic family (Dirk Bogarde, Ingrid Thulin and Helmut Berger) whose immense wealth derives from steel and armaments, director Luchino Visconti has fashioned a picture of the moral decadence within German society that made possible the rise of Hitler. The result has the primitive force of a Wagnerian opera in its mixture of fury and spectacle portraying the obscene lusts not only of the flesh, but of power and greed. Scenes of sexual perversity (incest, child molestation, homosexuality) are repulsive and anti-erotic, all part of a fabric that includes the obscenities of mass murder and unlimited violence on the part of those who ruled totalitarian Germany. Many will find this picture of evil a disquieting experience. A-IV (R) 18

Damned in the U.S.A. (1992) British television documentary on the 1990 controversy over the National Endowment for the Arts funding of sexually explicit and anti-religious works as well as the obscenity trial of the 2 Live Crew rap group. Director Paul Yule presents both points of view through TV news coverage of events, interviews with those against pornography (notably Rev. Donald Wildmon of the American Family Association) and those for free expression (notably Cincinnati museum director Dennis Barrie) and a running commentary on the issues by Boston topical humorist Jimmy Tingle. Some brief shots of the works in question and occasional rough language. A-IV (nr)

Dance of Death (1979) Claustrophobic rendering of Strindberg's play about an embittered army captain (Laurence Olivier) commander of a remote and unimportant fortress off the coast of Sweden and his love/hate relationship with his wife (Geraldine McEwan). Director David Giles preserves the relentless pessimism of the play, which expresses the dreary results of the couple's inability to find the grace of reconciliation. A-III (G/PG) A

Dances with Wolves (1990) Set in the Dakota Territory of the 1860s, the story centers on a soldier (Kevin Costner) at a deserted frontier fort who embarks on a voyage of self discovery when he is befriended by a Sioux tribe and falls in love with a white woman (Mary McDonnell) adopted by them. Also directed by Costner, the film's sensitive treatment of Native Americans, exceptional cinematography and fine performances compensate for its excessive three-hour-plus length. Much gory battlefield violence, minimal, restrained love-making and a flash of rear nudity. A-III (PG-13) 12

Dandy in Aspic (1968) A British secret agent (Laurence Harvey) also happens to be a Soviet double-agent but has become expendable to both sides. Directed by Anthony Mann the film is marked by interesting Berlin locales wasted on a confused plot that gets lost in its own web of intrigue. Stylized violence. A-III (br) A

Danger: Diabolik! (1968) Based on a European comic strip for adults, this campy Italian import features a cold, humorless thief and escape artist (John Philip Law) who confounds the police with his elaborate ploys and gadgetry. Its attitudes toward authority are cynical rather than satiric and many scenes are sexually suggestive. O (br) 15

Dangerous Game (1993) Dull movie-within-a-movie features a sex-obsessed director (Harvey Keitel) filming the story of a homicidal yuppie (James Russo) enraged that his wife (Madonna) is no longer willing to take part in drug-filled orgies. Abel Ferrara directs little more than one long shrill stream of curses, drugs, drinks, empty sex and repugnant characters. Recurring sexual violence against women including rape, some brief nudity, much substance abuse and incessant rough language. O (R) 18

Dangerous Liaisons (1988) In Paris before the French Revolution, a rogue aristocrat (John Malkovich) and his female counterpart (Glenn Close) weave a web of sexual intrigue and treachery to attain the lovers they covet and to destroy those who interfere. British director Stephen Frears portrays the psycho-sexual tug of war between the two selfish protagonists as devoid of moral or social considerations. Explicit sexual encounters with some nudity, acceptance of adultery as the norm within its historic context and much sexual innuendo. O (R) 15

Dangerous Woman, A (1993) A simple-minded woman (Debra Winger), raised by an overprotective aunt (Barbara Hershey), falls in love with an alcoholic drifter (Gabriel Byrne) who finally admits to fathering her child after she's institutionalized for killing a former co-worker (David Strathairn). Director Stephen Gyllenhall's unconvincing melodrama presents several well-meaning characters who make major mistakes in their lives, then concludes the story with a dreadfully unrealistic happy ending. A few bedroom scenes with fleeting nudity, brief gory violence, some heavy drinking and recurring rough language. A-III (R)

Dangerously Close (1986) Director Albert Pyun's hard-edged depiction of a high school breeding ground for Rambo-styled vigilantes is a disturbing look at what some fear may be a contemporary trend. Starring and co-written by John Stockwell, the drama has no message but its observation of the dread and menace caused by adolescent "law and order" fascists is a cautionary tale. Some violence, brutality and profanity. A-III (R)

Daniel (1983) Fictional treatment of the execution of Julius and Ethel Rosenberg for treason in the 1950s and its effect on their son (Timothy Hutton) as he grows into adulthood in the 1960s, determined to learn the truth about his parents' trial and their guilt or innocence. Sidney Lumet directs a well-intentioned but murky treatment of political events and personal relationships treated in a rather simplistic and romantic manner. It succeeds best, however, in showing the continuity of social justice issues and movements over the last half century. Graphic electrocution scene. A-III (R) 18

Danny (1979) A little girl (Rebecca Page) acquires a horse, nurses it back to health and then rides it to victory over the nasty and spoiled little rich girl who formerly abused it. Director Gene Feldman's simple tale about the positive effects of caring should appeal to a family audience wishing to sensitize youngsters to the virtues of gentility and compassion. A-I (G)

Danton (1984) Polish director Andrzej Wajda has made a stark and powerful film about the conflict between two leading figures of the French Revolution, the cold ideologue Robespierre (Wojciech Pszoniak) and the warm, passionate humanist Danton (Gerard Depardieu). The dubbed French production is essentially an intimate drama, revolving around the personality of its two protagonists. Although no prior knowledge of the intricacies of this revolutionary period is required, those who want to appreciate all the nuances of the situation may be motivated to do some reading in the history of the time. Some graphic violence. A-II (PG)

Danzon (1992) When her weekly dance partner disappears, a fortyish telephone operator (Maria Rojo) journeys from Mexico City to Veracruz in hopes of finding him but discovers instead a fresh perspective on her regimented life. Director Maria Novaro presents a sensitive but haltingly told story of assorted transients reaching out to help one another over the potholes on life's highway. Subtitles. An implied sexual encounter. A-III (PG-13)

Darby O'Gill and the Little People (1959) Though none believe his blarney about capturing the king of the leprechauns, wily old Darby (Albert Sharpe) has indeed bagged the magical trickster and won't let him go until granting a wish for his daughter (Janet Munro) and her young man (Sean Connery). Directed by Robert Stevenson, the Disney production spins a pleasing yarn of Irish fantasy that is both warmhearted and fun, though it has a few scary scenes to keep youngsters on the edge of their seats. A-I (G) U

Daredevil, The (1972) George Montgomery plays an aging, amoral dirt-track race driver forced by the mob to run heroin shipments across Florida and Terry Moore is the local school teacher who tries to reclaim him. Directed by Robert W. Stringer, the story and action are so inept that some will find it unintentionally entertaining. Some rough language. A-III (PG)

Daring Game (1967) Bubbly underwater action-adventure movie starring Lloyd Bridges, Nico Minardos and Joan Blackman who don rubber suits and flippers in an attempt to rescue a man held prisoner on a desert isle by a banana-Republic dictator. Director Laslo Benedek pumps up the action in attempting to supply some mediocre fun for all. A-I (br) U

Dark Avenger, The (see: "The Warriors").

Dark Command (1940) After losing both the job of sheriff and his girl (Claire Trevor) to a Texas hayseed (John Wayne), an embittered Kansas school teacher (Walter Pidgeon) heads a band of pro-slavery raiders as the Civil War nears. Director Raoul Walsh stages some sweeping action scenes and the supporting players (Roy Rogers, Gabby Hayes, Marjorie Main and Porter Hall) add flavor to a contrived but fanciful script. Stylized violence. A-I (br)

Dark Crystal, The (1983) Muppet masters Jim Henson and Frank Oz join in directing a Tolkein-like fairy tale about the restoration of a shattered crystal to wholeness that will bring about a never-ending reign of justice and peace. Although its story of good versus evil is a bit thin, the inventiveness of the puppetry and special effects is magical. Some scary moments for the very young. A-I (PG) A

Dark Eyes (1987) Aging philanderer (Marcello Mastroianni) shares reminiscences of his love-life unknowingly with the husband of the mysterious lover who abandoned him. Sumptuous Italian period romance from Russian director Nikita Mikhalkov is both an affectionate celebration and comic denunciation of the self-centered blindness of male chauvinism. A-III (nr)

Dark Half, The (1993) Half-baked psychological thriller in which an established author decides to stop writing sleazy but lucrative crime novels under a pseudonym, then finds himself implicated in a series of brutal murders that seem incredibly the work of his literary alias. Director George Romero works hard at creating a suitably eerie atmosphere and keeps the violent shocks largely off-screen but fails to make much sense out of Stephen King's novel involving a malignant twin brother with supernatural powers. Some graphic violence, much menace and occasional rough language and references. A-III (R)

Dark Journey (1937) Muddled spy melodrama of World War I follows two master agents (Vivien Leigh and Conrad Veidt) to neutral Stockholm where they fall in love, though on opposite sides. Director Victor Saville's shadowy tale of spy and counterspy is filled with period detail and a properly tense atmosphere but the bittersweet romance of the two secret agents seems as counterfeit as their assumed identities. Wartime menace and romantic complications. A-II (br) U

Dark Obsession (1991) Caring nothing that he has killed a woman in a hit-and-run accident and that one of the passengers (Douglas Hodge) may go to the police, a wealthy English aristocrat (Gabriel Byrne) is consumed by the fear that his wife (Amanda Donohoe) is unfaithful. Director Nick Broomfield's murky tale of violent sexual obsession offers a world of callous immorality where the sole well-intentioned character pays dearly for his pangs of conscience. A number of explicit sexual encounters, other scenes with nudity, implied incest, calculated indifference to human life and minimal rough language. O (NC-17)

Dark of the Night (1986) Lightweight Gothic tale about a woman (Heather Bolton) whose life is saved by the ghost of the former owner of her recently purchased vintage Jaguar. Directed by Gaylene Preston, the New Zealand import plays like a children's mystery devoid of any visual shocks and only mild suspense. A-I (nr)

Dark of the Sun (1967) Sleazy but gripping action-adventure melodrama about the efforts of mercenary soldiers Rod Taylor and Jim Brown to retrieve a fortune in uncut diamonds from their Congo employer's jungle outpost that has fallen into the hands of bloodthirsty rebels. British production directed by Jack Cardiff emphasizes gory slayings, tortures and some sexual situations. O (PG)

Dark Passage (1947) Offbeat crime melodrama about a man (Humphrey Bogart) who escapes prison, is sheltered by a woman (Lauren Bacall) who believes him innocent and has a plastic surgeon change his face in order to find the culprit who framed him. Directed by Delmer Daves, there are some interesting plot twists, fine use of San Francisco locations and a good gallery of intriguing characters. A-II (br)

Dark Places (1974) British horror movie about a man (Robert Hardy) who inherits the creepy estate of a wealthy maniac and then must defend it against outsiders (Joan Collins, Christopher Lee, and Herbert Lom) looking for the fortune stashed somewhere in the house. Directed by Don Sharp, the dark places are spooky enough for the undemanding horror buff. A dollop of blood and gore and some subtle sex. A-III (PG) A

Darker Than Amber (1970) Adaptation of a John MacDonald mystery with Rod Taylor as Travis McGee up to his neck in a tangle of brutal murders that begin when he falls in love with a woman (Suzy Kendall) he tries to protect from killers. Directed by Robert Clouse, the violence and brutality goes beyond bounds of taste and restraint, as do some sex scenes. O (R/GP) A

Darkman (1990) Extremely violent action thriller in which a scientist (Liam Neeson) seeks revenge on those who hideously disfigured him with acid by using his invention of synthetic skin to assume various identities in stalking his victims. Written and directed by Sam Raimi, the movie's production values add little to its dismal parade of grisly killings and human torture. Excessive violence and some rough language. O (R) 15

Darling (1965) Realistic British examination of the emptiness that characterizes the purposeless lives of the jet set. Directed by John Schlesinger with unrelenting honesty, the episodic movie follows the rise of a young woman (Julie Christie) through a series of affairs until she marries a wealthy prince whose palace becomes a sterile prison. A-IV (br) X

Darling Lili (1970) Uneven musical comedy set in World War I about a London music hall entertainer (Julie Andrews) who feigns romance with an Allied pilot (Rock Hudson) in order to ferret military secrets for the Germans. Produced and directed by Blake Edwards, Andrews' charming performance and the lavish re-creation of the period's rickety automobiles and biplane aircraft are generally pleasing, but some love-making scenes and a couple of strip-tease numbers place it in the adult category. A-III (G)

Darwin Adventure, The (1972) Jack Couffer directs an historical dramatization of the events that led to Charles Darwin (Nicholas Clay) writing "Origin of Species" with loving attention to the world of nature but little feel for the human conflicts and emotional crises aroused by the scientist's theories. A-II (G) U

D.A.R.Y.L. (1985) Sci-fi version of Pinocchio in which government scientists experimenting with artificial intelligence develop a robot that is like a boy in almost every respect. Some nasty higher-ups decide to put an end to the project when the robot transforms into a living boy with loving foster parents. Predictable storyline, but director Simon Wincer maintains interest and save for a few ill-considered vulgar expletives, it would have been quite suitable for young children. A-II (PG)

Das Boot (1982) Authentic World War II picture of a German submarine's final cruise in the North Atlantic where U-boats were the terror of Allied convoys. Director Wolfgang Petersen emphasizes the claustrophobic conditions and dangers of sub duty with creative camerawork and first-rate performances, especially that of Jurgen Prochnow whose haggard face as the captain is likely to haunt the viewer for some time. For all its virtues as a war movie, the moral dilemma of serving one of the worst causes in history is treated only indirectly. Subtitles or dubbed. Sexual references and crude language abound in this all-male environment. A-III (R)

Date with an Angel (1987) Plodding romantic comedy about a young man with a brain tumor (Michael E. Knight) who alienates his fiancee (Phoebe Cates) when he rescues an angel with a broken wing (Emmanuelle Beart). Writer-director Tom McLoughlin turns what might have been a lightweight, bouncy comedy into a leaden, earthbound fantasy. Some sexual innuendo, brief nudity and verbal vulgarities. A-III (PG)

Date with Judy, A (1948) Thin teenage romance with 16-year-old Santa Barbara high schoolers (Jane Powell in the title role with Elizabeth Taylor as her stuck-up rival) falling for a World War II veteran (Robert Stack) working his way through college as a soda jerk. Director Richard Thorpe's sentimental picture of small-town family life is invincibly innocent in its treatment of such contrivances as Judy's father (Wallace Beery) secretly taking lessons from a rhumba dancer (Carmen Miranda) in order to surprise his wife (Selena Royle) but causing Judy to fear he's having an affair. Adolescent mix-ups. A-I (br) U

Daughter, The (1970) Low-budget sex exploitation movie in which a daughter discovers that her moralizing mother is a sexual hypocrite and gets back at mom by experimenting wildly with all sorts of kinky sex practices. O (nr)

Daughters of Darkness (1971) Delphine Seyrig plays a glamorous 300-year-old vampire in a very bizarre but very stylish horror fantasy directed by Harry Kumel. The Belgian production is a nightmarish study in mood and atmosphere with contemporary settings used to brilliant effect, but its explicit treatment of the sexual perversity usually only implicit in such horror movies is offensive. O (R)

Daughters of Satan (1972) Philippine devil cult huff-and-puff their way through a ritual murder of the reincarnated Inquisitor responsible for the burning of three witches in 1592. Innocent of any coherence of plot, acting (Tom Selleck, Barra Grant, Tani Phelps Guthrie) or direction (Hollingsworth Morse), the movie carries the burden of several gratuitous scenes featuring sadism and nudity. O (R)

Daughters of the Dust (1991) Lyrical, feminist period piece set on an island off the South Carolina coast where a family clan descended from West African slaves gather on a summer's day in 1902 to discuss their plans for moving to the mainland. Writer-director Julie Dash's highly imaginative and very stylized work contrasts those who want to pursue the American dream with the majority who are adamant about preserving the African traditions and mystical tales that have sustained them through countless generations. Some familial bickering and mild sexual references. A-II (nr)

Dave (1993) Conniving White House Chief of Staff (Frank Langella) dupes a patriotic businessman (Kevin Kline) into impersonating the comatose President while the estranged First Lady (Sigourney Weaver) grows increasingly suspicious as the look-alike begins to reform the government. In typical Hollywood fashion, director Ivan Reitman's lightweight comedy affably presents populist themes and simplistic solutions grounded in feel-good fantasy. Brief bedroom scene, fleeting shadowed nudity and an instance of profanity. A-III (PG-13)

David and Bathsheba (1951) In Philip Dunne's somber biblical adaptation, King David (Gregory Peck) secretly orders one of his commanders (Kieron Moore) killed in battle so he can marry the man's widow (Susan Hayward), then faces God's wrath on him and his people. By avoiding the ostentatious spectacle usually associated with biblical epics, director Henry King weakens the impact of David's youthful triumphs shown in flashbacks but strengthens the narrative's main focus on the king's moral weaknesses and the complexity of their consequences—human and divine. Mature theme and treatment. A-III (br) A

David and Goliath (1961) Minor Italian production retelling the biblical story of David from boyish shepherd to manly Israelite champion (Ivo Payer) in the court of King Saul (Orson Welles). Directed by Richard Pottier and Ferdinando Baldi, the earnest but clumsy script is lost in hokey spectacle and bad acting. Stylized violence. A-I (br)

David and Lisa (1962) Two disturbed teenagers (Keir Dullea and Janet Margolin) in a mental institution form a loving relationship that helps each gain some emotional stability with the encouragement of a caring psychologist (Howard da Silva). Director Frank Perry with wife Eleanor's fact-based script turns the tale of damaged youths into an uplifting experience of love conquering despair, though some may find it all a bit too pat and unconvincing. Psychological problems of troubled adolescents. A-II (br) X

David Copperfield (1935) Classic adaptation of the Charles Dickens story about an orphan (Freddie Bartholomew) saved from the wicked designs of a cruel stepfather (Basil Rathbone) with the help of his aunt (Edna May Oliver) and a host of friends (Maureen O'Sullivan, Jessie Ralph, Lionel Barrymore, Herbert Mundin and others). Director George Cukor captures the flavor of Dickens' mix of whimsey and melodrama with the proper Victorian atmosphere and an outstanding cast portraying its rich ensemble of characters, not least of whom is W.C. Fields' Micawber besting Roland Young's Uriah Heep. Outstanding family fare. A-I (br)

Davy Crockett and the River Pirates (1956) Disney sequel directed by Norman Foster has Davy (Fess Parker) and his genial sidekick (Buddy Ebsen) in a Mississippi boat race against riverman Mike Fink (Jeff York), then the slapstick violence turns a little more serious when they tangle with some hostile Indians. Mostly unpretentious juvenile fun. A-I (br) U

Davy Crockett, King of the Wild Frontier (1955) Disney Western with coonskin-hatted Fess Parker as the Tennessee frontiersman of the title and Buddy Ebsen as his faithful partner in a series of adventures that end at the Alamo. Directed by Norman Foster, the setting is phony and the humor cornball but the camaraderie is appealing and the action exciting enough to hold interest. Stylized violence. A-I (br) U

Dawn of the Dead (1979) Survivors of a previous night of the living dead are now besieged in a shopping mall. George Romero's camp pulp yarn has metaphorical pretensions as social satire, but essentially what's on the screen, peppered with rough language, is a relentless exploitation of gore and violence and the repulsive effects of violence. O (R) 18

Day for Night (1973) Director Francois Truffaut presents an amusing day-to-day diary of how a melodrama gets filmed in a studio on the French Riviera and himself plays the role of the director battling production difficulties while trying to deal with various complications in the (mostly love) lives of his cast (Jacqueline Bisset, Jean-Pierre Leaud, Valentina Cortese and Jean-Pierre Aumont). It not only has some charming comedy, but it provides viewers with a real insight into how movies are made. A-II (PG) AA

Day in October, A (1992) A single Jewish family (Tovah Feldshuh, Daniel Benzali and Kelly Wolf) serves as the dramatic focus in this tribute to the people of Denmark who helped the vast majority of their Jewish fellow citizens escape to neutral Sweden in October 1943, a day before the Germans ordered the arrest of every Jew in Denmark. Director Kenneth Madsen's well-intentioned dramatization bogs down in a lethargic, cliche-ridden script about a wounded Danish resistance fighter (D.B. Sweeney) who is helped by the Jewish family and who in turn helps them. Extraordinary heroism in the context of wartime violence and a muted romantic scene. A-II (PG-13)

Day in the Death of Joe Egg, A (1972) Intense drama about the parents (Alan Bates and Janet Suzman) of a hopelessly retarded, spastic 12-year-old raises issues of abortion and euthanasia but is hardly a propaganda piece for either faction. Directed by Peter Medak, the ambiguities of its characters and situation are left unresolved and casual moviegoers are likely to find it a difficult, draining and confusing experience. A-IV (R) X

Day James Dean Died, The (see: "24 Hours of the Rebel").

Day of Anger (1969) Routine Italian western about a gunman (Lee Van Cleef) and his hero-worshipping young assistant (Giuliano Gemna) who take over a small town by blackmailing its leading citizens. Directed by Tonino Valeri, bullets fly quite readily, but the violence is controlled. A-III (PG)

Day of the Animals (1977) A depletion in the atmosphere's ozone layer provokes Rocky Mountain wildlife into a wholesale attack upon humans. There are some elemental terror and suspense in this silly plot premise, but director William Girdler quickly depletes the suspension of disbelief by ineptly staging the resulting violence, including an attempted rape. A-III (PG) 15

Day of the Dead (1985) Director-writer George Romero's third low-budget zombie chiller provides a loathsome and unimaginative mix of violence, blood, gore and some sexual references demeaning to women. O (nr) 18

Day of the Dolphin, The (1973) Dedicated scientist George C. Scott, privately funded and working in secret, has begun teaching a dolphin to talk. What he doesn't know is that he and the dolphin are being used by a mysterious clique of powerful officials in an assassination attempt. Director Mike Nichols' melodramatic plot about the corruption of the innocent is only intermittently interesting, but at least the movie serves as a reminder of the accelerated dangers of modern science. A-II (PG)

Day of the Evil Gun (1968) Routine but interesting western stars Glenn Ford as a long-lost rancher who returns home to find that his wife and child have been carried off by Apaches but that she was about to marry a neighbor anyway. Search for them he must, though, and director Jerry Thorpe packs the ensuing adventures with action, suspense and some stylized violence. A-II (G) A

Day of the Jackal, The (1973) Screen version of Frederick Forsyth's novel stars Edward Fox as a professional assassin hired by a rightist group of military officers to murder the President of France. Directed by Fred Zinnemann, this superbly crafted thriller succeeds not only as a gripping action movie but also as a serious probe into a theme of political expediency and amorality. A-III (PG) 15

Day of the Locust, The (1975) Aspiring artist (William Atherton) plumbs the emotional depths of the glittering 1930s' Hollywood in director John Schlesinger's adaptation of the Nathaniel West novel about the superficial values and exploitative relationships that bind the Tinseltown community together. Karen Black is one of the victims who works as an extra and is obsessed by the dream of future stardom. Provoking at times, but ultimately a disappointing melodrama, with unnecessarily graphic violence. A-IV (R) X

Day That Shook the World, The (1977) Yugoslavian re-creation of the 1914 assassination of the Archduke Ferdinand and his wife (Christopher Plummer and Florinda Bolkan) at Sarajevo, the tragic incident that triggered World War I. Director Veliko Bulajic captures the period atmosphere and historical background but fails to bring its characters to life, the result

being merely a colorful but unmoving pageant. Excessively graphic torture sequence. A-IV (R)

Day the Fish Came Out, The (1967) When dying fish surface around a small Aegean island teeming with tourists, it's the result of an accidently jettisoned nuclear weapon contaminating its waters and world doom is forecast. Michael Cacoyannis wrote, produced and directed this satiric morality play starring Candace Bergen and Tom Courteney that tries to do too many things and none of them well. Some sexual references concerning homosexuality. A-III (br) A

Daydreamer, The (1966) A little boy runs away from home and has a series of adventures, most of them taking place in his imagination. Jules Bass directs a part-animation, part live-action children's entertainment combining the biblical concept of Paradise with the fancy of Hans Christian Anderson and the result adds up to a diverting fantasy. A-I (br)

Daydreamer, The (1976) French comedy starring Pierre Richard (who also wrote and directed) as an eager but completely absent-minded art director for an advertising agency, where his wacky ideas prove so sensationally successful that they finally arouse the public to violence. In satirizing the vagaries of a consumer society, Richard's talent for remaining oblivious to all the chaos caused by his innocent eccentricities is in the best tradition of visual comedy. Minor romantic complications. A-III (PG)

Days and Nights in the Forest (1973) Indian movie about four men on holiday in a large forest preserve where they meet a number of interesting individuals, not least, two women of wit and intelligence. Director Satyajit Ray's character study offers very little of dramatic action, but it is fascinating to observe the interplay of characters who are as authentic as our own circle of friends. A-II (nr) A

Days of Heaven (1978) In a drama set in 1916, a Chicago mill worker (Richard Gere), his common-law wife (Brooke Adams) and his kid sister (Linda Manz) work their way West as migrant farm laborers until they are hired by a wealthy Texas wheat grower (Sam Shepherd). Directed by Terrence Malick, there is unfortunately not much in the characterizations or the plot's passionless romantic triangle to match the grandeur of Nelson Alemendros' camerawork and its visual homage to the land and those who work it. A-III (PG)

Days of Thunder (1990) Trained by a crusty racecar builder (Robert Duvall), a determined young driver (Tom Cruise) is pushed by his physician girlfriend (Nicole Kidman) to confront his fears head-on at

Stand + Deliver
Swing Boys
Lean on Me

MINNESOTA DEPARTMENT OF PUBLIC SAFETY
APPLICATION RECEIPT
DRIVERS LICENSE OR IDENTIFICATION CARD

RECEIVED OF _____

ADDRESS _____

CITY, STATE, ZIP _____

DATE OF BIRTH	COLOR EYES	HEIGHT	WEIGHT

Valid only for amounts circled or amount printed by cash register.

	Fee Paid
Classified Driver License ...... **$15.00** Classified Under 21 D.L. **$15.00**	
Classified Commercial D. L. ..... CC-**$19.00** B-**$26.00** A-**$34.00**	
Classified Under 21 Commercial D. L. C-**$19.00** B-**$26.00** A-**$14.00**	
Provisional Update to Under-21 D.L. Class C, B or A	**$5.00**
Duplicate Driver or Moped License	**$4.50**
Motorcycle Endorsement Renewal .... Additional Fee	**$6.00**
Motorcycle Endorsement Original .... Additional Fee	**$7.50**
Instructional Permit	**$6.00**
Moped	**$9.00**
Under-21 Moped	**$9.00**
Identification Card	**$9.00**
Identification Card Senior	**$7.50**
Identification Card Special Fee	**$ .50**

Date _____ Office _____ Sig. of Agent _____

This record was not checked before the Receipt was issued and is only valid as a
Temporary License if Record and Receipt indicates. If new license is not received
within 45 days, notify Department of Public Safety at 612/296-6911.

Driver and Vehicle Services
Transportation Building
St. Paul, MN 55155

PS-33088-13   № 8912958

the Daytona 500. Director Tony Scott surrounds Cruise's winning performance with wall-to-wall racing action in a formula underdog plot that builds to a rousing feel-good ending. Several sexual situations, a restrained bedroom scene, intense car crashes and a few instances of rough language. A-III (PG-13) 12

Days of Wine and Roses (1962) Sobering tale of alcoholism as public relations flack Jack Lemmon pulls wife Lee Remick into the bottle with him, then can't persuade her to quit when he joins Alcoholics Anonymous. Directed by Blake Edwards, the tragic narrative is rendered with harrowing realism but with enough compassion to earn sympathy for all involved. Many scenes of alcohol abuse and its consequences. A-II (br) X

Dazed and Confused (1993) A group of high school seniors (including, Jason London; Michelle Burke; Ben Affleck) honor the custom of taunting and beating incoming freshmen (including, Wiley Wiggins; Christin Hinojosa), first at school and then in an all-night pot-smoking, drunken beer bash. Writer-director Richard Linklater's plotless nostalgia about the excesses of free-spirited '70's adolescents is boringly inept, yet harmful in suggesting that doing drugs is simply a fun part of growing up. Constant teen drug and alcohol abuse, sexist attitudes, brief violence and much rough language. O (R) 18

D.C. Cab (1983) Fifth-rate taxi company on the verge of extinction suddenly shapes up and plays an heroic role in foiling a kidnapping. Cast includes Gary Busey, Adam Baldwin and Mr. T. Badly written and directed by Joel Schumacher, this vulgar comedy is dreary and unfunny, with foul language and some nudity. O (R)

De Sade (1969) The aging Marquis de Sade (Keir Dullea), in between bouts of prison and the insane asylum, returns to the decaying family mansion where he recalls significant events in his life. Instead of providing any insight into the relationships and misfortunes that formed his character, director Cy Enfield's kindergarten Freud lacks even a thread of intelligibility or coherence. Numerous orgy sequences and a leering depiction of sadism. O (R) X

Dead, The (1987) James Joyce's story of a family gathering on the Feast of the Epiphany in 1904 Dublin makes a small but beautifully crafted mood piece that ends somberly in the reverie of a wife (Anjelica Huston) on the long-ago death of a boy who was in love with her and the reflections of her husband (Donal McCann) on the transitory nature of love, life and the world.

Director John Huston's warm evocation of the period and its characters is enlivened by the excellent performances of a largely Irish cast. A few indelicate words and mature references. A-II (PG)

Dead Again (1991) A reincarnation theme fuels this slick romantic thriller in which a private eye (Kenneth Branagh) and a fearful amnesiac (Emma Thompson) use a hypnotist (Derek Jacobi) to uncover their past lives—which had intersected violently. Also directed by Branagh, it's an eerie, crackling-good suspense movie, only partially marred by a strident music score and gory climax. Some brief, intense violence, intermittent rough language and mild sexual innuendo. A-III (R) 15

Dead Are Alive, The (1972) Muddled European thriller about a series of murders occurring around the Etruscan excavations of an archaeologist (Alex Cord) who has some enemies (Samantha Eggar and John Marley). Director Armando Crispino's treatment of the story's abundant sex and violence can only be described as neo-paleolithic. O (R)

Dead-Bang (1989) Unsatisfying Los Angeles cop drama featuring a troubled homicide detective (Don Johnson) on the trail of a vicious cop killer who's tied to a grassroots white supremacist movement. Director John Frankenheimer fails to pull together the cop's messed up personal life and the growing threat of white racists in the Southwest. Much grisly violence, a gratuitous sex scene and profanity. O (R)

Dead Calm (1989) Australian director Philip Noyce turns in a taut psychological thriller about a couple (Sam Neill and Nicole Kidman) terrorized at sea by a psychopath (Billy Zane) who overtakes their sailing yacht. A real nail-biter with powerful technical effects and a refreshingly resourceful female heroine, but it's hampered by images of horrific violence and a brief but graphic sexual encounter. A-IV (R) 15

Dead End (1937) Gritty screen version of Sidney Kingsley's play about the cycle of poverty focuses on a fugitive gangster (Humphrey Bogart), an aspiring architect (Joel McCrea) and a union worker (Sylvia Sidney) worried over an adolescent brother (Billy Halop) who's hanging out with a gang of street toughs (Leo Gorcy, Huntz Hall, Gabriel Dell and others) in a New York City block of tenements next to a luxury apartment building. Directed by William Wyler, the story portrays a classic example of the slums as breeding ground for crime but ends with some hope of change. Stylized violence. A-II (br) PG

Dead Heat on a Merry-Go-Round (1966) Crass ex-con (James Coburn) engineers a bank robbery at the Los Angeles airport timed to coincide with the arrival the Soviet premier. Directed by Bernard Girard, the emphasis is less on the crime aspects than on depicting its amoral hero who not only gets the loot but ditches his girlfriend. Some violence. A-III (br)

Dead Image (see: "Dead Ringer").

Dead Men Don't Wear Plaid (1982) Steve Martin playing a 1940s' private-eye cavorts with famous stars of the period, thanks to some clever editing of footage from old Hollywood detective movies. Affectionate and moderately entertaining spoof directed by Carl Reiner, it's a one-joke movie, but the joke holds up fairly well. Some sexually oriented jokes. A-III (PG)

Dead of Night (1945) Classic British horror movie recounts five chilling tales, the best of which concerns the troubles of a ventriloquist (Michael Redgrave) with his dummy, unfolding within the frame story of an architect (Mervyn Johns) whose recurrent nightmare finally becomes a reality. Produced by Michael Balcon with various directors for the individual stories, the result is an eerie spellbinder, relying on the intelligence as well as the imagination of the viewer. Low-key menace and several instances of stylized violence. A-II (br) A

Dead of Summer (1971) Wealthy neurotic American (Jean Seberg), in a desolate Moroccan city beset by sweltering heat and a howling sandstorm, spends the day in her elegant apartment (with broken air conditioner) making various attempts to communicate with others. Director Nelo Risi's boring existential study has several needlessly extended erotic sequences. O (R)

Dead of Winter (1987) Aspiring actress becomes the pawn in a blackmail attempt that proves fatal to her captors and to the rich woman who's the target of their extortion. Director Arthur Penn's unconvincing thriller features Mary Steenburgen in a triple role. Unnecessarily explicit violence at the conclusion make the film unsuitable for youngsters. A-III (R) 15

Dead Poets Society (1989) A teacher (Robin Williams) returns in 1959 to the tony New England prep school for boys from which he had graduated, determined to turn his students on to poetry and into free-thinkers, but his unorthodox methods inspire the impressionable youths to take personal risks not always in their best interests. Director Peter Weir's thought-provoking period drama raises more questions than it answers in exploring such issues as peer pressure, child rights, values clarification, teen suicide and the price of nonconformity. Mild locker-room language and an unsettling, unresolved teen suicide. A-III (PG)

Dead Pool, The (1988) With some assistance from his Chinese-American partner (Evan Kim), San Francisco homicide detective "Dirty Harry" Callahan (Clint Eastwood) makes Swiss cheese out of both the mob and a psycho killer but is no match for a bomb-laden miniature sports car. Veteran stunt coordinator Buddy Van Horn directs the bloody action and graphic mayhem with a questionable sense of humor. Excessive violence and much profanity. O (R) 18

Dead Ringer (1964) Baldly contrived suspense thriller with Bette Davis in dual roles as an embittered sister who kills her treacherous twin, then assumes the sister's life as a wealthy widow. Directed by Paul Henreid, the paper-thin plot is given some class by Davis' highly charged performance until a good cop (Karl Malden) and a worthless womanizer (Peter Lawford) get in the way. Some stylized violence and implied marital infidelity. A-III (br)

Dead Ringers (1988) Twin gynecologists (Jeremy Irons plays both roles), unable to establish their own individual identities, ultimately find their lives and successful practice in ruins due to the love relationship between one brother and a strong-willed actress (Genevieve Bujold). Director David Cronenberg and actor Irons happily do not exploit the obvious horror-show potential of this chilling psychological thriller, but the explicit gynecological discussions of female anatomy and some graphic, kinky sexual encounters are excessive enough. Also much profanity and a gruesome, bloody finale. O (R)

Dead Run (1969) Petty German pickpocket steals some secret government papers and becomes the target for under-cover agents all over Europe. Humdrum foreign intrigue melodrama starring Peter Lawford and directed by Christian-Jacque, it's only saving feature is that it does not take itself seriously. Scenes of violence and torture and one featuring a strip tease. O (R) U

Dead Zone (1983) Good screen version of the Stephen King novel about a man (Christopher Walken) who awakens after being in a coma for five years to discover that he has the gift of second-sight enabling him to tell things of the future and past of anyone with whom he comes into physical contact. Such a gift has its drawbacks, of course, and director David Cronenberg does well in exploring them. More a psychological suspense thriller than a horror film, its strong supporting cast includes Brooke Adams, Tom Skerrit and Herbert Lom. Passably entertaining for a mature audience. A-III (R) 18

Deadfall (1968) Convoluted tale about a cat burglar (Michael Caine) who, linking up with a married couple of jewel thieves

(Eric Portman and Giavanna Ralli), falls in love with the wife, which is all right with the husband because he's a homosexual but, than again, maybe he's really her father. Obscure British production directed by Bryan Forbes fails both as action thriller and psychological drama with its implications of incest and homosexual relationships. O (br) X

Deadlier Than the Male (1967) Bulldog Drummond detective adventure starring Richard Johnson on the trail of a pretty pair of female assassins (Elke Sommer and Sylvia Koscina) whose specialty is murdering key executives involved in business mergers. Dim-witted British production directed by Ralph Thomas, it offers a frothy mixture of sex and violence adding up to some very distasteful entertainment. O (br) X

Deadline (1987) Reporter assigned to Beirut (Christopher Walken) not only loses his big story but gets caught between warring factions and has to flee for his life. Directed by Nathaniel Gutman, the personal story gets lost in the chaos and confusion of the war-torn city whose violence is depicted in realistic, stomach-churning fashion. Much bloody violence with vivid and gruesome scenes of the dead and dying. A-IV (R)

Deadly Affair, The (1967) Screen version of a John Le Carre novel about an aging government agent (James Mason) who, just before retirement, discovers he must carry out one last investigation that probably will shatter whatever small security he has left in life. Director Sidney Lumet gets fine performances from a cast that includes Simone Signoret, Harriet Andersson and Harry Andrews in this taut British spy thriller for grown-ups. A-III (br) 15

Deadly Fathoms (1973) Documentary explores the graveyard of sunken ships that were involved in the 23 atomic bomb tests in South Pacific waters near the atoll of Bikini. Despite a no-nonsense narration by Rod Serling, these grotesque monuments to the nuclear age often only serve the purposes of an underseas adventure directed by Michael Harris. A-I (G)

Deadly Friend (1986) A strange but mild-mannered horror movie about a teenager who brings his girlfriend back to life by implanting a computer chip in her brain. She thereupon kills her abusive father and the nasty old lady next door. Director Wes Craven makes little of this or anything else in a dull and pedestrian tale. Restrained violence. A-II (R) 18

Deadly Hero (1976) After killing an unarmed man (James Earl Jones) who has been terrorizing a cultured musician (Diahn Williams), a violence-prone New York policeman (Don Murray) becomes enraged when his career is put in jeopardy by her telling the truth. Director Ivan Nagy gets convincing performances and evokes the gritty atmosphere of the big city, but his creative energies flag midway and it becomes little more than another woman-stalked-by-terror movie relying on violence and the sexual menace it generates. O (R)

Deadly Trackers, The (1973) Excessively violent story of western revenge in which a sheriff (Richard Harris) sees his family murdered by a band of outlaws, follows them to Mexico and kills them one by one, until a Mexican sheriff, upholding law and order, kills the American sheriff. Directed by Barry Shear, much of the movie is devoted to bloody fights and shootouts as well as expounding a simplistic notion of law and justice. O (PG) X

Deadly Trap, The (1972) Frank Langella and Faye Dunaway play an uneasily married couple living in Paris and troubled by a series of peculiar occurrences that culminate in the disappearance of their two children. Badly failed French suspense thriller directed by Rene Clement, the plight of the two young children might be distressing for some pre-teens. A-II (PG) A

Deaf Smith and Johnny Ears (1973) Italian western filmed in sunny Spain and set in frontier Texas, where Anthony Quinn and Franco Nero spend most of their time preventing a particularly nefarious Mexican general from taking over the Southwest. Director Paolo Cavara provides numerous fistfights, shootouts, rattling Gatling guns and lots of explosions, with an occasional visit to the local bordello. A-III (PG)

Deal of the Century (1983) Chevy Chase and Gregory Hines play traveling salesmen selling bargain-basement weaponry to Third World governments and those who are trying to overthrow them. It might have worked as a satire on the illicit arms trade, but as a straight slapstick comedy, it is merely disappointing and only sporadically funny. Directed by William Friedkin, it is marred by some outrageous stereotyping of Hispanics, both in Latin America and in this country. A-III (PG)

Dealers (1989) British import takes a satirical look at the bankrupt ethic pushing high-powered financial traders to substance abuse and suicide in a story about the love-hate relationship between a flamboyant young trader (Paul McGann) and his new supervisor, a sexy American (Rebecca DeMornay) who's sleeping with their married boss. Directed by Colin Bucksey, the financial mumbo jumbo and male-female cat-and-mouse games divert attention from the pressures that drive such individuals to succeed at any cost. Brief sexual encounters and some scenes of drug abuse. A-III (R) 15

Dealing: Or The Berkeley-To-Boston Forty-Brick Lost-Bag Blues (1972) Harvard law student (Robert F. Lyons) flies out to Berkeley to pick up a marijuana shipment for the campus pusher (John Lithgow) and meets a liberated woman (Barbara Hershey) but they run into a corrupt cop (Charles Durning). Directed by Paul Williams, the supposed comedy views pot as amusing and contains nudity and rough language. O (R)

Dear America: Letters Home from Vietnam (1988) Based on the book of the same name, this feature-length documentary uses compelling newsreel footage to visualize the feelings and impressions recorded in the letters sent home by American soldiers who saw the war firsthand. Directed by Bill Couterie, the off-camera readers include a fine array of actors from Tom Berenger to Robin Williams and excellent use is made of the many songs engendered by the bitter conflict on the homefront. Realistic footage, some of it very intense, depicting the obscenity of war. A-II (PG-13)

Dear Detective (1978) Two former college classmates, now in their mid-40s', bump into each other (quite literally) and discover that he's still a bachelor (Philippe Noiret) and she's divorced (Annie Girardot). The main source of humor in this French comedy directed by Philippe de Broca is how their romance is complicated by each other's professions— he's a college professor and she's a police inspector. Cheerful little comedy with two charming, talented performers. Some Gallic wit about the war between the sexes and brief partial nudity. A-III (PG)

Dear John (1966) Swedish movie written and directed by Lars Magnus Lindgren is intended to explore the beginnings of a meaningful love relationship through a couple's physical experience of sex. It deals only superficiality with the human dimension of its characters and never gets much beyond the physical. Graphic portrayal of sexual activity. O (br) X

Death Becomes Her (1992) Satire and fantasy clash in this black comedy about two aging celebrities (Goldie Hawn and Meryl Streep) ready to kill each other over an alcoholic plastic surgeon (Bruce Willis). The humor is decidedly plastic in director Robert Zemeckis' frenzied movie, with Streep's finely nuanced performance the sole merit. Comic violence, some sexual references and a flash of nudity. A-III (PG-13) PG

Death Before Dishonor (1987) Trite, almost propagandistic account of hostilities between Arab terrorists and U.S. Marines assigned to protect a U.S. Embassy in a small Middle Eastern country. Fred Dryer is a clone of Clint Eastwood's "Heartbreak Ridge" gunnery sergeant in this failed drama replete with harsh language, violence and explicit brutality. O (R)

Death by Hanging (1974) Japanese movie made in 1968 presents a scathing attack on capital punishment with the subtheme of Japanese racist attitudes toward Koreans. Directed by Nagisa Oshima, its originality in structure and technique takes chances in combining documentary and dramatic styles but is unusually successful in making an exciting movie on a most provocative subject. A-III (nr)

Death Collector (1976) Crime syndicate melodrama about a rash but engaging young hoodlum (Joseph Cortese) who refuses to stay in line and suffers the ultimate penalty. Aided by some talented actors, director Ralph De Vito's effort, for all it's low-budget defects, has a tough sense of reality and some intelligence but resorts to excessive violence and some nudity. O (R)

Death Hunt (1981) Lee Marvin plays a grizzled Mountie tracking Charles Bronson, a wrongly accused fugitive, in the 1930s' Canadian backwoods, both men aware that they are the last of the old breed upon whom civilization is fast closing in. Routine outdoor melodrama directed by Peter R. Hunt with some rough language and violence. A-III (R) X

Death in Venice (1971) Fine adaptation of the Thomas Mann novel in which an artist (Dirk Bogarde), in the twilight of his career and unwilling to chance personal encounters with others, is taken with the beauty of a golden-haired youth, setting off within him an unresolved conflict between mind and body. Directed by Luchino Visconti, it is a movie of character and mood rather than of plot, with the interior drama being much more significant than any external actions. A-III (PG) AA

Death of a Bureaucrat (1979) Cuban director Tomas Gutierrez Alea fashions a satire on the hypocrisy of government bureaucracy. A widow must retrieve the work card buried with her husband in order to receive her pension. Black comedy with wry moments but a bit too sardonic and cynical for some tastes. A-III (nr)

Death of a Gunfighter (1969) Western town trying to attract eastern industry wants to get rid of its tough, old-fashioned sheriff (Richard Widmark) but he won't resign. So, in the interest of civic progress, the town fathers decide to have him gunned down. Though given little to do, Lena Horne as a madam who marries the sheriff is a real asset. This period of transition for the Old West makes an interesting setting for a movie that under Allen Smithee's direction is only fitfully successful either as a western or as a social document. Adult material and violence. A-III (PG) A

Death of a Hooker (see: "Who Killed Mary What's 'ername").

Death of a Jew (1973) Captured Israeli agent (Assaf Dayan) is befriended by an old Arab policeman (Akim Tamiroff), a promising situation that goes nowhere except to a very predictable conclusion. The 1970 Israeli production is a well-intentioned parable on the brotherhood of man, but it is without a shred of insight into people or politics and the direction of Denys de la Patalliere is hopelessly lackluster. A-III (PG)

Death of a Salesman (1951) Interesting adaptation of the Arthur Miller play charting the downward spiral of a middle-aged man (Frederic March) who cannot cope with the reality that his company and customers consider him redundant. Though the movie has limitations as popular drama, director Laslo Benedek generates empathy for the liked-but-not-well-liked salesman who relies on empty optimism to mask his growing doubts and then despair. The cautionary tale about defining one's life in terms of what one does for a living is too intense for children. A-II (nr) PG

Death of an Angel (1986) This unconvincing drama attempts to contrast a rationalistic vs. charismatic approach to matters of faith. An Episcopal priest (Bonnie Bedelia) confronts her doubts about her own religious belief and the integrity of a seemingly dishonest faith healer (Nick Mancuso) patronized by poor, destitute and crippled Mexican peasants. In addition to several instances of harsh language, writer-director Petro Popescu offers several scenes of needless sadistic brutality and ambiguous sexual references. O (PG)

Death of Tarzan, The (1968) This Czechoslovakian version of the Tarzan legend has the ape-man return to Europe in order to make its point that human society can be more predatory than that of the jungle. A dark comedy directed by Jaroslav Balik, it nevertheless demonstrates that love is a more basic part of human nature than greed or violence. A-II (br)

Death on the Nile (1978) An heiress (Lois Chilez) is murdered on a honeymoon cruise up the Nile and Hercule Poirot (Peter Ustinov), Agatha Christie's Belgian sleuth, is on hand to interrogate such suspects as Bette Davis, Angela Lansbury, Maggie Smith, Mia Farrow and George Kennedy. Directed by John Guillermin, it is an intricately plotted whodunit that plays the game fairly in laying out clues to challenge the mystery fan. A lavishly produced 1930s' period piece with exotic Egyptian locales, it's solid escapist entertainment for those who don't mind rather graphic depictions of murder. A-III (PG) A

Death Race 2000 (1975) Satire about the American passion for violence and speed set against the background of a transcontinental auto race in the year 2000 when America is ruled by a dictatorship whose main method of control is the bread and circus device. Director Paul Bartel exploits what supposedly he is satirizing, including a unneeded sampling of sex and nudity. O (R) 18

Death Rides a Horse (1969) After a gruesome opening in which a small boy watches his whole family brutalized and killed by outlaws, director Giulio Petroni's Italian western moderates the violence as it follows the pursuit of the killers by the boy (John Phillip Law) 15 years later. While it's somewhat lower on the violence scale than many others of the genre, it also registers fairly low on the scale of originality. A-III (M) PG

Death Ship (1980) George Kennedy and other unfortunates perform in a witless story about a Nazi ghost ship that roams the Atlantic ramming passenger ships and seeking the blood of the survivors to keep its ghoulish act going. Besides considerable gore and violence, director Alvin Rakoff's horror movie trades upon memories of the Holocaust to give substance to its cheap and grisly thrills. O (R) X

Death Valley (1982) Homicidal maniac (Steve McHattie) menaces a young boy (Peter Billingsley) in a terribly inept thriller that starts out like "Kramer vs. Kramer" and ends up like "The Texas Chainsaw Massacre." Directed by Dick Richards, it traffics in explicit violence, bloodshed and nudity. O (R) X

Death Warrant (1990) A spate of unexplained killings inside a Los Angeles prison prompts a former Canadian Mountie (Jean-Claude Van Damme) to pose as a newly arrived con and likely target for the next hit. Directed by Deran Sarafian, the routine kickboxing action movie features mediocre performances in a predictable plot with the expected pay-off of increasingly brutal, bloodthirsty fights. Excessive violence and some rough language. O (R) 18

Death Wish (1974) New York executive (Charles Bronson) sets about avenging the vicious assaults upon his wife and daughter by systematically doing away with the criminal population of the city. Director Michael Winner treats his judge-and-jury actions as if they were an admirable example of civic consciousness. Objectionable are not only the movie's incessantly bloody visuals but even more so its dangerous vigilante message. O (R) 18

139

Death Wish II (1982) Charles Bronson reprises his role of the decent citizen turned murderous vigilante in a sequel utterly condoning unlawful actions. Directed by Michael Winner with graphic violence, including sexual violence. O (R) 18

Death Wish III (1985) Urban vigilante Charles Bronson again mows down felons in this third outing directed by Michael Winner with a variation on the theme increasing the body count to the point of utter absurdity. Unremitting and exploitative violence, including sexual violence. O (R) 18

Deathmaster (1972) Stale story of a vampire (Robert Quarry) who employs brainless hippies to bring victims (Bill Ewing and Brenda Dickson) to his isolated beach mansion. Lifelessly directed by Ray Danton, the movie indulges in some raw dialogue and a bit of coy nudity. A-III (PG) X

Deathtrap (1982) A washed-up playwright (Michael Caine) contemplates murdering an up-and-coming one (Christopher Reeve) and stealing his play in this competent if uninspired movie version of Ira Levin's Broadway comedy-thriller. Though it drags and the ending is weak, director Sidney Lumet gets first-rate performances from a cast including Dyan Cannon and Irene Worth. Brutal murders and some rough language. A-III (PG) A

Debut, The (1971) Quiet little Russian comedy about a young woman worker who is selected to play Joan of Arc in a movie production and her affair with a married man. Director Gleb Pantilov gently contrasts proletarian life and attitudes with those of the official class of state artists and functionaries. A-III (nr)

Decameron, The (1971) Italian director Pier Paolo Pasolini's adaptation of some tales from Boccaccio's 14th-century volume of 100 stories is faithful to the original in burlesquing religious beliefs and practices in favor of the joys of the natural life, especially those relating to sex and greed. Though splendid in its robust evocation of Renaissance Italy, its explicit visualizations of sexual encounters is seriously offensive. O (X)

Deceived (1991) A young widow (Goldie Hawn) discovers that her museum curator husband (John Heard) was leading a double life, putting her and her little girl (Ashley Peldon) in mortal danger. Director Damian Harris' nifty thriller is packed with implausibilities but scores on atmosphere and emotionally involving suspense. Momentary violence and mild sexual innuendo. A-II (PG-13) 15

Deceivers, The (1988) Lackluster historical crime movie about a British officer (Pierce Brosnan) in 19th-century India who infiltrates and exposes a murderous cult that preys on unsuspecting travelers. Director Nicholas Meyer makes every effort to re-create the period and place but forgets to inject any energy into the scenario or examine the circumstances that fostered the cult. Much violence, brief flashes of nudity and a hallucinatory sexual encounter with a prostitute. A-III (PG-13) 15

Decline and Fall of a Birdwatcher (1969) Delightful screen version of Evelyn Waugh's 1928 novel about a naive school teacher (Robin Phillips) who becomes involved with the elegant Lady Margot Beste-Chetwynde (Genevieve Page) and her vice ring and winds up taking the rap for her and going to prison. Director John Krish has caught the satirically solemn flavor of the original and his fine British cast never cracks a smile in carrying on with Waugh's outrageous lampooning of English high and low life. Stylish comedy even for those who don't usually like British humor. A-III (PG) A

Decline of Western Civilization Part II, The: The Metal Years (1988) Penelope Spheeris' documentary focuses mostly on the posturing, wanton performers and fans in the L.A. heavy metal scene whose hedonistic and clearly self-destructive life-styles have nothing to commend them. Much profanity, bragging about sexual promiscuity, drug and alcohol abuse, some nudity and several sexually provocative scenes. O (R) 15

December (1991) Listless story tells of the effect the Japanese attack on Pearl Harbor has on five teens at a New England boys academy who stay up all night arguing about whether to enlist the next morning. Writer-director Gabe Torres' adolescent gab fest merely voices the boys' fears and naive patriotism without emotional involvement or any insights. Momentary violence. A-II (PG)

Deep, The (1977) Screen version of Peter Benchley's novel about an unmarried couple (Jacqueline Bisset and Nick Nolte) whose scuba diving on a Bermuda vacation leads to sunken treasure and the help of a salvage expert (Robert Shaw) in outwitting a crew of black villains (led by Louis Gosset). Simpleminded but clunky melodrama directed by Peter Yates, it has at least the Bermuda scenery and underwater photography to recommend it. Otherwise it makes much of a blissful premarital relationship, stereotypes blacks as threats, offers a particularly brutal fight scene and mixes an abundance of highly calculated titillation with sexual menace. O (PG) A

Deep Cover (1992) Violent, drug-themed movie has a corrupt attorney (Jeff Goldblum) outsmarted by an undercover narcotics cop (Larry Fishburne) who then succumbs to drugs and their profits when he becomes disillusioned. Director Bill Duke's thoroughly cynical movie sends the wrong message about the war against drugs and overdoses on gory killings. Excessive violence, morally ambiguous theme, sexually suggestive scenes and frequent rough language. O (R) 18

Deep End (1971) London adolescent (John Moulder-Brown) gets a job in a public bathhouse, becomes involved with one of the girl attendants (Jane Asher) and ruins his life and hers. Directed by Jerzy Skolimowski, the seedy environment is of more interest than the human characters within it. Some bizarre, graphic sex scenes. O (R) X

Deep in the Heart (1984) A rape victim (Karen Young) gains vengeance upon the rapist (Clayton Day), an amoral but respectable attorney who is a gun enthusiast, by learning how to use a pistol and then turning this symbol of male dominance against him. Directed by Tony Garnett, this British production relies on exploitative violence and nudity. O (R)

Deep Red (1976) David Hemmings stars in a badly acted, worse dubbed Italian horror movie in which director Dario Argento devotes most of his attention to depicting a series of gory, sadistic murders. O (R)

Deep Throat (1972) This is the first thoroughly hardcore porno feature to receive a sophisticated national promotion campaign, enabling it to reach beyond the porno theater circuit. It is not about cough remedies. O (X)

Deep Thrust—The Hand of Death (1973) Mindless Hong Kong Kung Fu story about a woman's revenge on the man who seduced her sister. Directed by Heang Feng, it is explicit in its physical violence almost to the point of nausea. O (R)

Deepstar Six (1989) Submerged for six months in the Pacific, some underwater experts unsettle a mysterious monster when they dynamite its sea cave for a U.S. missile site. Despite a likeable cast (Taurean Blacque, Nancy Everhard and Greg Evigan, among others) and the prerequisite monster of no known species, its mindless plot and unimaginative direction by Sean S. Cunningham generate about as much menace as a clogged drain. Some sexual suggestiveness, rough language and several incidents of gruesome gore. O (R) 15

Deer Hunter, The (1979) Three small-town steel-workers (Robert De Niro, Christopher Walken and John Savage) have their mettle tested by the horrors of Vietnam in director Michael Cimino's harsh evocation of the effects of war on friendship and spirit. Somewhat racist and chauvinistic treatment and the film's brutal and intense moments of violence play on gut emotions overriding any

serious intent to explore the painful tragedy of Vietnam. O (R) 18

Def by Temptation (1990) While visiting a friend (Kadeem Hardison) in the Big Apple, a southern divinity student (James Bond III) finds himself drawn to a beautiful sorceress (Cynthia Bond) who lures men into her bed before killing them. Bond III also wrote, produced and directed this comedy of horrors, which exploits sex and violence for shock value and cheap thrills. Excessive violence, fairly explicit sexual activity with frontal nudity and some rough language. O (R) 18

Defector, The (1966) Muddled espionage story about an American scientist (Montgomery Clift) recruited as a CIA spy and an East German scientist (Hardy Kruger) recruited by the Reds to get him to defect. Directed by Raoul Levy, the plot has some gaping holes and the Cold War politics are heavy-handed. Mild violence and romance. A-II (br) A

Defending Your Life (1991) After dying in separate accidents, a mild-mannered ad exec (Albert Brooks) and his new love interest (Meryl Streep) face individual trials in the afterlife, which will determine whether they progress to a higher life or return to Earth to try again. Also written and directed by Brooks, this vaguely defined comic fantasy is a smoothly soothing salute to the redemptive powers of love, given some needed sparks from Lee Grant and Rip Torn as trial prosecutor and defender. References to reincarnation and extremely mild sexual innuendo. A-II (PG)

Defenseless (1991) Lurid murder mystery has an L.A. police detective (Sam Shepard) tightening the screws on the attorney (Barbara Hershey) who is defending the wife (Mary Beth Hurt) of her murdered client-lover. Director Martin Campbell maintains suspense with a capable cast but favors the sensational in this dense and derivative plot. Intermittent gory violence, recurring sexual innuendo, fleeting partial nudity and some rough language. A-IV (R) 18

Defiance (1980) Young merchant seaman (Jan-Michael Vincent) leads the terrorized residents of a New York ghetto neighborhood in a vigilante assault on their tormentors. The oft-told tale, directed by John Flynn, is run-of-the-mill entertainment with some graphic violence. A-III (PG) X

Defiant Ones, The (1958) Interracial chase thriller in which a black convict (Sidney Poitier) and a Southern redneck (Tony Curtis) flee a chain gang shackled together and needing each other if they are to make good their escape. Director Stanley Kramer's message movie about the chains of prejudice may be a little too pat and melodramatic in developing the stark situation but the incidents along the way more than sustain interest until the finale. Some nasty stylized violence and racial epithets. A-III (nr) A

Degree of Murder (1969) German crime melodrama about a waitress who casually recruits two young men to help her dispose of the body of an ex-lover she has just as casually, though accidentally, killed. Director Volker Schlondorff's study of unfeeling, amoral youth emphasizes the matter-of-fact hedonism of the three as they enjoy themselves while going about their grisly errand. The treatment of these incidents is excessively graphic and undermines whatever serious intentions the movie may have had. O (R)

Delirious (1991) Weak comic fantasy in which an injured soap opera writer (John Candy) wakes up inside his own TV story and proceeds to write himself a role as a dashing hero to the two leading ladies (Emma Samms and Mariel Hemingway). Director Tom Mankiewicz spoofs nighttime soaps with a good cast but not enough wit to excuse its saccharine predictability. Infrequent slapstick violence, discreet sexual references and minimal profanity. A-II (PG)

Deliverance (1972) Challenging screen version of the James Dickey novel about four Atlanta businessmen (Burt Reynolds, Jon Voight, Ned Beatty and Ronny Cox) who decide to spend a weekend canoeing down a hazardous mountain river on a wilderness journey that turns into a nightmare. Director John Boorman's powerful and absorbing adventure piece tries fitfully to provide some insights on masculinity, civilization and nature. Those deciding to take the trip should be prepared for some harrowing violence and a brutal homosexual assault. A-IV (R) 18

Delta Force (1986) Lee Marvin and Chuck Norris replay the 1985 Lebanese hijacking of an American airliner in a fictional account portraying a U.S. Army Special Forces team successfully routing Arab terrorists while rescuing every American hostage. Excessive violence, unacceptably justified by patriotic fervor, runs consistently throughout the film. O (R) 18

Delta Force II (1990) An elite U.S. Army unit sends its most lethal muscleman (Chuck Norris) to capture a Latin American drug lord (Billy Drago) who is holding three Americans hostage. Director Aaron Norris' action movie is a strictly formula affair with hackneyed dialogue, no originality and an unending stream of machine gunfire and bloodied bodies. Excessive violence and occasional raw language. O (R)

Delusions of Grandeur (1975) Set in 17th-century Spain, this costume drama from director Gerard Oury stars Louis De Funes whose frenetic zest carries the comedy about avarice and pride. As the dismissed minister of finance for the Spanish king, he concocts an absurd plot whereby his valet (Yves Montand) is to make compromising advances to the beautiful queen. Innocent, light farce in French with English subtitles. A-II (PG)

Demolition Man (1993) An explosive L.A. cop (Slyvester Stallone) is pitted against a madman (Wesley Snipes) bent on mass destruction in the rigidly conformist society of 2032, where they are revived after having been cryogenically frozen 36 years earlier. Director Marco Brambilla's boring action flick is an overproduced assault on the senses that glorifies mindless mayhem and a sick, dehumanizing sense of humor. Excessive violence, some nudity and much rough language. O (R)

Demon (1977) Inept thriller about a New York detective (Tony Lo Bianco) trying to solve the mystery behind an outbreak of random murders in which the killers say that God told them to do it. Directed by Larry Cohen, the movie is marked by violence, nudity and a tawdry use of religious references. O (R) AA

Demon Seed (1977) Proteus IV, a thinking computer, focuses on the problem of giving its mind a body and propagating itself with the unwilling assistance of the wife (Julie Christie) of its creator (Fritz Weaver). The special effects are exceptional, but director Donald Cammell's treatment dwells on the vulnerability of a helpless woman, in the degrading context of its depiction of procreation via computer. Brief nudity and some profanity. O (R) AA

Demons (1974) Masterless samurai, duped by a woman out of the money he needs to redeem his honor, sets out on a rampage of violence to revenge himself on everyone associated with his betrayer. Directed by Toshio Matsumoto, its theme is the senseless wastefulness of any code of "honor" based on revenge. Stylized violence. A-III (R)

Dennis the Menace (1993) Hank Ketcham's comic-strip characters come to life with the cherubic-looking five-year-old (Mason Gamble) continually discombobulating his curmudgeonly neighbor (Walter Matthau) while unwittingly outwitting a dimwitted thief (Christopher Lloyd). Matthau's crotchety performance is the best thing in the comedy's aimless assortment of pranks, mischief and pratfalls blandly directed by Nick Castle and scripted by John Hughes who tacks on the same little-boy-vs.-nasty-thief situation from his earlier "Home Alone" movies. Momentary violence and many slapstick incidents.

Deranged (1974) Roberts Blossom plays an aging Mama's boy in a sick study of incestuous necrophilia, with Cosette Lee as the late object of his present affection, and a host of unknowns filling in as his erstwhile victims. Directed by Jeff Gillen, the grisly movie lives up to its title. O (R)

Derby (1971) Documentary by Robert Kaylor on the Roller Derby in Dayton, Ohio, focuses on the players, the hopefuls and the fans. Though it contains some unexpected humor and pathos, the violence and crude appeal of the sport is what it's all about. A-III (R/GP)

Dersu Uzala (1978) Russian production about the friendship that grows between a turn-of-the-century explorer in Siberia and his guide, an aging Tungus hunter whose name gives the film its title. Japanese director Akira Kurosawa concentrates on evoking the vast remoteness of the Siberian wilderness, a world the Russian finds forbidding but one in which the hunter is perfectly at home. Finely acted, beautifully photographed, it is an admiring portrait of a man living in harmony with nature and with his fellow hunters. A-I (G) U

Desert Bloom (1986) An idealistic young girl (Annabeth Gish) runs away from her family she has tried to keep together when she sees her father (Jon Voight) making a drunken pass at her visiting aunt (Ellen Barkin). Set in Las Vegas during the 1950s era of atomic testing, the movie by first-time director Eugene Coor expresses the adaptability and resilience of a compassionate teenager's growing maturity as she returns to try to bring her troubled parents back together. Brief scene of domestic violence. A-II (PG)

Deserter, The (1971) Cynical western about the U.S. Cavalry's recruiting an Indian-hating deserter (Bekim Fehmiu) to lead a raid against an Apache stronghold. Mediocre Italian production directed by Burt Kennedy, the movie exploits its subject for the sake of brutish violence. O (GP)

Deserter U.S.A. (1969) Swedish production about U.S. servicemen who defected during the Vietnam War to take refuge in Sweden is atrociously acted by the deserters themselves staging "typical" situations. Written and directed by Lars Lambert and Olle Sjogren, the pseudo-documentary's anti-American, anti-establishment bias is excessively heavy-handed and its production values are barely adequate. O (nr)

Desert Hearts (1986) Awaiting the finalizing of her divorce at a ranch near Reno, Nev., a 1950s' professional woman creates a new self-image during a sexual relationship with a younger woman. Director Donna Deitch's very personal romantic vision treats homosexuality as basically a matter of sexual preference and sex as the fundamental basis for a meaningful commitment between the film's main characters. Lengthy nude scene. O (R) 18

Desert Rats, The (1953) Standard war picture honors the exploits of an Australian battalion under an English officer (Richard Burton) during the 1941 siege of Tobruk by Desert Fox Rommel (James Mason). Directed by Robert Wise, the battle scenes are exciting but less than credible, further burdened by Burton who agonizes unconvincingly over his abilities as a commander. Wartime violence. A-I (br) U

Desire under the Elms (1958) Stagey adaptation of the Eugene O'Neill drama of greed and lust set in 19th-century New England where the angry son (Anthony Perkins) of a grasping, dour farmer (Burl Ives) falls in love with his father's new wife (Sophia Loren). Directed by Delbert Mann, the dramatic conflict between father, son and stepmother are treated in heavy-handed theatrical fashion that grows wearisome long before the conclusion's moral retribution. Mature themes, including infanticide. A-III (br) X

Desk Set (1957) It's mind over machine in this breezy romantic comedy about an eccentric automation expert (Spencer Tracy) who more than meets his match in the mental prowess of the woman (Katharine Hepburn) heading the TV network research department he's been hired to modernize. As directed by Walter Lang from William Marchant's play, the comic battle of wits between the two leads is charming, genial fun, abetted by the kooky hijinks of staff researchers Joan Blondell and Dina Merrill as well as some satirical jabs at corporate manners and mix-ups. A-II (br) U

Despair (1979) Expatriate White Russian (Dirk Bogarde) living in Berlin prior to Hitler's takeover, grows in madness and desperation, eventually killing a stranger and trying to change his identity. Portrait of a fragmented psyche from director Rainer Werner Fassbinder based on the Vladimir Nabokov novel also delves deeply and graphically into the anti-hero's sexual perversities. O (nr) AA

Desperados, The (1969) Substandard western about an outlaw family fathered by a mad, Bible-quoting parson (Jack Palance) who vows vengeance against his son (Vince Edwards) when he decides to go straight. Under Henry Levin's direction, everyone concerned looks embarrassingly ridiculous in a movie that emphasizes violence and toys with nudity, suggestive costuming, prostitutes and a little aberrant sex thrown in for good measure. O (M)

Desperate Characters (1971) Middle-class, childless couple (Shirley MacLaine and Kenneth Mars) live comfortably in New York City until urban realities of crime and vandalism begin to unravel their sense of security. Written and directed by Frank D. Gilroy, there is a hollow staginess about this affluent but loveless couple that makes it difficult to share their plight. Graphic, violent and, yes, desperate bedroom scene. A-IV (R)

Desperate Hours (1990) The home of an estranged couple (Mimi Rogers and Anthony Hopkins) is invaded by an escaped psychopathic killer (Mickey Rourke) who terrorizes them as he awaits the arrival of his lawyer/lover (Kelly Lynch). Director Michael Cimino's psychological thriller relies more on Rourke's chillingly nasty performance than on a coherent plot to carry the tale to its melodramatic finish. Some violence, much menace, occasional rough language and flashes of nudity. A-III (R) A

Desperate Journey (1942) Shot down over World War II Germany, a RAF bomber crew (notably Errol Flynn, Ronald Reagan and Arthur Kennedy) escape their Nazi captor (Raymond Massey) to commit various acts of sabotage while making their way back to England. Directed by Raoul Walsh, the brave derring-do has all the credibility of a romp with the Rover Boys and provides only dated wartime hokum today. Stylized violence with flagwaving rhetoric. A-I (br) A

Desperate Ones, The (1968) Uneven melodrama about two Polish brothers (Maximilian Schell and Raf Vallone) who escape from a Siberian labor camp during World War II and, as they make for the Afghanistan border, elude the NKVD, survive the elements and have improbable love affairs. Directed by Alexander Ramati, it has some good moments, but its sentiments are too often cloying. A-III (br)

Desperately Seeking Susan (1985) A New Jersey housewife (Rosanna Arquette) exchanges identities with a Manhattan playgirl (Madonna) in this screwball comedy directed by Susan Seidelman. Bright at moments but for the most part limp. Benign view of adultery and some exploitation of nudity. O (PG-13) 15

Destination Tokyo (1943) Wartime morale booster about an American submarine (captained by Cary Grant) sneaking into Tokyo Bay to guide bombers from nearby aircraft carriers in the first air attack on Japan's capital. Though dated by its patriotic rhetoric, this tribute to the "silent service" is directed by Delmer Daves with

credible attention to the tensions of duty aboard a sub, abetted by a good cast (Alan Hale, John Garfield and Dane Clark among them), suspenseful battle sequences and a textbook emergency appendectomy. Wartime violence and menace. A-I (br) U

Destry Rides Again (1939) Western sheriff (James Stewart) uses his wits rather than his dead aim with a six-shooter to rid a lawless town of its ruthless boss (Brian Donlevy). Director George Marshall mixes humor and action in equal measure abetted by a solid all-around cast, including Marlene Dietrich as a barroom singer ("See What the Boys in the Back Room Will Have") who shows her mettle in a knockdown brawl with Una Merkel. Stylized gunplay and fisticuffs. A-II (br) U

Destroy All Monsters (1969) It is 1999 and such monsters as Godzilla and Rodan have been exiled to Monsterland in remote Oceania from which they are unleashed by space aliens who want to make Earth their new home. Director Ishiro Honda's model work and special effects are unconvincing but fun for those who liked earlier editions of these Japanese monster movies. A-I (G)

Destroyer (1943) Patriotic World War II programmer from director William Seiter follows the course of a retired Navy seaman (Edward G. Robinson) who wangles sea duty on a troubled destroyer, bullies its crew (including Glenn Ford) but proves a hero under enemy fire. Wartime violence. A-I (br) U

Destructors, The (1974) Drug-syndicate thriller about a Paris-based U.S. narcotics agent (Anthony Quinn) who goes outside the law to nab the heads of rival syndicates (Michael Caine and James Mason). Directed by Robert Parrish, it is for those who like escapist action entertainment. Some violence in an amoral atmosphere. A-III (PG)

Detective, The (1954) British adaptation of the adventures of G.K. Chester-ton's amateur sleuth, Father Brown. Directed by Robert Hamer and with Alec Guinness in the title role, the movie offers a dandy mystery and some intelligent entertainment. A-I (br) 15

Detective, The (1968) Tough but honest New York cop (Frank Sinatra) has a number of problems, including railroading an innocent psychotic into the electric chair and a bad marriage to a nymphomaniac (Lee Remick). Gordon Douglas' flat-footed direction bludgeons home its condemnation of big city crime and corruption, mostly through rather lurid depictions of homosexual practices and much crude language. O (br)

Detective Belli (1971) Failed Italian crime melodrama in which crooked Rome cop (Franco Nero) supplements his paycheck by keeping the precocious son of a rich lawyer (Aldolfo Celli) out of harm's way. The plot is jumbled enough without director Romolo Guerreri adding to the confusion with jump cuts, flashy zooms and ragged editing. Stylized violence and brief nudity. A-III (R)

Detective Story (1951) Powerful adaptation of Sidney Kingsley's play about a day in a New York City police station beginning with the arrest of a shoplifter (Lee Grant) and ending with a dying cop's Act of Contrition. At the center of events is an idealistic but overbearing detective (Kirk Douglas) who brings in a petty thief (Craig Hill), slaps around an abortionist (George Macready), breaks up with his wife (Eleanor Parker) and stops an escaping crook (Joseph Wiseman). Director William Wyler keeps the set piece humming with finely honed character types including the weary precinct captain (Horace MacMahon) and a sympathetic cop (William Bendix). Veiled references to abortion and stylized violence. A-II (br) X

Detour (1969) Touching Bulgarian story of a chance meeting of two former lovers who had had a brief affair 17 years before when they were idealistic college students. Their nostalgic remembrances are told succinctly and with restraint, while their renewed affections and awkward present situations are handled sympathetically and with grace. A-III (PG) A

Detroit 9000 (1973) The title is the signal used by the Detroit police force to indicate an officer in need of assistance and the predictable story is of a cop (Alex Rocco) who doesn't want any assistance, let alone that of the black partner (Hari Rhodes) assigned him. Director Arthur Marks handles the action and supertough dialogue quite well, although the constant grittiness of both is eventually enervating. Excessive violence and brief nudity. O (R)

Devil and Daniel Webster (1941) Crackerjack adaptation of Stephen Vincent Benet's story about a New England farmer (James Craig) who sells his soul to the devil (John Huston), then hires lawyer Webster (Edward Arnold) to argue his case before a jury from hell. Directed by William Dieterle, it's a classic piece of regional Americana whose fantasy elements range from the sunny and playful to the dark and sinister, owing much of its success to Joseph August's evocative photography. Highly entertaining tussle between good and evil, though some fairly intense scenes for young children. A-II (br)

Devil and Max Devlin, The (1980) Sour owner of a rundown apartment house (Elliott Gould) plummets into hell after being struck by a bus while in pursuit of a jogger behind in his rent. Fiendishly unfunny fantasy has Satan's left-hand man (Bill Cosby) offer him a deal to escape damnation if he delivers the souls of three young people. Disney movie directed by Steven Hill Stern gives Cosby next to nothing to do and Gould, especially charmless here, has far too much. Some mild vulgarity. A-II (PG)

Devil by the Tail (1969) Breezy, exuberant French comedy about a once-noble family who maintain their ancient chateau by running it as a hotel, helped by the local garage mechanic's disabling passing automobiles, one of which belongs to a bank robber (Yves Montand) whose loot could permanently solve the family's financial woes. Directed by Philippe de Broca, the plot weaves in and out of comic situations with amazing speed and vivacity. Its amoral and unscrupulous stereotyped characters are in the great tradition of frothy farce. Adult situations. A-III (PG)

Devil Commands, The (1941) Low-budget horror movie directed by Edward Dmytryk with mad scientist Boris Karloff trying to establish contact with his dead wife through the brain waves of spiritualist Anne Revere and a coven of cadavers. Gruesome concept and treatment. A-III (br)

Devil Doll (1936) Using a deceased scientist's discovery for shrinking animals and people to fountain-pen size, Lionel Barrymore seeks revenge on his former banking partners who framed him and sent him to prison. Director Todd Browning's horror classic offers a fine cast in a good story supported by some ingenious special effects. A-II (br) X

Devil in Love, The (1968) An Italian comedy in which a devil (Vittorio Gassman), sent by Satan to provoke war between Renaissance Florence and the Papal States, falls in love with a princess and loses his diabolical powers. Directed by Ettore Scola, the movie has a sniggering script with a lascivious, overacted central character and nasty jabs at religious figures. Sexually suggestive situations and dialogue. O (br)

Devil in Miss Jones, The (1973) Hardcore porno item boasting limitless artistic pretensions and lush photography, but otherwise as totally degrading to watch as it must have been to enact. O (X)

Devil Is a Woman, The (1975) Italian potboiler with Glenda Jackson as the mother superior of what seems to be a cross between a medieval monastery and an early 1960s' Italian Holiday Inn. Director Damiano Damiani postulates institutional religion as a repressive force that stifles any sense of self-determination. Not only is the movie hopelessly adrift in depicting religious belief and practice, but its sexual implications are offensive. O (R)

Devil Rider (1971) Low-budget motorcycle movie about a biker gang hanging around Miami Beach and terrorizing two sisters and those who try to help them. Director Brad F. Grinter exploits an amateur cast with an emphasis on brutality and leering sex. O (R)

Devil within Her, The (1976) After many mysterious complications, a pregnant woman (Joan Collins) gives birth to a murderous baby in a clumsy, repulsive British horror movie directed by Peter Sasdy. Gore and nudity. O (R)

Devil's Bride, The (1968) Adequate British horror movie in which Christopher Lee is the hero in fighting a sect of devil worshippers. Directed by Terence Fisher, there is a lot of hokum about black magic, but the forces of good are more than equal to those of darkness. Mild violence. A-II (br)

Devil's Brigade, The (1968) World War II movie based on the training and battle experiences in Italy of the Special Service Force, the forerunner of the Green Berets. William Holden stars in the rather routine men-in-battle epic directed by Andrew V. McLaglen showing the hard work that prepares soldiers for the stress and grimness of combat. Wartime violence. A-III (br) A

Devil's Doorway (1950) Decorated for bravery as a Union soldier in the Civil War, a Shoshone Indian (Robert Taylor) returns to his Wyoming ranch but a fanatic Indian-hater (Louis Calhern) tries to drive him and his people off their fertile lands by stirring up a range war. Director Anthony Mann handles the Vanishing-American theme with much sympathy and plenty of action culminating in a truly tragic last stand. Stylized violence. A-I (br) U

Devil's Eight, The (1969) A federal agent (Christopher George) springs a group of convicts (led by Ross Hagan) from a Southern prison and cowers them into helping him crack a whiskey-running operation. Producer-director Burt Topper manages to mix questions of law enforcement, racial justice and the hippie philosophy together with scenes of violent action, fast cars and suggestions of promiscuity without any sense of priorities, taste or judgment. O (M)

Devil's Rain (1975) Routine horror movie stars Ernest Borgnine who gives an embarrassingly broad performance in his central role as a satanic recruiter. Director Robert Fuest's gimmick of having most of the cast melt away at the end is in keeping with his lack of interest in the logical and religious nuances of the subject in favor of simple gory visuals. A-III (PG)

Devil's Widow, The (see: "Tam Lin").

Devils, The (1971) Failed British adaptation of the Aldous Huxley novel about the demonic possession of a 17th-century French convent (led by Vanessa Redgrave) and the burning of a local priest (Oliver Reed) for his alleged commerce with the devil. Director Ken Russell's attempts to shock with scenes such as nuns cavorting at the altar in the nude are pathetic both in their imagination and in their execution. O (X/R) X

Dial M for Murder (1954) Talky suspense thriller from Frederick Knott's play about a London cad (Ray Milland) whose plan to murder his wealthy wife (Grace Kelly) boomerangs, thanks partly to a shrewd police inspector (John Williams) and the wife's ardent friend (Robert Cummings). Director Alfred Hitchcock handles the intricately plotted narrative deftly but without his usual flair for edge-of-the-seat tension. Intermittent menace and stylized treatment of a grisly murder. A-II (br) PG

Diamonds (1975) Dull jewel-heist caper with an ex-con (Richard Roundtree) and girlfriend (Barbara Seagull Hershey) being recruited by a wealthy London jeweler (Robert Shaw) to break into a mammoth jewelry exchange in Jerusalem. Director Menahem Golan succeeds much better as an Israeli travelogue than as crime melodrama with fleeting nudity and crude language. A-III (PG) A

Diamonds Are Forever (1971) This time James Bond's antagonist is intent on cornering the world diamond market in order to finance still worse villainy. British production directed Guy Hamilton lacks the wit and wizardry with which the 007 series began and everything about this entry seems tired including Sean Connery's performance. Usual stylized violence and sexual byplay. A-III (PG)

Diary of a Country Priest (1951) Director Robert Bresson's classic adaptation of the Georges Bernanos novel is a study in anguish, doubt and frustrated zeal set in the bleak Normandy countryside where a dedicated priest tries to revitalize a rundown parish but is regarded with suspicion by the locals. The diary format serves to evoke the interior life of a lonely soul who accepts his trials and ultimately finds peace within himself. The subtitled French production presents aspects of religious faith and human responses that make it ideal for study and discussion. A-II (br) U

Diary of a Mad Housewife (1970) Attractive Manhattan housewife (Carrie Snodgrass in a fine performance) rebels against her frustrating domestic life with an egotistical, social-climbing lawyer husband (Richard Benjamin) by acquiring a lover

(Frank Langella) who proves an equally unenlightened male chauvinist. Director Frank Perry's exercise in women's liberation issues is ultimately unsatisfying in its melodramatic conclusion with the mental breakdown of its affluent but unfulfilled housewife-victim. Some harsh language and brief nudity. A-IV (R) X

Diary of a Madman (1963) Pedestrian psychological thriller set in 19th-century France where a respected magistrate (Vincent Price) is driven to commit murder after he comes to believe he is possessed by a demon. Director Reginald Le Borg fails to create any sense of the supernatural and gets only limp suspense out of this talky exercise in horror. Overwrought menace and a few scenes of stylized violence. A-II (br) X

Diary of a Schizophrenic Girl (1970) Disappointing dramatization of the recovery of a mentally disturbed patient (Ghislaine D'Orsay) through the ministrations of a woman therapist (Margarita Lozano). Director Nelo Risi's plodding study spends too much time documenting the background and course of illness rather than on the cure. A-III (GP)

Diary of a Shinjuku Burglar (1973) Pretentious Japanese movie uses a young couple's confusion about their sexual identity to supposedly mirror the conflicting realities of the Tokyo student district of Shinjuku. Director Nagisa Oshima uses a number of confusing techniques that don't reflect much of anything for American viewers. Several very graphic sex sequences. O (nr) X

Diary of Forbidden Dreams (see "What?").

Dick Tracy (1990) Chester Gould's comic-strip detective (Warren Beatty, who also produced and directed) tries to get the goods on a mob syndicate headed by Big Boy Caprice (Al Pacino) with some help along the way from a seductive singer (Madonna), a streetwise orphan (Charlie Korsmo) and the hero's steadfast girlfriend, Tess Trueheart (Glenne Headley). Beatty deadpans his way through a plodding, threadbare cops-and-robbers script, Pacino chews up all the scenery in sight and a notable supporting cast languishes under mounds of make-up, leaving viewers disappointed with everything but Richard Sylbert's evocative 1930s' set designs. Several relatively mild double entendres and much comic-book violence ranging from menace to elaborate shoot-outs. A-II (PG)

Did You Hear the One about the Traveling Saleslady? (1968) A corny, cliche-ridden vehicle for comedienne Phyllis Diller who plays a player-piano peddler in a Missouri town circa 1910. Tedious. A-I (br) U

Die Hard (1988) When a band of savvy terrorists take over a L.A. high-rise on Christmas Eve, they're no match for a New York cop (Bruce Willis) who happens to be there visiting his estranged wife (Bonnie Bedelia). Director John McTiernan mixes thrills and chills with humorous banter and in-jokes, but its picture of conscienceless terrorist brutalities contains excessive graphic violence and rough language. O (R) 18

Die Hard II (1990) This time Det. John McClane (Bruce Willis) takes on an elite band of terrorists who have taken control of Washington D.C.'s Dulles airport while the plane his wife (Bonnie Bedelia) is in is rapidly running out of fuel in the raging blizzard overhead. As directed by Renny Harlin, this sequel matches the intense excitement, explosive special effects and welcome comic relief of the original film while surpassing its level of violence with constant, calculated and cold-blooded slaughters. Excessively graphic brutality and violence, much rough language and brief male nudity. O (R) 15

Die Laughing (1980) Young cabdriver (Robby Benson who also worked on the screenplay), accused of murdering a famous nuclear scientist, tries to clear himself with the aid of his girlfriend (Linda Grovenor) and a monkey. Directed by Jeff Werner, the lame comedy-mystery is mediocre entertainment in every respect. Violence. A-III (PG)

Die, Monster, Die (1966) Weak British horror movie directed by Daniel Haller with Boris Karloff playing a sort of contemporary wizard. Mild violence. A-II (br)

Different Story, A (1978) Failed romantic comedy in which boy meets girl (Perry King and Meg Foster) and, though both are homosexual, they settle down to a happily married life, complete with baby. Directed by Paul Aaron, there are few amusing lines and a good performance from Foster, but its rough language and a nude sequence are excessive. O (R/PG) AA

Digby, the Biggest Dog in the World (1974) British children's fantasy in which a lonely boy (Richard Beaumont) loses his dog when it consumes a secret growth chemical, expands to the size of three elephants and terrorizes the countryside. Director Joseph McGrath makes the most of a good cast of zanies (Jim Dale, Spike Milligan, Milo O'Shea and Victor Spinetti) who come to the lad's rescue in a shaggy dog story that relies on funny dialogue and comic gesture rather than transparent special effects. For the kids, but most parents will get some enjoyment too. A-I (G) U

Diggstown (1992) An ex-con (James Woods) outcons a con man (Bruce Dern) by betting millions on an aging ex-boxer (Louis

Gossett, Jr.) being able to beat 10 men in the ring in a single night. Director Michael Ritchie serves up lowest-common-denominator humor in brutally physical conflicts whose dramatic elements are sacrificed for cheap laughs. Extended bloody bouts, some sexual innuendo and recurring rough language. A-III (R)

Dillinger (1973) The crime odyssey of John Dillinger (Warren Oates) through the 1930s' Midwest is paralleled with the obsession of FBI agent Melvin Purvis (Ben Johnson) to capture the fear of criminals and the respect of the public. Written and directed by John Milius, the acting and period settings are very good and the special effects are appropriately brutal and eye-catching. Although extremely violent, one should emerge from the experience a little more reflective about our national fascination with guns. A-IV (R) X

Dimples (1936) Shirley Temple vehicle set in pre-Civil War New York where the little star plays a street urchin cared for by a rascally dishonest grandfather (Frank Morgan) until he's reformed by a wealthy matron (Helen Westley) interested in the girl's welfare. Director William A. Seiter peps up the sentimental plot with appealing musical numbers and colorful period settings, including scenes from "Uncle Tom's Cabin" with Shirley in the tragic role of Little Eva. Dated black stereotypes and Shirley in a blackface routine. A-I (br) U

Diner (1982) Low-keyed, humane and often very funny movie about several young men whose favorite hangout is a diner in 1959 Baltimore. Now in their early twenties, they still want to cling to the carefree life of high school days. Writer-director Barry Levinson has come up with an offbeat and entertaining piece that in its modest way is also a worthwhile one. A major portion of the dialogue is concerned with sex and there is a sequence involving a lewd practical joke. A-III (R) AA

Dinosaurus! (1960) Woefully inept fantasy directed by Irvin S. Yeaworth, Jr., takes place on a remote island whose inhabitants panic when a caveman and a couple of dinosaurs are dynamited out of their suspended animation and into the 20th century. Much silliness and some stylized violence. A-I (br)

Dionysus in '69 (1970) Filmed performance of an experimental play loosely based on Euripides depends mainly on its own uninhibited eroticism and the unrestrained participation of the audience. Director Brian De Palma records the proceedings in wave after wave of split-screen nakedness and orgiastic behavior that has little to do with art but seems more related to cheap exploitation. O (nr)

Dirt Gang, The (1972) Rampaging biker gang invades a western movie set and proceeds to terrorize and otherwise debauch the movie-makers until a movie stuntman (Michael Forest) pummels the gang's leader to death in a bike duel. Directed by Jerry Jameson, its combination of sex and violence is grossly offensive. O (R)

Dirty Dancing (1987) Coming-of-age story set in the 1960s about a middle-class girl (Jennifer Grey) and a local dancer (Patrick Swayze) who teaches her a few bold new steps. Director Emile Ardolino's lightweight effort at evoking the teen scene of a generation ago uses an ill-conceived plot contrivance about an abortion, brief nudity and an acceptance of casual sex. A-III (PG-13) 15

Dirty Dingus Magee (1970) Western spoof with Frank Sinatra in the title role as an outlaw involved with a town whose mayor (Anne Jackson) is also a madam whose brothel business thrives on a cavalry clientele and to keep them around she orders the sheriff (George Kennedy) to incite an Indian uprising. Director Burt Kennedy has a field day altering allegiances in a mad cacophony of discordant sequences that are juvenile in their attempts to ridicule the Old West and tiresome in their constant leering. Boisterous, bawdy and dumb. A-III (GP) AA

Dirty Dozen, The (1967) World War II story about a free-wheeling officer (Lee Marvin) and the dozen army convicts he trains to destroy the headquarters of the German General Staff. Directed by Robert Aldrich, the movie is savage in its violence, yet raises questions about authorized brutality. A-IV (br) 15

Dirty Game, The (1966) Jumbled European-produced espionage movie with Henry Fonda, Vittorio Gassman, Robert Ryan and directors Terence Young, Christian-Jaque and Carlo Lizzani. Some violence and sexual innuendo. A-III (br)

Dirty Hands (1976) Silly, convoluted plot about a wife (Romy Schneider) who plots with lover to murder drunken, maudlin husband (Rod Steiger in a self-indulgent performance). French production written and directed by Claude Chabrol is a sordid little story of marital infidelity and contains some nudity. O (R)

Dirty Harry (1971) Clint Eastwood stars as a hard-boiled detective of the San Francisco homicide squad who takes the law into his own hands when a psychotic killer is released on a technicality. Director Don Siegel keeps the action tightly wound and fast-paced, but his cynical superhero is basically irresponsible in endangering the lives of innocent people in his personal crusade against criminals. Harry is clearly dangerous and so is a movie that evades the complex legal problems and moral issues of vigilante justice. Sadistic brutality and graphic violence. O (R) X

Dirty Little Billy (1973) The story of how and why Billy the Kid (Michael J. Pollard) began his life of crime is told by director Stan Dragoti by making him the victim of the times and circumstances, an idea neither very new nor very stimulating and, at any rate, goes nowhere. Contains a barrage of gritty, peripheral sex and violence. A-IV (R) X

Dirty Mary, Crazy Larry (1974) Peter Fonda and Adam Roarke extort big money from supermarket executive Roddy McDowall, pick up Susan George, and destroy every car is sight while trying to escape with the cash. Directed by John Hough, it is thin action entertainment with an abundance of rough language. A-III (PG) X

Dirty O'Neil (1974) Small-town policeman (Morgan Paull) finds his job less challenging than trying to bed the area's entire female population until three thugs come to town and sodomize his steady girlfriend. Directors Howard Freen and Lewis Teague start with a sex farce that ends in sordid, sickening violence. O (R)

Dirty Outlaws, The (1972) Pallid Italian western directed by Franco Rossetti tells the story of a desperado (Chip Corman) who seeks gold and discovers that his heart is made of it. Some fairly benign violence. A-III (R)

Dirty Rotten Scoundrels (1988) Two rogues (dapper Michael Caine and slovenly Steve Martin) who specialize in conning women out of their money in a lucrative Riviera resort vie in a comic battle to bilk an American (Glenne Headly) out of $50,000. Director Frank Oz makes the most of his gorgeous Riviera setting, but the film lacks major laughs and a heart in its cynical attitude toward women as easily conned targets. Mild sexual innuendo and bathroom humor. A-III (PG)

Dirty Tricks (1981) Harvard history professor (Elliott Gould) and a television newswoman (Kate Jackson) are the unwitting targets of gangsters and government men in this inane comedy-thriller directed by Alvin Rakoff. Some leering humor. A-III (PG)

Dirtymouth (1971) At the time of his death, controversial comedian Lenny Bruce was the center of a legal storm that has far-reaching implications about the freedom of expression in modern society. Viewers of Herbert Altman's documentary will get little insight into the man and, more importantly, will come away without any perspective on his times. The failure exploits an already tragic career. O (nr)

Discreet Charm of the Bourgeoisie, The (1972) Director Luis Bunuel's surrealistic satire on the lives of the very rich presents an incredibly complicated series of events, such as dreamers dreaming of other dreamers, that grows more satisfying as the narrative becomes more outrageously illogical. The central recurring situation is that of six wealthy friends (Fernando Rey, Delphine Seyrig, Stephane Audran, Bulle Ogier, Jean-Pierre Cassel and Michel Piccoli) about to sit down to dinner but always being interrupted by something that prevents them from being able to proceed with the meal. The movie is meant to be enjoyed as something as playful as the title itself. A-III (PG) AA

Disorderlies (1987) The Fat Boys, a rap music group, star as health-care interns who unwittingly foil inept nephew Anthony Geary's plot to do in his wealthy uncle (Ralph Bellamy). Director Michael Schultz's not-exactly uplifting comedy relies on pure physical slapstick brought off amiably by the funky boys and is marred only by some mildly crude language and a brief nude swimming scene. A-II (PG)

Disorganized Crime (1989) Four seasoned cons (Ruben Blades, Fred Gwynne, Lou Diamond Phillips and William Russ) plan the heist of a small-town Montana bank without their ringleader (Corbin Bernsen) who is dodging the clutches of two dim-witted detectives (Ed O'Neill and Daniel Roebuck). Though all the disorganized running around makes for slapstick moments, director Jim Kouf doesn't take full advantage of his actors' potential. Rough language, cartoon violence and phoney glamorization of career criminals. A-III (R)

Distance (1976) Black sergeant (Paul Benjamin), on a Georgia army post in 1956, becomes estranged from his German wife (Eija Pokkinen), a woman desperately trying to save her marriage and her own sense of worth. With good acting, strong characterizations and period authenticity, Anthony Lover directs a meaningful story of alienation, but the fragile web of relationships that had been developing so well is finally overwhelmed by a needlessly melodramatic climax. Adult situations. A-III (R)

Distant Thunder (1975) Indian production about a young Brahman couple whose quiet, secure lives in a small Bengali village are disrupted and their modest expectations destroyed in the terrible famine of 1943 when more than five million people starved to death. Showing the gradual breakdown of village society as rice shortages and hunger grow, director Satyajit Ray makes the viewer share his compassion and anger for the fate of those anonymous victims of a catastrophe caused by World War II. Moving but unsentimental, it is also a cogent parable for our own times. A-II (nr) A

Distant Voices, Still Lives (1989) Visually beautiful but tedious autobiographical movie dramatizing filmmaker Terence Davies' working-class family roots in Liverpool, England, during the 1940s and 1950s. Impressionistic shots of various family rites of passage wear thin and ultimately tend to confound viewers about the family's troubled dynamics in which Catholic ritual and period music seem the only positive unifying forces. Several rough scenes of family violence and verbal abuse. A-III (PG-13) 15

Distinguished Gentleman, The (1992) Artificial comedy about a sleazy Florida con artist (Eddie Murphy) who gets elected to Congress, goes far on the government gravy train, then has an improbable change of heart by going public with evidence of graft on the part of his political mentor (Lane Smith). Director Jonathan Lynn plays "Mr. Smith Goes to Washington" for laughs but doesn't get many out of a clumsy comic vehicle for a performer who's made a career out of insincere grins and foul language. Comic depiction of a sexual encounter, much sexual innuendo and recurring rough language. A-III (R) 15

Diva (1982) Bright French production recounting the adventures of a romantic 18-year-old postman (Frederic Andrei), obsessed with an opera diva (Wilhelmenia Wiggins Fernandez), but when he records her performance at a concert, his tape gets mixed up with one incriminating some gangsters and the chase is on through the streets and subways of Paris. Jean-Jacques Beineix directs a diverting tongue-in-cheek thriller that's an all-style, no-substance entertainment. Violence and brief nudity. A-III (R) 15

Divine Mr. J., The (1974) Thoroughly mindless, abysmally inept, yawningly unfunny attempt to satirize the New Testament. Cast as a Flatbush-accented Virgin Mary, Bette Midler appears to be totally without any redeeming talent, a condition afflicting the rest of the cast in this low satire. O (R)

Divine Nymph, The (1979) Italian study of upper-class decadence after World War I from director Giuseppe Patroni Griffi tells the story of an insensitive woman (Laura Antonelli) who drives one lover (Terence Stamp) to suicide and another (Marcello Mastroianni) to join the Fascists. The theme of the destructive force of thwarted passion is given surface treatment as is the unclothed figure of its heroine. O (nr) A

Divorce American Style (1967) Dick Van Dyke and Debbie Reynolds have to decide whether to call it a day after 17 years of marriage and one of separation in their divorce-riddled California community. Producer-writer Norman Lear and director Bud Yorkin have come up with an entertaining satire that touches all the bases: the senseless rift, the well-meant advice, the legal razzle-dazzle, the shuffled offspring, the social plight of disconnected spouse, the financial bite. Well paced and occasionally very funny, it's a good try that largely succeeds. A-III (br) A

Do the Right Thing (1989) After 25 years of selling pizza in the same Bedford-Stuyvesant neighborhood, now black and Hispanic, Italian-American Sal (Danny Aiello) attempts to squash racial tensions before they destroy his family business. Writer-director-actor Spike Lee concocts a powerful look at racism with passionate characters, sharp satire, savvy musical counterpoints, theatricality and much humor. Its incendiary point of view—that violence may be a potentially justified means to an end—will unsettle many and force viewers to confront stereotypes. Heavy profanity, racial and ethnic slurs, intense climactic racial violence and a brief sexual scene with fleeting nudity. A-IV (R) 18

D.O.A. (1988) During an all-night drinking binge, a burned-out college professor (Dennis Quaid) somehow chugs a cocktail spiked with slow-acting poison and, with only 24 hours to live and the aid of a naive student (Meg Ryan), he maniacally tracks down his killer. Directed by British husband-wife team Rocky Morton and Annabel Jankel, the remake of the 1949 Hollywood thriller is entertaining but intense and not for the squeamish. Much violence and incidental profanity. A-IV (R) 15

Doberman Gang, The (1972) Enterprising gang (Byron Mabe, Julie Parrish and Hal Reed) uses a pack of doberman pinscher attack dogs in an intricate, highly orchestrated bank robbery. Director Byron Chudnow's inventive low-budget heist movie depends on an element of terror that attack dogs provide and has some mild love-making scenes. A-III (PG/G) U

Doc (1971) Stacy Keach stars as legendary gunfighter and gambler Doc Holliday. Director Frank Perry's re-creation of an oft-told tale attempts to turn the events leading up to the gunfight at the O.K. Corral into some sort of allegory about American involvement in Vietnam and the movie collapses under the weight of its pretensions. Considerable violence. A-III (PG) AA

Doc Hollywood (1991) Enroute to a lucrative plastic surgery practice in Beverly Hills, a young doctor (Michael J. Fox) is stranded by a car mishap in a folksy Southern town eager to keep him as their general practitioner. The corn is higher than an elephant's eye in director Michael Caton-Jones' syrupy, contrived and predictable tribute to small-town life. Scene with full frontal nudity and minimal vulgar language. A-III (PG) 12

Doctor, The (1991) Stricken with throat cancer, an arrogant physician (William Hurt) bristles at his treatment as a lowly patient but, inspired by a fellow sufferer (Elizabeth Perkins) and supported by his neglected wife (Christine Lahti), the experience unexpectedly enriches his life. Director Randa Haines gets some fine performances while fully developing the human element that often gets lost in modern, impersonal hospital settings. A suggestive song lyric, minimal rough language and graphic shots of open-heart surgery. A-II (PG-13) 12

Doctor and the Devils, The (1985) An often-too-gleefully gruesome dramatization of a famous 19-century case involving a prominent surgeon (Timothy Dalton) who refuses to inquire into the source of the cadavers furnished him for his lectures in anatomy. Though well-directed by Freddie Francis, with an exceptionally literate script by Ronald Harwood based on a Dylan Thomas scenario plumbing its theme of ends and means. Violent, sordid environment and brief nudity. A-III (R) 15

Doctor Blood's Coffin (1961) Pedestrian horror story in which a mad scientist (Kieron Moore) returns to his country village to use its abandoned tin mines as the site for ghoulish experiments in human transplants. Director Sidney Furie's low-budget British production is a poor Frankenstein variation that creates little sense of terror, though it does have an horrific finish. Stylized violence. A-II (br) X

Doctor Death: Seeker of Souls (1973) John Considine plays the dastardly doctor who specializes in giving a new lease on life to the ailing by finding a body into which his client's soul can be liberated. Directed by Eddie Saeta, it is so witless in plot and execution that its bloody excesses become equally meaningless and boring. A-III (R)

Doctor Detroit (1983) A mild-mannered but oddball English professor (Dan Aykroyd) assumes the role of Doctor Detroit, a real bad gangster, in order to protect four prostitutes who have been abandoned by their pimp (Howard Hesseman). The shuttle back and forth between the two identities is the basis for most of the comedy, but under Michael Pressman's direction the

laughs are infrequent and mild at best. Sexually oriented humor, brief shots from a pornographic movie and a benign view of drug use. O (R)

Doctor Dolittle (1967) Gentle, turn-of-the-century musical fantasy about an eccentric animal doctor's adventures searching for the Great Pink Sea Snail. Rex Harrison stars as the doctor who can talk to animals in an attractive but slow-moving production directed by Richard Fleischer. Movie musical purists may be disappointed in Leslie Bricusse's uninspired screenplay, music and lyrics, but others, especially children, may be charmed. A-I (br)

Doctor Faustus (1968) British adaptation of Christopher Marlowe's classic drama about the German university professor (Richard Burton) who sells his soul to the devil for knowledge, power and a woman (Elizabeth Taylor). Directed by Burton and Nevill Coghill, the result is something of a witch's brew of scenes depicting the emptiness of the world, the flesh and the devil. Brief nudity. A-III (br)

Doctor Glas (1969) In late 19th-century Stockholm, a physician (Per Oscarsson) sexually obsessed with a young woman (Lone Hertz) poisons her much older minister husband (Ulf Palme), but his undetected crime gains him nothing except a life of increasing loneliness and frustration. One may admire the icy precision of Oscarsson's performance and director Mai Zetterling's restrained treatment of the material, but it remains no more than a repugnant case history with little in the way of human insight, significance or even dramatic involvement. O (M)

Doctor, You've Got to Be Kidding (1966) Glamorized treatment of teenage pregnancy in director Peter Tewksbury's vacuous movie starring Sandra Dee and George Hamilton is offensive, especially considering the juvenile audience to which it is directed. O (br) AA

Doctor Zhivago (1965) Boris Pasternak's novel has been turned into a romantic epic of the Russian Revolution and its effects upon various individuals (Julie Christie, Omar Sharif and Alec Guinness) struggling to survive in difficult times. Adapted by Robert Bolt and directed by David Lean, the Revolution serves as a rich backdrop for a bittersweet love story reflecting the disruption of lives and values caused by the turmoil of the time. Restrained treatment of violence. A-II (PG) 15

Doctors' Wives (1971) Dyan Cannon and Richard Crenna star in an adult soap opera about doctors in a posh California medical clinic who dally with the nurses while their wives find diversion elsewhere.

A colleague's fatal heart attack provides the necessary scandal and shame to motivate everyone back into their proper and respective beds. Ploddingly directed by George Schaefer, the shenanigans are mostly off-camera and recounted in euphemistic dialogue. Gruesome open-heart surgical sequence, but the movie itself has no heart or any real emotion for that matter. O (R) 18

Dodge City (1939) Ex-Confederate officer (Errol Flynn) heads a cattle drive to the railhead in Dodge, becomes sheriff of the lawless town and takes on the entire gang of its worst badman (Bruce Cabot). Director Michael Curtiz's action-packed Western includes a cattle stampede, an epic barroom brawl and shoot-outs galore, given some pace by romantic misunderstandings (Olivia de Havilland) and rough frontier humor (Alan Hale, Frank McHugh and Guinn Williams). Stylized violence. A-I (br) A

Dog Day Afternoon (1975) Al Pacino stars as a hapless Brooklyn bank robber whose plans go awry when the police arrive before he and an accomplice can flee. A taut, well-acted drama with comic overtones, director Sidney Lumet is consistently entertaining in his treatment of this fact-based incident, but the bisexual character of the hero (who needed money for his partner's sex-change operation), the rough language and the disquieting look at the seamy side of life limit its appeal. A-IV (R) 15

Dog of Flanders (1959) In a turn-of-the-century Antwerp suburb, an old man (Donald Crisp) and his small grandson (David Ladd) rescue a dog left to die at the roadside. Produced by Robert B. Radnitz and directed by James B. Clark, the movie shows how unselfish love and understanding bring happiness even under conditions of dire poverty. Fine family fare. A-I (br) U

Dogfight (1991) Coming-of-age story about a teenage Marine (River Phoenix) who, on his last night stateside in 1963, finds friendship and romance with the shy waitress (Lili Taylor) he originally picked up as part of a game to find the ugliest date. Director Nancy Savoca examines male peer pressure and lances sexist attitudes with some sensitivity but gets only lukewarm results. Implied premarital encounter, some sexual innuendo and frequent rough language. A-III (R)

Dogpound Shuffle (1975) Tap-dancing vagrant (Ron Moody) teams up with an itinerant harmonica player (David Soul) in order to make enough money to retrieve his impounded dog. Director Jeffrey Bloom's frequently moving study of the interaction between the two has an affirmative, spunky quality marred by an unnecessarily bloody fight scene and a few expletives. A-II (PG)

Dogs of War, The (1981) Screen version of Frederick Forsyth's novel about mercenaries (headed by Christopher Walken) hired to oust a bloody West African tyrant in order to replace him with a man just as bad but one who will be more amenable to foreign business interests. Though the movie lacks sympathetic and well-defined central characters, the narrative's action is handled quite well by director John Irvin. The result is an interesting melodrama with serious but ambiguous implications and some graphic violence. A-III (R) 15

Dolemite (1975) Black exploitation movie about an army of women Kung Fu killers features violence, sex and an army of non-actors. Its production values are on a par with a badly done home movie. O (R)

Doll Face (1945) Brassy but sentimental low-budget clunker directed by Lewis Seiler transforms a burlesque queen (Vivian Blaine) into a Broadway musical star, despite misunderstandings with her manager boyfriend (Dennis O'Keefe). Romantic complications and sexual innuendo. A-III (br) U

Doll's House, A (1973) Director Patrick Garland interprets Ibsen's play as anything but a repudiation of the married state. Fine cast (Claire Bloom, Anthony Hopkins, Ralph Richardson) conveys those qualities of maturity, compassion, and respect for the integrity of the individual without which human growth and fulfillment in marriage is impossible. It is a film for women who yearn to be emancipated, for women who have been and for men who have wondered why Women's Lib was even necessary. A-II (G) A

$ (Dollars) (1971) Richard Brooks wrote and directed this only occasionally amusing Hamburg bank heist action drama that features Warren Beatty as the brains of the bank's security system and Goldie Hawn as his brainless, high-priced hooker accomplice. Unfortunately Brooks' fascination with electronic gadgetry impedes the pace of the action, which creaks along too implausibly to maintain much interest. Short on comedy and high on ugly twists and brutal turns, the movie has large doses of nudity, sexual innuendo and crude language. O (R)

Dominick and Eugene (1988) Lovely story of an unlikely pair of 25-year-old fraternal twins—a mentally damaged garbage man (Tom Hulce) and a moody medical student (Ray Liotta)—following the traumas and conflicts that threaten to disrupt their close sibling bond and the positive changes that result. Director Robert M. Young sensitively underplays a child abuse subplot and does not exploit the violent potential of several incidents. A few sexually sugges-

tive scenes and some profanity. A-III (PG-13)
Domino Principle, The (1977) Gene Hackman plays a convict recruited by a powerful and mysterious group to carry out an assassination whose intended victim apparently is the President of the United States. Director Stanley Kramer disappointingly fails to deal with the political paranoia of our times in any significant fashion, settling instead for another pointless and simple-minded melodrama with violence. A-III (R)

Don Giovanni (1979) Great voices and sumptuously romantic Italian landscapes predominate in director Joseph Losey's screen version of the Mozart opera about a jilted woman (Kiri Te Kanawa) obsessed with her husband's damnation. Realistic treatment of the Don's compulsive sexuality takes on Marxist significance as a reflection of the conflict of the old regime with the working class. A cultural artifact whose romantic vision of adultery requires a mature perspective. A-IV (nr) A

Don Is Dead, The (1973) Crime godfather (Anthony Quinn) suffers a heart attack, triggering a power struggle to fill the vacuum. Directed by Richard Fleischer, it is a dull, mindless variation on a theme. Excessive violence. O (R) X

Don Juan, My Love (1991) Riotous Spanish comedy in which the legendary 16th-century lover Don Juan escapes Purgatory to do good on earth and earn a heavenly reward, only to be mistaken for a look-alike, drug-smuggling actor (Juan Luis Galiardo in a dual role) who is playing the part of Don Juan in a Seville production rife with backstage amorous intrigues. Director Antonio Mercero handles this screwball bedroom farce in good taste and Galiardo fully captures both the gentler nature of the well-intentioned Don Juan and the arrogance of his latter-day counterpart. Some bawdy humor, frequent sexual innuendo and brief rear nudity. A-III (nr)

Don Quixote (1973) A performance by the Australian Ballet Company of the Cervantes classic, co-directed by Rudolf Nureyev and Robert Helpmann, with Helpmann in the title role and Nureyev dancing that of the young Basilio. A-I (G) U

Dona Flor and Her Two Husbands (1978) Brazilian sex fantasy about a remarried widow visited by the ghost of her first mate is interesting chiefly for its exotic locales and characters. Directed by Bruno Barreto, the slight Boccaccio-like anecdote employs several graphic sex scenes. O (nr) X

Donovan's Reef (1963) Throwaway situation comedy with World War II vets (John Wayne; Lee Marvin; Jack Warden) beachcombing on a South Pacific isle when the daughter (Elizabeth Allen) of one of them makes a surprise visit. Director John Ford plays around with his familiar themes of male camaraderie and manly rivalry as well as the freedom of nature versus the restraints of civilization, but the result is less than original and only fitfully engaging. Slapstick violence and comic bathos. A-II (br) U

Don't Cry with Your Mouth Full (1975) Pastoral symphony about a not very eventful summer spent by a family in the South of France is lovely to look at, but drama consists of more than holding a mirror up to reality. The only element of tension is the older teenage daughter's impending loss of virginity, but even this is not exploited and nothing is allowed to get beneath the shimmering surface of things. Beautiful, human, naturalistic but disappointing. A-IV (nr)

Don't Drink the Water (1969) Hapless Newark caterer (Jackie Gleason) tours Europe with wife (Estelle Parsons) and daughter (Joan Delaney), but in the process their plane is hijacked to Vulgaria, an Iron Curtain country, where the family is mistaken for American spies. Written by Woody Allen and directed by Howard Morris, the comedy's brightest moments come during the credits when the family is preparing for the trip, which itself proves less than memorable. Obligatory, but tastelessly handled, romance between the daughter and the American ambassador's son (Ted Bessell) brings the whole affair to its inevitable happy conclusion. A-III (G)

Don't Give Up the Ship (1959) Feeble comedy about a pea-brained naval officer (Jerry Lewis) accused of losing a destroyer escort. Directed by Norman Taurog, the episodic nonsense taxes the patience more than it tickles the funnybone. Sexual innuendo, especially wedding-night references. A-III (br) U

Don't Go in the House (1980) When a little boy whose mother burns him as punishment for being naughty grows up, he doesn't want to set the world on fire, only mama and every other woman who reminds him of her. Starring Dan Grimaldi and directed by Joseph Ellison, it's a grisly piece of trash exploiting violence and nudity. O (R)

Don't Just Stand There (1968) Brainless comedy in which two Americans (Mary Tyler Moore and Robert Wagner) in Paris deal with the problems caused by an authoress who has gone on a pleasure cruise leaving the last chapter of her new sex novel unwritten. Directed by Ron Winston, the plot complications don't make much sense and, even if they did, they are not very amusing. Excessive sexual innuendo. O (br) A

Don't Look Back (1967) Feature documentary on folk singer Bob Dylan produced by D.A. Pennebaker during Dylan's 1965 concert tour of England. Filming the singer in performance and off stage, the documentary records his expression of the doubts, depressions and joys of his generation without comment or explanation. Some crude language. A-II (br)

Don't Look Now (1969) Zany slapstick World War II comedy done with style by Terry Thomas, Bourvil and Louis de Funes about the confused attempts of the crew of a downed British bomber to escape from Occupied France. Written and directed by Gerard Oury, the comedy routines and sight gags may not be entirely new, but they are done imaginatively and with verve by three great film clowns. The period supplies suspense and is never used to make wartime look like a lark. The Disney release provides superior entertainment for audiences of all ages. A-I (G)

Don't Look Now (1973) English couple (Donald Sutherland and Julie Christie), distraught about the drowning of their only child, attempt to regain their emotional balance as he helps restore a crumbling church in Venice. Sutherland's gift of second sight is pivotal to both their dead child and their deteriorating marriage in this psychic potboiler directed by Nicholas Roeg with moody, atmospheric photography. Extended scene of explicit love-making. O (R) 18

Don't Make Waves (1967) California beach-blanket movie geared toward the easy-living teenage set revolving around the attempts of undernourished Tony Curtis to woo shapely Sharon Tate away from her muscle-bound surfer boyfriends. Directed by Alexander Mackendrick, the movie's light-headed attitudes toward teenage sexuality make it somewhat tainted fare, especially for impressionable viewers. O (br) A

Don't Open the Window (1976) Italian-Spanish horror movie set in England, starring Arthur Kennedy affecting a thick Irish accent while the rest of the cast of characters are dubbed with very British accents. Unpretentious and fairly competent production, but mainly preoccupied with setting up scenes of gore. O (R)

Don't Raise the Bridge, Lower the River (1968) Jerry Lewis stars in and directs a British-made comedy about a semi-shady promoter who likes to do things the hard way. Most of the humor is typical Lewis farce, with some really funny sight (and sound) gags, as well as some slack stretches. Gap-toothed Terry-Terry-Thomas, Bernard Crib-

bins and some other British comedy pros lend some extra spark. A-II (G) U

Don't Tell Her It's Me (1990) A meddling sister (Shelley Long) tries to make a writer (Jami Gertz) fall in love with her insecure brother (Steve Guttenberg) by coaching him in assuming a swaggering macho personality complete with motorcycle and foreign accent. The laughs are meager in director Malcolm Mowbray's dim-witted comedy whose sappy situations and dialogue are well below the talents of Long and Guttenberg. Sexual references and a discreet scene of unmarried intimacy. A-III (PG-13) 12

Don't Tell Mom the Babysitter's Dead (1991) With mom in Australia for the summer, five kids enjoy life without supervision when their elderly babysitter dies suddenly, leaving a 17-year-old (Christina Applegate) to juggle a fashion job and pay the bills. Director Steven R. Herek's contrived comedy is really a female adolescent success fantasy that sags for long stretches after its one-joke premise wears thin. Uncritical depiction of teens smoking pot as well as occasional sexual references and vulgarities. A-III (PG-13) 12

Doors, The (1991) Fact-based musical biography of the pivotal 1960s' rock band of the title, whose hedonistic leader Jim Morrison (Val Kilmer) died at age 27, following years of constant drug and alcohol abuse. Director Oliver Stone presents an overblown, self-important "rocku-mentary" detailing Morrison's endless sexual escapades, non-stop boozing and drug highs while treating him as the tragic rock poet and cultural demigod of the age. Much promiscuity with full nudity, pervasive substance abuse and continual rough language. O (R) 18

Dorian Gray (1971) Italian adaptation of the Oscar Wilde story about a young man (Helmut Berger) who watches a painting of himself take on the spiritual decay of his soul while his physical exterior remains unblemished. Director Massimo Dallamano treats the story's perversions, ranging from sodomy to murder, in such coy fashion that its hero's many vices are as lackluster as they are corrupting. O (R)

Dossier 51 (1979) Tediously subjective melodrama about a minor French diplomat harassed by all the technique and technology an intelligence agency can bring to bear against him. Director Michel Deville's deliberate but failed attempts at humor and extensive use of nudity make the unexciting plot even more mindless. O (nr)

Double Con, The (see: "Trick Baby").

Double Edge (1992) Provocative drama views the Palestinian-Israeli conflict through the helter-skelter experiences of a newspaper reporter (Faye Dunaway) on a three-week assignment in Jerusalem where she is romanced by an Israeli writer (Amos Kollek). Also written and directed by Kollek, the result tries to be even-handed in its treatment of both sides, including statements from actual leaders in the region, while showing how the news media are manipulated by all factions in the conflict. Realistic depiction of political tensions that occasionally erupt in violence, an implied sexual relationship and some rough language. A-III (PG-13)

Double Impact (1991) Bloody martial arts movie about identical twins (Jean-Claude Van Damme), separated as infants but reunited 25 years later in Hong Kong where they hunt down their parents' drug-dealing murderers. Director Sheldon Lettich grinds out another slick action movie that exists solely to showcase escalating, mindless violence in an heroic setting that justifies murder as righteous vengeance. Excessive violence, a scene with nudity and intermittent rough language. O (R) 18

Double Indemnity (1944) Dark crime classic adapted from James M. Cain's novel about a treacherous woman (Barbara Stanwyck) who conspires with an insurance agent (Fred MacMurray) to make her husband's murder look like an accident but before they can collect on his policy, a company investigator (Edward G. Robinson) begins to get wise. Directed by Billy Wilder, who also gets credit for co-writing the script with Raymond Chandler, the intricate plot centers on the furtive, greedy pair whose mistrust of each other finally ends in mutual betrayal. Riveting tale of crime and punishment, with hard-bitten performances, brightly cynical dialogue and darkly atmospheric imagery. A-II (br) A

Double Life of Veronique, The (1991) Two young women, one Polish and one French, are strangely linked by identical looks, musical talents and frail hearts. Director Krzystof Kieslowski's lyrical tale of unexplained spiritual bonding is given considerable emotional force by Irene Jacob's ethereal and haunting performance as the two Veroniques. Subtitles. A few restrained scenes of sexual encounters with some nudity. A-III (nr) 15

Double Man, The (1968) Routine spy thriller about a CIA agent (Yul Brynner) who ventures to the Swiss Alps to investigate his son's murder which, it turns out, was set up to lure him into a trap so that a look-alike (also played by Brynner) can take his place and infiltrate the U.S. intelligence network. British production directed by Franklin Schaffner, its intriguing premise had promise that is left largely unrealized. A-I (br) PG

Double Ransom (see: "The Terrorists").

Double Trouble (1967) Elvis Presley vehicle casts the singer as a nightclub entertainer playing London and pleasantly plagued by pretty, love-struck fan Annette Day. Directed by Norman Taurog, the plot includes a parental attempt to break up the romance, a spate of spies and nine well-swiveled song numbers. A-II (br)

Dove, The (1974) Fact-based odyssey of a 16-year-old (Joseph Bottoms) who sets out to sail around the world in a 23-foot sloop of the title until he meets an Australian girl (Deborah Raffin) and decides to marry, but she convinces him to complete his journey first. Directed by Charles Jarrott and beautifully photographed by Sven Nyquist, the entertaining adventure would appeal to youngsters, but the moral ambiguities of the early stages of the Bottoms-Raffin relationship warrant labeling it as adult fare. A-III (PG)

Down and Dirty (1979) Director Ettore Scola's Italian farce stars Nino Manfredi as a drunken, lecherous patriarch of an extended family of poverty-stricken street-folk trying to grab the insurance money he received after the loss of an eye. Irreverent, unkind attempt to derive comedy from human degradation and ignorance replete with sexual references. O (nr)

Down and Out in Beverly Hills (1986) Nick Nolte portrays a supertramp who relieves everyone's misery in a jaded and spoiled Beverly Hills household. Director Paul Mazursky's movie is an overly simplified tale of manners and morals poking fun at the tribulations of a suddenly rich family headed by Richard Dreyfuss and Bette Midler. Its farcical treatment of sex as a remedy for all ills marks it as a misguided burlesque, carefully avoiding any sense of conviction or consequence. O (R) 15

Down by Law (1986) This lighthearted comedy begins with a breezy introduction to three likeable but corrupt residents of Louisiana's bayou country. The friendship and humorous camaraderie that develop after they are wrongfully sent to jail propels them to escape detention and try to start new and more rewarding lives for themselves. Some profanity and nudity. A-III (R) 15

Down the Ancient Stairs (1975) Italian movie set in an insane asylum in the 1930s whose lecherous director (Marcello Mastroianni) gets his comeuppance from a new, no-nonsense assistant (Francoise Fabian). Director Mauro Bolognini draws a half-hearted parallel between the madness inside the asylum and the madness of an Italy rapt in Fascist frenzy, but he covers its flaws by baring a good deal of flesh. O (R)

Downhill Racer (1969) Robert Redford plays a surly American skier with enough recklessness and skill to challenge the best Europeans but is unwilling to listen to his team's tough, long-suffering coach (admirably played by Gene Hackman) in preparing for the big skiing competition. Though the personal drama follows the formula of such sports movies, director Michael Ritchie concentrates on providing a vivid overview of a dangerous and photogenic sport and the fallible people who compete in it for the psychological rewards that some find worth all its rigors and traumatic nervous strain. A-III (PG)

Downtown (1990) Hot-headed black cop (Forest Whitaker) and rookie white cop (Anthony Edwards) make a mismatched but likeable team in inner city Philadelphia as they investigate a psycho cop killer and a drug smuggling operation that smells like an inside job. Director Richard Benjamin injects some humanizing family touches and nutty humor, but the contrived drug bust scenario ambles along to a predictable grisly close that sees the good guys win validation for their unorthodox police work amidst much bloodshed. Much profanity laced with sexual vulgarities; grisly, gratuitous violence and a flash of nudity. O (R) 18

Dr. Bethune (1993) Fact-based story of the fiery Canadian surgeon (Donald Sutherland) who was considered a radical for promoting socialized medicine in the 1920s, served as a doctor with the anti-Franco forces in the Spanish Civil War and died in 1939 China while serving as chief medical officer in the Communist army. Despite the narrative's confusing chronology, director Phillip Borsos' international production offers a complex portrait of a selfless medical humanitarian who was also a hard-drinking womanizer as well as a lifelong political idealist. Some battlefield violence, alcohol abuse and sexual innuendo. A-III (nr)

Dr. Cyclops (1940) Fanciful low-budget thriller set in the Amazon jungle where a mad scientist (Albert Dekker) tries to hide his uranium experiments from unwanted visitors (Charles Halton, Janice Logan, Thomas Coley and Victor Kilian) by shrinking them to the size of dolls. Directed by Ernest B. Schoedsack, the uneven battle between the nearsighted doctor and his undersized victims is worked out rather neatly with simple but imaginative special effects. Occasional stylized violence and much menace. A-II (nr)

Dr. Frankenstein on Campus (1971) Contemporary namesake of the legendary scientist is a college student who doesn't fit in very well with the rest of the campus scene. Director Gilbert W. Taylor's attempt to update a classic story flounders in scenes more suited to sex exploitation movies than to the horror genre. O (R)

Dr. Giggles (1992) Grisly horror movie about an escaped lunatic (Larry Drake) who returns to his hometown to avenge the death of his physician father by murdering everyone in sight with specially designed medical instruments. Lame, sick humor predominates director Manny Coto's boring exercise in medical mass murder, unrelieved by any sense of drama or suspense. Excessive gory violence, heavy sexual innuendo, brief nudity and some rough language. O (R)

Dr. Jekyll and Sister Hyde (1972) British horror movie directed by Roy Ward Baker features Ralph Bates as Jekyll and Martine Beswick as his alter ego-ess. It is at its best when it slyly rings the changes on the 19th-century story, but it offers a lot of just-beneath-the-surface sexual ambience. A-III (PG)

Dr. Phibes Rises Again (1972) Vincent Price as Phibes is still trying to bring his beautiful wife back to life while he fends off Robert Quarry's devious attempts to locate the elixir of life beneath an Egyptian mountain. Directed by Robert Fuest, much of the fun comes from Phibes' ingenious manner of dispatching his enemies against Brian Eatwell's amusing art deco sets. Restrained violence. A-II (PG)

Dr. Strangelove or: How I Learned to Stop Worrying and Love the Bomb (1964) Peter Sellers is President of the United States, as well as the mad doctor of the title, when a fanatical general (Sterling Hayden) launches a nuclear bomber strike on the U.S.S.R. Director Stanley Kubrick's black comedy shows the absurdity of a world quaking under the threat of annihilation by its own artifacts. It may not be everyone's cup of tea, but sifting the leaves remains a provocative challenge even today. A-IV (PG) A

Dr. Who and the Daleks (1966) Derived from the British TV sci-fi series, the movie shows how the good Doctor (Peter Cushing) stops the Daleks, a tribe of mutants, from using their robot army to destroy their neighbors, the peaceful Thals people. Directed by Gordon Flemyng, the fantasy with all its colorful gadgetry will please the children and Dr. Who fans. A-I (br) U

Dracula (1992 version, see: "Bram Stoker's Dracula").

Dracula (1979) Clever British version of the horror story features Frank Langella re-creating his Broadway role as the ruthless vampire romantically obsessed with the daughter of a madhouse caretaker

(Kate Nelligan). Director John Badham's ill-considered use of violence directed against seemingly willing female victims and the gory and bloody killings of the Count's henchmen make the movie an exercise in excess. O (R) X

Dracula A.D. 1972 (1972) Fairly mild British horror movie in which the vampire count (Christopher Lee) returns to settle a score with the descendant (Peter Cushing) of the man who last put Dracula to sleep back in the 1870s. Director Alan Gibson holds attention with some gaudy twists and turns in the modern setting and with the usual amount of gory effects. A-III (PG) 18

Dracula Has Risen from the Grave (1969) When Dracula (Christopher Lee) is accidentally unentombed from a frozen mountain stream, he proceeds to take his revenge on the cleric (Rupert Davies) who exorcised his castle and barred its doors with a large cross. British production directed by Freddie Francis, this version of the old horror tale takes a much more sensual approach to the vampire's bloodlust and its young hero (Barry Andrews) is an outspoken atheist. Graphic blood and gore. A-III (G) 15

Dracula, Prince of Darkness (1966) Routine British vampire movie directed by Terence Fisher with Christopher Lee as the revived Count preying on unwary visitors to his castle. Mild violence. A-II (br) 15

Dragnet (1987) Dan Aykroyd plays police sergeant Friday, with Tom Hanks as his sidekick. Together they foil a group of PA-GANs (People Against Goodness and Normalcy) headed by a minister (Christopher Plummer) wishing to take over Los Angeles. Sarcastic putdowns of virginity, anti-pornography, government and personal integrity, combined with vulgar sexual gestures, rough language and brief nudity provide little genuine humor in director Tom Mankiewicz's updated spoof of the popular 1960s television show. O (PG-13) PG

Dragon: The Bruce Lee Story (1993) Fact-based biography of the late martial arts screen actor (played by Jason Scott Lee) tells of his relocation from Hong Kong to the U.S., interracial marriage, founding of his own martial arts academy and his imminent crossover to movie stardom at the time of his death under mysterious circumstances in 1973. Despite being based on the rose-tinted memoirs of Lee's widow, the Rob Cohen-directed film captures Lee's personal life and struggle against discrimination while blending in numerous intense but well-choreographed fight sequences. A discreet bedroom scene and several violent martial arts confrontations. A-III (PG-13)

Dragon Chow (1988) Two illegal Pakistani aliens (Bhasker and Buddy Uzzaman) attempt to settle into permanent homes and jobs in Hamburg, Germany. German director Jan Schutte offers a heartbreaking view of immigrants caught in a bureaucratic web of exploitation. Subtitles. Its theme and incidental rough language make it inappropriate for younger adolescents. A-II (nr)

Dragon Flies, The (1975) Martial arts story of a police inspector (Jimmy Wang Yu) in pursuit of the chief drug dealer in the Far East. It's all an excuse, of course, for running the gamut of Kung Fu brutality with some incidental interracial romance thrown in for good measure. Once again, however, the cardboard violence is vicious and the police are as reprehensible as the criminals. O (R)

Dragonfly (1976) Released from a mental institution where he was committed at age 13, a young man (Beau Bridges) is helped by a sympathetic woman (Susan Sarandon) to find out the truth about his past and the mother (Mildred Dunnock) he fears he has killed. Well-acted and sensitively directed by Gilbert Cates, the movie has much to recommend it, in spite of an uneven script and an overwrought conclusion that leaves some significant loose ends. Heavy-handed seduction scene. A-III (PG)

Dragonslayer (1981) Sorcerer's apprentice (Peter MacNicol) has to battle the fierce dragon terrorizing a distant kingdom in order to fulfill a promise made by his dead master (Ralph Richardson). Directed by Matthew Robbins, this above-average Disney co-production unravels in the latter third of the story, with showy special effects diminishing the simple human elements of romance and gallantry. Extremely unsettling sequence of a gory death, several other scenes of violence and very brief nudity. A-III (PG)

Draughtsman's Contract, The (1983) Mannered and pretentious period piece set in late 17th-century England, depicts an artist (Anthony Higgins) and the lady of a manor (Janet Suzman) caught up in a web of evil and hostility. Written and directed by Peter Greenaway, the period re-creation is stylish, but its too clever plot eventually becomes boring, undone by its carelessness and its airs. Considerable male nudity and a general air of amorality. O (R) 15

Dream a Little Dream (1989) Incomprehensible teen comedy-romance about a loving middle-aged couple (Jason Robards, Piper Laurie) who, through dream telepathy, swap psyches with a deadbeat teenage couple (Corey Feldman and Meredith Salenger) who redirect their adolescent anger into sweet romance and deflate their peers' anti-social behavior. Director Marc Rocco can't make sense out of the mess resulting from this misfire of the old-young body-switch gimmick. Much rough language laced with sexual vulgarities. A-III (PG-13)

Dream City (1977) A troubled artist and his wife are invited to join a utopian community hidden in a remote area of Africa but upon arrival, find that they are prisoners in an asylum run by the mad inmates. German production directed by Johannes Schaaf, this allegory on society and human nature is stunning to the eye but leaves the heart and imagination untouched. Several scenes are given a voyeuristic emphasis. O (R)

Dream Lover (1986) Psychological thriller starring Christy McNichol as a young girl tormented by a recurring nightmare in which she repeatedly stabs an intruder and potential rapist. Under a dream state induced to cure her, she envisions her own rape, the stabbing of her father and an unsuccessful leap off a 40-story building. Needless repetition of excessively violent acts. O (R) 18

Dream of Kings, A (1969) Uneven screen version of the Harry Mark Petrakis novel about a Greek American (Anthony Quinn in a larger-than-life performance) who, desperate for the money to take his terminally ill son to Greece to be cured by breathing the air of their noble ancestors, is caught cheating at dice and is brutally beaten. But his pride and dreams are saved by his long-suffering wife (Irene Papas). Daniel Mann's direction puts more emphasis on character study than on Chicago's Greek community, but the result has vitality and compassion for human struggle and endurance. A-III (R) X

Dream of Passion (1978) Aging international star (Melina Mercouri), back in her native Greece to play Medea, finds herself drawn to an American (Ellen Burstyn) imprisoned for killing her three children in revenge for her husband's infidelity. Director Jules Dassin's muddled attempt to give a modern slant to the Medea theme suffers from some dreadful acting (save for Burstyn), fatuous dialogue and a general mood of self-indulgence. Some rough language and violent emotions. A-III (R) X

Dream Team, The (1989) Contrived comedy about four mental patients (Michael Keaton, Christopher Lloyd, Peter Boyle and Stephen Furst) on the loose in New York City as they outwit murderous cops to save their comatose therapist (Dennis Boutsikaris). Valiant performances can't pump life into this uncomfortable mix of comedy and pathos about mental illness, leadenly directed by Howard Zieff. Brief violence, a flash of nudity and some rough language. A-III (PG-13) 15

Dreamchild (1985) A lovely movie full of genuine sentiment based upon the 1932 trip of 80-year-old Alice Hargreaves (Coral Browne)—the same Alice who inspired Lewis Carroll (Ian Holm) 70 years before—to New York City to celebrate the centenary of the author's birth. The trip unlocks a flood of memories in the old woman's mind as she recalls the past with a wisdom that comes only with age. Directed by Gavin Millar, the movie makes evident that the writer's love for the little girl, though kept within proper bounds, was more intense than it should have been. A-II (PG)

Dreamer, The (1970) Israeli story of a vague young handyman working in an old age home who, after a love affair with a woman visitor, decides he is happier with the old folks. It is a beautifully photographed, quiet paced study in loneliness, with gentle human and some winning emotions, but it lacks any sort of dramatic depth or narrative interest. A-III (R)

Dreamer (1979) Unranked amateur (Tim Matheson) becomes national bowling champ in director Noel Nosseck's insignificant little film about athletic determination. Implication of premarital sex further mars a bland plot and second-rate performances. A-III (PG)

Dreams of Glass (1969) Trite and banal romance between a rather irresponsible California youth (John Denos) and a charming Japanese girl (Caroline Barrett) whose trysting place in an abandoned warehouse is wrecked one day by a group of young thugs. Lacking a story with substance, director Robert Clouse relies on stylish camerawork and luscious photography. Visually beautiful but emotionally vapid. A-III (PG)

Dreamscape (1984) Absurd melodrama with a hero (Dennis Quaid) who enters the nightmares of disturbed people and performs instant repairs on their wounded psyches. Pulp fantasy movie directed by Joseph Ruben. A torrid but relatively restrained love scene. A-III (PG-13) 15

Dressed to Kill (1946) Modestly intriguing mystery as Sherlock Holmes (Basil Rathbone) and Dr. Watson (Nigel Bruce) seek to connect three music boxes made by a convict in Dartmoor prison with stolen Bank of England plates for printing five-pound notes. Directed by Roy William O'Neill, it was the 12th and final episode in the low-budget series of Holmes' modern adventures begun in 1942. Some menace and stylized violence. A-I (br)

Dressed to Kill (1980) Young prostitute (Nancy Allen) witnesses the brutal murder of a woman (Angie Dickinson) and, with the help of the woman's son (Keith Gordon), searches for the killer, a transvestite in a blond wig. An urbane psychiatrist (Michael Caine) is also part of the mix. Director Brian De Palma's suspense thriller, with its slipshod storyline, flat dialogue and paper-thin characters, is an empty, sterile exercise in fantasy sex and violence directed against women. O (R) 18

Dresser, The (1983) Albert Finney and Tom Courtenay score twin triumphs in a splendid adaptation of the play by Ronald Harwood on the symbiotic relationship between a vain, doddering Shakespearean actor (Finney) and his dresser (Courtenay). The main portion of the action takes place during a performance of "King Lear" given in the midst of an air raid in the darkest days of World War II. Peter Yates's direction helps greatly to make this an inspired adaptation of a stage play though for some tastes it may be too theatrical. A-II (PG)

Dressmaker, The (1989) Somber British movie about three troubled women living too close for comfort in a World War II Liverpool flat—two aging sisters (Joan Plowright and Billie Whitelaw) and their young niece (Jane Harrocks) whose failed romance with an American soldier has tragic consequences. Director Jim O'Brien's emphasis on mundane details of the women's everyday life detracts from illuminating the contradiction between one's outward appearance and actual character and the ultimate cost of repressed feelings and misdirected rage. A graphic scene of violence, sexual overtones and brief nudity. A-III (nr) 15

Drive, He Said (1971) Self-indulgent story of a college basketball star (William Tepper) who divides his time between working out in the gym and in the front seat of his car with the wife (Karen Black) of the drama prof (Robert Towne). Directed by Jack Nicholson, it is a mindless exercise in sexual explicitness and rough language. O (X/R) X

Drive-In (1976) Star-crossed teenagers, youth-gangs, inept armed robbers, nasty children and a variety of other characters converge upon a Texas drive-in to see a movie called "Disaster '76." Under Rod Amateau's direction, the results are sometimes amusing, but more often unfunny with some back-seat romancing and use of marijuana. A-III (PG) A

Driver, The (1978) In this somber crime movie, Ryan O'Neal plays a criminal who specializes in driving getaway cars and Bruce Dern is an obsessed detective out to get him even if he has to break the law to do it. Written and directed by Walter Hill, the confrontations between policeman and criminal lack any deeper resonances than that of other routine melodramas. Violence. A-III (R) A

Driver's Seat, The (1975) Uneven adaptation of Muriel Spark's story is a mood piece about a psychotic spinster (Elizabeth Taylor) who travels to the South of Italy to seek her lover-murderer . Director Giuseppe Patroni Griffi complicates the narrative by intercutting past and future scenes with the present and the result offers little insight into the characters' motives and actions. Its themes of alienation, the elusiveness of reality and the relationship between sexuality and violence will appeal only to a limited audience. A-IV (R)

Driving Miss Daisy (1989) Exquisite adaptation of Alfred Uhry's Pulitzer Prize-winning play about the growing friendship between a wealthy Jewish widow (Jessica Tandy) and her black driver (Morgan Freeman) that begins in 1948 and spans 25 years of turbulent change in the South. Without stooping to sentiment or racial and ethnic stereotypes, director Bruce Beresford sensitively tackles the issues raised by this whimsical friendship, including bigotry, the difficulties of change, the death of the old and birth of the new. The prejudices characterizing the period may be misunderstood by young children. A-II (PG) U

Drop Dead Fred (1991) A jilted wife (Phoebe Cates) moves back home to her tyrannical mother (Marsha Mason) and finds her horrid imaginary childhood pal (Rik Mayall) has reappeared to complicate her interpersonal relationships. Director Ate De Jong's failed fantasy is one long and boring parade of mindless mayhem not suitable for kids and too witless for grown-ups. Sporadic comic book violence and sexual references, a flash of nudity and occasional profanity. A-III (PG-13) 12

Drowning by Numbers (1991) As the movie's characters play endless games involving numbers, three related women (Joan Plowright, Juliet Stevenson and Joely Richardson) drown their husbands and get the coroner (Bernard Hill) to falsify the death certificates by implying possible sexual favors in return. British writer-director Peter Greenaway has nothing worthwhile to say in this pretentiously arty film that fails as black comedy and substitutes warped values for wit. Casual acceptance of murder, adultery and juvenile suicide, nude sexual encounters and minimal rough language. O (R) 18

Drowning Pool, The (1975) Uninspired adaptation of a Ross Macdonald mystery with Paul Newman as the low-key private-eye hired by frightened, rich Joanne Woodward. Director Stuart Rosenberg does better conveying the local flavor of New Orleans than he does stirring the plot's distasteful gumbo of corrupt police, sadistic oil men, blackmail and genteel depravity. The treatment of sexual elements in the story is marred by some ill-considered attempts at comic relief and by the use of a very young actress in an especially distasteful role. O (PG) A

Drugstore Cowboy (1989) Set in 1971 Portland, Oregon, this movie neither romanticizes nor condemns its protagonist—a drug-loving junkie who knocks off pharmacies to feed his habit and those of his pals. Director Gus Van Sant Jr. uses stark realism, jazzy music and hallucinatory flourishes to tell a tale of 1960s' hippie hold-outs whose renegade leader finally cleans up his act. Much profanity, some violence, incidental sexual innuendos and graphic scenes of drug abuse. A-IV (R)

Drum, The (see: "Drums"). 18

Drum (1976) Like "Mandingo," its sequel is an unsavory stew of sex and brutality that makes a ludicrous attempt to seem an earnest exploration into the evils of slavery. Directed by Steve Carver, it is a totally crass exploitation movie. O (R) X

Drum Beat (1954) Slow-moving story of an Indian fighter (Alan Ladd) sent by President Grant to make peace with the leader (Charles Bronson) of a renegade band of Oregon's Modoc Indians. Written and directed by Delmer Daves, it's an earnest effort to show that not all Indians were bad nor all whites good, but the Western action is unconvincing. Frontier violence. A-I (br) U

Drums (1938) Colorful adventure in India's Northwest Frontier where a young prince (Sabu) saves the British resident (Roger Livesey), his wife (Valerie Hobson) and a British garrison from being massacred by the lad's treacherous uncle (Raymond Massey). Director Zoltan Korda gets off to a slow start in setting the scene and relationships but the preliminaries pay off handsomely in the action-filled conclusion. Stylized violence. A-I (br) U

Drums Along the Mohawk (1939) Sparkling outdoor adventure saga of a colonial couple (Claudette Colbert and Henry Fonda) who settle in New York's Mohawk Valley where they are beset by Indian attacks led by English officers during the Revolutionary War. Directed by John Ford, the picture alternates lovely sequences of bucolic farming life with stirring action scenes and plenty of rough frontier humor. Some stylized violence but in a meaningful context holding appeal for all members of the family except pre-schoolers. A-I (br)

Drums of Africa (1963) Charting the course for a railroad through East Africa, a turn-of-the-century explorer and his ward (Frankie Avalon) wind up trying to free a woman (Mariette Hartley) captured by slavers. Director James B. Clark makes extensive use of stock footage trying to give some sense of adventure to an otherwise lackluster effort. Stylized violence and mild sexual innuendo. A-I (br)

Drums of Tahiti (1954) Routine programmer about an American expatriate (Dennis O'Keefe) smuggling arms for an 1877 Polynesian uprising against the French that is ended before it starts by a typhoon and volcanic eruption. Directed by William Castle, the movie's only bright spots are Patricia Medina as O'Keefe's battling bride and Francis L. Sullivan as the shrewd French police commissioner. Some stylized violence and romantic complications. A-II (br) U

Dry White Season, A (1989) Wrenching adaptation of Andre Brink's novel about the 1976 Soweto uprisings and a conscience-stricken white Afrikaner (Donald Sutherland) who becomes an anti-apartheid activist after his black gardener and the gardener's young son die from police brutality. Black woman director Euzhan Palcy depicts the moral bankruptcy of those supporting racist policies that lead to the slaughter of defenseless blacks. Brief but graphic scenes of violence. A-III (R) 15

Duck, You Sucker! (1972) Director Sergio Leone spins out another of his endless, blood-drenched western epics, this one telling how Rod Steiger and James Coburn win the Mexican Revolution. The story is far too long to hold up either its storyline or the viewer's sagging attention. Much preposterous violence. A-III (PG)

DuckTales: The Movie—Treasure of the Lost Lamp (1990) Meandering animated adventure involving a lost magic lamp whose genie takes refuge with Scrooge McDuck's clan to avoid capture by the evil sorcerer Merlock. Despite sprightly characters and busy storyline, the result is a rather lame feature cartoon stemming from the Disney television series. Produced and directed by Bob Hathcock, some of the highlights are Richard Libertini's sly voice as Merlock's lightfingered lackey and a few moments of striking animation. Minimum of scary menace. A-I (G)

Duel at Diablo (1966) Sidney Poitier, James Garner and Bibi Andersson star in a western rife with brutal killings and wife-kidnapping by Apache Indians, with Dennis Weaver as a vengeful husband who cannot forgive his wife for surviving her ordeal. Director Ralph Nelson disguises his movie's shortcomings with a complicated plot and larger-than-life characters but can't hide its violent excesses. O (br) A

Duellists, The (1978) Screen version of a Joseph Conrad story about two hussar officers in Napoleon's army (Keith Carradine and Harvey Keitel) who fight a series of duels over two decades. Director Ridley Scott excels in his re-creation of the settings, costumes and general flavor of the era and does well with a delightful supporting cast (notably Albert Finney and Diana Quick). These virtues cannot compensate, however, for a large hole at the center of the story due to inept performances by the two principals. Violence. A-III (PG)

Duet for Cannibals (1969) Young man and his girlfriend become involved with a fantasy-ridden political activist and his unstable wife in a relationship that becomes sexually bizarre and potentially murderous. Writer Susan Sontag's debut as a director is an interesting failure in its black-and-white variations on a theme of the corruption of innocence. A-IV (nr)

Duet for One (1987) Brilliant, world-renowned concert violinist (Julie Andrews) struggles to overcome the anger and depression she feels when her talents are diminished by multiple sclerosis. Frightened by the realization of her mortality, she finds consolation in her psychiatrist (Max von Sydow) only after two adulterous affairs and a failed suicide attempt. Director Andrei Konchalovsky stresses righteous indignation as a life-sustaining virtue over spiritual renewal. Alan Bates co-stars in this morbid and morally muddled melodrama. Brief nudity. O (R) 15

Duffy (1968) James Coburn plays a pop-erotic artist living in Tangiers who becomes involved in a complicated piracy plot with relatives of wealthy James Mason who has a few surprises in store for those trying to rob him. Instead of a sophisticated comedy, director Robert Parrish has come up with a shallow, low-grade bore whose sexual references are occasionally offensive. O (PG) A

Dulcima (1972) Rustic British movie traces the relationship between a cunning country lass (Carol White) who moves in as a "housekeeper" for a wealthy, much older farmer (John Mills), but the arrival of a handsome newcomer results in a shocking finale. Director Frank Nesbitt keeps things admirably subdued, although he is uncompromising in terms of the earthy language and lusty pursuits of his isolated characters. A-III (PG) A

Dumbo (1941) In this classic Disney animated feature, a baby elephant with oversized ears, the laughing stock of the entire circus troupe to which he belongs, is befriended by a sympathetic mouse. What happens to the diminutive pachyderm shows children how self-respect and self-confidence can be gained by making the most of one's imagination and inventive initiative. A-I (G) U

Dune (1984) Dark, quirky adaptation of Frank Herbert's science-fiction trilogy about four factions struggling for control of a desert planet and its wondrous spices. Directed by David Lynch, much of the story is incomprehensible to anyone who has not read the original and the staging of the action sequences is absurd rather than imaginative. Some graphic violence and vulgarity. A-III (PG-13) PG

Dungeonmaster (1985) Dreadful hodge-podge of a movie, with no less than seven directors, about a computer wizard who must overcome a series of challenges of the sort found in the game that gives this clunker its title. Sadistic violence. O (PG-13)

Dunwich Horror, The (1970) Young warlock (Dean Stockwell), despite the warnings of his grandfather (Sam Jaffe), strives to conjure up some devil-monsters from the underworld but is foiled by a prof of witchcraft (Ed Begley). Director Daniel Haller's weak horror movie has some sexually suggestive scenes. O (M) 18

Dusty and Sweets McGee (1971) Semi-documentary by Floyd Mutrux on the tragic lives of drug addicts and pushers parades the dehumanizing effect, the withdrawals and death that drugs produce. The result is a talk piece that poses tough questions about real people but gets nowhere in what ultimately proves to be a surface examination of substantive matters. A-IV (R)

Dutch (1991) Often tacky road movie in which the blue-collar boyfriend (Ed O'Neill) of a timid divorcee (JoBeth Williams) snatches her snobby adolescent son (Ethan Randall) from his Atlanta private academy to drive him home to Chicago for Thanksgiving dinner. Director Peter Faiman gets only cheap laughs from writer-producer John Hughes' simplistic and obvious comedy where rich is bad, poor is good and brawn wins over brains. Blatant sexual innuendo, intermittent sophomoric violence and an instance of rough language. A-III (PG-13)

Dutchess and the Dirt-Water Fox, The (1976) Western comedy about a bumbling gambler (George Segal) and a dance hall girl (Goldie Hawn) whose avarice brings them together in a series of cliched chases and misadventures. Director Melvin Frank's mostly unfunny effort collapses under the weight of incessant visual and verbal vulgarities, double entendres and some crude satire at the expense of Mormons and Jews. O (PG)

Dying Young (1991) A young man (Campbell Scott) stricken with leukemia hires a beautiful woman (Julia Roberts) to help him through chemotherapy treatment and encourages her love while misleading her about his condition. The emotional honesty of the characters in this compassionate movie from director Joel Schumacher eventually overcomes the romanticized Hollywood formula of poor girl meeting rich boy. Discreet unmarried sexual encounters, intermittent rough language and a flash of rear nudity. A-III (R) 15

Dynamite Chicken (1972) Director Ernie Pintoff's low-budget collection of skits on pot smoking, campus rebellion, Madison Avenue hucksterism, nudity, LBJ, Lenny Bruce and other dated topical items, is merely trite and self-consciously offensive. O (R)

E

Each Dawn I Die (1939) Crime melodrama about a crusading reporter (James Cagney) framed for manslaughter and sent to prison where he helps a gang leader (George Raft) who later helps the reporter clear his name. Directed by William Keighley, the conditions of prison life are harshly detailed but the plot is hackneyed and taxes credibility. Some hard-edged violence and ambiguous treatment of criminals. A-III (br) A

Eagle Has Landed, The (1977) Director John Sturges' lethargic adventure yarn based on the fictional premise involving a German plot to kidnap Winston Churchill during World War II is a conventional spy melodrama. Michael Caine, Robert Duvall and Donald Sutherland star in the suspenser, which is marred by some graphic violence, sexual byplay and profanity. A-III (PG) A

Eagle in a Cage (1971) Exiled after Waterloo on the barren isle of St. Helena in the middle of the South Atlantic, Napoleon wages an unequal contest of will with the English garrison and its overbearing commander. Director Fielder Cook's direction simply reflects the strength and weakness of an uneven script, though it does capitalize on the grandeur of the Yugoslavian location where it was filmed. A-III (GP) A

Early Spring (1974) Japanese study of a man's alienation from job and home until a series of events jolts him out of his benumbed apathy and he decides to make the best of things. Directed in 1956 by Yasujiro Ozu, the movie conveys the density of feeling and the richness of relationships that make up ordinary life. A-II (nr)

Earth Girls Are Easy (1989) When three fuzzy aliens crashland into a ditzy manicurist's pool, she (Geena Davis) is torn between her love for her philandering fiance (Charles Rocket) and her attraction to one of the aliens (Jeff Goldblum). Director Julien Temple's satire of California glitz, consumerism and grade-B alien movies sinks in a sea of poorly integrated musical numbers, sexual innuendos and an offensive, denigrating view of women. Endorses sexual promiscuity. O (PG)

Earth Is Our Sinful Song, The (1975) Director Rauni Mollberg's extraordinary picture of life in a Finnish Lapland village tells the story of a father's ill-considered act of vengeance provoked by the pregnancy of his unmarried daughter. The story taking place beneath the awesome, brooding northern sky has the authenticity of a documentary but also the power of drama about lust and love, passion and remorse. Some sexually graphic but not titillating scenes and some brutal but not gratuitous violence. Some may find this picture of another, more elemental, culture disturbing. A-IV (R)

Earthling, The (1981) Dying man (William Holden) teaches a lost orphan (Ricky Schroder) how to survive in the wilds of the Australian bush in this import from director Peter Collinson. The photography of Don McAlpine is outstanding with its lavish scenic splendor, but the story's stilted dialogue and sketchy characterizations make for a long sit. Mild profanity and threatening wild animals. A-II (PG)

Earthquake (1974) Moderately entertaining disaster spectacle of Los Angeles before, during, and after a cataclysmic earthquake. Directed by Mark Robson, Charlton Heston stars but is outclassed by the special effects. Unfortunately, in an attempt to include something for everyone, there is a seduction here, an attempted rape there, and a certain amount of strong language. A-III (PG) A

Earth's Final Fury (see "When Time Ran Out").

Easter Parade (1948) Irving Berlin musical about a vaudeville dancer (Fred Astaire) who loses one dancing partner (Ann Miller) but gains stardom with another (Judy Garland). Directed by Charles Walters, the story's little more than adequate but the principals make it all seem to matter and the songs and dance numbers are bright and cheery. A-I (br) U

Easy Living (1937) Pleasing screwball comedy about a secretary (Jean Arthur) whose chance meeting with a financier (Edward Arnold) over an errant fur coat leads to a wild variety of misunderstandings about their relationship, one of which happens to cause a stock market panic. Written by Preston Sturges and directed by Mitchell Leisen, the laughs are guaranteed by a solid cast including Luis Alberni as a desperate hotel owner and Ray Milland as an automat attendant who turns out to be the financier's son. Mild romantic situations. A-II (br) PG

Easy Money (1983) Happily married lout (Rodney Dangerfield), given to drinking, gambling, philandering and narcotics, is forced to clean up his act when wealthy mother-in-law (Geraldine Fitzgerald) leaves him a fortune on condition that he reforms completely. This dreary, witless failed comedy, directed by James Signorelli and written by Dangerfield and half a dozen others, passes off some nudity, obscenity and a benign attitude toward drugs as supposedly harmless gags. O (R) 15

Easy Rider (1969) Two drifters (Peter Fonda and Dennis Hopper), with a wad of cash from a drug transaction, motorcycle through the American Southwest on their way to New Orleans to celebrate. Along the way they encounter a disparate variety of American life, meet a small-town ACLU lawyer (Jack Nicholson in a fine performance) and wind up murdered for being different. Also directed by Hopper, the journey may lead nowhere but its use of the natural landscape brings beauty and lyricism to a work exploring the American Dream and its promise of individual freedom. A thoughtful, provocative movie, it is marred by some graphic violence, a foggy mixture of sex and religion and a benign view of drugs. A-IV (R) 18

Eat a Bowl of Tea (1989) Wry comedy about family life in New York's Chinatown circa 1949 depicting the pressures on one newly married Chinese-American couple (Russell Wong, Cora Miao) to have children. Because of immigration restrictions, Chinese-American communities of the period had many old men but few women, making the couple's marriage, child-bearing abilities and his impotence fraught with intergenerational and cultural pressures humorously and touchingly evoked by director Wayne Wang. Brief graphic violence, an adulterous liaison and some rough language laced with sexual innuendos. A-III (PG-13) 12

Eat My Dust (1976) Ron Howard stars in a brainless romp, a kind of live-action Roadrunner cartoon, about some youngsters obsessed with fast cars. Directed by Charles Griffith, it is an inane vision of youth culture and glorifies a dangerous pastime. A-III (PG) AA

Eating (1991) A group of women gather for a birthday party for three women (Lisa Richards, Mary Crosby and Marlena Giovi) which becomes a true confessions session exploring the partygoers' relationships to each other, to men and especially to food. Writer-director Henry Jaglom's lively, mildly insightful look at Americans' shallow obsession with being thin as a measure of self-worth makes its points well before the party's over. Several casual references to adultery and abortion, occasional rough language and momentary nudity. A-III (R)

Eboli (1980) The political exile of Italian anti-Fascist writer and artist Carlo Levi is the subject of director Francesco Rosi's warmly human dramatization. Though it does convey some of the complexities of Levi's social, political and artistic concerns, it is more interested in the man and his place in the context of the times. Serious subject matter and complex background

might be confusing for young viewers. A-III (PG)

Echo Park (1986) In a rare unglamorous view of Los Angeles, an aspiring actress (Susan Dey) who is a single parent finds security and devotion with a down-to-earth younger man (Tom Hulce). The gritty drama contrasts blind ambition and false illusions with the rewards of patience and kindness. Director Robert Dornhelm's harshly realistic but truthful treatment counterbalances a sexually explicit nude scene, some foul language and violence. A-IV (R) U

Echoes of a Summer (1976) Young girl (Jodie Foster) dying of a heart defect who conveys stoic acceptance of her condition and provides the inspiration for her family to deal gracefully with impending tragedy. Good cast with Lois Nettleton as the mother, Geraldine Fitzgerald as the tutor, and Richard Harris, who also co-produced, as the father. Director Don Taylor is a bit heavy-handed, but the sentiment is genuine. A-II (PG) A

Eddie and the Cruisers (1983) A reporter (Ellen Barkin) investigates the fate of a 1960s' rock group whose sudden disappearance raises questions about the apparent suicide of its lead singer (Michael Pare). Director Martin Davidson, hampered by a mediocre script, fails to create any visual or narrative interest. Mildly vulgar dialogue. A-II (PG)

Eddy Duchin Story, The (1956) Sentimental journey through the life and career of pianist Duchin (miscast Tyrone Power) who becomes a band leader in the 1930s, loses his wife (Kim Novak) in the 1940s and is crippled with leukemia in the 1950s. Director George Sidney overplays the innocence of the youthful Duchin, then his morose brooding over personal woes, relieved only by some bright musical numbers and occasional glimpses of the country's changing social context. Heavy-going for children. A-I (br) U

Edison, the Man (1940) Spencer Tracy plays the American go-getter who sells his first invention to Western Electric in order to set up his own laboratory, saves it by chancing upon the phonograph, then in 1886 achieves his dream of the electric light. Director Clarence Brown uses occasional comic touches to keep the idealized biography from getting too sentimental, but Tracy's likeable performance is what makes it worth watching. Its picture of science in the service of humanity as well as the virtues of dedication and hard work will not be lost on the young. A-I (br)

Educating Rita (1983) This British production adapted from Willy Russell's play and directed by Lewis Gilbert stars Michael Caine as a disillusioned, drunken professor of English in Dublin who becomes involved with a spunky housewife (Julie Walters) determined to get an education. The Pygmalion relationship has some charm, but Walter's characterization is somewhat crude and ethnically stereotyped. A-III (PG) 15

Education of Sonny Carson, The (1974) Screen biography of a black militant (Rony Clanton), graduating from the Brooklyn ghetto to reform school and prison, embittered by the brutal cops and uncaring parole officials. Directed by Michael Campus, this attempt to show a world of racial injustice suffers from an onslaught of foul language, disjointed episodes, jarring switches in movie styles and an excessively prolonged scene of a merciless beating by a racist cop. O (R)

Edvard Munch (1976) Written and directed by Peter Watkins, this is the story of the Norwegian artist Edvard Munch (1863–1944), who, as one of the founders of Expressionism, has had a great influence upon the direction of contemporary art. Watkins interweaves three main strands of narrative: the historical, the intellectual, and the personal. Beautifully photographed, with the feel of a semidocumentary, the movie's treatment of the tormented life of this artist is at times intense, but diffused by the cultural context. A-II (nr) A

Edward II (1992) Bizarre adaptation of Christopher Marlowe's 16th-century play about King Edward II (Steven Waddington), his male lover (Andrew Tiernan) and his wife, Queen Isabella (Tilda Swinton), who concocts a murderous revenge. British director Derek Jarman wallows in sexually violent images in a medieval story jarringly joined to scenes of modern-day gay bashing. Much sexual activity with nudity and bloody violence including scenes of torture and cannibalism. O (R) 18

Edward Scissorhands (1990) A gentle humanoid (Johnny Depp) with grotesque blades for hands is adopted by a family (Dianne Wiest, Alan Arkin and Winona Ryder) and prized by the community for his haircutting and lawn sculpting talents, until exploited by the daughter's boyfriend. Director Tim Burton's offbeat fantasy is an oddly appealing mix of mild comedy and mock tragedy despite its phony pastel suburban setting and stereotyped residents. Brief stylized violence and sexual innuendo. A-II (PG-13) PG

Effect of Gamma Rays on Man-in-the-Moon Marigolds, The (1972) Joanne Woodward stars in the screen version of Paul Zindel's play about a desperate middle-aged mother living in an urban hovel, abandoned by her husband and struggling to raise two teenaged daughters (Nell Potts and Roberta Wallach). Producer-director Paul Newman's ambitious but flawed exploration into the labyrinthian workings of the human heart is largely redeemed by Woodward's superb performance. A-III (PG) AA

Effi Briest (1977) Tragedy based on Theodor Fontane's 19th-century romantic novel about a 17-year-old girl, married to a middle-aged Prussian official, who makes the mistake of having an affair, ultimately leading to her destruction. Directed by Rainer Werner Fassbinder, the German production is a haunting black-and-white evocation of a by-gone age with some insight into the morals of the times. A-III (nr) U

Efficiency Expert, The (1992) Gentle Australian comedy about the irresistible effect of the human factor on a rigidly methodical management consultant (Anthony Hopkins) who has been hired to modernize a hopelessly out-of-date family-run shoe factory. Director Mark Joffe's sentimental fantasy centers in its good-natured depiction of the foibles and eccentricities of the factory workers and the idea that there is more to a business than making money. Some violence to property and minor romantic complications. A-II (PG)

Egg and I, The (1947) Postwar comedy in which a city couple (Claudette Colbert and Fred MacMurray) buy a broken-down chicken farm, then learn about country life the hard way from rustic neighbors Ma and Pa Kettle (Marjorie Main and Percy Kilbride). Directed by Chester Erskine, the fish-out-of-water proceedings provide mild fun, with Colbert especially good as the bemused, spunky wife, until taking a turn into melodrama for a sentimental finish. Domestic misunderstandings. A-II (br) U

Eiger Sanction, The (1975) An art professor (Clint Eastwood who also directed) moonlights as an assassin for an intelligence outfit run by a former Nazi. The movie is exploitative in its treatment of sexual promiscuity and brutality. O (R) AA

Eight Men Out (1988) Based on the 1919 scandal over bribe-taking Chicago White Sox players in the World Series won by the Cincinnati Reds is this morality tale about compromising a lifetime of professional credibility for big bucks and revenge on a stingy ballclub owner (Clifton James). Writer-director John Sayles does well contrasting honest and dishonest players, but the movie bogs down in too much detail and too many indistinguishable characters. Some locker-room language and a theme involving bribery and threats of violent retribution. A-III (PG)

8 Million Ways to Die (1986) In this heartless murder mystery, Jeff Bridges plays a reformed alcoholic ex-cop who breaks up a drug ring as he finds a prostitute's killer. Violence, ethnic stereotyping, extreme amounts of profanity and some nudity. O (R)

18 Again (1988) When a grandfather and grandson switch spirits after an almost fatal car crash, the 81-year-old grandpa (George Burns) manages to enjoy some college antics as an 18-year-old, while his grandson (Charlie Schlatter) learns a thing or two about social savvy from his grandfather's example. Directed by Paul Flaherty, the potentially sweet-natured comedy is marred by some off-color, sexist jokes with sexual inferences, sophomoric humor and brief nudity. A-III (PG)

80 Steps to Jonah (1969) Young drifter (Wayne Newton), innocently implicated in a car theft, takes refuge in a camp for blind children where he finds commitment and a new purpose in life. Romance and exoneration follow in director Gerd Oswald's simple, somewhat sentimental tale of spiritual renewal that has special appeal for youngsters. A-I (G)

84 Charing Cross Road (1987) Screen version of New Yorker Helene Hanff's autobiography telling of her 20-year transatlantic correspondence with a London bookseller, starting with an inquiry about some rare books in 1949 and ending with his death in 1969. Though they never meet, the book seller (Anthony Hopkins) and the book lover (Anne Bancroft) come sharply into focus through letters sharing their mutual love of literature and other cultural matters. Director David Jones does extremely well in conveying the spiritual meeting of minds underlying their long-distance friendship. This uplifting celebration of kind and gentle souls may be above the heads of the very young, but they would benefit from seeing it with their parents. A-I (PG) U

El Condor (1970) Big, bold Jim Brown joins up with skinny, mean Lee Van Cleef in this gory western about getting Maximilian's vast gold horde out of El Condor, which is guarded by cruel Patrick O'Neal. Director John Guillermin rightfully pays little attention to the shoddy script but, unfortunately, devotes his energies to heavy-handed violence and sex scenes. O (R) AA

El Dorado (1967) Western sheriff (Robert Mitchum), immobilized by drinking, is helped by his old partner (John Wayne), who suffers occasional spinal spasms, in fighting off a band of cut-throats terrorizing the town. Produced and directed by Howard Hawks, the movie has a good mixture of action, farcical situations and unconventional treatment to keep things moving at a good clip. Stylized violence. A-III (br) U

El Greco (1966) Mel Ferrer and Rosanna Schiaffino star in a very melodramatic romance based loosely on the life of the 16th-century Spanish painter. European production directed by Luciano Salce features beautiful location photography, but art is secondary to a presentation of the artist's tempestuous romance with a highborn lady. A-III (br) A

El Mariachi (1993) Increasingly violent comedy in which a mariachi guitarist (Carlos Gallardo) finds himself caught up in a killing spree when a series of menacing strangers mistake him for a vicious hit man (Reinol Martinez) out to murder a traitorous drug dealer (Peter Marquardt). Though its dark humor is occasionally funny, writer-director Robert Rodriguez' low-budget movie trivializes murder and the worth of human life. Subtitles. Much gratuitous violence and a conclusion justifying deadly violence to exact personal revenge. O (R)

El Norte (1984) Fleeing from terrorists who kill their father and kidnap their mother, two Guatemalan teenagers head toward "El Norte," meaning the U.S., where they hope to begin a new life free from fear and exploitation. After a journey with further terrors, they reach Los Angeles, get jobs and have a taste of the good life they have dreamed about before one becomes seriously ill and the other is deported as an illegal alien. Director Gregory Nava has made a splendid film about human dignity and the exploitation of undocumented workers, with some good-natured humor keeping matters from getting too solemn. Subtitles aplenty with much of the dialogue in Spanish and Mayan. Several scenes of intense violence. A-III (R) 15

El Super (1979) Unpretentious and affecting movie about a former Havana bus conductor (Raymundo Hidalgo-Gato) struggling to get through his 10th New York winter as a building superintendent, supported by his loving wife (Zully Montero) but troubled by their promiscuous, drug-taking daughter (Elizabeth Pena). Directed by Leon Ichaso and Orlando Jimenez-Leal, the slice-of-life portrait is brightened by wit and humor, bridging the gap between North American and Latin cultures with low-budget ingenuity and cultural integrity. A-II (nr)

El Topo (1971) Argentinian director Alexandro Jodorowsky's presents the story of a man's spiritual journey through life and the contradictions that arise between physical and moral power. The form is the time-honored western with its gunfighters, open landscapes, and frontier towns. But in addition to using the western conventions, the film also employs religious imagery, and sections of the Bible serve as its ideological frame of reference. Some will find its images of violence, sexuality and venality to be unsettling, if not offensive. A-IV (nr) X

Eldridge Cleaver (1970) William Klein's documentary on political refugee Cleaver, an American whose radical ideas are uncongenial to the majority of his fellow citizens, uses the rhetoric of violence in presenting his views on revolution. Viewers will make their own judgment about the validity of his statements according to their knowledge and experience. A-IV (nr)

Electra Glide in Blue (1973) Ironic slice-of-life movie about a motorcycle cop (Robert Blake) in a small Southwestern town who revels in his splendid uniform and rugged equipment but yearns for the status he might have as a detective. A short stint with the local marshal (Mitch Ryan) cures him of that and a botched twist ending leaves a bad aftertaste. Embarrassingly pretentious but empty movie, painfully directed by James Guercio, it contains violence, rough language and sexual references. A-III (PG) X

Electric Dreams (1984) Bland, innocuous British romantic comedy from director Steve Barron about a computer that falls in love with a woman. Youth-oriented movie features Lenny von Dohlen, Virginia Madsen and Bud Cort who manage to cavort in bed together, but this is implied rather than depicted. A-III (PG)

Electric Horseman, The (1979) Television reporter (Jane Fonda) teams up with over-the-hill rodeo star (Robert Redford) to save a gallant racehorse from commercial exploitation. Low-voltage but cheerful and unassuming movie directed by Sydney Pollack. Treatment of the romantic involvement between the two principals makes it mature viewing fare. A-III (PG)

Eleni (1985) A New York newspaper reporter (John Malkovich), born in Greece, returns to his native land to find the man responsible for the execution of his mother (Kate Nelligan) in the Greek Civil War 30 years earlier. Despite the emotional power intrinsic to its fact-based subject, director Peter Yates has made a flat and unmoving movie, due largely to a pedestrian script and miscasting. Some scenes of wartime violence. A-II (PG)

Elephant Boy (1937) Sturdy little adventure in the jungles of colonial India where a local youth (Sabu) helps a British hunting party on the trail of a great elephant herd. Co-directed by Robert Flaherty and Zoltan Korda, the simple story focuses on young Sabu's winning performance, though the film's semi-documentary style mixes the authentic with the phony, including making elephants appear to dance. For all its dated qualities, the movie still delights youngsters. A-I (br)

Elephant Called Slowly, An (1971) Director James Hill offers a rambling account of a return visit by Bill Travers and Virginia McKenna, the stars of "Born Free," to a Kenyan game preserve where they are befriended by a baby elephant. Nothing much happens, but this album of wildlife is so low-keyed and innocent that parents, especially accompanied by their youngsters, will find it a pleasant, relaxing experience. A-I (G)

Elephant Man, The (1980) Touching fact-based portrait of an impoverished man deformed by a rare disease who is rescued from a London freak show by a dedicated doctor only to become the curiosity of fashionable Victorian society. Directed by David Lynch with evocative black-and-white photography, it features a fine performance by Anthony Hopkins as the concerned physician who rehabilitates the outcast (John Hurt under great wads of make-up). Some intense scenes of brutality. A-III (PG) AA

Elephant Walk (1954) Heavy goings-on in Ceylon when a tea plantation owner (Peter Finch) brings home an English bride (Elizabeth Taylor) who can't understand his obsession with the colonial past and turns for sympathy to the plantation's manager (Dana Andrews). Directed by William Dieterle, the glossy romantic melodrama goes in circles until nature takes its revenge through drought, plague and an elephant rampage razing the planter's mansion and bringing him to his senses. Mild romantic triangle and stylized violence. A-II (br) U

Elmer Gantry (1960) Vivid dramatization of the Sinclair Lewis novel about a cunning sharpster (Burt Lancaster) who attaches himself to the entourage of a barnstorming evangelist (Jean Simmons) in the 1920s, then falls in love with her. In exploring the commercialization of religion and some of the techniques used by religious charlatans, writer-director Richard Brooks makes good use of the period's hypocrisy and people's credulity. Critical view of religion's exploitation, some sexual references and occasional stylized violence. A-III (br) A

11 Harrowhouse (1974) Routine caper movie in which jewel thieves (Charles Grodin and Candice Bergen) get some inside help from a dissident employee (James Mason). Director Aram Avakian does make the most of his London setting and especially the metallic glint of the sophisticated detection devices in the basement of the diamond exchange. A-II (PG)

Elvira Madigan (1967) Romantic 19th-century tale of a cavalry officer and a young circus performer who run away to the Danish countryside for a summer's idyll but, as the chill of fall sets in, realize their future is doomed. Director Bo Widerberg's sensitive, straight-forward version of a popular Swedish legend is lushly beautiful with a darkly somber ending. A-III (br) A

Elvira, Mistress of the Dark (1988) A buxom TV horror show hostess (Cassandra Peterson) gets into trouble trying to bankroll a Las Vegas song-and-dance act with her aunt's paranormal inheritance. Directed by James Signorelli, its wall-to-wall sex jokes, a tasteless orgiastic picnic and a tassle-twirling finale manage to reduce it to the level of soft-porn comedy. O (PG-13) 15

Elvis on Tour (1972) Pierre Adidge's documentary of a 15-day concert tour by Elvis Presley reveals nothing new about the man behind the legend, but devotees of the legend will find it entertaining enough. A-I (G) A

Elvis: That's the Way It Is (1970) Documentary profile of rock 'n' roll superstar Elvis Presley beginning with the rehearsals and exhausting preparations for a gala opening night performance at the International Hotel in Las Vegas. The performance itself is a winner giving fans of old swivel hips 30 songs to savor. Director Denis Sanders captures the quality of the man as performer and conveys that special Elvis magic that is part put-on and part solid singing conviction. A-II (G) U

Embalmer, The (1972) Ensconced in a sunken monastery beneath a fancy hotel in Venice, a psychotic frogman enshrines the beautiful women he has abducted and drowned in the canal until he tries to nab a lovely tourist who has caught the eye of a handsome reporter staying at the hotel. Dino Travella directs this failed 1966 Italian thriller with absolutely no imagination, but a few red herrings mildly seasoned with sexual innuendo. A-III (PG)

Embryo (1976) Scientist (Rock Hudson) injects a human embryo with a drug that speeds growth to save the baby of a woman who has committed suicide. The result is a young girl (Barbara Carrera) with a photographic memory that creates terrifying results. Director Ralph Nelson's sci-fi horror story contains graphic, but brief, nudity and a shockingly violent conclusion. O (PG)

Emerald Forest, The (1985) An American father (Powers Boothe) searches the Amazonian jungle for 10 years until he finds the son who was kidnapped by Indians. The boy, however, now a teenager, has no desire to return to civilization. Under John Boorman's direction, the exotic setting provides some interest to this simplistic and melodramatic story of noble and ignoble savages and the ravages wrought on nature by commercial exploitation. Passable entertainment, but strictly for mature audiences because of a great deal of nudity and some rather graphic violence. A-IV (R) 15

Emigrants, The (1972) Superb Swedish production starring Liv Ullmann and Max von Sydow about a young couple who leave their native land in the early 19th century to find a new home in Minnesota. Directed by Jan Troell, the re-creation of the era is finely detailed and the acting is first rate. A-II (PG) AA

Emil and the Detectives (1964) A group of boys play detective and thwart the plans of a trio of comically sinister bank robbers in West Berlin. Disney production directed by Peter Tewksbury may please the young and uncritical. A-I (br) U

Eminent Domain (1991) Bland cold war era drama in which a Polish Politburo member (Donald Sutherland) strikes back after he is summarily stripped of his position and power with disastrous results for his wife (Anne Archer) and child (Johdi May). A threadbare storyline and a lumbering pace make director John Irvin's movie a slack and tepid affair of minimal suspense. Momentary violence and an instance of rough language. A-II (PG-13)

Emitai (1972) Fact-based Senegalese movie about a small village whose men are conscripted by France during World War II but, when they refuse a year later to give up all their rice, the remaining villagers are massacred. Directed by Ousmane Sembene, much of the story is told solely through its expressive images, and these visuals are the great strength of the movie. The title is the name of one of the tribe's gods who represents the passage from one stage of life to a new and better one. Stylized violence. A-II (nr)

Emmanuelle (1975) French sex exploitation movie about a young woman's forays into the steamy regions of tropical sex in Thailand. O (X/R/X) 18

Emperor of the North (1973) Brutal, altogether unsubtle drama about a clash between a hobo (Lee Marvin) and a sadistic train guard (Ernest Borgnine) set in the era of the Great Depression. It captures some of the mood of the 1930s, with out-of-work men living in hobo camps and riding the rails, but this is only used as the context for director Robert Aldrich's myopic vision of the male mystique and the cult of violence. A-IV (PG) AA

Empire of the Sun (1987) Adventure saga of a British lad (Christian Bale) who has to learn how to survive on his own after being separated from his parents when the Japanese capture Shanghai and intern him for the duration of World War II. Director Steven Spielberg uses a large-scale canvas to depict with sensitivity and feeling the story of a youth growing up in the midst of wartime inhumanity. Some realistic violence and a scene indicating the boy's curiosity about sex. A-II (PG)

Empire Strikes Back, The (1980) Gallant intergalactic rebels led by Luke Skywalker (Mark Hamill), Hans Solo (Harrison Ford) and Princess Leia (Carrie Fisher) and lovable android companions continue the fight against the evil Empire aided by Yoda, a remarkable creature who safeguards the Force and teaches moderation in all things. Some intense fight sequences punctuate director Irvin Kershner's sci-fi fantasy action. A-II (PG) U

Enchanted April (1992) Charming period piece about the transformation four world-weary London women (Joan Plowright, Miranda Richardson, Josie Lawrence and Polly Walker) experience when they impulsively rent a medieval castle for a month in sunny Italy. Based on Elizabeth von Armin's 1922 novel, director Mike Newell offers up a sweetly fanciful film about characters removed from their drab routines who learn the value of tolerance and renewed commitment to relationships. Very mild sexual innuendo. A-II (PG) U

Enchanted Cottage, The (1945) Fragile romantic fantasy about a disfigured World War II veteran (Robert Young) and a plain-looking maid (Dorothy McGuire) who see the beauty of the other through the eyes of love. Directed by John Cromwell, the sentimentality is old-fashioned but the theme is universal. A-I (br) U

Enchantment (1948) Romantic melodrama centers on an aged British general (David Niven) who recalls the lost love (Teresa Wright) of his youth when visited during World War II by her son (Farley Granger) who falls for the daughter (Evelyn Keyes) of the general's mean-spirited sister (Jayne Meadows). Directed by Irving Reis, the parallel romances of past and present are neatly contrived and unabashedly sentimental. Tough sledding for children and non-romantics. A-I (br)

Encino Man (1992) Sophomoric comedy has two California teens (Sean Astin and Pauly Shore) unearthing a frozen caveman (Brendan Fraser) whom they defrost and pass off as a really cool high school exchange student. Director Les Mayfield's innocuous romp is just a drawn-out unreeling of gooney antics with no attempt at plot or characterization. Minor brawling and very mild sexual innuendo. A-II (PG)

End, The (1978) Except for the buffoonery of Dom Deluise, this is a painfully unfunny Burt Reynolds comedy about how not to commit suicide. Also directed by Reynolds, it contains an explicit love scene, some highly insulting ethnic jokes and disrespectful treatment of a religious rite. O (R) AA

End of a Priest (1970) Seriocomic Czechoslovakian tale about villagers rehearsing for a play during which the sexton becomes saintly playing the role of a priest and the teacher becomes an unimaginative buffoon in the role of mayor. The movie's theme is not the conflict between church and state but the difference between doing good and talking about it. Though it has a moral, director Evald Schorm is mainly concerned with its characters and the high comedy of the absurd. A-III (nr)

End of Innocence, The (1991) Rejected by her younger lover (Steve Meadows) and hooked on pills, a middle-aged woman (Dyan Cannon) begins to find herself after checking into a rehab center. Also written and directed by Cannon, the movie lacks any subtlety in its shrill look at one woman's long-overdue conclusion that she must accept herself. Discreet sexual encounters, recreational drug use, minor violence and rough language. A-III (R)

End of the Game, The (1976) Screen version of a Friedrich Duerrenmatt novel about a Swiss detective (Martin Ritt) who is obsessed with bringing to belated justice a former friend (Robert Shaw), now possessed of immense wealth and power, who 30 years earlier had killed a young woman. Director Maximilian Schell elicits strong performances from the cast, which also includes Jacqueline Bisset and Jon Voight, in this convincing crime melodrama about retribution and redemption. A-III PG) AA

End of the Line (1988) In order to protest the closing of their town's railyard, veteran Arkansas railroad workers (Wilford Brimley and Levon Helm) go to Chicago to confront the railroad's chairman of the board who helps them teach his weaselly son-in-law, the company president, a lesson in humanity. Director and co-writer Jay Russell and executive producer and co-star Mary Steenburgen have collaborated on an authentic and uncloying evocation of rural American life. Fine ensemble acting, but some rough language. A-II (PG)

End of the Road (1970) Screen version of John Barth's novel about a catatonic (Stacy Keach) who falls into the hands of a mad doctor (James Earl Jones) practicing multimedia shock treatment on his insane patients. Directed by Aram Avakian, vignettes of perversion, sadism, masochism and fetishism are woven into a story of adultery and exploitation, ending in a gross abortion sequence. O (X)

Endangered Species (1982) Ex-cop from New York City (Robert Urich) settles in Colorado to find peace and quiet but, instead, becomes involved in a bizarre case of cattle mutilations. Director Alan Rudolph manages to obscure a theme about chemical warfare by focusing upon the romance between the local sheriff (Jobeth Williams) and the boorish, foul-mouthed ex-cop. Some violence, nudity and rough language. A-III (R)

Endless Love (1981) Glossy fantasy about teenage love takes an inexplicable turn when the boy (Martin Hewitt) sets fire to the house in which the girl (Brooke Shields) and her family are sleeping. Directed by Franco Zeffirelli, the love-making scenes and needless nudity dissolve all pretense of sensitivity. O (R) AA

Endless Summer, The (1966) Two young experts (Robert August and Mike Hinson) travel to Africa, New Zealand, Tahiti and Hawaii in search for the perfect wave. Producer-director Bruce Brown pictures the pleasures of surfing with enthusiasm and humor. A-I (br) U

Enemies, A Love Story (1989) Brilliant adaptation of Isaac Bashevis Singer's novel about a troubled Holocaust survivor (Ron Silver) who shuttles between three wives (Margaret Sophie Stein, Lena Olin and Anjelica Huston) as he struggles with his indecision to choose one of them, his disillusionment with God and the chaos that his lies have caused. In capturing the feel of Jewish emigre life in 1949 New York City, director Paul Mazursky helps viewers empathize with the tragic flaws of the character and the courage of the women he loves. Sexually promiscuous protagonist, several sexual encounters with nudity, some violence and a climactic suicide. A-IV (R) 15

Enemy Mine (1985) In a science-fiction parable about the solidarity of intelligent life forms, a human (Dennis Quaid) and a reptilian alien (Louis Gossett, Jr.), enemies from warring star systems, find themselves marooned on an uninhabited planet where they must work together or perish. Plodding script by Edward Khmara and leaden direction by Wolfgang Petersen make the premise more silly than it might have been. Violence and a confusing sequence involving the reptilian reproductive process. A-III (PG-13) PG

Enforcer, The (1977) Clint Eastwood again plays Dirty Harry, the sadistic San Francisco policeman who, with a female partner (Tyne Daly) in tow, in on the job tracking down an underground terrorist group. Director James Fargo's crime melodrama has scant concern for plot consistency but just enough realism for its excessive violence to be offensive. O (R) X

England Made Me (1973) British screen version of the Graham Greene novel about a crooked Swedish tycoon (Peter Finch) and an ineffectual loser (Michael York) who gets in his way. By changing the locale from Depression Sweden to Hitler's Germany, director Peter Duffell focuses more on Nazi villainy than on the individual problems of the characters. The drama rejects the confused morality of its characters but lacks the sense of guilt that characterized Green's moral universe. A-IV (PG)

Enigma (1983) French-British production has an agent (Martin Sheen) sent on a perilous mission behind the Iron Curtain in this stodgy thriller directed by Jeannot Szwarc. Supporting cast, headed by Brigitte Fossey and Sam Neil, can do nothing to lift it above the conventional and mediocre. Some violence, brief nudity and a general air of moral ambiguity. A-III (PG) AA

Enough Rope (1966) French adaptation of a Patrica Highsmith mystery about a wife-killer (Gert Frobe), a man who would like to kill his wife (Maurice Ronet) and a police inspector (Robert Hossein) who gives them enough rope to wrap up his case. Directed by Claude Autant-Lara, the plot is intriguing in bringing together two strangers-in-crime, but the inspector's extra-legal methods are questionable. Mature themes. A-III (br)

Enter Laughing (1967) Autobiography based on comedian Carl Reiner's first break into showbiz. Reni Santoni is somewhat bland as the young comic, but Elaine May creates an outlandishly laughable neurotic, and Michael J. Pollard adds a fine folksy touch to the laughter. Also directed by Reiner, viewers will exit, if not laughing, at least smiling. A-I (br) U

Enter the Dragon (1973) Domestic martial arts exercise with Bruce Lee, Jim Kelly, and John Saxton as secret agents out to get the goods on a dope and prostitution ring by taking part in a Kung Fu competition staged by the gang. Directed by Robert Clouse, the complications are simply an endless repetition or brutal beatings, undifferentiated by the participant's race, creed or sex. O (R) X

Entertaining Mr. Sloane (1970) British screen version of Joe Orton's black comedy about an unscrupulous young man (Peter McEnery) being wooed and won simultaneously by a pathetic aging doxy (Beryl Reid) and her fastidious brother (Harry Andrews). Director Douglas Hickox gets too close to the corruption of human nature without the distancing of laughter that was intended, leaving most viewers incredulous about the film's surface reality and unconcerned about any inner meaning that might be there. A-IV (nr) X

Equinox (1971) The forces of good and evil emerge to do battle, this time in an inept and highly ludicrous story of devils and monsters and invisible castles. Directed by Jack Woods, this cornball exercise in fright and horror has phony special effects that could only scare the very young. A-II (PG)

Equinox Flower (1977) Gentle Japanese domestic comedy about a father's foolish concerns over his daughter's marriage. Directed in 1958 by Yusujiro Ozu, the story is infused with his loving brand of insight into character and situation that transcends national boundaries. A-II (nr)

Equis (1977) Director Sidney Lumet has brought Peter Shaffer's play to the screen with Richard Burton as the psychiatrist who treats a 17-year-old boy (Peter Firth) accused of blinding six horses. The tedium is made bearable only by Burton's presence and the work of a fine supporting cast. The fearful punishment that heterosexuality takes, the violence of the blinding, and the nude scene are unwarranted and insensitive. O (R) 15

Ernest Goes to Camp (1987) TV commercial legend Jim Varney plays the slaphappy goon of the title who bears the brunt of juvenile pranks and the callous villainy of some land developers in director John R. Cherry III's lame, often violently slapstick comedy set in a children's summer camp. Ex-football star Lyle Alzado's convincingly brutal beating of the Chaplin-like clown and Ernest's numerous pratfalls are too realistic to be funny. A-III (PG)

Ernest Goes to Jail (1990) When lovable, bumbling bank janitor Ernest (Jim Varney) switches places with a hardened death row inmate (also Varney), he must escape before he's electrocuted and his look-alike robs the bank. Director John Cherry keeps the slapstick gags flowing nonstop, including one with Ernest as a riotous human magnet and the silly antics of his yokel bank guard buddies (Gailard Sartain and Bill Byrge). Some prison menace and comic-book violence with extended scenes showing Ernest being zapped with electric shocks. A-II (PG)

Ernest Saves Christmas (1988) A Florida cabby (rubber-mouthed comic Jim Varney) picks up Santa (Douglas Seale) at the Orlando Airport and takes him into town in quest of a younger man to replace him at the North Pole, but they meet up with some disbelief. Directed by John Cherry, it's a holiday hoot with some good virtues for the youngsters. Some hectic traffic pile-ups and tense aerial moments. A-II (PG) U

Ernest Scared Stupid (1991) Child-kidnapping troll upsets the Halloween festivities of a small town until a slow-witted resident (Jim Varney) teams with an eccentric recluse (Eartha Kitt) to stop the supernatural monster. Director John Cherry's lame slapstick comedy gets precious few laughs from Varney's labored mugging and goofy anti-troll devices. Recurring threats to children, some frightening special effects and a few vulgar expressions. A-II (PG)

Erotic Three, The (see: "Scratch Harry").

Eroticon (1972) Barnard L. Sackett's sex exploitation movie interviews free love advocates, illustrating their views with hard-core pornographic footage and smutty songs. O (X)

Escape Artist, The (1982) Teenager (Griffin O'Neal), trying to measure up to his dead father's reputation as a magician, puts his lock-picking and wallet-lifting skills to good use in exposing a ring of corrupt politicians. Director Caleb Deschanel's offbeat adventure story has a rather underdeveloped plot, but what makes it worth seeing is O'Neal's precocious performance as the plucky youngster who beats an adult world at its own shady game. A-II (PG)

Escape from Alcatraz (1979) Clint Eastwood stars as a convict who attempts the impossible in a taut prison drama about one man's struggle to free himself from the conflicts and brutalities of the one-time island fortress known as the Siberia of prisons. Don Siegel's direction is grim but compelling. Some graphic violence. A-III (PG) 15

Escape from Fort Bravo (1953) A captured Confederate officer (John Forsythe) is helped by a friend (Eleanor Parker) to escape from a Union outpost in the Arizona badlands but are recaptured by a Yankee captain (William Holden), then ambushed by Mescalero Indians. Directed by John Sturges, the cliched story only comes to life in the climactic Indian battle amidst the rugged splendor of Death Valley locales. Stylized violence. A-I (br) U

Escape from New York (1981) Futuristic fantasy written and directed by John Carpenter imagines the island of Manhattan as a prison for incorrigible criminals who have taken captive the U.S. President (Donald Pleasence) and a seedy, cynical war hero (Kurt Russell) is sent in to bring him out. It's a clunker with excessive violence, brutality and sexual innuendo. A-III (R) AA

Escape from the Planet of the Apes (1971) Third in the series features Roddy McDowall and Kim Hunter as the upright apes from the future who whisk through the time barrier to land in the USA of today. The chaos resulting from man-kind's inhumanity to apes provides a so-so adventure that ends in tragedy but hope for the future in the birth a baby ape. The appeal of director Don Taylor's movie is less in its ragged story than in its creation of an imaginative situation and the zesty performances of its two leads. A-I (G) U

Escape to Athena (1979) Mediocre World War II movie has to do with a raid on a Nazi communications station in the Mediterranean led by some old familiar faces (Roger Moore, Telly Savalas, Elliott Gould and David Niven). British production directed by George Pan Cosmatos, it has considerable violence and a few brothel scenes. A-III (PG) A

Escape to Nowhere (1974) French spy thriller about a physicist (Lino Ventura) who is fleeing for his life from Soviet agents and whose only chance of survival is to trade a Soviet spy for his life. Director Claude Pinoteau has given new life to the old conventions of suspense, with menace and threat everywhere and the most ordinary places concealing potential dangers. A-II (PG)

Escape to the Sun (1972) Heavy, melodramatic escape adventure about a pair of Soviet Jews who hijack an Aeroflot jetliner to land at an abandoned airstrip and pick up a group of Jews hiding nearby. Director Menahem Golan's story is grim in outlook and execution, especially a long torture sequence, and its political implications require mature perspective and sensitivity. A-III (PG)

Escape to Witch Mountain (1975) Above average Disney adventure about two orphans with supernatural powers who become runaways sought by a greedy millionaire, muddled police, gangsters who think they are witches and even their own mysterious relatives from another solar system. Younger children will love the fantasy of kids having powers adults don't, but parents may wish that director John Hough had put a little more zest in the action. A-I (G)

E.T., The Extra-Terrestrial (1982) Ugly-duckling fable in which a boy (Henry Thomas) befriends a stranded alien creature from outer space and helps him return to his home. Director Steven Spielberg fashions an inspiring image of youthful innocence and courage in a story that some may find overly sentimental. Nevertheless, the childlike fantasy conveys some genuine emotion and a message of trust and peace that the family might enjoy sharing. A-I (PG) U

Eternally Yours (1939) Sour romantic comedy in which a daredevil magician (David Niven) tries to win back his ex-wife (Loretta Young) while she is honeymooning with her new husband (Broderick Crawford).

Director Tay Garnett plays up the stylish magic tricks and handcuffed parachute jumps but can't disguise the sentimental applesauce required in healing the broken marriage. Romantic complications and mild sexual innuendo. A-II (br) A

Ethan Frome (1993) Turn-of-the-century love triangle revolves around an impoverished New England farmer (Liam Neeson), his gloomy invalid wife (Joan Allen) and the tragedy that unfolds when her vibrant young cousin (Patricia Arquette) comes to care for her. Based on Edith Wharton's 1911 novel and directed by John Madden, the movie's skillful performances, exquisite cinematography and evocative music beautifully captures the moral dilemma of the farmer and his wife's cousin. Implied extramarital relationship. A-II (PG-13)

Eugenie (1970) Sex exploitation movie about a woman (Marie Liljedahl) who journeys into perversions perpetrated by satanists for the sex and violence trade. O (X)

Europa, Europa (1991) Stirring, fact-based story of a Jewish adolescent (Marco Hofschneider) who survives the Holocaust through an incredible series of events, including posing as an Aryan and being sent to an elite Hitler Youth school. Writer-director Agnieszka Holland's superb script is laced with ironic humor and a rich portrait of a youngster grappling with conflicting identities. Subtitles. Some wartime violence, fleeting sexual situations and occasional male nudity. A-III (R) 15

Europeans, The (1979) Screen version of the Henry James novel is a quiet comedy of manners about the unsettling effect of their European cousins (Lee Remick and Robin Ellis) upon the Wentworths, a proper Bostonian family. Though pleasant enough to watch, director James Ivory's moderately entertaining period piece lacks a sense of vitality and the feel for life that is to be found in the original. A-II (nr) U

Eve of Destruction (1991) Anti-terrorist expert (Gregory Hines) sets out to destroy a rogue robot that looks exactly like its creator (Renee Soutendijk) but is equipped with a nuclear capability that could destroy Manhattan. Duncan Gibbins directs an appallingly slick sci-fi thriller with little on its mind but assaulting viewers. Excessive violence, constant rough language, nasty sexual innuendo, brief nudity and menace to a child. O (R)

Evel Knievel (1971) Dramatization with George Hamilton playing a real-life character whose story this slapdash movie purports to be from growing up in Butte, Montana, and getting started on the motorcycle circuit to preparing for his impossible jump over 19 cars. Director Marvin

Chomsky's portrayal of a man driven by the desire to forever outdo himself in order to fend off personal insecurities has a passing interest, but Evel's amiable antics do not completely redeem the immaturity of his feelings about death or the cynical attitude of those fans who watch hoping for the worst. A-III (GP) A

Even Dwarfs Started Small (1972) Pretentious German movie in which the head of some kind of correctional institution is forced to barricade himself inside his office while crude male and female midget inmates wreak havoc upon the facilities and one another. Director Werner Herzog has come up with a visually striking, emotionally disturbing, curiosity piece that will tax the patience of most viewers. A-IV (nr)

Evening with the Royal Ballet, An (1965) Filmed on stage at the Royal Opera House in London, the work features Margot Fonteyn and Rudolf Nureyev in the performance of four ballets and two encores. Directed by Anthony Asquith and Anthony Havelock-Allan, it is a record of a prime ballet event marred only by static camerawork. A-I (br)

Event, An (1970) Yugoslavian adaptation of a short story by Chekhov relates a simple, tragic tale of a little boy and his grandfather who take a horse to the market and are waylaid on their return. Directed by Vatroslav Mimica, the hauntingly beautiful photography and credible acting of the small cast help make this small but terrible event an emotional experience of universal dimension. A-III (nr)

Events (1970) Feeble sex exploitation movie about a filmmaker making a stag movie to finance a serious movie. Director Fred Baker exploits a group of nonactors cavorting in graphic sexual excess. O (nr)

Everlasting Secret Family, The (1989) Unconvincing Australian drama about a government official (Arthur Dignam) who operates a secret society that procures young prep students for affluent homosexuals. Directed by Michael Thornhill, the movie largely romanticizes its story of sexual and political corruption. Some nudity in explicit, titillating homosexual encounters. O (nr) 18

Every Bastard a King (1970) Israeli movie set during the Six Day War is a contrived potboiler about an American journalist (William Berger) trying to understand the new society of Israel. Director Uri Zohar's title refers to the Israeli's spirit of democracy, but the movie itself manages to turn an interesting subject into a mediocre and incredibly muddled melodrama. A-III (GP)

Every Little Crook and Nanny (1972) The nanny of the title (Lynn Redgrave)

revenges the loss of her dancing school by kidnapping the young son of the crime boss responsible (Victor Mature). Director Cy Howard plays the situation comedy for dumb, at times coarse laughs. A-III (PG) A

Every Other Weekend (1991) Quiet, poignant French production in which a divorced actress (Nathalie Baye) impulsively takes her two young children out of Paris in violation of her custody agreement and heads for Spain with them with her anxious ex-husband (Miki Manojlovic) in pursuit. Director Nicole Garcia's melancholy first feature takes a vague and inconclusive look at a woman's self-absorption and the price she and her family pay for it. Subtitles. Family arguments with minor violence. A-II (nr)

Every Time We Say Goodbye (1986) Iowa minister's son (Tom Hanks) joins the British Royal Air Force during World War II, meets a Jewish-Hispanic girl living in Palestine and convinces her to wait for him to return. The glossy, overdone romance has some positive value in exploring the meaning of full commitment required for marriage. Bedroom scene and some violence. A-III (PG-13) 15

Every Which Way But Loose (1979) Clint Eastwood stars as a footloose trucker and barroom brawler who falls in love with a fickle country-western singer (Sondra Locke). Supporting characters includes an orangutan and Ruth Gordon as a foulmouthed old lady whose antics and vocabulary are supposed to be funny. Director James Fargo's slipshod movie features unremitting violence and sick humor. O (PG) AA

Everybody Does It (1949) Domestic comedy about a would-be singer (Celeste Holm) whose disapproving husband (Paul Douglas) is encouraged by an opera star (Linda Darnell) to become a professional singer. Directed by Edmund Goulding, this remake of "Wife, Husband and Friend" has a great cast, plenty of laughs but never quite pulls it all together. Romantic situations. A-II (br) U

Everybody Sing (1937) Fanciful Depression-era comedy about a wacky theatrical family (Billie Burke and Reginald Owen) saved from the poor house when their adolescent daughter (Judy Garland) teams up with the family's cook (Allan Jones) and maid (Fanny Brice) to stage a smash Broadway revue. Directed by Edwin L. Marin, the performances are spirited but the material is badly dated (including Garland's blackface number) and the songs unmemorable. More a curiosity piece than entertaining fare for youngsters today. A-I (br) U

Everybody Wins (1990) Sexually promiscuous, emotionally unstable New England woman (Debra Winger) baffles a private detective (Nick Nolte) with her puzzling offer to help him prove his client did not murder her physician. Scriptwriter Arthur Miller, director Karel Reisz and a gifted cast sustain the thriller's mood of intrigue but can't salvage the muddled exposition nor fill the holes in a plot involving judicial corruption. Some menace and promiscuity with veiled nudity, a graphic scene of violence and incidental rough language. A-III (R) 15

Everybody's All-American (1988) The 25-year-saga of the rise and fall of a Louisiana football hero (Dennis Quaid) and his Southern belle wife (Jessica Lange). Director Taylor Hackford's entertaining romance raises questions about hero worship and also touches on integration and other cultural changes affecting the South from 1956–1981. Brief sexual scenes, a flash of nudity, some bloody violence and vulgar language. A-III (R)

Everybody's Fine (1991) Poignant family drama follows an elderly Sicilian patriarch (Marcello Mastroianni) as he travels across Italy to visit his five grown children on a journey that proves full of bittersweet surprises and revelations. Director Giuseppe Tornatore blends Mastroianni's superlative performance into a wryly observed depiction of modern Italian life and personal predicaments. Subtitles. References to premarital pregnancy, promiscuity, suicide and a flash of nudity. A-III (PG-13) PG

Everything You Always Wanted to Know About Sex But Were Afraid to Ask (1972) Writer-director Woody Allen's take-off on Dr. David Reuben's book and the curiosity that made it a best-seller does better debunking sex obsessions than sex itself. The result is an uneven jumble of sketches, most of which go on too long, and range from the witty to the perverse, from hilarious sight gags to crudely offensive material. O (R) X

Everything's Ducky (1961) Mindless comedy drags out the slapstick efforts of numbskull sailors Mickey Rooney and Buddy Hackett to save a talking duck from being used in a Navy missile experiment. Directed by Don Taylor, the situation is tiresome, though the duck proves easier to take than his booby pals. Unimaginative fare without charm or appeal for young minds. A-I (br) U

Evil That Men Do, The (1984) Soldier-of-fortune (Charles Bronson) is hired to kill a political despot. Director Lee J. Thompson's violent action vehicle is set against the background of an oppressive regime in Central America, but sidesteps any serious political commentary in favor of the usual excessively brutal melodrama. O (R) 18

Evil Under the Sun (1982) Hercule Poirot (Peter Ustinov) is the thoughtful sleuth on a mission in the Adriatic in this fairly amusing adaptation of the Agatha Christie story. Director Guy Hamilton's British production turns the mystery into a travelogue which, lacking suspense, allows a talented cast free reign. The dialogue contains a few double entendres meant as witty insults. A-II (PG) A

Excalibur (1981) Long and lavish retelling of the legendary story of King Arthur (Nigel Terry) and his tutor Merlin (Nicol Williamson) is distinguished by an earnest sincerity and by its impressive settings, visual effects and cinematography. The treatment emphasizes the folk magic elements of the legend rather than its early Christian origin. In striving for effect, however, director John Boorman overdoes the sex and violence. O (R) 15

Execution Protocol, The (1993) Challenging documentary takes a clear-eyed view of what capital punishment means to those sentenced to die as well as to those responsible for executing them. Filmed by Steven Trombley at Missouri's Potosi Correction Center where the death sentence is carried out by a lethal injection machine, officials explain its humane application while death-row inmates describe it as "premeditated murder," leaving viewers confronting capital punishment not as a legal abstraction but as a troubling human reality. Grim subject and unsettling treatment. A-III (nr)

Executioner, The (1970) British spy thriller about an agent (George Peppard) who suspects a top level government security leak and takes it upon himself to execute the person he believes responsible. Director Sam Wanamaker emphasizes gray areas of conscience and morality in a setting of violence and intrigue, but the plot is unnecessarily complicated and lacking in subtlety, sympathy and credibility. A-III (GP) AA

Executive Action (1973) Failed political thriller about a conspiracy of right-wing millionaires who are behind the assassination of President John F. Kennedy neglects to offer any coherent, convincing demonstration of its fictional premise. Director David Miller wastes a good cast (Robert Ryan, Burt Lancaster and Will Geer) in a static movie that is disturbing only in its inability to stir even pathos for the fallen President. A-III (PG) A

Exodus (1960) Long and lavish adaptation of the Leon Uris novel about the birth of Israel follows the exploits of a Jewish underground leader (Paul Newman) in rescuing refugees interned by the British on Cyprus, freeing partisans from a British prison in Acre and saving a Jewish village from Arab attack after the 1948 U.N. partition of Palestine. Directed by Otto Preminger, the idealistic narrative is partly seen through the perspective of an American widow (Eva Marie Saint) whose visit to the Near East brings romance and an understanding of the need for a Jewish state. Some graphic violence including terrorist acts and sexual references. A-III (br) PG

Exorcist, The (1974) Screen version of the William Blatty novel about the demonic possession of a young girl (Linda Blair) and two priests (Jason Miller and Max von Sydow) who try to exorcize the devil from her. Directed by William Friedkin, the movie is on shaky ground theologically and its special effects are horrific, but it is exciting horror fantasy for those with strong stomachs. Its violence and obscenity as well as the powerful effect its subject matter and special effects could have on young viewers makes it strictly adult fare. A-IV (R) 18

Exorcist II: The Heretic (1977) It is four years later and Regan (Linda Blair), still bothered by a demon, is in the care of a psychiatrist (Louise Fletcher) and gets some help from a priest (Richard Burton) assigned to investigate the case. Director John Boorman's crass sequel, through simple ineptitude or outright ignorance, manages to denigrate a whole range of religious values. Some violence and profanity. O (R) X

Exorcist III, The (1990) Heavy-handed sequel pits an intelligent Georgetown detective (George C. Scott) against the diabolical deeds committed by an executed serial killer (Brad Dourif) whose soul has taken possession of the body of the priest (Jason Miller) who was killed at the conclusion of the original. Writer-director William Peter Blatty turns in a flawed horror movie with a slack plot but plenty of colorful characters and eerie photography. Several grisly scenes of demonic violence, many detailed verbal descriptions of bizarre murders and some instances of defiled religious symbols. A-IV (R) 18

Explorers, The (1985) Three 12-year-old boys, inspired by dreams, rig up their own spaceship and have some unusual close encounters. Moderately entertaining, but too much time is spent on the preliminaries with the outer-space payoff not packing the punch that it was meant to, namely some kind of profound lesson that lies beyond the cinematic vocabulary of director Joe Dante. Some profanity in the mouths of the young space cadets. A-II (PG) U

Explosion (1970) Canadian movie about a disturbed youth (Gordon Thomson) whose anti-Vietnam views supposedly cause him to rape a woman, flee to Canada and join a local hippie (Don Stroud) in an orgy of sex and violence through British Columbia. Director Jules Bricken's one-dimensional melodrama is hopelessly confused with flashbacks and fantasy sequences that rely for interest on bloodshed and nudity. O (R/GP)

Exposed (1983) Wisconsin farm girl (Nastassja Kinski) becomes a hot New York model and falls for a concert violinist (Rudolf Nureyev) who turns out to be a notorious terrorist tracking down his mother's murderer (Harvey Keitel). Director James Toback's shallow and silly vehicle exploits serious issues in an attempt to appear chic and witty. Excessive graphic sexuality. O (R) 15

Exterminating Angel, The (1967) A number of wealthy party guests find that after a long night in the home of their host, they are unable to leave, held by some mysterious force. In the days that follow, their veneer of politeness disintegrates until raw ego shows through. When finally released from each other's presence, they gather in a church to celebrate their deliverance only to discover themselves once again unable to leave. Director Luis Bunuel's 1962 surrealistic satire amusingly suggests that hell is other people. A-III (br) X

Exterminator, The (see: "The Inheritor").

Extraordinary Seaman, The (1969) World War II action fantasy in which a captain in the Royal Navy (David Niven) who died in 1914 is granted a celestial reprieve to vindicate an inglorious death by taking on the Japanese Navy with his dilapidated island steamer. Director John Frankenheimer fails in an embarrassingly bad effort to keep this seagoing bomb afloat. A-II (G) U

Extreme Close-Up (1973) Researching a story on electronic surveillance techniques, a reporter (James McMullan) becomes obsessed with the easily obtainable gadgets of the trade and their potential for invading the private lives of innocent people. Director Jeannot Szwarc uses Michael Crichton's screenplay simply as a vehicle for spying upon the sexual escapades of a rather dull group of characters. O (R)

Extreme Prejudice (1987) Nick Nolte plays a bulletproof Texas Ranger poised to stamp out a drug traffic kingpin (Powers Boothe) with the aid of a ruthless commando group made up of legally dead Vietnam vets headed by a double-crossing major (Michael Ironside). Director Walter Hill's lengthy sequences of excessively brutal gunplay and some nudity mark this as a conventional blood-and-guts timewaster. O (R) 18

Extremities (1986) A woman (Farrah Fawcett) is the target of a sadistic rapist (James Russo) whom she manages to restrain and molest in turn. Film plays upon the vulnerability of women in a man's world and suggests that fighting back is an essential survival tactic. It concludes somewhat weakly that justice must be tempered with mercy in spite of possible further endangerment. Instead of being thought-provoking, the film brutalizes the viewer with explicit scenes of sadism, violence and foul language. O (R) 18

Eye for an Eye, An (1966) Routine western directed by Michael Moore in which a former bounty hunter (Robert Lansing) teams with a young bounty hunter (Pat Wayne) to take revenge on the villains who brutally murdered his wife and son. Stylized violence and the revenge is accomplished through self-defense. A-II (br)

Eye of the Cat (1969) San Francisco mansion full of cats is the setting for the story of two nephews (Michael Sarrazin and Tim Henry) scheming to eliminate a rich, but ailing aunt (Eleanor Parker) and each other in order to inherit her fortune. Director David Lowell Rich manipulates the cats for shock and suspense effect but not enough to cover the gaping holes in the plot. Some violence and sexual implications. A-III (PG) X

Eye of the Devil (1967) The head of an aristocratic French family (David Niven) journeys to his ancestral chateau to offer himself as a victim in a religious rite practiced by his forbears. Under the direction of J. Lee Thompson, the performances of Niven and Deborah Kerr compensate for a plot that often strains credibility. A-III (br) X

Eye of the Needle (1981) Mediocre British screen version of Ken Follet's World War II thriller in which a coldly proficient German spy (Donald Sutherland) becomes distracted from his mission when he encounters a love-starved woman (Kate Nelligan) on a bleak island off the coast of Scotland. Directed by Richard Marquand, the unabsorbing melodrama combines a conventional espionage plot with a needlessly explicit depiction of a love affair. O (R) AA

Eyes of a Stranger (1981) Sadistic rapist-murderer (John DiSanti) stalks the blind adolescent sister (Jennifer Jason Leigh) of a television reporter (Lauren Tewes) in this sleazy, amateurish horror movie. Director Ken Wiederhorn's suspense thriller forfeits finesse in favor of stomach-churning violence and nudity. O (R)

Eyes of Laura Mars, The (1978) Failed thriller about a series of brutal murders that happens exactly as seen in the premonitions of a top New York fashion photographer (Faye Dunaway). The shallow, slick, kinky movie directed by Irvin Kershner leeringly exploits sex and violence. O (R) AA

Eyewitness (1981) A young janitor (William Hurt) falls in love with a television reporter (Sigourney Weaver) whom he has never met and, when she asks him questions about a murder committed in his building, he pretends to know more about the crime than he actually does. Director Peter Yates' romantic mystery succeeds better in terms of characterization of the young couple than its muddled attempts at suspense. Some violence and a rather graphic bedroom scene. A-III (R)

F

Fabulous Baker Boys, The (1989) Demoralized piano-playing brother team (Jeff and Beau Bridges) on the Seattle cocktail-lounge circuit briefly revitalize their stale act with a sultry female singer (Michelle Pfeiffer) who catalyzes the men to face some hard, personal realities. The acting of the principals is fine and writer-director Steve Kloves has a feel for these fringe performers and the poignant unraveling of family ties. Some profanity laced with sexual vulgarities and brief sexual situations with a flash of nudity. A-III (R) 15

Face to Face (1976) Stockholm psychiatrist (Liv Ullmann) discovers that she must heal herself when she suffers from a nervous breakdown in director Ingmar Bergman's clinical investigation into the realm of the feminine psyche. Ullmann's magnificent performance conveys the failure of psychiatry as a remedy to the disappointments and contradictions of her guilt-ridden life. The movie includes some harrowing scenes, including an attempted rape, but the emphasis is on the interior journey to peace of soul. A-III (R) X

Faces (1968) Director John Cassavetes intense study of the marital crisis of a middle-aged, middle-class couple (Gena Rowlands and John Marley) who discover that divorce isn't the answer to their personal emptiness and despairing search for meaning in life. Troubling, sardonic, somewhat depressing treatment of a mature theme that is part of so many contemporary relationships. Some rough language, sexual innuendo and a suicide attempt. A-IV (br) X

Faces of Love (1978) A movie director (Jean-Louis Trintignant) tries to win back his ex-wife (Delphine Seyrig) by starring her in an adaptation of Chekhov's "The Three Sisters" (with Lea Massari and Valerie Mairesse as the other leads). Swiss director Michael Soutter wastes a talented cast with what is in effect a shallow exercise in psychodrama. A-III (nr)

Fahrenheit 451 (1966) A fireman (Oskar Werner) reforms his book-burning ways in this adaptation of Ray Bradbury's science-fiction novel about a society that forbids the printed word. First rate performances by Julie Christie in a dual role as two women in the fireman's life and Cyril Cusack as a smiling fanatic help sustain the dream-like reality of director Francois Truffaut's allegorical fantasy. Menacing atmosphere. A-II (br) A

Fail Safe (1964) A mechanical failure makes impossible the recall of nuclear bombers headed for Russia in a movie questioning the ability of humans to control their inventions. Sidney Lumet directs Henry Fonda, Dan O'Herlihy and various machines with mounting suspense. A-II (br) PG

Falcon and the Snowman, The (1985) Some boyhood friends, now young men (Timothy Hutton and Sean Penn), sell secret data to the Soviets. How all this happened and why is an engrossing and very well-acted story, but director John Schlesinger has left too many loose ends and tends to sentimentalize these treasonous actions as mistaken idealism. Brief nudity, some drug use and ambivalent treatment of a complex subject. A-III (R) 15

Fall of the Roman Empire, The (1964) In this lavish historical re-creation, Rome's wise old emperor Marcus Aurelius (Alec Guinness) is poisoned by his corrupt son (Christopher Plummer) whose savage policies against the barbarians brings the teetering empire to its ruin. Directed by Anthony Mann, the three-hour dramatization has an autumnal splendor that one can admire, yet find the spectacle unmoving on a human level. Stylized battle scenes and other assorted violence may frighten young children. A-I (br) U

Falling Down (1993) Pointless, ugly saga of a bitterly divorced, unemployed defense worker (Michael Douglas) who freaks out one day and goes on a one-man killing spree in L.A. while a persistent cop (Robert Duvall) doggedly tracks him down. Director Joel Schumacher presents a repulsive view of contemporary America where murderous behavior is seen as an inevitable response to mundane frustrations of modern urban life. Trivialization of deadly violence and much rough language, including racial and ethnic epithets. O (R) 18

Falling from Grace (1992) Melancholy tale of a popular country singer (John Mellencamp) come home to rural Indiana where he cheats on his wife (Mariel Hemingway) with an old girlfriend (Kay Lenz) while considering how to proceed with the rest of his life. Also directed by Mellencamp, the ponderous story crawls along under the burden of static characters shuffling through midlife crises with little hint of resolution or personal growth. Discreet bedroom scene, references to adulterous affairs, fleeting violence and an instance of rough language. A-III (PG-13)

Falling in Love (1984) Two train commuters (Robert De Niro and Meryl Streep) fall in love, have a secret affair and part, never resolving their true feelings and their commitments to others. Although the story is essentially about adultery, the whole enterprise is so lacking in substance that moral principles hardly seem relevant. Director Ulu Grosbard fails to convey adequately the moral dilemma that was meant to be the core of the film's romantic theme. A-II (PG-13) PG

Falling in Love Again (1980) Elliott Gould plays the middle-aged owner of a Beverly Hills garment store who spends his time in nostalgic daydreams about his Bronx origins much to the chagrin of his wife (Susannah York) in this contrived and determinedly simple-minded little movie written and directed by Steven Paul. A bedroom sequence and a certain moral ambiguity makes this mature fare. A-III (PG)

Fame (1980) Irene Cara and several other talented youngsters from various ethnic and racial backgrounds learn the showbiz ropes studying in New York City's High School for the Performing Arts. Following them from audition to graduation, director Alan Parker's movie is a vibrant showcase for physical prowess not the least of which is demonstrated in some scenes involving nudity in a sexual context. Permissive sexual attitudes and irreverent treatment of religion overshadow the film's portrait of youngsters expressing their creativity and striving for professionalism. O (R) PG

Family, The (1987) Interesting Italian production recounting the lives of several generations of a family inhabiting an elegant apartment in Rome from the turn of the century to the present. Directed by Ettore Scola, the family portrait recalled by an aging man (Vittorio Gassman) is limited to the domestic life within the rooms of the apartment over the years. Many will find its fragmentary vignettes of personal drama surprisingly remote and lacking in emotional involvement. Some mature themes. A-III (PG)

Family Affair, A (1937) Fine old-fashioned and full-blooded family melodrama in which Judge Hardy (Lionel Barrymore) rescues the town from an aqueduct scam while saving the marriage of his eldest daughter (Cecilia Parker). Directed by George B. Seitz, the picture's strong success spawned 15 sequels in a series that came to focus more on the judge's teenage son (Mickey Rooney) than the role of sage family patriarch created by Barrymore but thereafter played by Lewis Stone. In 1942 the series received a special Oscar for "representing the American way of life." The original is dated entertainment but still of interest for its idealistic view of family life. A-I (br)

Family Business (1989) Muddled comedy-drama about a crooked grandfather (Sean Connery), his reformed son (Dustin Hoffman) and his bright grandson (Mat-

thew Broderick) who join forces to commit the perfect theft in an improbable caper that proves self-destructive for the entire family. Directed by Sidney Lumet, there is much father-son business to resolve but the poor script and oddball casting only get in the way. Much profanity, some sexual innuendo and an unresolved moral perspective on crime as a career. A-III (R) 15

Family Game, The (1984) Japanese director Yoshimitsu Morita fashions a gentle and noble comedy of family life and incisively chronicles their problems and how they resolve them. For those willing to read subtitles, the film will be an enjoyable as well as rewarding experience of the universality of family themes. A-II (nr)

Family Honor (1973) New York cop (Anthony Page) seeks revenge on the policemen who set up his father, also a member of the force, for opposing their taking payoffs from mobsters. Director Clark Worswick's crime movie is remarkable only in its consistent mediocrity, which follows a predictable course of killings, drug traffic, warehouse confrontations and corruption in high places. Some Italian Americans may be offended by ethnic stereotyping. A-III (R)

Family Plot (1976) Director Alfred Hitchcock turns in a below-par thriller about the efforts of a not-quite-bogus medium (Barbara Harris) and her not-too-bright boyfriend (Bruce Dern) to match wits with a pair of diabolically clever kidnappers (William Devane and Karen Black). The movie is peppered with profanity and unwitty double entendres, perhaps meant to inject some life into a slack picture. A-III (PG)

Family Prayers (1993) Melancholy tale set in 1969 as a sensitive Jewish boy (Tzvi Ratner-Stauber) prepares for his bar mitzvah while the marriage of his parents (Joe Mantegna and Anne Archer) unravels under the strain of his father's compulsive gambling. Despite its heartfelt intentions, director Scott Rosenfelt's earnest drama is a familiar story marred by flat direction and weak scripting. Minor violence and an ongoing sense of menace from loansharks. A-III (PG)

Family Way, The (1967) The lives of a young married couple (Hywell Bennett and Hayley Mills) are fraught with problems, including the groom's temporary inability to consummate their union. The groom's well-meaning but domineering father (John Mills) stands in his son's way, but it is the strengths of family life that save the day. Directed by Roy Boulting with musical score by Paul McCartney. A-IV (br) 15

Famine Within, The (1992) Thought-provoking documentary about female obsession with body shape examines how, increasingly, young girls and women are suffering serious eating disorders as they define their worth by their weight. Writer-producer-director Katherine Gilday perceptively questions society's adulation of ultra-thin models and actresses in disturbing interviews with young female bulimics and anorexics. Brief shower room nudity. A-II (nr)

Fan, The (1981) Young psychopath (Michael Biehn) stalks a glamorous star (Lauren Bacall) with whom he has become obsessed, striking with a razor at those whom he believes are preventing her from seeing him. Bacall is very good, but here she lends her presence and talent to a cheap, exploitative movie by director Ed Bianchi who seems obsessed with delivering brutal visual shocks. Extremely graphic violence. O (R) X

Fancy Pants (1950) Mistaken for an English butler, a jobless American actor (Bob Hope) is hired to bring some class to the household of a newly rich cattle baron whose sparky daughter (Lucille Ball) grows fond of the inept tenderfoot. Director George Marshall's enjoyable western comedy—a variation of "Ruggles of Red Gap"—offers a winning pair of screen clowns at the top of their form and a script that has room for wit as well as pratfalls. A-I (br) U

Fandango (1985) It's May 1971, and five new-minted Texas college graduates go off on a car trip to the Mexican border in search of their lost youth—fleeing Vietnam, marriage, regular jobs and other fearful spectres. Written and directed by Kevin Reynolds, the movie is sporadically amusing but more often sentimental, self-indulgent and tedious. Some brief nudity meant to be comic. A-II (PG)

Fando and Lis (1970) In an allegorical search for eternal happiness, Sergio Klainer and Diana Mariscal journey through a rocky, garbage-strewn landscape where a grotesque assortment of nightmarish characters confront them with sex and perversions. Scripted by Fernando Arrabal, directed by Alexandro Jodorowsky and filmed in Mexico, the bizarre narrative lacks coherence and is exploitative in its treatment of sex and violence. O (nr)

Fanny and Alexander (1983) Directed by Ingmar Bergman, this autobiographical mood piece set at Christmas in 1907 examines family ties through the eyes of a 10-year-old boy. Replete with the themes of earlier films, the period drama has none of the depth and perception of Bergman at his best but does offer the spectacle of a lavish re-creation. Scatological and sexually derived humor and some brief nudity set the naturalistic tone of this decidedly mature tale of Swedish provincial life. A-IV (R) 15

Fanny Hill (1969) Swedish exploitation movie directed by Mac Ahlberg about an inexperienced country girl (Diana Kjaer) who comes to the big city to find a job. The situation is used as the premise for a series of crudely explicit sexual encounters. O (R)

Fantasia (1940) Walt Disney's only excursion into the world of the fine arts presents eight selections of classical music, including Dukas' "Sorcerer's Apprentice" with Mickey Mouse and a bucket brigade of brooms, Stravinsky's "Rite of Spring" with its massive, earth-bound images and the macabre vision of Musorgsky's "Night on Bald Mountain." Using different approaches and animation styles for each separate section, it was not only Disney's most ambitious undertaking but it remains an enjoyably creative introduction to fine music, especially for youngsters. A-I (G) U

Fantastic Animation Festival (1977) Compilation consisting of 16 award-winning animated films. The majority are solidly entertaining, especially two featuring the clay figures of Will Vinton. For youngsters, it's a chance to view other approaches to the art of frame-by-frame movie making in contrast to Saturday morning cartoon fare. A-II (PG)

Fantastic Planet (1973) Lovely, haunting animated feature set in the far distant future where humans have become minuscule vermin in a world of purple reptilian giants that periodically exterminate the humans just as people today routinely exterminate roaches and rodents. For adults, this unusual picture, the creation of Rene Laloux and a Franco-Czech production team, can be a fascinating experience, heightened by its surrealistic imagery and eerie electronic soundtrack. Youngsters, however, might be disturbed by the occasional brutalities and the type of nudity associated with tribes living in a savage state. A-III (R/PG)

Fantastic Voyage (1966) The miniaturization of a medical team to the size of a molecule and their injection into a stroke patient's bloodstream is the only possible way to save the life of an important scientist. Director Richard Fleischer's incredible plot premise yields rich dividends in the form of exacting special effects re-creating the surreal world within the human body. A-I (br) A

Fantomas (1966) Gimmicky French-Italian superhero story about a master of disguise who battles all manner of Parisian criminals is directed by Andre Hanebelle in the melodramatic style of the old Saturday matinee adventure serials. Innocuous escapist fare. A-I (br) U

Far and Away (1992) Sprawling, brawling romantic adventure about the rebellious daughter (Nicole Kidman) of an Irish land-owner and a scrappy tenant farmer (Tom Cruise) who wind up in Boston where they share quarters in order to save enough to get to the 1893 Oklahoma land rush. Director Ron Howard orchestrates rousing, feel-good entertainment whose romanticized predicaments detract little from the spirited performances of the two principals. Some sexual innuendo and bloody fisticuffs. A-III (PG-13) 12

Far Country, The (1955) After taking a herd of cattle from Oregon to the gold camps of Alaska, a rancher (James Stewart) and aging sidekick (Walter Brennan) get in the way of a crooked judge (John McIntire) and his claim-jumping cohorts. Directed by Anthony Mann, the rugged setting appropriately frames the tough characters in an action picture that winds up with the usual shoot-out heroics. Some stylized violence and mild romance. A-I (br) U

Far from the Madding Crowd (1967) Excellent British screen version of Thomas Hardy's romantic melodrama of early Victorian country life with Julie Christie being pursued by Peter Finch, Terence Stamp and Alan Bates. Director John Schlesinger avoids the pitfalls of the formula blockbuster and comes up with a superbly realistic, atmospheric production filmed entirely on location in Hardy's Dorset. A-II (br) U

Far Horizons, The (1955) Colorful but wooden re-creation of the Lewis (Fred MacMurray) and Clark (Charlton Heston) expedition (1803-06) exploring the upper reaches of the Missouri River and across the Rockies to the Pacific Ocean. Directed by Rudolph Mate, the scenery is certainly picturesque but the adventure is too fanciful to be convincing, especially the hokey romance between Clark and the expedition's Indian guide, Sacajawea (a badly miscast Donna Reed). Some stylized violence and Native-American stereotypes. A-I (br) U

Far Off Place, A (1993) Contemporary African adventure with a 14-year-old American girl (Reese Witherspoon) and young friend (Ethan Randall) fleeing murderous ivory poachers by trekking 1000 miles across the Kalahari desert with only an African Bushman (Sarel Bok) as guide. Director Mikael Salomon combines a lively story, delightful cast and exquisite cinematography for an old-fashioned outdoor adventure with modern environmental sensibilities. Brief violence, occasional profanity and continuing menace. A-II (PG)

Far Out Man (1990) Terminally revolting movie about the aimless wanderings of an aging, leftover hippie (Tommy Chong) who takes to the road to forget his longlost wife and son but accidentally chances upon them. Chong wrote, directed and stars (along with assorted relatives) in this warped tribute to the drug culture and sexual promiscuity. Much rough language, sexually suggestive scenes with nudity, promotion of drug abuse and a variety of gross, violent and vulgar acts. O (R)

Faraway, So Close (1993) Poetic fantasy of invisible guardian angels watching over the untidy affairs of people living in contemporary Berlin, until one of them (Otto Sander) becomes a mortal man in order to save a child's life, then suffers a series of misadventures as a human. German director Wim Wenders' playfully creative but overlong journey is one of discovery in seeing modern life as experienced by a pure-hearted former angel trying to cope with such things as alcohol, pornography and arms trafficking. Subtitles. Some stylized violence and sexual references. A-III (nr)

Farewell My Concubine (1993) Long but colorful multi-leveled epic spanning the various political changes in China from 1925 to 1977 as seen in the lifelong friendship of two Peking Opera stars—one (Zhang Fengyi) famous for virile roles and the other (Leslie Cheung) for his performance of female leads—though the bond between them is strained after the former marries a prostitute (Gong Li). In intermixing the political with the personal, director Chen Kaige is particularly harsh on the excesses of the Cultural Revolution (1966–77), but his primary focus is on the world of the stage and those who make it their life. Subtitles. Some scenes of violence, sexual situations, including implications of homosexuality, and occasional rough language. A-III (R) 15

Farewell, My Lovely (1975) Hulking ex-convict (Jack O'Halloran) hires private investigator Philip Marlowe (Robert Mitchum) to find his girlfriend, though she hasn't bothered to write while he served a seven year sentence for bank robbery. Director Dick Richards' version of the Raymond Chandler mystery is skillfully crafted and Mitchum gives an outstanding performance. Some violence and incidental nudity. A-III (R) 15

Farewell to the King (1989) Epic set in the jungles of Borneo during the final months of World War II where an American survivor of Corregidor (Nick Nolte) winds up as the adopted "king" of a tribe of headhunters whom he tries to protect from annihilation when they are forced to fight against the Japanese by a British Special Forces unit. Director John Milius leaves little doubt about who the true savages are in this uncomplicated, old-fashioned adventure film. Intense battle carnage and minimal rough language. A-III (PG-13)

Farewell Uncle Tom (1972) Gualtiero Jacopetti and Franco Prosperi have been responsible for a long and dismayingly popular series of pseudo-documentaries but this time their subject is an historical one, slavery in the United States. Their voyeuristic treatment of the subject is simply vicarious flesh-peddling and the concluding section, specially prepared for the American version of this Italian film, can only deepen racial misunderstanding. O (X)

Farmer, The (1977) Revenge story of a World War II veteran (Gary Conway) has arty pretensions but not a spark of intelligence. Mechanically directed by David Berlatsky, it is excessively brutal and sexually degrading. O (R)

Fast Break (1979) Very funny movie about a new basketball coach (Gabe Kaplan) who recruits a motley collection of youths to give an obscure college a winning basketball season. Directed by Jack Smight, it contains some rough language and several mildly suggestive sexual scenes. A-III (PG)

Fast Charlie . . . The Moonbeam Rider (1979) Failed period road comedy about a World War I vet (David Carradine) who enlists the aid of some of his old buddies to help him enter a transcontinental motorcycle race. Director Steve Carver's thin story is amiable but not very funny. Permissive attitude toward casual sex. A-III (PG) U

Fast Forward (1985) Some bright and talented teenagers from Sandusky, Ohio, go to New York to win a dance contest without bothering to inform their parents. The poor kids have to hang on for a month or so before they make it to the top. Mediocre entertainment, disappointingly directed by Sidney Poitier. Some vulgar language, nose-thumbing at parental authority and teenage drinking presented as humorous. A-III (PG)

Fast Talking (1986) A modern artful dodger lies, cheats and steals his way out of high school and into the brave new world of self-sufficiency in reaction to flawed family, alienated friends and a social order that offers little positive encouragement. But it's hard to accept the amiable, resourceful teenager as someone incapable of finding positive options. The film points to the moral and political inadequacies of adult society but in less than constructive fashion. A-III (nr) 18

Fast Times at Ridgemont High (1982) Director Amy Heckerling's examination of teen mores in the suburban jungle of shopping malls, discos and the playing fields of Southern California has some insights. However, for the most part it is a crass, insensitive and superficial movie with an unsettling nastiness lurking just beneath its pleasant surface. Some extremely graphic nudity and a scene of adolescents discussing oral sex. O (X/R) 18

Fat City (1972) Complex character study of two boxers, one a has-been (Stacy Keach) and the other a youth of 19 (Jeff Bridges) whose prospects on the B-grade California boxing circuit are at best uncertain. Director John Huston's theme of wasted lives and loves and the hopes of youth for affluence and success (the ironic meaning of the title) are evocative but unsatisfying in terms of the dramatic whole. Well-staged, realistic fight sequences. A-III (PG)

Fat Man and Little Boy (1989) Fine production values and serviceable acting highlight this dramatization of the creation of the atomic bomb beginning in 1942 and focusing on the professional and personal agendas motivating the two key players, Gen. Leslie R. Groves (Paul Newman) and physicist J. Robert Oppenheimer (Dwight Schultz). Director Roland Joffe creates an air of scientific and historical accuracy together with a sense of visual tension and the result helps clarify the moral issues debated by those who made the bomb. An adulterous encounter with nudity, a grisly death from radiation and minimal rough language. A-III (PG-13)

Fata Morgana (1974) German director Werner Herzog's interior journey to Africa is a stunning portrait of the North African landscape where people are transformed into fragments of an alien, dreamlike world. For those adventurous enough to take a trip without the security of guideposts, it will most likely prove a consciousness-expanding experience. A-III (nr)

Fatal Attraction (1987) Ambitious, hard-driving but happily married lawyer (Michael Douglas) has a fling with a compulsive admirer (Glenn Close) and both suffer the dangerous consequences. Director Adrian Lyne's fatalistic romance begins as a moral tale and ends in a melodramatic bloodbath. Several graphic love-making scenes, but violence and rough language dominate. O (R) 18

Fatal Instinct (1993) Strained send-up of movie thrillers in which Armand Assante is the thoroughly dense object of affection and/or extinction by his wandering wife (Kate Nelligan), simpering secretary (Sherilyn Fenn) and kooky client (Sean Young). The slapstick and sight gags in director Carl Reiner's weak, goofy parody are only fitfully funny and often crude. Some vulgar sexual innuendo, brief nudity and sporadic violence played for comic effect. A-III (PG-13) 15

Father Goose (1964) An unusually disheveled Cary Grant plays a beachcomber reformed by a prim but high-spirited French schoolmarm (Leslie Caron) and her seven girl pupils when they are stranded together on a Pacific island during World War II. Director Ralph Nelson handles the romantic comedy deftly enough though the plot is entirely predictable in overcoming wartime dangers with affable, good-natured humor. A-I (br) U

Father of the Bride (1950) Delightful comedy from Edward Streeter's novel about a self-assured suburbanite (Spencer Tracy) suddenly thrust into the unfamiliar world of wedding preparations and financial obligations when his only daughter (Elizabeth Taylor) announces her engagement. Brightly directed by Vincente Minnelli, Tracy is superb as the caring but confused head of the household helped by patient wife Joan Bennett to come to terms with their daughter's vision of the perfect wedding. Amusing yet perceptive view of middle-class life and family values. A-I (br) U

Father of the Bride (1991) Trite remake of the 1950 Spencer Tracy-Elizabeth Taylor charmer this time has father Steve Martin battling the emotional loss of daughter Kimberly Williams while wife Diane Keaton tries to cushion the financial drain of a big wedding. A hilarious scene early on is outweighed by mawkish sentimentality in director Charles Shyer's drawn-out comedy. Fleeting sexual innuendo. A-II (PG)

Fathers and Sons (1992) Shallow drama of a widower (Jeff Goldblum) trying to help his teenage son (Rory Cochrane) confront the perils of contemporary urban life—gangs, drugs, alcohol, sex, cults and street crazies. Written and directed by Paul Mones, the well-intended effort realistically portrays the youth's problems while mawkishly handling the father's inept attempts to communicate with his son until a contrived ending. Restrained depiction of moral problems requiring a mature perspective. A-III (R)

Father's Little Dividend (1951) "Father of the Bride" cast returns in a heavy-handed sequel turning good old dad (Spencer Tracy) into an unsympathetic grouch dismayed by the demands of impending grandfatherhood. Nor does director Vincente Minnelli find much humor in the predictable problems of expectant parents Elizabeth Taylor and Don Taylor in naming the baby, false labors and in-law competition over the heir apparent. Confusing situations for youngsters. A-II (br) U

Fathom (1967) Mindless spy intrigue with Raquel Welch being pursued by plane, by boat, by harpoonist and by bull (both figuratively and literally). Directed by Leslie Martinson, the star vehicle becomes tiresome long before the ending. A-II (br) U

Fatso (1980) Actress Anne Bancroft fails to convey much sincerity or intelligence in her directorial debut. Her comedy stars Dom DeLuise as a compulsive eater who is so shocked by the early death of an obese cousin that he determines to lose weight. The humor is weighted down, however, by foul language and silly sight-gags in a social satire that provides little insight into a serious malady. A-III (PG) A

Favor, the Watch and the Very Big Fish, The (1992) Strained comedy has an earnest photographer (Bob Hoskins) of religious tableaux and the model he uses for Jesus (Jeff Goldblum) falling for the same woman (Natasha Richardson). Writer-director Ben Lewin's mildly naughty black comedy is too self-conscious and contrived to inspire more than forced laughter from the wacky situations. Much sexual innuendo, brief nudity, comic violence and minimal rough language. A-III (R) 15

Fear, The (1967) Greek movie directed by Costas Manoussakis centers on a retarded youth's morbid preoccupation with sex. Offensive because of its explicit treatment of erotic activities. O (br)

Fear City (1984) Psychotic killer of New York City strippers is hunted by an ex-boxer (Tom Berenger) and his exhibitionist girlfriend (Melanie Griffith) in a sleazy exploitation feature directed by Abel Ferrara. Excessive violence, much nudity and recurring rough language. O (R)

Fear Eats the Soul—Ali (1974) German movie in which a 60-year-old cleaning woman meets a young Moroccan mechanic, and out of mutual loneliness and a desperate need for some special other person, they marry and encounter the same rejection and discrimination suffered by minorities everywhere. Directed by Rainer Werner Fassbinder, the story is simply told and yet is profoundly human and affecting in its picture of two ordinary people persecuted by a hypocritical society. A-IV (nr)

Fear Is the Key (1973) Adaptation of Alistair MacLean thriller about an ex-salvage operator (Barry Newman) who, by reason of a wild and complex chain of events, finds himself in the palatial home of an oil heiress (Suzy Kendall) and given the task of dredging up a sunken treasure. Director Michael Tuchner's wildly improbable melodrama in which nothing is what it seems is moderately entertaining, mercifully short on sex and violence but awfully hard to swallow. A-II (PG) A

Fear No Evil (1981) Bright but popular high school student is possessed by the devil in this inept horror film written and directed by Frank Laloggia. Excessive violence, nudity and exploitation of religious themes. O (R)

Fearless (1993) In the months following a plane crash with many fatalities, a euphoric survivor (Jeff Bridges) feels disconnected from wife (Isabella Rossellini) and child, a situation aggravated by his determination to help a severely depressed survivor (Rosie Perez) adjust to the loss of her baby in the crash. Director Peter Weir realistically captures the spiritual anguish and psychological trauma of survivors trying to pull their lives together after a profound disaster completely changes their outlook on life. Violent aftermath of a crash with fleeting shots of the human carnage, minor sexual innuendo and occasional rough language. A-II (R) 15

Fearless Frank (1969) The Second City gang has put together a super-spoof of crime movies with some digs at sex and religion. Jon Voight plays Frank, a Superman character flying through the air and fighting evil wherever it rears its ugly head. Director Philip Kaufman's campy, superficial adult comedy is of limited quality and appeal. A-III (G)

Fearless Vampire Killers, The (1967) Offbeat horror spoof in which an old scholar of the occult (Jack McGowran) and his young assistant (Roman Polanski) seek out a vampire's castle in the hills of Transylvania, using the tools of garlic, the cross and a wooden stake in their research, but the vampires are released to spread throughout the world. Also directed by Polanski, it is imitation camp at best, all very short on humor, long on blood-drinking and sexual innuendo. A-III (br) A

Fedora (1979) Down-on-his-luck Hollywood producer (William Holden) journeys to the Greek island of Corfu to persuade a legendary actress (Marthe Keller) to come out of retirement and play the lead in his movie. German production directed by Billy Wilder is a failed curiosity piece about the old and the new wave of moviemakers. Some adult situations. A-III (PG)

Feds (1988) The saga of two women (Rebecca De Mornay and Mary Gross) determined to graduate from the male-dominated F.B.I. Academy takes some unexpected turns that upgrade it from mere fluff to a fairly respectable view of women in a traditionally male occupation. Directed by Dan Goldberg, it reverses the convention, in contrived humorous fashion, of weak-kneed women and super men. Some locker-room and sexually vulgar language. A-III (PG-13)

Fellini Satyricon (1970) Federico Fellini's self-indulgent vision of ancient Rome presents not a story but a series of sequences juxtaposed with little or no cause and effect relationship. Buried beneath its array of imagery ranging from the sensuous and opulent to the grotesque and orgiastic are such unconnected themes as youth's search for fulfillment, the destruction of the artist by his patrons and the collapse of a society burdened by the luxury of wealth. Though an extraordinary visual experience, it is disappointing in its lack of structure, logic and viewer engagement. Many scenes of sex and violence. A-IV (R)

Fellini's Casanova (1977) Director Federico Fellini's first English-language production concentrates on the sordid details of the sexual legend surrounding Giacomo Casanova without concern for any human dimensions of the worldly lover. Technically brilliant but lacking emotion, it is an empty work. Some nudity and consistently gross and perverse imagery becomes tedious and excessive. O (R)

Fellini's Roma (1972) Director Federico Fellini's imaginary tour of Rome is founded on an indulgent nostalgia for the 1930s and 1940s as against the city's present-day traffic jams, tourist traps and imported lifestyles. His dramatic re-creations of the past are at times heavy-handed (the pathetic contrast between cheap and high-class bordellos) or coy (an ecclesiastical fashion show) but, for the most part, they are fond and playful evocations of a Rome that no longer exists except in memory. Some grotesque images may be troubling. A-IV (R)

Female Animal, The (1970) Biographical account of a young woman (Arlene Tiger) who became a prostitute because of family and social pressures. Its gross treatment of basically immoral situations nullifies whatever social value it may have intended. O (nr)

Female Bunch, The (1972) Drugs, sex and sadism are the routine for a group of women at a remote ranch where some lustful admirers (Russ Tamblyn and Lon Chaney Jr.) become tortured victims of the gang. Sex exploitation western directed by Al Adamson and John Cardos. O (R)

Female Response, The (1972) Sex exploitation story of a newspaper lovelorn columnist (Raina Barrett) exploring the sex life of five women. Voyeuristic trash directed by Tim Kincaid. O (R)

Femme de Personne (1986) In a French production directed by Christopher Frank, four women try to work out their individual problems in relationships with stereotyped males in an overlong drama whose message is that men are a lost cause and women must sustain and support themselves. Promiscuity and infidelity are treated as positive strategies for women's survival in an alienating world of insensitive men. Some nudity. O (nr)

FernGully...The Last Rain Forest (1992) Animated children's fantasy tells how the tiny fairy Crysta (voice of Samantha Mathis) employs her magical powers to save a pristine forest and its lively creatures, including a wacky bat (voice of Robin Williams), from being destroyed by the pollution monster, Hexxon (voice of Tim Curry). Directed by Bill Kroyer, the animation of the natural world is lovely to see and the action is sufficiently fanciful, but the well-intentioned story is thin and its ecological message saccharine. Some tense scenes. A-I (G) U

Ferris Bueller's Day Off (1986) Director John Hughes turns in a lighthearted spoof about a teenager (Matthew Broderick) who has made a science out of truancy because he likes to take a break now and then to observe the world around him. The cheerfully implausible plot serves as the catalyst in changing the attitudes of his sister and best friend. Some vulgar language. A-II (PG-13) 15

Fever Heat (1968) Low-budget melodrama about a former stock-car racer (Nick Adams) who becomes romantically involved with the widow (Jeannine Riley) of a racer and she overcomes her fear of the dirt track. Director Russell S. Doughten Jr. does better with the world of racing than with the development of the personal relations of his characters. A-II (br)

Fever Pitch (1985) Sportswriter (Ryan O'Neal) addicted to gambling is sent to Las Vegas to do a story about compulsive gamblers. A well-intentioned drama about the evils of gambling that, unfortunately, becomes dull and repetitive, with a neat upbeat ending that undercuts the seriousness of the problem. Brief nudity and vulgar language. A-III (R)

Few Days with Me, A (1989) French director Claude Sautet tracks the travails of a depressed department store heir (Daniel Auteuil) who falls for a free-spirited young woman (Sandrine Bonnaire) but is unable to win her love. Despite hints of promiscuous relationships, this lightly comic tale is not about sex but about one frustrated man's inability to communicate love and affection for people in ways other than buying, selling and psychological manipulation. Minimal violence. A-III (PG-13)

Few Good Men, A (1992) Insecure but glib Navy lawyer (Tom Cruise), goaded by a strong-willed Internal Affairs attorney (Demi Moore), takes on the politically sensitive murder trial of two Marines (James Marshall and Wolfgang Bodison) who are being used as scapegoats by their commanding officer (Jack Nicholson). Director Rob Reiner's tautly-constructed courtroom drama bristles with intense performances while tackling prickly issues of honor, responsibility and personal integrity. An off-screen suicide, a blatantly sexist remark and intermittent rough language. A-III (R) 15

ffolkes (1980) Eccentric soldier of fortune (Roger Moore) and his crack team of underwater commandos are recruited by Her Majesty's Government to battle a sinister duo (Anthony Perkins and Michael Parks) and their dastardly gang of hijackers. Moore is in top form in director Andrew V. McLaglan's thriller which, unfortunately, has somewhat more graphic violence than necessary. A-III (PG)

Fiddler on the Roof (1971) Fine screen adaptation of Joseph Stein's Broadway musical about Tevye (Topol), a milk seller in a Czarist Russian village whose life of Jewish Orthodoxy is filled with joy and sadness but always buoyed by the human spirit and eternal hope. Struggling in a time of cultural and political flux to find suitable husbands for his three dowryless daughters, Tevye's faith and hope and sheer love of life and humankind keep him and the family going. Norman Jewison's direction does full justice to a rich and appealing musical that the whole family can enjoy. A-I (G) U

Field, The (1990) Obsessed with acquiring the field he has slavishly cultivated for his only surviving son (Sean Bean), an impoverished Irishman (Richard Harris) comes into mortal conflict with an American (Tom Berenger) who outbids him for the land. With Harris' commanding performance at the center, writer-director Jim Sheridan's extravagantly crafted morality tale fully exploits the austere beauty of the Irish landscapes to reflect the primal emotions that the story evokes. Intermittent violence and a very restrained sexual encounter. A-III (PG-13) 15

Field of Dreams (1989) When an Iowa farmer (Kevin Costner) begins hearing voices, he and his supportive wife (Amy Madigan) use the family savings to turn a cornfield into a baseball field, whereupon the spirit of Shoeless Joe Jackson (Ray Liotta) and others appear to play ball. Because Jackson was an idol of the farmer's deceased dad, it's apparent that the visions and voices will somehow enable a reconciliation between father and son. Adapted by director Phil Alden Robinson from W. P. Kinsella's novel, it's filled with happy, confounding surprises that some may dismiss as farfetched, heavy-handed fantasy. Others, however, will be refreshed by its positive point of view, wonderful mystical characters, love of baseball lore and respect for those who follow their dreams. Minor rough language. A-II (PG)

Fiendish Plot of Dr. Fu Manchu, The (1980) Peter Sellers, in his last movie, plays both the diabolical 168-year-old Fu Manchu and his now-retired nemesis, Nayland Smith of Scotland Yard. Seller's forte as a character actor is not supported by any comic imagination behind either the clumsy script or the flat direction of Piers Haggard. Some vulgar expletives and a mildly suggestive striptease. A-II (PG)

Fifth Floor, The (1980) A young woman (Diane Hull) is wrongly committed to an institution for the insane in this exploitation movie directed by Howard Avedis. Contains much nudity and violence. O (R)

5th Musketeer, The (1979) Uninspired Austrian remake of the 1939 American movie, "The Man in the Iron Mask," stars a miscast Beau Bridges in the dual role of Louis XIV and his twin brother, with aged musketeers Jose Ferrer, Cornel Wilde, Alan Hale Jr. and Lloyd Bridges assuring that the good twin ascends the throne. Director Ken Annakin's lackluster adventure includes some adult situations. A-III (PG)

55 Days at Peking (1963) With the encouragement of the Manchu dowager empress (Flora Robson), the forces of the 1900 Boxer Rebellion lay siege to the walled compound in the Chinese capital where the foreign community tries to hold out until an international relief force arrives. Director Nicholas Ray's widescreen spectacular has impressive sets and energetic action scenes but the cast (U.S. Marine officer Charlton Heston, British diplomat David Niven, Russian baroness Ava Gardner and the rest) are cardboard characters adding little human dimension to a script of limited historical proportion. Stylized violence and romantic interludes. A-I (br) U

52 Pick-up (1986) A wealthy industrialist and unfaithful husband (Roy Scheider), who dabbles in the sleazy underworld of drugs and sex, is taped in a liaison with a young girl that implicates him in her subsequent murder. The demand for blackmail motivates him to use his money to set the killers against themselves. The nasty peep-show ambiance of the proceedings, directed by John Frankenheimer, wallows in brutish violence, nudity, drugs and profanity. O (R) 18

Fighter Squadron (1948) Standard exploits of an Air Force unit (headed by Edmond O'Brien) in winning the war against the Luftwaffe despite the loss of brave pilots (notably Robert Stack). Director Raoul Walsh makes good use of actual combat footage but the movie flags on the ground with the usual arguments over tactics, conflicts with the brass and sporadic comic relief. Wartime violence. A-I (br) U

Fighting Back (1982) Inner-city Italian American (Tom Skerrit) organizes his neighbors to fight crime. Despite a muddled homage to the complexity of big city problems and an attempt to give some sort of moral perspective, the end result is the usual formula of simplistic violence as the way to solve all problems. Director Lewis Teague's movie is too morally confused to avoid giving the impression of extolling the virtues of vigilantism. Abundant violence. O (R) X

Fighting Prince of Donegal, The (1966) Young Irish prince tries to unite his country against the occupation by soldiers of Queen Elizabeth. Directed by Michael O'Herlihy, this Walt Disney production is an unpretentious action piece with adequate acting by its young leads, Peter McEnery and Susan Hampshire, and Gordon Jackson excels in the villainy department. A-I (br) U

Fighting Sullivans, The (see: "The Sullivans").

Figures in a Landscape (1971) Enigmatic chase movie begins with two escaped prisoners (Robert Shaw and Malcolm McDowell), hands bound, fleeing across a desolate Spanish countryside, pursued by a helicopter that occasionally shoots at them. Director Joseph Losey never explains who the fugitives are, nor from whom they are fleeing, in a movie that has only a middle, an unexplained antagonism between the principals and a landscape in which both figures and viewers become lost. A-III (PG)

File of the Golden Goose (1969) Yul Brynner portrays a tough, determined American CIA agent trying to infiltrate a British counterfeiting gang. Director Sam Wanamaker's rather pedestrian British spy thriller contains some rather gruesome killings, coarse language and homosexual references of questionable taste. A-III (PG) A

Fillmore (1972) Documentary record of the final days and closing night at Fillmore West, the pioneering San Francisco rock house, showing rock producer Bill Graham in action, for instance, haggling with the managers of groups he wants to perform in the farewell concert. Those who do include Jefferson Airplane, Santana, Quicksilver, New Riders of the Purple Sage and Hot Tuna. Director Richard T. Heffron has not only captured some of the bittersweet moments of a memorable event, but has made an enlightening work about the rock world. Scatter-shot profanity in an otherwise wholesome and entertaining movie. A-III (R)

Film Actress (1988) Japanese director Kon Ichikawa has fashioned an enlightening look at the life and times of film actress Kinuyo Tanaka (1909-1977), showing the rise and role of this strong-minded and talented female artist (played by Sayuri Yoshinaga) in the history of Japanese cinema through the early 1950s. Rather flat dramatized biographical segments are intercut with narrated documentary sequences that include excerpts from her movie performances. Subtitles. Premarital cohabitation. A-III (nr)

Film Portrait (1974) The year before his death in 1972, Jerome Hill put together this picture that consists of his reflections on the magic of cinema and on how his own life got so intimately bound up with it. Definitely for film students, but the casual moviegoer may also enjoy it because it's an interesting look at an individual taking stock of his life's work and finding it, on the whole, something still filled with wonder. A-I (nr)

Final Analysis (1992) Overripe Gothic thriller stars Richard Gere as a San Francisco psychiatrist duped into being a defense witness for a patient's sister (Kim Basinger) accused of murdering her abusive husband (Eric Roberts). Director Phil Joanou blends nifty plot twists with nicely shaded performances to heighten suspense, then drops the ball with a wildly melodramatic ending. Brief violence, short scene of adultery with nudity and intermittent rough language. A-III (R) 15

Final Chapter—Walking Tall (1977) Like the previous two movies about Tennessee Sheriff Buford Pusser and his fight against crime in McNairy County, Tennessee, director Jack Starrett's version is crude and simplistic in its good guys vs. bad guys approach. Bo Svenson in the Pusser role is a sensitive and appealing performer with a fine presence that, unfortunately, is wasted in the rigors of excessive violence and bloodshed. O (R)

Final Comedown, The (1972) Black exploitation movie with Billy Dee Williams as a young man on his way to death and destruction is a quite simple story cluttered unnecessarily by a raft of flashbacks. Written, produced and directed by Oscar Williams, the movie pits the violence of ghetto blacks against the fears of middle-class whites and relies on prejudice and stereotype for effect. Relentless stream of vile epithets and a generous helping of gratuitous nudity. O (R)

Final Conflict, The (1981) Lackluster concluding episode in "The Omen" trilogy with the now adult Damien (Sam Neill) growing desperate as his days as the Antichrist are drawing to an end. Graham Baker's plodding direction of Andrew Birkin's witless script strings together a boring series of scenes with gory violence. a touch of sadomasochistic sex and absurd theological allusions. O (R) 18

Final Countdown, The (1980) The premise of this film is clever even if a bit too reminiscent of "Twilight Zone" type television drama. Kirk Douglas, Martin Sheen and James Farentino are aboard the "U.S.S. Nimitz" when it slips through a time warp in the year 1980 and reappears at Pearl Harbor in December 1941. It is a clever premise, but the most interesting aspect of director Don Taylor's drama is the aircraft carrier itself, which photographed in detail, constitutes an overwhelming presence. Some brief, but intense violence. A-II (PG) A

Final Crash, The (see: "Steelyard Blues").

Final Option (1983) Elite anti-terrorist unit battles fanatical peace activists who take over an embassy in an extremely violent and simplistic melodrama directed by Ian Sharp from a screenplay by Reginald Rose. Mediocre entertainment with cardboard characters tries to justify excessive gunplay and brutal retribution for political crimes. A-III (R)

Find a Place to Die (1973) Routine Italian western about a disgraced Texas Ranger (Jeffery Hunter) who tries to regain his honor by helping a widow (Pascale Petit) recover the gold stolen by the outlaws who murdered her husband. Director Hugo Fregonese's film is notable only as the last performance of Hunter before his untimely death at age 40. Some brutal violence. A-III (R)

Finders Keepers (1984) Director Richard Lester's attempt at screwball comedy concerns a variety of characters (of which only David Wayne has a sense of comedy) trying to get their hands on a stolen $5 million in the course of a transcontinental train ride. The failed comedy revels in tastelessness, foul language and an offensively unfunny sexual sequence. O (R) 15

Fine Madness, A (1966) Sean Connery stars in a quaintly stereotyped role as an eccentric, romantically inclined Irish poet who is totally out of place in normal society. Unfortunately, director Irvin Kershner's movie places its emphasis on his promiscuity, which undercuts what might in other circumstances have been a very funny adult satire. O (br) A

Fine Mess, A (1986) When two friends (Ted Danson and Howie Mandel) win big money on a crooked horse race, they find themselves being chased by looney Mafia thugs (Stuart Margolin and Richard Mulligan) as well as the promiscuous wife (Maria Conchita Alonzo) of the Mafia boss (Paul Sorvino). Writer-director Blake Edwards turns the slapstick comedy into a burlesque of the sexual-tease variety. The result provides an unwholesome acceptance of social and sexual irresponsibility, largely in scenes of an adulterous affair. O (PG)

Fine Pair, A (1969) Square New York police detective (Rock Hudson) gets involved with a fey crook (Claudia Cardinale) and after innumerable plot complications they wind up as a couple of lighthearted jewel thieves.

Director Francesco Maselli's romance gets overly serious in its treatment of the supposedly idyllic love affair of the unprincipled principals, completely out of keeping with the movie's humorous intentions. O (PG) A

Fine Romance, A (1992) Middle-aged engineer (Marcello Mastroianni) and a doctor's wife (Julie Andrews) living in Paris meet to discuss the fact that their mates are having an affair and end up becoming romantically involved with each other. Director Gene Saks' slight comedy depends upon a frail sense of humor about marital infidelity and human weakness. Uncritical attitude toward extramarital affairs. A-III (PG-13)

Finest Hours, The (1964) British documentary on the life and times of Winston Churchill presents an overview of his accomplishments and defeats as statesman, orator, author, soldier and painter. Narrated by Orson Welles and good selection of photographs and newsreel footage. A-I (br)

Fingers (1978) Crude, pretentious crime melodrama with Harvey Keitel as a would-be concert pianist who supports himself by collecting bad debts for his loan-shark father (Michael V. Gazzo) and hotly pursues a blank-eyed young woman (Tisa Farrow). Directed by James Toback, the resulting confrontations, including random sex and violence, make no sense at all. O (R) X

Finian's Rainbow (1968) Screen version of a 1940s' Broadway musical is a variation on the girl-meets-boy plot, with a cantankerous father (Fred Astaire) and a lonely leprechaun (Tommy Steele) thrown in for good measure. Director Francis Ford Coppola brings off an enjoyable entertainment, not quite the lighthearted romantic fantasy that it might have been, but something that is pleasant to watch and, more especially, to listen to. A-I (G) U

Fire and Ice (1983) Animated feature created by Ralph Bakshi about a war between good and evil wizards—the good one's weapon is fire, the bad one's is ice—displays in abundant detail Bakshi's obsession with grotesque sex and extravagant violence. All the more disheartening is to see such material appearing in a format traditionally reserved for family entertainment. O (PG)

Fire and Ice (1987) Series of spectacular stunts on skis, bobsleds, wind sleds and skateboards is strung together by the flimsy device of a Canadian skier (John Eaves) searching for the girl of his dreams (Olympic skier Suzy Chaffee). German production photographed and directed by Willy Bogner offers plenty of winter feats with a pounding rock score and the limited dramatic talent of his principals. Some brief nudity in a bedroom scene. A-III (PG)

Fire Birds (1990) Brash Army helicopter pilot (Nicolas Cage) must convince his envious training instructor (Tommy Lee Jones) to select him for a dangerous air strike on a South American drug cartel, while coping with a feminist girlfriend (Sean Young) who despises his macho attitudes. Director David Green's rousing but simplistic tale of winning the drug war with a single military mission makes the characters secondary to the swooping aerial action and explosive special effects. Violent scenes of air combat, crude double entendres and a fairly restrained bedroom scene. A-III (PG-13)

Fire in the Sky (1993) Five Arizona loggers (led by Robert Patrick), suspected of murdering a vanished co-worker (D.B. Sweeney), are cleared when he returns to their midst five days later, dazed by terrifying memories of his abduction by a UFO. Director Robert Lieberman's dramatization of a supposedly fact-based 1975 incident uses imaginative special effects to suggest the alien encounter but avoids questions of extraterrestrial life by concentrating on the mundane plight of the loggers. A scene of menacing aliens physically abusing the main character. A-II (PG-13) 15

Fire with Fire (1986) Awkward teen romance with a bright and pretty convent schoolgirl (Virginia Madsen) being consumed by love for a boy (Craig Sheffer) from a nearby juvenile offenders' work camp. Directed by Duncan Gibbons, the plot of teenagers against a passionless adult world is dramatically unjustified. Instances of profanity and violence as well as scene of sexual gropings in a graveyard. A-III (PG-13)

Fire Within, The (1969) Taut, well-constructed and thoroughly engrossing French movie records two days in the life of an alcoholic ex-playboy (Maurice Ronet) desperately searching for security, understanding and meaning in his life. Director Louis Malle's 1963 drama presents a stinging indictment of upper middle-class life in a work whose theme is one of soul-searching despair. A-III (nr)

Fireball 500 (1966) Frankie Avalon plays a tough stock-car racer with Fabian Forte as his chief rival for the high racing stakes and for the dimpled hand of sweet Annette Funicello as well. William Asher directs this dumb, garden variety teenage vehicle that has everything that used to happen in those beach-blanket-bingo movies of the early 1960s, except that instead of bikinis the bouncing babes are wearing abbreviated racing duds. The giggles and inane songs are the same, though. A-III (br)

Firecreek (1968) Henry Fonda terrorizes the town where Jimmy Stewart is sheriff in a western reminiscent of the showdown situation immortalized in "High Noon," but it lacks that movie's punch. Director Vincent McEveety can't make up his mind whether the climactic shootout is a good thing or not so best not waste your time. Stylized violence. A-II (br)

Firefox (1982) Clint Eastwood stars as an American pilot traumatized by his Vietnam experiences who sneaks into the Soviet Union and steals a secret superplane. Also directed by Eastwood, the action movie is plodding and unexciting but does feature some graphic violence. A-III (PG) AA

Fireman's Ball, The (1968) Unpretentious Czechoslovakian comedy deals with the foibles of average people in the story of a small-town fire brigade's annual ball. Disorganized and inept, the brigade bungles through in the face of stolen raffle prizes, an embarrassing beauty contest and finally a real fire where the ball continues as if nothing had happened. Directed by Milos Forman, the film is done with such good humor and loving care that the viewer cannot help but enjoy its affirmation that people are good no matter how silly or stupid they may act. Some mature material. A-III (br)

Firepower (1979) Retired hit man (James Coburn) is recruited by the Justice Department to kidnap a crooked financier from his Caribbean sanctuary and bring him back to stand trial in the States. The lavishly mounted British production has lots of lovely scenery, but director Michael Winner's trite melodrama overdoses on heavy-handed action and violence, made even more repugnant by its sleazy moral outlook. O (R) 15

Firestarter (1984) Screen version of Stephen King horror story about a little girl (Drew Barrymore) who is kidnapped by a secret government agency who want to use her psychokinetic power to make things burst into flames. Martin Sheen and George C. Scott make an interesting contrast in villains, but director Mark Lester's treatment of the premise is more absurd than frightening. Youngsters, however, may be negatively influenced by and even delight in the film's theme of a child's revenge against a cruel adult world. A-III (R)

Firewalker (1986) Simple but plodding action-adventure yarn about a woman (Melody Anderson) who hires two soldiers-of-fortune (Chuck Norris and Louis Gossett Jr.) to hunt for ancient Mayan treasure in Central America. J. Lee Thompson's direction is amiable but slack in its treatment of the usual assortment of villains and plot complications. Stylized, almost slapstick, violence. A-II (PG)

Firm, The (1993) After accepting a lucrative job offer from a small Memphis law firm, a novice lawyer (Tom Cruise) discovers his bosses are laundering mob money and must decide whether to risk his life copying their files for the FBI or be indicted if he doesn't cooperate. Director Sydney Pollack translates John Grisham's bestseller into a tense thriller whose cat-and-mouse maneuverings are sometimes confusing, but whose wily performances by Cruise, Gene Hackman, Holly Hunter and Gary Busey are consistently absorbing. Brief violence, some sexual innuendo and intermittent rough language. A-III (R) 15

First Blood (1982) Sylvester Stallone plays John Rambo, a disillusioned Vietnam veteran who reacts to police brutality in a small northwestern town by waging a one-man war against the local police force and the National Guard. Though Ted Kotcheff's direction is effective in fashioning a quite brutal action melodrama, it offers nothing of substance about the plight of the Vietnam veteran. Violence and rough language. A-III (R) 15

First Charge of the Machete (1974) In 1868, Cuban nationalists declared their independence from the Spanish colonial regime and defeated the army sent against it by using machetes in hand-to-hand combat. Manuel Octovio Gomez re-creates this patriotic episode as if it were a documentary filmed as the events occurred, interviewing participants of both sides and using high-contrast photography to effect a period feeling. A-II (nr)

First Circle, The (1973) Screen adaptation of Russian author Aleksandr Solzhenitsyn's account of the spiritual and physical torments of a political prisoner under Stalinist oppression is a deeply felt one, but its meaning never gets beyond the literal level of story and dialogue. Director Alexander Ford's graphic depictions of sadistic brutalization and sexual degradation needlessly depart from the rest of the movie's stylized visualization of prison camp oppression. A-IV (R)

First Deadly Sin, The (1980) Frank Sinatra stars as an aging New York detective in pursuit of a deranged killer while worrying about his bed-ridden wife (Faye Dunaway). Brian G. Hutton directs a deeply flawed but entertaining enough crime melodrama with some gratuitous violence. A-III (R)

First Family (1981) Awkward, unfunny comedy starring Bob Newhart, Madeline Kahn and Gilda Radner as the U.S. presidential family. Buck Henry directs with total reliance upon humor derived from vulgar language and crude sight gags, combined with a few implicitly racist scenes. O (R)

First Love (1970) Romanticized German tale of fantasy and imagination in which a young lad falls in love with a slightly older flirt who has moved in next door, only to find out that his father (Maximilian Schell) is sleeping with the girl. Also directed by Schell, the movie concentrates on atmosphere and mood with bucolic settings and lush photography, but its lack of plot and shallow substance will leave most viewers yawning. A-III (R)

First Love (1977) College student (William Katt) looking for a lasting relationship catches a rich coed (Susan Dey), loses her to a married man, gets her back but then doesn't want her any more because the "magic" is gone. Director Joan Darling's overripe soap opera of instant gratification takes itself so seriously that it would be laughable if its nudity, simulated intercourse and coarse language were not so offensive. O (R) X

First Men in the Moon (1964) H.G. Wells' tale of an eccentric English inventor (Lionel Jeffries) who uses his discovery of anti-gravity to take a couple (Edward Judd and Martha Hyer) on a trip to the moon in 1899. Directed by Nathan Juran, the preliminaries are mildly amusing but matters turn serious after the trio find an advanced civilization of human-sized insects living in tunnels beneath the lunar surface. Some scary special effects by Ray Harryhausen. A-I (br) U

First Monday in October (1981) Walter Matthau and Jill Clayburgh star in this drama about the first woman appointed to the U.S. Supreme Court. On the surface director Ronald Neame's movie deals with liberal-conservative conflicts but essentially demonstrates that women have the same problems as men in dealing with the complex and often unfair American justice system. A pornography case involves a needless nude insert and mature line of dialogue. A-III (R) 15

First Nudie Musical, The (1977) Shoddy production about a producer who is inspired to put on a pornographic musical to save his seedy company from ruin. Directors Mark Haggard and Bruce Kimmel emphasize sophomoric vulgarities and exploit nudity. O (R) X

First Position (1973) Inside look at the training of ballet students in which the real test is whether they have sufficient talent and determination to devote their lives to the pursuit of artistic perfection. Produced and directed by William Richert, the documentary succeeds admirably in conveying the hard work that goes into the learning of any art and the self-doubts of students as they look to the future. A-II (nr)

First Power, The (1990) A Los Angeles homicide detective (Lou Diamond Phillips) and a psychic (Tracy Griffith) play cat-and-mouse games with the satanic spirit of an executed serial killer (Jeff Kober) who possesses the bodies of weak humans and keeps on killing. Writer-director Robert Resnikoff's inventive stunt work does not save this cop thriller from deteriorating into a predictable, overlong horror show. Much menace, grisly violence and bloody gore. O (R) X

First Time, The (1969) Empty-headed movie based on the supposition that the average American boy yearns to visit a house of prostitution and that listening to teenagers talk naively about sex is amusing. Directed by James Neilson, the treatment of characters and situation lacks any sensitivity or insight, and the movie is slapped together so badly as to give the impression of being an amateur production. O (M)

First Time, The (1978) Easygoing, highly indulgent memoir about a 16-year-old boy's first sexual encounter gives some warm and positive details of French family life, but the view of sex presented here is morally wanting. Directed by Claude Berri, the movie is further marred by offensive dialogue and graphic depictions of sexual behavior. O (X)

First Turn-On, The (1984) Exploitation film about a female guide and four teenage male campers who become trapped in a cave and pass the time describing their first sexual experiences. Nudity in a sexual context. O (R) 18

Firstborn (1984) Divorced mother (Terri Garr) falls for a brutish loser (Peter Weller) who moves in and precipitates domestic violence with resentful teenage sons. Trite melodrama directed by Michael Apted tries to be a cautionary tale about distraught women making desperate commitments to men before knowing anything about them. Brutality rules out youngsters. A-III (PG-13)

Fish Called Wanda, A (1988) Black comedy by veteran British director Charles Crichton involves an uptight barrister (John Cleese) with a bizarre gang of jewel thieves (Jamie Lee Curtis, Kevin Kline, Michael Palin) whose methods stop at nothing, including sex and violence. The comic performances are weakened by running gags offending animal lovers, stutterers and probably everyone else. Sexual promiscuity for laughs, much profanity and vulgar humor. O (R) 15

Fish Hawk (1980) The story of the friendship between a farmer's young son (Charlie Fields) and the lone Indian (Will Sampson) living in a white community in the Ozarks at the turn of the century is an unremarkable but pleasant and unpretentious entertainment directed by Donald Shebib. The acting is excellent and the outdoor adventures of the two principals will appeal to younger children. A-I (G)

Fish That Saved Pittsburgh, The (1979) Dreadfully inept comedy about the rejuvenation of a basketball franchise through applied astrology, with Stockard Channing as the team astrologer, has been thrown together in slapdash fashion by director Gilbert Moses. Several instances of vulgar language. A-II (PG)

Fisher King, The (1991) Extravagant fantasy about a guilt-ridden former talk show host (Jeff Bridges) and his feisty live-in love (Mercedes Ruehl) who try to help a tragically widowed homeless man (Robin Williams) win over a new love (Amanda Plummer). Director Terry Gilliam's exhuberant dramatic comedy is a boldly imagined and beautifully cast fable of redemption that lurches out of control as it nears its sentimental wrap-up. Momentary gory violence, a live-in relationship, frequent rough language and fleeting, shadowy nudity. A-III (R) 15

F.I.S.T. (1978) Sylvester Stallone stars in a deeply flawed, highly romanticized saga of the labor movement that draws heavily upon the history of the Teamsters Union and the rise and fall of James Hoffa. Director Norman Jewison works on a large canvas telling a story that begins with hope and ends in corruption. The violence along the way is set in the context of a well-intentioned theme of social justice. A-III (PG)

Fistful of Dollars, A (1967) The spaghetti western that launched Clint Eastwood's meteoric career as the squinting, black-hatted, cheroot-chomping gunslinger known as The Man with No Name who hires himself out to one side or the other, and occasionally both at once, in the settling of a border dispute. Directed with style by Sergio Leone, the action is swift, the violence plentiful and the vengeance all Clint's. O (br) 15

Fistful of Dynamite (see: "Duck, You Sucker!").

Fists of Fury (1973) Kung Fu artist Bruce Lee takes on a gang of Bangkok dope smugglers, dispatching them with axes and clubs, and in countless stabbings and slashings with knives and swords. Viewers will gasp at the gore more than at the hero's prowess in this inept action movie written and directed by Lo Wei. Excessive violence and nudity in a brothel scene. O (R)

Fists of the Double K (1973) Karate and Kung Fu are among the lethal means of killing people in this worthless action movie whose violence is bloody and interminable, interrupted only by some sex scenes by way of an attempted rape of a blind girl and a homosexual baddie. O (R)

Fitzwilly (1967) Breezy variation of the Robin Hood theme with a canny butler (Dick Van Dyke) running a thievery racket with other domestics in order to keep up the household of his once rich New York employer (Dame Edith Evans). Directed by Delbert Mann, it has its amusing moments but, in spite of a comment on the dishonesty of bilking insurance companies, it still implies that what people don't know won't hurt them. A-III (br) U

Five Bloody Graves (1971) Violent western in which foolhardy Robert Dix, trailing the Yaqui warrior who slaughtered his wife, encounters sneaky Indians, stubborn homesteaders, stranded stagecoach passengers, wily gunrunners and a half-breed renegade—all of whom dispatch one another before several suns have set. Women are not exempt from bullets or arrows, and producer-director Al Adamson treats one rape-murder in an especially cruel manner. O (R/GP)

Five Card Stud (1968) Mediocre Western mystery pits Dean Martin as a fast-talking, fast-loving gambler against Robert Mitchum as a hellfire preacher who also carries a gun. Director Henry Hathaway spins a simple story of retribution motivated by the lynching of a card cheat, but the identity of the revengeful killer is fairly obvious. Gory violence, sexual innuendo and a questionable use of religion. A-III (PG) A

Five Days One Summer (1982) Produced and directed by Fred Zinnemann, this is the story of a 1930s' romance set against the stunning background of the Swiss Alps where a man and his niece (Sean Connery and Betsy Brantley) try to pass themselves off as husband and wife during a skiing vacation. The well-crafted movie has very good acting and acknowledges in no-nonsense fashion, the existence of good and evil. Several love scenes handled with much restraint. A-II (PG)

Five Easy Pieces (1970) Jack Nicholson gives an outstanding performance as a young man who has lost his sense of identity and is wasting his life searching and unsatisfied. Directed with precision by Bob Rafelson, the movie's best scene is when Nicholson breaks down and confesses his loneliness to his stroke-victim father. The movie's moral ambiguity makes it more suitable for serious viewing rather than casual entertainment. A-IV (R) AA

Five Graves to Cairo (1943) Intriguing World War II thriller in which a British officer (Franchot Tone) masquerades as a porter in a Sahara Desert hotel occupied by Rommel (Erich von Stroheim) in order to learn where the Germans have hidden advance supply depots for invading Egypt. Director Otto Preminger relieves the tension with occasional humor in the relations between the bogus porter and the hotel staff (Akim Tamiroff and Anne Baxter), though the situation itself is less than credible. Wartime violence and menace. A-II (br) A

Five Heartbeats, The (1991) The career and personal lives of a fictional black singing group in the '60s is charted in this musical drama starring Robert Townsend, Michael Wright and Leon. Also directed by Townsend, the warm-hearted but vapid nostalgia trip has lots of corn but little bite. Considerable sexual innuendo, occasional violence and some rough language. A-III (R) 15

Five Man Army, The (1970) Peter Graves plays the leader of an odd collection of renegades whom he has brought together to rob a shipment of gold from the Mexican government at the turn of the century. Substandard western directed by Don Taylor has a lumpy double-cross plot that fails to bridge the credibility gap. Some of the violence gets a bit gruesome in spots. A-III (PG)

Five Million Years to Earth (1968) Above-average British science-fiction movie in which workers digging a London subway extension find skeletons and an indestructible spacecraft with a prehistoric secret that threatens the entire human race until a brave scientist (James Donald) discovers the origins and meaning of the craft. With good acting, dialogue and special effects, director Roy Ward Baker's unpretentious effort sustains interest and an air of plausibility. Mild violence. A-II (br)

Five on the Black Hand Side (1973) Good screen version of a play by Charlie L. Russell tells a simple but humorous story of the varying effect black awareness has on a middle-class family living in Los Angeles. Under the direction of Oscar Williams, the performances are warm and engaging, with Clarice Taylor and Leonard Jackson as the parents and Glynn Turman, Bonnie Banfield and D'Urville Martin as their grown children. The ultimate message is one of positive respect for oneself and others, which in turn leads to a sense of solidarity and community. A-III (G/PG)

5 Against the House (1955) Bored with college studies, three Korean War veterans (Brian Keith, Alvy Moore and Kerwin Matthews) concoct a "fool-proof" plan to rob a Reno gambling casino but need another vet (Guy Madison) and his girlfriend (Kim Novak) to pull it off. Director Phil Karlson's routine crime caper takes a long time getting away from the phony campus setting and some soggy romance before heading for Reno and a heist complicated by one of the vets being an ex-psychiatric case. Criminal situations and mild sexual innuendo. A-III (br)

5 Fingers of Death (1973) Hong Kong martial arts movie directed by Cheng Chang Ho shows the training of a young disciple of a Kung Fu master and their problems with thugs from a rival school. The atrocious dubbing of this thin effort makes the action seem at first to be played for laughs but it proves, unfortunately, to be deadly serious. Acrobatic violence. A-III (R)

Fixer, The (1968) Set during a time of pogroms in Czarist Russia, the movie tells the story of a simple carpenter (Alan Bates) who is falsely accused of the ritual murder of a young boy. The man's stubborn refusal to confess to the crime makes his case internationally famous and the country that holds him prisoner must force his confession in order to save its good name. Director John Franken-heimer's intense but thought-provoking adaptation of the Bernard Malamud novel confronts viewers with a universal theme of intolerance and abuse of power. Solid fare for adults and older adolescents. A-III (PG) X

Flame and the Fire (1966) French documentary about the Stone Age lives of primitive tribes in remote areas of South America, Africa and the Pacific. Directed by Pierre Dominique Gaisseau, it is not sensationalistic but some of its elements may prove distasteful or shocking to sensitive viewers. A-IV (br)

Flame in My Heart, A (1990) Sexually explicit black-and-white meditation on the drawbacks of obsessive love as observed in the life of a Parisian actress (Myriam Mezieres) who is stalked by one lover while she herself becomes obsessed with a casual stranger. While perhaps titillating to its Swiss director, Alain Tanner, this borderline porn movie is a hard-core bore and should be avoided at all costs. English subtitles. Numerous scenes of graphic sex including full frontal nudity. O (nr)

Flame of New Orleans, The (1941) Romantic comedy about antebellum foreign belle (Marlene Dietrich) who hooks a rich suitor (Roland Young) but can't land him because of the unwanted attentions of a dashing sea captain (Bruce Cabot). French director Rene Clair fails to get much mirth out of the silly situations, though Dietrich is fun to watch and the period costumes are eye-fetching. Borderline black stereotyping. A-II (br)

Flame Over India (1959) Rattling good adventure thriller follows a British officer (Kenneth More) escorting a six-year-old Hindu prince and his governess (Lauren Bacall) on a dangerous train journey to safety during a 1905 Moslem uprising on the Northwest Frontier. Directed by J. Lee Thompson, the well-paced narrative includes a traitor among the passengers (Herbert Lom, Wilfred Hyde-White, Ursula Jeans, et al.) in the prince's coach drawn by an antiquated steam engine with a personality all its own. Some reassuring humor and compensating values amidst the tale's suspense and stylized violence. A-I (br)

Flaming Frontier, The (1968) Ludicrous German western directed by Alfred Vohrer based on the Old Shatterhand character created by Karl May appears here as Old Surehand (Stewart Granger) who tries to keep peace between the Indians and frontier settlers. Mild violence. A-I (G)

Flamingo Kid, The (1985) Brooklyn youth of 18 (Matt Dillon) gains some maturity in the summer of 1963 while working at an affluent Long Island beach club, an experience that confirms his blue-collar father's traditional values over those of the would-be rich and famous. Director Garry Marshall's work is slickly fashioned but contrived and superficial. Sympathetic depiction of sexual promiscuity. O (PG-13) 15

Flanagan (1985) Middle-aged out-of-work actor (Philip Bosco), burdened with family and personal problems, is forced to drive a taxi while he struggles along trying to be ready to seize the big chance when it comes his way. Directed and co-scripted by Scott Goldstein, it's an interesting, often moving little film, though the script is too episodic and the happy ending is several shades too improbable. Mature treatment of the hero's marital problems and some rough language. A-III (R)

Flap (1970) Anthony Quinn plays Flapping Eagle in a seriocomic attempt to decry the mistreatment and indifference endured by today's Native Americans. Flap fights police prejudice and highway construction in trying to preserve his people's cultural heritage but, regrettably, the movie fails to confront far deeper issues of discrimination and, indeed, stereotypes Indians as deceitful, debauched (by Madam Shelley Winters and her girls) and destructive daredevils. British director Carol Reed's movie is an embarrassment that will seem funny only to the most ill-informed viewer. A-III (GP) A

Flareup (1969) Shallow chase film with little suspense and much trite characterization stars James Stacey as a mentally unbalanced, jealous husband who thinks go-go dancer Raquel Welch has broken up his marriage. Directed by James Neilson, the movie's bumbling treatment of violence, nudity, drugs and homosexuality only further encumber an already weak film. O (PG)

Flash of Green, A (1985) Reporter in a small Florida town lets himself be drawn into the orbit of a corrupt politician intent on enriching himself in fronting for an ecologically destructive resort development. An interesting, very well-acted but flawed movie based on a John D. MacDonald novel and directed by Victor Nunez. Violence and a fairly graphic bedroom scene. A-III (nr)

Flashback (1990) Mismatched-buddy picture that pits a wily old 1960s' radical (Dennis Hopper) against a young play-by-the-rules F.B.I. rookie (Kiefer Sutherland) assigned to escort the aging prankster to court. Director Franco Amurri badly juggles at least five themes-in-one here, including a buddy action-adventure, a generation-gap comedy, a drama about self-acceptance and an Abbott and Costello farce. Brief gratuitous violence, some sexual innuendo and profanity. A-III (R) 15

Flashdance (1983) Director Adrian Lyne romanticizes the rags-to-riches story of a working-class female (Jennifer Beals) who overcomes hardships to fulfill her dreams of becoming a professional dancer. Blatantly exploiting female anatomy, the musical tries to overcome the commercial sexism with a love story about self-reliance. Some nudity. O (R) 15

Flashpoint (1984) Two Border Patrol officers (Kris Kristofferson and Treat Williams) in a remote part of Texas find themselves the targets of ruthless covert agents after they discover a jeep long buried in the desert. Director Bill Tannen's moderately entertaining action adventure has restrained violence, but because of its somber mood and extremely rough language, it is not for younger viewers. A-III (R) 15

Flatliners (1990) Bizarre aftereffects plague ambitious medical students (Kiefer Sutherland, Julia Roberts, Kevin Bacon and others) when they engage in dangerous experiments aimed at taking them momentarily to whatever lies beyond death's threshold. Directed by Joel Schumacher, the pretentious fantasy thriller falls flat with illogical plot developments, frantically sound effects and generally unsympathetic characters. Rationalization of suicidal behavior, depictions of promiscuity, sporadic violence and some rough language. O (R) 15

Flavor of Green Tea over Rice (1973) Japanese drama shows the changes in the traditional view of marriage during the post-war era in the story of a woman's passage from indifference to rebellion and finally to a new appreciation of herself and her husband. Director Yasujiro Ozu's movie, made in 1952, is another of his quiet studies of family life, very intimate and warm with the special quality of humanity that Ozu manages to evoke from his characters. A-I (nr)

Flea in Her Ear, A (1968) Dull French bed-sitting room farce in which Rex Harrison and Rosemary Harris lead a parade of comically malcontent marrieds who get themselves into an essentially innocent tangle of mistaken identities and intentions that result in much door-slamming, sneaking around corners and hallway chases at a disreputable Paris hotel. Directed by Jacques Charon, the proceedings are energetic but lack the sense of timing and pace required for farce. A-III (PG) X

Flesh and Bone (1993) Emotionally scarred in childhood by a violent father (James Caan), a Texas loner (Dennis Quaid) becomes romantically involved with an abused wife (Meg Ryan), unaware they had met years earlier under deadly circumstances, which return to haunt him when his father reappears on the scene. Skillfully building on an atmosphere of menacing doom, writer-director Steve Kloves' contemporary film noir focuses on a well-meaning man who becomes unwittingly trapped in a moral dilemma. A few bedroom scenes with brief nudity, some violence and intermittent rough language. A-III (R)

Flesh and Fantasy (1943) Three moody stories of the supernatural tell of a Mardi Gras mask transforming a plain woman (Betty Field) into a beauty; a palm-reader (Thomas Mitchell) foretelling the terrible fate of a smug lawyer (Edward G. Robinson); and a tightrope walker (Charles Boyer) meeting the woman (Barbara Stanwyck) he dreamed caused his death. Director Julien Duvivier works up a lot of sinister atmosphere and tense suspense but the stories are only intermittently interesting and the limp comic wraparounds by Robert Benchley can't tie them together as a package. A-II (br) A

Flesh Gordon (1974) Witless spoof on both the old Flash Gordon and Buck Rogers serials and the new porno movies. Sophomorically smutty humor, nudity, rough language and cheap thrills. O (X/R)

Fletch (1985) This is a vehicle for comedian Chevy Chase to showcase several disguises and display his somewhat limited talent for accents. He plays a reporter trying to break a drug case with everybody against him, even his editors. Chase fans should enjoy this, but others are less likely to. The humor runs heavily to the vulgar side, with the emphasis on the scatological and the anatomical. A-II (PG)

Fletch Lives (1989) Cheesy comedy sequel with Chevy Chase reprising his role as a wise-guy investigative reporter who this time is up against a sinister plot to rid him of his inherited Louisiana plantation. Chase fans may chuckle over his nutty disguises, corny names and sappy one-liners, but director Michael Ritchie finds little humor, save in a satiric subplot about a sleazy TV faith healer (R. Lee Ermey). Rough language laced with vulgar references, sexual innuendos and a casual attitude toward sex. A-III (PG)

Flight of the Doves (1971) Young brother and sister (Jack Wild and Helen Raye) escape the crushing rule of their stepfather (William Rushton) in gray Britain for their dear granny (Dorothy McGuire) in green Ireland. Learning that the children are heirs to a large fortune, they are pursued by a menacing uncle (Ron Moody) who intends to dispose of them and claim the money for himself. Director Ralph Nelson, steering clear of the scary potential of the situation, produces a fancy, frothy entertainment package, stuffed with colorful set pieces, songs and sentimentality. The confection may be too sweet for adults, but young children will especially enjoy Moody's magic tricks and bag of disguises. A-I (G) U

Flight of the Eagle, The (1983) Swedish director Jan Troell's fact-based drama illustrates an ill-fated attempt to reach the North Pole by a group of explorers (Max von Sydow, Goran Stangertz and Sverre Anker Ousdal) making use of a hydrogen balloon. Though beautifully photographed and well-told, the somber nature of the story and the intensity of its treatment make it inappropriate for younger viewers. A-II (G)

Flight of the Innocent (1993) Engrossing fact-based story of feuding clans in southern Italy where a young boy flees for his life after his entire family is slaughtered, then finds he is being pursued for the ransom money paid the kidnappers of a rich man's son. Director Carlo Carlei turns the sympathetic youth's desperate attempts to escape his deadly trackers into a suspenseful chase movie that effectively condemns the culture of violence in which these events take place. Subtitles. Graphic violence, a youth in continuing jeopardy and occasional rough language. A-III (R) 18

Flight of the Intruder (1991) Demoralized by futile bombing missions over North Vietnam in 1972, a Navy pilot (Brad Johnson) and his bombardier (Willem Dafoe) defy their commander (Danny Glover) to bomb an off-limits weapons site in downtown Hanoi. Directed by John Milius, the predictable plot uses dazzling, high-flying visuals and rah-rah music to portray war as the ultimate macho adventure while skirting the story's moral conflicts. Intermittent aerial and battlefield violence, a restrained extramarital encounter and some crude bathroom humor. A-III (PG-13)

Flight of the Navigator (1986) A youngster (Joey Kramer) gets trapped in a time warp when he's transported to and from a distant world in the blink of an eye. Although he has not aged, he has been away from his family eight years and must decide if this is really home. The alien spacecraft that transported him figures prominently and humorously in this good-natured and unpretentious family movie directed by Randal Kleiser. A-I (PG) U

Flight of the Phoenix (1966) Uneven disaster movie in which an airplane with the usual motley collection of male passengers crashes in the Arabian desert somewhere off course and without a working radio. Their only chance of survival is to build a new plane from the wreckage of the old, which leads to friction between the pilot (James Stewart) and the German aircraft-designer who proposes to do it. Directed by Robert Aldrich, the situation is overly extended but provides enough suspense and excitement to please most old and young adventure fans. A-I (br) A

Flim-Flam Man, The (1967) Aging confidence man (George C. Scott) tutors a young Army deserter (Michael Sarrazin) in the subtle art of capitalizing on the greed of his fellow man as the unlikely pair go on some genuinely hilarious adventures across the Kentucky countryside. Scott plays the role with carefree flamboyance and glimpses of the pathos that is part of a drifter's loneliness, and Sarrazin is appealing as the AWOL farm boy who is finally brought to his senses by pretty Sue Lyon. Directed by Irvin Kershner, it has beautiful location photography, first rate dialogue and a uniformly capable supporting cast that help make the movie enjoyable for all but the very young. A-II (br)

Flipper (1963) After a young boy (Luke Halpin) rescues an injured dolphin, his fisherman father (Chuck Connors) releases it back into the sea but later, when his son's life is in danger, the grateful dolphin returns to save the lad. Directed by James B. Clark, the story is simple but well-told, the scene-stealing title character is as personable as any in the cast and the Florida nature footage, including a hurricane, is very watchable. Solid family fare, but especially appealing for youngsters. A-I (G) U

Flipper's New Adventure (1964) Lame sequel with the agile dolphin and his friend (Luke Halpin) saving a family whose yacht has been hijacked by escaped convicts. Directed by Leon Benson, the aquatic scenes are still lovely to watch but the story evokes little interest and less credibility. Some menace and fisticuffs. A-I (G)

Flirting (1992) Endearing Australian coming-of-age story set in the mid-1960s follows a stuttering Aussie lad (Noah Taylor) and an intellectual Ugandan girl (Thandie Newton) from neighboring private academies through the stages of interracial friendship and romance that gradually win the respect of their adolescent peers. Writer-director John Duigan treats the young characters with respect and affection in a story that gathers substance as the students mature beyond juvenile sexist and racist attitudes. An implied sexual encounter, flash of nudity and brief brawling. A-III (R)

Float Like a Butterfly, Sting Like a Bee (1970) Though boxing fans may be disappointed at the sparsity of ring action in this documentary on Muhammad Ali (a.k.a. Cassius Clay), it succeeds in being objective and entertaining while exploring the racial ramifications of Ali's success and notoriety, as well as providing insight into his life and character. A-III (nr)

Flowers in the Attic (1987) Failed suspense thriller about four youngsters locked in the upper story of a remote mansion where their lives are endangered by unknown hands. Writer-director Jeffrey Bloom's heavy-handed treatment of the situation becomes boringly repetitive long before the movie's grisly resolution. Mature themes and some violence. A-III (PG-13) 15

Fly, The (1986) Tender romance fades quickly when a biological experiment intermixing human and insect genes fails. The result is a mutant in the form of a sexually powerful human fly (Jeff Goldblum) who gets some compassion from his lover (Geena Davis) but his condition, like director David Cronenberg's beauty-and-the-beast allegory, degenerates into an unhealthy mix of sex, brutality and disgustingly grotesque imagery. Explicit sexual scenes, nudity and some profanity. O (R) 18

Fly II, The (1989) When the son (Eric Stoltz) of the original mutant fly-man grows up to realize that his body and brains are being exploited by a dastardly industrialist (Lee Richardson), the boy tries to free himself from his damaged chromosomes before it's too late. Remarkable creature effects and an involving struggle between good and evil don't make up for director Chris Walas' exploitation of gore and a frightening subplot about zapping test animals in microwave devices. Keep impressionable kids away from this or they may try something similar with family pets. Gratuitous sex, gore and some rough language. O (R) 18

Flying Leathernecks (1951) World War II Marine pilots fight the war in the Pacific while their commander (John Wayne) quarrels with his executive (Robert Ryan) about the best way to do it. Directed by Nicholas Ray, the extensive use of actual combat footage makes the script's heroics seem all the more hollow and phony. Documentary war footage and assorted stylized violence. A-I (br) PG

Flying Matchmaker, The (1970) Israeli musical comedy set in a 19th-century East European Jewish community with a busy matchmaker promoting happy weddings, but silly confusion runs rampant when an impersonator of a prospective groom shows up. Directed by Mordechai Navon, the colorful production stars Mike Burstein, Lillian Lux and Pesach Burstein, but the poorly dubbed comedy grows a bit tedious for those unaccustomed to its conventions. A-II (G)

FM (1978) Lightweight, derivative comedy about a popular radio station that is taken over by its disc jockeys because they refuse to contaminate their music with unsuitable commercials. Under John A. Alonzo's direction, the characters are uninteresting and the jokes feeble. Some highly suggestive dialogue. A-III (PG) A

Fog, The (1980) Victims of a century-old shipwreck caused by a false beacon stalk the descendants of their murderers under the cover of a lethal fog. Director John Carpenter's listless and heavy-handed thriller has little intelligence and much violence. A-III (R) AA

Folks! (1992) Aging parents (Don Ameche and Anne Jackson) persuade their cash-strapped son (Tom Selleck) that they must be killed so he can collect their insurance. Insensitivity toward the elderly abounds in director Ted Kotcheff's witless black comedy. Suicidal behavior and violence treated comically, mild sexual innuendo and minimal profanity. A-III (PG-13)

Follow Me (1969) Three American youths travel the globe in search of the perfect surfing wave in a movie that lacks any wit or style. Director Gene McCabe's material is so repetitious that one has time to question the young surfers' value system and sense of social consciousness. A-II (G)

Follow Me, Boys! (1966) Disney family movie with Fred MacMurray as a small-town Scoutmaster who devotes his life to helping the boys in his troop. Director Norman Tokar emphasizes the ideals of Scouting, has the period atmosphere of a generation ago and benefits from the capable acting of Lillian Gish and Charles Ruggles. Though a sentimental formula picture, it has more than enough spirited action to keep most viewer's interest. A-I (G) U

Follow That Bird (1985) In this first Sesame Street movie, a do-gooder type persuades Big Bird that he should be living with his own feathered kind and places him with the Dodo family in the distant Midwest. Pining for home, Big Bird heads East and immediately becomes the innocent object of a birdhunt. In Sesame Street style, the movie maintains a gentle, whimsical spirit rather than going for the big laughs. As such it will succeed best with younger children and least well with teenagers. A-I (G) U

Follow the Boys (1944) Patriotic World War II variety show in which a top screen hoofer (George Raft) organizes the show biz community to go on tours entertaining the troops, while his wife (Vera Zorina) smolders at his absences. As directed by A. Edward Sutherland, Universal Studio's tribute to Hollywood's part in the war effort features a lot of emotional applesauce along with such star turns as magician Orson Welles sawing Marlene Dietrich in half, W.C. Fields displaying his prowess at a pool table and tunes by the Andrew Sisters. Uneven assortment of period entertainment acts, double entendres and domestic misunderstandings. A-II (br) U

Follow the Fleet (1936) Sturdy musical about an easygoing sailor (Fred Astaire) trying to win back his former hoofing partner (Ginger Rogers) while her schoolteacher sister (Harriet Hilliard) pines for his shipboard buddy (Randolph Scott). Directed by Mark Sandrich, the appealing characters make the thin plot worth following, helped by some wry humor, delightful Astaire-Rogers dance routines and lively Irving Berlin songs. Romantic complications. A-I (br)

Food of the Gods, The (1976) Directed by Bert I. Gordon and loosely based on a H.G. Wells story, the gross sci-fi film delights in gore and vicious attacks by giant rats and insects on hapless explorers (Marjoe Gortner and Pamela Franklin). Excessive violence. O (R) X

Fool for Love (1986) Under Robert Altman's direction, Sam Shepard's adaptation of his own play about a brutalizing love-hate relationship between kissing cousins (Shepard and Kim Basinger) is unremittingly violent, both physically and psychologically. Sexual coarseness in dialogue and unresolved ambiguity of a theme of incest. O (R) 15

Fool Killer, The (1969) Young runaway (Edward Albert) escaping from severe foster parents meets a brooding war veteran (Tony Perkins) bitter about his own excessively strict religious upbringing, but the youth comes to find a home while the man is doomed to wandering. Although the comparatively lighthearted atmosphere of the first part of movie does not prepare the viewer for the darker tone of the later sequences, director Servando Gonzalez keeps the story consistently interesting. A-II (nr) X

Foolin' Around (1980) Failed update of 1930s' screwball comedy has a callow college freshman (Gary Busey) falling for an heiress (Annette O'Toole) and ruining her engagement to a boorish sophisticate. Directed by Richard Heffron, the slapstick overwhelms the few funny moments while an implication of pre-marital sex and some rough language rule out younger viewers. A-III (PG)

Fools (1970) Aging actor tired of being typed in low-budget horror movies (Jason Robards) and a rich girl drifting away from her status-seeking spouse (Katharine Ross) traipse around San Francisco feebly attempting to forget life's frustrations by hopping into bed half a dozen times. Directed by Tom Gries, the movie is singularly devoid of any feelings for humanity that might justify one's interest in the intimate affairs of the neurotic pair. O (GP) AA

Fools of Fortune (1990) After avenging the murder of his father and sisters, which caused the tragic suicide of his mother (Julie Christie), a young Irishman (Iain Glen) flees the law, leaving behind his pregnant lover (Mary Elizabeth Mastrantonio). Director Pat O'Connor's post-World War I historical drama is marred by jarring flashforwards, a profusion of characters and tedious pacing that detract from the film's primitive visual beauty and shimmering performances. Some violence with gore and a very restrained sexual encounter. A-III (PG-13) 15

Fools' Parade (1971) With money earned in prison, lovable ex-cons James Stewart, Strother Martin and Kurt Russell want to set up a general store but mean prison captain George Kennedy wants their dollars and their lives. Perhaps director Andrew McLaglen intended a cornball-campy spoof, but the result is a disappointing chase melodrama that is sometimes silly but only occasionally funny. Some violence with gore and sexual references. A-III (GP) AA

Footloose (1984) A city boy (Kevin Bacon), brought to live in a small Bible Belt town that has an ordinance against dancing in public places, promptly gets in trouble with the local preacher (John Lithgow) over seeing his daughter (Lori Singer), but eventually wins over the town. Director Herbert Ross tries to give the storyline as much weight as the dazzling scenes of acrobatic dancing, but the simplistic script's treatment of issues is woefully inadequate. A-III (PG) 15

For a Few Dollars More (1967) Spaghetti western directed by Sergio Leone with Clint Eastwood playing the cheroot-smoking Man with No Name and Lee Van Cleef, garbed all in black, as his not-to-be-trusted partner. Clint squints, Lee snarls and dozens of Mexican bandidos bite the dust in a routine shoot-em-up involving Clint's vengeance for a double-cross. A-III (br) 15

For All Mankind (1990) Original footage and audio from NASA's nine manned lunar flights (1968-1972) are edited together to create a composite lunar mission from lift-off to landing. Filmmaker Al Reinert provides glorious visuals and new astronaut interviews, but viewers will be confounded by his unidentified mix and melding of Apollo astronauts and launches into one mission. With clarifying introductory remarks, it may benefit young students of space exploration as well as interest veteran space buffs. A-I (nr)

For Better, For Worse (see: "Zandy's Bride").

For Keeps (1988) Romantic melodrama about two high school seniors (Molly Ringwald and Randall Batinkoff) whose plans for college and careers have to be deferred when they decide to face an unintended pregnancy by getting married and raising their child. Though the result is less than realistic in its treatment of the consequences of teen sex, director John G. Avildsen's movie is emotionally on the side of the miracle of human life and the value of the family bond. Some direct sexual references and a harrowing childbirth scene are not for the young and impressionable. A-III (PG-13)

For Love of Ivy (1968) Sidney Poitier plays a slick gambler who falls in love with a beautiful but ambitious maid (Abbey Lincoln), but what might have been an interesting romantic comedy is confounded by the overabundance of phony plot complications. As directed by Daniel Mann, whatever message the movie might have intended is lost in its glossy upper-class setting, pop songs and a pair of "hip" youngsters. Mature themes. A-III (G)

For Love or Money (1993) To gain financial backing for his dream hotel in New York City, an ambitious concierge (Michael J. Fox) agrees to look after the young mistress (Gabrielle Anwar) of a busy, older tycoon (Anthony Higgins)—with predictable results. Director Barry Sonnenfeld turns in a tired formula romantic comedy in which integrity belatedly conquers materialism and wedding bells peal. An implied affair and recurring sexual innuendo. A-III (PG)

For Me and My Gal (1942) Soppy romantic musical in which an ambitious song-and-dance team (Judy Garland and Gene Kelly) plan to wed once they've played the Palace, New York's vaudeville showcase, but World War I intervenes. Directed by Busby Berkeley, the sentimental story turns into patriotic mush as Kelly is transformed from heel to hero, though some first-rate musical numbers brighten the way. Romantic complications and a subplot about draft-dodging. A-II (br) U

For Pete's Sake (1974) Barbra Streisand vehicle about a Brooklyn housewife who borrows money to speculate on the commodities market in order to finance her husband's college diploma and then gets into trouble with a succession of unsavory characters who pressure her to pay back the loan. Director Peter Yates lets the promising comedy turn sour and not even a final hilarious chase sequence can save it. Some grim twists and bizarre plot turns, including the housewife taking a job as a part-time prostitute. A-III (PG)

For Queen & Country (1989) Grim drama about a black British soldier (Denzel Washington) returning to civilian life in his crime-ravaged London neighborhood where he resists illegal pursuits until he finds that, due to some legal loophole, he is no longer a British citizen. Director Martin Stellman stacks the cards against his ill-fated war hero and provides little insight into the grim community depicted. Profanity, sexual promiscuity and grisly scenes of street violence. A-IV (R) 15

For Sasha (1992) Tangled love story set on a kibbutz during Israel's 1967 Six-Day War involves a young woman (Sophie Marceau), the teacher (Richard Berry) she has followed there from Paris and three lifelong friends (Fabien Orcier, Niels Dubost and Frederic Quiring) who come to visit her. Alexandre Arcady directs a sentimental story of imperiled love that is more notable for its stirring portrayal of commitment to the Israeli cause. Subtitles. Fleeting sexual encounter and nudity, a live-in relationship, battlefield violence and suicidal references. A-III (nr)

For Singles Only (1968) Living in a swinging Southern California hotel for unmarrieds, a serious but poor graduate student (John Saxon) bets that he can seduce a high-principled coed (Mary Anne Mobley). She goes along because winning the bet will pay off his overdue tuition bills and then really cooperates because they are in love and are going to get married anyway. Directed by Arthur Dreifuss, the witless movie lacks any human texture or intelligence. Justifies premarital sex. O (br)

For the Boys (1991) Episodic melodrama about an earthy singer (Bette Midler) and a facile song-and-dance man (James Caan) who become a team entertaining the troops in World War II, then spend the next 50 years bickering on and off about their careers, families and personal relationship. Director Mark Rydell gets a standout performance from Midler as the gutsy entertainer at the center of events but the trivial show business story fails to gain any human or social significance by pegging it to milestones of the period. Several graphic sequences of battlefield violence, an adulterous liaison, some sexual innuendo and occasional rough language. A-III (R) 15

For the Love of Benji (1977) Extremely entertaining sequel with the lovable canine hero, this time on vacation in Greece, becoming the unwitting central figure in an international oil conspiracy and the chase is on through the streets and byways of picturesque Athens. Director Joe Camp's lively adventure is surefire entertainment for younger children and it goes down easily for parents as well. A-I (G) U

Forbidden Planet (1956) Engaging sci-fi outing with a space expedition (led by Leslie Nielsen) fighting unseen monsters of the Id on a planet where the powers of a superior, long-extinct civilization are being harnessed by a maverick scientist (Walter Pidgeon) with the help of his daughter (Anne Francis) and a very personable robot named Robby. Directed by Fred M. Wilcox, the premise echoes Shakespeare's "The Tempest" but the movie has its own suspenseful plot developments, intriguing gadgetry and colorful sets, flawed only by some clunky dialogue and desultory action. Occasional stylized violence and much menace. A-II (br) U

Forbidden Quest, The (1994) Drama in which a documentary filmmaker interviews an aged Irish sailor (Joseph O'Conor) who reveals what became of his ill-fated crewmates, all thought to be lost on the Hollandia's 1905-06 voyage from Norway to the South Pole. Dutch writer-director Peter Delpeut creates an atmosphere of mystery and suspense in telling the fictional story of a doomed ship by intercutting actual Antarctic exploration footage from the early 20th century with the old salt's crusty tale of a perilous and deadly voyage. Much menace and the shooting of a bear. A-II (nr)

Forbin Project, The (1970) An enormous self-sustaining and unjammable computer complex coordinating all U.S. military defenses locates a Soviet counterpart and together they plan a benevolent dictatorship guaranteeing peace and a better way of life for the peoples of the world at the expense of their freedom. A kind of horror film with contemporary allusions, director Joseph Sargent's movie has moments of genuine interest in its depiction of a modern electronic Frankenstein controlling humanity's fate but incapable of any human emotion or spiritual growth. Mild bedroom sequence. A-III (GP)

Force of One, A (1980) Run-of-the-mill melodrama about how karate champ Chuck Norris breaks up a narcotics ring. Justice triumphs by means of the martial arts instead of superior firepower with the violence being skillfully choreographed and kept in check by director Paul Aaron. A-II (PG)

Force 10 from Navarone (1979) Penny-ante sequel to "The Guns of Navarone" follows the mission of two American Rangers (Robert Shaw and Edward Fox) in Yugoslavia to blow up a bridge before the Germans can use it to attack the Partisans. Director Guy Hamilton's limp war movie is filled with cliches and occasional graphic violence. A-III (PG) 15

Foreign Affair, A (1948) Romantic intrigue in postwar Berlin with a visiting Iowan Congresswoman (Jean Arthur) falling for a U.S. officer (John Lund) who's involved with the wife (Marlene Dietrich) of a hunted Nazi criminal. Directed by Billy Wilder, the comedy is sharply barbed and often cynical, scoring best in the rivalry between homespun Arthur and sultry Dietrich. Much sexual innuendo. A-III (br) A

Foreign Correspondent (1940) With war threatening in Europe, a bumptious American newspaper reporter (Joel McCrea) stumbles upon a Nazi spy ring in Holland, escapes to London where he falls for the daughter (Laraine Day) of a peace leader (Herbert Marshall) and, after various attempts on his life, finally manages to get his story of a Nazi plot to the American public. Director Alfred Hitchcock turns in a masterful suspense thriller with some chuckles and a lot of clever business along the way, from an official's assassination amidst a rainswept maelstrom of umbrellas to a plane crash at sea, but the characters are cardboard and the script's anti-fascist rhetoric is dated. Much menace. A-II (nr) PG

Forever Darling (1956) Sentimental comic fantasy about the mid-life blues of a couple whose marriage is saved when the daffy wife (Lucille Ball) is persuaded by her guardian angel (James Mason) to join research chemist husband (Desi Arnaz) on a field trip testing a new insecticide. Directed by Alexander Hall, there are some playful moments in an otherwise routine domestic comedy whose fantasy device falls flat. A-I (br) U

Forever Female (1953) Stodgy romantic comedy in which a novice writer (William Holden) changes his play to suit a Broadway producer (Paul Douglas) who wants it tailored for his ex-wife (Ginger Rogers), then realizes the role requires a younger actress (Pat Crowley). Directed by Irving Rapper, the show business setting is more interesting than the predictable and largely unamusing romantic complications. Sexual innuendo. A-III (br) A

Forever Mary (1991) A caring teacher (Michele Placido) tries to make a difference at a boys' reformatory in Sicily where the staff and guards treat their adolescent charges like hardened criminals. Italian director Marco Risi's fact-based drama is a grimly moving expose of a harsh penal system that apparently writes off youthful first-time offenders thus encouraging their continued anti-social behavior. Subtitles. Scenes of brief but intense violence, occasional sexual harassment and innuendo and frequent vulgar language. A-III (nr)

Forever Young (1992) A secret experiment to briefly freeze a 1939 test pilot (Mel Gibson) goes awry and, instead, he wakes up 53 years later when a single mom (Jamie Lee Curtis) and her little boy (Elijah Wood) help him find someone from his past. Director Steve Miner's sweet old-fashioned romantic fantasy is resolved far too suddenly, blunting the story's emotional impact. Brief violence. A-II (PG)

Forever Young, Forever Free (see: "Lollipop").

For Your Eyes Only (1981) Uninspired, derivative spy caper with British agent James Bond (Roger Moore) out to retrieve a top-secret device from a sunken British ship. Directed by John Glen, the flimsy plot strings together a number of spectacular stunts amidst the tongue-in-cheek violence and disposable women, which are fixtures in the 007 fantasy world. Nudity in an underwater sequence. O (PG)

Fort Apache (1948) Elegiac Western in which a glory-seeking colonel (Henry Fonda) arrives from the East to command a cavalry post, arrogantly refuses the counsel of a seasoned subordinate (John Wayne) and leads his troop into a massacre by superior Indian forces. In contrasting the colonel's ignorance and scorn of the foe with the captain's experience and respect for the Indian, director John Ford acknowledges the reality of how the West was won while recognizing the need to turn it into a myth. Stylized violence. A-I (br) U

Fort Apache, the Bronx (1981) Paul Newman stars as a tough but compassionate police officer striving to do his job in a precinct that has the highest crime rate in New York City. Director Dan Petrie's standard urban melodrama is marked by excellent acting and fine cinematography but, though it has occasional insights, it tends to exploit a serious and tragic subject. Some tough scenes involving sex and violence. A-IV (R) AA

Fort Osage (1952) Formula Western programmer directed by Lesley Selander in which a frontiersman (Rod Cameron), despite bungling interference from the U.S. Cavalry, saves a group of settlers from an Indian uprising. Stylized violence. A-I (br)

Fortune, The (1975) Jack Nicholson and Warren Beatty play a bumbling pair of 1920s' con men and would-be murderers who try to do in heiress Stockard Channing. Director Mike Nichols' comedy is contrived, clumsy and only intermittently funny. Some sexual innuendo. A-III (PG)

Fortune and Men's Eyes (1971) Jailed on a minor narcotics rap, a young man (Wendell Burton) in fear of homosexual assault by the other prisoners lets a prison tough (Zooey Hall) protect him in return for exclusive rights to his body and eventually he himself becomes one of the brutalizers that he had once so feared. Directed by Harvey Hart, the movie examines homosexuality in prison not only as a sexual release but as a means of wielding power. The treatment, however, is heavy-handed to the point of exploiting an important subject. O (R) X

Fortune Cookie, The (1966) Shyster lawyer (Walter Matthau) gets brother-in-law (Jack Lemmon) to feign injuries in hopes of a million dollar settlement. Directed by Billy Wilder, the situation is at first amusing but grows increasingly cynical and mean-spirited. Vulgar language and low morals. A-III (br) U

Fortunes of Captain Blood (1950) The further adventures of the Irish doctor-turned-pirate (Louis Hayward) take him ashore in the Caribbean to rescue his men from a Spanish dungeon, then sail away in a captured galleon. Gordon Douglas directs the tame swashbuckler with little conviction and less interest. Stylized violence. A-I (br) U

Forty Carats (1973) Very slight romantic comedy about a 40-year-old divorcee (Liv Ullmann) who falls in love with a man (Edward Albert) half her age during a holiday in Greece. Directed by Milton Katselas, it's lighthearted and entertaining enough, thanks primarily to gorgeous Hellenic scenery and Ullmann's bright performance. A-III (PG)

40 Guns to Apache Pass (1967) Routine Western about a U.S. Cavalry captain (Audie Murphy) saving an Arizona outpost from marauding Apaches and a treacherous white man (Kenneth Tobey) by getting through with a shipment of repeating rifles. Directed by William Witney, the formula action scenes are held together by a cliched narration. Stylized violence. A-I (br)

48 Hrs. (1982) San Francisco police detective (Nick Nolte) springs a convict (Eddie Murphy) on a 48-hour pass in order to get his help tracking down some vicious killers. Directed by Walter Hill's slam-bang action thriller is filled with entirely disagreeable characters who indulge in extreme violence, crude sights gags and rough language. O (R) 18

Forty-Second Street (1933) Prototypical backstage musical in which a member of the chorus (Ruby Keeler) wins stardom when the frantic director (Warner Baxter) has her take over for the disabled leading lady (Bebe Daniels) on opening night. Directed by Lloyd Bacon, the Depression-era setting, slangy dialogue and zesty cast (Ginger Rogers, Una Merkel and Dick Powell, among them) are still fun, abetted by Al Dubin and Harry Warren's brassy music and topped off by Busby Berkeley's inventive production numbers for the title song,

"I'm Young and Healthy" and "Shuffle Off to Buffalo." Some romantic complications and mild sexual innuendo. A-II (nr) A

Foul Play (1978) Goldie Hawn and Chevy Chase are teamed in this comic melodrama about a feisty librarian and a police detective who foil a plot to assassinate the pope during a visit to San Francisco. Colin Higgins directs an above-average comedy that is frequently very funny but yet maintains enough tension to be enjoyable as a thriller too. Some crude language and a casual attitude toward premarital sex. A-III (PG)

Fountain of Love, The (1970) German sex farce about a little town that has a spring that bolsters the virility of all who bathe in it. The mayor's attempt to keep people from using it succeeds as badly as a meandering plot sprinkled with voyeurism and nudity. O (R)

Four Adventures of Reinette and Mirabelle (1989) Wispy French comedy tracking the friendship between a country girl (Joelle Miquel) and a Parisian college student (Jessica Forde) as they explore Mother Nature and the nature of rude city waiters, homeless panhandlers, shoplifters and a woman hustler in a train station. Director Eric Rohmer explores the contrasting thoughts and actions of the two young women—one innocent and rigidly didactic, the other more worldly and open-minded. A-II (nr)

4 Clowns (1970) Robert Youngson's compilation deals with the art of visual comedy as shown in the work of four of its leading buffoons:: Charley Chase, Buster Keaton, Stan Laurel and Oliver Hardy. The selection of excerpts is fine, the narration is helpful and the silent comedy is timeless. A-I (G) U

Four Deuces, The (1975) Apparently intended as a spoof, this clunker about gangland warfare during Prohibition gets its laughs all in the wrong places. Director William H. Busnell Jr. directs the lavish period sets better than he does his floundering cast and there is nothing funny about the movie's violent brutality and view of women as sex objects. A misdeal from the title on. O (R)

Four Feathers, The (1939) When his regiment is ordered to join Kitchener's 1895 campaign to recapture Khartoum, an officer (John Clements) resigns his commission, thereby earning white feathers of cowardice from three comrades (Ralph Richardson among them) and fiancee (June Duprez). How he redeems them by aiding his friends in the Sudan disguised as a native makes an exciting but farfetched adventure directed by Zoltan Korda with much spectacle, some good humor (notably C. Aubrey Smith's account of "the thin red line" at Balaclava) and no little flagwaving. Assorted stylized violence, but for a higher purpose than imperialism. A-I (br) A

Four Flies on Grey Velvet (1972) Italian director Dario Argento pursues his usual theme of homicidal paranoia in a story about a rock drummer (Michael Brandon) who, fearing his life is in danger, sends his raspy wife (Mimsy Farmer) out of town, seeks help from a bohemian friend (Bud Spencer), hires an effeminate private-eye (Jean-Pierre Marielle) and hops into the bathtub with his visiting cousin (Francine Racette). If anyone cares, there is unsettling violence, coarse language, illicit sex and a cast of unwholesome characters. O (PG)

Four for Texas (1963) Bloated comic Western about rival sharpsters (Frank Sinatra and Dean Martin) who fight for control of a Galveston gambling boat but unite against a crooked banker (Victor Buono). Producer-director Robert Aldridge gets little comic mileage out of his two stars who are more at home with double entendres than six-shooters. Stylized violence and sexual innuendo. A-III (br)

Four Friends (1981) Young immigrant from Yugoslavia (Craig Wasson) comes of age in 1960s' Indiana in Steve Tesich's uneven semi-autobiographical screenplay directed by Arthur Penn. Few effective moments are evident in this often outrageously sentimental melodrama that tries to evoke something of significance about the era and the Midwest. Permissive attitude toward adolescent sex and some brief nudity. A-III (R) AA

491 (1967) Spurious Swedish movie uses a rehabilitation program for incorrigible boys as an excuse for a parade of sadism, violence, vandalism and sexual perversity. O (br)

Four Men and a Prayer (1938) When their father (C. Aubrey Smith) is murdered, four English brothers (George Sanders, Richard Greene, David Niven and William Henry) set off to solve the crime, with some help from an American debutante (Loretta Young). Directed by John Ford, the uneven melodrama mixes in a arms-trafficking ring, a Latin American revolution and some silly romance, but it all works reasonably well thanks to a fine supporting cast (Barry Fitzgerald, Alan Hale, John Carradine). Sterling virtues triumph over stylized violence. A-I (br) A

Four Musketeers, The (1975) Oliver Reed, Raquel Welsh, Richard Chamberlain and Faye Dunaway star in director Richard Lester's sequel to his previous movie based on the Dumas novel. The style is halfway between spoof and in earnest with both pratfalls and bloodshed. The uneasy mix makes for rather uncertain entertainment and the violence makes it questionable fare for younger viewers. A-III (PG)

Four Nights of a Dreamer (1972) French adaptation of a Dostoevsky story about a lonely artist in need of someone to personify his ideals of beauty, saves a young woman from suicide and they meet for the next three nights to talk, but on the last night, the lover she thought untrue returns to claim her. The artist is again a solitary dreamer but now he has an ideal based upon reality. Directed by Robert Bresson, adults will find this a tender and loving film, and a warm, if predictable, exercise in romantic fantasy. A-III (nr)

Four Seasons, The (1981) Three couples (Alan Alda and Carol Burnett; Len Cariou and Sandy Dennis; Jack Weston and Rita Moreno) maintain a friendship despite various ups and downs, most having to do with marital problems. Written and directed by Alda, the entertaining but superficial comedy tries to elicit some sense of the complacency of middle-aged, middle-class suburban life-styles. Mature subject matter, some crude gags and profanity. A-III (PG) 15

1492: Conquest of Paradise (1992) Plodding chronicle follows Christopher Columbus (Gerard Depardieu) from his first voyage to the New World through his eventual fall from favor with the Spanish crown. Director Ridley Scott's hollow re-creation of history offers some breathtaking visuals but never probes very deeply into the character of the explorer or his times. Some savage violence, a common-law marriage and tribal nudity. A-III (PG-13) 15

Four Times That Night (1972) Footloose guy (Brett Halsey) picks up a poodle walker (Daniela Giordano) in the park one afternoon, and the next morning fabricates conflicting reports—she for her mother, he for his barroom buddies—about how they spent their evening together. A third version is supplied by the apartment house superintendent. Director Mario Bava's purported comedy, with an emphasis on nudity and perversions, is merely one more sex exploitation movie. O (R)

Fourth Protocol, The (1987) Searing spy suspenser about an attempt to detonate a small nuclear device at a U.S. military base in England in order to destroy the NATO alliance pits KGB agent Pierce Brosnan against British spychaser Michael Caine. Director John MacKenzie's realistic drama has enough nudity and brutal killings to make it off limits for youngsters. A-III (R) 15

Fourth War, The (1990) Lackluster Cold War thriller about maverick American and Soviet colonels (Roy Scheider and Jurgen

Prochnow) who personally battle it out on the 1988 West German-Czech border. Director John Frankenheimer fails to invest his infantile characters or their senseless actions with any interest or suspense. Some profanity and pointless violence. A-III (R) 15

Fox (1976) German melodrama directed by Rainer Werner Fassbinder tells of the rise and fall of a naive worker (played by Fassbinder himself) who is exploited by the bourgeoisie and then discarded when no longer useful. It's the old Hollywood story of the corruption of an innocent by the power placed within the context of the homosexual world. Devoid of any kind of sexual sensationalism, the movie is more about the evils of capitalism than about homosexuality. A-IV (nr)

Fox and the Hound, The (1981) A fox and hound raised as friends have to confront the consequences of the roles assigned them by humans and nature in this Disney animated feature directed by Art Stevens, Ted Berman and Richard Rich. Based on the book by Daniel P. Mannix, should make pleasant entertainment for the young, though its sentimentality and cloying cuteness will put off older and more demanding viewers. A-I (G)

Foxes (1980) Director Adrian Lyne's grim, depressing tale of four teenage girls (Jodie Foster, Marilyn Kagan, Cherie Currie and Kandice Stroh) left to their own devices amid the urban and moral squalor of Los Angeles. Fairly interesting, but the viewer stops caring about a third of the way through. Rough language and a superficial depiction of adult and youthful decadence. A-III (R) AA

Foxy Brown (1974) Pam Grier busts up a ring of ghetto drug dealers out of revenge in a movie directed by Jack Hill with more foul language, more horrible violence (rape and castration) and an even wider variety of sexual kinkiness than is usual for this kind of black exploitation movie. O (R)

Fragment of Fear (1971) When his aunt (Flora Robson) turns up strangled in the ancient ruins of Pompeii, a reformed drug addict (David Hemmings) resolves to track down her killer. Director Richard C. Sarafian initiates a crackling good study of the effect of the past on the present of a recovering addict, but those interested in it as a mystery thriller will be infuriated at its abrupt surprise ending. A-II (GP) 15

Fragrance of Wild Flowers, The (1979) Yugoslavian movie in which a successful actor gets fed up with life, takes up residence on a friend's river barge and winds up being celebrated by the media as a fashionable rebel, more in demand than ever. The alienation theme is a familiar one, but director Srdjan Karnovic handles it with incisive human detail and, amidst all the ironies, some warmly gentle humor. A-III (nr)

Framed (1975) Wronged man (Joe Don Baker) comes out of prison to wreck a quite literal bloody vengeance upon his oppressors. Directed by Phil Karlson, it is a vicious movie that goes all out in its depiction of brutal violence, especially against women. O (R) X

Frances (1984) Impassioned film biography of Frances Farmer, the 1930s' Hollywood starlet who bucked the system, got involved with alcohol, drugs and strange men and whose mother had her placed in a mental institution where she was abused, raped and received a lobotomy. Jessica Lange's fine performance makes this sincere, nonexploitative but rather plodding and episodic movie worth seeing. Director Graeme Clifford's depiction of Frances' suffering and fate is so unremittingly cruel, that the movie will be too harsh for many viewers. A-IV (R) 15

Frankenhooker (1990) Clunky horror farce about a "bio-electro technician" (James Lorinz) who saves his girlfriend's head after she is chewed up by a power mower and attaches it to various body parts selected from a bevy of Manhattan prostitutes. Directed by Frank Honenlotter, it's soft-core trash whose few droll moments are buried in low-budget gore. Repellent violence, sex scenes with nudity and drug abuse. O (nr) 18

Frankenstein and the Monster from Hell (1974) Peter Cushing again assumes the role of the mad doctor who, with his assistant (Shane Briant) assembles a creature from assorted parts they collect at the insane asylum in which they are residents. Directed by Terence Fisher, the gore is both sickening and sick. O (R) X

Frankenstein Must Be Destroyed (1970) Mediocre British installment in the Frankenstein saga with the mad doctor (Peter Cushing) fanatically intent on perfecting his experiments in brain transplants. Directed by Terence Fisher, the macabre setting and atmosphere are good but the gore, with heads being lopped off and blood splattering freely, is less effective than the earlier convention of suggesting such shock effects. A-III (PG) X

Frankenstein Unbound (see: "Roger Corman's Frankenstein Unbound").

Frankie and Johnny (1966) Elvis Presley vehicle with plenty of rock-'n'-roll music, fist-swinging action and cutsie-poo romance. Allegedly based on the famous folk ballad, Presley plays a two-timing but ultimately redemptive riverboat gambler with Donna Douglas as his tired-but-true love, Frankie. Directed by Frederick de Cordova, it's lightweight fun. A-II (br) U

Frankie and Johnny (1991) Moderately engaging love story about a fed-up-with-men waitress (Michelle Pfeiffer) in a Manhattan diner who doesn't want a relationship with the new cook (Al Pacino), an ex-con who wants to offer her love, marriage and a family. With Pacino in fine form here, producer-director Garry Marshall tackles themes of hope, renewal and family ties despite the confines of an overly talky romance. Brief shots of love-making, numerous sexual references and some rough language. A-III (R) 15

Frantic (1988) Well-crafted suspense thriller about an American couple (Harrison Ford and Betty Buckley) who on a visit to Paris get caught up in a dangerous game of international intrigue. Director Roman Polanski provides the chills and thrills with appropriately sinister camerawork and a strong performance by Ford, but several bizarre scenes involving drugs and a grotesque corpse are not for the squeamish. Restrained violence, drug use, brief nudity and some street language. A-III (R) 15

Fraternity Row (1977) Shallow and sentimental look at fraternity life in the mid-1950s in a story about an idealistic young man who becomes a pledge at a prestigious college fraternity and runs afoul of a sadistic bully. Director Thomas J. Tobin takes an uncritical view of the frat system on American campuses. Some sexual references. A-III (PG)

Fraternity Vacation (1985) Frat nerds place a wager on who will seduce Britt Ekland first. Directed by James Frawley, this "Animal House" clone offers nothing but the usual nudity and gross, vulgar humor. O (R)

Fraulein Doktor (1969) World War I German spy (Suzy Kendall) engineers the sinking of Lord Kitchener's ship, steals a poison gas formula from a French scientist (Capucine) and supervises the theft of the master battle plan from Allied headquarters in Belgium. Alberto Lattuada directs the movie in an almost documentary style that encourages a suspension of disbelief. Though uneven and deliberately devoid of emotional involvement, its events are often grimly absorbing and hard to dismiss. A-III (M) AA

Freaks (1932) Tod Browning, a director specializing in the field of horror and the grotesque, centered this story on a group of circus freaks who take in a normal woman in need of refuge but who betrays them. Browning endows the movie with an unusual sympathetic quality in not exploiting the deformities and monstrous appearance of his characters. The result is a unique film of the horror genre, a real classic of its kind, that is not easily forgotten by even the most sophisticated cinema-addict. A-II (nr)

Freaky Friday (1977) Mother and teenage daughter (Barbara Harris and Jodie Fos-

ter) vehemently wish to trade places for a single day, only to have the wish granted to their mutual discomfiture. Gary Nelson directs a typical Disney slapstick comedy bolstered by good performances in the leads. A-I (G) U

Freddy's Dead: The Final Nightmare (1991) Hideous Freddy Krueger (Robert Englund) continues to lure teenagers into suicidal nightmares until he is vanquished by his revenge-inspired daughter (Lisa Zane). Director Rachel Talalay spends more time on dream imagery and special effects than actual murders but the movie is still designed to invite laughter at adolescents being tortured and viciously slaughtered. Deadly violence depicted as entertaining and recurring rough language. O (R) 18

Free Willy (1993) After befriending a killer whale trapped in a cramped marine park, a rebellious 12-year-old (Jason James Richter) persuades his foster parents (Michael Madsen and Jayne Atkinson) and two park workers (Lori Petty and August Schellenberg) to help free the giant animal before it is killed for the insurance money. Director Simon Wincer's beguiling relationship story affirms family values, though it must be noted the adults cavalierly break the law in saving the whale. Fleeting violence. A-II (PG)

Free Woman, A (1974) German drama of a woman (Margarethe von Trotta) struggling for self-identity and fulfillment following her divorce and bitter court battle for custody of her little boy. Directed by Volker Schlondorff, it seethes with a restrained anger that leads to occasionally brutal characterizations of male stereotypes but avoids the pitfalls of exploiting women in the process. A-III (nr)

Freejack (1992) Ultraviolent, futuristic tale of a race car driver (Emilio Estevez) pursued by a ruthless killer (Mick Jagger) intent on selling the racer's body to a dying magnate (Anthony Hopkins). Director Geoff Murphy just marks time with his cast between the bloody shootouts that are the movie's only apparent reason for having been made. Excessive violence, implied live-in relationship and occasional rough language. O (R) 15

Freebie and the Bean (1974) Two freewheeling San Francisco cops career dangerously around the city to protect a mobster they plan to arrest when the time is ripe for a promotion. In director Richard Rush's failed comedy, Bean (Alan Arkin) and Freebie (James Caan) are gun-crazy psychopaths who enjoy indulging their penchant for foul language, ethnic slurs, kinky sex and beating up hapless individuals whenever they get a chance. O (R) X

Freedom to Love (1970) Presented in the form of a serious examination of sexual freedom, interspersed with some shallow commentary, the movie is merely a poor excuse to present scenes of graphic sex and nudity. O (nr)

Freeze-Die-Come to Life (1990) The foolhardy pranks of a young Russian boy (Pavel Nazarov) living nearby Stalin's World War II labor camps put him and his friend (Dinara Drukarova) in peril from both state authorities and a gang of cutthroat thieves. Director Vitaly Kanevski's grimly autobiographical account depicts life reduced to the level of self-preservation where children find little warmth and are quickly hardened. Subtitles. Several instances of violence, nudity and minimal rough language. A-III (nr)

French Connection, The (1971) Tough, unorthodox New York detective Popeye Doyle (Gene Hackman) and his partner (Roy Scheider) track down a massive heroin cache in this tense, exciting, very violent look at the darker side of law enforcement. Director William Friedkin makes excellent use of New York City locations in giving his fast-paced story the grimy look of reality and the acting of the leads is first-rate. The violent action and language are in the context of a sobering, perhaps shocking, portrayal of the kill-or-be-killed undercover world of cops and dope dealers. A-IV (R) 18

French Connection II (1975) Gene Hackman repeats his role as fanatical detective Popeye Doyle in a sequel set in France and directed by John Frankenheimer. Not nearly as successful as its predecessor, the movie is marred by its ambivalent attitude toward Doyle's ruthless methods, some strong violence and rough language. A-IV (R)

French Conspiracy, The (1973) Dramatic re-creation of the events in a political scandal that rocked the French government in the late 1960s when Ben Barka, a Moroccan revolutionary exile, was kidnapped in France with the apparent complicity and cooperation of some French officials. Directed by Yves Boisset, the result is not an espionage thriller, but rather a careful exposition of the intelligence community that operates beneath the surface of modern governments. Stars Gian-Maria Volonte, Michael Piccoli, and Jean-Louis Trintignant. A-II (PG)

French Cousins, The (see: "From Ear to Ear").

French Detective, The (1979) Gallic version of an American police thriller features a tough cop (Lino Ventura) and his young assistant (Patrick Dewaere) who encounter a dishonest political machine while investigating a murder. Director Pierre Granier-Deferre spends too much time on philosophical exchanges between his policemen

by Hollywood standards but its abuse of citizen's rights are familiar enough to American filmgoers. There is enough violence and moral ambiguity to make it adult fare. A-III (nr)

French Lessons (1986) Producer David Puttnam's somewhat anachronistic romance details the first sexual experience of a British exchange student in Paris. Jane Snowden gives a sensitive portrayal of the youth experimenting in adult responsibilities, but the dialogue is so awful and the script so woefully inadequate that the movie never achieves any credibility. O (PG)

French Lieutenant's Woman, The (1981) Scriptwriter Harold Pinter's adaptation of the John Fowles' novel uses a movie-within-a-movie gimmick so that the story of a wealthy gentleman's pursuit of a mysterious governess in the Victorian Age also becomes a tale of two performers carrying on an adulterous affair in the present. Meryl Streep and Jeremy Irons play the dual roles of the lovers. Director Karel Reisz' result is interesting, but too pretentious and humorless for its own good. Rather graphic bedroom scene. A-III (R) 15

French Postcards (1979) Lighthearted but aimless movie about a trio of American students in Paris (Miles Chapin, Blanche Baker, David Marshall Grant) and their various amorous misadventures. Director Willard Huyck's episodic, listless and anti-intellectual effort seeks unearned viewer sympathy for feckless youths whose acting ability seems more suited to amateur night at the fraternity house. The movie's implicit endorsement of sexual promiscuity makes it unacceptable entertainment. O (PG)

French Provincial (1976) Interesting French melodrama about a seamstress (Jeanne Moreau) who marries into a bourgeois family in the South of France and becomes the one who holds it together from the early 1930s to the 1970s. Director Andre Techine integrates the episodic family chronicle within the larger frame of the changes taking place within France during that period. A-III (nr)

French Way, The (see: "Love at the Top").

Frenzy (1972) Alfred Hitchcock's masterful suspense thriller focuses on a deranged strangler preying on women in contemporary London. The central character is an innocent man (Jon Finch) whose careless way of living implicates him as the serial murderer who dispatches his victims by means of a characteristic necktie, with accompanying perverse violence. The suspense is built on whether the wrong man will be punished for the crimes, something that is not resolved until the very last moment. Though of the same caliber as Hitchcock's best works, it lamentably resorts to some very explicit violence and brief nudity. A-IV (R) 18

Fresh Horses (1988) A college senior (Andrew McCarthy) drops his wealthy fiancee for a rural girl (Molly Ringwald) too young, uneducated and married to give him anything but grief. In this moodpiece about obsession, director David Anspaugh provides little understanding of the characters and ignores intriguing plotlines. Off-camera illicit sex, brief violence and minimal rough language. A-III (PG-13) 15

Freshman, The (1990) Shortly after arriving in New York City, a college freshman (Matthew Broderick) is bewildered to find himself involved with a Godfather-like businessman (Marlon Brando), his marriage-minded daughter, a giant lizard, federal agents and the threat of jail. Writer-director Andrew Bergman serves up an amiable comedy more distinguished by an amusing cast than the story's less-than-riveting dialogue and perfunctory pacing. Minimal rough language. A-II (PG)

Freud (1962) Earnest, plodding drama recounts the turning point for Dr. Sigmund Freud (Montgomery Clift) as a neurologist in 1885 Vienna where his treatment of a troubled patient (Susannah York) leads to his theory of childhood sexual repression, a concept rejected by his closest colleague (Larry Parks) and scorned by his peers. Director John Huston's dramatization of psychiatry's beginnings may be simplistic, especially the dream sequences, but demonstrates the limitations of the physical sciences in treating emotional disorders. Though handled with sensitivity, the subject matter may be distasteful for some viewers. A-IV (br) X

Friday Foster (1976) Director Arthur Marks wastes some talented performers (Yaphet Kotto; Godfrey Cambridge; Eartha Kitt; Pam Grier) in a black exploitation number adapted from a comic strip but without whatever depth and subtlety the original may have had. Excessive sex and violence. O (R)

Friday the 13th (1980) Homicidal maniac menaces teens at a summer camp. Crude, mindless exploitation cheapie directed by Sean S. Cunningham with much blood and violence and graphic sex scenes. O (R) X

Friday the 13th, Part II (1981) Disgusting horror sequel with the homicidal maniac once more stalking slow-witted camp counselors who have sex on their minds rather than self-preservation. Wholly uninspired direction and script are by Steve Miner and Ron Kurz, with the usual unhealthy mix of nudity and graphic violence. O (R) X

Friday the 13th, Part III (1982) The 3-D version directed by Steve Miner is no better than its predecessors in the blood and gore department. O (R) X

Friday the 13th—The Final Chapter (1984) The ghoulish maniac is on the loose again as director Joseph Zito fills the screen with the usual gore and violence mixed with crude language and much nudity. O (R) X

Friday the 13th, Part V—A New Beginning (1985) Directed by Danny Steinmann, this time out the maniac stalks a home for disturbed children. Violent, gory horror flick whose only goal is to shock. O (R) X

Friday the 13th, Part VI: Jason Lives (1986) The demonic killer is brought back from the dead via a lightning bolt to torment, terrorize and molest the descendants of his killers. This excessively violent sequel, written and directed by Tom McLoughlin, consists of little more than a succession of bloody slaughter scenes with a little explicit sex between minors thrown in for good measure. O (R) X

Friday the 13th Part VIII—Jason Takes Manhattan (1989) Sick horror show in which bionic corpse Jason (Kane Hodder) dismembers recent grads of Crystal Lake High on a tour ship bound for Manhattan and pursues the survivors into the subways and alleys of the Big Apple. Writer-director Rob Hedden zeroes in on every gory detail in a movie that also offers profanity, recreational teen cocaine use and fleeting nudity in a brief teen sexual encounter. O (R) X

Fried Green Tomatoes (1991) The youthful reminiscences of a nursing home resident (Jessica Tandy) about an unsolved, half-century-old murder mystery involving two spunky Alabama women (Mary Stuart Masterson and Mary-Louise Parker) inspire her newfound friend, a frustrated Southern housewife (Kathy Bates), to put her own house in order. An initially sluggish script hampers director Jon Avnet's beautifully acted movie but can't submerge its warm-hearted tribute to friendship, female solidarity and respect for people of color. Very brief violence and a few sexual references. A-II (PG-13) 12

Friend of the Family (1965) Weak French comedy directed by Robert Thomas about a toy inventor (Pierre Dux) and his wife (Danielle Darrieux) whose serenity is upset by a rival manufacturer (Jean Gabin) and his interest in their teenage daughter (Sylvie Vartan). A-III (br)

Friendly Persuasion (1956) Winning adaptation of Jessamyn West's novel about a Quaker household (Gary Cooper, Dorothy McGuire and Tony Perkins) at the time of the Civil War. Director William Wyler's lyric treatment of family life and human relationships heightens the conflict between the hard realities of the war and the pacifist convictions of the Quaker faith. Still a warm and cheering experience for family viewers. A-I (nr) U

Friends (1971) Soapy, sappy sudser about two unhappy teens (Sean Bury and Anicee Alvina) running away from cruel homes who meet in the Paris Zoo and flee to a seaside refuge where instead of being friends they become lovers and parents in the pseudo-lyrical style of director Lewis Gilbert. The explicitness of their barely post-pubescent sexual awakening is not only offensive but a saddening exploitation of minors in the name of box-office romance. O (R) X

Friends of Eddie Coyle, The (1973) Solid adaptation of a George V. Higgins' novel about a tired, small-time Boston crook (Robert Mitchum), who wants to retire on one last job but gets caught in the middle of con men, cops and criminals, and tries desperately to find an out. Directed by Peter Yates, the story is given a fine, naturalistic treatment, tough and complex, but tight. The powerful effect of the conclusion is achieved through the film's careful accumulation of detail, though some may be unwilling to wait for the final turn of events because of the harsh and uncompromising depiction of criminal life. A-III (R) X

Fright Night (1985) This horror movie attempts to evoke chills in a quite ordinary setting when a high school youth (William Ragsdale) becomes convinced that his new neighbor (Chris Sarandon) is a vampire. A major problem with writer-director Tom Holland's approach is its uncertain tone in veering between straight horror and a spoof of horror movies. The conclusion is dominated by gory pull-out-all-the-stops special effects. Benign view of extramarital sex. O (R) 18

Fringe Dwellers, The (1987) Insightful portrait of a young Australian aborigine girl's coming of age while struggling to break the cycle of poverty and oppression that crushes youthful ambition and enthusiasm. The contrived plot supplies an abrupt solution to a complex series of social and moral problems, but the overall perspective of director Bruce Beresford's movie provides an uplifting vision of community values and strong family ties. A-III (PG)

Frisco Kid, The (1979) A rabbi (Gene Wilder), sent cross-country on horseback during the Gold Rush to head a congregation in San Francisco, endures many misadventures that are potentially hilarious but prove only mildly funny in execution. Harrison Ford as the badman who brings him cross-country unscathed, makes the long journey as enjoyable as the material

allows. Contains some hard-edged violence and profanity. A-III (PG) A

Fritz the Cat (1972) Foul-mouthed comic book feline has been brought to the screen in an animated feature that lacks not only a clever script but a sense of humor. Under director Ralph Bakshi's slapdash direction, all attempts at satire regularly succumb to sexual sordidness, putting Fritz and his friends in the same category as the humans who toil in porno pictures. O (X)

Frogs (1972) Harmless looking frogs and toads send an army of snakes, leeches, snapping turtles and alligators to invade the home of Ray Milland on his swampy tropical island. Instead of playing the silly horror fantasy for laughs, director George McGowen tries for gasps in scene upon grisly scene with a transparent ecology message about nature taking its revenge. A-III (PG) X

From Beyond the Grave (1976) British horror movie composed of four tales linked together by the device of a sinister antique shop and its affable proprietor (Peter Cushing). Director Kevin Connor can't improve upon the weak script, but he gets some fine performances (Ian Bannen, Donald Pleasance and Margaret Leighton as an eccentric medium right out of Noel Coward). The blood flows a little too freely in one of the stories but, other than that, it's a relatively mild little chiller. A-III (PG) X

From Ear to Ear (1971) Tawdry French import offers a psychosexual thriller about two bisexual women who taunt a deeply disturbed wife into a drug-induced orgy that ends in murder. Director Louis Soulanes uses velvety amber photography to induce a mood of ennui and shrill music to suggest suspense, but its graphic sensationalism puts it in the sex exploitation category. O (X)

From Noon Till Three (1976) Seriocomic western about an outlaw (Charles Bronson) whose sexual dalliance with a zany widow (Jill Ireland) blossoms into true love. The cast's wooden performance, the script's utter banalities and Frank Gilroy's inept direction obscure the theme of mistaken identities and half-truths becoming the basis for a legend. Excessive sex scenes. O (PG) 15

From Russia with Love (1964) Stealing a top secret decoder from the Soviet Embassy in Istanbul, British superspy James Bond (Sean Connery) takes the Venice-bound Orient Express, fighting off a wicked assortment of assassins (notably Robert Shaw and Lotte Lenya) along the way. Directed by Terence Young, the slick, tongue-in-cheek espionage thriller is marred by some scenes of sadistic violence, casual sexual encounters and suggestive dialogue. O (PG)

From the Hip (1987) Law clerk (Judd Nelson) uses deceit and bravado to advance his career, but when he is given an unwinnable murder case, his defense of a psychotic literature professor (John Hurt) brings about a change of heart and conscience. Bob Clark directs this optimistic yuppie portrait with care and wit. Some vulgar language and a brief outburst of courtroom violence. A-II (PG) 15

From the Life of the Marionettes (1980) Disappointing exploration of the homicidal psyche details the killing and sexual violation of a prostitute by a sullen businessman. Director Ingmar Bergman's narrative is devoted to flashbacks and flashforwards that supposedly shed some light on the what caused this irrational act. Darkly clinical and emotionally sterile, the movie is obscure and troubling. Extensive nudity. O (R)

From the Mixed-Up Files of Mrs. Basil E. Frankweiler (1973) Two preteen runaways (Sally Prager and Johnny Doran) find a haven in New York City's Metropolitan Museum of Art until discovered by rich, eccentric recluse (Ingrid Bergman) from whom they learn a lesson in human integrity. In director Fielder Cook's well-intentioned but disappointing family movie, few things work the way they are supposed to, though young children may enjoy some of the midnight wanderings through the museum. A-I (G)

Front, The (1976) Tragicomedy set during the early 1950s about a born loser (Woody Allen) who fronts for blacklisted writers by submitting their work under his name until he himself is turned by a blacklisted actor (Zero Mostel) whose subsequent suicide is story's turning point. Many of those associated with the movie, including director Martin Ritt and writer Walter Bernstein, were themselves blacklisted during that period. It is an interesting look at a tragic era, but the drama and humor do not mix easily. Some rough language and comic sexual references. A-III (PG) 15

Front Page, The (1974) New edition of the Charles MacArthur-Ben Hecht play about tough Chicago newspapermen in the 1920s pits Jack Lemmon as the ace reporter against Walter Matthau as his wily editor. Directed by Billy Wilder, there is plenty of sharp, fast comedy straight out of the original, but nicely put over by a fine cast and a few neat touches of the director. Some, however, will be put off by the constant stream of pressroom profanity. A-III (R/PG appeal) AA

Frozen Dead (1967) Failed horror movie about a good-bad scientist (Dana Andrews) who thaws out former Nazi military leaders after their 25 years of deep freeze existence. Ineptly directed by Herbert J. Leder, its story of suspended animation and revivification is stupid but innocuous. A-I (br) X

F.T.A. (1972) Filmed record of performers Jane Fonda, Donald Sutherland and troupe staging a series of anti-war shows outside military bases in the U.S. and in the Pacific. The group as a whole looks rather sappy, but the show's politics, which is what it is all about, is as worthy of a platform as those of Bob Hope's Christmas troupe. A-III (nr)

Fuego (1969) Argentinian story of a nymphomaniac (Isabel Sarli) features a cliche-ridden plot, atrocious acting and a low level of technical competence. Written, produced and directed by Armando Bo, it is aimed squarely at the sex exploitation market. O (nr)

Fugitive, The (1947) Underrated screen version of Graham Greene's novel, "The Power and the Glory," about an all-too-human priest (Henry Fonda) who is hunted down by a puritanical officer (Pedro Armendariz) after the Mexican Revolution proscribes the free practice of religion. Director John Ford's flawed masterpiece uses deeply felt religious symbolism in telling the story of a weak man who, despite his fear of death, continues ministering to the spiritual needs of a poor community. Menacing atmosphere may be inappropriate for young children. A-I (nr)

Fugitive, The (1993) Having escaped while being transported to prison, a Chicago surgeon (Harrison Ford) convicted of murdering his wife must evade the ever-tightening net of a relentless U.S. marshall (Tommy Lee Jones) while desperately tracking down the one-armed man (Andreas Katsulas) who actually killed her. Director Andrew Davis knits together a strong narrative, crackerjack performances and taut editing for a fine thriller not dependent on constant, glorified violence for mounting suspense. Brief, sporadic violence. A-II (PG-13) 15

Full Life, A (1972) Japanese movie whose title indicates the goal that a young woman (Ineko Arima) sets for herself after leaving her worthless husband. Nothing very dramatic happens in director Susumu Hani's 1962 work, but the accumulation of small details of life in a large urban complex makes the woman's realization that she needs friends and social commitment seem quite real. A-III (nr)

Full Metal Jacket (1987) Director Stanley Kubrick's moody essay on the dehumanizing effects of basic training and combat during the Vietnam era traces the transformation of a typical Marine Corps recruit from observer to participant. Sexual come-ons by hookers, graphic bloodshed and excessive profanity provide the realistic texture for the expression of diminishing spiritual sensitivity and moral ambiguity. A-IV (R) 18

Full Moon in Blue Water (1988) The Mr. Nice Guy owner (Gene Hackman) of a rundown bar and grill on the Texas Gulf coast spends too much time mourning the loss of his wife and not enough time salvaging his business or courting the feisty woman who loves him (Teri Garr). Directed by Peter Masterson, the compact character study follows the nutty turn of events that motivate the laid-back hero to put the past to rest and get on with life. Constant stream of vulgar language spouted by the protagonist's senile father-in-law (Burgess Meredith) and implied sexual promiscuity. A-IV (R) 15

Fun with Dick and Jane (1977) Leaden comedy about an upwardly mobile suburban couple (Jane Fonda and George Segal) who suddenly find their direction reversed when the husband loses his job as an aerospace executive. After trying welfare and foodstamps, they take to armed robbery and succeed beyond all measure. Apparently director Ted Kotcheff was aiming at satire, a task too formidable for the modest talents involved. Besides the movie's general insensitivity to genuine social ills, it employs coarse language and a tasteless bathroom scene. O (PG) A

Funeral in Berlin (1967) In a sequel to the "Ipcress File," Michael Caine returns as the disreputable British intelligence agent, Harry Palmer. The plot's intermingling of German, Russian, British and Israeli spies defies synopsis, but the action is plentiful and exciting. The British production directed by Guy Hamilton succeeds in brilliantly contrasting the ways of life in East and West Berlin. A winner for those who enjoy undercover work. Restrained violence. A-III (br) PG

Funeral Parade of Roses (1973) Failed Japanese experimental work by Toshio Matsumoto is a mishmash of scenes filmed at a gay bar in Tokyo. Never have fragmented images of eroticism and bloodshed looked more boring than those concocted here in a venture that adds nothing to our understanding of human nature. O (nr)

Funhouse (1981) A monster stalks four extremely dim young people trapped in a carnival funhouse in a loathsome horror movie written and directed by Tobe Hooper. More likely to sicken than frighten, the film exploits sex and violence in grotesque and ugly ways. O (R)

Funniest Man in the World, The (1970) Douglas Fairbanks Jr. narrates a documentary on Charlie Chaplin's early career as shown through excerpts from his work at the Keystone, Essanay and Mutual studios and makes a good introduction to the comic art of silent comedy. Chaplin's admirers, however, may wince at the way some of his movies have been chopped up and comic routines presented out of context in a compilation assembled by Vernon P. Becker. A-I (nr) U

Funny about Love (1990) Touching comedy about a cartoonist (Gene Wilder) whose belated but overwhelming desire for fatherhood drives his wife (Christine Lahti) to leave him and results in a precarious relationship with a much younger woman (Mary Stuart Masterson). Though director Leonard Nimoy's comedy is fairly predictable, its humor, good-hearted characters and occasional sparkling dialogue make it lighthearted but strictly adult fare. Unmarried sexual relationships, several double entendres, a flash of nudity and minimal rough language. A-III (PG-13) PG

Funny Farm (1988) When a couple (Chevy Chase and Madolyn Smith) leave New York City behind for the joys of life in a Vermont farmhouse, their speedy disenchantment comes through many comic situations, some of them hackneyed. Though nicely acted, director George Roy Hill tends to let scenes drag on pointlessly. Some profanity and a skewed picture of rural folk as greedy nasties. A-III (PG)

Funny Girl (1968) Barbra Streisand musical is a sentimental treatment of certain aspects of the life of Fanny Brice, the Ziegfield Follies queen whose marriage to a gambler (Omar Sharif) fails in spite of their love. Director William Wyler turns Streisand's movie debut into a personal triumph. A-II (G) U

Funny Lady (1975) Barbara Streisand musical comedy in which she brings some depth to her portrayal of the maturing Fanny Brice trapped by her love for a professional gambler (Omar Sharif) and her attraction to a Broadway producer (James Caan) without losing any of her zest in interpreting the Billy Rose songs and elaborate dance routines. Directed by Herbert Ross, the serious moments tend to drag, but the comic ones are hilarious, and the verve and nostalgia of the revue help to conceal a flawed plot. Basic plot situations and some of the dialog are adult fare. A-III (PG)

Funny Thing Happened on the Way to the Forum, A (1966) Wacky and ribald Broadway hit about a cunning slave (Zero Mostel) in ancient Rome who has great fun in exploiting a series of mistaken identities and in misinterpreting various orders in an effort to gain his freedom. Director Richard Lester keeps the humor swift and visual, backed by such fine screen clowns as Buster Keaton, Phil Silvers, Jack Gilford and Michael Hordern in a crisp and stylish musical burlesque of ageless low comedy routines. A-III (br) PG

Funnyman (1971) Photographer-director John Korty applies his sensitivity and compassion to create a sort of fictional documentary about a young coffee-house comic (perfectly played by Peter Bonerz) who aspires to more intellectual work as a writer-actor and is forever feeling disappointed with himself. Matter-of-fact acceptance of casual sex and some lingering shots of an artist's nude model are questionable elements in an otherwise perceptive study of a talented young man's aspirations. A-IV (nr) A

Furies, The (1950) Overblown Western directed by Anthony Mann is mired in a convoluted narrative about a greedy cattle baron (Walter Huston) who double-crosses his iron-willed cowgirl daughter (Barbara Stanwyck) causing her to throw in with a bitter family enemy (Wendell Corey) to bring her father's ruin. Stylized violence, including hanging and disfigurement, assorted obsessive behavior and romantic complications. A-III (br) A

Further Adventures of the Wilderness Family, The (1979) A sequel to the 1976 film about a family who leaves Los Angeles to live in the Rocky Mountains. This time Dad (Robert Logan) is caught in an avalanche and jumped by a cougar. However, the main crisis involves Mom, who is coming down with double-pneumonia and visited by a nasty pack of wolves. None of these perils is treated realistically by director Frank Zuniga, however, and even the younger children should be able to bear up and enjoy them. A-I (G)

Fury (1936) Mistaken for a murderer, an innocent man (Spencer Tracy) escapes a small-town lynch mob and, despite his loving wife (Sylvia Sidney), becomes an embittered criminal obsessed with revenge. German director Fritz Lang's first Hollywood effort is a powerful picture of ordinary Americans struggling to survive hard times and hardened hearts during the Depression, though it falters in a melodramatic conclusion. The lynching sequence is a harrowing but classic portrayal of irrational mob violence. A-II (br) 18

Fury, The (1978) Kirk Douglas plays a man who tries to rescue his son from a sinister government agency that wants to use the boy's psychic powers for its own ends. Director Brian De Palma's crude, heavy-handed melodrama wallows in violence and gore. O (R) X

Futureworld (1976) Sequel to "Westworld" takes viewers back among those rambunctious robots. The plot gimmick this time is a scheme to replace world leaders with robots but enterprising journalists Peter Fonda and Blythe Danner foil the bad guys. Under Richard T. Heffron's direction, it's all pretty silly but mildly diverting entertainment, thanks mostly to Danner's decidedly nonrobotized performance. Some scenes involving sexually programmed robots. A-III (PG) A

Futz (1969) Filmed performance by New York's La Mama Repertory Troupe of a play by Rochelle Owens about a farmer who is murdered by the community because, failing to find human love, he loves his pig. Supposedly an allegory about freedom and personal responsibility, its deliberately shocking and disgusting elements are less intolerable than its pretentious air of self-righteousness. O (nr)

Fuzz (1972) Police satire about the bumbling crime-fighting antics of writer Ed McBain's mythical 87th Precinct in Boston where detective Burt Reynolds and subordinates Jack Weston, Tom Skerritt and Raquel Welch as a policewoman decoy fail to take seriously Yul Brynner's extortion demands. Their inept performances are about as laughable as director Richard Colla's inept comedy ever gets. Viewers who find murder, attempted rape and the burning of helpless hobos less than hilarious may wish to take a pass on this one. A-III (PG) X

F/X (1986) Tough suspense thriller concerning a movie special-effects expert (Bryan Brown) asked by a government agency to stage a fake killing but then finds himself hunted by the police for murder and shot at by unknown assassins. The plot is full of holes, but director Robert Mandel rivets attention on the action's twists and turns. There is some intense violence, but because the movie is about the trickery of special effects, the fake blood and gore are unlikely to offend most adult moviegoers. A-IV (R) 15

FX 2—The Deadly Art of Illusion (1991) A special effects expert (Bryan Brown) and a retired detective (Brian Dennehy) reteam to uncover why a cop (Tom Mason) was set up by his boss (Philip Bosco) to be rubbed out. Brown and Dennehy's appealing chemistry partially makes up for the contrived and convoluted plot in director Richard Franklin's rough, action-packed movie. Intermittent gory violence and brief shower nudity. A-III (PG-13) 15

G

Gable and Lombard (1976) Nostalgic love story about two famous Hollywood stars (James Brolin and Jill Clayburgh) is a slick but embarrassingly bad job of story-telling by British director Sidney J. Furie. Sympathetic and romanticized presentation of infidelity. O (R) AA

Gabriel over the White House (1933) Curious relic from Depression-era Hollywood in which a machine politician (Walter Huston) is elected President, then emerges from a brush with death to shed his party ties, suspend Congress and declare martial law. Using his executive powers, he puts the unemployed to work on federal construction projects, repeals Prohibition while crushing crime syndicates with Army tanks and uses a naval exercise of air power to cow foreign powers into signing a disarmament accord, with the money saved going to pay their U.S. war debts. Directed by Gregory La Cava, the political fantasy of a home-grown American dictator solving the desperate problems of the day takes plenty of strange turns, not least of which is draping its fascist hero in the mantle of Lincoln and linking his actions to the heavenly messenger of the title. Stylized violence, discreet sexual innuendo and rationalization of the end justifying the means. A-III (br) A

Gaby—A True Story (1987) Uneven dramatization of the story of Gabriella Brimmer (Rachel Levin), a successful Mexican writer who was born severely handicapped with cerebral palsy, and the peasant houseworker (Norma Aleandro) who became her nanny and eventually her guardian. The inspirational drama, as directed by Luis Mandoki, is somewhat frustrating in its failure to explore the motivations of a number of central characters, especially the mother (Liv Ullmann). Awkward and unnecessarily extended scenes of Gaby's attempts to express her sexuality. A-III (R) 15

Gaily, Gaily (1969) Ben Hecht, swaddled in adolescent innocence, makes his way to Chicago in 1910 and director Norman Jewison milks his autobiographical recollections into a nostalgic portrait capturing both the naivete of the young man and the corruption of the times. Illuminating satire stars Brian Keith, Beau Bridges and Hume Cronyn. A-III (M)

Galaxina (1981) Low-budget, tediously sophomoric spoof of science-fiction films stars Dorothy R. Stratten in the title role. Directed by William Sachs, Stratten is made the target for an unrelenting series of sexually suggestive remarks. A-III (R)

Galileo (1975) Producer Ely Landau's screen version of the Bertolt Brecht play about the 16th-century scientist (Topol) and his confrontation with the church and with his own conscience comes across brilliantly. Directed by Joseph Losey, the work present Galileo not as a hero but as a loving portrait of a great man who becomes the victim of ordinary creature comforts. A-III (PG) A

Gallipoli (1981) Enthusiastic young Australians (Mel Gibson and Mark Lee) enlist for service in World War I and soon have their romantic notions of the war as a glorious and noble adventure dissolved. Director Peter Weir contrasts naive patriotism with youthful idealism in this superbly rendered period drama. Intense battle scenes and a depiction of a brothel. A-III (PG)

Gambit (1966) Shirley MacLaine and Michael Caine set out to steal a priceless sculpture from wily Herbert Lom in the familiar plot about a perfect crime gone wrong. Director Ronald Neame comes up with a couple of new twists and some fine acting to distinguish it from a host of other romantic thrillers. A-I (br) U

Gambler, The (1974) Static story of a compulsive gambler (James Caan) who betrays his bookies (Paul Sorvino and Carmine Caridi), his too-forgiving mother (Jacqueline Brookes), his doting grandfather (Morris Carnovsky) and his lovely girlfriend (Lauren Hutton) as he degrades himself on the path to self-destruction. Directed by Karel Reisz, the story is obvious from the beginning and there is no attempt to make the viewer care a wit about the characters and their problems. A-III (R) X

Game Is Over, The (1967) French adaptation of an Emile Zola novel about a woman (Jane Fonda), married to a ruthless business man (Michel Piccoli), falls fatefully in love with her husband's son (Peter McEnery). Directed by Roger Vadim, the movie's emphasis on nudity and eroticism are excessive. O (br)

Games (1967) Mediocre thriller about a bored couple (James Caan and Katharine Ross) and a mysterious stranger (Simone Signoret) who introduces them to some macabre games that end in murder. Directed by Curtis Harrington, some viewers will feel cheated by the twist ending that explains the illogical situations that precede it. Mature themes and stylized violence. A-III (br) U

Games, The (1970) Ponderous Olympic marathon movie tracing the personal stories of various competitors, including an obnoxious American long-distance runner (Ryan O'Neal), his British counterpart (Michael Crawford), an exploited Australian aborigine (Athol Compton) and a patriotic Czech runner (Charles Aznavor). Forgettable British production directed by Michael Winner, it goes on and on to no point. Some sexual references. A-III (G)

Gandhi (1982) Superb portrait of India's great political and spiritual leader comes to life in Ben Kingsley's authoritative, yet sensitive performance. Director Richard Attenborough's epic-scale production re-creates Gandhi's life and times, especially his use of nonviolence and hunger strikes to bring together the diverse peoples of India and unify them as a nation. Though its scenes of violence are not for children, the movie's vision of justice and peace is for everyone else, especially young people. A-II (PG) A

Gang That Couldn't Shoot Straight, The (1972) Failed screen version of Jimmy Breslin's novel about a bunch of inept South Brooklyn hoods bent on "takin' ovah da territory" features ethnic humor that tends to give credence to the efforts of the Italian-American Anti-Defamation League. So inept are director James Goldstone's satirical irreverences that an adult perspective seems to be a basic requirement for viewing. A-III (PG) AA

Gang's All Here, The (1943) Wartime musical extravaganza in which a nightclub singer (Alice Faye) falls in love with a soldier (James Ellison) who is engaged to someone else. Directed by Busby Berkeley, things work out happily between the big musical numbers, including Carmen Miranda's "The Lady in the Tutti Frutti Hat." Innocent-but-dated fun. A-I (br) A

Ganja & Hess (1973) Mindless horror movie about an anthropologist who is addicted to human blood and a beautiful young woman who is both smitten and bitten by the evil doctor. The story never gets much beyond this, though director Bill Gunn adds a number of silly sex interludes suggesting even more unhealthy goings-on than plasma addiction. O (R)

Garbo Talks (1984) Sentimental comedy about a loving son (Ron Silver) who spares no effort to fulfill the wish of his dying mother (Anne Bancroft) to meet Greta Garbo. Directed by Sidney Lumet, it is modestly entertaining, but a little hard to take unless you share the Garbo mystique and don't mind watching a callous depiction of the collapse of a marriage. A-III (PG-13) 15

Garden of Delights, The (1971) Spanish director Carlos Saura has fashioned a quietly haunting, surreal black comedy about an aristocratic Madrid family perverted by greed. The story focuses on the aged family patriarch (Jose Luis Lopez Vasquez), struggling to regain his faculties after an auto accident; insightful study of a man coming to terms with the deceit and selfishness of loved ones. A-III (GP)

Garden of the Finzi-Continis (1972) Director Vittorio De Sica's drama about the effects of Fascist anti-Semitism on the Jewish community in a small Italian town tells the story of a poor Jewish college student (Lino Capolicchio) who loves the beautiful daughter (Dominique Sanda) of a wealthy Jewish family. Structured as a somber nostalgic romance in which old class divisions prove stronger than racial bonds, the movie develops into a disturbing elegy for the loss of human dignity. A-III (R) A

Gardens of Stone (1987) Director Francis Coppola's mildly nostalgic and insightful vision of the military as family contrasts the beliefs and aspirations of a decorated combat vet (James Caan) with those of a raw recruit (D.B. Sweeney) assigned to his Old Guard Arlington National Cemetery unit during the difficult Vietnam War years. Tragic story of the meaning of military service has some rough language and sexual situations marking it for mature audiences. A-III (R) 15

Gas Food Lodging (1992) Bittersweet tale of a starry-eyed teenage girl (Fairuza Balk) coming to accept the reality of life with her exhausted waitress mom (Brooke Adams) after her roaming dad (James Brolin) leaves and her rebellious sister (Ione Skye) runs away. Allison Anders directs a realistic drama of a broken home that is not without modest insights into female solidarity. A few discreet sexual encounters, brief nudity and minimal rough language. A-III (R) 15

Gas-s-s-s (1970) When the country's over-30 generation is wiped out by an accident with experimental nerve gas, a group of the under-30 crowd goes for a cross-country romp, encountering demented cowboys, motorcycle freaks, a paramilitary football squad, a teenage brain surgeon, and so on and on. Director Roger Corman's silly, disjointed fantasy ends in a harmonious youth celebration, long before which most viewers will have sought some fresh air. Some adult material. A-III (PG) AA

Gate, The (1987) Modern fairy tale for the younger set about the dangers of toying with the darker side. Pre-teens accidentally unleash suburban demons while parents are away and need a heavy-metal album, courage and pure hearts to chase them back through the "gate" from which they escaped. Director Tibor Takacs provides some mild scares in a simple good vs. evil tale. A-II (PG-13) 15

Gator (1976) Burt Reynolds stars in and directs this story of an undercover agent's attempt to send the Mr. Big of a corrupt Southern county to prison. Mediocre entertainment at best, the movie veers in mood from slapstick to melodrama to soap opera and back again. Violence. A-III (PG) AA

Gauntlet, The (1977) Not-too-bright Phoenix police officer (Clint Eastwood) goes to Las Vegas to extradite a convicted prostitute (Sandra Locke) only to discover that both of them have been marked for death. Eastwood also directed the shoddy, violent movie, which is little more than a pretext for an extravagant display of gunplay, a steady stream of verbal obscenities and a bit of sex and nudity. O (R) 18

Gay Deceivers (1969) Young men pose as homosexuals to avoid military induction, but the charade backfires when they have to convince parents, girlfriends and teachers that they are straight. Stereotyped characters may offend members of the gay community while the instances of nudity and love-making add little to director Bruce Kessler's muddled social satire. A-IV (R)

Gay Purr-ee (1962) Animated musical recounting the adventures of a country cat (voice of Judy Garland) who goes to Paris where she falls into the clutches of con artists (voices of Hermione Gingold and Paul Frees) until rescued by the cat (voice of Robert Goulet) she left behind. Director Abe Levitow's UPA cartoon feature has some pleasant but forgettable songs for older viewers and some broad comedy for the youngsters, but the story lacks strong appeal for either age group. A-I (G) U

Geisha Boy, The (1958) Jerry Lewis plays a fumbling out-of-work magician who gets into a wearisome series of jams as a member of a USO troupe entertaining troops stationed in Japan. Director Frank Tashlin mixes the usual Lewis pratfalls with cloying sentimentality over the rabbit used in his magic act and a sad Japanese boy who finds the gawky American hilarious. Mild sexual innuendo. A-II (br) U

General, The (1927) Epic silent comedy set in the Civil War has Buster Keaton as a Southern railroad engineer pursuing the Northern spies who have stolen his locomotive, outwitting them and driving it back in time to stop an attack by the Union Army. Keaton's mastery of physical comedy is seen at its best here as he stoically overcomes all manner of obstacles in the path of his speeding but recalcitrant locomotive. A beautifully crafted work, with an appropriate musical score, it's a treat for all ages. (br) U

General Idi Amin Dada (see: "Idi Amin Dada").

Generation (1969) Hippie (Pete Duel) and little rich girl (Kim Darby) move in together in Greenwich Village and decide to have a baby by natural childbirth. Anti-establishment comedy based on William Goodhart's play doesn't have the sharp edges of the original but preserves its wit and charm

thanks to director George Schaefer's toned-down treatment. A-III (PG) A

Genghis Khan (1965) Lumbering historical epic follows the Mongol warrior (Omar Sharif) who rises to head the Gobi Desert tribes by defeating his rival (Stephen Boyd) and marrying his wife (Francoise Dorleac). Director Henry Levin stages a lot of colorful action scenes but the script is cliched, the dialogue unintentionally funny and the acting overdone ham. Much stylized violence and some sexual situations. A-III (br)

Gentle Giant (1967) Engaging but less than credible adventure yarn about a young boy (Clint Howard) who rescues a bear cub in the Florida Everglades and raises him into a 650-pound house pet. Dennis Weaver is the boy's put-upon but understanding dad with Ralph Meeker as an antagonist of sorts. Directed by James Neilson, the problems of the situation are all very predictable, but they are still fun, especially for the youngsters. A-I (br) U

Gentle Sergeant, The (see: "Three Stripes in the Sun").

Gentleman Jim (1942) Period success story unfolds as James Corbett (Errol Flynn) rises from lowly San Francisco bank clerk to cocky prizefighter, ultimately winning the heavyweight championship in 1892 by knocking out John L. Sullivan (Ward Bond). Director Raoul Walsh alternates scenes of Jim's prowess in the ring with his relations, often comic, with his working-class Irish-American family and his on-again, off-again romance with a society debutante (Alexis Smith). Stylized boxing sequences and brawls. A-I (nr) U

George! (1973) The title character is a Saint Bernard whose clumsy exuberance embarrasses one and all, until he and his guardian (Marshall Thompson) rescue each other from an avalanche in the Swiss Alps. Director Wallace C. Bennett concentrates on the gorgeous Alpine locales, providing some distraction for audiences who may tire of watching actors engage in pratfalls for the benefit of a dopey, if lovable dog. A-I (G)

George Balanchine's The Nutcracker (1993) Shimmering movie version of Tschaikovsky's Christmas-themed ballet (performed by the New York City Ballet) in which a little girl (Jessica Lynn Cohen) dreams her nutcracker toy soldier comes to life (as Macaulay Culkin), rescues her from the giant Mouse King and transports her to the enchanted Land of Sweets where magical fairies enchant them with dances. With Kevin Kline's brief narration setting the scenes, director Emile Ardolino presents a straightforward filming of Balanchine's choreography in a production captivating for its glorious music and splendid dancers; though without any dialogue, small children and some adults may get restless. A-I (G)

Georgia, Georgia (1972) Written by Maya Angelou and directed by Stig Bjorkman, this story of a beautiful black singer on tour in Sweden quickly lapses into a romantic interracial interlude between the singer (Diana Sands) and a photographer (Dirk Benedict). Clumsy insertion of coy material focusing on the homosexual appetites of the singer's manager and a jarring climax that shocks but without providing an adequate resolution. A-IV (R)

Georgy Girl (1966) Tragicomedy of a good-hearted, awkward young woman (Lynn Redgrave) who tries to make a life of her own after her friends (Alan Bates and Charlotte Rampling) break up and leave her to care for their neglected child. Under Silvio Narizzano's direction, Redgrave brings warmth and credibility to the title role, with James Mason adding a wry, slightly self-mocking performance as the aging millionaire who has long pursued her. Frank treatment of sexual matters. A-IV (nr) X

Geronimo: An American Legend (1993) Leaden Western about the efforts of General Crook (Gene Hackman) and two of his officers (Jason Patric; Matt Damon) to recapture Geronimo (Wes Studi) and his small band of renegade Apaches hiding out on the Arizona–Mexico border in 1885-86. In pretentious, stilted fashion, director Walter Hill alternates scenes of brutal shootouts by both sides with the depiction of the government's unjust treatment of Native Americans. Frequent bloody violence. A-III (PG-13)

Get Carter (1971) Violent British crime melodrama in which Michael Caine plays a gangland killer-enforcer whose investigation into his brother's death finds him in and out of danger, bed and dens of rival gangsters. Directed by Mike Hodges, the movie's principle is kill or be killed in coldly brutal, cruel style, varied only by scenes of graphic sex and nudity. O (R) X

Get Charlie Tully (1977) Tedious British comedy directed by Cliff Owen about two con men who, after bilking a foreign industrialist, find themselves on the run from the mob. A plot gimmick about the numbers of a secret Swiss account tattooed where anyone familiar with this kind of British humor can probably guess is the occasion for a good deal of female nudity. O (PG)

Get Out Your Handkerchiefs (1979) Very uneven French comedy in which a not-too-bright but good-natured husband (Gerard Depardieu) is willing to go to any lengths to cure his wife (Carole Laure) of a galloping case of boredom, even to propositioning a stranger (Patrick Dewaere) on her behalf. While entertaining a few clever moments, director Bertrand Blier's attempts to sustain

the one-joke affair are more frantic that successful and its nudity and sexual immorality are seriously offensive. O (R)

Get to Know Your Rabbit (1972) Inane sex farce features Tom Smothers as a high-powered corporate dropout who turns road magician and lover to a veritable parade of naked females. Director Brian De Palma's self-indulgent comedy is an utterly sophomoric burlesque posing as a spoof of conventional comedy. O (R) AA

Getaway, The (1972) Released from prison through the connivance of a crooked politician, Steve McQueen has to return the favor by robbing a bank and sharing the proceeds. When the heist goes bad, McQueen and Ali MacGraw skip town with the law in hot pursuit. The movie, however, goes nowhere under Sam Peckinpah's heavy-handed direction, which resorts to some fairly ugly violence and a little sex. A-IV (PG) X

Getting It Right (1989) Coming-of-age British comedy directed by American Randal Kleiser about the social and sexual blossoming of a shy hairdresser (Jesse Birdsall) who loses his virginity to a lonely older woman (Lynn Redgrave), befriends a wacky heiress (Helena Bonham Carter) and finally takes a proper bride (Jane Horrocks). It's well-acted, often engaging material, with astute nuances about the wounded humanity of its characters. Suggestive sexual banter and an adulterous encounter with brief nudity. A-IV (R) 15

Getting of Wisdom, The (1980) Spirited Australian girl (Susannah Fowle) at a stuffy academy for young women in turn-of-the-century Sydney gives teachers, classmates, long-suffering mother and various other people a run for the money before she settles down and graduates with honors. Unfortunately, director Bruce Beresford's heroine remains unlikeable and self-absorbed from first to last, making the result less than engaging entertainment. A-II (nr)

Getting Straight (1970) Superficial survey of some elements of campus unrest in the story of a graduate student (Elliott Gould) and his encounters with sloganeering students, black militants, self-satisfied professors, insensitive administrators, bloodthirsty riot police, promiscuity, narcotics use, draft-dodging, profanity. Directed by Richard Rush, the movie exploits serious social issues, without any attempt to put them in context or provide a perspective for trying to understand them. O (R)

Gettysburg (1993) Long but compelling historical re-creation of the Civil War battle of Gettysburg focuses on the decisive action of Union general Buford (Sam Elliott) in seizing the high ground at the start, the role of Union colonel Chamberlain (Jeff Daniels) in holding the Little Round Top and the disastrous charge led by Confederate general Pickett (Stephen Lang) that ended the battle. Adapted by director Ronald F. Maxwell from Michael Shaara's novel *The Killer Angels,* the military actions are depicted on an epic scale that succeeds as spectacle but only occasionally as human drama. Much battlefield carnage. A-II (PG)

Ghetto Freaks (1972) Young people preach to each other, between rounds of dancing and heavy drug-taking, about the joyful simplicity of urban communal life. It ends in a nude psychedelic orgy sufficiently explicit to relegate the movie to the exploitational junk pile. O (R)

Ghidrah, the Three-Headed Monster (1965) Japanese rubber-suited monsters threaten miniatures of Tokyo in a standard fantasy thriller directed by Inoshiro Honda. Stylized violence. A-II (br)

Ghost (1990) The ghost of a murdered young banker (Patrick Swayze) uses a phony spiritualist (Whoppi Goldberg) to warn his lover (Demi Moore) that she too is in deadly peril until he can discover why he was killed and stop those responsible. Director Jerry Zucker's offbeat but uneven blend of fantasy, horror and comedy is an engagingly sentimental thriller plump with quirky characters and edgy performances. Some grisly violence, acceptance of premarital sex and occasional profanity. A-III (PG-13) 12

Ghost and Mr. Chicken, The (1966) Don Knotts comedy vehicle in which he spends a night in a haunted house is ineptly directed by Alan Rafkin. A-I (br) U

Ghost Breakers, The (1940) Comic chiller in which a witless radio crime reporter (Bob Hope) flees an irate gangster for Cuba where he helps an heiress (Paulette Goddard) move into a creaky old castle complete with a resident zombie, assorted spooks, secret passageways and a hidden treasure. Director George Marshall plays the eerie situation mainly for laughs, though with mild frights and a few scares along the way. Still a lot of fun for those in the mood, but small children may need the reassuring presence of an older viewer. A-I (br)

Ghost Dad (1990) Drawn-out, one-joke comedy about a widower (Bill Cosby) who is the victim of a fatal car accident but whose spirit returns determined to ensure the financial security of his three orphaned children. Director Sidney Poitier relies on broad, often vulgar visual gags and inconsistent use of the ghost gimmick, but the silly plot is occasionally brightened by Cosby's likeable performance as a caring father and some special effects wizardry that might frighten young children. A number of vulgarities, some sexual references and several instances of profanity. A-II (PG)

Ghost in the Machine (1993) Absurd sci-fi horror tale in which the brain of a serial killer lives on in a computer mainframe, tracking the movements of his next victim (Karen Allen) and her teen-age son (Wil Horneff) while a computer expert (Chris Mulkey) works feverishly to prevent the killings. Director Rachel Talalay tosses together routine suspense elements with lots of razzle-dazzle computer graphics and high-tech lingo in a story so silly it would be funny were it not so pathetic. Intermittent stylized violence, fleeting sexual innuendo and an instance of rough language. A-III (R)

Ghost Story (1981) Fred Astaire, Melvyn Douglas, Douglas Fairbanks Jr., John Houseman and Patricia Neal appear in director John Irvin's lavishly produced but intellectually impoverished film version of Peter Straub's novel about a vengeful spirit (an extremely fleshy spirit) stalking four old codgers who sent her to the bottom of a Vermont pond 50 years before. Ectoplasmic nudity and graphic spooky sexuality. O (R) X

Ghostbusters (1984) Three parapsychologists (Bill Murray, Dan Aykroyd, and Harold Ramis), bounced from Columbia University because of the dubious nature of their research, go into private practice as ghost exterminators and find that all hell is about to break loose, quite literally. There are some very funny moments, largely due to Murray, but director Ivan Reitman lets the spectacular special effects begin to dominate midway and the humor fades. Some adult ribald jokes. A-III (PG)

Ghostbusters II (1989) Has-been Manhattan spook chasers (Dan Aykroyd, Bill Murray, Harold Ramis and Ernie Hudson) reunite to save the same lady in distress (Sigourney Weaver) from losing her baby to a 16th-century evil spirit (Wilhelm Von Homburg). The ghostly special effects are comical and mostly nonmenacing, the guys are funny and director Ivan Reitman satirizes the Big bad Apple and yuppie trends without a heavy hand. Some sexual innuendo and mildly vulgar language. A-II (PG)

Ghosts Italian Style (1969) Italian romantic comedy about newlyweds trying to save their sputtering marriage by living rent-free in a decaying baroque mansion haunted by a womanizing Count. Sophia Loren and Vittorio Gassman turn social satire into farce as director Renato Castellani tries to make something out of a story about false impressions and mistaken identities. A-III (G)

Ghoulies (1985) Shameless, thoroughly inept rip-off of "Gremlins." Directed by Luca Bercovici, it has some brief partial nudity and gore but not too much in the way of real violence. A-III (PG-13)

Giant (1956) Sentimental but stylish adaptation of Edna Ferber's sprawling family saga of life and love in Texas oil country from the turn of the century to the early 1950s, with Dennis Hopper as the clean-cut, intense son of Texas patriarchs Elizabeth Taylor and Rock Hudson, while James Dean gives his most moving performance as the inarticulate cowhand who strikes it rich. Directed by George Stevens, the plot is less important than its themes of changing times, the generation gap, racial prejudice, the waste of war and marital incompatibility. Over three hours long, children may find it a taxing experience. A-I (G) A

Giant of Thunder Mountain, The (1992) When a little girl (winningly played by Noley Thornton) befriends a lonely, oversized woodsman (Richard Kiel) living on a nearby mountain, the villagers determine to drive him away but have a change of heart when he saves them from a gang of cutthroats. Written by Kiel and directed by James Roberson, the story of a child's ability to see the goodness in a man foolishly misjudged by her elders is ultimately heartwarming and certainly eye-filling in its turn-of-the-century Western setting but suffers from a lumpy plot with too much violent action. Initial scenes of parents being killed by a grizzly bear, life-threatening situations involving children as well as adults and frightening scenes of vigilante justice. A-II (PG)

Gilda Live (1980) Concert film by director Mike Nichols of comedienne Gilda Radner's Broadway stage show should appeal to fans of "Saturday Night Live," but leave others flat. Most of the amusing moments come from Don Novello as Father Guido Sarducci. Some rough language and Novello's occasional (and highly original) ventures into theology make this mature fare. A-III (R)

Gimme Shelter (1970) Straightforward documentary gives an honest picture of what it was like to tour America with the Rolling Stones rock group and their notorious Altamont Speedway free concert where a fan was beaten to death by a member of the Hell's Angels. Directed by David Maysles, Albert Maysles and Charlotte Zwerin, it is a disturbing picture of the dark side of the American Dream. A-IV (R)

Ginger (1971) Cheri Caffaro plays the female private-eye of the title who has a yen for sadistic revenge. Her methods range from castration to outright murder as she disrobes and dispatches a nasty band of sex merchants. Directed by Don Schain, it's another tired sex and violence exploitation film. O (R)

Ginger and Fred (1986) Ginger (Giulietta Masina) and Fred (Marcello Mastroianni), a former vaudeville team who imitated Hollywood's Rogers and Astaire, are invited to perform in a Christmas television special. In this Italian production about the disappointments of old age and the commercialization of contemporary life, director Federico Fellini pays homage to performers important in his career, while at the same time indulging his penchant for visual cascades of freakish humanity. Some earthy proverbs about sex and several ambiguous references to religion. A-III (PG-13)

Girl and the General, The (1967) Muddled Italian movie set in World War I in which an Austrian general (Rod Steiger) is captured by an Italian private (Umberto Orsini) and a peasant waif (Virna Lisi). Directed by Pasquale Festa Campanile, it has wartime violence and brief nudity. A-III (br) AA

Girl from Petrovka, The (1974) Romance between a Russian woman (Goldie Hawn) and an American journalist (Hal Holbrook) based in Moscow blossoms into true love, but she is picked up by the police while on an errand of mercy and sentenced to prison. Directed by Robert Ellis Miller, the story is thin and watery and treated in ponderously sentimental style. Some ludicrously inappropriate nudity. A-III (PG) AA

Girl Getters, The (1966) British look at contemporary society through the eyes of young rebels without goals. Michael Winner's direction of Peter Draper's episodic script captures something of the cynical innocence of its subject. A-III (br)

Girl in Blue, The (1974) David Selby crisscrosses picturesque Ontario looking for the blue-clad girl (Maud Adams) he encountered long ago. He also lives with his girlfriend (Gay Rowan) just in case the girl in blue never materializes. Directed by George Kaczender, the hackneyed exercise in romantic sentimentality is so slight and silly that even the occasional expletive and glimpse of nudity seems innocuous. A-III (nr)

Girl Named Tamiko, A (1962) Unsavory sudser about an embittered Eurasian (Laurence Harvey) working as a photographer in Tokyo but trying to use a rich American (Martha Hyer) as his passport to the U.S. until falling for the lady of the title (France Nuyen). Directed by John Sturges, the only thing authentic about this ludicrous, anti-romantic account of a mean-spirited opportunist is the beautiful Japanese location photography. Implied sexual encounters. A-III (br) A

Girl of the Golden West, The (1938) Wildly fanciful Nelson Eddy-Jeanette MacDonald musical set in California pioneer days when a notorious bandit leader (Eddy) is reformed by the love of a good woman (MacDonald) who runs the saloon in a rough mining town where the sheriff (Walter Pigeon) hopes to marry her and hang the bandit. Directed by Norman Z. Leonard, the creaky melodramatic plot is helped by a bizarre assortment of characters, though the Sigmund Rohmberg-Gus Kahn songs are entirely forgettable. Old-fashioned escapist fare with well-intentioned ethnic stereotypes. A-I (br)

Girl on a Motorcycle, The (1968) The woman of the title (Marianne Faithfull) relives her past as she speeds down the highway early one morning to meet her lover and her fate. Failing to come to grips with the motivation of the character's past actions, director Jack Cardiff understandably concentrates on the travelogue aspects of a ride through the beautiful French and German countryside. Frequent and explicit depictions of scenes of physical intimacy are dramatically as well as morally unjustified. O (X/R) X

Girl Who Couldn't Say No, The (1969) Bland Italian comedy of a young surgeon (George Segal) who frequently falls in and out of love with an energetic Virna Lisi who's a soft touch for distressed persons. Directed by Franco Brusati, its permissive attitude toward sex is treated farcially but with excessive detail. O (PG) AA

Girl Who Knew Too Much, The (1969) Mystery story about a hired gun (Adam West) caught between the love for a slain crime boss' girl (Nancy Kwan) and his job of uncovering a Communist plot to take over the syndicate. Director Francis D. Lyon features a full-length strip-tease to enliven the dull, but brutally violent proceedings. O (R)

Girl with Green Eyes (1964) British coming-of-age drama about a naive young country girl (Rita Tushingham) who, on her first experience of living on her own away from home, becomes infatuated with a middle-aged writer (Peter Finch). Directed by Desmond Davis, the tale is slight but the acting is fine and the girl's problems quite convincing. Sexual situations. A-IV (br) PG

Girlfriends (1978) Director Claudia Weill's contrasting portrait of two New York women and the measures they take to find romance and commitment. Realistic treatment of sex and use of profanity override what little sensitivity and insight the film conveys. O (PG) AA

Girls Are for Loving (1973) In this latest chapter in the apparently ceaseless adventures of Ginger, our heroine breaks up a nasty extortion-kidnapping plot in high places and low. Once again Cheri Caffaro

and writer-director Don Schain outdo themselves as the perfect husband-wife team of voyeur and exhibitionist working the sexploitation-action flick market. O (R)

Girls Just Want to Have Fun (1985) Standard teen movie in which two plucky, cleancut kids (Sarah Jessica Parker and Lee Montgomery) win a dance contest. Competent but mediocre light entertainment. A-II (PG)

Girly (see: "Mumsy, Nanny, Sonny and Girly").

Give 'em Hell, Harry (1976) James Whitmore gives his interpretation of Harry Truman in a film recording of his one-man performance in the Samuel Gallu play. Directed by Steve Binder, Whitmore brings a passion, a conviction and a dauntless energy that engenders some understanding for the man and his controversial political career. The language is sometimes rough, but it is in the service of honest emotions. A-II (PG)

Give Her the Moon (1970) Unpretentious French comedy in which an American industrialist is so determined to get a French maid (Marthe Keller) that he transports her entire village to New York, where culture shock becomes amusingly apparent. Though there is some romance, director Philippe de Broca concentrates on the contrasting life-styles with some gentle satire of both. Its an old-fashioned escapist movie that may be lost on the young. A-II (G)

Gizmo (1980) Howard Smith's delightfully zany little film uses newsreels from the 1920s and 1930s to chronicle the dogged if flawed ingenuity of a host of inventors whose creations did not become household words. Very entertaining. A-I (G)

Glacier Fox, The (1979) Outstanding Japanese wildlife documentary, narrated by Arthur Hill, presents the story of a glacier fox, his mate and their five pups who live on the Okhotsk Sea coast of Hokkaido, a region blasted in winter by frigid winds that blow down from Siberia. Directed by Koreyoski Kurahara, the photography is stunning as it captures the intrinsic drama and humor in the life cycle of this fox family. Though it does not shy from some of the grimmer aspects of life in the wild, there are no visuals that might prove too strong for younger children, making it perfectly suited for the whole family. A-I (G)

Gladiator (1992) Routine prizefight picture in which a venal promoter (Brian Dennehy) pits a Chicago high schooler (James Marshall) against his best friend (Cuba Gooding, Jr.) in illegal boxing matches so the youth can pay off his father's gambling debts. Capitalizing on the popularity of the two young actors, director Rowdy Herrington goes down for the count with this strictly formula story. Brief teen bedroom scene, much graphic violence in the ring and intermittent rough language. A-III (R) 15

Glass Bottom Boat, The (1966) A secretary (Doris Day) and a scientific genius (Rod Taylor) get involved with each other and assorted spies, gadgets and contrivances. The comedy has a number of good sight gags, some clever situations and a fine supporting cast. As put together by director Frank Tashlin, it adds up to a lot of fun. A-II (br) U

Glass Houses (1972) Broken family seeks self-revelation through group encounter therapy at a California spa. Director Alexander Singer's ill-conceived satire features Jennifer O'Neil as a mistress and Deirdre Lenihan as the daughter of a business type who contend for his sexual attention. Most viewers will experience a gagging sensation rather than a catharsis. O (R)

Glass Key, The (1942) Hard-boiled crime picture from the Dashiell Hammett novel about a machine politician (Brian Donlevy) saved from a murder rap by his right-hand man (Alan Ladd), despite various complications created by the dead man's sister (Veronica Lake). Directed by Stuart Heisler, the murder mystery is less perplexing than the relationships between the principals and the efforts of the hoods (Joseph Calleia and William Bendix) to benefit from the situation. Stylized violence, some of it quite nasty, and romantic complications. A-II (br) A

Glass Slipper, The (1955) Pretty-looking but stilted rendering of the Cinderella story, this time with a waif (Leslie Caron) suffering under an ill-tempered stepmother (Elsa Lanchester) until the magic powers of a local eccentric (Estelle Winwood) help her win the love of a handsome prince (Michael Wilding). Director Charles Walters' slow-moving narrative is brightened by some elaborate fantasy numbers but there is little magic or humor in this version of the classic romance and the songs are strictly forgettable. For romantics of any age, though a long sit for children. A-I (br) U

Glass Sphinx (1968) Inept European production directed by Luigi Scattini about an archaeological expedition led by Robert Taylor in searching the Egyptian desert for a lost tomb containing the art treasure of the title. Some violence and sexual innuendo. A-III (br)

Gleaming the Cube (1989) When an alienated teen (Christian Slater) decides to investigate the death of his adopted Vietnamese brother (Art Chudabala), he employs daredevil skateboard wizardry against the many meanies who get in his way. Set in a Southern California Vietnamese community, director Graeme Clifford's contrived murder mystery uses a lot of fancy footwork to divert attention from its flimsy plot. Mild rough language, some violence and comic-book menace. A-II (PG-13) PG

Glen and Randa (1971) After a thermonuclear apocalypse has destroyed contemporary civilization, two lost innocents (Steven Curry and Shelly Plimpton) live like primitive natives among the debris of Howard Johnson restaurants and deserted superhighways. Director Jim McBride's failed allegory about the primacy of animal passions becomes pretentious in execution and offensive in treatment, employing crude sex scenes and frontal nudity. O (X/R)

Glengarry Glen Ross (1992) Screen version of David Mamet's play about four real estate salesmen (Jack Lemmon, Al Pacino, Ed Harris and Alan Arkin) who, under threat of being fired unless they close some deals within the week, commit desperate acts which ultimately backfire. James Foley's tautly directed movie delivers intense performances with blistering dialogue while depicting the characters' moral disintegration in a dehumanizing pressure-cooker where money is everything. Much rough language and some sexual references. A-III (R) 15

Glenn Miller Story, The (1954) James Stewart gives an ingratiating performance as the trombone player who starts his own band, discovers the "sound" that makes it a national favorite, then dies in a World War II flight over the English Channel. Directed by Anthony Mann, the story's interesting and the acting good (June Allyson as his supportive wife) with plenty of examples of Miller's music and appearances by many of the era's musicians. A-I (br) U

Gloria (1980) Independent filmmaker John Cassavetes tries to transport a 1930s' crime melodrama to the 1980 streets of New York in the story of a middle-aged gun moll (Gena Rowland), retired from the mob, suddenly finds herself responsible for a young boy marked for death by her old gang. The movie's strength lies in the extraordinary performance of Rowland, which more than makes up for some of the narrative's incoherence. A-III (PG)

Glory (1989) The story of the 54th Regiment of Massachusetts Volunteer Infantry, the first black fighting unit raised during the Civil War, focuses on its enlightened white commander (Matthew Broderick) who molded field hands and runaway slaves into proud, heroic Union soldiers. Director Edward Zwick raises consciousness about the little-known regiment and re-creates some harrowing battle scenes but, unfortunately, gives shallow attention to the themes of racism and the obscenity of war. Stereotyping of key black characters, much grisly wartime violence and some profanity. A-III (R) 15

Glory Boy (1971) World War II vet (Michael Moriarty) returns to the family farm with two of his buddies (William Devane and Mitchell Ryan) with the intention of proving to his patriotic father (Arthur Kennedy) that there is no glory on the battlefield but things get out of hand. Director Edwin Sherin's movie about the dehumanizing effects of war goes to excess in depicting rape and murder and its use of nudity and foul language. O (R)

Gnome-Mobile, The (1967) A lumber baron takes his two grandchildren to one of his forests, discovers some lonely gnomes and helps them find another gnome-infested forest. Walter Brennan is excellent in a dual role as the kindly grandfather and a waspish, irascible little old man. Robert Stevenson directs the colorful Walt Disney fantasy whose good humor and many finely executed special effects will divert just as many adults as children. A-I (G) U

Go-Between, The (1971) British period romance features Michael Redgrave reminiscing about his childhood role as the innocent messenger between lovers (Julie Christie and Alan Bates) who are separated by the gulf of social class. Director Joseph Losey handles with sensitivity the boy's growing awareness of the nature of the couple's relationship and how, on his 13th birthday, he is directly confronted with the physical realities of adult life. A-III (PG) AA

Go for Broke (1951) Worthy, entertaining World War II account of a Japanese-American infantry unit's exploits on the battlefields of Italy and France. Writer-director Robert Pirosh provides a convincing picture of the unit's perseverance not only against the enemy but also in the face of prejudice from fellow Americans, including one of their own officers (Van Johnson). Wartime violence. A-I (br) A

Go Tell the Spartans (1978) Burt Lancaster plays an overage major who commands a small American cadre working with a motley collection of regular Vietnamese troops, mercenaries and militia in the hostile countryside during the early days of the Vietnam involvement. Director Ted Post handles the action sequences extremely well and, as a whole, the movie is intelligent, well-acted and moving. Violence and rough language, but conveys the contradictions and pathos of the Vietnam struggle. A-IV (R) X

Goal! (1967) Good sports documentary highlights the skill and endurance of the champion soccer teams that vied for the 1966 World Cup in England. Octavio Senoret's production does well in showing the differences in the style of play of the 16 coun-

tries represented and Nigel Patrick's narration helps explain the worldwide popularity of a sport in which no substitutions are allowed during the game. A-I (br)

Goat Horn, The (1974) Bulgarian folk tale set during the time of Turkish rule when a goatherd raises his daughter as if she were a boy so that she will never be the victim, as was her mother, of the lust of their despotic master. Though it all ends badly, director Metodi Andonov conveys the sense of powerlessness of a subject people, not through dialogue, but through small details showing the daily life of the period. A-IV (nr)

Gobots, Battle of the Rock Lords (1986) This animated action-adventure film features constant combat between humanoids, robots and other silicon-based life forms, perpetuating the exploitation of the pre-teen market. Parents should consider the merits of further exposure of the very young to increased levels of hostility depicted in this movie. A-II (G)

God Forgives, I Don't (1969) Professional gambler (Terence Hill) tracks down a notorious outlaw for personal reasons rather then to bring him to justice. Directed by Giuseppe Colizzi, the tale of a personal vendetta has little action or sense, but maintains an atmosphere throughout of brutality and needless violence. O (M)

Goddess, The (1958) Episodic story follows the unhappy formative years of a young woman (Kim Stanley) who goes on to movie stardom, growing more self-destructive with each success. Scripted by Paddy Chayevsky and directed by John Cromwell, the period details of the 1930s-50s provide a credible context for this psychological probe of a troubled woman driven by the need to be loved yet unable to believe that she deserves anyone's love. Mature themes and treatment. A-III (br) A

Godfather, The (1972) Blockbuster screen version of the Mario Puzo novel about a Mafia family's rise, decline and resurgence in the murderous world of New York racketeering. Marlon Brando plays the aging but indomitable don, with James Caan and Al Pacino as leading family members. Francis Ford Coppola's direction is a study in control and pacing with all the right touches in establishing the proper 1940s' ambience. The murders are plentiful and gruesome, with little spared in detailing the intricacies of mob life. A-III (R) X

Godfather, Part II, The (1974) Lacking the original's grace, majesty and energy, the sequel follows the rise to power of a crime boss (Robert De Niro) and the subsequent use of that power by his son (Al Pacino). Produced and directed by Francis Ford Coppola, the unmanageably complex scenario shifts interminably from Lake Tahoe to the Kefauver hearings, from the lower East Side to Florida base of a crime kingpin (Lee Strasberg). The effect is unsettling and there is much graphic violence. A-III (R) X

Godfather Part III, The (1990) Having shed all ties with the underworld, Michael Corleone (Al Pacino) seeks respectability and profits by investing in a Vatican holding company run by corrupt financiers whose business tactics include murder. Directed by Francis Ford Coppola, the narrative strives for tragedy but settles for melodrama after losing its way in the vague, shadowy world of international finance and the intrigues of certain church officials. Some scenes of intense violence, the twisted morality of criminal retribution, rough language and an unedifying fictional depiction of some religious figures. A-IV (R) 18

Gods and the Dead, The (1972) Brazilian turn-of-the-century drama about cocoa plantation owners who try to destroy each other with the ultimate survivor being a peasant who discovers that, just as he has been victimized by the owners, so too they were victimized by international business interests. Director Ruy Guerra's movie about the unequal distribution of wealth is filled with poetic imagery of the struggle for social justice. A-III (nr)

Gods Must Be Crazy, The (1983) An African bushman discovers a discarded Coke bottle and, after it causes dissension among his people, undertakes a trek to throw it off the edge of the world, but in the course of the journey he runs into some very peculiar civilized people. Director Jamie Uys' simple comedy-adventure explores amiably the cultural differences between industrial society and ritualized tribal folkways. Some violence. A-II (PG) A

Gods Must Be Crazy II, The (1990) Mildly amusing but overly contrived sequel set in Africa's Kalahari Desert where three different sets of strangers (a pair of poachers, two soldiers from opposing sides and a couple whose plane has crashed) get lost but are helped periodically by a bemused bushman (Nixau) looking for his two missing children. Written and directed by Jamie Uys, the South African production has much broad visual comedy and some charming moments with the lost youngsters, but the endless predicaments of the strangers strain patience and credibility. Bare-bottomed Bushmen and several gags involving a woman's undergarments. A-II (PG)

Gods of the Plague (1977) German crime melodrama made in 1969 about a young gangster who teams up with a killer for another robbery but is betrayed by one his girlfriends. Director Rainer Werner Fassbinder overdoes the murky underworld atmosphere, in which violence needs no motivation or justification, and the film has little point other than as an exercise in criminal brutality. O (nr)

Godsend, The (1980) Foundling with a nasty disposition knocks off, one by one, the natural children of her foster parents, who seem to be inordinately slow to get the drift. Director Gabrielle Beaumont's tepid British thriller has little to recommend it and, though all of its violence is off-camera, it creates a foreboding atmosphere and features a rather graphic birth scene. A-III (R)

Godson, The (1972) Chilling psychological study of a lonely criminal (Alain Delon) whose life is held in a delicate balance between the gang and the law. French director Jean-Pierre Melville unfolds this lone wolf's struggle to survive police pursuits, the distrust of his gangland associates and the false sympathy of a woman in a restrained and highly visual manner without the violent excesses associated with gangster films. A-II (PG)

Godspell (1973) Sparkling screen version of musical based loosely on the Gospel according to Matthew, featuring an off-Broadway cast with Victor Garber as the Christ figure and David Haskell as both John the Baptist and Judas. What makes the movie so high-spirited is director David Greene's turning the entire city of New York into a giant stage set, with its buildings, streets and parks all strikingly used for great effect. The parables are presented in imaginative skits, many of which serve as springboards for the irresistible tunes, such as "Day by Day" and "God Save the People!," that made the play so popular. A-I (G) U

Godzilla (1985) You can't keep a good monster down and Japan's favorite has risen again, along with his old pal Raymond Burr, in a fairly competent new version. Godzilla fans everywhere should have reason to be happy with the results, though all the crashing and banging might frighten young children. A-II (PG)

Godzilla vs. the Smog Monster (1972) Godzilla tangles with a smog monster that bloats itself on factory and automobile wastes, and succeeds in frustrating its ambition to feed on the sacred fumes of Mt. Fuji. Wry social satire on pollution from director Yoshimitu Banno whose use of blurry, grainy, anemic color photography here is for once thematically motivated. A-I (GP/G)

Godzilla's Revenge (1971) Young boy's conversation with Godzilla (who is in retirement on Monster Island) and also with his son teaches him a few tricks that help thwart a pair of bank robbers who are hiding near his home. Director Ishiro Honda resurrects his collection of monsters for another round of campy adventures. A-I (G)

Goin' All the Way (1982) Shoddy exploitation movie about the sexual yearnings of some high school students, not one of whom looks a day under 25. Directed by Robert Freedman with crass vulgarity, abundant nudity and graphic sexuality. O (R)

Goin' Down the Road (1970) Canadian movie in which two Nova Scotians come to Toronto in search of a better life but soon find themselves back on the highway, a little less likely of ever finding their place in the world. Directed by Donald Shebib, it is best in its celebration of the city and its environs, but its young people (Doug McGrath, Paul Bradley and Jane Eastwood) are so sincere and earnest in their idealism that they almost overcome the handicap of stereotyped roles. A-III (R/GP)

Goin' South (1978) Jack Nicholson directs his own performance as a raffish outlaw who is saved from hanging when a young woman (Mary Steenburgen) agrees to marry him. Her sole interest is a hired hand to help her work a supposedly exhausted gold mine, but, naturally, romance blooms in the desert air. Moderately entertaining comedy Western with some sexually oriented humor. A-III (PG) A

Going Ape! (1981) Three orangutans provide the madcap antics in director Jeremy Joe Kronsberg's inept and witless situation comedy about a young man (Tony Danza) who inherits a fortune with the requirement that he care for the apes. Danny De Vito helps him protect the beasts from a greedy zoological society that also tries to get the dough. Much vulgarity and frequent profanity. A-III (PG)

Going Berserk (1983) Collection of skits loosely joined together by the gimmick of having television comic John Candy handcuffed to an escaped convict. Written and directed by David Steinberg, the farce offer little other than much foul language and some gross sexually oriented humor. O (R)

Going Hollywood (1933) Slight but bubbly musical romance in which a teacher (Marion Davies) falls for the voice of a radio crooner (Bing Crosby), follows him to Hollywood, then tangles with his tempermental French co-star (Fifi D'Orsay). Directed by Raoul Walsh, there's still some fun in its spoof of period radio shows and moviemakers but, despite a good supporting cast (Ned Sparks, Stuart Erwin and Patsy Kelly) and bouncy production numbers, the hokey Cinderella romance has aged rather badly. Some sexual innuendo, an implied liaison and a comic blackface routine. A-III (br) U

Going Home (1971) Jan-Michael Vincent plays a man who as a young child saw his father (Robert Mitchum) kill his mother in a drunken rage and now seeks to avenge her by raping the paroled father's new bride-to-be (Brenda Vaccaro). Producer-director Herbert Leonard's failed drama deals in the cliches of abnormal psychology without any serious analysis of characters and their actions nor is there any meaningful resolution of its muddled plot. Some violence. A-III (GP) X

Going in Style (1980) Three oldsters on pension (George Burns, Art Carney, and Lee Strasberg), fed up with feeding pigeons in a Queens park, decide to rob a Manhattan Bank. Only George Burns' fine performance makes director Martin Brest's flat and uninspired geriatric farce at all worth watching. Some rough language and its benign view of the crime. A-III (PG)

Going My Way (1944) Bing Crosby ambles amiably through the role of Father O'Malley, the crooning curate sent to assist the aging, crotchety pastor (Barry Fitzgerald) of a poor parish in need of change. Director Leo McCarey's sentimental story is well paced with humor and songs such as "Swinging on a Star," but at its sugary center is the theme of new ways replacing the old as conveyed amusingly but with feeling by the two principals. The definitive Hollywood version of Catholic life in an age of innocence, the picture retains appeal today mainly as a well-crafted vehicle of popular entertainment. A-I (nr) U

Going Places (1974) Pair of petty thieves (Gerard Depardieu and Patrick Dewaere) graduate to auto theft, kidnapping and assault as they wander aimlessly through the French countryside, with a sex encounter of some sort at every stop. Directed by Bertrand Blier, the movie's amoral view of life is conveyed in gross language and even grosser, occasionally degrading. images. O (R)

Gold (1974) Though its plot is a rather tiresome affair about the manipulations of an international gold syndicate, this large-scale disaster movie offers an exotic catastrophe (the flooding of an entire gold mining area), fresh South African locations and some gripping action sequences and spectacular special effects. Director Peter Hunt, however, fights a losing battle against an inept script. Some double entendres and an illicit romance make it inappropriate for youngsters. A-III (PG) A

Gold Rush, The (1925) Classic silent comedy with Charlie Chaplin as the Little Tramp searching for gold in the Klondike where he gets snowed in with a starving prospector (Mack Swain) and has a bittersweet romance with a dance hall girl (Georgia Hale).

It's Chaplin at his best, with memorable comic highlights including a tilting cabin perched on the edge of a precipice, a Thanksgiving dinner made out of a boiled shoe and a charming dance performed by bread rolls. Delightful family fare. A-I (br)

Goldbergs, The (see: "Molly").

Golden Boy (1939) Clifford Odets' romantic melodrama about a Depression youth (William Holden) who turns in his violin for boxing gloves, then falls for the girlfriend (Barbara Stanwyck) of his manager (Adolphe Menjou). Directed by Rouben Mamoulian, the ham-fisted story of material wealth versus human values is earnest but obvious, though its critical attitude towards prizefighting is quite effective. Stylized treatment of violence in the ring and romantic entanglements. A-II (br) A

Golden Calf, The (1974) The stratagems of a confidence man (Sergei Yursky) in the Soviet Union of the late 1920s backfire with slapstick regularity and when one of his schemes finally brings in a million rubles, he learns that money does not buy happiness and returns to his con games. Directed by Mikhail Shveitser, it is an amusing change of pace from the usual socialist realism of Soviet cinema. A-I (nr)

Golden Child, The (1986) A private detective (Eddie Murphy) is charged with rescuing from evil kidnappers a Tibetan toddler, revered by a cult as their sacred leader. A tiresome Murphy vehicle, more irreverent than funny, replete with some unwholesome seduction humor, many indecent expressions and other harsh language as well as much violent action and gruesome images. O (PG-13)

Golden Hawk, The (1952) Slapdash 17th-century swashbuckler directed by Sidney Salkow features a womanizing French privateer (miscast Sterling Hayden) who's rebuffed by an attractive English pirate (Rhonda Fleming), then wins her love and aid in sacking the Spanish stronghold at Cartegana. Stylized violence, sexual situations and marital infidelity. A-III (br)

Golden Needles (1974) Fair adventure movie in which Elizabeth Ashley, acting for aging millionaire Burgess Meredith, hires Joe Don Baker to obtain an Oriental statuette whose seven gold needles are said to be able to restore youth and virility to its possessor. Directed by Robert Clouse, it has generous helpings of kung fu and karate fights and enough love scenes to put it in the adult class, but otherwise it is an escapist movie that doesn't take itself seriously. A-III (PG) AA

Golden Raiders, The (see: "Escape to Athena").

Golden Seal, The (1983) Isolated by a storm, a lonely boy (Torquil Campbell) living on an island in the Aleutians befriends a mother seal and protects it from family and poachers. There is a lot of profanity, including some dark pearls from the mouth of our young hero, and a bit of violence. A-II (PG)

Golden Voyage of Sinbad, The (1974) John Phillip Law as Sinbad sails off to find the Fountain of Destiny, harassed by a variety of demons and other nasty types conjured up by Ray Harryhausen's imaginative special effects that upstage the human cast. Director Gordon Hessler's lighthearted and entertaining adventure movie brings a treat for youngsters and those adults who wish to recapture some of the magic of childhood. A-I (G) U

Goldengirl (1979) Muddled potboiler about the merchandising of an Olympic sprinter (Susan Anton) by a promoter (James Coburn) who discovers that her scientist father (Curt Jurgens) has been giving her periodic injections of a dangerous growth hormone. Directed by Joseph Sargent, the movie is against the commercialization of sports and the manipulation of human beings but compromises itself by attempting to merchandise an attractive model as an actress. A number of rather crude sexual references. O (PG)

Goldfinger (1964) British superagent James Bond (Sean Connery) is on the trail of international smuggler Goldfinger (Gert Frobe) and his chief henchman, Oddjob (Harold Sakata), and with a little help from the ladies (Shirley Easton and Honor Blackman), he thwarts their plan to rob Fort Knox. Directed by Guy Hamilton, the fast-paced plot contains the usual assortment of gimmicky action and tongue-in-cheek sexual references, but adults who enjoy escapist entertainment will find it harmless campy fun. A-III (GP) PG

Gone With The Wind (1939) Epic historical romance spanning 20 years in the troubled lives of its southern heroine (Vivian Leigh), the man she loves (Leslie Howard) and the man she marries (Clark Gable). Produced by David O. Selznick and directed Victor Fleming, the movie re-creates not the history but the myth of the Old South and its destruction in the Civil War and Reconstruction. Though blacks are treated in the stereotyped fashion of its time, the picture is sympathetic toward its main black characters, particularly Hattie McDaniel who received an Academy Award for her performance. A-II (G)

Gong Show Movie, The (1980) Chuck Barris' television game show featuring outtakes too deplorable to show on television form the basis for this monument to bad taste and witless vulgarity. O (R)

Good Father, The (1987) Middle-aged executive, troubled and resentful because of his broken marriage, uses his anger and a male-dominated legal system to pressure an unhappy friend into divorce and a child custody battle in Mike Newell's somber drama. Anthony Hopkins' statement about lost idealism is conveyed with quiet rage as he rejects the feminism he once championed and seeks vengeance vicariously through the court battle of another, gaining only a greater sense of remorse. A-II (R) 15

Good Guys and the Bad Guys, The (1969) Aging marshal Robert Mitchum joins forces with aging outlaw George Kennedy to thwart a train robbery in this tongue-in-cheek tribute to the senior side of the generation gap. Director Burt Kennedy's entertaining, energetic western spoofs the New West of inept bad men, greedy politicians and complacent townspeople. Its aging stars' heroics are more slapstick than swashbuckling. A-III (PG) A

Good Guys Wear Black (1979) Mediocre action adventure directed by Ted Post concerns the vengeful exploits of the leader (Chuck Norris) of an elite unit that was betrayed and almost wiped out in the last days of the Vietnam War. Standard violence and sexual hijinks in the service of eye-for-an-eye justice. A-III (PG)

Good Morning, Babylon (1987) The Taviani brothers take us on an operatic tour of the early days of Hollywood as two Italian brothers learn that creativity and passion don't last as long as movies and cathedrals. This homage to the silent era and celebration of brotherhood and paternal obligations has some brief nudity, but is, otherwise, emotionally and visually engaging. A-III (PG-13) 15

Good Morning, Vietnam (1987) Robin Williams stars as a wacky U.S. Armed Forces radio disc jockey brought to boost troop morale in 1965 Vietnam, but his unmilitary sense of humor brings him into conflict with those in charge of the station. Directed by Barry Levinson, the seriocomic movie has some hilarious routines but also considerable raunchy sexual humor, rough language and irreverences, only somewhat redeemed by being placed within the context of the obscenity of war. A-IV (R) 15

Good Son, The (1993) Staying with relatives after his mother's death, a distraught youth (Elijah Wood) becomes convinced that his young cousin (Macaulay Culkin) is evil and bent on murder, but no one will believe him. Director Joseph Ruben's atmospheric thriller is handsomely shot and nicely acted, though the contrast between angelic and diabolic boys is overly simplistic and the denouement unnerving. Brief violence, menace to children and an instance of rough language. A-III (R)

Good, the Bad, and the Ugly, The (1968) Typically cynical, brutal Spaghetti western with Clint Eastwood, Lee Van Cleef and Eli Wallach looking for some stolen gold at the time of the Civil War. Directed with some class by Sergio Leone, the movie's good is overwhelmed by the bad and the ugly. O (br) X

Good Times (1967) Sonny and Cher star as themselves in a spoofy, puffy vehicle allowing them to try out various types of Hollywood roles and generally have a lot of fun fooling around in fancy costumes on colorful sets. Directed by William Friedkin, it's a cheerful, unassuming little film. A-I (br) U

Good Wife, The (1987) Seemingly faithful and modest wife (Rachel Ward) tries to overcome a sexual crisis in her marriage by having an affair with her brother-in-law and succumbing to the temptations of an aggressive stranger (Sam Neill). Bryan Brown is the unexciting lumberjack who suffers through his wife's sexual odyssey with the hope of putting their marriage back together. Director Ken Cameron makes it trashy with too many simulated sex scenes and confused moral perspective. O (R) 15

Goodbye, Columbus (1969) Uncompromising screen version of Philip Roth's novel about the generation gap in early 1960s America in a story about an affluent Jewish family whose daughter (Ali MacGraw) is pursued by an ambitious young man (Richard Benjamin). The conflicting social and generational attitudes result in general disillusionment for almost everyone involved. Directed by Larry Peerce, the young couple's sexual relationship is treated quite frankly. A-IV (R/PG) X

Goodbye Gemini (1970) Surrounded with an aura of evil and perversion, maladjusted twins (Judy Geeson and Martin Potter) take up residence in a London fantasy world of their own making and become involved in a series of senseless and promiscuous escapades ending in murder. Director Alan Gibson's foul black comedy is replete with rape and other violence, nudity and implied incest. O (R) X

Goodbye Girl, The (1977) Aspiring actor from Chicago (Richard Dreyfuss) sublets a New York apartment from a friend and finds it already furnished with a 33-year-old divorcee (Marsha Mason) and her 10-year-old daughter (Quinn Cummings). Neil Simon's romantic comedy, directed by Herbert Ross, is pleasant and entertaining. though unfortunately flawed by occasional vulgarities and the acceptance of premarital sex. O (PG)

Goodbye, Mr. Chips (1939) Warmly affectionate, occasionally humorous story spans 50 years in the life of a dedicated but stodgy classics teacher (Robert Donat) whose love of learning eventually wins the respect and devotion of students, faculty and the woman who becomes his supportive wife (Greer Garson). Directed by Sam Woods, this tribute to the teaching profession still touches the emotions, largely because of Donat's charmingly low-keyed, Oscar-winning performance. A-I (nr)

Goodbye, Mr. Chips (1969) Musical version of the James Hilton novel with Peter O'Toole as the distracted, unbending schoolmaster who is set upon, conquered and finally humanized by a hoydenish music hall performer (Petula Clark). Director Herbert Ross shifts the focus from the academic to the happy marriage of such unlikely opposites. Leslie Bricusse's songs are pleasantly unobtrusive in the enjoyable old-fashioned romance, that some will find quite moving. Youngsters, however, are more likely to find it sentimental and overlong. A-I (G) U

Goodbye, Norma Jean (1976) Director Larry Buchanan's obsessive exploitation of the speculative and sordid details of Marilyn Monroe's rise to stardom is a dreadful little film trading on tabloid sensationalism, sexual intimacies and demeaning images of women. O (R)

GoodFellas (1990) The heady rise—and eventual downfall—of three Brooklyn hoods (Ray Liotta, Robert De Niro and Joe Pesci) are shown from one gangster's warped point of view in this fact-based story spanning 30 years. Director Martin Scorsese synthesizes flowing cinematography, an eye for details and commanding performances into a chilling re- creation of the empty glamor, endless greed and sick violence that characterizes mob life. Much graphic violence and rough language. A-IV (R) 18

Goonies, The (1985) A gang of kids searchs for pirate treasure to save their homes from foreclosure. A scaled-down version of "Indiana Jones" aimed squarely at children, but many parents will have reservations about exposing their pre-teens to the vulgar expletives that pepper the dialogue, supposedly as all part of the fun. A-II (PG)

Gordon's War (1973) Former Green Beret captain (Paul Winfield) declares war on Harlem drug pushers with the help of three other Vietnam vets (Carl Lee, Tony King and David Dowling). It is unfortunate that the movie dishes up so much unrelenting street violence, frank nudity and unconscious acceptance of the hero as righteous avenger, because director Ossie Davis obviously has a moral point to make about the social evil of substance addiction. O (R) X

Gorgo (1961) A sea captain (Bill Travers) captures a gigantic prehistoric monster off the coast of Ireland and sells it to a London circus, but not even Britain's military might can save the city from destruction when the monster's mother comes looking for its missing youngster. Directed by Eugene Lourie, the British production's low-budget special effects suit the unpretentious nature of the fantasy and, indeed, add a measure of sympathy, if not charm, to the put-upon monsters. Tense crowd scenes and much damage to models of London landmarks. A-I (br) X

Gorgon, The (1964) Sluggish British horror movie in which the ancient Greek monster of the title takes over the body of a young woman (Barbara Shelley) in a turn-of-the-century German town and begins turning its residents to stone. Director Terence Fisher concentrates on the clash between the town doctor (Peter Cushing) who wants to hush matters up and a university professor (Christopher Lee) who wants to stop them. Unconvincing menace and occasional stylized violence. A-II (br) X

Gorillas in the Mist: The Adventure of Dian Fossey (1988) Sigourney Weaver stars as Dian Fossey whose dedication over 18 years to saving the endangered mountain gorillas of central Africa alienated many and ended tragically in her murder in 1985. Sensitive direction by Michael Apted and Weaver's fine performance make this an inspiring but heartrending account of human courage and an unwavering commitment to wildlife preservation. An adulterous love affair, much rough language and explicit attacks against gorillas. A-III (PG-13) 15

Gorky Park (1983) Disappointing adaptation of the Martin Cruz novel about murder in Moscow with William Hurt playing the honest, apolitical detective in charge of the investigation, but his listless, mannered portrayal proves deadening. Director Michael Apted reduces Cruz's ingenious story to a run-of-the-mill mystery with a brief but graphic love scene, some violence and several gruesome sequences involving corpses. A-IV (R)

Gospel According to St. Matthew, The (1966) Straight-forward Italian dramatization of the evangelist's account of the life of Jesus and His message of salvation. It succeeds exceptionally well in placing the viewer within the Gospel events, avoiding the artificiality of most biblical movie epics. Director Pier Paolo Pasolini is completely faithful to the text while employing the visual imagination necessary for his realistic interpretation. English subtitles. A-I (nr) U

Gospel According to Vic, The (1987) Tom Conti is a schoolmaster teaching learning-impaired children in a school in Scotland. Pride and public opinion lead him to believe that he's a miracle worker, but he slowly discovers that his special gifts of love, courage and generosity are so rare that they are often mistaken for divine providence. Some profanity and implied sex impose upon an otherwise thoroughly gentle and uplifting story. A-III (PG-13)

Gospel Road (1973) Produced by Johnny Cash and filmed in locales around Jerusalem, the movie is a very personal and sincere interpretation of the public ministry of Jesus Christ. Directed by Robert Elfstrom (who is often seen as the Christ figure), it avoids for the most part a literal portrayal of the events of the New Testament and wisely opts for a symbolic visualization. Cash appears as on-screen narrator as well as vocalist backed by a country-folk musical score and the result reflects, better than most, the spirit of the Gospels. A-I (G)

Gotcha (1985) A college boy (Anthony Edwards), eager to rid himself of his virginity, vacations in Europe, meets an agreeable older woman but becomes the target of real bullets instead of the liquid air-gun pellets used in a campus game called "gotcha." Director Jeff Kanew's sophomoric fantasy is neither funny nor exciting. Benign view of sexual promiscuity. O (PG-13)

Gothic (1987) Director Ken Russell's muddled exploration of the nightmarish roots of creativity is set during a Victorian era weekend visit by poet Percy Shelley and fiancee Mary to the weird villa of Lord Byron. This grotesque vision of the darker side of the imagination features an unpleasant mix of nudity in a sexual context, images of death, deprivation and degeneracy. O (R) 18

Grace Quigley (1985) Aged widow (Katharine Hepburn) hires a professional hitman (Nick Nolte) to do her in and then becomes his agent. A satiric comedy that went dreadfully wrong, despite the efforts of director Anthony Harvey and talented cast. Because of the movie's ineptness and its lack of satiric point, the view of suicide is more benign than not. O (PG) 15

Graduate, The (1968) Fresh out of college, an aimless middle-class youth (Dustin Hoffman) is seduced by a suburban housewife (Anne Bancroft) but redeemed by his love for her daughter (Katharine Ross). Directed by Mike Nichols, this satiric tale of an innocent in a corrupt world harpoons the emptiness of materialistic values but offers little in its place. Questionable treatment of adultery and some strong language. A-IV (PG) AA

Graffiti Bridge (1990) A brooding musician (Prince) and a rival rock artist (Morris Day) compete over ownership of a dance club and the attentions of an elusive girl (Ingrid Chavez). Also written and directed by Prince, this vanity production is simply a feature-length music video with sleekly expressionistic visuals, catchy choreography and awful acting. Females depicted primarily as sex objects and suggestive dancing. A-III (PG-13) 12

Grand Canyon (1991) Contemporary drama featuring an ensemble cast (Danny Glover, Kevin Kline, Steve Martin, Mary McDonnell and Alfre Woodard) grappling with increasing lawlessness in a big city as they weather personal mid-life crises. Though the pace is sluggish, director Lawrence Kasdan credibly blends some dozen characters and situations for a sobering but ultimately hopeful look at the fragility of modern life. Brief violence, adulterous references, momentary nudity and recurring rough language. A-III (R) 15

Grand Prix (1967) Large-scale production takes viewers around the 10 courses of Europe's Grand Prix auto-racing circuit that conveys in almost documentary fashion the experience of racing. Director John Frankenheimer interweaves the story of four drivers (Yves Montand, James Garner, Brian Bedford and Antonio Sabata) but is less successful with their off-track romances. A-III (br) A

Grand Slam (1968) European production in which a retired teacher (Edward G. Robinson) plans the complex robbery of a Brazilian diamond firm during the time of the Rio Carnival and with some inside assistance (Janet Leigh). Tautly directed by Giuliano Montaldo, crime does not pay but a seduction scene is not for youngsters. A-III (br) A

Grapes of Wrath, The (1940) Outstanding adaptation of John Steinbeck's novel about an Okie family who lose their farm and join other Dust Bowl refugees on the road to exploitation as migrant workers. Told with gritty realism but with a compassion that still engages viewers a half century later, director John Ford's definitive portrait of uprooted and dispossessed Americans during the Depression features compelling performances by a superior cast, including Henry Fonda as young Tom Joad, perplexed and angry that people are starving in a land of plenty, and Jane Darwell as the formidable Ma Joad whose perseverance and optimism keep the family together. Brutalizing conditions of poverty and some violence. A-II (nr) PG

Grasshopper, The (1970) Small-town Canadian girl Jacqueline Bisset comes to Los Angeles for romance but ends up as a showgirl who becomes an executive's mistress and then a prostitute. Director Jerry Paris' sordid and pessimistic melodrama resorts to frequent use of nudity. O (R) X

Grave Secrets (1990) Muddled thriller directed by Donald P. Borchers goes nowhere with the dull tale of a psychic researcher (Paul LeMat) aiding a woman (Renee Soutendijk) haunted by a headless ghost. Off-screen murder and infanticide, with a few spooky special effects. A-III (R)

Graveyard Shift (see: "Stephen King's Graveyard Shift").

Gravy Train, The (1974) Pair of brothers from the hills of West Virginia (Stacy Keach and Frederic Forrest) join in a complex armored-car robbery only to be ripped off by the caper's mastermind (Barry Primus). What follows is a downhill race against time to intercept the loot before it is sold to a fence. Director Jack Starrett has an eye for pell-mell action and an ear for racy backwoods expletives and witticisms. But the killings and cursing, plus a gratuitous massage parlor visit, tends to put a sour edge on the action. A-IV (R)

Gray Lady Down (1978) Reconditioned nuclear submarine on a shakedown cruise is struck by a freighter and sinks into a deep sea canyon from which the Navy tries to rescue the survivors. Charlton Heston, as the sub commander, and Stacy Keach, as the officer in charge of the rescue operation, are properly taut-jawed and grimly heroic, while for variety's sake, David Carradine is relaxed and cheerfully heroic as the pilot of a small experimental submarine. Director David Greene plumbs the depths and comes up with some fairly good entertainment. A-II (PG) A

Grayeagle (1978) A dying Indian chief commissions a warrior to kidnap a supposed white woman who is in fact his daughter so that he might see her before he dies. Not even the presence of Ben Johnson helps this embarrassingly bad western written, produced and directed by Charles B. Pierce (who also does some dreadful acting in it). Violence and some partial nudity make it a tall tale for adults. A-III (PG)

Grazie Zia (1969) Ironic Italian fable about a rich young psychopath (Lou Castel) who torments his attractive aunt (Lisa Gastoni), a doctor trying to cure his affliction. Director Salvatore Samperi reduces the theme of good and evil to an unrelenting series of sexual games and perverse role-reversals ending in self-destruction. O (PG)

Grease (1978) Nostalgic 1950s' musical romance in which John Travolta plays the leader of a slick-haired, leather-jacketed gang, and Olivia Newton-John is a sweet high school transfer student from Australia whose attraction for him transforms her into a tough, sensual leather groupie. Though director Randal Kleiser plays it for simple-minded fun, the teen fantasy glamorizes negative role models and is preoccupied with sex in its dialogue and lyrics. O (PG) A

Grease II (1982) Taking up where the original musical left off, an English youth (Maxwell Caulfield) enrolls at Rydel High School and learns to ride a motorcycle to impress his girlfriend (Michelle Pfeiffer). Set in the 1960s, director Patricia Birch's movie is bland and synthetic, but its gaping moral vacuum, emphasis on conformity at all costs and sexual innuendo in the lyrics make it unsuitable for younger viewers. A-III (PG) A

Greased Lightning (1977) The usually comic Richard Pryor gives an extremely restrained and effective performance as a stock car racer in the Deep South who has to overcome racial prejudice to succeed. Despite director Michael Schultz's blunting of the story's conflict and tension by inappropriate humor, Pryor's charm and skill along with an excellent supporting cast provide some buoyant and entertaining moments. A-II (PG) A

Greaser's Palace (1972) Director Robert Downey's wacky fable juxtaposes the Old Movie West with the Second Coming of Christ (by parachute), a comic concept that deteriorates into a meandering string of sight gags. Those who find nothing funny in religious irreverence should be warned that this is definitely not their movie. Some explicit sexual and scatological references are excessive. O (nr)

Great Balls of Fire! (1989) Director Jim McBride's biography of rock legend Jerry Lee Lewis (Dennis Quaid) sacrifices a serious look at the troubled musician for glossy, pop entertainment. Little is made of the fact that radio stations in the late 1950s banned his records for being sexually suggestive. Also glossed over is his controversial marriage to his 13-year-old second cousin (Winona Ryder), which led to his career doldrums. Sexual innuendo, brief violence and a sexually suggestive encounter. A-III (PG-13) 15

Great Bank Hoax, The (1979) Fine but ill-used cast headed by Ned Beatty, Burgess Meredith and Michael Murphy is unable to get anything but a mild chuckle or two from this leaden-paced, awkward comedy about an attempt to cover up an embezzlement by staging a mock robbery. Director Joseph Jacoby adds an adult flavor to the jokes and slapstick situations. A-III (PG) U

Great Bank Robbery, The (1969) Sophomoric western spoof stars Zero Mostel and Kim Novak as the Rev. Pious Blue and Sister Lyda who try to save a small western town from themselves as well as from some bandits. Directed by Hy Averback, a seduction sequence, a tasteless comic nude scene and double-entendre sermonizing are not for youngsters, and probably most adults. A-III (PG)

Great Battle, The (1974) Inept Soviet dramatization depicting the bitter and dramatic siege of the Russian city of Kursk by German forces in 1943. The badly dubbed movie has little interest either historically or dramatically, and its scenes of carnage are not for young children. A-II (PG)

Great Catherine (1969) Chaotic flight-of-fancy based on George Bernard Shaw's bedroom farce opposes Peter O'Toole, as a British Dragoon, and Jeanne Moreau, as the 18th-century Russian Empress. Director Gordon Flemyng manages to erode Shaw's fragile, pungent satire of pompous British aristocracy and unbridled Russian passion with slapstick humor, frantic chases and crude caricatures. A-III (G) U

Great Dictator, The (1940) In this satirical indictment of Hitlerian totalitarianism, writer-producer-director Charles Chaplin plays dual roles as Hynkel, the mimi-moustachioed dictator of Tomania and as the Little Fellow in the form of a Jewish barber. As his lady love, Paulette Goddard shines luminously, even when she's banging storm troopers over the head with her frying pan. Because of its subject and themes, the movie is less likely to engage the interest of the very young. A-II (G) U

Great Man, The (1957) Talky melodrama about a radio journalist (Jose Ferrer) hired to do a memorial program on a popular network broadcaster after his sudden death, who then has qualms of conscience when interviews with those who knew him reveal that the man was a heel and his career a fraud. Also directed by Ferrer, it's a smug variation on "Citizen Kane" without the flashbacks and moral ambiguity, despite a standout bit from Ed Wynn as a decent human being in the broadcast business. Private vices of a public figure. A-II (br) A

Great Escape, The (1963) Thrilling rendition of a fact-based story about an elaborate escape of Allied prisoners from a German P.O.W. camp during World War II. Steve McQueen is the most ambitious of a crew that includes James Garner, Charles Bronson, James Coburn and Richard Attenborough as they plot a mass escape that results in an intriguing, highly entertaining suspense gripper. With John Sturges directing, it all builds to a stunning, sobering climax that both tugs at the heart and keeps it racing. A-I (br) PG

Great Gatsby, The (1974) Lavish but disappointing screen version of F. Scott Fitzgerald's novel about the fatally ill-matched love of a millionaire (Robert Redford) for another man's wife (Mia Farrow). Director Jack Clayton's lush production gives more attention to the movie's set design and costuming than to Francis Ford Coppola's very literate but frequently literal adaptation. The result is beautiful to watch but proves an empty experience. Mature themes. A-III (PG) A

Great Imposter, The (1960) Intriguing fact-based story of Ferdinand W. Demara, Jr. (Tony Curtis), who carried off his curious compulsion to assume false identities with convincing assurance as military officer, Trappist novice, prison warden, doctor on a Canadian warship and school teacher. Director Robert Mulligan uses a fine supporting cast to give weight to the circumstances of each impersonation, with Curtis easy to take in the role of a likeable fraud who uses bogus credentials in ways that help others. Some menace and mild romantic complications. A-II (br) U

Great McGinty, The (1940) Wacky political spoof in which an enterprising soup-line refugee (Brian Donlevy) is hired as a muscleman by a big-city machine boss (Akim Tamiroff), then takes over the organization, gets elected governor and is undone only when he decides to run an honest administration. Written and directed by Preston Sturges, the daffy turns of fortune are as incongruous and untidy as the political corruption they satirize, all of which is treated with bemused wonderment rather than cynical disdain. Tongue-in-cheek electoral hijinks and minor stylized violence. A-II (br)

Great McGonagall, The (1975) Spike Milligan directs and stars in an offbeat movie about a poor 19th-century Scottish weaver who late in life gives up everything to write truly atrocious poetry and dies unknown and impoverished. Milligan's comedy lacks the anarchistic zest of his glory days on BBC radio and only occasionally reflects the madcap fancy of simpler times. A brief nude dance only compounds the movie's many problems. O (nr) AA

Great Mouse Detective, The (1986) Disney animated feature relates the adventures of Basil of Baker Street (voice of Barrie Ingham), the Sherlock Holmes of mouseland, while rescuing a little girl mouse's kidnapped father from the nefarious Professor Ratigan (voice of Vincent Price). While not one of Disney's finest, producer/co-director Burny Mattinson's sprightly take-off on the Holmes stories still manages charming characterizations throughout. A-I (G) U

Great Muppet Caper, The (1981) Jim Henson directs his incomparable cast of muppets as wisecracking Kermit and song-and-dance lady Miss Piggy lead the troupe off to England to thwart Charles Grodin's plan to rob fashion queen Diana Rigg of her jewels. Great silly fun for adults and children. A-I (G) A

Great Northfield, Minnesota Raid, The (1972) Western melodrama about one of the last of the great outlaw bands contrasts the nonviolent, philosophical Cole Younger (Cliff Robertson) and the murderous, Bible-spouting Jesse James (Robert Duvall). Director Philip Kaufman's mix of character study and a demythologizing of the frontier experience has many good moments but is flawed and derivative. Graphic violence and some incidental nudity. A-III (PG) X

Great Outdoors, The (1988) Director Howard Deutch chronicles the botched summer vacation spent by two mismatched brothers-in-law (John Candy and Dan Aykroyd) and their families in the Canadian North Woods. Scripted by John Hughes, the humor comes from its two stars whose characters seem to be hilarious retreads from "Saturday Night Live." Some vulgar language. A-II (PG)

Great Race, The (1965) Slapstick potpourri of sight gags and broad characterizations abound in a turn-of-the-century automobile race from New York to Paris via Alaska, Russia and Western Europe. While Tony Curtis and Jack Lemmon ham it up outrageously as the chief racing rivals, Blake Edwards directs the low comedy farce in high comedy style. A-I (nr) U

Great Santini, The (1980) Solid portrait of a gung-ho but aging Marine fighter pilot (Robert Duvall) who, having no war to fight in 1962, brings his own war home to cause conflict with his wife (Blythe Danner), and especially his teenage son (Michael O'Keefe). Though flawed with some heavy melodrama and a contrived resolution, director John Lewis Carlino's story of family life has much heart, strong values, warm humor and three marvellous performances to more than compensate. Some rough language and the intensity of emotional family conflict. A-II (PG)

Great Scout and Cathouse Thursday, The (1976) Lee Marvin plays a veteran scout out to avenge a swindle worked on him by former partner Robert Culp, but in the process he falls in love with a young prostitute. Director Don Taylor's western spoof is tedious, unfunny, occasionally brutal and unremittingly vulgar in its attempts at bawdy hijinks. O (PG) AA

Great Spy Chase, The (1966) Flat French spy spoof directed by Georges Lautner in which the world's leading secret agents pursue the blonde widow (Mireille Darc) of a manufacturer who left her his papers on a devastating new weapon. Much sexual innuendo. A-III (br)

Great Texas Dynamite Chase, The (1977) Two young women carry out a bank-robbing spree and live happily ever after. Despite oafish attempts at tongue-in-cheek satire, director Michael Pressman's farce sinks into gratuitous sex and violence with degrading female stereotypes. O (R)

Great Train Robbery, The (1979) Sean Connery stars as a debonair Victorian con man who carries off the first high-speed train robbery in history with the aid of accomplished locksmith Donald Sutherland and girlfriend Lesley Anne Down. British production boasts hair-raising hijinks and an impressive re-creation of the period by director-writer Michael Crichton. There is a fair amount of lighthearted double-entendres and an acceptance of less than virtuous behavior. A-III (PG)

Great Waldo Pepper, The (1975) Robert Redford stars as a 1920s stunt pilot who realizes his fantasy of meeting a great German ace in air combat. Director George Roy Hill's movie is rather flat, but its aerial photography of the great old biplanes is entertainment enough. Some strong language. A-III (PG)

Great Wall, A (1986) Gentle but keenly observed comedy of cultural collision when a Chinese-American family visits relatives in Peking. First U.S. feature produced in mainland China. Directed by Peter Wang, the movie provides entertaining and informative dissection of humorous pitfalls of stereotyping. A-I (PG)

Great Waltz, The (1972) Failed musical extravaganza tracing the life and times of 19th-century German composer Johann Strauss Jr., from when he first eclipsed his father as the most popular songwriter of Old Vienna, through the middle period when Strauss chased skirts and the muse with equal fervor, to his moment of triumph when he presented "On the Beautiful Blue Danube" at the 1872 Boston World Peace Jubilee. Horst Bucholz as Strauss looks like he is ready to gag on a steady diet of producer-writer-director Andrew L. Stone's preposterous dialogue. And the audience might gag on the saccharine treatment of this controversial composer's life. A-II (G) U

Great White Hope, The (1970) Fictionalized but hardly sanitized story based on the life of prizefighter and onetime heavyweight champion of the world, Jack Johnson, here named Jack Jefferson. Set in the early decades of the century, the narrative traces the swift rise and sudden, prolonged fall of the giant black boxer, played with burning intensity by James Earl Jones. Directed by Martin Ritt, the movie is a stinging indictment of the racial attitudes of the time. A strong film both visually and verbally, it should be approached with clear eyes and an open mind. A-III (GP) 15

Great Ziegfeld, The (1936) The life of Broadway producer Florenz Ziegfeld (William Powell) is told in terms of the various performers he turned into headliners, including wives Anna Held (Luise Rainer) and Billie Burke (Myrna Loy). Directed by Robert Z. Leonard, the result is an eye-filling cornucopia of musical extravaganzas, stylish show girls and vintage acts, including Fanny Brice and Ray Bolger as themselves. Mild sexual innuendo and romantic complications. A-II (br) U

Greatest, The (1977) Entertaining but rather flat and patched together film version of Muhammad Ali's autobiography with Ali playing himself. Director Tom Gries' dramatization seems to have simplified a great deal, and the effect is to show the heavyweight boxing champion with no warts at all. Ring violence and religious stereotyping. A-III (PG) A

Greatest Story Ever Told, The (1965) While it is obviously not the greatest movie ever made, director George Stevens' vision of the Gospel story presents a consistent, traditional view of Christ as the God Incarnate. The movie, despite its epic Hollywood scale, is well-acted, tastefully and realistically written, beautifully photographed and Max von Sydow's believable portrayal of the Christ is the most essential element in its success. A-I (G)

Greek Tycoon (1978) Tabloid melodrama in which a Greek shipping magnate (Anthony Quinn) woos and wins the chic widow (Jacqueline Bisset) of an assassinated president of the United States. Directed by J. Lee Thompson, the movie is trashy to the core in its shameless trafficking in actual events viewed through the distorting glass of malicious gossip and innuendo, compounded by rough language and a graphic nude scene. O (R) AA

Green Berets, The (1968) John Wayne stars in and co-directs (with Ray Kellogg) this ghastly commercial for U.S. involvement in Vietnam. Based on the popular Robin Moore novel, the movie follows Wayne and his green-bereted force as they slaughter wave upon wave of slant-eyed commies. Racial stereotyping and wartime violence depicted in much the same manner as the old Hollywood World War II movies set in the Pacific. A-III (G) A

Green Card (1990) Unexpected romance develops after two strangers marry in name only so he (Gerard Depardieu) can remain in the U.S. and she (Andie MacDowell) can move into a marrieds-only apartment. Written, produced and directed by Peter Weir, the outcome is never in doubt, but the rocky road to love makes a sweet journey in this light-as-air romantic comedy. Mild sexual innuendo and minimal rough language. A-III (PG-13) 12

Green Fire (1954) Soggy adventure in Colombia's backcountry where a pair of engineers (Stewart Granger and Paul Douglas) tunnel into a mountain searching for a lost emerald mine despite bandits, cave-ins and the owner (Grace Kelly) of a coffee plantation in the valley below. Though director Andrew Marton makes the action in the wilderness setting seem credible, there is little he can do with an unconvincing plot and its cardboard characters. Some stylized violence, menacing situations and mild romantic complications. A-II (br) U

Green Mansions (1959) Overcooked version of W.H. Hudson's turn-of-the-century romance about a political refugee (Anthony Perkins) who escapes into the Amazonian jungles where he falls in love with a young woman (Audrey Hepburn) feared as an evil spirit by the local natives. Directed by Mel Ferrer, the romantic pretensions of the narrative are undone by the overacting of the principals, including Sessue Hayakawa and Henry Silva as tribal notables. Stylized violence and ethnic stereotyping. A-I (br) U

Green Pastures, The (1936) Warmly sympathetic, gently humorous fantasy from Marc Connelly's Pulitzer Prize-winning play portraying stories from the Old Testament as imagined in the cultural idiom of black youngsters in a rural Sunday school of a long-ago segregated South. Directed by Connelly and William Keighley, the all-black cast carries off the narrative's mixture of whimsy and reverence in high style, with a commanding performance by Rex Ingram as De Lawd and appropriate gospel music by the Hall Johnson choir. Considered a positive portrayal of black folk culture and religious feeling by audiences of the time, the work still has considerable charm and emotional appeal today, especially for those interested in the history of the African American community. Parents, however, should be sensitive that its picture of blacks may be misunderstood as patronizing or demeaning unless seen in historical context. A-I (br) U

Green Room, The (1979) French director Francois Truffaut's adaptation of two short stories by Henry James is a philosophical meditation on the subject of death and the transcendence of the human spirit. Truffaut himself plays the World War I soldier who returns safely from the trenches to find that his wife has died. A masterful exercise in the cinema of atmosphere and characterization, but some may find the hero's obsession with death morbid. A-III (PG) A

Green Slime, The (1969) A big mushroom from outer space plays the title role, with support from earthlings Robert Horton and Richard Jaeckel. Forgettable Japanese sci-fi movie directed by Kinji Fukasaku. A-I (G)

Green Wall, The (1972) Young couple have carved out a homestead in the jungle of Peru's interior, fighting the lush vegetation for each acre of arable land. When their young son is bitten by a poisonous snake, the movie becomes a race to get the vaccine that will save the child, underlining the isolation of every frontier community. Writer-director Armando Robles Godoy has constructed his script around that one fateful day, with flashbacks filling out the story. Discreet love-making scene. A-III (R)

Greetings (1968) Brian De Palma directs a way-out satire on draft-dodgers, computer dating and other aspects of 1960s' society. The effort is sometimes humorous but when wit fails, it turns to sex, nudity and tasteless situations. O (X)

Gregory's Girl (1982) A charming movie about the travails of adolescence in urban Scotland. Written and directed by Bill Forsyth, it retains to the end its capacity to surprise with its daffy, yet at times touching incongruity. A-II (PG) A

Gremlins (1984) Bouncy, but often repulsively dark comedy about nasty little creatures spawned by a cute, furry little Christmas gift an inventor (Hoyt Axton) buys for his son (Zach Galligan). A strained moral tale about the consequences of not following directions, the fantasy directed by Joe Dante is steeped in fierce, violent, savage sight gags that lead to mindless mischief, mayhem and murder. A-III (PG) 15

Gremlins II: The New Batch (1990) This time the fearsome creatures run amuck in a Manhattan skyscraper where the adolescents (Zach Galligan and Phoebe Cates) from the original must save the day or the vicious gremlins will overrun the Big Apple during the night. Despite an elaborate visual design and wacky sight gags, director Joe Dante's sequel is a rather drawn-out testament to murderous mayhem, with plodding predictability, insipid characters and an overkill quotient of violence disguised as nasty fun. Many scenes of intense menace and violence. A-III (PG-13) 12

Grey Fox, The (1983) Stagecoach robber (Richard Farnsworth), released after 30 years in prison into a world without stagecoaches, heads for Canada and starts robbing trains. Leisurely directed by Philip Borsos, the beautiful locales and some fine acting obscures the Canadian production's basically anti-social theme. A-III (PG)

Grey Gardens (1976) Documentary about two women, an aging mother and a middle-aged daughter, once wealthy but who now live as recluses in a crumbling man-

sion in an exclusive community that wants them out. Directed by Albert and David Maysles, the often moving, often troubling portrait of rugged individualism invades their privacy but presents them as noble and heroic women who refuse to compromise their ideals to the standards of society. A-III (PG)

Greyfriars Bobby (1961) Disney movie about a 19th-century dog in Scotland whose faithfulness in staying by his master's grave in an Edinburgh cemetery make him a town legend. Director Don Chaffey's fine cast (Donald Crisp, Alex MacKenzie, Laurence Naismith, Gordon Jackson) and solid staging make it superior family entertainment that young children especially will enjoy. A-I (br) U

Greystoke: The Legend of Tarzan, Lord of the Apes (1984) Director Hugh Hudson's visually stunning, extremely intelligent, well-acted retelling of the Edgar Rice Burroughs popular classic about a boy raised by apes and returned to civilization only to recoil from its moral savagery. The violence in the jungle sequences is very strong stuff, and there is also a brief bedroom sequence and some male nudity. A-III (PG)

Grifters, The (1990) A mother (Anjelica Huston), her son (John Cusack) and his lover (Annette Bening) are con artists in a bizarre triangle that gets deadly when the two women turn on each other. Director Stephen Frears' tale of twisted relationships presents a totally bleak view of humanity where decency, conscience or even hope have no place. Intermittent intense violence, casual promiscuity with nudity and minimal rough language. O (R) 18

Grimm's Fairy Tales for Adults (1971) Pretentious sex fantasy with two impotent bumpkins seeking their fortune in the deep woods where they have encounters with Snow White, Sleeping Beauty and Cinderella. Director Rolf Thiele allays his own subconscious anxieties by lacing the uncouth undoings with gory details in a German-produced strudel full of raw and rotten apples. O (nr)

Grissom Gang, The (1971) Perverse tale of a poor little rich girl (Kim Darby) who finds true love with one of her kidnappers (Scott Wilson) in director Robert Aldrich's excessively violent movie set in Prohibition-era Kansas City. O (R) X

Grizzly (1976) Inept action thriller about a 15-foot grizzly bear attacking unwary campers in a national park. Starring Christopher George and directed by William Girdler, it is no more than a tedious exercise in special-effects mayhem, totally inappropriate for youngsters. A-III (PG) A

Grizzly Adams (see: "The Life and Times of Grizzly Adams").

Groove Tube, The (1974) Satirical skits spoofing the state of television programming by imagining what it would be like if there were no sacred cows and the predominant color were blue. Directed by Ken Shapiro, the result is wild satire, mad slapstick and, as might be expected, adolescent smut, gross scatological humor and a garden variety of tastelessness. O (X/R)

Gross Anatomy (1989) Seriocomic look at the trials and tribulations of first-year medical students with focus on an obnoxious class clown (Matthew Modine) and the dissection professor (Christine Lahti) who inspires his overnight, unlikely transformation into a responsible student. Directed by Thom Eberhardt, it features a tensionless plot and unappealing, one-dimensional characters. Some rough language and an off-camera sexual liaison. A-III (PG-13)

Groundhog Day (1993) Lightweight romantic fantasy in which a sarcastic weatherman (Bill Murray) slowly goes bonkers when inexplicably caught in a time warp in Punxsutawney, Pa. where, in daily reliving the same Groundhog Day, he gradually falls in love with his sweet-natured producer (Andie MacDowell). Despite appealing performances and numerous chuckles, director Harold Ramis' comic invention falls victim to the movie's own theme of repetitiveness. Occasional sexual innuendo and comic treatment of theft and suicide. A-II (PG)

Ground Zero (1988) Poorly realized political thriller about the British testing of atomic bombs during the 1950s and 1960s in the Australian desert and the military cover-ups that hid the tests' toll on soldiers and aborigines. Political fact and fiction is made so indistinguishable here by Australian directors Michael Pattinson and Bruce Myles that this unfortunately can too easily be dismissed as escapist fare. An overall sense of menace culminating in climactic violence and death, with a brief unsettling shot of stockpiled corpses. A-III (PG-13)

Groundstar Conspiracy, The (1972) Mediocre espionage thriller about a plot to sabotage an important government nuclear research center focuses mainly on George Peppard's ruthless, amoral methods of flushing out the traitor at the top. Directed by Lamont Johnson, the movie's hazy philosophical-political attitudes, as well as a romantic subplot, are not for the immature. A-III (PG) AA

Group, The (1966) Screen version of Mary McCarthy's novel about the private lives of eight Vassar girls capitalizes on the comeliness of its principals, particularly Candice Bergen, Elizabeth Hartman and Johanna Pettit, to the detriment of real dramatic interest and human values. Lumpily directed by Sidney Lumet, the screen adaptation emphasizes the young ladies' sexual proclivities as they pursue husbands and careers in the 1930s. O (br) X

Groupies (1970) Director Ron Dorfman's movie about the idolization of pop musicians by the young seems less a documentary than a put on with the kids acting up for the camera in amateur fashion. It is exploitation masked as celebration of the uninhibited, irresponsible life-styles of the rock music subculture. O (X)

Grumpy Old Men (1993) A half-century rivalry between two old pranksters (Walter Matthau; Jack Lemmon) escalates when an attractive widow (Ann-Margret) moves in across the street from them. Director Donald Petrie's contrived romantic comedy benefits greatly from the veteran actors' crusty portrayals despite the formula script and a feel-good finish. An implied sexual encounter, some crude sexual references, mild menace and a few instances of profanity. A-III (PG-13)

Guardian, The (1990) Failed horror film about a supernatural being (Jenny Seagrove) who masquerades as a nanny in order to steal infants and sacrifice them to some woodland deity. Director William Friedkin works hard at building an eerie, foreboding atmosphere, but the story is a clunker that doesn't make much sense and the special effects of a tree whose limbs kill people isn't worth the effort. Excessive gory violence, extended nudity and an explicit sex scene. O (R) 18

Guelwaar (1993) When the body of a murdered political activist in Senegal disappears just before his Catholic burial, his upset family and friends go to the Muslim cemetery where they believe he was mistakenly interred but meet armed Muslims who will not allow the grave in question to be disturbed. Writer-director Ousmane Sembene touches upon religious animosities, widespread political corruption and the need for African self-sufficiency in a straightforward narrative that is rich in complex characters and cultural observations. Subtitles. Some sexual innuendo, brief nudity and momentary violence. A-III (nr)

Guernica (1976) Fernando Arrabal's movie presents a surrealistic history of the Spanish Civil War, making grotesques out of the Nationalists and idealizing the Republicans. It is basically a series of theatrical set pieces whose best images are filled with pain, sadness and longing, but the imagery frequently operates on the level of shocking violence and anti-religious references. O (nr)

Guess What We Learned in School Today? (1971) Pretending to parody puritanical attitudes toward the sex education of the young in affluent suburbia, director John

G. Avildsen's satire teaches its paltry lessons mainly with redundant nudity and protracted promiscuity. The movie's various sex-obsessed caricatures are embodied by passable unknown performers. O (R)

Guess Who's Coming to Dinner (1967) Pat comedy starring Spencer Tracy and Katharine Hepburn as parents whose daughter (Katharine Houghton) suddenly announces her plans to marry a distinguished black physician (Sidney Poitier). Directed by Stanley Kramer, the movie has some good comic moments and by showing the efforts of both families to cope with the racial issues and the generation gap, it achieves a dimension of truth. A-II (nr) PG

Guilty as Sin (1993) A defense attorney (Rebecca De Mornay) discovers her wily client (Don Johnson) is in fact a ladykiller who can frame her as an accomplice if she doesn't get him off the hook. Despite an implausible plot, director Sidney Lumet still manages to inject some suspense into the cat-and-mouse proceedings of this sinister courtroom melodrama. Briefly intense violence, an implied sexual encounter and intermittent rough language. A-III (R)

Guilty by Suspicion (1991) The House Un-American Activities Committee in the early 1950s pressures a director (Robert De Niro) to name Communist sympathizers in the movie industry or face the complete destruction of his career. Directed with empathy by Irwin Winkler, the movie is a compelling and sobering look at the profound effect the loss of jobs and friends had on members of the Hollywood community who were blacklisted during the McCarthy era. Scene of suicide and occasional rough language. A-II (PG-13) 15

Gulliver's Travels (1939) Max Fleischer's animated version of Jonathan Swift's tale of the shipwrecked Englishman who is washed ashore in Lilliput, a diminutive land by whose scale Gulliver is a full-blown giant. The adaptation still goes over well with youngsters bemused by the images of tiny people coping with an oversized man, the movie's comic invention more than compensates for the silly subplot of neighboring kingdoms warring over a royal wedding and the songs are pleasant if not memorable. A-I (br)

Gulliver's Travels Beyond the Moon (1966) Young children will like this Japanese-produced but Western-geared animated feature about a little boy, a pup dog and a tin soldier who join forces with old Lemuel Gulliver on an adventuresome trip by spaceship to the distant star of Hope. Charming and worthwhile. A-I (br)

Gumball Rally, The (1976) Mindless cross-country car race featuring a cast of characters led by Michael Sarrazin. Stunt coordinator-turned-director Chuck Bail tries some leering sex at the pit-stops. O (PG) A

Gumshoe (1972) British movie in which Albert Finney plays a man who imagines himself as a hard-boiled private-eye of the Raymond Chandler and Dashiell Hammett school and these fantasies get him involved in a nasty but highly implausible case of gun-running and murder. Directed by Stephen Frears, the movie is fun at first, but it lacks a solid plot and therefore bogs down very quickly in its nonstop allusions to old detective movies. Violence and sexual innuendo. A-III (GP) 15

Gun Glory (1957) Stewart Granger plays a gunfighter who wants to hang up his six-shooter but can't until he stops the cattleman (James Gregory) terrorizing the local sod-busters. Director Roy Rowland can't work up much interest in tired situations and formula plot, though Chill Wills does a nice turn as a down-to-earth preacher. The violence makes it unlikely children's fare. A-I (br) U

Gunfight, A (1971) Retired gunfighters Kirk Douglas and Johnny Cash have little more to look forward to than an inevitable showdown with each other or with a younger, faster gun so they stage their own final shootout. Director Lamont Johnson aiming at audience participation in the ambiguous outcome settles for heavy symbolism spotted with some rough language and a brief nude scene. A-III (PG) A

Gunfighter, The (1950) Pensive tale of an aging 1880s' gunslinger (Gregory Peck) who is looking to outrun his reputation and settle down but his past fame makes him a target for every aspiring gunman in the Southwest. Director Henry King delivers an intelligent Western drama with plenty of atmospheric Americana and fine performances from Peck, Millard Mitchell as the local sheriff and Richard Jaeckel and Skip Homeier as would-be gunfighters. Some tense menace and stylized violence. A-I (br) A

Gunfighters of Casa Grande (1964) Routine European-made Western in which a gringo gunman (Alex Nichol) offers his gang to help protect Mexican ranchers from a bandit horde while planning to steal their cattle herds himself. The usual stylized violence and an off-screen rape. A-II (br)

Gung Ho (1986) Michael Keaton stars in this comedy about the reluctance of U.S. workers to accept the standards of performance imposed upon them when a Japanese management team takes over a defunct auto manufacturing plant in a small Pennsylvania town. Offering a multitude of stale one-liners and sight gags, the script seems somewhat insensitive in the stereotyping of Japanese businessmen as obsessively concerned with efficiency and saving face. Failed comedy with low humor, harsh language and ethnic stereotyping. A-III (PG-13)

Gunga Din (1939) Classic adventure yarn loosely based on the Rudyard Kipling poem about a water carrier (Sam Jaffe) in Victoria's India who here dies a hero with a bugle warning British forces of an ambush. Director George Stevens focuses the action on three seasoned sergeants (Victor McLaglen, Cary Grant and Douglas Fairbanks Jr.) whose bickering comradeship provides some hardy fun while fighting Thugs, a long-suppressed murder cult led by a formidable foe (Eduardo Ciannelli). Celebrates such "manly" virtues as loyalty, courage and steadfastness, though with plenty of stylized violence. A-I (br) U

Gunman's Walk (1958) Tough-minded Western in which a pioneer rancher (Van Heflin) comes to regret being too indulgent in raising his motherless boys after the elder son (Tab Hunter) becomes a remorseless killer and the younger (James Darren) sides with the sister (Kathryn Grant) of an Indian his brother murdered. Director Phil Karlson relies on the clash of sharply contrasting characters to sustain interest in the contrived proceedings till the final showdown between father and trigger-happy son. Tragic family theme with cold-blooded though stylized violence. A-III (br) A

Gunn (1967) Seamy, occasionally brutal feature based on the once-popular "Peter Gunn" TV detective series features Craig Stevens as impeccable as ever in the title role. It's a minor effort from director Blake Edwards, offering little more than routine private-eye segments, a passel of cameo appearances by screen stars and an unoriginal twist ending. Excessive violence and sexual situations. O (br) A

Gunpoint (1965) Substandard western directed by Earl Bellamy in which Audie Murphy plays a lawman chasing an outlaw band. Stylized violence. A-I (br) U

Guns for San Sebastian (1968) Mexican rebel (Anthony Quinn), mistaken for the priest expected by the inhabitants of a village ravaged by Indians and bandits, teaches them how to fight back and drive off the marauders. Directed by Henri Verneuil, the 18th-century setting is beautifully evoked but the story is somewhat far-fetched and on the sentimental side. Stylized violence. A-II (br) A

Guns of a Stranger (1973) Boring western in which Marty Robbins plays a straight-shooter who comes to the rescue of a damsel-in-distress (Dovie Beams) whose boozy grandfather (Chill Wills) is about to lose his ranch to a cattle baron (William Foster). Robert Hinkle directs Robbins, who is a singer but no cowboy, and certainly no actor. A-I (G)

Guns of August, The (1965) Based on Barbara Tuchman's study of how World War I started, this documentary popularizes the scholarly story of diplomatic blunders and political miscalculations. Director Nathan Kroll and his film researchers have accumulated a mass of familiar and unfamiliar footage on the outbreak of the war, presented in a straight-forward, factual manner. A-I (br)

Guns of Fort Petticoat, The (1957) With their men away fighting for the Confederacy, a bevy of Texas women (Kathryn Grant, Hope Emerson and others) are helped by a Union officer (Audie Murphy) to defend themselves against an Indian uprising. Director George Marshall has trouble sustaining interest in the women's plight, though he stretches it out with broad humor, a band of outlaws and an action-packed ending. Stylized violence and Indian stereotypes. A-I (br) A

Guns of Navarone, The (1961) Oversized World War II action yarn from Alistair MacLean's novel about Allied commandos (Gregory Peck, David Niven, Anthony Quinn, Stanley Baker and Anthony Quayle) sent to destroy a German artillery emplacement atop a Greek island. Director J. Lee Thompson notches the suspense tightly along the way to a bang-up finish but the spectacle's impact is lessened by scant attention to the tale's human dimension. Wartime violence. A-I (br) U

Guns of the Magnificent Seven (1969) Mercenaries try to outwit superior forces in this sequel set in revolutionary Mexico. Plot operates on the level of gunfights rather than coherent story, with George Kennedy trying hard but simply not the taciturn strong-man type. Best is the historical background that director Paul Wendkos occasionally brings in. A-II (G) A

Gun That Won the West, The (1955) Two veteran plainsmen (Dennis Morgan and Richard Denning) leave a Wild West show to serve as Indian scouts for a troop being equipped with a new model Springfield rifle. Directed by William Castle, the story is pure Hollywood hokum which recycles action footage from earlier, better Westerns. Indian stereotyping and stylized violence. A-I (br)

Guru, The (1969) English pop singer (Michael York) journeys to Bombay to learn to play the sitar where his teacher (Uptal Dutt) tries but fails to convert him to the spiritual values of the East. Rita Tushingham plays a wandering hippie fleeing Western materialism. Director James Ivory's uneven story is essentially a study in contradictions, with humorous overtones, between two cultures and their outlook on life. A-II (G) U

Guru, the Mad Monk (1971) The title character is a maniacal chaplain of a prison island where Central Europe sends its prisoners to be tortured and executed. The film's blood and sex diversions are complicated with a silly vampire and a hodgepodge of religious symbolism offensive to all faiths. O (nr)

Gus (1976) Above average Disney comedy about a mule who kicks field goals. Vincent McEveety directs the lively, fast-moving entertainment, especially suitable for children. A-I (G)

Guyana: Cult of the Damned (1980) Dull fact-based dramatization of the 1978 Jonestown tragedy in which 900 followers of the Reverend James Jones went to their death with their deranged leader. Stuart Whitman stars as the false prophet in director Rene Cardona Jr.'s Mexican production, which is not as sensational as it might have been, but neither does it have the least merit. A scene featuring nudity and another involving physical punishment are gratuitous and offensive. O (R)

Guys and Dolls (1955) Overstuffed screen version of Jo Swerling and Abe Burrows' stage musical based on Damon Runyon's colorful 1920's Broadway types in the story of a bet by a two-bit gambler (Frank Sinatra) that leads ultimately to the reformation of a big-time gangster (Marlon Brando) by a Salvation Army lass (Jean Simmons). Directed by Joseph L. Mankiewicz, the result is an uneven mix of Hollywood and Broadway styles, with some bright production numbers and Frank Loesser tunes, notably Stubby Kaye's "Sit Down, You're Rocking the Boat," but the parts never quite jell into a satisfying whole. Considerable sexual innuendo. A-III (br)

Gypsy Girl (1966) Slight British story of a retarded girl (Hayley Mills), fatherless and neglected by her alcoholic mother, whose tragic young life is changed when a handsome gypsy pays attention to her and she learns what it means to be loved. Directed by John Mills, it is a well-done study of the simplicity of childlike people. The girl's prolonged sadness and her fights with her mother make it inappropriate for young children. A-II (br)

Gypsy Moths, The (1969) Burt Lancaster, Gene Hackman and Deborah Kerr star in this unusual action movie about a rough-and-tough team who makes a living skydiving at state fairs across the Midwest. Director John Frankenheimer's aerial photography, especially the actual dive sequences, is absolutely breathtaking, but the dramatic portions unfolding on terra firma, having to do with the personal lives and problems of the divers, lack credibility. A-III (R) A

H

Hagbard and Signe (1968) Scandanavian medieval romance based on the Romeo and Juliet theme is set against the stunning landscape of Iceland. Though there is much that is compelling and authentic in director Gabriel Axel's beautifully crafted movie, its treatment is regrettably marred by excessive nudity and graphic depictions of brutality. O (br)

Hail, Hero (1969) Generation-gap movie about a college dropout (Michael Douglas) who returns to the ranch to announce to his indifferent parents that he's joining the Army. Character portrait from director David Miller conveys an overly optimistic embodiment of joyous vitality and spiritual awareness. Disjointed comments about family ties, first love, prejudice and war. A-III (M)

Hail! Mafia (1966) Forgettable crime melodrama directed by Raoul Levy about a paid killer involved in a gang war. Violence. A-III (br)

Hail Mary (1985) The Gospel account of the Incarnation and Virgin Birth is updated to present-day Switzerland in this French production. Though seriously intended, director Jean-Luc Godard's movie is not only tedious and disjointed, but its extensive use of nudity and extremely rough language in a context so sacred to Christians will be offensive to many. O (nr)

Hail the Conquering Hero (1944) Wacky homefront comedy about a World War II recruit (Eddie Bracken) who is rejected by the Marines because of chronic hay fever but, thanks to some veterans of the fighting in the Pacific (led by William Demarest), returns home a reluctant war hero and is elected mayor in spite of himself. Written and directed by Preston Sturges, the tongue-in-cheek premise relies on the comic interplay between Bracken's mousy, nonheroic civilian, Demarest's tough, brassy veteran and the patriotic fervor of a small American town whose sensible values emerge happily in the end. Memorable for its witty dialogue and slapstick situations. A-II (nr) U

Hail to the Chief (1973) Occasionally hilarious, more often sophomoric spoof of Presidential politics stars Dan Resin as the nation's Chief Executive who is more than slightly demented about stamping out dissent in the land. Directed by Fred Levinson, there are some sterling gags of sight and sound but also a malicious sense of humor in regard to American politics. A-III (PG)

Hair (1979) Key Broadway musical of the 1960s was as much a slick exploitation of the flower children phenomenon as it was a celebration of it. Director Milos Forman's 1970s' screen version keeps intact its virtues, including its measure of sincerity, and its defects, including its large dose of showbiz phoniness. For the most part, Forman does not romanticize his characters (John Savage, Treat Williams, Beverly D'Angelo, Charlotte Rae), though there are huge, lavish dance numbers and a restrained depiction of scenes with drugs, promiscuity, nudity and some rough language. A-IV (PG) AA

Hairspray (1988) Underground writer-director John Waters makes a successful transition into the mainstream with this campy musical comedy tracing the rise of a chubby teenager (Ricki Lake) as the unexpected star of a 1962 Baltimore TV dance show. The storyline includes teen rivalry, outrageous stage parents and a nice subplot about integration, all of which is enlivened by toe-tapping period music and rousing dance numbers. Some off-color remarks. A-II (PG)

Half a Sixpence (1968) Director George Sidney's expanded version of the stage musical stars Tommy Steele as an exuberant dancing, singing draper's clerk who pledges his love to a girl of his own background, Ann (Julia Foster), inherits a fortune, nearly marries a society girl and goes back to faithful Ann, a bit sadder and wiser. Though overlong and somewhat lacking in variety, its handsome sets and soft lens photography give the movie an Edwardian storybook quality that most viewers should find delightful. A-I (br) U

Half Moon Street (1986) Intelligent and attractive woman (Sigourney Weaver) supplements her meager salary as a London researcher by working as a part-time prostitute for upper-class clients. When one of them (Michael Caine) falls in love with her, she finds herself in the middle of a Middle-Eastern power struggle that nearly costs her her life. Director Bob Swaim's routine tale of scandal among the British power elite apparently intends to show how badly women are exploited but it only does more of the same. Violence, nudity and simulated sex. O (R) 18

Hallelujah, I'm a Bum (1933) Fine musical comedy about the Depression stars Al Jolson as the Mayor of Central Park, a bum respected by every tramp in New York City until he falls in love and gets a regular job. Directed by Lewis Milestone, the movie is one of a kind in providing a socially conscious rather than escapist Hollywood musical. A-III (nr) U

Halloween (1978) Criminally insane patient escapes to his hometown on Halloween, the 15th anniversary of the brutal murder for which he was locked up, and becomes a deadly menace to unsuspecting babysitters in director John Carpenter's low-budget horror show. Mixture of some nudity with much violence. O (R) 18

Halloween II (1981) The further adventures of the homicidal maniac and his relentless pursuit of babysitter Jamie Lee Curtis. Directed by Rick Rosenthal, it is just as bad as the original with its nauseating violence, sadism, tastelessness and general senselessness. O (R) X

Halloween III: Season of the Witch (1982) Director Tommy Lee Wallace's sequel uses a plot about a fiendish toy manufacturer (Dan O'Herlihy), intent upon giving the tots of America a Halloween to remember, as an excuse for trotting out the usual sickening special-effects violence and gore as well as some nudity. O (R) 15

Halloween IV: The Return of Michael Myers (1988) Michael (George P. Wilbur) is back in Haddonfield, Ill., and this time he's escaped the mental ward to kill his little niece (Danielle Harris) on Halloween despite his psychiatrist (Donald Pleasence). Director Dwight H. Little is unsuccessful in trying to turn the formula plot into a psychological thriller. Excessive violence, intense menace, a brief sex scene and fleeting nudity. O (R) 18

Halloween V: The Revenge of Michael Myers (1989) Dominique Othenin-Girard directs this film that senselessly exploits Michael's psychic power over his young niece (Danielle Harris), who survived last year's installment and is once again her uncle's major target when he returns to terrorize young, Halloween revellers in Haddonfield, Ill. Mindless menace, remorseless violence and a sexually suggestive encounter. O (R)

Halls of Anger (1970) Sixty white students are bused to a large, all-black high school where the lid is kept on by a disciplinarian who happens to be a former athlete (Calvin Lockhart). Director Paul Bogart handles the desegregation issue with some authenticity but resorts to typical cliches and easy solutions. Much violence and brief nudity. A-III (PG)

Hamburger Hill (1987) A group of American grunts rest, recuperate, talk about their differences, while making failed attempts to capture a Vietnamese-held hilltop before a final bloody assault. Directed by John Irvin, it is more a testament to blind obedience and the absurdities of war than to the virtues of teamwork and determination. Excessive violence and profanity, some nudity and false stereotyping. O (R) 18

Hamburger ... The Motion Picture (1986) Former football star Dick Butkus is the harsh and talkative coach teaching management techniques to trainees at a special college dedicated to Lyman Funk's All Bull Buster Burgers. What begins as social satire upon callous commercialism quickly collapses into an unfunny sex farce with profanity, nudity and violence. O (R)

Hamlet (1969) Director Tony Richardson's intimate rendering of the Shakespearean tragedy emphasizes personal confrontations, heroic solitude and, in the title role, Nicol Williamson's penchant for caustic repartee. Some omissions detract from the spirit of the original text, but this occasionally boisterous version still provides a poignant portrait of a man's obsessive search for truth. Stylized violence. A-II (G) U

Hamlet (1990) Crazed by grief, the despairing Prince of Denmark (Mel Gibson) seeks the truth surrounding the death of his father (Paul Scofield) and the precipitous marriage of his mother (Glenn Close) to his murderous uncle (Alan Bates). Franco Zeffirelli's fluid direction of Shakespeare's classic is emotionally charged, cinematically beautiful and boasts uniformly superior acting. Stylized violence. A-II (PG) U

Hammer (1972) Black exploitation movie about an ex-dockworker (Fred Williamson) who becomes a boxer but when the mob wants him to take a dive, he takes them on and lays them out. Directed by Bruce Clark, the production values are good and the violence is toned down, but it suffers from weak characterization and too-familiar storyline. Some raw sex scenes and rough language. O (R)

Hammer of God, The (1973) Mindless martial arts movie about Japanese karate fighters who slaughter students of a Chinese kung-fu school, but a survivor bolsters himself with iron fist techniques and takes revenge on the baddies. Usual amount of violence except for a savage rape of a woman who has nothing to do with the story. O (R)

Hammerhead (1968) An American soldier of fortune (Vince Edwards) and his companion (Judy Geeson) spend most of their time tracking down an international spy posing as an art collector (Robert Vaughn). Sluggish espionage melodrama directed by David Miller. Nasty violence and sexually suggestive treatment. O (R) A

Hammersmith Is Out (1972) Sluggish variation on the Faust legend in which a psycho-ward attendant (Beau Bridges) is promised strength, wealth and a hashhouse waitress (Elizabeth Taylor) if he will let an inmate (Richard Burton) escape. From there it is a murderous journey to the upper reaches of corruption in a movie directed by Peter Ustinov with a total lack of wit and vigor. Some graphic sex and violence and much crude language. O (R) X

Hammett (1983) Mediocre melodrama about Dashiell Hammett (Frederic Forrest), the creator of Sam Spade, getting started as a writer in 1928 San Francisco but becoming sidetracked by a murder case in which he absorbs the same kind of punishment that would later appear in his hard-boiled detective stories. Directed by Wim Wenders, the result proves to be a pretentious, sentimental and uninspired tribute to old Hollywood murder mysteries, and at times borders on self-parody. Some vulgar expletives and some violence. A-II (PG) AA

Hand, The (1981) Successful cartoonist (Michael Caine) loses his drawing hand in a freak accident and then imagines that the severed hand, never recovered, is pursuing him and threatening those who arouse his anger, especially his restless wife (Andrea Marcovicci). Director Oliver Stone achieves some scary effects, but it's otherwise a gloomy, depressing story with cardboard characters. Some graphic sex and violence. O (R) 18

Hand in Hand (1960) A British movie about the childhood friendship between a Catholic boy and a Jewish girl who discover that God is everywhere, watching over everyone. Directed by Philip Leacock, it is a fine little film, especially for family audiences. A-I (br) U

Hand That Rocks the Cradle, The (1992) Callous suspense movie has an infant and a little girl (Madeline Zima) entrusted to a psychotic nanny (Rebecca De Mornay) out to kill the brood's young mother (Annabella Sciorra). Curtis Hanson directs a manipulative, highly contrived and predictable thriller emphasizing violence and menace to helpless children. Exploitation of violence to women and children, occasional nudity, sexual references and some rough language. O (R) 15

Handful of Dust, A (1988) Based on Evelyn Waugh's 1934 novel satirizing the British upper classes in the guise of a beautiful young couple (James Wilby and Kristin Scott Thomas) whose contented country life is destroyed by the wife's infidelity. Directed by Charles Sturridge, it plays more like romantic tragedy than social satire, with the wife as an especially remorseless, conscienceless character. A-III (PG)

Handle with Care (1977) Good-natured, warm-hearted little comedy set in a small California town where a Citizens Band radio enthusiast (Paul Le Mat) dashes about rescuing people and doing other good deeds, though not always with the approval of his pensive girlfriend (Candy Clark). Director Jonathan Demme contrives an ending that tries to pull all his diverse story elements

together, but it's forced and out of keeping with the relaxed mood of the rest of the movie. A subplot about a bigamous trucker and his two wives is adult fare. A-III (PG)

Handmaid's Tale, The (1990) Muddled fable about a fascist state of the near future where pollution and radioactivity have made most women barren and the fertile few are enslaved as "handmaids" to breed children for the state's rulers. Though director Volker Schloendorff's visuals summon up the image of Nazi Germany, the story of one particular handmaid (Natasha Richardson) gets lost in a dreary depiction of a dehumanized, male-dominated world. Several excessively graphic simulations of sexual intercourse, brief nudity, some rough language and an ambiguous treatment of religion as contributing to a repressive society. O (R) 18

Hands across the Table (1935) Light romantic comedy about a manicurist (Carole Lombard) out to marry for money instead of love, but the rich man's son (Fred MacMurray) she's after proves penniless and himself seeking a wealthy spouse while the crippled millionaire (Ralph Bellamy) who truly loves her waits patiently in the wings. Director Mitchell Leisen keeps the frothy plot bubbling with comic wit and slapstick pranks as the cheerfully hard-boiled gold-diggers charm each other and the viewer until an agreeably sentimental ending. Romantic complications and situations. A-III (br) A

Hands of the Ripper (1972) A pioneer psychoanalyst (Eric Porter) tries to cure the daughter of Jack the Ripper (Angharad Rees) who has inherited her father's tendency to slash things in moments of stress. Fairly well-done British horror movie, but too violent for younger viewers. A-III (R) X

Hang 'em High (1968) Vigorous western starring Clint Eastwood as a former lawman who journeys into the Nebraska Territory where he is promptly hanged—but not high enough to keep him from coming back to enforce a rough version of justice on the range. Directed by Ted Post, the result is clever without being campy and, unusual for an action-packed Eastwood vehicle, without too much violence. A-III (M) 18

Hangar 18 (1981) Within the title edifice are the remains of a wrecked flying saucer kept undercover as part of a government cover-up in this anemic little movie directed by James Conway and starring Darren McGavin and Robert Vaughn. Some incidental violence. A-II (PG) A

Hangman's Knot (1952) After robbing a Union gold shipment, a Confederate major (Randolph Scott) and his small band (including Lee Marvin and Claude Jarman

Jr.) learn the war is over and they are being hunted as outlaws. Directed by Roy Huggins, the action centers on a stagecoach relay station where the group is besieged by local gunmen after the gold. Stylized violence and several muted sexual references. A-II (br)

Hanky Panky (1982) Limp and tedious comedy-adventure in which a mild-mannered architect from Chicago (Gene Wilder) finds himself suspected of murder and pursued by all sorts of hostile people, among them a mystery woman (Gilda Radner). Directed by Sidney Poitier, the poor effort contains a scene involving the beating and murder of a woman and some strong language. A-III (PG) 15

Hanna's War (1988) Based on the short, courageous life of World War II martyr Hanna Senesh (Maruschka Detmers), a Hungarian Jew who relocated to Palestine after high school graduation in 1938 but returned to Hungary on a secret RAF mission to help save her fellow Jews. Director Menahem Golan's glossy, superficial epic leaves more questions than it answers about Hanna's courageous life in Palestine and Hungary during the war. Intense prison scenes and brutal off-camera torture. A-III (PG-13) 15

Hannah and Her Sisters (1986) Writer-director Woody Allen's disappointing treatment of infidelity and adultery in the lives of three sisters (Mia Farrow, Dianne Wiest and Barbara Hershey). Although it shows the struggle and disappointments of people searching for a better life, it romanticizes amoral behavior and dishonesty as a natural consequence of contemporary urban life-styles. A-IV (PG-13) 15

Hannibal Brooks (1969) British World War II P.O.W. (Oliver Reed) escapes in the company of an elephant to Switzerland. Director Michael Winner's pacifist fable resorts to some large-scale but graphically restrained guerrilla warfare to conclude the escape but preserves the lighthearted adventure motif of this generally amiable satire. A-II (M) U

Hannie Caulder (1972) A rancher's wife (Raquel Welch) learns to take justice and a six-shooter into her own hands after being raped and widowed by three bumbling bandits (Strother Martin, Ernest Borgnine, Jack Elam). Director Burt Kennedy's erratic western focuses on a simple-minded and unquestioned theme of vengeance. Exploitative rape sequence, violence and coarse language. O (R) 15

Hanoi Hilton, The (1987) Michael Moriarty is the Christ-like crucified leader of a group of U.S. POWs tortured by callous North Vietnamese until their release at the end of the war. Canadian director Lionel Chetwynd intends this as a tribute to their uncommon bravery but manages to convey an insidious jingoistic notion that duty to country is equal to Christian virtue. Profanity, male nudity and scenes of brutality and torture are more prominent than religious references. O (R)

Hanover Street (1979) Dashing American bomber pilot (Harrison Ford) falls in love with a married woman (Lesley Anne Down) during a 1943 London air raid, they have an affair and then he winds up on a secret mission in France with her nice-guy husband (Christopher Plummer). Written and directed by Peter Hyams, it is an inept attempt to make an old-fashioned wartime romance without the skill or intelligence to evoke any genuine emotions or feelings. Though it does not condone adultery, its glossy and graphic treatment of it is offensive. O (PG)

Hans Christian Andersen (1952) Pleasant family musical based on the life of the Danish author (1805–75) whose fairy tales are among the favorites of children's literature. Directed by Charles Vidor, the biography is pure Hollywood hokum but Danny Kaye is particularly good as the gentle storyteller and Frank Loesser's delightful musical numbers, including "Thumbelina," "The Ugly Duckling" and "The King Is in the Alltogether," are simple, singable and just plain fun. Best for young children, though their elders will find sufficient charm in the proceedings to offset the sentimentality. A-I (nr) U

Happiest Millionaire, The (1967) Musical biography of Anthony J. Drexel Biddle (Fred McMurray), an eccentric turn-of-the-century millionaire who kept alligators as pets, collected prizefighters and alternated a family program of physical fitness with hymn-singing. Directed by Norman Tokar, it has all the usual Disney staples: some innocent romance, a sentimental view of family life and amusing animals. It is, however, over-long and the music by Richard and Robert Sherman is undistinguished. A-I (br) U

Happily Ever After (1990) Snow White and her Prince are about to be married, but the dead Queen's evil brother intervenes, casting a spell on the Prince and dooming Snow White unless the Seven Dwarf's cousins, the Dwarfelles, can rescue them. Filmation Studio's animated sequel to the Grimm Brothers fairy tale fails to capture the magic of the 1937 Disney classic, but zippy pacing, the musical numbers and positive messages for children make it lighthearted family fare. This was re-released in 1993 under the same title. A-I (G)

Happiness (1934) Soviet silent slapstick comedy about a peasant misfit who is put in the Czarist army but after the Revolution returns home to what is now part of a collective farm where he is as much of a misfit as ever. Directed by Alexandre Medvedkine, the action has the zany absurdity that is universal to visual comedy, though the ending is predictably didactic as the peasant learns that happiness is working for the common good. Some earthy humor. A-III (nr)

Happiness Cage, The (1972) Army private (Christopher Walken) receives some experimental brain wave treatment to control his schizophrenic behavior, administered by a neurosurgeon (Joss Ackland) who is trying to learn how to rehabilitate undesirables. Directing an adaptation of Dennis Reardon's play, Bernard Girard fails to provide enough information or human feeling about the scientific conditioning process to make the movie anything more than an old-fashioned horror movie. Patients rant and curse periodically. A-III (PG)

Happy Birthday Gemini (1980) Screen version of Albert Innaurato's play about a poor Italian-American youth (Alan Rosenberg) who receives a surprise visit on his 21st birthday from two wealthy classmates, a brother and sister, but he thinks he loves the brother more than he does the sister. Directed by Richard Benner, the youth's sexual ambivalence is used as the hook upon which to hang all sorts of vignettes of working-class life, but the movie is loud, messy and overacted. Lacks any moral perspective on the sexual identity question, and features crude ethnic stereotypes, vulgarity and profanity. O (R)

Happy Birthday to Me (1981) Simpleminded Canadian horror movie about a disturbed student (Melissa Sue Anderson) at an exclusive school whose friends start disappearing. The climax is her birthday party, at which they all show up rather the worse for wear. Directed by J. Lee Thompson, it is senselessly nauseating in its gore and violence. O (R) 18

Happy Birthday, Wanda June (1971) Screen version of the Kurt Vonnegut Jr. play in which an explorer (Rod Steiger), presumed dead after disappearing in the Amazon jungles eight years before, returns home to discover that his wife (Susannah York) is about to marry a doctor (George Grizzard). Director Mark Robson's stagebound adaptation is a muddled black comedy about the destructive he-man image of masculinity, the nature of aggression and the status of women. Though there are some amusing bits, they do not add up to a coherent whole and the number of verbal obscenities becomes needlessly excessive. O (R)

Happy Ending, The (1970) The movie begins with a disillusioned couple (John Forsythe and Jean Simmons) out of love on the morning of their 16th wedding anniversary and, after various complications, concludes with the wife asking whether, if her husband had to do it over again, he would marry her. Directed by Richard Brooks, it is as unenlightening as it sounds and more than a little cliched. A-III (PG)

Happy Hooker, The (1975) Lynn Redgrave struggles gamely to give some life and glamour to the essentially sordid trade of prostitution. Though there are some humorous touches and a minimum of offensive graphics and vulgar speech, director Nicholas Sgarro's movie fails to justify its existence as either art or entertainment. O (R) X

Happy Mother's Day . . . Love, George (1973) A young lad (Ron Howard) searching for his unknown father comes to a New England fishing village inhabited by a bizarre set of characters (Cloris Leachman, Patricia Neal and Tessa Dahl). Ineptly directed by Darren Mc-Gavin, the film's gory violence, supposedly motivated by sexual repression, is an unsavory fantasy. O (PG)

Happy New Year (1973) French comedy about a pair of jewel thieves (Lino Ventura and Charles Gerard) who meticulously plan a heist on New Year's Eve, set it in action and have it fail because one of them falls completely for the charming owner (Francoise Fabian) of an antique shop next door. Director Claude Lelouch succeeds in presenting a crime caper in a human context that has some moral weight to it. A-III (PG) A

Happy Years, The (1950) A mischievious youth (Dean Stockwell) is sent by his exasperated father (Leon Ames) to a boys' boarding school where he is straightened out by classmates (Darryl Hickman, Scotty Beckett and numerous other juveniles) and a caustic but fatherly Latin teacher (Leo G. Carroll). Director William A. Wellman stresses the healthy nature of the boys' hijinks while poking some gentle fun at the manner and mores of 1896 New Jersey society. Pleasant exercise in nostalgia with special appeal for young viewers. A-I (br) U

Hard Contract (1969) Hired gun James Coburn gets amorously sidetracked by Lee Remick on his way to murder three people in Europe. He has a change of heart but struggles with his own lack of sensitivity. Talkathon by director-writer S. Lee Pogostin questions how much authority figures are responsible for society's dehumanization. A-IV (R) X

Hard Promises (1992) Lifeless romantic comedy concerns a young mother (Sissy Spacek) torn between marrying her solid, dependable fiance (Brian Kerwin) or taking back her dashing ex-husband (William Petersen) who shows up on the eve of the wedding. Aside from its trite characters and sheer predictability, director Martin Davidson makes positive values look positively dull. Some sexual references, momentary fisticuffs and occasional profanity. A-II (PG)

Hard Ride, The (1971) Vietnam vet (Robert Fuller) escorts home the body of his black buddy who had wanted his motorcycle pals to be present at his funeral but, in trying to fulfill this request, he is killed in a bikers' brawl and is buried with his friend. Directed by Burt Topper, the movie mutes the usual sex and violence to make the point that being a road bum is a senseless way of life. A-III (GP)

Hard Target (1993) Hard-core violence is a constant in this repulsive tale of an unemployed New Orleans merchant sailor (Jean-Claude Van Damme) determined to singlehandedly stop a pack of sadistic killers who hunt down and slaughter homeless veterans for sport. Director John Woo assaults viewers with deafening sounds of human torture and death as violence and vengeance are glorified to a sickening degree. Nonstop graphic mayhem and much rough language. O (R) 18

Hard Times (1975) Tough loner (Charles Bronson), down on his luck during the Depression, picks up money by street fighting, an elemental no-holds-barred kind of contest whose payoff comes from the bets wagered. Director Walter Hill gets the period right and does well with the New Orleans locales, but the movie has no pretensions to being anything but good pulp fiction and it succeeds on this level. Some brutal fighting scenes. A-III (R/PG)

Hard to Hold (1984) A rock star (Rick Springfield) falls madly in love with a sophisticated lady (Janet Eilber) whom he meets in a traffic accident. Director Larry Peerce's listless, awkward movie features bad acting by all concerned. A benign view of sex outside of marriage and some rough language are adult fare. A-III (PG)

Hard to Kill (1990) L.A. detective (Steven Seagal) awakens from a coma to avenge the bloodthirsty slaughter of his family seven years before by agents of a corrupt Congressman. Though martial arts master Seagal is depicted as a loving family man, director Bruce Malmuth emphasizes his grisly means of retribution. Excessive graphic violence and acts of vigilantism. O (R) 18

Hard Traveling (1986) Dan Bessie directs a grim, fact-based story of the Depression years about a down-and-out farmer convicted of murder. Although this movie offers a depressing vision of social injustices and their causes, its sensitive portrayals and strong period details lessen its pessimistic outlook. A-III (PG)

Hard Way, The (1991) Workaholic macho cop (James Woods) on the track of a serial killer (Stephen Lang) is stymied by his happy-go-lucky temporary partner (Michael J. Fox), a movie star along for the ride as he prepares for a new role. Director John Badham's formula comedy of stick figures and car chases is helped by its fast pace and lively climax of cliffhangers. Recurring stylized violence and rough language with vulgar expressions. A-III (R) 15

Hardbodies (1984) California smut-in-the-sun movie about three middle-aged lechers who engage a teen-age Lothario (Grant Cramer) to instruct them in the art of seduction. Badly directed by Mark Griffiths, it features abundant nudity, graphic sex and utter disregard of every moral consideration. O (R)

Hardcore (1979) Deeply committed Christian from the Midwest (George C. Scott) hires a Los Angeles detective (Peter Boyle) to find his 15-year-old daughter who has disappeared while attending a religious youth convention in California. When she turns up in a porno film, Scott is plunged into the pornographic underworld trying to find her. Writer-director Paul Schrader's movie deals with a serious subject, but on the whole is crude and simplistic, its characters shallow and its melodramatic resolution unbelievable. Nudity and frequent rough language. O (R) 18

Hardys Ride High, The (1939) When Judge Hardy (Lewis Stone) learns he may be the heir to a $2 million estate, he takes the family to Detroit to verify his claim. Directed by George B. Seitz, the episode is unusually playful in testing the family's small-town values when faced with sudden wealth as well as providing some romance for Andy's maiden aunt Millie (Sara Hayden). A-I (br)

Harder They Come, The (1973) The movie, in English but frequently subtitled because of the thickly accented Jamaican speech, stars Jimmy Cliff as a country boy come to Kingston town seeking fame and fortune and winding up with the wrong sort of the one and none of the other. Directed by Perry Henzell, the result is a fast-paced picture full of color and action, sometimes violent and harsh, occasionally confusing, but constantly bursting with energy and interest. A-III (R)

Harder They Fall, The (1956) Crooked fight promoter Rod Steiger hires veteran sportswriter Humphrey Bogart to build interest in a musclebound Argentinian boxer who's being set up to lose big. Director Mark Robson gets convincing performances from a strong cast in an adaptation of Budd Schulberg's novel about the callous types behind the brutal fight racket. Some menace and stylized ring violence. A-II (br) 15

Hardly Working (1981) Jerry Lewis directs as well as stars in the role of an out-of-work circus clown who tries to hold down a string of varied jobs, ranging from chef to postman, with predictably disastrous results. As usual in his comedies, there are some genuinely funny moments, but otherwise this is for die-hard Lewis fans only. Some mild and incidental profanity. A-II PG

Hardware (1990) Horrific sci-fi tale in which a scrap metal sculptress (Stacey Travis) is given discarded robot parts by her lover (Dylan McDermott), unaware that the parts will reassemble into a rampaging, merciless killer-cyborg. Writer-director Richard Stanley captures the stark ugliness of a ravaged, futuristic society, but his nihilistic story concentrates on constant, unrelenting gore. Excessive violence, an extended sex scene with nudity, recreational drug use and rough language. O (R) 18

Harlan County, U.S.A (1977) Filmed during a bitter 13-month coal strike in eastern Kentucky, the documentary examines the strike's origins, the working and living conditions of the miners and the violence that breaks out between the pickets and the strikebreakers. Though flawed by a clumsy narrative structure that is sometimes confusing, filmmaker Barbara Kopple's stirring picture of the still-unfinished struggle for labor justice has the raw power of reality and the passion of the worker's cause. A-II (PG)

Harlem Nights (1989) Action comedy set in 1938 Harlem pits black nightclub owners (Richard Pryor and Eddie Murphy) against a bloodthirsty white gangster (Michael Lerner) and his cop henchman (Danny Aiello). Written, produced and directed by Murphy, the uninspired, derivative movie is saved from tedium by nutty running gags from a notable supporting cast (Redd Foxx, Della Reese, Stan Shaw and Arsenio Hall). Excessive profanity, racial epithets, comic violence and suggestive sexual encounters. O (R) 18

Harley Davidson and the Marlboro Man (1991) Ultraviolent action movie about a biker (Mickey Rourke) and a cowboy (Don Johnson) whose bungled armed robbery sets a corrupt banker and a quintet of killers on their trail. Pedestrian direction by Simon Wincer glamorizes trashy macho heroics while rationalizing murderous behavior. Excessive violence, positive depiction of crime as well as vigilante justice, brief nudity and frequent rough language. O (R) 12

Harold and Maude (1971) Bud Cort plays an immature youth who finds a sympathetic older woman to help him grow up in the person of an eccentric woman bordering on 80 (Ruth Gordon). Cort is a neurotic smothered by the love of his mother (Vivian Pickles) upon whom he takes his revenge by acting out all kinds of elaborate fake suicides. Hal Ashby directs with a good photographer's eye, but his emphasis on the cute is out of place. A-III (PG) 15

Harper (1966) Paul Newman stars as a hard-boiled private-eye hired to track down a missing millionaire and his various leads include Lauren Bacall, Shelley Winters, Robert Wagner and Julie Harris. Director Jack Smight's mystery thriller has an intricate plot that sustains interest, solid performances by a good cast and a satisfying pay-off. Restrained violence. A-III (br)

Harper Valley P.T.A. (1979) When the hypocritical board of a small-town P.T.A. sends a nasty letter to a fun-loving widow (Barbara Eden), scolding her for her behavior and threatening to expel her daughter from junior high school, they get much more than they bargained for. Based upon a hit song of the late 1960s, this unsophisticated comedy is standard drive-in fare, though the actors add an enjoyable zest to the proceedings. Some vulgar and risque humor. A-III (PG)

Harrad Experiment, The (1973) James Whitmore plays the dean of an experimental coed college at which controlled group experience in premarital sex is the major item of the curriculum. Directed by Ted Post, the movie has much unintentional comedy, but its message of sexual indulgence as primal cure for all attitudinal problems comes off as such sentimental hogwash that only the most naive college freshman will be deceived. Some nudity. O (R)

Harrad Summer (1974) Those boring, sexually liberated students from Harrad are adrift for the summer and two couples travel together as a quartet, keeping their respective journals as summer homework. Directed by Steven H. Stern, the result is low-grade exploitation that will disappoint the voyeur trade and put everyone else to sleep. O (R/PG)

Harry and Son (1984) Meant to be a warm-hearted comedy that tugs at the heart-strings, this woeful misfire about a laid-off construction worker (Paul Newman, who also produced, directed and did the screenplay) and his sensitive son (Robby Benson) is painful to sit through. Not the least oppressive element is Benson's insufferably cloying acting style. Aside from some rough language, the movie would be entirely innocuous if the filmmakers had not tried to get some comic mileage out of a sexually liberated secretary bestowing her favors on the heroes. O (PG) 15

Harry and the Hendersons (1987) When John Lithgow and family come across a bigfoot primal creature they name Harry, they try to protect him from the media, the police and a French-Canadian hunter while, along the way, learning a bit about the human links to the animal kingdom. Director William Dear's Northwestern fantasy tale has some violent auto chases but otherwise is a mild-mannered presentation of family values and the virtues of teamwork. A-II (PG)

Harry and Tonto (1974) Art Carney stars as Harry, the 72-year-old retired teacher who, after being evicted from his New York apartment, takes to the road with his cat Tonto, sees different aspects of contemporary American life and reaches California to continue his struggle alone. Written, produced and directed by Paul Mazursky, the subtle, sensitive, bittersweet comedy about old age and loneliness is marred only by the needless inclusion of many vulgarisms that may not be suitable for the young. A-III (R) A

Harry and Walter Go to New York (1976) James Caan is crafty Harry and Elliott Gould is guileless Walter, two safecrackers so inept that, according to gentleman safecracker Michael Caine, "they would require practice to become oafs." But that doesn't stop them from trying to beat Caine to the biggest safe of them all, with the competent assistance of Diane Keaton. Director Mark Rydell's slack, tepid gaslight-era comedy has overcooked a satirical breast fetish scene and some crude verbal gags. A-III (PG) U

Harry in Your Pocket (1973) James Coburn fills the title role as a pickpocket working some of the Northwest's most photogenic watering places in collusion with Walter Pidgeon and Trish Van Devere. Directed by Bruce Geller, it misses as an offbeat crime movie but does offer lovely travelog footage of the posh resorts visited by the gang, and some silly romantic sex and hip humor. A-III (PG)

Harvey (1950) Amusing adaptation of the Mary Chase play about affable imbiber Elwood P. Dowd (James Stewart) whose drinking companion is an invisible six-foot rabbit, which leads to some zany mix-ups when Elwood's slightly dotty sister (Josephine Hull) tries to have her brother committed. Directed by Henry Koster, the comedy is stagy but amiable and centers on Stewart's charming performance as the good-natured eccentric with much goofy byplay from a fine supporting cast, especially the incomparable Hull, Cecil Kellaway as the bemused asylum director and Jesse White as an attendant. A-II (br) U

Hatchet for the Honeymoon (1973) Spanish-Italian movie about a bridal wear designer (Stephen Forsyth) who cannot bear to see his young models leave to get married because at age 12, the poor paranoiac hacked up his mother when she remarried, and ever since—well, never mind. Badly directed by Mario Bava, the bloodier frames have been chopped from the picture, leaving only a stuffy sexual aura to put adults to sleep. A-III (GP)

Haunted Honeymoon (1986) Light and uneventful horror spoof written and directed by Gene Wilder with silly performances by Wilder, Gilda Radner and Dom DeLuise as radio actors. When Wilder develops a strange malady, some of his friends try to frighten him out of it during his honeymoon at his aunt's weird mansion. Slapstick violence and a bit of rough language. A-II (PG)

Haunting, The (1963) Eerie version of Shirley Jackson's novel about Hill House, an isolated 19th-century New England mansion where reports of psychic phenomena are investigated by a parapsychologist (Richard Johnson), a skeptic (Russ Tamblyn) and two potential psychic mediums (Julie Harris and Claire Bloom). Director Robert Wise generates mounting tension from the spooky atmosphere of the long-empty house and the terror of unseen forces lurking within it. Scary proceedings, mostly in the imagination but no less effective for that. A-II (br) X

Haunting of Julia, The (1981) Mia Farrow, playing a grief-stricken mother who has just lost her young daughter in a tragic accident, moves into an old house that comes completely furnished, including just the kind of unholy secret one would expect to find in this kind of place and this kind of movie. Director Richard Loncraine's muddled and tedious movie utterly lacks the inner logic that a good ghost story must have. Some violence. A-III (R)

Havana (1990) On the eve of the Cuban Revolution, an American gambler (Robert Redford) gets caught up in rescuing the beautiful wife (Lina Olin) of a wealthy revolutionary (Raul Julia). Director Sydney Pollack has fashioned an intriguing though overlong love story, bolstered by strong performances and scenes of a decadent Havana overrun by American gangsters. Restrained sexual references, minor violence and occasional rough language. A-III (R) 15

Hawaii (1966) Big, boring movie based on the sweeping epic by James A. Michener concentrates on the struggle between missionary Max von Sydow and the islands' pagan way of life. Von Sydow does as well as possible in his one-dimensional role of religious fanatic, while Julie Andrews is patient and long-suffering and Jocelyne Le Garde is delightful as the Hawaiian ruler.

Though the spectacular re-creates its locale convincingly, it romanticizes the natives and vilifies the missionaries. Some nudity and harrowing childbirth scene. A-III (br) A

Hawaiians, The (1970) Readers of James A. Michener's sweeping novel, "Hawaii," will be disappointed that almost none of its spirit and style has survived in this sequel. Its witless, wordy screenplay avoids every opportunity for action in telling the potentially lively story of the lusty sea captain (Charlton Heston) who brought the pineapple to Hawaii. Though at times showing a nice sense of place, the lethargic direction of Tom Gries fails to do much with his cast. Silly nude bathing scene. O (GP)

Hawk, The (1993) Overwrought British thriller in which a woman (Helen Mirren) comes to suspect her travelling salesman husband (George Costigan) is a serial killer but, given her history of mental illness, the police discredit her story with tragic results. Director David Hayman's attempts to reveal the woman's increasingly shaky state of mind never get far beyond booming music and exaggerated sound effects. Brief violence, some sexual references and intermittent rough language. A-III (R) 15

Hawks (1989) Manic British lawyer (Timothy Dalton) and depressed American football hero (Anthony Edwards), both terminally ill, team up for one last adventure in an Amsterdam bordello but are instead sidetracked into a journey of self-discovery by two offbeat, refreshing women (Janet McTeer and Camille Coduri). Director Robert Ellis Miller's black comedy about death and dying is quirky, bittersweet and poignant. Much vulgar humor, profanity, sexual innuendo and incidental nudity. A-IV (R) 15

Hawks and the Sparrows, The (1967) Italian movie about the human journey on the road of life is a simple but strikingly photographed allegory in two acts that reject both Christian and Communist ideologies in favor of a very earth-bound vision of humanity. Director Pier Paolo Pasolini offers a sketchy probe rather than a finished statement and it is an interesting challenge for seasoned moviegoers. A-IV (br)

Hawmps (1976) The Army's attempt to replace horses with camels in the rugged terrain of the Southwest was ended by the Civil War and the railroad. Director Joe Camp's comic version of that attempt does have its occasional moments, but the humor never gets beyond the level of silliness. The camels steal every scene they're in, and only character actor Jack Elam comes close to out-mugging them. Children will find it fun, but parents may wish for a little less slapstick. A-I (G)

Hazel's People (1978) When a New York hippie goes to rural Pennsylvania for the burial of a student activist friend, he finds himself at home with the simple, anti-materialistic people of the local Mennonite community, but finally leaves to find his own way. What the film lacks in moviemaking polish, it makes up for in sincerity, photogenic locale and superb performances by Pat Hingle and Geraldine Page. A-II (PG)

He Knows You're Alone (1980) Psychotic killer of young brides-to-be is the focus of director Armand Mastroianni's low-budget exploitation thriller. Physical and psychological violence, sexual titillation and occasional profanity. O (R) X

He Said, She Said (1991) Two rival journalists (Kevin Bacon and Elizabeth Perkins) who are live-in lovers analyze their rocky relationship from their separate points of view. As co-directed from the male perspective by Ken Kwapis and from a female vantage by Marisa Silver, the movie's self-absorbed yuppie couple presents a talky, sometimes tacky and insipid look at the war of the sexes. Acceptance of promiscuity and cohabitation and a flash of nudity. A-III (PG-13) PG

He Who Must Die (1957) French drama adapted from the Nikos Kazantzakis novel about the inevitable fate of some Greek refugees in a Turkish occupied village. Whether seen as religious allegory or political tract, director Jules Dassin has made an emotionally arresting motion picture. A-III (br)

Head (1968) Flashy vehicle for the Monkees musical group (Peter Tork, Davy Jones, Mickey Dolenz and Michael Nesmith) juxtaposes a nonsensical melange of scenes against a background chromatically and acoustically gone berserk. Directed by Robert Rafelson, the Monkees themselves are simply four very ordinary young men trying to imitate the Beatles but without the British group's spontaneity and sense of fun. Some tasteless spoofs. A-II (G) PG

Head Over Heels (1979) Minor bureaucrat (John Heard) has had a brief affair with a married woman (Mary Beth Hurt) but, when she returns to her husband, he is obsessed to win her back. Directed by Joan Micklin Silver, the story is told in a series of flashbacks interspersed with scenes of the poor fellow's cheerless present life. All in all, it is a deadly dull affair. A-III (PG) A

Hear My Song (1992) Jaunty comedy follows a conniving London concert promoter (Adrian Dunbar) back to Ireland to lure a famous tenor (Ned Beatty) out of retirement for a reunion with his old flame (Shirley-Anne Field). Director Peter Chelsom's scenic joyride across Ireland is littered with plucky characters, romantic sentiment and broad humor that's as silly as it is charming. Fleeting bedroom scene with nudity, momentary violence and occasional rough language. A-III (R) 15

Hear No Evil (1993) Unaware that a priceless stolen coin has been hidden in her pager, a deaf woman (Marlee Matlin) and her boyfriend (D. B. Sweeney) face mortal danger from the corrupt cop (Martin Sheen) who orchestrated the theft and wants the coin back. Director Robert Greenwald delivers only mild suspense in a thriller which gets sidetracked by a dull romance. Intermittent violence, a discreet bedroom scene, fleeting nudity and minimal rough language. A-III (R)

Hearse, The (1980) Supernatural thriller starring Trish Van Devere who is recovering from a nervous breakdown and haunted by visions of a hearse. Directed by George Bowers, there is some graphic violence and devil worship figures in the plot. A-III (PG) 15

Heart and Souls (1993) Schmaltzy comedy-fantasy in which a yuppie banker (Robert Downey Jr.) becomes the reluctant medium for four strangers (Charles Grodin; Alfre Woodward; Kyra Sedgwick; Tom Sizemore) killed in a bus crash, each of whom uses him to complete some unfinished business before moving on to the afterlife. Director Ron Underwood's tiresome fantasy is as inept as it is doggedly warm-hearted, straining to wring rich emotions out of contrived situations. Some sexual innuendo, fleeting violence and an instance of profanity. A-III (PG-13)

Heart Beat (1980) Anemic screen biography of 1950s' writer Jack Kerouac (John Heard) focuses on his friendship with fellow Beat Generation figures, Neal and Carolyn Cassady (Sissy Spacek and Nick Nolte). John Byrum's simplistic script and direction waste superficial performances and suggest nothing of the force and passion that must have driven Kerouac. Some use of nudity and a muddled moral outlook. O (R) X

Heart Condition (1990) Bigoted slob of a Los Angeles vice cop (Bob Hoskins) is hounded by the ghost of his heart transplant donor (Denzel Washington), a slick black attorney out to protect his heart and solve his murder. Writer-director James D. Parriott skirts over the crime-thriller aspects of the story to focus on the comic antagonisms between the two offbeat characters and, along the way, make some valid points about healthy hearts and racial stereotypes. Some sexually suggestive scenes involving prostitutes, climactic violence and rough language, including racial slurs. A-III (R) 15

Heart Is a Lonely Hunter, The (1968) Sensitive adaptation of a Carson McCullers story about a deaf-mute (Alan Arkin), his frustrations in trying to help others and his friendship with a teenager (Sondra Locke), which is not enough to compensate for his isolated world of utter silence. Director Robert Ellis Miller successfully treads the line between sentiment and sentimentality. A-II (G) A

Heart Like a Wheel (1983) Fact-based story of Shirley Muldowny, who overcame prejudice in a man's profession, achieving success as a racing car driver. But her career triumphs cost heartbreak and bitterness in her personal life. With Bonnie Bedelia giving a wonderful performance in the role, director Jonathan Kaplan catches the human level of the story in moving and poignant fashion. Because adultery figures in the plot, it is not for younger viewers. A-III (PG)

Heart of Dixie (1989) 1950s' Deep-South saga in which a college coed (Ally Sheedy) blossoms from shallow sorority sister into a vocal integrationist under the tutelage of a worldly photojournalist (Treat Williams) who has returned to his home turf to document civil rights activity. Directed by Martin Davidson, the characters in this soapy stew are so thin and stereotyped and the pivotal issues of sexism and racism are so poorly developed that this scattershot tale is best forgotten. Much sexual innuendo, some vulgar references and brief violence. A-III (PG)

Heart of Glass (1978) German movie about a town of glass blowers in the 18th century who find their livelihood threatened when the secret of a unique scarlet glass dies with a master craftsman. Werner Herzog directs a muddled parable so ponderous and dense, so inane in storyline and dialogue that the whole enterprise lies beyond parody. A-III (nr) A

Heart of Midnight (1989) Inheriting a former sex club from her sleazy uncle (Sam Schacht), a disturbed young woman (Jennifer Jason Leigh) hopes to turn it into a classy nightclub but is tormented by unseen demons that seem to haunt the place or her mind. An empty-headed psychological thriller with muddled artsy direction by Matthew Chapman. Includes a brief but brutal rape, sexually suggestive scenes, nudity, profanity, intense menace and gratuitous grisly violence. O (R) 18

Heartbeeps (1981) Dreadful futuristic comedy about two robots who fall in love and run off together is an endless one-joke situation with no place to go. Andy Kaufman and Bernadette Peters have an impossible task as the romantic robots, and the banality of John Hill's script is underscored by the ineptness of Allan Arkush's direction. To be avoided at all costs. A-I (PG)

Heartbreak Hotel (1988) Hoping to cheer up his ditzy mother (Tuesday Weld), a teenager (Charlie Schlatter) kidnaps Elvis Presley (David Keith) after a 1972 concert and the singer rejuvenates the boy's troubled family by injecting some clean-living values, self-respect and hope where none existed before. Though well-intended by writer-director Chris Columbus, the first half of this fable has a decidedly nasty tone. Some rough language and implications of illicit sexual liaisons. A-III (PG-13) 15

Heartbreak Kid, The (1973) Adult comedy about an immature Jewish bridegroom (Charles Grodin) who is stung by a WASP (Cybill Shepherd) on his Miami Beach honeymoon with his ill-fated bride (Jeannie Berlin) is a marvelous but uneven combination of strengths, especially those of Elaine May's deft direction. The movie bristles with telling barbs about contemporary life, some of which are merely entertaining, but many of which are truly enlightening and occasionally frightening. A-III (PG)

Heartbreak Ridge (1986) Flag-waving portrait of a Marine sergeant (Clint Eastood, who also directed), a hardened veteran whose last assignment before retirement is to train a reconnaissance troop for combat. His brutal methods and end-justifies-the-means philosophy supposedly prepare his troop for victory in Grenada. Violent combat footage, scenes of dramatic brutality and excessive profanity and vulgar language. O (R) 15

Heartbreakers (1985) Two friends (Peter Coyote; Nick Mancuso) in the throes of mid-life crisis share everything, even their girlfriends. Shallow, unsympathetic characterizations under the direction of Bobby Roth. Nudity and a graphic sex scene. O (R) 18

Heartburn (1986) Meryl Streep and Jack Nicholson are professionals whose marriage dissolves over his infidelity. Director Mike Nichols' essentially pessimistic view of the contemporary state of romance in the 1980s implies more than it expresses but focuses amiably on the plight of women who must find options to the American male's fear of commitment and responsibility. Adult theme, harsh language and sexual innuendo. A-III (R) 15

Heartland (1981) Poor widow (Conchata Ferrell) takes her 7-year-old daughter to Wyoming in the first decade of the century where she has signed on as housekeeper of a dour and laconic Scotsman (Rip Torn) on a remote ranch. During the long months of a hard and terrible winter, they realize that life would be better together and the rancher proposes marriage. Director Richard Pearce's optimistic conclusion doesn't seem justified by the couple's poor circumstances, but this low-budget effort is unusually effective both in its emotional force and fine performances by Ferrell and Torn.

Extremely realistic birth sequence and some scenes of slaughtering farm animals are inappropriate for younger viewers. A-II (PG) A

Hearts and Minds (1975) Hard-hitting documentary on the Vietnam War avoids the political realities that shaped the conflict and polarized the nation, presenting instead a painful picture of American soldiers lost in a moral quagmire. Director Peter Davis has compiled a selective history of the war as a visceral experience that may touch some hearts and open some minds about the moral paradox that Vietnam represented for the American people. Graphic scenes of battlefield carnage with military and civilian casualties, as well as some explicit scenes of prostitution. A-IV (R)

Hearts of Darkness: A Filmmaker's Apocalypse (1991) Documentary on the making of "Apocalypse Now"—the 1979 Vietnam War movie loosely based on Joseph Conrad's novel, "Heart of Darkness"—shows how the production ballooned from modest-budget project into high-cost epic as director Francis Ford Coppola struggled with his ambitions, complicated logistics on Philippine locations and an incredible run of bad luck. In their fascinating behind-the-scenes account, Fax Bahr and George Hickenlooper make extensive use of footage shot during the course of production by Coppola's wife, Eleanor, and recent interviews with many of those involved in what proves a fascinating account of a creative moviemaker on the edge of self-destruction. Sporadic violence, recreational drug use, rough language and a flash of rear nudity. A- (R) 15

Hearts of the West (1975) Would-be writer of westerns (Jeff Bridges) gets a job in 1930s' Hollywood as a cowboy extra, but on his rise to stardom he has to dodge some crooks who are out to recover the loot he took by mistake. Director Howard Zieff's old-fashioned narrative makes an enjoyable comedy of character and situation, though for a film based on the innocence of its young hero, the needless scene of a stag party with a stripper interrupts the fun and makes it adult fare. A-III (PG) U

Heat (1972) Sylvia Miles, Joe Dallesandro and Andrea Feldman play characters living on the fringes of Hollywood and using sex to help their careers or assuage their loneliness. Director Paul Morrissey has made the "Sunset Boulevard" of independent cinema, but his characters here drown in a heavily convoluted and sexually explicit narrative. O (R)

Heat (1987) An extremely dull and pointless exercise in violent self-defense as Burt Reynolds, playing a compulsive gambler, slays the son of a crime boss and his hired thugs who are bent upon revenge for a previously murderous encounter. Contrasts two kinds of revenge, both equally demented. O (R) X

Heat and Sunlight (1989) Self-indulgent film directed by and starring Rob Nilsson as a troubled photojournalist who agonizes through the last 16 hours of his affair with a dancer (Consuelo Faust). It's not clear why their relationship is on the skids or why he is still depressed by a Biafran photo assignment 20 years before. Graphic sexual encounter with much frontal nudity and some profanity laced with sexual vulgarities. O (nr)

Heathers (1989) Disturbing satire of remorseless, self-serving, compassionless adolescents who seek revenge on equally nasty peers by murdering them and passing off the deaths as suicide. Winona Ryder is excellent as the movie's muddled voice of reason, but her character never quite makes sense nor does the ease with which she conspires with the school psychopath (Christian Slater). Director Michael Lehmann has a feel for teenage narcissism, but this grisly account of it seems pointless. Much intense profanity, teen promiscuity and mocking the value of human life. O (R) 18

Heaven and Earth (1991) Historical epic set in feudal Japan traces rivalry of two fierce samurai (Takaaki Enoki, Masahiko Tsugawa) to become the most powerful warlord of the day. Director Haruki Kadokawa paints a colorful canvas of pageantry and immense battle scenes of interest to armchair warriors and students of Japanese history. Subtitles. Intermittent battlefield violence. A-II (PG-13)

Heaven and Earth (1993) Growing up during the Vietnam War, a peasant girl (Hiep Thi Le) sees her family torn apart and is herself brutalized by both sides, then faces continuing problems after settling in San Diego as the wife of a Marine sergeant (Tommy Lee Jones) suffering post-war trauma. Writer-director Oliver Stone's fact-based dramatization paints a vivid portrait of a woman—and symbolically of her country—victimized and devastated by the ravages of war, but the movie's anti-war theme is overwhelmed by its narrow focus on the lurid and melodramatic aspects of her story. Much wartime violence including rape and torture, brief bedroom scenes and nudity, off-screen suicides and recurring rough language. A-III (R)

Heaven Can Wait (1943) After a lifetime which he sums up as "one continuous misdemeanor," a deceased but still dapper playboy (Don Ameche) seeks accommodations from the Devil (Laird Cregar) rather than applying "upstairs." Director Ernst Lubitsch's zesty comedy of family life in late 19th-century New York makes good use of a splendid cast (Gene Tierney, Charles Coburn, Eugene Pallette and Marjorie Main) and a witty script with a droll after-life fantasy opening and close. Mild sexual innuendo. A-II (br) A

Heaven Can Wait (1978) Charming remake of the 1941 comedy "Here Comes Mr. Jordan," has a past-his-prime quarterback (Warren Beatty) die prematurely, but the bungling angel responsible (James Mason) places him in the body of an eccentric millionaire just as he is done in by his wife (Dyan Cannon) and her lover (Charles Grodin). Enlisting the aid of his former coach (Jack Warden) to get his new body into playing form, the now rich quarterback returns to the gridiron and wins the love of a good woman (Julie Christie). Co-directed by Beatty and Buck Henry, the entertainment succeeds in being very innocent and yet wise and funny. A-II (PG)

Heaven Help Us (1985) The adventures of four desperate misfits in a Catholic boys' school in 1965 Brooklyn. Though Catholic education of the era does take its lumps, the underlying feeling is one of affection. Written by Charles Purpura and directed by Michael Dinner, the movie is flawed, especially with regard to its fragmented storyline, but the overall result is moderately entertaining. Some rough language and sexually oriented humor. A-III (R)

Heaven with a Gun (1969) Glenn Ford plays a gunslinging preacher who mediates between feuding ranchers and sheepherders, punctuating his sermons with gunplay. Director Lee Katzin trades on the family-type western to introduce a sexually oriented saloon encounter, a graphic rape scene and a brief but totally gratuitous nude scene. A-III (M) X

Heaven's Gate (1980) Bloated western written and directed by Michael Cimino takes up the familiar theme of ranchers versus settlers and is set in late 19th-century Wyoming with lavish and exhausting attention to period authenticity. However, the characters are shallow, the story lacks dramatic force and the whole thing becomes a pretentious bore. Extravagant nudity in one bedroom scene and lacks any moral frame of reference. O (R) 18

Heavenly Bodies (1985) Canadian movie directed by Lawrence Dane in which rival aerobic academies face off in a winner-take-all marathon workout. This "Flashdance" clone is so vapid, banal and brainlessly cheerful that it makes the original look like a somber work of art. Excessive sex and nudity and some foul language. O (R)

Heavenly Kid, The (1985) Feeble effort telling of a teenager who had been killed in the early 1950s and sent back to Earth in the 1980s to earn his wings by helping a gawky teen to become a success with the girls. Written and directed by Gary Medoway, the movie is contrived, clumsy, not very funny and manipulatively sentimental. A-III (PG-13)

Heavy Metal (1981) Feature-length cartoon made in a variety of styles and backed by the music of various rock groups offers six sci-fi tales loosely tied together by the appearance of a malevolent green sphere of death and destruction. The animation is far more imaginative than the narratives themselves, which never rise above the elemental level of pulp comic books. Abundance of cartoon sex and violence. O (R) AA

Heavy Petting (1989) Nostalgic, relatively nonjudgmental compilation movie that looks back at the forces shaping and controlling teen sexuality and dating mores during the 1950s. Directors Obie Benz and Josh Waletzky use clips from old sex ed and Hollywood teen films, topical period news and TV footage to catalog the type of propaganda used to contain teen libidos of the period. Incidental explicit sexual terminology and some reminiscences about sexual promiscuity. A-III (R)

Heavy Traffic (1973) Director Ralph Bakshi and producer Steve Krantz animated feature about black and white love in the gritty streets of New York is infantile in technique and scabrous in theme and image. The film seems to have set out to offend just about everybody, and has generally succeeded with a constant flow of racial, ethnic, sexual and religious slurs. O (X/R)

Heidi's Song (1982) Hanna-Barbera's animated, musical version of the popular story about an orphan girl who brings cheer into the life of her grandfather, a crippled child and all sorts of other people, is an entertaining film for younger children. A nightmare sequence in which Heidi is menaced by rats might be rather scary for the very young. A-I (G) U

Helga (1968) German sex education motion picture is too superficial for adults, too detailed for adolescents and has no place in movie theaters. It might have use in a classroom or the home where parents could put the material in a moral context. A-IV (br)

Hell Boats (1970) Routine World War II story about an American (James Franciscus) in the British navy whose difficult mission is to destroy a German base on Sicily that has proven impenetrable from the sea and the air. The focus in on the American's relationship to the men under his command and a romantic involvement with his superior's wife but, though the acting leaves a bit to be desired, action

buffs should be pleased with the special effects. A-III (PG) A

Hell in the Pacific (1968) Two enemy soldiers (Lee Marvin and Toshiro Mifune), marooned on a Pacific island during World War II, struggle against each other until they form a tentative friendship and begin building a raft together. Directed by John Boorman, the cast of two are not only contrasts in culture but also in acting styles and this helps make very watchable what is essentially an allegory on the nature of aggression and the will to survive. A-II (G) A

Hell Up in Harlem (1974) Fred Williamson fights his way to the top as a black mobster before turning onto the straight and narrow and becoming a family man of sorts. Larry Cohen's writing and direction are third-rate and the acting of Williamson and cast is even worse. Excessive violence. O (R) 15

Hell with Heroes, The (1968) Cynical World War II veteran (Rod Taylor) needing cash to bail out the air freight business he started in Algeria, gets involved with a black marketeer (Harry Guardino) and then falls for the criminal's mistress (Claudia Cardinale). Directed by Joseph Sargent, the entirely predictable melodrama has some excessive brutality and sexually suggestive scenes. O (br)

Hellbound: Hellraiser II (1988) Blood oozes from every frame of director Tony Randel's horror movie sequel in which a teenager (Ashley Laurence) is tagged for evisceration by the skinless souls of the nether world who have been released from hell by an ancient puzzle box. Excessive, senseless and repulsive gore, some simulated sex, brief nudity and periodic profanity. O (R) 18

Hellfighters (1968) John Wayne heads an oil well firefighting team whose highly dangerous profession takes them worldwide at a moment's notice, but his worries are about his daughter (Katherine Ross) whose marriage is in danger of winding up like that of his estranged wife (Vera Miles). Directed by Andrew McLaglen, the marital comparisons are strained and of less interest than the grand pyrotechnics of flaming oil wells and vintage Wayne action, including the expected but totally irrelevant barroom brawl. A-II (G) U

Hellions, The (1962) Nasty clunker about a demented outlaw (Lionel Jeffries) and his four brutish sons terrorizing a frontier town and its one police officer (Richard Todd) in 1860's South Africa. Directed by Ken Annakin, the plot is as ludicrous as the acting is hammy. Much senseless violence and some sexual references before the inevitable retribution. A-II (br) A

Hell's Angels on Wheels (1967) Overly violent motorcycle gang movie directed by

Richard Rush exploits sex and brutality for their own sake. O (br) 18

Hell's Angels 69 (1969) Two wealthy playboys (Tom Stern, Jermey Slate) infiltrate the Hell's Angels in order to use them as a diversionary front to pull off a casino heist. Biker girl (Conny Van Dyke) upsets the plan and the rather dull climax of director Lee Madden's cycle flick is bumpy cross-country chase ending in death. Notable only in that the real Hell's Angels tried a stint at acting. A-III (M)

Hell's Belles (1969) A young roughhewn, stoic rancher (Jeremy Slate) sets out alone to retrieve his valuable bike and the girl (Jocelyn Lane) swapped for it, from the lawless gang that stole it. Director Maury Dexter's motorcycle epic features violent action and a moral theme, but the film is too steeped in adolescent rat-pack thinking. A-III (M)

Hell's Bloody Devils (1971) The title characters are beefy motorcyclists in the pay of a German counterfeiter who has a deal with Las Vegas mobsters to help finance a worldwide resurgence of Nazism. Director Al Adamson tosses into this noxious mix some FBI agents, wily blondes and a Jewish woman searching for the war criminal who executed her parents. Much violence and gratuitous sex. O (GP)

Hello Again (1987) Failed romantic comedy about a housewife (Shelley Long) brought back from the dead by an occult incantation of her sister (Judith Ivey) to find that her husband is now married to her best friend. Frank Perry's pedestrian direction of a rather dull and unimaginative script provides few laughs and almost no romance. Some sexual innuendo, vulgar situations and coarse language. A-III (PG) U

Hello Dolly (1969) Zesty New York Jewish widow and matchmaker (Barbra Streisand) gets emotionally involved with a rich client (Walter Matthau). Lavish musical extravaganza is a vehicle for Streisand's melodious talents staged and directed by Gene Kelly with exhilarating, albeit synthetic, Hollywood effervescence. Thornton Wilder's play is memorably infused with Jerry Herman's music. A-I (G) U

Hello Down There (1969) An Ivan Tors production with plenty of marine life to entertain the kiddies, the adventure yarn situates a family with three teenagers complete with guitars in an experimental undersea house to sample living on the ocean floor and save their father's job. Plot centers on how the youngsters will get their music published while down under. A-I (G) U

Hello-Goodbye (1970) Languid European triangle features Curt Jurgens as a baron with a love for antique autos, Genevieve Gilles as a baroness with a roving eye and Michael Crawford as a lover of ladies and fine cars. Millions were spent on the cars, sets and costumes but not a penny's worth of action, dialogue or characterization to break up the sheer boredom. Director Jean Negulesco's agonizing pace makes both the inept acting and slack moral values all the more apparent. O (PG) AA

Hellraiser III: Hell on Earth (1992) Revolting horror tale continues the gruesome killing spree of satanic monster Pinhead (Doug Bradley) as he vies with a TV newswoman (Terry Farrell) over a magical box that can return him to Hell. Director Anthony Hickox fills the screen with an incessant parade of young people being tortured, murdered and mutilated. Excessive dehumanizing violence, crude mockery of religion, a sex encounter with nudity and intermittent rough language. O (R) 18

Hellstrom Chronicle, The (1971) Odd mixture of fascinating yet unsettling documentary footage of insect life in all its forms, from kindly moths and lady-bugs to deadly fire ants and black widow spiders. Unfortunately, the movie as directed by Walon Green, uses scare tactics in arguing that the world is on the brink of an ecological disaster from which insects will emerge as the dominant form of life. Though the information is neither startling nor precise, the insect footage is stunning. A-II (G)

Help! (1965) Madcap musical comedy with the Beatles on the run from Oriental religious fanatics (Leo McKern and Eleanor Bron) seeking a ring which Ringo can't get off his finger. Director Richard Lester uses a lot of clever editing but the chase's frantic pace eventually grows tiresome, not that Beatles' fans will mind a whit. Comic menace and slapstick violence. A-I (br) U

Hennessy (1975) Routine thriller about an Irishman (Rod Steiger) who decides to blow up Parliament after seeing his family killed by the British, but trying to stop him are a brutal British police officer (Richard Johnson) and an Irish widow tired of all the bloodshed (Lee Remick). Director Don Sharp works every conceivable variation on the chase, but the thrills aren't there and the result is quite ordinary melodrama. A-III (PG)

Henry & June (1990) Boring dramatization of the adulterous affair between writers Anais Nin (Maria de Medeiros) and Henry Miller (Fred Ward) in 1931 Paris. Director Philip Kaufman's dull and pretentious account alternates Nin's breathless musings about "sexual liberation" with scenes of simulated sex acts, lesbian as well as heterosexual. In attempting to justify a promiscuous life-style, the treatment resorts to explicit depictions of sex and much rough language. O (NC-17) 18

Henry: Portrait of a Serial Killer (1990) Former cellmates (Michael Rooker and Tom Towles) team in videotaping the tortured death throes of their random victims until one murderer kills the other. Director John McNaughton's pointless exercise in sadistic mayhem is little more than a voyeur's guide to psychopathic behavior. Excessively graphic scenes of brutal slayings, torture, dismemberment, rape and necrophilia. O (nr) 18

Henry V (1989) This version of the Shakespeare play features a powerful performance by Kenneth Branagh in the title role and makes good use of close-ups to bring intimacy and immediacy to Henry's mission to reclaim the French throne. Also directed and adapted by Branagh, the St. Crispin's Day speech of unity and the bloody battle at Agincourt are especially memorable, driving home the fact that war is hell and that faith is a strong instrument in survival. Graphic hanging scene and an intense, bloody climactic battle. A-II (PG)

Henry VIII and His Six Wives (1974) Keith Michell gives a memorable performance in a role that spans Henry's entire reign from the boyish energy of the young king to the quiet suffering of an amorous man betrayed by age and disease. Director Waris Hussein turns the historical events into personal drama, with each of the wives getting their fair share of attention, and the result proves as satisfying for the average viewer as for the specialist in Tudor history. A-II (PG) A

Her Alibi (1989) A novelist (Tom Selleck) suffering from writer's block acts as an alibi for a beautiful Romanian murder suspect (Pauline Porizkova) intending to use her as a subject for his next book and they end up falling in love despite their mutual distrust and lack of chemistry. Ineptly directed by Bruce Beresford, it's a poor excuse for a romantic thriller. Mild sexual innuendo, incidental vulgar references and some minor comic-book violence. A-III (PG)

Her and She and Him (1970) Boring French sex exploitation movie about a young woman student, her lesbian lover and the male companion of a homosexual painter, all four of whom offer endless apologies for their devious behavior while engaging in boudoir episodes under the direction of Max Pecas. O (R)

Herbie Goes Bananas (1980) The little car with a personality takes a Caribbean cruise to Panama this time, where it and its young owners become involved with villains looting ancient ruins. Director Vincent McEveety's effort is dismal, the Disney production is substandard and it is hard to see how children would like it any more than their parents. Sprinkling of double-entendres, presumably for adults accompanying their tots. A-I (G) U

Herbie Goes to Monte Carlo (1977) Disney's "Love Bug" Volkswagen with a personality makes a comeback to win the Trans-France car race, a feat complicated by a diamond theft and his falling in love with a sleek sports car. Director Vincent McEveety makes the mildly amusing fantasy with the two cars much easier to take than the human actors (Dean Jones, Don Knotts and Julie Sommars). Strictly for the kids. A-I (G) U

Herbie Rides Again (1974) Sequel to "The Love Bug" with Herbie the lovable Volkswagen back not as a race car but as the well-kept companion of eccentric dowager Helen Hayes who is trying to keep her home from being bulldozed by snarling land developer Keenan Wynn. Directed by Robert Stevenson, it's all lots of witless fun in the standard Disney vein. A-I (G) U

Hercules (1983) Lou Ferrigno, better known as the Incredible Hulk, brings his massive pectorals to the role of the classic strongman, but not even Ferrigno's muscles can hoist John Thompson's languid direction and Lewis Coates's silly script out of the slough of mediocrity. Some mild violence. A-II (PG)

Here Come the Girls (1953) Lame Bob Hope vehicle places him on turn-of-the-century Broadway as a ham actor whose attempts to woo an actress (Arlene Dahl) rile her murderous boyfriend (Robert Strauss). Director Claude Binyon's comedy has a flat script and unappealing characters, despite some good musical numbers with Rosemary Clooney. Unamusing sexual innuendo and comic violence. A-III (br) A

Here Come the Waves (1944) Stale musical comedy directed by Mark Sandrich has Navy recruits (Bing Crosby and Sonny Tufts) at cross purposes romancing twin-sister Wave recruits (Betty Hutton in a dual role). Bing sings, Tufts connives and Hutton gets to play a prim brunette as well as her usual daffy blonde in this wartime morale booster. The usual romantic mix-ups. A-II (br) U

Here Comes Every Body (1973) British filmmaker John Whitmore photographed a week's worth of encounter therapy at California's Esalen Institute where participants are encouraged to remove their clothing as part of the treatment. The mostly young group grope frantically and vituperate fiercely but seem to be acting more for the camera than to learn anything about themselves. Exploitative nudity. O (nr)

Here Comes Mr. Jordan (1941) Whimsical fantasy in which a saxophone-playing prizefighter (Robert Montgomery) is saved just before dying in an plane crash by an over-eager novice angel (Edward Everett Horton) and then has to find a new body in which to live his allotted span. Directed by Alexander Hall, the quest for a suitable replacement may not be very logical but is lots of fun, thanks chiefly to its comic twists, otherworldly special effects and a fine cast, including James Gleason as an incredulous boxing manager and Claude Rains in the title role as the head angel. Not for literal-minded youngsters. A-II (nr) A

Here Comes the Groom (1951) Affable journalist (Bing Crosby) comes home with two war orphans after three years in France to find his long-suffering fiancee (Jane Wyman) about to marry a genial millionaire (Franchot Tone). Director Frank Capra's musical comedy suffers from a surfeit of cuteness, a tired plot and an aging Crosby, though Wyman is surprisingly good in a lightweight role and Alexis Smith scores as a stuffy heiress who learns to unbend. Romantic complications. A-II (br) U

Here We Go Round the Mulberry Bush (1968) British sex comedy in which a 17-year-old lad (Barry Evans) wants to to be initiated into the mysteries of sex, gets involved with a string of girls who are easily available, but when he gets the one pure girl who is not, she turns out to be no better than the rest. Directed by Clive Donner, the predictable course of the story tries to hide behind overdone optical effects and its humor tends toward the sordid. Unnecessary prolonged nude sequence. O (br) X

Here's Your Life (1969) Exceptional seriocomic coming-of-age Swedish film about an idealistic youth's (Eddie Axberg) experiences, beautifully evoked with period and location details, shortly before World War I. Director Jan Troell's gentle, warm and sincere drama reveals the youthful search for the spiritual significance of life, sex and brotherhood. Brief nudity in a sexual situation. A-III (PG)

Hero (1992) After rescuing 54 passengers from a crashed, burning jetliner, a small-time crook (Dustin Hoffman) is cheated out of a million-dollar reward when a homeless man (Andy Garcia) takes credit and is lionized by a TV reporter (Geena Davis). Director Stephen Frears' stylish comedy about heroism and media manipulation blends its flawed characters into an intricate plot that is both thoughtful and entertaining. Some morally ambiguous situations and minimal rough language. A-III (PG-13)

Hero, The (1972) Richard Harris stars as an aging footballer with feet of clay who is befriended by a 10-year-old runaway (Kim Burfield). Produced in Israel, the banality

of the script by Wolf Mankowitz is exceeded only by the ineptness of its direction by Harris. A-II (PG)

Hero Ain't Nothin' But a Sandwich, A (1978) Benjie (Larry B. Scott) is a black 13-year-old living with his mother (Cicely Tyson) and grandmother (Helen Martin) in a Los Angeles ghetto and his inability to accept his mother's lover (Paul Winfield) leads to school problems, the wrong companions and drug addiction. Produced by Robert Radnitz and directed by Ralph Nelson, the movie deals realistically with the ghetto environment whose problems go far beyond those of drugs, but it does so from a perspective of hope and human potential. Some coarse street language and the depiction of Benjie shooting heroin and the agony of withdrawal. Good for parents to see with their older children and discuss afterwards. A-III (R/PG appeal)

Hero and the Terror (1988) Los Angeles detective (Chuck Norris) comes up against a psychotic murderer (Jack O'Halloran) of almost superhuman strength. Director William Tannen attempts to turn karate champ Norris into a sensitive, reluctant hero whose lady love (Brynn Thayer) and their new baby are as important as his job, but it just doesn't wash. Numerous graphic neck-breaking scenes, gruesome half-naked corpses, the hero's unwed union and some locker-room language. O (R)

Hero at Large (1980) Disarming romantic comedy about a struggling young actor (John Ritter) who, returning from a job still dressed in a superhero costume, routs a pair of thugs robbing a grocery, becomes a media celebrity and is then exploited by a smooth public relations man (Bert Convy). Director Martin Davidson's contrived story runs out of invention about two-thirds of the way through, but it has the prime asset of Ritter's warm appeal in the role and Anne Archer is extremely likable as the disdainful neighbor eventually won over by his charm and decency. Despite its melodramatic ending, the comedy has a generous amount of good humor and the romance is unabashedly sentimental. Occasional burst of rough language. A-II (PG) A

Heroes (1977) Henry Winkler plays a mentally disturbed Vietnam War veteran who treks cross-country with Sally Field to meet old buddies and set up a worm farm. Director Jeremy Paul Kagan tries for seriocomic social relevance but manages only some underdeveloped ideas about the psychic toll wrought by war. Violent fight scene makes this less suitable for youngsters. A-III (PG) AA

Heroes of Telemark, The (1966) Norwegian resistance fighters (Kirk Douglas, Richard Harris and Ulla Jacobson) try to stop the

Nazis from developing the atom bomb. Director Anthony Mann accomplishes a lot with the action scenes, but the storyline keeps getting in the way. Stylized violence. A-II (br) U

Hester Street (1975) Lively tale of Jewish immigrant life in New York's Lower East Side just before the turn of the century tells of the conflict between a husband (Steven Keats) who wants to forget all traces of his origins and his wife (Carol Kane) who refuses to abandon the Russian Jewish traditions in which she was raised. Directed by Joan Micklin Silver, it is a film to be seen as a piece of Americana but also to be savored for the many brilliant little scenes that comprise a pulsating mosaic of the immigrant experience shared by so many Americans of diverse national origins. A-III (PG) U

Hex (1973) Motorcycle gang led by Keith Carradine falls upon a little Nevada town on their way to California but is decimated by two comely farm girls (Hilarie Thompson and Tina Herazo). The year is 1919 and the girls are daughters of an Indian medicine man whose legacy to them is the power of witchcraft. Directed by Leo Garen, the unintentionally comic proceedings are distinguished only by its attempt to an erotic atmosphere that is as silly as it is unnecessary. O (PG)

Hexed (1993) Crude spoof of violent thrillers in which a bored hotel clerk (Arye Gross) assumes a fake identity and gets romantically involved with a homicidal model (Claudia Christian). Writer-director Alan Spencer's emphasis on shrill, vulgar and nasty humor is a cheap substitute for comic wit. Extended sex scene, much nudity and rough language and frequent comic violence. O (R)

Hey Good Looking (1982) Animated feature by Ralph Bakshi about juvenile gang warfare in Brooklyn in the 1950s is extremely ugly and distasteful. It has an unremitting emphasis upon sex and violence. O (R) 18

Hi, Mom! (1970) After failing as a porno-filmmaker, a serious young lad (Robert De Niro) finds success as an urban guerrilla. Director Brian De Palma's movie is a put-on put-down of present American customs and culture. However, its clumsy satirization of contemporary fads and fashions will also outrage the moral sense of some of its viewers. O (R) AA

Hickey and Boggs (1972) When Los Angeles private-eyes Bill Cosby and Robert Culp take a simple case of finding a missing person, they are soon embroiled in a sticky mess involving murder, a fortune in stolen currency, Chicago bank robbers, the Mafia, brutal cops and black militants. Also directed by Culp, the movie starts promisingly enough but soon bogs down in plot complications and ends on a bitter, hopeless note. Hard-edged look at the tribulations of crime-fighting, it is extremely violent. A-IV (PG) AA

Hidden, The (1987) An alien inhabits the bodies of a series of individuals, turning them into homicdal maniacs until it is finally stopped by a good alien (Kyle MacLachlan) and a Los Angeles detective (Michael Nouri). Jack Sholder directs all the mayhem with mindless gusto. Excessive violence, brief nudity and rough language. O (R) 18

Hidden Agenda (1990) Fictionalized though fact-based political thriller about a British policeman (Brian Cox) sent to Belfast to investigate the slaying of an American civil rights lawyer (Brad Dourif) by Ulster security forces whom he discovers are systematically terrorizing the populace with the secret complicity of the British government. Director Ken Loach's chilling indictment of British policy in Northern Ireland is fueled by republican sympathies, but there is little reference to the I.R.A.'s men of violence to balance its picture of Orange fanaticism and a heavy-handed ending about a fascist conspiracy among Britain's top leaders. Some graphic violence and brutalizing tension, a few instances of rough language and references to an illicit sexual relationship. A-III (R) 15

Hide in Plain Sight (1980) Taut, fact-based story about a divorced factory worker (James Caan) whose two small children disappear when the government gives a new identity to his ex-wife's new husband who has turned state's witness against the mob. Also directed by Caan, the emphasis is upon characterization rather than action and the acting is uniformly convincing. The measure of its success is its ability to convey an authentic sense of reality with but the most sparing use of violence and rough language. A-II (PG)

Hideaways, The (see: "From the Mixed-Up File of Mrs. Basil E. Frankweiler").

Hiding Place, The (1975) Interesting story of two Dutch Christians, Corrie and Betsie ten Boom, who gave shelter to Jews during the Nazi occupation but, when discovered, one of them (Julie Haris) was sent to her death in Ravensbruck, while her sister (Jeannette Clift) was released by mistake. Produced by Billy Graham's World Wide Pictures and directed by James F. Collier, the movie is quite well done, though the script belabors the theological questions raised by the evil of fascism to the point of becoming preachy. Harsh violence. A-III (PG)

High Anxiety (1978) Mel Brooks spoof of suspense thrillers has Brooks as the new director of the Institute for the Very, Very Nervous, the unwitting target of a staff (Harvey Korman and Cloris Leachman) who want him out of the way so they can continue to rip off wealthy patients. Though dedicated to Hitchcock, the entirely predictable plot consists of one liners, outrageous slapstick and a mixture of sexual and tasteless humor that some may find offensive. A-IV (PG) A

High Commissioner, The (1968) Entertaining crime melodrama in which Rod Taylor plays an Australian policeman sent to London to arrest his country's leading diplomat (Christopher Plummer) for murder but thwarts a plot to assassinate him instead. Directed by Ralph Thomas, the action holds one's attention, the acting is more than adequate and it accomplishes its purpose of painless diversion. Stylized violence. A-III (br)

High Fidelity—The Adventures of the Guarneri String Quartet (1989) The musicians who comprise the oldest and most successful string quartet performing today are the subject of a spirited documentary in which the four men recall how they met and how they've managed to co-exist and flourish as a team for 25 years. Director Allan Miller offers a relaxed blend of biography, backstage banter, bickering and virtuoso performances that most fans of good music will enjoy. Some mild profanity. A-II (nr)

High Heels (1991) Unappealing Spanish melodrama about an estranged mother and daughter (Marisa Paredes and Victoria Abril), both of whom are suspected of murdering the daughter's husband (Feodor Atkine) who was also the mother's lover. None of the sappy, manufactured emotions rings true in writer-director Pedro Almodovar's kinky soap opera whose comic overtones fall distinctly flat. Subtitles. Brief sex scene with fleeting nudity plus lesbian and sexual references. A-III (R) 18

High Hopes (1989) Low-key British satire focuses on one working-class couple (Ruth Sheen and Philip Davis) and their interaction with family members and wealthy neighbors who don't share their concern about economic reform. Writer-director Mike Leigh offers an especially savage portrait of nouveau riche relatives, snooty yuppies and a painfully real family dynamic in which communication and love play minimal roles. Some rough language laced with sexual vulgarities, brief abuse within an adulterous liaison and a common-law cohabitation. A-IV (nr) 15

High Noon (1952) Message Western in which a veteran sheriff (Gary Cooper) is left on his own to face four vengeful gunmen when the citizens of the town he had freed of outlaws refuse to get involved. Tautly directed by Fred Zinnemann, the isolated frontier setting is used to probe the psychology of fear which immobilizes a law-abiding community before the inevitable showdown whose outcome will affect them all. Stylized violence. A-II (br) U

High Plains Drifter (1973) Clint Eastwood directs and stars in a pretentious, if not perverse tale of a stranger with no name who destroys a town for its cowardly collaboration in the murder of a marshal opposing the local mining company's appropriation of federal land. Eastwood's celebration of sadistic vengeance applied by an individual outside the law features repeated graphic brutalities and a sexist attitude toward women, in particular the male fantasy that women cannot fail to respond to rape. In short, an utterly despicable movie. O (R) 18

High Risk (1981) American adventurers (James Brolin, Bruce Davison and Cleavon Little) meddle in the affairs of a Latin American drug ring in a trite melodrama directed by Stewart Raffill. Excessive violence. O (R) AA

High Road to China (1983) Spoiled rich girl Bess Armstrong, 1920s' vintage, hires hard-drinking, disillusioned World War I ace Tom Selleck to fly her from Turkey to China to find her father (Wilford Brimley) who has disappeared in the midst of a civil war. Jack Weston is good as Selleck's mechanic-sidekick and Brian Blessed scores as a vividly nasty war lord. Director Brian G. Hutton's consistently entertaining adventure movie does not rely upon sex and extravagant violence to keep the viewers interest. A-II (PG)

High Spirits (1988) When an impoverished Irish nobleman (Peter O'Toole) attempts to save his rotting, debt-ridden ancestral castle by luring American tourists with a promise of ghostly sightings, he doesn't bargain for the arrival of the real ghosts of his ancestors (Daryl Hannah and Liam Neeson) who meet and co-mingle with his guests. Writer-director Neil Jordan's noisy, haphazard farce has few likeable characters and the sexual co-mingling of humans and ghosts is a tad dopey. Much foul language laced with sexual vulgarities, explicit sexual seduction and the implied deflowering of a would-be priest. O (PG-13)

High Street (1977) Belgian movie of the Holocaust that has the haunting central figure of a woman (Annie Cordy) whose Jewish husband was taken one night to the camps and their child killed in the confusion. Twenty years later, living in a Brussels slum and regarded as a harmless eccentric, she awaits her husband's return, irrationally screaming profanities at passersby, until an expatriate American artist (Mort Shuman) befriends her and shares her plight with the world. Told simply but with emotional directness, director Andre Ernotte's powerful indictment of people's unconcern for the suffering of others is an eloquent reminder of the indifference that made the Nazi camps a tragic part of human history. A-III (nr)

High Time (1960) Tired vehicle for Bing Crosby in the role of the wealthy founder of a burger-restaurant chain who goes back to school as a 51-year-old college freshman and proves he's not too old to make the grade scholastically or romantically with French prof Nicole Maurey. Director Blake Edwards injects some energy through zippy montages of college life, concluding with Crosby's sappy but soaring graduation valedictory. Youthful hijinks and frolicking co-eds. A-I (br) U

High, Wild and Free (1968) Fairly interesting documentary about fishing and hunting in British Columbia and Alaska with sportsman Gordon Eastman as the guide, director and narrator. The emphasis is on the beauty of nature, conservation and ecology. A-I (br)

High Wind in Jamaica, A (1965) Some children fall into the hands of pirates (Anthony Quinn and James Coburn) who see to it that they are unharmed in the hazardous events that follow. Director Alexander Mackendrick's exciting adventure is an excursion into the uncertain world of childish logic but the action is too intense for younger children. A-II (br)

Highlander (1986) Action adventure fable of good conquering evil offers a positive hero (Christopher Lambert) as one of group of immortals who must battle to the death throughout history until only one survives. Director Russell Mulcahy's mix of action and diverse period settings lift the movie somewhat above the average for this kind of escapist fantasy. Some foul language, brief nudity and several less than realistic decapitations. A-III (R) 15

Highlander 2: The Quickening (1991) Attempting to release the Earth from the force shield destroying its atmosphere, two extraterrestrials (Christopher Lambert and Sean Connery) are confronted by an archenemy (Michael Ironside) from their home planet. The dark, flashy visuals and overused special effects in director Russell Mulcahy's lame sequel only magnify the wooden acting and plot incoherences. Intermittent violence and minimal rough language. A-III (R) 15

Highway 61 (1992) Drug-smuggling roadie (Valerie Buhagiar) cons a naive musician (Don McKellar) into driving a corpse from Ontario to New Orleans, then meet enroute a devil-obsessed crackpot (Earl Pastko) who steals the body. Director Bruce McDonald's surreal vision of America is an exasperating assortment of lost souls on the road to nowhere. Brief sexual encounter, momentary nudity, minimal violence and occasional rough language. A-III (R)

Hill, The (1965) World War II British military prison is the setting for a story of human injustice with Sean Connery as a prisoner who bucks the system and Harry Andrews as the chief warder. Sidney Lumet directs a tightly wound script that is a brutal, agonizing experience, yet a meaningful one. A-IV (br) X

Hills Have Eyes, The (1977) Amateurish little horror about a family on a trip who are attacked by some very nasty people but whom they eventually beat at their own game. Director Wes Craven overdoes the blood and gore. O (R) X

Hills Run Red, The (1967) Bottom-drawer Italian Western directed by Lee W. Beavers (aka Carlo Lizzani) tells of an ex-Confederate soldier (Thomas Hunter) seeking vengeance on a double-crossing compatriot. The usual assortment of meaningless violence. A-III (br)

Hindenburg, The (1975) Based upon the ill-fated last voyage of the famous German zeppelin in May 1937, the movie half-heartedly proposes that the disaster was caused by anti-Nazi sabotage. Director Robert Wise's thin plot and its Grand Hotel collection of passengers is of less interest than the majestic airship in flight (the special effects are quite effective). The final tragedy is too intense for youngsters. A-II (PG) A

Hired Hand, The (1971) Offbeat, sensitive and quiet little western directed by and starring Peter Fonda. The tale of a young man turning away from his life as a drifter in order to return to the wife, child and farm he deserted years before is probably too slow for most western fans. But those who stick with it will find the movie rewarding in the way it attempts to sort out human values and relationships. Warren Oates as Fonda's sidekick gives a subtle performance and figures in a gentle resolution that follows a climactic outburst of frontier violence. A-III (GP) AA

Hireling, The (1973) Superb British screen version of the L. P. Hartley novel about a high-born lady (Sarah Miles) recovering from a breakdown who hires a brooding World War I veteran (Robert Shaw) to drive her to her mother's house in Bath. Thus begins a slow and somber character study that under the painstaking direction of Alan Bridges results in a painful awareness of the tragic limitations of a class-conscious society. Mature themes. A-III (PG)

His Double Life (1933) Famous English painter (Roland Young) lets the public believe him dead in order to settle down to a life of domestic bliss with a devoted wife (Lillian Gish)—until his new paintings give him away. Directed by Arthur Hopkins, the dated satire has some good moments, such as attending his own funeral at Westminster Abbey and his trial as forger and bigamist, but it's mostly a pedestrian affair. A-III (br)

History of the Blue Movie, A (1970) Blurry 16mm stag films are not only hard on the eyes but quite deadening to the spirit, especially when accompanied by dreary, pseudo-sociological commentary. Alex de Renzy's compilation is really nothing more than a long advertisement for the more technically proficient pornography that he is in the business of putting out. O (nr)

History of the World, Part I (see: "Mel Brooks' History of the World, Part I").

Hit! (1973) Billy Dee Williams plays a hard-nosed federal agent whose daughter's death from an overdose determines him to mastermind a plot to exterminate the entire drug syndicate of Marseilles. Director Sidney J. Furie's movie uses all the essential story devices of the traditional detective movie but needlessly laced with casual sex, nudity and rough language. O (R) X

Hit Man (1973) Bernie Casey plays a hood stalking the killer of his brother through some of the seamier sites of East Los Angeles where his quest takes him into the arms of some of the ghetto's most unliberated but libidinous ladies. George Armitage's sharp direction is well above black exploitation standards, but it is squandered in a plot featuring graphic sex and super-graphic violence. O (R)

Hitcher, The (1986) Homicidal maniac (Rutger Hauer) terrorizes a teenage driver (C. Thomas Howell) who has unwisely given him a lift one rainy night on a lonely southwestern highway. Director Robert Harmon makes excessive use of violence and scenes of bloodshed to propel the narrative to its gory conclusion. O (R) 18

Hitchhikers, The (1973) Pregnant runaway (Misty Rowe) finds happiness with a group of hippies who subsist by seducing and robbing lonely motorcyclists. Its a bum trip of sex and violence from low-budget filmmakers Ferd and Beverly Sebastian. O (R)

Hitler: The Last Ten Days (1973) The paradox of this movie directed by Ennio de Concini is that, while it is very well made and has an excellent performance by Alec Guinness as Hitler, it misses the boat historically by getting all the details right but without giving them the meaning of their context. The result is a faithful but impossibly constricted dramatization that re-duces a genuine monster to a figure of morbid curiosity and becomes little more than a footnote to a much more complex and significant chapter of human history. A-II (PG) A

HMS Defiant (see: "Damn the Defiant!").

Hoa-Binh (1971) Low-key French drama about life in a Vietnamese village as seen through the eyes of an 11-year-old boy. The child, who has never known a day of peace, loses his sick mother to death, and all that keeps the boy going is his hope that some day he and his sister will be reunited with their father who is presumed to have joined the Viet Cong. Directed by Raoul Coutard, it is a film of compassion and not polemics. A-II (GP)

Hocus Pocus (1993) Three witches (Bette Midler, Sarah Jessica Parker and Kathy Najimy), brought back to life in a Halloween prank by teenagers, scour a New England village for children whose life force they need to survive beyond the break of day. Directed by Kenny Ortega, the spooky comedy misfires by lavishing its attention on ghoulish special effects, rather than the contrived predicaments of silly youngsters and dopey adults. Multiple vivid frights and some sexual innuendo. A-II (PG)

Hoffa (1992) Key moments in the career of Teamster Union boss Jimmy Hoffa (Jack Nicholson) are recalled by a long-time aide (Danny DeVito) as they wait for a meeting with a powerful crime lord (Armand Assante) on the last day of their lives. Also directed by DeVito, the energetic but erratic production has its center in Nicholson's convincing performance as a man of action, equally willing to use his fists or cut a deal to achieve his ends, but precisely what they were and what Hoffa wanted out of life remains an enigma. Some graphic violence, several sexual situations, brief nudity and recurring rough language. A-III (R) 15

Hold Me, Thrill Me, Kiss Me (1993) After accidentally killing his girlfriend (Sean Young), a thief (Max Parrish) hides out in a trailer park, where he gets involved with a crude stripper (Andrea Naschak), her younger sister (Adrienne Shelly) and other nasty types. Writer-director Joel Hershman's vicious comedy is a degrading parade of mean-spirited characters in ugly relationships that are pointedly unfunny. Much promiscuity and rough language, comic depiction of murders and frequent nudity. O (nr)

Hold On (1966) Mindless youth film directed by Arthur Lubin about a rock music group is utterly innocuous and eminently forgettable. A-I (br)

Hold That Co-Ed (1938) Wacky comedy in which a governor (John Barrymore) running for the Senate bets the election on the outcome of a college football game in which a woman student (Joan Davis) makes the key play. Directed by George Marshall, there's a little bit of romance (George Murphy-Marjorie Weaver and Jack Haley-Davis), some musical numbers and a lot of funny business with Barrymore as a flamboyant politician. A-I (br)

Hold That Ghost (1941) In one of their better efforts, Bud Abbott and Lou Costello are part of a group of strangers (including Richard Carlson, Joan Davis and Marc Lawrence) stranded in a spooky, abandoned hotel where a fortune in criminal loot is hidden. Directed by Arthur Lubin, the mystery comedy gets double mileage out of a setting honeycombed with sliding panels and secret passages abetting both the eerie goings-on, including a peripatetic corpse, and the wacky hijinks of Costello and Davis at her best. Comic menace and slapstick violence. A-I (br) A

Holiday (1938) Sophisticated romantic comedy in which an honest go-getter (Cary Grant) becomes engaged to a millionaire's glamorous but materialistic daughter (Doris Nolan) only to discover he's really in love with her more intelligent and winningly down-to-earth sister (Katharine Hepburn). George Cukor directs the Philip Barry play in high style and the fine cast (including Lew Ayres, Edward Everett Horton and Ruth Donnelly) easily ridicule the emptiness of upper-class pomposity in favor of the more substantive values of ordinary people. Entertaining, meaningful fare for all but the very young. A-I (nr)

Holiday Inn (1942) Easy-going musical romance with two veteran song-and-dance men (Bing Crosby and Fred Astaire) who fall for the same woman (Marjorie Reynolds) while performing together in a rural inn open only on holidays. Directed by Mark Sandrich, the slim plot mainly provides an amiable context for Astaire's eye-fetching dance numbers and Crosby's crooning some pleasant Irving Berlin songs, including "White Christmas" for the first time. Romantic complications. A-I (br) U

Hollywood Babylon (1972) Director Van Guylder's movie uses a few photos and brief footage of famous silent film personalities, then dresses up actors of no ability to resemble them and stages reenactments of their reputed escapades. Wallowing in explicit sex sequences, it is solely of prurient interest. O (nr)

Hollywood Blue (1971) Crude compilation of hard-core pornographic footage interspersed with sidewalk interviews of people giving their opinion of the social value of such movies. Sheer exploitation. O (nr)

Hollywood Horror House (1975) Miriam Hopkins plays an aging, former movie star whose reveries are interrupted by a psychopathic visitor (John David Garfield) to her remote Beverly Hills estate. Thoroughly B-grade film with sex and violence directed against women. O (R)

Hollywood Knights (1980) Writer-director Floyd Mutrux's vulgar attempt at slapstick comedy recounts the misadventures of a cretinous Beverly Hills car club on Halloween night. The film's crudity and graphic sexuality are seriously offensive. O (R)

Hollywood or Bust (1956) Anemic comedy about the misfortunes of an unlucky gambler (Dean Martin) while driving from New York to L.A. with an idiotic movie fan (Jerry Lewis), his Great Dane and a shapely singer (Pat Crowley). Director Frank Tashlin fails to get many smiles from the witless clowning of Lewis while Martin's supposed romantic charm has even less appeal than the unmemorable songs. Tiresome sexual innuendo. A-III (br)

Hollywood Shuffle (1987) Writer-producer-director Robert Townsend provides satirical comment on black stereotyping in the movie business while contrasting career aspirations with his character's sense of dignity. The low-budget feature is informed social satire with limited scope but right-minded intention of racial self-reflection. Much profanity treated within the context of streetwise social conventions of the environment. A-II (R)

Holocaust 2000 (see: "The Chosen").

Holy Outlaw, The (1971) Documentary about Daniel Berrigan, Jesuit priest, poet and pacifist, examines the man's personal witness against human indifference and the horror of war. Filmmakers Don Lenzer and Lee Lockwood rely mainly on interviews with Father Berrigan, members of his family, close friends and his religious superior, during a four-month period when the FBI was seeking to arrest him. A-II (nr)

Homage to Chagall: The Colours of Love (1977) Documentary on the occasion of Marc Chagall's 90th birthday pays tribute both to the beauty of his art and the humanity of the artist. With a script based upon Chagall's own writing and featuring hundreds of his paintings, murals and stained-glass windows, director Harry Rasky searches for the vision that inspired their creation, a quest helped immensely by a remarkable interview with Chagall himself. A-I (nr)

Hombre (1967) White man living as an Apache (Paul Newman) is on an ambushed stagecoach with people he neither likes nor trusts and who neither like nor trust him but, in the course of a struggle for survival, he wins their admiration. Directed by Martin Ritt, its story of injustice is brutal in spots but it serves a purpose in this above-average western. A-II (br) A

Home Alone (1990) A large family takes off for Christmas in Paris accidentally leaving behind their timid 8-year-old (Macaulay Culkin) who becomes very resourceful in defending the house against a persistent pair of bungling burglars (Joe Pesci and Daniel Stern). The laughter ebbs and wanes in director Chris Columbus' contrived comedy, but the pace is peppy and family message heartwarming. Minor violence and robbery played for laughs. A-II (PG)

Home Alone 2: Lost in New York (1992) Formula sequel places the resourceful 10-year-old (Macaulay Culkin) on his own in the big city, this time determined to prevent the same bone-brained bandits (Joe Pesci and Daniel Stern) from ripping off a toy store on Christmas Eve. Writer-producer John Hughes and director Chris Columbus repeat their popular comic paces in a similar lively adventure similarly hampered by exaggerated comic violence and cloying sentiment. Much slap-stick violence and some menace to a child. A-II (PG)

Home and the World, The (1985) Indian director Satyajit Ray's screen version of Nobel laureate Rabindranath Tagore's novel set in 1907 Bengal centers on a triangle involving a wealthy and idealistic landowner, his willful and naive wife, and his best friend, a charismatic revolutionary who has feet of clay. Though static and talky, it provides a fascinating glimpse into a bygone era and aspects of human nature that are universal. A-II (nr) U

Home Movies (1980) Failed attempt at a screwball comedy about a high school student (Keith Gordon) who tries to become something more than "an extra in my own life" by turning it into a film about himself with the help of an instructor (Kirk Douglas). Director Brian De Palma's embarrassingly bad movie achieves the level of an almost unwatchable student film exercise. Sexual nature of some of the gags is adult fare. A-III (PG)

Home of Our Own, A (1993) Leaving Los Angeles for rural Idaho in 1962, a penniless mother of six (Kathy Bates) tries to make a home for her family out of a crumbling shack, with the reluctant help of her 15-year-old (Edward Furlong) and the generosity of the landowner (Soon-Tek Oh). Tony Bill directs a gritty, often downbeat story of a loving but dictatorial matriarch who scorns charity as well as religion, but vividly instills the work ethic in her children so the family can stay together under their own roof. Fleeting violence and

sexual innuendo, occasional profanity and the mother's antagonistic attitude toward organized religion. A-III (PG)

Home of the Brave (1986) In a concert performance, composer-director Laurie Anderson offers a musical diversion for the cultivated few who appreciate Far Eastern-inspired pointilist melody, Dadist minimalism and the poetry of alienation. Musically and visually dull, the concert does not demonstrate the potential of its all-digital sound track. A-II (nr)

Homebodies (1974) Handful of oldsters living in a creaking Cincinnati tenement doomed to be torn down rebel against the wrecker's ball, first by sabotaging the encroaching construction sites, then by taking more direct guerrilla actions that culminate in murder. Thanks to a sprightly set of aging character actors (Paula Trueman, Frances Fuller, Peter Brocco), it is a gripping and macabre little slice of black comedy. Director Larry Yust's ending is as grisly as it is illogical, yet its theme that the lives of old people, like those quaint Victorian houses, are all too often wasted in the face of "progress" remains to haunt the viewer. A-III (PG)

Homer (1970) Midwest farm boy (Don Scardino) likes to swill cheap wine, spark his girl (Tisa Farrow), smoke a little pot and bug his dad by refusing to get a haircut and staging a one-man anti-war demonstration outside the local VFW Hall. Before mercifully ending the picture by running away, Scardino manages to sing or listen to enough songs to fill a soundtrack album, which seems about all that director John Trent has on his mind. A-III (PG)

Homer and Eddie (1990) Lovable brain-damaged man (James Belushi) and homicidal maniac with a brain tumor (Whoopi Goldberg) team up in a search for long-lost parents and $87 in stolen cash. Director Andrei Konchalovsky builds no empathy for Goldberg's repulsive role and, despite Belushi's endearing performance, the result is little more than a parade of brain-damaged freaks. Much profanity and some grisly, pointless violence. A-III (R)

Homeward Bound: The Incredible Journey (1993) Left temporarily with a friend, an aging golden retriever (voice of Don Ameche), a sassy cat (voice of Sally Field) and a frisky bulldog puppy (voice of Michael J. Fox) embark on a perilous journey across the wilds of the Sierra Mountains to get home to the family they so desperately miss. In this remake of a 1963 Disney feature, director Duwayne Dunham's lethargic pacing weakens the appeal of a mostly charming live-action animal adventure that stresses perseverance and the importance of family and friendship. A-I (G)

Homicide (1991) Powerful drama centering on an inner-city cop (Joe Mantegna) who belatedly identifies with his Jewish heritage when investigating a murder with possible anti-Semitic overtones. Writer-director David Mamet's riveting action thriller resonates with added layers of depth as the cop faces a moral dilemma that threatens to destroy all that he has steadfastly believed in. Intermittent brutal violence and much rough language. A-III (R)

Hondo (1953) Lean Western about a hard-riding, straight-shooting cowboy (John Wayne) who gives up his independent ways to stand by a woman (Geraldine Page) whose husband has abandoned her and their young son during an Apache uprising. Directed by John Farrow, the obligatory action scenes of fistfights, cavalry patrols and Indian battles are less interesting than Wayne's strong title performance as the mythic Western hero who respects women, children and the Indian way of life. Frontier violence. A-I (br) U

Honey, I Blew Up the Kid (1992) When a two-year-old toddler is accidentally enlarged to a 112-foot giant by his inventor dad (Rick Moranis), he tucks his teenage brother and babysitter (Robert Oliveri and Keri Russell) into his pocket and heads for the bright lights of the big city. Director Randal Kleiser's sequel makes the most of a one-joke premise with amiable characters and amusing special effects. Comic treatment of the destruction and menace caused by the giant child. A-II (PG) U

Honey, I Shrunk the Kids (1989) A nutty professor (Rick Moranis) mistakenly throws out his own and his neighbors' youngsters with the garbage after one of his inventions accidentally shrinks them to a quarter-inch in height. Director Joe Johnston does a great job concocting a backyard full of hurdles, including giant insects, for these miniature kids to conquer on their way back to the house. Very young children may be frightened, but older ones will enjoy the dizzy array of special effects and appealing young actors. Witless parents, some menace and minimal sexual innuendo. A-II (PG) U

Honey Pot, The (1967) Pretending to be dying, a bachelor (Rex Harrison) summons three women (Susan Hayward, Edie Adams and Capucine) from his past and says that one of them will become his sole heir. Intricate plot twists and a murder in his Venetian palace reveal his real motives. Typically witty, urbane performance by Harrison, who also manages to make the cynical and crafty bachelor a touching fig-ure as well. Written and directed by Joseph L. Mankiewicz, the movie's mixture of satire and suspense doesn't quite jell but will please sophisticated tastes. A-III (br) A

Honeycomb (1972) Spanish psychological study of a young wife (Geraldine Chaplin) who is emotionally still a child and of her middle-aged husband (Per Oscarsson) whose chief interest is business. Directed by Carlos Saura, the story takes place over the course of a weekend during which their suppressed marital discontents emerge through dreams, fantasies and murderous games in a destructive pattern worthy of an abnormal psychology textbook. Intense psychological and some physical violence. A-IV (PG)

Honeymoon Academy (1990) Failed attempt at slapstick comedy has a honeymooning ex-State Department courier (Kim Cattrall) and her naive husband (Robert Hays) pursued around Madrid by brainless foreign agents and sinister figures, all searching for counterfeit currency plates that could ruin the U.S. economy. Writer-director Gene Quintano lacks any subtlety in treating cartoonish characters with utterly predictable reactions, strained chase scenes and routine shootouts. Several abrupt deaths and an instance of rough language. A-II (PG-13)

Honeymoon in Vegas (1992) Hours before the wedding, the prospective groom (Nicolas Cage) squares his losses in a Vegas card game by loaning his fiancee (Sarah Jessica Parker) for a platonic weekend with a wealthy, older man (James Caan) who really wants to marry her himself. Writer-director Andrew Bergman's slight comedy uses a convention of international Elvis impersonators as a diverting gimmick but the story sometimes lags behind the laughs. An unmarried sexual relationship, flash of nudity and an instance of rough language. A-III (PG-13) A

Honeymoon Killers, The (1970) Fact-based story of a professional gigolo and the 200-pound nurse he loves as they bilk and kill off a number of female victims responding to lonely hearts club letters. Without any real distinction on the part of the actors (Tony LoBianco and Shirley Stoler) or director (Leonard Kastle), the movie quickly descends into a quagmire of sick, morbidly sexual and violent situations, offensive both in theme and treatment. O (R) 18

Honeymoon Machine, The (1961) Naval officer (Steve McQueen) and computer expert (Jim Hutton) join in a scheme to beat the roulette wheel at a Venice casino but their girlfriends (Paula Prentiss and Brigid Bazlen) and an admiral (Dean Jagger) complicate matters. Director Richard Thorpe's lightweight romantic comedy has a few good moments but should have had more.

Harmless escapist fare. A-I (br) U

Honeysuckle Rose (1980) Boring romantic triangle involves a singing star (Willie Nelson), his wife (Dyan Cannon) and a young musician (Amy Irving). The three principals give good performances but are up against a trite script, uninspired direction (Jerry Schatzberg) and poor editing. Course language, the use of marijuana and an adult theme. A-III (PG) A

Hong Kong (1951) Formula melodrama directed by Lewis R. Foster in which a down-on-his-luck American (Ronald Reagan) tries to steal a valuable statuette from a little orphaned Chinese refugee but the heel is transformed by the love of a Red Cross worker (Rhonda Fleming). Stylized violence and various threats to a child. A-I (br) U

Hong Kong Cat, The (see: "Karado, the Hong Kong Cat").

Honkers, The (1972) James Coburn, free spirit and sometime rodeo performer, returns to sometime wife Lois Nettleton and son Ted Eccles in between one-night stands. Directed by Steve Ihnat, the movie gives no reason why viewers should be expected to sympathize with an aging adolescent loser who is incapable of making responsible decisions or understanding their consequences. A-III (GP) AA

Honky (1972) Black teenager (Brenda Sykes) and a white classmate (John Neilson) fall in love, cut class to hustle some pot, crack up daddy's flashy car and split for the Coast where the girl is raped and the boy beaten to a pulp. Director William A. Graham's story of adolescent folly is a shallow dramatic effort with a matching moral sensibility in its treatment of drugs and sex, teen irresponsibility and parental unresponsiveness. O (R)

Honky Tonk Freeway (1981) Converging on a small Florida town that is trying to effect its own exit ramp from a new superhighway are a dozen or so uninteresting motorists, including some New York bank robbers, a would-be writer, a cocaine-sniffing hitchhiker, a Kentucky waitress and other vacationers. Director John Schlesinger's failed satire of American road culture is an incoherent hodgepodge of silly sight gags and insulting stereotypes. A number of scenes involve casual sex. O (PG) 15

Honkytonk Man (1982) Hard-living, hard-drinking honkytonk singer-composer (Clint Eastwood), accompanied by his 14-year-old nephew (played by Eastwood's own son, Kyle), goes to an audition in Nashville for the Grand Old Opry. A brink-of-death recording session ensures supposedly a measure of posthumous glory. Also directed by Eastwood, there are some good moments, but most of it suffers from self-

indulgence. Not only does the hero go to bed with a 16-year-old girl, but he pays a prostitute to introduce his nephew to sex. O (R) 15

Hook (1991) Enormously elaborate modern fairy tale in which a grown-up workaholic Peter Pan (Robin Williams) is spirited back to Neverland by tiny Tinkerbell (Julia Roberts) to rescue his kids (Charlie Korsmo and Amber Scott) from the dastardly Captain Hook (Dustin Hoffman). Director Steven Spielberg goes overboard on story embellishments, extravagant set designs and dizzying production numbers, almost burying the positive family message in the visual spectacle of his high-flying adventure. Some swashbuckling violence, a juvenile death and brief toilet humor. A-II (PG) U

Hook, The (1963) Tense Korean War moral poser in which a veteran sergeant (Kirk Douglas) and two enlisted men (Robert Walker Jr. and Nick Adams) take a captured North Korean pilot aboard a freighter evacuating their gasoline supply depot, then receive a radio message from headquarters directing them to execute their prisoner. Director George Seaton sustains interest in a situation revolving around an unjust order, military discipline and human nature until the melodramatic, cop-out ending. Much menace and wartime violence. A-II (br) A

Hook, Line & Sinker (1969) Informed by his doctor that he has only a few months to live, Jerry Lewis embarks on a trip around the world in order to indulge his favorite sport—fishing. Director George Marshall's alleged comedy also involves his wife (Anne Francis) and doctor (Peter Lawford) attempting to cash in on the peripatetic fisherman's large insurance policy by pulling a switcheroo in the local morgue. Unfunny stuff. A-II (G) U

Hooker's Revenge (see: "They Call Her One Eye").

Hooper (1978) Aging Hollywood stuntman (Burt Reynolds) faces competition from a young newcomer (Jan-Michael Vincent) who is seeking to displace him, just as he had done to a top stuntman (Brian Keith) 20 years earlier. Directed by former stuntman Hal Needham, the movie is little more than a succession of stunts (barroom fights, car crashes, helicopter jumps, chariot races and so on) set within a film-within-a-film being directed by Robert Klein. Bawdy humor, rough language and seems to justify the reckless endangerment of life for profit. O (PG)

Hoosiers (1987) Dedicated but dictatorial coach (Gene Hackman) leads a small town high school basketball team to the 1952 Indiana state championship while effecting some attitude adjustments in the community and rebuilding his self-esteem along the way. Director David Anspaugh's film recalls and celebrates a vanishing American rural ethic where integrity is everything and winning is the spice of life. Brief instances of mildly vulgar language and a courtside scuffle. A-I (PG)

Hope and Glory (1987) Fine British dramatization about a young boy growing up amid the terror and excitement of the London blitz during World War II Director John Boorman's fact-based re-creation eloquently expresses a child's sense of wonder and hopefulness in contrast to the anxiety-ridden, pessimistic and socially conscious lives of the adults around him. Seriocomic treatment of several restrained sexual scenes and some rough language. A-III (PG-13) 15

Hopscotch (1980) When a veteran CIA agent (Walter Matthau) is demoted by his incompetent superior (Ned Beatty), he goes underground to write an exposé of international covert operations, trying to stay one step ahead of liquidation by the world's spy organizations. Matthau is in top form as the maverick agent and Glenda Jackson is fine as his helpful friend in a highly entertaining chase thriller directed by Ronald Neame. It has intelligence and wit, but also some rough language. A-III (R) 15

Horn Blows at Midnight, The (1945) Trumpet-playing angel (Jack Benny) is sent to Earth to destroy the troublesome planet by tooting a few notes from the top of a New York skyscraper but his good intentions—and two fallen angels—get in the way. Director Raoul Walsh's whimsical fantasy features Benny in a role well-tailored to his deadpan style of comedy but the humor of the situation fades well before the sentimental ending. Apocalyptic premise may be confusing for youngsters. A-II (br)

Hornet's Nest (1970) Trapped behind enemy lines in Italy during World War II, rugged Marine Rock Hudson assembles a rag-tag army of kids too young to join the Resistance but old enough to smell blood, Hollywood-style. Phil Karlson directs an improbable and confused war adventure movie that resorts to several rape scenes and excessive gore, made all the more gruesome by using youngsters in violent, foul-mouthed roles. O (M) AA

Horoscope (1970) Slow-paced Yugoslavian movie about some aimless young men in a sweltering small town on the Adriatic who for want of anything better to do try to seduce a pretty new shopkeeper with tragic results. Without becoming overly moralistic, director Boro Draskovic provides an engrossing vignette of youth trapped in a wasteland of inactivity. A-IV (nr)

Horror House (1970) When Frankie Avalon leads a group of youths in exploring an old house, one of them is killed and the audience is led to believe that the psychopath responsible is the lover of one of the girls, but Frankie finally unmasks the mental case. Directed by Michael Armstrong, there's lots of tension, plenty of false alarms and a couple of bloody murders. A-III (PG)

Horror of Blackwood Castle, The (1973) German murder mystery spoof about a retired ship's captain (Otto Stern) whose apparent demise brings daughter and former crew members to search for pirated jewels. Directed by Alfred Vohrer, its good fun with an intricate, fast-moving plot, a bushel of snakes and scary props, at least three surprise endings and a batch of frisky characters. A-II (PG)

Horror of Frankenstein (1971) When the monster finally appears in this fresh reworking of the Mary Shelley classic, he is considerably less frightening than his creator (Ralph Bates) whose total lack of human feeling is chilling. Directed by Jimmy Sangster with understated black humor, whose tone is established by Dennis Price as a discreet grave robber, this proves to be witty, literate and a cut above the usual horror fare. A-III (R) X

Horror of the Blood Monsters (1971) After arriving by plastic rocketship on a planet remarkably like Earth, astronaut John Carradine tussles with the Tubertons, fang-toothed archetypal vampires. Meanwhile, mission controllers Robert Dix and Vicki Volante take time out to engage in electronically controlled lovemaking. Producer-director Al Adamson has slapped together a flimsy sci-fi adventure that is not worth anybody's traveling time. A-III (GP)

Horror on Snape Island (1972) Archaeological expedition searches a long-abandoned island off the English coast for a Phoenician burial site after some youths are found there slaughtered by ancient weapons. Unfortunately, British writer-director Jim O'Connolly, unable to sustain much suspense with his story, settles for a tacky mixture of nudity and mayhem. O (R)

Horse in the Gray Flannel Suit, The (1968) Weak Disney comedy about the problems of a widowed advertising man (Dean Jones) in finding ideas for his client, a horse for his daughter and a romance for himself. Directed by Norman Tokar, there is colorful photography and some trained horses, but parents will likely find it a long sit. A-I (G)

Horsemen, The (1971) Failed adventure movie filmed in the mountains of Afghanistan about a man who is driven to prove his bravery but in the process loses his leg and ultimately his pride. Directed by John

Frankenheimer, the narrative is incongruous and its movie stars (Omar Sharif, Leigh Taylor-Young, Jack Palance) are ridiculously out of place among the rugged mountain tribesmen. What it offers is plenty of violent action and feats of horsemanship. A-III (GP) PG

Hospital, The (1971) Uneven black comedy about a series of deaths in a big-city hospital whose chief of surgery (George C. Scott) begins to suspect that what is going on is not simply gross medical incompetence but the work of a madman on the loose. Brilliantly written by Paddy Chayefsky and well directed by Arthur Hiller, some of the situations are hilarious, but the feeling is one of giddiness, followed by the bite of terror. Language and uncompromising situations make it for adult patients only. A-III (GP)

Hot Box, The (1972) Philippine production in which four foul-mouthed nurses become tortured objects of lust, first at the hands of jungle revolutionaries who kidnap them, then at the hands of government troops who rescue them. Director Joe Viola simply alternates scenes of nudity with displays of bloodshed. O (R)

Hot Dog . . . The Movie (1984) Featuring Patrick Houser and Tracy Smith, this Animal-House-on-skis is about a rivalry between clean-cut but lecherous American skiers and some sneaky, unsportsmanlike Europeans. Director Peter Markle's mindless diversion features action on the slopes by day and in hot tubs by night. Graphic sex and nudity. O (R)

Hot Lead and Cold Feet (1978) Poor Walt Disney western satire in which twin brothers of markedly different character (both played by Jim Dale) inherit a vast fortune with the stipulation that they engage in a winner-take-all competition. The talented Jim Dale does as well as he can with the script's slapstick cliches and the cast support offered by Karen Valentine, Don Knotts and Jack Elam. But not even children are likely to enjoy director Robert Butler's effort very much; the very young won't understand the jokes and the older children won't find them very funny. A-I (G)

Hot Millions (1968) Deft British comedy in which an embezzler (Peter Ustinov) takes revenge on the computer system that caused his previous imprisonment by setting up phony companies for which he has programmed the computer to make regular payments. Aiding and abetting the comedy are Maggie Smith, Karl Malden and Bob Newhart, with director Eric Till contributing some fine comic visuals and gags. Mild romantic complications. A-II (G) U

Hot Pants Holiday (1971) Harried New York housewife (Tudi Wiggins) on holiday in the Caribbean shares lust with native sex symbol (Christopher St. John), but after a voodoo ceremony as inept as it is lewd, housewife discovers that her native is two-timing her. Directed by Edward Mann, there are no surprises here. O (X/R)

Hot Pursuit (1987) Weak attempt to build romance around the madcap efforts of a college student (John Cusack) to catch up to his girlfriend's vacationing family stretches credibility. Director Steve Lisberger's contemporary comedy adventure set in the West Indies has some ambiguities about drugs, premarital sex and heroism that are further obscured by improbable plot devices and concluding gunplay. A-III (PG-13) 15

Hot Rock, The (1972) Lighthearted caper in which four bumbling crooks (Robert Redford, George Segal, Ron Leibman and Paul Sand) are hired by an African diplomat (Moses Gunn) to steal a huge uncut diamond that was taken from his country and now resides inside a heavily guarded display case in the Brooklyn Museum. Directed by Peter Yates, the fast-paced entertainment has a number of intriguing twists, but Gunn and Zero Mostel steal the picture in their supporting roles. A-II (GP) U

Hot Rod Action (1969) Feature documentary celebrating America's penchant for speed and danger uses footage from Indianapolis, Daytona and other speedways without commentary or narrative structure. For racing car buffs and anthropologists. A-I (G)

Hot Shots! (1991) Mildly entertaining spoof has daredevil Navy pilot (Charlie Sheen) rescuing a jinxed mission under the bumbling command of a scatterbrained admiral (Lloyd Bridges). Director Jim Abraham's lightweight comedy doesn't stay aloft long with leaden Sheen in the cockpit and the helter-skelter inclusion of unrelated scenes spoofing other movies. Intermittent sexual innuendo, minor slapstick violence and an instance of rough language. A-III (PG-13) 12

Hot Shots! Part Deux (1993) Goofy spoof in which a love-scarred Marine (Charlie Sheen) heading a hostage-rescue mission in the Middle East stumbles upon an old flame (Valeria Golino) in the thick of the fray which turns into an assassination plot led by the numbskull U.S. President (Lloyd Bridges). Director Jim Abrahams' silly but scrappy sequel is a potluck grab bag of rapid-fire sight gags, spills, shootouts and visual jokes spoofing earlier movies. Much comic violence, a racy bedroom scene, some toilet humor and an instance of rough language. A-III (PG-13)

Hot Spot, The (1990) A bank robber (Don Johnson) falls for a teenage blackmail victim (Jenifer Connelly) while trying to conceal his crime from his boss's sex-crazed wife (Virginia Madsen). Limply directed by Dennis Hopper, the slow-moving narrative lacks the subtlety and character interest needed to overcome holes in the plot. Adulterous relationship, recurring partial nudity, brief violence, occasional rough language. O (R) 18

Hot Stuff (1979) Routine comedy directed by Dom DeLuise, who also has the leading role, about a police burglary task force who set up a phony fencing ring to ensnare thieves and run afoul of the Mafia. Some adult humor and an abundance of profanity. A-III (PG) AA

Hot to Trot (1988) Loony young man (Bob Goldthwait) inherits a talking horse named Don (voiced by John Candy) and, amidst some hair-raising moments, the horse comes up with stock tips and a winning racing form to help out its dim-witted owner. A knuckle-headed insult to Mr. Ed fans, director Michael Dinner's unfunny comedy features some embarrassing performances by Dabney Coleman, Virginia Madsen and Cindy Pickett. Much rough language laced with sexual vulgarities. A-III (PG)

Hotel (1967) Screen version of Arthur Hailey's novel about a New Orleans hotel famous for its old-fashioned hospitality but losing money and facing a take-over. Richard Quine directs an old-fashioned melodrama using the hotel as the site for dramatic events in the lives of those staying there. Standing out among the large cast of stars are Melvyn Douglas as the aristocratic hotel owner and Karl Malden as a sneak thief. Escapist entertainment with some adult situations. A-III (br) A

Hotel New Hampshire (1984) Eccentric New England family (Nastassja Kinski, Jodie Foster, Beau Bridges and Rob Lowe) jokes and cavorts in the face of human mortality in this glib and shallow adaptation of the John Irving novel adapted and directed by Tony Richardson. A kind of absurdest "You Can't Take It with You," it affects a benign view of all sorts of sexual activity, including incest. O (R)

Hotel Paradiso (1966) British bedroom farce set in Paris at the turn of the century has a fine cast (Alec Guinness, Gina Lollobrigida, Robert Morley and Akim Tamiroff) and a plot filled with mistaken identities and broad characterizations. Unfortunately, Peter Glenville's direction lacks the fast pace and timing required by this sort of comedy. A-III (br) A

Hotel Terminus: The Life and Times of Klaus Barbie (1988) Four-and-a-half-hour documentary by Marcel Ophuls about the infamous war criminal termed the "Butcher of Lyons" for his brutal crimes against humanity in 1944-45 France as well as on his work after the war under the protection of a U.S. agency. Relying mainly on interviews with Barbie's victims and co-workers, there are some redundancies and much sarcasm. Explicit recounting of Nazi torture. A-III (nr)

Hound of the Baskervilles, The (1939) The first and one of the best in a series of adaptations of the cases of Sir Arthur Conan Doyle's Victorian detective featuring Basil Rathbone with Nigel Bruce as Dr. Watson. Directed by Sidney Lanfield, the story has mysterious murders on the moors, a baying hound, old cemetery ruins, ancestral curses, eccentric neighbors, a young couple in love and an escaped convict on the prowl. Engrossing and entertaining thriller, but a little scary for young children. A-II (nr) A

Hound of the Baskervilles, The (1977) Failed British spoof directed by Paul Morrissey stitches together a series of wildly eccentric skits with Peter Cook as Holmes, Dudley Moore as Watson and a badly used supporting cast (Terry-Thomas, Hugh Griffith and Joan Greenwood among them), leaving the hound literally to steal the picture. Much sexual innuendo, comic vulgarities and unamusing sallies in bad taste. A-III (nr) A

Hour of the Gun (1967) Standard western about Marshal Wyatt Earp (James Garner) defending Tombstone against the Clantons (led by Robert Ryan) in the famed gunfight at the O.K. Corral. After the bloody shootout, Earp begins taking the law into his own hands until Doc Holliday (Jason Robards) straightens him out. John Sturges directs with a steady hand for convincing action sequences. A-II (br)

House (1986) Director Sean Cunningham's parody of "Poltergeist" has some fun and fright in this story of a divorced novelist (William Katt) who rescues his captive son from angry spirits that are infesting his grandmother's house. Unfortunately, there is excessive gore and harsh language in Vietnam War flashbacks that flow, intermittently, from the hero's memory. O (R) 15

House II: The Second Story (1987) Inventive fantasy with touches of horror in which Arye Gross digs up his ancestor Royal Dano, kept alive for a century by a magical skull. Director Ethan Wiley takes the funhouse approach, which wrecks more terror upon the cast than on the young audience that the movie's weirdness is certain to engage. Brief violence, ghoulish faces and silly female stereotypes. A-II (PG-13)

House by the Lake, The (1977) Four hoodlums terrorize a couple in an isolated villa only to have the woman (Brenda Vaccaro) wreak revenge on each of them. Canadian exploitation movie directed by William Fruet focuses on rape and bloodletting. O (R)

House Calls (1978) Walter Matthau plays a doctor who enthusiastically pursues women after the death of his wife, only to get his comeuppance from an independent-minded divorcee (Glenda Jackson). Director Howard Zieff's tepid little comedy looks like a slipshod reworking of "Cactus Flower" and is thoroughly adult in theme and dialogue. A-III (PG)

House of Cards (1968) Handsome, footloose American tutor (George Peppard) is up against fanatical Algerian ex-patriots. Good wins over evil despite conventional mystery-melodrama trimmings from director John Guillermin who uses the commonplace as a source of horror. Attractively lush Parisian milieu, some spurts of violence and gratuitous, silly attempts at sexual titillation. A-III (G) A

House of Cards (1993) Traumatized by her father's sudden death, a six-year-old (Asha Menina) withdraws into a silent dreamworld from which her mother (Kathleen Turner) tries to extricate her using her own intuitive approach which clashed with the more traditional methods of a skeptical child psychiatrist (Tommy Lee Jones). Writer-director Michael Lessac mixes elements of mystery and near-mysticism in a visually lovely movie that compares medical science unfavorably with a loving mother's desperate attempts to save her child from becoming autistic. A child's emotional trauma and a few scenes of a youngster in mortal danger. A-II (PG-13)

House of Dark Shadows (1970) Movie version of a daytime television series about a family of vampires features Jonathan Frid re-creating his role of Barnabas, the 175-year-old owner of the spooky Collinwood estate, with Joan Bennett and Grayson Hall as residents. Directed by Dan Curtis, the melodrama often slips into a mire of gushing blood and gore amidst all the vampire lore required by die-hard horror fans. Others are likely to be repulsed. A-III (PG)

House of Exorcism (1976) Playing the role of a suave butler in a sinister mansion is Telly Savalas, who seems to be making it up as he goes along, in a standard Italian Gothic horror filled with gore and nudity, and innocent of the least trace of taste or wit. O (R)

House of Games (1987) Eminent psychiatrist (Lindsay Crouse) becomes involved with a con artist (Joe Mantegna) and some of his shady games of deception with disastrous results for both. Writer-director David Mamet succeeds fairly well in conning the viewer with a plot in which nothing is quite what it seems. Some brutal violence, rough language and a restrained bedroom scene. A-III (R)

House of Missing Girls, The (1972) French movie with Anna Gael as a salesgirl who freely exhibits her own contours in a sordid adventure that has her fleeing a band of abusive slavers and finding refuge with a hermit-like musician. Jean-Francois Davy directs the English-dubbed exploitation import. O (R)

House of Whipcord (1974) British sex exploitation movie about a woman (Penny Irving) who is kidnapped and held prisoner by some demented types who torment and degrade. Director Pete Walker's flimsy story is only an excuse for an unhealthy fantasy of sex and violence. O (R)

House on Carroll Street, The (1988) Romantic thriller set in 1951 New York features a gutsy, blacklisted photo editor (Kelly McGillis) who uncovers a politically sanctioned conspiracy aimed at hiding Nazi war criminals in the U.S. Hitchcockian influence poorly realized by director Peter Yates in a stylish-looking but far-fetched film about political hypocrisy, scripted by once blacklisted screenwriter Walter Bernstein. Brief nudity and some graphic violence. A-II (PG)

House on Chelouche Street, The (1974) Israeli movie about a widow (Gila Almagor) in 1946 Tel Aviv who decides to remarry to give her family some security, but her adolescent son (Ophir Shalitan) resents her choice, has a brief affair with an older woman (Michal Bat-Adam) and learns something about adult responsibilities. Written and directed by Moshe Mizrahi, it proves an engaging and interesting portrayal of human problems and makeshift solutions in a time of great turmoil. A-III (PG)

House Party (1990) Grounded by his well-meaning dad (Robin Harris), a black, middle-class teenager (Christopher Reid) is determined to attend a pal's house party. Black director Reginald Hudlin plays up the comic obstacles that get in the way, including a gang of toughs and some buffoonish white cops. Though this growing-pains comedy has a clear anti-drug and alcohol message, it also implies that the kids are sexually active. Nonstop rough language with much sexually explicit dialogue and black rap, some bathroom humor and incidental cartoon violence. A-IV (R) 15

House Party 2 (1991) Vulgar sequel follows a black youth (Christopher Reid) to college, where he discovers his tuition check has been stolen, prompting his playboy buddy (Christopher Martin) to throw a steamy pajama party on campus to raise the needed cash. Producers-directors Doug McHenry and George Jackson inject lots of bouncy energy into the rapping and dancing but the racial and sexual stereotyping defeat the movie's attempt at comedy. Much rough language and sexual innuendo, racial stereotyping, implied sexual encounters, a flash of nudity and brief violence. A-IV (R)

House Party 3 (1994) Vulgar sequel in which a black youth (Christopher Martin) sets up a raunchy bachelor party for a friend (Christopher Reid) after they take money from a music promoter for a singing act they can't deliver. Director Eric Mesa throws together a rap music sit-com whose marginal humor is sexist, mean-spirited and features a trio of very young boys who are casual lawbreakers. Implied promiscuity, partial nudity, many racial slurs and sexist insults, comic violence and much rough language. O (R)

House That Dripped Blood, The (1971) Four tired tales of the preternatural are linked by the weak device of a haunted house that supposedly influences the behavior of its inhabitants. British director Peter Duffell fails to develop the least sense of dread and the only surprise is that the screenplay is by veteran horror writer Robert Bloch. A-II (GP) X

House That Screamed, The (1971) Lilli Palmer plays the turn-of-the-century proprietress of a French finishing school for wealthy girls and, while her 15-year-old son (John Moulder-Brown) pursues the girls, they pursue the local deliveryman. The promiscuous pursuits at the school are finally relieved by several bloody murders but, by then, director Narciso Ibanez Serrador's attempts at horror are lost in a sophomoric sex teaser. O (GP)

Household Saints (1993) Multi-generational story set in New York City's Little Italy, where a superstitious mother-in-law (Judith Malina) frightens her son's pregnant wife (Tracey Ullman), who subsequently bears a daughter (Lili Taylor) so obsessed with serving God that she eventually loses touch with reality as well as morality. Director Nancy Savoca's confusing treatment of the role of Catholicism in the life of an Italian-American family robs the drama both of human credibility and a positive spiritual dimension. A few bedroom scenes, fleeting nudity, a suicide, gory shot of a stillborn baby and superstitions depicted as part of Catholicism. O (R)

Housekeeping (1987) Interesting seriocomic probe into small-town family life in the 1950s tells the story of two girls who, after their mother's suicide, are raised by their aunt (Christine Lahti), a woman of somewhat strange and erratic behavior. Scottish director Bill Forsyth's look at growing up in an unconventional American household, frowned upon by conformist neighbors, is quite often amusing and frequently very touching. The movie's portrayal of the tension between individual and social values may be confusing for children. A-II (PG)

Housesitter (1992) Kooky pathological liar (Goldie Hawn) pretends she's married to an architect (Steve Martin) who hopes to make his ex-girlfriend (Dana Delany) jealous. Director Frank Oz's misguided comedy features perky performances but falls flat with phony motivations and contrived sitcom humor. An implied bedroom encounter and much sexual innuendo. A-III (PG)

Housewife (see: "Bone").

How Do I Love Thee? (1970) Long-suffering, Bible-thumping wife (Maureen O'Hara) desires only to instill a fear of God in her college professor son (Rick Lenz) and to pray for the conversion of her atheist husband (Jackie Gleason) who is fooling around with a client (Shelley Winters). Director Michael Gordon, failing to elicit any depth or purposeful narrative, settles for prolonged and vacuous discussions of religion, remarkably tasteless sexual innuendo and a generally witless sense of the comic. O (PG) AA

How Funny Can Sex Be? (1976) Tedious Italian sex farce starring Giancarlo Giannini in a series of six ribald stories that under Dino Risi's direction vie with one another in lack of wit and general tastelessness and feature considerable nudity. O (R)

How Green Was My Valley (1941) Nostalgic chronicle of family ties based on the Richard Llewellyn novel about a Welsh coal-mining village at the turn of the century trying to maintain its traditional way of life despite changing industrial times and the power of the mine owners. Director John Ford's episodic picture of a community in transition is depicted largely through an emotionally rich, often sunny but sometimes tragic portrait of the close-knit Morgan family and its proud father (Donald Crisp) who rejects his five sons when they join the union, the mediating mother (Sara Allgood) who reconciles them, the daughter (Maureen O'Hara) who marries unhappily when rebuffed by the village's new minister (Walter Pidgeon) and the youngest of the Morgans (Roddy McDowall) recalling the family's past as a grown man leaving his beloved but now-depressed valley. Muted treatment of romantic complications and some stylized violence including the sadistic caning of a youth and a harrowing mine disaster. A-II (nr) U

How I Got into College (1989) Mediocre high school senior (Corey Parker) aims to be accepted by the same top college that his secret heartthrob (Lara Flynn Boyle), the smartest and most popular girl in his class, hopes to attend. Directed by Savage Steve Holland, it's an innocuous, pleasant teen comedy about the very real anxieties suffered by college hopefuls and their parents. Mild rough language and sexual innuendos. A-II (PG-13)

How I Won the War (1967) Unusual British anti-war movie ridicules the military concept of war as a noble game and debunks the cliches and slogans of belligerents. Michael Crawford stars as an inexperienced lieutenant assigned to build an advanced cricket field in World War II North Africa, with John Lennon as the compliant everyman of the unit that deserts at the Rhine. Directed with comic ingenuity by Richard Lester, its pacifist view of war may be controversial but it is neither anti-religious nor anti-patriotic, and it merits attention and reflection. Stylized violence. A-II (br)

How Sweet It Is! (1968) James Garner and Debbie Reynolds star in a comedy-melodrama about a crazy, mixed-up American family sight-seeing in Europe. Basically a happy couple, in the midst of complications caused by their son and his girlfriend, they find themselves on the brink of extra-curricular flirtations. Forgettable froth directed by Jerry Paris. A-III (br) X

How Tasty Was My Little Frenchman (1973) Brazilian movie set in the early colonial times when a Frenchman is taken captive by a cannibal tribe and is held for execution at an upcoming festival. The final horror (and key to the title) in this black comedy is the cheerful smile of the young girl who has been his native wife as she prepares to eat her allotted portion of his dead body. Director Nelson Pereira Dos Santos does not romanticize nor sentimentalize the savages or the Europeans, but neither does his movie miss the joy of life that exists in every culture. Scenes of nudity in this semi-ethnographic movie are without any sense of sexual exploitation. A-IV (nr)

How the West Was Won (1962) Sprawling Cinerama epic tracing the way West from the mountain men (James Stewart and Henry Fonda) to the settlers coming by river boat (Karl Malden and Agnes Moorehead), wagon train (Debbie Reynolds and Gregory Peck) and railroad (Richard Widmark and George Peppard), with a Civil War stopover at Shiloh (John Wayne and Henry Morgan). Mostly directed by Henry Hathaway, with John Ford directing the Civil War sequences and George Marshall the railroad segment, the result is picturesque entertainment, stereotyped history and bloated melodrama, chiefly of interest as a compendium of Western

screen conventions. Some tense but stylized violence. A-I (br) PG

How to Beat the High Cost of Living (1980) Three housewives (Susan Saint James, Jane Curtin and Jessica Lange) conspire to replenish their depleted finances by stealing the money displayed in a huge plastic ball in a shopping center promotion. Director Robert Scheerer's comedy has some tart humor but is pretty mediocre going and sometimes mean-spirited to boot. Adult humor and situations. A-III (PG) AA

How to Commit Marriage (1969) When the daughter of real estate agent (Bob Hope) and his wife of 19 years (Jane Wyman) learns that her parents are about to be divorced, she goes off to live out of wedlock with the son of a cynical agent for rock groups (Jackie Gleason). How everyone, including Gleason and his girlfriend Tina Louise, is eventually legally united or re-united might have been the basis for some good satire, but director Norman Panama treats both his characters and the institution of marriage in a consistently grotesque and sleazy fashion. Though there are a few scattered laughs, this is not a funny picture. O (PG)

How to Frame a Figg (1971) Dim-witted City Hall clerk (Don Knotts) accidentally uncovers some shady dealings by the boys in the back room who promote him to a high-pay, no-sweat job, but eventually he figures out why and then blows the whistle on the corrupt officials. The comedy's humor revolves around the inane personality of Knotts, as well as around the far-fetched situations he bumbles into and out of. Alan Rafkin directs the appropriately juvenile script as if it were an extended TV sitcom. A-I (G)

How to Get Ahead in Advertising (1989) Biting British satire of the advertising business centers on an ad-man burnout (Richard E. Grant) who grows a talking boil on his neck with which he carries on a running debate over the evils of the ad game. Although writer-director Bruce Robinson's work is thought-provoking and technically sound, the satire deteriorates into a manic mad show starring a ghoulish boil. Much profanity, sexually vulgar language and an intense, though humorous, depiction of madness. A-IV (R) 15

How to Make Love to a Negro Without Getting Tired (1990) Offensively titled French-Canadian production takes a lightweight look at racial and sexual stereotypes in Montreal where a black Haitian immigrant (Isaach de Bankole) engages in writing a novel while enjoying the sexual favors of several white women. Based on Dany Laferriere's 1985 novel and directed by Jacques

Benoit, the result is superficially entertaining but rarely thought-provoking and blatantly exploitative in its positive portrayal of casual sex and promiscuity. Several fairly explicit simulated sex scenes, petty thievery shown as fun and minimal rough language. O (nr)

How to Save a Marriage...and Ruin Your Life (1968) Eli Wallach and Anne Jackson play an adulterous couple under investigation by bachelor Dean Martin who mistakenly identifies Stella Stevens as Wallach's compliant girlfriend in a divorce action. Fielder Cook directs a not-so-funny marriage-go-round comedy that goes cheerfully around in circles leading nowhere. A-III (br) X

How to Seduce a Woman (1974) Witless one-joke sex comedy with Angus Duncan is ineptly directed by Charles Martin. O (R)

How to Steal a Million (1966) Audrey Hepburn as the daughter of art forger Hugh Griffith desperately tries to steal his bogus masterpiece from a museum exhibit before it can be revealed as a fraud. Peter O'Toole stages the caper, foils art dealer Charles Boyer, and wins the hand of the fair lady from Eli Wallach. William Wyler directs the romantic comedy with sophisticated elegance. A-I (br) U

How to Succeed in Business Without Really Trying (1967) Robert Morse and Rudy Vallee whoop it up at the World Wide Wicket Company in a zestful adaptation of the Broadway musical about an ex-window-washer's schemes to reach the top of a big corporation in the shortest possible time. Director David Swift's sharp, witty spoof retains most of the original's running gags and Frank Loesser's music. A-II (nr) U

Howard the Duck (1986) This caustic, cynical and malevolent fantasy-adventure features a fully costumed duck from outer space trying to find his way home after having been accidentally transported to a hostile Earth. Director Willard Huyck fills the screen with too much vulgarity, violent destruction and sadistic humor to make the movie of interest to any sensitive earthling. O (PG)

Howards End (1992) Exquisitely done drama based on E. M. Forster's novel about an aristocratic widower (Anthony Hopkins) in turn-of-the-century England who cheats a young woman (Emma Thompson) out of property left her by his wife (Vanessa Redgrave) but then falls in love with her, much to the dismay of her egalitarian younger sister (Helena Bonham Carter). Enhanced by the ensemble cast's splendid performances, the sensitive collaboration of director James Ivory, producer Ismail Merchant and screenwriter Ruth Prawer Jhabvala does justice to Forster's ironic and witty story of class distinctions and their sometimes tragic outcomes. Discreet sexual innuendo and fleeting violence. A-II (PG)

Howling, The (1981) Trashy but flashy horror movie written by John Sayles and directed by Joe Dante in which a television newswoman (Dee Wallace) finds herself in dire straits when her companions at a psychiatric retreat turn out to be a pack of werewolves. The special effects by Rob Bottin are remarkable, but not enough to justify what is essentially a sex-and-violence exploitation movie. O (R) 18

Huckleberry Finn (1931) Creaky version of Mark Twain's adventure story directed by Norman Taurog follows Huck (Jackie Coogan) on his Mississippi River adventures with escaped slave Jim, including their encounter with the Lost Dauphin (Eugene Pallette). Dated as a movie production but still some fun. A-I (br)

Huckleberry Finn (1939) Still one of the best screen adaptations of the Twain classic with Mickey Rooney properly scrappy in the title role and Rex Ingram strong and dignified as his companion, the freedom-seeking Jim, with Walter Connolly and William Frawley as the confidence men they meet along the river. Director Richard Thorpe captures much of the youthful wonderment and the spirit of adventure that makes the original such enjoyable reading. Fine family fare. A-I (br) U

Huckleberry Finn (1974) Sugary musical version of the Twain classic, with script and lyrics written by the Sherman Brothers, features Jeff East in the title role and Paul Winfield as Jim. Directed by J. Lee Thompson, it contains a clutter of supremely forgettable musical numbers, entirely misses the book's point and adds up only to a minor children's matinee entry. A-I (G) U

Hudson Hawk (1991) A reformed cat burglar (Bruce Willis) and his pal (Danny Aiello) are coerced into stealing art objects from the Vatican for a power-crazed couple (Sandra Bernhard and Richard E. Grant) while an undercover nun (Andie MacDowell) tries to foil the plan. Director Michael Lehmann's turkey crashlands with a maddeningly overwritten script cluttered with underdeveloped characters and moronic musical duets. Much cartoon violence and rough language. A-III (R)

Hugh Hefner: Once Upon a Time (1992) Uncritical documentary chronicles the millionaire publisher's Methodist upbringing, marital dissatisfactions, the growth and eventual decline of his "Playboy" business up to his present May-December marriage and second shot at fatherhood. Robert Heath's unctuous direction and a fawning narration voiced by actor James Coburn attempt to lionize Hefner for supposedly liberating a generation of sexually repressed males but, in the process, unintentionally reveal the man's enormous ego and spiritual emptiness. Acceptance of promiscuity, sexist attitudes, frequent nudity and minimal rough language. O (R)

Hugs and Kisses (1968) Swedish movie about a triangular relationship that develops between a woman, her husband and his bumbling friend. Written and directed by Jonas Cornell, the fragmentary story and its seriocomic incidents are at best ambiguous in developing a theme about human relationships. Unnecessarily graphic nude sequence. O (br) X

Human Factor, The (1975) When the family of a computer expert (George Kennedy) at a NATO base in Naples is murdered by international terrorists, he tracks down the villains and slaughters them in an orgy of violence. Despite the title and Kennedy's efforts to give his role some human dimension, Edward Dmytryk directs his story of vigilante vengeance with little feeling for any of its characters. O (R) 18

Human Factor, The (1980) Nicol Williamson plays a quiet family man, working for British Intelligence but also leaking information to the Russians, who has a crisis of conscience that causes him to risk everything. Also with Richard Attenborough and Derek Jacobi, the performances are excellent and Tom Stoppard's too literal adaptation of the Graham Greene novel and Otto Preminger's plodding direction results in movie that entertains, but does not excite or have the moral complexity of the original. Suggestive nightclub dance scene. A-III (R) 15

Human Revolution, The (1974) Japanese dramatization of the 1930s' beginnings and beliefs of the Nichiren Shoshu Academy (a Buddhist sect numbering some 20 million adherents). Directed by Toshiro Masuda, it's a handsome and intelligent production whose philosophical rather than religious message is that the world can only become better through the inner change of each individual. A-II (G)

Humanoids from the Deep (1980) Meddling scientists tampering with genetic laws turn some prehistoric creatures, who are minding their own business at the bottom of the sea, into sex maniacs. Directed by Barbara Peeters, the penny-ante dreadful contains excessive violence and nudity. O (R) X

Hunger, The (1983) Catherine Deneuve and David Bowie play vampires whose love has stood the test of time until he, after dining on punk rockers, begins to die and she falls in love with the doctor (Susan Sarandon) called in to try to save him. This relentlessly slick and shallow movie, as directed by Tony Scott, consists of elegant surroundings and extravagant doses of blood and gore, nudity, graphic sexuality and not one bit of plausibility. O (R) X

Hunger for Love (1973) Brazilian drama presents a socio-psychological survey of contemporary values in the story of a young man who decides to run away with the wife of his best friend. Directed in 1969 by Nelson Pereira Dos Santos, the beautifully crafted movie will appeal most to those interested in themes of social justice. A-III (nr)

Hunt, The (1967) Spanish film in which three old friends spend a day hunting rabbits while the pressure of resentments caused by changed fortunes grows in each until the occasion culminates in senseless tragedy. Director Carlos Saura's veiled political allegory about the Spanish Civil War makes a subtle anti-fascist statement. A-III (br)

Hunt for Red October, The (1990) Cold War thriller based on Tom Clancy's novel tracks the near clash of U.S. and U.S.S.R. submarines in the Atlantic when a maverick Soviet sub captain (Sean Connery) plots to defect. Director John McTiernan captivates viewers with the suspenseful story, fine ensemble cast and masterful production design without resorting to gratuitous violence for thrills and chills. Some intense menace and climactic violence. A-II (PG)

Hunter, The (1980) Steve McQueen plays a modern-day bounty hunter hired by bail bondsmen to bring back clients who have jumped bail. Though McQueen is very good, director Buzz Kulik's action movie is put together in slipshod fashion with an excess of plot threads that never come together. Good deal of violence. A-III (PG) 15

Hunting Party, The (1971) Repulsive western about a wife (Candice Bergen) kidnapped by a sex-crazed outlaw (Oliver Reed) and pursued by bloodlusting husband (Gene Hackman). Directed by Don Medford, its depiction of sex and nudity is mild in comparison to its graphic presentation of senseless violence and sadistic brutalities. O (R)

Hunting Scenes (1970) German movie about a young man who becomes the object of ridicule in his small village when a rumor starts that he is a homosexual. In a vain attempt to escape his persecutors, he kills someone. Writer-director Peter Fleischmann's story is not about homosexuality but about a tightly knit community whose fear of those who are different unites them, and may be seen as referring to Hitler's popular support. A-III (nr)

Hurricane (1979) Listless, mediocre remake of the 1937 John Ford movie about ill-fated South Sea lovers (Mia Farrow and Dayton Ka'Ne) was filmed in Bora Bora, but the spectacle of the climatic hurricane does not measure up to the Hollywood original. Director Jan Troell's melodramatic script and its shallow characterizations waste a good cast including Jason Robards, Max Von Sydow and Trevor Howard. Erotic dance sequences and distasteful pre-marriage ritual. O (PG) A

Hurry Sundown (1967) Michael Caine plays a Cockney-accented cracker and Jane is his somewhat bruised Georgia peach. Director Otto Preminger's superficial depiction of social, marital and racial unrest in a small Southern town during the 1940s is patronizing in its treatment of racial attitudes and also demeaning in its approach to sex. O (br) A

Hurry Up, or I'll Be 30 (1973) A young Brooklynite (John Lefkowitz), crushed by thoughts that he is almost 30, tries vainly to break out of his sterile life-style. Director Joseph Jacoby's generally sappy narrative involves the ypung man's frustrating job in his father's small print shop and a brief affair with an aspiring Broadway actress (Linda DeCoff). Entirely predictable movie about boring people. Occasional gratuitous nudity. O (R/GP)

Husbands (1970) Long Island commuters (John Cassavetes, Ben Gazzara and Peter Falk) attend the burial of a mutual friend suddenly carried off by a coronary, and their own sense of mortality becomes both the catalyst and context for the drunken antics, middle-aged frustrations and inarticulate revelations that follow. For all of its ex-cesses, from a lavatory vomiting scene to a crude sex romp in a London hotel, director John Cassavetes injects a compassion for his male misfits that redeems many of the glaring faults in his treatment of the proceedings. A-III (PG)

Husbands and Wives (1992) An insecure and childless couple (Mia Farrow and Woody Allen) starts questioning their own marriage when their close friends (Sydney Pollack and Judy Davis) separate after 20 years and rush into hasty affairs. Also written and directed by Allen, the movie presents a cynical view of the permanence of love while deftly skewering older mens' flirtations with much younger women. Theme of marital disharmony and infidelities, with some rough language. A-III (R) 15

Hush . . . Hush, Sweet Charlotte (1965) Creaking suspense thriller about a neurotic recluse (Bette Davis) haunted by 30-year-old memories of the hatchet murder of her fiance and smothered by the attentions of her cousin (Olivia de Havilland). Directed by Robert Aldrich, the cast is better than the bogus plot and its belabored sinister atmosphere. Much psychological menace. A-III (br)

Hustle (1975) Los Angeles detective (Burt Reynolds), whose mistress is an expensive call girl (Catherine Deneuve), finds nothing but corruption in places high and low during his investigation of a young girl's death. Director Robert Aldrich's muddled movie is not above purveying a bit of the corruption it seems to be decrying. Excessive sex and violence. O (R) X

I

I Am a Dancer (1973) Pierre Jourdan's documentary records Rudolf Nureyev as he rehearses, in performance and working with promising novices. John Percival has written a reverent, rather adulatory, narration for the movie, which is pleasantly read by Bryan Forbes. A-I (nr)

I Am Curious (Blue) (1970) The Blue version is just as boring as its Yellow predecessor. Though it contains fewer erotic sequences, its social and political subject matter is as intemperate, irrelevant and uninteresting to an American audience as previously. O (nr)

I Am Curious (Yellow) (1969) Failed social commentary by Swedish director Vilgot Sjoman tries to find a metaphorical link between the ills of Swedish society and the sexual problems of a young woman. The theme of smug complacency boils over into a sensationalized exploitation of nudity. O (X)

I Am the Cheese (1983) Story of an adolescent's identity crisis adapted from the novel by Robert Cormier presents a rather bleak and depressing portrait of the hurt child under psychiatric care. Director Robert Jiras has some insight into ways children might deal with the loss of parents, but it is not a movie youngsters will find engaging. A-II (PG)

I Come in Peace (1990) A Houston cop (Dolph Lundgren) teams with an obnoxious FBI agent (Brian Benben) to track down a serial killer who is actually an intergalactic drug dealer (Matthias Hues). Director Craig R. Baxley's routine action flick limps from one violent scene to the next and the wooden acting doesn't help an already ludicrous plot. Excessive violence, much rough language and partial nudity. O (R)

I Could Never Have Sex with Any Man Who Has So Little Regard for My Husband (1973) Dreary, psuedo-sophisticated sex comedy written by Dan Greenburg and directed by Robert McCarty is set on a rainy Martha's Vineyard where Carmine Caridi, Cynthia Harris, Andrew Duncan and Lynne Lipton play strip hide-and-seek while they wait for the weather to clear. Monogamy wins in the end but till then, it's a low comedy exercise in sexual brinkmanship. A-III (R)

I Don't Give a Damn (1988) Disappointing Israeli melodrama about the emotional and physical problems of a wounded soldier (Ika Sohar) who despairs of adjusting to life as a paraplegic. Director Samuel Imberman centers on the soldier's fears of sexual inadequacy with little subtlety or insight. Several fairly explicit bedroom scenes, brief nudity and much rough language. A-IV (R)

I Drink Your Blood (1971) Low-budget horror movie exploiting the hippie and drug scene begins with some phony occult rites and ends in a ridiculous rabies epidemic. Directed by David Durston, it is devoid of style and notable only for the way in which it proceeds to turn trash into garbage. O (X/R)

I Eat Your Skin (1971) Routine horror movie is set on a mysterious island with voodoo ceremonies, secret medical experiments and roaming zombies. It has all been done before and with much more dash than writer-producer-director Del Tenney has been able to come up with, though the zombie make-up does add a little craft to tiresome proceedings. A-III (GP)

I Escaped from Devil's Island (1973) Held prisoner in the forbidding French penal colony circa 1918, Jim Brown and Christopher George are brutalized by sadistic guards until they flee through shark-infested waters and the teeming jungle. Director William Witney's tough and sweaty movie has excessive violence and a lengthy nude scene. O (R) X

I.F. Stone's Weekly (1973) Fine documentary by Jerry Bruck Jr. is primarily a study of Stone as a reporter's reporter, whose labors have made him an ebullient force in contemporary journalism. Not least of the film's virtues is its rare picture of a man who truly enjoys what he does for a living and even feels a little guilty that he gets paid for it. A-II (nr)

I Love My Wife (1971) Selfish, overgrown adolescent surgeon (Elliott Gould) spends increasing amounts of time with his mistresses while ignoring his wife (Brenda Vaccaro) who had put him through medical school and whom he loves deep down inside. Director Mel Stuart indulges Gould's shaggy-panda style, which generates the barest number of painful laughs and a great deal of embarrassment at his frantic sex life. O (R) X

I Love You (1982) Vapid and pretentious Brazilian movie about two bored members of the privileged class (Sonia Braga and Paulo Cesar Perelo) acting out their fantasies at tedious length in a luxurious Rio high rise. Director Arnaldo Jabor presumes to deal with politics in sexual terms but succeeds only in producing a boring exercise in soft-core pornography. O (R)

I Love You, Alice B. Toklas (1968) Peter Sellers plays a Beverly Hills attorney drawn by love into the hippie life-style in what begins as an amusing satirical farce harpooning both the establishment as well as the counter-culture. Directed by Hy Averback, it eventually turns into a sex comedy with graphic sexual scenes, hash parties and coarse language. O (R) X

I Love You, I Kill You (1972) German movie set in the future where there is a village existing only to maintain a game preserve for the ruling class and whose inhabitants are kept happy by popping pills. Written and directed by Uwe Brandner, the movie operates on many levels of love-hate relationships, but it is primarily a political parable about fascism and freedom. For those who have the inclination to interpret its languid, dreamlike visuals, it is a demanding exercise but worth the experience. A-IV (nr)

I Love You, Rosa (1973) Israeli movie about an 11-year-old boy who wants to marry his brother's widow (Michal Bat-Adam) and as he grows older and more insistent, she finally has to take him seriously. Writer-director Moshe Mizrahi's story is set in late 19th-century Jerusalem and is told with a charmingly poetic, humorously sentimental glow that romantics will find hard to resist, though it does indulge in some nudity, crude dialogue and has a casual attitude about premarital sex. A-IV (nr)

I Love You to Death (1990) One-joke film about a loving wife (Tracey Ullman) who tries and fails to murder her philandering Italian husband (Kevin Kline). As directed by Lawrence Kasdan, this fact-based scenario is cartoonish at best, with oddball casting that showcases Joan Plowright as the Lothario's murderous Yugoslavian mother-in-law and buries William Hurt and Keanu Reeves as two nitwit, drug-addicted assassins. Jokey attitude toward adultery and a cavalier acceptance of murder as a viable solution, some rough language and fleeting nudity in a sexual context. O (R) 15

I Married a Monster from Outer Space (1958) Low-budget clunker directed by Gene Fowler Jr. in which a woman (Gloria Talbott) marries the man of her dreams (Tom Tryon) only to discover that he and the rest of the town's male population are being replaced by alien creatures seeking to continue their species. Silly "Body Snatcher" rip-off with few chills and no thrills. A-II (br) X

I Married You for Fun (1969) Monica Vitti displays comic flair as the "kooky" swinging wife of a young man from an absurdly stuffy background in this Italian sex farce posing as a satire on marriage. Director Luciano Salce opens with a suicide attempt and goes on to employ a decadent orgy scene and nudity in a sexual context. O (X)

I Never Promised You a Rose Garden (1977) The parents of a teenage schizophrenic (Kathleen Quinlan) reluctantly place her in a mental institution. Quinlan and Bibi Andersson as the psychiatrist give superb performances in this drama of mental illness directed by Anthony Page. The too realistic depiction of the teenager's fantasy world and some brief nudity are sufficiently graphic to be inappropriate for youngsters. A-III (R) 18

I Never Sang for My Father (1970) Gilbert Cates directs a solid adaptation of the Robert Anderson play about a grown son (Gene Hackman) who is forced to come to some decision about how to care for his aging father (Melvyn Douglas). Both give remarkable performances filled with compassion and understanding and their scenes together are charged with the love and hate that simultaneously bind them together and make them strangers. It would be fine for adolescents save for a rather frank bedroom scene. A-III (GP) A

I Ought to Be in Pictures (1982) Superficial seriocomic Neil Simon story about a teen (Dinah Manoff) who reunites with the father (Walter Matthau) who had deserted her in order to become a Hollywood writer. Directed by Herbert Ross, the movie tries to make light of an adulterous, misguided character, and says very little of import about parent-child relations. Because of a brief scene involving nudity and the father's dealings with a mistress (Ann-Margret), it is mature fare. A-III (PG) 15

I Remember Mama (1948) Engaging, warm-hearted version of the John Van Druten play in which a daughter (Barbara Bel Geddes) recalls the nurturing influence of her mother (Irene Dunne) on her Norwegian-American brood in San Francisco circa 1910. Produced and directed by George Stevens, the interplay of family life is richly depicted through good times and bad, convincingly portrayed by a cast including Oscar Homolka as the family patriarch, Ellen Corby as the spinster aunt and Edgar Bergan as her mousey beau. Sincere, affecting and universal in theme and appeal. A-I (br) U

I, the Jury (1982) Gross remake of the 1953 Mickey Spillane private-eye melodrama features Armand Assante as the sullen Mike Hammer out to avenge a dead friend by smashing a rogue CIA operation that uses a sex clinic as a front. Director Richard T. Heffron makes unbridled use of a repulsive mix of sex and violence. O (R) X

I Walk the Line (1970) Taking its title from a bittersweet Johnny Cash country-western song, the film concerns a redneck Tennessee sheriff (a miscast Gregory Peck) and his romance with a moonshiner's daughter (Tuesday Weld). Director John Frankenheimer reduces the story to a series of heavy, melodramatic surface strokes, avoiding the issues of life's social and moral complexities, resulting in a movie without any substance. A-III (GP) 15

I Wanna Hold Your Hand (1978) Three New Jersey high school girls enact an elaborate scheme to get to see their heroes (the Beatles) on the day the singing group is to appear on the Ed Sullivan Show in 1964. Director Robert Zemeckis' farcical style, rough language and a tasteless scene with a prostitute make it a decidedly adult comedy. A-III (PG) A

I Want What I Want (1972) Anne Heywood playing both the before and after role in the story of a transsexual struggles sincerely, if not quite convincingly. Directed by John Dexter, the result is wanting in such basics as dramatic interest and literacy, as well as depth in the psychological, medical and moral areas it opens up. A-III (R) X

I Will, I Will . . . For Now (1976) Limp sex farce about sexually based marital problems stars Elliott Gould and Diane Keaton. Directed by Norman Panama, the movie's tasteless humor is structured as a parody of a sex manual with vulgar jokes and negative female stereotypes. O (R) X

I'd Rather Be Rich (1964) Plodding remake of "It Started with Eve" in which a dying millionaire (Maurice Chevalier) is rejuvenated when his granddaughter (Sandra Dee) introduces a stranger (Robert Goulet) as her fiance. Directed by Jack Smight, the merriment of the original is missing and Chevalier comes nowhere near matching Laughton's mischievous humbug. Romantic complications. A-II (br) U

I'll Never Forget What's 'isname (1968) Failed British melodrama about an advertising whiz (Oliver Reed) who, disillusioned with success, an unsatisfying marriage and two mistresses, decides to throw it all up and return to making an honest living but learns one can't recapture a lost innocence. Directed by Michael Winner, there is some satirical goring of TV commercials and the emptiness of affluence, but the plot goes nowhere and ends in cynicism. Excessive gory violence and graphic sex scenes. O (br) X

I'll See You in My Dreams (1951) Sentimental biography of songwriter Gus Kahn (Danny Thomas) tracks his start during World War I, marriage (to Doris Day) and Tin Pan Alley triumphs, then Depression doldrums until renewed success in Hollywood. Directed by Michael Curtiz, the engaging performance by Thomas almost overcomes the script's showbiz cliches and formula obstacles, but Day is credible as the supportive wife and along the way is an enjoyable review of Kahn lyrics, including the title song. Restrained treatment of

marital misunderstandings and domestic difficulties. A-II (br) U

I'm Dancing as Fast as I Can (1982) Disappointing movie version of television producer Barbara Gordon's account of her struggle to overcome an addiction to tranquilizers. Jill Clayburgh's characterization casts little light upon why she is so driven to drugs, the result being an unnerving melodrama rather than anything deeper. Director Jack Hofsiss details the horrors of quitting "cold turkey" and uses violence and rough language to realistic effect. A-III (R)

I'm Gonna Git You Sucka (1989) Writer-director Keenen Ivory Wayans also stars in this comic parody of 1970s' black-exploitation films that sees a former wimp (Wayans) avenge the death of his brother with the help of some over-the-hill black heroes (Bernie Casey, Issac Hayes, Jim Brown, among others). Tacky, too self-mocking and unfocused, it will hardly inspire audiences to question the media's role in perpetuating offensive black stereotypes. Much profanity laced with sexual vulgarities and intense comic-book violence. O (R) 15

Ice (1970) Writer-director Robert Kramer has made a fictional movie with a documentary look about shadowy revolutionary groups joining together to plan and then carry out a regional show of force in preparation for a nationwide uprising. Though its surface realities seem to have little connection with any actual violence of radical groups, it does offer a chilling picture of the fantasies engendered in those frustrated by their hopes for social change. A-IV (nr)

Ice Castles (1979) When a talented young ice skater (Lynn-Holly Johnson) training for the Olympics is blinded in an accident, her father (Tom Skerritt) and boyfriend (Robby Benson) persuade her to resume her career. Director Donald Wrye gets good performances in this mildly inspirational tale, but the movie is undone by frequent rough language and its sympathetic attitude toward premarital sex on the part of its teenage heroine. O (PG) A

Ice Pirates, The (1984) Lackluster sci-fi story about the hijacking of spaceships that supply ice to waterless planets tries but fails to get by as a spoof. Directed by Stewart Raffill and starring Robert Urich and Mary Crosby, it has some sexually oriented humor, a relatively mild bedroom sequence and an air of pervasive vulgarity. A-III (PG)

Ice Station Zebra (1968) Uneven screen version of an Alistair MacLean thriller in which a nuclear submarine captain (Rock Hudson) is ordered to bring a British spy (Patrick McGoohan), a friendly Russian (Ernest Borgnine) and a detachment of Marines to an Arctic weather station where a Russian surveillance satellite has landed, but the Russians are already enroute. Directed by John Sturges, there are double agents and a Cold War showdown to keep up adult interest and plenty of adventure for the youngsters. A-I (G) U

Iceman (1984) Talented Australian director Fred Schepisi has too little to work with in a script by Chip Proser and John Drimmer about an Arctic expedition revivifying a frozen Neanderthal man (John Lone). There is a running argument between a scientist-humanist (Timothy Hutton) and a more clinical type (Lindsay Crouse) as to what to do with him, but it fails to generate enough heat to thaw out anything. Some mild vulgarities. A-II (PG)

Ichabod and Mr. Toad (see: "The Adventures of Ichabod and Mr. Toad").

Icy Breasts (1975) French suspense movie set on the Riviera in winter when a hack writer (Claude Brasseur) sees a striking blonde (Mireille Darc) with a hurt, gamin-like quality, and sets out in pursuit but is stopped by her lawyer (Alain Delon) who tells him she is unstable and a murderess. Director Georges Lautner has made a taut, spare thriller with talented performers and luxurious settings. Some brief nudity that the context makes far from erotic. A-IV (R)

Identification Marks: None (1969) Impressionistic Polish drama about a youth waiting to enter military service. Directed by Jerzy Skolimowski, the movie poetically evokes the confusions and personal conflicts of young people in a bleak, repressive society. A-III (nr)

Idi Amin Dada (1976) Self-portrait of the Ugandan leader shows Amin as a dangerous dictator perhaps more effectively than if director Barbet Schroeder had been permitted to make his own objective documentary. Its display of the ruler's gross self-indulgence in the midst of such an impoverished nation is of value for future historians, if not contemporary viewers. A-II (nr)

Idol, The (1966) Self-centered American art student in England (Michael Parks), pursued by his friend's girlfriend, is more interested in seducing his pal's mother (Jennifer Jones). Director Daniel Petrie fails to make clear why anyone would find his confused, boorish hero of the slightest interest, let alone appeal. Adult themes and treatment. A-III (br)

Idolmaker, The (1980) Ray Sharkey turns in a fine performance as a Svengali-like manager who turns two marginally talented youngsters (Peter Gallagher and Paul Land) into rock stars in the early 1960s. Although the film runs out of energy and interest about two-thirds of the way through, director Taylor Hackford's portrait of the power-hungry is superior entertainment up till then. Some sexual references. A-III (PG) 15

If (1969) British schoolboys (among them, Malcolm McDowell) rebel against the abuses of a social and educational system out-of-step with their yearnings and fantasies for a life of freedom from unenlightened authority. Director Lindsay Anderson's complex fable halfheartedly accepts violence as a means to social change and uses nudity as a symbol of liberation. A-IV (X/R) X

If a Man Answers (1962) Dull romantic comedy in which a wealthy debutante (Sandra Dee) marries a struggling fashion photographer (Bobby Darin), then tries to keep him from straying by inventing an imaginary lover. Directed by Henry Levin, the glossy proceedings have little humor and no wit. Sexual situations and comic treatment of infidelity. A-III (br) A

If Ever I See You Again (1978) Self-indulgent story about a hugely successful commercial songwriter (Joe Brooks) who after 12 years rediscovers, loses and, at movie's end, wins his college sweetheart (Shelley Hack) while echoes of "Venite Adoremus" are heard on the sound track. Also directed by Brooks, it is so gloppy it makes "Love Story" look like a Tolstoy novel. Some scenes, by suggestion at least, are adult. A-III (PG)

If He Hollers, Let Him Go (1968) Black auto mechanic (Raymond St. Jacques), wrongly convicted of a capital crime, escapes prison and saves the life of a wealthy woman (Dana Wynter) who offers all the financial aid necessary to prove his innocence. Written, produced and directed by Charles Martin, its story of racism and injustice is little more than a cheap exploitation of explicit sex and brutality. O (R)

If I Had a Gun (1973) The setting is a small rural village in Slovakia, the state created after the Nazi occupation of Czechoslovakia, during the last years of World War II. The central figure is a young boy living through the normal problems of early adolescence, which are compounded by the extraordinary conditions of wartime. Director Stephen Uher does not sentimentalize his subject but suggests that the effect of violence upon the young is the most terrible heritage that the adult world has to bestow. A-III (nr)

If It's Tuesday, This Must Be Belgium (1969) Drip-dry comedy about American tourist stereotypes, camera and luggage ladened, on an economy tour of Europe. Both the people and the places make easy targets for director Mel Stuart to poke fun at. Less funny is a romantic complication involving tourist Suzanne Pleshette, who tries a fling with grabby guide Ian McShane. A-III (G) A

If I Were King (1938) Stylish tale of 14th-century vagabond poet Francois Villon (Ronald Colman) who saves Louis XI (Basil Rathbone) and Paris from Burgundian invaders by leading an army of the city's poor against the enemy. Director Frank Lloyd displays some wit in the shifting relationship between crafty king and bright commoner but the historical pageantry is pure Hollywood hokum. Stylized violence and mild romantic complications. A-II (br)

If Looks Could Kill (1991) Mistaken for an American secret agent, a high school senior (Richard Grieco) in Europe with his French class, is called upon to save the continent from the murderous machinations of a madman (Roger Rees). Director William Dear's spectacularly awful spy movie spoof is a grab bag of screen cliches, all the more pronounced by the script's being underdeveloped and overacted. Much comicbook violence and some sexual innuendo. A-III (PG-13)

If You Could See What I Hear (1982) Based upon the college experiences of blind singer-entertainer Tom Sullivan (Marc Singer), this muddled movie offers both crude slapstick and pathos with very little in between. Sullivan's pursuit of women and an off-again, on-again religious dimension is conveyed in a crude, insensitive manner by director Eric Till. A-III (PG)

If You Don't Stop It . . . (1975) Montage of ancient dirty jokes acted out and trying to pass itself off as a movie. Often enough, it is merely vulgar, an aspect not nearly as offensive as its cynical exploitation of female nudity. O (R)

Il Bidone (1965) Italian drama about a confidence man (Broderick Crawford) who begins to realize that he is too old for the small-time rackets in which he is engaged. Directed by Federico Fellini, the 1955 production is episodic and the characters (including Giulietta Masina, Richard Basehart and Franco Fabrizi) somewhat sentimentalized. Subtitles. Mature themes. A-III (br)

I'll Cry Tomorrow (1955) Strong fact-based story of singer Lillian Roth (Susan Hayward), a child vaudeville star pushed by her mother (Jo Van Fleet) to Hollywood and Broadway fame in the 1930s but, after romantic disappointments and a disastrous marriage (to Richard Conte), winds up an alcoholic on Skid Row from which she emerges with the help of an Alcoholic Anonymous worker (Eddie Albert). Director Daniel Mann depicts with harrowing realism the effects of compulsive drinking as well as the courage needed for rehabilitation, but much of the credit for the movie's emotional impact belongs to the performances. Effective cautionary tale with discreet treatment of sordid details, including suicidal despair. A-II (br) X

Il Ladro di Bambini (1993) Assigned to escort two youngsters to a distant children's home after their mother is arrested on a morals charge, a young policeman is at first exasperated, then appalled at their sullen, withdrawn behavior and endangers his career by responding to their desperate need for someone to trust and make them feel safe. Director Gianni Amelio's engrossing Italian production offers a small but emotionally rich story of an ordinary man whose sense of decency compels him to try to help undo the damage done abused youngsters robbed of childhood's innocence. Subtitles. Veiled references to the sexual exploitation of a minor. A-II (nr)

Illustrated Man, The (1969) Failed attempt to tie in three unrelated tales with the story of a man (Rod Steiger) whose body is covered from head to foot with tattoos in which others see their future. Directed by Jack Smight, the movie wavers between horror, thriller and science fiction with unsatisfying results. Some violence and brief nudity. A-III (PG) 15

Ilsa, Harem Keeper of the Oil Sheiks (1976) The moral cretins who brought "Ilsa, She-Wolf of the SS" to the screen offer another sex exploitation movie with the same low-budget production values. O (R)

Images (1972) Psychological thriller in which events are seen through the eyes and mind of a troubled woman (Susannah York) and leaving, until the final shot, the audience to determine which of her perceptions are real and which are imaginary. Director Robert Altman demonstrates a technical mastery of his medium, a willingness to take chances in achieving an effect and a talent for eliciting strong performances from his actors. Mature themes. A-III (R) X

Imagine: John Lennon (1988) Director Andrew Solt's documentary intersperses interviews with film footage to provide a portrait of the prolific singer, songwriter and ex-Beatle. There's a lot of great music, but as much about the fans and the period in which the music was written as about Lennon who comes across as a mature, positive image late in life. Some rough language and fleeting nudity. A-III (R) 15

Immediate Family (1989) In an open-adoption arrangement, a childless middle-class couple (Glenn Close and James Woods) take in a pregnant working-class teenager (Mary Stuart Masterson) and while nervously awaiting the arrival of the child, they interact tentatively and with conflicting emotions. Director Jonathan Kaplan's predictable, bittersweet story shows adoption as neither an easy solution for the childless couple nor an easy way out for the pregnant teen. Minor rough language laced with sexual innuendos. A-III (PG-13) 15

Imitation of Life (1959) Tawdry romantic claptrap about a struggling actress (Lana Turner), the self-effacing black woman (Juanita Moore) who becomes her best friend and their daughters, one of whom (Sandra Dee) falls for her mother's beau (John Gavin) while the other (Susan Kohner) tries desperately to pass for white. Director Douglas Sirk's silly tearjerker changes the credible premise of the 1934 original for an empty scenario full of bad acting and bogus sentimentality. Some sexual innuendo, violence and unenlightened racial attitudes. A-III (br) U

Immortal Bachelor, The (1980) Claudia Cardinale serves on the jury trying the case of a charwoman (Monica Vitti) on trial for murdering her philandering husband. Vitti's defense is that she could not possibly murder a man who was unequaled among lovers. Director Marcello Fondato's mood of artificiality undercuts the social satire while his emphasis upon marital infidelity makes this adult fare. A-III (PG)

Immortal Story (1969) Orson Welles directs as well as stars in this solemn tale about a merchant baron's grotesque obsession with transforming pretense into reality. Jeanne Moreau appears in a cameo in this haunting, elusively obscure fable about the futility of wealth and power to provide fulfillment. A-III (nr) X

Impasse (1969) Salvage company owner (Burt Reynolds) reassembles four members of an Army detail that had buried a fortune in gold bullion in the tunnels of Corregidor just before its surrender to the Japanese. What could have been an interesting action melodrama in Philippine locales is ruined by a confused screenplay, formula characters and the unsavory cynicism with which director Richard Benedict treats a love affair that eventually causes failure for the entire operation. Some violence, coarse language and a rather graphic love-making scene. O (M) A

Imported Bridegroom, The (1990) Thinking it will earn him a place in paradise, a pompous Jewish businessman (Eugene Troobnick) brings a bashful Talmudic scholar (Avi Hoffman) from Poland to marry his social-climbing Bostonian daughter (Greta Cowan). Produced and directed by Pamela Berger, the film is an affectionate look at a turn-of-the-century Jewish household with humorously ethnic dialogue, but the film is diluted by the actors' studied and self-conscious performances. A-I (nr)

Impossible on Saturday (1966) Mediocre French import. A-II (br)

Impossible Years, The (1969) Sappy situation comedy about a university professor (David Niven), a supposed authority on teenage behavior, who is unaware that his own teenage daughter (Christina Ferrare) is secretly married (to Chad Everett). The girl's permissive standards of conduct become the source of irreverent generation-gap humor, which director Michael Gordon plays badly as adult farce. A-III (G) AA

Impromptu (1991) Enchanted by Chopin's music, female novelist George Sand (Judy Davis) sets her sights on having an affair with the sickly musician (Hugh Grant), unaware that the jealous mistress (Bernadette Peters) of Franz Liszt (Julian Sand) has thrown a wrench in the works. Despite of an appealing cast, director James Lapine's comedy fails to rise beyond being a silly period piece. Minor violence, casual acceptance of affairs and minimal rough language. A-III (PG-13) 15

Improper Channels (1981) Alan Arkin stars as a screwball architect who is unjustly accused of child abuse when his five-year-old daughter hits her head and a social worker misjudges the situation. Canadian production directed by Eric Till elicits a few comic moments but refuses to deal with the real questions of domestic violence and children's rights. A-II (PG)

Impulse (1984) Young couple (Meg Tilly and Tim Matheson) return to her home town to find that everyone has gone berserk, indulging in bloody violence and promiscuous sex. Director Graham Baker's horror film is as ridiculous as it is vicious. O (R) 18

Impulse (1990) Murky crime drama about a Los Angeles undercover female vice cop (Theresa Russell) whose distorted priorities, problems with men and near burnout become life-threatening when she's almost killed during a drug sting. Despite its intriguing female protagonist and impressive direction by Sondra Locke, the script is clumsily plotted and strangely lacking in female perspective. Some profanity, grisly violence and a sexual encounter with shadowed nudity. A-III (R)

Impure Thoughts (1987) Four recently deceased friends are reunited in purgatory and reminisce about their 1960s' Catholic upbringing. Some mildly irreverent humor is offset by director Michael Simpson's exploration of religious values and family life. Some crude language and sexual references. A-III (PG)

In Celebration (1975) British adaptation of the David Storey play about three sons (Alan Bates, James Bolam and Brian Cox) who return home to a coal-mining town to celebrate their parents' 40th wedding anniversary. Director Lindsay Anderson's incisive portrait of family relations and each individual's struggle to cope with the bonds of the past is emotionally powerful and will deeply involve most viewers. Mature themes. A-III (PG) A

In Cold Blood (1967) Meaningful screen version of Truman Capote's nonfiction novel about the senseless 1959 slaying of a Kansas family and the apprehension and hanging of their killers (Robert Blake and Scott Wilson). Director Robert Brooks takes a semi-documentary approach in re-creating these events with shattering realism but with compassion and a notable lack of sensationalism. It also explores the backgrounds and the motivations of the two criminals as well as scrutinizes the practice of capital punishment. Strong stuff but the experience is thought-provoking. A-III (br) X

In Country (1989) Old wounds are opened when a recent high school grad (Emily Lloyd) begins to question her grandmother (Peggy Rea) and uncle (Bruce Willis) about her father who died in Vietnam before her birth. Director Norman Jewison's poignant drama about how one rural Kentucky family deals with the unfinished business and personal tragedy caused by the unpopular conflict also includes the crucial element of healing that must occur within all individuals touched by war. Sexual involvement by the young, female protagonist, some rough language laced with sexual innuendo and brief wartime violence. A-III (R) 15

In Enemy Country (1968) Limp World War II spy thriller about the exploits of a French intelligence agent (Tony Franciosa) behind German lines. The mediocre effort is directed by Harry Keller with no moral considerations beyond that of all is fair in love and war. Some violence and sexual situations. A-III (br) A

In God We Trust (1980) Marty Feldman's inept and hugely unfunny comedy, intended as a satire on the exploitation of people in the name of religion, displays a tasteless, irreverent, crude mocking of religious beliefs. O (PG) AA

In Harm's Way (1965) Bloated World War II saga of U.S. naval operations in the Pacific after Pearl Harbor centers less on military action than on the personal lives of its characters, particularly an extramarital affair between a tough commander (John Wayne) and a sympathetic nurse (Patricia Neal). Producer-director Otto Preminger churns the emotions in grand soap-opera fashion but to little purpose and only empty effects. Stylized violence and sympathetic treatment of sexual liaisons. A-III (br) AA

In Praise of Older Women (1979) Hopelessly episodic, shallow and sexually exploitative Canadian movie about a young Hungarian emigre (Tom Berenger) and his amorous adventures with the likes of Karen Black and Susan Strasberg. Directed by George Kaczender, events never stray far from the bedroom. O (R)

In Search of Gregory (1970) British female Don Quixote fantasy set in the 20th century centers on a young woman (Julie Christie) who is told by her wealthy father (Adolfo Celi) and neurotic brother (Peter Hurt) about a young man (Michael Sarrazin) who will bring romance and fulfillment into her life. Directed by Peter Wood, the story is so murky and its execution so undisciplined that its moral about not taking fantasy for reality becomes bogged down in its own tedium, making the occasional nudity and brother-sister incest theme even more offensive than they might have been. O (PG) X

In Search of Historic Jesus (1980) Pseudo-documentary by Henning G. Schellerup moves from a summary of the life of Jesus to a detailed examination of the significance of the Shroud of Turin, believed by many to be Jesus' burial cloth. Ludicrous dramatizations and dubious embellishments of the gospel story suggest parental discretion in exposing youngsters to such a grab-bag selection of material, no matter how orthodox it is in regard to Christian doctrine. A-I (G)

In Search of Noah's Ark (1977) Semi-documentary sets out to prove the literal truth of the biblical account of the Flood, basing its case largely on conjecture and hypothesis. Directed by James Conway, its inept dramatization of the building and stocking of the Ark makes it appear ridiculous and undercuts the religious significance of the biblical story. A-I (G)

In Search of the Castaways (1962) Disney adventure fantasy from Jules Vernes story of a girl (Hayley Mills) and two siblings searching for their missing explorer father with the help of an eccentric professor (Maurice Chevalier). As the 19th-century expedition makes its way from South America to Australia, director Robert Stevenson pays less attention to the characters than to the excitement along the way with natural disasters, strange creatures and exotic natives. Youngsters in peril. A-I (br) U

In the Heat of the Night (1967) One steamy night, an industrialist is murdered in Sparta, Mississippi, and the local police chief (Rod Steiger) has to rely on the scientific experience of a black homicide expert (Sidney Poitier) who is passing through town. Though the movie begins with a very suggestive sex scene, the superior acting of the two principals and the sure hand of director

Norman Jewison turn a rather muddled detective plot into a balanced and significant expression of the complex racial, legal and intellectual prejudice permeating many areas of American life. A-III (br) 15

In the Line of Fire (1993) While bragging about his imminent plans to assassinate the incumbent President, a methodical killer (John Malkovich) taunts an aging Secret Service agent (Clint Eastwood) on the phone about his failure to save JFK in Dallas and promises history will repeat itself. Director Wolfgang Petersen's cat-and-mouse thriller is far better on characterization than on action as Eastwood and Malkovich's exchanges are shrewdly revealing, but the climax is unconvincingly staged. Intermittent violence; some rough language. A-III (R)

In the Mood (1987) Teenage Lothario (Patrick Dempsey) hits the headlines during the mid-1940s' war years by running away with an older married woman—twice. Fact-based farce from director Phil Aiden Robinson romanticizes adultery and derides the idea of matrimony. Some implied sex scenes involving a minor. O (PG-13)

In the Name of the Father (1974) Italian drama about a boys' school run by a corrupt religious order into which comes a new teacher (Yves Beneyton), a man of efficiency, pragmatism and scientific bent, who dedicates himself to reforming the old ways and introducing a new regime. Director Marco Bellocchio's talent is everywhere in evidence, though his political allegory about fascism will probably seem to viewers with little knowledge of Italian culture as a rather strange and tedious fable. A-III (nr)

In the Name of the Father (1993) Based on the 1975 case of the "Guildford Four," the narrative centers on an aimless Belfast lad (Daniel Day-Lewis) grabbed by the British police and tortured into confessing complicity in an IRA bombing for which he is sentenced to life—with long prison terms for other falsely accused co-defendants, including his father (Pete Postlethwaite)—until 15 years later when his lawyer (Emma Thompson) uncovers proof of his innocence hidden from the court by the police. Director Jim Sheridan focuses on the human dimensions of this political miscarriage of justice but spends more time exploring the generational conflicts between the imprisoned father and son than on the larger issues of the Ulster conflict and the battle to win public opinion. Recurring menace and violence, unresolved justice questions and occasional rough language. A-III (R) 15

In the Realm of the Senses (1977) Japanese director Nagisa Oshima's study of perverse sex and its consequences is a tale of a former prostitute working as a maid whose affair with the owner of an inn culminates in her killing him and mutilating his body in horrible fashion. Pretentious mix of violence and eroticism. O (nr)

In the Shadow of Kilimanjaro (1986) Gritty wildlife adventure, based on an actual event at a game preserve in Kenya during a severe drought, turns into a gruesome carnage as thousands of starving baboons attack humans. Timothy Bottoms and John Rhys-Davies are featured in the bloody rampage, which relies too heavily on visual shock, including gory scenes of dismemberment. A-III (R)

In the Spirit (1990) Spacey New-Age widow (Marlo Thomas) patches up her differences with a spoiled matron (Elaine May) in order to join forces in trapping a murderous stalker. Director Sandra Seacat misses a grand opportunity to explore intriguing questions about women and middle-age, friendship and self-reliance in this otherwise disjointed female buddy caper comedy. Some rough language laced with explicit sexual references. A-III (R) 18

In the Year of the Pig (1969) Emile de Antonio's documentary recounts the political history of Vietnam from French colonial days to the American military involvement. Less an anti-war tract than a lucid examination of the complex political realities that have made Vietnam an American tragedy, it's a valuable document worthy of retrospective scrutiny. A-II (nr)

In-Laws, The (1979) Prominent New York dentist (Alan Arkin) and a seedy CIA agent (Peter Falk) are brought together when their children are engaged and the hapless dentist finds himself unexpectedly plunged into a wild adventure in a corrupt Central American dictatorship. Directed by Arthur Hiller, the pairing of Arkin and Falk is bright and the comedy frequently hilarious. Some comic violence and a few mild vulgarities. A-II (PG) A

Inadmissible Evidence (1968) Mid-life crisis of a successful London lawyer (Nicol Williamson) triggers fears of an unsure future and concerns about failures of the past, especially his relations with women. Director Anthony Page's adaptation of the John Osborne play is claustrophobic and introspective, but it is Williamson's tortured performance that makes it worth seeing. A-IV (br) AA

Inchon (1982) Expensively staged but wretched retelling of General Douglas MacArthur's amphibious victory in the early stages of the Korean War. Though Laurence Olivier plays MacArthur, supported by an international star cast, director Terence Young can't overcome the poor script, leaving only wartime melodrama and pyrotechnics for interest. A-III (PG)

Incident, The (1967) Dynamic social drama about a group of passengers riding the New York subway late at night and being terrorized by two hoodlums (Tony Musante and Martin Sheen). Tautly directed by Larry Peerce, it is not a pleasant story, but gripping and thought-provoking. A-IV (br)

Incident at Oglala (1992) Documentary recounts events culminating in the 1975 killing of two FBI agents on South Dakota's Pine Ridge Sioux reservation and argues that the subsequent conviction of Leonard Peltier for the crime is a miscarriage of justice. Directed by Michael Apted and narrated by Robert Redford, the film's use of newsreel footage and interviews with many of the principals succeeds in explaining the context of violence on the reservation and the disputed evidence used to convict Peltier. Raises contemporary justice issues in realistic fashion. A-II (PG)

Incorrigible (1980) French director Philippe De Broca's wan comedy in which a hyperactive flimflam artist (Jean-Paul Belmondo) meets his match in a lovely and quick-witted social worker (Genevieve Bujold). The dash and charm of these two actors are the saving grace of the movie. Some sexual references. A-III (nr)

Incredible Journey, The (1963) Fact-based Walt Disney story of a 250-mile trek through the Canadian wilds undertaken by an English bulldog, a Labrador retriever and a Siamese cat to rejoin their owner who had left them with friends while on vacation. Director Fletcher Markle allots most of the time to his four-footed actors who prove more engaging than the human characterizations and an overcute narration. A-I (G) U

Incredible Sarah, The (1976) Pop bio of actress Sarah Bernhardt (Glenda Jackson) lacks the warmth or stateliness that might have conveyed the magnetism of the reputedly great performer. Incredibly misdirected by Richard Fleischer and filmed in England with little sense of the misfortune in her life and career. A-II (PG) A

Incredible Shrinking Man, The (1957) Imaginative sci-fi tale from Richard Mathesen's novel about an ordinary fellow (Grant Williams) whose boating encounter with a radioactive mist starts him shrinking away to nothing, his diminishing size making him the target of the family cat and eventually a basement spider. Director Jack Arnold keeps viewer interest in the poor man's predicament by a judicious use of perspective, oversized props and special effects. Some tense scenes. A-I (br) A

Incredible Shrinking Woman, The (1981) Lily Tomlin plays a harried suburban housewife and mother who suddenly finds that she is shrinking due to an allergy from all the chemical additives in her household products. Strained allegorical slapstick comedy directed by Joel Schumacher falls far short of satire despite its jibes at consumerism and its consequences. Mild sexual innuendo. A-III (PG) A

Incredible Two-Headed Transplant, The (1971) Disappointed medical student (Bruce Dern) grafts the head of a homicidal maniac onto the shoulders of a retarded brute and the maniac takes over, escapes and is not caught until he has committed half a dozen murders. Director Anthony Lanza's low-budget horror movie supplies only a few grisly laughs here and there. A-III (GP)

Indecent Proposal (1993) Trite romantic triangle involves a wealthy stranger (Robert Redford) who pays a cash-strapped married couple (Demi Moore and Woody Harrelson) a million dollars to sleep with the wife for one night, then continues his romantic pursuit of the woman as her marriage crumbles. Director Adrian Lyne's thoroughly transparent and suspenseless movie revolves around cardboard characters who rationalize their every act without ever considering the moral dimensions of their behavior. Materialistic view of life, brief bedroom scene, fleeting nudity and occasional rough language. O (R) 15

Independence Day (1983) Small-town girl (Kathleen Quinlan) yearns for success as a photographer in Los Angeles and must choose between love and ambition. Director Robert Mandel's predictable story has a subplot of wife abuse, but only Quinlan's vibrant performance is of interest. There is a love affair and a relatively sympathetic depiction of suicide. A-III (R) 15

Indian Paint (1965) Naive, sometime dramatically inept account of the testing of an adolescent Indian brave (Johnny Crawford). Directed by Norman Foster, the movie's chief interest is in its authentic native lore and insights into the honorable values of another culture. A-I (br)

Indian Runner, The (1991) Violence-prone Vietnam veteran (Viggo Mortensen) returns to Nebraska in the late '60s, marries his pregnant girlfriend (Patricia Arquette) and settles down, yet remains a walking time bomb despite the best efforts of his patrolman brother (David Morse). Writer-director Sean Penn paints a moving portrait of a tortured soul and the effect he has on those around him, but the plot is too drawn-out to sustain its paltry insights. Some brutal violence including suicide, brief male nudity, a graphic birth scene, much rough language and a glimpse of recreational drug use. A-III (R) 15

Indian Summer (1993) Seriocomic ensemble piece concerns an aging summer camp owner (Alan Arkin) who holds a week's reunion for his seven favorite campers of the past (notably, Elizabeth Perkins; Vincent Spano; Kevin Pollak; Diane Lane) during which they act like kids while evaluating their adult lives. Writer-director Mike Binder's nostalgia-drenched story offers situations of limited interest and characters whose puerile pranks soon grow tiresome. Brief recreational drug use, an implied sexual encounter and an instance of rough language. A-III (PG-13)

Indiana Jones and the Last Crusade (1989) The adventure trilogy ends by pairing Indy (Harrison Ford) with his father (Sean Connery), a medieval scholar trying to save the Holy Grail from 1930s' Nazis. Director Steven Spielberg's eye-popping stunts and intense comic-book violence are balanced by the humorous interaction between father and son whose survival depends on their resolving long-standing conflicts. Exhilarating, old-fashioned action movie, much too intense for youngsters but less threatening to older adolescents. Minor sexual innuendo and rough language. A-III (PG-13) PG

Indiana Jones and the Temple of Doom (1984) Director Steven Spielberg's sequel to "The Raiders of the Lost Ark" has Indiana (Harrison Ford), with the help of a chorus girl (Kate Capshaw) and a Chinese war orphan (Ke Huy Quan), rescue a stone from a nasty Indian sect and return it to its rightful owners. Nonstop stunts take precedence above all else, making it entertaining for action fans, but the comic-book violence is a little intense, especially a sequence involving the removal of a human heart. A-III (PG)

Indochine (1992) Romantic family saga set in 1930s' French Indochina where a rubber plantation owner's daughter (Catherine Deneuve) has a brief affair with a French naval officer (Vincent Perez) but her adopted Vietnamese daughter (Linh Dan Pham) falls in love with him and the two wind up fleeing the French authorities by hiding out with Communist revolutionaries. Director Regis Wargnier maintains interest in the romantic storyline by developing it in tandem with the changing political balance between French colonists and Vietnamese nationalists. Subtitles. Mature themes and treatment. A-III (PG-13)

Infinite Tenderness, An (1973) French documentary on the world of a brain-damaged, physically handicapped child confined to a wheelchair, unable to speak but trying desperately to communicate with his nurse and the other children in the hospital. It chron-icles his friendship with another youngster even more crippled than himself, their joy in being together, their little spats and, finally, the termination of their friendship by death. Directed by Pierre Jallaud, it is a remarkable achievement, treating its subject creatively yet with complete integrity. There is no commentary, no dialogue, only the natural sounds of the children and their environment. A-II (nr)

Informer, The (1935) Powerful adaptation of Liam O'Flaherty's novel about oafish Gypo Nolan (Victor McLaglen) who betrays a comrade (Wallace Ford) to the Black and Tans for the reward, then squanders the blood money on drink trying to drown his guilty conscience and fear of being found out by the rebel organization. Director John Ford's poetic evocation of 1922 strife-torn Dublin builds pity for the slow-witted Gypo but only revulsion for his deeds in a tightly wound story of betrayal, retribution and forgiveness. Stylized violence and veiled references to prostitution. A-II (br)

Inga (1968) Swedish sex exploitation import directed by Joseph W. Arnbo details the initiation of a young girl (Marie Liljedahl) into a life of promiscuity. O (R)

Inheritor, The (1973) Slick French mystery adventure in which a ne'er-do-well play-boy (Jean-Paul Belmondo) investigates the circumstances of his industrialist father's death and his search leads to some dark secrets in his own family as well as to the top leadership of Europe's industrial giants. Director Philippe Labro takes some elegant jabs at high society and the swaggering Belmondo has some discreet fun with the ladies. A-III (PG)

Inn of the Sixth Happiness, The (1958) Ingrid Bergman gives a warmly sympathetic performance as a Christian missionary in 1930's China where her patience and sincerity gradually win over the district's crafty mandarin (Robert Donat), his people and a cynical Eurasian army officer (Curt Jurgens), until the Japanese invasion forces her to lead a column of orphans across the mountains to safety. Director Mark Robson finds some delicious humor in the worldly mandarin's increasing bafflement at the woman's selfless kindness, then grows quite serious as her spiritual convictions are tested midst the ravages of war. Despite tense moments and wartime violence, it's rewarding family fare. A-I (br) U

Inner Circle, The (1991) Life in the Soviet Union from 1939 to 1953 as seen by Stalin's personal movie projectionist (Tom Hulce) whose faith in the dictator is unshaken despite party purges, the persecution of his neighbors, the suicide of his wife (Lolita Davidovich) and the blighted life of an orphan (Bess Meyer) befriended by his wife. Directed by Andrei Konchalovsky, the Italian production was filmed inside the Kremlin and around Moscow with a largely Russian cast that gives its picture of a totalitarian state more interest than the dramatic contrivances of the narrative. Some brief but strongly felt violence, a restrained bedroom scene and some rough language. A-III (PG-13) 15

Innerspace (1987) Martin Short is the victim of industrial espionage as he tries to safely return the miniaturized capsule floating through his body and piloted by Dennis Quaid to the lab that created it. Madcap comedy from director Joe Dante falls short of large laughs but has some genuinely charming, albeit dumb, moments of clean fun. A-II (PG)

Innocence Unprotected (1971) Yugoslavian director Dusan Makavejev's 1968 work is a documentary about the making of the first Serbian talking feature (done in 1942 under the nose of the Nazis). The central figure is acrobatic strongman Dragoljub Aleksic, a national hero whose feats of strength have to be seen to be believed. Makavejev captures the warmth and vitality of the 1942 filmmakers so that his movie becomes a commentary on society's changing values with a nostalgia for the innocence that is missing from our own "enlightened" times. A-II (nr)

Innocent, The (1979) Italian director Luchino Visconti's last movie tells of a turn-of-the-century Roman aristocrat (Giancarlo Giannini) who makes no secret of his infidelities to his wife (Laura Antonelli) until she pursues an affair of her own, which has tragic consequences. Although the feel for the period and place is assured, the suicide of a major character is completely unmotivated. Extravagant, at times ludicrously so, use of nudity. O (R)

Innocent Blood (1992) Violent, trashy vampire parody features an undercover cop (Anthony LaPaglia) who risks having sex with a vampire (Anne Parillaud) while pursuing a mobster-turned-vampire (Robert Loggia) who is preying on other gangsters. Director John Landis is at his heavy-handed worst treating a gross parade of vicious killings as a comic lark. Extended kinky sex scene, much gory violence, rough language and recurring nudity. O (R) 15

Innocent Bystanders (1973) Substandard British spy movie in which an aging agent (Stanley Baker), in order to save his job, has to find a scientist escaped from a Siberia camp before other agents do. Peter Collinson's awkward direction highlights the story's violence, sadism and cynical view of humanity. Particularly distasteful

is a just off-screen torture sequence involving Geraldine Chaplin. O (PG) 18

Innocent Man, An (1989) Wrongfully accused and convicted citizen (Tom Selleck) ends up in maximum security prison where he is beaten and forced to kill another inmate (Bruce A. Young) to survive. Directed by Peter Yates, Selleck's transition from nice guy to tough dude is laughable. The plot's far-fetched premise strains credibility in its cartoonish depiction of our judicial and penal systems. Racist undertones, vigilante ending, grisly violence and profanity. O (R) 18

Inserts (1976) There are fitful glints of serious intent amid the dreary chaos of this vulgar, pretentious movie about a once-brilliant Hollywood director (Richard Dreyfuss) reduced to making stag movies. Though Dreyfuss gives a convincing portrayal of a man bored with himself, director John Byrum has made nothing of consequence out of the movie's vulgarities and considerable nudity. O (X)

Inside Daisy Clover (1966) Cute 15-year-old starlet (Natalie Wood) is exploited by suave 1930s' Hollywood producer (Christopher Plummer). Though it has its moments, director Robert Mulligan's oft-told story of the empty lives of media stars is itself empty, if not dull. Mature themes. A-III (br) X

Inside Moves (1980) Director Richard Donner's melodrama is set in a neighborhood bar patronized by men who have physical disabilities but who team up to help each other. Crippled John Savage regains his love of life and goes on to play pro basketball. Some rough language and crude sexual references mar an otherwise articulate story about regaining one's self-esteem. A-III (R/PG) AA

Inspector Clouseau (1968) Miscast Alan Arkin gamely plays the role Peter Sellers made his own but is let down by an unfunny script and lethargic direction by Bud Yorkin. Those with a taste for simple pratfalls may find some amusement in this crime comedy. A-III (G) U

Inspector General, The (1949) Uneven Danny Kaye costume vehicle places him at the center of all manner of comic misunderstandings when the corrupt officials (Gene Lockhart, Alan Hale, etc.) of a Central European town mistake a meek vagabond (Kaye) for the Emperor's feared inspector. Directed by Henry Koster, the 19th-century Gogol story is turned into a musical farce, broadly played by Kaye and company often to the point of tedium. Mild romantic subplot. A-I (br) U

Interiors (1978) Written and directed by Woody Allen, the plot involves three sisters (Diane Keaton, Marybeth Hurt and Kristin

Griffith), their mother (Geraldine Page), their father (E. G. Marshall) and his new wife (Maureen Stapleton). Save for the last named, all the rest of the characters are locked in their narcissistic prisons, the exquisite interiors Allen strives mightily to explore, but the dense theme often leaves the viewer staring into space rather than focusing on the profound. The claustrophobic and pessimistic movie communicates a sense of nihilistic ennui. A-IV (PG) 15

Interlude (1968) Married orchestra conductor (Oskar Werner) conducts both the Royal Philharmonic and an affair with a London reporter half his age (Barbara Ferris). Director Kevin Billington's romantic tearjerker treats adultery as a bittersweet affair. A-III (br) A

Internal Affairs (1990) When an L.A. detective (Andy Garcia) in the department's Internal Affairs Division begins to investigate a routine misconduct case, he uncovers a web of police corruption masterminded by a well-respected veteran cop (Richard Gere). British director Michael Figgis creates a dark but shallow thriller depicting women as sexual playthings and exploiting the corrupt cop's pathological acts of blackmail, seduction and murder. Much sexual promiscuity including a flash of nudity, graphic violence and sexually vulgar language. O (R) 18

International Velvet (1978) Lavishly produced and entertaining sequel to "National Velvet" (1944) now has the adult Velvet (Nanette Newman) living with a writer (Christopher Plummer) and her newly orphaned niece from America (Tatum O'Neal) who goes on to win the gold medal in the Olympic equestrian competition. Directed by Bryan Forbes, there is a little violence and the unmarried state of the two adults raises questions of propriety for younger viewers. A-II (PG)

Interplay (1970) By the time the long-suffering heroine of this clumsy movie has tried and rejected group sex in affluent suburbia, the hapless viewer has been subjected to a series of immoralities as boring as they are unconvincing. Directed by Albert T. Viola, it's an inept exploitation of contemporary moral confusion. O (X/R)

Intersection (1994) A successful Vancouver architect (Richard Gere) vacillates about whether to build a new home with his lover (Lolita Davidovich) or to return to the life he has built with his estranged wife (Sharon Stone) and 13-year-old daughter (Jenny Morrison) until a car crash figures into the mix. The shallow central characters make director Mark Rydell's exploration of a tortured romantic triangle slow going, though the final ironies are a nice touch. Marital

infidelities, flashes of nudity and minimal rough language. A-III (R)

Interval (1973) Sentimental romance with Merle Oberon as an unattached woman traveling through an amber-colored Yucatan while fending off any number of mature males who become enchanted with her ageless beauty, one of whom (Robert Wolders) finally catches up with her. Aside from some quite pleasant travelogue footage of Mayan ruins, director Daniel Mann's movie is so trite as to be an embarrassment, and all the gauze over the close-up camera lens and the fireworks at climactic moments of passion only serve to emphasize its dated soap opera origins. A-III (PG)

Intervista (1992) In this 1987 Italian production, director Federico Fellini takes viewers on an imaginative tour of moviemaking at the famed Cinecitta Studios in the suburbs of Rome. Fellini's leisurely paced valentine to the joys and confusion of the filmmaking process radiates a fondness for all around him but is best energized in scenes of a nostalgic reunion with his "La Dolce Vita" (1961) stars, Marcello Mastroianni and Anita Ekberg. Subtitles. A flash of shadowy nudity, some vulgar references and minimal rough language. A-III (nr) 18

Intimate Lighting (1969) A Prague cellist together with his girlfriend returns to his hometown for a few days and stays with a childhood chum and his family. Director Ivan Passer's loving portrait of Czech life, culture and people is done with affection and earthy humor. A-III (nr) A

Into the Night (1985) A man (Jeff Goldblum), bored with such problems as insomnia and an unfaithful wife, finds life noticeably more exciting when a beautiful woman (Michelle Pfeiffer) dives into his car with a quartet of assassins in hot pursuit. Crude, unimaginative effort from director John Landis with excessive violence and nudity. O (R) 15

Into the West (1993) When a magnificent white horse wanders into their Dublin slum, two motherless waifs (Ruaidhri Conroy; Ciaran Fitzgerald) ride off into the countryside, pretending to be Wild West cowboys, with their sobered father (Gabriel Byrne) and the police in hot pursuit. Director Mike Newell presents a sensitive yet rousing tale of emotionally neglected children whose fertile imaginations help them transcend an impoverished home. Fleeting violence, children in jeopardy and a few profanities. A-II (PG)

Intruder in the Dust (1949) Engrossing social drama from William Faulkner's novel about an aloof black farmer (Juano Hernandez) arrested for killing a white man, then saved from lynching by a Southern mob after an earnest youth (Claude Jarman Jr.) and an elderly lady (Elizabeth Patterson) prove his innocence. Director Clarence Brown uses the puzzling murder mystery to hold interest while exploring the motivations of the characters and the ethos of a small town (filmed in Oxford, Miss.) where racial prejudice is an accepted way of life. Excellent study of racial attitudes and human rights, though some scenes may be too intense for young children. A-I (br) A

Invaders from Mars (1986) Inferior remake of the 1953 original about a little boy (Hunter Carson) who tries to warn his parents that their neighbors are being taken over by Martians. Director Tobe Hooper concentrates on the period settings to the detriment of some talented performers (Laraine Newman and Timothy Bottoms). Although the movie resorts to bullets as the answer to a communication problem, the movie is light enough for family entertainment. A-I (PG)

Invasion of the Blood Farmers (1973) Moronic movie about descendants of an ancient Druid cult who depopulate a rural area of upstate New York searching for the perfect specimen whose transfused blood would revive their catatonic queen. Director Ed Adlum's low-budget horror involves a cast of amateurs in excessively gory murders and tortures, with some teasing sexual allusions. O (GP)

Invasion of the Body Snatchers (1956) Classic sci-fi thriller in which a small-town doctor (Kevin McCarthy) and his girlfriend (Dana Wynter) discover that their fellow citizens are being replaced by pod people from outer space. Tautly directed by Don Siegel, the nightmarish concept becomes frighteningly credible as the townspeople gradually turn into their emotionless alien counterparts bent on keeping the terrified pair from escaping to warn the outside world. Mounting suspense, menacing atmosphere and an incidental marital complication. A-II (br) PG

Invasion of the Body Snatchers (1979) Mediocre remake of the 1956 thriller in which aliens from outer space take over the identity of earthlings through a pod producing a double of the sleeping victim. Its basic failing is director Philip Kaufman's inability to turn the banal pod people into villains worth rooting against. Donald Sutherland and Brooke Adams try to stem the tide, but Kevin McCarthy and Dana Wynter did it better in the low-budget, yet more imaginative original. Some excessive scenes of blood and gore and gratuitous nudity. O (PG) 15

Invasion U.S.A. (1985) Group of Soviet terrorists sneaks ashore at Miami Beach and proceeds to wreck havoc until stopped by karate champion Chuck Norris and director Joseph Vito's simple-minded script. Unremitting violence. O (R)

Investigation of a Citizen Above Suspicion (1970) Italian drama of a police chief (Gian Maria Volonte) who murders his girlfriend (Florinda Bolkan), then leaves a trail of evidence that inescapably reveals his identity. Director Elio Petri's narrative interweaves the investigation of the crime with flashbacks establishing its motivation. The engrossing thriller has many implications about the role of authority in maintaining an ordered society, but some may find its realistic scenes of sex and violence rather unsettling. A-IV (R)

Invisible Kid, The (1988) Failed teen comedy about a youth (Jay Underwood) who discovers his deceased father's secret formula for invisibility and uses it for a series of adolescent hijinks, including a foray into a girls' locker room and the bedroom of a pretty cheerleader neighbor. Written and directed by Avery Crounse, the potential for humor in the dull-witted situation is stretched painfully thin. A-III (PG)

Invisible Man, The (1933) Gripping adaptation of the H. G. Wells story about a scientist (Claude Rains) who succeeds in perfecting a serum making him invisible but loses his sanity in the process and winds up terrorizing the countryside as an unseen menace. Directed by James Whale, Rains is impressive though his performance consists mostly of a maniacal disembodied voice, neatly abetted by convincing special effects and suitably terrified extras. Excellent fantasy fare with minimal stylized violence. A-I (br)

Invisible Man Returns, The (1940) In an uneven sequel to the 1933 original, a man (Vincent Price) convicted of murdering his brother uses the invisibility serum in order to bring the real killer to justice. Directed by Joe May, the plot nicely balances the invisible gimmickry with the wry ingenuity of the police inspector (Cecil Kellaway) in charge of the case. Some stylized violence. A-I (br)

Invitation, The (1975) Pleasant little Swiss film about a shy, awkward bachelor (Michel Robin) who invites his fellow office workers to a Sunday afternoon gathering at his rather plush home. Though everyone gets a little drunk, nothing much really happens in director Claude Goretta's adroitly precise celebration of ordinary people and their mundane foibles. A-III (nr)

Ipcress File, The (1965) Story of spy and counter-spy that amuses as it confuses, deglamorizing the business of undercover work to some extent with humor while the story moves by tricky plot twists, some of which do not bear later examination. Michael Caine is excellent as the uncertain hero and director Sidney Furie holds everything together with a lightly satiric touch. A-II (br) A

Iphigenia (1977) Greek adaptation of Euripides' play faithfully retells the story of King Agamemnon (Costa Kazakos), who is told to sacrifice his daughter, Iphigenia (Tatiana Papamoskou) in order to assure safe passage for his fleet to Troy. Considering the difficulties inherent in bringing Greek tragedy to the screen (not just translating one art form to another but overcoming the cultural diversities of two millenia) producer-director Michael Cacoyannis' work represents a considerable accomplishment. Mature theme and some incidental nudity. A-III (nr)

Iron & Silk (1991) A 22-year-old American (Mark Salzman) arrives in China in 1982 to teach English and absorb the culture, but spends much of his time training under the skeptical eye of a famed kung fu master (Pan Qingfu). Producer-director Shirley Sun's fact-based account of the youth's two years in China alternates martial arts sequences with an earnest, low-keyed glimpse of Chinese society that hints at the government crackdown to come at decade's end. Restrained kung fu segments. A-II (nr)

Iron Eagle (1986) Taking his high school commencement speech about accepting adult responsibilities seriously, Air Force brat (Jason Gedrick) steals a Phantom jet fighter and, with a little help (Lou Gossett Jr.), blasts his way through an unfriendly Arab country to free his captive father. Self-righteous adolescent fantasy directed by Sidney J. Furie justifies excessive violence in the service of youthful idealism. Negative role model and extremely foul language. O (R) PG

Iron Eagle II (1988) The sequel tracks the U.S. and Soviet brass as they unite misfit American and Soviet pilots in a joint mission to knock out a hot nuclear warhead in the Middle East. With Lou Gossett Jr., in a respectable reprise of his original role, director Sidney J. Furie's sincere but cliched effort offers an innocuous vision of international cooperation and world peace. Cartoon violence and some locker-room language. A-II (PG)

Iron Eagle III (see: "Aces: Iron Eagle III").

Iron Maze (1991) Unsavory tale of the attempted murder of a Japanese businessman (Hiroaki Murakami) as recounted to the Pennslyvania police in contradictory versions by the victim, his U.S. bride (Bridget Fonda) and her volatile lover (Jeff Fahey). Director Hiroaki Yoshida's clumsy melodrama sheds little light on the nature of truth or

the clash of cultures and is further marred by choppy exposition and underdeveloped characters. Repeated staging of a violent confrontation, restrained lovemaking and recurring rough language. A-III (R)

Iron Will (1994) Old-fashioned underdog tale in which a South Dakota youth (Mackenzie Astin) in 1917 attempts to save the family farm and earn college tuition by competing for the $10,000 prize in a gruelling, 522-mile dogsled race from Winnipeg to St. Paul, Minnesota, in the dead of winter. Director Charles Haid's outdoors adventure is rousingly rendered despite downright corny dialogue and several cardboard villains. Some menace and brief violence. A-II (PG)

Ironweed (1987) Story set in 1936 Albany, N.Y., about a hobo (Jack Nicholson) who visits the wife (Carroll Baker) and family he had deserted 22 years before after having drunkenly caused the death of his infant son. Scripted by William Kennedy from his own novel and directed by Hector Babenco, the result is less the story of a few days in the life of a Depression-era bum than it is a challenging meditation on the quality of lost souls. Some adults will be repelled by its depiction of the brutalizing conditions in which derelicts live as well as several needlessly explicit sex scenes. A-IV (R) 15

Irreconcilable Differences (1984) Pre-teen girl (Drew Barrymore) sues to be free of her parents (Ryan O'Neal and Shelley Long) who have been driven to distraction by life in the Hollywood fast lane. Some parents may be chagrined over the legal and emotional precedent of the child rights issue, but director Charles Shyer can't choose whether this is light comedy or fairly serious drama. Very brief nudity in a comic context. A-III (PG) 15

Is Paris Burning? (1966) Rene Clement directs this epic tribute to the French people who fought valiantly to save their city from the senseless destruction ordered by Hitler. In concentrating on the sweep of events rather than on the many individuals involved, the movie is convincing history but fails as human drama. Wartime violence. A-I (br) A

Is There Sex After Death? (1971) Writer-director Alan Abel plays a sexologist who, when not attending local patients, roams the country asking pointed questions of people on the street. A few familiar personalities contribute risque routines or scatological interviews, but for the most part the porno parade is strictly amateur night. O (X/R)

Isabel (1968) French Canadian story of a young woman (Genevieve Bujold) who returns to a stifling back country environment upon the death of her mother and finds herself unable to escape from her strange family whose history is tied to the land. Written, produced and directed by Paul Amond, it has plenty of lushly beautiful country scenes but its moody, sinister interiors with their turgid, murky implications of incest don't add up to a satisfying experience. A-III (br)

Isadora (see: "The Loves of Isadora").

Ishtar (1987) Warren Beatty and Dustin Hoffman play failed songwriters who find themselves pawns in a dangerously ironic game of international intrigue in director Elaine May's failed buddy comedy set in the Moroccan desert. Essentially a story about the saving grace of brotherly love, the exotic romantic adventure has some rough language, brief slapstick violence and a momentary flash of nudity. A-II (PG-13) PG

Island, The (1980) Clumsy, brutish thriller about a writer (Michael Caine) and his young son who inadvertently come across the descendents of 16th-century pirates still plying their bloodthirsty trade in the shelter of the Bermuda Triangle. Director Michael Ritchie's fantasy veers wildly between the cruel, ridiculous and downright nasty. Excessive violence, some nudity and profanity. O (R) X

Island at the Top of the World, The (1974) Disney version of a Ian Cameron novel about an American archaeologist (David Hartman) and a British adventurer (Donald Sinden) who journey to the Arctic where they discover a tropical island atop a polar ice cap inhabited by the descendents of the Vikings. Directed by Robert Stevenson, it is burdened by a ragged screenplay, some lackluster special effects and many atrocious performances. Harmless family fun, but it could have been so much better. A-I (G) U

Island of Dr. Moreau, The (1977) Second screen version of H. G. Wells' novel about a scientist's obsession to turn animals into human beings starts out promisingly enough with a shipwrecked engineer (Michael York) finding himself on a remote Pacific island presided over by a kind but somewhat sinister doctor (Burt Lancaster). Once Moreau's secret is out, however, director Don Taylor's movie degenerates into rather clumsy and ineffective melodrama with considerable violence and bloodshed. The 1933 version with Charles Laughton is the one to see. A-III (PG) 15

Island of the Blue Dolphins (1964) Engrossing adaptation of Scott O'Dell's children's story about the 19th-century adventures of a young Indian girl (Celia Kaye) who learns to fend for herself when stranded on a remote island off the coast of California.

Produced by Robert B. Radnitz and directed by James B. Clark, the movie captures the wondrous beauty of nature and its sense of ecology provides a delightful lesson for youngsters. A-I (br) U

Island of the Burning Damned (1971) Standard British sci-fi programmer with Christopher Lee and Peter Cushing combating extraterrestrial beings who invade a country inn. Director Terence Fisher engenders as much suspense as possible with invaders who resemble nothing so much as bubbling, crawling neon pancakes. A-III (GP)

Islands in the Stream (1977) George C. Scott stars as an expatriate American living in the Bahamas who is jolted out of his self-pitying sense of failure as a man and as an artist by the demands of World War II. Franklin Schaffner has directed this adaptation of the posthumous Ernest Hemingway novel with considerable success in focusing upon the interior world of the central character, the prototypical Hemingway hero acting with style under pressure. A-II (PG) A

Isle of the Dead (1945) Science faces the supernatural during the 1912 Balkan War when a stern Greek general (Boris Karloff) quarantines an island beset by plague and gripped by the fear of a vampire. Producer Val Lewton and director Mark Robson team to fashion a fairly effective tale of psychological dread filled with talk of evil spirits and dark, moody photography. Spooky effects and stylized violence. A-II (br) X

It! (1967) Hokey horror with Rabbi Loew's Golem turning up in a British museum where loony assistant curator Roddy McDowall brings it to life but can't control it. Writer-producer-director Herbert J. Leder updates the Golem legend with snatches of other horror movies, including "Psycho," but with little sense of suspense or credibility. Stylized violence and sexual situations. A-III (br)

It Happened Here (1966) Imagining what life might have been like if Hitler had succeeded in invading Great Britain is shown in the story of a nurse who is drawn into collaboration with the puppet regime under the German Occupation. Directed by Kevin Brownlow and Andrew Mollo, it is an interesting inquiry into the nature of Nazi totalitarianism, with some scenes of brutality that, though not vivid, are extremely realistic and not for children. A-II (br) A

It Happened One Night (1934) Delightful romantic comedy in which a just-fired reporter (Clark Gable) sees a scoop in helping a runaway heiress (Claudette Colbert) escape her father (Walter Connolly), detectives and the press by roughing it from

Miami to New York via buses, roadside tourist cabins and even on foot. Director Frank Capra's screwball Depression roadshow has the charm of matching opposites in Gable's hardboiled working man and Colbert's spoiled rich girl whose unsentimental journey ends with the falling "Walls of Jericho," a running gag which finally brings them together. Memorable romantic classic with plenty of fun as well as social and personal values. A-II (br) U

It Happens Every Spring (1949) Lightweight but very enjoyable comedy about a chemistry professor (Ray Milland) who concocts a wood-repellent formula that makes baseballs immune to contact with bats. Directed by Lloyd Bacon, the comic premise turns the prof into a big-league star whose pitches defy batters and confound his catcher (Paul Douglas). Fun for all. A-I (br) U

It Lives Again (1978) Cheap and shoddy horror movie about an epidemic of monstrous infants who kill with superhuman force. Director Larry Cohen's blood-and-gore thriller is excessive not only in its concept but also its graphic visuals. O (R)

It Lives by Night (1974) When a honeymooning couple (Steward Moss, Marianne McAndrew) run into a bat while frolicking in a western cave and the husband is bitten, he goes around by night killing people, including the local tourist trade. Directed by Jerry Jameson, it is an innocuous bottom-drawer horror movie, but a love scene and some grisly details make it inappropriate fare for the youngsters. A-III (PG)

It Only Happens to Others (1971) Written and directed by Nadine Trintignant, this is a very personal movie about the loss of a child (the Trintignant's lost their child when Jean-Louis was filming "Z"). With Marcello Mastroianni and Catherine Deneuve playing the grieving parents, the result is a movie that seems to mourn over the loss of a sweet, precious toy rather than for a human life. The director seems to have kept her own feelings private while distracting viewers with both the luminous personalities of her players and the glossy plastic backgrounds against which they emote. A-III (GP)

It Started with Eve (1941) When a dying millionaire (Charles Laughton) insists on meeting his son's fiance, the dizzy lad (Robert Cummings) brings home a hatcheck girl (Deanna Durbin) and the confusion contributes to the old man's recovery. Directed by Henry Koster, Laughton steals the picture in a sly performance that goes from death bed to dance floor, imparting much needed charm to an otherwise artificial romantic comedy. A-I (br)

It's a Mad Mad Mad Mad World (1963) Overlong, overdone comedy spectacular about a random assortment of ordinary citizens who become greedy competitors in a madcap race to recover a fortune hidden by a bank robber (Jimmy Durante). Producer-director Stanley Kramer misuses practically every Hollywood comedian of the period (from Buster Keaton and Jack Benny to Jonathan Winters and Carl Reiner, not to mention actors such as Spencer Tracy and Peter Falk) in a ponderous attempt to wring laughs from car crashes and other forms of slapstick carnage. The main value of this misguided effort is its all-star gallery of comics who manage to keep the heavy-handed vehicle at least fitfully funny. A-I (br)

It's a Wonderful Life (1946) Seasonal favorite about the joys and trials of a good man (James Stewart) who, facing financial ruin on the eve of Christmas, contemplates suicide until his guardian angel (Henry Travers) shows him how meaningful his life has been to those around him. Director Frank Capra's unabashedly sentimental picture of mainstream American life is bolstered by a superb cast (including Lionel Barrymore as a conniving banker) and a wealth of good feelings about such commonplace virtues as hard work and helping one's neighbor. Young children may find the story's dark moments unsettling. A-II (br)

It's Alive (1977) Thoroughly nauseating movie in which a newborn baby turns out to be a bloodthirsty monster who kills some 20 people before the police stop it. Director Larry Cohen is most interested in using gore and graphic brutality for shock value alone. O (PG)

It's My Turn (1980) Jill Clayburgh plays an intelligent independent woman who meets an out-going man (Michael Douglas) and knows enough to dump the man she has been living with (Charles Grodin). Director Claudia Weill's attempt at a Tracy-Hepburn romantic comedy lacks the essential chemistry between the principals and its delineation of sexual as well as feminist themes requires a mature perspective. Some rough language. A-III (R)

It's Showtime (1976) Compilation of excerpts from Hollywood movies whose stars were four-footed, furry, winged or other varieties of the animal kingdom. The clips have charming appeal in their lively and nostalgic remembrance of a time when movies were perhaps less sophisticated, but definitely more fun. Good family viewing. A-I (G)

It's Your Thing (1970) Produced by brothers Ronald, Rudolph and O'Kelly Isley who also topline the marquee and perform the title number, the movie records a June evening in 1969 when New York's Yankee Stadium shook with the gospel singers and pop groups who strut and stomp inexhaustibly. Jackie "Moms" Mabley steals the show with a heartfelt interpretation of "Abraham, Martin and John." Some revealing costumes, suggestive lyrics and movements. A-III (G)

Italian Connection, The (1973) German-Italian B-grade gangster film about a Milan pimp (Mario Adorf) who has been set up by the mob as scapegoat for a missing shipment of heroin sought by two American hit men (Henry Silva and Woody Strode) and the result is endless mayhem and violence. Director Fernando Di Leo punctuates the physical action with lots of sex and nudity. O (R)

Italian Job, The (1969) Tongue-in-cheek spoof of heist thrillers follows the hijacking of $4 million in gold as it is being transferred from the Turin airport to bank by staging the world's most spectacular traffic jam. Michael Caine organizes the job for mastermind Noel Coward who operates from an English prison. Before director Peter Collinson brings it all to a close with a maniacal, hair-raising auto chase, there's some good visual satire and a lot of busy acting to make up for the loose ends in the plot. A-II (G) U

Italiano Brave Gente (1965) The plight of Italian soldiers fighting on the Russian front during World War II is portrayed in the fate of four individuals, with Peter Falk and Arthur Kennedy as part of an impressive international cast. Director Giuseppe De Santis' large-scale epic manages to retain some feeling for the human pain of war. Fairly intense battle scenes. A-III (br)

Ivanhoe (1952) The age of chivalry is revisited in this version of Sir Walter Scott's novel about 12th-century England where Saxon knight Ivanhoe (Robert Taylor) battles a host of Norman nobles, wins the hand of his lady fair (Joan Fontaine) and rescues a Jewish merchant (Felix Aymler) and his comely daughter (Elizabeth Taylor). Director Richard Thorpe's good cast does well in a story chock-full of romance, ideals, villainy and medieval derring-do, including tournaments, the storming of a castle and the ransom of good King Richard. Stylized violence. A-I (br) U

Ivanhoe Donaldson (1965) Feature documentary about the work of Donaldson, field secretary of a civil rights organization, as he helps conduct voter-registration drives, freedom marches and rallies in the South during 1963. Its footage showing the sincere commitment of those involved and their reliance on nonviolence in the face of provocation makes it a valuable part of the record of the times. A-II (br)

Ivory Hunter (1952) With the moral support of wife (Dinah Sheridan) and young son, a British game warden (Anthony Steel) perseveres in establishing East Africa's first wildlife preserve, despite pestilence, bureaucrats, native resistance and greedy poachers. Writer-director Harry Watt's earnest drama features colorful action in the bush as well as an inspiring story with humane values. Entertaining family fare. A-I (br)

J

Jabberwocky (1977) British farce inspired by some lines of Lewis Carroll and shaped by the comic spirit of the Monty Python gang tells of a medieval country bumpkin (Michael Palin) who suffers all manner of indignities until he finally becomes a hero by slaying a monster. Directed by Terry Gilliam, much of the humor is of the British bathroom variety, with some comic gore and brief nudity adding up to a movie less offbeat than it is offensive. O (PG)

Jack and the Beanstalk (1952) Pedestrian comic fantasy in which Lou Costello falls asleep on a babysitting job and, together with sidekick Bud Abbott, enters the fairy tale as the lad who bests the giant and escapes with his riches. Directed by Jean Yarbrough, the fantasy portion is filmed in color but that doesn't make the forgettable songs and slapstick routines any brighter. Innocuous entertainment for young children. A-I (nr)

Jack and the Beanstalk (1976) Japanese animated musical version of the childhood classic has insipid songs and rather primitive animation. Still, it moves along at a lively enough pace and may amuse younger children. A-I (G) U

Jack the Bear (1993) A boozy, grieving widower (Danny De Vito) moves his two young sons (Robert J. Steinmiller Jr.; Miko Hughes) to northern California where a sinister neighbor (Gary Sinese) decides to kill the boys after an imagined hurt. Director Marshall Herskovitz treats deadly danger to children with the same weight as the father's comic antics as a TV monster-show host and one son's case of puppy love, making for a jumbled, disturbing movie. Continuing menace, brief but nasty violence directed at a child and an instance of rough language. A-III (PG-13) 12

Jack Frost (1966) Russian version of the Cinderella story with wicked stepmother, beautiful maid and handsome prince set in a wintery countryside and told with charm. Adults will enjoy the gorgeous scenery, colorful costuming and doll-like performances even if they don't appreciate the old fairy tale as much as the youngsters do. A-I (br)

Jack of Diamonds (1967) Mild suspense thriller about a suave international jewel thief (George Hamilton) who plans a big haul at a posh Bavarian ski resort lodging Zsa Zsa Gabor, Carroll Baker, Lilli Palmer and their jewelry boxes but meets a rival in pretty Marie Laforet who's equally adept at light-fingering the ice. Directed by Don Taylor, it's diverting if familiar entertainment. A-II (br)

Jack the Giant Killer (1961) When an English princess (Judi Meredith) is stolen away by an evil sorcerer (Torin Thatcher), a country youth (Kerwin Matthews) battles his way through an assortment of magic spells, witches and giant creatures to rescue her—with the help of a wee leprechaun. Directed by Nathan Juran, the Edward Small production features some dandy special effects and fanciful settings, though the story and acting are pedestrian. Stylized violence and some scary moments. A-I (br)

Jacknife (1989) While an old Vietnam War buddy (Robert De Niro) tries to jolt a depressed friend (Ed Harris) out of drowning his memories of the war in drink and drugs, a tender middle-aged love story unfolds between the visitor and the troubled vet's shy sister (Kathy Baker). Director David Jones does a subtle job of weaving this low-key story to its conclusion in a well-acted slice of war-at-home life that sensitively explores the ghosts haunting Vietnam vets. Some profanity, brief violence and a discreetly filmed bedroom scene. A-III (R) 15

Jackson County Jail (1976) While driving cross-country to a new job, a young woman (Yvette Mimieux) is raped by a small-town sheriff whom she kills in self-defense and then flees with an accused murderer (Tommy Lee Jones). Director Michael Miller conveys with some care and sensitivity a fugitive's view of ruthless authority and the rape scene, though intense, is treated as a repugnant act of violence. A-IV (R) X

Jacob the Liar (1977) East German film about Polish Jews forced to serve the Nazis as laborers whose spirits are kept up by reports on advancing Allied troops by one of their number who pretends to have a secret radio. Under Frank Beyer's direction, Vlastimil Brodsky's acting in the title role helps to redeem a somewhat thin storyline, though its theme of hope born of invention has universal appeal. Stylized violence. A-II (nr)

Jacob's Ladder (1990) A Vietnam vet (Tim Robbins) suspects the Army is behind the terrifying hallucinations that are plaguing him and others in his unit. It's a case of style over substance in director Adrian Lyne's atmospheric thriller that jumpstarts from one menacing scene to the next showcasing eerie cinematography but coming up short on satisfactory storyline. Intermittent gory violence and rough language, recurring partial nudity and a live-in relationship. A-III (R) 18

Jacqueline Susann's Once Is Not Enough (1975) Kirk Douglas stars as a washed-up movie producer who marries rich Alexis Smith so he can continue providing motherless daughter Deborah Raffin with a luxurious life-style, even though he realizes that his new wife is having a lesbian affair with Melina Mercouri who is sleeping with George Hamilton. Directed by Guy Green, the movie is simple-minded trash whose formula is to reduce every human relationship to its genital components. O (R)

Jacques Brel Is Alive and Well and Living in Paris (1975) Lively, freewheeling collage of bittersweet romantic songs written and composed by Brel makes a charming piece of cabaret entertainment. Directed by Denis Heroux, it has a good cast, including Elly Stone, Mort Schuman, Joe Masiell and, of course, Jacques Brel. A-III (PG)

Jacquot (1993) Warmly nostalgic re-creation of the formative years of filmmaker Jacques Demy (1931-90) follows his childhood in Nantes during World War II, enthrallment with marionettes, operettas and then movies, teen attempts at filming with an amateur camera and, finally, making his father realize he does not want to become a mechanic but go to film school in Paris. Directed by Agnes Varda, the 1991 French production is not only a loving tribute to her husband, playfully exploring the sources of his creative imagination by intercutting excerpts from his movies with episodes of his youth, but it also beautifully evokes the universal passage from childhood to the brink of adulthood. Subtitles. Wartime destruction and tensions, minor domestic disputes and several scenes of youthful curiosity about sex. A-III (PG)

Jagged Edge (1985) Woman attorney (Glenn Close), defending a client (Jeff Bridges) accused of murdering his wife, begins to fall in love with him while becoming increasingly convinced of his guilt. Director Richard Marquand tries for Hitchcock-style suspense, but the plot line is implausible and the ending disappointing. Graphic violence, foul language and nudity. O (R) 18

Jail, The (1974) Documentary, originally aired on public television, takes viewers within the walls of San Francisco County Jail to experience the daily life of the inmates and guards. Filmmakers Michael Anderson, Paul Jacobs, Saul Landau and Bill Yahraus have collaborated in an effort to show that even in a relatively humane prison, keeping people locked away behind bars is an inhuman condition. A-III (nr)

Jail Bait (1977) German film about a 14-year-old girl who has an affair with a 19-year-old boy, gets pregnant and persuades the boy to kill her father for trying to keep them apart. Director Rainer Werner Fassbinder's unsavory tale about adolescent relationships and middle-class hypocrisy is seriously marred by excessive nudity. O (nr)

Jake Speed (1986) Self-indulgent action-adventure yarn in which a deadpan, not-too-perfect hero (Wayne Crawford) saves a college coed (Karen Kopins) from white slavers. Filmed in Zimbabwe, director Andrew Lane's pulp drama lacks comedic flair that might have saved its stodgy characterizations. Comic-book violence. A-II (PG) 15

Jamilya (1972) Lyric Russian movie evoking the life of a peasant village during World War II in which a 12-year-old parts with his childhood as he witnesses his sister-in-law's clandestine affair with a convalescent soldier and their subsequent flight from her ruthless husband. Director Irina Poplavskaya paints her celluloid picture in predominantly sepia tones reflecting the primitive locale and a people whose personal emotions are habitually overshadowed by communal devotion to duty. A-III (nr)

Janis (1975) Documentary on blues singer Janis Joplin is less a coherent chronicle of a life or a pop music era than an assemblage of available footage, some of it quite elegant, but much rough-edged film clips people were willing to let directors Howard Alk and Seaton Findlay use in their musical portrait. The segments don't add up to a whole person (none of the personal problems that contributed to her death of a drug overdose in 1970 are broached), but it does have some of her finest numbers as seen in performance. Some rough language. A-III (R)

January Man, The (1989) Implausible N.Y. cop thriller about a serial strangler wastes its time on the eccentric antics of a super-sleuth investigator (Kevin Kline), his possibly crooked brother (Harvey Keitel), the frustrated women in their lives (Susan Sarandon; Mary Elizabeth Mastrantonio) and the loud-mouthed Mayor (Rod Steiger) orchestrating the investigation. Irish director Pat O'Connor fails to mesh an erratic portrait of irreverent Irish-American New Yorkers with a crime story of serious intent. Excessive profanity laced with sexual vulgarities, sexual promiscuity; some nudity. O (R) 15

Jason Goes to Hell: The Final Friday (1993) Mindless horror sequel in the "Friday the 13th" series with its unkillable killer (Kane Hodder) on another murderous rampage until stopped by a female relative (Erin Gray) plunging a magic dagger through the monster's heart. Directed by Adam Marcus, the repetitious action of the formula script is as tiresome as its gory variations of special-effects mayhem are repulsive. Excessive violence, sexual situations, gross humor and rough language. O (R) 18

Jaws (1975) Solid thriller about a killer shark first establishes the monster's reality by the effect of its attacks on the tourist trade of a seaside community and then becomes the all-out battle of three men (Roy Scheider, Robert Shaw and Richard Dreyfuss) against a malignant force of nature. Aided by good acting and superior special effects, Steven Spielberg directs the hunt and killing of the monster with sustained and riveting dramatic intensity. Graphic scenes of the shark attacks may be far too strong for younger viewers. A-III (PG)

Jaws II (1978) Roy Scheider re-creates his role of an embattled sheriff pitted against a great white shark in this dull sequel directed by Jeannot Szwarc. Violence, teenage promiscuity, vulgar language. A-III (PG)

Jaws 3-D (1983) This second sequel to the big blockbuster only demonstrates there is a world of difference between technology and creativity. The 3-D effects are really rather effective in a grisly sort of way, but the movie itself is slow-moving, talky and generally dull. The big fish inspires little fear, the plot inspires little excitement and director Joe Alves tries to rescue his mediocre effort by emphasizing the violence. A-III (PG)

Jaws: The Revenge (1987) The great white shark tries to eat up the remainder of the Brody family but can't get past Mom (Lorraine Gary). Failed attempt by director Joseph Sargent to milk the suspense and shock of Steven Spielberg's original offers only mild scares for the small fry and dull, repetitive bloody visual effects. A-II (PG-13) 15

Jayhawkers, The (1959) Twisted tale of friendship focuses on the ruthless gunman (Jeff Chandler) whose band is terrorizing 1850s' Kansas and an outlaw (Fess Parker) who agrees to betray him in return for a pardon. Director Melvin Frank fails to give much credibility to a convoluted plot which gallops off in too many directions, though individual action scenes are memorable. Stylized violence, some of it nasty, and sexual references. A-III (br) A

Jazz Singer, The (1980) Neil Diamond stars as the cantor's son who pursues a career in show business, with Laurence Olivier as his grieving father and Lucie Arnez as the woman who promotes the son's career. Director Richard Fleischer's dim, sentimental tearjerker has more cliches than either the 1927 or 1953 version. A-III (PG)

J.C. (1971) Strange biker movie about an itinerant preacher (William F. McGaha) whose motorcycling congregation share his rootless, searching way of life and return with him to his Alabama home town. Its redneck sheriff (Slim Pickens) torments them and the story quickly resolves itself by violent confrontations ending in death. Also produced and directed by McGaha, the movie may

strike some as an interesting parable about an outcast heralding peace, while others will dismiss it as glamorizing an irresponsible vision of life. A-IV (R)

J.D.'s Revenge (1976) The vengeful spirit of a slain hoodlum takes control of a cleancut black law student who becomes a vicious sadist. Director Arthur Marks' tale of demon possession is a tiresome and disagreeable affair revolving around sex and violence. O (R)

Je T'Aime, Je T'Aime (1972) French film about a failed suicide (Claude Rich) who agrees to participate in a scientific experiment aimed at sending him one year into the past where he becomes lost in the labyrinth of bits and pieces of his life, centering mostly in the tragic love affair that led to his attempted suicide. Director Alain Resnais dazzles viewers with mental gymnastics and some uncharacteristic humor, but this excursion into the memories of a man who has no future is only a minor exercise by a major director marking time. A-II (nr)

Jean de Florette (1987) The first in a two-part adaptation of Marcel Pagnol's novel about a crafty farmer (Yves Montand) who in the early 1900s cheats a man from the city (Gerard Depardieu) out of the farm he has inherited by blocking the spring that is its only source of water, a wrong righted in the second part, "Manon of the Spring." Directed by Claude Berri, the French production is beautifully crafted and its sympathetic characterizations make the suffering and final tragic ruin of the city man, his wife and their small daughter all the more affecting. Realistic depiction of the unfortunate family's hardships and a passing sexual reference. A-II (PG)

Jennifer (1978) Mediocre thriller about a poor girl (Lisa Pelikan) in a posh private school on a scholarship who gets her revenge on the vicious and snobbish girls persecuting her by using her family training in snake-handling. John Gavin and Nina Foch in supporting roles lend whatever dignity there is to director Brice Mack's low-budget effort whose violence makes it adult fare. A-III (PG)

Jennifer 8 (1992) Obsessed with trying to protect his blind girlfriend (Uma Thurman) from a serial killer of blind women, a northern California cop (Andy Garcia) finds himself framed for the murder of his partner (Lance Henriksen). Writer-director Bruce Robinson's limp thriller finally falls apart in a ludicrous ending. Brief violence, some menace, a flash of nudity and much rough language. A-III (R) 15

Jennifer on My Mind (1971) Pretentious story starts with the death of a young woman (Tippy Walker) and then proceeds through flashbacks and tape recordings to chronicle the life of cute pot smokers and heroin shooters. Director Noel Black has rendered something that would have been merely boring as straightforward narrative into something insipid and absurd. Its most serious flaw is a total absence of any perspective, moral or otherwise. A-III (R)

Jenny (1969) Marlo Thomas stars in the title role as a patient, intelligent, resolute girl who intends to keep her baby even though born out of wedlock. She meets and marries Alan Alda, a self-centered filmmaker trying to avoid the draft. Director George Bloomfield's superficial melodrama reverses itself and manages to demonstrate how familiarity slowly leads to mutual respect and responsibility, and ultimately a deep regard and tender affection. A-III (PG)

Jeremiah Johnson (1972) Robert Redford stars in the story of a 19th-century mountain man from his arrival in the Rockies through his years as a self-sufficient trapper, then as family man and, finally, a Crow Indian fighter of legendary proportions. Director Sydney Pollack's story offers the awesome natural spectacle of the mountain locales, the swift frontier action, intense cultural conflict and colorful characters rendered without the burdens of sentimentality and contrivance. Stylized violence. A-II (GP) PG

Jeremy (1973) Robby Benson stars in the title role as a shy New York high school sophomore who finds true love with a pretty senior transfer student (Glynnis O'Conner), but they are parted when her father gets his old job back in Detroit. Directed by Arthur Barron, the slickly sentimental tearjerker is so phony in its contrivances that it should make any self-respecting teenager retch. A-III (PG) A

Jerk, The (1980) Steve Martin plays a poor sharecropper who goes from rags to riches in a dreary, relentlessly vulgar and foulmouthed comedy directed by Carl Reiner. Sexual innuendo and racial stereotyping. O (R) 15

Jerusalem File, The (1972) Idealistic American student (Bruce Davison), against the advice of his college professor (Nicol Williamson) and an Israeli intelligence officer (Donald Pleasence), sets up a tragic meeting between some moderate Arab nationalists and a group of Israeli students. Director John Flynn handles the mechanics of the espionage caper adequately enough but cannot disguise what ultimately is a naive, unnecessarily muddled narrative. A-III (PG) A

Jesse James Meets Frankenstein's Daughter (1966) Laughable horror movie in a western setting and ineptly directed by William Beaudine with an amateur cast. A-II (br)

Jesus (1979) Originally intended for educational purposes, this screen version of the Gospel of St. Luke is more a picture album illustrating the *Good News Bible* translation than a creative attempt to use the power of the film medium. Directed by Peter Sykes, the presentation is more likely to provoke boredom than stir admiration among young viewers. A-I (G)

Jesus Christ Superstar (1973) Screen version of the Andrew Lloyd-Webber/Tim Rice musical adds a completely new dimension and drive to the music by cinematography that enhances the original songs but also threatens to overwhelm them. Director Norman Jewison presents a visual recording, with optical embellishment, of a performance of the rock opera based on the last days of Christ's life on earth, ending in his crucifixion. Entertaining as musical theater, it can also be seen as a sincere if naive effort to tell the story of Jesus in contemporary musical and ethical terms. Some scenes require a mature perspective. A-III (G) A

Jesus of Montreal (1990) Challenging French-Canadian drama about a young actor (Lothaire Bluteau) who takes seriously an invitation to modernize a traditional Passion Play staged annually at a local shrine and, though his new version is a dramatic success, its unorthodoxy causes the shrine's religious authorities to withdraw permission for future performances, resulting in a crisis for all concerned. Written and directed by Denys Arcand, this provocative movie places the gospel story in the midst of the contemporary world, suggesting parallels to events in the life of Christ with what happens to the dedicated young actor. While some viewers may be dismayed by the work's critical attitude toward the institutional church and its intermingling of the historical Jesus with unseemly aspects of modern life, others may gain some refreshing insights and perspectives on Christianity's continuing relevance in our own times. A-IV (R) 18

Jet Pilot (1957) Addled cold-war drama in which a U.S. Air Force officer (John Wayne) is vamped by a Soviet spy (Janet Leigh) masquerading as a defecting Russian aviator. Directed by Josef von Sternberg, the slack proceedings grow increasingly dim with silly on-again, off-again romancing and dull ideological clashes that wind up in a preposterous All-American finish. Sexual situations and innuendo. A-III (br) U

Jetsons: The Movie (1990) Feature-length cartoon based on the popular television series about a space-age family follows George Jetson into outer space where Mr. Spacely's sprocket factory is under siege by little creatures bent on sabotage. The producer-director team of William Hanna and Joseph Barbera sustain the upbeat personalities of the gadget-crazy Jetsons but fail to mesh two opposing animation styles—the characteristically flat Jetsons look alongside the more dimensional, computerized animation. Musical interludes sung by teen pop stars Tiffany and Shane serve only as forgettable fillers. A-I (G) U

Jewel of the Nile, The (1985) Jack and Joan (Michael Douglas and Kathleen Turner) take off in their yacht for the Middle East to rescue a special kind of "jewel" in this disappointing sequel to "Romancing the Stone." The zest of adventure has faded and even the comic touches seem forced in a ponderous plot with endless chase sequences and little suspense. Some mature subject matter and mild vulgarity. A-III (PG)

Jewish Gauchos, The (1976) Entertaining Argentinian movie about a group of Jewish refugees from pogroms in Czarist Russia who settle in the ranchlands of Argentina. A nostalgic version of immigrant history not too far different from our own, it tells the story of how these Jewish gringos become gauchos with robust action, comedy and romance, helped by some lovely songs sung by Ginamaria Hildalgo. Restrained but intense scene of violence. A-II (PG)

JFK (1991) Choppy dramatization chronicles the efforts of New Orleans District Attorney Jim Garrison (Kevin Costner) to refute the Warren Commission's conclusion that Lee Harvey Oswald (Gary Oldman) was the sole assassin of President Kennedy and instead charges conspiracy at the highest levels of government by bringing to trial a local gay businessman (Tommy Lee Jones) with alleged CIA connections. Director Oliver Stone freely mixes fact with speculation to validate Garrison's views in a long, unwieldy movie that is dramatically persuasive in relentlessly reconstructing its version of a crime that may never be adequately explained. Brief but recurring shots of violence including staged and documentary footage of the assassination and subsequent autopsy, fleeting scene of a homosexual party and intermittent rough language. A-III (R) AA

Jigsaw Man, The (1984) Laurence Olivier, Michael Caine and Susan George are wasted in a dismal spy movie pitting a Soviet double agent against British Intelligence. Director Terence Young fails to make all the intrigue and plot contrivances of the slightest interest. A-II (PG)

Jim, the World's Greatest (see: "Story of a Teenager").

Jimi Hendrix (1974) Documentary on pop singer Hendrix who died tragically in 1971, ending at age 27 his meteoric rise in the glittering constellation of rock music. An unusual and occasionally profound work assembled by Joe Boyd from mostly familiar footage of Hendrix performances interspersed with interviews and reminiscences of people who were close to him. Some rough language and crude gestures. A-III (R)

Jinxed (1982) Unhappy wife (Bette Midler) of a seedy gambler (Rip Torn) teams up with a blackjack dealer (Ken Wahl) to get rid of her unwanted husband whom the dealer believes is a jinx. Director Don Siegel's attempt at black comedy is an embarrassing disaster, resorting to vulgarity and profanity as sources of humor. A-III (R)

Jo Jo Dancer, Your Life Is Calling (1986) Richard Pryor directs as well as stars in a tragicomic story of a comedian on his deathbed, reliving his past, assessing what went wrong and finally affirming the value of his life. Pryor takes some chances, with what many will see as autobiographical material, as he exposes the hurt and anger that was the source of the comedian's personalized brand of humor. Excessive harsh language and some nudity, but utilized as an authentic reflection of the environment in which the action takes place. A-IV (R)

Joanna (1968) Pretentious British movie about a 19-year-old innocent (Genevieve Waite) who comes to London to live with her grandmother and study art but the wrong friends and the urban life-style lead her astray. Directed by Michael Sarne, the movie is supposedly about the need for an authentic value system, but its graphic sex scenes are excessive. O (R) X

Jock Petersen (1975) Australian sex exploitation movie directed by Tim Burstall is distinguished only by some pretty travelogue footage of Quantas-land. O (R)

Joe (1970) Low-budget look at a blue-collar worker (Peter Boyle) whose hatred of hippies leads him to join in the search of an executive (Dennis Patrick) for his lost daughter and in their forays into the youth subculture, they participate in orgies of promiscuity and pot smoking with tragic results. Written by Norman Wexler and directed by John G. Avildsen, the movie deals with the conflict between rebellious youth and conventional society in terms of stereotypes, yet Boyle's performance as a bigoted hard-hat has a three-dimensional quality. A-IV (R) X

Joe and Maxi (1980) Documentary made by Maxi Cohen about her father, Joe, who during the filming learned he was dying of cancer. The result is utterly lacking in style and point of view, raising only questions of the propriety in continuing a project that the dying man insists be stopped. Perhaps it has some educational use in classroom discussions of death and family relationships. A-II (nr)

Joe Hill (1971) Turn-of-the-century labor saga of an itinerant union organizer for the International Workers of the World (I.W.W. or more commonly, the Wobblies), about whom little is known except that he wrote a number of songs popular in the labor movement. Swedish director Bo Widerberg has taken this almost mythical character and fleshed out a personality that is more poetic than real, yet Tommy Berggren's appealing performance as Joe makes credible his dedication to society's unfortunate and downtrodden. A-II (GP)

Joe Kidd (1972) Predictable western in which an eastern landgrabber (Robert Duvall), needing to get rid of the Mexican American (John Saxon) standing in the way of his scheme, hires a shiftless gunman (Clint Eastwood) who eventually gets around to seeing that justice is done his way. Directed by John Sturges, the justice-of-the-gun theme is distanced by the western myth and can be dismissed as simple fantasy. A-III (PG) 15

Joe Versus the Volcano (1990) When a burned-out romantic (Tom Hanks) learns that he has only six months to live, he quits his grim job and jumps at an offer to spend 20 carefree days on a remote South Seas island after which he will serve as a human sacrifice to the island's volcano. As written and directed by John Patrick Shanley, this delightful comic fantasy about realizing one's dreams before it's too late recalls earlier Hollywood fantasies with its magical set design, nutty romantic touches and endearing performances. Some minor sexual innuendos. A-II (PG)

John and Mary (1969) Dud melodrama focusing on the relationship between two young singles (Mia Farrow and Dustin Hoffman) after they spend the night together. Director Peter Yates' essay on sexual morality in a liberated age raises questions about love and commitment but capitalizes on nudity and bogs down in endless discussions about sex. O (R/PG) AA

Johnny Angel (1945) The mystery of a deserted freighter adrift on the high seas is solved by the thin-lipped merchant-ship captain of the title (George Raft) in this tale of smuggled gold, double-crossers, a two-timing wife (Claire Trevor) and a fearful witness (Signe Hasso). Director Edwin L. Marin keeps the mystery afloat with shady characters and taut action until the final showdown. Stylized violence. A-II (br) A

Johnny Apollo (1940) In trying to get money to spring his embezzler father (Edward Arnold) from prison, a devoted son (Tyrone Power) turns to an influential gangster (Lloyd Nolan), becomes his front man and winds up in prison along with dad. Director Henry Hathaway's tough crime melodrama takes some nasty turns, including an ice-pick murder, before the son is reformed by prison and a good-hearted woman (Dorothy Lamour). Stylized violence and sympathetic treatment of criminals. A-III (br)

Johnny Be Good (1988) When a top high school quarterback (Anthony Michael hall) is courted by sleazy college football recruiters promising fame and fortune, he exposes their slimy tactics by choosing to play for a school where he'll get a good education. Badly directed by Bud Smith, the movie has much jock humor and rough language, several situations that vulgarize women and brief nudity. A-III (PG-13)

Johnny Belinda (1948) Sensitive turn-of-the-century drama about the transformation of a deaf mute (Oscar-winning performance by Jane Wyman) when taught to read and sign by the new doctor (Lew Ayres) in a poor Nova Scotia community, but then is raped by a drunken fisherman (Stephen McNally) and threatened with the loss of the child she bears as a result. Director Jean Negulesco makes good use of the isolated rural setting in telling the story of a young woman who overcomes the inner isolation of her physical disability as well as the unenlightened prejudices of her neighbors. Several scenes of stylized violence and an off-screen rape. A-II (br)

Johnny Cash: The Man, His World, His Music (1970) Documentary follows Cash on his tours, at home and behind the scenes in warm, intimate sessions with friends and admirers. There is plenty of music for the fans, and its above average production values contribute to an enjoyable and entertaining movie. Some passages of dialogue are not for youngsters. A-II (GP)

Johnny Concho (1956) Bogus western about a puny parasite (Frank Sinatra) who bullies a town cowed by his gunfighter brother until a mean hombre (William Conrad) shows up with the news that he's just killed the feared gunman. Under Don McGuire's uncertain direction, the script's contrived transformation of a nasty little coward into a righteous citizen is unearned, unconvincing and, even worse, uninteresting. Stylized violence. A-II (br)

Johnny Dangerously (1984) Michael Keaton stars as a man who turns to crime in order to pay for his mother's multiple medical crises. Director Amy Heckerling's spoof of 1930s' gangster movies, with Keaton doing a take-off on James Cagney, is defeated by an unfunny script emphasizing vulgar language and sexual situations. A-III (PG-13):

Johnny Got His Gun (1971) Dalton Trumbo directs his own adaptation of his 1938

novel about the hideous ironies of war, specifically the limbless, faceless, senseless but conscious trunk that is all that remains of a World War I soldier (Timothy Bottoms). The story of an innocent sent out by his elders to make the world safe for democracy is told in straightforward, homey flashback scenes with a warmth and poignancy that makes ordinary American life wondrously appealing. It is remarkable for its achievement as a disturbing moral statement about the immorality of war, though many will turn away from its uncompromising treatment. A-IV (R/GP) X

Johnny Handsome (1989) Downbeat drama about a disfigured felon (Mickey Rourke) who is given a second chance at life by a plastic surgeon, but even a new face, an honest job and the love of a good woman (Elizabeth McGovern) do little to turn this low-life around. Director Walter Hill's grisly, pointless effort also features a sadistic pair of nasties (Ellen Barkin and Lance Henriksen). Assorted violence, much profanity and brief nudity. O (R) 15

Johnny Minotaur (1971) Sojourning on Crete with the intention of making a movie about the myth of the Minotaur, surrealist poet and painter Charles Henri Ford evidently became preoccupied with the shiftless life-style of some young Greeks he retained to help with his project. The result is an amateur movie documenting homosexual diversions in graphic detail. O (nr)

Johnny Nobody (1965) Unusual British mystery about a priest (Nigel Patrick) who becomes an amateur sleuth when a writer is murdered in front of him and his entire congregation. Also directed by Patrick, the plot has some some suspenseful twists and the star is quite credible as a clergyman. A-II (br) U

Johnny Reno (1966) Low-budget western ineptly directed by R.G. Springsteen about a sheriff (Dana Andrews) trying to keep a prisoner from being lynched by the townspeople. Stylized violence. A-II (br)

Johnny Stecchino (1992) Italian comedy of mistaken identity concerns a mild-mannered bus driver who looks like a gangster-turned-informer (Roberto Benigni in a dual role) whose wife (Nicoletta Braschi) sets up the busman to be killed by the mob instead. As also written and directed by Benigni, the madcap movie's manic energy tends to compensate for the thin premise. Subtitles. Comic depiction of gunplay, drug abuse and insurance fraud, mild sexual innuendo and minimal rough language. A-III (R)

Johnny Suede (1992) Vacuous story of a vain would-be country singer (Brad Pitt) who drifts through intimate relationships, gaining no insight into himself or his pa-

thetic schemes. Writer-director Tom DiCillo's ironic humor doesn't overcome a pointless script that treats the lead character's continual promiscuity with great bemusement. Several promiscuous relationships, sexist attitudes, minor violence and frequent rough language. O (R)

Johnny Tiger (1965) Set in Florida Everglade country is the story of a half-breed Seminole Indian (Chad Everett) and a teacher (Robert Taylor) who tries to help him in a mediocre melodrama directed by Paul Wendkos. Some violence and mature themes. A-III (br)

Joke, The (1970) Czechoslovakian story of a man (Josef Somr), sent to prison and his career ruined for holding political ideas that 20 years later have become fashionable, determines to take revenge on those mouthing the new line as glibly as they had the old. Director Jiromil Jires infused his 1966 movie with a sense of quiet outrage, a sour and acerbic protest against the intolerance of the past and a warning for the present. A-III (nr)

Joke of Destiny, A (1984) Director Lina Wertmuller's satire on modern life and Italian politics is a disappointing misfire. Plodding and heavy-handed, the movie's comic invention fails badly after a brilliant opening. Adult situations. A-III (PG)

Jokers, The (1967) British comedy about two brothers (Michael Crawford and Oliver Reed) who concoct a scheme to steal the crown jewels from the Tower of London, but the zany lark gets out control when one brother double-crosses the other. Director Michael Winner keeps the plot boiling all the time, not in the least concerned that there are a number of gaping holes in it. Viewers who like fast-paced humor won't mind either, especially with the picturesque London setting. A-II (br)

Jonah Who Will Be 25 in the Year 2000 (1976) Whimsical, very talky and coolly detached movie from Swiss director Alain Tanner about the effects of today's sexual and political upheavals on the life-styles of several young adults. Its focus is on the future and, as its title implies, it is fundamentally optimistic about people and their ability to survive. Some frank talk about sexual relationships; brief nudity. A-IV (nr) X

Jonathan (1973) German horror film about an isolated area where Dracula maintains a reign of terror until a student leads the villagers in a raid driving the vampire hordes to their destruction in the sea. Writer-director Hans W. Geissendorfer's plot is secondary to its theme that total helplessness leads ultimately to revolt. Highly stylized but graphic images of the bizarre and the demonic. A-IV (nr)

Jonathan Livingston Seagull (1973) Richard Bach's pretentious little fable about a seagull who makes a number of discoveries, personal and cosmic, has been turned into a big pretentious film. Director Hall Bartlett's reverential treatment of Bach's jumbled bits and scraps of mystical adages only highlights the weaknesses of the source, an effect helped not at all by the drone of Neil Diamond's uninspired ballads. A-I (G) U

Joni (1982) Fact-based story of Joni Eareckson, a talented athlete who breaks her neck a month after graduation from high school and is doomed to a wheelchair for the rest of her life. Director James F. Collier details her fight to rebuild her life and the central part played by her religious conversion. Inspiring and often deeply moving, it is made quite special by Eareckson's performance as herself. Restrained but realistic hospital scenes. A-I (G)

Jory (1972) Dim western with Robby Benson in the title role as a 15-year-old who witnesses his father's murder, avenges it, repeats the pattern for a friend and gets involved in a range war before riding off into the sunset. Directed by Jorge Fons, the tale of a youth coming to renounce violence by first bathing in blood is familiar to the point of being trite as well as poorly done. Stylized violence. A-II (PG)

Joseph Andrews (1977) Failed British adaptation of Henry Fielding's 18th-century farce about a virtuous servant lad (Peter Firth) beset by lustful females (Ann-Margret among them). Director Tony Richardson offers little more than a tedious and distasteful exercise in period lechery with gratuitous nudity and rough language. O (R) AA

Josh and S.A.M. (1993) Shuttled between divorced, self-absorbed parents (Stephen Tobolowsky and Joan Allen) two unhappy youngsters take off cross country for Canada because the 12-year-old (Jacob Tierney) has convinced his 7-year-old brother (Noah Fleiss) that he is a U.S. government humanoid rigged with a secret weapon that will detonate unless he escapes the country. Director Billy Weber's concern about neglected children of divorce being used as pawns by parents gets lost in an increasingly bizarre narrative that utterly defies credibility. Brief violence, frequent juvenile theft and lying, some menace to children and sexual references. A-II (PG-13)

Joshua Then and Now (1985) Jewish writer (James Woods) from Montreal finds true love in London with a woman (Gabrielle Lazure) who comes from one of Montreal's first families but, upon returning to Canada, their happy marriage threatens to come apart under pressure of their quite different social and religious backgrounds. Directed by Ted Kotcheff, it is an entertaining if uneven and often awkward film that occasionally presents some serious ideas in provocative fashion. Extremely crude and vulgar language and situations, including brief nudity. A-IV (R)

Journey into Fear (1942) Uneven suspense thriller in which an American munitions expert (Joseph Cotton) becomes a bewildered pawn in the deadly game of international espionage played out on board a Black Sea freighter with an odd lot of mysterious passengers (including Delores Del Rio, Agnes Moorehead and Jack Moss), one of whom is a Nazi agent. Adapted from Eric Ambler's exotic tale of foreign intrigue, it is a curious mixture of menace and muddlement, much of it directed by Orson Welles (who also plays a cunning Turkish intelligence officer) though finished by the studio and credited to Norman Foster. Sinister atmosphere and stylized violence. A-II (br) A

Journey into the Beyond (1977) Shoddy documentary that purports to be a serious inquiry into life-after-death is little more than tabloid exploitation of footage that is by turns tedious and revolting. O (R)

Journey of Hope (1991) The dream of a better life in Switzerland for a Turkish couple (Necmettin Cobanoglu and Nur Surer) and their little boy (Emin Sivas) is shattered when smugglers leave the three in the frozen Alps to find their own way across the border. Swiss director Xavier Koller's Oscar-winning fact-based drama is a powerful, straightforward appeal to the emotions regarding the plight of desperate, easily exploited immigrants from Third World countries. Subtitles. A violent beating and scenes of intense menace. A-II (nr) PG

Journey of Natty Gann, The (1985) Courageous young girl (Meredith Salenger) searches for her father on a dangerous but wondrous trek cross-country, accompanied by a protective drifter (John Cusack) amidst the political unrest, social upheaval and economic hardship of the 1930s' Depression. Though unabashedly sentimental, this Disney movie under the direction of Jeremy Kagan is enjoyable family entertainment, filled with life-affirming people and situations. A-I (PG)

Journey Through Rosebud (1972) Well-intentioned but inept movie about an Indian tribe's refusal to accept U.S. government restrictions on their hunting rights involves a draft dodger (Kristoffer Tabori) who unwittingly causes the suicide of the tribe's demoralized leader (Robert Forster). Written by Albert Ruben and directed by Tom Greis, the movie's attempt to explore the causes of the Indians' bitter behavior gets lost in a welter of history, psychology and contemporary sociology that most will find difficult to unravel. A-III (GP)

Journey Through the Past (1974) Basically a home movie for the fans of rock superstar Neil Young, vaguely structured and larded with interview clips and lots of musical numbers recalling Young's early work with other groups. Its scenes showing his relationship with a screen actress are of dubious taste if not morality. A-IV (R)

Journey to Shiloh (1967) Seven young Texans join the Confederate Army to take part in what they believe will be a grand and glorious adventure, but soon become disillusioned with the war and all but one (James Caan) are killed at the bloody Battle of Shiloh. Directed by William Hale, the melodramatic story is carelessly patched together and ineptly told, especially the badly handled battle action. Violence and a bedroom scene. A-III (br)

Journey to the Far Side of the Sun (1969) Sci-fi melodrama about a deep-space journey to explore a newly discovered planet. Theme contends with dangers of space-age technology. Above average attempt to probe the vast mysteries of new worlds from director Robert Parrish. A-II (G) A

Jovita (1970) Polish story of illusion and ennui about a young long-distance runner who meets a girl at a masquerade party and, in his attempts to find her again, makes a few self-discoveries along the way. Directed Janusz Morgenstern, the simple romance has a bit of athletics and classical music but is chiefly of interest as one of the last performances of its star, Zbigniew Cybulski. A-III (nr)

Joy Luck Club, The (1993) A San Francisco bon voyage party becomes the occasion for four immigrant Chinese mothers (France Nuyen; Lisa Lu; Kieu Chinh; Tsai Chin) to reflect on their past lives and present prickly relationships with their Americanized daughters (Rosalind Chao; Lauren Tom; Tamlyn Tomita; Ming-Na Wen). Wayne Wang directs the adaptation of Amy Tang's novel with considerable sensitivity, insightfully exploring the love and pain that go into nurturing mother-daughter bonds complicated by parent and child having grown up in vastly different cultures. Brief violence including a suicide, a restrained sexual encounter, much sexual innuendo and minimal rough language. A-III (R)

Joy of Living (1938) Wacky romantic comedy about a down-to-earth Broadway musical star (Irene Dunne) and a rich nonconformist (Douglas Fairbanks Jr.) who insists she drop her career and bevy of idle relatives to sail away for a carefree life as his wife on their own island in the South Seas. Director Tay Garnett keeps the odd-couple situation amusing as practical star resists free-spirited suitor until the inevitable becomes unavoidable. Romantic complications. A-II (br)

Ju Dou (1991) Set in a Chinese village in the 1920s, a young bride (Gong Li) is abused by her aged, impotent husband (Li Wei) but finds refuge in the arms of his adopted nephew (Li Baotian), and the son they conceive brings disaster to all of them. As directed by Zhang Yimou, the melodrama is a beautifully shot, bittersweet love story condemning the Chinese feudal society that so regimented people's lives. Subtitles. Discreet sexual encounters; some restrained violence. A-III (nr) 15

Judex (1966) French-Italian action melodrama about a daredevil champion of justice (Channing Pollack) who fights crime in the era just before World War I. Directed by Georges Franju, it will appeal to those who enjoy the innocent adventures of the superheroes of yesteryear. Stylized violence. A-II (br) A

Judge Hardy and Son (1939) While the judge (Lewis Stone) saves an old woman (Maria Ouspenskaya) from losing her home, Mom Hardy (Fay Holden) battles pneumonia and Andy (Mickey Rooney) has his usual trouble with the girls. Directed by George B. Seitz, the point of the episode is that parents must be honored and listened to, as Andy does in one of the longest man-to-man talks in the series. A-I (br)

Judge Hardy's Children (1938) Judge Hardy (Lewis Stone) takes son Andy (Mickey Rooney) and family to Washington, D.C. for a patriotic excursion in the Hardy series under the direction of George B. Seitz. A-I (br)

Judgment Night (1993) While taking a shortcut through a dark, deserted Chicago slum, four pals (Emilio Estevez; Cuba Gooding Jr.; Jeremy Piven; Stephen Dorff) happen upon a murder, then are pursued by the killer (Denis Leary) and his goons. Director Stephen Hopkins' edgy thriller tempers scenes of violence with fitful attempts to portray the positive nature of masculinity and the bonds of friendship. Much violence and rough language. A-III (R)

Judith (1966) Sophia Loren plays a concentration-camp refugee in Palestine after the war who joins an anti-Arab group in order get revenge on her ex-husband (Hans Verner), a former Nazi working for the Arabs. Directed by Daniel Mann, it's melodramatic hokum, though some may enjoy its picturesque locales and supporting cast (Peter Finch and Jack Hawkins). Restrained violence. A-II (br) A

Judo Saga (1972) Japanese movie about the moral discipline necessary for a student of judo to best the rival followers of jujitsu is set in 1882 when Japan was emerging from feudalism under the Meiji restoration and contrasts the changes of the period with the constant values of a moral code. Directed by Akira Kurosawa in 1943, his first movie already reveals the characteristic narrative style that so distinguishes his later, internationally popular works. A-I (nr)

Juggernaut (1974) A demolition expert (Richard Harris) tries to disarm seven bombs placed by a madman aboard Omar Sharif's luxury liner carrying some 1200 passengers. Director Richard Lester deftly turns a routine thriller into grand, fast, suspenseful entertainment. A-II (PG)

Juice (1992) Unrelentingly ugly story of four young Harlem thieves, one of whom (Tupac Shakur) relishes killing and turns with deadly force on his three friends (Omar Epps, Jermaine Hopkins and Khalil Kain). Director Ernest R. Dickerson presents a shrill movie where hatred, violence and drug use is the norm and has no moral implications. Mindless violence, momentary bedroom scene, some casual drug use and sexual references and constant rough language. O (R) 15

Julia (1977) Recollections by writer Lillan Hellman (Jane Fonda) of her friendship with Julia (Vanessa Redgrave), an extraordinary Englishwoman whose struggle to help Jews and anti-Nazis flee Hitler's Germany ends in tragedy. Directed by Fred Zinnemann, it is rather slow-moving, but its good acting and stress on human dignity in the face of inhumanity compensate for its dramatic flaws. A-II (PG)

Julia and Julia (1988) Failed thriller about a young widow (Kathleen Turner) inexplicably reunited with her husband six years after his death and pulled unnervingly between two worlds, until finally pushed to murder and mental collapse. Despite its eerie Italian setting and Turner's valiant effort to reflect the terror felt by her character, director Peter Del Monte is unable to combine the psychological and supernatural in a plausible narrative. Considerable nudity, graphic sex and some violence. O (R)

Julia Has Two Lovers (1991) A young man (David Duchovny) who gets his kicks sweet-talking strangers on the phone, then seducing them in their homes, falls for his latest victim (Daphna Kastner) just as she is about to marry her callous lover (David Charles). Director Bashar Shbib's low-budget movie traps the viewer into hearing details of the pathetic characters' perverse sexual encounters. Much sexual exploitation and recurring nudity. O (R) 15

Juliet of the Spirits (1965) Federico Fellini's first movie in color centers on a middle-aged woman (Giulietta Masina) trying to take stock of her life by sorting through her problems, memories and illusions. Fellini's imaginative imagery and Masina's aging gamin make the reveries and evocations a delight to the eye and the spirit. Ambiguous treatment of mature themes. A-IV (br) X

Juliette De Sade (1970) Sex exploitation movie about a young girl's desires to be initiated into a life of unrestricted sex and crime. The plot, dialogue and acting are of poor quality, with no other aim than titillation. O (R)

Julius Caesar (1970) Failed version of Shakespeare's tragedy directed by Stuart Burge with awkward staging, uniformly poor performances (Charlton Heston as Antony and Jason Robards as Brutus) and gauche Roman costuming right out of an Italian muscle movie. Even a desperate teacher, willing to try anything to motivate English students, had best beware this slack effort. A-II (PG) U

Jumbo (see: "Billy Rose's Jumbo").

Jumpin' Jack Flash (1986) Whoopi Goldberg plays a compassionate but fiercely independent computer operator who saves the life of a British intelligence agent trapped in an Iron-Curtain country when she communicates with him via her computer terminal. This raucous but lighthearted spoof of the spy genre as directed by Penny Marshall is chilled by an extraordinary amount of sexually derived expletives. A-III (R) 15

Jun (1980) Japanese movie about a maladjusted Tokyo worker who gives vent to his frustrations by molesting women on crowded commuter trains. Written and directed by Hiroto Yokoyama, its pretentious vision of urban alienation becomes a heavyhanded display of graphic sexual excesses. O (nr)

Jungle Book, The (1942) Uneven adaptation of the Rudyard Kipling story in which an infant boy (Sabu) is raised by wolves in the wilds of India, then protects an ancient treasure from a trio of greedy villagers (led by Joseph Calleia). Directed by Zoltan Korda, the jungle with its exotic animals has greater appeal than the village and its human tribe. Some graphic violence. A-II (br)

Jungle Book, The (1967) Rudyard Kipling's adventures of Mowgli, a boy-child reared by obliging wolves in the jungles of India, has been freely but nicely adapted in this animated feature in Disney's best traditions. Using contemporary humor and the voices of Phil Harris as Baloo, a lovable bear, George Sanders as Shere Khan, a suave, menacing tiger and Sterling Holloway as an opportunistic python, the movie will amuse everyone in the household. A-I (G) U

Jungle Fever (1991) A married African American architect (Wesley Snipes) becomes an outcast to his Harlem family as does his Italian Catholic girlfriend from Brooklyn (Annabella Sciorra) when their interracial affair is exposed. As written, produced and directed by co-star Spike Lee, the ugliness of racism is provocatively exposed and the human toll of drug addiction is harrowingly portrayed while religion comes off as something ineffectual or negative. An adulterous relationship, short outbursts of violence, brief partial nudity and much rough language. A-IV (R) 18

Junior Bonner (1972) Aging cowboy Steve McQueen has one big challenge left to meet in the form of a brahma bull that nearly killed him last time around. The film is stolen, however, by Robert Preston as Junior's wild Pa and Ida Lupino as his heartbroken, long-suffering but tough Ma in their superb and emotionally wrenching scenes together. Unlike some of his violent westerns, director Sam Peckinpah has here devoted his talents to constructing a well-balanced, well-paced and well-acted rodeo movie. A-II (PG) A

Jupiter Menace (1983) Narrated by George Kennedy with a straight face, this is one of those psuedo-scientific, quasi-religious documentaries that forecasts the end of the world. It may scare the wits out of those not inclined to take it all with several grains of salt, but then, fear is sometimes good for the soul. A-II (PG)

Jurassic Park (1993) A bizarre theme park featuring genetically re-created dinosaurs becomes a potential deathtrap when the carnivorous monsters break loose, endangering some visiting scientists (Sam Neill, Laura Dern and Jeff Goldblum) and two very frightened young children (Joseph Mazzelo and Ariana Richards). Director Steven Spielberg's monster fantasy downplays plot and characterization in favor of spectacle and horrific special effects in which the realistic-looking creatures hunt down their human prey. Much intense menace to children and several stylized scenes of violent death. A-II (PG-13) PG

Just Another Girl on the I.R.T. (1993) Gritty cautionary tale of a bright but flip African American teen (Ariyan Johnson) who aims to go to college and become a doctor but falls for a jock with a jeep (Kevin Thigpen), gets pregnant and winds up a single mother enrolled in a community college. Writer-director Leslie Harris's low-budget account of coming of age in Brooklyn's public housing projects makes good use of the harsh urban landscape and blighted social conditions but fails to create much sympathy for the girl's character and provides little insight in her predicament. Some restrained bedroom scenes, explicit discussions of contraception and abortion, an intense birth scene, attempted infanticide and much rough language. A-IV (R)

Just Around the Corner (1938) After her architect father (Charles Farrell) loses his job in the Depression, his little girl (Shirley Temple) helps him get it back by appealing to a millionaire (Claude Gillingwater) whom she mistakes for Uncle Sam. Director Irving Cummings pads out the formula plot with a little comic relief (Bert Lahr and Joan Davis) and some musical numbers with Shirley and Bill Robinson. Thin sentimental fare for the undemanding. A-I (br) U

Just Before Nightfall (1975) French psychological melodrama in which an ordinary man (Michel Bouquet) murders his mistress and then, overcome by guilt, decides to confess, but his wife (Stephane Audran) takes steps to prevent him from disgracing the family name. Director Claude Chabrol tells his story of conscience and middle-class morality with one ironic twist after another, confronting viewers with an ambiguous conclusion that implicitly indicts the emptiness of materialistic values. Brief nudity. A-IV (PG)

Just Between Friends (1986) Marital infidelity is the starting point for a seriocomic treatment of the relationship between a naive housewife and an independent career woman. When the man in their lives is killed in an accident, the wife (Mary Tyler Moore) discovers his affair with her friend (Christine Lahti) who is now pregnant with his child. The women ultimately find grounds for reconciliation and mutual support after the baby's birth. Directed by Allan Burns, the sitcom format and soap-opera characterizations offer little inspiration and less justification for a frivolous handling of a serious theme. A-III (PG-13) 15

Just Like at Home (1979) Hungarian director Marta Meszaros explores the relationship between a precocious 11-year-old girl (Zsuzsa Czinkoczy) and a rash and bedeviled man in his 30s. A flawed but nonetheless absorbing movie, it conveys the somber texture of life in contemporary Hungary. Mature themes. A-III (nr)

Just One of the Guys (1985) An ambitious high school girl (Joyce Hyser) who wants to be a journalist decides that no one takes her work seriously because she's too pretty and so she disguises herself as a boy. Director Lisa Gottlieb's plodding, mediocre comedy has a heavy emphasis on vulgarity and sexually oriented humor. Worse, outright promiscuity is portrayed as perfectly normal. O (PG-13)

Just Tell Me What You Want (1980) Long-time mistress (Ali MacGraw) of a greedy tycoon (Alan King) tries to break away by marrying a New York playwright (Peter Weller). The tycoon's devious efforts to get her back provide the thrust of the plot in this sour, vulgar comedy directed by Sidney Lumet. Though it has a lot of action, it has little purpose and no heart. Condones immoral actions and features foul language. O (R)

Just the Way You Are (1984) Crippled musician (Kristy McNichol) beds a succession of men both at home and on a vacation at a Swiss ski resort, where she hides her affliction with a plaster cast. Directed by Eduard Molinaro, the dull and listless attempt at light romance takes an entirely benign view of the heroine's promiscuous behavior. O (PG)

Just You and Me, Kid (1979) Retired comedian (George Burns) finds a teen-age girl (Brooke Shields) in the trunk of his vintage Pierce-Arrow clad in nothing but an old inner tube. Neither the plot explanation nor the attempts at humor are convincing in director Leonard Stern's generation-gap bore that has some brief laughs from John Schuck and Andrea Howard as nosey neighbors. Some violence and strong language. A-II (PG) A

Justine (1969) The last days of the British involvement in Egypt frame this complicated story featuring Anouk Aimee as the somber, crafty medium of the title, Michael York as a spineless schoolmaster and Anna Karina as the tubercular dancer he comes to love. Director George Cukor uses the city of Alexandria to convey the social and moral decadence of the late-1930s. Graphic rendering of homosexality; excessive use of nudity. O (R) A

J.W. Coop (1972) Cliff Robertson plays a rugged rodeo champ fresh out of prison after serving 10 years for forging a check and raring to get back on the circuit to catch up with his life and the times. Also written, produced and directed by Robertson, the success story may be a bit long in the telling, but its picture of a man who grits his teeth and gets on with the job of regaining a hold on life provides reasonably intelligent entertainment. Questionable romantic entanglement. A-III (GP)

K

K2 (1992) The lifelong friendship of two amateur mountain climbers (Michael Biehn and Matt Craven) is put to the ultimate test in the Himalayas where they become stranded atop the world's most dangerous mountain peak. While the physical dangers in this adventure movie are predictable, director Franc Roddam enhances the spectacular action sequences with gripping character studies of the two men as they face impending death. Some sexual innuendo, rough language and a flash of nudity. A-III (R)

K-9 (1989) Lame story of a hotheaded San Diego narcotics cop (James Belushi) and his police dog partner. Director Rod Daniel tracks this unlikely team as they corner a slick drug czar (Kevin Tighe). Much of this comedy caper focuses on implausible macho heroics. Intense comic-book violence, rough language, vulgar sexual innuendos. A-III (PG-13)

Kafka (1991) Interesting excursion into the dark imagination of absurdist author Franz Kafka (Jeremy Irons) whose dull duties as an insurance clerk in 1919 Prague spark nightmare images of an oppressive regime secretly operating from the medieval castle overlooking the city. Directed by Steven Soderbergh, the narrative is by turns moody, bizarre and ironic but never quite achieves the dreamlike logic that would make it work as something more than an elaborate exercise of the emotions. Morosely unsettling atmosphere, some nasty stylized violence and a glimpse of a nude photo. A-III (PG-13) PG

Kaleidoscope (1966) Warren Beatty and Susannah York star in a sophisticated comedy-thriller having to do with the big con games of a gambler on the loose in London and on the Continent. Beatty is miscast as a suave playboy, but the largely British cast is excellent. The plot is complicated, but director Jack Smight keeps it diverting enough for those who like this kind of derring-do. Moderate violence. A-III (br)

Kalifornia (1993) Violent road movie in which a cash-strapped couple (David Duchovny; Michelle Forbes) unwittingly share cross-country car expenses with a dimwitted innocent (Juliette Lewis) and her boyfriend (Brad Pitt), a cold-blooded murderer. Director Dominic Sena allows the drama to wallow in the vicious brutality of a callous killer and the conversion of a normal guy into a vengeful executor, depicting it all with flippant black humor. Excessive violence, graphic sexual encoun-ters, nude photos and occasional rough language. O (R) 18

Kama Sutra (1971) Exploitation movie using the Hindu sexual manual as an excuse for graphic sex scenes and frequently ludicrous commentary. O (X/R)

Kamouraska (1975) French-Canadian film set in the early 19th century in which a passionate and headstrong young woman (Genevieve Bujold) marries the boorish master of a remote estate (Philippe Leotard), leaves him to return to civilization and has a romance with a doctor (Richard Jordan) that ends in murder. Directed by Claude Jutra, the movie captures a vanished era, has excellent acting and the beauty of its settings, but its story of hot passion in a cold climate is heavily melodramatic. Some incidental nudity and scenes of questionable taste. A-IV (R)

Kansas City Bomber (1972) Raquel Welsh plays a top skater on the Roller Derby scene with Kevin McCarthy as the team owner trying to promote a bigger and better franchise. Burdened with some unconvincing, if decorative, performances, director Jerrold Freedman's inept and shallow melodrama manages to make the Roller Derby look boring. Some rough language. A-III (PG) 15

Kaos (1986) Comprised of four fables of Italian peasant life drawn from Luigi Pirandello's short stories, this Italian production by the Taviani brothers offers a range of sensitive characterizations expressing simple but profound truths. Each segment is a self-contained tale on a social, political or moral theme. Visually rich and dramatically provocative, the film's life-affirming narrative is well worth its running time of over three hours. A brief shot of partial nudity and a gruesome shot of a decapitated head punctuate an otherwise pastoral vision. A-III (R) 15

Karado, the Hong Kong Cat (1973) Martial arts champion returns to the island of his birth and finds himself between two opposing factions. Nonstop violent encounters in which everything from chain whips to revolvers come into play, as well as some sex scenes. O (R)

Karate Kid, The (1984) High school student (Ralph Macchio) learns about life, friendship and the martial arts from a kindly Japanese-American gardener (Pat Morita) who shows him how to deal with the bullies tormenting him. Directed by John G. Avildsen, the movie is made extremely appealing by the performances of the two principals despite its message that violence solves all ills. Parents should be sure that their youngsters realize karate is considerably more lethal than depicted here. A-II (PG) 15

Karate Kid Part II, The (1986) Repeating his role in the sequel, Pat Morita gives a winning performance as the martial arts teacher who brings his young student (Ralph Macchio) to Okinawa in a gentle story reaffirming the importance of devotion, loyalty and the sweet-and-sour of life as seen from the perspective of old age. Unabashedly moralistic without being didactic, it is high-spirited, engaging entertainment. A-I (PG)

Karate Kid Part III, The (1989) Against the wishes of his karate mentor (Noriyuki "Pat" Morita), young Daniel (Ralph Macchio) is coerced by sleazy martial artists into defending his championship title. Director John G. Avildsen puts more emphasis on the smirking heavies and grisly brutality than on the antiviolence values of the earlier series. The exploitative nature of the violence is unsuitable for preteens or impressionable younger adolescents. A-III (PG)

Katerina Izmailova (1969) Russian production of Shostakovich's opera features the performance of Galina Vishnevskaya, first soprano of the Bolshoi. Director Mikhail Shapiro provides a fluid rendering of tragic lovers who resort to murder to preserve their relationship but imprisoned in Siberia, love gradually turns, through mutual recriminations and the man's infidelity, into hatred. Dreary moral tale in Russian with English subtitles. A-III (nr)

Kaya, I'll Kill You (1969) Yugoslavian import conveys the simplicity of life in a pre-war Croatian village and the terror that is unleashed by the emergence of its own hometown fascists inebriated by power. Symbolic narrative set in exotic locales and directed by Vatroslav Mimica makes obscure points about the nature of violence and militarism. A-III (nr)

Kazablan (1974) Israeli musical pits the Sephardim against Ashkenazim in the Jaffa slums of Tel Aviv, telling the story of two lovers from different sides of the ethnic gap. Director Menahen Golan's economy-sized extravaganza of dancing and singing has some natural charm and its salty taunting and gesture is submerged in its theme of finding one's heart by relaxing one's prejudices. A-III (PG)

Keep, The (1983) Nazi unit guarding an ancient fortress in Romania runs into some odd events in this arty, pretentious and thoroughly muddled drama of the supernatural written and directed by Michael Mann, and starring Scott Glenn and Ian McKellan. Vicious rape scene and some graphic sex. O (R) 18

Keep On Rockin' (1974) Documentary of the 1969 Toronto Rock and Roll Revival features performances by Chuck Berry, Little Richard, Jerry Lee Lewis and Bo Didley. Made by D. A. Pennebaker, the film captures the infectious energy of the performers, and the drive of their music. A-II (PG)

Keeper of the Flame (1942) Contrived melodrama in which a journalist (Spencer Tracy) sets out to gather material for a tribute to a late public leader, falls for his widow (Katharine Hepburn), then discovers the truth about the man's death and secret subversive plans. Director George Cukor's woolly tale of home-grown fascism starts slowly and grows increasingly portentous until ending in typical period flag-waving. Muddled attempt to justify murder. A-III (br) A

Keetje Tippel (1976) Dutch drama about a 19th-century woman, forced by her mother into prostitution to support the family, who learns from a middle-class lover how to act and dress like a lady, and eventually marries a wealthy social reformer. Director Paul Verhoeven's masterful depiction of the terrible poverty of the working class and their first stirrings of revolt are overshadowed by obsessive detailing and graphic treatment of sexual encounters. O (nr)

Kelly's Heroes (1970) Clint Eastwood and Telly Savalas lead a group of U.S. soldiers (including Don Rickles and Donald Sutherland) 30 miles behind German lines to pull off a gold heist. Directed by Brian Hutton, the movie's premise is that all Germans are stupid, that American pragmatism is invincible and that the realities and deadly rituals of warfare make engrossing entertainment. A-III (PG)

Kentuckian, The (1955) Rough-hewn but unconvincing frontier tale of an 1820s backwoodsman (Burt Lancaster) torn between starting a new life in Texas with a servant girl he's rescued (Dianne Foster) or settling down in a small Kentucky town with a schoolteacher (Diana Lynn). Also directed by Lancaster, the plot is a haphazard series of complications delaying the predictable choice between frontier and civilization until the final scene. Assorted violence, some of it quite nasty, and romantic complications. A-III (br)

Kentucky Fried Movie, The (1977) Unfunny collection of sketches spoofing television and movies, especially movie trailers. Director John Landis finds vulgarity a proper source of humor, but even on a simple slapstick level his satire is often tasteless and sexually exploitive. O (R) X

Kes (1970) British movie set in a small, drab Yorkshire coal mining town tells the story of a lonely, sullen boy (David Bradley) whose life is momentarily given meaning by his experience in raising and training a baby kestrel, a European falcon. Directed by Ken Loach, the movie is a compassionate study of the blighted conditions and brutalizing life of this youth that in its final scenes indicates the possibility of his rising above his environment. Fine experience for adults and older adolescents. A-III (PG) U

Key Exchange (1985) Young novelist (Ben Masters), unsure of his feelings about a young woman (Brooke Adams), joins a friend (Dan Jenny), whose wife deserted him, in prowling the singles bar jungle before the inevitable happy ending. A very slight sex farce with little wit or charm, directed by Barnet Kellman. Nudity, graphic depiction of sex, benign view of adultery and fornication. O (R)

Keys of the Kingdom, The (1944) Underrated adaptation of A. J. Cronin's novel about a Scottish priest (Gregory Peck) sent to China at the end of the 19th century where he rebuilds a ruined mission, endures misunderstanding, war and disease but perseveres through humility and cheerful service to win many converts and friends until retirement in Scotland fishing for supper rather than souls. Directed by John Stahl, the narrative is interestingly contrived and Peck's characterization is entirely likeable and sincere though, like so many vintage Hollywood pictures about religion, lacking much spiritual depth. A-I (br) A

Khartoum (1966) Exciting action adventure with modern overtones about the British involvement in the Sudan during the 19th-century pits the Empire's most famous general (Charlton Heston) against the ferocious leader of the desert tribes (Laurence Olivier). Directed by Basil Dearden, the movie has the sweep of history and some good characterizations. Stylized violence. A-I (br) PG

Kickboxer (1989) Belgian martial-arts whiz Jean-Claude Van Damme is pitted against a deadly Thai kickboxing champ (Tong Po) who crippled his brother in the ring. Featuring some amateurish acting, melodramatic scripting and heavy-handed direction by David Worth and Mark DiSalle, the film is entertaining when it focuses on Van Damme's strict training sessions with a mysterious Thai mentor (Dennis Chan), but the kickboxing fight scenes are brutal. Intense ring violence and profanity. O (R) 18

Kid Blue (1973) Petty outlaw (Dennis Hopper) gives up on crime to make his way honestly in the little Texas town of Dime Box, whose single industry is a ceramic novelty factory, finds honesty hard work and decides to rob the factory payroll. James Frawley's direction makes the most of the comic potential of an uneven script that stretches to make contemporary references to everything from the drug culture to the plight of the American Indian. Brief but explicit seduction scene. A-III (PG) A

Kid from Spain, The (1932) After being expelled from college for a prank in the women's dorm, an overaged zany (Eddie Cantor) winds up in Mexico helping a friend (Robert Young) by masquerading as the son of a famous bullfighter. Director Leo McCarey wrings some laughs from predictable situations, aided by a good cast and inventive Busby Berkeley production numbers. Some sexual innuendo and comic menace. A-III (br)

Kid Millions (1934) Vintage Eddie Cantor musical follows him to Egypt to claim a fortune left by his archeologist father, but along the way he has to fend off an assortment of other claimants (Ethel Merman, Warren Hymer, Ann Sothern and George Murphy). Directed by Roy Del Ruth, the plot is sappy and the songs forgettable but it's a lot of silly fun, including the final reel with Eddie's ice cream factory in Technicolor. Some stylized violence and mild sexual innuendo. A-II (br)

Kid Rodelo (1966) Passable melodrama about a drifter (Don Murray) who is forced to protect a young woman (Janet Leigh) from a rough band of former convicts who are looking for gold. Director Richard Carlson moderates the violence in favor of the action adventure. A-II (br) U

Kidnapped (1938) Melodramatic adaptation of Robert Louis Stevenson's tale of an 18th-century orphaned youth (Freddie Bartholomew) befriended by a Scottish rebel (Warner Baxter) who tries to help the lad gain his stolen inheritance while fighting the English. Director Alfred L. Werker's good vintage cast (John Carradine, C. Aubrey Smith, Nigel Bruce and Reginald Owen) keep the adventure exciting, if not quite what Stevenson had mind. Stylized violence. A-I (br) U

Kidnapped (1948) Low-budget version of Robert Louis Stevenson's classic adventure in 18th-century Scotland with William Beaudine directing Roddy McDowall as the wronged youth and Dan O'Herlihy as the anti-English rebel in a generally lackluster production. Stylized violence. A-I (br) U

Kidnapped (1960) Disney version of the Robert Louis Stevenson adventure classic about a 18th-century Scottish youth (James MacArthur) done out of his inheritance and sold into servitude as a cabin boy by his treacherous uncle, then rescued by a dashing Jacobite rebel (Peter Finch) during the course of his battles with the English. Director Robert Stevenson is faithful to the spirit of the original, though some of the action may be a bit too intense for the pre-teen crowd. Stylized violence. A-I (br)

Kidnapped (1972) British adaptation of the Robert Louis Stevenson story of the young David Balfour (Lawrence Douglas) who is rescued from the villainy of his uncle (Donald Pleasence) by Alan Breck (Michael Caine), the heroic Stuart who opposes English rule over Scotland. Directed by Delbert Mann, it's still a classic children's adventure story, though there is some violence that might disturb young children. A-II (G) U

Kidnapping of the President, The (1980) South American terrorist (Miguel Fernandes), laden with dynamite, handcuffs himself to the President of the United States (Hal Holbrook), but the villains are no match for the head of the Secret Service (William Shatner). Canadian director George Mendeluk's routine suspense thriller features unnecessarily graphic violence in the opening sequence. A-III (PG) X

Kids Are Alright, The (1979) Performance and interview film featuring the antics and music of the British rock group, The Who. Director Jeff Stein's poorly organized documentary is marked by very little revelation, some vulgar language and sexual references. A-III (PG)

Kill a Dragon (1967) Run-of-the-mill action adventure movie set in the Orient with contrived plot and unbelievable scenes of bravado. Directed by Michael Moore, it follows a predictable course of sex and violence. A-III (br)

Kill and Kill Again (1981) Martial arts master (James Ryan) is hired to rescue a scientist from the clutches of a villain who wants to control the world in this slapdash, simple-minded melodrama produced in South Africa. Directed by Ivan Hall, the movie's violence is far less fierce than the accompanying grunts and groans. A-III (PG)

Kill-Off, The (1990) A bedridden crone (Loretta Gross) indulges in malicious phone gossip and before long the objects of her invective, including her younger, unfaithful husband (Steve Monroe), are thinking deadly thoughts about silencing her. Jim Thompson's hard-boiled novel is lifelessly directed by Maggie Greenwald with plodding pace, hesitant acting and heavy-handed music. Intermittent partial nudity, fairly restrained violence and minimal rough language. A-III (R)

Kill Them All and Come Back Alone (1970) Italian western in which Chuck Conners heads a band of Confederate renegades out to steal gold from a Yankee mining camp. Director Enzo G. Castellari lets the killings run their course until only anti-hero Conners remains. Extreme violence. O (R)

Killer Elite, The (1975) James Caan and Robert Duvall give fine performances as professional assassins working for a secret government agency in a suspense drama directed by Sam Peckinpah. Though flawed and lapsing into melodrama at times, the film raises questions of undercover agencies. Some brutal violence. A-III (PG) X

Killer Force (1976) Peter Fonda plays the leader of a raid on the vaults of a diamond mine in South Africa and after much muddlement escapes with the loot. Directed by Val Guest, the plot twists in this movie are so arbitrary that they are not worth following. Excessive gory violence. O (R)

Killer Grizzly (see: "Grizzly").

Killer Klowns from Outer Space (1988) The aliens of the title turn the residents of a small town, most notably a disagreeable police officer (John Vernon), into pods of fodder. Directed by Stephen Chiodo, the inane thriller is silly and nasty by turns. Much noisy violence, some of it quite bloody, and occasional vulgar language. A-III (PG-13)

Killers, The (1946) Convoluted thriller from the Ernest Hemingway story starts with a former prizefighter (Burt Lancaster) being killed by two hitmen, leaving a puzzled insurance investigator (Edmond O'Brien) to search for the woman (Ava Gardner) involved. Directed by Robert Siodmak, one clue leads to another as the ex-boxer's part in a payroll heist and its aftermath is reconstructed in flashbacks that ultimately end in some measure of justice. Stylized violence and some menace. A-II (br) A

Killing Fields, The (1984) Powerful and visually overwhelming film about the friendship of an American correspondent (Sam Waterston) and his Cambodian assistant (Haing S. Ngor) set against the background of the fall of Cambodia and the slaughter of millions by the Khmer Rouge. Director Roland Joffe's fact-based drama makes an extraordinary human document in the tragic history of an entire nation. Graphically realistic but not overdone scenes of carnage. A-II (R) 15

Killing Floor, The (1984) Arresting, meaningful drama of a black sharecropper (Damien Leake) who comes to Chicago during World War I, gets a job in the stockyards, joins the union and becomes an organizer until the union is crushed in the race riots of 1919. Directed by William Duke, the personal drama has considerable force in the context of the union's struggle to achieve ethnic and racial solidarity in its battle against the meatpackers. Period racism and some nasty stylized violence. A-II (PG)

Killing Game, The (1968) Pretentious French murder mystery directed by Alain Jessua has excessive nudity. O (br)

Killing of a Chinese Bookie, The (1976) Owner of a cheap nightclub (Ben Gazzara) undertakes a murder to pay off the gambling debt he owes gangsters. Director John Cassavetes' quest for authenticity and spontaneity takes an indecorous turn down a blind alley at the end of which one becomes sand-bagged by sex and violence in a tedious drama that doesn't ring true. O (R) AA

Killing of Sister George, The (1969) British story about a fading soap-opera actress (Beryl Reid) whose lover (Susannah York) has been seduced by another woman (Coral Browne). Director Robert Aldrich fails to treat lesbianism with any depth, opting instead for heavy-handed melodrama and a rather clinical demonstration of love-making with ample peek-a-boo nudity. O (X/R) 18

Kim (1950) The orphaned son (Dean Stockwell) of an English soldier in Kipling's India is befriended by a Tibetan lama (Paul Lucas), sent briefly to military school and then introduced to the "great game" of British intelligence by a dashing native agent (Errol Flynn). Directed by Victor Saville, the young lad's adventures in Queen Victoria's colonial empire are colorful enough but the movie suffers from a plodding script and lackluster action. Some stylized violence. A-I (br) U

Kindergarten Cop (1990) Posing as a kindergarten teacher, an undercover cop (Arnold Schwarzenegger) tries to protect a mother (Penelope Ann Miller) and her little boy from her ex-husband, a deadly drug dealer (Richard Tyson). Misleadingly marketed as a kid-appeal comedy, director Ivan Reitman has produced an unsettling mix of menace, mirth and contrived romance that repels as often as it entertains. Recurring violence with menace to children and brief sexual innuendo. A-III (PG-13) 15

King and Country (1966) The court martial and execution of a British deserter during World War I is the grim story told by this impressive indictment of war and its injustices. Tom Courtenay is the passive and withdrawn victim of the military system and Dirk Bogarde plays his sincere but ineffectual defense counsel. Director Joseph Losey's anti-war statement at times stretches for symbols but its sense of moral outrage is perfectly clear. A-III (br) PG

King and I, The (1956) Imaginative screen version of the Rodgers and Hammerstein musical tells the story of a 19th-century British governess (Deborah Kerr) who comes to Thailand as tutor to the large brood of children in the royal court but finds her biggest job is enlightening its obstreperous King (Yul Brynner). Director Walter Lang creates a lovely fantasy version of an Asian kingdom, Kerr nicely abets Brynner's Oscar-winning performance and the songs, especially the sweeping "Shall We Dance," are delightful. Fine family fare with some solid moral values. A-I (nr) U

King David (1985) For half its length, this is a superb biblical film in which the sex, violence and pageantry usually emphasized in this genre do not obscure the central theme of God's intervention in humanity's messy affairs. However, the last half of director Bruce Beresford's work seems badly truncated which, together with a miscast Richard Gere in the title role, makes it a severely flawed film, but nonetheless one worth seeing. There is some nudity and considerable violence, but they are subordinated to the theme and not exploitative. A-III (PG-13) PG

King in New York, A (1957) Produced, written, and directed by Charles Chaplin, the movie is a rather mild satire of the 1950s' witch hunts and black listings, as well as some of the foibles in American life. It is a less than profound work but a reminder of a past political hysteria that barred a great comedian from working in America. A-I (G) U

King Kong (1933) The screen's best remembered monster takes on New York City in a desperate attempt to regain the blonde beauty (Fay Wray) lost by the beast when captured on an uncharted island by an intrepid showman (Robert Armstrong). Produced and directed by Merian C. Cooper and Ernest B. Schoedsack, this classic adventure fantasy succeeds largely because of the giant ape's sympathetic treatment and Willis H. O'Brien's imaginative special effects in animating Kong and the prehistoric world of Skull Island. Scary situations and stylized violence, some of it quite brutal. A-II (br) PG

King Kong (1977) The Empire State Building and Fay Wray are in no danger of being outdone by the World Trade Towers and Jessica Lange in a moderately entertaining but uninspired remake of the 1933 classic. Director John Guillerman's lack of creative energy contrasts unfavorably with the naive vigor of the original. Some semi-nudity and graphic violence. A-III (PG) A

King Kong Escapes (1968) Japanese monster movie directed by Inoshiro Honda has a modern setting but unwisely goes out of its way to try to duplicate a number of sequences from the 1933 original and comes up looking somewhat ludicrous. For the undemanding only. A-I (G)

King Kong Lives (1986) After an open-heart operation revives his comatose state, Kong returns to find a mate, father a child and be killed in a better-safe-than-sorry military action. Needlessly detailed and extended scenes of bloodshed, both of the heart operation and fight sequences, and a very suggestive sexual encounter. A-III (PG-13) PG

King Lear (1971) Director Peter Brook's adaptation of Shakespeare's tragedy is a brilliant, stunning production, almost overwhelmingly powerful, owing to the combined strengths of the bold direction and the brilliance of a cast boasting Paul Scofield as Lear, Irene Worth as Goneril, and Alan Webb as Gloucester. It stands as one of the screen's most striking homages to the Bard of Avon. A-II (GP)

King Murray (1969) Semi-documentary centers on Murray King, an overbearing, loud-mouthed Long Island insurance agent who caters exclusively to a wealthy clientele. Director Jonathan Gordon's fictionalized reenactment follows King through business deals, lunch breaks and finally a Las Vegas excursion replete with obscene stories and the typical vulgarities of character the film suggests go hand-in-hand with a dehumanizing profession. O (nr)

King of Comedy (1983) Robert De Niro plays an aspiring stand-up comedian who kidnaps a famous talk show host (Jerry Lewis) in order to obtain an appearance on his show. Director Martin Scorsese transforms an act of desperation into a black comedy in an offbeat and menacing study of a social misfit. Attempted seduction scene is done with restraint. A-III (PG)

King of Hearts (1966) Seriocomic commentary on the insanity of war makes its point in a World War I story of a sane British soldier (Alan Bates) who happens upon a town taken over by the inmates of a lunatic asylum after the villagers have fled. Directed by Philippe De Broca, the French production's awkward interplay of realism and fantasy just barely manages to avoid both sheer comedy and fresh insight. A-III (br) A

King of Kings (1961) Stolid screen spectacular presents the life of Christ within the historical context of Jewish resistance to Roman rule. Uncomfortably cast in the title role is Jeffrey Hunter, though more effective are Siobhan McKenna as his mother, Robert Ryan as John the Baptist, Hurd Hatfield as Pilate, Rip Torn as Judas and Harry Guardino as Barabbas. Directed by Nicholas Ray, the script is preoccupied with the period's political unrest but treats the gospel account reverentially, if with more dramatic license than some might find acceptable. A-IV (br) U

King of Marvin Gardens, The (1972) Jack Nicholson and Bruce Dern play two brothers who get together for a reunion in wintry Atlantic City to muse about their problems and wander around the near-deserted resort with girlfriends (Ellen Burstyn and Julia Anne Robinson) in tow. Directed by Bob Rafelson, nothing much happens, but the setting and situation seem to suggest that life is a game, and a fixed one at that. Several sexual scenes. A-IV (R)

King of New York (1990) Vigilante cops target a well-connected psychopath (Christopher Walken) who is killing off New York City's drug lords in order to take over the trade and use its profits to fund a children's hospital. Director Abel Ferrara's stylishly photographed nighttime cityscapes mask a bleakly nihilistic vision of a doomed city where life is cheap, lawlessness is everywhere and police readily resort to murder. Excessive violence, glamorized drug use, some nudity and intermittent rough language. O (R) 18

King of the Grizzlies (1970) Disney adventure about a 1,300-pound mountain bear who roams the Canadian Rockies and his friend, a young Cree Indian of the bear clan, who must choose between his sympathy for the animal and his position as foreman of a cattle ranch. Ron Kelly directs with fine wildlife footage and a mildly dramatic story suitable for youngsters. A-I (G) U

King of the Gypsies (1978) Young N.Y. Gypsy (Eric Roberts) is appointed king of the clan by his grandfather (Sterling Hayden), passing over his father (Judd Hirsch) who hires two men to kill him. Sven Nykvist's beautifully photographed vision of a little-known world directed by Frank Pierson conveys a wholly negative portrait of Gypsy life characterized by rough language and brutal violence. O (R)

King of the Hill (1993) Depression-era drama in which an impoverished 12-year-old schoolboy (Jesse Bradford) lives by his wits out of a shabby St. Louis hotel room after his mom (Lisa Eichhorn) is put in a sanitorium, his kid brother (Cameron Boyd) is sent to live with an uncle and his father (Jeroen Krabbe) goes on the road selling door-to-door. Writer-director Steven Soderburgh's adaptation of A.E. Hotchner's childhood memoir captures the pervasive hard times and growing desperation of its characters while revealing the resourcefulness of a child coping courageously with basic survival and hopes of reuniting his family. A suicide, brief violence and discreet sexual innuendo. A-II (PG-13) 15

King of the Mountain (1981) Banal and pretentious movie whose anemic plot concerns the empty-headed romance between a woman singer and a young mechanic who loves to race his Porsche down a treacherous California road. Director Noel Nosseck celebrates the teen obsession with death-defying speed and takes a permissive attitude toward casual sex. A-III (PG)

King of the Wild Stallions (1958) Standard Western directed by R.G. Springsteen in which a cowboy (George Montgomery) and his old pard (Edgar Buchanan) save a widow (Diane Brewster) from losing her land to a crooked rancher. Youngsters may be more interested in scenes of the wild herd and the role of the widow's young son in capturing the horse of the title. Minimal stylized violence. A-I (br)

King, Queen, Knave (1975) Gawky, naive nephew (John Moulder-Brown) is initiated into the ways of love by his earthy aunt (Gina Lollobrigida) while his urbane uncle (David Niven) tends to his own affairs. Director Jerzy Skolimowski turns Vladimir Nabokov's novel into a sex farce lacking in humanity and humor. O (R) X

King Ralph (1991) The throne of England is inherited by a good-hearted American slob (John Goodman), who chases a common shopgirl (Camille Coduri) much to the dismay of his most proper royal secretary (Peter O'Toole). Writer-director David S. Ward's clash-of-cultures comedy is a lightweight effort, equal parts affable and forgettable. Occasional vulgar expressions, double entendres and flash of rear nudity. A-II (PG)

King Rat (1965) Japanese prisoner-of-war camp with George Segal as the American opportunist of the title and James Fox as the British officer who tries to befriend him. Director Bryan Forbes' story of the human spirit under duress does not gloss over the rigors of captivity and its depiction of degradation is strong fare. A-III (br) A

King Solomon's Mines (1950) Rousing good version of the H. Rider Haggard adventure saga about an English woman (Deborah Kerr) who hires a guide (Stewart Granger) to search for her lost brother (Richard Carlson) in the African jungle where they also find fabulous diamond mines. Directed by Compton Bennett and Andrew Marton, the picturesque sights and colorful action make this a first-rate family safari. A-I (br) U

Kingdom in the Clouds (1971) Rumanian fairy tale about a young man who goes in search of a fabulous kingdom where no one ever grows old, survives various tests on the way and at last wins the hand of the princess of the deathless kingdom. Adequately directed by Elisabeta Bostan, it has colorful characters in picturesque locales that will satisfy younger members of the audience. A-I (G)

Kingdom of the Spiders (1978) Complacent community in Arizona finds itself suddenly besieged by a horde of hungry mutant tarantulas. Director John Cardos' camp chiller features William Shatner and Tiffany Bolling trying to stop the revolt-of-nature nightmare in a fairly routine but mindless entertainment for the undemanding. A-II (PG)

Kings of the Road (1976) German story about a movie projector repairman and a hitchhiker who share their dissatisfaction with contemporary life and search for some way to change things. Director Wim Wenders's exploration of alienation reaches toward positive affirmation about the future. Some matter-of-fact nudity and a scene depicting a bodily function that would affront some viewers. A-IV (nr) AA

Kinjite: Forbidden Subjects (1989) When a Los Angeles detective (Charles Bronson) is ordered to find a missing Japanese girl, he must stifle his bigotry to help the girl's family get her back before a pimp (Juan Fernandez) turns her into a big-buck call girl. Director J. Lee Thompson plays up suggestions of exotic sex to titillate viewers and exploits the violence used to crush the baddies. Much gratuitous violence, rough language and sexually suggestive scenes with some nudity. O (R)

Kipps (see: "The Remarkable Mr. Kipps").

Kiss, The (1988) Cliched vampire film about a curse passed down from aunts to nieces that makes a New York teenager (Meredith Salenger) the target of her afflicted aunt from the Belgian Congo (Joanna Pacula). Directed by Pen Densham, there is much grisly violence, nudity within several graphic sex scenes and some rough language. O (R)

Kiss Before Dying, A (1991) Refusing to believe that her twin sister committed suicide, a young bride (Sean Young) uncovers a trail of murders that lead back to her own husband (Matt Dillon). Writer-director James Dearden delivers an engrossing thriller, carefully scripted, sleekly shot and nicely acted but the death scenes are unnecessarily gruesome. Some gory violence, several bedroom scenes with brief nudity and minimal rough language. A-III (R) 18

Kiss Me Goodbye (1982) Dull, plodding remake of a popular Brazilian sex farce in which an about-to-be-married widow (Sally Field) is haunted by the ghost of her dead husband (James Caan) who tries to scare off the fiance (Jeff Bridges). Directed by Robert Mulligan, the situation is so poorly contrived as to be embarrassing. Restrained sex scene. A-III (PG)

Kiss Me Kate (1953) Halting version of Cole Porter's musical comedy about the backstage bickering between husband and wife (Kathryn Grayson; Howard Keel) starring in a Broadway production of Shakespeare's "The Taming of the Shrew." Director George Sidney gets lost in low comedy routines with an aspiring starlet (Ann Miller) and a gangster duo (Keenan Wynn; James Whitmore) while Porter's musical numbers are squandered in raucous style. Sexual innuendo and domestic turmoil. A-III (br) U

Kiss of Death (1947) Tough crime story about a crook (Victor Mature) who informs on his gang after they harm his family, but he needs more than police protection when a crazy killer (Richard Widmark) comes gunning for him. Though it's a fairly standard melodrama of the bad-man-goes-straight variety, director Henry Hathaway achieves a suitably gritty atmosphere by filming on the mean streets of New York City and Widmark's performance as the gunman with a maniacal laugh is still chilling. Some nasty stylized violence. A-II (br) A

Kiss of the Spider Woman (1985) Brazilian political prisoner (Raul Julia) shares a cell with a relatively flamboyant homosexual (William Hurt) who helps both of them pass the time by giving detailed descriptions of old Hollywood movies. Much musing about politics and sex, about verities of love and of betrayal, but there is not enough intelligence and wit in the script to carry off the high purpose that Argentinian director Hector Babenco obviously had in mind. Mature subject matter. A-IV (R) 15

Kiss the Girls and Make Them Die (1966) Failed Italian spy spoof about a CIA agent (Michael Connors) on the trail of a power-mad industrialist (Raf Vallone) who has developed a satellite that can render the entire world sterile. Directed by Henry Levin, the result is largely unamusing and mildly sexually suggestive. A-III (br)

Kiss the Other Sheik (1968) Italian sex farce about a husband (Marcello Mastroianni) who sets out to sell his wife to a rich sheik but she winds up selling him into a homosexual harem. Director Luciano Salce's heavy-handed treatment is flat and extremely vulgar. O (PG)

Kissin' Cousins (1964) Silly Elvis Presley vehicle about rebellious Tennessee mountaineers blocking the Army's plan to build an ICBM missile site in the Great Smoky Mountains. Directed by Gene Nelson, the dumb yokel humor is tiresome, the songs forgettable and Elvis is doubly bad in dual roles. Sexual innuendo. A-III (br) U

Kitchen Toto, The (1988) A 12-year-old Kikuyu boy (Edwin Mahinda) is tragically caught between his devotion to a kind British police chief (Bob Peck) and the 1950 terrorist Mau Maus fighting to liberate Kenya from British rule Director Harry Hook shows how children are victimized by political strife. Some grisly violence and an adulterous affair. A-III (PG-13) 15

Kitty Foyle (1940) Subtitled "The Natural History of a Woman," the dated tearjerker spins the tale of a "white-collar girl" (Ginger Rogers) torn between the rich, handsome man of her dreams (Dennis Morgan) and the steady, down-to-earth beau (James Craig) who wants to marry her. Directed by Sam Woods, Rogers won an Oscar in the role of a woman who refuses to compromise her

working-class principles to the upper-class snobbery of Philadelphia mainliners. Sexual situations and innuendo. A-III (br) A

Klansman, The (1974) Adaptation of William Bradford Huie's novel about white-garbed fanatics set upon preserving racial purity by stopping a voter registration rally. Director Terence Young and his cast (Richard Burton, Lee Marvin and O. J. Simpson) can do nothing with a dated scenario placed in a contemporary setting. It is an irresponsible premise for a repellent motion picture that makes rape, castration, murder and racist terror into spectator sports. O (R)

Klute (1971) Taut thriller about a savvy yet pathetic call girl (Jane Fonda) and an unruffled, methodical private-eye (Donald Sutherland), whose lives intersect when he comes to New York to search for a missing friend and uncovers a sadistic murderer (Charles Cioffi). Director Alan J. Pakula takes a serious, unflinching view of his characters, their actions and the dark world they inhabit. Challenging subject matter but not treated exploitatively. A-IV (R) 18

Knife in the Head (1980) Swiss drama in which a totally apolitical scientist (Bruno Gans) becomes the political pawn of leftists and police while recovering from a police gunshot wound that has left him an amnesiac. Director Reinhard Hauff focuses on the man's lonely struggle to regain his identity and personality in an alienated world. Violence and frank treatment of sex. A-IV (nr)

Knightriders (1981) Writer-director George A. Romero's lengthy and overambitious attempt to re-create the Arthurian legend in the saga of a troupe of daredevils who joust on motorcycles instead of horses. The idea is promising and the acting is appealing enough, but the plot is simpleminded at best, with too little action and too much gratuitous sex. O (R) PG

Knights of the Round Table (1953) Stiff costume drama about the rise of Camelot and its fall after Lancelot (Robert Taylor) is banished by Arthur (Mel Ferrer) because of his love for Guinevere (Ava Gardner). Director Richard Thorpe's picture of King Arthur's court is pretty but lifeless, save for the villainy of Modred (Stanley Baker) and some battle scenes. The ideals of chivalry are wrapped up in empty spectacle and stylized violence. A-I (br) U

Kona Coast (1968) Lurid melodrama with Richard Boone playing a brutally vengeful father out to crush the dope peddlers responsible for his daughter's death. The lush Hawaiian setting is the movie's only asset as director Lamont Johnson's treatment of drug trafficking lacks substance and credibility. Tends to condone taking the law violently into one's own hands. O (br)

Korczak (1991) A humanitarian doctor (Wojtek Pszoniak) heroically struggles to save the lives of 200 doomed orphans in Warsaw's Jewish ghetto during the Nazi occupation. A moving testament to one person's indomitable spirit, Polish director Andrzej Wajda's starkly powerful chronicle of this horrific fact-based story is at odds with its surreal fantasy ending. Subtitles. Brief wartime violence and shots of discarded nude corpses. A-II (nr) PG

Kotch (1971) Walter Matthau captures to perfection the eccentric but lovable grandfather who adores children and befriends an unwed teenage mother (Deborah Winters) when his son (Charles Aldman) places him in an old age home. Directed by Jack Lemmon, it's an old-fashioned sentimental melodrama, full of warmth and fun, but avoids some of the serious implications of the situation. A-III (GP) AA

Krakatoa, East of Java (1969) Lavish disaster movie built around the 1883 eruption of a small volcanic island in the Dutch East Indies features the skipper (Maximilian Schell) of a vessel searching for sunken treasure but also transporting a gang of convicts to an island prison. Directed by Bernard L. Kowalski, the grand scale of the eruption is awesome on the big screen, but the cliche-studded story that precedes it is a yawner. Its terribly melodramatic dialogue and some romantic liaisons make it less appropriate for youngsters. A-II (G) U

Kramer vs. Kramer (1979) Superficial treatment of child custody battle between angry wife (Meryl Streep) and resentful husband (Dustin Hoffman). Director Robert Benton conveys the tragedy of divorce by putting the emphasis on the father's attempts at parenting but neglects the child's perspective. Some harsh language and a sex scene witnessed by the young child. A-IV (PG)

Krays, The (1990) Harrowing fact-based drama about twin brothers (Gary and Martin Kemp) who ruthlessly murder their way to the top of the London crime scene in the 1960s while maintaining a slavish devotion to their overprotective mother (Billie Whitelaw). With excellent performances by the Kemp brothers, director Peter Medak's coldly fascinating portrait captures the twins's rise from lower-class origins and domineering females without glamorizing the lurid crimes that eventually caught up with them. Occasional graphic violence, homosexual innuendo, intermittent rough language and a flash of nudity. A-III (R) 18

Kremlin Letter, The (1970) Screen version of Noel Behn's spy novel about a scramble among the world's intelligence agencies to obtain a letter outlining U.S. policy in case of war between Russia and Red China. Director John Huston has fashioned a complex, action-packed and occasionally very cruel and violent Cold War thriller whose twists and turns leave nearly all its characters, which include Patrick O'Neal, Richard Boone, Nigel Green, Dean Jagger, and George Sanders, either murdered or revealed as double or even triple agents. A-III (PG) 18

Krull (1983) Director Peter Yates cannot quite bring into focus his tale of a mythical land, an enchanted weapon and an evil monster. There are too many characters (a cyclops, a wizard, a spiderwoman, a magician, a seer, etc.), too many illogical jumps in the plot and the familiar quest to save a damsel in distress has been done better before by others. A-II (PG)

Krush Groove (1985) Backstage saga of the rap music scene, featuring some dynamic young performers under the direction of Michael Schultz. Disarming and energetic, the movie nevertheless suffers from a weak storyline and the very specialized nature of music that is for rap fans only. Some vulgar language. A-II (R)

Kuffs (1992) Addle-brained comedy about an irresponsible young man (Christian Slater) who becomes a cop to avenge the murder of an older brother (Bruce Boxleitner) killed in the line of duty. Director Bruce A. Evans uses a clumsy Slater-talking-to-the-camera technique as moronic humor trivializes the graphic shootouts. Excessive violence, positive portrayal of vigilante justice and premarital and adulterous affairs and minimal rough language. O (PG-13) 15

Kung Fu Master! (1989) French import about an implausible infatuation between a 40-year-old divorced mother (Jane Birkin) and the 15-year-old friend (Mathieu Demy) of her adolescent daughter. Director Agnes Varda provides no clue to this woman's amoral obsession for a youth who's obsessed with the "Kung Fu Master!" video game. Numerous AIDS warnings are inexplicable public service messages. No onscreen sex, but the cuddling and chaste kisses are unsettling. O (R)

Kwaidan (1966) Japanese fantasy composed of three ghost stories set in the days of the samurai will engross, if not enthrall viewers. Directed by Masaki Kobayashi, the narratives are so simple, direct and carefully paced that one is lulled into acceptance of their eerie logic. The stories are by Lafcadio Hearn, an American who went to live in Japan at the turn-of-the-century and wrote many stories based upon their legends and the movie helps one see why he found their culture so fascinating. A-II (br) X

L

L.A. Story (1991) A TV weatherman (Steve Martin) is chased by a bouncy blonde (Sarah Jessica Parker) while, with a little help from a magical freeway sign, he pursues a reserved English journalist (Victoria Tennant). As written by Martin and directed by Mick Jackson, a wry eye is cast upon the trendy populace of Los Angeles, which is more diverting than the fairly bland fantasy-romance storyline. Casual attitude toward premarital sex and minimal rough language. A-III (PG-13) 15

La Bamba (1987) Pop biographical homage to teenage rock singer Ritchie Valens (Lou Diamond Phillips). Director Luis Valdez sets Valens meteoric success and tragic death against the poverty and oppression of the barrios of Southern California and ethnic bias of middle-class suburbia. Effective study of Valens' struggle against cultural stereotyping and his relationship with his wayward brother (Esai Morales). Scenes of domestic violence, a brief instance of nudity and some profanity are overcome by the film's overall inspirational tone and depiction of positive youthful aspirations. A-II (PG-13)

La Boca del Lobo (1989) Gripping Peruvian production about a civilian atrocity committed by government forces in their struggle to crush the rebel movement known as the Shining Path. Director Francisco J. Lombardi centers the narrative on a young city-bred recruit (Antonio Vega) whose growing sympathy for the Indians being victimized by both army and terrorists causes him to refuse to obey the order to fire on a group of peaceful villagers. Some graphic depictions of violence. A-III (nr)

La Boheme (1965) Puccini's opera as performed on stage by the La Scala Opera company with musical direction by Herbert Von Karajan and stage direction by Franco Zeffirelli. The singing apparently was recorded separately with the result that the excitement associated with a live performance is missing. A-II (br)

La Boheme (1989) Lackluster, updated adaptation of the Puccini opera about the frail, impoverished Mimi (Barbara Hendricks) whose love affair with the penniless poet Rodolfo (Luca Canonici) is doomed by her health, but not before we hear them sing of love, jealousy, heartbreak and watch as their playful bohemian friends fall in and out of love. Unimaginatively directed by Luigi Comencini, the classic work is plagued with bad lighting, stiff performances and choppy editing. Implied sexual liaisons. A-III (nr)

La Bonne Soupe (1966) This French film's graphic portrayal of the details of prostitution is offensive. O (br)

La Cage Aux Folles (1979) Transvestite nightclub owner (Ugo Tognazzi) lives with the club revue star Zaza (Michel Serrault), a situation he wishes to conceal from his son who returns to announce his marriage to the daughter of a sanctimonious town official. A comedy of deceptions and misconceptions, this French farce directed by Eduard Molinaro uses homosexuality as the context for poking fun at moralistic hypocrites, flamboyant transvestites and society in general. A-IV (R)

La Cage Aux Folles II (1981) Sequel to the popular French comedy about a homosexual couple isn't up to the original. But thanks to Ugo Tognazzi and Michel Serrault, re-creating their original roles, director Eduard Molinaro's movie has some diverting moments before getting bogged down in an improbable plot that has the heroes becoming involved in a counterespionage operation. A-IV (R)

La Chamade (1969) Bland, menage-a-trois melodrama with Catherine Deneuve as mistress to both wealthy graying Michel Piccoli and young, handsome and not-so-wealthy Roger Van Hool. Adapted from a Francoise Sagan novel and directed by Alain Cavalier, there is little to recommend in its frothy cliches, stock characters and passionless bedroom scenes, but its moral meaning is clear: such vapid relationships are unfulfilling and provide no real meaning or stability to one's life. A-IV (R)

La Chienne (1976) A drab accountant and hen-pecked husband (Michel Simon) falls hopelessly in love with a crass prostitute who is only interested in getting every cent he has. A familiar story of passion and ruin, the 1931 French production is of interest chiefly for Simon's rich performance and as an example of the early sound work of director Jean Renoir. A-III (nr)

La Collectionneuse (1971) French story of a stuffy young wastrel (Patrick Bauchau) who meets an attractive woman (Haydee Politoff) staying at his friend's country estate, becomes totally infatuated but, in the end, through a quirk of fate and not entirely of his own volition, he rejects her. Director Eric Rohmer's third in his series of "Six Moral Tales" presents a picture of a not very sympathetic male chauvinist who has to rationalize the woman's lack of interest in him. A-III (nr)

La Discrete (1992) A wily publisher (Maurice Garrel) convinces a self-important writer (Fabrice Luchini) to select a woman at random, seduce and abandon her (Judith Henry), then publish the intimate details of the affair. French director Christian Vincent plays the writer for a fool in a sluggish, talky movie whose only charm is Henry's gently dignified performance. Subtitles. An unmarried sexual relationship and references to previous affairs. A-III (nr)

La Femme Infidele (1969) French director Claude Chabrol manages to generate suspense with many layers of tension, ambiguity and passion seething under a placid surface. Here he examines the apparently happy suburban marriage of insurance man Michel Bouquet and wife Stephane Audran, but the husband's growing suspicions of his wife's infidelity are confirmed and he confronts and kills the other man (Maurice Ronet). Though Chabrol's style is coolly detached, viewers will be caught up in an inquiry into the human potential for evil. A-III (R)

La Femme Nikita (1991) A convicted killer (Anne Parillaud) working as an assassin for the French government wants out when she falls for an innocent store clerk (Jean-Hughes Anglade). Writer-director Luc Besson's sleek action thriller goes somewhat overboard on violence during the protagonist's journey to redemption via the healing power of love. Subtitles. Some grisly violence, a live-in relationship, flash of nudity and occasional rough language. A-IV (R)

La Fuga (1966) Italian dramatization of the psychiatric treatment of a disturbed 27-year-old wife whose marital problems are related to latent lesbian tendencies. Directed by Paolo Spinola, the effort is well-intentioned but the graphic treatment of several sexual scenes is excessively explicit. O (br)

La Lectrice (1989) French literary comedy in which a woman (Miou-Miou) fantasizes that she is the heroine of a novel about a woman who makes a living as a professional reader. Directed by Michel Deville, the dual role leads to some delightful vignettes about the woman's interaction with her eccentric clients and the literary works she deems suitable for each. The charm wears off, however, when she becomes both reader and sex surrogate to a frustrated client. Several gratuitous sexual encounters. O (R)

La Mandragola (1966) Italian adaptation of a Machiavellian satire whose theme is adultery and whose treatment is steeped in prurience and cynicism is unrelieved by any redeeming qualities. O (br)

La Peau Douce (see: "The Soft Skin").

La Prisonniere (1969) French import about a woman who finds herself first intrigued by, and then hopelessly attracted to an art dealer (Laurent Terzieff) who proves to be a sadistic voyeur incapable of love. Director Henri-Georges Clouzot affects a detached, noncommital attitude toward his subject, forcing viewers to share the voyeurism that his characters are experiencing. O (nr)

La Rupture (1975) Contrived French mystery about a woman (Stephane Audran) seeking a divorce from her deranged husband in order to protect herself and her child without realizing that her rich father-in-law (Michel Bouquet) will stop at nothing to get custody of his grandson. Director Claude Chabrol has used the theme of social decadence and moral corruption to better effect in other movies, but this one is little more than an interesting exercise in the modern-Gothic imagination. A-III (nr)

La Salamandre (1972) Engrossing Swiss drama about the collaboration between a journalist and a fiction writer on a television play based on a recent case of a young woman's shooting of a relative, but when they finally meet her (Bulle Ogier) she is too chameleon-like for them to continue the project. Director Alain Tanner's story seems on the surface an amusing anecdote about whether imagination or fact reveals the truth better, but underneath is the question of survival in a destructive postindustrial society, where by movie's end it is clear that the woman has made the most progress toward self-liberation. Mature themes and treatment. A-III (nr)

La Strada (1956) Two-bit strongman (Anthony Quinn) adds a simple-minded peasant (Giulietta Masina) to his circus act, treating her badly until a tragic encounter with a bantering acrobat (Richard Basehart) who tries to help her. Italian director Federico Fellini's somber picture of lost souls on the backroads of life has its emotional center in Masina's Chaplinesque performance as the poor waif struggling to keep her spirit from being crushed by the brute she serves. Subtitles. Some stylized violence and brutalizing conditions of life. A-III (br)

La Tia Tula (1965) Delicate Spanish tale of a beautiful woman (Aurora Bautista) who rejects the love of her late sister's husband, then comes to regret her proud aloofness too late. Director Miguel Picazo treats the woman's fears of marriage in the context of her cultural and religous upbringing, investing the character with a tragic human dimension that earns respect and leaves a sense of loss. Subtitles. Sexual situations, including an attempted rape. A-III (br)

La Vie De Chateau (1967) Set in Normandy just before D-Day, the story is about a wealthy orchard farmer (Philippe Noiret), his lively wife (Catherine Deneuve), a lovelorn leader of the Resistance (Henri Garein) and a detachment of German soldiers quartered there. Some haphazard heroics take place on the beautiful old estate before it finally becomes the landing point for Allied paratroopers. A-II (br)

La Visita (1966) Middle-aged spinster (Sandro Milo) uses the personal columns to arrange a meeting with a seemingly eligible suitor (Francois Perier). The day they spend together is both amusing and touching as they come to discover the truth about their personalities. Director Antonio Pietrangeli's seriocomic tale is minor but deftly played. A-III (br)

Labyrinth (1986) Menagerie of muppet goblins and related little folk tries to defer a young girl from solving the puzzle of the labyrinth and saving her infant brother from the snare of the Goblin King (David Bowie). Directed by Muppet-master Jim Henson, the movie is a colorful but overlong intricate visual romp for the young. Some bathroom humor. A-I (PG) U

Labyrinth of Passion (1990) Spanish farce portraying the interaction of various sexually promiscuous and perverse characters in the streets, clubs and boudoirs of Madrid. Director Pedro Almodovar pokes fun at incest, rape, nymphomania, bisexuality, transvestism, homosexuality, frigidity, infertility, psychotherapy and plastic surgery, most of which are acted out on camera. Despite the frothy satiric point of view, its graphic depiction of sexual acts, as well as a particularly gross bathroom joke, are excessive. O (nr) 18

Lacemaker, The (1977) The heroine of Swiss director Claude Goretta's film is an 18-year-old Parisian (Isabelle Huppert) who falls in love with wealthy, educated gentleman (Ives Beneyton) and their relationship results in her mental breakdown. It's a carefully etched melodrama about class consciousness, false impressions and male irresponsibility. A-IV (nr) AA

Lacombe, Lucien (1974) Excellent French World War II drama about a 17-year-old farm boy (Pierre Blaise) who wants to join the Resistance but, when he is turned down as too young and irresponsible, joins the French collaborators of the local German police. Directed by Louis Malle, the movie succeeds admirably as a chilling story of an immature youth, but it also adds considerable insight to our knowledge of the history of this period. A-II (nr)

Lad: A Dog (1962) With the blessings of his owners (Peter Breck and Peggy McCay), the champion collie of the title and his two pups help a crippled little rich girl (Angela Cartwright) walk again, despite the canine phobia of her stuffy father (Carroll O'Connor). Directed by Aram Avakian and Leslie H. Martinson, the sentimental tale is plain and simple but too threadbare for older viewers, even with some menace supplied by a disgruntled poacher who sets fire to the barn housing the pups. For wee ones and Lassie fans. A-I (br)

Ladies and Gentlemen, the Rolling Stones (1975) Pop concert documentary with Mick Jagger and crew at their slightly satanic but self-parodying best. Directed by former ad man Rollin Binzer, it is bright, swift and irresistible for adult rock fans. A-III (PG)

Lady and the Tramp (1955) Walt Disney's animated feature about a cute little cocker spaniel in a Victorian family who loses her place in the couple's affections with the birth of their first child but who is reinstated through the efforts of a freedom-loving mongrel. The cast of lovable dog characters and some delightful songs by Peggy Lee still appeal to youngsters. A-I (G) U

Lady Beware (1987) A window dresser (Diane Lane), with a penchant for the erotic, decides to turn the tables on a psychotic admirer who terrifies her. Director Karen Arthur's clumsy chiller relies heavily on male and female nudity rather than developing any feminist insights. O (R)

Lady Caroline Lamb (1973) Robert Bolt wrote and directed this vehicle for Sarah Miles about a high-born but promiscuous lady who consorts with poets and other male playthings during the early 19th century. Miles' nonacting is complemented by Richard Chamberlain's nonlimping parody of Byron, and the sincere efforts of Jon Finch as her stoical husband Willie cannot offset the movie's overall absurdity. Brief nudity. A-III (PG) A

Lady Chatterley's Lover (1982) French director Just Jaeckin's skin-deep adaptation of the D. H. Lawrence novel, with Sylvia Kristel and Nicholas Clay, is a dulling exercise in commercial eroticism. Graphic sex. O (R) 18

Lady Frankenstein (1972) When her fanatic father (Joseph Cotton) dies at the hands of the demented creature he created, his daughter (Sara Bey) vows to create a perfect superman to destroy her father's murderer. Unfortunately in this Italian penny-dreadful directed by Mel Welles, she has to seduce her subjects for surgery and graphic sex sequences only detract from the blood-drenched horror fantasy. O (R)

Lady Ice (1973) Middling diamond heist caper in which an insurance investigator (Donald Sutherland) gets involved with a diamond fence (Jennifer O'Neill) and a hard-bitten U.S. Justice Department agent (Robert Duvall) who adds a bit of class but his scenes get lost in the shuffle. Directed by Tom Gries, the complex, and at times, confusing plot doesn't add up to much. A-II (PG) AA

Lady in Cement (1968) Hard-boiled private detective (Frank Sinatra) gets involved in the murder of a woman in the title, but director Gordon Douglas provides neither credibility nor atmosphere in the rambling, loosely plotted proceedings that create an ersatz excitement only by resorting to brutal violence and some sleazy sexual distractions. O (R/PG) X

Lady in the Car with Glasses and a Gun, The (1970) Failed mystery thriller in which Samantha Eggar takes a holiday drive in the South of France and, after a number of puzzling incidents happen to her, she discovers a body in the trunk of the car she got from her boss (sinister Oliver Reed). Director Anatole Litvak goes overboard trying to create some suspense, but the result of all his efforts is no more than pure cleverness and empty contrivance. Some adult mayhem. A-III (R) AA

Lady in White (1988) Supernatural thriller about a small-town boy (Lukas Haas) who comes face to face with the ghost of a girl murdered 10 years before—as well as with her murderer. With breathtaking special effects and cinematography, director Frank LaLoggia's unique fantasy attains wonderful interplay between the boy, his family and the ghosts in a lovely re-creation of life in 1962. Graphic violence directed toward children and some particularly chilling supernatural occurrences. A-III (PG-13). 15

Lady Jane (1986) The innocence and altruism of youth are contrasted with the deceit and treachery of the adult world in this period drama about the religious power struggle following the reign of King Henry VIII. Its romantic treatment of adult themes contains a brief scene of nudity and a brutal scene of flogging. A-III (PG-13) PG

Lady L (1966) Tasteless British comedy set in 1920s' Europe stars Sophia Loren and under Peter Ustinov's direction is excessive in its sexual emphasis. O (br) A

Lady Liberty (1972) When Sophia Loren flies into JFK Airport to rejoin her fiance, she has a 20-pound mortadella sausage under her arm and the crisis this causes at Customs promises one of those coarse peasant comedies the Italians do so well. Unfortunately, director Mario Monticelli presents a freak show of grisly New York stereotypes in a cynical blend of contempt, distrust and generally low opinion of humanity. A-IV (PG)

Lady of Monza, The (1970) Sordid Italian melodrama supposedly based on a 17th-century incident in which the lover of a Spanish nun was beheaded and she was walled up alive. Directed by Eriprando Visconti, the film's production values are as minimal as its ludicrous nude love scenes. O (R)

Lady on the Tracks, The (1968) Czechoslovakian musical fantasy about a lady streetcar driver in Prague (Jirina Bohdalova) who mounts a campaign for women's rights when she discovers her husband's love affair. Directed by Ladislav Rychman, its musical numbers are done in 1930s' Hollywood style and the result is a warm and humorous tale of one woman's dreams of glory. A-II (br)

Lady Sings the Blues (1972) Diana Ross stars as Billie Holiday in a screen biography that reduces the famous singer's life to a series of cliches and soap opera theatrics. A very good performance by Ross can't save director Sidney J. Furie's failed movie. Rough language and sordid situations. A-IV (R) X

Lady Yakuza (1974) Japanese gangster movie in which a young woman (Junko Fuji) takes over the leadership of a gang after her father's murder and ultimately is able to avenge his death. Directed by Kosaku Yamashita, there is plenty of violence but used within a context of group loyalty and personal friendship. A-III (nr)

Ladybugs (1992) A salesman (Rodney Dangerfield) whose promotion depends on successfully coaching his company-sponsored all-girl soccer team gets his fiancee's son (Jonathan Brandis) to play disguised as a girl in order to ensure a winning season. Sidney J. Furie directs a genial sports comedy peppered with Dangerfield's snappy one-liners. Mild sexual innuendo and double entendres. A-II (PG-13) PG

Ladyhawke (1985) Medieval sword-and-sorcery epic looks beautiful but tells a silly story of a curse that changes two true lovers into a hawk (Michelle Pfeiffer) and a wolf (Rutger Hauer). Directed by Richard Donner, it is rife with bad dialogue, bad acting and anachronisms. Aside from some violent swordplay, it is innocuous. A-II (PG-13)

Lair of the White Worm, The (1988) Director Ken Russell's update of a 1911 Bram Stoker novel has a vampire (Amanda Donohoe) lure humans into the lair of an ancient serpent still living in an English town with two sisters (Catherine Oxenberg; Sammi Davis) as key targets. The satiric elements are diluted by Russell's fascination with sexual debauch, involving dream sequences of the blood-splattered rape of nuns by pagan soldiers in front of a serpent-draped cross. Explicit sexual seduction, fleeting nudity and intense vampire attacks. O (R) 18

L'Amour (1973) Andy Warhol's counter-culture denizens flutter around Paris in this generally vapid put-on that Warhol co-directed with Paul Morrissey. In tune with Warhol's philosophy, the camera-work is grainy, the color is anemic and the parade of verbal and visual vulgarities is constant. O (R)

Lambada (1990) High school math teacher (J. Eddie Peck) moonlights in an East Los Angeles barrio disco where he dances and educates young Latinos so they can pass their high school equivalency exams. Director Joel Silberg plays up the gyrations of the scantily clad female dancers as well as a student's lust for her teacher in this cut-and-paste exploitation of adolescent male sexual fantasies. Much sexual innuendo and vulgar language. A-III (PG) 12

Lancelot of the Lake (1975) French director Robert Bresson takes the Arthurian legend and interprets it in austere realistic fashion, focusing on the decline of the Knights of the Round Table after their failure in the quest of the Grail. His treatment purges the legend of its magic and romance, searching for some historical substance, which for some will have more interest than the story. Some realistic violence. A-III (nr) A

Lancer Spy (1937) World War I tale of a British agent (George Sanders) arriving in Berlin in the place of a lookalike captured German spy and using a beautiful woman (Delores Del Rio) as an unwitting accomplice in ferreting out war secrets. Director Gregory Ratoff builds the cat-and-mouse suspense as the agent arouses the growing suspicions of the German military (Peter Lorre, Joseph Schildkraut and others). Implausible but diverting enough espionage thriller. A-I (br)

Land Before Time, The (1988) Delightful animated feature about the exploits of five young dinosaurs of differing species who band together for survival. Plagued by hunger and threats from meat-eating dinos, the leaf-eating tykes make their way to the Great Valley for food. Director Don Bluth offers some cute little characters, quality animation and a lovely message of solidarity and courage. A brief, nicely handled sequence of a mother dino's death. A-I (G) U

Land of the Pharaohs (1955) Uneven tale in which a ruler of ancient Egypt (Jack Hawkins) forces a captive architect (James Robertson Justice) to build a great pyramid housing a tomb that proves spacious enough not only for the pharaoh but also for his greedy, treacherous second wife (Joan Collins). Director Howard Hawks turns in an historical spectacle on a scale far grander than required for the soap opera antics of a conniving royal golddigger. Stylized violence and sexual situations. A-III (br) U

Land Raiders (1970) Telly Savalas plays a loud, overbearing rancher who stirs up trouble with a local Indian tribe, is discovered to have killed his brother's girl and gets his just desserts when the Indians go on the warpath. Directed by Nathan Juran, it's a poorly done Western with some gory violence and sexual references. A-III (PG)

Land That Time Forgot, The (1975) Doug McClure, John McEnery and Susan Penhaligon are among the survivors of a World War I U-boat attack who find themselves in a strange land filled with prehistoric beasts. Routine British fantasy adventure directed by Kevin Connor. Restrained violence. A-II (PG)

Landlord, The (1970) Rich young man (Beau Bridges) becomes a ghetto landlord in some vague hope that by renovating a decaying Brooklyn brownstone, tenanted by justly suspicious blacks, he can rebuild his empty life. Directed by Hal Ashby, the seriocomic drama has some good performances (Diana Sands and Lou Gossett) and lyric photography but lacks depth and coherence. Interesting failure with some mature themes. A-IV (R/PG) X

Landscape After Battle (1978) Polish drama directed by Andrzej Wajda is a compilation of short stories by Tadeusz Borowski, survivor of Auschwitz and suicide victim. Some brief nudity, but the somberness of the theme makes this a movie for mature viewers. A-III (nr)

Landscape in the Mist (1990) Two runaways, a girl (Tania Palaiologou) and her little brother (Michalis Zeke) hitchhike and sneak onboard trains all across Greece in a pitiful attempt to reach Germany where they seek the father they have never seen. Director Theo Angelopoulos' film is rich in striking imagery and symbolism, but its ponderous pace and theme of innocents set adrift in a world of mostly hostile adults is a decidedly downbeat experience. Greek production with English subtitles. Off-screen rape of the girl. A-III (nr)

Language of Love (1971) Swedish exploitation import is a crudely done series of demonstrations of sexual techniques that will offend any who consider sex a private human expression of love rather than a perfectible mechanical task. O (nr)

Las Vegas Hillbillys (1966) Ferlin Husky comes out of the hills and gains success in Las Vegas in a mindless story directed by Arthur C. Pierce. A-I (br)

Lassie Come Home (1943) Before television, the faithful collie got her start in this story of a poor English family who have to sell their dog, Lassie, but the canny canine crosses the Scottish highlands, despite the elements and all manner of hazards, to return to the little boy (Roddy McDowall) who loves her. Directed by Fred M. Wilcox, the movie's charm holds up quite well as family entertainment, especially for youngsters enthralled by Lassie's intelligence and perseverance. A-I (nr) U

Lassiter (1984) Tom Selleck stars as a womanizing detective forced to become a spy in this espionage thriller directed by Roger Young and set in London just before

THE COUNSELOR'S MAILBOX

Guidance and discussion on issues concerning personal and spiritual growth

Please send your questions and comments to The Counselor's Mailbox, LIGUORIAN, One Liguori Drive, Liguori, MO 63057. All letters will be acknowledged and considered for publication.

Unfaithful spouse

I am in my sixties now, and for the last twenty-five years my marriage has been celibate—though not through any choice of mine. Our marriage started out happy, but then my husband simply "lost interest" in me. He was a great father and a good provider, so I blamed myself for being unattractive or undesirable to him (while the truth is that I was, and still am, attractive and intelligent). Through all these years, he has enjoyed a social life totally apart from me. He also traveled frequently in connection with his work, always without me. With him retired now and our children gone, I have with much shock come to know of his infidelities—which are still ongoing. Of course, he fell away from the Church years ago.

To him, counseling is an unnecessary waste of time because he is happy with his life and tells me that I had better "make a life" for myself. I went for counseling and was told that I could either divorce him or live with the situation. Do you agree with this advice?

Heartache in the South

Dear Heartache,

Judging from what you've told me about your situation, *you have no marriage* (except in a legal sense). It would seem that your husband has no intention of being faithful or of reconciling with you; furthermore, he seems to be urging you to leave him. Why would you ever want to stay in such a situation? Now that you know the truth about his behavior and intentions, you will only be hurt again and again.

Divorce is not your only alternative however. Separation without divorce is also a possibility. Bear in mind too that many relationships such as yours have been annulled by the Church.

What do you need to do to take care of yourself in this painful which is an indictment of Christianity. I was delighted to find two recent films, *Babette's Feast* (go rent it; it not only makes you hungry but feeds your spirit as well!) and *The Mission,* with its moving story of spiritual conflict.

Under "Values" are films you would expect to find, like *Gandhi* and *Schindler's List,* but you'll also find *It's a Wonderful Life* and the recently deceased Louis Malle's *Au Revoir, Les Infants* (also in video stores). Under "Art" are the great *Citizen Kane,* Fellini's *La Strada* and *8 1/2,* and Chaplin's *Modern Times.* But to give some indication of the breadth of the selections, also listed are one of the first vampire films, *Nosferatu;* and the magnificent silent epic *Napoleon,* as well as *Fantasia, The Wizard of Oz, 2001: A Space Odyssey,* and Cukor's *Little Women.*

In all, a balanced selection, a mix of family and adult fare, films both inspiring and upsetting, controversial and mainstream. And one that reminds you of how penetrating and insightful—and also how enjoyable—a good movie can be!

Religion

  Andrei Rublev
  The Mission
  The Passion of Joan of Arc
    (1928)
  La Passion Pathé
  The Flowers of St. Francis
  The Gospel According to St.
    Matthew
  Thérèse
  Ordet
  The Sacrifice
  Francis
  Ben-Hur (1959)
  Babette's Feast
  Nazarin
  Monsieur Vincent
  A Man For All Seasons (1966)

Values

  Gandhi
  Intolerance
  Il Decalogo
  Au Revoir, Les Enfants
  Dersu Uzala
  The Tree of Wooden Clogs

  Open City
  Smultronstallet
  The Seventh Seal
  Chariots of Fire
  The Bicycle Thief
  It's a Wonderful Life
  Schindler's List
  On the Waterfront
  The Burmese Harp (1956)

Art

  2001: A Space Odyssey
  La Strada
  Citizen Kane
  Metropolis
  Modern Times
  Napoleon (1927)
  8 1/2
  Grand Illusion
  Nosferatu (1922)
  Stagecoach (1939)
  The Leopard
  Fantasia
  The Wizard of Oz
  The Lavender Hill Mob
  Little Women (1933)

World War II. Lauren Hutton is the German Mata Hari with a kinky appetite for blood, sex and brutality. Violence and nudity. O (R) 18

Last Action Hero (1993) Overproduced parody of action movies follows an 11-year-old boy (Austin O'Brien) as he magically enters the movie he's watching to join his hero, a trigger-happy cop (Arnold Schwarzenegger), in countless chases and shootouts. Director John McTiernan does little but stitch together the mindless mayhem wrought by assorted weapons and the pyrotechnics engineered by the special effects unit for a clunky and uninvolving pastiche that glamorizes violence and equates heroism with macho posturing and big guns. Much mean-spirited comic violence, positive treatment of phony male heroics, sexist images of women and an instance of rough language. O (PG-13) 15

Last Adventure, The (1968) Episodic French movie about the comradeship between two men (Alain Delon; Lino Ventura) and a young woman (Joanna Shimkus) with the trio winding up on a dangerous search for sunken treasure. Directed by Robert Enrico, the emphasis is less on their adventures than on the qualities of loyalty and respect that keep the three together. A-II (br)

Last American Hero, The (1973) Story of champion stock-car driver Junior Johnson (Jeff Bridges) who evolved from running corn whiskey over the backroads of North Carolina to earning $100,000 a year racing cars. Directed by Lamont Johnson, the film's gritty atmosphere is evoked beautifully, supported by a fine cast (Art Lund, Geraldine Fitzgerald, Gary Busey and Ned Beatty). A-III (PG) AA

Last Boy Scout, The (1991) A former Secret Service agent (Bruce Willis) and a drug-addicted ex-football player (Damon Wayans) constantly court death while attempting to stop the assassination of a corrupt Senator. Director Tony Scott's sleazy bloodbath is an affront to human sensibilities disguised as slick action entertainment. Excessive violence, incessant rough language and brief nudity. O (R) 18

Last Days of Man on Earth, The (1977) Failed British satire set against the background of a post-nuclear disaster in which a group of scientists led by a ruthless woman (Jenny Runacre) force a brilliant young man to help them in an attempt to create a new breed of superhumans. Directed by Robert Fuest, the exotic settings are far more interesting than the action occurring in them. Excessive nudity. O (R)

Last Detail, The (1974) Career sailors (Jack Nicholson and Otis Young), assigned to escort a young seaman (Randy Quaid) to the Marine brig, stop off along the way to give him a last fling, which proves to be his first. Directed by Hal Ashby, it is fairly consistent but very coarse adult entertainment. Brothel scene with brief nudity and unrelenting flow of rough language are part of the movie's apparent definition of manliness. A-IV (R) X

Last Dragon, The (1985) A kind of black Kung Fu movie that doesn't take itself too seriously. Although it has a banal storyline about a good martial arts expert vanquishing a nasty one, director Michael Schultz is helped out by lively high-spirited performers. Some restrained violence and vulgar language. A-II (PG-13) 15

Last Embrace (1979) Florid melodrama directed by Jonathan Demme about a government agent (Roy Scheider) who has a mental breakdown after his wife is killed in a shootout in which he inadvertently involved her. A mysterious graduate student (Janet Margolin) is somehow involved in a flimsy plot loaded with red herrings. Generous doses of brutality and sexual scenes. O (R) X

Last Emperor, The (1988) Sweeping historical saga of Pu Yi (1906–67) who, after being crowned emperor of the fading Manchurian dynasty at age 3, becomes a passive pawn amidst political power plays until ending his life as a humble gardener under Chinese Communist rule. Italian director Bernardo Bertolucci's movie boasts exquisite historical detail, beautiful costumes, extraordinary location sets in the Forbidden City and breathtaking pageantry, but oddly lacks dramatic punch. Some scenes of violence, sex and opium smoking, though brief and integral to the cultural context. A-III (PG-13) 15

Last Escape, The (1970) Stuart Whitman leads an Allied operation in the final months of World War II to smuggle a leading rocket scientist out of war-scarred Germany while the Russians are attempting to do the same. Director Walter Grauman compensates for an obvious script and wooden acting by a lot of wartime action scenes with remarkably little bloodshed. A-II (G) U

Last Exit to Brooklyn (1990) Repugnant view of working-class life during a 1952 shipping strike in a waterfront neighborhood where thugs amuse themselves terrorizing passersby, the local union strike leader (Stephen Lang) destroys himself in a homosexual affair, and an aspiring hooker (Jennifer Jason Leigh) winds up the victim of a stand-in-line gang rape. Director Uli Edel's dark picture of human degradation makes several feeble gestures affirming the values of family and union solidarity, but they ring hollow and fail to add any significance to the dehumanized proceedings. Excessive violence and sexual exploitation. O (R) 18

Last Flight of Noah's Ark (1980) Elliott Gould agrees to fly missionary Genevieve Bujold and a menagerie of domestic animals to a South Pacific island but, when the plane crash lands, they discover two child stowaways (Ricky Schroder and Tammy Lauren). Directed by Charles Jarrott, the Disney production is disarming and has a lighthearted grace that is irresistible. Appealing fare for young and old. A-I (G) U

Last Grenade, The (1970) British agent Stanley Baker tramps up and down the hills bordering Hong Kong in pursuit of Alex Cord, a grinning sadist working for the other side. Director Gordon Flemyng's chase story, in which an adulterous affair plays a part, doesn't make much sense and the movie is a dud. A-III (M) A

Last Hard Men, The (1976) Ugly, distasteful Western about an escaped convict (James Coburn) who is determined to get revenge upon the retired sheriff (Charlton Heston) who put him in jail. Coburn manages to be interesting and Michael Parks contributes a few bright moments, but all director Andrew V. McLaglen's movie really has on its mind is the usual rape and other brutalities that go with simple-minded debasements of the western myth. O (R) X

Last House on the Left, The (1972) Two teenagers (Lucy Grantham; Sandra Cassel) are kidnapped, tormented, raped and slaughtered while a foolish sheriff bungles his investigation and the parents of one girl take their own brutal revenge. Written and directed by Wes Craven, this lurid movie indulges in gore, sex and profanity. O (R) 18

Last Hunt, The (1956) In the 1880s, with the last of the great buffalo herds nearing extinction, a cynical gunman (Robert Taylor) persuades a veteran hunter (Stewart Granger) to join him in going after buffalo hides, with predictably disastrous results. Director Richard Brooks reduces the plot to a simplistic contrast between the noble hunter and the cold-blooded gunman who not only kills people as wantonly as buffalo but also brutalizes an Indian woman (Debra Paget) he has taken captive. Much stylized violence and sexual situations. A-III (br) A

Last Hurrah, The (1958) Uneven screen version of Edwin O'Connor's novel about the end of a colorful era in urban machine politics as seen in the final campaign of fictional Boston Mayor Frank Skeffington (Spencer Tracy). Directed by John Ford, the story's contrast between the old and the new TV breed of politicians is less interesting than its nostalgia for a more human, if much flawed American past as evoked by a cast of veteran character actors (Pat O'Brien, Frank McHugh, James Gleason) as well as some of Ford's own stock company (Donald Crisp, Jane Darwell, John Carradine) who balance the thick sentimentality with broad humor. Lingering demise of main character. A-II (br) U

Last Married Couple in America, The (1980) George Segal and Natalie Wood begin to doubt the validity of their own relationship when the marriages of all their friends shatter around them. Directed by Gilbert Cates, it is a clumsy, shapeless affair, poorly scripted and badly acted. Some nudity and a great deal of foul language. O (R) X

Last Metro, The (1981) Uninvolving wartime melodrama directed by Francois Truffaut about a harried actress-theater manager (Catherine Deneuve) who tries to keep her theater open and her Jewish husband (Heinz Bennent) hidden during the German Occupation of Paris. It's a romantic and sophisticated production lacking depth and passion. Adultery figures in the plot. A-III (PG)

Last Movie, The (1971) Failed story about the bizarre and tragic effects a movie company has on a community of primitive Peruvian Indians whose village they use as a location. Directed by Dennis Hopper, who also stars, the movie's concept is an intriguing one that, unfortunately, is not realized in a work totally out of control with incredible lapses of logic and jumbled time sequences. Graphic scenes of sexual encounters and a demeaning attitude toward Indian culture and religious beliefs. O (R) X

Last of His Tribe, The (1992) Stolid human drama based on the book by anthropologist Alfred Kroeber (Jon Voight) about his 1911 discovery of Ishi (Graham Greene), the last survivor of the Yahi, an Indian tribe long thought extinct, and his work in trying to preserve its language and culture. Director Harry Hook gives a rather flat account of an aboriginal man's learning to live in the 20th century and Kroeber's attempts to reconstruct the lost Yahi way of life. Some heart-rending scenes of violence and a restrained sexual episode. A-III (PG-13)

Last of Sheila, The (1973) Film producer (James Coburn) invites some friends (Richard Benjamin, Joan Hackett, Dyan Cannon, James Mason, Raquel Welch and Ian McShane) for a week's cruise in the Mediterranean celebrating the first anniversary of the hit-and-run killing of his wife, whose name graces both the yacht and the movie's title. Director Herbert Ross is so busy being slick and clever in his parody of Hollywood types, that he creates an elaborate hoax rather than a plausible whodunit. A-III (PG)

Last of the Comanches (1952) After Comanches massacre a troop of U.S. Cavalry, six survivors (led by Broderick Crawford) take refuge in an abandoned mission and hold off waves of attackers until reinforcements arrive. Directed by Andre de Toth, the result is little more than standard action fare ending in a tribute to the bravery of the fallen. Frontier violence. A-I (br) U

Last of the Finest, The (1990) Suspended veteran Los Angeles cop (Brian Dennehy) and his three young cronies bust a bigtime drug and money laundering racket tied to Central American gunrunners. Directed in plodding, unimaginative fashion by John MacKenzie, this implausible cop adventure justifies vigilantism as patriotism. Some profanity, sexual expletives, bathroom humor and explosive comic-book violence. A-III (R)

Last of the Mobile Hot-Shots (1970) Failed screen version of a play by Tennessee Williams presents a muddled and superficially symbolic story of Southern racial attitudes involving James Coburn, Robert Hooks and Lynn Redgrave. Directed by Sidney Lumet, this talky affair has an excess of crude dialogue and several unnecessarily explicit sex scenes in the flashbacks. O (X/R)

Last of the Mohicans, The (1992) When the French and Indian War erupts on New York's colonial frontier, heroic woodsman Hawkeye (Daniel Day-Lewis) cannot save a British force from being massacred in the wilderness but at least he's able to rescue its commander's daughter (Madeleine Stowe) from a wicked Huron warrior (Wes Studi). In adapting the James Fenimore Cooper classic to the screen, director Michael Mann updates its romanticized version of pioneer life amidst noble woodland savages by dwelling in realistic detail on the inhuman cruelties of hand-to-hand combat. Many graphic depictions of deadly violence and bloodshed. A-III (R) PG

Last of the Red Hot Lovers (1972) Failed screen version of the Neil Simon comedy about a man (Alan Arkin) who uses his unsuspecting mother's apartment for sex in the afternoon. Directed by Gene Saks, it tries desperately to be amusing but, except for the occasional one-liner, it is boring when it's not irritating in its search for euphemisms for sin. A-III (PG)

Last of the Renegades (1966) Routine European-made western directed by Harald Rinl is an old-fashioned cowboy and Indian movie with Lex Barker and Anthony Steel trying to avert an Indian war while both pursuing the same Indian maiden (Karin Dor). Stylized violence. A-I (br)

Last of the Secret Agents?, The (1966) Stupid undercover spoof directed by Norman Abbott features the tiresome slapstick antics of comics Marty Allen and Steve Rossi. Overemphasis on the sexually suggestive. O (br) U

Last Outpost, The (1951) Raiding Union supply lines along the Santa Fe Trail, a Confederate officer (Ronald Reagan) comes across his brother (Bruce Bennett), who happens to be a Yankee officer, and the two join forces to stop an Apache uprising. Director Lewis R. Foster, treats the farfetched yarn as if it were a Rover Boys adventure in blue and gray. Stylized violence. A-I (br) U

Last Picture Show, The (1971) Bleak picture of life in a dust-stricken and culturally depressed little town in 1951 Texas. Director Peter Bogdanovich captures brilliantly the banal details of time and place but portrays the town's inhabitants (Timothy Bottoms, Jeff Bridges; Cybill Shepherd; Ellen Burstyn; Cloris Leachman; Ben Johnson) as a hopeless lot whose only interests are sexual experimentation and watching TV soap operas and quiz shows. There's more to life than that, even in a small town. Brief nudity. O (PG) X

Last Rebel, The (1971) Joe Namath smirks his way through a puerile western as an ex-Confederate adventurer who shoots up a few rivals, hustles some local pool sharks and makes merry with ladies high and low. Director Denys McCoy's movie has crude language, stylized violence and brief nudity, but its major offense is being so witless and dull that an adult will find it hard to sit through. A-III (GP)

Last Remake of Beau Geste, The (1977) Witless and boring spoof of a classic adventure movie stars Ann-Margret and Michael York who are less embarrassing to watch than the struggle of a cast of comedians in the clutches of a dreary script. Director Marty Feldman relies almost solely on vulgar sight gags and crude humor to keep the French Foreign Legion afloat. A-III (PG)

Last Resort (1986) Charles Grodin takes his movie family on an island resort vacation in this failed satire about the crude excesses of the travel business. The sex maniacs who run the resort manage to corrupt the middle-class values of mom, dad and the kids in this unfunny farce obsessed with crude sexual innuendo and sight gags, the drug-and-booze culture and profanity. O (R)

Last Rites (1988) Donald P. Bellisario directs a trashy, twisted tale of a New York priest (Tom Berenger) who falls in love with a woman (Daphne Zuniga) seeking his protection from a Mafia gang headed by the priest's father (Dane Clark). Several simulated sex scenes, some bloody violence and occasional rough language. O (R) 18

Last Romantic Lover, The (1979) French sex farce begins with a male beauty contest sponsored by a women's magazine and ends with the runner-up romancing the supposedly liberated woman editor with such old-fashioned techniques as tenderness. The movie is directed by Just Jaeklin with all the gloss and glamour that he learned as a fashion photographer. Except for some partial nudity, it is a throwback to an earlier age of sexual comedy that feminists may find more objectionable than moralists. O (R)

Last Run, The (1971) George C. Scott plays an old-time professional getaway driver hired to break out a young convict (Tony Musante), and he handles all the ensuing ambushes, chases and double-crosses with credible assurance. Directed by Richard Fleischer, the flawed narrative is of less interest than Scott's bravura performance. Some violence and sexual references. A-III (GP) 18

Last Safari, The (1967) Mediocre British adventure directed by Henry Hathaway with Stewart Granger as a safari guide. The original version featured extensive nudity that was edited out of the American release. A-I (br) A

Last Shot You Hear, The (1969) Unintriguing thriller dealing with a renowned marriage counselor (Hugh Marlowe) who, after refusing to give his wife a divorce, is murdered by her lover. Director Gordon Hessler's movie concludes fatuously attempting to elicit sympathy for the murderers. O (PG) 18

Last Starfighter, The (1984) High school senior (Lance Guest), a whiz at electronic games, finds himself defending the frontiers of the universe against ruthless space invaders in a touching, romantic, humorous fantasy from director Nick Castle. Some of the violence might be too much for younger viewers. A-II (PG)

Last Summer (1969) Suntanned teenagers (Richard Thomas, Bruce Davison and Barbara Hershey) exploring adolescent limits of mutual trust and confidence and the tragic destruction of a self-possessed young girl (Kathy Burns) form the background and structure of the movie. Director Frank Perry's vision of upper-class youths contending with their curiosity about each other's physique and psyche features a terrifying rape sequence in which the antics and silliness in the first part of the film turn to dread. Though its use of nudity is questionable, this journey of sorts into self-discovery is a provocative examination of physical and spiritual maturation. A-IV (X/R/GP/R) X

Last Tango in Paris (1973) Middle-aged man (Marlon Brando), numb with despair at the suicide of his wife, happens upon a woman (Maria Schneider) inspecting a vacant apartment, and they immediately engage in sex. She returns again and again to the apartment for further encounters, but when he eventually proposes marriage, she runs away and in pursuing her he is killed. Directed by Bernardo Bertolucci, the romantic twaddle about tortured, alienated people adds up to very little, and the sex scenes, while not pornographic are needlessly extended and explicit. O (X/R/X)

Last Temptation of Christ, The (1988) Deeply flawed screen adaptation of the Nikos Kazantzakis novel probing the mystery of the human nature of Jesus Christ, the Son of God, fails because of artistic inadequacy rather than anti-religious bias. Director Martin Scorsese's wrong-headed insistence on gore and brutality, as well as a preoccupation with sexual rather than spiritual love, is compounded by screenwriter Paul Schrader's muddled script, shallow characterizations and flat dialogue delivered woodenly by William Dafoe in the title role. Excessively graphic violence, several sexually explicit scenes and some incidental nudity. O (R) 18

Last Tycoon, The (1976) Uninspired film version of an unfinished F. Scott Fitzgerald novel about an Irving Thalberg-like producer (Robert De Niro), who slowly works himself to death. Despite the handsomely mounted production, director Elia Kazan runs out of creative ideas of what to do with a cast (Robert Mitchum; Jeanne Moreau; Tony Curtis) seemingly adrift in the setting. Occasional rough language and an overextended nude sequence. A-IV (PG) 15

Last Unicorn, The (1982) Animated feature about a lonely unicorn (voice of Mia Farrow) who goes off in a quest to learn what happened to the others of her kind. Though the animation is not very imaginative, the Rankin and Bass production has some superb voice-over talent (Alan Arkin; Angela Lansbury; Keenan Wynn; Christopher Lee; Tammy Grimes) and the story itself is likeable enough. The result provides some pleasant fantasy for younger children. A-I (G)

Last Valley, The (1971) Omar Sharif plays a man of letters, fleeing the 17th-century wars of religion and nationalism in the Germanies, who takes refuge in an out-of-the-way, untouched village, but soon it is also found by a band of freebooters (led by Michael Caine). Written, produced and directed by James Clavell, it is of more historical than dramatic interest and its scenes of mass slaughter and individual cruelty coupled with the moral ambiguities of life under duress make it decidedly mature fare. A-III (GP) AA

Last Voyage, The (1960) When the boiler in an aging ocean liner blows, the captain (George Sanders) delays evacuating the sinking vessel while his chief engineer (Edmond O'Brien) tries to contain the damage. Writer-director Andrew L. Stone's so-so disaster movie centers on the plight of a trapped woman (Dorothy Malone) whose husband (Robert Stack) gets help from one of the crew (Woody Strode). Much menace, including a terrified child. A-I (br) A

Last Waltz, The (1978) This is a cinematic record of the last concert given by a rock group called The Band. Supplemented by interview footage and some numbers shot in a studio, director Martin Scorsese has put it all together extremely well, but its primary appeal is to rock fans. Some coarse language and an amoral attitude on the part of some of the performers. A-III (PG)

Last Wave, The (1979) Staid Australian lawyer (Richard Chamberlain) defends four aborigines accused of murder, but a mysterious tribal seer divines that the lawyer is the precursor of some cycle-ending event of cataclysmic proportions. Director Peter Weir evokes a strangely eerie sense of the aborigine's transcendental link with nature in stark contrast to the sterile mechanistic environment of the city in which the trial takes place. Increasingly heavy atmosphere of the occult and foreboding of human disaster. A-III (PG) AA

L'Atalante (1934) Lyrically romantic French classic in a newly restored print tells of a barge captain (Jean Daste) who brings his country bride (Dita Parlo) to live aboard his boat, but when they reach Paris, she goes off to see the sights and gets left behind until the crusty old mate (Michel Simon) reunites the unhappy couple. Director Jean Vigo's simple tale of love and its complications is marked by strange yet lovely surreal passages, Simon's masterfully eccentric performance and Boris Kaufman's poetic photography of life along the river. Several references to prostitution and a scene of erotic yearning. A-III (nr)

Late Autumn (1973) Fine Japanese drama made in 1961 about a young woman who rejects marriage because she does not wish to leave her widowed mother alone, but the mother tricks her into getting engaged. Director Yasujiro Ozu lightens the mood with some gentle humor, especially pointed at insufferable male smugness in a society in which women are dependent upon men. A-I (nr)

Late for Dinner (1991) Silly fantasy about a young family man (Brian Wimmer) frozen with his mildly retarded brother-in-law (Peter Berg) in 1962 and thawing 29 years later to return to his now middle-aged wife (Marcia Gay Harden) and grown daughter (Colleen Flynn). Producer-director W. D. Richter's inept attempt at heartfelt drama, comedy and fantasy overplays the story's sappy sentiment. Momentary violence. A-II (PG)

Late Great Planet Earth, The (1979) Screen version of a book proving the imminent destruction of earth using prophecies from the Old and New Testament is a mishmash of interviews with experts of greater and lesser authority, portentous narration and stock newsreel footage, with a touch of pseudo-biblical drama thrown in. Its distorted idea of the nature and purpose of biblical prophecy makes it unsuited to young and impressionable viewers. A-III (PG)

Late Liz, The (1973) Anne Baxter plays a hard-drinking woman who sifts through multiple marriages and attempted suicide before salvation hits her through the guidance of a local clergyman. Directed by Dick Ross, its rather bogus sentimentality and adult situations make it adult fare. A-III (GP)

Late Show, The (1977) Art Carney as the aging private-eye (who spends most of his time watching old movies on television) feels compelled to solve the murder of his old partner (Howard Duff) who shows up on his doorstep with a fatal bullet wound. Lily Tomlin teams up in the sleuthing and the result is an above-average crime entertainment directed by Robert Benton. Occasional violence and crude language. A-III (PG) 15

Late Spring (1972) Japanese story of a dutiful daughter who refuses to leave her widowed father until he finally is forced to trick her into marriage. Director Yasujiro Ozu's 1949 movie is a lyric study of the abiding strength of family life and relationships, warmly told and universal in its values. A-I (nr)

Latitude Zero (1970) Japanese science-fiction movie with Joseph Cotton and Cesar Romero pitted against each other as the classic counterparts of good and evil. Directed by Inoshiro Honda, an underwater city in the Jules Verne vein, grotesque monsters, and some excellent miniature work make it a must for sci-fi fans. A couple of grisly scenes are inappropriate for small children. A-II (PG)

Laughing Policeman, The (1973) Detective thriller about a brutal mass murder on a San Francisco bus that veteran detective Walter Matthau pursues because his partner is one of those killed and the clues point to a previous unsolved murder case. There's the basis for a good yarn here, but director Stuart Rosenberg puts too much emphasis on violence, crude language and an exploration of the city's tawdry side. O (R) X

Laughter in the Dark (1969) British drama about a man of some intelligence and breeding being destroyed by his infatuation for an unscrupulous schemer. The performance of Nicol Williamson, as the titled art dealer victimized by a dreadful cinema usherette (Anna Karina) is skillful, and Tony Richardson's direction evidences serious intentions, but the cumulative effect is merely ludicrous with more than a little nudity and explicit depiction of sex. O (X)

Laura (1944) Sparse mystery embroidered with moody romance from Vera Caspary's novel about a police detective (Dana Andrews) investigating the reported murder of the beautiful title character (Gene Tierney) whose rise in the New York social set was aided by an influential radio commentator (Clifton Webb at his waspish best). Things, of course, are not what they seem as director Otto Preminger probes the dark side of high society life while focusing on the dour detective's growing fascination with the glamorous Laura and the vitriolic journalist's feelings for his former protege. More for romantics than mystery fans, there are some scenes of menace, stylized violence and implied sexual encounters. A-II (nr) U

Laurel and Hardy's Laughing Twenties (1966) Affectionate look back at the great comedy team of Stan Laurel and Oliver Hardy in a collection of excerpts from their silent two-reelers. The narrative is helpful and the sight gags irresistible. A-I (br) U

Law and Disorder (1974) A taxi driver (Carrol O'Connor) and a hairdresser (Ernest Borgnine) form a number of their New York neighbors into an auxiliary police force to put a stop to an invasion of muggers, thieves and exhibitionists. Directed by Ivan Passer, there is some sharp satire on contemporary urban crime and middle-class frustrations. Some intense violence, very rough language and a number of embarrassing sexual references. A-IV (R) 18

Law and Jake Wade, The (1958) Contrived western in which an outlaw (Richard Widmark) seeks revenge on a one-time partner (Robert Taylor) who ran out on him with the loot from a bank robbery, then settled down as sheriff of a small town. Directed by John Sturges, the clumsy narrative has the lawman and his fiance (Paricia Owens) taken captive and forced to lead the outlaw's gang to the missing loot on a journey ending in a ghost town during a Comanche uprising. Stylized violence and much menace. A-II (nr)

Lawless Street, A (1955) Cliched western in which a veteran marshal (Randolph Scott) outguns all his foes and wins back the wife (Angela Lansbury) who had left him years before because she distained bloodshed. Director Joseph H. Lewis is more interested in shootouts and barroom brawls than in trying to make some sense out of a silly plotline. Much violence and implied adultery. A-III (br)

Lawman (1971) Straight-shooting marshal (Burt Lancaster) attempts to round up seven murder suspects in a town where longtime sheriff (Robert Ryan) has learned to compromise with local cattle baron (Lee J. Cobb). The situation results in bloodshed with justice depending upon the fastest, surest gun. Director Michael Winner seems to have pretensions about examining what or who is the law, but the conclusion solves nothing. Stylized violence and bloodshed. A-III (GP) PG

Lawnmower Man, The (1992) Failed sci-fi film about a driven doctor (Pierce Brosnan) whose experiments turn a retarded man (Jeff Fahey) into a killer with psychic powers. Directed by Brett Leonard, it's little more than a computer-graphics variation on the mad scientist theme with thoroughly unappealing characters and images. Recurring violence, including a sadistic cleric, brief sexual encounters with momentary nudity and some rough language. A-III (R) 15

Lawrence of Arabia (1963) Set within the frame of a grand adventure is this interesting study of British hero-author T. E. Lawrence (Peter O'Toole), whose World War I exploits in leading the Arabs against the Turks made his literary works popular in the 1920s. In a 1989 restoration of the original wide-screen print, director David Lean focuses on the diverse aspects of the man with an ambiguity suitable to the mystery still surrounding this mythic figure. Bloody wartime battles and implication of a homosexual incident. A-II (PG)

Laws of Gravity (1992) Shrill drama about two hot-tempered Brooklyn thugs (Peter Greene and Adam Trese) trying to hold on to their women (Edie Falco and Arabella Field) while secretly conniving to rip off a cache of stolen guns. Writer-director Nick Gomez blunders through a meaninglessly violent story of brutish, boastful thieves, told in ear-splitting obscenities. Some graphic violence, including abuse of women, much heavy drinking and nonstop rough language. O (R)

Lawyer, The (1970) Routine crime melodrama in which a hotshot lawyer (Barry Newman) races around California in his beat-up camper trying to get his client, philandering Dr. Jack Harrison (Robert Colbert), off the hook for murdering his wife. Directed by Sidney J. Furie, it contains frequent nudity and crude dialogue. O (R) X

Le Beau Mariage (1982) French comedy of manners and morals from director Eric Rohmer proves to be an amusing yet perceptive exploration of courtship rituals and mating practices not far different from our own. Its young heroine (Beatrice Romano), fed up with the complications of her affair with a married man, decides to get married and sets out to find her own husband. The result is a comedy of situations seen from a feminine perspective. A-III (PG)

Le Boucher (1972) Excellent psychological thriller about a schoolteacher (Stephane

Audran) and the butcher of the title (Jean Yanne) who live in a small French village where a series of insane murders has taken place. Written and directed by Claude Chabrol, the script is marvelously tight and disciplined and the characterizations have an unusually solid psychological foundation. There are some shocks, but they are done with all the authority of the old master, Hitchcock himself. A-III (GP)

Le Chat (1975) French study of a couple (Simone Signoret and Jean Gabin) who have been married for 25 years but whose ardor has cooled and turned to rancor. Directed by Pierre Granier-Deferre, the script is one of unrelieved bleakness, yet the two principals invest their roles with a rich human dimension as two imperfect individuals who stubbornly go on, fueled by hate, but they sometimes remember love. A-III (nr)

Le Depart (1968) Belgian story of an assistant hairdresser (Jean-Pierre Leaud) who is so obsessed with the idea of entering an upcoming motor rally that he neglects his girlfriend in trying to find a suitable car. Director Jerzy Skolimowski treats his self-indulgent youth with stinging humor but also with some sympathy. A-III (br)

Le Magnifique (1976) Jean-Paul Belmondo stars in a failed satire of superspy adventures of the James Bond variety. Forgettable French production directed by Phillipe de Broca. A-III (nr)

Le Mans (1971) Steve McQueen combines his acting and racing skills in a convincing portrait of a driver in the famed Le Mans competition in France. Directed by Lee H. Katzin, the drama is on the track and racing fans will find much satisfaction in the authenticity of the driving and in the beauty of the machines A-I (G)

Le Petit Theatre de Jean Renoir (1969) Three short nostalgic sketches present a Christmas fantasy, a wildly funny opera-bouffe and a tribute to the French game of boules. A charming interlude, sung by Jeanne Moreau, complements this homage to life by director Jean Renoir who introduces each of his tales with an unpretentious explanation of his reasons for bringing it to life on film. Lovely, quaint and sentimental by turn, but with some mature themes. A-III (nr)

Le Retour D'Afrique (1973) Swiss drama about a young couple who decide to join a friend in Africa to help fashion a better world. After a final farewell party, a telegram arrives from their friend telling them not to come and that the explanation is in the mail. Awaiting the letter in their empty flat, they begin to confront themselves and their relationship to society. Director Alain Tanner's theme of real change coming only from within is a bit pretentious and stilted, yet it does raise questions about coping in a post-industrial society. A-III (nr)

Le Sex Shop (1973) Unfunny French sex farce about the owner of a failing book store (Claude Berri) who opens a shop selling erotic books and related mechanical contraptions and then becomes obsessed with his merchandise and starts experimenting. Also written and directed by Berri, what might have been a satire on contemporary sexual mores itself becomes obsessed with the subject and the explicit nature of its treatment is at best tasteless and at worst grossly offensive. O (X/R)

Le Trio Infernal (1974) Failed French black comedy depicting the moral bankruptcy of society following World War I, the plot details the murder-for-profit of two German sisters (Romy Schneider and Mascha Gomska) by a French war hero (Michel Piccoli). Directed by Francis Girod, what begins as a Gallic sex farce soon becomes mired in details of ghoulish dismemberments and bizarre sex. O (nr)

Leadbelly (1976) Screen biography tracing the troubled life of neglected Huddie Ledbetter, legendary black folk singer and master of the twelve-string guitar whose work became part of the post-World War II folk renaissance. Director Gordon Parks downplays the racial themes in favor of a musical tribute while eliciting a colorfully authentic performance from Roger E. Mosley as Huddie. A-III (PG)

League of Their Own, A (1992) In a spirited, often amusing drama about the formation of a women's professional baseball league during World War II, the narrative follows the course of a season with a team whose odd assortment of players includes sibling rivals (Geena Davis and Lori Petty), a backwoods slugger (Megan Cavanagh), street-wise fielders (Madonna and Rosie O'Donnell) and a washed-up rummy as manager (Tom Hanks). Directed by Penny Marshall, the story uses the baseball diamond as an arena of team solidarity and personal self-discovery rather than as an ideological soapbox, though its feminist perspective is abundantly evident. A few mild sexual references, some vulgar language and occasional tasteless humor, including a toilet joke. A-II (PG)

Lean on Me (1989) Formula feel-good bio of controversial Paterson, N.J., high school principal Joe Clark (Morgan Freeman) focuses on his mission to clean up the crime and graffiti-infested school, restore student self-pride and raise their abysmal reading scores. Fearless, funny and nasty, Freeman is a stand-out as he rejuvenates the school. Director John G. Avildsen's cartoon movie heroics may be simplistic and the screenplay may play fast and loose with the facts, but the film should speak to older urban adolescents faced with similar school blight. Much rough language, some violence and menace and a flash of nudity. A-III (PG-13)

Leap of Faith (1992) During a three-day revival in a backwater Kansas town, a bogus faith healer (Steve Martin) and his mercenary manager (Debra Winger) each experience minor transformations when he witnesses a possible real miracle and she is moved by the decency of the local sheriff (Liam Neeson). Director Richard Pearce's seriocomedy of religious hucksterism has few laughs and little meaning, made all the more unsatisfactory by a vague, feel-good ending. Comic depiction of religious sentiment exploited for profit and an implied sexual encounter. A-III (PG-13) PG

Learning Tree, The (1969) Director Gordon Park's lifeless cinematic version of his autobiographical novel is a highly romantic, colorful recreation of a black adolescent's coming-of-age in a mixed atmosphere of gentleness and violence, honesty, hypocrisy and bigotry. The result has more a sense of a photographic essay than of a realistic portrait of the rural black experience. A-III (PG)

Leather Boys, The (1966) British story of a failed marriage with Rita Tushingham as a teenager who weds to escape her appalling home, Colin Campbell as the immature husband and Dudley Sutton as his calculating friend. Though the episodic story is loosely motivated, the acting is first-rate and Sidney Furie's direction has the ring of authenticity. A-III (br) X

Leathernecks Have Landed, The (1936) Dated pulp adventure in movieland China where an ex-Marine (Lew Ayres) turns gunrunner, then winds up back in the Corps by saving his former buddies from a rebel attack. Director Howard Bretherton does little with the standard melodramatics, though a likeable cast (James Ellison, Isabel Jewell and Ward Bond) makes it relatively painless. Stylized violence. A-I (br)

Leaving Normal (1992) A runaway battered wife (Meg Tilly) and a hard-bitten cocktail waitress (Christine Lahti) hitchhike to Alaska in hopes of finally putting down roots. Director Edward Zwick's combination female buddy and road movie is too contrived to be convincing. Recurring rough language and some sexual innuendo. A-III (R)

Legacy (1976) Middle-aged woman (Joan Hotchkis) is too busy to notice that she is on the verge of a breakdown in director Karen Arthur's attempt to turn a myriad of feminist themes into a movie. Her treatment of a woman's repressed sexuality and guilt feelings about her life might have some use for women's discussion groups but not as a popular entertainment. O (R)

Legacy, The (1979) Inferior horror movie of the satanic, let's-make-a-deal subgenre depicts the misadventures of a bright, unmarried young couple (Katharine Ross and Sam Elliot) in a Gothic English manor. Directed by Richard Marquand, the story is extremely silly and excessively gory. O (R) X

Legal Eagles (1986) Robert Redford tries his best to be funny, charming and resourceful as the lawyer whose political ambitions get sidetracked when two women, a lawyer (Debra Winger) and her client (Daryl Hannah), implicate him in an art fraud that turns into a murder case. Director Ivan Reitman's shallow comedy is marred by female stereotyping and casual sex. A-III (PG)

Legend (1986) Director Ridley Scott's sumptuous fairy tale contrasts exceptionally cruel evil with extraordinarily sweet innocence in a quest to redeem a frozen world from the control of the Lord of Darkness. Tom Cruise is the hero who vanquishes the devil (Tim Curry) in an astonishing visual delight, but some instances of grotesque imagery, especially the Lord of Darkness may frighten very young children. A-II (PG)

Legend of Billy Jean, The (1985) Four teenagers unwittingly become outlawed folk heroes. The value system represented is so confused that the movie is inappropriate for its intended adolescent audience. Some vulgar language. A-III (PG-13) 15

Legend of Boggy Creek, The (1973) Little town in Arkansas is bothered by a hairy monster, with a dubious footprint or two as evidence of its existence. In the fictionalized speculations about the monster's attacks, an actor made up with a lot of hair is photographed from the rear and sides in shadowy condition; he is as skillful at evading pursuing dogs and townsmen as he is the camera. A-I (G)

Legend of Hell House, The (1973) Good British horror movie in which a skeptical physicist (Clive Revill), his wife (Gayle Hunnicutt) and two mediums (Pamela Franklin and Roddy McDowell) attempt to unravel the source of the ghastly murders that occurred when a previous group of scientists attempted to penetrate the mysteries of a deserted Gothic mansion on the outskirts of London. Directed by John Hough, it has plenty of atmosphere, not a little suspense but also some intense violence and a suggestion of perverse sexuality. A-III (PG) X

Legend of Lylah Clare, The (1968) Sudsy, sentimental soap opera in which a young starlet (Kim Novak) is coached by a has-been movie director (Peter Finch) who exhibits untoward interest in her that leads to tragedy. Directed by Robert Aldrich, it's a clunker with sexually suggestive scenes. O (R) X

Legend of Nigger Charley, The (1972) Runaway slaves (Fred Williamson, D'Urville Martin and Don Pedro Colley) are pursued by a bloodthirsty slave-tracker (Keith Prentice). Directed by Martin Goldman, the mindless action film indulges in some foul language and incidental nudity. A-IV (PG)

Legend of the Lone Ranger, The (1981) Klinton Spilsbury portrays the masked champion of justice who, with the aid of Tonto (Michael Horse), rescues President Grant (Jason Robards) from the clutches of a badman (Christopher Lloyd). While moderately entertaining, director William A. Fraker's western has considerable violence and occasional rough language. A-III (PG)

Legend of Tom Dooley, The (1959) Unaware of Lee's surrender, Confederate raiders (including Michael Landon) attack a Union coach, kill some passengers and become fugitives from Northern justice. Directed by Ted Post, the narrative is clumsily pegged to a song about doomed lovers, but the action is largely unconvincing. Stylized violence and romantic complications. A-II (br) U

L'Elegant Criminel (1992) Before he is guillotined in 1836, a notorious French murderer (Daniel Auteuil) writes his memoirs rationalizing his life of crime. Director Francis Girod's overlong, fact-based period film leaves several key characters unexplained and fails to come to grips with what motivated the killer's callous behavior. Subtitles. Occasional violence and fleeting bedroom shots. A-III (nr)

Lemon Drop Kid, The (1951) Frantic adaptation of a Damon Runyon story in which a small-time bookie (Bob Hope) schemes to raise the money owed a gangster by setting up bogus sidewalk Santa Clauses supposedly collecting money for an old people's home. Directed by Sidney Lanfield, the script is tailored to suit Hope's talents for sight gags and one-liners but the humor is too fitful to sustain the cumbersome plot and phony Christmastime sentimentality. Mild sexual innuendo. A-II (br) A

Lemon Sisters, The (1990) Three lifelong girlfriends (Diane Keaton; Carol Kane; Kathryn Grody), self-dubbed Atlantic City's singing "Lemon Sisters," support each other through personal and career crises. Director Joyce Chopra's comedy features endearing performances and some heartwarming moments but is so lightweight it never gets beyond being a sentimental tribute to friendship. Brief instances of rough language. A-II (PG-13)

Lenny (1974) Screen version of Julian Barry's play about comic Lenny Bruce's problems with drugs and obscenity prosecution of his routines takes a semi-documentary stance by way of interviews with Bruce's widow, mother, agent and others. Bob Fosse has directed an intelligent, complex and often disturbing film, with Dustin Hoffman extraordinarily fine in the title role. No viewer should be surprised to hear a good deal of crude language. A-IV (R) 18

Leo and Lorrie (1980) A young actor and actress (Danny Most and Linda Purl), struggling for fame in television, fall in love, and encourage and console each other in this featherweight romantic comedy directed by Jerry Paris. The unabashed approval of unmarried cohabitation has enough substance to be morally offensive. O (PG)

Leo the Last (1970) The title character (Marcello Mastroianni), the last of an exiled European royal line, lives in the elegant family mansion in the heart of London's West Indian ghetto. When Leo realizes that the family fortune depends entirely on the rental income from these ghetto flats, he leads a peasant's revolt to blow up his mansion. The final frames show those who took part milling aimlessly around the rubble, wondering along with the audience what purpose director John Boorman's symbolic gesture served. Several relatively graphic sex scenes. A-IV (R)

Leolo (1993) A dreamy young boy (Maxime Collin) growing up in a strict Montreal family plagued by mental illness escapes his troubled surroundings by acting out murderous and sexual fantasies before going completely over the edge. Writer-director Jean-Claude Lauzon's self-indulgent and ugly view of life makes almost no human connections and gains added repulsion when seen through a child's eyes. Subtitles. Fierce murderous attacks, sexual perversions, some nudity, very crude toilet humor and rough language. O (nr) 18

Leon the Pig Farmer (1993) After learning that he is the product of artificial insemination in which the test tubes were accidentally switched, a Jewish Londoner (Mark Frankel) moves in with his natural father (Brian Glover), an earthy pig farmer in Yorkshire. Produced and directed by Gary Sinyor and Vadim Jean, the social comedy relies heavily on the contrasts between Jewish and gentile stereotypes for its satirical edge, but its exaggerated humor manages to be fitfully funny without being meanspirited. Discreet bedroom scene with fleeting nudity and an irreverent depiction of religious traditions. A-III (nr) 15

Leopard Man, The (1943) Producer Val Lewton's dark, eerie thriller is set in a New Mexico town where a singer's agent (Dennis O'Keefe) rents a leopard as a publicity stunt but the animal's escape is followed by a series of deaths which the agent begins to suspect are the work of a madman. Director Jacques Tourneur overcomes a weak plot by using the power of suggestion to fill the situation with dread and suspense, while making good use of the Hispanic locale and character, including a religious procession in the climax. Menacing atmosphere. A-II (br)

Lepke (1975) Crime melodrama about a top Jewish member (Tony Curtis) of Murder Inc. who has the unenviable distinction of being the only upper-echelon gang leader to suffer capital punishment. Directed by Menahem Golan, the problem of working up sympathy for a ruthless criminal, though a dedicated family man, is not surmounted by the talents involved. The treatment is restrained except for one excessive scene combining both sexuality and violence. O (R) 18

Les Biches (1968) Corruption is the theme of this subtle French production about the complicated relationship between a man and two women. Director Claude Chabrol is above all a moralist in telling the story of an innocent artist destroyed by the lavish excesses of wealthy society. Its context is psychologically ambiguous and seemingly amoral and it ends in an outburst of madness. Chabrol's work raises questions about life rather than resolves them and for this reason will not be very satisfying for the casual filmgoer. Others, however, will find it a thoughtful experience. A-IV (br)

Les Demoiselles de Rochefort (see: "The Young Girls of Rochefort").

Les Enfants Terribles (1975) Jean Cocteau's story about the perennial revolt of youth against all that established society represents was brought to the screen in 1950 by director Jean-Pierre Melville. A remarkable achievement in many ways, some of its themes of alienation and self-destruction are troubling and even anarchistic but serve as a reminder that life is not as tidy and rational as one might wish. A-IV (nr)

Les Gauloises Bleues (1968) While his wife is giving birth in the hospital, the husband (Jean-Pierre Kalfon) waits, his thoughts of his own unhappy childhood and troubles as a young man. Written and directed by Michel Cournot, the surrealistic flow of these memories reflect the man's insecurity about himself and his relations with others, but many viewers will be put off by the obscurity of much of it. A-III (G)

Les Parapluies de Cherbourg (see: "The Umbrellas of Cherbourg").

Les Violons du Bal (1974) French director Michel Drach has constructed a film-within-a-film dealing with the various problems he encountered in making a feature based upon his World War II memories of a Jewish childhood. The essential merit of this work lies in its strong evocation of the love uniting a family caught up in the terrors of the Nazi era. It succeeds admirably as a fragmentary remembrance of a child's struggling to cope with events beyond his comprehension. A-III (nr)

Less Than Zero (1987) Failed cautionary tale about the terrible consequences of the drug scene for three bright high school students in an affluent California community. Director Marek Kanievska spends most of his energies depicting the high gloss drug scene so that none of the main three earn viewer sympathy or interest. Several excessive scenes of simulated sex and a pervasive atmosphere of the sordid depths of the drug culture. O (R)

Let Him Have It (1991) Plodding, fact-based drama about the 1952 London murder of a policeman by a teenager (Paul Reynolds) too young to be executed although his 19-year-old accomplice (Chris Eccleston), who did not participate in the shooting, was hanged. A snaillike pace and unanswered questions mar director Peter Medak's miscarriage-of-justice movie that makes a strong case against capital punishment. Brief violence and recurring rough language. A-III (R) 15

Let It Be (1970) Filmed practice session of The Beatles as they rehearse various songs and clown around a bit. Directed by Michael Lindsay-Hogg in semi-documentary fashion with no real focal point or direction, but does give an interesting and informal low-key look behind the scenes. A-I (G)

Let Joy Reign Supreme (1976) French director Betrand Tavernier details the abuses of the aristocratic regime that led to the French Revolution. Philippe Noiret, Jean Rochefort and Jean Pierre Marielle tend to get lost in a narrative preoccupied with noblemen's debauchery and clergymen's corruption in a manner closer to the excesses of sex farce than historical drama. O (nr)

Let the Good Times Roll (1973) Director Sid Levin's documentary shows the story of the Golden Age of Rock, and does it with a dazzling array of stars and an extraordinary balance of intelligence, artistry and warm good humor. Stars include Chuck Berry, Little Richard, Fats Domino, Chubby Checker, Bill Haley and the Comets and Bo Diddley. A-II (PG)

Lethal Weapon (1987) Mel Gibson is a deadly effective Los Angeles cop almost psychotically ruthless in getting his job done. He's teamed with a veteran policeman (Danny Glover) whose family is threatened by drug dealers headed by a former Vietnam Special Forces and CIA operative. Gibson's square-jawed version of a legalized Rambo and Richard Donner's powerfully frenetic direction festers with excessive violence, brutality and profanity. O (R) 18

Lethal Weapon II (1989) Mindless, excessively violent sequel has the black-white cop team (Danny Glover and Mel Gibson) turn vigilante to squash a ruthless South African diplomat (Joss Ackland) behind a Los Angeles drug operation. Director Richard Donner forgoes human interest and suspense by stringing together an endless stream of intense chases, death-defying stunts and numbing, bloody carnage. Some profanity and a sexual encounter with shadowed nudity. O (R) 18

Lethal Weapon 3 (1992) Tired sequel has two L.A. detectives (Mel Gibson and Danny Glover) out to get stolen, high-powered weapons off the streets—with a little help from an Internal Affairs officer (Rene Russo) and an overeager real-estate agent (Joe Pesci). Director Richard Donner's dull formula story and lame macho humor descends into a series of meaningless, glorified shootouts. Excessive violence, an implied sexual encounter and much rough language. O (R) 15

Let's Do It Again (1975) Sidney Poitier (who also directed) and Bill Cosby play two lodge brothers from Atlanta who, in order to get money for a new meeting hall, get involved in a prize fight and the gangsters who go with it. Once the situation is set up, the comedy begins to flag and the gags become repetitive. It would be fine for children except for two sequences involving illicit love-making and an off-color verbal exchange. A-III (PG) U

Let's Get Lost (1989) Disturbing documentary portrait of jazz trumpet great Chet Baker in youth and tragic middle-age. Director Bruce Weber includes much performance footage and interviews with drug-dazed Chet at the end of his life as well as with his wives, lovers, colleagues and family. Though Baker's self-destructive life-style is not romanticized, there are explicit references to sexual promiscuity, drug and spouse abuse and other anti-social behavior. A-IV (nr)

Let's Kill Uncle (1966) Offbeat British thriller about a young boy (Pat Cardi) who finds out his uncle (Nigel Green) is plotting to murder him and so contrives with his girlfriend (Mary Badham) to kill uncle. Produced and directed by William Castle, Green is excellent in the preposterous situation, but children may find the suspense a bit too intense. A-II (br) A

Let's Make Love (1960) Clumsy romantic comedy about a billionaire playboy (Yves Montand) who falls for an actress (Marilyn Monroe) in a comedy revue, gets a role in the show and then hires Bing Crosby, Gene Kelly and Milton Berle to teach him to sing, dance and tell jokes. They can't and that's about as amusing as it gets in director George Cukor's laborious quest to wring some smiles out this lackluster star vehicle. Some sexually suggestive musical numbers. A-III (br) U

Let's Scare Jessica to Death (1971) Zohra Lampert plays a young woman who goes to a remote farmhouse to recover from a nervous breakdown only to find herself beset with eerie voices from beyond the grave. Unpretentious little horror movie directed with some intelligence by John Hancock. Some instances of sudden, graphic violence. A-III (GP) X

Let's Talk About Men (1976) Italian director Lina Wertmuller's 1965 movie with four vignettes depicting the foibles of the male gender is a moderately entertaining parable with Nino Manfredi playing five roles that humorously contrast definitions of manhood. A-III (PG)

Letter, The (1940) In a Singapore courtroom, the wife (Bette Davis) of a rubber plantation owner (Herbert Marshall) stands trial for killing a man she claims tried to assault her but his Eurasian widow (Gale Sondergaard) turns up with a letter proving it was an act of murder. Under William Wyler's moody direction, Davis gives a chilling performance as the coldly unsympathetic role as the faithless wife who ruins her life and the happiness of those around her. Restrained treatment of infidelity and its consequences. A-III (br) PG

Letter to Brezhnev (1986) Two tough working-class girls in Liverpool search for romance and a way out of the narrow confines of dull lives. This uncompromisingly realistic but lighthearted slice-of-life comedy, directed by Chris Bernard, features Peter Firth as a Russian sailor who provides a possible new direction for one of the girls (Alexandra Pigg). Harsh language and sexual innuendo. A-III (R) 15

Leviathan (1989) Tedious deep-sea monster movie in which an aborted Russian genetic experiment dooms a U.S. mining team, turning most of its divers into amphibious beasts. Director George P. Cosmatos renders his cast (Richard Crenna, Amanda Pays, Peter Weller and Daniel Stern) comatose long before the big pay-off where the moral issue of using human guinea pigs loses out to showcasing the monsters. Moderate grisly gore and profanity. A-III (R) 18

Lianna (1983) Young wife (Linda Griffiths) falls in love with another woman (Jane Hallaren) and impulsively abandons her philandering husband and two children only to find that she has traded one set of problems for another. Written, produced and directed by John Sayles, it is a sensitive account of a lesbian relationship but lacks any but the most rudimentary of moral perspectives. Graphic and unnecessarily extended love-making sequence. O (R) 18

Liberation of L.B. Jones, The (1970) Melodrama about the determined efforts of an upright black undertaker (Roscoe Lee Browne) to get a divorce from his unfaithful wife whose lover happens to be the white deputy of the little Tennessee town in which they live. Though perhaps overlong and cluttered with subplots, director William Wyler tells his story of racial justice in straightforward and dignified fashion. A-III (R) AA

Libertine, The (1969) Young widow (Catherine Spaak) avenges her late husband's sexual indulgences by experimenting with a host of graphically portrayed sadistic perversions. Posing as a spoof of exploitation films, this Italian sex farce from director Pasquale Festa-Campanile succumbs to the same indecent cliche it has chosen to mock. O (X)

Libido: The Urge to Love (see: "The Sensuous Teenager").

License to Drive (1988) After failing his driver's exam, a 16-year-old (Corey Haim) borrows his grandfather's car to take out the girl of his dreams (Heather Graham). In the ensuing havoc, director Greg Beeman highlights the follies of peer pressure, puberty and driving without a license. Fleeting rough language and a tasteless sex reference. A-II (PG-13) PG

Licence to Kill (1989) British agent James Bond (Timothy Dalton) has a personal vendetta as he tracks down a sadistic Latin American drug lord (Robert Davi). As directed by John Glen, the usual nutty stunts, mechanical gizmos and various Bond in-jokes fail to perk up this clone of every other Ramboesque action-adventure movie currently on the market. Grisly deaths by torture, intense chases, explosive violence and implied sexual promiscuity. O (PG-13) 15

Lickerish Quartet, The (1970) Producer-director Radley Metzger's dreary sex melodrama is set in a decaying Italian castle occupied by a decadent husband, wife and son who spend their time watching porno movies and having sex with a house guest (Silvana Venturelli). O (R)

Liebestraum (1991) Morbid melodrama about a love triangle (Kevin Anderson; Pamela Gidley; Bill Pullman) that develops much like a decades-old murder mystery recalled by a dying woman (Kim Novak). Written and directed by Mike Figgis, this dark and plodding tale shows more style than substance as it winds down to an unsatisfying conclusion. Brief adulterous encounters, a flash of nudity, minimal stylized violence and recurring rough language. A-III (R) 18

Lies My Father Told Me (1975) Warm, lyric picture of a boy's growing up in Montreal's Jewish ghetto with a careful exploration of the customs and values of a ritualistic culture. Directed by Jan Kadar, it is a delicate poem about being Jewish and, at the same time, about being human. Some sexual elements make it mature fare. A-III (PG) A

Life and Nothing But (1990) A war-weary major (Philippe Noiret) in post-World War I France finds unexpected romance when a wealthy woman (Sabine Azema) enlists his help in locating her husband, who was reported missing in action and presumed dead. Director Bertrand Tavernier's uneven film makes pointed anti-war statements in an ironic context, but the movie is drearily drawn-out and mostly of interest for the principals' assured and impassioned performances. A minimum of vulgar expressions. A-II (PG)

Life and Times of Grizzly Adams, The (1976) Dan Haggerty stars as a late 19th-century trapper who lived with and befriended the animals of the Rocky Mountains. Directed by Richard Friedenberg, the film is less a story than an occasion to show sun-drenched photography of picturesque landscapes and frolicsome animals that will appeal to very small children and undemanding adults. A-I (G) U

Life and Times of Judge Roy Bean, The (1972) Director John Huston has a great deal of fun with this seriocomic tale of frontier justice as administered by the legendary "hanging judge" of Vinegaroon, Texas (Paul Newman). Some viewers, however, may not be as readily amused by its loud, coarse and bawdy humor or repetitive use of fantasy violence. A-III (PG) A

Life at the Top (1966) Laurence Harvey continues his callow progress in a sequel to "Room at the Top." Directed by Ted Kotcheff, the movie's realistic treatment of his groping for some kind of personal integrity in a rootless and corrupting society will seem excessive to some. A-IV (br) X

Life Begins for Andy Hardy (1941) The Hardy boy (Mickey Rooney) leaves Carvel to prove he's a man by getting a job in New York City, spurns help from a wealthy friend (Judy Garland) and learns the hard way that he's not ready for independence. Directed by George B. Seitz, this edition of the Hardy series is a bit more realistic than the others but equally sentimental about small-town virtues. A-I (br)

Life Is a Long Quiet River (1990) Two families react quite differently when told that each has a child that belongs to the other family. Director Etienne Chatiliez uses the plot primarily to pinpoint unflattering contrasts in the life-styles of a smugly wealthy bourgeois family and a lower class family of thieves whose greed is boundless. Some unwholesome sexual references and occasional vulgar expressions. A-III (nr) 15

Life Is Cheap . . . But Toilet Paper Is Expensive (1990) Disjointed story of a Chinese American (Spencer Nakasako) wandering through the strange byways of contemporary Hong Kong's commercialized culture. Directed by Wayne Wang, the fictional situation is undeveloped and the movies's critical perspective of this culture is superficial. Some very graphic violence and brief clinical nudity. O (nr)

Life Is Sweet (1991) Richly observed story of good-natured English parents (Alison Steadman and Jim Broadbent) and their totally dissimilar twin daughters—one a placid plumber (Claire Skinner), the other (Jane Horrocks) a secretive anorexic hostile to one and all. Director Mike Leigh sensitively blends his characters' comic eccentricities with the heartfelt misery of a young woman's frightened search for herself made bearable by her supportive family. Brief bedroom scene with nudity and occasional rough language. A-III (nr)

Life, Love, Death (1969) French director Claude Lelouch examines the apprehension, trial and execution of a murderer (Amidou). The drama indicts capital punishment suggesting that it dehumanizes those who demand it, and especially, those who carry it out. Coldly intellectual, his treatment responsibly distances the viewer from a subject easily sensationalized. A-III (R)

Life, Loves, and Operas of Giusepppi Verdi, The (1974) Mediocre European dramatization of Verdi's career with Tito Gobbi and Mario Del Monaco appearing in excerpts from his major works. The production is lavish, the personal dimension is not interesting but the music is for all who love opera. A-I (nr)

Life of Brian (1979) Monty Python movie about a hapless fellow named Brian, a contemporary of Jesus, who is mistaken for the Messiah and eventually crucified by the Romans. The nihilistic, anything-for-laughs thrust of director Terry Jones's comedy deliberately exploits much that is sacred to Christian and Jewish religious tradition. Especially offensive is the mocking parody of the crucifixion scene. O (R) 15

Life of Riley, The (1948) Screen version of a popular radio comedy series about a working-class family headed by a good-hearted but dim-witted factory worker (William Bendix) whose constant mixups are smoothed over by his sage wife (Meg Randall). Written, produced and directed by Irving Brecher, the plot revolves around Riley's money problems and the romantic concerns of his college-age daughter (Rosemary DeCamp). Still some fun, despite dated family stereotypes. A-I (br) U

Life on the Edge (1992) Witless satire about the Southern Californian life-style is set at a trendy L.A. party where the shallow guests (including Jeff Perry; Jennifer Holmes; Andrew Prine) must cope with the aftermath of an earthquake. Director Andrew Yates turns out an amateurish comedy whose characters' predictable sexual escapades are of little interest and no value. Adulterous theme, lesbian encounter with nudity, some violence and occasional rough language. O (nr)

Life Stinks (1991) Betting he can live for 30 days on L.A.'s skid row without any money, a cocky billionaire (Mel Brooks) finds love with a bag lady (Lesley Ann Warren) and becomes a crusader for the homeless. When not chewing up the scenery, producer-director Brooks' absurd populist fantasy offers occasional moments of madcap lunacy that sparkle in an otherwise forgettable comedy. Implied sexual encounter, comic-book violence and an instance of rough language. A-III (PG-13) 12

Life Study (1973) Low-budget feature directed by Michael Nebbia tells the story of a girl chasing a reluctant boy encompasses 30 years of screen cliches done with such awkward sincerity as to evoke laughter in all the wrong spots. A-IV (nr)

Life with Mikey (1993) An irresponsible former child star (Michael J. Fox) becomes a substitute father figure when he turns a sassy, 10-year-old pickpocket (Christina Vidal) into a cookie commercial star in hopes of salvaging his nearly bankrupt juvenile talent agency. Director James Lapin gets limited comic mileage out of the odd coupling though the twosome's positive changes become mildly heartwarming. Dysfunctional family circumstances. A-II (PG)

Lifeforce (1985) Vampires from outer space wreak havoc in director Tobe Hooper's disjointed sci-fi end of the world movie that tries to sell itself by exploiting sex, nudity and gore. O (R)

Lifeguard (1976) This is a paean to arrested adolescence, an uninspired soap opera on the beach. Director Daniel Petrie's bland, morally insensitive account of the growing pains of a 32-year-old lifeguard (Sam Elliott) is sheer male romanticism with a dash of nudity. A-III (PG) 15

Light at the Edge of the World, The (1971) Brutal adaptation of a Jules Verne story about a lighthouse keeper (Kirk Douglas) whose rock-ribbed Cape Horn isle is invaded by blood-thirsty pirates (under Yul Brynner) who, after impaling Douglas' co-workers, hack apart the hapless passengers aboard the first ship they manage to drive upon the rocks. Samantha Eggar is preserved, however, for a series of fates worse than death. Produced by Douglas and directed by Kevin Billington, it's literal visualizations of violence are excessive. O (GP) A

Light of Day (1987) A brother-sister music team (Michael J. Fox; Joan Jett) have their self-centered attitudes toward life changed when faced with the death of their mother (Gena Rowlands). Awkward but naturalistic portraits of misdirected young adults in this film spotted with rough language are somewhat elevated by Rowlands' exquisite cameo performance. A-III (PG-13) PG

Light Sleeper (1992) Veteran drug dealer (Willem Dafoe) takes desperate action when his shrewd boss (Susan Sarandon) decides to start a legitimate business without him and his ex-girlfriend (Dana Delany) meets a sudden, drug-related death. Writer-director Paul Schrader trivializes the harmful consequences of the drug culture with characters whose supposed transformation rings hollow. Narcotic trafficking shown as easy and highly profitable, brief violence, a sexual encounter with nudity and much rough language. O (R) 15

Lighthorsemen, The (1987) Unable to dislodge the Turks from Gaza during World War I, the British mount a surprise attack on Beersheba in a daring frontal assault by an Australian troop of Light Horse Infantry. Director Simon Wincer's Australian production is a visually compelling picture of war in the desert, with mass formations of soldiers riding to battle or marking time in camp, though its focus on several troopers (Jon Blake and Peter Phelps) and their problems is less than interesting. Stylized violence and several flashes of rear nudity. A-II (PG)

Lights of Variety (see: "Variety Lights")

Lightship, The (1986) Obscure drama centered in a contest of wills between a Coast Guard skipper (Klaus Maria Brandauer) and a Southern con man (Robert Duvall) who needs the skipper's boat to make a getaway. Aiming at a parable about freedom and determination, the movie has a dark and foreboding air, some explicitly violent murders and some harsh language as it builds up to an abrupt and muddled conclusion. A-III (PG-13) 15

Like Father Like Son (1987) Fantasy about father-son role reversals brought about accidentally when the father (Dudley Moore) ingests a brain-transference potion. Director Rod Daniel's sitcom conveys the neces-sity for understanding and love between parents and children but has some rough language, a failed seduction scene and some brief violence. A-II (PG-13) PG

Like Water for Chocolate (1993) Culinary magic is the main ingredient in this romantic melodrama set in 1910 revolutionary Mexico where a family's youngest daughter (Lumi Cavazos) cooks up all manner of mischievous dishes for her family when her beloved (Marco Leonardi) asks her hand but is made to marry her older sister (Yareli Arizmendi) instead. Mexican director Alfonso Arau cleverly blends comedy and tragedy into this beguiling period movie about repressed love sublimated into a passion for cooking. Subtitles. A few bedroom scenes, some nudity and minor violence. A-III (R)

Li'l Abner (1959) Flat-footed musical based on Al Capp's comic-strip yokels who save their Southern town of Dogpatch from becoming an A-bomb test site. Written by Norman Panama and Melvin Frank with Panama producing and Frank directing, the stagebound proceedings are generally witless, with clunky choreography and wooden acting (especially by Peter Palmer as Abner and Leslie Parrish as Daisy May), though Stubby Kaye puts over a couple of catchy Johnny Mercer songs. Much sexual innunedo and barnyard humor. A-III (br)

Lilies of the Field (1963) When an itinerant jack-of-all-trades (Sidney Poitier) stops to help a group of German nuns newly arrived in New Mexico, his cheerful generosity is disdained by the stern, demanding Mother Superior (Lilia Skala) until he builds them a chapel with the aid of the local Mexican-American community. Directed by Ralph Nelson, the movie's simple little story of the triumph of faith coupled with goodwill has enormous charm in the winning performances of the two principals, some good-natured comedy and an infectious theme song that will leave viewers humming "Amen." A-I (nr) U

Lily in Love (1985) Stage actor (Christopher Plummer) disguises himself to get the romantic movie role for which his screenwriter wife (Maggie Smith) thinks he's entirely unsuited and she begins falling in love with her husband's new persona. Witty, sophisticated comedy from Hungarian director Karoly Makk, it's a game of who's playing a trick on whom. A-II (PG-13)

Limbo (1972) Sincere tearjerker based on the stateside emotional and financial hardships of a group of Vietnam POW-MIA wives (Kathleen Nolan, Katherine Justice and Kate Jackson). Despite its obvious melodrama, director Mark Robson makes the situation ring true much of the time by showing the human side of women trying to keep their family and emotional lives intact without any certainty about their husbands or the future. Nolan's performance, strong yet vulnerable, is worth seeing. Mature themes. A-III (PG)

Limelight (1952) Written, produced and directed by Charles Chaplin, the story is about a World War I music hall comic (Chaplin) who helps a ballerina (Claire Bloom), but its importance resides in the light it casts on Chaplin as an artist and a man. It is deeply steeped with Victorian sentimentality and is centered in a naive belief in nature's goodness, something modern audiences will have to conjure with but something that is sincere, deeply felt and enduring. Well worth seeing. A-II (G) U

Limit, The (1972) Yaphet Kotto gets in over his head as writer, director, and star in a film about a Los Angeles cop having trouble justifying his job and the special demands it makes on him because he is black. As a director, Kotto is unable to overcome the insurmountable problems of an underdeveloped script and an obviously bargain-basement budget. Some mature themes. A-III (PG)

L'Immortelle (1969) Director Alain Robbe-Grillet's existential love story set in Istanbul about a man who dies trying to unravel the mystery behind the woman he loved and lost in a car accident. Narrative unfolds jumping back and forth in time and space in an attempt to make a cinematic (and philosophical) comment upon the nature of illusion and reality. An exercise for film buffs and poets. A-III (nr)

Lincoln Conspiracy, The (1977) Revisionist account of Lincoln's assassination alleges that Secretary of War Stanton and other high officials were involved in the plot directed at the President. As history, the movie relies upon still questionable documentation. As entertainment, director James L. Conway's stiff, instructive treatment would be more suited to a slide lecture. A-II (G)

Lion Has Seven Heads, The (1974) Brazilian production about African neo-colonialism and revolution told not in narrative form but through a series of highly stylized scenes conveying various forms of social, economic and ideological exploitation. Directed by Glauber Rocha, one may object to some of the excesses in imagery, but there is no question it does contribute a sense of the revolutionary ferment in underdeveloped parts of the world. A-IV (nr)

Lion in Winter, The (1968) Toward the end of her life, Eleanor of Aquitane (Katharine Hepburn) engages in a running duel with her husband, Henry II of England (Peter O'Toole), over which of their sons should ascend the throne. Director Anthony Harvey does not allow history to get in the way of the principals whose full-blown performances make absorbing entertainment. Adult themes. A-III (PG) 15

Lion of the Desert (1981) Director Moustapha Akkad's homage to Libyan hero, Omar Mukhtar (Anthony Quinn), who defied Mussolini's forces for 20 years until his capture and execution in 1931. Some of the desert battle scenes and those involving Italian reprisals are both extremely violent and poorly staged. A-III (PG) AA

Lion's Love (1969) French director Agnes Varda's homage to and criticism of the Hollywood ethos is little more than a series of cameos with show business types and pop art personalities who seem terribly phony trying to act genuine. The amoral life-style espoused by its principals severely limits the movie's appeal and acceptability. O (nr)

Lionheart (1991) A French Foreign Legionnaire (Jean-Claude Van Damme) goes AWOL to L.A. to provide for his murdered brother's wife (Lisa Pelikan) and child by fighting a series of high-stakes, no-holds-barred bouts. Director Sheldon Lettich's pulpy plot has all the cheap trimmings—destitute widow with cute tot, bloodthirsty crowds and animal-like brutality. Excessive violence, much rough language and rear nudity. O (R)

Lipstick (1976) Lamont Johnson directs this tawdry melodrama in which a woman (Margaux Hemingway), after being raped by a man who is freed and later attacks her younger sister (Mariel Hemingway), takes justice into her own hands. Exploitation of serious social problems offers only violence and brutality instead of insight. O (R) 18

Liquidator, The (1966) British spy thriller directed by Jack Cardiff about a tough intelligence agent (Rod Taylor) assigned to liquidate a number of folks the agency considers to be security risks. One of them is Jill St. John, and this complicates things, much to boss Trevor Howard's dismay. Routine action movie with stylized violence. A-III (br) A

Listen, Let's Make Love (1969) Inept Italian soap opera directed by Ferdinando Scarfiotti purports to describe the pitfalls and insecurity of a young gigolo enmeshed in the opulent decadence of Milanese society. Excessive sexual depictions. O (R)

Listen to Me (1989) Campus hijinks at a posh California college focus on the school debating team that at the end of the year vies for a national championship led by two freshman (Kirk Cameron and Jami Gertz) arguing in the affirmative that abortion is wrong. Written and directed by

Douglas Day Stewart, the movie laboriously delays the inevitable romance between its two principals and plays both sides of the street on the abortion issue, though it ends affirming the pro-life view. Contains several suggestive sex scenes, sophomoric sex jokes and a bit of rough language but seen from a perspective critical of contemporary moral permissiveness. A-III (PG-13)

Listen Up: The Lives of Quincy Jones (1990) Portrait of the composer-producer's musical development and career achievements plus details of his personal life, including a harsh ghetto background and failed marriages. The colorful, kaleidoscopic "rockumentary" from director Ellen Weissbrod is done via interviews with Jones, his daughter and famed musical collaborators in a somewhat lengthy and reverential study of what makes Quincy Jones tick, tempered by his refreshingly honest self-appraisal. Minimal rough language and racial epithets. A-II (PG-13)

Little Ark, The (1972) Director James B. Clark tells the story of two children (Philip Frame and Genevieve Ambas) who are separated from their parents during the 1953 floods in northern Holland. It has an intelligent message about human community, but the children face some intense dangers best left unexperienced by small children. A-II (G) A

Little Big Man (1970) Dustin Hoffman as the sole survivor of Custer's Last Stand relives the story of his life and times on the frontier. Although not tightly conceived or executed, director Arthur Penn's large canvas provides a major overview of the Old West and its conflicts between Indians and pioneers. A-III (GP) AA

Little Cigars (1973) Sadistically abused woman (Angel Tompkins) takes refuge with a group of midgets in a traveling side show where she runs an aphrodisiac candy bar, while having an affair with the head midget (Billy Curtis). Directed by Chris Christenberry, it is an utterly cruel and tasteless movie, with the worst big-woman, little-man joke ever devised. O (PG)

Little Darlings (1980) Silly but nasty little movie wasting the talents of young Kristy McNichol and Tatum O'Neal in a story that has to do with a group of girls at a summer camp making a bet that places loss of virginity into the category of a competitive sport. Besides some distasteful visuals and offensive language, director Ronald F. Maxwell's movie condones immoral behavior despite some moralistic hedging at the end. O (R) AA

Little Drummer Girl, The (1984) Lackluster screen adaptation of the John Le Carre novel about an actress (Diane Keaton) recruited by Israeli agents to trap a terrorist. Director George Roy Hill appears unconcerned for politics, characterization or moral details. Considerable violence, some nudity and rough language. A-III (R) 15

Little Fauss and Big Halsy (1970) Routine motorcycle-racing movie that dotes upon the idiosyncrasies of one of its stars (Michael J. Pollard) and the good looks and sexual prowess of the other (Robert Redford). Sidney J. Furie directs an undistinguished clunker that has a permissive attitude toward casual sex. A-IV (R) X

Little Foxes, The (1941) Engrossing adaptation of Lillian Hellman's play about a woman (Bette Davis) and her two brothers (Charles Dingle and Carl Benton Reid) who conspire to get the money needed for a business deal from her estranged but wealthy, seriously ill husband (Herbert Marshall). Directed by William Wyler and strikingly photographed by Gregg Toland, the post-Civil War drama centers on the Southern family's conniving among themselves and ultimately against each other, with Davis memorable as the shrewd, conscienceless wife. Fascinating portrait of self-defeating greed. A-II (br) PG

Little Girl Who Lives Down the Lane, The (1977) Jodie Foster plays a mysterious, self-sufficient 13-year-old in a Maine village who is befriended by a teenage boy (Scott Jacoby) and threatened by an unstable adult (Martin Sheen) because she has something to hide. Pat, unbelievable Canadian melodrama directed by Nicholas Gessner, the movie condones teenage promiscuity and makes an adolescent the object of sexual titillation. O (PG) AA

Little Man Tate (1991) Poignant drama concerns a lonely, genius-level 7-year-old (Adam Hann-Byrd) torn between his love for his unmarried, barmaid mom (Jodie Foster) and the intellectual stimulation offered by a book-bound psychologist (Dianne Wiest) who takes him away from home. Also directed by Foster, the movie presents an affecting story about the emotional vs. intellectual needs of one gifted child but cops out with a typical Hollywood happy ending. Brief bedroom scene. A-II (PG)

Little Man, What Now? (1934) With his wife (Margaret Sullavan) pregnant, an insecure clerk (Douglass Montgomery) desperately seeks work in the depths of Weimar Germany's economic depression. Director Frank Borzage depicts the couple's problems realistically within the context of Germany's social and political turmoil but the sentimental treatment weakens the story's impact today. Marital problems, some sexual innuendo and unsavory characters. A-III (br)

Little Mermaid, The (1989) Enchanting Disney animated feature adds a hopeful, happy ending to the Hans Christian Andersen fairy tale about a feisty mermaid (voice of Jodi Benson) who falls in love with a human prince. Written and directed by John Musker and Ron Clements, the characters are delightful, the music is exhilarating and the underwater animation is magical. Youngsters will love how its enterprising heroine faces up to typical parental pressures and learns to take responsibility for her own choices. A-I (G) U

Little Miss Marker (1980) Adaptation of the Damon Runyon story about a six-year-old (Sara Stimpson) who is left as security (a marker) for a bet with a bookie (Walter Matthau). Although director Walter Bernstein's reliance upon one-liners keeps the movie lively and his treatment of the romance between Matthau and Julie Andrews is light, the original 1934 version remains unequalled by this remake. Occasional rough language. A-II (PG) U

Little Monsters (1989) Sophomoric comedy about a sixth-grader (Fred Savage) who befriends a 200-year-old monster (Howie Mandel) from the demon world beneath his bed where the boy almost becomes a monster himself. Directed by Richard Alan Greenberg, the plot is witless and the fantasy effects are nothing special. Bad taste abounds in its crude, at times gross, humor, comic violence and coarse language. A-III (PG)

Little Mother (1973) Exploitative fictional life of Eva Peron hypothesizes a woman's rise to power in Argentinian politics through the use of her body and various forms of murder, torture and brutality. Director Radley Metzger's ridiculous sexual obsessions will satisfy neither voyeurs nor students of Latin American politics. O (R)

Little Murders (1971) Screen version of Jules Feiffer's black comedy about an apathetic man (Elliott Gould) who is awakened to a need for personal relationships by an aggressive young woman (Marcia Rodd), but when she is senselessly murdered by a sniper, he joins in the insanity that surrounds him. Directed by Alan Arkin, the film's object apparently is to sensitize its audience to the alienation of urban life by shocking it with sudden violence and a barrage of profanity. Viewers willing to undergo such an experience will find enough insights to justify the approach. A-IV (R/PG) X

Little Nemo: Adventures in Slumberland (1992) Animated tale about the dreams of a boy at the turn-of-the-century who in his sleep enters Slumberland where he must rescue kindly King Morpheus from the evil clutches of the Nightmare King. Based on Winsor McCay's classic comic-strip, directors Masami Hata and William Hurtz's delicate backdrops are visually pretty, but the many characters and busy story may not hold small children's attention. A-I (G)

Little Night Music, A (1978) Screen version of the Broadway musical about ill-matched spouses and lovers who sort out their differences and find happiness in the coarse of a turn-of-the-century summer night. Harold Prince's uninspired direction and some unfortunate casting (Elizabeth Taylor is sadly unsuited to the central role of the charming and magnetic Desiree) cause what should have been a light and airy sophistication to become rather earthbound. The situations and dialogue make it mature viewing fare. A-III (PG) AA

Little Nuns, The (1965) Sentimental Italian comedy about two persistent nuns (Didi Perego and Catherine Spaak) who get an airline to change the route of its planes from passing over their orphanage. Director Luciano Salce treats the naivete of provincial sisters in sophisticated Rome with broad visual comedy yet with enough charm to make the situation pleasantly diverting. Dubbed. Unpretentious entertainment. A-I (br)

Little Prince, The (1974) Screen version of the Alan Jay Lerner and Frederick Loewe musical made from Antoine de Saint Exupery's classic fable about a planet-hopping child prince (Steven Warner) who relates his adventures to a crash-landed pilot (Richard Kiley). Directed by Stanley Donen, the story ends with a gentle let-down that may bring a wee tear to the eye of the very young but, overall, it is warm and upbeat, with engaging acting, pleasant music and clever dancing. A-I (G) U

Little Princess, The (1939) Delightfully sentimental children's story of a poor little rich girl (Shirley Temple) put to work as a servant in a ritzy boarding school when her father (Ian Hunter) is reported dead during the Boer War but she persists in searching for him among the convoys of wounded. Directed by Walter Lang, the story is not only a good heart-tugger but gives Shirley a chance to sing, dance and dream of being a queen. Charming family movie. A-I (br) U

Little Romance, A (1979) Romantic comedy about two teenagers in Paris—an American girl (Diane Lane) and a French boy—who run away to Venice to kiss under the Bridge of Sighs in fulfillment of a legend told to them by a romantic pickpocket (Laurence Olivier). Director George Roy Hill's treatment of adolescent love is affectionately tender with only two risque asides about human anatomy conveyed in the context of honest curiosity. A-II (PG) U

Little Sex, A (1982) Romantic comedy about a newly married young man (Tim Matheson) who has trouble remaining faithful to his wife (Kate Kapshaw). Director Bruce Paltrow's nearsighted sexual soap opera offers a sniggery bit of irreverent cynicism. O (R) 15

Little Shop of Horrors (1986) The wit and charm of the stage musical's black comedy about a carnivorous plant has been mistaken for the theater of cruelty. Director Frank Oz concentrates on literal depictions of the plant's feeding sessions and use of foul language, the sadism and masochism of various characters, including Steve Martin in a madcap cameo, and constant references, both visual and verbal, to killing and brutality. O (PG-13) PG

Little Thief, The (1989) Opening in a rural village in 1950, this curious bittersweet French movie about a 16-year-old (Charlotte Gainsbourg) follows her life of lies and petty theft after being abandoned by her parents to the care of grim relatives. Directed by Claude Miller, it's a sensitive character study of a postwar survivor, adrift without love or guidance, although her miraculous change-of-heart at final fade-out is mere fairy tale. Teenage promiscuity, adultery, brief nudity, some violence, rough language. A-IV (R)

Little Treasure (1985) An erotic dancer (Margot Kidder) and a down-on-his-luck ex-seminarian (Ted Danson) team up in Mexico to find the loot from a Depression-era bank robbery her father had buried there. Alan Sharp wrote and directed a morality tale with serious overtones but not enough substance, despite some good acting and dialogue. Dance sequence involving nudity and some rough language. A-IV (R)

Little Vera (1989) Nonpolitical Russian movie about an aimless high school graduate (Natalya Negoda) who feigns pregnancy to get her working-class parents to consent to her marrying a playboy student (Andrei Sokolov) and, when he moves in with them, her father's alcoholism and mother's nagging end the relationship. Director Vasily Pichul's frank look at an imperfect Russian family and teen sexuality is convincing, though melodramatic. An explicit sex scene with nudity, occasional locker-room language and some violence. A-IV (nr) 15

Littlest Horse Thieves, The (1977) Directed by Charles Jarrott this Disney production is set in England around 1909 in a coal mining town in Yorkshire. Three children (Andrew Harrison, Chloe Franks, and Benjie Bolgar) try to save the ponies who haul the coal from the mines and who are about to be taken to the slaughterhouse and replaced by machinery. There is an ingenious twist, however, that provides a happy ending, though with a bittersweet touch. A-I (G)

Littlest Rebel, The (1935) The Civil War serves as a vehicle for a Shirley Temple heart-tugger in which she plays the daughter of a Confederate officer (John Boles) condemned to death as a spy until she wheedles a reprieve from Abraham Lincoln. Director David Butler's sentimental melodrama creaks with slave stereotypes (notably Stepin Fetchit) but is saved by Bill Robinson's dignified portrayal of a trusted servant whose song-and-dance routines with Shirley are not to be missed. Clear anti-war theme but youngsters may need help with the movie's racial overtones. A-I (br) U

Live a Little, Love a Little (1968) Elvis Presley puts some new twists into his 28th screen effort, directed by Norman Taurog, his 9th collaboration with Presley. The gyrations are vintage swivel hips, but there's an attempt to update the stock dialogue and situations with the introduction of double entendre and sexual titillation. A-III (PG)

Live a Little, Steal a Lot (1975) Failed crime melodrama about the petty thief, Murph the Surf (Don Stroud), who stole the Star of India from New York's Museum of Natural History is a yawner. Directed by Marvin Chomsky, it tries to glamorize its immature hero and the peek-a-boo sex is dreary going. O (PG) 15

Live and Let Die (1973) James Bond (Roger Moore) takes on hokey mixture of Harlem hoods (led by Yaphet Kotto) and Caribbean voodoo worshippers, all eager to chop him up before he blows the whistle on their plan to saturate the U.S. with heroin. Directed by Guy Hamilton, the plot is preposterous, the humor more tasteless than spicy and the special effects department works overtime to hold the spectator's flagging attention. A-III (PG)

Live for Life (1967) Long rambling story about the late maturing of a French photographer (Yves Montand) and his wife (Annie Giradot) after his affair with a model (Candice Bergen). Director Claude Lelouch sustains interest in a superficial, sentimental story with beautiful photography, locales, music and talented actors. A-III (br)

Lives of a Bengal Lancer, The (1934) Gary Cooper and Franchot Tone play British officers who save the colonel's son (Richard Cromwell) and the honor of the regiment by quelling a rebellion on India's Northwest Frontier. Directed by Henry Hathaway, the rousing military adventure features a tall but lively tale of comradeship and bravery with some good action sequences and not a little humor. Stylized violence including a torture scene. A-I (br) U

Livin' Large (1991) Strained comedy about a young black man (T. C. Carson) whose overnight success as a TV reporter goes to his head and results in an identity crisis. Michael Schultz directs a situation comedy whose early promise disintegrates into an extended, one-joke routine, punctuated by some wry observations about today's ratings-mad TV news coverage. Fleeting sexual encounter, a very crude double entendre and some rough language. A-III (R)

Living Daylights, The (1987) Timothy Dalton plays the new, more altruistic James Bond who foils an arms and drug-dealing scheme by KGB bigwig Jeroen Krabbe and ruthless dealer Joe Don Baker. Mellow treatment of spy thriller by director John Glen includes a conventional romance with agent Maryam d'Abo and violence toned down to a level more acceptable for adults and mature teens. A-II (PG)

Living Free (1972) Sequel to Joy Adamson's "Born Free" tells of her attempts to rescue a trio of Elsa's orphaned lion cubs. Many adults will find their patience in short supply as Adamson (Susan Hampshire) and her gamekeeper-husband (Nigel Davenport) pursue their silly and sentimental ends in the name of humanitarianism while the cubs damage property and endanger themselves. Children, however, will only see cute wildlife antics. A-I (G)

Lizard in a Woman's Skin (1971) Italian clunker about a detective (Stanley Baker) investigating a series of murders finds the clues pointing toward a psychotic woman (Florinda Bolkan). Director Lugio Fulci's treatment of the heroine's real and imagined sexual perversions and the grisly representation of several murder victims are exploitative. O (R)

Liztomania (1975) Ken Russell directs an extravagant tribute to composer Franz Liszt whom he presents as a 19th-century pop star (Roger Daltrey) whose concerts are mobbed by shrieking teenage girls who teeter on the verge of hysteria whenever his fingers touch the piano keys. Though there is much here that is good, funny and on-target, the movie flounders in excesses of every variety, most frequently sexual. O (R)

Local Hero (1983) Hotshot young executive (Peter Riegert) comes to buy up a remote Scottish village to turn it into an oil refinery but goes native, while the natives themselves pant after the millions he came to give them. Director Bill Forsyth's delightful comedy keeps taking strange but enjoyable turns and the prevailing mood is low-keyed zany. Some mild adult humor. A-II (PG)

Lock Up (1989) Sylvester Stallone plays another violent cartoon-hero in a behind-bars drama pitting good prisoners against bad prison officials (notably warden Donald Sutherland). Directed by John Flynn, Stallone's Mr. Nice Guy is appealing, but the grisly violence that befalls him and his inmate cohorts make this especially off-limits for youthful Rocky fans. Intense, sadistic violence and some profanity. O (R) 18

Lock Up Your Daughters (1969) Musical farce about three sex-starved sailors is a blend of two British Restoration comedies with their stock characters and scenes cluttering its ribald scenario of permissive wenching. Christopher Plummer stars and Peter Coe directs the slapstick action and humor at the level of TV sitcom. Some nudity and sexual jokes. O (R) X

Logan's Run (1976) Futuristic social order is a hedonistic paradise except that its citizens are automatically exterminated at age 30. Instead of submitting, Michael York and Jenny Agutter make a run for it, pursued by zealous policeman Richard Jordan. Director Michael Anderson's rather simpleminded sci-fi chase movie is made moderately entertaining by its sets, special effects and the talents of its three principals. Some incidental nudity and disappointing downbeat conclusion. A-III (PG)

Lola (1971) Charles Bronson, terribly miscast as an aging American writer living in Britain, is smitten with a 16-year-old girl (Susan George) and marries her with predictable results. Directed by Richard Donner, the story has some interest but ultimately fails on the dramatic levels of coherence and acting. A-III (GP)

Lola Montes (1969) Heavily romantic treatment of the life of the 19th-century's most famous courtesan (Martine Carol) and her romance with King Ludwig of Bavaria (Anton Walbrook). Produced in 1955, director Max Ophul's visually masterful and lavish evocation of the Age of Romanticism plays down the heroine's amorality and paints, instead, a compassionate portrait of a pathetic and tragic figure who ends as a circus attraction for the curious. A-IV (nr) A

Lolita (1962) Mangled, meandering adaptation of Vladimir Nabakov's controversial novel about a mild university professor (James Mason) and his passion for a 14-year-old girl (Sue Lyon). Director Stanley Kubrick uses a comic menace (Peter Sellers) to surface the professor's guilt and shame at his vague, undefined obsession but the result leads nowhere. Mature themes related to abnormal psychology. A-IV (br) X

Lollipop (1976) Ailing white orphan (Norman Knox) from a Catholic mission in South Africa flees from his Afrikaner grandmother to the hills where he nearly freezes to death. Director Ashley Lazarus tells a poignant tale about racial prejudices and interracial brotherhood, somewhat sentimentalizing his stereotyped characters, yet for many reasons, it is rewarding fare for young viewers. A-I (G)

Lollipop Cover (1966) Retired prizefighter (Don Gordon) and a 9-year-old girl (Carol Selfinger) help each other come to terms with their problems. The low-budget production is directed by Everett Chambers and the fine acting of the principals helps keep the slight but uplifting story convincing. A-II (br)

Lolly-Madonna XXX (1973) Two neighboring Tennessee mountain families (headed by Rod Steiger and Robert Ryan) engage in a modern-day Hatfield-McCoy feud over a piece of pasture land and an innocent passerby (Season Hubley) is held captive by one clan who thinks she belongs to the other. Directed by Richard C. Sarafian, the self-indulgent movie seems only interested in graphic displays of violence, including rape and the threat of rape. O (R/PG) PG

Lone Wolf McQuade (1983) Martial arts star Chuck Norris plays a modern Texas Ranger out to get a nasty arms smuggler (David Carradine) with Barbara Carrera on hand to look sultry and utter her share of the sappy dialogue. There is considerable violence, though treated by director Steve Carver in rather stylized and unrealistic fashion. A-III (PG) 18

Loneliness of the Long Distance Runner, The (1962) British reform school inmate (Tom Courtenay) mulls over his troubled past while making practice runs in training for the big cross-country race that the institution's head (Michael Redgrave) wants him to win. Alan Sillitoe's story of a working-class youth's rebellion against authority is directed by Tony Richardson with a gritty social realism that convincingly reflects, if not explains, the boy's alienation from a hypocritical adult world. Bleak study of the making of a juvenile delinquent. A-III (br) 15

Lonely Are the Brave (1962) Thoughtful contemporary Western in which a free-spirited cowboy (Kirk Douglas) tries to break a pal out of jail, then gallops off for the protective wilderness of the mountains as a police manhunt (led by Walter Matthau) closes in. Director David Miller's engrossing narrative provides a penetrating character study of a nonconformist who has to pay the penalty for his refusal to adapt to changing times. Stylized violence. A-II (br) A

Lonely Guy, The (1984) Steve Martin plays a writer of greeting-card verses, thrown out by his lover and wandering in Central Park where he meets Charles Grodin who initiates him into the Lonely Guy fraternity. Director Arthur Hiller's comedy has sparse

humor, stemming mainly from the encounters between Martin and Grodin. Some mild sexual humor. A-III (PG)

Lonely Lady (1983) Screen version of Harold Robbins' novel stars Pia Zadora as a young writer who cannot find happiness as she wins fame and fortune in Hollywood. Crass, sleazy vanity production directed by Peter Sasdy has graphic sex scenes and much nudity. O (R) 18

Lonely Passion of Judith Hearne, The (1987) Disappointing movie version of the 1955 Brian Moore novel about a middle-aged Dublin spinster (Maggie Smith) who mistakes a gentleman's attentions as romantically intended and suffers a nervous breakdown when she discovers the truth. Elegantly directed by Jack Clayton, the novel's religious dimension is underdeveloped and the spinster becomes a pathetic figure of sheer desperation. Some sexual scenes involving a teen-aged maid. A-III (R)

Lonely Woman Seeks Life Companion (1990) Somber Soviet comedy about a 43-year-old woman (Irina Kupchenko) who posts signs around her Moscow neighborhood for a mate and then is harassed by a drunken respondent. Directed by Viacheslav Krishtofovich, this is grim stuff with a stereotypic portrait of a single woman as desperate, cranky and past consideration as a potential mate. Minimal rough language and some sexual innuendos. A-III (nr)

Lonesome Cowboys (1969) Minimal western spoof from pop artist Andy Warhol treats its homosexual characters with repellent cruelty and is little more than an adolescent peep-show exhibition of sexual acts. O (nr)

Long Ago, Tomorrow (1971) British love story of a man (Malcolm McDowell), paralyzed from a soccer injury, and a quiet, attractive polio victim (Nanette Newman) who reside in a nursing home for the disabled. Director Bryan Forbes' story of their determination to marry in spite of their limitations is cut short by her death, but the movie handles a delicate subject with great sensitivity. A-III (GP)

Long Day Closes, The (1993) Uneventful, impressionistic look at life in mid-1950s' Liverpool through the eyes of an 11-year-old lad as he takes part in the daily routines of his working-class family and neighbors. Writer-director Terence Davies' autobiographical movie is warmly nostalgic in treating his Catholic childhood, loving mother and older siblings, but the period music and visually arresting images do not sustain what amounts to a slow-moving, highly personal reminiscence. Several racist references. A-II (PG) 12

Long Day's Dying, The (1968) British World War II drama about three soldiers

(David Hemmings; Tom Bell; Tony Beckley) trying to get back to their lines with a German prisoner. Directed by Peter Collinson, the realistic brutality used in this anti-war movie to convey the horror of war will strike some as excessive. A-IV (br) X

Long Duel, The (1967) British India is the setting for this stiff-upper-lip story starring Trevor Howard as a nonconformist official who wants to treat even an outlaw native chief (Yul Brynner) with man-to-man justice. British production directed by Ken Annakin is routine escapist affair. A-II (br)

Long Good Friday, The (1982) Tough British gangster movie in which Bob Hoskins gives a remarkable performance as a London gang lord down in by his own pride. Director John MacKenzie invests his brutal underworld story with grim but intelligent realism that some will find unnerving. Some intense scenes of violence. A-IV (R) 18

Long Goodbye, The (1973) Raymond Chandler's private-eye, Philip Marlowe (Elliott Gould), by helping a friend out of a jam, finds himself picked up by the police and booked as an accessory to murder and left to sort through a tangle of murder, deception, robbery, suicide and double-crossing. Directed by Robert Altman, the action is handled quite well as is the tacky atmosphere, but Marlowe and his moralities are hopelessly confused. Some rough language and brief nudity. A-IV (R) 18

Long Ride from Hell, A (1970) Steve Reeves stars in an Italian western as a man bent on revenge for a horse theft and the death of his brother. Directed by Alex Burks, the movie makes up in blood and sadism what it lacks in wit and talent. O (R)

Long Ride Home, The (1967) Vicious psychological triangle set at the end of the Civil War pitting Union officer Glenn Ford against Confederate counterpart George Hamilton with Inger Stevens in the middle. Dwarfed by the magnificence of its Grand Canyon locations, the characters lack human interest and director Phil Karlson's movie ends up somewhere between muddled comment on the brutality of war at best and distorted, misguided melodrama at worst. A-III (br)

Long Riders, The (1980) Slow-paced, somber western starring the Carradine, Keach and Quaid brothers reenacting the James and Younger gangs' disastrous raid on the bank in Northfield, Minnesota. Though it has its moments, director Walter Hill's effort is a little too pretentious to be really entertaining or enlightening. Some graphic violence and a realistic bordello scene. A-IV (R) 18

Long Voyage Home, The (1940) Compelling dramatization of four one-act plays by Eugene O'Neill about merchant seamen (Thomas Mitchell, Barry Fitzgerald, Ward Bond and John Wayne, among them) sailing on a British tramp freighter from a Caribbean port of call to the U.S. where they take on a cargo of munitions and head through the war zone for London. Director John Ford fashions an emotionally involving picture of life at sea, focusing on the camaraderie of the crew as they face the voyage's dangers from nature and human folly as well as the temptations ashore at journey's end. Some menace and sexual references. A-II (nr) A

Long Walk Home, The (1990) The 1955 bus boycott by blacks in Montgomery, Alabama, forces a wealthy white socialite (Sissy Spacek) to see her long-suffering black maid (Whoppi Goldberg) as a person and not just a personal convenience. Directed by Richard Pearce, the leads give shining performances, but its attempt to contrast a black and a white family is flawed by one dimensional characterizations. Numerous racial epithets and brief violence. A-II (PG)

Longest Yard, The (1974) Burt Reynolds stars as an imprisoned ex-pro quarterback who leads a team of fellow convicts against a team of guards. Directed by Robert Aldrich, the movie has a careless, slapped-together look and relies heavily on violence and foul language. A-III (R)

Longtime Companion (1990) Moving but somewhat idealized portrait of how the AIDS epidemic affected the lives of three homosexual couples in New York City from 1981 to 1989. Directed by Norman Rene, the movie captures the human dimension of the illness without sensationalism or sentimentality, using understated performances to reveal the everyday heroism of "longtime companions" caring for their terminally ill loved ones. Frank depiction of homosexual life, including male kissing and embraces, casual drug use and sporadic rough language. A-IV (R) 15

Look Who's Talking (1989) Lame comedy about an unmarried career woman (Kirstie Alley) whose married lover (George Segal) leaves her pregnant and searching for the perfect father (John Travolta) for her baby son who "talks" (voice of Bruce Willis) to the audience as he evolves from energized sperm and embryo through birth and toddler stages. Writer-director Amy Heckerling manages through the baby's sarcastic comments to vulgarize the process of conception, trivialize childbirth and make a three-ring fantasy out of single parenthood. Much vulgar sexual humor, some rough language and a cavalier attitude toward adultery. O (PG-13) 15

Look Who's Talking Now (1993) Witless sequel in which two family dogs (voices of

Danny DeVito and Diane Keaton) trade insults while the husband (John Travolta) fends off a lecherous boss (Lysette Anthony) determined to keep him away from worried wife (Kirstie Alley) and children over Christmas. Director Tom Ropelewski's comedy clunker tacks a talking-dogs gimmick onto a contrived marital crisis of insipid sitcom proportions. Some sexual innuendo, crude remarks and an intense dogfight. A-II (PG-13)

Look Who's Talking Too (1990) Silly sequel in which busy toddler Mikey (voice of Bruce Willis) confronts toilet training, a new baby sister (voice of Roseanne Barr) and his mom (Kirstie Alley) being on the outs with his new dad (John Travolta). Since virtually nothing happens in the movie, director Amy Heckerling is reduced to stringing together a lot of adorable baby shots until the grownups get their act together. Minor fantasy violence, sexual references and much bathroom humor. A-III (PG-13) 12

Looker (1981) Beverly Hills plastic surgeon (Albert Finney) uncovers a plot by a conglomerate (headed by James Coburn) to hypnotize television viewers into buying products advertised in commercials. The scheme involves the murder of several actresses who are turned into computerized images. Writer-director Michael Crichton's confused story substitutes superficiality for social satire and flashiness for mystery. Some violence and brief nudity. A-III (PG) 15

Lookin' to Get Out (1982) Two luckless gamblers (Jon Voight; Burt Young) in debt to gangsters flee New York for Las Vegas where they stake a down-on-his-luck gambling whiz (Burt Remsen) to one last try at the jackpot. Director Hal Ashby's movie written by Voight is a total disaster, utterly lacking in charm, with unremitting vulgar language, some brief nudity and a benign view of the easy sex to be had in a resort. A-III (R) 15

Looking for Mr. Goodbar (1977) Director Richard Brooks' harrowing account of some of the consequences of the sexual revolution stars Diane Keaton as a wildly self-destructive young single on the prowl for love and commitment. Drama tries to evoke the moral confusion that pervades the lives of young people caught up in the liberated life-styles of the 1970s but says little about the options open to them. Details of the singles drug and sex scene including a graphic rape and murder hammer home the obvious. O (R) 18

Looking Glass War, The (1970) Failed screen version of John Le Carre's story of a Polish national (Christopher Jones) who jumps ship in Britain and is promised asylum by a group of British intelligence agents (led by Ralph Richardson) who cynically plan to use him for their own espionage ploys. Directed by Frank R. Pierson, the adaptation misses the interest and suspense of the original by bogging down in unmotivated and barely credible incidents, including his affair with a German woman (Pia Degermark). A-III (PG)

Looking Up (1977) Documentary directed by Linda Yellen offers a fragmented chronicle of the lives of three generations of a Jewish family seeking upward mobility and success in America. Although used to establish character, there are instances of vulgar language that may offend some viewers. A-III (PG)

Looney Looney Looney Bugs Bunny Movie, The (1981) Compilation of vintage Warner Brothers cartoon shorts with some new material. The art work and the style of the animation are light years removed from the crude fare offered a new generation watching Saturday morning television. A-I (G)

Loose Cannons (1990) Witless action comedy about two screwball cops (Gene Hackman and Dan Aykroyd) whose investigation of a bizarre murder case leads to a sleazy porno king (Dom DeLuise) linked to foreign agents seeking a lost reel of Nazi pornography. Director Bob Clark's sophomoric exercise in minimalist comedy strings together a series of dumb gags, weak spoofs, sex jokes and special-effects mayhem. Much demeaning sexual humor, senseless violence and some very offensive language. O (R) 15

Loot (1972) British black comedy by Joe Orton in which a mortician-bank robber (Hywel Bennett), his adoring pal (Roy Holder), the pal's freshly widowed father (Milo O'Shea), the dead wife's piously amoral nurse (Lee Remick) and a batty Scotland Yard inspector (Richard Attenborough) get mixed together in a tacky Brighton hotel with a fresh but rapidly stiffening corpse. Directed by Silvio Narizzano, the result is flat, chewy but indigestible. O (R/PG) X

Lord Jim (1965) Disappointing screen version of Joseph Conrad's novel about courage and cowardice as seen in the Far Eastern adventures of a British sailor (Peter O'Toole), a flawed hero driven to redeem himself in his own eyes. Directed by Richard Brooks, the theme is lost in a superficial and disjointed pageant, though handsomely photographed and containing many effective individual scenes. Some scenes of violence. A-II (nr) PG

Lord Love a Duck (1966) Uneven black comedy about high school kids in Southern California that tries to offer some bitng commentary on the meaningless lives of a certain segment of contemporary society. Starring Roddy McDowall and Tuesday Weld, there are some good laughs at the expense of ready targets, but George Axelrod's direction is frank and adult in terms of treatment and dialogue, including a plot complication involving hypnosis to regulate the love lives of students. A-IV (br)

Lord of the Flies (1990) Pointless remake of William Golding's 1954 novel about a contingent of schoolboys who deteriorate quickly into savages while marooned on an uninhabited tropical island. With too much emphasis on the island's lush wildlife and not enough on the characters, director Harry Hook's use of novice performers, Americanisms and popular culture asides detracts from the story's parable of good vs. evil. Much profanity and some grisly, conscienceless violence between the adolescents. A-III (R) 15

Lord of the Rings, The (1978) Ralph Bakshi's animated film version of the J.R.R. Tolkien epic of Middle Earth deals with the darker side of the trilogy. Since the monsters, and not the Hobbits, make a stronger impression, parents may want to think twice about their smaller children seeing this often frightening film. A-II (PG) 15

Lords of Discipline, The (1983) David Keith stars as a decent young cadet at a Southern military academy who tries to stop the hazing of a black freshman by a brutal clique trying to force him to quit the academy. Director Franc Roddam uses some fairly graphic violence and very rough language in depicting the ravages of prejudice and abuse of power. A-III (R) 15

Lords of Flatbush, The (1974) Small saga of leather-jacketed kids coming of age in Brooklyn in the late 1950s. Co-directed by Stephen F. Verona and Martin Davidson, it is not very probing, but it does have some good performances by Perry King, Sylvester Stallone and Henry Winkler as well as offering considerably more humanity and substance than most such nostalgia films. Some graphic depiction of sexual encounters and crude language. A-III (PG) 15

Lords of the Deep (1989) Set in the underwater world of 2020 when Earth has become virtually uninhabitable due to environmental disasters, a motley crew of scientists meet a colony of friendly aliens who settled at the bottom of the sea when their planet was similarly destroyed. Low-budget ecological warning produced by Roger Corman suffers from cheesy sets and costumes, derivative script and amateurish direction by Mary Ann Fisher. Mild rough language, sexual innuendo and comic-book menace. A-II (PG-13)

Lorenzo's Oil (1992) Confronted with the devastating news that their five-year-old son (Zack O'Malley Greenburg) is dying of a rare terminal disease, his desperate parents (Nick Nolte and Susan Sarandon) defy medical science by setting out on their own to find some way to prolong their boy's life. Without shielding viewers from the relentless progress of the child's degenerative illness, director George Miller presents a grueling but incredible fact-based story of a couple who, with no medical training and while agonizing over their son's constant suffering, beat tremendous odds in discovering a treatment that has since saved hundreds of afflicted boys. Harrowing scenes of a child's physical deterioration and some intense arguments. A-II (PG-13) 12

Losers, The (1970) Motorcycle gang goes to Vietnam and they blast their way into a Viet Cong stronghold to rescue a CIA official. Director Jack Starrett's action movie is appalling in its excessive bloodshed, glamorized violence, cheap moralizing and phony patriotism. O (R)

Lost and Found (1979) George Segal, a widowed professor of English at a second-rate university, meets sharp-tongued divorcee Glenda Jackson while on a sabbatical in Europe. They marry, return to the States, only to have everything fall apart. Melvin Frank's uninspired direction doesn't help the offhanded message that commitment dulls romance. A few vulgar turns of dialogue and some cynical humor concerning marriage. A-III (PG) AA

Lost Angels (1989) Aimless but gifted Los Angeles youth (Adam Horovitz) pals around with his delinquent older brother (Don Bloomfield) and ends up being sent to a private mental hospital for adolescents where an overburdened therapist (Donald Sutherland) tries to help him. British director Hugh Hudson paints a grim, at times heavy-handed, picture of upper-class parents whose broken marriage and self-involvement have disastrous consequences for their kids. Much profanity, some intense violence and a brief graphic sex scene. A-IV (R)

Lost Boys, The (1987) Strained parable of the evils of drugs and sex couched in a story about a gang of teenage vampires headed by Kiefer Sutherland trying to get the new kid in town (Jason Patric) to join them. Director Joel Schumacher leaves it up to pre-teens to foil the pack via the gruesomely violent, albeit traditionally effective, stake-in-the-heart bit. A-III (R) 15

Lost Command, The (1966) French paratroopers retaliate by atrocity and torture against the terrorists whom they are fighting in Algeria. Directed by Mark Robson, the politics may be muddled, but the acting is good (Anthony Quinn and Alain Delon) and the action well-staged with realistic violence. A-III (br) 15

Lost Continent, The (1968) British horror movie in which a ship, beleaguered in the Saragasso Sea, finds a centuries-old Spanish galleon whose strange occupants (Hildegard Knef; Daryl Read; Eddie Powell) are the descendents of the original crew and passengers. Director Michael Carreras offers a senseless mix of threatening violence and sexual innuendo. A-III (br) X

Lost Flight, The (1971) Innocuous little melodrama about a planeful of people marooned on a remote South Sea island as a result of engine failure. Gallant pilot Lloyd Bridges tries to maintain peace among his passengers while awaiting rescue from various plot contrivances under the uninspired direction of Leonard J. Horn. A-II (G)

Lost Honor of Katharina Blum, The (1976) Written and directed by Volker Schlondorff and Margarethe von Trotta, this is a plodding adaptation of Heinrich Böll's 1974 novel about an ordinary citizen (Angela Winkler) who is victimized by the police and the press because they mistakenly believe she is part of a terrorist group. Overall, the movie makes it too easy to condemn police excesses while not clearly defining its complex political theme. A-III (PG)

Lost Horizon (1937) Producer-director Frank Capra's classic yarn about the kidnapping of a British consul (Ronald Colman) who is brought to Shangri-La, a thriving utopian community in the High Himalayas, as the chosen successor to its dying leader (Sam Jaffe). Restored in 1986 as closely as possible to the original release print, its picture of an ideal society whose people live in peace and harmony has as much meaning for our own troubled times as it did for audiences on the eve of World War II. A-I (nr) U

Lost Horizon (1973) Producer Ross Hunter's mammoth, lavish musical version of the 1937 Frank Capra classic is an enormous dud. Director Charles Jarrott wastes a fine cast and good story in a welter of forgettable Burt Bacharch-Hal David tunes. Charles Boyer as the ancient High Lama wisely succumbs midway. A-I (G) U

Lost in Alaska (1952) Routine Bud Abbott and Lou Costello comedy directed by Jean Yarbrough with the boys in 1890s' San Francisco where they save a despondent prospector, then help him search for his lost gold mine in the frozen North. Comic menace and mild sexual innuendo. A-II (br)

Lost in America (1985) Slight comedy about a yuppie couple (Albert Brooks and Julie Hagerty) who buy a Winnebago and go off in search of America when he's fired instead of promoted at the ad agency. Also written and directed by Brooks, their misadventures lead to no greater insight than his going back to the ad game, though

viewers will see the emptiness of their materialistic values. Some rough language in a humorous context. A-II (R)

Lost in Yonkers (1993) When their father must take a job on the road for almost a year, two teenagers (Brad Stoll; Mike Damus) move in with a fearsomely cruel grandmother (Irene Worth), a ditzy romantic aunt (Mercedes Ruehl) and a shady uncle (Richard Dreyfuss) hiding out from gangsters. Adapted from Neil Simon's World War II-era play, director Martha Coolidge's drama of comic one-liners is unabashedly sentimental in its humanist treatment of a flawed family struggling to accept each other despite varied emotional problems. Fleeting violence, mild sexual references and minimal profanity. A-II (PG)

Lost Man, The (1969) A decent man (Sidney Poitier) engages in robbery to get money needed for the families of jailed black militants. Director Robert Alan Aurthur's movie refuses to grapple with the real issues posed by the black movement yielding only a mixed-up story of revolution born of despair and an ethic based on the end justifying the means. A-III (PG) A

Louisiana Story (1948) Robert Flaherty's evocative documentary about life deep in the Louisiana bayous revolves around a Cajun youth whose first contact with the outside world comes when an oil company begins drilling in the area. With music by Virgil Thompson and photography by Philip Leacock, the story contrasts the boy's easy relationship with nature and his innocent wonderment at the modern utilities and new ways brought by the oil drillers. Lyrical blending of the primitive and the modern with an optimistic sense that progress is more beneficial than destructive. A-I (br) U

Love (1973) Hungarian drama about the wife (Mari Torocsik) of a man imprisoned by the Stalinist regime who tries to keep her aged mother-in-law (Lili Darvas) from learning the truth about her son's absence. Director Karoly Makk's work is simple, unpretentious and quite honest in its celebration of such sentiments as love, fidelity and sacrifice. Subtitles. A-I (nr)

Love and Anarchy (1974) Seriocomic Italian story of an anarchist (Giancarlo Giannini) who decides to avenge a friend murdered by Fascists by journeying to Rome to assassinate Mussolini, staying with a prostitute (Mariangela Melato) whose life has been ruined by Blackshirts. Directed by Lina Wertmuller, the movie's vulgar humor clashes uneasily with the serious tragedy being played out. Some ribald bordello scenes are certainly not glamorized and anything but attractive. A-IV (R)

Love and Death (1975) Ambitious and delightful spoof of Russian literature with

Woody Allen turning his wit on the most turgid aspects of Dostoevski and Tolstoy, mocking both the characters and the heavy philosophy. It's a rather rarefied comedy trying perhaps a little too hard to be naughty and nice, funny and ferocious. Given the context and some knowledge of the subject of the satire, it should not offend mature viewers. A-III (PG)

Love and Marriage (1966) Italian movie presents a quartet of stories making fun of marital fidelity. O (br)

Love and Money (1982) Silver magnate (Klaus Kinski) hires a troubleshooter (Ray Sharkey) to persuade a Latin American dictator (Armand Assante) to give back his mines. Scripted by Sharkey and directed by James Toback, it's a dreadful little movie with the depth of a television pilot. Prolonged and extravagant sex scenes. O (R)

Love and Pain and the Whole Damn Thing (1973) Aging, ailing, inhibited English spinster (Maggie Smith) meets an inarticulate young American (Timothy Bottoms) on a bus tour of Spain and the summer friendship turns into a love affair. Director Alan J. Pakula succeeds with poignant comic sequences as the unlikely pair get to know each other, but the romantic ending turns the movie into routine soap opera. A-III (R/PG) A

Love at First Bite (1979) Dracula (George Hamilton) comes to New York and falls in love with a glamorous model (Susan St. James) in this uneven, essentially one-joke comedy directed by Stan Dragoti. Several graphic love-making scenes and blacks are made the butt of some jokes. O (PG) AA

Love at Large (1990) Entertaining romantic spoof of 1940s' private-eye movies tracks the exploits of a rumpled gumshoe (Tom Berenger) who's supposed to be following the sinister boyfriend of a mysterious femme fatale (Anne Archer) but mistakenly trails the wrong man (Ted Levine). Writer-director Alan Rudolph has a ball with these offbeat characters whose love lives are a mess of contradictions and lost causes. Much sexual innuendo, a subplot about bigamy and comic-book violence. A-III (R) 15

Love at the Top (1975) Frothy, stylish French comedy that bounces from slapstick to vitriolic satire in telling the story of a young man (Jean-Louis Trintignant) climbing the ladder of success by exploiting a long line of women. Director Michel Deville has his tongue firmly in cheek, but some viewers may find the darkness of the comedy too bleak, the general amorality of the characters offensive and the casual nudity too pervasive. A-IV (R)

Love Bug, The (1969) Disney comedy about a sentient Volkswagon named Herbie who adopts a has-been, egotistic racing driver (Dean Jones) and drives him to victory and the altar (with Michele Lee). Mildly diverting fantasy from director Robert Stevenson, but it's mostly for the kids. A-I (G) U

Love Child (1982) Amy Madigan makes an impressive screen debut as Terry Jean Moore, a troubled, unloved teenager who undergoes a remarkable transformation by learning to love. Thrown into prison, she becomes pregnant by a prison guard (Beau Bridges) and fights for her right to keep her baby. The film is worth seeing for Miss Madigan's performance. Director Larry Peerce's fact-based somewhat sentimental drama has a relatively graphic scene involving sex and nudity. A-IV (R)

Love Clinic, The (1971) The title says it all in this hard-core pornography that apparently is also circulating in a soft-core porno version. O (nr)

Love Crimes (1992) Sleazy would-be thriller has a Georgia prosecutor (Sean Young) using herself as bait to nail a man (Patrick Bergin) posing as a famous photographer who attacks women after getting them to pose nude. With blank performances and an undeveloped plot, director Lizzie Borden presents nothing more than a pointless, dehumanizing peep show. Much nudity, violence against women and recurring rough language. O (R) 18

Love Doctors, The (1971) These doctors run a friendly neighborhood sex laboratory where they conduct clinical sex experiments involving various combinations of men, women, and machines. Thoroughly cheap and offensive. O (X/R appeal)

Love Field (1992) A well-intentioned but interfering white woman (Michelle Pfeiffer) en route to JFK's funeral in 1963 ends up protecting a black man (Dennis Haysbert) and his little girl (Stephanie McFadden) from federal authorities after she mistakenly reports him as a kidnapper. Director Jonathan Kaplan injects this interracial road movie with drama and humor, then damages its credibility by unnecessarily developing an unconvincing romantic angle. An ambiguous sexual situation and brief violence. A-III (PG-13)

Love Finds Andy Hardy (1938) Winding up with two dates (Ann Rutherford and Lana Turner) for the high school Christmas ball, Andy (Mickey Rooney) is saved from disaster by a new girl in town (Judy Garland). One of the better efforts in the Hardy series, director George B. Seitz's family comedy gets help from songs by Garland, especially her Clark Gable ballad. A-I (br)

Love God?, The (1969) Leaden comedy in which the editor (Don Knotts) of a bankrupt birdwatching magazine becomes a sex symbol when tricked into selling his fourth class mailing permit to a publisher of pornography. Director Nat Hiken makes up in tastelessness what the satire lacks in wit, making obscenity legislation, civil liberties and public morality all seem as silly as the movie itself. A-III (M) A

Love in Our Time (1969) Psuedo-documentary purports to explore contemporary sexual mores in Britain by examining the cases of eight volunteer couples. Director Elkan Allen employs graphic reenactments of marital problems that focus on cruel and unusual sex acts. O (X)

Love in the Afternoon (1957) Overlong, undernourished romantic bauble follows the improbable escapades of a 19-year-old Parisian music student (Audrey Hepburn) in winning the affections of a rich American roue (Gary Cooper). Director Billy Wilder gets an appealing performance from Hepburn as the "susceptible" young thing but Cooper never seems comfortable as the aging womanizer and the only thing sophisticated about this story of illicit trysts is the decor of the Ritz Hotel suite in which they take place. Comic treatment of sexual relationships. A-III (br) A

Love Is a Funny Thing (1970) French romance about a film composer (Jean-Paul Belmondo) and a film actress (Annie Giradot) who meet on a Hollywood set and initiate a casual affair. The actress admits the situation to her husband in Paris, not knowing that for the composer it's all a game and she is being taken for a ride. Directed by Claude Lelouch, there's some funny spoofing of Hollywood, but the story moves too slowly in parts and the characterizations too facile to be either effective or affecting. A-III (PG)

Love Laughs at Andy Hardy (1946) Army vet Andy (Mickey Rooney) goes to college on the G.I. Bill but is crushed when his heartthrob (Bonita Granville) marries another man. Director Willis Goldbeck evokes few smiles in overseeing the demise of a series that outlasted its popularity. Mild romantic complications. A-I (br)

Love Letters (1945) Contrived romance of a soldier (Joseph Cotten) and the girl (Jennifer Jones) he has wooed through letters written for his buddy during the war. Directed by William Dieterle, the muddled plot revolves around his comrade's murder and the girl's loss of memory. Phony sentimentality. A-II (br) A

Love Letters (1984) Jamie Lee Curtis plays a disc jockey who becomes involved in an obsessive affair with a married man. She is inspired to risk all for love, it seems, by the discovery of some old letters that indicate that her dead mother also had a great love in her life. Contrived, sentimental film directed by Amy Jones has extensive nudity and graphic sexuality. O (R) 18

Love Machine, The (1971) Screen version of Jacqueline Susann's raunchy novel about high-powered sex and corporate intrigue is just as raunchy with John Phillip Law as the ruthless young executive, Robert Ryan as his corporate head, David Hemmings as his swishy confidant and Dyan Cannon as only one of the innumerable mistresses who help him earn his mechanical nickname. Directed by Jack Haley Jr., it is laughably stupid and banal, qualities that only partially relieve the boredom. O (R)

Love Nest (1951) Slight domestic comedy about an Army veteran (William Lundigan) whose wife (June Haver) has bought a run-down apartment house with all kinds of problems, including a tenant who's an aging lothario (Frank Fay). Directed by Joseph M. Newman, the situation meanders fitfully and to little comic effect, with Marilyn Monroe and Jack Paar wasted in bit parts. Romantic complications. A-II (br) U

Love Object, The (1971) Graphic demonstration of what a pretty but basically untalented young woman must do in order to get her start in the New York Theater. The producers have recruited Kim Pope, a pretty but basically untalented young woman who seems to know what she must do in order to get into movies. O (R)

Love on the Run (1979) Francois Truffaut's fifth film about Antoine (Jean-Pierre Leaud), now feckless and boring at age 33, in the midst of an affair and about to get a divorce from his wife (Claude Jade). Shallow and vapid exercise in middle-age melodrama whose point seems to be the inevitability of divorce. A-III (nr) A

Love Potion #9 (1992) Comic complications result when two scientists (Tate Donovan and Sandra Bullock) use themselves as guinea pigs in testing a magic love potion obtained from a gypsy (Anne Bancroft). Writer-producer-director Dale Launer's romantic fantasy begins agreeably enough but rather quickly flattens out to a banal, contrived comedy. Frequent sexual innuendo with implied affairs. A-III (PG-13)

Love Songs (1986) French drama about a woman (Catherine Deneuve) who balances the responsibilities of motherhood with her biological needs by sexually exploiting a younger man (Chris Lambert) whom she coldly leaves when she decides to go back to her husband. Directed by Elie Chouraqui, the movie treats infidelity not as a moral issue but rather as a device to explore some muddled ideas about the nature of the family bond from a feminist perspective. Justifies casual sex. O (nr)

Love Story (1970) Supersuds screen version of Erich Segal's romantic melodrama about a rich youth (Ryan O'Neal) and a rough-talking baker's daughter (Ali MacGraw) whose Harvard-Radcliffe courtship and marriage survive their social and cultural differences until her early death from some sort of dread ailment. Director Arthur Hiller skillfully and shamelessly manipulates viewer emotions in a sentimental, old-fashioned tear-jerker. Some rude language. A-III (GP) PG

Love Under 17 (1973) German exploitation import directed by Wolfgang von Schiber combines roving reporter interviews with soft-core episodes of young women seeking to satisfy their sexual appetites. O (R)

Love Without Pity (1991) Living off his drug dealing teen-age brother (Jean Marie Rolin), a shiftless Parisian (Hippolyte Giradot) listlessly pursues an affair with a brainy interpreter (Mireille Perrier). French writer-director Eric Rochant sympathetically portrays the smugly self-absorbed brothers without offering any hope for their improvement in this dark and sullen study of alienated youth who are society's parasites. Subtitles. Casual depiction of drug use, drug dealing and petty thievery, implied sexual encounters and occasional rough language. O (R)

Lovely Way to Die, A (1968) B-grade thriller concerning an ex-cop (Kirk Douglas) hired by a district attorney (Eli Wallach) as a bodyguard for a New York socialite (Sylvia Koscina) accused of murdering her husband. Directed by David Lowell Rich, the proceedings are crudely violent and sexually suggestive. O (br)

Lover, The (1992) Empty, soft-core tale of the steamy affair between a bored 15-year-old schoolgirl (Jane March) and an idle rich Chinese (Tony Leung) in 1920s French Indochina. Derived from Marguerite Duras' novel and directed by Jean-Jacques Annaud, the result is little more than a lethargic exercise in voyeurism. Numerous explicit sexual couplings, occasional drug abuse, fleeting violence and some racial slurs. O (R) 18

Loverboy (1989) Tasteless comedy about a dopey college student (Patrick Dempsey) who earns his fall tuition by parlaying his summer pizza delivery route into a sex-for-hire service to unhappy Hollywood wives (Barbara Carrera, Kirstie Alley and Carrie Fisher). Directed by Joan Micklin Silver, the movie never seems to question the morality of its promiscuous proceedings. O (PG-13) 15

Lovers (1992) Fact-based melodrama set in mid-1950s' Spain where a manipulative landlady (Victoria Abril) seduces her young border (Jorge Sanz), gradually convincing him to rob his innocent fiancee (Maribel Verdu) of her life savings and her life. Director Vincente Aranda's depiction of desperate lust taken to murderous extremes plays up the erotic sex scenes, virtually ignoring the tragic human consequences of sexual obsession. Subtitles. Some graphic sex scenes with nudity and brief violence. O (nr)

Lovers and Other Strangers (1970) Seriocomic view of love and marriage told through a series of vignettes of the unhappy experiences of those taking part in the wedding of a young couple (Michael Brandon and Bonnie Bedelia). Directed by Cy Howard, the bittersweet currents that underlie the slick, surface witticisms seem to suggest that even as characters deny their love for one another, they share something deeper than a sexual attraction. A-IV (R/GP) AA

Loves and Times of Scaramouche, The (1976) Moronic Italian slapstick comedy directed by Enzo Castellari with Michael Sarrazin in the title role as a farcical rogue whose sexual exploits, primarily with Ursula Andress, are embroiled in the intrigues of Napoleon's court. Exploitative nudity. O (PG)

Loves of a Blonde (1966) Czechoslovakian movie about the lesson in life that a shy young girl learns from her first disillusioning experience with romance. Director Milos Forman's otherwise sensitive treatment indulges in an unnecessarily graphic seduction sequence. O (br)

Loves of Isadora, The (1969) Spectacular and poignant dramatization of the life of Isadora Duncan, one of modern dance's daring pioneers and free spirits. Director Karel Reisz focuses on the colorful (and ultimately tragic) career of the artist, with special emphasis on her vigorous and unorthodox romantic life. Vanessa Redgrave carries the title role and her dancing is surprisingly graceful and appealing. Some sexually frank dialogue and suggestive visuals. A-III (PG)

Lovesick (1983) Dudley Moore plays a married psychiatrist on Manhattan's Upper East Side who falls in love with a patient (Elizabeth McGovern), which isn't a problem because his wife is having an affair with a deranged painter. Predictable and unfunny romantic comedy directed by Marshall Brickman takes a benign view of adultery. A-III (PG) 15

Lovin' Molly (1974) Adaptation of the Larry McMurtry western novel in which the earth mother of the title (Blythe Danner), who lives and loves with the same abandon, gives her favors freely to two men (Anthony Perkins and Beau Bridges) before and after her marriage to a third. Director Sidney Lumet focuses most on her two lovers, thus leaving a good deal of Molly's motivation obscure, at best. Some nudity and much earthy language. A-IV (R) AA

Loving (1970) Flawed but interesting study of a commercial illustrator (George Segal) who fancies the ladies and himself as an artist condemned to drawing trucks and who finally goes overboard when, during the course of a party, he is monitored on closed circuit television making love to a neighbor's wife. Directed by Irvin Kershner, the movie succeeds best in placing its aimless hero in the context of affluent, materialistic suburbia. Needlessly extended sex scene. O (R) X

Loving Couples (1980) Director Jack Smight's comedy about mate swapping, featuring James Coburn, Shirley MacLaine, Susan Sarandon and Stephen Collins, is only intermittently funny. Though it is innocuous for the most part, its implication that such behavior can have a therapeutic effect on a marriage is objectionable. O (PG) AA

Lt. Robin Crusoe, U.S.N. (1966) Dick Van Dyke stars as a navy pilot marooned on a Pacific Island in this mindless Disney comedy directed by Byron Paul without the slightest subtlety of any sort. A-I (br) U

Lucas (1986) Bright 14-year-old boy nearly kills himself trying to impress his best and only friend, a 16-year-old girl who is attracted instead to one of the school's football stars. This teen drama offers thoughtful and sensitive characterizations and insightful depiction of high school socializing. Its gentle tone is slightly jarred by some foul language and locker-room hijinks. A-II (PG-13) 15

Lucia (1974) Unusual Cuban movie with three different stories told from the perspective of three different women in three entirely distinct styles are united by the theme of Cuban revolutions in 1895 against the colonial Spanish rulers, in 1933 against the dictator Machado and finally the Castro revolution in the 1960s. Director Humberto Solas demonstrates not only technical virtuosity but his real accomplishment is in the vigor with which he expresses the humanity of his characters. Some shocking brutalities and some confusing historical material. A-IV (nr)

Luck of Ginger Coffey, The (1964) Splendid adaptation of Brian Moore's novel set in Montreal where an irresponsible dreamer (Robert Shaw) goes on a spree after being fired from his newspaper job, gets arrested and, facing the laughter in court the next morning, begins to realize how he has failed his wife (Mary Ure). Director Irvin Kershner succeeds in a probing character study of human weaknesses that is presented with feeling but without pity. Domestic strife and some coarse earthiness. A-III (br) A

Luck of the Irish, The (1948) When an Irish-American reporter (Tyrone Power) happens to help a leprechaun (Cecil Kellaway) recover a pot of gold, the friendly old fellow reciprocates by turning up in New York to save his benefactor from working for an unsavory publisher (Lee J. Cobb) and to wed a proper colleen (Anne Baxter). Henry Koster directs the sentimental blarney with a leaden hand and little imagination, though Kellaway gives an endearingly droll performance as one of the wee people. It's a long sit for children and a matter of taste for others. A-I (br) U

Luckiest Man in the World, The (1989) When a wealthy man (Philip Bosco) who has spent his life in quest of power and selfish pleasures is jolted into realizing the harm he has caused family, friends, mistress, business partner and employees, his attempt to make amends are left to being determined off-camera by his lifelong victims. Playwright Frank D. Gilroy concocts a somewhat pedestrian look at one nasty man's search for redemption. Rough language laced with sexual vulgarities. A-III (nr)

Lucky Lady (1976) Failed crime melodrama spoof in which small-time 1920s' bootleggers (Gene Hackman, Burt Reynolds and Liza Minelli), at war with rival mobsters and the U.S. Coast Guard, find time to engage in some kinky sex. Director Stanley Donen seems to have choreographed all the action to a musical whose songs have been edited out. Much sexual innuendo and frequent profanity. O (PG) AA

Lucky Luciano (1974) Francesco Rosi's dramatization of the most wily of America's wily Mafiosi never manages to bring the facts of Luciano's life into focus, especially with Gian Maria Volonte's detached performance in the title role. The result is a disjointed and confusing portrait of a complex figure, ineffective as a movie entertainment and as history. Stylized violence and profanity. A-III (R)

Ludwig (1973) Director Luchino Visconti presents the story of the mad German ruler (Helmut Berger) of the 19th-century Austrian Reich as a companion piece to his depiction of the madness of the Third Reich in "The Damned." Severed from any political or social purpose, the work is a pointless exercise in pictorial opulence and rococo style, with questionable implications that latent homosexuality was the reason for Ludwig's problems. A-IV (R/PG)

Lulu the Tool (1975) Italian dramatization of a political theme illustrating the dehumanization of a worker (Gian Maria Volonte) being driven mad by his assembly-line job. Director Elio Petri's movie is a cry of moral outrage, a reminder that people are more than machines. There is strong material in its depiction of economic injustice, particularly brutish living conditions, with some vulgar language and a pathetic seduction scene some may find offensive. A-IV (nr)

Lumiere (1976) Subtle French exploration of the varieties of femininity as mirrored by four actresses (Jeanne Moreau, Lucia Bose, Francine Rachette and Caroline Cartier) who share their insecurities about men, career and family. Written and directed by Jeanne Moreau, the psychosocial portrait exudes a cool detachment concerning adult themes of love, seduction, suicide and ambition. A-III (R)

Luna (1979) Italian director Bernardo Bertolucci treats the subject of incest in this story of a recently widowed opera star (Jill Clayburgh) who drags her 15-year-old son (Matthew Barry) off on an Italian tour. This sullen, self-indulgent film is an unmitigated disaster for all involved. Some violence and graphic sexual scenes. O (R)

Lupo! (1971) Israeli comedy revolving around an honest, earthy man who acts from the heart without attention to protocol or official regulations, thereby embarrassing his daughter and friends. It is a refreshingly entertaining, low-key comedy with quiet humor and some charm. A-II (G)

Lust for a Vampire (1971) Teacher Ralph Bates eyes comely student Yutte Stensgaard at a finishing school for young ladies, but she has only fangs for him. This film is at best a teasing corruption of the vampire genre, introducing some graphic situations of casual nudity and a touch of lesbianism. O (R) X

Lust in the Dust (1985) Director Paul Bartel's attempt at a satirical western is just relentlessly tasteless and unfunny. Among other things, its crude humor is directed at women and religious groups. O (R) 15

Luv (1968) Uneven, occasionally tasteless screen version of Murray Schisgal's Broadway comedy about the marital mix-ups of a New York couple (Peter Falk and Elaine May) and a talkative loser (Jack Lemmon). Director Clive Donner tries everything from burlesque to satire but is unable to elicit much more than stock reactions from its stock situations about love and marriage. A-IV (br) X

M

M. Butterfly (1993) A French diplomat (Jeremy Irons) in 1964 China is drawn into a secretive affair with a Chinese opera singer, unaware his lover is actually a male (John Lone) spying for the Chinese government, which results in the Frenchman's conviction for espionage in Paris years later. Neither Irons nor Lone can do anything with their unconvincing roles in director David Cronenberg's fact-based movie that fails to make the situation credible and leaves many questions unanswered. Extramarital affair with a few discreet bedroom scenes, brief nudity, a suicide and an instance of rough language. A-III (R) 15

Mac (1993) Like his Italian immigrant father before him, a master carpenter (John Turturro) demands perfection in his craft and from his younger carpenter brothers (Michael Badalucco and Carl Capotorto), alienating them by assuming the role of benevolent dictator within the family as well as in the family homebuilding business. As also directed by Turturro, the sometimes shrill movie salutes a sadly vanishing era when a man was respected more for the quality of his work than the size of his paycheck. Minor violence and sexual innuendo, brief nudity and frequent rough language. A-II (R)

Macao (1952) Contrived crime melodrama set in the Portuguese colony on China's coast where an American expatriate (Robert Mitchum) gets involved with a singer (Jane Russell) whose hardened boss (Brad Dexter) mistakes him for a detective (William Bendix) after him for a stateside crime. Directed by Josef von Sternberg, the thin plot offers little beyond an exotic setting, plenty of sinister atmosphere and amoral characters. Stylized violence, menace and sexual innuendo. A-III (br) A

MacArthur (1977) Gregory Peck plays the title role in this sprawling screen biography of World War II hero General Douglas MacArthur, giving equal time to both sides of his public image as ruthless egotist and noble patriot but without providing any key to the real man. Capable if unspectacular dramatization directed by Joseph Sargent, it's basically a one-man show with the lesser roles devoid of substance. Restrained wartime violence. A-II (PG)

MacArthur's Children (1985) The changes in the life of a Japanese fishing village under the American Occupation are seen through the wondering eyes of a fifth-grader (Takaya Yamauchi) whose teacher (Masako Natsume) is a war widow lusted after by her brother-in-law. Though the narrative is episodic and melodramatic, director Masahiro Shinoda excels at showing the human impact of Japan's military defeat and occupation as the villagers strive to retain their traditional values while accommodating those imported from America, including democracy, coeducation, swing music and, especially, baseball. Subtitles. Implied rape, several discreet sexual references and a few adolescent vulgarities. A-III (PG)

MacKenna's Gold (1969) Gregory Peck stars as a former prospector, now marshal, forced by outlaw Omar Sharif to lead his gang to a hidden Valley of Gold sacred to the Indians but which Peck insists doesn't exist. Interminable complications set in as gold fever corrupts all in a story of cruelty, betrayal and vengeance. J. Lee Thompson directs an episodic work whose theme of universal greed is morally unappealing and dramatically boring. Frequent violence and brief nudity. O (M)

Macaroni (1985) Breezy Italian comedy in which an uptight American (Jack Lemmon) on a business trip to Naples is confronted by the brother (Marcello Mastroianni) of a woman with whom the American had had a wartime romance and, in the process of fulfilling the forgotten woman's expectations, the two men become friends. Under Ettore Scola's deft direction, the cheerful proceedings result in a charming little slice of Neapolitan life. Mildly profane language. A-III (PG)

Macbeth (1972) One of Shakespeare's most violent dramas has been visualized on the screen in an extremely realistic manner, turning the tragedy's verbal imagery of evil acts and brutal deeds into a real-life horror show that is neither convincing as human experience nor dramatically necessary. Yet director Roman Polanski's version of the play does have its virtues in being faithful to the text, in creating the primitive time period in Welsh and Northumberland locations and in a very capable supporting cast for the unfortunately miscast leads (Jon Finch in the title role and Francesca Annis as Lady Macbeth). A mixed-bag with some graphic violence and brief nudity. A-IV (R) AA

Machine Gun McCain (1970) Paroled convict John Cassavetes pulls off a one-man heist of a Las Vegas gambling casino and is subsequently tracked down by the Syndicate who disapprove of such private initiatives. Mediocre Italian production directed by Giuliano Montaldo with cast mostly from Italian B-grade movies. Some violence and ethnic stereotyping. A-III (PG) 15

Macho Callahan (1970) After a gutsy escape from a grisly Confederate prison, outlaw David Janssen kills the husband of

Jean Seberg who puts up a reward and then hunts him down herself. She finds him irresistible, but their relationship is finally terminated when his past and the bounty hunters catch up with him. Bernard L. Kowalski misdirects a twisted exercise in brutality and violent sex. O (R) 15

Mack, The (1973) Black exploitation movie about an ex-con (Max Julien) who claws his way to the top in the mink coat, customized limo world of a big-time ghetto pimp in Detroit. Directed by Michael Campus, the shoddy production views prostitution as an economic necessity. Excessive violence and sexual references. O (R)

Mack the Knife (1990) Cheesy, tedious adaptation of "The Threepenny Opera," the 1929 Brecht-Weill musical about the downfall of MacHeath (Raul Julia), a despicable womanizer and criminal in London's underworld of beggars, whores, murderers and thieves at the time of Queen Victoria's coronation. Writer-director Menahem Golan misses the point of the original's social commentary by stuffing this forgettable film with unimaginative musical numbers, a grey-on-grey color scheme and overacting. Some sexual innuendo, crude language and violence. A-III (PG-13)

Mackintosh & T. J. (1976) Returning to the screen after an absence of more than 20 years, Roy Rogers is back in the saddle as a washed-up rodeo cowboy of stern moral principles who befriends a young boy (Clay O'Brien in a good performance). Amiable, old-fashioned western entertainment directed by Marvin J. Chomsky, it has an absurd subplot involving a sex maniac but nothing that would be too strong for most teenagers. A-II (PG)

Mackintosh Man, The (1973) Paul Newman stars in a suspense thriller about a plan to capture a master spy who is a British politician. Though directed by John Huston and filmed on quite enchanting Irish and Maltese locations, it is no more than routine spy fare until the climax, which emphasizes the indistinguishable morality of spies, whatever their allegiance. A-III (PG) 15

Macon County Line (1974) Cluttered suspense thriller about brothers (Alan and Jesse Vint) driving through the South during the 1950s with a hitchhiker (Cheryl Waters) who find themselves wrongly accused of murdering the wife of a county deputy (Max Baer) and flee for their lives from his bloody rampage. Director Richard Compton supplies the gritty effects, but writer-producer Baer is responsible for the bizarre twist ending to this tangled tale, supposedly based on a true incident. Excessive violence and exploitative nudity. O (R) X

Macunaima (1972) Brazilian satire about a modern Don Quixote who rambles through a series of often-contradictory adventures that takes him from primitive jungle to industrialized metropolis and back again. Told in crude but colorful folkloric style, with a melange of symbolic characters and unrelated episodes, the point of it all seems to be that poor nations destroy themselves in their quest for commercial growth. Written and directed by Joaquim Pedro de Andrade, the movie might be likened to the theater of the absurd, but some casual nudity and lewd sight gags prove more offensive than humorous. O (nr)

Mad Adventures of 'Rabbi' Jacob, The (1974) Madcap is the word for this zany French production that begins on New York's Lower East Side from which Rabbi Jacob departs for Paris to attend the bar mitzvah of a favored nephew. What happens after that is a delightful, nonstop romp with Louis de Funes as an idiotic anti-Semite whose prejudices lead him into, among other things, a bubblegum vat and a rabbinical disguise. Under the deceptively casual direction of Gerard Oury, bigotry is thoroughly ridiculed with very controlled and funny slapstick humor. The result is a comedy that the whole family can enjoy. A-I (G)

Mad Dog (1976) Writer-director Philippe Mora's ragged account of the career of a 19th-century Australian outlaw (Dennis Hopper) squanders a good re-creation of the era because of its incoherent narrative, undue attention to the effects of violence and some brief nudity. O (R)

Mad Dog and Glory (1993) After a nasty loanshark (Bill Murray) sends a beautiful debtor (Uma Thurman) to spend a week with the timid cop (Robert De Niro) who saved his life, the sleazy shyster is enraged because the cop falls in love with her. Director John McNaughton employs a slickly sick sense of humor in a mean-spirited comedy replete with casual violence and women who are willingly victimized. Some brutal violence, a demeaning and sexist depiction of women, an extended sexual encounter and much rough language. O (R) 15

Mad Dogs and Englishmen (1971) Performance documentary of 1970 American tour by Joe Cocker's musical group. Director Pierre Adidge also spends some time documenting the communal life-style of Cocker's troupe as a warmly sympathetic, but doubtless for many, shockingly irresponsible experiment in human relations. Rather graphic description of a sexual encounter by a groupie, some flashes of nudity, as well as the musicians' nonconformist life-style require an adult perspective. A-III (nr)

Mad Max (1980) Australian action melodrama set in the near future when the world has lurched a little further toward chaos and nomadic motorcyclists and a brutal police force fight it out on desert roads. Mel Gibson stars as the decent cop who tries to fight within the system until his wife and daughter are brutally killed and he goes on a bloody rampage. Director George Miller stages the action sequences quite impressively, but characterizations count for nothing and the poor dubbing of American voices is distracting. Excessively graphic violence. O (R) 18

Mad Max Beyond Thunderdome (1985) Solitary, two-fisted roamer of the post-Armageddon Australian Outback, Mad Max (Mel Gibson) chances upon a backward settlement where he is forced to fight in its arena (the Thunderdome), goes on to becomes a hero figure for a tribe of lost children and then has a final showdown with the settlers, involving the usual collection of bizarre vehicles. With the backgrounds showing the appalling consequence of nuclear holocaust, there is more than a touch of solemnity to the proceedings. Directed by George Miller and George Ogilvie, it's all rather violent, but not excessively so, and action fans will find it fairly intelligent entertainment. A-III (PG-13) 18

Mad Miss Manton, The (1938) Minor screwball comedy in which a rebellious socialite (Barbara Stanwyck) pursues a murderer despite interference from an amorous newspaper editor (Henry Fonda) and an irascible police detective (Sam Levene). Directed by Leigh Jason, the mystery plot takes a backseat to the opposites-attract romance and the comic turns of a talented cast, including Hattie McDaniel and Grady Sutton. Comic menace and mild romantic situations. A-I (br) 15

Mad Monster Party? (1967) Animated horror spoof with Dr. Frankenstein (voice of Boris Karloff) hosting a gathering of movie monsters in order to name his successor. Produced by Arthur Rankin Jr. and directed by Jules Bass, the result is more silly than scary. Mild menace and stylized violence. A-II (br)

Mad Room, The (1969) After having killed their parents, two children committed to a home for the mentally insane are released as teenagers (Barbara Sammeth and Michael Burns) in the custody of their older sister who lives with her disagreeable, unsuspecting employer. The outcome of this psychological thriller is predictably dire, but writer-director Bernard Girard's disappointing adaptation of a real chiller, "Ladies in Retirement," is clumsy and only infrequently establishes the required mood of suspense. Restrained violence. A-III (M) X

Madame Bovary (1991) Faithful adaptation of Gustave Flaubert's 1856 novel about a restless Frenchwoman (Isabelle Huppert) who, bored in her marriage to a doltish

physician (Jean-Francois Balmer), precipitates her own downfall by adulterous infatuations and compulsive expenditures. As adapted and directed by Claude Chabrol, the melodramatic story offers a visually engaging but emotionally distant picture of a relentlessly self-absorbed woman. Subtitles. Restrained treatment of extramarital affairs and a suicide. A-III (PG-13)

Madame Rosa (1978) Memorable performance by Simone Signoret as an aging former prostitute and survivor of Auschwitz who makes a living of sorts by running a foster home for the children of prostitutes in her sixth-floor walk-up in a rundown Parisian neighborhood. As her health deteriorates, she develops a relationship of need with a 14-year-old Algerian boy (Samy Ben Youb). French production directed by Moshe Mizrahi, its Arab-Jewish jokes quickly wear thin and its evocation of the horror of Auschwitz and persecution is far too superficial. Mature theme and atmosphere. A-III (PG) AA

Madame Sousatzka (1988) Madame Sousatzka (Shirley MacLaine) is an eccentric musical artiste who achieves her greatest glory as a teacher not performer. Past middle age, she focuses on her talented piano students, in this case a virtuoso 15-year-old Indian boy (Navin Chowdhry). MacLaine is terrific in this rich character role warmly directed by John Schlesinger. Off-camera adulterous affair and some rough language. A-III (PG-13) 15

Maddalena (1971) Italian soap opera about a passionate woman (Lisa Gastoni) and her destructive love for a priest (Eric Woofe) contents itself with wallowing in extensive nudity, pulp psychology and phoney pathos. Talented Polish director Jerry Kawalerowicz has turned a potentially interesting theme into a boring feature that has little to offer but sensationalism. O (R)

Made for Each Other (1971) Italian boy and Jewish girl find each other at a group therapy session and shout and fight their way across the city into matrimony. The film's few virtues and many faults are all attributable to Renee Taylor and Joseph Bologna, who both wrote and star in what one may assume is something of a real-life experience. As directed by Robert B. Bean, the movie's contrast of ethnic value systems and traditions provides some humor but cloaks its lack of depth in some puerile sentimentality. A-III (PG)

Made in America (1993) Clunky romantic comedy in which a resourceful African-American teen (Nia Long) discovers that her sperm-donor father is a white used-car salesman (Ted Danson), a revelation that infuriates her mother (Whoppi Goldberg) until she discovers that he's not as obnoxious as he appears. Director Richard Benjamin's one-joke premise is stretched to the limit in a predictable, formula sitcom built around lamely contrived relationships. Some sexual innuendo, fleeting nudity and a few racial stereotypes. A-III (PG-13) 12

Made in Heaven (1987) Failed romantic fantasy about a youth (Timothy Hutton) who dies and goes to heaven, falls in love with an unborn soul (Kelly McGillis) and then pursues her when she is sent to earth. Director Alan Rudolph's fantasy lacks imagination and the romance lacks any appeal or interest. Some restrained love scenes and rough language. A-III (PG)

Made in Italy (1967) Series of semi-documentary vignettes of Italian life, exploring such topics as work, women, customs, the family, politics and religion. The episodes, which feature some leading Italian and French performers, are directed by Nanni Loy with humor, affection and pathos. Standout is Anna Magnani as a mother determined to get her family across an auto-jammed highway, a triumph both hilarious and moving. Older adolescents might enjoy this beautifully photographed, very human work. A-III (br)

Mademoiselle (1966) Lurid French movie about a woman who uses her sexuality for evil ends. O (br)

Madhouse (1974) Undistinguished horror melodrama but some fun because its storyline is about a faded horror movie star (Vincent Price) whose attempts to get a leading part in a new TV horror series are thwarted by a fellow actor (Peter Cushing) who starts killing off Price's friends and leaving evidence implicating Price as the murderer. Directed by Jim Clark, the plot is a jumble, not helped much by the inclusion of a number of clips from old horror movies, but there are enough grisly murders for the horror trade. A-III (PG) 18

Madhouse (1990) Humorless comedy in which houseguests from Hell (actually New Jersey) descend upon a Los Angeles couple (John Larroquette and Kirstie Alley) who have just settled into their first real home. Writer-director Tom Ropelewski leaves no crass stone unturned as the houseguests systematically turn their hosts into raving maniacs. Some suggestive sexual situations, vulgar jokes and cat abuse. A-III (PG-13) 15

Madigan (1968) Fast-moving crime thriller featuring Richard Widmark and Harry Guardino as New York City detectives who spend a couple of frenzied days trying to redeem themselves by recapturing the psychotic killer they let escape. Vividly directed by Donald Siegel, the focus is on the details of routine police work rather than on re-solving its numerous plot complications and moral ambiguities. Some tough violence. A-III (br) X

Madigan's Millions (1969) Botched comedy with Dustin Hoffman playing a bumbling U.S. treasury agent sent to locate a million dollars smuggled into Italy by deported gangster Cesar Romero. Ineptly directed by Stanley Preger, the silly plot has a few amusing moments but the rest is woefully unfunny. A-II (G)

Mado (1978) Long, rambling tale of a pure-of-heart prostitute (Ottavia Piccolo) whose devotion to her working-class friends and lack of greed are a constant reproach to her most enamored patron, a wealthy businessman (Michel Piccoli). The inconsequential French comedy directed by Claude Sautet gets muddled in corrupt business deals but has the good sense to drop them for a country outing, a driving rainstorm, and huge quantities of mud in some dim metaphorical resolution. Sexual situations and some gratuitous nudity. O (nr)

Madonna: Truth or Dare (1991) Self-serving documentary-style footage of the rock star's 1990 Blond Ambition concert tour, focusing mostly on her outrageous backstage pronouncements and manipulative encounters with family and tour members. As directed by Alek Keshishian, the result is a boring, self-obsessed descent into vulgar exhibitionism that, far from an honest revelation of the pop icon, is just one more calculating pose. Incessantly crude sexual innuendo with some homosexual references, brief nudity and much rough language. O (R)

Madron (1971) Low-budget western about an Indian fighter (Richard Boone) who rescues a nun (Leslie Caron) left for dead by Apaches after a stagecoach attack. Together they wend their way through the desert, fighting off Indians and outlaws, until eventually Sister lets her long hair down and seems to anticipate a love scene that never fully materializes. As directed by Jerry Hopper, the principals play their sharply contrasting roles with an undeserved verve and the ultimate discretions of the silly script render the movie an innocuous exercise. Some violence and tasteless treatment of religious elements. A-III (GP)

Madwoman of Chaillot, The (1969) Katharine Hepburn, Richard Chamberlain and Danny Kaye play slightly daft Parisian idealists who rally the poor and simple of the city to foil an insane plot to destroy Paris for the sake of oil deposits deep beneath its streets. Director Bryan Forbes has made a beautiful-looking but sluggish screen version of the delightful Jean Giradoux play in which the mad are really sane and the supposed sane are quite mad. Disappointing, but has plenty of good moments. A-III (G) U

Mafia (1969) Italian crime melodrama with Lee J. Cobb as the head of the local syndicate controlling a Sicilian town where an uncooperative businessman is murdered and the husband of Claudia Cardinale disappears. The efforts of the local police to solve the crimes are thwarted in an involved plot sluggishly directed by Damiano Damiani. Violence. A-III (M)

Magic (1978) Anthony Hopkins stars in this dull and brutal melodrama about an unbalanced ventriloquist who tends to get into arguments with his dummy. Burgess Meredith plays his manager who inadvertently sets off a series of tragic events for all concerned, including Ann-Margret as an unhappily married woman. Director Richard Attenborough falls far short of the modest goal of making an entertaining thriller. Violence, a bedroom sequence and sympathetic attitude toward adultery. O (R) 15

Magic Christian, The (1969) Film version of Terry Southern's novel about a wealthy tycoon (Peter Sellers) who sets out to prove that money means everything and everyone has his price. Directed by Joseph McGrath, this establishment spoof has some humorous situations, but the film's satirical intent is largely unrealized. Some homosexual innuendo, nudity and off-color language. O (PG) 15

Magic Flute, The (1975) Director Ingmar Bergman presents this opera by Wolfgang Amadeus Mozart as an actual performance on a cramped 18th-century stage, boldly taking viewers into a world of illusion, stagecraft and mystery. Originally produced for Swedish television, its stress on the theatricality of Mozart's fairy-tale operatics is to the advantage of a pretty silly libretto. Bergman's austere yet ingratiating visual style suitably complements Mozart's beautifully intricate music. It is a classic that might serve as a good introduction to opera for young people, though parents should be aware that it contains some sexual allusions and a brief close-up of an erotic drawing. A-III (G) U

Magic Garden of Stanley Sweetheart, The (1970) Exploitative melodrama about a college student (Don Johnson) who gradually retreats from reality as he becomes dependent upon sex and drugs. Director Leonard Horn stages an interminable series of explicit sexual encounters and pot parties without providing the least insight into the youth's problems or reasons for his downslide into sexual aberrations and drugged lethargy. O (R)

Magic of Lassie, The (1978) The celebrated collie returns to foil the bad guy (Parnell Roberts) in his attempt to steal James Stewart's ranch. Good production of a standard plot and solid supporting cast includes Mickey Rooney and Alice Faye. Though director Don Chaffey elevates Lassie's human qualities to new heights of absurdity, younger viewers will take much delight in the adventures of this canine movie legend. A-I (G) U

Magic of the Kite, The (1971) Children's adventure movie, with beautiful location photography in France and China, follows the odyssey of a young lad and his little sister in search of the owner of a magic kite. The imaginative French production (dubbed in English) features flying bedsteads, a colorful Chinese magician and two charming youngsters, presented with enough flair and fantasy to captivate the small fry. A-I (G)

Magic Sword, The (1962) Halting medieval fantasy in which the foster son (Gary Lockwood) of a good witch (Estelle Winwood) sets off to rescue a princess (Anne Helm) from being fed to a two-headed dragon by a villainous wizard (Basil Rathbone). Unimaginatively directed by Bert I. Gordon, the threadbare story features some lackluster special effects but not much else of interest. Stylized violence and assorted villainy. A-II (br) U

Magician of Lublin (1979) Failed screen version of the Issac Bashevis Singer novel about an irreligious, woman-chasing, Jewish magician (Alan Arkin) in turn-of-the-century Poland who convinces a Warsaw theater manager (Lou Jacobi) that he can fly but then squanders the money he receives on a countess (Louise Fletcher). Director Menachem Golan's crude and plodding effort misses the religious theme of the original and Arkin is badly miscast as the magnetic, erotic and ultimately spiritually tormented hero. Some extravagant nudity and graphic sexuality. O (R) 15

Magnificent Obsession (1954) Sappy remake of the 1935 tearjerker in which a playboy (Rock Hudson) devotes himself to helping others after causing an accident blinding the woman he loves (Jane Wyman). Director Douglas Sirk emphasizes the artificial sentimentality of the sudsy script, though the cast tries gamely not to notice. High-minded romance but flatly unconvincing. A-II (br) U

Magnificent Seven Ride!, The (1972) After his wife is kidnapped, raped and murdered, Lee Van Cleef sets out to find those responsible. When the trail leads to a large and vicious band of renegades, he gathers his old comrades—the Magnificent Seven—five of whom are in prison. Director George McCowan's sequel is a standard western, though the climactic showdown, as might be expected, is violent in the extreme. A-III (PG) A **Magnum Force** (1973) Clint Eastwood returns as San Francisco detective "Dirty Harry" Callahan, this time taking on a group of renegade rookie cops who are systematically murdering the city's mobsters. Harry stops them by taking the law into his own hands, though viewers may have difficulty distinguishing between his brand of fascism and theirs. Ted Post directs an irresponsible movie celebrating the vigilante spirit. Graphic violence and incidental sexual references. O (R) 18

Magus, The (1968) British teacher (Michael Caine), escaping the marriage plans of his mistress (Anna Karina), comes to a Greek island where he happens upon a practitioner of the occult (Anthony Quinn). As the young teacher becomes sexually involved with one of the magician's followers (Candice Bergen), the movie shifts from reality to self-indulgent fantasy. Director Guy Green's screen version of the John Fowles novel is not only pretentious but hopelessly muddled and ultimately senseless. Explicit sex and nudity. O (PG) X

Mahanagar (see: "The Big City").

Mahler (1976) British production about the Austrian composer constructed out of a series of recollections triggered in Mahler's mind by his triumphant return to Vienna just before his death in 1911. Attempting to show the source of the composer's creative inspiration, director Ken Russell succeeds in linking a personality to a body of music, though there is an excess of Jewish stereotyping and references to the proto-Nazi tendencies of the period. A-IV (PG) AA

Mahogany (1975) Talented Diana Ross is wasted in a story about a black woman's rise from sales clerk in Chicago to famous model and fashion designer in Rome where she becomes disillusioned and returns to Chicago and the arms of her rejected lover (Billy Dee Williams). Directed by Berry Gordy, this Cinderella variation starts well enough but soon becomes mired in soap opera histrionics and sexual stereotyping. A-III (PG) AA

Maid in Sweden (1971) Swedish production about 17-year-old country girl (Christina Lindberg) who, on an innocent visit to her big sister in Stockholm, undergoes a prolonged bout of sexual awakening and initiation, thanks to the tutorial efforts of the sister and her boyfriends. Directed by Floch Johnson, the movie is little more than a vehicle for some grossly offensive nudity and simulated sex. O (R)

Maid to Order (1987) Spoiled Beverly Hills heiress (Ally Sheedy) learns a lesson in humility and caring when forced to work as a maid for a zany, garish couple (Dick Shawn and Valerie Perrine). Director Amy Jones sets the appropriate tone of fantasy for this romantic fable, which has a brief moment of comic nudity and some rough language. A-II (PG)

Maiden for a Prince, A (1967) Based on an historical incident, this bawdy Italian comedy in which the virility of a prince is put to an absurd test by his prospective in-laws satirizes Renaissance manners and morals. Some viewers may not find the subject particularly amusing or appropriate screen entertainment. A-IV (br)

Maids, The (1975) Screen version of the Jean Genet play about two maids (Glenda Jackson and Susannah York) who, whenever their mistress (Vivian Merchant) is absent, act out their hatred of her in little dramas of revolt that always climax in her murder. The last time they go into their act, one of them really dies, or so it seems. Directed by Christopher Miles, three talented actresses are wasted in a hopeless effort to find some meaning in a boring, repetitive drama that takes perverse pleasure in sadomasochistic cruelties. A-IV (PG) AA

Maidstone (1971) Novelist Norman Mailer made this movie by having a group of actors and nonactors improvise dialogue and action around a story of a movie director (Mailer) who decides to run for President. The result, unfortunately, is a tedious, self-conscious vanity production in which nothing much happens, unless one considers Rip Torn's violent on-screen fight with Mailer notable. Some graphic nudity; rough language. O (nr)

Mail Order Bride (1964) Uneven Western in which a retired lawman (Buddy Ebsen) tries to get a dead friend's wild son (Keir Dullea) to settle down by importing a needy widow (Lois Nettleton) and her young boy from Kansas City, but it will take more than marriage to make a man out of the callow lad. Writer-director Burt Kennedy sets up an intriguing situation with strong characters but then goes sentimental until the baldly contrived ending. Some stylized violence and numerous sexual situations and references. A-III (br) U

Main Chance (1966) British crime story in which a gambler outwits a group of international jewel smugglers and makes off with a fortune in diamonds. Director John Knight proves there is no honor among thieves rather smartly but tends to glamorize the amorality of the cardsharp hero. A-III (br)

Main Event, The (1979) Barbra Streisand, a high pressure perfume executive, finds that her accountant has absconded with her funds, leaving her but a single asset—the contract of a reluctant prizefighter, Ryan O'Neal. Attempting to recoup her losses, she forces him into the ring and their antagonism soon transmutes itself into true love. Erratic and not very funny comedy directed by Howard Zieff. Several sexually suggestive scenes. A-III (PG) 15

Maitresse (1976) French movie about a love affair between a country lout (Gerard Depardieu) and a city girl (Bulle Ogier), who works very hard at her chosen profession in which, clothed all in leather, she whips wealthy masochistic clients and provides whatever they request in brisk, businesslike fashion. Director Barbet Schroeder records these sessions with plodding, uncritical fidelity, showing far less interest in developing any credibility to the love affair. Tedious, ill-conceived movie with baldly explicit scenes of sadomasochism. O (R)

Major Dundee (1965) Muddled Western in which a glory-seeking cavalry officer (Charlton Heston) takes a command of misfits and Confederate prisoners-of-war on a raid across the Mexican border to destroy a band of rampaging Apaches who have taken refuge there. Directed by Sam Peckinpah, the Civil War setting makes for all kinds of complications and unconvincing characterizations, though the action scenes are well done if implausible. Frontier violence. A-II (br)

Major League (1989) Lighthearted comedy about misfit Cleveland Indian baseball players who rally for one last hurrah when they learn the team's new owner (Margaret Whitton) is trying to engineer a losing season in order to move the franchise to Miami. Although strapped with a feel-good plot as old as the hills, writer-director David Ward keeps his action fun and funny with a top-notch cast of losers (Tom Berenger, Charlie Sheen, Corbin Bernsen, Wesley Snipes and James Gammon). Much locker-room language and implied sexual trysts. A-III (R)

Make a Face (1971) Independent production about the lonely existence of a young woman (Karen Sperling who also produced and directed) near the border of schizophrenia, increasingly losing hold on what is real and what is fantasy. The more deeply troubled she becomes the more fragmented the movie and the more erratic and inexplicable are the events. An intriguing concept, it flounders in self-absorbed sexual fantasies and the limitations of low-budget filmmaking. A-IV (nr)

Making It (1971) Kristoffer Tabori plays a high school Lothario whose aim is to make love with every female around. His irresponsible view of life is made all the worse by the movie's portrayal of adults and life in general as thoroughly rotten, apparently justifying the contempt expressed by the boy's sexual vengeance. Director John Erman plays up the exploitative possibilities of the story at the expense of any moral relevance. Though there is nudity and coarseness, what offends most is the lack of any human values. O (R)

Making Love (1982) Predictable, uninspired triangle story about a husband (Michael Ontkean) who leaves his wife (Kate Jackson) for another man (Harry Hamlin). Under Arthur Hiller's flat direction, the romantic melodrama manages to work up no emotional power whatsoever, partly because homosexuality (a term that is never used and the word "gay" appears only once) is presented as nothing more than an acceptable variation of normal sexuality. This attempt to forestall moral implications and human consequences is as obviously fabricated as the rest of the movie. O (R)

Making Mr. Right (1987) Young professional woman giving up on romance finds true love in the arms of an android, made to resemble a real human being and for which she has been hired to program with the required social graces. Ann Magnuson and John Malkovich are the unlikely couple in director Susan Seidelman's social satire that has most of its focus on sexual matters. The movie manages to convey issues important to women but lacks a balanced approach to the relative importance of sex and love in a lasting relationship. Some crude language and sexual innuendo. A-III (PG-13) 15

Making the Grade (1984) Wretched little film about an obnoxious rich kid who hires a tough city kid to go to prep school for him. Directed by Dorian Walker, it is crude, tasteless and sexually exploitative. O (R)

Malaya (1949) World War II story begins promisingly as Spencer Tracy and James Stewart concoct a plan to smuggle rubber out of Japanese-occupied Malaya, then turns into a stale tale of wartime adventure. Director Richard Thorpe wastes a good cast, including Sydney Greenstreet, Valentina Cortese and Gilbert Roland, in patriotic derring-do that rings hollow today. Stylized violence. A-II (br) A

Malcolm (1986) A clever and affable story about a misunderstood young man (Colin Friels) who puts his mechanical abilities to work by teaming up with a pair of small-time felons. An Australian production directed by Nadia Tass and David Parker, it is an entertaining social comedy. Some harsh language and sexual references. A-III (PG-13) 15

Malcolm X (1972) Documentary based on the autobiography of Malcolm X offers some selections from the black liberation leader's book (sensitively read by James Earl Jones) played against stock footage intended to sketch in Malcolm's early years.

The film's main substance, however, comes from newsreel interviews made after he had become a major public figure. Produced by Marvin Worth and Arnold Perl, the film suffers from the paucity of visual materials documenting Malcolm's life, but at least the interviews let Malcolm speak for himself, and viewers who wish to know more can read his extraordinary autobiography. A-II (PG)

Malcolm X (1992) Uneven, overlong screen biography of the African American (1925-65) who rose from a sordid background to become the chief spokesman for the separatist Nation of Islam but, after breaking with its leaders and starting his own movement, was cruelly assassinated. Though director Spike Lee indulgently romanticizes Malcolm's criminal record and rise to national prominence, Denzel Washington's riveting performance in the title role captures the mature Malcolm's charismatic personality, intellectual depth and oratorical skill in attacking racism in American society. Occasional stylized violence and substance abuse, some sexual references and minimal rough language. A-III (PG-13) 15

Male of the Century (1976) French production directed by Claude Berri in which he also stars as the jealous husband whose wife (Juliet Berto) is taken hostage in a bank holdup. The movie flounders between comic vulgarity and soap opera histrionics before a final lunge into a moralistic conclusion about learning to live with our human imperfections. Failure in Gallic wit and taste in dealing with sexual matters. A-III (nr)

Malice (1993) Convoluted plot involves campus murders and a college dean (Bill Pullman) whose wife (Nicole Kidman) leaves him after a botched hysterectomy, performed by his arrogant doctor friend (Alex Baldwin). Director Harold Becker mixes unrelated murders with an implausible medical story, but assembles enough slippery plot twists to fashion an adult escapist thriller of passing interest. Brief violence, a few bedroom scenes with shadowed nudity and intermittent rough language. A-III (R) 15

Malizia (1974) Italian sex comedy about a pretty young girl from the provinces (Laura Antonelli) who becomes the housemaid for an all-male household in Palermo, where all from widowed father to a brat in kneepants make eyes at her. Directed by Salvatore Samperi, the movie relies upon comic inversion so that by the conclusion it is clear that the seemingly sweet young thing is the dominant figure who has been doing the seducing. Graphic sexual initiation of an adolescent. O (R)

Maltese Bippy (1969) Feeble horror comedy in which Dan Rowan and Dick Martin are victims of a conspiracy to steal a priceless gem hidden somewhere in their decaying Victorian mansion near a cemetery with walking corpses. Director Norman Panama seldom achieves anything more than an isolated funny line or sight gag. Mild sexual innuendo. A-II (G)

Maltese Falcon, The (1941) Dashiell Hammett's private detective Sam Spade (Humphrey Bogart) gets involved with a crafty trio of crooks (Mary Astor, Sidney Greenstreet, Peter Lorre) each trying to outswindle the other in quest of the priceless statue of the title. But all the hardboiled gumshoe wants is to nab the one who murdered his partner (Jerome Cowan). Writer-director John Huston's classy crime melodrama has taut pacing, snappy dialog, wry characterizations and an unsentimental pay-off. Though there's some menace and violence, it's mainly a mind-over-muscle caper. A-II (br) PG

Mama, There's a Man in Your Bed (1990) Wildly romantic French comic fantasy about the head of a yogurt company who falls helplessly in love with the black woman who cleans his firm's offices at night after she reveals the plot that almost causes its financial ruin. Written and directed by Coline Serreau, the comedy has some delicious moments of devious corporate backstabbing, but the romance is so outrageously unlikely that one can't take it seriously. Subtitles. Several discreet bedroom scenes and brief partial nudity, thought the movie's moral is clearly that people are more important than material riches. A-IV (nr)

Mambo Kings, The (1992) A failed romance haunts two Cuban brothers (Armand Assante and Antonio Banderas) who arrive in New York in 1952 with dreams of becoming the leading mambo band. Directed by Arne Glimcher, the period movie exudes a Latin beat in capturing the emotional conflicts of the close but radically different siblings. Momentary violence, brief bedroom shots with flashes of nudity and an instance of rough language. A-III (R) 15

Mame (1974) Lucille Ball gives a game but disappointing performance as the flamboyant Auntie Mame in director Gene Saks' overblown screen version of the Broadway musical hit. Though the fun of the original is still there, it is obscured by an overly lavish and slow-paced production that robs the material of any spontaneity. Mediocre entertainment at best. A-II (PG) U

Man, The (1972) Intelligent adaptation of mushy Irving Wallace novel scores as a melodrama about a black man thrust into the White House by a freak accident. The story concerns no real political issues, but it is absorbing to watch the character of the new President (James Earl Jones in a fine performance) develop from figurehead to forceful chief executive. Rod Sterling gets credit for wresting a credible screenplay from the Wallace original and Joseph Sargent directs with a sure sense of popular entertainment. A-II (G)

Man, a Woman and a Bank, A (1979) Routine bank heist movie about an engineer (Donald Sutherland) and an old friend (Paul Mazursky) who join forces to rig the workings of the bank's computer and the photographer (Brooke Adams in a bright performance) who is on to them. Directed by Noel Black, the predictable plot moves at a sluggish pace with little to recommend it save some picturesque views of Vancouver and Macao. Acceptance of casual sex and frequent rough language. A-III (PG) AA

Man and a Woman, A (1967) The soap opera sudsiness of this tender, optimistic love story about a widowed auto test-driver (Jean-Louis Trintignant) and a widowed script girl (Anouk Aimee) is enhanced by the lush cinematic style of director Claude Lelouch and a haunting musical background. In a graphic sexual encounter, virtue triumphs in effect, but rather slowly for the sensibilities of some viewers. A-III (br) 15

Man and a Woman: 20 Years Later, A (1986) Director Claude Lelouch's sequel has none of the charm and appeal of the original. Instead, he has made a glossy-looking movie about filmmaking that has its clever moments but lacks any humanity in its characters. Permissive attitude toward sexual affairs. A-III (PG) 15

Man and Boy (1972) Western about a black ex-cavalry man (Bill Cosby) who struggles to maintain his homestead in spite of racial tensions after the Civil War. Most of the picture, however, deals with the odyssey of father and young son trying to recover a stolen horse. Directed by E. W. Swackhamer, the racial dimension is handled quite well and the story has a certain gritty honesty, but the plot has some gaping holes and foggy motivations, especially in a climactic shootout. Some salty dialogue may be inappropriate for pre-teens. A-II (G)

Man Bites Dog (1993) Failed black comedy supposedly about media's complicity in society's rising tide of violence follows the daily rounds of a moronic serial killer as recorded by a documentary film crew who gradually begin helping him commit crimes. Directed by Remy Belvaux, the French-language Belgian production is a slap-dash low-budget affair with a lot of brutal mayhem but little sense or purpose beyond affording novice moviemakers a chance to indulge themselves in a simple-minded, inept exercise trivializing a serious subject. Repellent graphic violence,

including a rape, incessant criminal rationalizations too stupid to be amusing and occasional rough language. O (NC-17) 18

Man Called Adam, A (1966) Muddled, melodramatic story with Sammy Davis Jr. as a jazz musician struggling against his own personal problems and racial prejudice. Unfortunately, the film is not helped by director Leo Penn's heavy-handed treatment of mature themes. Some sexual innuendo. A-III (br)

Man Called Dagger, A (1967) Low-budget spy story about an agent (Jan Murray) who thwarts a scheme by neo-Nazis to conquer the world. Ineptly directed by Richard Rush, it is excessively violent and sexually suggestive. O (br)

Man Called Flintstone, The (1966) Big-screen version of the Hanna-Barbera television cartoon series about the Flintstone family in which Fred's resemblance to a secret agent results in his being sent to Paris on a spy mission. Harmless slapstick fun, though some adults may find it a bore. A-I (br) U

Man Called Horse, A (1970) Richard Harris plays a wealthy Englishman who is captured by Sioux Indians and, after undergoing a painful and humiliating captivity, wins the respect of his captors and is ultimately accepted as a member of the tribe. Director Elliot Silverstein succeeds to a large extent in attempting to portray Native Americans as something more than Hollywood stereotypes. In doing this, however, the dramatization includes some nudity and a number of scenes of torture, scalping and painful rites of initiation. A-IV (PG) 15

Man Called Sledge, A (1971) Routine caper movie with James Garner playing the title character, a hard-bitten, semi-respectable outlaw who'd rather rob than kill, but who has been forced for economic reasons to do both. With sidekick Dennis Weaver, Garner and his gang set out to pull off a fantastic gold heist. As directed by Vic Morrow, however, the story heavily accents the violence, including a brutal rape that occurs in a desecrated church. O (R) 15

Man Could Get Killed, A (1966) James Garner plays an innocent American banker who gets embroiled in one mysterious situation after another in this caper spoof featuring Melina Mercouri in an inernational smuggling ring. There is nothing new here, but what gives the comedy some class is the stylish tongue-in-cheek direction under Ronald Neame and Cliff Owen. Some comic violence. A-II (br) U

Man for All Seasons, A (1966) Engrossing drama of the last seven years in the life of Thomas More, Henry VIII's chancellor, who met a martyr's death rather than compromise his conscience during a period of religious turmoil. Robert Bolt's script is masterfully directed by Fred Zinnemann, with a standout performance by Paul Scofield in the title role, among other notable performances from a uniformly fine cast. The historical dramatization achieves an authentic human dimension that makes its 16th-century events more accessible and its issues more universal. Profoundly entertaining, but heavy-going for children. A-I (G) U

Man Friday (1976) Defoe's story about two men's survival on a desert island is turned into a moralistic attack on the evils of civilization as Crusoe (Peter O'Toole) attempts to infect the noble savage Friday (Richard Roundtree) with such ignoble concepts as master and servant, personal property, competition, greed and sexual guilt. Despite some occasional humor, director Jack Gold cannot sustain credibility in the movie's sophomoric central thesis, let alone its bloody conclusion, which turns the 19th-century adventure classic on its head. A-III (PG)

Man from Colorado, The (1948) After the Civil War, an unstable Union colonel (Glenn Ford) goes completely bonkers as a federal judge who rules the Colorado Territory at the end of a rope until his best friend (William Holden) turns against him. Directed by Henry Levin, the plot centers on a mining war and the rivalry of the two men over a lady (Ellen Drew), but Ford's portrayal of a psychopath is the movie's chief interest. Much stylized violence. A-II (br)

Man from Laramie, The (1955) Uneven Western opens with a stranger (James Stewart) arriving in a prairie town on the trail of his brother's killer whom, after repeated run-ins with a local rancher (Donald Crisp), his loco son (Alex Nicol) and devious foreman (Arthur Kennedy), he finally finds selling repeating rifles to Apaches. Directed by Anthony Mann, the plot is familiar but the action scenes are done with style and conviction, helping sustain interest until the predictable outcome. Stylized violence, some quite nasty, and mild romantic complications. A-II (br)

Man from O.R.G.Y., The (1970) Robert Walker Jr., supersleuth from the Organization for the Rational Guidance of Youth (O.R.G.Y.), must uncover three lost ladies of easy virtue whose branded behinds prove them beneficiaries of their deceased madam's will. Directed by James Hill, the movie veers into a series of vicious murders and inane burlesque skits relying heavily on nudity and racial slurs. O (R)

Man from Snowy River, The (1983) Australian western about a young man (Tom Burlinson) who tames a herd of wild horses and wins the love of a spirited young woman (Sigrid Thornton). Kirk Douglas is on hand in a dual role playing twin brothers. The scenery is impressive and so are the horses, but director George Miller fares less well with the humans in this moderately entertaining, but far from inspired movie. Some restrained violence. A-II (PG)

Man Hunt (1941) Dandy adaptation of Geoffrey Householder's cat-and-mouse suspense story, "Rogue Male," pits an English sportsman (Walter Pidgeon) against a fanatical Nazi (George Sanders) as a "stalking hunt" of Hitler turns into the real thing. Director Fritz Lang packs a lot of anti-Nazi fervor in a fast-paced narrative featuring Joan Bennett as a cockney waif, John Carradine as a relentless villain and Roddy McDowall as a brave little cabin boy. Much menace and stylized violence. A-II (br)

Man in the Glass Booth, The (1975) Screen version of Robert Shaw's play about a Jewish survivor of the Nazi death camps who becomes a wealthy New York businessman until arrested and put on trial in Israel as a Nazi war criminal. Edward Anhalt's script shifts the emphasis from the question of the man's true identity to his motivation in testifying about the irrational prejudice that caused the Holocaust. Though director Arthur Hiller fails to integrate all of the themes, including that of a Christ figure, and Maximilian Shell's performance in the title role is uneven, the movie's effort to evoke a more human response to the enormity of the Nazi crimes is of more than passing merit. Mature themes would be accessible to most older teenagers. A-III (PG)

Man in the Gray Flannel Suit, The (1956) Earnest melodrama based on Sloan Wilson's novel in which a novice broadcasting executive (Gregory Peck), torn between the needs of family and job, faces a crisis with his wife (Jennifer Jones) when he learns that he fathered a child in a brief affair during the war. Directed by Nunnally Johnson, the plot is as obvious as the situations are contrived, but fine performances from Frederic March as the unhappy boss and Lee J. Cobb as a kindly judge help keep the picture of interest. Though the story and treatment are dated, the conflict between material success and personal integrity remains valid. A-II (br) A

Man in the Moon, The (1991) The close relationship between adolescent sisters (Reese Witherspoon and Emily Warfield) in 1950s rural Louisiana comes unglued when both fall in love with the 17-year-old boy (Jason London) who moves in next door. With an assist from Sam Waterston and Tess Harper as the girls' finely drawn parents, director Robert Mulligan captures the period and region in exquisite detail but is especially successful in the warm portrayal of a family coping with heartache and forgiveness. An implied sexual encounter, flash of nudity and brief violence. A-III (PG-13) PG

Man in the Saddle (1951) Routine western in which a small rancher (Randolph Scott) refuses to knuckle under to the strongarm tactics of a would-be cattle baron (Alexander Knox). Directed by Andre de Toth, the range war is muddled by a romantic triangle though the dour proceedings are enlivened by some robust action scenes and the outdoor locations are worth a look. Stylized violence. A-II (br) U

Man in the Wilderness (1971) Richard Harris plays a frontiersman abandoned in hostile Indian country by a trapping expedition after being mauled by a bear. Recovering, he treks through the wilds seeking revenge on the expedition's leader (John Huston). Richard C. Sarafian's direction becomes tiresome in cutting back and forth between tracker, Indians and struggling expedition and the final confrontation is jarringly anti-climactic. The movie's rewards are in its photography of the great, rugged wilderness conveying nature's power and dignity, as well as several sights along the way, notably the trailside birth of an Indian baby, that have their own stunning, eerie beauty. Considerable violence. A-III (GP) A

Man Inside, The (1990) Crusading journalist (Jurgen Prochnow) infiltrates Germany's leading newspaper to expose its reprehensible practices and its link to a high government official. The interesting, fact-based story is rendered in curiously flat fashion by director Bobby Roth, due chiefly to Prochnow's bloodless performance and stiff, methodical pacing. Some violence and an unmarried live-in relationship. A-III (PG)

Man Is Not a Bird (1974) Excellent Yugoslavian drama about a middle-aged engineer whose work takes him to a small town for a couple of weeks where he passes the evenings in a brief affair that ends badly. Director Dusan Makavejev creates a picture of people mesmerized by the daily routine of their lives from which they escape only through momentary diversions. Though produced in a socialist country, its mood of quiet desperation could be mirrored in any industrialized country of the world. A-III (nr)

Man of a Thousand Faces (1957) Screen biography of silent movie actor Lon Chaney (James Cagney) from childhood with loving deaf-mute parents and early success in vaudeville, through a troubled marriage to a singer (Dorothy Malone) who leaves him and their young son, to his remarriage (Jane Greer) and Hollywood stardom in a series of eccentric roles. Directed by Joseph Pevney, the scenario is riddled with showbiz cliches but Cagney and a fine supporting cast (though Robert Evans as Irving Thalberg is a hoot) give some human dimension to the domestic woes and career ambitions of those involved. Mature themes and treatment. A-III (br)

Man of Aran (1934) Jutting from the sea off the western coast of Ireland rise the sheer cliffs of the Aran Islands whose inhabitants over the centuries have eked out their livelihood fishing and growing potatoes on barren rock heaped with seaweed. Documentary filmmaker Robert Flaherty depicts the life of the islanders as a daily struggle against an incredibly hostile environment, reinforcing the theme with some re-creations of an earlier era and awesome photography of fishermen risking their lives in puny boats on the often violent sea. A-I (br) U

Man of Iron (1982) Polish production directed by Andrzej Wajda presents a powerful account of the confrontation between Solidarity labor union and Poland's Communist regime at the Gdansk shipyards that ended in Solidarity's victory in August 1980. Though the mix of real characters and documentary footage with a fictional storyline isn't as smooth as it might be, the result is a dramatic and courageous movie in its own right, one that will have a continuing significance for those concerned about human rights. A-II (PG)

Man of La Mancha (1972) Disappointing screen version of the Dale Wasserman musical about Cervantes transforming his Inquisition cell into the world of Don Quixote preserves enough of the music and lyrics to please most admirers of the original, but just barely. Peter O'Toole in the title role and Sophia Loren as Aldonza/Dulcinea are miscast. Even worse, director Arthur Hiller's tight, literal camera and endless pans work against the romantic poetry of the story and, by dwelling on its adventure aspects, misses the work's emphasis on the power of ideals and the artistic spirit. Mature themes. A-III (PG)

Man of the Year (1973) Witless Italian sex farce about the misadventures a poor Sicilian (Lando Buzzanca) with a genital deformity that makes him irresistible to women. Produced, written and directed by Marco Vicario, it's a low-budget one-joke movie that never rises above the level of adolescent sex fantasy. O (R)

Man on a Swing (1974) The brutal murder of a young girl has the police baffled until a clairvoyant comes forward with some information about the crime that could only be known to the murderer. Good performances by Cliff Robertson as the dogged police chief and Joel Grey as the wildly erratic clairvoyant, but director Frank Perry's drama is full of holes, false clues and an abrupt ending that will satisfy only those interested in parapsychology and the fact that it is difficult to distinguish genuine mediums from fakers. A-III (PG)

Man on the Roof (1977) Deceptively simple, straightforward crime thriller about the murder of a police inspector and the subsequent siege of the heavily armed killer who takes to a roof top and cuts down the policemen attempting his capture. Swedish production directed by Bo Widerberg, its attention to detail and urban environment give the sometimes melodramatic events an emotional impact that places it in a class far above the conventional thriller. Its dramatic credibility is helped also by the performances of a superior cast headed by Carl-Gustaf Lindstedt. Some scenes of graphic violence. A-III (R) AA

Man They Could Not Hang, The (1939) Plodding, low-budget horror movie directed by Nick Grinde about a mad doctor (Boris Karloff) who's executed for murder, then brought back to life by his own resuscitation device to take revenge on those who sent him to the gallows. Ghoulish concept and treatment. A-III (br) A

Man Trouble (1992) Dreadfully dumb comedy about a con man (Jack Nicholson) who sells an attack dog to a frightened female (Ellen Barkin), then falls in love with her. Director Bob Rafelson has a half-dozen story threads unravelling in this embarrassingly barren comedy of errors. Brief violence and an implied extramarital affair. A-III (PG-13) 15

Man Who Came to Dinner, The (1941) Screen version of the Broadway comedy by George S. Kaufman and Moss Hart in which an acerbic network radio personality (Monty Woolley), forced by a broken hip to spend Christmas with a small-town Ohio family, contrives to keep his secretary (Bette Davis) from getting married while withering all around him with his insufferable sarcasm. Director William Keighley's stagey production gets sure-fire laughs from the fish-out-of-water situation, witty dialogue and zany characters (Jimmy Durnate, Reginald Gardiner and Ann Sheridan), though some viewers may tire of Woolley's irascible egomania and the dated topical humor. Mild sexual innuendo. A-II (br) U

Man Who Could Work Miracles, The (1936) Intriguing fantasy from the H. G. Wells story in which an ordinary British clerk

(Roland Young) suddenly finds he has the power to do whatever he wishes, tries to use his gift to better the world, then almost destroys it by turning his power to selfish ends. Directed by Lothar Mendes, the story has its context as a test of human responsibility by the gods but the British production is content to play around with simple yet effective camera tricks that seem to turn the ordinary into the miraculous. Minor stylized violence. A-II (br) U

Man Who Fell to Earth, The (1976) Arty sci-fi movie about a visitor from outer space (David Bowie) who has left his own drought-stricken planet in an effort to save his dying wife and child, but how is never quite clear. Director Nicholas Roeg, a former camera-man, prefers flashy visual effects rather than less picturesque exposition that would better advance the storyline and develop characterization. Several scenes of nudity in a sexual context. O (R) 18

Man Who Had Power Over Women, The (1970) Rod Taylor stars as the London-based manager of a bratty rock star, but he has grown sick of his lucrative job and a marriage that has soured. When he becomes romantically involved with the wife (Carol White) of his best friend, a happy ending is hard to contrive. As directed by John Kish, the well-acted, potentially interesting melodrama concentrates on the slick and flashy rather than facing up to the moral questions, including abortion, that it raises. A-III (R) 15

Man Who Haunted Himself, The (1971) Stuffy British executive Roger Moore has no difficulty getting back into the swing of things following a nasty auto accident, but he does develop a problem in trying to cope with a look-alike double who is out to smash Moore's career and marriage. Moore is quite good as the confused businessman, but director Basil Dearden's psychological drama lacks tautness and relies upon too many plot contrivances. Adult situations. A-III (PG) A

Man Who Loved Cat Dancing, The (1973) Sarah Miles, running away from her husband in the Old West, is picked up by Burt Reynolds' outlaw band. After being humiliated, menaced, brutalized and finally raped, she at last finds true love and the strength to kill her husband. Directed by Richard C. Sarafian, the movie never gets below the surface of its inept plot, so burdened is it with complications often bordering on the ridiculous. Long-drawn out scenes of sexual menace and the implication that rape has served to "liberate" this woman from her sexual fears constitute a male fantasy that should be put to rest. O (PG) 18

Man Who Loved Women, The (1977) Trivial French production about a man (Charles Denner) whose single passion is his pursuit of women is little more than a loosely tied collection of bland vignettes, which are seldom amusing and never moving. Directed by Francois Truffaut, it is a weak and shallow effort, especially because the activity of its title character is given no moral context whatsoever. Some gratuitous nudity. O (nr) X

Man Who Loved Women, The (1983) Burt Reynolds plays a famous sculptor whose insatiable pursuit of women is eventually and quite literally the death of him. The story is told in flashbacks by his psychiatrist (Julie Andrews), incessantly droning on with some of the most banal insights ever set to film. Directed by Blake Edwards, the limp comedy is a poor remake of a 1977 French movie. Some extremely crude sexual sequences. O (R) 15

Man Who Skied Down Everest, The (1976) In 1970, Japanese skier Yuichiro Miura set out from Katmandu, Nepal, for Mt. Everest where his objective was not to make an ascent to the peak but to reach a ledge 400 yards short of the crest from which he would ski down to the valley that lay more than a mile below. What happened during this dangerous undertaking may be seen in a splendid Academy Award-winning documentary with a narration adapted from Miura's diary, giving Western viewers some insights into this feat as a quest in achieving harmony with nature. An exciting adventure documentary, filled with dazzling scenic beauty, it is absorbing fare for the entire family, including those unconcerned with the paradoxes of Eastern and Western philosophy. A-I (G)

Man Who Wasn't There, The (1983) Gimmicky 3-D movie about a liquid that makes the drinker (Steve Guttenberg) invisible and free to explore a women's locker room—among other things—while eluding various American and foreign agents. Amateurishly directed by Bruce Malmuth, the film has little plot, humor or excitement. In 3-D, a bad movie simply gains another dimension of awfulness. Exploitative nudity. O (R)

Man Who Would Be King, The (1975) Sean Connery and Michael Caine star as highly imperfect heroes in an adaptation of Rudyard Kipling's story about two 19th-century British soldiers who pursue their dangerous dream of founding a kingdom of their own in the remote mountains of northern India. Director John Huston has fashioned a vigorous saga of romantic adventure tinged with realism and some fine acting, including that of Christopher Plummer as Kipling who, one suspects, would have thoroughly enjoyed the movie version. Some hard-edged violence and sexual references. A-III (PG)

Man with Connections, The (1970) French anti-war comedy about an enterprising draftee (Guy Bedos) who wins the respect of his military superiors by claiming to be a personal friend of Brigitte Bardot, but even this fails to save him from being sent to the front, where he serves more time in the stockade than in defending his country. Director Claude Berri's lightly humorous, occasionally caustic and witty, account is too loosely plotted and nostalgically self-indulgent to be completely satisfying. A-III (R)

Man with One Red Shoe, The (1985) An innocent bystander (Tom Hanks), mistaken for an enemy agent by the CIA, goes through his daily routine blissfully unaware that he is in mortal danger from various and sundry agents who are following his every move. Directed by Stan Dragoti, this comedy is an innocuous remake of the stylish French farce, "The Tall Blond Man with One Black Shoe." Comic violence and a bit of sexual innuendo. A-II (PG)

Man with the Balloons (1968) Failed Italian story about a man (Marcello Mastroianni) who goes bonkers when his girlfriend (Catherine Spaak) leaves him. Directed by Marco Ferrari, the story treatment exploits nudity. O (br)

Man with the Glass Eye, The (1972) Confused mystery yarn about a rash of murders decimating a gang of weird characters who use a vaudeville troupe as a cover for their dealings in white slavery and heroin smuggling. Badly dubbed German import directed by Alfred Vohrer relies on grotesque characterizations in a story punctuated by sex and gore. A-III (PG)

Man with the Golden Arm, The (1955) Dreary screen version of Nelson Algren's novel about a drug addict (Frank Sinatra) whom a friend (Kim Novak) helps to kick the habit by going cold turkey. Producer-director Otto Preminger fails to make either the milieu or the characters credible. Sordid atmosphere and characters. A-III (br) X

Man with the Golden Gun, The (1974) Rather tired spy adventure with James Bond (Roger Moore) as the target for a million-dollar assassin (Christopher Lee) who uses golden bullets. Director Guy Hamilton offers the standard Bond mayhem, including a spectacular auto stunt, but the once brittle and bright double-entendres are now merely tasteless and smutty remarks. Maud Adams and Britt Ekland are the decoratively exploited females. A-III (PG) A

Man with Two Brains, The (1983) Brilliant brain surgeon (Steve Martin) is married to a woman (Kathleen Turner) who has a beautiful body but loathes him, while the woman who loves him is a bodyless brain being kept alive by a mad scientist (David Warner). Guess what happens? Director Carl Reiner has a lot of good fun with such things as

Warner's Frankenstein-style layout in a sleek condominium and a very tough Austrian test for drunk drivers, but the silliness does pall after a while. Some rather explicit sexual byplay and nudity. O (R) 15

Man Without a Face, The (1993) A fatherless 12-year-old (Nick Stahl), ignored by his self-centered mother (Margaret Whitton) and harassed by an older half-sister (Fay Masterson), persuades a disfigured recluse (Mel Gibson) to tutor him for a boarding-school entrance exam, leading to ugly rumors in their coastal Maine community. Also directed by Gibson, the relationship which transforms the lonely child and outcast adult is convincingly rendered in earnestly sentimental terms without substantially detracting from the uplifting narrative. Fleeting bedroom scene, some homosexual innuendo, minor violence and an instance of rough language. A-III (PG-13) 15

Man Without a Star (1955) Uneven western in which a top cowboy (Kirk Douglas) on a big spread run by a woman (Jeanne Crain) throws in with some small ranchers. Directed by King Vidor, the predictable proceedings huff and puff but add up to little. Much stylized violence and some sexual implications. A-III (br) A

Man Without a World, The (1992) Using the conventions of the silent movie era, the work re-creates a nostalgic melodrama of Jewish life in an East European *shtetl* (village) where a simple love story is hopelessly complicated by the arrival of a Gypsy troupe, the exorcism of a wandering spirit from a mad girl, religious and political rivalries, murder and flight to the big city. Written, produced and directed by Eleanor Antin, this is a labor of love that pays tribute to the craft of the silent cinema while creating an imaginative memorial for a richly human world snuffed out in the Nazi death camps. Some stylized violence including murder and the brutal rape of a young girl, several seduction scenes and a few flashes of nudity. A-III (nr)

Man, Woman and Child (1983) Sappy screen version of a soppy novel by Erich Segal about a perfect American couple (Martin Sheen and Blythe Danner) and their two perfect children, all living in perfect bliss until Sheen finds out he is the father of a bastard son conceived during a weak moment while in France a decade earlier. The waif is brought to California where he turns out to be perfectly irresistible and all ends predictably. Director Dick Richards' slick and manipulative melodrama leaves a soapy aftertaste. Glossy depiction of the affair (in flashbacks). A-III (PG)

Man's Best Friend (1993) Repugnant horror fantasy written and directed by John Lafia unleashes a genetically engineered guard dog whose killer instincts threaten to disembowel a lightheaded TV reporter (Ally Sheedy), her cloddish live-in boyfriend (Fredric Lehne), a mad vivisectionist (Lance Henriksen) and numerous other victims. Mindless graphic violence, an extended bedroom scene, some coarse language and occasional profanity. O (R) 15

Manchurian Candidate, The (1962) Fine political spine-tingler with Laurence Harvey playing a Korean War P.O.W. transformed by Red Chinese hypnosis into a deadly instrument of assassination before his return to the U.S. during a Presidential campaign. By the time an Army psychiatrist (Frank Sinatra in a solid performance) figures out the reason for his strange behavior toward wife and family, a major manhunt and race with time are on. Director John Frankenheimer has fashioned a superior suspense movie with a growing intensity that adults and older teenagers may appreciate. A-III (PG-13) A

Mandabi (1970) From Senegal comes a small gem of a tale about a money order (which is what the title means) for a small amount of money sent from France by a hard-working young man to his uncle in Dakar whose attempts to cash it become an odyssey through the senseless byways of modern bureaucracy. Even when it despairs, the film is balanced by humor and belief in the eventual triumph of human righteousness. Very convincing performances by a nonprofessional cast in a very professionally made movie directed by Ousmane Sembene. A-II (nr)

Mandingo (1975) Old South plantation owner (James Mason) runs a "breeding farm" for black slaves, a business allowing his son (Perry King) to take his choice of black women when not off setting up fighting matches for his full-blooded Mandingo slave (Ken Norton) with whom his wife (Susan George) takes to sleeping out of pique at her husband's infidelity. Directed by Richard Fleischer, it's sordid melodramatic trash, forgettable save for its cynical box-office manipulation of racial tensions in sexual contexts. Violence, sadism, nudity and graphic sex. O (R) 18

Manhattan (1979) Successful TV comedy writer (Woody Allen), whose wife (Meryl Streep) has left him for another woman, is having an affair with a 17-year-old high school girl (Mariel Hemingway) but then gets involved with the lover (Diane Keaton) of his best friend (Michael Murphy). Greatly aided by romantic black-and-white photography and a lush Gershwin score, director Allen has made a small but clever bittersweet comedy about sexual relationships, often amusing, but just as often flat. Though the film's moral vision puts a premium on being faithful and really caring about people, it seems largely to excuse its characters' sexual weaknesses. A-IV (R) 15

Manhattan Melodrama (1934) Boyhood buddies from the slums remain best friends even after one becomes a gangster (Clark Gable) and the other a district attorney (William Powell) who marries his erring pal's girl (Myrna Loy) and later puts him on trial for murder. Directed by W. S. Van Dyke II, the colorful story and breezy performances overcome all the plot contrivances and hokey ending. Stylized violence and sympathetic treatment of a criminal. A-III (br) A

Manhattan Murder Mystery (1993) Breezy comic mystery concerns a husband (Woody Allen) who becomes increasingly nervous when his wife (Diane Keaton) decides their next-door neighbor (Jerry Adler) murdered his wife and sets out to prove it with the help of their flirtatious, newly divorced buddy (Alan Alda), whom the husband has been trying to distract with a colleague (Anjelica Huston) who prefers the husband. Director Allen amusingly combines a rectangular relationship movie with a rather flimsy mystery, but the result is a good-natured look at the fluctuating fortunes of love and life in the "Big Apple." Fleeting violence, a few sexual references and occasional profanity. A-III (PG)

Manhattan Project, The (1986) Overlong melodrama, loosely based on fact, about a teenager (Christopher Collet) who builds an atomic bomb at home to protest the construction of a nuclear plant near his home. A physicist from the lab (John Lithgow) tries to save the boy—and the New York area—from potential disaster. Failed social commentary, token teen romance and a single harsh expletive. A-II (PG-13) PG

Manhunter (1986) The twist in this crime thriller is in following an FBI agent (William Peterson) who uses both imagination and intuition to reconstruct the mind of a serial killer in order to track him down. Director Michael Mann emphasizes the psychological elements of detection rather than resorting to the more conventional means of guns and brawn. Glimpses of grisly photos of murder victims, a bedroom scene and some foul language. A-III (R) 18

Manitou, The (1978) A 500-year-old Indian medicine man comes back to life and wreaks all sorts of havoc in this inept and ludicrous horror movie starring Tony Curtis and Susan Strasberg. Director William Girdler's otherwise innocuous effort contains violence and nudity. O (PG) 18

Mannequin (1987) A stock boy (Andrew McCarthy) has his life changed when the mannequin he created comes to life (Kim Cattrall) and falls in love with him while helping to foil a villainous attempt to buy out the store for which he works. Michael Gottlieb directs a romantic fantasy in which Miss Cattrall, an older woman, seduces the younger, seemingly innocent youth. Characterizations stressing the physical aspects of the relationship, sexual references, crude jokes and poorly executed slapstick comedy. A-III (PG)

Mannequin Two: On the Move (1991) A pretty maiden (Kristy Swanson) wakes up from a thousand year spell to the adoring gaze of a department store employee (William Ragsdale) who must rescue her from being restored to her mannequin status and whisked off to a faraway kingdom. Director Stewart Raffill's silly slapstick fantasy is a fairly innocuous sequel but decidedly moronic in content and treatment. Mild sexual innuendo and brief, cartoon-like violence. A-II (PG)

Manon of the Spring (1987) The conclusion of a two-part adaptation of Marcel Pagnol's novel about French country life in the early decades of the century details the revenge of a young woman (Emmanuelle Beart) on the farmer who ruined her family and on the community who let him get away with it, as told in the first part, "Jean de Florette." Directed by Claude Berri, the story of long-overdue retribution builds to a powerful conclusion in which wrongs are righted and justice finally served. Subtitles. Mature treatment and brief nudity. A-III (PG)

Manson (1973) Filmmaker Laurence Merrick's exploitative documentary supposedly examining the social ills behind the crimes committed by the hippie clan led by Charles Manson exposes little more than the director's own cynicism and the morbidity of its intended audience. Relentlessly foul language and occasional matching visuals further emphasize this work's moral vacuum. O (R)

Manufacturing Consent: Noam Chomsky and the Media (1993) Dense 167-minute documentary on the life, times and political commitment of linguistics scholar Chomsky who, since voicing opposition to the Vietnam War in 1969, has written much and spoken often against American foreign policy, transnational economic elites and abuses of power around the world. Canadian filmmakers Mark Achbar and Peter Wintonick concentrate on Chomsky's analysis of the media as ideological agents of "thought control in a democratic society," with a case study comparing the U.S. press coverage of genocide in Cambodia with that of East Timor. Raises provocative questions about contemporary justice issues. A-II (nr)

Many Rivers to Cross (1955) Western misfire with a Kentucky frontiersman (Robert Taylor) running from the Shawnees and a marriage-minded backwoods maiden (Eleanor Parker). Director Roy Rowland's mangled romantic comedy is a howler that makes everybody look like ancestors of the comic-strip Yokum clan. Stylized violence and sexual references. A-III (br) U

Map of the Human Heart (1993) Clash-of-culture melodrama spanning several decades and continents involving an Eskimo (Jason Scott Lee), a Canadian who is half-Indian (Anne Parillaud) and a World War II pilot (Patrick Bergin) who comes between them. Directed by Vincent Ward, the international production makes good use of stark Arctic settings, the wartime era and well-observed racial themes but bogs down in story coincidences and unconvincing romances. Some subtitles. A sexual encounter with fleeting nudity, wartime violence and minimal rough language. A-III (R) 15

Mara Maru (1952) Slack adventure features a salvage operator (Errol Flynn), a greedy crook (Raymond Burr), several murders and a sunken treasure in Manila Bay. Directed by Gordon Douglas, the murky intrigue goes around in circles until ending in the tunnels beneath an old church. Stylized violence. A-II (br) A

Mara of the Wilderness (1966) Tall yarn set in northern Alaska where an orphaned child is raised by wolves until as a 19-year-old woman (Linda Saunders) she is saved from an evil trapper (Theo Marcuse) by a park ranger (Adam West). Director Frank McDonald's low-budget production hardly does justice either to the world of nature or that of humans. Stylized violence. A-I (br)

Marathon Man (1976) Dustin Hoffman stars as an introspective student who finds himself involved with a terrifying fugitive Nazi (Laurence Olivier). Director John Schlesinger has made a shrewd, hollow and profoundly anti-human thriller, heavy on violence and exploiting the tragedy of the Holocaust. O (R) X

Marauders, The (1955) Bottom-drawer Western about an Arizona squatter (Jeff Richards) facing a motley gang of paid guns led by a psychopath (Dan Duryea). Directed by Gerald Mayer, the feeble plot is as meaningless as the acting is ludicrous, with a silly ending to boot. Stylized violence and brutality. A-III (br) A

March of the Wooden Soldiers (1934) Classic screen version of the Victor Herbert operetta, "Babes in Toyland," features Laurel and Hardy as toyshop workers who rescue the winsome Bo-Peep (Charlotte Henry) from the evil Barnaby (Henry Brandon) and save Toyland from invading Bogeymen. Produced by Hal Roach and directed by Gus Meins and Charles Rogers, the antic silliness of the bumbling duo adds to the fun of a musical fantasy whose nursery rhyme characters, sentimental songs and fanciful storyline should entertain the youngsters while charming their elders. Delightful family fare. A-I (br)

March or Die (1977) Dick Richards directs a muddled action adventure epic starring Gene Hackman as a cynical major in the French Foreign Legion who, following action in World War I, is given the task of protecting an archaeological expedition in the Sahara led by Max Von Sydow. Among a cast including Catherine Deneuve, only Terence Hill manages to come out of this cliche-ridden melodrama with any amount of luster. Violence and brutal view of life. A-III (PG)

Marco (1974) Disappointing musical treatment of Marco Polo's success story has a number of amusing moments, supplied principally by the uncontrollable mugging of Zero Mostel as the naughty-but-nice Kubla Khan, and Cie Cie Win as his nice-but-naughty warrior-daughter. As the intrepid Marco, Desi Arnaz Jr.'s role demands little acting but lots of cheery grinning. Directed by Seymour Robbie, the funny bits and pieces cannot overcome the dull stretches in a drawn-out, generally slack production. Some risque byplay and mild double-entendres. A-II (G)

Marco the Magnificent (1966) Disappointing adventure movie based on the adventures of Marco Polo (Horst Buchholz) in carrying a message from the pope to Kubla Khan in China. Directed by Denys De La Patelliere and Noel Howard, the plodding and episodic script is of less interest than the spectacle and beautiful photography. Some violence. A-II (br)

Margo (1971) Israeli production about a stodgy university professor (Oded Teomi) who is brought out of his shell by a country girl (Levanna Finkelstein) who gives him the maternal care, zest for life and simple pleasures that his swinging, pseudo-sophisticated wife can't. Lacking wit and originality, director Menahem Golan's effort just romanticizes adultery and divorce in sun-drenched Jerusalem with little rhyme or reason. O (R)

Maria's Lovers (1985) World War II veteran (John Savage) returns from a prisoner-of-war camp to marry his childhood sweetheart (Nastassja Kinski), but when he can't consummate the marriage, she is courted by a host of suitors. In a ponderous slow-moving melodrama, director Andrei Konchalovsky generates far less emotion than needed to keep it from being a bore. Some too-graphic bedroom sequences. O (R) 15

Marie (1985) Following the true story of Marie Ragghianti, a divorced mother of three children and the first woman to head the Tennessee Board of Pardons and Paroles, the movie details her courage in refusing to cooperate in the graft and corruption of the governor who appointed her to office. Directed by Roger Donaldson, this inspiring film portrait owes much to a superb performance by Sissy Spacek in the title role. Several scenes of violence. A-II (PG-13) 15

Marie Antoinette (1938) Historical extravaganza follows the tribulations of the Austrian princess (Norma Shearer) in the French court of Louis XV (John Barrymore), married to his dull-witted son (Robert Morley), their succession to the throne and execution in the French Revolution. Director W.S. Van Dyke II alternates scenes of elaborate spectacle with sympathetic vignettes of the queen, her well-meaning but ineffectual husband Louis XVI and the queen's lifelong admirer (Tyrone Power), with the script attributing their downfall to the treacherous Duke of Orleans (Joseph Schildkraut). Long and stodgy but occasionally moving Hollywood rewrite of history, with plenty of court intrigues and revolutionary violence. A-II (br) A

Marines Have Landed, The (see: "The Leathernecks Have Landed").

Marjoe (1972) Documentary look behind the gaudy facade of the evangelical "business" in the Southwest, focusing on the spotted career of itinerant preacher Marjoe Gortner, a young man who began big-time tent preaching at the age of 4 and who now, in his mid-20s, wants to cash in his ministry and expose himself and his fellow evangelist-hustlers. When filmmakers Howard Smith and Sarah Kernochan get away from Marjoe's somewhat suspect self-confessions, they find a chilling system of religious exploitation based on a fundamentalist fear of God, and viewers will have to decide for themselves how unbiased is their portrayal of the dark underside of that old-time religion. A-III (PG)

Mark of the Devil (1972) Wretched little horror movie about a 16th-century witch hunter (Herbert Lom) and his young assistant (Udo Kier) who go from town to town searching out evidence of witchcraft. Director Michael Armstrong spends a good deal of time in the torture chamber demonstrating the uses of such instruments as tongue extractors, thumb screws, racks and spiked chairs, torturing not only a host of hapless actors but also the audience. Extreme violence, a few rapes and some nudity. O (R)

Mark of Zorro, The (1940) Dashing tale of Old California in which a well-bred caballero (Tyrone Power) turns bandit in order to free Los Angeles from its greedy governor (J. Edward Bromberg) and his ruthless commander (Basil Rathbone). Directed by Rouben Mamoulian, the period action piece is strikingly photographed with Power easy to take as the Spanish Robin Hood masquerading as a foppish dandy. Some stylized violence and mild romance. A-II (nr)

Marked for Death (1990) Trite action flick has a burned-out DEA agent (Steven Seagal) retiring to Chicago where his pal (Keith David) enlists him as a vigilante to blow away a gang of Jamaican drug dealers. Director Dwight H. Little's strictly formula film lacks imagination and credible acting, with little attention to all but sleeze and butchered bodies. Constant violence, intermittent rough language and recurring nudity. O (R) 18

Marked Woman (1937) Dated but sturdy crime melodrama in which a nightclub hostess (Bette Davis) blames her criminal boss (Eduardo Ciannelli) for the death of her younger sister (Jane Bryan) and gets her roommates to join in helping the D.A. (Humphrey Bogart) convict him. Director Lloyd Bacon's formula proceedings retain their edge today principally due the movie's strong portrayal of women's solidarity in the face of male oppression. Stylized violence, menace and veiled sexual inferences. A-II (br)

Marlene (1984) Unconventional documentary on the life and career of screen star Marlene Dietrich (1902–1992) uses the usual movie excerpts and newsreel footage but spends much time listening to director Maximilian Schell's futile tape-recorded efforts at interviewing the retired actress and his failure to persuade her to appear on camera. With Dietrich dismissing most of his questions as "rubbish," Schell winds up making a documentary in which he co-stars as the frustrated director struggling to win the confidence of a feisty 84-year-old who stubbornly refuses to participate in the project on any but her own terms. Some subtitles. Mature themes. A-III (nr) PG

Marlowe (1969) James Garner stars as Raymond Chandler's hard-boiled detective, Philip Marlowe, in a complicated plot that involves blackmail and ice-pick murders. Garner's Marlowe relies on whimsey but lacks the inner toughness that is an essential of this school of private-eye. Director Paul Bogart and cast (including William Daniels and Jackie Coogan) try hard but can't quite bring the movie off as a cohesive whole. Sensationalistic treatment with nudity in story's conclusion. O (PG) A

Marnie (1964) Flawed but masterfully eccentric thriller stars Tippi Hedren as a compulsive thief caught in the act by wise and worldly journalist Sean Connery. Instead of turning her in, he marries the disturbed girl and tries to discover the reasons for her irrational behavior. Director Alfred Hitchcock explores the theme of the redeeming power of love with some compassion, but the treatment is adult. A-III (PG) 18

Maroc 7 (1967) Agent Gene Barry tracks international jewel thief Cyd Charisse to Morocco where she plans her next robbery in director Gerry O'Hara's dull and implausible crime story. Excessive sexual innuendo and some violence. O (br) A

Marooned (1969) Space mission goes awry when three astronauts (Gene Hackman, Richard Crenna and James Franciscus) get stranded on a space station and ground control (headed by Gregory Peck) tries to get a rescue rocket ready in time to save them. Under the direction of John Sturges, what could have been a gripping adventure yarn bogs down in some fine space and electronic effects that detract interest from the human dimension of the plot and the moral questions raised by it, such as risking the rescue mission in an unproven craft. A-II (PG) U

Marquise of O . . ., The (1976) French adaptation of a 19th-century novel by Heinrich von Kleist about a woman (Edith Clever) who is rescued from enemy soldiers by seemingly virtuous count who takes advantage of her sedated sleep as he guards her through the night. Director Erich Rohmer has fun with the conventions of the time but does not betray Kleist's characters and their concerns. A-II (PG)

Marriage Came Tumbling Down, The (1968) The focus of this slight but beautifully tender little French movie is Michel Simon's performance as an aging, earthy, yet wise and loving grandfather who helps save his philandering grandson's marriage. Unfortunately, director Jacques Poitrenaud fails to give much substance to the young couple's roles so that their final reconciliation has small significance. However, the lovely countryside of Provence and Simon's sensitive and profoundly human characterization make it well worth viewing. A-II (G)

Marriage Italian Style (1965) Dark comedy about an amoral man (Marcello Mastroianni) who is tricked into marrying the woman (Sophia Loren) with whom he has lived for 20 years. Directed by Vittorio de Sica, the movie sparkles with biting satire and sophisticated humor about the battle of the sexes. Subtitles. Centers on sexual innuendo. A-IV (br)

Marriage of a Young Stockbroker, The (1971) Failed satire about a neophyte broker (Richard Benjamin) who is a failure in his attempts to control his compulsive voyeurism, which cause endless professional and marital problems, until his realization at movie's end that he need not be ruled by society's conventions. For all of its humorous digs at social conformity, director Lawrence Turman fails to elicit any sympathy for his alienated young man whose real problem is a complacent smugness that makes him and the movie a bore. Its treatment of women is consistently demeaning, for example, the sordid scene with a nymphomaniac should have been played for compassion instead of snickers. O (PG) X

Marriage of Maria Braun, The (1979) German melodrama about a woman (Hanna Schygulla) whose husband returns from a Russian P.O.W. camp after World War II to discover she is having an affair with an American soldier, kills him and goes to prison. Vowing to have a fortune waiting when he gets out, she rises to be top executive at a textile firm through an affair with its owner. Directed by Rainer Werner Fassbinder, this hard-edged portrait of pragmatic amorality seems to be saying that postwar Germany, like Maria, lost its soul in the struggle for material prosperity. Some rough language and brief nudity. A-IV (R)

Married Couple, A (1970) Canadian documentary about the marital games that go on within a troubled Toronto household in which husband and wife act out their inner frustrations and conflicts for the benefit of a movie crew. Directed by Allan King, the film might serve a psychologist or marriage counselor as a point of departure for discussion purposes, but in itself it lacks the coherence to justify the extremities of emotion, rough language and nudity it displays. A-IV (nr)

Married to It (1993) After a PTA meeting, three vastly dissimilar married couples (Beau Bridges and Stockard Channing; Mary Stuart Masterson and Robert Sean Leonard; Cybill Shepherd and Ron Silver) instantly bond as close friends and see each other through their marital crises. Director Arthur Hiller's well-intentioned but unconvincing comic drama affirms commitment in marriage even as it battles lame dialogue and contrived situations. Discreet bedroom scene and frequent rough language. A-III (R)

Married to the Mob (1988) Director Jonathan Demme's antic comedy focuses on a Long Island mob widow (Michelle Pfeiffer) who tries to start a clean new life with her son on New York's Lower East Side in spite of a lusty mob boss (Dean Stockwell), his jealous wife (Mercedes Ruehl) and a nerdy FBI undercover agent (Matthew Modine). Fine performances make Demme's oddball characters and offbeat subject shine. Some graphic rubouts handled with a humorous touch, much profanity and brief nudity within an implied illicit dalliance. A-III (R) 15

Marry Me, Marry Me (1969) French production about an amiable but aimless young man (Claude Berri) who is so uncertain about marrying his already pregnant fiancee (Elizabeth Wiener) that he has a quick affair before going through with the ceremony. A fatuous epilogue suggests the hero's fears of marriage to have been unjustified. Also directed by Berri, the story is as aimless as its self-absorbed central character, but in the background are some interesting aspects of Jewish life, especially the wedding feast and a certain sense of sadness at the erosion of Jewish traditions in the affluent, socially permissive present. A-III (PG)

Marrying Man, The (1991) A playboy (Alec Baldwin) falls for a cabaret singer (Kim Basinger) and despite their differences marries her time and time again. Best moments are attributable to Neil Simon's witty script in this otherwise brisk but fluffy fare directed by Jerry Rees. Acceptance of premarital sex and chauvinist references, some comic violence and occasional rough language. A-III (R)

Marty (1955) Low-key tale of a 34-year-old butcher (Ernest Borgnine) who falls for a shy science teacher (Betsy Blair) despite the disapproval of his mother (Esther Minciotti) and his Bronx buddies. Written by Paddy Chayevsky and directed by Delbert Mann, the story of two lonely people who've come to think of themselves as losers only to discover they're not is told with honesty and warmth, gaining much credibility from the realistic treatment of its urban ethnic setting. Excellent fare for teens. A-II (br) U

Martyr, The (1976) Israeli-German screen biography of a Polish physician and educator, Dr. Janusz Korczak, who in 1942 accompanied a group of wartime orphans to the Warsaw Ghetto and then to the extermination camp of Treblinka where they all perished together. Directed by Alexander Ford, it is a rather plodding and unimaginative dramatization, but the concluding scene of the children with Dr. Korczak (Leo Genn in a very credible performance) at their head, marching with dignity to the train that will take them to Treblinka, is heart-rending and unforgettable. A-II (nr)

Martyrs of Love (1969) Czechoslovakian movie offering three surrealistic episodes on the theme of frustrated desire focusing on the monotonous life of a junior clerk, the aristocratic dreams of a servant girl and a lonely man's need to feel part of a family. Directed by Jan Nemec, its serio-comic mixture of reality and fantasy is very effective, but many will find its absurd logic and bizarre scenes pointless, if not unsettling. A-III (nr)

Mary of Scotland (1936) Literate adaptation of Maxwell Anderson's play recounting the political intrigues against Scotland's Catholic Queen Mary Stuart (Katharine Hepburn), driving her protector Bothwell (Fredric March) into exile and Mary to the execution block under England's Queen Elizabeth (Florence Eldridge). Director John Ford puts a fine cast through their dramatic set-pieces, with occasional flourishes of pageantry to supply the historical atmosphere. Stylized violence and complicated motivations make it unlikely fare for young children. A-I (br) U

Mary Poppins (1964) Walt Disney's musical adaptation of P.L. Travers children's classic about the primly perfect nanny of the title (Julie Andrews) who uses her magical powers and common sense to straighten out the disorderly children and preoccupied parents of a London household at the turn of the century. Director Robert Stevenson fancifully integrates songs, dance numbers, animated characters and marvelous special effects into the live-action story that features a bright performance by Dick Van Dyke as a Cockney worker who also does a comic turn as a bank president. Entertaining family fantasy. A-I (G) U

Mary, Queen of Scots (1971) Historical drama details the downfall of the Scottish queen (Vanessa Redgrave) in a 16th-century power struggle with Elizabeth of England (Glenda Jackson). Charles Jarrott directs the fascinating story of two strong women, both utterly egotistical but otherwise completely opposite personalities, slugging it out dramatically and politically in a contest of wits and wills. Besides a slice of history, the movie's value is to afford two accomplished actresses the opportunity to play against one another. A-II (GP) A

M*A*S*H (1970) Anti-war comedy about a Mobile Army Surgical Hospital during the Korean War where a trio of skilled battle surgeons (Donald Sutherland, Elliott Gould and Tom Skerritt) maintain their sanity by engaging in crazy hijinks outside the operating room. Robert Altman directs Ring Lardner Jr.'s episodic screenplay with an uneven mixture of comic styles, leaning heavily on irreverence and ridicule of authority figures. Good cast also includes Robert Duvall as a pious hypocrite and Sally Kellerman as the head nurse. Gory operating room sequences and sexually oriented humor. A-IV (PG) 15

Masala (1993) Failed surrealist drama about an alienated Indian youth (Srinivas Krishna) who was raised in Canada but feels an outsider both in the New World and among the Hindu community of Toronto. Also produced, written and directed by Krishna, the result is multicultural confusion that does best with the comic incongruities of immigrant life but lacks narrative coherence and dramatic substance. An explicit bedroom scene, numerous sexual references, some irreligious remarks and sporadic rough language. O (nr) 18

Mask (1985) Sentimental, slow-moving story of a youth with a deformed face who makes a happy life for himself with the help of his understanding mother (Cher). Director Peter Bogdanovich offers a relatively benign view of the life-style of a motorcycle gang, involving drug abuse and sexual promiscuity. A-IV (PG-13) 15

Masquerade (1988) Thriller using the old romantic plot about a naive, young heiress (Meg Tilly) set upon by gold diggers has all sorts of plot twists and characters who are not what they seem. A handsome rogue (Rob Lowe) becomes the love of the heiress' life amidst a lovely beach setting in the Hamptons, an eerie score by John Barry and Bob Swaim's fine direction. Unfortunately marred by a few scenes of graphic violence and several explicit sexual encounters. O (R) 15

Mass Appeal (1984) Screen version of Bill C. Davis' stage comedy about the pastor (Jack Lemmon) of an affluent suburban parish who is assigned to take an outspoken young seminary student (Zeljko Ivanek) under his wing. Davis' play is really about two characters much alike in everything but age who have suffered through unhappy childhoods and never established a good relationship with their families. For them the priesthood is a refuge from the harsh complexities of life. Since the inaccuracies about the Catholic Church (and there are many) are innocuous, this is for adults and adolescents. A-II (PG) 15

Massacre in Rome (1973) On March 23, 1944, Italian partisans attacked a column of SS police troops marching through the center of Rome and killed 33 of them. Within 24 hours, 335 Italians were dead, executed in reprisal on the direct orders of Hitler. Director George Pan Cosmatos effectively sets up this specific moment in history and the motivations of the various characters involved, capably performed by a strong cast including Richard Burton, Marcello Mastroianni and Leo McKern. The provocative re-creation, based on the book by Robert Katz, avoids the easy oversimplifications of most such movies to pose troubling issues of moral responsibility for war-time atrocities that deserve thoughtful consideration by its audience. A-III (PG) 15

Master Gunfighter, The (1975) American gunslinger and samurai-sword fighter (Tom Laughlin) marries into an aristocratic Spanish family in Old California but has to fight their son (Ron O'Neal) when he takes to stealing gold and killing Indians in order to pay the Yankee taxes on the family hacienda. Directed by Frank Laughlin, the result is a tedious, pretentious, badly acted but lushly produced western whose theme of anti-violence is conveyed mostly through violence. A-III (PG) AA

Masters of Menace (1990) Loutish comedy about a spacy biker (David Rasche) and his moronic motorcycle gang trashing the landscape as they flee a court order and overzealous cops. Director Daniel Raskov's sophomoric exercise in crudity can't be taken seriously by adults but may be by some adolescents. A-III (PG-13)

Masters of the Universe (1987) Live-action sci-fi fantasy based on the Mattel toy line and TV cartoon series about the ongoing conflict between heroic warrior He-Man (Dolph Lundgren) and power crazed Skeletor (Frank Langella). Gary Goddard directs using ample comic-book stylized violence in this purely escapist zapfest that might adversely affect the very young. A-II (PG)

Matador (1988) Director Pedro Almodovar's slick, seriocomic look at a couple of kinky individuals—a high-class lawyer (Assumpta Serna); a retired matador (Nacho Martinez)—whose respected positions in Madrid society cloak their search for a deadly sexual high. Despite serious-minded philosophical and political asides on the connections between sex and death, the film includes explicit, often violent sexual encounters, much nudity and profanity. Subtitles. O (nr)

Match Factory Girl, The (1992) Ignored and exploited at home and dehumanized by her assembly-line job, a love-starved young woman (Kati Outinen) exacts merciless revenge after she spends the night with a man (Vesa Vierikko) who then cruelly rejects her. Finnish writer-director Aki Kaurismaki pointedly evokes the misery of a loveless existence in a dark drama with bleakly comic undertones. Subtitles. An implied sexual encounter and several poisonings. A-III (nr)

Matchless (1968) Steely-eyed Patrick O'Neal is an espionage agent of passing skill in this intermittently comic spy melodrama with an invisible man gimmick. He gets by with a little help from secret agent Ira Furstenburg and the stupidity of heavies Donald Pleasence and Henry Silva. Italian production directed by Alberto Lattuada has some violence, but its suggestive costuming and situations are excessive. O (br)

Matewan (1987) Arriving in the coal fields of West Virginia after World War I, a union organizer (Chris Cooper) tries to help the miners win a bitter, bloody strike. Written and directed by John Sayles, the fact-based movie is admirable in its idealistic picture of the workers' solidarity in standing together against the company's reliance upon force. Some graphic violence and a verbal account of a sexual assault. A-III (PG-13) 15

Matilda (1978) Elliott Gould plays a seedy promoter who discovers a down-at-the-heels kangaroo act and with the help of sportswriter Robert Mitchum steers the beast to a bout with the heavyweight champion of the world. Director Daniel Mann's mirthless, blindingly dumb comedy is an embarrassment to sit through. The realistic violence of the final boxing match is not the sort of thing most parents would want their younger children exposed to. A-II (PG) U

Matinee (1993) Nostalgic period comedy set in Key West during the Cuban missile crisis as a horror movie director (John Goodman) tries out his gimmick-laden monster movies on an audience of kids already jumpy about a possible nuclear attack on the area. Joe Dante directs a flighty and fitfully funny look back at the era of radiation-mutation movies and backyard fallout shelters. Brief menace to children and comic treatment of monster movie violence. A-II (PG)

Mating of Millie, The (1948) Sappy romantic comedy in which a single woman (Evelyn Keyes) seeking a husband in order to adopt an orphan falls for a bachelor (Glenn Ford) who insists he's not the marrying kind. Directed by Henry Levin, the coy romance and its predictable outcome is as dated as its disapproving attitude toward single parents. A-II (br) U

Mattei Affair, The (1973) Enrico Mattei, head of the state's oil cartel, was perhaps the most powerful man in Italy when he died under mysterious circumstances in a 1962 plane crash. In following his career and in examining the contradictory evidence about the crash, this Italian dramatization is as dynamic as Mattei himself, played by Gian Maria Volonte with the complete assurance of the self-confident man who relishes competition. Implicit throughout director Francesco Rosi's fast-moving, impressionistic re-creation are questions about the wider issues of social justice that are seldom raised in the ruthless battle to control the world's oil resources. Some scenes of stylized violence. A-III (R)

Matter of Days, A (1969) French student activist studying in Prague, believing the Czech liberalization to be tainted with bourgeois materialism, returns to Paris during the May 1968 student riots. Though the Soviet invasion a few months after the completion of the movie proved her political views wrong-headed, the drama is of some interest for its picture of 1960s' youth with their easy comradeship, their insatiable quest for new values and their inevitable sexual candor. A-IV (R)

Matter of Innocence, A (1967) Failed British adaptation of a Noel Coward story about a young girl (Hayley Mills) being raised by her reprobate uncle (Trevor Howard). Guy Green's heavy-handed direction makes even more offensive scenes of her learning about sex, alcohol and larceny. O (br)

Matter of Time, A (1976) Well-intentioned but hopelessly sentimental and disjointed treatment of the Cinderella theme defeats the best efforts of Liza Minnelli, Ingrid Bergman and Charles Boyer. Directed by Vincente Minnelli, the inept Italian production has some occasional rough language and a comically meant attempted rape scene. A-III (PG)

Maurie (1973) Fact-based dramatization of Cincinnati Royals basketball player Jack Twyman (Bo Svenson) who devoted himself to caring for teammate Maurice Stokes (Bernie Casey) after a 1957 head injury during a game resulted in total paralysis. The result is a saga of determination, love, and endless hours of pain from expensive treatments that gradually brought back his powers of speech and partial control of body movement. Though director Daniel Mann's movie is slow, it is never tedious in recounting without sentimentality but plenty of honest emotion the story of teammates who summoned the inner strength necessary to surmount a time of deep crisis. A-I (G)

Max Dugan Returns (1983) A long absent father (Jason Robards) turns up at the home of his daughter (Marsha Mason), an impoverished widow with a teenage son (Matthew Broderick). He has only six months to live, is remorseful and also has more than a half-million in cold cash of dubious origin neatly packed in one of his suitcases. Bland, contrived comedy written by Neil Simon and directed by Herbert Ross, it is mildly amusing thanks to the skill and personality of its performers. Some mild verbal vulgarities and a fuzzy moral stance toward stealing, but it's basically innocuous. A-II (PG)

Max Havelaar (1979) Dutch drama about a brave, exuberantly idealistic government official (Peter Faber) in mid-19th-century Java who almost single-handedly takes on the entrenched exploiters of the native population until the authorities finally send him back to Holland. Director Fons Rademakers has succeeded admirably in his re-creation of a little-known bygone era, with Faber giving a vital, wholly convincing performance as the anti-colonial hero. Engrossing and largely entertaining—but with several instances of brutal violence. A-III (R)

Maxie (1985) A young couple (Glenn Close and Mandy Patinkin) rent a house that had once belonged to a promising Hollywood starlet named Maxie (Close in dual role). Seeing her second chance at stardom, Maxie's spirit inhabits the wife's body with comic results. Directed by Paul Aaron, the movie almost succeeds in reviving the madcap verve of the 1930s' screwball comedies. Several restrained bedroom scenes. A-III (PG)

Maximum Overdrive (1986) Writer-director Stephen King's malevolent allegory about strange disturbances that turn every machine and truck in a small town into a murderous entity is preoccupied with the demonic. Virtually nonstop images of death and destruction, gore, violence and profanity. O (R)

May Fools (1990) While the turmoil of the May 1968 students' strike in Paris spreads, greedy relatives gather in the picturesque French countryside when the family matriarch dies, and her distraught son (Michel Piccoli) fears they will insist on selling his lifelong home as part of the estate. Not one of director Louis Malle's most insightful works, the film nonetheless is evocative of the gentler, bygone life-style of the rural bourgeoisie, and intermittently droll as the family members feverishly pursue the dead woman's belongings. Several explicit sexual references, including a lesbian relationship, and partial female nudity. A-IV (R)

Maya (1966) American boy (Jay North) discovers mystery in India when he visits his big-game hunter father (Clint Walker). John Berry directs the action adventure in a simple, fast-moving manner that emphasizes the sights and sounds of a fabled land. For the younger members of the family. A-I (br) U

Mayerling (1968) Mushy, overlong, lavishly costumed tearjerker starring Catherine Deneuve and Omar Sharif in the story of the tragic royal romance between Austrian Crown Prince Rudolph and his young mistress that ends in double suicide in the royal lodge at Mayerling in 1889. British production directed by Terence Young has all the trappings of a good soap opera version of the life and leisure of the ruling class but comes up boring and emotionally empty. A-III (PG) A

McCabe and Mrs. Miller (1971) Warren Beatty and Julie Christie star in a western examining the reality of American frontier life in a story about a petty gambler who opens a brothel in a boom town and it becomes so successful that eastern business interests decide to take it over. Director Robert Altman's effort has many interesting segments but fails to come together as a cohesive whole. Rough language and some graphic nudity in brothel scenes. O (R) X

McCullochs, The (1975) Strong, self-made trucking magnate (Forrest Tucker) has built a successful career but at the expense of not spending enough time with his growing children and their problems. Produced, written, and directed by Max Baer, this sentimental chronicle of family life in the early 1950s offers no new insights into its characters or their times. Some macho brawling and boozing. A-III (PG)

McKenzie Break, The (1970) Absorbing though familiar World War II story manages to avoid most of the cliches inherent in prison camp pictures. Centered on two strong personalities (Brian Keith, a hard-boiled career officer sent to quell a riotous prison camp for Nazi officers, and Helmut Griem, an indomitable German officer fomenting trouble to cover up escape attempts), director Lamont Johnson's movie is nicely paced, with strong performances, a credible script and an attempt at characterization uncommon in this type of story. Tight, coherent and thoroughly intelligent contest of wills. Some violence. A-III (GP) AA

McMasters, The (1970) After the Civil War, black Union soldier Brock Peters returns to his former, aging employer Burl Ives, who makes him co-owner of his ranch. This act of friendship incites the bigotry of neighboring ranchers, led by ex-Confederate officer Jack Palance. To further complicate matters, the local down-trodden Indians help out with the ranch chores and give Peters a squaw (Nancy Kwan). The inevitable showdown is long and violent. A conventional western ably directed by Alf Kjellin. Its attempt to deal with an interracial justice theme makes it noteworthy. A-III (PG) X

McQ (1974) John Wayne stars as a Seattle policeman so determined to nail a notorious drug dealer that he turns in his badge and initiates justice on his own terms. Director John Sturges offers the usual brand of Wayne frontier justice updated to an urban setting. Violence and some sexual references. A-III (PG) 15

Me (1970) Quiet, unpretentious French drama about a 10-year-old boy (Michel Terrazon), an unwanted child shuttled from foster home to foster home, never fully trusted, loved or understood. By movie's end, though he has been returned to the institution, he has at last experienced affection and friendship from an aged grandmother who has taken the time to break through his defensive shell. Maurice Pialat's direction is restrained and unsentimental, while gently probing beneath the surface of events with a rare understanding of childhood and human nature in general. In distancing his subject matter he has re-created an all too real world of loneliness and hope, for the tender chords he strikes are at the heart of the human condition. A-II (nr)

Me, Natalie (1969) Patty Duke plays an unhappy but spunky teenage "ugly duckling" struggling to fend for herself in New York's Greenwich Village. Directed by Fred Coe, the movie either overstrains for laughs or settles for the cliches of sentimental melodrama, such as her affair with a married architect (James Farentino). Some entertaining moments but few serious insights. A-III (PG) AA

Mean Frank, Crazy Tony (1977) Mediocre Italian production about a deported American gang lord (Lee Van Cleef) who teams up with a bumbling, would-be gangster (Tony Lo Bianco) to knock over a really nasty mobster. Though director Michele Lupo treats the story in tongue-in-cheek fashion, there is still a great deal of graphic violence. O (R)

Mean Season, The (1985) A psychotic killer (Richard Jordan) stalks Miami and chats occasionally with the reporter (Kurt Russell) covering his crimes. A melodrama directed by Philip Borsos with ciphers for characters, it is of no more consequence than a ride on a roller coaster. Some bloody violence, premarital sex and brief nudity. A-III (R) 15

Mean Streets (1973) Robert De Niro and Harvey Keitel star in director Martin Scorsese's drama about small-time crime in New York's Little Italy. The drama has moments of power and effectiveness, mostly in its depiction of an authentic ethnic neighborhood, but it too often degenerates into a kind of bizarre freak show. Some intense violence, nudity and rough language. A-IV (R) 18

Meanest Man in the World, The (1943) In this creaky adaptation of a play by George M. Cohan, radio comedian Jack Benny plays an unsuccessful lawyer besieged by clients after a newspaper story reporting that he took candy from a child. Director Sidney Lanfield's low-budget comedy yields few laughs, despite a hard-working cast including Eddie Anderson as Benny's servant and Priscilla Lane as the romantic interest, with results only of interest to Benny fans and social historians. Mild romantic complications. A-II (br) U

Meatballs (1979) Bill Murray cavorts as the director of a haplessly ill-organized summer camp. Canadian production ineptly directed by Ivan Reitman contains some relatively mild off-color jokes and sex-oriented pranks. A-III (PG) 15

Mechanic, The (1972) Twisted, ironic, somewhat depressing chiller about a cynical, cold-blooded Mafia hit man (Charles Bronson) who takes on an apprentice (Jan-Michael Vincent). Betrayal is in the wind,

however, but from what direction isn't clear until the twist ending. Director Michael Winner has turned out a slick, suspenseful and not very pleasant crime movie. Several grisly murders. A-III (PG) 15

Medea (1971) Italian dramatization of the Medea myth, going beyond the confines of Euripides' tragedy by sketching in some of the background of a violent time and place. The focus, however, is on the title character and as performed by Maria Callas, the evil of this witch-goddess figure becomes increasingly palpable. Though some may fault the film for its departures from the classic tradition, few will deny the power of director Pier Paolo Pasolini's visualization of the ancient Greek world. A-III (nr) PG

Medicine Ball Caravan (1971) Documentary directed by Francois Reichenbach recording the travels of a musical troupe (including among others, B. B. King, Alice Cooper, Delaney and Bonnie) across the U.S. during the summer of 1970, promoting peace, love and music. Judging from the evidence on the screen, one would conclude that all counter-culturists know how to do is freak out, hassle with the fuzz and swim naked. Most of this is merely irritating, but viewers should know that Warner Brothers paid for both the tour and the movie that features many of their slower-selling recording artists, another example of the movie medium's potential as an instrument of commercial exploitation. A-IV (R)

Medicine Man (1992) Belabored drama has Sean Connery as an eccentric medical researcher in the endangered Brazilian rain forest forced to enlist the help of an unwelcome assistant (Lorraine Bracco) sent from the States to check up on him. Lush cinematography and Connery's considerable screen presence do not compensate for a tedious script and Bracco's dreadfully shrill performance. Some tribal nudity, very brief violence and an instance of rough language. A-II (PG-13) PG

Mediterraneo (1992) Stranded on a remote Greek island during World War II, eight Italian soldiers lay down their arms and embrace the peaceful life of the villagers. Director Gabriele Salvatores' charmingly simplistic and bittersweet comedy positions war as a man-made folly in light of our shared humanity. Some sexual innuendo with implied encounters, occasional nudity and minimal rough language. A-III (nr) 15

Medium Cool (1969) Television news cameraman (Robert Forster) has no interest in the effect of the stories he covers until he falls in love with a young widow (Verna Bloom) whose son is a runaway. His views change as he helps her search for her son in the midst of the violence and confusion of police-yippie confrontations during the 1968 Chicago Democratic Convention. Director Haskell Wexler's powerful movie intertwines staged drama and documentary footage in a convincing, seamless style that gives point to the work's probing into the ethics of news coverage. It is unfortunate that a bedroom romp with total nudity mars a significant attempt to question the role the media play in the violence of today's society. O (X/R) X

Medusa Touch, The (1978) Richard Burton plays a man who can destroy others just by willing their death, a telekinetic power that psychiatrist Lee Remick discovers to her horror. Though the plot device is extremely implausible, director Jack Gold makes the most of it in turning out a well-acted, superior thriller. Some rather frightening violence and occasional anti-God rantings. A-III (PG) 15

Meet John Doe (1941) An unassuming hobo (Gary Cooper) is hired to embody the average American but when he discovers that his media-created popularity is being used to further the ambitions of a home-grown fascist politician (Edward Arnold), he decides to commit suicide. Director Frank Capra plumbs the darker side of the American character in an interesting but ultimately heavy-handed story about the dangers of media manipulation. A-II (br) U

Meet Me in St. Louis (1944) Nostalgic musical placed in St. Louis on the eve of the 1903 World's Fair celebrates the old-fashioned virtues of close-knit family life as domestic complications beset parents (Leon Ames and Mary Astor), grandpa (Henry Davenport), teenage daughter (Judy Garland) and the boy next door (Tom Drake). Director Vincente Minnelli lightens the sentiment with good-natured humor. Judy's numbers include "The Trolley Song" and "Have Yourself a Merry Little Christmas." Tiny Margaret O'Brien steals the show with her Halloween pranks. Appealing family fare. A-I (nr) U

Meet the Applegates (1991) Giant bugs disguised as typical Americans (Ed Begley Jr. and Stockard Channing) plot the meltdown of an Ohio nuclear plant to protest the destruction of the Brazilian rain forest that is their home. Directed by Michael Lehmann, the initially amusing satire soon nosedives into ugly stereotypes and unamusing tastelessness. Rape scene, several extramarital encounters, recreational drug use, cartoon violence, constant off-color references and intermittent rough language. O (R) 15

Meeting Venus (1991) An international production of Wagner's "Tannhauser" in the Paris Opera House presents its little-known Hungarian conductor (Niels Arestrup) with a slew of petty problems, not the least of which is an unexpected love affair with a volatile diva (Glenn Close). Hungarian director Istvan Szabo offers scattered but shallow charms in a movie intended as a metaphor for the problems facing European unification. An adulterous affair, assorted references to sexual promiscuity and a brief shot of drug abuse. A-III (PG-13) 12

Meetings with Remarkable Men (1979) Surface treatment of the formative years of Russian mystic G. I. Gurdjieff who before World War I discovered, hidden deep in the Asian hinterlands, an ancient monastic order in whose keeping were the secrets of the universe and the meaning of life. Directed by Peter Brook, the natural spectacle of the rugged mountainous landscape of Afghanistan is more remarkable than any of the movie's portentous encounters or pretentious dialogue. A-III (G)

Megaforce (1982) Tongue-in-cheek adventure about an elite force put together by the nations of the free world to combat oppression. Directed by Hal Needham, it has a solid plot and there is a certain charm in its lack of pretension. Barry Bostwick carries off the hero's role with panache and just a touch of self-mockery, while Henry Silva, less burdened than he usually is as the heavy, gets a chance to lighten things up as a not-too-bad villain. Despite much cannon and rocket fire, there's not a drop of blood spilled or even an elbow dislocated during all the spectacular derring-do. Several mild double-entendres. A-II (PG)

Melinda (1972) Black exploitation movie with Calvin Lockhart as a radio disk jockey whose casual acquaintance with Vonetta McGee pits him against Syndicate boss Paul Stevens because of an incriminating tape recording in her possession. Directed by Hugh A. Robertson, the muddled plot follows the formula of alternating violence with a smattering of soft-core sex and climaxing in a bloody showdown with the crime kingpin. O (R)

Melo (1988) Dated French period-piece about a tragic love affair in which the wife (Sabine Azema) of a mediocre pianist (Pierre Arditi) falls in love with a concert violinist who is her husband's best friend (Andre Dussollier). Based on Henry Bernstein's 1929 play, director Alain Resnais' movie emphasizes its stage origins by stylized acting and theatrical effects that some may find needlessly affected and historically remote. Mature subject and treatment. A-III (nr)

Melody (1971) Unpretentious little movie about two London schoolboys (Mark Lester and Jack Wild) whose friendship is threatened when one of them develops a crush on 11-year-old Melody (Tracy Hyde). Puppy love leads to the announcement of their plans to marry, confounding parents and ending in a free-for-all at school between students and teachers. Sensitively directed by Waris Hussein, the engaging story of fantasy and romance presents a child's view of the adult world with much humor and gentle ironies that will appeal as much to parents as to pre-teens. A-II (G) PG

Melvin and Howard (1980) A supreme American loser and a supreme American winner forge a bond based upon mutual respect in this touching comedy about a gas station attendant (Paul LeMat) who discovers he is among the heirs of eccentric millionaire Howard Hughes (Jason Robards). Director Jonathan Demme's movie makes viewers feel a little better about this crazy, mixed-up but unique and quite wonderful country of ours. Some incidental nudity and some profanity. A-III (PG) AA

Member of the Wedding, The (1952) Stagey yet evocative portrait of adolescent turmoil from Carson McCullers' story about a lonely 12-year-old (Julie Harris) whose only friends are her widowed father's housekeeper (Ethel Waters) and an 8-year-old boy from next door (Brandon de Wilde). Director Fred Zinnemann succeeds well with the trio's kitchen dialogues but the larger picture of the girl's uneasy relations with father, relatives and peers as well as her coming-of-age experiences in the finale are less than convincing. Intense yet insightful picture of teenage anxieties. A-II (br) A

Memoirs of a River (1992) Fact-based drama of a simple Jewish logger (Sandor Gaspar) and other innocents, both Christians and Jews, who face torture and death during an outburst of anti-Semitic violence in the Austro-Hungarian Empire of 1882. Written and directed by Judit Elek, the Hungarian production gets off to a slow, somewhat confusing start in establishing the historical circumstances, then becomes a riveting account of the terror unleashed by the spread of a rumor about a Jewish ritual murder of a Christian child. Much tension and some grisly scenes of torture and brutalization. A-III (nr)

Memoirs of an Invisible Man (1992) Strained comedy about a West Coast businessman (Chevy Chase) accidentally made invisible who, with his girlfriend (Daryl Hannah) in tow, is on the run from a power-crazed government agent (Sam Neill). The funny moments tend to vanish quickly in director John Carpenter's awkward romantic comedy. Restrained bedroom scene, occasional sexual innuendo, stylized comic

violence and an instance of rough language. A-III (PG-13) PG

Memories of Me (1988) Cardiac surgeon (Billy Crystal), felled by his own heart attack, decides to head West and make peace with his dad (Alan King), a lifelong movie extra and embarrassment. It takes the surgeon's girlfriend (JoBeth Williams) and another critical illness to bring them to play the roles of father and son for the first time in their lives. Uninspired direction by Henry Winkler and a too facile ending do not detract from the entertaining performances and touching concept. Rough language, sexual references and a brief premarital sex scene. A-III (PG-13)

Memories of Underdevelopment (1973) Cuban production directed by Tomas Gutierrez Alea about the day-to-day recollections of an upper-middle class Cuban (Sergio Corrieri) who refused to join his family's flight from Castro by emigrating to Miami, but who also refuses to take part in a revolution that is distasteful to him personally and intellectually. Seen through the eyes of this alienated outsider are the changes taking place under the Marxist regime, but the film's relaxed, sometimes comic, presentation of revolutionary deficiencies helps give its picture of present Cuban life a sense of credibility instead of propaganda. A-III (nr)

Memory of Justice, The (1976) Documentary on the Nuremberg Trials of Nazi war criminals and whether they established a legal precedent for judging the wartime conduct of all nations. After an extensive examination of the Nuremberg process for trying crimes against humanity, producer-director Marcel Ophuls goes on to ask some uncomfortable questions about offenses committed by the Allies during the World War II and the Occupation, the conduct of the French military during the Algerian War and Americans during the Vietnam War. Ophuls brings patient intelligence and concern for human dignity to a four-and-a-half-hour demonstration of the difficulty but the necessity of establishing accountable standards of international conduct. Unflinching look at death camp atrocities and an unnecessary use of nudity. A-IV (PG)

Memphis Belle (1990) Fact-based World War II drama about a B-17 bomber and its 10-man crew embarking on their final and most dangerous mission over Nazi Germany. Director Michael Caton-Jones turns in an unabashedly old-fashioned aerial war movie that, while offering nothing fresh or original, does convey the extreme pressures and fears faced by young soldiers. Wartime violence, mild sexual innuendo and minimal rough language. A-II (PG-13)

Men (1986) Another round in the battle of the sexes is provided in this German production about a woman who, tired of her successful businessman husband, has an affair with a nonconformist musician. The husband moves in with his wife's lover and slowly transforms him into a hard-working ad agency executive, thereby saving his marriage. Director Doris Dorrie's comedy of manners and morals concentrates more on the male camaraderie of the odd-couple relationship than on the wife's infidelity. Mild sexual innuendo. A-III (nr)

Men, The (1950) Brooding in a Veterans Administration Hospital, a bitter World War II paraplegic (Marlon Brando) resists all attempts at rehabilitation for civilian life until a dedicated doctor (Everrett Sloane) and his loving fiancee (Teresa Wright) make him face the future. Directed in semi-documentary style by Fred Zinnemann, the story amply demonstrates the psychological dimensions of devastating injuries but it is Brando's powerful, convincing performance that makes the movie a vivid experience. A-II (br) PG

Menage (1986) French import about a couple who have their marriage turned inside out when a homosexual friend falls for the husband (Michel Blanc) who will do anything for his wife (Miou-Miou) who, it turns out, is infatuated with the friend (Gerard Depardieu). Director Bertrand Blier's gentle bedroom farce turns nasty as it depicts the treachery, deceit and brutality inevitable in the situation. Nudity, explicit sex and rough language. O (nr)

Men at Work (1990) Feeble action comedy about two garbage men (Emilio Estevez; Charlie Sheen) who get stuck with the corpse of a corrupt politician while trying to find his murderer, a sleazy toxic-waste kingpin (John Getz). Also written and directed by Estevez, the result is a sophomoric vanity production, relying on anti-establishment posturing rather than substantive social persective in its condescending depiction of blue-collar workers, minorities, police officers and fears of pollution. Cartoon violence, occasional profanity, bathroom humor and vulgar situations. A-III (PG-13) 15

Men Don't Leave (1990) Realistic, unsentimental portrait of a family in crisis after the sudden death of her husband leaves the mother (Jessica Lange) and her two young sons to cope with the shock, grief and change of life-style that result. Director Paul Brickman shows the difficulty of their struggle to survive as a family in a financially strapped environment, a situation made believably poignant by a fine cast. Though the sexual involvement of the 17-year-old son is inappropriate for younger adolescents, parents may wish to share this otherwise relevant film with their older offspring. Some sexual situations and rough language. A-III (PG-13) 15

Men in White (1934) Dated medical melodrama from the Sidney Kingsley play about a dedicated intern (Clark Gable) whose plans for further studies are complicated by a rich socialite (Myrna Loy) and a lonely nurse (Elizabeth Allan). Directed by Richard Boleslawski, its idealized treatment of dedicated doctors is cloying, despite a tragic romantic subplot. Veiled reference to abortion. A-III (br)

Men of Respect (1991) When a Bronx Mafia don (Rod Steiger) is murdered by his own lieutenant (John Turturro), a torrent of mob reprisals engulfs the killer and his manipulative wife (Katherine Borowitz). Director William Reilly's updated version of "MacBeth" scores on acting and intrigue but its chosen form of lurid melodrama yields little moral insight. Some grisly violence, intermittent rough language and momentary nudity. A-IV (R) 18

Men of the Fighting Lady (1954) U.S. aircraft carrier's doctor (Walter Pidgeon) recounts the brave acts of its fighter pilots (Van Johnson, Frank Lovejoy, Keenan Wynn, etc.) during the Korean War. Directed by Andrew Marton, the routine All-American script is helped by filming aboard an actual carrier and much use of official combat footage. Wartime violence. A-I (br)

Menace II Society (1993) Ultraviolent drama set in Watts unreels the fate of an African American youth (Tyrin Turner) who learns the drug trade early on, graduates to murder, but is almost saved by a good woman (Jada Pinkett) before becoming just another statistic of revenge-motivated, drive-by shootings. In allowing the fatalistic youth to rationalize his murderous behavior, directors Allen and Albert Hughes leave the impression that society, not the individual, must take full blame for spiraling crime in the inner city. A nihilistic view of life, excessively graphic bloodshed, a brief bedroom scene, many degrading sexist references and incessant rough language. O (R)

Mephisto (1982) Hungarian-German production directed by Istvan Szabo is an extremely interesting film about the temptation of power. A provincial German actor (Klaus Maria Brandauer) whose forte, ironically enough is playing the great tempter Mephisto, allows himself to be taken under the wing of a prominent member of the rising Nazi party and, when they come to power, becomes director of the Berlin National Theatre. The film lacks dramatic force, but it is nonetheless fascinating, especially Brandauer's brilliant performance as the good-hearted but feckless hero. Some rather graphic nudity. A-IV (R) 15

Mephisto Waltz, The (1971) Mediocre horror movie about a dying master pianist (Curt Jurgens) who befriends a young journalist (Alan Alda) because he needs a suitable body in which to continue his existence as a follower of Satan. Once this is established the suspense is over and the rest is a tiresome exercise in routine scenes of witchcraft rituals. Director Paul Wendkos works hard to create the reality of his occult world, but what was needed was a little subtlety and imaginative suggestion. Some violence. A-III (R)

Mercenary, The (1970) Loosely plotted Italian spoof of spaghetti westerns revolving around the waxing and waning fortunes of a taco-brained Mexican revolutionary (Tony Musante) and a stoic soldier-for-hire (Franco Nero) who is pitted against the sinister arch-villain of the piece (Jack Palance). Musante garners most of the laughs as the grinning fool of a would-be general leading an equally inept, rag-tag band of peasants. Directed by Sergio Corbucci, the frequently hilarious goings on should not be taken too seriously, especially all the shooting and bright red paint splattering everyone. Brief nudity. A-III (GP)

Merchant of Four Seasons, The (1973) German drama about a misfit who after many failures in life becomes a fruit peddler, but his family's malice and his wife's infidelity destroy his last spark of independence. Director Rainer Werner Fassbinder offers a depressing but valid picture of the dehumanizing effects of modern society's materialistic values upon the human spirit. Subtitles. Graphic sexual encounter. A-IV (nr)

Mermaids (1990) An adolescent girl (Winona Ryder), troubled by her attraction to a 26-year-old man (Michael Schoeffling), is even more embarrassed by her flamboyant single mom (Cher) who has taken up with the local shoestore owner (Bob Hoskins). The baldly contrived storyline in director Richard Benjamin's limp comedy trivializes a young girl's religious leanings while managing to make her promiscuous mom seem hip. Acceptance of promiscuous and premarital sexual relationships. O (PG-13) 15

Merry Christmas, Mr. Lawrence (1983) David Bowie and Tom Conti star in an English-Japanese production about the clash of cultures in a Japanese camp for British prisoners during World War II. At war's end, with the Japanese prisoners of the British, there is an indication that perhaps humanity can bridge such cultural chasms. The subject is almost a movie

cliche and others have done it much better. Directed by Nagisa Oshima, the movie features much hard-edged Samurai-code violence and an ambivalent attitude toward homosexuality. A-IV (R) 15

Merry Go Round (1976) Starring Senta Berger and Helmut Berger, this is an inane, tedious, badly dubbed remake of the turn-of-the-century Schnitzler play about a series of sexual relationships coming full circle. O (R)

Merry Wives of Windsor, The (1966) Undistinguished British production of Otto Nocolai's opera based on Shakespeare's comedy about the buffoonish Falstaff (American bass Norman Foster) who is made sport of by two mischievous wives. Directed by George Tressler, it might be of interest to students of music but not drama. A-II (br)

Message, The (see: "Mohammad, Messenger of God").

Message from Space (1978) Mediocre Japanese production offering a pint-sized variation on the "Star Wars" theme with some plucky youngsters teaming up with an old-timer (Vic Morrow) to save the universe from intergalactic villains. Other familiar elements include a captive princess dressed in white, a cute little robot, two hotshot pilots and some bargain-basement mysticism. Directed by Kinji Fukasaku, the special effects are satisfactory, though the storyline is cluttered and the comic relief not very amusing. A-II (PG)

Meteor (1979) Sean Connery and Natalie Wood star as scientists attempting to deflect a huge meteor heading for the earth and whose impact might bring on another Ice Age, among other calamities. Though ladened with disaster movie cliches, director Ronald Neame makes the premise into surprisingly good entertainment thanks to a good cast and several plot twists more sophisticated than is usual for this kind of movie. Some profanity. A-III (PG)

Meteor Man, The (1993) Comic-book adventures of a mild inner-city shoolteacher (Peter Townsend) who, after being hit by a meteor, finds he has superhuman powers which he uses to help his neighbors clear out the hoodlums and drug traffickers. Also written and directed by Townsend, the superhero fantasy is played for good-natured laughs with a solid supporting cast (including Bill Cosby; James Earl Jones; Robert Guillaume; Marla Gibbs) and plenty of rap music. Fantasy violence in a realistic context of street crime. A-II (PG)

Metropolitan (1990) An outsider (Edward Clements) who claims to detest social snobbism is admitted to the nightly Manhattan soirees of seven wealthy youngsters and soon finds his life revolving around them.

Whit Stillman's directorial debut is marked by a lighthearted comedy of manners that is well-acted and enlivened by witty dialogue, but leaves many unanswered questions about the privileged characters' pointless partying and aimless life-styles. References to promiscuous relationships. A-III (PG-13) 15

Miami Blues (1990) Colorful black comedy tracks the battle of wills between a seedy homicide detective (Fred Ward) and a psychopathic ex-San Quentin inmate (Alec Baldwin) who cross paths in Miami. Director George Armitage makes the most of these losers on the fringe of a cotton-candy world and his actors, especially Jennifer Jason Leigh as the part-time prostitute with a yen for marriage, is bright and often surprising. Some grisly violence, several highly suggestive sexual encounters with some nudity and occasional rough language. A-IV (R) 18

Michael and Helga (1969) Soporific German sex-education movie uses impersonal diagrams and silly dramatizations to treat too many complicated biological, psychological and social aspects of its subject so that it tends to confuse more than enlighten viewers. Much too diffuse for parents to use in acquainting their offspring about the facts of life. A-IV (R)

Mickey One (1965) Muddy tale of a small-time stand-up comic (Warren Beatty) on the run from some threatening mobsters without ever learning precisely why they are after him. Director Arthur Penn succeeds best with the moody location filming in Chicago but the volatile theme of alienation dead-ends in a murky, undefined plot. Some stylized violence and much menace. A-III (br) A

Micki and Maude (1985) Broadcast journalist (Dudley Moore) marries his pregnant mistress (Any Irving) before divorcing his pregnant wife (Ann Reinking) because he loves them both. Director Blake Edwards comes up with a few funny moments, but the sentimental treatment of the situation makes the movie's attempts at farce unsatisfactory, if not dishonest. Sympathetic depiction of adultery. O (PG-13) PG

Midas Run (1969) British secret service officer (Fred Astaire) concocts an elaborate scheme to hijack a large gold shipment he is supposed to be guarding. Jumbled script and plodding direction by Alf Kjellin make the caper tiresome long before the end. Lengthy and overdrawn scene of love-making. O (PG) A

Middle Age Crazy (1980) Successful contractor (Bruce Dern) with a gorgeous wife (Ann-Margret), a son who loves and admires him, a beautiful home and a host of friends but, in an oft told story, as he approaches 40, things start to fall apart for him. Directed by John Trent, it has fine performances from its principals and the familiar situation is treated with an unusual moral sense that makes it well worth seeing. Mature theme with some rough language and harsh satire. A-III (R) AA

Middle of the World, The (1975) Swiss drama about a bright married engineer (Phillipe Leotard), chosen by party regulars to run for office, who pursues an indiscrete affair with a young waitress (Olimpia Carlisi) until she rejects his callous use of her. Directed by Alain Tanner, the movie proves a wise, humane parable about a comfortable, materialistic society that has lost its soul and sense of the dignity of the individual. It is somewhat ironic, however, that the narrative, in making a strong statement against the exploitation of women, is itself guilty of using an unnecessary amount of nudity in detailing the adulterous affair. O (nr)

Midnight Clear, A (1992) Highly stylized anti-war movie focuses on the insane outburst of violence engulfing a reconnaissance squad (including Ethan Hawke, Ayre Gross and Gary Sinise) in the Ardennes Forest in December 1944 when an equally small unit of German soldiers tries to arrange a surrender. Adapted from William Wharton's novel by director Keith Gordon, the action is more symbolic than credible, though admirable in using an isolated snowbound setting to suggest a surreal situation transcending all wars. Graphic wartime violence, a highly romanticized sexual encounter and minimal rough language. A-III (R) 15

Midnight Cowboy (1969) A Texas bumpkin (Jon Voight) comes to New York City expecting to make his fortune as stud to what he believes are its endless supply of lonely women. In trying to cope with reality of urban life, he relies on his friendship with another loser, a small-time con artist (Dustin Hoffman) crippled physically and emotionally with a hopeless dream of escaping to the sun. Director John Schlesinger treats with compassion this odyssey of two alienated outcasts blindly groping for some redemptive human fellowship in a society that values sex and money more than human beings. Some may find its realistic depiction of a sordid environment, with a graphic sexual encounter and a brutal outburst of violence, quite reprehensible. Others will find merit in its attempt to recognize the resilience of the human spirit and the dignity of the individual. Challenging fare, not for the casual viewer. A-IV (X/R) A

Midnight Crossing (1988) Trashy adventure story about a man (Daniel Travanti) who returns to retrieve a fortune in stolen money he had helped hide 30 years before on an island off Cuba. Ineptly directed by

Roger Holzberg, the ranks of those who become involved are decimated by greed, lies, attempted murder and a storm at sea. Some bloody violence, some brief but graphic sexual scenes with fleeting nudity and incidental profanity. A-III (R) 18

Midnight Express (1978) Wildly melodramatic movie directed by Alan Parker about the imprisonment of an American youth in a Turkish prison for narcotics smuggling. Wallows in bloody violence and cruelty, an indulgence hardly justified by its human rights plea. Further marred by sexual references, nudity. O (R) 18

Midnight Lace (1960) Doris Day screams, cries, whines and whimpers her way through this suspense thriller as a rich American married to a suave Englishman (Rex Harrison) living happily in London until a series of threatening telephone calls turns her into a basket case. Directed by David Miller, it's a slickly done, highly manipulative affair which depends largely on one's tolerance of women-in-peril situations. Much menace heightened by a little stylized violence. A-II (br) A

Midnight Madness (1980) Rival teams of college students compete in a dead-of-the-night treasure hunt in this slapdash effort at zany comedy written and directed by David Wechter and Michael Nankin. The laughs are few and the goings-on get tiresome. Some mild sexual innuendo in the dialogue. A-II (PG)

Midnight Man, The (1974) Burt Lancaster plays a brutal ex-cop employed as security chief for a Midwestern college campus where there is a bisexual counselor (Susan Clark), a sexpot student (Catherine Bache) who gets murdered, and a corrupt sheriff (Harris Yulin). Director Roland Kibbee's confused plot is full of numbing twists and inconsistencies, leaving little justification for its violence and sexual references. O (R) X

Midnight Run (1988) An embezzler (Charles Grodin), on the run from mobsters and the law, is nabbed in New York by a bounty-hunter (Robert De Niro) who attempts to escort him back to Los Angeles alive to collect $100,000. With humor and some sentiment, director Martin Brest charts the growing camaraderie between this odd couple as they dodge dangers along the way. Much profanity and some comic-book violence. A-III (R) 18

Midsummer Night's Dream, A (1967) The N.Y. City Ballet in its first feature-length presentation, conceived and choreographed by the company's artistic director, George Balanchine, with Suzanne Farrell as Titania, Edward Villella as Oberon and Arthur Mitchell as Puck. A treat for those who couldn't otherwise see this lavish, seldom-performed ballet with the music of Felix Mendelssohn. A-I (br)

Midsummer Night's Sex Comedy, A (1982) Woody Allen directs and stars in this slight little comedy of manners set in a Victorian house in rural New York at the turn-of-the-century. Mia Farrow, Jose Ferrer and Mary Steenburgen are among the three couples who switch, or consider switching, partners in the course of a summer's day and night. There are few jokes, and just about all of them are about sex. Mature subject matter. A-III (PG) 15

Midway (1976) Charlton Heston, Henry Fonda and Glenn Ford head an all-star cast in this occasionally effective re-creation of the most decisive naval battle of World War II. Unfortunately, director Jack Smight is unable to overcome the shallow fictional subplots that supposedly were meant to add human interest but which instead blunt the emotional potential of historical material capable of standing on its own. Wartime violence and some rough language. A-II (PG) A

Mighty Ducks, The (1992) Loud, obnoxious story of a mean yuppie lawyer (Emilio Estevez) and a bunch of nasty juveniles being transformed by working together to win a pee-wee hockey championship. Director Stephen Herek's oft-told tale of the character-building potential of team sports offers bogus characters in bogus situations that earn little sympathy or respect before the predictably bogus outcome. Bone-crunching violence of a contact sport, nasty youthful pranks and coarse language. A-II (PG)

Mighty Quinn, The (1989) The murder of a white businessman on an exotic Caribbean island pits an honest Chief of Police (Denzel Washington) against white and black powerbrokers who would like to pin the murder on a local ne'er-do-well (Robert Townsend). Director Carl Schenkel dilutes the suspense with meandering subplots that enhance the film's local color but do nothing for the crime at hand. Some grisly violence, rough language and sexual innuendo. A-III (R) 15

Mikado, The (1967) Gilbert and Sullivan's timeless comic operetta about the son who defies his emperor father and wins his love, Yum-Yum, in a wonderful stage production of Japanese make-believe. Pleasant story, lovely costuming, wit, laughter and song by the D'Oyly Carte Opera Company adds up to excellent entertainment for everyone. A-I (br) U

Mike's Murder (1984) When Debra Winger's boyfriend, Mike (Mark Keyloun), is murdered, she investigates and learns about the drug trade and the seamy side of Los

Angeles life. Winger has little to do in a listless melodrama, written and directed by James Bridges, that is as flat as its title. A-III (R) 18

Mikey and Nicky (1977) Nicky (John Cassavetes) is a bookie who steals some money from his boss and, fearing he is marked for death, contacts the only man he can trust to help him, his boyhood friend Mikey (Peter Falk). The narrative consists of their odyssey through the course of one wild evening whose complications are, unfortunately, entirely predictable. Though the acting of the principals is excellent, especially in their interplay, director-writer Elaine May fails to offer enough substance to engage the viewer's emotions in any significant way. Some violence, rough language and a frank treatment of sex. A-III (R)

Milagro Beanfield War, The (1988) Honest but flawed attempt to depict the cultural strength of a poor Hispanic community in the Southwest when it bands together against greedy Anglo land developers. Directed by Robert Redford, the feel-good plot is rendered in broad, melodramatic strokes, saving most of its energies for illustrating the foibles of a large cast of colorful characters, among them Chick Vennera, Christopher Walken, Sonia Braga and John Heard. Some violence, rough language and muted sexual references. A-III (R) 15

Mildred Pierce (1945) Misplaced ambition fuels James M. Cain's dark story of a driven woman (Joan Crawford) who shucks a useless husband (Jack Carson) in rising from waitress to head a restaurant chain, then falls for a scoundrel (Zachary Scott) who turns his attentions to her adolescent daughter (Ann Blyth). Directed by Michael Curtiz, it's an acerbic tale of how obsession with material success ultimately destroys its misguided heroine, not the least of whose mistakes is raising her only child to be a spoiled brat. Mature theme and treatment. A-III (br) A

Miles from Home (1988) Two brothers (Richard Gere and Kevin Anderson) burn down their Iowa farm rather than turn it over to the bank, but the shock of losing their family's once proud farmstead leads them to a life of aimlessness, one step ahead of the cops. Gary Sinise directs a heartbreaking story of two young men whose rising reputation as folk heroes doesn't ease their sense of family loss. Adult themes and some rough language. A-III (R) 15

Milestones (1975) Fictional documentary about what happened to those involved in the protest movements of the 1960s whose failed efforts at changing the nature of the American politics and society led them inward, banding together in little groups for mutual support and survival. Interweaving the activities of some 50 characters may be confusing for those uninterested in political alienation, but filmmakers Robert Kramer and John Douglas have documented how a lost segment of a generation sees itself that has importance for future historians. Unconventional views, some nudity and a graphic birth sequence make this mature fare. A-IV (nr)

Milk and Honey (1989) Leaving her native Jamaica for work as a nanny in Toronto, a poor woman (Josette Simon) and her young son hope for eventual citizenship, but bigotry and immigration red tape lead them into an underground life of fear and deceit. Canadian directors Rebecca Yates and Glen Salzman deliver a sensitive, carefully etched study of one black woman's determination to make a better life without compromising her dignity or values. Some vulgar sexual innuendos. A-III (nr)

Milky Way, The (1969) French production directed by Luis Bunuel about a pilgrimage made by two men to the shrine of St. James the Apostle in Spain, the road to which is known as "the Milky Way." It is an extraordinary journey of faith, ranging not only from place to place but from century to century as the pilgrims encounter advocates of past heresies and those who are true believers in orthodoxy. Bunuel provides a lively mixture of pious Christian traditions and superstitious beliefs through an episodic and absurdly humorous series of adventures that challenges the serious viewer with its ambiguous reflections on the relevance of religion in contemporary life. A-IV (PG) A

Millennium (1989) Inept science-fiction excursion a thousand years into the future from which time travelers return to the 20th century seeking to retrieve an object left behind on a previous visit. Veteran director Michael Anderson tries to work up some tension in a muddled plot involving a romance between an aircrash investigator (Kris Kristofferson) and a traveler from the 30th century. Some fairly graphic violence and several restrained sex scenes. A-III (PG-13) PG

Miller's Crossing (1990) Tough Prohibition-era gangster movie about a mob war in which the right-hand man (Gabriel Byrne) of the city's top boss (Albert Finney) goes to work for the opposition after the two have a falling out over a woman (Marcia Gay Harden). Written, produced and directed by the brothers Joel and Ethan Coen, the hard-boiled story has some interesting twists about personal loyalty and the criminal code, the melodramatic performances and the period setting go well together and the hard-edged violence is neatly stylized for the most part.

Considerable violence and menace, references to illicit sexual relationships and occasional profanity. A-IV (R)

Millhouse: A White Comedy (1971) Documentary on the life and career of Richard Millhouse Nixon begins with Nixon's 1962 "last" press conference and then returns to his origins and six political crises (including the famous 1956 "Checkers" speech), his role in the 1964 campaign and finally his election as President in 1968. Based solely on newsreel footage (and a few out-takes), the satiric intent of director Emile de Antonio's partisan selection of material can only amuse anti-Nixonites but will not convince his supporters of the shallowness and ineptness that de Antonio finds in the visual record. Lack of explanatory historical background limits its usefulness for young viewers. A-III (G)

Million Dollar Mystery (1987) Fluffy comedy adventure filled with car chases and demolition features an ensemble cast of new faces on a greedy search for $4 million in hidden pay-off money. Director Richard Fleischer makes the most of the stark Southwest landscape shot exquisitely by Jack Cardiff as backdrop for the slapstick antics and dangerous stunts that form the substance of the movie. Some coarse language and sexual sight gags are brief and restrained. A-II (PG)

Mind of Mr. Soames, The (1970) Offbeat story about the education of a 30-year-old man (Terence Stamp) who, until a delicate brain operation restores consciousness, has been in a coma since birth. A compassionate physician (Robert Vaughn), realizing the man-child's need for tenderness and the simple pleasures of childhood, opposes the unyielding authoritarian rigors of the neurophysiological hospital staff in whose charge he has been placed. Though raising some provocative questions about the learning process and responsibility, director Alan Cooke's work is too episodic and diffuse to provide many insights. A-II (PG) AA

Mini-Skirt Mob, The (1968) Honeymooning couple (Ross Hagen and Sherry Jackson) are terrorized by motorcycle gang in a tawdry action film directed by Maury Dexter. Excessive sadistic violence and sexual innuendo. O (br)

Ministry of Fear (1944) Moody version of Graham Greene's novel about an Englishman (Ray Milland) who stumbles onto a Nazi spy ring during the London Blitz, then finds himself framed for murder and on the run from the police. Directed by Fritz Lang, it's a nightmare situation with an innocent man uncertain of what he's gotten into or whom he can trust. Much menace, some stylized violence and murky references to a mercy killing. A-III (br) A

Minnie and Moskowitz (1972) Improbable romance of a zany parking-lot attendant (Seymour Cassel) and a museum assistant (Gena Rowlands), carried on in shouting matches throughout Los Angeles. Minnie with her history of failed masochistic relationships and Moskowitz with his utter lack of direction are so unsuited for each other that the ending is sheer Hollywood romantic fantasy. Director John Cassavetes in characteristic improvisational style has made a wry, harshly shot but warmly acted contemporary version of the old saw about the attraction between opposites. Some rough language and sexual references. A-III (PG) AA

Minute to Pray, a Second to Die, A (1968) Routine Italian western directed by Franco Giraldi about an outlaw hero (Alex Cord) who, fearing he has epilepsy, tries to go straight. Much standard violence. A-III (br)

Minx, The (1969) Sex exploitation movie about business executives planning a corporate merger during a stag weekend at a hunting lodge. Poorly staged and acted, it is punctuated with double crosses, orgies and voyeuristic fantasies. O (R)

Miracle, The (1991) A motherless teenager (Niall Byrne) in Bray, an Irish seaside resort town, finds himself strongly attracted to a visiting U.S. actress (Beverly D'Angelo) old enough to be his mother, despite the vehement objections of his alcoholic father (Donal McCann). Irish-born writer-director Neil Jordan's inconclusive melodrama toys with incest and is overwhelmed by its drawn-out predictability, though the setting and some nice performances provide marginal interest. Brief sexual encounter, occasional rough language and minor violence. A-III (R) 15

Miracle in Milan (1951) Marvellous Italian fable about an unspoiled youth (Francesco Golisano) who leaves the orphanage in which he was raised and, on the outskirts of post-World War II Milan, chances upon an encampment of homeless whose impoverished lives are transformed by his simple, unassuming joy of life. Directed by Vittorio de Sica, the movie looks beyond the miserable conditions of poverty to see the humanity of the poor, pokes satire at the rich and ends in the happy fantasy of a fairy tale. Subtitles. A-II (nr) U

Miracle Mile (1989) Writer-director Steve DeJarnatt's woefully ill-conceived story about a promising romance between two strangers (Anthony Edwards and Mare Winningham) loses its quirky appeal when it diverts from giddy romance to far-fetched doomsday thriller played out on the mean streets of Los Angeles. Much gratuitous, grisly violence exploiting the horror of a pending nuclear disaster and profanity laced with sexual vulgarities. O (R) 15

Miracle of Fatima (see: "The Miracle of Our Lady of Fatima").

Miracle of Love, The (1969) German sex-education movie that confuses providing information about sex with prolonged demonstrations of sexual behavior and the depiction of erotic fantasies. Worthless. O (X)

Miracle of Marcelino, The (1955) A foundling left at a Franciscan monastery in 19th-century Spain is spoiled by the attention of all the monks who raise him until, as a mischievous five-year-old (Pablito Calvo), the lad's disobedience leads to a miraculous encounter with the crucified Christ. Directed by Ladislao Vajda, the Spanish production's story of childhood innocence and the power of faith is told simply but with sincerity and good humor. Dubbed in English, the movie's miracle may tax the credibility of some, but all can enjoy its picture of a child in unusual circumstances. A-I (nr)

Miracle of Our Lady of Fatima, The (1952) When a young girl reports seeing a vision of the Blessed Mother in 1917 Portugal, she is harassed, then arrested by atheistic government officials but nothing can stop the crowds of faithful from coming to the site in expectation of a miracle. Directed by John Brahm, the religious story is treated with reverence yet is dramatically interesting with such characters as the good-hearted thief (Gilbert Roland) who helps her. Inspirational fare. A-I (br) U

Miracle of the Bells, The (1948) Sticky cardboard tale of a parish priest (Frank Sinatra) presiding over the burial of a former movie star in a played-out mining town where a media-hyped "miracle" rejuvenates the community. Director Irving Pichel stumbles through the contrived story until an unconvincing ending few will find inspirational. Good intentions but bogus results. A-I (br) A

Miracle of the White Stallions (1963) Disney drama about the World War II attempt to smuggle the Spanish Riding School's prize Lipizzaner stallions out of Vienna before the city is occupied by the Russians. Directed by Arthur Hiller, the precision riding sequences show the great training of these famed horses, though their evacuation by military trucks is delayed somewhat by a bloodless battle sequence at the Czech border. Worthwhile family fare. A-I (br)

Miracle on 34th Street (1947) Familiar seasonal favorite follows a department store Santa (Edmund Gwenn) as he strives to convince a lonely little girl (Natalie Wood) that he's the genuine article, despite the objections of her rigidly pragmatic mother (Maureen O'Hara) and a court trial that hinges on the U.S. Post Office. Director George Seaton's amusing romantic fantasy has its sentimental moments while spreading a reasonable amount of holiday cheer, largely due to Gwenn's charming performance as Kris Kringle. Problems of single parenthood. A-II (br) U

Mirage (1965) Gregory Peck plays an amnesia victim who is being stalked by a killer, Diane Baker is a woman out of his past, Walter Matthau is a private detective and, shrouded in the background, is a world peace organization. Directed by Edward Dmytryk, the ingredients of this suspense-filled puzzle may be familiar, but their solution is intriguing and nicely integrated in the N.Y. setting. A-II (br) A

Mirror Crack'd, The (1980) Agatha Christie mystery with Miss Marple (Angela Lansbury) solving a murder committed while an American movie company is on location in England. Despite a valiant cast (Tony Curtis, Rock Hudson, Kim Novak and Elizabeth Taylor), director Guy Hamilton fails to supply any pace, style or suspense to the proceedings. Some mild profanity and stylized violence. A-II (PG)

Misadventures of Mr. Wilt, The (1990) British black comedy about a Walter Mitty-like college professor (Griff Rhys Jones) caught in a bizarre set of circumstances involving his missing wife (Alison Steadman) and a dim-witted police inspector (Mel Smith) who's convinced that the prof has murdered her. Directed by Michael Tuchner, the farcical proceedings are intermittently amusing and have some wit, though much depends on one's tolerance for rude humor, saucy situations and outrageous misunderstandings caused mostly by an inflatable woman-sized doll of the sex-shop variety. Some rough language and sexual references. A-IV (nr)

Mischief (1985) The class nerd (Doug McKeon) and a cool newcomer (Chris Nash) team up to pursue girls in a small-town high school in 1950s' Ohio. Directed by Mel Damski, it's a sloppily executed affair in which all adults are depicted as semi-morons. Its idea of humor is obscene language and boys peering up girl's dresses. Excessively graphic bedroom scene. O (R)

Misery (1990) Injured in a car crash, a romance novelist (James Caan) is rescued by his Number One fan (Kathy Bates) who keeps him in her remote farmhouse and becomes his deadly tormentor. Stephen King's horror story becomes a tautly edited, gripping psychological thriller in the hands of director Rob Reiner, who coaxes top-notch performances from the chilling Bates, the terrorized Caan and a crafty sheriff (Richard Farnsworth). Climactic graphic violence and minimal rough language. A-III (R) 18

Misfits, The (1961) After getting a Reno divorce, a free but lonely woman (Marilyn Monroe) takes up with a cowboy (Clark Gable) and other inveterate loners (Eli Wallach, Montgomery Clift and Thelma Ritter), then is appalled by a round-up of wild horses. Written by Arthur Miller and directed by John Huston, the theme seems to have something to do with the fear of being trapped in romantic relationships, though the treatment is obscure, if not muddled. Some sexual inferences. A-III (br) PG

Mishima: A Life in Four Chapters (1985) Writer-director Paul Schrader attempts to do justice to the complex and flamboyant Japanese writer Yukio Mishima, who committed suicide by military ritual in 1970. The result is flat and listless, an illustrated slide lecture that doesn't come close to capturing the enigmatic Mishima. Brief nudity and violence. A-III (R) 15

Miss Firecracker (1989) Lifetime outcast (Holly Hunter), living in the shadow of her beautiful older cousin (Mary Steenburgen), tries to win her town's annual 4th of July beauty pageant. Adapted by Beth Henley from her play and directed by Thomas Schlamme, the result reveals an eye and ear for life lived off the beaten track in the Deep South. Its characters never lack dignity no matter how wacky or how unrealistic their hopes and dreams. Some sexual innuendo; minimal fisticuffs. A-III (PG)

Miss Grant Takes Richmond (1949) Dippy comedy in which a gambler (William Holden) hires a secretarial-school novice (Lucille Ball) as part of a cover operation, then is undone by her zeal to make good. Directed by Lloyd Bacon, the funny business with Ball's dumb but honest secretary is ably abetted by a solid supporting cast but the contrived situation becomes tiresome. Comic treatment of illegal activities. A-II (br) U

Miss Mary (1986) British governess (Julie Christie) recalls the years she spent in Buenos Aires caring for the children of a wealthy family. The real interest of this Argentinian production, directed by Maria Luisa Bemberg, is its depiction of the politically confused and socially demoralized climate prior to the Peron dictatorship. Mature themes including several sexual encounters. A-III (R) 15

Missing (1982) Director Costa-Gavras in his first American movie presents a taut and powerful drama based upon an actual event, that of an American father's search for his son, a 31-year-old writer living with his wife in a Latin American country, who has disappeared in the midst of the brutal repression following a right-wing coup. Jack Lemmon and Sissy Spacek are outstanding as the concerned father and his daughter-in-law, with John Shea giving capable support as the missing man. Significant and absorbing work on a topical and important theme of human rights. General atmosphere of menace, a depiction of the aftermath of bloodshed and occasional profanity. A-II (PG) AA

Missing in Action (1984) Chuck Norris stars in a hokey, derivative movie directed by Joseph Vito about a commando operation mounted to rescue Americans still held prisoner in Vietnam. Gene Hackman did it better in "Uncommon Valor." Graphic wartime violence, rough language and Asian stereotyping. A-III (R) 15

Missing in Action II: The Beginning (1985) In a sequel with even more violence than its violent predecessor, this time around the blank-faced hero (Chuck Norris) is a prisoner of war in Vietnam a few years prior to the original. Directed by Lance Hool, this run-of-the-mill war movie overdoses on graphic depictions of brutality and sadism. O (R) 18

Mission, The (1986) In the 1750s, the large and prosperous Jesuit Indian missions of South America were divided between Spain and Portugal. In retelling these events, Robert Bolt's screenplay focuses not on the religious but on the sociopolitical dimension of the colonial era and its injustices. The epic production is visually splendid, but Roland Joffe's direction is erratic and bogs down in contrasting a nonviolent priest (Jermey Irons) and one (Robert De Niro) who leads the Indians against a colonial army. Although flawed, the work recalls a past that provides a context for current Latin American struggles. Violence and ethnographic nudity. A-III (PG)

Missionary, The (1982) Writer-producer Michael Palin (of the Monty Python troupe) also stars as the Rev. Charles Fortescue, a missionary sent to the slums of London by his bishop (Denholm Elliot) to open up a home for fallen women, and with Lady Ames (Maggie Smith) as his patron, he has great success. Unfortunately, there is a rather snide quality to the comedy's religious and social criticism and there is one incredibly crude exchange between Mr. Fortescue and a tough prostitute. Some obscene language. O (R) 15

Mississippi (1935) Affable period melodrama with comedy supplied by W. C. Fields as a showboat captain and some Rodgers-and-Hart songs crooned by pistol-packing Bing Crosby who plays the Singing Killer. Director Edward Sutherland succeeds far better with Fields' comedy routines than Crosby's romantic problems with two sisters (Joan Bennett and Gail Patrick). Some comic violence. A-II (br)

Mississippi Burning (1988) Fictionalized version of the 1964 murder of three young civil rights activists in Mississippi focuses on the conflict between two FBI agents (Gene Hackman and Willem Dafoe) over how to handle the investigation. Director Alan Parker powerfully re-creates the brutal racist climate of the times, but the questionable vigilante tactics used to crack the case may confuse those unfamiliar with the real events. Unrelenting atmosphere of violence and racist rhetoric, together with much profanity. A-IV (R) 18

Mississippi Masala (1992) Upbeat interracial love story involving a young woman (Sarita Choudhury) with family roots in India and an enterprising African American (Denzel Washington) whose romance is opposed by the families and friends of both. Only a sluggish pace detracts from director Mira Nair's warm-hearted exploration of racial taboos and family values. Very brief bedroom scene with a flash of nudity, momentary violence and minimal rough language. A-III (R) 15

Mississippi Mermaid (1970) Disappointing French melodrama about the mail-order bride (Catherine Deneuve) of a rich planter in the tropics (Jean-Paul Belmondo) who proves to be an imposter when she cleans out his bank account and disappears—but not for very long. A minor effort from director Francois Truffaut, it pays tribute to the old Hollywood action adventures while at the same time satirizing them with an incredibly absurd plot made worse by being badly dubbed into English. For Truffaut fans only. Brief nudity. A-III (GP)

Missouri Breaks, The (1976) Jack Nicholson heads a band of rustlers and Marlon Brando is the ruthless killer hired to hunt them down. Director Arthur Penn's failed western is full of loose ends and fey dialogue, an embarrassing muddlement that lumbers to a brutal conclusion for want of anything better to do. Excessive violence. O (PG) 15

Mister Buddwing (1966) Forgettable melodrama about an amnesia victim (James Garner) whose career ambitions and marital woes are shown in flashbacks and dreams as his memory returns. Directed by Delbert Mann, the story is needlessly confusing in the use of three actresses in the role of his wife and the result doesn't add up to much. Mature sexual themes including abortion. A-III (br)

Mister Johnson (1991) In 1923 British colonial West Africa, a native clerk (Maynard Eziashi), who fancies himself a true English gentleman, wrecks his cherished relationship with his British boss (Pierce Brosnan) by his carefree thieving ways. Bruce Beresford directs a charmingly realized period piece full of wry observation of British colo-

nialism, but the effect is marred by some cardboard characters and ponderous pacing. Minimal stylized violence and some racial epithets. A-II (PG-13)

Mister Music (1950) Lackluster musical comedy directed by Richard Haydn concerns a lazy veteran songwriter (Bing Crosby) whose producer (Charles Coburn) hires a no-nonsense college grad (Nancy Olson) to oversee his work schedule, the result of which is a hit musical and a May-December romance. Silly romantic complications. A-II (br)

Mistress (1992) Flat satire of the movie business centers around the compromises made by a failed producer-director team (Martin Landau and Robert Wuhl) when three backers (Robert De Niro, Danny Aiello and Eli Wallach) of their proposed movie insist their girlfriends be given starring roles. Director Barry Primus' sluggish mix of comedy and drama is damaged by stale characterizations and lead actor Wuhl's dull performance. Much sexual innuendo and some rough language. A-III (R) 15

Misty (1961) The story of some children who fall in love with a wild horse captured on an island off the Atlantic coast is tinged with history and a respect for nature. Produced by Robert B. Radnitz and directed by James B. Clark, the movie is beautifully done, the youngsters appealing and the result is superior family entertainment. A-I (br) U

Misunderstood (1984) Gene Hackman plays a widower who is slow to come to terms with his loss and make a new life for himself and his two young sons (Henry Thomas and Huckleberry Fox). Director Jerry Schatzberg's picture is pleasant enough, with competent acting and exotic settings (Tunisia), but there are no dramatic sparks to speak of until a contrived tearjerker of an ending. Some vulgar language. A-II (PG)

Mitchell (1975) L.A. police detective (Joe Don Baker) pursues two suave lawyers (Martin Balsam; John Saxon) mixed up in the heroin trade by using unorthodox methods that look suspiciously like police brutality. Directed by Andrew V. McLaglen, it's a fairly silly, slapped-together affair whose thin plot is nothing more than an excuse to string together a series of routine chases. Most, but not all, of the rough stuff is kept off-camera, substituting instead some sexual exploitation scenes. O (R) A

Mixed Company (1974) Joseph Bologna and Barbara Harris star in a sentimental comedy drama about a couple who decide to augment their family, which already includes three children, with three more, each from a different race. Melville Shavelson directs a good-natured movie that carefully avoids any realistic situations of racial tension. Mildly entertaining, sometimes funny and touching, it seems like something made for television except for its strong language. A-III (PG)

Mo' Better Blues (1990) Self-absorbed jazz trumpeter (Denzel Washington) remains loyal to his inept manager (Spike Lee) while studiously avoiding commitment to either of his impatient lovers (Joie Lee and Cynda Williams) until his manager's gambling ways change all of their lives. Lee also produced, wrote and directed this tale of interwoven relationships that features Washington's finely shaded performance as a character who gradually comes to terms with his egotism. Much casual use of rough language, fairly explicit treatment of sexual relationships and a graphic scene of gut-wrenching violence. A-IV (R) 15

Mo' Money (1992) A con artist (Damon Wayans) disappoints his younger brother (Marlon Wayans) by taking a straight job at a credit card company to impress a girl (Stacey Dash), then gets involved in a bigtime scam ripping off the firm. Director Peter Macdonald's sluggish and predictable comedy pulverizes the work ethic while it exalts stealing as the only cool way to beat the system. Grand theft glamorized, some exploitative violence, sexist attitudes with implied encounters, recurring rough language and racial stereotyping. O (R)

Mobsters (1991) Glossy Prohibition-era gangster movie follows the bloody rise to power of young thugs Lucky Luciano, Meyer Lansky, Bugsy Siegel and Frank Costello (Christian Slater, Patrick Dempsey, Richard Grieco and Costas Mandylor) by murdering the two reigning dons (Anthony Quinn and Michael Gambon). Director Michael Karbelnikoff glamorizes the killers all through this humdrum rehash of far better gangster movies of yesteryear. Excessive violence, uncritical portrayal of murderers, much rough language, a restrained bedroom scene and occasional nudity. O (R)

Moby Dick (1956) Uneven adaptation of the Herman Melville classic follows the vengeful course of Captain Ahab (miscast Gregory Peck) in quest of the Great White Whale. Co-scripted by Ray Bradbury and director John Huston, it captures well the details of 19th-century whaling life but the voyage of the Pequod at the center of the story is curiously slack and largely uninvolving. Stylized violence. A-I (br) U

Model Shop, The (1969) French romantic drama about a brief encounter between an alienated Los Angeles dropout (Gary Lockwood) and an attractive model (Anouk Aimee) who takes him to bed, tells him her life story and he gives her money for her fare back to France. Though beautifully produced and mildly appealing, the movie lacks the charm and novelty of director Jacques Demy's earlier works and their unabashed romantic exuberance. A-III (PG) X

Modern Problems (1981) Chevy Chase plays an air traffic controller possessed of extrasensory powers that are put to no good use in a dreary, slipshod comedy that intersperses long boring stretches with only a few patches of fitful humor. Directed and co-written by Ken Shapiro, it has some vulgarity and incidental sexual byplay. A-III (PG)

Modern Romance (1981) Obsessive and insecure film editor (Albert Brooks) has an on-again, off-again relationship with his girlfriend (Kathryn Harrold), but he can't break this recurring cycle of misery. Also written and directed by Brooks, it is a sometimes very funny movie, but suffers from a lack of structure and too much Brooks. Still, two hilarious sequences in the cutting room might make some viewers willing to forgive the movie's frequent slow stretches. Some brief semi-nudity, occasional rough language and a muddled view of sexual morality. A-III (R) 15

Modern Times (1936) Written, produced and directed by Charles Chaplin, this insightful fable of man against machine features some of the great buffoons of the silent era and marks the last appearance of Chaplin's little tramp character. A model of comedic technique and refined slapstick humor, the movie deals with the consequences of industrialized society and the anxieties of Depression-era audiences as the little fellow dances his way through the hazards of a factory assembly line. For his final walk down the long empty road, Chaplin is accompanied by Paulette Goddard, who added an element of freshness to Chaplin's old-fashioned romance. A-I (G) U

Moderns, The (1988) Set in Paris in 1926, this romantic drama follows the travails of some American expatriates, chief among them a struggling painter (Keith Carradine), his estranged wife (Linda Fiorentino), her nouveau riche companion (John Lone) and a frustrated society columnist (Wallace Shawn). Director Alan Rudolph re-creates a wonderful sense of the period and the artistic milieu that flourished then. Some nudity, brief violence and implications of sexual hedonism. A-III (nr) 15

Modesty Blaise (1966) Monica Vitti, Terence Stamp and Dirk Bogarde in a plot about a shipment of diamonds that is merely an excuse for a series of impossible adventures and characters that parodys the cliches of popular culture. The opulent sets, costumes and gadgets are stylishly photographed and the dialogue and situations are outrageously exaggerated. Director Joseph Losey obviously enjoyed spoofing areas of the dark world that he has treated seriously so often before. A-III (br) PG

Mohammad, Messenger of God (1977) Dramatic re-creation of the years from A.D. 610, when Mohammad was driven from Mecca for claiming to have received a new religion from the Angel Gabriel, to A.D. 630 when the victory of Islam was assured. The best feature of this religious epic directed by Moustapha Akkad is its sincerity in recounting the birth of Islam and some of the essential tenets of the Moslem religion. An international cast includes Anthony Quinn, Irene Papas and Michael Ansara. Some scenes of restrained violence. A-II (PG) A

Molly (1950) When Molly Goldberg (Gertrude Berg) plays matchmaker, it threatens a business deal made by her husband Jake (Philip Loeb). Walter Hart directs the TV cast of "The Goldbergs," which began as a daytime radio serial about the domestic ups-and-downs of a loving Jewish family in the Bronx. Though its production values are rudimentary, its picture of family life still has charm. A-I (br)

Molly Maguires, The (1970) Fact-based, hard-hitting drama set in the Pennsylvania coal mining fields during the 1880s when the mine owners hire an undercover agent (Richard Harris) to ferret out the leaders (Sean Connery and Anthony Zerbe) of a secret band of miners known as the Molly Maguires who resort to terrorist tactics to force better pay and working conditions. Director Martin Ritt has made a thoughtful movie about the futility of using violence to redress injustices. More menace than bloodshed. A-II (PG)

Mom and Dad Save the World (1992) Silly sci-fi comedy about a far-distant planet's dictator (Jon Lovitz) who magnetically draws a suburban California couple (Teri Garr and Jeffrey Jones) to his kingdom planning to force the wife to marry him. A witless script and Greg Beeman's heavy-handed direction produce a contrived, artificial spoof that quickly fizzles. A few off-color references. A-II (PG)

Moment by Moment (1978) Middle-aged Beverly Hills housewife (Lily Tomlin) succumbs to the charms of a young drifter (John Travolta). Devoid of dramatic action, save for scenes of love-making punctuated by little spats of no consequence, writer-director Jane Wagner's movie has hardly a glimmer of wit, intelligence or credibility. Graphic and glossy depiction of adultery. O (R) AA

Mommie Dearest (1981) Faye Dunaway plays Joan Crawford in this unpleasant screen version of the harsh biography written by her adopted daughter, Christina. Director Frank Perry alternates heavy doses of sensation and sentimentality without really getting at anything that might make its subject credible. Only occasionally does the episodic and overlong movie rise above the level of verge-of-hysteria soap opera. Some brief but graphic violence, rough language and vulgarity. A-III (PG) 15

Mona Lisa (1986) Love-starved small-time tough (Bob Hoskins in a memorable performance) falls in love with the prostitute (Cathy Tyson) he chauffeurs around town, only to be victimized by his own blind trust and devotion. This British production's depiction of underworld violence, deception and betrayal leads nowhere. Brutal violence, brief nudity and some profanity. O (R) 18

Money Jungle, The (1968) Routine detective melodrama about a private-eye (John Ericson) who is hired to solve the mysterious murders of four geologists working aboard an offshore oil rig. Intriguing but predictable plot competently directed by Francis D. Lyon. Violence. A-III (br)

Money Man (1993) Documentary follows self-proclaimed artist J.S.G. Boggs as he painstakingly creates counterfeit currency which he then tries to get people to accept at face value, not as legal tender, but as a works of art. Writer-director Philip Haas looks at this dubious art form mainly through the perspective of Boggs, striking more of a whimsical note than a balanced look at whether he is in fact an artist or a con artist. Some morally ambiguous situations. A-III (nr)

Money, Money, Money (1973) Amusing but overlong French comedy about a ragtag band of con artists, petty thieves, bank robbers and other paunchy, middle-aged underworld types (among them, Lino Ventura, Jacques Brel and Charles Denner) adapt to changing times by turning to kidnapping political figures and extorting high ransoms from embarrassed governments. Directed by Claude Lelouch, the source of the comedy is how the inept misfits complement each other's foolishness and become so rich and successful that they themselves are kidnapped. The Gallic humor, including a Tahitian vacation among semi-clad native beauties, may escape some viewers. A-III (PG)

Money Pit, The (1986) A young engaged couple (Tom Hanks and Shelley Long) buy a mansion and suffer humorous consequences when trying to fix it up. The strained comedy resorts to heavy doses of slapstick and the deteriorating condition of the house comes to mirror their increasingly exasperated relationship. Some sexually suggestive scenes are handled within the context of their successful efforts to build trust and strengthen commitment. A-II (PG)

Money Talks (1972) Using the same formula as his popular "Candid Camera" TV show, director Allen Funt presents a series of trite sketches and allegedly spontaneous routines designed to show how ordinary people react to situations involving money. Among the offerings, one can watch men pluck, with varying degrees of hesitancy, a dollar bill taped to the backside of a sweet young thing, or listen to Funt interview his pretty three-year-old daughter, who openly exhibits a preference for being rich. At least she's candid about it. A-II (PG)

Monique (1970) British exploitation film about a French *au pair* girl (Sibylla Kay) hired to care for a young couple's boisterous children and instead seduces first the husband, then the wife and finally the trio wind up in bed together. Low-budget production directed by John Brown, it contains nudity in a sexual context. O (X/R)

Monitors, The (1969) Failed satire about a police force of the future that relies on thought control to bring peace and order in a society beset by violence, brutality and rapaciousness. Directed by Jack Shea, a talented cast headed by Guy Stockwell, Susan Oliver and Keenan Wynn try desperately but fail to find anything humorous in a plot both tedious and inane. A-III (M)

Monkey Business (1931) The four Marx Brothers (Groucho; Chico; Harpo; Zeppo) cause all manner of havoc as stowaways aboard an ocean liner and even more among some gangsters ashore. Directed by Norman Z. McLeod, the manic absurdity of the wacky sight gags and verbal mayhem keep the nonsensical situation from growing tiresome. Slapstick comedy and zany dialogue, including absurd double entendres. A-I (br) U

Monkey Hustle, The (1977) Black exploitation comedy about some supposedly lovable con artists who rally an inner-city neighborhood threatened by highway construction. Director Arthur Marks gets some good acting (Yaphet Kotto, Rosalind Cash, Kirk Calloway and Randy Brooks) but not much else. Some rough language and a frank treatment of sexual matters. A-III (PG)

Monkey Shines: An Experiment in Fear (1988) Director George Romero's attempt to upgrade his exploitation image flops with this tasteless effort that sees a lab-tortured monkey turn killer after being trained to serve the needs of a paraplegic (Jason Beghe). Graphic injection scenes, grisly murders and mayhem, much menace and an explicit kinky sex scene. O (R) 18

Monkeys Go Home (1967) Disney comedy in which ex-GI Dean Jones inherits an olive farm in France, retrains four Space Program astro-chimps to help out when a shortage of local olive pickers develops and outwits a conniving real estate man with the aid of a refreshing lass (Yvette Mimieux) and the village priest (Maurice Chevalier). Andrew V. McLaglen directs a slapdash plot with monkeyshines galore that will appeal more to youngsters than their parents. A-I (br) U

Monsieur Hire (1990) Intriguing psychological puzzler about a pathetic loner (Michel Blanc) who spends his nights spying on a young woman (Sandrine Bonnaire) in an apartment across the way, but when he meets and falls in love with her, the results are tragic. Directed by Patrice Leconte, the French production subtly unfolds a strange, obsessive love story that starts with a murder investigation and ends plumbing the depths of a desperate soul. Subtitles. Mature themes in a highly charged erotic atmosphere. A-III (PG-13) 15

Monsieur Verdoux (1947) Written, directed and produced by Charles Chaplin, the fact-based black comedy stars Chaplin in the title role as a French Bluebeard who marries women and then murders them for their money. Though his first serious role understandably disappointed audiences of its day, Chaplin as a performer was never better in the subtlety of gesture and expression. There is much sharp wit in the action but also some great slapstick, notably from Martha Raye who proves impervious to all murderous stratagems. Subtitled "A Comedy of Murder," the movie is a critical statement about the hypocrisy of society, neither cynical nor nihilistic, but attempts to punctuate a serious message with humor. A-III (nr) A

Monsignor (1982) Christopher Reeve plays an American priest with a graduate degree in finance who rises in the church hierarchy when he gets the Vatican involved with the Mafia, but who pauses on the ladder of success to have an affair with a Carmelite postulant (Genevieve Bujold). Directed by Frank Perry, the film's melodramatic account of an ambitious cleric is so simple-mindedly wrong-headed that it would be howlingly funny if it were not so grossly insulting to clergymen and institutional religion. Some gratuitous nudity. O (R) 15

Monster in a Box (1992) Monologuist Spalding Gray relates how writer's block chained him to a monster—the huge, autobiographical manuscript which he toted around for years before completing. As directed by Nick Broomfield, writer Gray's darkly funny one-man show generally overcomes the limitations of its form to engage audiences with lively storytelling and sharp observations. Mild sexual innuendo and references to his mother's suicide. A-II (PG-13)

Monster Squad, The (1987) Pre-teens foil Count Dracula's attempt to destroy an amulet bearing positive energy in this visually stunning mock horror flick from writer-director Fred Dekker. Lots of fun and frolic but explosively realistic demise of the monsters may chill the very young. A-II (PG-13) 15

Monster Zero (1970) Routine Japanese science-fiction fantasy in which the title monster, Ghidrah, teamed with Godzilla and Rodan, attempt to conquer Earth for their masters on Planet X while Nick Adams leads a force of astronauts out to stop them. Directed by Inoshiro Honda, the movie's special effects will hold the attention of young viewers while grown-ups will chuckle at the anthropomorphic monsters. A-I (G)

Monte Walsh (1970) Once the Wild West was tamed, cowboys like Monte Walsh (Lee Marvin) found it hard to adapt to the demands of society. Jeanne Moreau and Jack Palance join Marvin in strong performances in a seriocomic study of ordinary cowpokes put out of work by a changing cattle industry that director William Fraker makes interesting despite a weak and aimless script with a hopelessly melodramatic climax. Some Hollywood heroics featuring fist fights and gun play. A-III (PG) A

Monterey Pop (1969) Eye-staggering, ear-popping souvenir of the June 1967 Monterey Music Festival briefly captures the spirit of an age and a generation. The performers include The Mamas and the Papas, Jefferson Airplane, The Who, Janis Joplin, Jimi Hendrix and Ravi Shankar, who closes the concert with his extraordinary sitar playing. Some sexually suggestive lyrics and gestures. A-III (nr) A

Monty Python and the Holy Grail (1975) Departing from their BBC television format of unconnected skits, the Python comedy troupe zero in on the single subject of King Arthur and his dim-witted knights of the roundabout table. As directed by the Python's Terry Gilliam and Terry Jones, the episodic narrative strings together a series of gags, most of which are allowed to cross the threshold of boredom and then are repeated to test one's patience further. Their brand of irreverent humor is an acquired taste, appealing to those who can find amusement in the concept of a feisty knight whose extremities are being lopped off one by one gamely urging a superior but reluctant opponent to fight on. Comic violence and sexual references. A-III (PG) 15

Monty Python's The Meaning of Life (1983) The Python troupe (John Cleese; Terry Gilliam; Eric Idle; Michael Palin; Terry Jones, who also directed) breaks new ground, not in terms of satire, but of grossness for its own sake. There are indeed some very funny moments, but much of it is vile bile, the product of bright, well-bred but naughty boys who bear a lot of minor grudges, but lack the satiric ability to do a proper job on their targets. Graphic nudity and an attack on formal religion. O (R) 15

Moon Over Parador (1988) American actor in a Caribbean country (Richard Dreyfuss), strong-armed by the local chief of police (Raul Julia) into impersonating its newly deceased dictator, soon grows to love the power trip and the dead leader's mistress (Sonia Braga). Writer-director Paul Mazursky never quite decides whether he's making a slapstick comedy about the acting profession or a satire about Latin American politics with unfocused and unfunny results. Lusty, clothed bedroom scene and other sexual innuendo played for laughs. A-III (PG-13) 15

Moon Zero Two (1969) British science-fiction yarn in which a woman (Catherine von Schell) enlists the aid of a space pilot (James Olson) to find her brother who is missing from his mining claim on the moon. Directed by Roy Ward Baker, the plot is that of a conventional claim-jumping western with good special effects and little violence. A-II (G) U

Moonlighting Mistress (1972) Wolfgang Becker directs an English-dubbed German exploitation movie about a husband who underestimates his wife's cleverness when he conspires with his mistress to murder her. O (R)

Moonraker (1979) British agent James Bond (Roger Moore) teams up with a CIA operative (Lois Chiles) to save the world from a deadly shower launched from outer space by a madman (Michael Lonsdale). Director Lewis Gilbert offers the usual Bond fare with the usual mix of stylized sex and violence. A-III (PG)

Moonshine War, The (1970) Internal revenue agent Patrick McGoohan and a murderous gang led by Richard Widmark go after poor country moonshiner Alan Alda who has inherited 150 barrels of perfect "white lightning" from his dear departed dad. Director Richard Quine conveys a sense of Depression-era nostalgia but heavy-handedly injects farcial sex vignettes and a slapstick parody of mass killing to conclude a pointless plot. AIII (PG) AA

Moonstruck (1987) Charming romantic comedy set in an Italian-American neighborhood in Brooklyn where a widow (Cher) accepts the proposal of a fastidious bachelor (Danny Aiello) but falls in love with his darkly emotional younger brother (Nicolas Cage). Director Norman Jewison concentrates more on the comedy of character than on incident and the result is pleasantly amusing, emotionally operatic and humanly uplifting. Several restrained scenes implying sex, but the movie's moral perspective is implicit throughout. A-III (PG)

Moonwalk One (1973) Documentary recording man's first visit to the moon on Apollo II in 1969 is first-rate in explaining the technology of space flight, as well as imparting some of the wonderment and sense of history involved in this accomplishment. NASA-produced film, directed by Theo Kamecke, is a fine tribute to a scientific achievement that is truly awesome. A-I (G)

More (1969) Drug and sex melodrama about a German student's progressive addiction from marijuana to heroin to LSD and his fatal love affair with an attractive American woman. Director Barbet Schroeder never gets beyond a surface rendering of the descent into the world of addiction, using it mainly as a pretext to portray unnecessarily explicit scenes of sex and perversion. O (nr)

More American Graffiti (1979) Auto racing, Vietnam combat, peace demonstrations and Flower Children constitute the four facets of the sequel whose characters are now a few years older, have gone their separate ways but have still kept in touch. The acting (Bo Hopkins; Ron Howard; Candy Clark; Paul Le Mat) is quite good, but director B.W.L. Norton's effort seems simply to trade on late-1960s' nostalgia without any of the wit and feeling of the original. Some rough language, the use of drugs and the shallow treatment of serious issues, such as the Vietnam conflict. A-III (PG) AA

More Dead Than Alive (1969) Standard western about a notorious gunfighter (Clint Walker) who gives up his trade by becoming a sharpshooter in a travelling sideshow (run by Vincent Price) but is gunned down by the son of one of his former victims. Directed by Robert Sparr, the melodrama's anti-violence message is unconvincing, especially in view of its excessively gory visual effects. A-III (PG) X

More Than a Miracle (1967) Uneven Italian-French romance set in the 17th century in which a Spanish prince (Omar Sharif) marries a Cinderella (Sophia Loren), with witches and saints helping matters along. The episodic storyline with none-too-noble nobles and the all-too-common commoners, the bawdy earthiness of a few incidents and director Francesco Rosi's association of witchcraft with religion makes it all pretty hard to swallow. A-III (br)

Morgan! (1966) Young London nonconformist (David Warner), likeable but hard to understand, tries to win back his estranged wife (Vanessa Redgrave) but increasingly gets lost in his own fantasies, shown by scenes from old movies and camera effects. Director Karel Reisz has achieved a strange mixture of comedy and social comment, effectively brought off by the fine performances of the principals. A-III (br)

Morgan Stewart's Coming Home (1987) Jon Cryer is the wise son and Lynn Redgrave is the overly sophisticated, domineering mother and political power-broker who make a loving compromise when the family is duped by the father's unscrupulous campaign manager in director Alan Smithee's comedy of manners and teen coming-of-age story. Two shower-room sight gags and some concluding rough language are brief and restrained comic asides in this movie that shows that patience and understanding help rebuild family ties. A-II (PG-13)

Morire Gratis (1969) Italian production about a sculptor (Franco Angeli) driving a load of narcotics from Rome to Paris and the woman he picks up along the way (Karen Blanguernon). Director Sandro Franchina prepares for the journey's inevitable tragic ending with a number of scenes of violence encountered along the way. Though it raises moral questions, it lacks depth and its perspective tends to be pessimistic. A-IV (nr)

Morituri (1965) Murky World War II espionage thriller about an unwilling German pacifist (Marlon Brando) forced by a British agent (Trevor Howard) to undertake the disablement of a Nazi freighter (captained by Yul Brynner) on the high seas. Director Bernhard Wicki gets plenty of tension aboard ship but never seems quite certain whether he's making an action picture or some kind of allegorical statement on war. Stylized violence, drug use and sexual situtions. A-III (br)

Morning After, The (1986) A fading actress (Jane Fonda), prone to one-night stands and alcoholic blackouts, wakes up one morning in bed with a dead man. Director Sidney Lumet's thriller solves the murder mystery, but it's a rather empty exercise in style without substance. Implied sex and some rough language. A-III (R) 15

Mortal Thoughts (1991) Two best friends (Demi Moore; Glenne Headly) come under close scrutiny by a police detective (Harvey Keitel) when they try to cover up the accidental killing of one's husband (Bruce Willis). Fine acting generally compensates for director Alan Rudolph's unduly drawn-out suspense movie of female friendship and betrayal. Some gory violence, abuse of women and much rough language. A-III (R) 15

Moscow on the Hudson (1984) Robin Williams stars as a jazz-playing Russian musician who falls in love with a department store salesclerk and finds a safe haven and the American Dream in New York City. Somewhat funny and vulnerable performance by Williams fails to save director Paul Mazursky's comic study of defection and exile in a movie that resorts to some nude bedroom scenes to heat up the action. O (R) 15

Moses (1976) Theatrical version of a European television mini-series on the Book of Exodus has serious shortcomings in its level of acting, especially Burt Lancaster's soporific performance as Moses, as well as in the script's plodding rationalizations of the appearance of the divine in human events. Directed by Gianfranco De Bosio, the dramatization is unconvincing; its secular interpretation of the Bible story lacks depth; its spectacle is low-budget and unimaginative. Some brief but graphic violence. A-III (PG)

Mosquito Coast, The (1986) Dissatisfied with the ills of modern civilization, an American intellectual (Harrison Ford) takes his family to a tropical wilderness but finds that life in this new Eden is no better than that which he fled. Adapted from Paul Theroux's novel and directed by Peter Weir, the movie's rather cynical outlook makes it less entertaining than thought-provoking fare. Mature themes. A-III (PG) 15

Mosquito Squadron (1970) World War II adventure with David McCallum leading a squadron of RAF fighter-bombers across the channel to destroy the Nazi center developing a super V-2 rocket and save one bomb to open up the POW-packed chateau next door. Director Boris Sagal handles the heroics as melodramatically as possible so that even the model planes used in re-creating the air battles seem to be overacting. A-I (G)

Most Beautiful Age, The (1970) Low-keyed Czechoslovakian drama about the generation gap in various levels of society, set in a sculpture studio where the interplay between students, teachers, models and visitors occasion humorous, ironic, and even tragic observations on the human condition. Director Jaroslav Papousek has an eye for detail that lends substance and depth to the film and makes it a rewarding entertainment. Mature themes. A-III (nr) U

Motel Hell (1980) Totally unappetizing horror film with Rory Calhoun as a motel keeper whose sideline is selling smoked meat made out of humans whose vocal cords have been cut while being fattened before butchering. The grisly horror story is made all the more repugnant because director Kevin Connor apparently thinks it's a comedy. Excessively graphic violence and some nudity. O (R) 18

Mother (see: "The Toy Grabbers").

Mother and the Whore, The (1974) Provocative French drama about the self-deceptions of a pseudo-intellectual (Jean-Pierre Leaud) who, though kept by an older woman (Bernadette Lafont), gets involved with a young nurse (Francoise Lebrun) bent on marriage. The ambivalent, shifting relationships between the three are seen as basically dishonest, showing especially the man as a perpetual adolescent torn between the two aspects of the title. Director Jean Eustache has chosen a documentary approach to his material, filming in the less fashionable bistros and tenements frequented by his characters, using rough street language and explicit depiction of sexual relationships, challenging viewers about the contradictions of modern life-styles. A-IV (nr)

Mother, Jugs & Speed (1976) Bill Cosby, Raquel Welch and Harvey Keitel respectively play the title characters in a failed comedy about a private ambulance service on the verge of bankruptcy and locked in a frantic rivalry with a competing service. Director Peter Yates stages some spectacular scenes of violent action, but none of it comes off as particularly amusing. Crude, tasteless and vulgar, especially in its sexual references. O (PG)

Mother Teresa (1986) Feature documentary by Ann and Jeanette Petrie on the life and work of a Catholic nun in India whose tireless efforts for the poorest of the poor have earned her the Nobel Peace Prize and recognition as a media star and secular saint. Inspirational portrait of a contemporary woman. A-I (nr)

Mother's Day (1980) Bloody shocker about a demented mother and her two cretinous sons who wreak all sorts of horrors on three young women. Poorly written and amateurishly directed by Charles Kaufman, it features excessively graphic violence and some nudity. O (PG)

Mountain Family Robinson (1979) After building a cabin on a mining claim in the Colorado Rockies, the family is informed that unless they mine their claim, they will lose their home. Though director John Cotter's simplistic plotting and saccharine characters are overly familiar, its vistas of nature and abundance of wildlife will satisfy young viewers. A-I (G) U

Mountain Men, The (1980) Charlton Heston plays a trapper who has outlived his era with the decline of the fur trade and arrival of wagon trains of settlers in the Old West. Richard Lang's leaden direction of a cliched script centering on a Blackfoot warrior's attempt to revenge himself on the trapper for taking his squaw flounders in graphic violence, an extended rape scene and foul-mouthed profanity. O (R) 15

Mountain Road, The (1960) James Stewart plays a demolitions expert who tries to block a Japanese offensive in 1944 China by blowing up a refugee-clogged road. Directed by Daniel Mann, the story is earnest and well-crafted but rather pointless. Stylized violence. A-II (br) U

Mountains of the Moon (1990) Epic docudrama recounts the 19th-century expeditions to discover the source of the Nile made by British explorers Richard Burton (Patrick Bergin) and John Hanning Speke (Iain Glen). Director Bob Rafelson's period piece ably reflects the obsession of the explorers and the beauty as well as savagery of the African wilderness. Its masterful mix of entertainment, education and biography may be accessible for older adolescents, though integrated in the context are intense scenes of violence, some nudity and an implication of homosexuality. A-III (R) 15

Mouse and His Child, A (1978) Animated feature about the adventures of a mechanical mouse and his son in the forbidding world outside of their toy store where their friends help them defeat their chief persecutor, a rat (voiced by Peter Ustinov), and gain self-winding status. Directed by Fred Wolf, the movie has its bright and clever moments, but is too often serious, if not downright somber, with many of the jokes and references not at all relevant for youngsters and too juvenile for adults. A-I (G)

Mouse That Roared, The (1959) Wry British comedy about the tiny, bankrupt duchy of Grand Fenwick whose prime minister (Peter Sellers) convinces the Grand Duchess (also Sellers) to declare war on the U.S., then surrender and accept post-war aid. Director Jack Arnold keeps the comic premise bubbling along as Fenwick's general (Sellers again), unaware of the plan, invades New York and captures a scientist's new secret weapon. The political satire is less amusing today but Sellers' triple performance and the clever sight gags are as funny as ever. A-I (br) U

Move (1970) Dim-witted comedy about a professional dog-walker and occasional porno pulp writer (Elliott Gould), in the midst of moving wife (Paula Prentiss), St. Bernard and their belongings to another apartment, dashes headlong from one unfunny noncrisis to another, including a casual dalliance with a model (Genevieve Waite). Directed by Stuart Rosenberg, the vulgar level of humor reaches rock bottom with a shot of Gould urinating in the kitchen sink to spite the landlord. Sexual references and nudity. O (R) X

Movers and Shakers (1985) A limp satire on Hollywood movie making, written and produced by actor Charles Grodin (who also stars) and directed by William Asher. Some mild vulgarities and some tasteless humor. A-II (PG-13) 15

Movie, Movie (1978) Producer-director Stanley Donen has contributed a comic valentine to 1930s Hollywood movies by re-creating a modern version of the era's double features, pairing a black-and-white boxing melodrama and a musical in color, using virtually the same cast for both (George C. Scott, Trish Van Devere, Eli Wallach, Art Carney and others). The gentle parody captures well the innocent fantasies of a less sophisticated age, not to make fun of past movie conventions but to enjoy them in a more knowing way. Some ring violence and a sensuous nightclub dance. A-II (PG) A

Moving Violations (1985) The feeble premise for director Neal Israel's failed comedy is the gathering together of some diverse types who must attend driving school to get back their licenses. Emphasis on sexually oriented humor. O (PG-13) 15

Mr. & Mrs. Bridge (1990) Fascinating portrait of a World War II-era, uppercrust Kansas City family, dominated by a rigidly narrow-minded father (Paul Newman) whose submissive wife (Joanne Woodward) is at a loss to draw emotional warmth from her husband or three grown children. Director James Ivory's film is a minor masterpiece of superb characterizations and extraordinary performances, accentuated by fine dialogue and rich imagery. Instances of promiscuity and fleeting shot of female nude photos. A-III (PG-13) PG

Mr. Baseball (1992) When a fading major league player (Tom Selleck) is traded to a Japanese team, his flippant attitudes antagonize his new club's team-spirited manager (Ken Takakura) and the player's fiery girlfriend (Aya Takanashi). Fred Schepisi directs a comedy of clashing cultures that drops the ball with its superficially developed one-joke premise. Some subtitles. Benign attitude toward premarital sex, a few off-color references and some male rear nudity. A-III (PG-13)

Mr. Billion (1976) Poor Italian mechanic (Terence Hill) inherits the controlling interest in a vast American corporation, provided he can reach San Francisco by a certain day. Villainous Jackie Gleason hires Valerie Perrine to impede him, but, predictably enough, she switches sides. Pleasant and diverting, if more than slightly sappy, comedy directed by Jonathan Kaplan. Some limited violence. A-II (PG) A

Mr. Blandings Builds His Dream House (1948) Wry view of postwar middle-class yearnings as seen in the rising discontent of a $15,000-a-year Madison Avenue executive (Cary Grant) and his wife (Myrna Loy) at life with two daughters in a cramped four-room city apartment and their escalating woes after they decide to move to a country house in Connecticut. Director H.C.

Potter's droll satire of a first-time property owner's bewildered encounters with real-estate agents, architects and contractors has plenty of funny business, compounded by the know-it-all comments of the family's lawyer and bachelor friend (Melvyn Douglas). Domestic squabbles and misunderstandings. A-II (br) A

Mr. Deeds Goes to Town (1936) When a small-town writer of greeting-card verses (Gary Cooper) inherits a fortune, he moves to New York City where he is made into a front page laughingstock by a two-timing reporter (Jean Arthur) and his plans to help the poor embroil him in a sanity hearing. Director Frank Capra deftly juggles romance and humor in this entertaining Depression-era tale of an ordinary American whose home-spun virtues triumph over big-city cynicism and greed. A-II (nr)

Mr. Destiny (1990) Anemic fantasy about an average Joe (Jim Belushi) whose life is magically reinvented by a bartender (Michael Caine) so that suddenly he finds himself wealthy, married to the prom queen and, as the despised president of a business, longing for his old life. Sluggishly directed by James Orr, the flat comedy is harmless but insipid entertainment without wit, grace or mirth. Minor stylized violence, mild sexual innuendo and a few vulgar expressions. A-II (PG-13) PG

Mr. Jones (1993) Downbeat drama in which a manic-depressive (Richard Gere) resists taking medication or opening up to a psychiatrist (Lena Olin) who unprofessionally allows herself to fall in love with him. Gere's nuanced performance elicits much sympathy for those afflicted with mental illness, but the point of director Mike Figgis' uneven movie is unclear and further muddled by the glossy romance between doctor and patient. Fleeting violence, a suicide, sexual innuendo and frequent rough language. A-III (R)

Mr. Klein (1977) French drama about a dealer in art objects (Alain Delon) who buys family heirlooms from Jews needing cash to escape the Nazi terror, but then he himself is mistaken for a Jew and handed over to the Germans, as were 13,000 others on what is known as Black Thursday, July 16, 1942. Directed with great sensitivity by Joseph Losey, it is exceptional in viewing the Holocaust as a universal experience, as meaningful to gentiles as to Jews. The nature of the theme, and some incidental nudity, make this a film for serious viewers. A-III (PG) A

Mr. Love (1986) In this quirky British romance a timid gardener (Barry Jackson) who is caught in an unhappy 28-year marriage decides he must find love at least once before he dies. Director Roy Battersby's gentle satire implies that the self-indulgence of one's passions justifies infidelity. Romanticization of immoral behavior. O (PG-13)

Mr. Majestyk (1974) Charles Bronson stars as an embattled ex-convict determined to protect his farm from the inroads of mob-instigated labor problems. Director Richard Fleischer helps divert attention from an overly familiar story by making the most of the scenic Colorado hills and desert locations. Some violence; strong language. A-III (PG) X

Mr. Mom (1983) When a father of three (Michael Keaton) loses his job, he takes over the household chores while his wife (Teri Garr) goes back to work. In handling the comic complications of the role-reversal plot, director Stan Dragoti is helped greatly by the likeable leads who manage to turn saccharine-coated problems into genial comedy. Toys with but firmly rejects several plot lines leading toward infidelity. A-II (PG)

Mr. North (1988) Smarty-pants Yale grad (Anthony Edwards) raises havoc among the wealthy citizens of 1926 Newport, R.I., because of his peculiar talent for giving electric shocks. Based on Thornton Wilder's last novel, the breezy, technically uneven movie is directed by Danny Huston, son of the late director, John Huston, who is credited as producer. Lively character performances but some vulgar references. A-II (PG)

Mr. Quilp (1975) Uninspired British musical version of Charles Dickens "The Old Curiosity Shop" about the villainous usurer, Quilp (Anthony Newley), the put-upon Little Nell and her improvident grandfather (David Warner). Directed by Michael Tuchner, it is a colorless, undistinguished effort that substitutes sweetness and light for Dickens' gritty melodrama. It may divert the very young but won't satisfy their older siblings and parents. A-I (G) U

Mr. Ricco (1975) Routine police thriller about a San Francisco lawyer (Dean Martin) who gets his client off a murder rap but comes to regret it when he winds up in the middle between the authorities and a black activist cell. Directed by Paul Bogart, the movie has some suspense, occasionally clever dialogue and a good supporting cast, but there's nothing here that hasn't been seen before. A-III (PG) AA

Mr. Saturday Night (1992) Bittersweet comedy traces the career of a caustic, stand-up comedian (Billy Crystal) whose insatiable need for center stage hurts his neglected family and brother-manager (David Paymer). Also produced and directed by Crystal, despite many good comic moments, it proves a long haul with a nasty central character who stubbornly resists insights until the overly sentimental ending. Some rough language, minor violence and numerous off-color jokes. A-III (R) 15

Mr. Smith Goes to Washington (1939) Classic piece of Americana in which an idealistic junior Senator (James Stewart) stages a one-man filibuster to stop the corrupt machinations of his political mentor (Claude Rains). Director Frank Capra's paean to American democracy has a solid plot, fine acting from a memorable cast, including Jean Arthur and Thomas Mitchell, as well as a lot of heartfelt patriotic sentiment that few will find dated. A-II (br) U

Mr. Wonderful (1993) Flat romantic tale of a cash-strapped blue-collar worker (Matt Dillon) seeking to set up his ex-wife (Annabella Sciorra) with eligible men in hopes of ending his alimony payments, though they secretly still care for each other. Director Anthony Minghella's contrived movie limps along to its forgone conclusion while relying on lame stereotypes of its Italian-Catholic characters. Implied sexual encounters, a violent workplace accident and occasional rough language. A-III (PG-13) 12

Mrs. Brown, You've Got a Lovely Daughter (1968) Delightful British comedy in which some working-class youths turn to performing professionally to support a racing greyhound, named Mrs. Brown, whose puppy gets lost during an unfortunate expedition to London. The plot, however, is only a nonsensical peg on which to hang a number of pleasant songs by the teenage pop singing group, Herman's Hermits, who here display some irresistible high spirits plus an offbeat decency and good sense. A-I (br) U

Mrs. Doubtfire (1993) Limited by court order to seeing his three children only once a week, a resourceful father (Robin Williams) disguises himself as a matronly British housekeeper, gets hired by his estranged wife (Sally Field), then tries to dissuade her from romance with a wealthy former beau (Pierce Brosnan). Directed by Chris Columbus, the sweet but one-joke comedy is carried by Williams who manages to make the zany situation both hilarious and heartfelt. Frequent though mild sexual innuendo. A-II (PG-13)

Mrs. Pollifax: Spy (1971) Rosalind Russell plays a woman free of family commitments who satisfies a lifelong ambition to become a spy by joining the CIA and winding up imprisoned with accomplice Darren McGavin on an Albanian mountain top from which she must effect a daring escape. Director Leslie Martin-son's adventure spoof is laced with warm humor and clever situations and features a winsome performance by its star in her last screen appearance. A-II (G)

Mrs. Soffel (1985) Turn-of-the-century story about a woman (Diane Keaton), married to a prison warden (Edward Herrmann), who falls in love with a condemned convict (Mel Gibson) and helps him escape.

Director Gillian Armstrong's powerful, well-acted movie balances sympathy for its doomed principals with a clear-eyed depiction of the devastation caused by the wife's betrayal of her family and herself. Adultery, though clearly depicted as wrong, is a major plot element. A-IV (PG-13) PG

Much Ado About Nothing (1993) While a pair of tart-tongued sparring partners (Kenneth Branagh and Emma Thompson) are tricked into confessing mutual love, the wedding of two other lovebirds (Robert Sean Leonard and Kate Beckinsale) seems doomed when the maiden is falsely accused of foul betrayal. Director Branagh's screen adaptation of Shakespeare's lusty comedy is a fresh and playful romp over the rocky road to love, enhanced by period Italian countryside settings and a breathless pace culminating in a heady tribute to chastity and marital vows. Brief group nudity and a fleeting bedroom scene. A-III (PG-13) PG

Muhair (1970) Argentinian sex melodrama with Isabel Sarli as the object of passion and antagonism between a father and son. Exploitative nudity. O (nr)

Mummy, The (1959) Slack British remake of the 1932 original about the vengeance taken by a 4,000-year-old mummy (Christopher Lee) on the archeologists (notably Peter Cushing) who violated the tomb of which it was the guardian. Directed by Terence Fisher, the narrative plods along with little action or tension until the mummy shows up in 1898 England. Some stylized violence and menace. A-II (br) X

Mummy's Shroud, The (1967) Plodding horror film directed by John Gilling follows the fate of a 1920 British expedition after it returns to Cairo with the remains of a pharaoh's son. Intermittent hokey menace with the usual stylized violence. A-II (br) X

Mumsy, Nanny, Sonny and Girly (1970) The odd quartet of the title live in an out-of-the-way Victorian mansion to which they lure unsuspecting strangers to play "games" with them that end in their being murdered in one ghoulish way or another. British horror movie directed by Freddie Francis, it lacks any story development or suspense, fails to elicit sympathy for its looney protagonists and falls flat as comedy, though the dialogue is frequently unintentionally amusing. Violence. A-III (R) X

Munster Go Home (1966) Big screen version of a popular TV horror comedy series in which the Munster family inherit a English manor but have to eject the gang of counterfeiters occupying it. Earl Bellamy directs the TV cast (Fred Gwynne, Yvonne De Carlo, Al Lewis) with less attention to the plot than the gags. Mildly entertaining but mostly for the show's fans. A-I (br)

Muppet Christmas Carol, The (1992) In this sprightly version of Charles Dickens' "A Christmas Carol," Muppets Kermit, Miss Piggy, the Great Gonzo, Rizzo the Rat and Fozzie Bear have incidental roles as Michael Caine portrays skinflint Ebenezer Scrooge, who is visited by the spirits of Christmas Past, Present and Future so he can learn the true spirit of Christmas. Director Brian Henson retells the holiday classic with delightful musical numbers, though with less frenzied fun than the usual Muppet outings. A-I (G) U

Muppet Movie, The (1979) After a chance encounter with a Hollywood talent scout Dom DeLuise, Kermit the Frog abandons his soggy swamp for a movie career, taking the entire Muppet crew on a heart-warming cross-country jaunt, but it is Miss Piggy who saves the day by getting Kermit his Hollywood audition. In their first appearance on the big screen, Jim Henson's Muppet characters seem right at home and director James Frawley's location filming gives them the world as a stage. Charming and delightful entertainment for all. A-I (G) U

Muppets Take Manhattan, The (1984) Kermit and Miss Piggy emulate Mickey Rooney and Judy Garland in this spoof of old-time Hollywood musicals. Under Frank Oz's direction, the third screen outing of Jim Henson's Muppets offers some highly entertaining musical numbers, much witty comedy and a lot of fun. Highly recommended for family viewing. A-I (G) U

Murder Ahoy (1964) Agatha Christie's sleuthing Miss Marple (Margaret Rutherford) finds the solution to a murder committed ashore by going on board a naval training ship where her snooping unsettles crew and captain (Lionel Jeffries). Directed by George Pollock, the mystery formula has been diluted with too much feeble comedy and even Rutherford seems bored by the lackluster proceedings. Minimal stylized violence. A-I (br) U

Murder by Death (1976) Eccentric criminologist (Truman Capote) invites five master detectives and assistants (including David Niven, Maggie Smith, Eileen Brennan and James Coco) to his sinister mansion, intending to confound them with a crime they cannot solve. Neil Simon's script owes much to Agatha Christie's "Ten Little Indians," but its attempt to spoof whodunit movies is badly wide of the mark. Director Robert Moore fails to find much humor in the flimsy plot, multiple inconsistencies and flat dialogue. Even the broad performances of a capable cast don't help matters much (Alec Guinness is wasted in a butler part). Adult and frequently vulgar humor. A-III (PG)

Murder by Decree (1979) Sherlock Holmes meets Jack the Ripper in this handsome, expensively mounted period piece in which Holmes (Christopher Plummer) and Dr. Watson (James Mason) trace a series of murders to a high personage in Queen Victoria's England. Directed by Bob Clark, a preposterous and incredibly untidy plot is overcome by the fine acting of the principals supported by such nonpareils as John Gielgud and Anthony Quayle. Harmless but somewhat violent and gory entertainment not meant for younger viewers. A-III (PG) 15

Murder Czech Style (1968) Weak Czechoslovakian satire manifests a cynical view of marriage. O (br)

Murder, He Says (1945) Eccentric comedy in which an opinion pollster (Fred MacMurray) is forcefully detained by a murderous family of hayseeds headed by a wacky inventor (Porter Hall) and his bullwhip-wielding wife (Marjorie Main) as they search for a fortune hidden in a backwoods house. Though the plot is as nonsensical as the silly rhyme holding the secret to the treasure, director George Marshall has a lot of fun with the zany characters and screwball situations. Comic violence and mild romance. A-II (br) A

Murder Most Foul (1964) Agatha Christie's Miss Marple (Margaret Rutherford) causes a hung jury in a murder trial and then tracks the real killer to a theatrical troupe headed by a ham actor (Ron Moody). Directed by George Pollack, there are the usual assortment of suspects and red herrings but the stage setting is rather fun and gives Rutherford the opportunity to recite "The Shooting of Dan McGrew." Enjoyable mystery fare and the violence is minimal. A-I (br) U

Murder, My Sweet (1944) Raymond Chandler's hard-boiled detective, Philip Marlowe (Dick Powell), sets out to find a missing person but the trail leads to a widening mystery involving a stolen jade necklace, a blackmail ring and assorted mayhem. Directed by Edward Dmytryk, the crime story offers a lot of gritty atmosphere, tough characters (Claire Trevor, Mike Mazurki and Otto Kruger), imaginative plot twists and snappy period dialogue. Justice prevails over all the stylized violence. A-II (br)

Murder on the Orient Express (1974) Stylish screen version of the Agatha Christie mystery with Belgian detective Hercule Poirot (Albert Finney) solving the murder of a man (Richard Widmark) whom everyone on the train apparently had good reason to kill. Set in the 1930s, director Sidney Lumet emphasizes the elegance of the period, has an enthusiastic all-star cast (Ingrid Bergman, Wendy Hiller, Vanessa Redgrave, Lauren Bacall, John Gielgud, et al.) and is faithful to the original's wit and verve. Exceptionally well-done escapist entertainment for those who enjoy murder mysteries, but the murder here is rather brutal and definitely not for pre-teens. A-II (PG)

Murderer's Row (1966) Dean Martin as Matt Helm, the poor man's James Bond who specializes less in espionage than in booze and broads. Its plot about a kidnapped scientist is meant to be a spoof of spy-spoof movies but offers little more than a leer-filled bag of crude sexual innuendo and puerile naughtiness with Martin's lumbering characterization providing a paltry few unintentional guffaws. O (br) PG

Murders in the Rue Morgue (1971) Poor adaptation of the Poe story with a wooden performance by Jason Robards matched by those of Christine Kaufmann and Herbert Lom. Director Gordon Hessler provides little tension in what was intended as a horror story, though he keeps the make-up artists and special effects department busy with a plethora of acid murders, decapitations and dream sequences. A-III (PG) 15

Murmur of the Heart (1971) French drama about the sexual maturing of a precocious adolescent in an upper middle-class family whose comfortable materialism is more offensive than the youth's sexual initiation in a brothel or the salvation-through-incest resolution of the story. Directed by Louis Malle, the movie has some light humor and fine performances but depicts the sexual and social antics of the disinterested father (Daniel Gelin) and the disorganized mother (Lea Massari) and their three parasitic sons as both healthy and amusing. Amoral treatment of sexual promiscuity and a bogus sense of social values. O (nr)

Murph the Surf (see: "Live a Little, Steal a Lot").

Murphy's Law (1986) A ruthless felon (Carrie Snodgrass), determined to even the score with the men who sent her to prison, goes on a killing spree for which she frames a cop (Charles Bronson). J. Lee Thompson's direction succeeds only in exploiting vulgarity and violence for simplistic shock value. Profanity and nudity further mar the film. O (R) 18

Murphy's Romance (1986) It isn't until movie's end that Sally Field in the role of a divorcee and James Garner as a widower twice her age realize that all their previous bickering means that they're in love, long after all but middle-aged romantics will have lost interest. Intruding into director Martin Ritt's mostly genial fantasy romance is some rough language and an inconsistent view of sexual morality. A-III (PG-13) 15

Murphy's War (1971) Offbeat drama about merchant seaman Peter O'Toole, sole survivor of a German submarine attack off South America near the end of World War II, who is picked up by barge owner Philippe Noiret and patched up by Quaker missionary Sian Phillips. O'Toole seeks to sink the U-boat by bombs from an ancient airplane, ramming it with the old barge and is still at it when the war ends. Director Peter Yates fails to make his implausible revenge tale exciting, let alone interesting. Some intense scenes of wartime violence. A-III (GP) A

Music Box (1989) Prominent Chicago attorney (Jessica Lange) successfully defends her father (Armin Mueller-Stahl) against accusations of World War II crimes committed in his native Hungary, but then a startling cycle of events suggests that he may, in fact, be guilty. Instead of exploring the daughter's dilemma whether to believe his denials or turn him in, director Costa-Gavras spends most of the movie on tedious, surprisingly suspenseless courtroom proceedings that do, however, raise some justice issues worth pondering. Rough language and explicit courtroom testimony about a gang rape and other wartime atrocities. A-III (PG-13) 15

Music Lovers, The (1971) British film of the tormented life of the 19th-century Russian composer Peter Ilyich Tchaikovsky (Richard Chamberlain) places too much stress on trying to link his music to his sexual disorientation and unconsummated marriage to a woman (Glenda Jackson) who, in a grisly set of sequences, goes quite mad. Directed by Ken Russell with characteristic visual extravagance and narrative weaknesses, the movie's Freudian approach is questionable, but its interplay with realism and surrealism, objectivity and subjectivity succeeds to a surprising degree. Mature themes and some nudity. A-IV (R) 18

Music Man, The (1962) Rousing screen version of Meredith Willson's Broadway musical about Professor Harold Hill (Robert Preston), a smooth-talking con-man who tries to swindle an Iowa community by spinning dreams of a school marching band, but love pushes larceny out of his heart when he falls for the town librarian (Shirley Jones). Directed by Morton Da Costa, the show revolves around the irrepressibly energetic Foster, supported by a strong cast (Pert Kelton, Paul Ford and little Ronny Howard), nostalgic bits of 1912 Iowa corn and Wilson's lovely yet lively song-and-dance numbers, including the show-stopping "76 Trombones." Fine family fare, though a bit long for small attention spans. A-I (G) U

Music of Chance, The (1993) Seedy gambler James Spader and ex-firefighter Mandy Patinkin lose all in a high-stakes card game to eccentric millionaires Charles Durning and Joel Grey, then set to working off their debt by building a massive stone wall on the winners' secluded estate under the watchful eyes of smilingly sinister groundskeeper M. Emmet Walsh. Directed by Philip Haas, the psychological tale of cunning characters trying to outfox each other is interesting to watch but leads nowhere and in the end seems pointless. An implied sexual encounter, several off-screen beatings and intermittent rough language. A-III (nr)

Music Teacher, The (1989) Turn-of-the-century story of an opera star (Jose Van Dam) who retires at the peak of his career to become the singing teacher of two unlikely young students (Anne Roussel and Philippe Volter). Belgian director Gerard Corbiau fashions the movie around opera singer Van Dam and the result will entrance opera buffs with its wall-to-wall music but may distance others with its passionless, ambiguous character study. Implied sexual encounter. A-III (PG) U

Mustang Country (1976) Joel McCrea plays an aging cowboy who is joined by a little Indian boy (Demetri Mina) in attempting to capture a wild horse while eluding a three-toed grizzly, the villain of the piece because he kills more than he eats. Directed by John Champion, the result is a predictable wildlife adventure movie for family viewers, but one that youngsters will especially enjoy. A-I (G) U

Mutations, The (1974) Disagreeable British horror movie about a mad doctor (Donald Pleasence) whose attempt to create a new form of life that is both plant and animal requires experimental candidates that a sadistic freakshow owner (Tom Baker) helpfully supplies. Humorlessly directed by Jack Cardiff, the movie's collection of human mutants varies from the merely gruesome to the baldly disgusting, with a layer of coy nudity to add the final insult. O (R) 18

Mutiny on the Bounty (1962) The remake is a much more handsome production than the original but, despite Trevor Howard's steely performance as the notorious Captain Bligh, Marlon Brando sinks the enterprise by turning Fletcher Christian into an effete snob rather than a leader of men. Director Lewis Milestone turns an exciting story of conflict between duty and humanity into a good-looking but leaden exercise. Sexual innuendo and stylized violence. A-II (br) A

My American Cousin (1986) A Canadian pre-adolescent (Margaret Langrick) is lifted out of the boring doldrums of 1950s' Vancouver when her teenage American cousin (John Wildman) visits her staid, conventional family. Writer-director Sandy Wilson scores with a light and tender reminiscence

of puppy love and new awakenings the outside world. Although there are some scenes of passionate cuddling, it's an essentially innocent treatment of youthful affection. A-II (PG)

My Best Friend Is a Vampire (1988) Humorless comedy in which a nerdish but likeable teenager (Robert Sean Leonard) is seduced and bitten by a new neighbor who turns out to be a vampire. Much offensive sexist humor, some profanity and disconcerting visuals of the newly vampired teen biting necks and guzzling blood. O (PG)

My Bloody Valentine (1981) Low-budget Canadian exploitation film about a demented coal miner who stalks his attractive young victims with a pick ax on Valentine's Day. Directed by George Mihalka, the absurd plot offers violence and vast amounts of flowing blood. O (R)

My Blue Heaven (1990) Big-city mob informant (Steve Martin), relocated to the suburbs by the Witness Protection Program, masterminds a romance between an FBI agent (Rick Moranis) and an assistant district attorney (Joan Cusack), while they have their hands full trying to reform the happy-go-lucky hoodlum. Director Herbert Ross turns in a minor-league comedy notable chiefly for Martin's riotous performance as the tough New Yorker bored to death by laid-back Californians. Cartoon-style shoot-outs; comic treatment of theft and bigamy; an instance of rough language. A-II (PG-13) PG

My Bodyguard (1980) Young transfer student (Chris Makepeace), bullied by a neighborhood gang of toughs, hires a hulking, brooding classmate (Adam Baldwin) to act as his bodyguard. Some effective moments, but it takes some uncertain turns before reaching a violent and far-fetched conclusion. Some sexual references and its simplistic solving of a problem by resorting to violence makes it dubious fare for young viewers. A-III (PG)

My Boyfriend's Back (1993) Witless comedy about a lovestruck teen (Andrew Lowery) who comes back from the dead as a reluctant flesh-eating zombie so he can go to the prom with the girl (Traci Lind) he died saving during a botched convenience store hold-up. Director Bob Balaban delivers a sophomoric horror comedy that might amuse 10-year-olds, were it not for the adult level of the double-entendres. Comic depiction of violence and much sexual innuendo. A-III (PG-13)

My Brilliant Career (1980) Bright Australian dramatization of a autobiographical novel about a young farm girl (Judy Davis in a dazzling performance) raised in poverty but determined to make a life of her own as a writer at the turn of the century. Gillian Armstrong directs a work that besides being very funny, very human, very touching and always entertaining, is a tribute to the human spirit and the artistic imagination. Exhilarating family fare. A-I (G) U

My Cousin Vinny (1992) Tough-talking comedy has New York college students Ralph Macchio and Mitchell Whitfield improbably charged with murder in the deep South, then defended by rookie Brooklyn lawyer Joe Pesci with a little help from girlfriend Marisa Tomei. Relying on blue-collar and Southern stereotypes, director Jonathan Lynn fashions a fitfully funny, fish-out-of-water courtroom comedy. Much rough language, a few double-entendres and an implied premarital relationship. A-III (R) 15

My Demon Lover (1987) Scott Valentine is the youth with the Romanian curse that makes him turn into a beast whenever he thinks about sex. A noble act frees him into the arms of true love, but director Charles Loventhal exploits sexual situations and bedroom scenes for one-joke humor about demonic violence. O (PG-13)

My Fair Lady (1964) Screen version of the Lerner and Loewe Broadway musical based on George Bernard Shaw's play, "Pygmalion," the story concerns Eliza Doolittle (Audrey Hepburn), a Covent Garden flower girl who longs for a better life and the egotistical bachelor Professor Henry Higgins (Rex Harrison) who bets a friend that he can transform Eliza's Cockney speech and manners so that she can pass for a lady at the upcoming Royal Ball. Predictably, it is not always the professor who gives the lessons. George Cukor's nimble direction, Cecil Beaton's stunning sets and costumes, the charming performances and the wonderful music add up to splendid family entertainment. A-I (G) U

My Father, My Master (1977) Somber Italian production about a Sardinian youth, an illiterate shepherd until military service opens his eyes to a wider world, studies for a high school diploma and eventually obtains a degree in linguistics. Directed by Paolo and Vittorio Taviani, the emphasis is on the simple but backward life of rustic peasants where the family patriarch has total authority. The cruel beatings that the lad endured as a child and the dark and violent passions that permeate the culture in which he grew up make it a film for none but mature viewers. A-IV (nr)

My Father's Glory (1991) At the turn of the century, a young lad from Marseilles (Julien Ciamaca) spends an idyllic summer with his family in rustic Provence learning about nature's wonders from a local boy (Joris Molinas) and about life from his schoolteacher father (Philippe Caubere). Directed by Yves Robert and based on the reminiscences of French author Marcel Pagnol, the result is a lyrical, conflict-free tribute to family life in a simpler, bygone era (companion to "My Mother's Castle"). Subtitles. Brief shot of nude boys. A-I (G) U

My Favorite Spy (1951) Middling comedy in which a stand-up comic (Bob Hope), sent to Morocco to impersonate a look-alike spy, outbluffs the villains to get the goods and the real spy's girl (Hedy Lamarr). Directed by Norman Z. McLeod, the vehicle is not one of Hope's best but there are enough laughs to pass the time until the madcap chase wind-up. Some stylized violence and double entendres. A-II (br)

My Favorite Year (1982) Peter O'Toole plays a fading movie star who agrees to appear on a show in the early days of television comedy and a young gag writer (Mark Linn-Baker) is assigned to keep the drunken, womanizing actor in line. Director Richard Benjamin's comedy is bright and entertaining as long as talented, charming O'Toole is on screen, but when he's off, the picture quietly dies. Because the humor revolves around the hero's pursuit of women and the bottle, as well as some rather vulgar gags, it is not for younger viewers. A-III (PG)

My Friend Flicka (1943) After a horse rancher (Preston Foster) gives his young son (Roddy McDowall) a wild colt to care for as his own, the untamed horse causes much grief to both until ultimately responding to the boy's steadfast love and devotion. Directed by Harold Schuster, there's nothing fancy about this heartwarming family story of a youngster's growth in responsibility but most viewers will find the boy's adventures with his colt in the scenic wilds of the ranch reason enough to watch. Fine family fare but especially appealing for children. A-I (br) U

My Friends (1976) Italian comedy concerning the juvenile pranks of four middle-aged practical jokers for whom nothing is sacred except their own bond of camaraderie. Their idea of a good time, for example, is to go to the railroad station and slap the faces of people looking out the windows of departing trains. Directed by Mario Monicello, the movie's attitude toward people in general, and women in particular, is downright nasty, with nudity and vulgar language compounding the tastelessness. O (PG)

My Girl (1991) Heartwarming drama in which an imaginative 11-year-old (Anna Chlumsky), whose widowed father (Dan Aykroyd) operates a funeral parlor out of their home, confronts some of her worst fears when her dad's attention is drawn to the new cosmetologist (Jamie Lee Curtis) and she loses her best friend (Macaulay

Culkin). Director Howard Zieff handles childhood traumas with humor and sensitivity in an evocative story of memorable characters and life-affirming relationships. Brief but disturbing sequence of a juvenile's death, discreet scene about menstruation and a drug reference. A-II (PG)

My Left Foot (1989) Powerful dramatization of the life of Irish writer-artist Christy Brown (1932–1981), born with cerebral palsy to a large, impoverished Catholic family, shows his triumph over physical disabilities as the creative intelligence bottled up inside his young, twisted body finds expression, thanks in large part to his mother's love and encouragement. Jim Sheridan's sensitive, unsentimental direction and brilliant acting by Hugh O'Conor and Daniel Day-Lewis as the young and the adult Christy provide a testament to the power of the spirit over adversity and a tribute to a mother's unquestioning belief in her child. Some violence, rough language and sexual innuendo. A-III (R) 15

My Life (1993) High-powered but terminally ill business executive (Michael Keaton) experiences emotional and spiritual healing during the process of making an autobiographical video for his pregnant wife (Nicole Kidman) to show their unborn son in later years. Writer-director Bruce Joel Rubin explores the personal growth of a man who has repressed his feelings until coming to terms with his impending death in a drama that resists tugging on the tearducts until the closing scenes. Family confrontations and an instance of rough language. A-II (PG-13) 12

My Life as a Dog (1988) When his mother becomes seriously ill, a fatherless 12-year-old (Anton Glanzelius) finds himself packed off to spend the summer with his uncle in the country where he comes to feel at home amidst the colorful characters living and working nearby. Swedish director Lasse Hallstrom delivers a lovely, spirited and hopeful movie about how people survive life's tragedies and loneliness. Subtitles. Fleeting shot of a nude model and several scenes depicting children's curiosity about sex. A-III (nr) 15

My Love Has Been Burning (1979) Elegant Japanese production about a pioneer for women's rights in the 1890s. Kinuyo Tanaka plays the daughter of a wealthy family who through bitter personal experience of male domination of society becomes a dedicated feminist who founds a school for the education of women. Directed in 1949 by Kenji Mizoguchi, it is a feminist tract more than a credible drama, but one that has considerable historical interest in terms of the development of women's rights in Japan. A-II (nr)

My Lover, My Son (1970) Failed British melodrama dealing with the sexual attraction a mother (Romy Schneider) develops for her understandably confused adolescent son (Dennis Waterman). Directed by John Newland, whose main object seems to be gaudiness, the screenplay all but drowns its principals in cheap melodramatic thrills, and neither the mother's ultimate comeuppance nor the son's more natural romance with a local girl can save the movie from deserved oblivion. O (R)

My Michael (1976) Screen version of the Amos Oz novel, set in Israel during the 1950s, about a marriage that has withered because it never had a chance to grow. Understanding how the young couple's life together goes on unraveling in estrangement and alienation is possible only if seen as reflecting the embattled Israeli state, not at war but certainly not at peace, in their own land. While all the dimensions of this ambitious theme are not completely realized, director Don Wolman had made a challenging drama about the special complexities of Israeli life that is worth the attention of serious moviegoers. A-III (nr)

My Mother's Castle (1991) Continuing the story of "My Father's Glory," a young boy in pre-World War I Marseilles (Julien Ciamaca) has his first case of puppy love and his schoolteacher father (Philippe Caubere) risks his job by sneaking the family across private property to shorten their miles-long walk to a summer weekend cottage in Provence. French author Marcel Pagnol's joyous childhood memories are beautifully realized under Yves Robert's direction which casts a kindly eye on its characters' well-observed foibles. Subtitles. Ambivalent discussion of father's atheism. A-II (PG)

My Name Is Nobody (1974) Henry Fonda and Terence Hill star in a lavish spoof of spaghetti westerns, produced by Sergio Leone and directed by Tonino Valeria. Fonda is a laconic, aging marshal with the reputation of being the fastest gun in the West. Actually the sly, kinetic Hill is faster and saves the lawman from any number of mishaps on his last assignment before retirement. Though there are some charming comic bits, the movie's one-joke concept can only be characterized as a good-natured waste of time. A-II (PG) A

My Neighbor Totoro (1993) Mildly entertaining animated feature from Japan recounts the adventures of two small girls when their family moves to an old rural house where they discover, among other things, the fat, furry creature of the title whose magical powers at first frighten, then delight them. Directed by Hayao Miyazaki, the 1988 production does best with its fantasy of spirit creatures, some spooky but most benign, and there are some lovely vistas of nature, especially when Totoro flies them over the countryside, but like the dubbing, the storyline is rather forced and artificial. Some fun for the very young and those young in spirit. A-I (G)

My New Gun (1992) Subservient housewife (Diane Lane) bullied by obnoxious husband (Stephen Collins) into keeping a handgun for protection becomes romantically entangled with a strange neighbor (James LeGros) who steals the weapon to protect his goofy mom (Tess Harper). Writer-director Stacy Cochran's stab at sly, suburban satire is a minor effort showcasing amusingly quirky characters in wry situations. Implied affair, comic violence and occasional rough language. A-III (nr)

My Night at Maud's (1970) After resolving to marry a religiously devout student (Marie-Christine Barrault) he has never met, a 34-year-old engineer (Jean-Louis Trintignant) happens to meet a sensuous woman (Francoise Fabian) with whom he spends the night in talking about everything from literature and mathematics to politics and religion. Intriguing French movie directed by Eric Rohmer, the intellectual talkathon focuses on the cerebral quest for life's meaning while indicating the difficulty of people to live up to the practical aspects of idealism and dogma, whether Christian or Marxist. The third in Rohmer's series of "Six Moral Tales," it has the ambiguity of real life and is a perfect discussion piece. A-III (GP) U

My Old Man's Place (see: "Glory Boy").

My Own Private Idaho (1991) Perverted tale of two young male prostitutes (River Phoenix and Keanu Reeves) who hustle their way from the Northwest to Italy in a futile search for one's homicidal mom. Writer-director Gus Van Sant's disjointed story is a smug and ugly commentary on friendship and family life. Frequent sordid sexual references and allusions to incest, brief shots of gay and heterosexual encounters with momentary nudity and much rough language. O (R) 18

My Secret Life (1971) Canadian version of a book of Victorian pornography consists of a singularly dreary flood of sexual description vapidly read and illustrated with visuals that are numbing in their dullness. Directed by Leland R. Thomas, whatever its poetic aspirations, it is only a pretentious bore. Nudity in a sexual context. O (X)

My Side of the Mountain (1969) Toronto youth journeys into the Quebec wilderness to prove that he can take care of himself, adapts quite easily to life in the forest and is befriended by a migrant folk singer (Theo-dore Bikel) who eventually rescues him during a snowstorm. Produced by Robert B. Radnitz and directed by James B. Clarke, its intriguing story has substance instead of cliches, in addition to magnificent photography capturing the beauty of its natural setting. Intelligent family fare whose spirit of adventure and youthful independence can be enjoyed by all. A-I (G)

My Stepmother Is an Alien (1988) Cosmic clinker in which a shapely alien (Kim Basinger) saucers to Earth to find and conquer the scientist (Dan Aykroyd) who is zapping her planet with his zany experiments. Director Richard Benjamin's humorless comedy becomes lurid in depicting her sexual attempts to distract her homeland's tormentor. Explicit seduction scenes, much sexual innuendo and a child's encouragement of her parents' sexual misconduct. O (PG-13)

My Sweet Charlie (1970) Two fugitives—a frightened pregnant girl thrown out by her family (Patty Duke) and a black lawyer (Al Freeman Jr.) on the run for killing a white man in self defense—find themselves taking refuge in a vacant Southern beach house. The relationship has nothing to do with sex or sensationalism but with basic emotions of fear and prejudice that ultimately lead to honesty and recognition of each other as human beings. Director Lamont Johnson avoids melodramatic sentimentality, helped by sharp performances from his two principals and an intelligent script based on David Westheimer's novel. One of those rare made-for-television movies that earned subsequent distribution to movie theaters, it still has something relevant to say about ordinary people as well as social justice. A-II (G)

My Sweet Little Village (1987) Czech director Jiri Menzel creates a gentle fable about fellowship and brotherhood in a tiny worker's commune. Imbedded in the narrative is a sly comment upon socialist ideals and an affirmation of the joys of a simple rural life. A-II (PG)

My Uncle Antoine (1972) Canadian movie centering on a Christmas Eve during the 1940s when an adolescent gets his first glimpse of adulthood after he and his inebriated uncle lose a corpse they are transporting to the funeral parlor during a snowstorm and arrive home in the early morning to chance upon his aunt's act of infidelity. Directed by Claude Jutra, the film looks with clarity and compassion at the world of a small French-Canadian mining village and its vibrant community of characters seen in a montage of portraiture and vignette. Though rooted in a specific ethnic tradition, its perspective is universal enough to strike chords celebrating our common humanity. A-III (nr)

My Way (1974) Muddled South African melodrama about the highly strained relations within the family of a success-driven building contractor (Joe Stewardson), a former marathon runner who demands success from his three sons, and the predictable conflicts and lapses that result. Directed by Emil Nofal, it is notable only for its complete absence of blacks, even in crowd scenes. Domestic violence. A-III (PG)

Myra Breckinridge (1970) Screen version of Gore Vidal's novel about a sex change operation turns satire into burlesque and, in trying to show how society has accepted the false values of Hollywood image-making, makes gross caricatures out of the notable (John Huston and Mae West) and less than notable (Rex Reed). Directed by Michael Sarne, the treatment is thoroughly distasteful and at times repulsive. Sexual innuendo, nudity, vulgar sight gags and rough language predominate. O (R) 18

Mysteries of the Organism (1971) The title refers to the fanciful theories of Wilhelm Reich, psychologist convicted of fraud in selling scientifically repudiated apparatus. Yugoslavian director Dusan Makavejev uses Reich as the central image in a movie devoted to contemporary sexual politics, and perhaps the only group that won't be offended by it are anarchists. Some of the bizarre sexual material is at best crude, and the result is less a commentary on the sexual confusion of the age than itself a product of it. O (nr)

Mysterious Island (1961) Escaping a Confederate prison in an observation balloon, five men (led by Michael Craig and Gary Merrill) wind up on a Pacific island where they encounter giant-sized animals, a shipwrecked Englishwoman (Joan Greenwood) and her niece, pirates, an erupting volcano and the helping hand of Captain Nemo (Herbert Lom). Director Cy Enfield's sequel to Jules Verne's "20,000 Leagues under the Sea" is a rousing adventure tale with intriguing plot twists and imaginative special effects by Ray Harryhausen but the ending flags. Despite the usual stylized violence and menace, the result is exciting family fare with an anti-war message. A-I (br) U

Mysterious Island of Captain Nemo, The (1974) The famed Nautilus of Jules Verne has been dry-docked and is being used solely as a kind of plush houseboat by the mysterious Captain Nemo (Omar Sharif) who deters visitors by blasting them from afar with his robot ray guns. Curiously disjointed European co-production directed by Juan Antonio Bardem and Henri Colpi mixes a thin plot and some lovely scenery with a torrent of mushy dialogue and low-grade acting that results in less than enthralling children's fare. A-I (G)

Mystery Date (1991) Bloated suspense comedy has a naive young fellow (Ethan Hawke) mistaken for his hotly pursued criminal older brother (Brian McNamara) while trying to impress his perplexed date (Teri Polo). As the number of situations and characters increase, director Jonathan Wacks' muddled movie sinks into oblivion. Recurring nasty menace with some violence and dead bodies. A-III (PG-13)

Mystery of Kaspar Hauser, The (1975) Compelling German drama about the discovery in the town square one morning in 1828 of a teenage boy capable of speaking but a few words, barely able to walk and apparently without any experience of human society. The mystery of his origins was never solved, but he became an object of curiosity, exhibited in a sideshow and studied by scientists and philosophers until his equally mysterious murder in 1833. Director Werner Herzog is not interested in rational explanations of these fact-based events but in portraying the injustices committed against a totally innocent outsider by a complacent, self-satisfied society. A-III (nr)

Mystery of Thug Island, The (1966) Failed European adventure story ineptly directed by Nino Battiferri with Guy Madison fighting an outlaw cult operating under the direction of a pseudo-goddess in India. Stylized violence. A-II (br)

Mystery Train (1989) Writer-director Jim Jarmusch has concocted a trio of lightly comic tales set on the back streets of Memphis that offhandedly invoke the memory and spirit of Elvis Presley. An offbeat road picture in which locals and foreigners mix in search of themselves and the ghost of Elvis. Some violence, sexual innuendo and profanity. A-III (R)

Mystic Pizza (1988) Three young Portuguese-American women (Julia Roberts, Annabeth Gish, Lili Taylor) live in the seaport town of Mystic, Conn., and work in a pizza parlor known for its secret pizza sauce and warmhearted owner (Conchata Ferrell). Directed by Donald Petrie, the coming-of-age story might work as a TV series minus the focus on the girls' indiscriminate sex lives. Explicit sex banter and off-camera sex. O (R) 15

N

Nada Gang, The (1974) French film about a small motley band of political extremists whose kidnapping of the American Ambassador leads authorities to use extreme counterterrorist tactics, ultimately forcing the band's fanatic leader (Fabrio Testi) to conclude that violence from the left is as self-defeating as from the right. Directed by Claude Chabrol, the individual characterizations of a fine cast overcome stereotyped roles to involve viewers in the movie's obvious antiterrorist message. Violent action and atmosphere. A-IV (nr)

Nadine (1987) Warmhearted comedy romance about a zany, fumbling couple (Kim Basinger and Jeff Bridges) whose marriage is reconciled after dangerously failed attempts to exploit profit from a set of highway plans. Writer-director Robert Benton's southern gentility shows brightly through Basinger's frothy portrait of a 1950s' working-class woman. A-II (PG)

Naked (1993) Seamy picture of a wild-eyed vagrant (David Thewlis) who steals a car in Manchester to drop in on a former girlfriend (Lesley Sharp) in London where he beds her spaced-out roommate (Katrin Cartlidge), then takes to roaming the streets until beaten up by hoodlums, which brings him back to be patched up by the girlfriend and steal off with a large sum of money. Writer-director Mike Leigh looks at the dark side of human nature in his portrait of a young man gone bad but gives no insight into the cause for his self-destructive behavior or that of the other characters. Graphic sex scenes, stylized violence and recurring rough language. O (nr) 18

Naked Among the Wolves (1967) Tender German movie about a little Jewish boy smuggled by a prisoner into a concentration camp where the child's survival becomes a symbol of the struggle between the inmates and their Nazi guards shortly before the camp's liberation by American troops. Directed by Frank Beyer, the movie has warmth, compassion and optimism about the survival of the human spirit even in the most inhuman of circumstances. Restrained treatment of Nazi atrocities. A-II (br)

Naked Ape, The (1973) Failed screen version of the popular anthropology book by Desmond Morris uses live action segments and cartoon fantasies to illustrate the human evolution from the primate order, with emphasis on pair-mating. Adapted and directed by David Driver, it is a mishmash of mindless shards seeking desperately to congeal into a whole, though Victoria Prin-cipal and Johnny Crawford are attractive as naked apes going bananas over each other. Inept treatment of an inert movie property relies on heavy-handed sexual humor. A-III (PG)

Naked Gun: From the Files of Police Squad, The (1988) Silly comedy abounds in this nutty farce about the bumbling attempts of a L.A. police lieutenant (Leslie Nielsen) to clear the tarnished name of his partner (O.J. Simpson) and save the life of Queen Elizabeth II (Jeannette Charles). Director David Zucker's parody of classic detective yarns is for those who enjoy mindless pratfalls, chases and other sight gags. Some particularly vulgar bathroom and sexual humor. A-III (PG-13) 15

Naked Gun 2 1/2: The Smell of Fear, The (1991) The comic misadventures of a bumbling cop (Leslie Nielsen) continue as he discovers that a business magnate (Robert Goulet) who's subverting the government's energy policy is also stealing his girlfriend (Priscilla Presley). The sight gags are fast and scattershot in director David Zucker's slapstick sequel that is mostly harmless nonsense with only occasional lapses in taste. Intermittent sexual innuendo, mildly vulgar humor, comic violence and minimal rough language. A-III (PG-13) 12

Naked Hearts (1970) French film about a group of aimless boys who band together for kicks and occasionally get into trouble, with the focus on one boy more sensitive, yet ultimately as irresponsible as his companions. French director Eduard Luntz captures a mood of loneliness and frustration, emphasized by harsh black-and-white photography of an alienating industrialized environment with its factory smoke stacks, seedy tenements and dirty streets. The reality of characters and situations requires a mature perspective. A-III (nr)

Naked Jungle, The (1954) Turn-of-the-century romantic thriller centers on a sour plantation owner (Charlton Heston) who imports a mail-order bride (Eleanor Parker) to his South American backwater, then faces the fight of his life trying to save his lands from an invasion of soldier ants. Directed by Byron Haskin, the climax pitting Heston against a ferocious army of insects is edge-of-the-seat fare, thanks to George Pal's convincing special effects. Initial romantic complications swept away by the growing menace of a natural disaster. A-II (br) A

Naked Lunch (1991) Punk adaptation of William S. Burrough's bizarre 1959 novel about a drug-abusing insect exterminator (Peter Weller) who kills his cheating wife (Judy Davis) and subsequently experiences grotesque hallucinations relating to his sexual identity, writing ambitions and substance addiction. Writer-director David Cronenberg's unpalatable, surreal procession of depraved humans and hideous monsters attempts sly, counterculture humor but delivers only pointless and boring excess. Gross sexual imagery, much homosexual innuendo and drug abuse, extramarital encounters, occasional violence and some rough language. O (R) 18

Naked Prey, The (1965) Brutal picture of 19th-century Africa in which natives cruelly massacre a hunting safari, then give its guide (Cornel Wilde) a headstart before sending their best warriors to hunt him down for sport. Also produced and directed by Wilde, the life-and-death action is vigorous, the tactics of surviving in the savage wilderness are inventive but the result proves little more than an ultimately disappointing exercise in menace. Savage violence and racial stereotyping. A-III (br)

Naked Runner, The (1967) Frank Sinatra plays an American ex-sharpshooter in exile, who is manipulated by British intelligence agents to kill an enemy agent in this suspenseful but wildly improbable yarn taken from the Francis Clifford novel. Director Sidney J. Furie is most concerned with the official ruthlessness that reduces people to instruments of power and, though the plot may be muddled, it is an interesting premise. Some violence. A-III (br) PG

Naked Spur, The (1953) Bounty hunter (James Stewart), aided by an old sourdough (Millard Mitchell) and a cashiered Army officer (Ralph Meeker), gets his man (Robert Ryan) but bringing him in for the reward is complicated by the badman's girl (Janet Leigh) and a band of Indians. Director Anthony Mann's tough-minded Western centers on the theme of greed, abetted by an effective performance from Ryan as the smiling outlaw who turns his three captors against each other. Some stylized violence and much menace. A-II (br) A

Naked Tango (1991) Baroque potboiler set in 1920s Argentina where a young bride (Mathilda May) of an old judge (Fernando Rey) assumes a new identity in a bordello where she becomes obsessed with a tango-mad killer (Vincent D'Onofrio). Writer-director Leonard Schrader crams his lurid melodrama with violent and voyeuristic images and little else of note. Callous exploitation of women, rape scene, recurring nudity, gory violence and minimal rough language. O (R) 18

Name of the Rose, The (1986) Darkly envisioned murder-mystery set in a medieval monastery features a Franciscan friar (Sean Connery) who uses logic to uncover the cause of a mysterious death among a Fellini-like assortment of grotesque and repulsive monks, all of whom appear to be either homicidal or homosexual. A freak show is all that emerges from this badly bungled adaptation of Umberto Eco's intriguing novel. Explicit sex scene, violence and burnings at the stake. O (R) 18

Namu, the Killer Whale (1966) Simple story of a fishing village set in an ocean cove where the local fishermen learn that killer whales are dangerous only if attacked. Directed by Laslo Benedek, it is wholesome children's fare and parents can enjoy the beautiful ocean setting, if not its pleasant but unremarkable tale. A-I (br)

Nana (1971) Swedish production directed by Mac Ahlberg exploits Emile Zola's novel about a 19th-century French courtesan (Anna Gael) in a ridiculous updated film version. Excessively graphic sex and nudity. O (X)

Nanami (1969) Japanese story about two young people groping toward pure love despite their sordid environment starts well, but their plight and aspirations are soon overpowered by arbitrary and confused melodrama and director Susumu Hani's lack of restraint in several sex scenes. O (nr)

Napoleon and Samantha (1972) Disney comedy details the story of a young man (Michael Douglas) who gets involved with an orphaned little boy (Johnny Whitaker), his pet lion and his seven-year-old playmate (Jodie Foster). Among the problems are the burial of the boy's grandfather (Will Geer) and a menacing homicidal maniac. The movie could do without the latter, but Geer's death is handled in a sensitive manner that provides a gentle lesson about the passage from life. Appealing performances from Geer and the children under the competent direction of Bernard McEveety make it an enjoyable family movie. A-I (G) U

Narrow Margin, The (1952) Tightly wound thriller takes place aboard a Chicago-to-Los Angeles train carrying a hard-boiled cop (Charles McGraw), the reluctant witness (Marie Windsor) he's escorting back to testify against the mob and some gunmen sent to silence her. Director Richard Fleischer makes the trip a suspenseful one, with plenty of edgy menace, a bit of comic relief and topped off by an edge-of-the-seat surprise finish. Threatening situations and stylized violence. A-II (br) A

Narrow Margin (1990) Two mob hitmen (James B. Sikking and Nigel Bennett) close in on a Deputy D.A. (Gene Hackman) who is concealing a murder witness (Anne Archer) aboard a Vancouver-bound train. Written, photographed and directed by Peter Hyams, this remake of a 1952 movie is a sleek, compact thriller that, save for one overly violent shoot-out early on, concentrates on stylish visuals, convincing acting and razor-sharp editing to tell its suspenseful story. Intermittent menace, some violence and minimal rough language. A-III (R) 15

Nashville (1975) Robert Altman's ambitious backstage epic about the careers of the people who make the capital city of country music come alive is a consistently entertaining, at times enlightening, look at an uniquely American phenomenon. Unfortunately, in reaching for something more—an indictment of sorts of contemporary America—Altman lapses into a series of cliches regarding political elections, violence, Vietnam, etc., that is quite unworthy of his film at its best. Fine performances by Ronee Blakley, Henry Gibson, Lily Tomlin, Michael Murphy and many others in a large and talented cast. Some of the subject matter and its naturalistic treatment make this a movie not for casual viewers. A-IV (R) AA

Nashville Girl (see: "New Girl in Town").

Nasty Girl, The (1990) Dark German comedy about a woman (Lena Stolze) who starts out to write a short essay on her Bavarian town during the Nazi era but, encountering a collective amnesia on the part of those who lived through the period and denied access to the town records, she becomes obsessed with the need to find the truth. Writer-director Michael Verhoeven uses a variety of comic techniques and dramatic styles in telling his fact-based story, which has more to do with modern Germany than with the Third Reich. Subtitles. Mature themes, some racial epithets and a flash of nudity. A-III (PG-13)

Nasty Habits (1977) Clumsy screen version of "The Abbess of Crewe," Muriel Spark's satire paralleling the Watergate scandal with wiretapping in a Philadelphia convent. Directed by Michael Lindsay-Hogg, with Glenda Jackson as the autocratic abbess and Sandy Dennis as her kooky aide, the movie's jabs at institutional power vary from slapstick to long, talky sketches with occasional tastelessness. Though the film goes out of its way to insist that this order of nuns is not officially recognized, some may find the treatment of women religious and convent life offensive. A-IV (PG) A

National Lampoon's Animal House (1978) After being expelled from college, the members of a rowdy fraternity get revenge on the school's administration and a rival fraternity by disrupting the homecoming parade. Directed by John Landis, the mindless, unfunny exercise in grossness tries to pass itself off as an anti-establishment comedy, despite reserving some of its most tasteless jibes for blacks and women. Exploitative sex and nudity. O (R) AA

National Lampoon's Christmas Vacation (1989) In the third Griswold family saga,

dizzy dad Clark (Chevy Chase) aims to create an old-fashioned Christmas at home despite his clumsy pratfalls and short-fuse patience pushed to the limit by wife (Beverly D'Angelo), kids, in-laws and assorted relatives. Director Jeremiah S. Chechik keeps the gags moving quickly past the double entendres and gets some laughs from Clark's bumbling attempts to enjoy Christmas. Some rough language laced with vulgarities and sexual innuendos. A-III (PG-13) PG

National Lampoon's Class Reunion (1982) The 10th annual reunion of the class of '72 at Lizzie Borden High School is enlivened by a prowling homicidal maniac. Director Michael Miller's comedy is not even mildly funny in its reliance on extremely coarse humor and some nudity. O (R) 15

National Lampoon's European Vacation (1985) The family that cavorted their way across America on their first film vacation does so again, this time in Europe. Chevy Chase and Beverly D'Angelo repeat their roles as the parents in a movie that is witless, vulgar, unfunny and in consistently bad taste. Nudity and sexually oriented humor. O (PG-13) 15

National Lampoon's Loaded Weapon 1 (1993) Freewheeling spoof of recent violent action blockbusters teams a burnt-out cop (Emilio Estevez) with a ready-to-retire partner (Samuel L. Jackson) on a murder-drug conspiracy case of ludicrous proportions. Writer-director Gene Quintano keeps up a stream of sight gags, ditzy dialogue and star cameos that wryly mock the excesses of macho action movies. Much cartoonish violence, numerous off-color and sexual references and a flash of nudity. A-III (PG-13) PG

National Lampoon's Vacation (1983) Chevy Chase stars in this comic saga of a family's misadventures driving from Chicago to a California amusement park. As in any trip there are moments of fun and humor and long stretches of dull, tedious travel. Directed by Harold Ramis, there is some tasteless humor involving a corpse, some sexual innuendo and brief nudity. A-III (R) 15

National Velvet (1944) Warmly sentimental story of an English country girl (Elizabeth Taylor) who sets her heart on entering her spirited horse Pie in the Grand National Steeplechase, England's most challenging race, and with the help of an ex-jockey (Mickey Rooney) and supportive parents (Anne Revere and Donald Crisp), her great expectations are finally realized. Directed by Clarence Brown, it is a fine picture of youthful ambition and determination fostered within a caring, loving home. A family classic with special appeal for youngsters. A-I (br) U

Natural, The (1984) Screen version of the Bernard Malamud novel about a phenomenal baseball player (Robert Redford) is as much a fable about the temptations of worldly glory and the flesh as it is a red-blooded sports saga. Directed by Barry Levinson, it has a strong supporting cast (Robert Duvall, Glenn Close, Wilford Brimley) but muddles the story's underlying themes of self-deceit, evil and mortality. Promiscuity figures in the plot but is treated with restraint. A-II (PG)

Natural Enemies (1979) Successful magazine editor (Hal Holbrook) decides to shoot his wife (Louise Fletcher) and three teenage children but his best friend (Jose Ferrer) tries desperately to argue him out of it. Written, produced and directed by Jeff Kanew, this story of marital breakdown is a cold and superficial exercise. Needlessly explicit brothel scene that includes partial nudity. O (R)

Navajo Joe (1967) Fed by the hatred of their half-breed leader, a gang of outlaws become compulsive Indian-killers until one heroic Indian (Burt Reynolds) outwits and destroys most of them when they try to rob a train. Routine spaghetti western directed by Sergio Corbucci has an excess of wanton killings, brutality and sadism. O (br)

Navigator: An Odyssey Across Time, The (1989) New Zealand director Vincent Ward weaves a visually exquisite but muddled tale traveling from the 14th century to modern times and back again. The imaginative but demanding fable concerns a 9-year-old English lad (Hamish McFarlane) whose visions of a church steeple in a strange new world send him on a journey to the 20th century to save his medieval village from the Black Death. The role of faith is obvious and some may see connections with AIDS, but the rest is tenuous. Some intense menace and scenes of death. A-III (PG)

Navy SEALs (1990) U.S. Navy anti-terrorist team (headed by Charlie Sheen and Michael Biehn) is sent into war-torn Beirut to neutralize a cache of stolen American Stinger missiles. Director Lewis Teague delivers a standard action yarn packed with macho stereotypes, daredevil stunts, ferocious explosions and predictable casualties and triumphs. Much violence and rough language. A-III (R) 15

Nazarin (1968) Mexican story set in 1905 when a young priest comes into disfavor with his inflexible religious superiors, the civil authorities and even the poor among whom he tries to live a life of simplicity, poverty and charity. Though director Luis Bunuel's work is not very optimistic about the possibility of idealism winning over the world, it's not critical of religion, only pious hypocrisy. English subtitles. Perplexing themes. A-III (br) A

Nea (1978) When a rich and nasty 16-year-old girl (Ann Zacharias) writes a successful erotic novel, her lover-editor (Sammy Frey) claims credit and she exacts a cruel revenge. French director Nelly Kaplan evidently had social satire in mind, but the movie's exploitation of sex is more in evidence than any wit or insight. O (R)

Necessary Roughness (1991) Formula football comedy about a hopeless Texas college team whose coaches (Hector Elizondo and Robert Loggia) recruit a 34-year-old freshman (Scott Bakula) to be their star quarterback. Director Stan Dragoti manages to extract some laughs from an otherwise routinely contrived storyline. Implied sexual affair, some slapstick violence and minimal rough language. A-III (PG) 12

Necromancy (1972) Pamela Franklin finds herself the latest candidate to play at witchcraft in a creepy little California village owned and completely dominated by Orson Welles, toy manufacturer and master of the occult. Written, produced and directed by Bert I. Gordon, it's not very scary but is slightly amusing in its ineptness and desperate attempts at plot twists and shocks. Innocuous save for some brief nudity and a nasty attack by rats. A-III (PG) X

Ned Kelly (1970) Uneven but engrossing British production about an Irish outlaw gang led by Kelly whose exploits in 1870s' Australia grew in legend after betrayal by one of their own led to their capture and execution by the Crown. Mick Jagger in the tile role gives a successful portrayal as the embittered, hardened man-child outlaw. Tony Richardson's bold and sweeping direction, the beautifully muted color photography, and the bittersweet ballads about the now folk hero sung by Waylon Jennings (and composed by Shel Silverstein) are more than enough to recommend it. Some fairly graphic violence. A-III (PG) AA

Needful Things (1993) Disguised as a sympathetic antiques shopowner, the devil (Max Von Sydow) goes about slyly manipulating the good people of a New England town to go on an ugly killing spree until the sheriff (Ed Harris) calls them to their senses and the devil smugly goes on his merry way. Fraser C. Heston directs this adaptation of a Stephen King novel, a boring and mean-spirited horror comedy whose glib message is that evil will always triumph in the end. Recurring nasty violence, mindless mayhem and frequent rough language. O (R)

Neighbors (1981) Director John G. Avildsen's screen version of Thomas Berger's black comedy about a staid suburbanite (John Belushi) who is driven crazy by a looney neighbor (Dan Aykroyd) is a muddled, dismal failure devoid of both laughs and insight. Senseless scene of seduction, much sexual innuendo and unusually crude language. O (R) 15

Nelson Affair, The (1973) Boudoir history of Admiral Lord Nelson's (Peter Finch) scandalous behavior with his beloved and presumably bewitching mistress Lady Emma Hamilton (Glenda Jackson in an eccentric performance). Scripted by Terence Rattigan and directed by James Cellan Jones, it is a literate if somewhat bland treatment of the stormy love affair. A-III (PG)

Neptune Factor, The (1973) Ben Gazzara heads the rescue submarine racing to recover the men trapped in an undersea research lab by a volcanic eruption in the North Atlantic. Canadian production directed by Daniel Petrie, the routine underwater adventure relies heavily on the special sub's scientific gadgetry and the exotic deep sea creatures, which will engage the interest of younger viewers, but adults may prefer staying on dry land. A-I (G) U

Nest of Vipers (1979) Italian film about a callow piano student (Christian Borromeo) who has an affair with the mother (Senta Berger) of a fellow student and then abandons her for a beautiful young heiress (Ornella Muti). Director Tonino Cervi's story of jealousy and revenge is mired in graphically depicting the affairs as well as others including incest, lesbianism and homosexuality. O (R)

Network (1976) When a TV anchorman (Peter Finch) has a breakdown and rants and raves on camera, his ratings soar and an ambitious network executive (Faye Dunaway) centers a new program concept on him over the protests of a more humane executive (William Holden). Written by Paddy Chayefsky and directed by Sidney Lumet, the heavy-handed satire on the evils of television and its effects on the public misses as often as is on target. Needless subplot involves an adulterous affair with an explicit scene of love-making. O (R) AA

Nevada Smith (1966) Well-made western about a youth (Steve McQueen) who, after his mother and father are tortured to death by three outlaws looking for gold, tracks them down, killing them one by one. Directed by Henry Hathaway, the revenge story is told in very violent fashion and there are some sexual references. A-III (br) A

Never a Dull Moment (1968) Well-paced gangster spoof about a TV actor (Dick Van Dyke) who is mistaken for a killer and has to turn on all of his tough guy mannerisms while looking for a chance to escape a colorful mob of would-be art thieves (led by Edward G. Robinson). Though there's nothing he can do to avoid the museum heist, it winds up a harmless caper in the pop art department. Jerry Paris directs a likable bit of light entertainment from the Disney Studio that will go down as easily with parents as with their children. A-I (G) U

Never Cry Wolf (1983) A government naturalist (Charles Martin Smith) who is sent to the Canadian Arctic to determine if wolves are responsible for decimating the once abundant caribou herds, learns instead a lesson in survival and self-knowledge. Director Carrol Ballard's fact-based Disney drama allows the viewer to feel the wonder and excitement of the wilderness with insightful humor and stunning visuals. Some scenes of Smith eating mice and going naked in barren Arctic landscape. A-II (PG)

Never Give an Inch (see: "Sometimes a Great Notion").

Never Let Me Go (1953) Fanciful cold war clunker about an American reporter (Clark Gable) getting a British seaman (Bernard Miles) to sail him to the U.S.S.R. in an attempt to smuggle his Russian ballerina bride (Gene Tierney) out of the country. Director Delmer Daves takes a pedestrian look at Soviet intransigence in a dated period piece of possible interest to social historians. Ideological stereotypes and dangerous doings. A-I (br) U

Never Say Die (1939) Frenetic comedy set in a Swiss spa where an American millionaire (Bob Hope), mistakenly told he has only 30 days to live, jilts a gun-toting socialite (Gale Sondergaard) to wed an oil man's daughter (Martha Raye) who's unhappily betrothed to a penniless count (Alan Mowbray), intending to leave her a wealthy widow able to marry the man she loves—a Texas bus driver (Andy Devine). Directed by Elliott Nugent, the good cast provides occasional splashes of humor but the wacky characters and zany situations grow increasingly tiresome. Romantic complications galore and some sexual innuendo. A-III (br) U

Never Say Never Again (1983) Aging Agent 007 (Sean Connery), who was shunted aside by a new chief, is called back to retrieve two nuclear warheads stolen by a charming and sinister villain (Klaus Maria Brandauer). Director Irvin Kershner's version of the Bond mystique goes overboard in treating violence as spectacle and promiscuity as hyperactive heroism. O (PG)

Never Too Late (1965) Uneven adaptation of the Broadway comedy about a couple who late in life have another child and the complications this causes in their lives. Under Bud Yorkin's direction, Paul Ford is practically the whole show as he tries in his hard-hearted but soft-headed way to cope with the situation. A-III (br) A

NeverEnding Story, The (1984) While hiding out from class bullies, a schoolboy reads a storybook that propels him into its fantasy world where his imagination runs wild and his courage is tested. German director Wolfgang Peterson delivers a work filled with murky metaphysical references, vividly grotesque creatures and a concluding literary-inspired act of retribution that adults may appreciate more than younger viewers, although there is more than enough fairy-tale ambiance to hold their interest. A-I (PG) U

NeverEnding Story II: The Next Chapter, The (1991) A young boy (Jonathan Brandis) enters a fairy tale storybook to help the characters save their planet from an evil sorceress (Clarissa Burt). Though director George Miller's fantasy-adventure sequel is visually captivating, its bland storyline holds little interest for adults and its monsters might scare preschoolers. Some menacing characters and fantasy violence. A-I (PG) U

New Adventures of Pippi Longstocking, The (1988) Cheesy, cloying English-language adaptation of the Astrid Lindgren children's books sees high-spirited Pippi (Tami Erin) housed briefly in an orphanage after being washed overboard from her father's (John Schuck) ship. Peppy music, bad acting and unimaginative direction by Ken Annakin. A-I (G)

New Angels, The (1966) Quasi-documentary with 9 vignettes showing the life of Italian young people attempts to make a serious social statement, but its emphasis on the erotic details of sexual situations undermines the theme of director Ugo Gregoretti's effort. O (br)

New Centurions, The (1972) Screen version of Joseph Wambaugh's novel about a veteran police sergeant (George C. Scott) who schools a rookie cop (Stacy Keach) in handling Los Angeles street crime. Director Richard Fleischer's diffuse and episodic melodrama reduces characters and social issues to simple good-guy, bad-guy dramatics. Some bleary-eyed nightclub philosophizing comparing the collapse of law and order in Rome to present society (presumably symbolized by a topless dancer in the background) is the key to the movie's easy sympathies for the police taking the law into their own hands. Violent action and atmosphere. A-IV (R) AA

New Girl in Town (1977) Sympathetic account of the rise of a young woman (Monica Gayle) to stardom in the world of country western music. Under the direction of Gus Trikonis, however, the heroine spends a great deal of time taking off her clothes on camera, making doubtful the movie's sincerity of purpose. O (R)

New Jack City (1991) Ruthless gang leader (Wesley Snipes) muscles in on the drug traffic while two honest cops (Ice T, Judd Nelson) fight the system to bring him to justice. Director and co-star Mario Van Peebles makes an anti-drug statement by exploiting the seamiest aspects of drug addiction in the ghetto. Excessive violence, sexual exploitation, some nudity and incessant rough language. O (R) 18

New Land, The (1973) Sequel to "The Emigrants" continues its story of a Swedish family (Max von Sydow and Liv Ullmann) after they and a small band of farmers arrive in the Minnesota wilderness of the 1850s and set to work establishing homesteads, cultivating the land, raising their families and acclimatizing themselves to life in the New Land. Superbly directed by Jan Troell, the historical re-creation is an extraordinary achievement in conveying a sense of the pioneer spirit out of which our nation grew. A-II (PG)

New Leaf, A (1971) A slick, money-grubbing cad (Walter Matthau) courts and marries a wealthy spinster (Elaine May) whose passion is botany. She comes to love him dearly but undeservedly as he tries various schemes to kill her until an increasing glimmer of affection rises in his own heart. Witty and fast-paced comedy, also written and directed by May, is frequently hilarious and often biting in its moral satire. A-III (G) U

New Life, A (1988) Workaholic Wall Street broker (Alan Alda) and wife (Ann-Margret) split up after 26 years of marriage and nervously enter into the singles' scene and commitment to difficult new relationships. Writer-director Alda takes full advantage of the seriocomic elements found in the somewhat predictable plot that benefits from fine acting and characterizations. Some rough language and discreet nudity in several sexual situations. A-III (PG-13) 15

New Life Style, The (1970) Trashy German production about a conservative travel agent (Horst Tappet) who attends a business convention at the seashore and is soon having a whirl with a comely blonde (Renata Van Holt). Around them, swinging couples frolic freely and interchangeably according to their perverse preferences. Presented by Peter Savage, this burlesque is badly dubbed into English, further marring a bad experience. O (nr)

New Moon (1940) One of the sillier Nelson Eddy-Jeanette MacDonald costume musicals is set during the French Revolution when a nobleman-turned-pirate (Eddy) captures a ship bearing an aristocrat's daughter (MacDonald) who spurns his love until marooned on an uninhabited island. Directed by Robert Z. Leonard, the turns of plot are outlandish but the romance is sappily endearing backed by Sigmund Romberg-Oscar Hammerstein songs, including "Stout-Hearted Men" and "Lover, Come

Back to Me." Some romantic mush with unlikely appeal for youngsters. A-I (br)

New York, New York (1977) Nostalgic musical romance about a 1940s' showbiz couple (Liza Minnelli and Robert De Niro) who seek stardom and pay the price in an adulterous affair, drugs and alcohol abuse before achieving success. Directed by Martin Scorsese, the big budget musical is technically impressive but dramatically off key in its depiction of the trials and tribulations of marriage. A-III (PG) A

Newman's Law (1974) George Peppard plays an incorruptible Los Angeles cop who, on the verge of arresting a drug ring, is framed on a drug charge, causing him to go off on his own to clear his record and knock off the villains to boot. Directed by Richard Heffron, the routine crime plot moves swiftly to its predictable bloody climax. The plot's justification—taking the law into one's own hands—would be troubling if it were not so unbelievable as presented here. Some violence and rough language. A-III (PG) AA

Newsfront (1979) Australian production about the lives and careers of a veteran newsreel cameraman (Bill Hunter) and his assistant (Chris Haywood) from 1948 to 1956 when the nightly television news made the weekly newsreel redundant. Writer-director Philip Noyce pays more attention to the craft of the newsreel and its content during the era of its glory than to the private lives of its characters, which receive rather soap opera treatment in marital problems and love affairs. Interesting re-creation but shallow human dimension. A-III (PG) A

Newsies (1992) Run-of-the-mill musical about New York City newsboys (including Christian Bale and David Moscow) going on strike in 1899 to protest higher newspaper prices decreed by publisher Joseph Pulitzer (Robert Duvall). Though it offers some skillful choreography and a sprightly musical score, director Kenny Ortega develops little dramatic interest in the characters or their predicaments. Brief violence. A-II (PG)

Next! (see: "The Next Victim").

Next Man, The (1976) Spoiled rich girl (Cornelia Sharpe) works as an assassin for a terrorist group, seducing and liquidating her victims in exotic corners of the world, but meets her match in a visionary Arab diplomat (Sean Connery). Director Richard C. Sarafian's mediocre, high gloss thriller offers little besides mindless violence, some gratuitous nudity and a brutal ending. O (R) PG

Next of Kin (1989) Savvy Chicago cop (Patrick Swayze) is torn between the law and his family's backwoods code of justice when his older brother (Liam Neeson) comes to town to avenge the murder of their younger brother (Bill Paxton) by the mob. Director John Irvin attempts to contrast the feuding ethics of hillbilly and mobster clans, but the numerous plot gaps, ethnic caricatures and deterioration into vigilantism weaken the effort. Much profanity. Some grisly violence. O (R) 15

Next Stop, Greenwich Village (1976) Jewish youth (Lenny Baker) leaves his blue-collar Brooklyn neighborhood in 1953 to seek fame as an actor in Greenwich Village. His growth both on the stage and as a person is chronicled by director Paul Mazursky in a series of incidents that are often quite amusing and sometimes extremely touching. Though soft and sentimental in its portrayal of the young man and overly nostalgic about the era, the movie is positive in its assertions of values and sense of ethnic roots. One notable exception is its acceptance of abortion. A-IV (R)

Next Summer (1986) In a story about three generations and how each defines the nature of loving relationships, this French production features an impressive cast, including Claudia Cardinale, Jean-Louis Trintignant, Philippe Noiret and Fanny Ardant. Directed with charm and humor by Nadine Trintignant, each member of this family saga is shown grappling with the many facets of love, sex and marriage from the perspective of strengthening or weakening family ties. Adult theme. A-III (nr)

Next Victim, The (1971) Italian-Spanish co-production about a succession of young ladies who lose their lives to a savage razor-wielder whose real object is to terrorize one particularly fickle young lady (Edwige Fenech). Directed by Sergio Martino, the badly dubbed terror mystery has an obvious twist ending, predictable suspense and abundant nudity. O (R)

Next Voice You Hear, The (1950) The lives of an average American worker (James Whitmore), his pregnant wife (Nancy Davis) and their young son are transformed when they hear God speaking to the world on the radio. Directed by William Wellman, the intriguing and well-intentioned concept falls flat because of the banality of the radio message directing people to perform "miracles" of "peace and loving kindness" and the clumsy day-by-day portrayal of how the father gradually changes over the course of a week. It's not silly, but it's not very credible. A-I (nr) A

Nice Girl Like Me, A (1969) Boring British melodrama about an unwed mother (Barbara Ferris) who conceives one child in Paris, another in Venice and acquires a third infant when it is dumped in her arms by a desperate Italian mother. Directed by Desmond Davis, there is a lot of lush photography of European cities and pastoral landscapes, but the story lacks any social or moral perspective that might have given it some significance. A-III (PG)

Nicholas and Alexandra (1971) British epic offers the spectacle of glittering palaces, splendid pageantry and larger-than-life characters in ornate costumes but misses the historical context making understandable why this couple were the last of the Romanovs to rule Russia. Directed by Franklin J. Schaffner, the focus is on the domestic lives of the Tsar (Michael Jayston) and Tsarina (Janet Suzman) with occasional fragmentary scenes indicating the revolutionary events that were to sweep away the entire epoch. Grand-scale romance set against a turbulent but fuzzy background, with only Rasputin's rampant sexuality to give children pause, though all will wince at his brutal murder. A-II (PG)

Nickel Ride, The (1975) Aging, small-time operator (Jason Miller) gets into a tight spot trying to put together a deal for the crime syndicate and tries to avoid his inevitable fate. Though the narrative is somewhat muddled, director Richard Mulligan's treatment of the central issue of the man's survival is taut and powerfully done, with nicely nuanced characterizations and atmosphere of menace. Element of human compassion elevates it above standard crime movie. A-III (PG) AA

Nickelodeon (1977) Mildly humorous slapstick drama about the pioneer days of silent films stars Ryan O'Neal as young lawyer turned writer-director and Burt Reynolds as his star. Director Peter Bogdanovich's story has some amusing moments but is rather thin in dramatic developments, leaving the main focus on movie memorabilia. A-II (PG) U

Night and the City (1992) A second-rate lawyer (Robert De Niro) invites disaster by borrowing money from the jealous husband (Cliff Gorman) of his girlfriend (Jessica Lange) to put on a boxing tournament in a venue controlled by a crooked promoter (Alan King). Writer-director Irwin Winkler's profane, edgy movie captures the hustling spirit of New York City lowlifes while leaving their intersecting relationships too vague to be dramatically satisfying. An adulterous relationship, brief violence, some sexual innuendo and much rough language, including racial slurs. A-III (R) 15

Night at the Bijou, A (see: "The Three Stooges Follies").

Night Call Nurses (1972) Sex comedy about nurses (Patricia T. Byrne, Alana Collins and Mittie Lawrence) who temper the needling they receive from psychotic doctors and patients by indulging in gratuitous sex relations with them. Directed by Jonathan Kaplan, it's exploitation drivel. O (R)

Night Caller (1975) Unsavory French film about a police inspector (Jean-Paul Belmondo) whose methods in trying to catch some bank robbers and a deranged serial murderer are both brutal and lack any sense of legal niceties. Director Henri Verneuil's disjointed crime thriller lacks any elements of tension or suspense. Violence, rough language and elements of sexual perversion. O (R) AA

Night Crossing (1982) Disney fact-based drama about two families (John Hurt, Jane Alexander, Beau Bridges, Glynnis O'Connor) who make their way to freedom from East Germany by way of a hot air balloon. While there are some moments of suspense and entertainment, director Delbert Mann doesn't deal adequately with the foreign setting, culture and people. Nevertheless, it provides the family audience with a harrowing reminder of the price of freedom. A-I (PG) A

Night Digger, The (1971) British psychological thriller about an aging spinster (Patricia Neal), long dominated by a tyrannical adoptive mother, who falls in love with a psychotic killer twenty years her junior (Nicholas Clay). Good acting gives credibility to a rather preposterous situation, allowing director Alistair Reid the intriguing opportunity to probe into the darker corners of the human mind and soul. The result is a mixed bag, caught somewhere between a taut chiller and a human interest story. Some flashbacks indicating the killer's twisted sexuality and several grisly murders with oppressive sexual overtones. A-IV (R) X

Night Evelyn Came Out of the Grave, The (1972) Italian production about an Englishman (Anthony Steffen) who is haunted by the ghost of his unfaithful wife and lapses into periods of insanity during which he becomes a sadistic libertine. Directed by Emilio P. Miraglia, the murder mystery is secondary to the sexual aspects that feature nudity. O (R)

Night Eyes (1990) Security guard (Andrew Stevens) falls for the rich divorcee (Tanya Roberts) he's guarding and winds up being made the patsy in a murder case. Ineptly directed by Jag Mundhra, the story is made out of cardboard with characters to match. Graphic sex scenes with some nudity, occasional violence and rough language. O (R)

Night Flight from Moscow (1973) Convoluted espionage story about a glowering Russian spy (Yul Brynner) who defects to the West and the CIA official (Henry Fonda) whose task is to determine whether the defector is an honest turncoat or a double agent. French production directed by Henri Verneuil has interesting details about counter-intelligence methods, but the slow pace of the international yarn makes it a yawner. Some violence. A-III (PG)

Night Full of Rain, A (1978) The unhappy marriage of a rich American (Candice Bergen) and an Italian Communist journalist (Giancarlo Giannini) forms the basis for director Lina Wertmuller's story of their violent meeting and courtship told in flashbacks. Some nudity, sexual by-play and crudities. O (R)

Night Game (1989) Tedious serial-killer thriller unfolds in a colorful Gulf-Coast setting with a burned-out cop (Roy Scheider), his ill-suited fiancee (Karen Young) and an implausible scenario about a maniac who kills young blonds whenever the Houston Astros' star pitcher wins a game. Director Peter Masterson's effort strikes out. Some profanity, menace and grisly shots of mutilated corpses. A-III (R)

Night Games (1980) Ludicrous and inept melodrama about a wife (Cindy Pickett), traumatized by a girlhood assault, who is cured of her frigidity by having sex with a stranger dressed in feathers. Listlessly directed by Roger Vadim, the acting is embarrassingly bad. Nudity and graphic sexuality abound. O (R) 18

Night Has Eyes, The (1942) Romantic British chiller in which school teachers (Joyce Howard and Tucker McGuire) trace a missing friend to the Yorkshire moors where they stumble upon a spooky mansion inhabited by a strange composer (James Mason) and two servants (Wilfrid Lawson and Mary Clare). Written and directed by Leslie Arliss, the plot's suspense doesn't measure up to the eerie atmosphere of the fog-shrouded setting and Mason's wild-eyed portrayal of a shattered veteran of the Spanish Civil War. Menacing situations. A-II (br) A

Night in Casablanca, A (1946) Tame Marx Brothers comedy has Groucho managing the hotel where Sig Ruman and other fugitive Nazis have stashed stolen loot but, when they try to escape with it, Chico and Harpo ground their plane. Directed by Archie L. Mayo, the script is awfully thin and the old zany flair of the Brothers' antics is barely visible. Comic violence and mild sexual innuendo. A-II (br) U

Night in Heaven, A (1983) Married school teacher (Lesley Ann Warren) has an affair with a student (Christopher Atkins) who works as a male exotic dancer. Directed by John Avildsen, the crude effort emphasizes nudity and graphic sex while disparaging marital fidelity. O (R)

Night Moves (1975) Gene Hackman stars as an L.A. private-eye who traces a 16-year-old runaway to Florida living with her stepfather and his mistress who are both involved in a smuggling operation. Director Arthur Penn's muddled, badly acted detective melodrama features some brutal murders and resorts to sexual exploitation, especially of the girl, to keep things moving. O (R) X

Night of Bloody Horror (1970) Gross horror movie about a mother who mummifies dead members of the family and her manic-depressive son suspected of three sensational murders. Producer-director Joy N. Houck Jr., while suggesting these may have been cases of accidental fratricide and paternal suicide, concentrates on explicit love-making, ax-wielding, and quarts of blood-letting. O (nr)

Night of Counting the Years, The (1975) Unusual Egyptian film about a poor village whose livelihood depends upon periodically selling archaeological treasures they have discovered in an unlooted royal tomb ingeniously hidden in the rocky heights above the Valley of the Kings on the Upper Nile. Writer-director Shadi Abdelsalam links the grandeur and beauty of the age of the pharaohs with the stark poverty of their black-robed descendents in a brilliantly photographed drama filled with many poetic and lyric passages evoking a sense of mystery appropriate to the land of the Sphinx. A-II (nr) A

Night of Dark Shadows (1971) Spooky doings in a sequel to "House of Dark Shadows" center on Quentin (David Selby), the last of the Collins heirs who returns to the family mansion with his bride (Kate Jackson) and falls victim to reincarnations of his ancestors. Producer-director Dan Curtis dredges up a bushel of scary chestnuts for those who enjoy such things. Minimal gore, but some sexual allusions suggest an adult perspective. A-III (GP)

Night of the Blood Monster (1972) Cut-rate British costume melodrama with Christopher Lee as a lecherous witch hunter under James II. Lee gets his just desserts when William of Orange invades and wins the throne. Directed by Jess Franco, this is a talkie with a lot of posturing and little action. The sex and violence is mostly implied by using victims of rape and torture as background decoration. A-III (PG)

Night of the Comet (1984) Two teenage California Valley girls (Catherine Mary Stewart, Kelli Maroney) survive the passing of a comet that has reduced nearly everyone else to red dust. Some bright moments in this tongue-in-cheek disaster thriller from director Thom Eberhardt, but silly zombie attacks and a benign view of promiscuity mars the film's value as simple diversion. O (PG-13) 15

Night of the Executioners (see: "The Cop").

Night of the Following Day, The (1969) Failed crime melodrama in which four Americans (Marlon Brando, Jess Hahn, Richard Boone and Rita Moreno) concoct a scheme to kidnap a wealthy youth (Pamela Franklin) on her arrival in France. Directed by Hubert Cornfield, the plot is implausible and the characterizations are wildly unconvincing. Some violence, sex and graphic drug use. A-III (R) X

Night of the Generals, The (1967) A detective story without much mystery but unusual because the suspects are World War II German Army generals (Donald Pleasence, Charles Gray and Peter O'Toole). Detective Omar Sharif plods along after his man with amiable determination, but director Anatole Litvak's straightforward narrative does not arouse much interest. Some brutal violence. A-III (br) A

Night of the Grizzly, The (1966) Unpretentious western directed by Joseph Pevney about a ranch family (Clint Walker, Marta Toren) who is trying to raise livestock on a range at the foot of the Rockies, but their ranch draws an enormous grizzly bear that eludes every effort to trap him. Wholesome outdoor adventure fare for the family. A-I (br) U

Night of the Hunter, The (1955) Powerful chiller from David Grubb's novel in which a berserk backwoods preacher (Robert Mitchum) learns of money stolen by a dying convict, marries his widow (Shelley Winters) to find it, then pursues her two frightened youngsters until they find sanctuary with a frail but resourceful matron (Lillian Gish). The only movie directed by actor Charles Laughton, the dark tale of suspense builds a truly frightening picture of a homicidal fanatic whose righteous facade is finally shattered by the innocence of children and the common sense of a determined woman. Much menace, some stylized violence and muted sexual references. A-III (nr) 15

Night of the Juggler (1980) A Psychotic (Cliff Gorman) kidnaps the teenage daughter of an ex-policeman (James Brolin) and the desperate father tracks down the killer himself, a chase that takes him into a very rough and sordid part of town. Director Robert Butler's moderately exciting thriller is marred by graphic violence, rough language and gratuitous nudity. O (R)

Night of the Lepus (1972) Zoologists Stuart Whitman and Janet Leigh, experimenting with hormones to reduce the rabbit population, accidentally produce a whole Arizona desert full of rabid cottontails as big as cattle who terrorize the countryside. Directed by William F. Claxton, the monster bunnies loom large on miniature sets, but not large enough to hide the inanities of the script. Still, this hare-raising tale delivers more chuckles than chills. A-II (PG) X

Night of the Living Dead (1968) Low-budget horror movie whose plot centers on a group of strangers barricaded in a farmhouse while radiation-animated corpses who feed off the living try to storm in for their prey. Directed by George Romero, the unpolished look of the production (grainy black-and-white photography and use of local Pittsburgh residents) has a makeshift quality helping to sustain the dimension of nightmarish unreality. Every once in a while, there is some unconscious humor that nicely relieves the tension and helped earn its cult reputation. Several fleeting but graphic scenes of ghouls gnawing on various parts of the anatomy. A-III (nr) 18

Night of the Living Dead (1990) Color remake of the 1969 low-budget cult classic about flesh-eating zombies converging on a rural farmhouse with six frantic adults and one injured child trapped inside. Director Tom Savini's rehash of Romero's original stomach-wrencher is superior only in its production values, but its nihilistic conclusion is much nastier. Grisly violence, momentary rear nudity and minimal rough language. O (R) 18

Night of the Shooting Stars, The (1983) In the chaotic final days of World War II, some Italian peasants flee their villages and hide out in the woods, trying to avoid both retreating German soldiers and vengeful Fascists. Directed and written by Paolo and Vittorio Taviani, the narrative is seen through the perspective of a 6-year-old girl who, years later, relates her impressions of war's absurdities to her young son. Visually stunning, often lyric essay on hope and human resilience. Brief, but intense violence. A-II (R)

Night of the Witches (1970) Failed horror movie about a venal preacher, a naive young man, and a cult of astrologers who kill people with bad horoscopes. Keith Erik Burt directs a tiresome exercise, relying solely upon sexual innuendo for energy. O (PG)

Night on Earth (1992) Amusing look at five distinctly different cab rides occurring on the same night in Los Angeles, New York, Paris, Rome and Helsinki. With delightful performances from Gena Rowlands, Winona Ryder and Armin Mueller-Stahl, these wry anecdotes by writer-producer-director Jim Jarmusch playfully capture the universal nature of people despite differing cultures. Some subtitles. Numerous sexual references and recurring rough language. A-III (R) 15

Night Passage (1957) Accordion-playing troubleshooter (James Stewart), hired to protect a railroad payroll from Colorado train-robbers, comes up against his outlaw younger brother (Audie Murphy). Director James Neilsen's predictable Western works up some interest in the moral struggle between good and bad siblings and its effect on an impressionable youth (Brandon de Wilde). Some menace and stylized violence. A-I (br) U

Night Patrol (1985) Stupid hijinks in the police department are the sole feature of this vulgar, sexually exploitative clone of "Police Academy." O (R)

Night Porter, The (1974) Dirk Bogarde plays the porter in a Viennese hotel who resumes the sadomasochistic relationship he began years before with a woman inmate (Charlotte Rampling) of a concentration camp where he was a Nazi officer. Director Liliana Cavani claustrophobically dissects the terror and thrill of a renewed and sick lust that both know will ultimately destroy them. Though done with some artistic integrity, this exercise in abnormal psychology lacks dramatic coherence or human insight. Several explicit scenes of a sexual nature involving nudity and sadistic brutality. O (R) X

Night Shift (1982) Night crew at the N.Y. City morgue (Henry Winkler and Michael Keaton) turn the place into a call-girl service. The situation allows for little but smirks and the few laughs are sight gags about life in the big city. Under Ron Howard's heavy-handed direction, Winkler is overshadowed by Keaton's fine performance as a frenetic zany. Romanticizes prostitution and some brief nudity. O (R) AA

Night Stalker, The (1987) Demented crime melodrama about an alcoholic vice-squad detective (Charles Napier) on the trail of a psychopathic serial killer of hookers. Director Max Kleven's tired plot features an excess of bloody violence, nude corpses and profanity. O (R)

Night the Lights Went Out in Georgia, The (1981) Dennis Quaid and Kristy McNichol play a brother and sister who dream of being big-time country-western singers in Nashville but face the predictable problems of earning a living in a small Georgia town. Director Ron Maxwell's attempt to cash in on the hit song of the title is mediocre at best. A-III (PG)

Night the World Exploded, The (1957) Pulp doomsday tale about a scientist (William Leslie) and his assistant (Kathryn Grant) seeking the cause of increasing underground pressures which threaten to blow up the world. Directed by Fred F. Sears, the plot is hilariously hokey and the acting wooden but it may please viewers looking for a simple-minded exercise in the absurd. A-I (br)

Night They Raided Minsky's, The (1968) Because this film celebrates the crude lustiness that characterized burlesque in the 1920s, some may find it an honest relief from the present era's overglamorization of sex. As directed by William Friedkin, the movie's stand-out performance is by Norman Wisdom as a sad little comic, with Bert Lahr's last movie appearance adding some pathos and nostalgia to the proceedings. Unfortunately, however, the long-awaited "accident" that led to the first strip-tease gets most of the emphasis. O (PG) A

Night Visitor, The (1971) A double murder disrupts a quiet Scandinavian countryside and the man under suspicion (Per Oscarsson) tells the police inspector (Trevor Howard) that the murders could only have been done by his brother-in-law (Max von Sydow) who resides in an escape-proof cell in an insane asylum. Directed by Laslo Benedek, this modern Gothic tale uses von Sydow's gymnastic skills and menacing presence to achieve a near perfect combination of thriller and mystery. Some violence. A-III (PG) X

Night Watch (1973) Disappointing British murder melodrama revolves around whether Elizabeth Taylor is actually mad or only pretends to be in order to avenge herself on husband Lawrence Harvey for plotting to get her enormous wealth by doing away with her and marrying Billie Whitelaw. Under Brian Hutton's uncertain direction, Taylor's performance is a monotonous mixture of screechy emotional outbursts and frumpish attempts at feline sensuality, even as the muddled plot lurches toward its throat-slitting climax. A-III (PG) X

Night We Never Met, The (1993) Time-sharing a Manhattan apartment with two men she has never met, a married woman (Annabella Sciorra) decides to have an affair with one of them (Matthew Broderick) but accidentally sleeps with the wrong guy (Kevin Anderson). Writer-director Warren Leight's dreary mistaken-identity comedy takes a contrived situation and beats it to death with charmless characters and numbingly dumb dialogue. Benign treatment of casual sex, brief nudity, heavy drinking and some rough language. O (R)

Night Zoo (1988) French-Canadian crime film about an ex-con (Gilles Maheu) trying to stay alive in Montreal's sleazy underworld while being pursued by two drug-dealing cops he has double-crossed. Written and directed by Jean-Claude Lauzon, its hard-edged depiction of criminal excesses is softened somewhat by a subplot involving a growing reconciliation between the ex-con and his father (Roger Le Bel in a fine performance). Excessively violent treatment, several explicit sex scenes and rough language. O (nr) 18

Nightbreed (1990) A young man (Craig Sheffer) and his girlfriend (Anne Bobby) race to save a legendary city of dead souls from invading human nut cases, including a psycho psychoanalyst (David Cronenberg), a fascist cop (Charles Haid) and a spineless priest (Malcolm Smith). Writer-director Clive Barker's muddled horror movie features a haphazard collection of gruesome freaks, nightmare imagery and make-up wizardry. Excessive images of grisly human slaughter, some profanity and nudity. O (R) 18

Nightcomers, The (1972) Based on the Victorian characters in Henry James' supernatural story, "The Turn of the Screw," the film ends where the original began and imagines the dark events transpiring between the groundskeeper (Marlon Brando) and his mistress (Stephanie Beacham) that leave two very troubled children for the new governess who arrives at the beginning of the James' story. Director Michael Winner dramatizes literally the perverse tendencies and violent events (bizarre sadomasochistic games), which only lurked beneath the surface of the original James story. Climatic gore, nudity in a sexual context and a theme of evil in innocence. O (R) X

Nightfall (1956) Tough crime thriller of an innocent man (Aldo Ray) pursued by a cop (James Gregory) who wants him for murder and a bankrobber (Brian Keith) who wants the loot he's lost. Director Jacques Tourneur makes it all the more intriguing by doling out the story with flashbacks as needed and the cast makes it seem convincing enough. Stylized violence. A-II (br) A

Nighthawks (1981) Intense thriller with Sylvester Stallone playing a N.Y. City policeman assigned to an anti-terrorist unit whose mettle is tested by a clever and utterly ruthless German terrorist (Rutger Hauer). Director Bruce Malmuth fails to invest any human dimension to all the violence and counterviolence that transpires, using the situation merely as the basis for exciting melodrama. Brutal violence and rough language. A-III (R) X

Nightmare Before Christmas, The (1993) Minor fantasy of the macabre with puppet animation telling the tale of Halloweentown's skeleton king replacing the kidnapped Santa Claus and spreading Christmas fear with scary toys until stopped by a missile, then returning home to free Santa in time to make his accustomed rounds. Producer Tim Burton's story centers in the dark world of hobgoblins and monsters suddenly intruding on the bright expectations of St. Nick's annual visit but the narrative proves tiresome in padding out the thin concept, despite all its stylish puppetry and ghoulish humor. Considerable menace and threatening atmosphere. A-II (PG)

Nightmare in Wax (1969) Old-fashioned horror movie about a psychotic wax museum curator (Cameron Mitchell) who seeks vengeance on some old associates for having humiliated and disfigured him. Director Bud Townsend bridges the gaps in the storyline with a little morbid humor, some mild horror and playful settings. A-II (M)

Nightmare on Elm Street, A (1984) Freddy (Robert Englund), a long-dead child murderer, haunts the dreams of some high school students who also die from them. Directed by Wes Craven, the horror movie relies on graphic gore, sexual references and images of uncaring parents for the purpose of eliciting shock and irreverent humor. O (R) 18

Nightmare on Elm Street II: Freddy's Revenge, A (1985) Foiled in the original, the slashing monster returns in this sequel, directed by Jack Sholder, to again take possession of a teenager so that he can do some further cutting up. More blood and gore mixed with sexual titillation aimed at teenagers. O (R) 18

Nightmare on Elm Street III: The Dream Warriors, A (1987) A group of youngsters are terrorized in their dreams by a restless, evil phantom who returns to avenge his fiery death at the hands of their parents. Director Chuck Russell's worn-out plot relies on gory special effects and sadistic violence with no other purpose but to shock. O (R) 18

Nightmare on Elm Street IV: The Dream Master, A (1988) Another inept sequel about a child murderer (Robert Englund) who takes revenge for his death by invading the dreams of his teenage victims. Directed by Renny Harlin, the plot is an unhealthy brew of gruesome, gory visuals with some nudity and rough language. O (R) 18

Nightmare on Elm Street V: The Dream Child, A (1989) Freddy Krueger (Robert Englund) is back, and this time he is stalking teenage Alice (Lisa Wilcox) through the dreams of her unborn, illegitimate child. Directed by Stephen Hopkins, there are gruesome flashbacks recalling Freddy's conception and birth as the son of a nun raped by psychos in an insane asylum, as well as Freddy's usual sadistic teen-stalking. O (R) 18

Nightwing (1979) An Indian deputy sheriff (Nick Mancuso), the deputy's girlfriend (Kathryn Harrold), and an obsessed scientist (David Warner) team up to track down and destroy a colony of ravenous, plague-bearing vampire bats. Director Arthur Hiller's modest thriller relies on an interesting mix of Indian mysticism and scientific facts, but the action leads only to an anticlimax. Rather graphic violence and the use of drugs for religious purposes. A-III (PG) AA

Nijinsky (1980) Biographical dramatization about legendary ballet dancer Vaslav Nijinsky (George de la Pena) and impresario Sergei Diaghilev (Alan Bates) places less emphasis upon ballet itself than upon their master-protege relationship and its homosexual dimension. Director Herbert Ross presents an elegant re-creation of pre-World War I Europe and the acting is of high order, but some may find the pace of the drama far too languid and others will be uncomfortable with the frank, if nonexplicit manner in which the homosexual relationship is depicted. Graphic but brief scene of heterosexual love-making. A-IV (R)

9 1/2 Weeks (1986) Director Adrian Lyne delivers a passionless expression of erotic fantasy in his sexually explicit depiction of a sadomasochistic love affair between an art gallery manager (Kim Basinger) and a financier (Mickey Rourke). Nudity and simulated sexual activity. O (R) 18

Nine Lives of Fritz the Cat, The (1974) Based on R. Crumb's comic-strip adventures of a funky feline whose primitive vulgarity and social irreverence some found refreshing, this inept animated version by Robert Taylor throws together a batch of disjointed and unimaginative episodes in a manner too literal and witless to be taken as satire. Its excesses of racial animosity and sexual exploitation go beyond questions of taste and tend to be socially destructive rather than purgative. O (R)

9.30.55 (see: "24 Hours of the Rebel").

9 to 5 (1980) Dolly Parton, Jane Fonda and Lily Tomlin play a trio of harassed, exploited secretaries who rise up in revolt against an autocratic boss (Dabney Coleman). Director Colin Higgins' promising satire becomes sheer silliness and then begins to drag. Some rough language, a pot-smoking scene and a sexually oriented dream sequence in which the male-dominance theme is inverted. A-III (PG) AA

1918 (1985) Mortality presses in upon ordinary happiness in a small Texas town as World War I is coming to an end in Euope and a killer flu epidemic rages at home. Written by Horton Foote and directed by Ken Harrison, it is an excellent movie that catches in wonderfully evocative fashion the terror and beauty of daily life. Though the setting is a vanished era, it nonetheless gives some rich insights into one's own life. There is nothing in it harmful to youngsters, but only children of a certain level of maturity will be able to appreciate it. A-I (nr)

1984 (1984) Uninspired screen version of George Orwell's foreboding vision of a totalitarian state crushing the individual rights of its hapless citizens loses here both the original's passionate idealism and sense of immediacy. Director Michael Radford's dryly somber work lacks the sense of human nobility that is the story's thematic core, but it does offer a nuanced performance by Richard Burton as a Big Brother surrogate and John Hurt as the rewriter of history. Some violence and brief nudity. A-III (R) 15

1941 (1979) Japanese submarine sighted off the coast of Southern California in the early days of World War II starts a panic with rumors of an invasion. Director Steven Spielberg wastes the comic talents of Dan Aykroyd and John Belushi in a vulgar, tedious, supremely unfunny comedy. Sexual connotations abound and there is some slapstick nudity. O (PG) A

1900 (1977) Sprawling, disjointed narrative spanning 70 years of Italian history seen through the eyes of two men born in 1901, one an aristocrat (Robert DeNiro), the other a Marxist (Gerard Depardieu). Director Bernardo Bertolucci's view of history lacks dramatic force and the human frame of reference is chiefly sex and politics. Extravagant depiction of violence and exploitation of nudity. O (R) X

1969 (1988) This sentimental reflection on the pivotal year of the Vietnam War era follows two small-town 19-year-olds (Kiefer Sutherland and Robert Downey Jr.) who as college students struggle to balance their fears about the draft with their desire to enjoy their last summer of teenage freedom. Writer-director Ernest Thompson's contrived memory play fails to flesh out his one-dimensional characters or inject the story with anything more than superficial period hype. Locker-room language, full frontal nudity in a brief, nonsexual scene and some drug abuse. A-III (R) 15

90 Days (1986) A young Canadian has three months in which to decide if he will marry the Korean woman he has sent for via a mail-order service. Director Giles Walker's small Canadian comedy explores the pitfalls of the male ego with charm and subtlety while showing that happiness and commitment can develop without premarital sex. A few harsh expletives and running gag about artificial insemination. A-III (nr) 15

99 and 44/100% Dead (1974) Silly, badly done gang-war movie starring Chuck Conners, Richard Harris, Edmond O'Brien and Bradford Dillman as various mobster types. As directed by John Frankenheimer, the movie fails to be either a serious crime melodrama or a comic-strip crime spoof, and consequently leaves the audience feeling uncomfortable about its realistic scenes of shootouts and sadistic brutality. A-III (PG) AA

99 Women (1969) Crude European exploitation film, directed by Jess Franco, centers on the more sordid aspects of life in a women's prison. Merely an excuse to portray nudity and perversion. O (R)

92 in the Shade (1975) Peter Fonda and Warren Oates play fishing boat owners competing for the tourist trade in the Florida Keys. The only elements that works in this failed comedy by writer-director Thomas McGuane are Fonda's madcap father (William Hickey) and his goatish grandfather (Burgess Meredith) Some exploitative sexual elements. O (R)

Ninth Configuration, The (1980) Stacy Keach plays a government psychologist trying to determine if the inmates of an asylum housed in a Californian Gothic castle are really psychological casualties of the Vietnam War or fakes. Writer-director William Blatty attempts to explore more than the nature of mental illness by introducing such issues as the existence of God, but the drama gets mired down in the more graphic aspects of insanity and unorthodox therapy. Disturbing and provocative movie with suicide as a plot device, some extreme violence and rough language. A-IV (R) X

No Blade of Grass (1970) Ecological disaster destroys all varieties of grasses and drives a London family to flee to a relative's farm in the north. Along the way the father (Nigel Davenport) kills anyone who stands in his way, but when they finally arrive at the farm they are faced with the father's brother waving a machine gun against unwelcome guests. Unsubtle melodrama directed by Cornel Wilde bludgeons viewers with assorted violence, blood and gore, a motorcycle gang rape and a very realistic birth sequence. Cruelly cynical conception of the anarchy and inhumanity resulting from the spectre of doomsday. O (R) AA

No Deposit, No Return (1976) Disney film with a better than average cast (David Niven, Herschel Bernardi and Darren McGavin) about two kids who stage their own kidnapping in order to join their mother in Hong Kong. Director Norman Tokar's plot is as old as O'Henry's "The Ransom of Red Chief," but that won't bother youngsters. A-I (G) U

No Drums, No Bugles (1971) Small, unpretentious Civil War drama about a West Virginia farmer (Martin Sheen) who rather than take up arms, leaves his wife and child for a solitary three-year self-imposed confinement in the backwoods. The substance of the movie is taken up with his techniques for survival in the forest through the changing seasons and Sheen makes it an absorbing experience in a tour de force performance. Written, produced and directed by Clyde Ware, it is not a tract against the evils of war but a comment on the sacrifices that must be made by those who place themselves outside the accepted standards of the community. Some motivations are unclear and an ambiguous ending make it best suited for an adult audience, but it is certainly one that could be appreciated by older teenagers. A-III (G)

No Holds Barred (1989) Strongman Hulk Hogan grunts, winks and stomps through his role as a TV superstar wrestler fending off bids from a sleazy rival network. Directed in gratuitous fashion by Thomas J. Wright, the movie's dumb material includes black stereotyping, excessive comic-book violence, some rough language and vulgar bathroom humor. O (PG-13) 15

No Man of Her Own (1932) Amusing romantic melodrama in which a crooked New York gambler (Clark Gable) marries a small-town librarian (Carole Lombard) on the flip of a coin, then becomes intrigued with the notion of going straight. Director Wesley Ruggles keeps the situation light and lively with snappy dialogue, a dandy supporting cast (notably Grant Mitchell, Elizabeth Patterson and J. Farrell MacDonald) and the sparks generated by the principals. Some sexual innuendo and criminal activity. A-III (br) A

No Man of Her Own (1950) Melodramatic tale in which a desperate unwed mother (Barbara Stanwyck) assumes the identity of a wealthy woman killed in a train wreck, then faces exposure unless she pays off her blackmailing ex-boyfriend (Lyle Bettger). Director Mitchell Leisen drags out the contrived suds as the woman's plight deepens until a sordid murder solves her immediate problems. Moral complications arising from the deception and some nasty menace. A-III (br) A

No Mercy (1986) Chicago cop (Richard Gere) avenges the murder of a fellow officer by using a beautiful Cajun (Kim Basinger) as the bait to smoke out and kill a crime boss of the Louisiana bayous. Director Richard Pearce's nasty, brutish thriller with implied sexual and explicit physical violence and excessive profanity. O (R) 18

No Small Affair (1984) When a 16-year-old boy (Jon Cryer) gives a boost to the career of a young singer (Demi Moore), she takes him to bed in gratitude. Director Jerry Schatzberg's limp romantic comedy is filled with unpleasant characters in an uninvolving plot. Endorses sexual promiscuity. O (R)

No Time for Breakfast (1978) French tearjerker about a witty, vivacious woman (Annie Girardot), senior physician at a Paris hospital, an ideal wife and extraordinary mother, who has an affair and develops a cancer that goes into remission when family ties are restored. Director Jean-

Louis Bertucelli coats the fact-based story with melodramatic overtones. Casual acceptance of infidelity and a nude bathtub scene. O (nr)

No Time for Sergeants (1958) Drafted into the Army, a Southern yokel (Andy Griffith) gets through boot camp only with the desperate assistance of his long-suffering sergeant (Myron McCormick). Director Mervyn LeRoy's one-joke comedy hinges on Griffith's hilarious performance as the well-intentioned rube which finally wears out its welcome in a tiresome, overlong ending. Wholesome service comedy except for a vulgar latrine routine and minimal fisticuffs. A-I (br) U

No Way Out (1975) Predictable Italian crime melodrama about what happens to a decent, hard-working family man (Alain Delon) when he tries to retire from his job as a Mafia hit-man. Director Duccio Tessari's dreary, mediocre film deals in standard violence of the genre, though women are treated especially brutally. Contains a gratuitous lesbian scene. O (R)

No Way Out (1987) Three-way power struggle erupts when a high-ranking politico (Gene Hackman) and his chief counsel (Will Patton) try to cover up the accidental death of a party girl (Sean Young) unknowingly shared by the politician's CIA liaison officer (Kevin Costner). Director Roger Donaldson's taut tale of betrayal and the abuse of power is marred by a fairly graphic lovemaking scene. A-III (R) 15

No Way to Treat a Lady (1968) Rod Steiger plays a madman with a severe mother complex who changes disguises for five compulsive murders, while a likeable police detective (George Segal) tries to outwit him. Director Jack Smight provides an effective mixture of adult comedy, psychodrama and an upbeat love story. A-III (br) X

Nobody Waved Goodbye (1965) Perceptive Canadian drama about a know-it-all adolescent (Peter Kastner) whose mounting troubles with middle-class parents, teachers and pregnant girlfriend (Julie Biggs) end with his running away. Directed in semi-documentary fashion by Don Owen, the result has a sense of spontaneity and unpretentious realism that makes it convincing both as drama and as social commentary. Assorted problems of a troubled youth. A-II (br)

Nobody's Fool (1986) Abandoned by her boyfriend when she becomes pregnant, a teenager (Rosanna Arquette) is befriended by a local theater director (Eric Roberts) who helps her refocus her life after giving up her baby for adoption. Directed by Evelyn Purcell, the movie is more about building one's self-esteem and trust than about sexual relationships. Implied sexual en-

counter and brief scene of violence. A-II (PG-13) U

Noises Off (1992) On the opening night of a Broadway comedy, its panicked director (Michael Caine) recalls the chaotic road-show rehearsals while the backstage infighting of the cast (Carol Burnett, John Ritter, Christopher Reeve and Denholm Elliott) noisily spills onstage. Peter Bogdanovich directs an overwrought, British-inspired sex farce of split-second timing whose frantic pranks and pratfalls entertain for a while, then are repeated to death. Some sexual innuendo, double entendres and an instance of rough language. A-III (PG-13) 15

Nomads (1986) A French anthropologist (Pierce Brosnan) is tormented by punk-rocker demons who invade his L.A. home. After the evil spirits are transferred at his death to his doctor (Lesley-Anne Down), the malevolent punkrockers scare her out of California. Profanity, brief nudity and scenes of violence. O (R) 15

None But the Brave (1965) Frank Sinatra directs as well as stars in this anti-war movie set in World War II on an out-of-the-way Pacific island where the crew of a downed American plane are pitted against a small Japanese outpost. The story's message of brotherhood is clearly stated but a bit too violently. A-II (nr) A

None But the Lonely Heart (1944) Darkly muddled story of a British drifter (Cary Grant) who returns to his home in the London slums to look after his dying mother (Ethyl Barrymore) but can't resist the easy money offered by a local mobster (George Coulouris). Written and directed by Clifford Odets, not even the square-jawed Grant can make the shallow lead sympathetic, though Barrymore copped an Oscar for her shining performance as his longsuffering yet ever hopeful mom. Brief stylized violence. A-II (br) A

Norma Rae (1979) Inspiring drama with Sally Field in the title role as an Alabama textile worker recruited by a tenacious labor organizer (Ron Liebman) to help rally her exploited co-workers into forming a union in the face of tough tactics by an unenlightened management. Director Martin Ritt's dramatic expose of injustices in the workplace gives viewers some characters and a cause to cheer about. Absorbing, thoughtful entertainment, but there are some frank references to sexual misconduct. A-III (PG) AA

Norman Is That You? (1976) Failed sitcom about a father (Redd Foxx) who discovers that his son is a homosexual. Though the visual elements are restrained, director George Schlatter's film stereotypes blacks, women and homosexuals; conveys a smug contempt for parental authority and affection; and exploits a serious theme in a witless manner. O (PG) X

Norseman, The (1978) Viking chieftain (Lee Majors) leads his men to the shores of the New World to rescue his father (Mel Ferrer), who is held prisoner by the Indians. Director Charles B. Pierce's low-budget, low-IQ saga presents Indians as the treacherous, bloodthirsty stereotypes that one would have thought had passed from the screen forever. Generous amount of violence and bloodshed. A-III (PG) A

North Avenue Irregulars, The (1979) Standard Disney comedy about a minister (Edward Herrmann) who takes over a failing parish in a small town and, along with other revitalizing measures, mobilizes a predictably zany collection of church women to put some illegal gamblers out of business. Director Bruce Bilson concludes the action with a car-crunching slapstick chase. Fair family fun, but less than appealing view of women. A-I (G) U

North by Northwest (1959) Stylish tongue-in-cheek thriller in which a suave advertising executive (Cary Grant), mistaken for a spy by foreign agents (James Mason and Martin Landau) and suspected of murder by the police, is chased from the United Nations to Mount Rushmore, with some time out along the way for romance with a double agent (Eva Marie Saint). With the plot serving only to string together a dandy series of suspense sequences (most memorable, the deadly crop-dusting plane in the middle of nowhere), director Alfred Hitchcock is at his most playful in manipulating the viewer through his intricate maze of menaces. Stylized violence and discreet sexual references. A-III (br) PG

North Country (1972) Ron Hayes is a bush pilot who delivers mail-and-supplies to those rugged individualists who have chosen to live off the land in the lonely, lovely wilds of Alaska. Functioning as a filmmaker in his spare time, Hayes conceived and photographed this documentary view of the modern pioneer on America's last frontier. Its blending of scenery, rare wildlife and the people who live in the land of the Eskimo make an outdoor adventure that is unusually satisfying family fare. A-I (G)

North Dallas Forty (1979) Nick Nolte and Mac Davis star as professional football players who love the game but not what commercialism has done to it. Nolte is excellent and director Ted Kotcheff's expose of the hypocrisy and violence of professional sports has some very effective moments, especially the effects of drug abuse, but its focus becomes obscured in promiscuous sex and the athletes' propensity for pranks. Some nudity and much rough language. O (R) 18

Northwest Frontier (see: "Flame Over India").

Northwest Passage (1940) Colorful, large-scale adaptation of Kenneth Roberts's novel about a rugged company of colonial backwoodsmen led by Captain Robert Rogers (Spencer Tracy) deep into hostile country to destroy an enemy stronghold during the French and Indian War. Directed by King Vidor, the narrative's violent frontier action is well paced with humor and pathos, mainly involving two novice Rangers (Walter Brennan and Robert Young), but in celebrating the brave exploits of a tiny band of colonial patriots against a wilderness foe, the movie is woefully dated in its depiction of Indians as brutal savages. Though there is much good in this historical adventure, its violence and ethnic stereotypes make it questionable fare for young children. A-I (nr)

Norwood (1970) Corny but entertaining Glen Campbell vehicle following his misadventures after military service as he innocently transports some stolen cars to N.Y., has a one-night stand with a pretty hippie in Greenwich Village, meets Kim Darby on a bus and brings her back to his Southern home along with a midget and a performing rooster. Campbell's fans will enjoy the romp, though some may be put off by the salty dialogue and tasteless but brief situations. A-III (G) A

Nosferatu, the Vampire (1979) Slow but stylish German version of the vampire legend, patterned on F. W. Murnau's 1922 classic film, relies upon mood and atmosphere to create an eerie sense of evil and terror rather than resorting to cheap tricks and shock effects. Under Werner Herzog's direction, Klaus Kinski is suitably malevolent in the title role, with Isabelle Adjani and Bruno Ganz offering fine support. The overt sexual references and nightmarish quality of the visuals make it unsuitable for youngsters. A-III (PG) AA

Not as a Stranger (1955) Fitful melodrama about a blonde nurse with a terrible Swedish accent (Olivia de Havilland) who marries an impoverished medical student (Robert Mitchum), pays his way through school and, when he begins practice as a rural doctor, helps him face his arrogance, fallibility and attraction to another woman (Gloria Grahme). Producer-director Stanley Kramer does best with the travails of medical school but matters get soapier after the doctor hangs up his shingle. Mature themes. A-III (br) A

Not on Your Life (1966) Spanish-made black comedy about aa good-natured Madrid undertaker (Nino Manfredi) who is persuaded to take the vacant post of state executioner. Directed by Luis Berlanga, the film satirizes government bureaucracy, human foibles and, quite grimly, capital punishment. A-III (br)

Not Without My Daughter (1990) An American wife (Sally Field) attempts to escape fanatically fundamentalist Iran with her little girl (Sheila Rosenthal) after her husband, an Iranian-born doctor (Alfred Molina), tricks her into a one-way trip to the virulently anti-American country. As directed by Brian Gilbert, the main character's compelling, fact-based story is a real eye-opener, with a bravura performance by Miss Field, but marred by the cartoonish depiction of most of the Iranians in the film. Scenes of domestic violence. A-II (PG-13) 12

Nothing but a Man (1965) Black railroad worker (Ivan Dixon) tires of life on the rails and settles down in a southern town where he and his wife (Abbey Lincoln) are confronted by a hostile community that deprives him of one job after another. Directed by Michael Roemer and Robert Young, the movie is episodic and anything but slick, yet it has the ring of documentary reality as well as a story that has universal implications about human dignity. Some intense violence and a few profanities. A-III (br) A

Nothing but Trouble (1991) A decrepit, demented judge (Dan Aykroyd) and his police chief grandson (John Candy) detain a guileless couple (Chevy Chase and Demi Moore) speeding through their zany little burg. Aykroyd's writing and direction is heavy-handed and muddled resulting in an uneven mishmash of mindless mayhem. Comic book violence, brief sexual innuendo and minimal rough language. A-II (PG-13) U

Nothing by Chance (1975) A group of pilots try to recapture the pre-war barnstorming days in which biplanes toured rural America giving farmers and townspeople the opportunity of experiencing the pleasures of flying in an open-cockpit. Though it has some picturesque aerial photography, William Barnett's documentary will disappoint nostalgia and aviation buffs because of its concentration on the touring pilots and a pretentious narration written by Richard Bach. A-I (G)

Nothing in Common (1986) A wonderfully witty and wise portrait of a young ad agency superstar (Tom Hanks) who must settle accounts with his divorcing parents (Jackie Gleason and Eva Marie Saint) before it's too late. Director Garry Marshall's seriocomic film features warm and insightful performances by the three principals as they try to reconcile their differences. Some profanity and sexual scenes. A-III (PG) 15

Nothing Personal (1980) Romantic screwball comedy about a militant college professor (Donald Sutherland) who goes to Washington to battle a giant corporation bent on the slaughter of baby seals. The insincere social commentary is overpowered by a seduction scene in which Suzanne Sommers as the helpful lawyer further obscures Sutherland's motives. A-III (PG)

Notorious Gentleman (1945) Satiric British tale of a 1930s upper-class idler (Rex Harrison) who leads a self-indulgent life sponging off others until the irony of a hero's death in World War II. Directed by Sidney Gilliat, Harrison's witty but unlikeable opportunist reflects the turmoil of British life between the wars. Amoral attitudes and anti-social behavior. A-III (br)

Now You See Him, Now You Don't (1972) Although apple-cheeked college boy Kurt Russell doesn't know how he invented a chemical that makes people invisible, he does realize it will come in handy against gangster Cesar Romero. Robert Butler directed the carefully homogenized Disney production that, although morally unimpeachable, nonetheless continues the Disney tradition of setting usually inane comedies in a safe, largely white, middle-class context whose values, if they exist at all, are purely material, bereft of any spiritual or even social dimension. A-I (G) U

Now, Voyager (1942) Classy tearjerker follows a repressed Bostonian spinster (Bette Davis) from a sanatorium where she gains some self-confidence to an ocean cruise where she falls for an unhappily married man (Paul Henreid) but sublimates her love for him by giving a home to his love-starved pre-teen daughter. Directed by Irving Rapper, Davis' transformation from milksop to socialite is winning, Gladys Cooper makes a fine ogre as her domineering mother and Henreid's routine in lighting two cigarettes is classic Hollywood schmaltz. The doomed love affair is handled most discreetly. A-II (br) PG

Nowhere to Run (1993) Formula movie about an escaped con (Jean-Claude Van Damme) coming to the aid of a widow (Rosanna Arquette) with small children who is being forced to sell her land to a murderously corrupt real estate developer (Joss Ackland). Director Robert Harmon's attempts to turn action-movie star Van Damme into a brooding romantic hero fall flat in this routine tale of cardboard good guys and bad guys. Intermittent violence, fleeting bedroom scene, brief nudity and minimal rough language. A-III (R) 15

Nude Bomb, The (see: "The Return of Maxwell Smart").

Number One (1969) Charlton Heston plays an aging, once-great quarterback who after some humiliating failures on the field is emotionally torn over retiring. His inability to communicate with his career-oriented wife (Jessica Walter) leads to a one-night stand with a more than cooperative lady sports enthusiast. Director Tom Gries does as well as he can with a story that offers not enough football for the fans and not enough human interest for nonfans. A-III (PG) A

Nun, The (1971) French dramatization of Diderot's 18th-century novel about a young girl (Anna Karina), forced by her mother into the convent, who in desperation escapes with a discontented priest and ultimately destroys herself. Although the narrative's exaggerations and stereotyped characters and situations may annoy or disturb some, director Jacques Rivette's main theme is the arbitrary exercise of power, which in the historical context of this period is not without interest. Mature themes. A-IV (PG)

Nun at the Crossroads (1970) When a Belgian nun (Rosanna Schiaffino) becomes pregnant after being raped during a 1960s uprising in the Congo, her stern superiors in Brussels prefer that she leave the convent and so she brings up the child alone while engaging in missionary work as a lay woman. Italian-Spanish co-production directed by Julio Buchs with a heavy hand and little help from a generally unconvincing cast. Superficial melodrama. A-III (PG)

Nun's Story, The (1959) Sent by her religious community to be a nurse in the Belgian Congo, a young nun (Audrey Hepburn) resists her feelings of love for the doctor (Peter Finch) with whom she works, returns to Belgium and, after struggling with the routine of convent life, leaves for the world beyond the wall. Sensitively directed by Fred Zinnemann, the fact-based story focuses on the interior conflict between the nun's idealism and her growing sense of her own needs as an individual. Convincing portrayal of religious life as a vocation requiring more than good intentions. A-II (nr) U

Nuns on the Run (1990) Lightweight British comedy about two genially daft gangsters (Eric Idle, Robbie Coltrane) who masquerade as Catholic nuns while using a convent as a hide-out from the police and two rival gangs. Written and directed by Jonathan Lynn, the ridiculous situation of men in religious drag offers much irreverent—though good-natured—humor that may rub some the wrong way while providing others with some healthy laughter about Catholic life and foibles. A-IV (PG-13) 15

Nunzio (1978) Often moving story of a retarded young man (David Proval) whose loving mother (Morgana King) indulges his fantasies of being Superman while his tough truck driver brother (James Andronica) tries to protect him from abuse in their ethnic Brooklyn neighborhood. Director Paul Williams' concentrates on character and setting, gradually building through incident and dialogue a convincing picture of the love that binds a family together. Unfortunately, a needlessly graphic rape scene, omitted from the original release, has been inserted subsequently. O (PG/R)

Nutcracker Prince, The (1990) Animated fantasy about a young girl helping a lad who was transformed into a nutcracker-toy soldier to break the spell he's under and vanquish the wicked Mouse king. Uninspired animation from director Paul Schibli's Lacewood Productions neither enhances Tchaikovsky's famous ballet score nor brings to life Hoffman's classic story, but children may be amused by the fairy tale. Minor menace and an evil-looking Mouse king. A-I (G)

Nutcracker, The Motion Picture (1986) Tchaikovsky's fairy-tale ballet, a perennial Christmas favorite, has been given a darker interpretation as representing a young girl's sensual daydreams that are part of the fears and doubts of coming of age. Performed by the Pacific Northwest Ballet, the movie version's psychological implications will elude younger members of the family. A-II (PG/G appeal) U

Nuts (1987) Barbra Streisand stars as a high-priced prostitute charged with manslaughter but whose competency to stand trial is at issue. Director Martin Ritt's highly contrived courtroom drama spends more time trying to manipulate viewers' emotions than it does in trying to probe the issues facing women in a male-dominated society. Much sexually explicit language and references. A-IV (R) 18

O

O Dad, Poor Dad, Mama's Hung You in the Closet and I'm Feeling So Sad (1966) Failed screen version of Arthur Kopit's play about an overpowering mother (Rosalind Russell) and her inhibited son (Robert Morse). Richard Quine's direction of the black comedy tends to be more offensive than funny and some of the tasteless treatment plays with the prurient. O (br)

O Lucky Man! (1973) British surreal allegory about a young innocent (Malcolm McDowell) whose attempts to succeed in a world he can't understand result in an absurd series of misadventures involving Ralph Richardson, Rachel Roberts, Arthur Lowe, and Mona Washbourne. The targets of director Lindsay Anderson's satiric jabs include corrupt officials, military xenophobia, medical experimentation, sex clubs and a host of other aspects of irrational social activity. Some will find its narrative disjointed and senseless, while others will welcome its pro-human, pro-individual stance. It is quite discreet in handling sex and violence, using such scenes only to make a point. A-IV (R)

Object of Beauty, The (1991) The relationship of a high-living American couple (John Malkovich and Andie MacDowell), stranded in their London hotel suite without funds, is tested when their only hope for conversion to quick cash—a Henry Moore sculpture—is stolen by the maid (Rudi Davies). Writer-director Michael Lindsay-Hogg dishes out a mildly entertaining send-up of the materialistic yuppie mentality, but it is so vaguely focused the performers appear to waft through their roles without conviction. Acceptance of extramarital relations and insurance fraud, a flash of nudity and minimal rough language. A-III (R) 15

Oblomov (1981) Russian dramatization of Ivan Goncharov's 19th-century novel about an absentee landlord who has made sloth his life's work. Oleg Tabakov is excellent in the title as the lazy hero whose pampered upbringing leaves him ill-prepared for even the moderate rigors of adulthood as a member of a privileged class. Director Nikita Mikhalkov's puts too much effort into atmospheric effects and not enough into moving the overlong story forward. Still, the marvellous re-creation of late-19th-century Russian life is engrossing and worth seeing. A-II (nr)

Oblong Box, The (1969) Weak British horror movie loosely based on an Edgar Allen Poe story in which a man (Alastair Williamson), horribly disfigured by an African spell, is kept locked up by his brother (Vincent Price), but when he breaks out, terrible things happen in the neighborhood. Directed by Gordon Hessler, the hazy narrative relies solely on visuals of blood and gore for effect, with little attempt at building suspense. A-III (M) X

Obsession (1976) On a business trip to Italy, widower Cliff Robertson falls in love with Genevieve Bujold because she resembles his wife who, along with their daughter, had been killed in a kidnapping 15 years before. This sets up a plot reminiscent of Hitchcock's "Vertigo," but director Brian De Palma attempts to pump romance into Robertson's Italian affair and an absurd conclusion make the result a disappointing miscalculation. Some violence and a muted incest theme. A-III (PG) X

Octopussy (1983) Superagent James Bond (Roger Moore) is once again on the trail of an international conspiracy, this time involving an East German circus, a maverick Soviet general, an Asian dealer in counterfeit gems and an Oriental ring of women. Like previous Bond outings, the plot is less important than director John Glen's tongue-in-cheek treatment of the unflappable, fantasy hero surrounded by curvaceous women, cartoon violence, mechanical gimmickry and exotic locales. The venerable formula succeeds only intermittently, partly because of heavy-handed double-entendres and sexual encounters. A-III (PG)

Odd Couple, The (1968) Two men separated from their wives and sharing an apartment discover what incompatibility is all about. One is obsessively neat (Jack Lemmon) and the other is a compulsive slob (Walter Matthau). The story is a nice twist on the adjustments people have to make in life as well as marriage and both principals take good advantage of the comic potential of teaming a disparate pair. Director Gene Sacs relies on Neil Simon's adaptation of his own stage play and the result is often hilarious comedy. Some sexual references. A-III (G) A

Odd Man Out (1947) After being shot and left behind in the bungled robbery of a Belfast firm, a mortally wounded IRA leader (James Mason) spends the night seeking shelter from a variety of people until finally cornered by the Ulster police. Directed by Carol Reed, the movie features a strong cast, many from the Abbey Theatre, in a challenging story that is less about the dying fugitive than about the few who try to help him, the many who don't want to get involved and the several who only want to use him for their own ends. Stylized violence, including a murder and a suicide. A-III (br) PG

Ode to Billy Joe (1976) Based on a popular Bobbie Gentry song about two Mississippi Delta teenagers (Robby Benson and Glynnis

O'Connor) whose brief romance, in the long-ago summer of 1953, ends in tragedy when the boy throws himself off the Tallahatchie Bridge. Not even the considerable charm of the acting nor the beauty of the Delta setting can help director Max Baer overcome the thin, contrived plot and insufferably cute dialogue. A-III (R/PG)

Odessa File, The (1974) Screen version of the Frederick Forsyth thriller about a German journalist (Jon Voight) who seeks to track down a Nazi war criminal (Maximilian Schell) and comes into conflict with the dreaded Odessa, a secret Nazi organization bent on regaining power. Too heavy and slow moving to be an effective melodrama, director Ronald Neame has made a run-of-the-mill entertainment with serious overtones. Some violence. A-III (PG) A

Oedipus, the King (1968) Static British version of the Greek tragedy by Sophocles features Christopher Plummer and Lilli Palmer under the direction of Philip Saville. A-II (G)

Of Mice and Men (1992) Flat version of the John Steinbeck novel about the tragic circumstances of a Depression-era migrant (Gary Sinise) who looks after a simple-minded, trouble-prone buddy (John Malkovich) until the poor soul accidentally kills someone. Also directed by Sinise, the story is still powerful in its depiction of those on the margins of society struggling to survive hard times but the result here is somewhat on the stagey side and lacking in emotional involvement and impact. Some brutal violence, including murder in the plot resolution, and occasional coarse language. A-III (PG-13)

Off Beat (1986) Judge Reinhold plays a loser who impersonates a N.Y. police officer, foils a bank robbery and falls in love with a female cop (Meg Tilly) while rehearsing for a police dance benefit. Weak romantic comedy with narrow emotional range and improbable storyline. Brief nudity and some harsh language. A-III (PG)

Off Limits (1988) A salt 'n' pepper military police team (William Dafoe and Gregory Hines) in 1968 Saigon stumbles into a series of sadomasochistic murders of prostitutes and is stymied at every turn by cover-up attempts when the prime suspects prove to be high-ranking Army officers. Directed by Christopher Crowe, the movie fails to take its cliched storyline beyond the chase to explore its larger implications within the Vietnam War. Many scenes of extreme violence, wall-to-wall profanity, some nudity and several suggestive scenes with prostitutes. O (R)

Offence, The (1973) Veteran London police detective (Sean Connery), in interrogating a man picked up for the rape murder of a number of school girls, pummels the taunting suspect to death and his world crumbles. Director Sidney Lumet compassionately explores the man's psychological and spiritual disintegration through flashbacks and flash-forwards, actual events and fragmentary memories of the detective's past experiences. Casual moviegoers may find it a difficult, distasteful experience, but it has value as a picture of the results of constant exposure to violence and sordid criminality that are a part of law enforcement. Challenging but thoughtful mature fare. A-III (R) X

Officer and a Gentleman, An (1982) Bitter loner (Richard Gere) enters officer candidate school with the dream of becoming a Navy pilot, but he and a buddy (David Keith) are given a hard time by a tough drill sergeant (Louis Gossett Jr.) and further complicate their lives by getting involved with two local women (Debra Winger and Lisa Blount). Though a suicide puts a pall over the proceedings, director Taylor Hackford's romance is old-fashioned enough to contrive a happy ending but not enough to avoid steamy sex scenes and rough language. O (R) 15

Official Story, The (1985) An upper-class Argentine wife (Norma Aleandro) whose wealthy husband is a friend of the powerful, begins to suspect that her adopted daughter might be the child of a mother victimized by the right-wing government's reign of terror five years before. The Argentinian production, directed and co-scripted by Luis Puenzo, is a extraordinary work that subordinates politics to human characterizations of anguish and nobility. Some brief violence and rough language. A-II (nr) 15

Oh! Calcutta! (1972) Poor quality videotaped stage performance of an erotic revue consisting of a series of vignettes intending to reflect both the sexual obsessions and hang-ups of society, but its heavy reliance on nudity never gets much further than exhibitionism. O (nr)

Oh, God! (1977) California supermarket manager (John Denver) becomes a middle-class Moses when chosen by God (George Burns) to tell the world that he is alive and well. As might be expected, no one believes him and complications arise. The gentle comedy, written and directed by Carl Reiner, has its heart in the right place and provides some effective moments, Burns and Denver both being very appealing performers. Reiner's idea of a nonsectarian God who denies original sin, pronounces morality to be entirely subjective and says that Jesus is his son only in the sense that God is the father of all presents a special problem for parents of young viewers who might not understand the fantasy nature of the comedy. Moreover, while sparing other religious groups, the movie makes a

Billy Graham-style evangelist into a gross caricature. A-III (PG) A

Oh, God! Book II (1980) George Burns returns as the Almighty, his comic timing as quasi-omnipotent as ever. This time he teams up with an 11-year-old schoolgirl whom he persuades to launch an ad campaign promoting him. Directed by Gilbert Cates, it is entertaining, if only mildly funny fare. Though there is less of the secular humanism that marred the original, the concept of Burns as God together with a bit of mild vulgarity may not suit all tastes. A-II (PG)

Oh, God! You Devil (1984) George Burns is back as the Divinity with an infinite number of one-liners. This time he gets to double as the devil and play poker for an errant soul. Director Paul Bogart fashions a comedy that is only mildly amusing and what humor there is comes from Burns. A few sexual references in the dialogue, but otherwise innocuous. A-II (PG) 15

Oh, Heavenly Dog (1980) A murdered detective (Chevy Chase) is reincarnated as a lovable mutt (Benji) whose mission is to solve the crime. Jane Seymour provides some romantic interest. Director Joe Camp's canine movie is sometimes amusing, but slow paced, overly cute and, in general, pretty tepid stuff. Some double-entendres; significant amount of profane language. A-III (PG)

Oh! What a Lovely War (1969) British musical version of World War I covers events from Sarajevo to America's entrance in the conflict as told in a series of sketches conveying the mood, motives and attitudes of the British government, military, clergy, common soldier and the folks at home. Directed by Richard Attenborough, with a large and talented British cast, the ambitious but largely successful work intermixes song and comedy with the ugly reality of the battlefield. Its anti-war perspective emphasizes the futility and waste of a war in which a generation of young men sacrificed their lives. A-II (G) A

Oklahoma! (1955) Stunning, delightful yet surprisingly serious screen version of the classic Rodgers and Hammerstein musical set in the relatively innocent days when Oklahoma was getting ready to join the Union and everything was up-to-date in Kansas City. Shirley Jones is absolutely winsome as the fresh-as-milk farm girl, Gordon MacRae almost outsmarts himself as her cowpoke-beau Curley and Rod Steiger is downright malevolent as would-be suitor Jud Fry. The plot is corny as all get-out, the music and dance numbers charming and memorable, but the melodrama tends to be a tad too heavy. A-II (br) U

Oklahoma Crude (1973) Turn-of-the-century man-hating oil prospector (Faye Dunaway) reluctantly accepts help from her ne'er-do-well father (John Mills) and a drifter (George C. Scott), in order to keep the big oil combine's enforcer (Jack Palance) from jumping her claim. Her wildcat well, naturally, comes up a gusher as does her emotional turnabout toward reformed daddy and newfound friend. Directed by Stanley Kramer, there's plenty of old-fashioned action and melodrama here, making fairly solid entertainment for adults who don't mind some Oklahoma crude violence and language. A-III (PG) AA

Old Boyfriends (1979) Recently divorced woman in her 30s (Talia Shire) tries to make sense out of her life by hitting the road in her Firebird and looking up old boyfriends (Richard Jordan and John Belushi). A third, she discovers, has died in Vietnam and she quickly transfers her affections to his mentally disturbed younger brother (Keith Carradine). Directed by Joan Tewkesbury, the dreary story suffers from the same malaise that afflicts the heroine. Some rough language and adult situations. A-III (R) X

Old Curiosity Shop, The (see: "Mr. Quilp").

Old Dracula (1976) Director Clive Donner's spoof of the classic horror tale portrays women as sex objects and becomes little more than a sex farce using brief nudity and crude sight gags for humor. Unfortunately, the presence of David Niven in the cast may arouse unwarranted expectations that the movie offers more than cheap thrills. O (PG)

Old Gringo (1989) Lumpy adaptation of the Carlos Fuentes novel about three very different rebels—a repressed American school teacher (Jane Fonda), noted American writer Ambrose Bierce (Gregory Peck) and a general in Pancho Villa's army (Jimmy Smits)—who paths in 1913 during the Mexican Revolution. Directed by Luis Puenzo, the movie sacrifices substance for style and the intriguing protagonists can't make up for its confusing depiction of the era. Lengthy, grisly battle scene, point-blank murders and discreetly filmed sexual encounters with fleeting nudity. A-III (R) 15

Old Gun, The (1976) French drama set during World War II about a doctor (Philippe Noiret) who sends his wife and child to the countryside far from the fighting, but on a visit finds that they have been killed in a massacre by a Nazi unit that becomes the target for his revenge. Director Robert Enrico's use of flashbacks recalling details of the doctor's marriage may be sentimental, but they are effective in conveying the outrage that motivates his vengeance. Strong images of wartime violence. A-III (R)

Old Yeller (1958) Dorothy McGuire, Fess Parker and Chuck Connors star in this Disney movie about a lovable mongrel that proves a loyal, selfless companion for the youngsters of a frontier Texas family. Directed by Robert Stevenson, the nostalgic fun is mixed with some poignant moments that may be tough-going for young children. A-I (G) U

Oliver! (1968) Rousing British musical drawn from the Charles Dickens classic, "Oliver Twist," but bearing little resemblance to the original. Lionel Bart's adaptation borrows only the chief characters and turns them loose in what amounts to a colorful, swirling-stomping-singing Cockney street show. As Fagin, rubber-faced Ron Moody carries most of the burden as if it were light as a feather, with Mark Lester perfectly winning as Oliver, Jack Wild stealing scene after scene (along with handy wallets) and Harry Secombe as a bumbling Mr. Bumble. Under Carol Reed's direction, it all adds up to delightful fare for the entire family. A-I (G) U

Oliver and Company (1988) Colorful, toe-tapping animated musical frolic updates Charles Dickens' "Oliver Twist" to New York City where an orphaned kitten named Oliver (voice of Joey Lawrence) gets caught up in the shenanigans of a human con artist (voice of Dom DeLuise) and his rowdy band of rogue dogs who steal for him, including the terrier Dodger (voice of Billy Joel). Directed by George Scribner, it's a children's movie that parents can enjoy, with just the right balance between pathos, action, comedy and music. Some menace from animated Dobermans and peril on an elevated subway track. A-I (G) U

Oliver's Story (1979) Listless romantic melodrama, a sequel to "Love Story," takes up the life of widowed Oliver Barrett (Ryan O'Neal) whose father-in-law (Edward Binns) urges to start anew, which he does by having an affair with a rich WASP (Candice Bergen). Director John Korty has difficulty fleshing out the characterizations of the two principals in their ambiguous affair, which ultimately becomes tiresome. A-III (PG)

Olivier Olivier (1993) Discovered on the streets of Paris six years after having disappeared in the French countryside, a 15-year-old boy (Gregoire Colin) is returned to this jubilant mother (Brigitte Rouan), though his older sister (Marina Golovine) sullenly suspects that the youth is not her brother. Writer-director Agnieszka Holland fashions an eerie tale of complex familial relationships that range from unhealthy emotions to unconditional love as the family members struggle to sustain one another. Subtitles. Mature themes, including child molestation and possible incest, several sexual encounters, brief nudity, fleeting vio-

lence and minimal rough language. A-IV (R) 15

Omar Khayyam (1957) Persia's 11th-century poet-astronomer (Cornel Wilde) helps the son (John Derek) of the Shah (Raymond Massey) defeat a secret cult of assassins led by a power-mad court official (Michael Rennie). Director William Dieterle's lackluster costume picture suffers from a predictable plot and unconvincing action. Stylized violence and period sexism. A-I (br) U

Omega Man, The (1971) Post-nuclear holocaust movie about the apparently last healthy man on earth (Charlton Heston) wandering around downtown Los Angeles by day and by night trying to fend off bands of radiation-diseased ghouls. Directed by Boris Sagal, the situation becomes little more than a shallow, garden-variety romantic melodrama with the hero teaming up with some refugee kids hanging out in the hills and the only untainted woman around (Rosalind Cash) with whom he has some coyly ludicrous love scenes. A-III (PG) A

Omen, The (1976) The American ambassador to Great Britain (Gregory Peck) finds himself the foster father of the anti-Christ in director Richard Donner's slick, expensively mounted but essentially trashy horror show. Though it refers to scripture and religious beliefs, its only interest in religion is in terms of its exploitation potential. Some intense violence. O (R) 18

On a Clear Day You Can See Forever (1970) Screen version of a Lerner-Lane musical about a Brooklyn coed (Barbra Streisand) who is cursed with ESP and memories of a past incarnation as a 19th-century coquette with whom her psychiatrist-teacher (Yves Montand) falls in love. Under Vincent Minnelli's direction, Streisand shines. The rest, however, is glossy romantic fluff. Brief seduction scene. A-II (G) U

On Any Sunday (1971) Written, produced, directed and narrated by Bruce Brown, this enthralling documentary on motorcycle racing may popularize this endurance sport in the same way that Brown's "The Endless Summer" glorified surfing. Filmed in five countries, the emphasis is on the action and the racers, including top professionals Mert Lawwill and Malcom Smith, as well as actor Steve McQueen. A-I (G)

On Golden Pond (1981) Warm movie about the bickering relationship of an aging couple (Katherine Hepburn and Henry Fonda) at the lakeside vacation home where they have spent their summers for four decades. Visiting is their divorced, middle-aged only child (Jane Fonda), forever at odds with her cantankerous father. Directed by Mark Rydell, the sentimental story revolves around Henry Fonda who gives a fine performance (his last), despite the shallow, caricature-like nature of the role. Too much of the humor leans upon the device of putting vulgarities in the mouth of either the old man or a 13-year-old boy visitor. A-III (PG)

On Her Majesty's Secret Service (1969) This caper takes James Bond (George Lazenby) to the Swiss Alps where he uncovers an insidious plan to threaten the world with genetic extinction. Director Peter Hunt makes a conscious effort to outdo its predecessors in scope, excitement and visual effects, but only succeeds in presenting more of the same formula of fantasy sex and violence. A-III (PG)

On My Way to the Crusades I Met a Girl Who . . . (1969) Completely unfunny Italian comedy about an upstart knight (Tony Curtis), his enterprising bride (Monica Vitti) and a chastity belt, the device allegedly employed by departing crusaders to insure their wives' faithfulness. Directed by Pasquale Feste Campanile, the tastelessness of the story calls for little more than one-dimensional lechery from its participants. O (R)

On the Edge (1986) Bruce Dern plays a long-distance runner who 20 years after being unjustly denied a chance at Olympic competition determines to prove his talent and integrity in the toughest race of his career. Filmed on location in the beautiful Mill Valley region of northern California, the movie is an impressionistic, somewhat rambling essay on the male jock mentality. Some partial nudity and brief profanity. A-II (PG-13)

On the Nickel (1980) Ralph Waite stars in this story (which he also wrote and directed) of the Los Angeles Skid Row, known as "The Nickel," a place where society's dropouts drown their despair in alcohol. While an admirable attempt to define the helplessness of these unfortunates, the movie is far too long, the action quite repetitive and the use of comic relief is unfortunate. Depiction of sordid environment is not too strong for older teenagers. A-III (R)

On the Right Track (1981) A small boy (Gary Coleman) who lives in a locker at Chicago's Union Station makes a living as a shoeshine boy with a psychic ability to pick winning horses. Directed by Lee Phillips, the cluttered plot of this thin comedy throws the whole burden upon the young actor, and some may find his charm not enough to sustain it. Adult romantic complications are inappropriate in a movie aimed at children. A-III (PG)

On the Waterfront (1954) Classic labor film about a punched-out boxer (Marlon Brando) who, despite the machinations of his shifty brother (Rod Steiger) and with some encouragement from the woman (Eva Marie Saint) he loves as well as a waterfront priest (Karl Malden), decides to stand up to the criminal boss (Lee J. Cobb) of a corrupt union of dock workers. Based on fact, Budd Schulberg's original script is directed by Elia Kazan with stand-out performances and a gritty realism grounded in a working-class milieu, abetted by Leonard Bernstein's rousing score and Boris Kauffman's atmospheric photography. Much menace and some violence. A-II (nr) A

On the Yard (1979) Screen version of Malcolm Brady's prison novel centers on a wheeler-dealer (Thomas Waites) who rules over the other inmates until a determined rival inmate (John Heard) brings about his downfall. Subplots involve a prisoner desperate for parole (Mike Kellin) and the obsession of another (Joe Grifasi) to escape in a balloon he is secretly building. Raphael D. Silver's direction is too uncertain and his characterizations too sketchy to achieve anything more than a realistic depiction of the violent world of prison. A-III (R)

On Valentine's Day (1986) After shocking a small Southern town with their elopement, a young couple find reconciliation with their parents and friends. Horton Foote's contemplative little movie covers wide-ranging emotional ground in its exploration of small-town intimacies and the erosion of traditions through careful characterizations of one family. The semi-autobiographical narrative is propelled, albeit slowly, by a spirit of unbridled loyalty and devotion tinged with a sense of loss for pre-World War I ways of life. A brief but brutal suicide scene. A-II (PG)

Once Around (1990) Lovestruck, middle-aged salesman (Richard Dreyfuss) takes a young bride (Holly Hunter) whose parents (Danny Aiello and Gena Rowlands) and sister (Laura San Giacomo) can't stomach his overbearing ways. Despite a positive message, the touching moments in director Lasse Hallstrom's family drama are diluted by heavy-handed characterizations, sappy dialogue and drawnout situations. Acceptance of premarital sex, vulgar jokes and casual rough language. A-III (R)

Once a Thief (1965) Listless crime story of an ex-crook (Alain Delon) who has married (Ann-Margret) and settled down but is hounded by the police (Van Heflin) and a gangster brother (Jack Palance) needing his help for a big-time robbery. Director Ralph Nelson gets good performances and uses the San Francisco settings well but the loosely plotted proceedings are entirely predictable. Stylized violence and drug usage. A-III (br) A

Once Before I Die (1966) John Derek and Ursula Andress spend much of their time in this attempt at a World War II thriller making love just out of range of the camera and the advancing Japanese tanks and artillery. Derek gets killed but Andress carries on, ultimately giving significance to the coy title by taking a young soldier into her arms one fateful night. Overblown and undernourished. O (br) X

Once Bitten (1985) A vampire (ineptly played by Lauren Hutton) must find a teenage virgin male in order to preserve her youth. He in turn must lose his virginity to escape the curse of the undead. Lots of tasteless humor and mindless sexual innuendo. O (PG-13) 15

Once in Paris (1978) Frank D. Gilroy wrote, produced and directed this romance about the relationship between a screenwriter (Wayne Rodgers), an heiress (Gayle Hunnicut) and a chauffeur (Jack Lenoir). Filmed in Paris, the lame and languid story condones infidelity and adultery. O (R/PG appeal)

Once Is Not Enough (see: "Jacqueline Susann's Once Is Not Enough").

Once Upon a Crime (1992) Limp comedy revolves around five innocent Americans (John Candy, James Belushi, Cybill Shepherd, Sean Young and Richard Lewis) suspected of murdering a wealthy dowager in Monte Carlo. Eugene Levy's directorial debut is a forgettable, failed farce filled with overly broad acting and predictable situations. Some comic violence and brief sexual innuendo. A-II (PG)

Once Upon a Forest (1993) Animated tale in which three animal youngsters—a hedgehog, a mole and a wood mouse—face various dangers in obtaining herbs from a distant meadow needed to cure their sick badger friend. Director Charles Grosvenor turns in a blandly sweet Hanna-Barbera production that ambles along rather listlessly, save for one highly engaging musical number, "He's Gone – He's Back." Best for the very young. A-I (G)

Once Upon a Time in America (1984) Italian director Sergio Leone has attempted to make an American urban crime epic, but his melodramatic tale of Jewish gangsters (Robert De Niro and James Woods) is dull and lifeless in spanning 30 years in the lives of characters impossible to be concerned about, not only because their actions are so brutal but also because their motivations never rise above the most elemental. Excessive violence and a crude and brutalizing depiction of sex. O (R) 18

Once Upon a Time in the West (1969) Any movie with such a plainly mythic title can't be all bad and this one really isn't bad at all. Epic, stately spaghetti western directed by Sergio Leone, its wispy plot concerns hired killer Henry Fonda's pursuit of outlaw Charles Bronson and widow Claudia Cardinale's land, but it contains a whole encyclopedia of western cliches and stereotypes that are irresistible for western buffs. Others may enjoy it as a knowing spoof but one that is overlong and featuring some rather intense violence. A-III (PG) 15

Once You Kiss a Stranger (1969) Failed thriller about a psychopathic young woman (Carol Lynley) who murders one golf pro in order to blackmail a competing pro (Paul Burke) into murdering her psychiatrist. Mindless script ineptly directed by Robert Sparr. A-III (M)

One and Only, The (1978) Henry Winkler plays a boorish college dropout in the 1950s who goes to New York to become a Broadway star but, to avoid starvation, becomes a wrestler and wins fame and fortune in the ring. Director Carl Reiner tries very hard for the proper blend of humor and nostalgia, but his egotistical hero lacks the essential charm the role intended. The lightweight comedy has a heavy load of crude sexual and scatological references. A-III (PG) A

One and Only Genuine Original Family Band, The (1968) Uneven Disney musical about a family (grampa Walter Brennan, Janet Blair, Buddy Ebsen and eight kids) who emigrate from Nebraska to the Dakota territory just in time to get embroiled in partisan politics over Dakota's proposed statehood and the presidential race between Grover Cleveland and Benjamin Harrison. Behind its overcute tendencies and oversentimental songs by the Sherman brothers, the movie has some infectious high spirits, but director Michael O'Herlihy might have done a better job mining the genuine lode of Americana to be found in the book by Laura Van Nuys. A-I (G)

One Brief Summer (1972) Talky British soap opera about a middle-aged financier (Clifford Evans) who carries on a torrid romance with a 17-year-old girl (Felicity Gibson) vacationing on his estate. Director John MacKenzie photographs the boring affair in musty blue hues and glazes the superficial characterizations with bits of gratuitous nudity and kinky eroticism. O (R) AA

One Crazy Summer (1986) Absurdest comedy replete with tiresome bathroom humor, profane gestures and vulgar sight gags has a group of high school grads saving the ancestral home of a streetwise girl (Demi Moore) from a ruthless developer and his son. The movie is essentially pulp entertainment, vapid enough to cause goof-ball behavior in the young and immature. A-III (PG)

One Day in the Life of Ivan Denisovich (1971) British screen version of Russian novelist Alexander Solzhenitsyn's account, based on his own experience, of what daily life meant to a prisoner of a forced labor camp in the Soviet penal system. Directed by Casper Wrede, Tom Courtney excels in the title role, conveying the feeling of a prisoner trying to survive each day by keeping alive the hope of freedom. A powerful indictment of Soviet oppression, it is filled with gloomy images of human suffering and hardship, but it also details the little victories that lessened the pain of injustice. A-II (G) A

One False Move (1992) After murdering six people in L.A., two icy-veined killers (Billy Bob Thornton and Michael Beach) follow a girlfriend accomplice (Cynda Williams) to her Arkansas hometown whose action-starved sheriff (Bill Paxton) awaits their arrival with mixed emotions. Carl Franklin directs a realistically violent drama that raises some serious questions about contemporary race relations and the spread of crime to rural areas. Intermittent graphic violence, occasional drug abuse and some rough language. A-IV (R) 18

One Flew Over the Cuckoo's Nest (1975) Screen version of the Ken Keasy novel about an abortive rebellion in a mental institution led by a drifter (Jack Nicholson) feigning mental illness to avoid being sent to a prison farm. Director Milos Forman's smooth, low-keyed movie about life in an asylum is filled with colorful, often amusing incidents and characterizations, but the central confrontation between the sane drifter and the repressed and repressing nurse (Louise Fletcher) is too contrived to evoke a strong emotional response. Some violence, very rough dialogue and an incident presenting loveless sexual intercourse as therapeutic. A-IV (R) 18

One from the Heart (1982) Teri Garr and Frederic Forrest fall out of love and back into it in this lavishly produced musical that seems more interested in its technical effects than in its story of a young couple's relationship. Directed by Francis Ford Coppola, the result is artificial and tedious. Some partial nudity, sexual byplay and profanity. A-III (R)

One Good Cop (1991) When a widowed New York City narcotics detective (Anthony LaPaglia) meets a violent death, his partner (Michael Keaton) boldly steals a cache of drug money so he can afford to adopt his dead pal's three little girls. Writer-director Heywood Gould's intense action drama savagely juxtaposes wrenching scenes of tenderness with horrific violence, wrapping up the story with a morally questionable fantasy ending. Considerable violence with recurring rough language and drug abuse. A-IV (R)

101 Dalmations (1961) Puppy parents Pongo and Perdita (voices of Rod Taylor and Cate Bauer) rush to rescue their 15 dalmatian offspring from the evil Cruella De Vil (voice of Betty Lou Gerson) who has stolen 99 puppies to make a polka-dot fur coat. Walt Disney's animated canine caper, with art direction and production design by Ken Anderson, maintains its appeal as heartwarming family entertainment. A-I (G) U

100 Rifles (1969) Arizona deputy (Jim Brown) tracks a bank robber (Burt Reynolds) into Mexico where ultimately he takes a leading part in an uprising by the Yaqui Indians against the central government. Director Tom Gries pulls out all the stops in orchestrating the horse opera's violence, ranging from fist fights to total massacre. Overemphasis on brutal action wastes potential of plot and characters. O (PG) X

One Is a Lonely Number (1972) Intelligent soap opera about a housewife (Trish Van Devere), devastated by a bitter divorce from a philandering husband, who gets some inspiration and hope from a kindly old grocer (Melvyn Douglas). Director Mel Stuart's treatment vacillates between being simplistic and tough, harsh and sentimental, but there are some worthwhile insights along with all the superficialities. A-IV (PG) AA

One in a Million (1936) In her movie debut, Sonja Henie stars as a Swiss skater whose Winter Olympics gold medal is jeopardized by charges of her having skated professionally for an American promoter (Adolphe Menjou) but a love-smitten newsman (Don Ameche) clears her name and makes her fortune. Director Sidney Lanfield surrounds the Danish star with a seasoned cast and some comic relief from the Ritz Brothers among others, but the lackluster plot has aged rather badly. Wholesome though dated entertainment. A-I (br) A

One Little Indian (1973) Above-average Disney adventure set in the Old West about a U.S. Calvary corporal (James Garner) on the run from an unjust court martial, a white boy being raised by the Indians and a pretty widow lady (Vera Miles) who helps both of them. Directed by Bernard McEveety, what makes the movie of more than average interest is that the corporal's predicament is for disobeying orders by defending Indian women and children during a no-prisoner raid. What makes it fun is that his escape across the desert is by camel, a temperamental beast responsible for much of the film's comedy. A-I (G) U

One Magic Christmas (1985) Failed Disney movie directed by Philip Borsos lets materialistic values predominate in a story starring Mary Steenburgen and Gary Basaraba supposedly learning about "the true spirit" of Christmas. A-II (G)

$1,000,000 Duck (1971) Disney situation comedy about a Peking duck who lays golden eggs, but when its owners (Sandy Duncan and Dean Jones) try to turn them into cash, they get in trouble with the Treasury Department. Director Vincent McEveety offers standard animal antics and climactic chase sequence that will divert, if not delight pre-teens. A-I (G)

One Minute to Zero (1952) An Army colonel (Robert Mitchum) wins the heart of a U.N. relief worker (Ann Blyth) during the U.S. retreat in the early months of the Korean War. Directed by Tay Garnett, the patriotic but plodding tale includes some implausible derring-do and the colonel's firing on Korean refugees being used as a shield by infiltrating enemy troops. Wartime violence. A-I (br) A

One More Saturday Night (1986) Director Dennis Klein overcomes a weak script and subject matter to provide an affectionate glance at the adaptability and resourcefulness of less-than-articulate teenagers (and some adults) who struggle during a typical weekend date night in contemporary suburbia. Some rough language and a brief instance of nudity in a sexual context are offset by honest and objective performances. A-III (R)

One More Time (1970) In a sequel to "Salt and Pepper," comedy duo Peter Lawford and Sammy Davis Jr. chase about the English countryside in a contrived and irrelevant diamond smuggling plot that is terribly forced and unfunny. Directed by Jerry Lewis, the timing of all the gags is off, the plot predictable and the dialogue stupid. Some sexual innuendo. A-III (PG) A

One More Train to Rob (1971) Slack western with George Peppard as ex-con returned to take revenge on his partner (John Vernon) who double-crossed him by not only taking the gold but also his girlfriend (Diana Muldaur). Director Andrew V. McLaglen offers more cliches than action, but its bawdy language and violent situations are not for youngsters. A-III (GP) AA

One Night at Dinner (1971) Italian production about a dramatist (Jean-Louis Trintignant) who decides to base his next play on the personal affairs of his seductive wife (Florinda Bolkan), his friend (Tony Musante) who is pursuing her and the bisexual stage star (Lino Capolicchio) on whose affections they both trade. Directed by Giuseppe Patroni Griffi, the movie tries to justify infidelity and promiscuity but offers only teasing eroticism. O (R)

One of Our Aircraft Is Missing (1942) Hit during a raid on Nazi Germany, a British bomber crew (Godfrey Tearle, Eric Portman, Bernard Miles and others) bail out over Holland and are helped by Dutch patriots (including Peter Ustinov as a local priest) to reach the coast and embark for England. Directed by Michael Powell and Emeric Pressberger, the airmen's predicament behind enemy lines is tense but lightened by occasional humor, some of it directed at British conceits. Wartime violence. A-I (br) U

One of Our Dinosaurs Is Missing (1975) Walt Disney romp set in London during the 1920s with a gang of nannies, headed by Helen Hayes, and a clutch of Oriental villains, led by Peter Ustinov, vying with each to recover a secret Chinese formula hidden in a dinosaur skeleton. Directed by Robert Stevenson, the slapstick affair will appeal to the very young, but the Oriental stereotypes may not amuse adults. A-I (G) U

One on One (1977) Robby Benson stars as a hotshot basketball player recruited by a college coach who tries to make him give up his scholarship when he doesn't measure up to expectations. Directed by Lamont Johnson, the cluttered storyline makes only a token gesture toward exposing the corruption of college sports. Glossy, sympathetic depiction of a casual sexual relationship. O (PG)

One Potato, Two Potato (1964) Sincere melodrama about the problems faced by a shy divorcee (Barbara Barrie) after she marries a black co-worker (Bernie Hamilton). Director Larry Peerce's low-budget movie is flawed dramatically but raises some important questions about the problems facing an interracial couple. A-II (br)

One Sings, the Other Doesn't (1977) French production about the women's liberation movement centering on the developing relationship between two women (Therese Liotard and Valerie Mairesse) through identity crises, abortion and career changes. Director Agnes Varda has made a thesis film with considerable charm and appeal but little insight into its theme of the relativistic nature of sexual morality. O (nr)

One Spy Too Many (1966) Secret gas is stolen from an Army testing unit and agents Solo (Robert Vaughn) and Kuryakin (David McCallum) set off in pursuit of the thief (Rip Torn). Directed by Joseph Sargent, the third movie derived from the TV series, "The Man from U.N.C.L.E.," is one too many. Stylized violence. A-II (br) A

1000 Convicts and a Woman (1971) When the trusty warden's lusty daughter (Alexandra Hay) comes home from school on holiday, all manner of havoc breaks loose on dad's normally quiet prison farm. The exploitation movie's ridiculous ineptness fails to mitigate the unsubtle titillation. O (R)

One Trick Pony (1980) Singer-composer Paul Simon stars as a band leader whose marriage is on the rocks and whose group is breaking up. An ambitious movie, directed by Robert M. Young and written by Simon, it is very knowing about the tensions in the popular music industry between those who run the business and those who provide the talent, but less sure about the personal problems of those involved. Several sexually explicit scenes, nudity and gross language. O (R)

One Woman or Two (1987) Ex-model (Sigourney Weaver) impersonates a patroness of the sciences (Dr. Ruth Westheimer) to escape a pesky ex-lover. Gerard Depardieu and Michael Aumont are the duped scientists who discover the remains of a 2-million-year-old woman as well as the deception. The conclusion of director Daniel Vigne's dizzy romantic comedy has brief nudity in a sexual context. A-III (PG-13)

Onion Field, The (1979) Two petty criminals (James Woods and Franklyn Seales) kidnap two policemen, brutally murdering one of them (Ted Danson), and the consequences nearly destroy the surviving officer (John Savage) in this somber, slow-moving but gripping movie version of Joseph Wambaugh's novel. Director Harold Becker conveys the grim reality of police work and the varied, intensely human character of those involved on both sides of the law. Violence, rough language and frank depiction of the seamy details of criminal life. A-IV (R) 18

Only Angels Have Wings (1939) A stranded American entertainer (Jean Arthur) gets stuck on the leader (Cary Grant) of a bunch of daring aviators trying to win a government contract flying the mail over a dangerous South American route. Director Howard Hawks' classic story of men whose bond of camaraderie transcends the dangers of their profession is conveyed by a fine cast including Noah Berry Jr. and Allyn Joselyn as devil-may-care pilots, Thomas Mitchell as the flier with failing eyesight and Richard Barthlemess as a disgraced pilot trying to prove himself. A-II (br) A

Only Game in Town, The (1970) Two lonely people in Las Vegas, a mixed-up compulsive gambler (Warren Beatty) and a hefty chorus girl (Elizabeth Taylor), meet by chance, take up residence together and ultimately fall in love. Though overlong and lacking comic flair, director George Stevens' movie offers some interesting delineations of character and excursions into motive and meaning but never with any real depth or emotion. A-III (PG) A

Only the Lonely (1991) A 38-year-old Chicago cop (John Candy) vacillates in his struggle to free himself from the manipulative domination of his mother (Maureen O'Hara) as he seeks a last chance at love with a shy mortuary cosmetician (Ally Sheedy). Writer-director Chris Columbus scores with a top-notch cast in a warmhearted story that casts a wry eye on Irish Catholic mores. Implied

premarital sexual encounter, minimal slapstick violence, flash of nudity, a few ethnic slurs and an instance of rough language. A-III (PG-13) 15

Only When I Larf (1968) Three con artists (Richard Attenborough, David Hemmings, and Alexandra Stewart) pull some neat capers on a variety of victims ranging from gullible New York stock speculators to army officers from an emerging African nation. For the most part Basil Deardon directs the international swindles with a light, witty touch, but in following the novel by Len Deighton, there are some slow moments with a love triangle and assorted jabs at contemporary social values. A-III (G) A

Only When I Laugh (1981) Marsha Mason plays a successful actress who is a reformed alcoholic whom circumstances conspire to push to the brink once more. Contributing to her problems are her daughter (Kristy McNichol), a homosexual actor (James Coco) and a rich man's wife (Joan Hackett) who is pathologically afraid of growing old. Written by Neil Simon and directed by Glenn Jordan, it's a moderately entertaining blend of laughs and seriousness. Aside from some occasional foul language, the contrived plot is innocuous. A-II (R)

Open Doors (1991) Ignoring public outcry and pressures from the Fascist regime in 1937 Italy, a judge (Gian Maria Volonte) refuses to mete out the death penalty to a fired civil servant (Ennio Fantastichini) convicted of murdering his wife, ex-boss and his replacement. Director Gianni Amelio evokes strong performances from the leads, but the snail-like pace of the film and its exploration of capital punishment are generally unsatisfying. Restrained depiction of a triple murder and adulterous references. Subtitles. A-III (nr)

Open Season (1974) Grisly plot about three war buddies (Peter Fonda, John Phillip Law, Richard Lynch) who, on their annual people-hunting trip, kidnap a couple (Albert Mendoza and Cornelia Sharp) for a week of rape and mayhem before the father (William Holden) of a previous victim puts a revengeful stop to it. Directed by Peter Collinson, the exercise in sadism has nothing to redeem it. O (R) X

Opening Night (1978) Director John Cassavetes explores the terrors of aging in the story of a popular stage actress facing her first role as an older woman, and the prospect of a future limited to character parts. Gena Rowlands' performance as a woman on the edge is universal in capturing the dread and fear of a person making the passage to a new stage in life. An exceptional supporting cast (Joan Blondell, Paul Stewart; Ben Gazarra) is pushed to the limits of their craft. Mature themes. A-III (PG-13) AA

Operation Crossbow (1965) Colorful adventure story about an Allied espionage mission to destroy German long-range missiles in the final days of World War II. Directed by Michael Anderson, there's plenty of tension and interesting characterizations from an international cast headed by George Peppard, Tom Courtney, Sophia Loren and Lilli Palmer. Wartime violence. A-I (br) A

Operation Kid Brother (1967) Inept spy spoof about an international scheme to hypnotize the world's great powers into surrendering most of their gold reserves to a gang of crooks. Neil Connery, Sean's younger brother, apparently was never told that he was acting in a take-off and hence he doesn't. A-II (br)

Operation Leontine (1973) In this zany French spoof of the crime genre, Francoise Rosay plays a feared former gang leader who emerges from retirement for one last caper and outwits and outguns all her gangster opponents. Directed by Michel Audiard, the stylish, well-acted movie adds up to little more than a collection of sight gags (some quite hilarious) and adult fantasies revolving around rival gang's double-crossing one another. A-III (M)

Operation Petticoat (1959) Belabored World War II comedy aboard a patched-up submarine whose captain (Cary Grant) depends upon a cunning officer (Tony Curtis) to find the parts to keep it running, despite the complications caused after evacuating five Army nurses from a Japanese-threatened island. Directed by Blake Edwards, the best jokes come from the frantic efforts to keep the broken-down sub operational, with the usual sexist jokes occasioned by the nurses in close quarters with the crew. Much sexual innuendo. A-III (br) U

Operation S.N.A.F.U. (1974) Failed World War II comedy about some unwilling Allied soldiers (Jason Robards, Martin Landau, Peter Falk) sent into German-held Sicily to destroy artillery positions impeding a seaborne invasion. Filmed in Italy and Yugoslavia, director Nanni Loy's slapstick treatment of a cornball plot is rarely amusing. Some rough language and raunchy humor. A-III (nr)

Operation Thunderbolt (1978) Director Menahem Golan's dramatization of the heroic rescue by Israeli commandos of the Jewish hostages at Entebbe Airport perhaps errs on the side of being too scrupulous in avoiding the sensational. Thus there is considerable plodding and skimping on characterization, but the subject itself has enough excitement and heroism to make it an entertaining and quite moving viewing experience. A-II (PG)

Ophelia (1974) Modern version of "Hamlet" attempts to make the audience question its initial sympathy for the title character (Andre Jocelyn) and prepare it for an ending that Shakespeare never envisioned. Director Claude Chabrol turns the original into a study of destructive obsessions involving such themes as family tensions, middle-class materialism, the sense of the irreparable and emotional ambivalence. While not entirely successful, the adaptation has brilliance and imagination. A-II (nr)

Opium War, The (1978) Chinese production about the early 19th-century imperial commissioner sent from Peking to put a stop to the opium trade at the port of Canton but instead sets off a war between China and Great Britain. Director Chen Chunli's highly romanticized and stylized dramatization gives only sketchy details of the conflict but is worth seeing for its spectacle and sheer novelty, if nothing else. A-II (nr)

Opportunity Knocks (1990) Humorless rags-to-riches comedy about a Chicago con artist (Dana Carvey) who falls for the daughter (Julia Campbell) of his rich victim (Robert Loggia). Uninspired direction by Donald Petrie and a hackneyed script do little for TV comic Carvey's first starring vehicle on the big screen. Some comic-book violence and bathroom humor. A-II (PG-13)

Optimists, The (1973) Aged ex-vaudevillian (Peter Sellers), reduced to entertaining on the London streets with his scruffy little trained dog Bella, gradually develops a cherished friendship with two young slum children (played delightfully by Donna Mullande and John Chaffey). The British production, warmly directed by Anthony Simmons, has much to say about the world of children and the importance of the magical and the incongruous in their world. Meaningful family entertainment. A-I (PG)

Orca (1977) Shark-hunter Richard Harris decides to go after bigger game and, in attempting to catch a killer whale, kills its pregnant mate, thus incurring the wrath of the male. Charlotte Rampling is on hand as a whale specialist who seems to have a soft spot in her heart for big brutes of all sorts. Director Michael Anderson's seafaring adventure has some scenic beauty, but its story is mediocre entertainment at best. Some rather graphic violence. A-III (PG)

Orchestra Rehearsal (1979) Italian production about an orchestra whose members are constantly being distracted by each other and the inane questions of a television crew. A union dispute leads to violence and ultimately chaos. Director Federico Fellini's failed fable about the tension between authority and the individual becomes a disjointed series of gags and jabs at music, nationality, television, art, sports, sex and other perennial favorites.

Minor work from a great director. A-III (R)

Ordinary People (1980) Donald Sutherland and Mary Tyler Moore give fine performances as confused and troubled parents trying to cope with the psychological aftershocks that result when the older of two sons dies in a boating accident and the surviving son (Timothy Hutton) attempts suicide. Directed by Robert Redford, the movie hints that the characters' complacent and wholly materialistic environment may have contributed to the family's instability, but these aspects remain underdeveloped. The problems are very real, but the movie is strangely cool and distanced from them. Due to the heaviness of the theme and some instances of rough language, it is for mature viewers. A-III (R) 15

Organization, The (1971) Sidney Poitier in a third outing as Lt. Virgil Tibbs of the 1967 movie, "In the Heat of the Night," finds himself involved in a situation where the police are using extra-legal methods to apprehend a gang trafficking in heroin. Directed by Don Medford, the thriller concentrates on chase scenes without any attempt at characterization or addressing the moral and legal issues inherent in the plot. Physical and psychological violence. A-III (R) AA

Organizer, The (1964) Prime Italian import about underpaid factory workers in turn-of-the-century Turin as they try to form a union with the help of a teacher-turned-labor organizer (Marcello Mastroianni). Directed by Mario Monicelli, the production is steeped in a sense of social justice, clearly showing management's exploitation of the workers and the blighted lives of their impoverished families. Subtitles. Earthy treatment and vulgar language. A-III (br)

Orlando (1993) British adaptation of Virginia Woolf's feminist fantasy about the curious experiences of an Elizabethan noble (Tilda Swinton) who lives for 400 years, the first 100 years or so as a man and the rest as a woman. Adapted and directed by Sally Potter, the result is always pretty to look at but not particularly amusing or enlightening as the centuries roll by slowly with few insights on the unequal social conditions that till recently had been women's traditional lot. Momentary frontal nudity and a few circumspect scenes of lovemaking. A-III (PG-13) PG

Orpheus (1949) Startlingly designed, exquisitely photographed version of the classic myth about the relationship between love and death visualized with haunting beauty in this French movie directed by artist and poet Jean Cocteau. A-II (br)

Oscar, The (1966) One-dimensional story of the efforts of a psychopath (Stephen Boyd) to achieve Hollywood stardom has all the empty glitter of Tinsel Town, but director Russell Rouse goes to excess in sexual suggestiveness. O (br) X

Oscar (1991) The efforts of a Prohibition-era gangster (Sylvester Stallone) to turn over a new leaf are continuously complicated by skeptical cops, greedy bankers, his larcenous accountant (Vincent Spano) and his scheming daughter (Marisa Tomei). Director John Landis' attempt at farce is only modestly entertaining with generally unfunny performances and methodical pacing. Very mild sexual innuendo. A-II (PG)

Osterman Weekend, The (1983) Screen version of Robert Ludlum's espionage thriller about a television talk-show host (Rutger Hauer) who is used by a CIA agent (John Hurt) in a ruse to discredit the head of intelligence (Burt Lancaster). Directed by Sam Peckinpah, the convoluted plot serves up a thoroughly distasteful stew of gratuitous violence and sex, with not a trace of human feeling. O (R) 18

Otello (1986) Franco Zeffirelli's lavish production of the Verdi opera, with Placido Domingo in the title role, emphasizes the visuals at the expense of the rather depressing libretto, based on Shakespeare's play about jealousy leading to murder and suicide. A-II (PG) U

Othello (1966) British adaptation of Shakespeare's play with Laurence Olivier as the epileptic general whose jealousy and passion destroy him, abetted by Frank Finlay as Iago and Maggie Smith as Desdemona. Directed by Stuart Burge, it's a photographed performance in which simple stage backgrounds, stage movements and camera close-ups focus all attention on the lead actor and Shakespeare's language. A-II (br) U

Other, The (1972) Sleepy Connecticut farm in the summer of 1935 is the setting for a tale of horror and suspense involving the possession of an innocent child by the evil spirit of his dead twin. Director Robert Mulligan gets the proper atmosphere, but the story, based on the Thomas Tryon novel, gets so convoluted in the deaths of family members that it becomes a bit unbelievable and more than a touch too gruesome. A-III (PG) X

Other People's Money (1991) Disappointing comedy stars Danny DeVito as a Wall Street corporate raider in love with the lawyer (Penelope Ann Miller) representing the New England company he is trying to wrest from its benevolent chief exec (Gregory Peck). Director Norman Jewison blunts the potential for rich social commentary by stressing the unconvincing romance. Some crude sexual references and minimal rough language. A-III (R) 15

Other Side of Midnight, The (1977) Screen version of Sidney Sheldon's novel about a poor French girl (Marie-France

Pisier) who is jilted and left pregnant by a romantic American World War II pilot (John Beck), who becomes the mistress of a Greek tycoon (Raf Vallone) and seeks revenge on the faithless American. Directed Charles Jarrott's vulgar, trashy melodrama features a great deal of nudity and explicit sex. O (R) X

Other Side of the Mountain, The (1975) Good telling of the fact-based story of Jill Kinmont (Marilyn Hassett), a young skier who, completely paralyzed from the chest down after a 1956 fall in pre-Olympic competition, overcame her handicap to make a new life for herself as a grade-school teacher. Director Larry Peerce at times veers into sentimentality, but for the most refrains from tampering with the emotional power inherent in the story of an individual's achievement over cruel odds. Very appealing young cast also includes Belinda J. Montgomery and Beau Bridges. A-II (PG) A

Other Side of the Mountain, Part II, The (1978) This film sequel about paralyzed skier Jill Kinmont (Marilyn Hassett) takes up the events leading to her marriage to John Boothe (Timothy Bottoms). Though lacking the drama of the original, director Larry Peerce's movie is consistently entertaining and, at times, quite moving, chiefly because of Hassett's superb performance. Brief sequence involving premarital sex. A-III (PG)

Other Voices (1970) Documentary by David Sawyer and Robert Elfstrom details the confrontational "verbal shock" therapy used on mentally ill patients at the Delaware Valley Mental Foundation. Suicide prevention is a primary objective of the treatment, but the movie's realistic observation of the private lives of these patients offers the lay audience little insight into the complexity of the social and moral problems of mental health care. A-IV (nr)

Otley (1969) Sardonic British satire about a drifter (Tom Courtenay) who muddles his way into the middle of an espionage caper, winds up being pursued by two rival spy organizations and falls for a temptress with ambiguous allegiances (Romy Schneider). As directed by Brian Clement, the story gets lost in its own intrigues, but Courtenay holds it together with a likeable comic performance and some sharp comments on the times and people's lack of integrity. A-III (PG)

Our Hearts Were Young and Gay (1944) Slight but engaging comedy from Cornelia Otis Skinner's tale of the misadventures she (Gail Russell) and college chum Emily Kimbrough (Diana Lynn) encounter on a trip to Europe in the 1920s, the highlight of which is being locked overnight in Notre Dame's belltower. Directed by Lewis Allen, the predicaments of the young ladies are delightfully innocent in keeping with period proprieties, with a capable supporting cast (notably Charles Ruggles and Dorothy Gish as Skinner's parents) adding to the fun. The silliness of the situations will amuse youngsters while their elders are more likely to be charmed by the period characters. A-I (br) U

Our Latin Thing (1972) Latino music documentary filmed in and around New York City's Cheetah nightery, the Leon Gast production fills the screen with people enjoying the vibrant sounds of Johnny Pacheco, Willie Colon, El Conde and many other performers (there are no subtitles for the Spanish lyrics). Though partly a plug for the record company issuing works by these performing artists, it stands on its own as a lively, appealing musical celebration of life. A-II (nr)

Our Little Girl (1935) Low-budget Shirley Temple vehicle directed by John Robertson has the charming moppet run away from her troubled home, thereby saving her miserable parents (Rosemary Ames; Joel McCrea) from a divorce neither really wants. Heavy-handed domestic strife. A-II (br) U

Our Man Flint (1966) Spy spoof with James Coburn as an agent with an eye more for the ladies than the job in hand has been directed by Daniel Mann with a heavy emphasis on sexually suggestive situations and references. O (br) A

Our Mother's House (1967) Disturbing British movie about seven children who, to avoid being sent to an orphanage, bury their deceased mother secretly and hold seances in which they continue to invoke her advice. When their long absent father (Dirk Bogarde) turns up and announces he is going to sell "our mother's house," the children deal forcefully with the situation. Director Jack Clayton effectively tells a rather chilling parable of the influence, for good or evil, exercised on children by their elders. A-III (br) AA

Our Time (1974) Set unconvincingly in 1955, this film coyly depicts the frantic sexual experimentation of two WASP schoolgirls (Pamela Sue Martin and Betsy Slade), which for one leads to abortion and death. Directed by Peter Hyams, the tearjerker's contrast between the good girl who pays with her life for making a mistake and the more calculating, unscathed friend conveys a sour, half-hearted lesson in life. A-IV (PG)

Our Town (1940) Fine adaptation of Thornton Wilder's play about two families in a small New Hampshire town circa World War I, centering in the romance between the daughter (Martha Scott) of one family and the son (William Holden) of the other. Directed by Sam Wood, the result is prime

Americana, with Frank Craven re-creating his role as narrator in pointing out the virtues of the community and the values of its individual members. The whole family can enjoy this look back at a simpler age and more wholesome way of life. A-I (br) A

Our Winning Season (1978) High school senior (Scott Jacoby) trains earnestly to win the mile run in the season's finale, but in the interim the movie marks time with a string of less-than-compelling vignettes of school life. Director Joe Rubin's only attempt at deeper significance involves an affair between the hero's best friend and his sister before the friend goes off to die in Vietnam. Banal in every department. A-III (PG)

Out Cold (1989) Offbeat black comedy about two California butchers (John Lithgow and Bruce McGill) whose longtime business partnership ends abruptly when one is frozen to death in a meat locker by his wife (Teri Garr) who also bumps off the nitwit gumshoe (Randy Quaid) she has hired to track her philandering husband. Director Malcom Mowbray understates just about everything in this humorless effort, except his cliched characters. Casual treatment of adultery, some flashes of nudity and profanity. A-III (R) 15

Out for Justice (1991) Enraged at the murder of his partner by a childhood bully (William Forsythe) from their old neighborhood, a Brooklyn cop (Steven Seagal) sets out to kill the punk before the police or the Mafia can get to him. There's more than gritty urban realism in director John Flynn's bloody exploitation film—namely, relentless ultraviolence on the road to vigilante justice. Excessive violence, sexual exploitation of women, incessant rough language, recreational drug use and brief nudity. O (R) 18

Out on a Limb (1992) Action-comedy clunker in which a hapless yuppie (Matthew Broderick) finds himself up to his neck in murderous mayhem while visiting his kid sister (Courtney Peldon) in a remote logging town. Director Francis Verber's numbingly sophomoric plot strings together an odd assortment of klutzy characters, silly shootouts and crashing cars. Much mindless slapstick violence. A-III (PG)

Out of Africa (1985) Slow-moving narrative and beautiful photography characterize this dramatization of storyteller Isek Dinesen's (Meryl Streep) years as a plantation owner in East Africa and her love affair with a hunter (Robert Redford). Produced and directed by Sydney Pollack, the film celebrates the African mystique rather than the muddled romance of its two main characters. Romanticized treatment of adultery. A-IV (PG)

Out of Bounds (1986) An Iowa farmboy (Anthony Michael Hall) is hunted by drug peddlers, police and corrupt narcs when he picks up the wrong bag upon arriving in Los Angeles to visit his brother. Derivative script and melodramatic treatment. Profanity and needlessly extended violence and bloodshed. O (R)

Out of It (1969) Story of a shy adolescent (Barry Gordon) who is inept in dealing with girls has some funny and perceptive moments but not enough substance for a feature-length movie. Director Paul Williams makes things worse by pretentious and obtrusive camera techniques. A-III (PG)

Out of Sight (1966) Spies vie with rock music group in director Lennie Weinrib's innocuous entry for the youth market. A-II (br)

Out-of-Towners, The (1970) Midwestern couple (Jack Lemmon and Sandy Dennis) on a business trip to New York City try to cope with an hilarious series of mishaps, including a garbage strike, a snafu with hotel reservations, a rainy night in Central Park, a mugging to go with it, the siege of the Cuban U.N. embassy and a stolen car chase. Arthur Hiller's spirited direction of Neil Simon's script provides lots of fun at the expense of big-city life for family viewers. A-I (G) U

Out West with the Hardys (1938) Judge Hardy (Lewis Stone) takes wife (Fay Holden), daughter Marian (Cecilia Parker) and son Andy (Mickey Rooney) on an excursion in a typical episode of the Hardy family series directed by George B. Seitz. A-I (br)

Outback (1971) On his way from a backcountry one-room schoolhouse to Sydney for the Christmas holidays, a naive young teacher (Gary Bond) falls in with a depraved and besotted one-time doctor (Donald Pleasance) who insists on showing him some of the perverse ways he passes his time, the highlight of which is a drunken kangaroo hunt slaughtering the defenseless animals for amusement. Directed by Ted Kotcheff, this is a disturbing picture of life in Australia's outback that, unfortunately, provides little positive insight to justify its tasteless language and brutal visuals. A-IV (R)

Outfit, The (1974) Two born losers, an ex-con (Robert Duvall) and an ex-torpedo (Joe Don Baker), team up to take over the gang (headed by Robert Ryan), methodically mowing their way up the mob ranks and robbing syndicate operations for ready cash. An action-packed, B-grade, old-time gangster movie with plenty of violence, but under John Flynn's direction there is such a dreamlike 1950s nostalgia coating the entire proceedings, that none of it can be taken seriously. A-III (PG) 15

Outland (1981) It's high noon on a moon of Jupiter with Sean Connery playing a beleaguered federal marshal involved in an old-fashioned western shoot-out with a team of killers sent to stop his investigation of Peter Boyle's deadly mining operation. Written and directed by Peter Hyams, the sci-fi movie lacks energy and imagination but does have a sympathetic depiction of the friendship that grows between the marshal and space doctor Frances Sternhagen. Moderately entertaining but has scenes of intense violence. A-III (R) 15

Outlaw Blues (1977) Peter Fonda and Susan Saint James star in a comic chase adventure about a singer-songwriter on the run after being framed for a crime. Directed by Richard T. Heffron, it is an amiable and fairly entertaining movie, but the romantic relationship between the principals is rich in sexual innuendo. A-III (PG) 15

Outlaw Josey Wales, The (1976) At the outbreak of the Civil War, northern guerrillas slay the wife and young son of a Missouri farmer (Clint Eastwood who also directs), leaving him for dead. He settles the score by wreaking havoc as a Confederate guerrilla who befriends a strange assortment of colorful characters along the way. A graphic scene of attempted rape. In addition, the film lacks any moral perspective to balance the unremitting slaughter. O (PG) 18

Outrageous! (1977) Canadian production about a young mental patient (Hollis McLaren) who escapes and takes refuge with a homosexual hairdresser (Craig Russell) who helps her to cope with the demons of her schizophrenia and she, in turn, encourages him to embark upon a new career as a satiric female impersonator. Director Richard Benner's movie is alive with humor, vitality, and warmth thanks to some witty dialogue and two superb performances by the principals. Frank, thoroughly objective presentation of the homosexual subculture. A-IV (R) X

Outrageous Fortune (1987) Arthur Hiller directs Bette Midler and Shelley Long as aspiring actresses who single-mindedly seek revenge when they learn that they have been betrayed by the same man with whom each is having an affair. Negative stereotyping of women, a casual attitude toward sex and rough language leave no room for genuine comedy. O (R) 15

Outside Chance of Maximilian Glick, The (1989) When his family in a rural Canadian town of the 1960s squashes his friendship with a Catholic girl (Fairuza Balk) who is his partner in a piano competition, a 12-year-old Jewish youth (Noam Zylberman) is troubled by the hypocrisy and prejudice that he discovers within the local Jewish and Christian communities. Directed by Allen Goldstein, the slickly produced story too easily resolves the issue of ingrained religious prejudice,

though it does not sugar-coat the Jewish point of view and clearly evokes the confusion faced by children too young to understand or accept the concept of prejudice. Fine for interfaith parent-child audiences. A-I (G)

Outside Man, The (1973) Jean-Louis Trintignant plays a hired killer brought to Los Angeles to knock off a mob biggie, but then finds himself being hunted by an equally faceless killer. Ann-Margret is cast as a friend-of-a-friend who gets dragged into the confusion by her pretty heels, and Roy Scheider plays the sadistic silent type on Trintignant's tail. Director Jacques Deray's intriguing melodrama of a stranger in a strange land is packed with sly comic touches and has restrained, but continuous tension and violence. A-III (PG)

Outsider, The (1980) Thriller about an Irish-American youth (Craig Wasson) who leaves his affluent Detroit family to fight in Belfast with the Provisional IRA. Blinded by the love of an Irish girl (Patricia Quinn), he is unaware that he is being used as a pawn in their dangerous game. Director Tony Luraschi gets excellent performances from a fine Irish and English cast. The movie shows the grimy details of life in war-torn Belfast and is a thoughtful commentary on the victimized people of Ulster and the injustices on both sides. A-III (R)

Outsiders, The (1983) Screen version of S. E. Hinton's novel about three youths (Matt Dillon, C. Thomas Howell, Ralph Macchio) growing up in Tulsa, Okla., during the 1960s. Director Francis Coppola's fragile mood piece can't quite connect the youth's violent ways with their discussions of "Gone with the Wind" and Robert Frost's poetry. The violence in a fight between rival gangs is very pronounced. A-III (PG)

Over the Brooklyn Bridge (1984) A Brooklyn luncheonette owner (Elliott Gould) yearns to open a restaurant in Manhattan, but his rich uncle won't come across with the financing unless he gives up his WASP girlfriend (Margaux Hemingway) and marries a nice Jewish girl (Carol Kane). Director Menahem Golan's failed ethnic comedy drama is embarrassingly bad on all counts. Much sexually oriented humor and some rough language. A-III (R) 15

Over the Top (1987) A truck driver (Sylvester Stallone) tries to win back the son he abandoned by showing off his physical prowess. Limp, unconvincing drama directed by Menahem Golan says little about the nature of father-son relationships and opts instead for the goofy contortions of an arm-wrestling championship. Some mildly vulgar language and momentary violence. A-II (PG)

Overboard (1987) When a rich lady (Goldie Hawn) suffers amnesia, a rough carpenter

(Kurt Russell) claims her as his wife and the mother of his four unruly children. Directed by Garry Marshall, the tasteless sex farce relies on the suggestiveness of a situation that makes light of adultery and uses vulgar language and references. O (PG)

Overcoat, The (1965) Fine adaptation of the Gogol short story of a poor clerk (Roland Bykov) in desperate need of a new coat to get through the Russian winter. Director Aleksei Batolov's 1959 production runs its inevitably tragic course with genuine pathos, some gentle humor and much satire poked at office bureaucracy. A-II (br)

Overlanders, The (1946) Fearing a Japanese invasion of northern Australia in 1943, a small band of riders (headed by Chips Rafferty) herd 1,000 head of cattle 1,500 miles to Queensland. Writer-director Harry Watt's fact-based story convincingly details the physical and spiritual courage needed to overcome the dangers of the drive across desert wasteland and mountainous terrain. Epic cattle drive with an Aussie accent. A-I (br)

Over-Exposed (1956) Weak programmer follows an ambitious young photographer (Cleo Moore) who wants to get to the top fast, turns to blackmail but is saved by her reporter boyfriend (Richard Crenna). Directed by Lewis Seiler, there's nothing new or interesting here. Mild stylized violence. A-II (br) U

Overseas (1991) The lives of three French sisters (Nicole Garcia, Marianne Basler and Brigitte Rouan) are individually portrayed as each copes with domestic crises in the midst of the 1950s' Algerian War. Also directed by Rouan, the lyrical tri-part story builds interest as the war takes its sobering toll on the stalwart sisters and their loved ones. Subtitles. Momentary violence and fleeting nudity. A-III (nr)

Owl and the Pussycat, The (1970) Barbra Streisand plays a would-be model who is working as a part-time hooker and George Segal is a would-be writer who is working in a bookstore. When both are kicked out of their apartments, they find themselves the oddest of bedfellows. Director Herbert Ross undercuts the situation's potential for lighthearted comedy by giving it an overly realistic treatment, emphasizing its acceptance of casual sex. O (R) X

Ox, The (1992) Fact-based Swedish period piece begins in 1868 when a young man (Stellan Skarsgard) is sentenced to life imprisonment for slaughtering his employer's ox to feed his starving family but the village vicar (Max Von Sydow) perseveres in a years-long effort to get him released and restored to his tormented wife (Ewa Froling). Director Sven Nykvist's drama of justice and compassion captures the diverse humanity of its characters with spare dialogue, expert acting and achingly beautiful images. Subtitles. Minor violence and an implied sexual encounter. A-III (nr) 12

Oxford Blues (1984) Director Robert Boris badly bungles this remake of "A Yank at Oxford" (1938) by making its hero (Rob Lowe) such a dislikable heel that most American viewers probably will cheer for the British when he takes on the upper-class establishment. Favorable attitude toward sexual promiscuity. O (PG-13) 15

P

Pacific Heights (1990) After moving into their newly purchased Victorian home, a young couple (Melanie Griffith and Matthew Modine) rent its studio to a devious sociopath (Michael Keaton) who twists the law in hopes of wresting the house's ownership from them. Director John Schlesinger's psychological thriller is full of dark doings and murky motivation, but only the good performances lift it beyond run-of-the-mill fare. Some violence, acceptance of premarital sex, brief nudity and occasional rough language. A-III (R) 15

Pacific Vibrations (1971) Producer-director John Severson's documentary presents a colorful and musically pulsating portrait of the West Coast surfer. His treatment, however, tries a bit too hard to deemphasize the joyousness of this obviously fun sport and to elevate it into something of sociological significance and ecological importance in the battle to save the California coastline. Some discussion of hedonistic life-styles. A-II (G)

Package, The (1989) In an otherwise middling espionage thriller, Gene Hackman gives a sterling performance as an Army sergeant whose search for an escaped prisoner uncovers an international military conspiracy. Director Andrew Davis fails to evoke much suspense in proceedings that ultimately target a world leader for assassination, but gets a truly sinister performance from Tommy Lee Jones as Hackman's principal adversary. Some intense violence and profanity. A-III (R) 15

Pad and How to Use It, The (1966) Weak sex comedy adapted from a Peter Shaffer play about an inept young man (Brian Bedford) and his pursuit of a swinger (Julie Sommars). Directed by Brian G. Hutton, it makes extensive use of sexual innuendo. A-III (br) A

Paddy (1970) Irish production about a supposedly likeable but totally irresponsible Dublin lad (Des Cave) who alternately services a middle-aged widow (Judy Cornwell), indulges in occasional orgies and fathers a child with a girlfriend (Dearbhla Molloy) whom he abandons. Directed by Daniel Haller, the episodic movie wanders about aimlessly, uncertain of its theme, statement or sympathies in telling the story of an immature teenager. O (PG)

Pain in the A—, A (1975) French farce in which a professional assassin (Lino Ventura) checks into a hotel to carry out a job but the bungling attempts at suicide by the man in the next room (Jacques Brel) distract him with a series of frenetic mishaps. Director Eduard Molinaro keeps things moving at a good pace, with some fine comic moments, until the one-joke situation finally wears thin. Brief but graphic violence and a comically intended nude scene. A-III (PG)

Paint Your Wagon (1969) Screen adaptation of the Lerner and Loewe musical about two mining partners (Lee Marvin and Clint Eastwood) who "marry" the discarded second wife (Jean Seberg) of a pioneer Mormon, though monogamy triumphs in the end. Director Josh Logan's lavish production has plenty of lush scenery and swirling action to go with the lively songs and dances, but it's all pretty earthbound entertainment. Some frontier humor and ambiance are not for all tastes. A-III (M) A

Painters Painting (1973) Documentary on the post-war rise and influence of N.Y. as a center of the art world. Consists mainly of interviews with many of those who contributed to this development from de Kooning to Warhol, as well as some prominent dealers and collectors. Produced and directed by Emile De Antonio, it's a valuable resource for the history of contemporary American art. A-I (nr)

Palaces of a Queen (1967) Documentary tour of Buckingham Palace, St. James Palace, Windsor Castle, Kensington Palace and the Palace of Holyroodhouse in Edinburgh, showing the art treasures, architecture and furnishings of a royal way of life long past. Directed by Michael Ingrams and narrated by Sir Michael Redgrave, it is an agreeable way to renew a sense of history, though most youngsters will find it a long sit. A-I (br)

Pale Flower (1974) This 1964 Japanese gangster melodrama tells the story of a hit man (Ryo Ikebe) who gets out of prison, meets a beautiful but compulsive gambler, pulls another job and returns to jail. Director Masahiro Shinoda builds up the alienated ambiance of the Tokyo criminal underworld into an exotic but convincing picture of crime familiar the world over. A-III (nr)

Pale Rider (1985) Clint Eastwood plays a mysterious stranger who helps a group of embattled miners in their struggle with a brutal magnate determined to take over their claims. In all essentials a remake of "Shane" updated by resort to a little sex and a lot more violence. O (R) 15

Palm Beach Story, The (1942) Daffy romantic comedy in which a wife (Claudette Colbert) tries to help her penniless inventor husband (Joel McCrea) by leaving him for a millionaire (Rudy Vallee) who has a marriage-minded sister (Mary Astor), but the husband's only concern is getting his wife back. Written and directed by Preston

Sturges, the comic premise sets up a wacky variety of witty confusions and funny incidental characters, but the empty-headed, conniving wife adds a sour note to the otherwise entirely frivolous proceedings. Comic treatment of marriage. A-III (br) U

Palomino, The (1950) Simple story of a cattleman's son (Jerome Courtland) who helps save a Chicano horse ranch by finding its prize palomino and the thieves who stole it. Directed by Ray Novarro, the thin plot and perfunctory acting won't keep youngsters from enjoying the antics of a palomino colt and the majesty of its sire. A-I (br)

Pancho Villa (1973) Telly Savalas plays the Mexican revolutionary as a blithering idiot who forces his advocates to watch home movies of his exploits when he is not abusing women or cynically executing opponents. Director Gene Martin occasionally interrupts the juvenile horseplay to stage some tiresome shoot-outs and a head-on train collision. There's more entertainment in Villa's encyclopedia entry. A-III (PG) AA

Panic in Needle Park, The (1971) Grim and harshly realistic love story about a wasted junkie (Al Pacino) struggling to survive in New York City's underworld of drugs and his doomed romance with the girl (Kitty Winn) he introduces to hard drugs and who then turns tricks to feed their habit. Directed by Jerry Schatzberg, the drama convincingly shows the horrors of drug addiction and its toll on human potential. Much brutality and foul language, with graphic depiction of heroin injections and occasional nudity. A-III (R/PG) X

Papa's Delicate Condition (1963) Nostalgic melodrama about a turn-of-the-century Texas family whose railroad executive father (Jackie Gleason) does strange things, such as buying a circus, when he overimbibes—the condition of the title. Directed by George Marshall, the potential charm of the family story is often stifled by scenes overindulging the star for whom this served as a vehicle. Comic intemperance. A-I (br) U

Paper Chase, The (1973) First-year Harvard law student Hart (Timothy Bottoms) quickly finds himself torn between the cool, cruel competitive life of the intellect, personified in distinguished law contracts prof. Kingsfield (John Houseman who steals the show), and the warm, sensuous spontaneous life of the body, personified in Kingsfield's daughter (Lindsay Wagner). Director James Bridges conveys well the pressures of campus life, especially in Hart's study group with students whose varied personalities and weaknesses represent a cross section of humanity. Mature treatment although accessible for older teenagers. A-III (PG)

Paper Lion (1968) Alan Alda stars as journalist George Plimpton investigating the world of professional football by actually playing quarterback for the Detroit Lions. Directed by Alex March, it's a fairly interesting football movie for those who don't normally follow the sport. A-I (G)

Paper Mask (1992) Murky psychological drama has an ambitious hospital orderly (Paul McGann) successfully assuming the identity of a deceased doctor until his nurse-girlfriend (Amanda Donohue) learns the truth and must decide what to do. British producer-director Christopher Morahan's initially interesting tale of deadly deception steadily falters until its flimsy conclusion. Brief bedroom shots with nudity and minimal violence. A-III (R) 15

Paper Moon (1973) Entertaining period comedy in which a bumbling con man (Ryan O'Neal finds himself saddled with a 9-year-old girl (Tatum O'Neal) who proves to be more adept at his profession than he is. Directed by Peter Bogdanovich, there is occasional rough language and adult references. A-III (PG) A

Paper Tiger (1976) David Niven plays a mild-mannered school teacher tutoring the young son of a Japanese official (Toshiro Mifune) when terrorists strike and kidnap both of them. Although the film is sentimental and poorly directed by Ken Annakin, it conveys effectively the influence upon a youngster of an imaginative adult who proves heroic when put to the test. The movie's realistic treatment of terrorist violence may adversely affect its intended preteen audience. A-II (PG)

Paper Wedding, The (1991) An unplanned romance develops when a Canadian immigration official suspects that a Montreal schoolteacher (Genevieve Bujold) has married a swarthy dishwasher (Manuel Aranguiz) in order to save him from political persecution back in Chile. Director Michel Brault's unpretentious movie is a slight but rather sweet love story that gradually brings out the best in its varied characters. Subtitles. An extramarital affair and flash of nudity. A-III (nr)

Paperhouse (1989) Troubled by her mother's minimal attention and her father's lengthy absences, an 11-year-old (Charlotte Burke) is consumed with her drawings of an odd, isolated house inhabited by a crippled boy (Elliott Spiers) that are translated into frightening dreams when she comes down with a fever. British director Bernard Rose imbues his haunting psychological drama with riveting, surreal visuals, some unanswered questions and a far-fetched ending. Intense climatic violence, ongoing menace and some rough language. A-III (PG-13) 15

Papillon (1973) Steve McQueen and Dustin Hoffman star in this generally entertaining drama of one man's daring attempts to escape from Devil's Island, an inhumane penal system designed to break both body and spirit. Director Franklin Schaffner neatly balances adventure and spectacle with a vivid depiction of the horrors of prison life. Viewers may not appreciate some of the brutality and references to masturbation and homosexuality, yet such scenes are necessary to the factual description of the convict's world and are in no way sensationalized. A-III (PG) 18

Parades (1972) Muddled film-within-a-film story follows the making of a documentary about a pacifist soldier's suicide that triggers a riot and the massacre of protesting students outside a military stockade. Though well-intentioned, director Robert J. Siegel's dramatization is artificial and unconvincing while the issues it raises are treated inadequately. Some sadistic violence and coarse language. A-III (R)

Paradise (1982) Two teenagers (Phoebe Cates and Willie Aames) survive an attack on their caravan and find bliss in various lushly appointed oases in director Stuart Gillard's shoddy, trashy little movie that attempts to do the "Blue Lagoon" number with camels. Exploitative nudity and graphic sex. O (R) 12

Paradise (1991) Touching story of a young boy (Elijah Wood) who comes to live with an emotionally estranged couple (Melanie Griffith and Don Johnson) mired in individual grief over the loss of their toddler son. Writer-director Mary Agnes Donoghue's well-acted picture interweaves several stories about relationships for an evocative look at childhood fears and adult pain. Fleeting shot of a sexual encounter, glimpse of nudity and several sexual references. A-III (PG-13)

Paradise Alley (1978) Sylvester Stallone (who also wrote and directed), stars as one of three tough brothers from the New York slums trying for big money in the wrestling ring in the 1940s. Rivalry between brothers and the machinations of a petty gangster (Kevin Conway) complicate matters. Though the movie has a few good moments, it never rises above the level of pulp melodrama and sometimes sinks to that of a cartoon. The violence of the wrestling sequences make this mature viewing fare. A-III (PG) A

Paradise, Hawaiian Style (1966) Innocuous Elvis Presley vehicle directed by Michael Moore in another Hawaiian musical romance. A-I (br) U

Parallax View, The (1974) Gripping thriller about an unorthodox reporter (Warren Beatty) whose investigation of a senator's assassination leads him to suspect that the murder was the work of a nationwide con-spiracy. Though it's bit too contrived, director Alan Pakula keeps the action tense and taut until the sudden, smashing climax. The result is a first-rate suspense chiller that makes clever use of a number of political conspiracy theories without pretending to be a serious statement on the subject. Some violence and rough language. A-III (R) AA

Paranoia (1969) Italian-French import with Carroll Baker and Lou Castel in a cliched plot mixing rich, neurotic widow, lonely villa and masterful stranger in a tiresome ritual of sex and violence plot directed by Umberto Lenzi. O (R)

Parasite (1982) Robert Glaudini plays a scientist with nothing better to do than developing creatures that fasten onto people, propagate and burst out at odd moments through various sections of their victim's anatomy. Directed by Charles Band, it is a loathsome exercise in nausea. Excessively graphic sex and violence. O (R)

Paratrooper (1953) Routine war story with an angry young Yank (Alan Ladd) joining an elite British airborne unit in 1940 and his difficulties with the outfit until proving his leadership on the battlefield. Director Terence Young is helped by a fine stiff-upper-lip cast (Leo Genn, Harry Andrews and Stanley Baker) but is hampered by the script's focus on the American's struggle with his personal problems. Wartime violence. A-I (br)

Pardon Mon Affaire (1977) French sex farce about a middle-aged man (Jean Rochefort) who is encouraged by his friends to seduce a beautiful model (Anny Duperey) and his infidelity leads to a comic expose in full view of television news cameras. Director Yves Robert has a difficult time striking the proper balance between the comic and the serious in a story devoted to an adulterous situation. O (PG) AA

Parent Trap, The (1961) Identical twins (Hayley Mills), raised separately by parents (Maureen O'Hara and Brian Keith) who split up shortly after their birth, only learn of the others existence at boarding school and they concoct an elaborate scheme to get Mom and Dad back together again. Typical sentimental Disney family comedy, with parents having the IQ of domestic pets and no match for precocious youngsters. Still, it's genial and mostly heart-warming with good acting thrown in for good measure. A-I (br) U

Parenthood (1989) Disappointing comedy-drama about four generations of one troubled American family centering on a 35-year-old (Steve Martin) and his father (Jason Robards). Director Ron Howard catalogs some very real problems faced by modern single- and two-parent households but, much like sitcoms, the vignettes have no depth or follow-through. Much sexual innuendo; vulgar language; some female stereotyping. A-III (PG-13) 15

Parents (1989) Corny satire of 1950s' suburbia employs a grisly theme of cannibalism as practiced by a supposedly perfect mom (Mary Beth Hurt) and dad (Randy Quaid) whose morose son (Bryan Madorsky) turns out to be the only sane one in the family. Director Bob Balaban carefully creates a sense of menace in picture postcard 1950s' America, but destroys it all with an unpalatably bloody ending. Much climatic gore and stomach-turning implications of suburban cannibalism. O (R) 18

Paris Blues (1961) Expatriate jazz musicians Paul Newman and Sidney Poitier pair up with tourists Joanne Woodward and Diahann Carroll, sharing the sights of the Paris and their beds. Director Martin Ritt's bittersweet romance has a fine jazz score but bogs down in self-conscious soul-searching about love, musical genius and race relations. Implied sexual relationships. A-III (br) X

Paris Holiday (1958) Leaden comedy about an American comedian (Bob Hope) whose life is threatened when he goes to France to buy a hot script. Directed by Gerd Oswald, the international cast (Fernandel, Anita Ekberg and Marta Hyer) never jells in a slapdash narrative whose highlight is Hope's stay in a mental clinic. Occasional slapstick violence and double entendres. A-I (br) U

Paris, Texas (1984) Father and son are reunited and then son and mother are reunited as dad rides off into the sunset. Directed by Wim Wenders, it is a pretentious and boring effort with a hero (Harry Dean Stanton) who at first won't talk and then won't stop talking. Some rough language. A-II (R) 15

Paris vu Par . . . (see: "Six in Paris").

Parson and the Outlaw, The (1957) After hanging up his guns for good, Billy the Kid (Anthony Dexter) comes out shooting when his preacher friend (Buddy Rogers) is ruthlessly gunned down. Directed by Oliver Drake, it's a clunker despite character actors Sonny Tufts, Bob Steele and Marie Windsor. Stylized violence overcomes pacifist premise. A-II (br)

Part II, Sounder (1976) Tepid sequel continuing the story of a black family of sharecroppers in the rural Louisiana of the 1930s focuses on how the father (Harold Sylvester) rallies his neighbors to build a new school that will keep the teacher (Annazette Chase) from leaving for a better job in the North. Produced, as was the original, by Robert B. Radnitz and directed by William A. Graham, the plot is disappointingly predictable, but some fine acting, the beauty of the setting, and its earnest sense of humanity make it above average family entertainment. A-I (G)

Part II, Walking Tall (1975) Sequel, far more restrained and low key than its violent predecessor, picks up the story of Sheriff Buford Pusser as he searches for the criminals who killed his wife but, by sequel's end, the man responsible is still at liberty. Capably directed by Earl Bellamy, Svenson's characterization of the fighting sheriff is much more credible than the melodramatic script. A-III (PG) AA

Partner (1974) Heavy-handed Italian production about a schizophrenic drama teacher (Pierre Clementi) whose other personality is that of a violent revolutionary. Directed by Bernardo Bertolucci in the heat of the political upheavals of 1968, the drama tries to relate art to politics, making an unconvincing statement about revolution as a creative act. Suicide figures into abstract plot line. A-III (nr)

Partners (1982) Ryan O'Neal and John Hurt star as detectives, one of them homosexual, who are assigned to pose as a homosexual couple in order to investigate a murder in a stupid comedy directed by James Burrows. O'Neal and Hurt admirably struggle with an underdeveloped script that turns homosexual and heterosexual characters alike into insulting stereotypes. Exploitative nudity. O (R) AA

Party, The (1968) Well-meaning, disaster-prone actor from India (Peter Sellers), instead of receiving a pink slip for his unwitting sabotage on a remake of "Gunga Din," gets an invitation to the producer's home for a pretentious Hollywood party that he turns into total chaos. Director Blake Edwards borrows liberally from the situations and sight gags of silent slapstick, but in the thin, one-joke context of a hopeless bungler, the hilarity soon gives way to tedious repetition, especially in a prolonged and tasteless bathroom sequence. A-III (br) PG

Party Girl (1958) Mediocre crime film set in Prohibition-era Chicago where a mobster's mouthpiece (Robert Taylor) turns on his boss (Lee J. Cobb) in order to save his showgirl lover (Cyd Charisse). Director Nicholas Ray finds few fresh angles in a hackneyed story of shifting loyalties. Nasty stylized violence and sexual innuendo. A-III (br) A

Pascali's Island (1988) Adaptation of Barry Unsworth's novel set on an Aegean island in 1908 where a Turkish spy (Ben Kingsley) comes under the spell of a fast-talking but secretive British archaeologist (Charles Dance). Director James Dearden slowly unfolds his plot of a man who has dealt so long in deceit that he ultimately cannot trust those who would save his life. Fleeting nudity and a bloody climax. A-III (PG-13) 15

Passage, The (1979) World War II story about a fiendish Nazi (Malcolm McDowell) who pursues an escaping scientist (James Mason) and his family across the Pyrenees where they get help from a stalwart Basque guide (Anthony Quinn). Mediocre British production directed by J. Lee Thompson, it is filled to excess with sadistic violence and brutality. O (R) X

Passage to India, A (1984) Screen version of the E.M. Forster classic about the inability of two diverse cultures to have any but perilous contact in the British-ruled India of the 1920s as seen in a story centering on a question of rape. Though painstakingly crafted by director David Lean and superbly acted by an outstanding cast (Judy Davis, Victor Banerjee, Dame Peggy Ashcroft, James Fox and Alec Guinness), the movie fails to dramatize convincingly the mysticism at the heart of its theme. Flawed but culturally rich entertainment. A-II (PG)

Passed Away (1992) Ensemble comedy concerns the reunion of a bickering Irish-American family (Pamela Reed, Bob Hoskins, William Petersen and Frances McDormand) upon the sudden death of their father (Jack Warden). Writer-director Charlie Peters turns in a fitfully funny movie whose one-dimensional characters are entirely predictable. Frequent sexual innuendo and an instance of rough language. A-III (PG-13)

Passenger, The (1970) Polish production about two women who meet by accident on an ocean liner, triggering memories of their days in a concentration camp together: one a Nazi officer, the other a prisoner. Both stories are related subjectively in flashback and their differing perspectives become both fascinating and disturbing. Although director Andrej Munk died before the movie's completion, what he did accomplish are brilliant fragments in a compelling exploration of human motivation and justification. A-III (nr) X

Passenger, The (1975) Empty Italian drama in which a TV journalist (Jack Nicholson), exasperated by an assignment in North Africa and acting on impulse, switches passport photos with a European who dies of a heart attack and finds that he has assumed the identity of an international gun runner. Director Michelangelo Antonioni has made a visually stunning work, yet its plot contrivances are more irritating than mysterious and its delving into the interior of its characters is without interest. A-III (PG)

Passenger 57 (1992) Standard action yarn pits a ruthless British terrorist (Bruce Payne) against an airline security expert (Wesley Snipes) onboard a hijacked L-1011 as the lives of 200 passengers hang in the balance. Director Kevin Hooks delivers a fast-moving, somewhat muddled plot in which violence is an inevitable but not unduly glamorized ingredient. Much menace with frequent violence and some rough language. A-III (R) 15

Passion Fish (1992) A former TV soap opera star (Mary McDonnell), embittered by an accident that left her a paraplegic, is cared for by a no-nonsense nurse (Alfre Woodard) who is secretly battling her own demons. Writer-director John Sayles' intimate portrait of the anguished, interior struggles of two women is unsentimental and affecting when not bogged down by its sleepy pace. An implied sexual encounter and intermittent rough language. A-III (R)

Passion of Anna, The (1970) Swedish production about a human cipher (Max von Sydow), living hermit-like on a small island, who becomes friendly with a cynical architect (Erland Josephson), his wife (Bibi Andersson), and their close friend, Anna (Liv Ullmann). Eventually he and Anna share their loneliness and then part even more hopeless than when they first met. Director Ingmar Bergman's bleak vision of people unable to find salvation from existential despair questions the meaning of life. A suicide and brief shots of mutilated animals combined with the moral ambiguity of the brief affair make this adult fare. A-III (R)

Passover Plot, The (1977) Dramatization of a book by biblical archaeologist Hugh J. Schonfield presents Jesus as a good and pious man who believed himself to be the Messiah but his plan to fake his death by Roman crucifixion failed, leaving his disciples to invent the story of his resurrection. Directed by Michael Campos, the movie is deeply flawed in narrative construction, acting and production values, but many Christians will find its muddled attempt to demythologize the Gospels repugnant. O (PG)

Pastime (1991) Old-fashioned sports story set in the mid-1950s when an over-the-hill minor league baseball pitcher (William Russ) befriends an insecure black rookie (Glenn Plummer) ignored by his teammates. Directed by Robin B. Armstrong, the heartwarming if simplistic story of black and white heroes and villains is soft on dramatic tension but strong on sentiment and values. Brief fisticuffs and a veiled sexual reference. A-I (PG)

Pat and Mike (1952) Offbeat romantic comedy teams veteran sports promoter Mike (Spencer Tracy) with top amateur athlete Pat (Katharine Hepburn) who's aces in any competition except when her beau (William Ching) is around. Directed by George Cukor, it's Hepburn's picture with Tracy cheering her on as she goes through her winning pace in such scenes as that of Pat saving Mike from two thugs. Feminist twist on the battle of the sexes. A-II (br) U

Pat Garrett and Billy the Kid (1973) The story of Garrett (James Coburn), in the hire of ruthless cattlemen, tracking down his old saddle mate Billy (Kris Kristofferson) is intended to show the slow passing of the western frontier in the 1880s. The end result is a ponderous and depressing study of men whose time has past. It's a familiar theme for director Sam Peckinpah who, once again, cannot resist graphic depictions of blood-spattered killings and various characters' rough use of women. O (R) 18

Patch of Blue, A (1965) A blind girl (Elizabeth Hartman), living in a dismal tenement, falls in love with the gentle black neighbor (Sidney Poitier) who befriends her, despite the shrill opposition of her mother (Shelley Winters). Director Guy Green takes an honest look at racial relations, avoids most of the obvious cliches and scores some points for human values. Mature theme. A-III (br) A

Paternity (1981) Callous egomaniac (Burt Reynolds) decides he wants a son and sets about interviewing prospective surrogate mothers. Beverly D'Angelo, a musician working as a waitress, gets the job and foolishly falls in love with the boor. Directed by David Steinberg, the ill-conceived romantic plot results in a slack and listless comedy of sexual politics with a false female stereotype and some rough language. A-III (PG) 15

Pathfinder, The (1952) James Fenimore Cooper's title character (George Montgomery) offers to guide a French force in the American wilderness of 1754 in order to betray them to the English. Director Sidney Solkow's low-budget effort turns the frontier into the usual stereotyped entertainment, however with notably unconvincing action scenes. Stylized violence. A-I (br)

Paths of Glory (1957) The terrible slaughter of World War I is re-created in this fact-based story of a French colonel (Kirk Douglas) who tries to save his men from being court-martialed for cowardice in a failed attack that should never have been ordered. Director Stanley Kubrick's anti-war classic contrasts the horrors of trench warfare at the front with the indifference and incompetence of the generals (Adolphe Menjou and George Macready) safely quartered in the rear. Graphic battlefield violence and a harrowing execution by firing squad. A-II (nr)

Patrick (1979) Tacky little thriller from Australia about a young man (Robert Thompson) who, while being kept alive on a support system, develops a "seventh sense" that enables him to perform all sorts of disgusting stunts when he becomes attached to a pretty nurse (Susan Penhaligon). Directed by Richard Franklin, it is a painful experience in every respect, with violence and a graphic depiction of some alleged medical techniques. A-III (PG)

Patriot Games (1992) Suspenseful thriller from Tom Clancy's novel about an ex-CIA agent (Harrison Ford) who returns to the fold to protect his wife and child (Anne Archer and Thora Birch) from a revenge-crazed IRA terrorist (Sean Bean). Director Phillip Noyce rivets attention on the family's vulnerability but doesn't shield viewers from brutal terrorist executions and violent shootouts. Much violence, a brief bedroom scene and minimal rough language. A-IV (R) 15

Patsy, The (1964) After a famous comedian dies in an accident, his staff (John Carradine, Peter Lorre, Everett Sloane, Keenan Wynn and Ina Balin) decide to turn a hotel bellboy (Jerry Lewis) into his successor. Also written and directed by Lewis, the slack plot and klutzy slapstick action can only appeal to fans of the star's goonish brand of comedy. Mild slapstick violence. A-I (br) U

Patti Rocks (1988) Boring, pretentious and ultimately repellent movie about a married clod (Chris Mulkey) who cajoles a friend (John Jenkins) into coming with him to help persuade his pregnant, out-of-town girlfriend to have an abortion. Directed ineptly by David Burton Morris, the movie consists of little more than an interminable car ride with two adolescent males talking dirty about sex and women, with the payoff being a romp in the girlfriend's bed. Unremittingly rough language and a simulation of sex. O (R) 18

Patton (1970) George C. Scott's complex portrayal of World War II General George S. Patton conveys a paradoxical, multifaceted character whose love of the fray and intense will to win was grounded in a deep-seated hatred of war itself. Director Franklin Schaffner's powerful dramatization is neither a glorification of war nor an anti-war tract but pays homage to a career officer who, unfortunately, could only achieve his destiny in wartime. Violence and profanity within a realistic context. A-II (PG)

Patty Hearst (1988) The 1974 kidnapping of heiress Patty Hearst (Natasha Richardson) from her Berkeley apartment by the Symbionese Liberation Army is told from her point of view in an intense docudrama directed by Paul Schrader. Richardson's mesmerizing performance conveys the brutality and brainwashing Hearst had to endure. Much conscienceless violence, a continuing sense of menace and wall-to-wall profanity. A-IV (R) 18

Paul and Michelle (1974) Noxious sequel to "Friends" returns to the perils of Paul (Sean Bury) who finds Michelle (Anicee Alvina) living with their young daughter and an understanding American (Keir Dullea). They fly off to Paris to resume their lives in a morass of sickly-sweet dialog, carefully photographed nudity, Michelle's abortion of the American's baby, and Paul's fat allowance being cut off by Daddy—and they separate yet again. Directed by Lewis Gilbert, it's sheer exploitation without pretense of moral perspective. O (R)

Paula (1952) Soggy tearjerker in which the barren wife (Loretta Young) of a college professor (Kent Smith) accidentally runs down a young orphan (Thomas Rettig) leaving him unable to speak but, with the help of her doctor (Alexander Knox), she adopts the mute boy and teaches him to speak again. Directed by Rudolph Mate, the melodramatic contrivances keep getting in the way of Young's showy display of surface emotion. Delicate treatment of infertility and a youth's protracted trauma. A-II (br) A

Pauline at the Beach (1983) French comedy about six oddly assorted lovers and would-be lovers who pursue and flee one another at a seaside resort in Brittany in late summer while talking endlessly about the nature of love. As with director Eric Rohmer's better movies, it is never dull, never less than diverting, but is satisfied with clever surfaces rather than underlying meaning. Extremely mature subject matter. A-IV (R)

Pawnbroker, The (1966) Holocaust survivor (Rod Steiger) runs a pawnshop in Harlem in a movie intermingling his experiences of oppression with those of the inhabitants of a black ghetto. Directed by Sidney Lumet, it is a powerful, effective parable on human solidarity and the pain of life. Adult treatment. A-III (br) X

Payday (1973) Gritty study of second-rate country-western singer (Rip Torn), whose career has peaked without his even knowing it, and whose life is about to go right over the edge in a series of one-night stands, cheap motel rooms, good bourbon, popped uppers and downers and a ragged assortment of groupies and hangers-on. Director Daryl Duke's picture of the tormented, self-destructive anti-hero on a lonesome road with nothing at the end has the tragic sense of reality. Some rough language and brief nudity. A-IV (R) X

Payment in Blood (1969) Dreary Italian western set right after the Civil War when disbanded military freebooters (led by Guy Madison) terrorized the Southwest. Director E. G. Rowland's badly staged violence and even worse acting is a tiresome bore. A-III (R)

Peace Killers, The (1971) Brutal motorcycle gang makes war on a commune of peaceful pot-smokers when one of the gang's women trades in her backseat on a cycle for a snug little sleeping bag at the commune. Directed

by Douglas Schwartz, the resulting reprisals would make grown men blanch at scenes of utter brutality, torture, gang rape, and general mayhem. O (R)

Peach Thief (1969) Disappointing Bulgarian import tells a World War I story about a frustrated young wife (Nevena Kokanova) who has a foredoomed affair with a Serbian prisoner-of-war (Rade Markovich). The meager and predictable story lacks individuality and human resonance. A-III (nr)

Pedestrian, The (1974) Demanding German drama about an aging industrialist (Gustav Rudolf Sellner) who is tortured by guilt and fear that his secret crime as a Nazi officer responsible for an atrocity is about to be made public because of the digging and sifting into the incident by a German news magazine. Director Maximilian Schell questions what might be called a moral statute of limitations in his complex probing of personal and collective guilt. Strong subject not for casual moviegoers. A-III (PG)

Pee-wee's Big Adventure (1985) Comic personality Pee-wee Herman's search for his stolen bike takes him on a madcap chase from the Alamo in Texas to Hollywood. Directed by Tim Burton, the humor is puerile with occasional slapstick violence. A-II (PG) U

Peggy Sue Got Married (1986) A middle-aged mom (Kathleen Turner), about to be divorced from her unfaithful husband (Nicolas Cage), relives her past when she faints at a class reunion and discovers that the person she was and has become are one and the same. Director Francis Ford Coppola carefully controls the sentimental romanticism inherent in this story, showing the continuum of values through the course of an individual's life. A brief scene of love-making and some rough language. A-II (PG-13) 15

Pelican Brief, The (1993) With her life in grave danger after figuring out who was behind the assassination of two Supreme Court justices, a New Orleans law student (Julia Roberts) turns to an investigative reporter (Denzel Washington) to get her incriminating brief in print. Abetted by exceptional performances from a fine supporting cast, director Alan J. Pakula's spiky thriller maintains suspense despite a convoluted plot. Some restrained violence and an instance of rough language. A-III (PG-13)

Pelle the Conqueror (1988) Unsentimental Danish film follows a turn-of-the-century elderly widower (Max von Sydow) and his young son (Pelle Hvenegaard) from their arrival on Danish shores in search of a better life to their many hardships as stablehands on a farm. Directed by Bille August, this is long and grim, but imbued with a strong feel for the landscape and low level of humanity on the farm as well as the life-sustaining love of a father for his young son. Subtitles. Brief, graphic images implying the results of incest, infanticide and castration, some violence and vulgar language. A-III (nr) 15

Pendulum (1969) George Peppard, Jean Seberg and Richard Kiley star in a fast-paced crime thriller about a dedicated cop (Peppard) who within the space of a few weeks finds himself on both sides of the issues surrounding civil rights of accused criminals. With strong performances and fine location photography of the nation's capital, director George Schaefer's work poses some tough questions about law enforcement and the justice system, providing enough material for viewers to draw their own conclusions. A-II (M) AA

Penitentiary (1980) A young black (Leon Issac Kennedy), wrongly convicted and sent to prison, takes up boxing and battles his way to vindication. The mediocre melodrama, written and directed by Jamaa Fanaka, provides an excessively graphic depiction of the corruption, brutality and homosexuality pervading prison life. O (R) X

Penitentiary II (1982) Young convict (Leon Isaac Kennedy) gains freedom and respectability by his boxing skills. Director Jamaa Fanaka's sequel, however, falls far short of the barely competent standards of the original. Repulsive, brutal mess with excessive violence. O (R)

Penitentiary III (1987) A boxer (Leon Isaac Kennedy) fights his way out of a prison dominated by a wealthy degenerate inmate (Tony Geary) but can't overcome the nightmarish plot absurdities and writer-director Jamaa Fanaka's near farcical excesses of violence and brutality. O (R)

Penn & Teller Get Killed (1989) Pointless black comedy enmeshes the comic magicians Penn and Teller in a web of self-inspired practical jokes that become more and more macabre until they backfire and snuff them out. Directed by Arthur Penn, the school-boy gags involve lots of fake blood and grisly pranks. Cavalier attitude toward death and suicide, much profanity and some sexual innuendo. A-III (R)

Pennies from Heaven (1981) Comedian Steve Martin plays a straight role in this almost unqualified disaster. As an unsuccessful peddler of sheet music in the Depression era, Martin is beastly to women and takes refuge from harsh reality by imagining lavish Busby Berkley-style production numbers. Neither director Herbert Ross nor writer Dennis Potter seem to have any idea how to adapt the story and concept for a feature movie. Besides the amorality of the hero, the plot contains scenes dealing with prostitution and abortion. A-III (R)

Penthouse, The (1967) Failed adaptation of a play by C. Scott Forbes in which two psychopaths keep a man (Terence Morgan) and his mistress (Suzy Kendall) prisoner in their penthouse apartment, the woman in the bedroom and the man tied to a chair. Director Peter Collinson's attempt to make a statement about hypocrisy and disillusionment fails because of its contrived and melodramatic treatment and becomes little more than a tiresome exercise in sadism. O (br) X

People Against O'Hara, The (1951) Aging lawyer who's a recovering alcoholic (Spencer Tracy) agrees to defend a neighborhood youth (James Arness) accused of murder but when the trial goes badly, he puts his career on the line by bribing a witness. Director John Sturges' slack courtroom drama is less interesting than Tracy's arresting portrayal of a faltering veteran doing his best for a client he knows is innocent. Legal complications involving a lawyer's unethical conduct. A-II (br) A

People Next Door, The (1970) J. P. Miller's adaptation of his award-winning television play about a middle-class teenager (Deborah Winters) who grooves with the boys and trips on LSD to escape the reality of her hypocritical parents (Eli Wallach and Julie Harris). Drearily moralizing, one-dimensional melodrama contrasts parents who drink and hide their sexual indiscretions with youngsters who smoke dope and flaunt theirs. Director David Greene's treatment fosters false stereotypes, uses unnecessary nudity and fails to deal adequately with the serious problem of drug abuse in suburbia. O (R) X

People of the Wind (1976) British documentary follows the annual trek of a nomadic tribe in southern Iran that each spring must bring their sheep and cattle from winter quarters to fresh grazing lands on a journey through perilous mountain terrain. Directed by Anthony Howarth, it is the record of a fiercely independent people who accept such dangers as the price of remaining free from the influences of the outside world. A-I (nr)

People That Time Forgot, The (1977) Rescue attempt on a prehistoric island brings viewers back to the same ice-bound fastness teeming with prehistoric monsters and cavemen depicted in "The Land That Time Forgot." Directed by Kevin Connor, the British production is lackluster, with tepid acting from Patrick Wayne and Doug McClure, but its silly special effects may amuse youngsters. A-II (PG) U

People Under the Stairs, The (1991) Revolting horror comedy in which a ghetto kid (Brandon Adams) gets trapped in a creaky mansion populated by a cannibalistic couple (Everett McGill and Wendy Robie), their abused daughter (A. J. Langer) and a cellar full of rampaging ghouls. Writer-director Wes Craven wallows in gore and sick humor about child abuse in a drawn-out, badly-acted terror tale. Excessive violence, some racial slurs and sexual references and occasional rough language. O (R) 18

Pepi, Luci, Bom (1992) Vicious black comedy centers on the gleefully sadomasochistic activities of three women (Carmen Maura, Eva Siva and Olvido Gara). Written and directed by Pedro Almodovar, this 1980 Spanish production celebrates the abuse of women and treats rape as a joke. Subtitles. Scenes of rape and other violence, sexual encounters with nudity, recreational drug use and occasional rough language. O (nr)

Peppermint Soda (1979) French production about two sisters in 1963, one of whom is 15 and trying to cope with love, politics and anti-Semitism while her 13-year-old sister wants to follow her example but is not quite ready. Directed by Diane Kurys, the beautifully made movie is about people in the midst of life, but many viewers may find the pace too leisurely for enjoyment. A-III (nr) AA

Perceval (1978) Stylized French production based on the medieval romance about the knight (Fabrice Luchini) who joins King Arthur's court, fails to claim the Holy Grail when he has the chance, and is punished for his ignorance. Directed by Erich Rohmer, the visuals beautifully evoke the world of the Middle Ages and its code of chivalry as well as the conflict in Christendom between the spiritual and temporal. A-II (nr)

Percy (1971) Witless British sex farce about a young man (Hywel Bennett) with a genital transplant that fascinates both the medical world and several young ladies who discover his new acquisition. Directed by Ralph Thomas, its snickering tone is even more offensive than such scenes as a nurse doing a striptease to test his convalescence. O (R) X

Perfect (1985) Rolling Stone reporter (John Travolta) becomes involved with an aerobics instructor (Jamie Lee Curtis) while researching a story on health clubs. Director Jim Bridges' muddled and pretentious movie offers a favorable view of promiscuity and includes a thoroughly distasteful sequence with a male stripper. O (R) 15

Perfect Couple, A (1979) Middle-aged, brow-beaten son of a wealthy, conservative Greek family (Paul Dooley) uses a computer dating service that matches him with an aspiring rock singer (Marta Heflin). They surmount all difficulties, proving that director Robert Altman has a heart and the title is not ironically meant. The film does have some cheerful moments, and the acting is quite good, but the whole thing is so inconsequential that it often seems in danger of evaporating. A-III (PG) AA

Perfect Friday (1970) British caper movie tries to liven up the muddled plot revolving around bank teller Stanley Baker's clever bank robbery with an incoherently staccato narrative, false plot twists and shots of accomplice Ursula Andress undressed. Director Peter Hall's sense of timing and humor is as badly off the mark as the movie's sense of moral perspective. O (R) AA

Perfect Weapon, The (1991) Seeking the mob boss killer (James Hong) of his mentor (Mako), a kenpo karate expert (Jeff Speakman) is tricked into thinking the gangster's archrival is the guilty party. Director Mark DiSalle's standard action yarn is a yawn that could pass for an episode of a private-eye TV series, simply stretched out to accommodate more karate bouts. Intermittent martial arts violence and an isolated instance of rough language and drug use. A-III (R)

Perfect World, A (1993) Hard-edged adult thriller about an escaped convict (Kevin Costner) taking a 7-year-old hostage (T. J. Lowther) on a blood-splattered ride as he tries to elude the pursuit of a veteran Texas Ranger (Clint Eastwood) and a young criminologist (Laura Dern). Also directed by Eastwood, the story's tension revolves around the menacing situations in which the young boy is placed as he witnesses deadly violence and then participates in it. Intense menace to a child, graphic violence, sexual references and coarse language. A-III (PG-13) 15

Perfectly Normal (1991) A young loner (Michael Riley) jettisons his plans to build a house when a flamboyant stranger (Robbie Coltrane) persuades him to spend his inheritance on a restaurant where the two would sing Italian operas to the clientele. Director Yves Simoneau's offbeat, fitfully funny comedy endearingly portrays eccentric characters who happily change each other for the better. Restrained love scene with brief nudity and some rough language. A-III (R) 15

Performance (1970) A hood (James Fox), on the run from the mob, takes refuge with a temporarily retired pop singer (Mick Jagger) awaiting the return of his inspiration in the company of several fans (Anita Pallenberg and Michele Breton). Bizarre British drama directed by Don Cammell and Nicholas Roeg is a pseudo-sophisticate's vision of evil with the kind of slick gimmickry that promises revelations but never rises above its shallow fascination with the perversities it supposedly explores. It's a morass of unrelieved violence, drug use, sex and grotesque immoralities. O (R) 18

Perils of Gwendoline, The (1985) Coy, fly-blown adventure movie, by French director

Just Jaeckin, about a trio of explorers in a land ruled by warrior women. Obviously meant to be satirical and sexy, it's merely distasteful and boring. O (R)

Perils of P. K., The (1986) Amateurish, low-budget sex farce centering on a neurotic middle-aged woman recounting her sexual daydreams and memories to a psychiatrist. Vulgar sight gags and crude gestures, foul language and off-color sexual jokes. O (R)

Permanent Record (1988) The repercussions of a popular high school senior's suicide are followed as the boy's friends attempt to deal with their grief, rage, guilt and bewilderment over his senseless death. Director Marisa Silver sensitively explores the emotional turmoil experienced by adolescents in facing such a tragedy, though the movie is weakened by a pat resolution. Unsettling theme, incidental drug and alcohol abuse and some profanity. A-III (PG-13) 15

Persecution and Assassination of Jean-Paul Marat as Performed by the Inmates of the Asylum of Charenton under the Direction of the Marquis De Sade, The (1967) The play by Peter Weiss examines the conflict between the political autocracy of the French revolutionary Marat and the social anarchy of De Sade. Peter Brook directs the Royal Shakespeare Company in a screen version that is not so much a record of its staging and performances as it is a surprisingly good movie that never quite overcomes the weaknesses of its material. Complex, sometimes shocking, the drama's criticism of social, political and religious conventions will agitate some but give others a number of insights into the conflict between freedom and authority. A-IV (br)

Persona (1967) Swedish drama about an actress (Liv Ullmann) who suddenly cannot speak, fails to respond to psychiatric treatment and is sent to a seaside villa for a rest in the care of a talkative, sympathetic nurse (Bibi Andersson). There the two women seem to change roles and their personal identities become strangely intermingled. Directed by Ingmar Bergman, it is intensely personal, largely obscure and not a little disturbing. A-IV (br) X

Personal Best (1982) Two female track stars (Mariel Hemingway; Patrice Donnelly) carry on a homosexual affair in a dull, unbelievably crude and relentlessly simple-minded film written and directed by Robert Towne. Excessive nudity. O (R) 18

Personal Services (1987) Wry British sex farce about a waitress (Julie Walters) who turns to running a brothel catering to the whims of the upper class. Despite some barbs at the hypocrisy of the toffs, director Terry Jones insists on romanticizing an immoral profession. Kinky sex, arrogant bawdiness and nudity are used as sources of humor. O (R) 18

Personals (1972) Sex-exploitation director Armand Weston stages hard-core demonstrations to complement his interviews with people who advertise their appetites in sex-oriented publications. O (nr)

Pet Sematary (1989) Failed horror movie about a Maine family living near a dangerous highway and two cemeteries—one for family pets and the other for those who want their loved ones to return from the dead. Adapted by Stephen King from his best-seller and directed by Mary Lambert, the film is peppered with loose ends and gratuitous climatic gore. While relevant questions about the finality of death are raised by the family's six-year-old (Blaze Berdahl), her toddler brother's afterlife transformation into a gruesome slasher is depicted in horrific, graphic detail. O (R) 18

Pet Sematary Two (1992) Buried on supposedly cursed ground by teenaged buddies (Edward Furlong and Jason McGuire), a vicious stepfather (Clancy Brown) and a dog return as fiendish zombies on a murderous rampage. Mary Lambert directs a drawn-out and consistently predictable horror sequel with a death-affirming theme. Numerous grisly killings, brief nudity and some rough language. O (R) 18

Pete 'n' Tillie (1972) Awkward and at times grating seriocomedy in which Pete (Walter Matthau) meets Tillie (Carol Burnett) in sunny California, bed down, get married, raise a son only to lose him to leukemia, separate and finally reunite. Director Martin Ritt proceeds with a wildly inappropriate mixture of sardonic humor, slapstick, stark tragedy, heavy melodrama and cheap soap operatics. Lapses in taste include an excessive amount of profanity and a shrill bit of blasphemy. A-IV (PG) AA

Pete Seeger . . . A Song and a Stone (1972) Documentary on one of the bedrock figures of American folk songs shows him in performance and conversation about his music and its relation to such issues as ecology. The stone in the title represents the only weapon Seeger has ever carried, a little one he keeps in his banjo, symbolic of breaking Establishment windows. Seeger's songs and his little stone are at the core of this engaging and rewarding work directed by Robert Elfstrom. A-II (nr)

Pete's Dragon (1977) Pete, a young orphan (Sean Marshall), and Elliot, an amiable dragon, are befriended by a lighthouse keeper's daughter (Helen Reddy) in a small Maine fishing village at the turn-of-the-century. Disney musical fantasy, directed by Don Chaffey, combines live-action with animation. The dragon's ability to become invisible is the chief source of humor in a slow-moving film that also features Mickey Rooney, Red Buttons and Shelley Winters. A-I (G)

Peter Pan (1953) Walt Disney's animated feature is a delightful adaptation of Sir James M. Barrie's 1904 play about an impish 12-year-old boy (voice of Bobby Driscoll) who refuses to grow up. Directed by Hamilton Luske, Clyde Geronimi and Wildred Jackson, it offers dreamy fantasy panoramas of London and Never-Never Land, Tinker Bell as a feisty pixie and innocuous, mostly unmemorable music. Some dated sexist (jealous women) and racial (Native Americans) stereotypes are wrong-headed and should be noted as false to children. A-I (G) U

Peter Rabbit and Tales of Beatrix Potter (1971) British ballet production conjures up Beatrix Potter's delicate animal fables and through Frederick Ashton's choreography enables them to dance and pantomime their way into the hearts of story lovers. Director Reginald Mills frees the work from the stage by photographing it in a picturesque English countryside and patterns the costumes on the soft, cuddly textures and pale pastels of the famous Potter sketches. A beautiful way to introduce youngsters to the world of Peter Rabbit and the art of the ballet. A-I (G)

Peter's Friends (1992) British seriocomedy about six university classmates (Kenneth Branagh, Emma Thompson, Stephen Fry, Alphponsia Emmanuel, Hugh Laurie and Imelda Staunton) who, a decade after graduation, reunite at an English manor for a New Year's weekend of carefree catching-up and unexpected soul-searching. Producer-director Branagh's derivative situation is sporadically entertaining as it charts the shifting personal relationships of friends who are each facing turning points in their lives. Fleeting bedroom shot, flash of rear nudity and frequent rough language. A-III (nr) 15

Petulia (1968) An affair between a discontented wife (Julie Christie) and a divorced doctor (George C. Scott) is ended when her husband (Richard Chamberlain) finds out and brutally beats her. In picturing a sick society, director Richard Lester follows the story's alienated characters as they check in and out of a San Francisco hospital where it is easier to mend broken bodies than damaged lives. The humor is dark, but the effect is stunning. A-III (R) X

Peyton Place (1957) Trashy soap opera from the Grace Metalious novel about the bedroom affairs of a hypocritical small town in Maine until culminating in the trial of a young woman (Hope Lange) for murdering her stepfather (Arthur Kennedy). Director Mark Robson dresses up the one-note scenario in a glossy production that makes it seem all the more tawdry. Muted treatment of a variety of sexual wrongdoing, stylized violence and a veiled reference to abortion. A-III (br) 15

Phantasm (1979) Dreadfully amateurish attempt to cross comedy with horror in a story about two brothers in a graveyard battle with brown-robed dwarfs and a fiendish undertaker on the lookout for bodies, dead or alive. Directed by Don Coscarelli, the movie employs excessive violence, gore and nudity. O (R) 18

Phantasm II (1988) Two teenagers (James Le Gros and Paula Irvine) and a middle-aged cohort (Reggie Bannister) track and attempt to kill a ghoulish mortician (Angus Scrimm) who can't get his fill of corpses. Director Don Coscarelli's sequel has no redeeming qualities. Excessive blood and gore, some profanity and a kinky sex scene. O (R) 18

Phantom of Liberty, The (1974) French production freely shifts through a series of loosely connected vignettes beginning as a costume drama set in Toledo during the Napoleonic era returning to contemporary scenes of political, social and religious satire. Directed by Luis Bunuel, the narrative's general complexity as well as its anti-clerical references, casual nudity and mature sexual motifs, make this surrealistic work not for all audiences. A-IV (R)

Phantom of Terror, The (see: "The Bird with the Crystal Plumage").

Phantom Tollbooth (1970) When a tollbooth appears in his bedroom, a rather listless youngster (Butch Patrick) escapes through it into a world of fantasy where he meets an assortment of allegorical figures and learns the value of using time well and making the most of his schooling. Director Chuck Jones' feature-length cartoon makes playful, intelligent use of visual metaphors and clever word-turns that may motivate some youngsters' interest in reading and writing. A-I (G) U

Phantom of the Opera, The (1943) His face disfigured by acid, an embittered musician (Claude Rains) hides behind a mask in the cavernous rooms beneath the Paris Opera from which he terrorizes the company into making his protege (Susanna Foster) a star despite her love for a weak tenor (Nelson Eddy). Director Arthur Lubin's lush period costumer lavishes more attention on stilted opera scenes than the sinister activities of the menacing phantom. Some stylized violence and moody atmosphere but few scares. A-II (br) A

Phantom of the Paradise (1974) Loosely based on "The Phantom of the Opera," the updated version is about an aspiring rock composer (William Finley) whose face is mutilated by a recording press and his rock cantata on the Faust legend is stolen by a ruthless music producer (Paul Williams) who wants it for the opening of his new house, the Paradise. The composer seeks revenge by terrorizing those working in the Paradise in an effort to have his one love (Jessica Harper) sing his cantata. Director Brian De Palma uses the almost surrealistic plot to concoct a unique combination of horror and comedy, avoiding excess while making some incisive comments about the state of modern music. A-III (PG) AA

Phar Lap (1984) Rousing, wholesome entertainment from Australia about a famous Depression-era racehorse who meets a tragic end. Though not especially dramatic, director Simon Wincer's work with Tom Burlinson, Martin Vaughan and Ron Liebman is nonetheless interesting family entertainment. A-I (PG)

Phase IV (1974) Sci-fi tale of the world being taken over by ants acting out of mass instinct. The photographic techniques somehow make the ants and their colony a much more believable world than that of the cast of human characters (Nigel Davenport, Michael Murphy and Lynne Frederick). Although artist-director Saul Bass's ending is a little muddled, getting there is half the fun. A-II (PG) A

Phedre (1973) Marie Bell, the legendary actress of the Comedie Francaise, plays the tragic queen in Racine's 17th-century version of the Greek myth of Theseus, the prince torn between two loves. Director Pierre Jourdan has tried to do more than record a stage performance, yet the play is necessarily artificial and stage-bound. Though the English subtitles give only a suggestion of Racine's complicated romantic verse, the work is of interest to students of French culture and drama. A-II (PG)

Phffft! (1954) Leaden romantic comedy about a couple (Judy Holliday and Jack Lemmon) who get divorced for no good reason, then can't adjust to the complications of single life and decide to get back together. Director Mark Robson gets no laughs from his heavy-handed treatment of the mating game, which here has little to do with love, much less fidelity. Recurring sexual references. A-III (br) A

Philadelphia (1993) After abruptly being fired for incompetence, a homosexual lawyer (Tom Hanks) dying of AIDS hires an attorney (Denzel Washington) to sue his former boss (Jason Robards) for discrimination. Directed by Jonathan Demme, the emotionally manipulative script and Hanks' restrained, powerful performance reduce complex social issues to the personal level of one victim's humanity and search for justice. Sympathetic depiction of gay relationships, fleeting nudity and a few sexist

and sexual slurs. A-IV (PG-13) 12

Philadelphia Experiment, The (1984) Routine time-travel adventure with Michael Pare and Bobby Di Cicco playing World War II sailors projected into the present. Directed by Stewart Raffill, the result is innocuous and moderately entertaining. A-II (PG)

Photographer, The (1975) Demented photographer (Michael Callan), who hates his mother, murders his models while taking pictures of their death agonies, until murdered by a model who hates her father. Pointless, absurd and relentlessly violent story. O (PG)

Phynx, The (1970) Intended as a satire of both foreign intrigue movies and popular music, director Lee H. Katzin's story about a group of rock musicians who are sent to Albania to rescue some American show people is merely dull and boring, save for the brief appearances of some famous performers of the past (Ruby Keeler, Dorothy Lamour, Busby Berkely, Leo Gorcey, Huntz Hall and many others). Some slapstick violence and sexual references. A-III (PG)

Physical Evidence (1989) A hard-living, veteran detective (Burt Reynolds), accused of murdering a crook known to have had many enemies, is represented by a yuppie public defender (Theresa Russell) who's stymied in her efforts to clear her client. Director Michael Crichton fails to rev up his derivative scenario with thrills or star chemistry. Some profanity and bloody violence. A-III (R) 18

Piaf—The Early Years (1982) Disappointing dramatization of French singer Edith Piaf's life from her birth in 1915, through her formative years in the seedy underworld of criminals and prostitutes who helped her eke out a living as a street singer until her success as a top Paris entertainer in the 1930s. Director Guy Casaril has trouble maintaining interest in the muddled continuity of the narrative, but Brigitte Ariel in the title role is moderately successful in overcoming this handicap. Rather romantic treatment of Piaf's affairs of the heart. A-III (PG)

Piano, The (1993) A Scottish mute (Holly Hunter) with a 9-year-old child (Anna Paquin) arrives in 19th-century New Zealand bush country for an arranged marriage but, after her new husband (Sam Neill) sells her beloved piano, she and its new owner (Harvey Keitel) fall in love. Writer-director Jane Campion's striking film explores the intensity of sexual desire and love without placing it in a moral context. Brief bedroom scene with full nudity, fleeting violence and an instance of rough language. A-IV (R) 15

Pickpocket (1969) Alienated youth turns to petty crime as a kind of lark but, not very good at it, is caught and sent to prison where he is visited by a young woman who cares for him and will be waiting when he is released. French production directed by Robert Bresson in 1956, the work has nothing to do with crime thrillers but is an austere look at a lost soul and his possible chance of redemption. Challenging but worthwhile fare for reflective viewers. A-II (nr)

Pickup Artist, The (1987) Unintelligent late-teen romance about an aggressive womanizer (Robert Downey) and promiscuous museum guide (Molly Ringwald) who take a tumble in the front seat, solve father Dennis Hopper's gambling debt to tough Harvey Keitel and find true love without much happiness or a solution to their bad habits. Director James Toback indulges in TV superficiality and tired stereotyping in this lazy tale that endorses gambling and recreational sex. A-III (PG-13) 15

Pickup on 101 (1972) College coed (Lesley Warren) heading toward a New Mexico commune and a rock guitarist (Martin Sheen) on his way to Los Angeles are brought together on the road by a an old hobo (Jack Albertson) whose redemptive quality brings the young couple to transcend their own selfishness and learn that love means more than sex. Director John Florea has a script loaded with simplistic and pietistic preachments, but at least it tries for something a bit more substantial than the usual sentimental romance. A-III (PG) A

Picnic at Hanging Rock (1979) On a sunny St. Valentine's day in 1900, a group of Australian schoolgirls go off on a picnic to a strange and foreboding place called Hanging Rock where three of the girls and one teacher disappear without a trace. Director Peter Weir's fact-based, never-solved mystery creates an eerie, otherworldly atmosphere as the girls explore the ledges and recesses of the ancient rock formation. The somberness of the theme and an emphasis on suppressed sexuality make it mature fare. A-III (PG) A

Picture Mommy Dead (1966) Suspense melodrama about a young heiress (Susan Gordon) who returns to the house where her mother had burned to death many years before and, in the company of her father and stepmother (Don Ameche and Martha Hyer), strange things begin happening to her. Director Bert I. Gordon tries to do something with all the frights and hallucinations contained in the script, but the result borders on the absurd. Stylized violence. A-III (br) X

Piece of Pleasure, A (1976) French drama about a "liberated" husband (Paul Gegauff who also wrote the script) who pushes his less-educated wife (Danielle Gegauff) into a chaos of sexual experimentation with pre-dictably tragic results. That people are capable of destroying themselves by their own self-deceptions may sound like a fairly banal theme, but director Claude Chabrol presents it as a harrowing truth, with a level of human involvement, yet distancing itself from their excesses. A-IV (R)

Piece of the Action, A (1977) Two smooth con men (Bill Cosby and Sidney Poitier) are blackmailed by a retired police detective (James Earl Jones) into working for a youth center devoted to educating ghetto youngsters and getting them jobs. Directed by Poitier, the comedy-melodrama quickly exhausts the situation and is only mildly entertaining. Strong language and a muddled sense of morality (the two criminals show no signs of remorse and Poitier lives in unwedded bliss). A-III (PG) A

Pieces of Dreams (1970) A troubled, lonely pastor (Robert Forster), out of touch with his people and bored with the routine chores of parish life, leaves the priesthood and marries a divorced social worker (Lauren Hutton). Director Daniel Haller fails to get inside the personal world of his characters and their spiritual conflicts, leaving one with the impression that the priest's ultimate decision was motivated by little more than a tumble in the hay. A-IV (PG)

Pied Piper, The (1972) British production filmed in Germany by French director Jacques Demy results in a confused retelling of the medieval tale about the piper (folk singer Donovan) who comes to save the hamlet of Hamelin from the Black Plague by leading a parade of rodents down to the river to drown but unpaid returns to spirit the town's children away to a happier clime. It mixes childlike fantasy with such a cluttered picture of the people and artifacts of medieval life that its simple storyline is often difficult to follow. A-II (G) PG

Pierrot le Fou (1969) Unconventional French melodrama about a man and a woman (Jean-Paul Belmondo; Anna Karina) whose relationship is based upon misunderstandings and boredom. Director Jean-Luc Godard's highly subjective, stream-of-consciousness lacks narrative coherence yet conveys the need people have for ideals in a world of absurdity. A-IV (nr) A

Pigeons (1971) Trite and silly story about aimless urban youth, here a yuppie New York cab driver (Jordan Christopher) who falls for a cute neighbor (Jill O'Hara), but their romance withers on a trip to the suburbs to meet his neurotic folks. Directed by John Dexter, the story is overly familiar and the treatment overly cute. Some relatively innocuous nudity. A-III (R)

Pillow Talk (1959) Slick but sappy romantic comedy starts with an interior decorator (Doris Day) berating an amorous song writer (Rock Hudson) for hogging the telephone party-line they share, then being tricked into falling in love with him and his days as a bachelor are doomed. Directed by Michael Gordon, the contrived situation is decked out in plush settings and comic support by Tony Randall and Thelma Ritter, but the weak results don't justify the effort. Comic treatment of sexual situations. A-III (br) U

Pin (1991) A disturbed young man (David Hewlett) who believes a ventriloquist's dummy to be real goes over the edge when the boyfriend (John Ferguson) of his sister (Cyndy Preston) suggests he be committed. Director Sandor Stern's drawn-out thriller is a low-budget, predictable affair of little tension or distinction. Brief violence, references to promiscuity and abortion and momentary nudity. A-III (nr)

Ping Pong (1987) Young Chinese law clerk (Lucy Sheen) rediscovers her cultural roots and inadvertently reunites a fragmented family while executing the will of a wealthy Chinese businessman. British import from director Po Chih Leong deals affectionately with the social and cultural pressures that alienate westernized foreign nationals and erode their family ties. Charming but slow-moving portrait. A-I (nr) PG

Pink Cadillac (1989) A bail bondsman's skip-tracer (Clint Eastwood) falls for his prey, a dizzy bail jumper and devoted mom (Bernadette Peters) wrongfully arrested for hiding her husband's counterfeit cash. On the run from the law and her husband's white supremacist gang of ex-cons, the duo manage to put a little life into a suspenseless scenario sluggishly directed by Buddy Van Horn. Much comic-book violence, some rough language and a brief sexual encounter. A-III (PG-13) 12

Pink Floyd (1974) The musical group of the title in a sophisticated, heavily electronic rock concert that their fans will appreciate, though others may be put off by the intensity of sound and artiness of image (most of it was filmed in an amphitheater amid the ruins of Pompeii). Directed by Alan Parker, it features Bob Geldof, Eleanor David, Christine Hargreaves, James Laurenson, and Bob Hoskins. A-II (G) 15

Pink Jungle, The (1968) Amusing comedy-adventure with a twist ending in which a photographer (James Garner) and pretty model (Eva Renzi) helicopter into a Latin American jungle for a lipstick ad layout, are mistaken for spies and get involved with a flamboyant wheeler-dealer (George Kennedy) searching for a lost diamond mine. Directed by Delbert Mann, it's generally fast-paced and funny, if a trifle conde-

scending toward that nameless Latin government, and Kennedy nearly steals the show. A-II (br) U

Pink Narcissus (1971) The phallic fantasies of a young homosexual introvert assembled by an anonymous filmmaker who uses tumultuous music and no dialogue to accompany a hothouse montage of floating doilies and bizarre superimpositions. The lugubrious exercise incorporates indecent exposures of the anatomy. O (nr)

Pink Panther, The (1964) Farcical comedy introduces the accident-prone French policeman, Inspector Clouseau (Peter Sellers), in Switzerland on the trail of a suspected English jewel thief (David Niven) after the fabled jewel of the title. Directed by Blake Edwards, the comic caper complications are broad and zesty, ranging from unsubtle sight gags and silly puns to bedroom hanky-panky, with the clumsy antics of the dim Clouseau amusing enough to sustain six sequels. Slapstick violence, sexual situations and double entendres. A-III (br) A

Pink Panther Strikes Again, The (1977) Peter Sellers returns as Inspector Clouseau, but the one-joke nature of his success through bungling has worn rather thin, especially the running gag of karate assaults by his Oriental servant. The plot revolves around the machinations of Clouseau's former superior (Herbert Lom) who, driven mad by the constant incompetence of his underling, has gotten control of a doomsday machine. Director Blake Edwards achieves some good comic bits but mainly relies on slapstick violence and sexually derived humor. A-III (PG) U

Pink Telephone, The (1977) French production about an American conglomerate (run by Michel Lonsdale) that tries to induce an aging French factory owner (Pierre Mondy) to sell out by setting him up with a call girl (Mireille Darc) with whom he falls in love. Director Eduard Molinaro and writer Francis Verber resist a pat sentimental and moralistic ending and concentrate on illustrating the lack of values operating in an amoral environment. Well-acted and directed, the movie's adult theme contains brief nudity and rough language. A-IV (R)

Pinocchio (1940) Walt Disney's animated classic about a wooden-headed puppet (voice of Dick Jones) who wants to be a real boy but keeps getting into trouble by listening to foxy Honest John (voice of Walter Catlett) instead of appointed conscience Jiminy Cricket (voice of Cliff Edwards). The fantasy quality of the story is made all the more delightful by superb animation and such lovely songs as "When You Wish Upon a Star," though small fry may get some frights on Pleasure Island and in the sea depths with Monstro the Whale. One of Disney's grandest contributions to family entertainment. A-I (G) U

Pipe Dreams (1976) Going to Alaska in an attempt to win back her estranged husband, a woman (Gladys Knight) gets involved in breaking up a teenage prostitution ring. The failed romantic melodrama is poorly directed and carelessly edited by Stephen Verona. Some violence, rough language and a scene of an attempted abortion. A-III (PG)

Pirate, The (1948) Stylish musical romance set in the 18th century on a Caribbean island where a traveling performer (Gene Kelly) woos a well-bred senorita (Judy Garland) by pretending to be the dashing pirate she secretly admires. Directed by Vincente Minnelli, the stage-bound story is an uneasy mix of comedy and sentimentality, though the sets, costumes and choreography are lovely to look at and the Cole Porter songs easy to take, especially the "Be a Clown" finale. Romantic situations. A-II (br) U

Pirate Movie, The (1982) Incompetent movie musical revolves around contemporary characters (Kristy McNichol and Christopher Atkins) who find themselves in the world of Gilbert and Sullivan's "The Pirates of Penzance." Filmed in Australia by director Ken Annakin, the movie desperately tries to evoke laughter at any cost, relying mainly on pratfalls, vulgar language and crude double-entendres, but nothing can save it from its own ineptitudes. A-III (PG) A

Pirates (1986) Director Roman Polanski's obsessively detailed and ornamental portrait of the era when galleons feared ships flying the Jolly Roger features Walter Matthau as an irascible pirate captain determined to possess a solid gold throne. Unfortunately, the overblown action epic leaves little room to develop a somewhat whimsical plot. Vulgarity, brutality and disproportionate amounts of realistically staged sea battles. A-III (PG)

Pirates of Blood River, The (1961) Pulp British adventure yarn about a 17th-century Huguenot colony being invaded by pirates (led by Christopher Lee) searching for treasure. Directed by John Gilling, the hokey proceedings make as little sense as the bad acting. Stylized violence. A-II (br) U

Pirates of Penzance, The (1983) Screen adaptation of a N.Y. staging of the Gilbert and Sullivan operetta has a fine cast headed by George Rose, whose rendition of "A Modern Major General" is easily the best moment. Linda Ronstadt is Mabel and Kevin Kline is the Pirate King. As directed by Wilford Leach, it is good family entertainment, though some may find it much too stage-bound. A-I (G) U

Pirosmani (1978) Russian import about an obscure Georgian painter whose work has grown in stature since his death in 1919. Director Georgy Shengelaya employs beautifully stark images to show how the artist's imagination was rooted in his rural environment and time period, one that is rather exotic because so unfamiliar. His kind of folk art appealed to the common people because of its traditional ethnic and religious themes and symbolism. A-II (nr) U

Pixote (1982) Harrowing and poignant Brazilian drama about a gang of nomad boys in Rio and the terrible things they do to survive. Directed by Hector Babenco, this powerful movie is definitely not for the faint of heart or weak of stomach because it involves sordid violence and graphic sexuality. A-IV (nr) 18

Pizza Triangle, The (1970) Stylish Italian satire about a tragic love affair involving a Marxist bricklayer (Marcello Mastroianni) who leaves his wife for a cemetery flower peddler (Monica Vitti) and then becomes insanely jealous when she in turn falls in love with a pizza cook (Giancarlo Giannini). Director Ettore Scola is not interested in his hackneyed romantic plot except as a device supporting a pastiche of comic styles and sensibilities poking fun at movie cliches and stereotypes as well as Italian life and institutions. Some rough language. A-III (R)

Place Called Glory, A (1966) Undistinguished western directed by Ralph Gideon with Lex Barker as a gunfighter who joins a pal in cleaning out a town full of bad men. Stylized violence. A-II (br)

Place Called Today, A (1972) The stakes are the mayor's office in a racially polarized New Jersey city, but the issues are buried in an onslaught of unrelenting violence and explicit nudity. Written and directed by Don Schain and starring his wife, Cheri Caffaro, there is no reason for others to share their voyeur-exhibitionist relationship. O (X)

Place for Lovers, A (1969) Lovely American (Faye Dunaway) initiates an affair with a romantic Italian (Marcello Mastroianni) who learns only after falling hopelessly in love that she is doomed by a fatal disease. Directed by Vittorio De Sica, the melodrama's amoral approach to love and life is handled in a heavy, pretentious manner. A-III (R) X

Places in the Heart (1984) Sally Field plays a young widow struggling to keep her family together and her integrity intact after her husband's death in rural Texas during the Depression. Under the direction of Robert Benton, Field's performance winningly conveys a character of strong faith and goodwill in the face of adversity. A-II (PG)

Plague of the Zombies, The (1966) Routine British horror film directed by John Gilling about a man (Andre Morell) who can turn people into the walking dead. Restrained gore. A-II (br) 15

Plainsman, The (1936) Wild and woolly Western adventure yarn in which Wild Bill Hickcok (Gary Cooper) teams up with Calamity Jane (Jean Arthur) and Buffalo Bill Cody (James Ellison) to stop a traitor (Charles Bickford) from selling repeating rifles to the Indians. A rousing and often agreeable entertainment directed by Cecil B. DeMille, the result has plenty of outdoor action but little sense of Western history. Woefully stereotyped Indians and stylized violence. A-I (br) U

Plainsman, The (1966) Director David Lowell Rich's undistinguished remake of the 1936 original features Don Murray as Hickok, Abby Dalton as Calamity Jane and not much more. For patient youngsters and undemanding adults. A-I (br)

Planes, Trains and Automobiles (1987) Steve Martin plays a hapless traveler trying to get from New York to Chicago in time to have Thanksgiving with his family but, among other disasters and discomforts, planes are grounded, trains break down and even automobiles catch fire. Adding to the disagreeable experiences of the journey is fellow traveler John Candy in director John Hughes' comedy that, though uneven, does have its truly hilarious moments. Some very rough language and sexual references. A-III (R) 15

Planet of the Apes (1968) Charlton Heston plays the leader of a space expedition who lands his craft on an unnamed planet in the constellation of Orion where he discovers a civilization of apes trying to domesticate a species of human beings. Director Franklin J. Schaffner's entertaining screen version of Pierre Boulle's novel is an allegorical warning to a destruction-prone world. Some violence and mature themes. A-III (G) PG

Plastic Dome of Norma Jean, The (1974) The media's inevitable victimization of the personalities that they create is the theme of this story about a young woman (Sharon Henesy) whose gift of clairvoyance is used to popularize an exceptionally undistinguished rock group. The script and direction by Juleen Compton prove simply inadequate to the ambitions of what proves to be a terribly flawed movie. Mature themes. A-III (nr)

Platoon (1986) The Vietnam War as experienced by a raw recruit (Charlie Sheen) is evoked with relentless realism in scenes of battle and brutality in writer-director Oliver Stone's haunting reminiscence of its horrors and inhumanity. Its excessive violence, unrelenting profanity and graphic depiction of representative atrocities are stomach-churning, but serve as a corrective to Rambo-style romanticizations of the war. A-IV (R) 15

Play Dirty (1969) British World War II story about a motley collection of criminals sent behind German lines in North Africa under the command of an inexperienced but decent officer (Michael Caine). Andre de Toth's direction emphasizes the ugly realities of survival in the desert, but its anti-war message suffers from overkill and borders on a cynical destruction of all values. Strong graphic violence. A-III (PG) AA

Play It Again, Sam (1972) Woody Allen plays a balding, bespectacled loser who grooves on Humphrey Bogart movies (and even conjures Bogey up for on-the-spot advice in touchy situations). When his beautiful, brainy wife (Susan Anspach) walks out on him, his best friends (Diane Keaton and Tony Roberts) devote themselves to setting up blind dates (Jennifer Salt, Viva and Joy Bang). A very funny comedy directed by Herbert Ross, it's not a family film, but one most older teens and adults will thoroughly enjoy for some witty insights into the mating game. A-III (PG) 15

Play It As It Lays (1972) Failed exploration of contemporary womanhood and decadent movie industry folk based on the Joan Didion novel. Tuesday Weld is the unsuccessful actress, neglected wife and mother on a Hollywood odyssey into self-realization. Director Frank Perry envisions life as a crap game, but doesn't see beyond the superficial characters whose confusion he portrays. A suicide and marital problems are central to the plot. A-IV (R) X

Play Misty for Me (1971) Slick disk jockey (Clint Eastwood, who also directs) has a near-tragic romantic involvement with one of his fans, a severely disturbed woman (Jessica Walter) who is given to very dangerous fits of jealousy. Eastwood's performance is less wooden than usual though still lethargic, and it's up to Walter to supply the spark, here of manic menace. Gripping but flawed psychodrama lacks any sense of the moral implications of the situation. Violence and gore with brief nudity. A-IV (R) 18

Playboys, The (1992) An Irish village in the 1950s is beset by scandal when a middle-aged constable (Albert Finney) and a traveling theatrical troupe's leading man (Aidan Quinn) compete for the affections of a fiercely independent unwed mother (Robin Wright). Director Gillies MacKinnon's romantic triangle is sensitively played out without glossing over the moral considerations of the woman's predicament. A few discreet sexual encounters, a suicide and brief fisticuffs. A-III (PG-13) 12

Player, The (1992) Incisive satire of the Hollywood moviemaking scene revolves around a studio executive (Tim Robbins) whose murder of an insulting screenwriter (Vincent D'Onofrio) concerns him less than the continual power plays inherent in his job.

Director Robert Altman deftly skewers Hollywood's shallowness with sharply observed characterizations brimming with cynical wisdom. Momentary violence, a discreet encounter, flashes of nudity and some rough language. A-III (R) 15

Players (1979) Ali MacGraw plays the contented, middle-aged mistress of magnate Maximilian Schell, but she falls in love with young tennis hustler Dean-Paul Martin and has to choose between security and romance. Directed by Athony Harvey, the turgid melodrama deals in simplistic love-hate characterizations consistent with its muddled conclusion. Condones an illicit sexual relationship. O (PG)

Playing for Keeps (1986) A teenager elicits the help of friends to convert a dilapidated hotel his mom has inherited, foiling attempts by unscrupulous real estate agents to convert the site into a secret toxic waste dump. Predictable and simplistic in plot, the movie highlights matter-of-fact acceptance and depictions of casual sex relations between the kids. O (PG-13)

Playtime (1973) Monsieur Hulot (Jacques Tati) wanders through various vignettes with characteristic absentmindedness, totally unsurprised by any absurdity that crosses his path. The 1967 French comedy is a loose-collection of anecdotes about the depersonalized steel-and-glass environments comprising the urban landscape, a Parisian maze that writer-producer-director Tati treats with the humor of the urban commonplace. A-I (nr) U

Plaza Suite (1971) Walter Matthau plays the central character in each of three segments about successive occupants of the same suite in New York's famed Plaza Hotel. Directed by Arthur Hiller, derived from the Broadway play by Neil Simon, the lame comedy matches Matthau's penchant for mugging with Simon's middlebrow humor resulting in only a passing diversion. Mature themes. A-III (PG)

Please Don't Eat the Daisies (1960) Overwrought screen version of Jean Kerr's amusingly anecdotal book of family life as wife (Doris Day) of New York drama critic Walter (David Niven). Director Walter Lang gets few smiles from the frenetic goings-on in a household of busy parents, rambunctious boys, long-suffering maid (Patsy Kelly) and neurotic dog during the transition from cramped city apartment to affluent suburban home. Domestic misunderstandings and mild sexual innuendo. A-II (br) U

Plenty (1985) Impressionistic chronicle of the growing disillusionment and mental instability of an English woman (Meryl Streep), a heroin of the French Resistance, over the course of the two decades following World War II. Directed by Fred Schepisi, the sole bright spot in this cold, tedious, unfocused and intellectually muddled movie is John Gielgud's performance as a befuddled but honorable diplomat. Some fairly graphic bedroom scenes. A-IV (R) 15

Plot Against Harry, The (1990) Originally filmed in 1969, the whimsical tale tells of a small-time Jewish numbers racketeer (Martin Priest) who loses his Bronx turf after a 9-month stint in prison. Director Michael Roemer's slice of Jewish Americana and New York mob life uses black-and-white photography to capture the environment as well as the humorous situation of a has-been whose family tries to steer him straight. Minimal rough language and some casual involvement with prostitutes. A-III (nr) PG

Plymouth Adventure (1952) Hokey history of the Pilgrims' voyage to the New World aboard the "Mayflower" whose hard-drinking, double-dealing captain (Spencer Tracy) pursues the wife (Gene Tierney) of the colony's leader (Leo Genn), then blames himself for her suicide. Director Clarence Brown's talky script, sporadic action and melodramatic treatment add up to disappointing results. Stylized violence, including an off-screen suicide. A-II (br) U

Pocket Money (1972) Slight but often amusing contemporary western in which a down-on-his-luck cattleman (Paul Newman) is hired by a shady operator (Strother Martin) to buy rodeo bulls in Mexico, enlists the help of an old friend (Lee Marvin) to bring them back but encounters some double-dealing along the way. Directed by Stuart Rosenberg, the meandering buddy movie has some fine rodeo action and occasional adult humor. A-III (PG) A

Pocketful of Miracles, A (1961) Colorful Damon Runyon story about how a band of Manhattan hoods and grifters (headed by Glenn Ford) turn poor old Apple Annie (Bette Davis) into a socialite so her daughter can marry into a wealthy family. Director Frank Capra's last movie is an embarrassingly sentimental remake of his 1933 "Lady for a Day" and, despite the fine cast, seems little but silly. A-II (br) U

Poetic Justice (1993) A beautician (Janet Jackson), mourning her murdered boyfriend, cautiously allows herself to open up to a South Central L.A. postal worker (Tupac Shakur) while they are on a trip to Oakland with a shrilly argumentative couple (Regina King and Joe Torry)—until more deadly violence nearly deep-sixes the new couple's budding romance. Writer-director John Singleton focuses on the relationships of four foul-mouthed and often boring characters, but the ultimate message is that love is possible and worthwhile, even in the most menacing environments. Some nasty violence, a discreet sexual encounter, coarse sexual references and constant rough language. A-IV

Point Blank (1967) Double-crossed in a robbery by a friend who takes not only the loot and his wife but also leaves him for dead, tough guy Lee Marvin comes back to uncover an underworld connection, which he destroys man by man until all responsible are dead. Director John Boorman's brutally violent and illogical crime thriller is handled with a technical virtuosity that is sometimes effective but frequently pretentious and overblown in its graphic depiction of violence. O (br)

Point Break (1991) Ultraviolent action thriller in which a rookie FBI agent (Keanu Reeves) befriends a surfer-guru (Patrick Swayze) suspected of masterminding a string of California bank robberies. Director Kathryn Bigelow's splashy surfing footage and razzle-dazzle camerawork doesn't erase the plot inconsistencies, hackneyed romantic subplot or uncritical portrayal of extremely macho behavior. Excessive violence and rough language, implied promiscuity and suicide and brief nudity. O (R) 15

Point of No Return (1993) A convicted killer (Bridget Fonda), turned into a skilled assassin by a government agent (Gabriel Byrne) for a covert organization, takes on a high-risk mission hoping if she succeeds to be allowed to retire and wed her lover (Dermot Mulroney) who knows nothing of her past. Director John Badham shortchanges the supposed reformation of the central character for a steady stream of graphic violence. Excessive violence, brief bedroom shots, fleeting nudity and much rough language. O (R)

Point of Terror (1971) Pop singer (Peter Carpenter) plays up to the lusting wife of the crippled owner of a record company but, when she refuses to marry him after he kills her spouse, he switches his affections to her comely daughter who has reaped the lioness' share of Daddy's inheritance. The sordid melodrama depends totally upon crude sensationalism for cheap thrills. O (R)

Poison Ivy (1992) Sleazy melodrama about a conniving high school girl (Drew Barrymore) who moves into her friend's (Sara Gilbert) home where she seduces the girl's father (Tom Skerritt), murders her mother (Cheryl Ladd) and drives her distraught friend into a killing rage. Director Katt Shea's death-embracing movie is darkly atmospheric but comes up short on intelligence and moral perspective. Several adulterous encounters with brief nudity, occasional violence, alcohol abuse and some rough language. O (R)

Police Academy (1984) Reluctant police recruit (Stephen Guttenberg) finds that law enforcement can be fun in this dismal, failed comedy directed by Hugh Wilson. It relies heavily on sexually oriented humor, some nudity and rough language to convey its crude message of social irresponsibility. O (R) 15

Police Academy II: Their First Assignment (1985) Sequel directed by Jerry Paris is somewhat less vulgar than the original but vulgar enough, as well as altogether lackluster and unfunny. Sexually oriented humor. A-III (PG-13)

Police Academy III: Back in Training (1986) Police recruits try to save the prestige of the training academy's aging director in a tasteless movie whose failed humor is derived chiefly through sadistic violence, lewd jokes and slapstick stunts. O (PG)

Police Academy IV (1987) Limp plot and lame script with unfunny Keystone Cop slapstick antics by Steve Guttenberg, Bobcat Goldwait and company is featured in this edition, which deals with the academy's post-graduate project involving a citizens action group. Tame in language and sexual references, director Jim Drake's movie emphasizes aerial and ballooning chase sequences. Mild-manered but sophomoric entertainment. A-III (PG) U

Police Academy V: Assignment Miami Beach (1988) The Police Academy graduates return to honor soon-to-be-retired Commandant Lassard (George Gaynes) as Policeman of the Decade at a police chief's convention in Miami Beach. Directed by Alan Myerson, the boys and girls in blue frolic on the beach and, among other things, foil a kidnapping plot. Dumb but innocuous fun, though some brief sexist visuals. A-II (PG) U

Policy Academy VI: City Under Siege (1989) The crackpot cop squad is back, this time to rid the city of an insidious gang of thieves. Though the gals and guys in blue have more dignity this time around, director Peter Bonerz's tired sequel provides more than enough time to snooze and schmooze. Minimal vulgar references and some comicbook violence. A-II (PG)

Police Call 9000 (see: "Detroit 9000").

Police Connection, The (see: "Badge 373").

Policeman, The (1972) Israeli import features Shay K. Ophir as a Jaffa policeman whose 20-year career is distinguished only by its lack of arrests. Learning that Ophir is about to be fired, some crooks stage a heist to save his job. Director Ephraim Kishon uses a number of sweet, light, and warm moments to celebrate human solidarity. A-II (nr)

Policewoman (1974) Sondra Currie and her distaff detective squad turn the underworld upside down by outdoing their brothers in blue. Director Lee Frost's mindless female crime-stopper movie offers a variety of wild fights, hints of sadism, endless car chases, undeleted expletives and a sprinkling of coy nudity. O (R)

Pollyanna (1960) Heartwarming Disney dramatization of the Eleanor Porter children's classic about a turn-of-the-century orphan (Hayley Mills) who comes to live with her stern New England aunt (Jane Wyman), then proceeds to brighten the lives of all in the vicinity with her sunny disposition and penchant for looking on the bright side. Director David Swift has the benefit of Mills' sweet performance with a contrasting cast of grumps (notably Wyman, Adolphe Menjou and Karl Malden), though youngsters may find the proceedings overlong and their elders put off by the sugar-coated treatment. A-I (br) U

Poltergeist (1982) Suburban couple (Jobeth Williams; Craig T. Nelson) find their cozy existence disturbed when their five-year-old daughter gets trapped in the television screen and a parapsychologist (Beatrice Straight) is called in to retrieve her. Along the way to the burial grounds, producer Steven Spielberg and director Tobe Hooper treat viewers to some special effects violence and gore, teenage sexuality and a benign look at Mom and Dad smoking marijuana at bedtime. O (R/PG appeal) 15

Poltergeist II: The Other Side (1986) Angry spirits led by a demonic minister (Julian Beck) return to torment and terrorize the Freeling family just when they thought it was safe to leave grandma's house. The family has become more cynical, and the effects less frightening but more disgusting, in this sequel. The Vomit Creature sequence may be too gruesome for the very young in an otherwise mild-mannered Gothic tale. A-II (PG-13) 15

Poltergeist III (1988) Impossibly silly sequel sees little Carol Anne (Heather O'Rourke) spending some time in a Chicago high-rise with her mother's sister (Nancy Allen), her new husband (Tom Skerritt) and his teenage daughter (Lara Flynn Boyle). The potential of their glass and mirrored high-tech environs are utilized by the ghouls who continue to hound the little girl in a far-fetched and gruesome movie directed by Gary Sherman. Much grisly violence and frightening special effects that are specially aimed at destroying a youngster and some teenagers. O (PG-13)

Polyester (1981) Saga relating the sorrows of Francine Fishpaw, an overweight suburban matron (played by female-impersonator Divine) and the man (Tab Hunter) who seems to be the answer to her dreams. Baltimore writer-director John Waters often shows real satirical flair, but he too often tries to get laughs by appealing to the sadistic streak in an audience. Romantic homosexual aspect figures in the plot. O (R) X

Pony Express (1953) Standard Western heroics with Buffalo Bill Cody (Charlton Heston) and Wild Bill Hickok (Forrest Tucker) fighting off badmen and Indians to open the route for riders carrying the mail from Missouri to California. Directed by Jerry Hopper, the action features some fanciful derring-do but the ladies (Rhonda Fleming and Jan Sterling) are purely decorative and expect no surprises along the way. Frontier violence and mild romantic complications. A-II (br) U

Poor Cow (1968) British story of life in London's slums where an impoverished, too-young mother (Carol White) drifts into degrading situations, even posing for lecherous amateur photographers while her husband (John Bindon) and lover (Terence Stamp) are in prison. Directed by Kenneth Loach, the stuff of social protest is certainly here, but artistic discipline is lacking in such matters as a gory scene of childbirth and several erotic sequences whose point is less dramatic than exploitative. O (br) 15

Poor Little Rich Girl (1936) Dated but enduring Shirley Temple vehicle in which she pretends to be an orphan, gets taken in by a song-and-dance vaudeville team (Jack Haley and Alice Faye), then charms a crusty soap manufacturer (Claude Gillingwater) into sponsoring their radio show. Directed by Irving Cummings, little Shirley troupes through the formula sentiment in winning fashion, though the bald plot contrivances may hinder the enjoyment of some viewers. A-I (br) U

Popcorn (1969) Loud, cluttered documentary with pop music groups, such as the Vanilla Fudge, the Rolling Stones, the Bee Gees and a host of others, performing amid psychedelic lights and wildly fast editing. Some extremely fleeting nudity and a suggestive performance involving Jimi Hendrix make it inappropriate for youngsters. A-III (G)

Popcorn (1991) Film students (Tom Villard and Jill Schoelen) and their teacher (Tony Roberts) stage an all-night horror filmfest which is punctuated by as much mayhem and murder off-screen as on. Director Mark Herrier's attempt to create a campy spoof mostly bombs out with a convoluted plot, corny dialogue and choppy editing—which just may make it a cult favorite on video. Some violence and minimal rough language. A-III (R)

Pope Joan (1972) Legendary tale of a 9th-century woman (Liv Ullmann) who disguised herself as a man and worked her way up to the papacy. Directed by Michael Anderson, the British production is both a dramatic clunker and an historical yawner that fails to convey any sense of the life and experience of Christianity in the early Middle Ages. Graphic rape scene and the suggestion of lesbianism in the convent. A-IV (PG) AA

Pope Must Die, The (1991) Flaccid British farce in which a bumbling country priest (Robbie Coltrane) is mistakenly named pope only to discover an unholy alliance of cardinals and crooks as well as a pre-seminary girlfriend (Beverly D'Angelo) who announces he has a rock musician son. Director Peter Richardson's witless spoof of Vatican officialdom is a one-joke affair that grows tiresome with silly sight gags, one-liners and incongruities so outrageous that they cannot be taken seriously, yet done in such bad taste as to offend many. Some rough language, comic violence and sexual references with a flash of nudity. A-IV (R) 15

Pope of Greenwich Village, The (1984) Two amateur hustlers (Mickey Rourke and Eric Roberts) run afoul of both the mob and corrupt police. Though it lacks dramatic power, director Stuart Rosenberg's movie presents a sensitive study of a streetwise collection of characters made interesting because of good acting and perceptive script. Some scenes of restrained sex and violence. A-III (R) 15

Popeye (1980) Disappointing attempt to bring Popeye and the Thimble Theater gang to the screen is clever and sometimes mildly amusing, but never very funny. Robin Williams works valiantly as the hero, but neither director Robert Altman nor writer Jules Feiffer have given him much to do. The songs and dances are leaden and witless. Some slightly naughty visuals and expletives dragged in for no good purpose. A-II (PG) U

Popi (1969) Puerto Rican widower (Alan Arkin), struggling to give his sons something of a decent life amidst the slums of New York City, finds that he can't make it even with his three jobs as handyman, bus boy and hospital orderly. Director Arthur Hiller skirts sentimental melodrama and Arkin's comic lightness keeps viewers engaged in a potentially tragic story, the point of which is that there are no fantasy solutions to the hard realities of poverty. Some brutal aspects of slum life. A-II (G) A

Porky's (1982) Sex-obsessed adolescents cavort at a Florida high school during the Eisenhower era. Director Bob Clark's extended dirty joke is made even more offensive by some ill-advised stabs at seriousness. Witlessly vulgar movie. Much nudity, graphic sexuality and an almost nonstop flow of verbal obscenities. O (R) 18

Porky's II: The Next Day (1983) Sequel dishes up more of the same elaborate but boring hijinks of sex-crazed Florida high school boys, most of whom look old enough to play their teachers. Directed again by Bob Clark, it differs from the original only in having an even more muddled and disjointed storyline. Excessive nudity and scabrous dialogue. O (R) 18

Porky's Revenge (1985) The old gang at Angel Beach High who now look old enough, if not bright enough, to be out of graduate school are at it again. This effort directed by James Komack, like the previous ones, is beneath contempt. Exploitative nudity and tedious, mindless vulgarity. O (R) 18

Portnoy's Complaint (1972) Sneering, caustic and self-defeating adaptation of the Philip Roth novel about the sexual fetishes and fixations of a Jewish youth (Richard Benjamin). Produced and directed by Ernest Lehman, its social satire is an extraordinarily repulsive mix of vulgar sight gags, crude bathroom humor, sexual escapades and profanity that add up to a demeaning stereotyped portrait of Jewish family life. O (R) X

Portrait of the Artist as a Young Man, A (1979) Screen version of James Joyce's autobiographical novel about his aesthetic and philosophical development during his school and university years before departing for Paris. Director Joseph Strick's uninspired, talky drama has a number of good performances, the most memorable of which is John Gielgud as the Jesuit retreat master delivering the famous sermon on hell. The tension between religious faith and literary aspirations is at the heart of the adaptation and is treated in serious and mature fashion. A-IV (nr)

Poseidon Adventure, The (1972) Massive tidal wave overturns ocean liner, leaving just enough survivors to exemplify every stereotype and cliche expected by disaster movie fans. Gene Hackman plays a liberal minister leading his instant flock of Hollywood stars to the deepest part of the overturned hull where there is an air pocket and chance of escape. Ronald Neame directs the mushy but occasionally gripping tale for viewers seeking escapist fare. Stylized violence, a few sexual references and some profanity. A-III (PG)

Posse (1975) Kirk Douglas plays a politically ambitious U.S. marshal in late 19th-century Texas who battles outlaws by means of his own well-trained, fanatically loyal posse but runs into trouble when he brings in a popular train robber (Bruce Dern). Also directed by Douglas, the simplistic morality tale is heavy-handed in its use of violence and offensive in a needless bit of sexual exploitation. O (PG) A

Posse (1993) Returning from fighting in the Spanish-American War in 1898 Cuba, a small band of African American soldiers (headed by Mario Van Peebles) and a white comrade (Stephen Baldwin) head West to settle a score with the sheriff (Richard Jordan) who murdered their leader's peace-loving father. Also directed by Van Peebles, the movie certainly doesn't skimp on shootouts and portrays vigilante justice uncritically, but it also reminds viewers of the not insignificant presence of African American settlers in the development of the West and of the particular hardships they encountered. Much stylized violence, a bedroom scene, brief nudity and some rough language. A-IV (R)

Possession of Joel Delaney, The (1972) Strained horror movie with some pretensions to social commentary tells the story of an affluent N.Y. divorcee (Shirley MacLaine) and her brother (Michael Hordern), seemingly possessed by the malevolent soul of a dead Puerto Rican youth who had brutally murdered several women. The social dimension shows the cultural gulf between the Park Avenue rich and those living in Spanish Harlem. Director Waris Hussein resorts to shock tactics considerably lessening the intensity of his film's serious subject matter by punctuating action with beheaded nude bodies and a climax that is as berserk as poor Joel. A-IV (R) X

Postcards from the Edge (1990) Dramatic comedy about a young actress (Meryl Streep) forced to confront long-standing conflicts with her hard-drinking moviestar mom (Shirley MacLaine) in whose care she is released following drug rehabilitation. Written by actress Carrie Fisher and directed by Mike Nichols, the stylishly mounted look at mother-daughter relationships features splendid performances by the two leads representing the old and the new Hollywood. Comic treatment of drug and alcohol abuse, intermittent rough language and several references to promiscuous relationships. A-III (R) 15

Postman Always Rings Twice, The (1981) Failed screen version of James M. Cain's bleak, Depression-era tale of passion and retribution about an adulterous couple (Jessica Lange and Jack Nicholson) who conspire to kill the woman's husband. Directed by Bob Rafelson, the slow-moving, uninvolving movie devotes most of its energy to conveying in needless detail, the sadomasochistic sexual relationship between the two principals, neither of whom give very convincing performances. Excessively graphic display of sex. O (R) 18

Pound (1970) Absurdest social satire in which actors assume the roles of dogs waiting in the city pound to be destroyed. These sad, lonely, unfulfilled social outcasts are potential elements for a meaningful exploration of one or another aspect of the human condition. Unfortunately, director Robert Downey's improvisational approach lacks any insight and the content consists of little else but gross crudities played simply for irreverent and tasteless humor in a style that is more asinine than canine. O (X)

Power (1986) Richard Gere stars as a public-relations expert and power broker in this glamourized depiction of the media process that creates and manipulates the image of politicians. The drama asserts that television is the major influence in molding public opinion. The narrative is spotted with a profanity unnecessary for characterization. O (R) 15

Power, The (1967) As his colleagues die mysteriously, scientist George Hamilton has to discover which of those involved in his pain-resistance experiment is a super-intelligent being. The thriller has an interesting premise, but suspense drains off through credibility gaps in the plot and Byron Haskin's slack direction. Benign attitude toward premarital sex. A-III (br) AA

Power of One, The (1992) Touching drama about a white orphan's experiences growing up English in South Africa at the time the German-speaking Afrikaners were gaining enough political power to make apartheid the law of the land in 1948. Under John G. Avildsen's less-than-subtle direction, the action scenes of boxing bouts and racial bloodshed threaten to overshadow the inspirational story of the young boy developing courage and a keen sense of social justice. Frequent bloody violence and racial slurs. A-II (PG-13) 12

Powwow Highway (1989) A philosophical conflict emerges on a journey from Montana to New Mexico between two Native Americans, one of whom (A. Martinez) dismisses Cheyenne tradition and culture as irrelevant in pulling the tribe up from Third-World poverty, while the other (Gary Farmer) cherishes Cheyenne legends and longs to become a spiritual warrior. Though director Jonathan Wacks injects little suspense into his low-key road picture, it highlights the personal and political struggles being waged within the Native American community to regain and sustain their fast-disappearing culture. Some profanity, violence and a flash of nudity. A-III (R) 15

Practice Makes Perfect (1980) Jean Rochefort plays a famous pianist, a conceited self-centered woman chaser, who gets a mild comeuppance when he tries to abandon his second wife (Nicole Garcia) and their three children by running off with the granddaughter (Catherine Le Prince) of an old flame (Danielle Darrieux). French sex farce directed by Philippe de Broca, it's all very light, very sentimental and passably droll for adults who enjoy such fare. A-III (nr)

Prancer (1989) Sweet-natured Christmas story about a spirited 8-year-old farm girl (Rebecca Harrell) who cares for an injured reindeer believing it is one of Santa's team. While this "E. T." clone may have its fill of cranky adults and earnest moments, John Hancock's direction has a feel for rural community life that will please older viewers while younger ones will love the reindeer and the praise lavished on the spunky heroine for revitalizing the town's Christmas spirit. A-I (G) U

Prayer for the Dying, A (1987) A political assassin (Mickey Rourke) seeks redemption while fleeing killers from the IRA to which he belonged, a mobster (Alan Bates) who wants his services and the police. A priest (Bob Hoskins) helps and comforts him in director Mike Hodges' heavy-handed drama saved by Rourke's skin-tight portrayal. Some violence and profanity cut with black humor. A-III (R) 15

Predator (1987) Elite commando rescue team on a mission into the Latin American tropics becomes the prey of a superhuman predator who fights it out to the death with Arnold Shwarzenegger. Director John McTiernan builds suspense in his nightmarish depiction of the hunt, but the landscape is strewn with skinned, bloodied victims. Profuse profanity and gruesome stylized violence. A-III (R) 18

Predator II (1990) Sci-fi horror tale set in 1997 Los Angeles where a hot-headed cop (Danny Glover) ignores the hands-off orders of a top federal agent (Gary Busey) and vows to personally exterminate the powerful alien killer (Kevin Peter Hall) who has slaughtered his colleagues. In spite of clever lighting and special effects, director Stephen Hopkins cuts straight to the jugular with no pretense at character build-up in a grisly bloodfest devoid of human dimension. Excessive, graphic violence, full frontal nudity and continuous rough language. O (R) 18

Prelude to a Kiss (1992) When they kiss at her wedding, a bride (Meg Ryan) and an elderly stranger (Sydney Walker) magically switch personalities, leaving the groom (Alec Baldwin) to figure out how to get the woman he loves out of the old man's body. Director Norman Rene's featherweight fantasy barely sustains a contrived romantic comedy about the transcending power of love. An implied premarital relationship. A-III (PG-13)

Premonition, The (1976) Unconvincing thriller concerns a parapsychologist's attempt to find a missing child through the foster mother's psychic contact with the child's dead mother. Though it has some eerie moments and suggests some gory

horrors, one doesn't have to be clairvoyant to perceive how badly director Robert Allen Schnitzer has missed the mark. A-III (PG)

President's Analyst, The (1968) James Coburn plays shrink to the Commander-in-Chief who develops a case of the jitters when the revelations that relieve the President's tensions also happen to be state secrets. But he also discovers that he is being pursued by agents and double-agents who alternately want him to keep the lid on or blow it off. Director Theodore J. Flicker's comedy has some adult humor. A-III (br) A

Presidio, The (1988) An army officer (Sean Connery) based at the Presidio and a San Francisco police inspector (Mark Harmon) who once served under him jointly investigate a murder on the base, but their past conflicts and the cop's brewing relationship with the officer's sexy daughter (Meg Ryan) complicate matters. Director-cinematographer Peter Hyams handles the car pile-ups better than he does the actors and their relationships. Several intense chase sequences culminating in brutal death and destruction, much profanity and a fairly explicit sexual encounter. O (R) 15

Presumed Innocent (1990) A prosecuting attorney (Harrison Ford) becomes the prime suspect in his own investigation of a sensational murder case in which the victim (Greta Scacchi) was a colleague as well as his ex-lover. Director Alan J. Pakula's darkly absorbing courtroom drama weaves an intricate plot around adultery and criminal complicity while presenting a disturbing picture of the manipulation of the criminal justice system by those who administer it. Ambiguous treatment of the justice theme, some scenes of an adulterous relationship and occasional rough language. A-IV (R)

Pretty Baby (1978) The story of a 12-year-old girl (Brooke Shields), born and raised in a house of prostitution, who eventually marries historical figure E. J. Bellocq (Keith Carradine), a photographer who first came to photograph her mother (Susan Sarandon). Director Louis Malle's listless, dubiously nostalgic tour of a bordello relies on extravagant nudity and the flagrant exploitation of a 12-year-old girl. O (R) X

Pretty in Pink (1986) Self-sufficient, self-assured teenager (Molly Ringwald) goes to the junior prom alone when let down by the boy who was to take her. Director John Hughes provides a positive portrayal of a teenager who maintains a wholesome sense of her own identity despite the peer pressures and scorn of some of her classmates. Sexual innuendo and harsh language. A-III (PG-13) 15

Pretty Maids All in a Row (1971) Failed sex farce stars Rock Hudson as a high school guidance counselor who cures the coeds' hang-ups by couch therapy, and solves sophomore John David Carson's perpetual erection by introducing him to teacher-sexpot Angie Dickinson. As some of the pretty coeds wind up as corpses, super-sleuth Telly Savalas questions the student counselor's methods. Directed by Roger Vadim, there is little comedy or mystery in a work whose sole purpose seems to be to exploit sex. O (R) X

Pretty Poison (1968) Psychological terror movie about a mad youth running murderously amok is of only routine interest, but director Noel Black has gotten subtle and chilling characterizations from Anthony Perkins as a crazed killer and Tuesday Weld as the perverse teenage nymph who inspires him. A-III (R) X

Pretty Woman (1990) Entertaining romantic confection about a smarmy corporate raider (Richard Gere) and a feisty street walker (Julia Roberts) who fall in love against their better judgment and are transformed into good, wholesome people. The contemporary fairy tale, a meld of Pygmalion and Cinderella, shines due to its likeable characterizations and sentimental touches injected by director Garry Marshall. Strictly adult comedy fare with a romanticized view of prostitution, several suggestive sexual encounters and some rough language laced with sexual innuendo. A-III (R) 15

Prettykill (1987) When the life of a N.Y. call-girl (Season Hubley) is threatened by the schizophrenic Southern charmer (Suzanne Snyder) she has taken under her wing, she seeks help from her long-time boyfriend, a police detective (David Birney). Director George Kaczender's failed thriller plays more like a distorted caricature of a romance. Unwholesome mix of sex and violence, with some nudity. O (R)

Prick Up Your Ears (1987) Harshly realistic depiction of the doomed love affair between British playwright Joe Orton (Gary Oldman) and his collaborator Kenneth Halliwell (Alfred Molina). Uncompromising direction by Stephen Frears dwells too vividly on the details of sordid homosexual encounters and a concluding bloody murder and suicide scene. Vanessa Redgrave co-stars in the British production, which has brief male nudity and vulgar language. O (R) 18

Pride of St. Louis, The (1952) The life and times of baseball pitcher Jerome "Dizzy" Dean (Dan Dailey) whose Arkansas twang and garbled syntax make him a beloved sports announcer after his glory years on the mound for the Cardinals during the 1930s. Directed by Harmon Jones, Daily gives a likeable performance as the clowning ballplayer whose biggest fan is his wife (Joanne Dru), while the pitching career of

his brother "Daffy" (Richard Crenna) becomes one of his major concerns. A-I (br) U

Pride of the Yankees, The (1942) Fine drama of N.Y. Yankee first baseman Lou Gehrig (Gary Cooper), who never missed a game in 14 years of outstanding play until forced to retire in 1939 by an incurable disease, which has since borne his name. Directed by Sam Wood, the result has interest beyond the story of a baseball hero because it captures the universal qualities of character and spirit underlying the career of a man who gave his unfailing best for team, fans and family. Memorable movie even for those who don't like baseball. A-I (br) U

Priest and the Girl, The (1973) The story told by this 1966 Brazilian drama is of a young priest, overwhelmed by the poverty and injustice of the backward community to which he has been sent, blindly runs away in the company of a sensual young girl who looks to him for protection from her brutal guardian. Director Joaquim Pedro de Andrade's slow-moving study of spiritual aridity is less concerned with his two central characters than in the barren lives of the people who inhabit a desolate part of the world. A-III (nr)

Priest's Wife, The (1971) Careless Italian romp stars Sophia Loren as a suicidal pop singer and Marcello Mastroianni as the priest who becomes the object of her attentions. What begins as a rather lighthearted spoof of the issue of priestly celibacy, ends up as a humorless and bitter indictment of church law. While the viewer is mercifully spared the visual aspects of the pair's sexual relationship, director Dino Risi's irreverent and occasionally tasteless humor is more an insult to one's intelligence than to one's religious convictions. A-IV (PG)

Prime Cut (1972) Tough slice-of-crime melodrama about a hired killer (Lee Marvin) sent to extol tribute from a double-crossing Kansas City gangster (Gene Hackman) who sells beef and women. As directed by Michael Ritchie, the fast-paced action becomes a senseless nightmare of white slavery, drugs and meat-packing treated with blood, gore, nudity and foul language. O (R) 18

Prime of Miss Jean Brodie, The (1969) Poignant screen version of Muriel Spark's novel about a lovable, eccentric school teacher (Maggie Smith in a grand performance) who just doesn't fit in with the faculty or administration at the conservative Edinburgh girls' school in the 1930s. She's demanding but her "gurrls" love her until one them (Pamela Franklin) betrays her. Director Ronald Neame handles with great sensitivity the moral ambiguities of the teacher's odd personal traits as well as that of her precocious student who poses in the nude for the art teacher. A-III (PG) 15

Prince and the Pauper, The (1937) Durable version of the Mark Twain classic in which an English prince (Bobby Mauch) switches places with a lookalike urchin (Billy Mauch) for a lark that could prove fatal unless a would-be usurper (Claude Rains) is undone by a mettlesome commoner (Errol Flynn). Director William Keighley's melodramatic style only slows the pace of the boys' misadventures after swapping the dangers of the Tudor court for the squalor of the London slums and vice versa. For all the aristocratic villainy and some minimal stylized violence, it's an enjoyable period adventure for family viewers. A-I (br) U

Prince of Darkness (1987) Failed horror movie about the discovery by a priest (Donald Pleasence) that a secret vault in a Los Angeles church contains an ancient jar holding a cosmic force that if let loose will become the Son of Darkness. Directed self-indulgently by John Carpenter, the boring and pretentious movie talks itself to death but sprinkles in enough blood-and-gore scenes and vomiting zombies to bludgeon moral sensibilities. O (R) 18

Prince of the City (1981) Treat Williams plays a N.Y. City detective who, tormented by guilt, comes forward to cooperate with federal authorities investigating police corruption. Director Sidney Lumet succeeds in portraying the human complexity in this flawed but gripping drama that has some of the inexorable force of Greek tragedy. Williams is particularly fine among a strong cast, with many excellent performances. Though the violence is extremely restrained, a somber and difficult theme with much rough language. A-III (R) X

Prince of Tides, The (1991) Hoping to help his suicidal sister, an estranged husband (Nick Nolte) relates their troubled family history to her psychiatrist (Barbra Streisand) and the two become romantically involved, profoundly affecting each other and both of their families. Also produced and directed by Streisand, the emotionally complex drama muddies the question of infidelity but is rich in themes of interpersonal communication and familial forgiveness. Momentary but violent rape scene, discreet bedroom scenes, adulterous and homosexual references and some rough language. A-IV (R) 15

Princes in Exile (1991) A 17-year-old boy (Zachary Ansley) finds romance and a new attitude at a summer camp for youngsters struggling with cancer. Humor and hope come shining through this moving film from Canadian director Giles Walker, who keeps excess sentimentality at bay with honest performances from the young cast.

Disturbing subject matter that may be frightening to small children; mild sexual references. A-II (PG)

Princess, The (see: "A Time in the Sun").

Princess Bride, The (1987) Affectionate, lighthearted parody of romantic medieval adventure in which a young beauty (Robin Wright) is saved from a forced marriage to a nasty prince (Chris Sarandon) by a farm boy turned pirate (Cary Elwes). Director Rob Reiner plays with scriptwriter William Goldman's verbal wit as comically delivered by Elwes, Mandy Patinkin, Wallace Shawn and Billy Crystal. Some comic-book violence. A-II (PG)

Princess Comes Across, The (1936) Fitful comedy combining murder and romance aboard an ocean liner whose passengers include a girl from Brooklyn (Carole Lombard) trying to get to Hollywood by masquerading as a princess from Sweden, a band leader (Fred MacMurray) aware of the ruse but sweet on its perpetrator, top detectives from around the world and an escaped killer. Director William K. Howard can't quite make it all work but Lombard has a lot of fun spoofing Garbo and Alison Skipworth shines as her brassy lady-in-waiting. Mild romance and some menace. A-I (br) A

Princess Yang Kwei Fei (1972) One of the most beautiful color movies ever made, this 1955 Japanese production retells a Chinese legend about a graceful princess who dies for her emperor and whose love lives on after death. Directed by Kenji Mizoguchi, the narrative is slow and measured, but the interest lies less in its traditional story than in the beauty and grace of its presentation done with an artistry that is genuine and universal. A-II (nr)

Principal, The (1987) A rowdy, inept teacher (James Belushi) becomes a dedicated administrator who takes it upon himself to tame the drug dealing felons who rule an inner-city high school. Director Christopher Cain milks an improbable plot for violence and brutality failing to provide a balanced forum for the real and pressing issues of crime in the schools. O (R) 18

Prison Guard (1973) Surrealistic Czech drama about institutional dehumanization tells the story of a young prison guard in the 1920s whose experiences teach him that brutality is the best way to deal with prisoners. Having previously taken out his frustrations on his dog, the guard turns to beating the inmates when one of them runs off with his wife. Director Ivan Renc's characters are strange and disturbing inhabitants of a bleak terrain that corresponds to the barrenness of their lives. A-III (nr)

Prisoner of Second Avenue, The (1975) Uneven screen version of Neil Simon's

Broadway comedy about a middle-aged New Yorker (Jack Lemmon) who loses his job, gets mugged while his apartment is robbed and endures all sorts of other urban traumas with the help of his sensible, down-to-earth wife (Anne Bancroft). Director Melvin Frank pumps up all the life possible in a script hinged on situations that aren't very amusing and wisecracks that are only occasionally witty. Intermittent profanity. A-III (PG)

Prisoner of Shark Island, The (1936) Sentenced to life imprisonment for setting the broken leg of Lincoln's assassin, Dr. Samuel Mudd (Warner Baxter) is sent to an island fortress off the Florida coast where he earns a pardon after risking his life to save others during a yellow fever epidemic. Director John Ford's fact-based story of a doctor who became an innocent victim of his times achieves considerable impact from its credible evocation of the period and its human context. Miscarriage of justice and brutal mistreatment. A-I (br) A

Prisoner of Zenda, The (1937) Grand romantic adventure from the Anthony Hope novel of a mythical Central European kingdom where a vacationing Englishman (Ronald Colman) saves the throne of his distant royal cousin (also Colman) who's been kidnapped by a villainous stepbrother (Raymond Massey) and his chief henchman (Douglas Fairbanks, Jr.). Directed by John Cromwell, the late-19th-century setting nicely suits the tale of loyalty and honor amid court intrigues, desperate forays and the bittersweet romance of commoner and princess (Madeleine Carroll). Some stylized violence and romantic complications. A-I (br) U

Prisoner of Zenda, The (1952) Color remake of the 1937 version has Stewart Granger in the dual role as the Englishman who saves a lookalike European crown prince from a ruthless usurper (James Mason), then loses his heart to the king's intended bride (Deborah Kerr). Director Richard Thorpe's turn-of-the-century costume romance has plenty of regal spectacle, though the bittersweet love story is somewhat stilted and Mason nearly steals the show as the nasty plotter whose downfall in the big action finish is entirely satisfying. Some stylized violence and romantic complications. A-I (br) U

Prisoner of Zenda (1979) Peter Sellers plays the dual role of the foppish King Rudolph of Ruritania and the stout-hearted Englishman who takes his place to foil a plot against the throne. As directed by Richard Quine, the action and pageantry in gorgeous settings are treated realistically rather than as fantasy, with the result being that the film is neither funny enough nor romantic enough. A-II (PG)

Prisoners of the Sun (1991) International political considerations after World War II impede the efforts of a tenacious lawyer (Bryan Brown) to bring to trial the Japanese officers responsible for the torture and execution of more than 300 Australian prisoners-of-war. Directed by Stephen Wallace, the earnest, fact-based drama suffers from lugubrious pacing and uninvolving characters but poses some intriguing moral questions about justice. Some wartime violence and an instance of rough language. A-II (R)

Private Benjamin (1980) When her husband dies on their wedding night, the distraught bride (Goldie Hawn) joins the New Army as an impossibly inept recruit whom boot camp changes into a person able to look after herself, until she meets a rich, handsome French doctor. Some good laughs from old military jokes updated to the coed Army, with Eileen Brennan especially funny as a wacky martinet. Sexual morality is ridiculed in a number of scenes and there is brief nudity and some rough language. O (R) 15

Private Duty Nurses (1972) Doctors and patients concerned about such matters as racial discrimination, military service and water pollution in sunny Santa Monica devote equal time to gratuitous sexual pursuits with student nurses in waterbeds. Directed by George Armitage, the failed sex farce is devoid of wit, taste and interest. O (R)

Private Eyes (1981) Anemic little slapstick comedy stars Tim Conway and Don Knotts as a Sherlock Holmes–Dr. Watson duo solving a murder in a spooky old house. Director Lang Elliot serves up all the predictable comic cliches of the genre, but none of them are very funny. Several mild vulgarisms. A-II (PG)

Private Function, A (1985) With rationing in effect at the end of World War II, an English couple (Michael Palin and Maggie Smith) steal the pig that local dignitaries are secretly fattening up for a banquet celebrating Princess Elizabeth's wedding. The English comedy, directed by Malcolm Mowbray, is slow-moving and leans heavily on vulgar humor some may find offensive. Restrained bedroom scene. A-III (R) 15

Private Lessons (1981) Housekeeper Sylvia Kristel gives the master's teenage son a hands-on course in sex. Directed by Alan Myerson, it's a failed little exploitation comedy with nudity and graphic sex. O (R)

Private Life of Sherlock Holmes, The (1970) Plodding spy melodrama without much mystery to it takes some extreme liberties with the Conan Doyle character by making the Victorian detective not only a cocaine addict but sexually ambiguous as well. Directed with a heavy hand by Billy Wilder, the lightweight case involves Holmes (Robert Stephens) and Dr. Watson (Colin Blakely) in the search for the missing husband of a mysterious woman (Genevieve Page), with some assistance from Holmes' brother, Mycroft (Christopher Lee). Lacking lightness and imagination, it will irritate Holmes' fans and disappoint others. Some sexual innuendo. A-III (GP) PG

Private Navy of Sgt. O'Farrell, The (1968) Unfunny World War II comedy set on a Pacific island where O'Farrell (Bob Hope) tries to raise morale on an Army-Navy base by importing some nurses who turn out to be all male except for Phyllis Diller. Director Frank Tashlin can't get much out of the situation except to parody some other films. A-II (G) U

Private Parts (1973) Creepy, campy, sex-and-horror movie about a teenage girl who becomes a more or less willing victim to an assortment of sinister types inhabiting a creaky flea-bag hotel managed by her crazed aunt. Directed by Paul Bartel, nudity and cheap thrills abound. O (R)

Private School (1983) Self-described comedy is no more than a B-grade sexploitation movie, from the vulgar lyrics of the opening song to the closing scene, where the graduating class simultaneously indulges in an obscene gesture to their headmistress. Directed by Noel Black, the film consists of an unremitting stream of sexual scenes, jokes and dialog. O (R)

Privates on Parade (1984) Uneven British satire about a motley collection of misfit soldiers who, under the flamboyant leadership of a homosexual director (Dennis Quilty), put on a variety show for troops fighting Communist guerrillas in 1948 Malaya. Thanks to the invincible stupidity of their unit commander (John Cleese), they become directly involved in the conflict. Director Michael Blakemore scores enough satiric hits to overcome the film's excess of double-entendres, a bit of blasphemy, a brief bedroom scene involving nudity and an abundance of homosexual references. A-III (R) 15

Privilege (1967) Uneven British cautionary tale about the use of the mass media to manipulate and control public opinion, as seen in the case if a pop singing star (Paul Jones). Directed by Peter Watkins, there is more flash than substance, so that its unfocused indignation blunts its criticism and ultimately leaves viewers without a constructive point of view. A-IV (br)

Prizzi's Honor (1985) Middle-aged man (Jack Nicholson) falls in love with a beautiful, mysterious woman (Kathleen Turner) and she with him. It turns out they are both in the same line of work, but since that happens to be killing people, it makes for complications once they are married. Though this very black comedy is directed

with great skill and flair by John Huston, its level of violence makes it extremely mature fare and not suited to everybody's taste. A-IV (R) 15

Problem Child (1990) Dumb one-joke comedy in which a would-be dad (John Ritter) and his social-climbing wife (Amy Yasbeck) adopt a sweet-looking 7-year-old (Michael Oliver), unaware that he is the bane of the nuns at the orphanage and that his pen-pal is an escaped killer. Directed by Dennis Dugan, the comic fantasy rarely rises above the level of nasty, often vulgar pranks and overblown characterizations, except for the performances by Ritter and the youngster. Stylized violence intended for comic effect, crude expressions and bathroom humor. A-II (PG)

Problem Child 2 (1991) After moving to a new town, bratty Junior (Michael Oliver) runs into an even brattier girl (Ivyann Schwan) as he tries to prevent his divorced dad (John Ritter) from having any dates. Director Brian Levant's sequel is mired in shrill toilet humor and dangerously unfunny pranks. Brief adolescent sexual innuendo, much coarse humor and mindless comic-book violence. A-III (PG-13) PG

Prodigal, The (1983) Produced by the Rev. Billy Graham's organization, the movie is a modern retelling of the parable about the repentance of a man who squandered his inheritance but, despite some fine acting and good intentions, it doesn't quite come together as persuasive drama. Its shortcomings, however, do not keep it from being inspirational family entertainment. A-II (PG)

Producers, The (1967) Farce about an accountant (Gene Wilder) who gets involved with would-be producer (Zero Mostel) of a buoyant musical based on the life of Hitler. Some of the laughs are a little sick around the edges, but those who don't mind bawdy and blatant satire should survive the experience. Director Mel Brooks gets a brilliant comic performance from Mostel, well supported by Wilder. Matter of comic taste. O (br) PG

Professionals, The (1966) Four soldiers of fortune (Lee Marvin, Burt Lancaster, Woody Strode, Robert Ryan) are hired to rescue a woman (Claudia Cardinale) being held for ransom by a Mexican bandit (Jack Palance). What raises this above the level of average action-adventure is the stylish manner and steady pace of director Richard Brooks' homage to the specials skills of a group. Some brutal violence, coarse language and several sensuous scenes. A-III (br) A

Program, The (1993) Predictable tale of a college football coach (James Caan) and his team of troublesome players, including an alcoholic quarterback (Craig Sheffer), a steroid-taking defensive tackle (Andrew Bryniarski) and a freshman tailback (Omar Epps). Directed by David S. Ward, the story portrays the multiple ills of collegiate sports while focusing its sympathies on those involved in breaking the rules. Bone-crunching violence on the field, an attempted rape, substance abuse and occasional rough language. A-III (R)

Project X (1968) Futuristic, sci-fi reconstruction of the 22nd century, in which the quality of life has drastically changed but the ideological tensions between East and West have persisted. In the end, it turns out that the film's pretensions and sometimes effective special effects are used for nothing more than a routine secret agents melodrama that might as well have taken place in the present. A-II (br) AA

Project X (1987) Unpleasant military monkey business is challenged by altruistic recruit with a social conscience (Matthew Broderick) in this story about lovable chimps used for flight simulation testing. His attempt to help them escape nearly causes a nuclear disaster. Director Jonathan Kaplan's lightweight tale of youthful idealism vs. duty is shareable family entertainment, though there is a touch of rough language. A-II (PG)

Projectionist, The (1971) Chuck McCann runs the projector in a N.Y. movie theater and is given to lapsing into movie-based fantasies in which he becomes Capt. Flash, converses with Bogart, feasts in Babylon, shoots down Ming's space ship and cavorts with King Kong. Directed by Harry Hurwitz, the collection of movie nostalgia is somewhat self-indulgent but should delight buffs. Enough offbeat comedy for the uninitiated; brief sexual fantasies. A-III (GP)

Prologue (1970) Stilted, uneven, and technically inferior study of war dissenters during the riots at the Chicago Democratic Convention in 1968. Directed from a Canadian perspective by Robin Spry, the black-and-white semi-documentary pretentiously contrasts the brutality of the police with gentle lovemakers in a commune. Gratuitous nudity. O (nr)

Prom Night (1980) Mad killer seeks revenge by stalking high school students on the night of the big dance and slashing their throats whenever they stray from the dance floor. Directed by Paul Lynch, the horror story is more dumb than nasty, but some of its grisly scenes are excessively graphic. O (R)

Promise, The (1979) A silly tearjerker in which a woman (Kathleen Quinlan) who is disfigured in an auto accident is separated from her lover (Stephen Collins) by his wealthy mother (Beatrice Straight), who offers to pay for expensive plastic surgery, provided the woman never sees her son again. Directed by Gilbert Cates, this sentimental, overwrought melodrama displays a permissive attitude toward premarital sex. A-III (PG) A

Promise at Dawn (1970) French adaptation of novelist Romain Gary's memoir of his boyhood days and aspirations living with his loving mother (Melina Mercouri) in the Leningrad of the 1920s. Directed by Jules Dassin, these poignant recollections become a buoyantly human portrait, rich in the cultural humor and solid values that stoke the human spirit's inexhaustible striving for identity and achievement. A scene dealing with the boy's sexual awakening and his mother's response require a mature perspective. A-III (GP)

Promise Her Anything (1966) Mediocre romantic comedy about a recent widow (Leslie Caron), on the lookout for a new father for her young son, who settles first on her boss (Robert Cummings) but then finds true love with a low-budget moviemaker (Warren Beatty). Director Arthur Hiller's predictable story offers little new in an old scenario. A-III (br) A

Promised Lands (1974) Directed by Susan Sontag, this documentary about Israel at the time of the October War proves a poetic and moving meditation on the tragedy of a nation's struggle for existence in a land claimed by others. From its opening shots of the diverse cultural traditions that coexist in Israel to its concluding episode of a soldier being treated for battle trauma, the film's images connect repeatedly with the precise detail or telling scene to express the bewildering complexity of the problems facing this beleaguered state. A-II (nr)

Promises in the Dark (1979) Counterpointing the decline of a 17-year-old terminal cancer patient (Kathleen Beller) with her doctor's (Marsha Mason) renewed interest in romance after the experience of bitter divorce, producer-director Jerome Hellman offers us a sentimental melodrama that contains scattered bits of insight. The movie does not go too deeply into the complex moral problems it raises, notably the cutting off of life-sustaining systems when life ceases to be viable. A-IV (PG)

Proof (1992) Absorbing psychological drama about a blind, emotionally fragile photographer (Hugo Weaving), his new friend (Russell Crowe) who describes the content of his photos and a jealous housekeeper (Genevieve Picot) who is determined to wreck their friendship. Writer-director Jocelyn Moorhouse builds an eerily suspenseful story out of the strange dynamics motivating this odd triangle of troubled adults learning to relate to one another. Fleeting sexual encounter, flash of nudity and minimal rough language. A-III (R) 15

Prophecy (1979) When a health department doctor (Robert Foxworth) takes his pregnant wife (Talia Shire) on an assignment checking the environmental effects of a paper mill in the Maine woods, they become the target of an exceptionally ill-tempered mutant. Everything about director John Frankenheimer's ecological shocker is so ludicrous and inept that it overwhelms the ecological message it's supposedly plugging. Some intense violence. A-III (PG) X

Protector, The (1985) Two N.Y. policemen (Jackie Chan; Danny Aiello) wreak havoc in Hong Kong, where they have gone to break up a drug ring. Mindlessly violent movie written and directed by James Glickenhaus. Besides the violence there is some exploitative nudity. O (R)

Protocol (1984) Dizzy cocktail waitress (Goldie Hawn) becomes a national heroine when she thwarts the assassination of a visiting Arab leader, which gives some nasty State Department types the idea of using her as a diplomatic pawn. Directed by Herbert Ross, it's a routine comedy vehicle for its star who would be better if the role was just a bit less lovable and cute. Sexually oriented humor, including depicting Arabs throughout as oversexed buffoons. A-II (PG)

Proud Rebel, The (1958) Coming to the Midwest in search of a doctor able to cure his mute son (David Ladd), an ex-Confederate officer (Alan Ladd) gets caught in a land war between a mean sheepman (Dean Jagger) and a spinster farmer (Olivia de Havilland). Directed by Michael Curtiz, the post-Civil War conflict between the adults is heavy-going at times, but the boy and his smart sheep dog will appeal to the youngsters. Some stylized violence, with several scenes quite harrowing for children. A-I (br) U

Providence (1977) Uneven British drama about a 78-year-old novelist (John Gielgud) trying to come up with a story interweaving fantasies about his son (Dirk Bogarde), his son's wife (Ellen Burstyn), her friend (David Warner) and his son's imaginary mistress (Elaine Stritch). Director Alain Resnais fails to create any consistent emotional mood for scriptwriter David Mercer's indulgent jumping back and forth in time and space to indicate a failing imagination. Gielgud's character is not only foul-mouthed and lecherous but is excessively graphic in his complaints about failing bodily functions set against unpleasant shots of his autopsy. O (R) X

Prudence and the Pill (1968) Brittle British comedy with Deborah Kerr and David Niven dealing with the advent and repercussions of the contraceptive pill in a manner that overlooks the basic issues of premarital sex, adultery and divorce. When two households take to underhanded pill-swapping for various reasons, the final result is two marriages, two divorces and remarriages and babies under every cabbage leaf. Despite a few smiles, director Fielder Cook gets them by ignoring the emotional upheaval that such finagling would produce. O (R) X

Psych-Out (1968) Cliched story of hippie life in San Francisco's Haight-Ashbury district with Susan Strasberg as a deaf teenage runaway and Dean Stockwell as a freaked-out guru. Director Richard Rush tries to balance his picture of the dropout life-style but conventional society is shown as responsible for such alienation. Confused treatment of violence, sex and drugs. A-III (br) X

Psychic Killer (1976) Lightweight horror movie about a man (Jim Hutton) who projects mental powers to avenge his unjust incarceration in a mental institution. Director Raymond Danton uses parapsychology to explain the plot's series of gruesome murders, but nothing can justify the bloody detail, the nudity or the movie's resolution in vigilante justice. O (PG)

Psycho II (1983) Norman Bates (Anthony Perkins) is declared sane and comes home after more than 20 years in a mental institution. This time poor Norman is the victim of a mother and daughter (Vera Miles and Meg Tilly) who are determined to push him over the edge again so that he has to be recommitted. Director Richard Franklin diminishes tensions by the broad in-joke quality of the whole enterprise, but the conclusion is explicitly graphic in its bloody violence. O (R) 15

Psycho III (1986) Tony Perkins directs and stars in this intense, brutally sardonic drama in which Norman Bates once again goes over the edge providing the audience with a parade of gruesomely victimized women in various states of undress. Excessive mix of sex and violence. O (R) 18

Psychopath, The (1966) Mild British mystery, directed by Freddie Francis, in which the investigation of four murders leads a London police inspector (Patrick Wymark) to the strange house of widow (Margaret Johnston), who is confined to a wheelchair. Stylized violence. A-II (br) X

Psychout for Murder (1971) Rossano Brazzi as the head of a wealthy, but depraved, Italian family has a luscious daughter (Adrienne La Russa) whose heart, deep down inside, belongs only to Daddy. Directed by Edward Ross, this sordid story of revenge and incest has no redeeming elements. O (R)

Public Enemy (1931) Classic gangster melodrama about a young hoodlum (James

Cagney) during Prohibition who rises up the gang ladder until a mob war shows that he "ain't so tough." Directed by William A. Wellman, Cagney gives his definitive performance as the cocky tough in an era of lawlessness spawned by the demand for illegal booze. Stylized violence and implied promiscuous relationships. A-III (br) A

Public Eye (1972) Witty British production about an insecure newlywed (Michael Jayston) who hires a private-eye (Topol) to tail his capricious wife (Mia Farrow). Detective and wife flirt innocently after they discover a bond of attraction in their mutually unorthodox personalities. Director Carol Reed proves his adeptness at handling romantic comedy as he blends the sprightly performances of the three stars with a sumptuous tour of London. A-II (G)

Public Eye, The (1992) A lonely free-lance tabloid photographer (Joe Pesci) in 1942 New York City tries to help a glamorous nightclub owner (Barbara Hershey) from a mob takeover, then stumbles on a syndicate plot to control wartime gas rationing. Writer-director Howard Franklin weaves together a gangster story and an intriguing character study in a downbeat picture with more gritty style than substance. Some stylized violence, several grisly corpse shots, discreet sexual innuendo and minimal rough language. A-III (R) 15

Puerto Rican Mambo, The (1992) Incisive humor highlights the monologues and skits of stand-up comedian Luis Caballero, who bemoans what he perceives to be the lowly status of Puerto Ricans in this country. Produced and directed by co-star Ben Model, the increasingly amusing look at common ethnic stereotypes channels Caballero's frustrations into wry, insightful commentary. Mild sexual references and minimal rough language. A-II (nr)

Pufnstuf (1970) Director Hollingsworth Morse's merry romp of song, dance and adventure features young Jack Wild as a human visitor to the magical land of Living Island, home of a dotty assortment of colorful stuffed animals overseen by their gentle dragon of a mayor, the Hon. H. R. Pufnstuf. Kids will enjoy the antics, although the flute-napping Witchiepoo (Billie Hayes) makes up in decibels what she lacks in scariness. Grown-ups might enjoy it too, especially those who like the idea of an absent-minded owl who sounds like Ed Wynn, a blind bat-messenger who keeps banging into walls, and a cheerful lion who does a pretty good turn at W. C. Fields. A-I (G) U

Pulp (1972) Michael Caine plays a hack author hired to ghost-write the memoirs of aging gangster-movie actor Mickey Rooney, but soon discovers himself in the middle of a murder caper not unlike the plots of any number of his own cheap novels. Though occasionally very funny, director Michael Hodges cannot sustain his spoof on old Hollywood crime movies as a coherent whole. Some mature references. A-III (PG) AA

Pump Up the Volume (1990) Painfully shy teenager (Christian Slater) secretly develops a hip alter-ego as Hard Harry during his nightly broadcasts on a pirate radio band, and the show's influence on his impressionable peers turns the entire community on its ear. Written and directed by Allan Moyle, the plot touches on teenage problems of loneliness, emerging sexuality, alienation and suicide, though its insensitivity in treatment of these important issues is likely to prove more of a barrier for some than a bridge to meaningful insights. Positive depiction of radio piracy, simulated masturbation, frequent rough language and a flash of nudity. A-IV (R)

Pumping Iron (1977) Unassuming documentary about the world of body-builders, singling out for major consideration Austrian-born Arnold Schwarzenegger, six-time winner of the "Mr. Olympia" title. Directed by George Butler and Robert Fiore, the film has some human touches that are entertaining and sometimes moving, but its adulation of Schwarzenegger's limited view of life and his blunt advocacy of hedonism makes this questionable material for younger viewers. A-III (PG) A

Pumping Iron II: The Women (1985) Mostly boring documentary by George Butler and Charles Gaines (who also made the original) about women body-builders participating in Las Vegas competition. Snide approach to its subject leaves a bad taste. Some brief partial nudity and a general air of vulgarity. A-III (nr) PG

Punchline (1988) A frustrated New Jersey housewife (Sally Field) and a manic medical student (Tom Hanks) aspire to become stand-up comics in a seedy Manhattan comedy club. Writer-director David Seltzer fails to bring the two into focus as unlikely friends, though each creates a quirky but interesting characterization. Much profanity, sexually explicit humor and vulgarities, including a male comic dressed as a nun. A-IV (R) 15

Punishment Park (1971) Social drama imagines a kangaroo court of conservative Americans conducting the trials of an assortment of conscientious objectors, hippies and peaceniks in a tent on the edge of the Mojave Desert whose heat is part of the terrors awaiting those sentenced for punishment. Directed by Peter Watkins, the nearsighted political tract about repression and dissent is steeped in brutality and foul language that antagonize rather than inspire, provoke disdain rather than assent. A-IV (R)

Puppet On a Chain (1972) British adaptation of Alistair MacLean's novel about Interpol agents (Sven-Bertil Taube and Barbara Parkins) assigned to uncover the Amsterdam drug connection. Directed by Geoffrey Reeve, the movie's high point is a speedboat chase through the canals of Amsterdam, but the rest of it goes from run-of-the-mill to dull. Some sadistic violence is not redeemed by its sophomoric preaching on the fate of a teenage drug addict who figures in the plot. A-III (PG) AA

Pure Country (1992) Flat story of a disillusioned country singer (George Strait) who falls in love with a rancher (Isabel Glasser) while on the lam from a possessive manager (Lesley Ann Warren) and her bookings of huge, impersonal concerts. Corny dialogue and Christopher Cain's consistently drab direction reduce this vehicle for country star Strait to little more than trite schmaltz backed by a fine soundtrack. Minor sexual innuendo, an instance of drunkenness and brief fisticuffs. A-II (PG)

Pure Luck (1991) Amiable but lame comedy teaming a detective (Danny Glover) with an accident-prone accountant (Martin Short) who career across Mexico in search of a missing amnesiac (Sheila Kelley). The many mishaps and pratfalls eventually wear thin in director Nadia Tass' faint-hearted attempt at slapstick. Minor violence, minimal profanity and a discreet sexual allusion. A-II (PG)

Purple Hearts (1984) Mediocre Vietnam War soap opera about the efforts of a Navy doctor (Ken Wahl) and nurse (Cheryl Ladd) to resolve all the obstacles that stand in the way of the inevitable clinch. Directed by Sidney J. Furie, the film's sentiments are about as genuine as the contrived and improbable dialogue that passes here for the utterances of brave men under fire. Premarital sex figures in the theme and there is one restrained bedroom scene in addition to some very rough language. A-III (R)

Purple Rain (1984) Rock star Prince's film debut features graphic sex, nudity, and an outrageous treatment of women that goes beyond anything demanded by plot considerations. O (R) 15

Purple Rose of Cairo, The (1985) Woody Allen comedy about a Depression-era housewife (Mia Farrow), married to an insensitive brute (Danny Aiello), whose only solace is going to the movies. One day, while watching a romance, its handsome young hero (Jeff Daniels) steps out of the screen into the audience and tells her that he loves her. There are some good moments

and some laughs, but the comedy is not especially inspired and its rather grim, realistic mood suggests pretensions to seriousness that the movie is incapable of supporting. A-II (PG)

Pursuit of D. B. Cooper, The (1981) Slapdash chase-comedy inspired by a successful 1971 airplane hijacking and robbery, is such mediocre fare that even so capable an actor as Robert Duvall looks bad in his role of determined insurance investigator. Treat Williams fares even worse as the happy-go-lucky criminal who is less than endearing. Though director Roger Spottiswoode's movie plays on a cartoon level, its benign attitude toward crime and an amorous sequence are adult material. A-III (PG) AA

Pursuit of Happiness (1971) Failed melodrama about a campus drop-out (Michael Sarrazin), who has turned his back on both his WASP background and synthetic college radicals, winds up in jail and in the end decides to escape to Canada with his girlfriend (Barbara Hershey). Directed by Robert Mulligan, the manipulative plot loads the deck against society, making it to blame for the problems of this misguided, misunderstood young man. There are some real issues here, but they are treated only superficially. Several silly nude scenes. A-IV (GP) X

Pussycat, Pussycat, I Love You (1970) Utterly dismissable sex farce about a writer (Ian McShane) who cheats on his wife (Anne Calder-Marshall) and her retaliation in kind. Written and directed by Rod Amateau, this is a totally inept production devoid of any but sophomoric humor. Adulterous theme, with some nudity and tasteless sight gags. O (PG)

Putney Swope (1969) Uneven satire in which blacks take over a Madison Avenue advertising agency and, despite their ban on alcohol, cigarette and war-toy advertising, their basic philosophy is as money-oriented as their white predecessors. Director Robert Downey's offbeat, irreverent humor uses a machine-gun barrage of complex irony and slapstick imagery, only some of which hit their intended targets. Very casual approach to sex, some scenes of extensive nudity and rough language. O (R) X

Puzzle of a Downfall Child (1970) Tired melodrama starring Faye Dunaway in the story of a fashion model's rise to the top where she leads a life of illusion and delusion. The tale has been told too many times and in too many better versions than this particularly hollow attempt by director Jerry Schatzberg. Some nudity and sexual references. A-III (R) X

Pyx, The (1973) Montreal hooker (Karen Black) falls to her death from a high rise, clutching a pyx (a container holding communion wafers) and wearing an inverted cross around her neck. Investigating her death, a detective (Christopher Plummer) uncovers a strange underworld in which drugs, prostitution and religious perversion go hand in hand. Directed by Harvey Hart, the occult mystery's treatment of the diabolic makes a fairly intriguing horror fantasy, though its inversion of religious symbols is disturbing and at times repulsive. A-IV (R)

Q

Q (1982) Failed horror movie about the feeding habits of a giant predatory bird, once an Aztec god but now reduced to living in a cramped nest in the peak of the Chrysler Building and grabbing a bite wherever she can. David Carradine, Candy Clark and Michael Moriarty are featured in this lackluster, ludicrous chiller produced and directed by Larry Cohen. Some disgusting violence, brief nudity and much foul language. O (R) 18

Q & A (1990) Blatantly racist N.Y. cop (Nick Nolte) murders an Hispanic hood and gets a reputable District Attorney (Patrick O'Neal) to push for an open-and-shut case of justifiable homicide. Writer-director Sidney Lumet tautly follows the investigation of the case by an idealistic assistant D.A. (Timothy Hutton), who uncovers a chain of sleazy witnesses and high-level judicial corruption. Intense profanity, including racial and ethnic slurs and vulgar sexual references, much grisly violence and graphic scenes involving sexual come-ons. A-IV (R) 18

Q Planes (see: "Clouds over Europe").

Quackser Fortune Has a Cousin in the Bronx (1970) He also has an unusual profession collecting horse manure in the Dublin streets for sale to gardening ladies, an offbeat girlfriend (Margot Kidder) and all of the bluff humor, warmth, rascality and pathos too often assigned to movie Irishmen. Fortunately, Quackser (so dubbed because of the duck sounds he made as a wee babe) is played by Gene Wilder, and without him, director Waris Hussein's movie would be just another charming but slight slice of Irish life. Some fairly graphic love scenes make it adult fare. A-III (R/PG) A

Quadrophenia (1979) British musical (whose title comes from "The Who" album that serves as the score) re-creates in gritty, vital fashion the world of the Mods and the Rockers, rival youth gangs of the 1960s who affected different versions of rebellion against the values of their working-class parents. Director Frank Roddam fails to offer any perspective on the characters and environment he has so skillfully evoked and the movie ends in an anarchistic, morally ambiguous scene. Graphic depiction of drug abuse and sexual promiscuity as well as rough language. A-IV (R) X

Quarrel, The (1992) A chance meeting in 1948 between a Yiddish writer (R. H. Thomson) and a Hasidic rabbi (Saul Rubinek) reunites two old friends from Eastern Europe, each of whom thought the other had perished in the Holocaust, and they soon pick up where they had left off in their youthful, pre-war disputations about God, Jewish identity and the mystery of evil as personified by the Nazis. Adapted by David Brandes from a play by Joseph Telushkin and directed by Eli Cohen, the outdoor setting on Montreal's Mount Royal gives some visual relief to the deftly performed series of verbal exchanges ranging from the intensely cerebral to the deeply emotional as the rabbi tries to persuade the writer to return to his orthodox religious roots. Some complicated but universal questions of faith and a discreetly handled sexual reference. A-II (nr)

Queen of Blood (1966) Routine horror movie written and directed by Curtis Harrington features a futuristic gimmick and stars Basil Rathbone and John Saxon. A-I (br)

Queen of Hearts (1989) British love story and sweeping family saga about an Italian couple (Anita Zagaria and Joseph Long) who run off to London to marry, raise a family and flourish as owners of a cafe until their past comes back to haunt them. Told through the eyes of their endearing youngest son (Ian Hawkes), the movie is a warm comedy-drama filled with many surprises. Director Jon Amiel nicely connects old and young, past and present, and shows the power of the family bond to transcend sorrow. Minimal violence, some menace and sexual innuendo. A-III (PG)

Queens, The (1967) Italian movie with four stories directed by Mauro Bolognini, Mario Monicelli, Antonio Pietrangeli and Luciano Salce tends to be dehumanizing in its one-sidedly negative view of women (Monica Vitti, Claudia Cardinale, Raquel Welch and Capuchine). O (br)

Queens Logic (1991) Longtime friends in a New York City neighborhood reexamine their relationships when one couple (Joe Mantegna and Linda Fiorentino) separates and the wedding of another couple (Chloe Webb and Ken Olin) is jeopardized. Steve Rash's direction of this ensemble cast produces a few good characterizations, though it is hampered by its talky, drawn-out predictability. A live-in relationship, some rough language and a shadowy flash of nudity. A-III (R)

Quentin Durward (1955) Indifferent adaptation of Sir Walter Scott's novel about an adventurous Scot (Robert Taylor) righting wrongs in the French court of Louis XI (Robert Morley). Directed by Richard Thorpe, the costumed derring-do only occasionally comes to life, though there's plenty of 15th-century pageantry to watch. Stylized violence. A-II (br)

Quest for Fire (1982) Ludicrously serious prehistoric adventure tale about three warriors (Everett McGill, Ron Perlman, Nameer Eli-Kadi) whose search for fire when that of their clan has been extinguished by a marauding band of Neanderthals leads to a humanizing encounter with a more culturally advanced girl (Rae Dawn Chong), who helps them learn to laugh and even to fall in love. Directed by Jean-Jacques Annaud who coscripted with Gerard Brach, its attempts at authenticity are made even more ludicrous by brutal sex scenes, violent combat and other assorted caveman antics. O (R)

Quick Change (1990) Disguised as a clown, Bill Murray and his accomplices Geena Davis and Randy Quaid pull off an ingenious million-dollar bank robbery in the Big Apple, only to find that their complicated caper was a breeze compared to getting to the airport. Co-directed by Murray and Howard Franklin, the result is a sporadically funny attempt at screwball comedy with the madness of New York City serving as a backdrop for understated performances by Murray and Davis, abetted by Quaid's slapstick goofiness. Some rough language, references to an unmarried sexual relationship and crime treated as a lark. A-III (R) 15

Quick Gun, The (1964) A reformed gunslinger (Audie Murphy) is treated as an outcast in his home town until he saves it from a band of desperados (led by Ted de Corsia). Director Sidney Salkow's slack Western has no particular merit or interest. Stylized violence. A-II (br) A

Quicksilver (1986) Ill-conceived youth film in which a young stockbroker (Kevin Bacon) has a run of bad luck, quits the market to become a bicycle courier and saves his new working-class friends from dope pushers, loan sharks and dead-end jobs. Directed by Tom Donnelly, it is a phony picture of a teenage hero demonstrating that immaturity and juvenile behavior can lead to success. A-III (PG)

Quiet Cool (1986) When a gang of dope addicts brutally murder a peaceful family, they themselves are hunted down and killed in an extraordinarily violent, sadistic manner. The crude and bloody story encourages vigilantism. O (R)

Quiet Days in Clichy (1970) Screen version of a Henry Miller novel about the dehumanized sexual adventures of two writers down and out in Paris. The result is human debasement, made all the worse by an irrelevant scatological music-lyric soundtrack supplied by Country Joe McDonald. O (nr)

Quiet Earth, The (1986) New Zealand scientist (Bruno Lawrence) awakes one morning to discover that he is the last man alive after a U.S. celestial experiment goes haywire. Director Geoff Murphy's quaint science-fiction mystery has some suspense and a warning against tampering with the laws of nature. Several scenes with nudity. A-III (nr)

Quiet Man, The (1952) When a retired Irish-American boxer (John Wayne) buys a plot of Irish land and courts a lovely colleen (Maureen O'Hara) to go with it, his stubborn bride insists he collect her dowry from her mean-spirited brother (Victor McLaglen). Director John Ford's grand celebration of all-too-familiar Irish stereotypes, ranging from a fondness for spirits to the love of a good fight, is delivered with much broad humor but the movie's universal appeal lies in the robust romance at the heart of the good-natured, old-fashioned story. Comic violence. A-II (br) U

Quiet Place in the Country, A (1970) When a troubled abstract-expressionist artist (Franco Nero) is placed in an institution (a nice quiet place in the country) by his mistress (Vanessa Redgrave), his madness crystallizes into an object of tediousness rather than of possible interest. Director Elio Petri chooses to use tricky nude shots and violent erotic dreams to hold attention, but the movie crumbles as it goes all out for slick sensationalism. O (R)

Quigley Down Under (1990) An American cowboy (Tom Selleck), hired as a sharpshooter in the 1860s' Australian Outback, turns against his villainous boss (Alan Rickman) in defense of the native aborigines and a slightly mad young woman (Laura San Giacomo). Director Simon Wincer gives a fresh spin to the traditional western and backs it with interesting plot developments, credible performances and breathtaking Australian locales. Intermittent violent shoot-outs, occasional menace and shots with tribal nudity. A-II (PG-13)

Quiller Memorandum, The (1967) Resurgence of Nazism in post-war Germany is the background for this spy story starring George Segal, Max von Sydow, Senta Berger and Alec Guinness in a cameo. Director Michael Anderson gets some suspenseful moments in a convoluted thriller that is spun out beyond its limits. A-III (br) A

Quintet (1979) Director Robert Altman's failed futuristic fable about six citizens of an ice-bound, dying world engaged in a lethal cat-and-mouse game of survival that gives the movie its title. Paul Newman, Bibi Andersson, Fernando Rey, and Vittorio Gassman head the fur-swathed cast of an ambitious but hapless attempt to philosophize about the meaning of life. Graphic depiction of brutal killings. O (R) AA

Quo Vadis (1951) Roman general (Robert Taylor) falls in love with Christian maid (Deborah Kerr) but matters get complicated when the looney emperor burns Rome and blames the Christians. In director Mervyn LeRoy's version of the Henryk Sienkiewicz novel, the epic production overpowers the pallid love story and the conflict between Christianity and paganism proves less interesting than that between the mad Nero (Peter Ustinov) and his rationalist advisor (Leo Genn). A mixed bag of religious fervor and pagan frolics, there's a lengthy suicide scene, some sexual innuendo and stylized violence. A-I (br) PG

R

Ra Expeditions, The (1972) Documentary record of anthropologist Thor Heyerdahl's voyage from Africa to the Americas in a papyrus reed boat called the Ra, the name of an Egyptian god. Using a reed craft of early Mediterranean design, Heyerdahl set out to demonstrate that such a ship could stand the long voyage between hemispheres, and does on a second try. Produced and directed by Lennart Ehrenberg, the documentary enables a vicarious sharing of adventure on high seas. A-I (G)

Rabbit, Run (1971) Failed screen version of John Updike's dark and brooding novel probing the shadowed corners of the mind of an irresponsible young man (James Caan) who persists in chasing illusions and women with equal fervor, resulting in a ruined marriage and shattered dreams. Director Jack Smight dissipates the novel's passionate intensity by concentrating on the surface level of the action. Graphic sexual depictions. O (R)

Rabbit Test (1978) Failed sex farce about the world's first pregnant man is comedienne Joan Rivers' debut as a director. Posing a feminist satire, the effort lacks the wit and satiric nuance that might have saved it from being ploddingly tasteless and offensive. Unfunny jokes about religious beliefs are scattered throughout this indelicate comedy. O (PG)

Rabid (1977) Canadian production about a young woman (porno star Marilyn Chambers) who undergoes plastic surgery only to find herself turned into a vampire who soon has a good portion of the population of Montreal going green in the face, frothing at the mouth and biting one another. Directed by David Cronenberg, it's a nauseating, gory piece of trash. O (R) 18

Race for Your Life, Charlie Brown (1977) Feature cartoon based on the Charles M. Schulz comic strip that tells of the adventures and perils that the Peanuts characters encounter while spending the summer at a wilderness camp out West. Though little of the subtlety of Schulz at his best is represented, the film will entertain younger children. A-I (G) U

Race with the Devil (1975) Businessmen (Warren Oates and Peter Fonda) on a vacation trip with their wives inadvertently come upon some Satanists at their rituals and then are pursued across Texas by the vengeful cultists. Directed by Jack Starrett, the silly horror movie has a bad script, a few scares and some bloodshed. A-III (PG) 15

Rachel and the Stranger (1948) A widower (William Holden) raising a son on the Kentucky frontier marries a bondswoman (Loretta Young) but only appreciates her when his best friend (Robert Mitchum) tries to win her affections. Directed by Norman Foster, the odd triangle leads Young to reject both men as wanting a servant rather than a wife but a Shawnee attack resolves the dilemma. Quasi-feminist theme with conventional romantic ending. A-II (br) A

Rachel, Rachel (1968) Joanne Woodward plays a painfully lonely and somewhat repressed woman teaching school in a small Midwestern town and concerned about becoming a dowdy spinster. When an old school chum (James Olsen) visits, she falls hopelessly in love and has a brief, intense affair that ends harshly and with bitterness. Directed by Paul Newman, the story is poignant and terribly human with excellent performances. A-III (R) X

Racing with the Moon (1984) Likable teenager (Sean Penn), finishing high school during World War II, falls for a winsome California beauty (Elizabeth McGovern) and both try to get money for a friend's abortion. Nostalgic romance from director Richard Benjamin captures the atmosphere and the mood of the period but concentrates too heavily on the sexual nature of youthful relationships. Some nudity and a benign view of premarital sex. O (R/PG appeal) 15

Rad (1986) Talia Shire stars in her own production of a story about a teenage bike enthusiast who overcomes an unscrupulous businessman's plot to keep him from winning a national championship race. Directed by Hal Needham, it is a pretentious and simplistic tale and its execution is graceless and unrewarding. Several obscene gestures by Ray Walston in a cameo role and some rough language by a little girl seem quite unnecessary. A-II (PG)

Radio Days (1987) Writer-director Woody Allen celebrates the positive impact of radio on the lives of a New York family in the story of two women (Dianne Wiest and Mia Farrow) seeking romance via different paths. This nostalgic look at the 1940s indicates that the values of that era have been lost and even the fond memories are fading. A-II (PG)

Radio Flyer (1992) Sensitive but jumbled drama about two kid brothers (Elijah Wood and Joseph Mazello) who build a wagon that can fly so the younger boy can escape their brutally abusive, alcoholic stepfather (Adam Baldwin). Director Richard Donner mixes a serious story about child abuse with elements of magical fantasy that don't successfully mesh. Continual menace to children and momentary graphic violence. A-II (PG-13)

Radioactive Dreams (1986) Two youths leave their bomb shelters after 15 years to explore the post-nuclear world outside. Passing through a desolate and bleak landscape, they encounter a vile assortment of mutants and perverted road life. Many visual effects are used by director Albert Pyun simply to frame violence, brutality, nudity and profanity. O (R)

Rafferty and the Gold Dust Twins (1975) Bumbling Los Angeles driving-test examiner (Alan Arkin) is kidnapped by roving hippies (Sally Kellerman and MacKenzie Phillips) and forced at gunpoint to drive them to New Orleans. Directed by Dick Richards, everything about this predictable heart-tug road movie is bogus, including the realistic language and frequently sordid situations. O (R)

Raffles (1930) Ronald Colman turns on the charm as the gentleman thief who steals a valuable necklace to help a needy pal, then has to outwit Scotland Yard's bulldog sleuth (David Torrence). Directed by Harry D'Arrast and George Fitzmaurice, the picture of an honorable crook is dated and its treatment creaky, but still fun for all that. A-II (br)

Raffles (1940) Playful gentleman thief (David Niven) steals a jeweled necklace from under the nose of a Scotland Yard inspector (Dudley Digges) and the chase is on. Directed by Sam Wood, Niven's bright performance as the lightfingered Raffles sparkles in its stuffy British society setting but the period plot fairly creaks and the action is disappointingly slack. Justice prevails implicitly. A-II (br)

Raga (1971) American documentary provides an historical introduction to the musical heritage of India and Ravi Shankar's part in introducing it to Western audiences. Produced and directed by Howard Worth, the account is filled with insights about the individual and the cultural diffusion engendered by modern world communications. A-I (nr)

Rage (1966) Muddled melodrama set in a remote area of Mexico where an alcoholic doctor (Glenn Ford) is bitten by a dog with rabies, then delivers a poor woman's baby before racing the clock to get the serum needed to save his life. Directed by Gilberto Gazcon, the dubbed Mexican production is hardly credible, especially with Stella Stevens' role as the doctor's would-be girlfriend. Much menace, a complicated childbirth and some sexual innuendo. A-III (br)

Rage (1972) After camping out with his boy one night, an Arizona sheep farmer (George C. Scott) wakes to the horror of finding his son and flock dying in convulsions. When he finally learns that a secret military test of nerve gas is responsible, he goes berserk and sets out to destroy those he considers responsible. The story of a decent man crushed by a technocracy unconcerned with the individual is told by Scott in his debut as a director in purely melodramatic terms with two-dimensional figures and plot contrivances. Yet it is close enough to reality to trouble any viewer's complacency, though its violent conclusion undercuts the meaning of what precedes these scenes of destruction. A-III (PG) 15

Rage in Harlem, A (1991) Toting a trunkful of stolen gold, a scheming sexpot (Robin Givens) hooks up with a gullible chump (Forest Whitaker) but is tracked down by her furious ex-lover and partner in crime (Badja Djola). Bill Duke directs an overproduced potboiler awash in brutal characterizations and sleazy situations. Excessive, gory violence, some promiscuity and nudity and much rough language. O (R) 18

Rage in Heaven (1941) Labored adaptation of the James Hilton novel in which a cracked millionaire (Robert Montgomery) kills himself so that it appears he has been murdered by a friend (George Sanders) he suspects is in love with his wife (Ingrid Bergman). Directed by W. S. Van Dyke II, the fine cast seems hopelessly adrift in this static, unconvincing melodrama. Unsettling atmosphere and a suicide. A-II (br) A

Rage of Paris, The (1938) Flimsy romantic comedy directed by Henry Koster in which a Frenchwoman (Danielle Darrieux) stranded in New York agrees to trick a millionaire (Louis Hayward) into marriage, then falls for his even wealthier friend (Douglas Fairbanks Jr.). Romantic situations and some sexual innuendo. A-III (br)

Raggedy Ann and Andy (1977) Feature-length musical cartoon inspired by the long-time childhood favorites is, unfortunately, distinguished more by the technical excellence of Richard Williams' animation than by any real creative verve or even sense of imagination. The songs are mostly forgettable and there is no storyline of any significance to keep children's attention. A-I (G) U

Raggedy Man (1981) A young divorcee (Sissy Spacek) in a small Texas town during the Second World War has a brief romance with a sailor passing through (Eric Roberts) and fends off the unwelcome attentions of two local louts who threaten her and her two boys. Director Jack Fisk fails badly in the attempt to mix childlike whimsey, light romance and Gothic terror. Some violence and premarital sex are central to the plot. A-III (PG) 15

Raging Bull (1980) Hard-edged, uncompromising portrait of former middleweight boxing champ Jake La Motta (Robert De Niro in an outstanding performance) and his agonizing relationship with his second wife (Cathy Moriarity) and his brother (Joe Pesci). Director Martin Scorsese's stark black-and-white treatment conveys La Motta's often grim, violently hostile personality, which the film suggests was born of sexual problems. Brutal fight scenes, a graphic bedroom sequence and rough language. A-III (R) 18

Ragman's Daughter, The (1974) British bittersweet romance between a young tough who steals out of need and his hopelessly middle-class girlfriend who does it for kicks. Scripted by Alan Sillitoe and directed by Harold Becker, the predictable plot lacks energy and drive as well as credibility. A-III (nr) X

Ragtime (1981) Loose, sporadically effective adaptation of the E. L. Doctorow patchwork novel about some representative Americans at the turn-of-the-century. Notable among them are James Cagney as the police commissioner of N.Y. City and a black piano player (Howard E. Rollins Jr.) who turns into a revolutionary combating social injustice. Directed by Milos Forman, it succeeds as a lavish historical re-creation but gets low grades in the matter of credible characterization. An excessively extended sequence involving partial nudity and some rough language. A-IV (PG) AA

Raid on Rommel (1971) World War II adventure gasps along with Richard Burton's commandos as they fight Rommel's Afrika Korps across the Sahara and through Tobruk to an awaiting rescue unit, leaving a path of mayhem and devastation in their wake. Directed by Henry Hathaway, the action sequences are made up of stock footage and darkened sequences lifted from the 1966 "Tobruk." Ludicrous desert action histrionics. A-III (PG) 15

Raiders of the Lost Ark (1981) Tongue-in-cheek action melodrama about Indiana Jones, an archeologist-adventurer (Harrison Ford), and his feisty girlfriend (Karen Allen) who save the biblical Ark of the Covenant for the good old USA despite the worst efforts of a clutch of Nazi villains. Director Steven Spielberg's attempt to recapture the excitement of the old movie serials becomes tiresome and repetitious in its reliance upon constant action. Intense violence, gruesome special effects and a questionable use of something as sacred as the Ark as a source of destructive power. A-III (PG)

Railroad Man, The (1965) Series of misfortunes plagues a working-class family in Italy after World War II. The sincerity of the characterizations more than outweighs the contrivances of the plot. Pietro Germi both directs and stars as the head of the family,

but it is a child actor (Eduardo Nevola) who will steal the affection of even the most cynical viewer. A-II (br)

Railway Children, The (1971) Three children (Jenny Agutter; Sally Thomsett; Gary Warren) and their mother (Dinah Sheridan) are forced to move from their comfy Victorian mansion to an austere cottage in the country along the railway tracks while they wait expectantly for their Daddy to be cleared of false charges. Directed by Lionel Jeffries, the entire production is colored with an instinctive, childlike innocence and loyalty providing viewers of all ages with a warming and reassuring conviction that even in the most adverse times hope and love can, indeed must, exist. A-I (G) U

Rain for a Dusty Summer (1972) Humberto Almazan, a popular Mexican actor who retired from the screen at the age of 35 to become a missionary priest, returns to portray Father Miguel Pro, a Mexican priest whose ministry during a time of religious oppression in the 1920s made him a folk hero and, ultimately, a martyr. Unfortunately, Arthur Lubin's heavy-handed direction of an oversimplified, melodramatic script makes the religious theme appear absurd and prevents a talented cast (including Ernest Borgnine as the dictator) from developing any but superficial characterizations, especially with the flat, expressionless dubbing of the mostly Spanish-speaking cast. Restrained violence. A-II (GP)

Rain Man (1988) A shady L.A. car dealer (Tom Cruise) loses the family inheritance to an older brother (Dustin Hoffman) who suffers from irreversible autistic savant syndrome and has been institutionalized most of his life. On a cross-country auto journey, the younger brother drops his plans for a custody battle when he learns to love his brother despite his disability. Under the direction of Barry Levinson, the brothers' intense and sometimes comical interaction during the life-affirming journey is wonderful, but the rest of the film is less satisfying and detracts from the character study. Much profanity, a few intense but brief emotionally unhinged outbursts by the autistic protaganist and a fleeting off-camera sex scene. A-III (R) 15

Rain People, The (1969) Shirley Knight plays a pregnant woman fleeing husband and home to come to terms with her womanhood and incomplete sense of fulfillment. Written and directed by Francis Ford Coppola, the movie's theme of flight from responsibility is treated with poetic intensity and subtle nuance. Some violence and sexual references. A-III (PG) AA

Rain Without Thunder (1993) Dreary talking-heads feature offers a series of repetitious interviews about the case of a woman (Ali Thomas) convicted of fetal murder in the year 2042 after a Constitutional Amendment has made abortion illegal. Instead of a movie, writer-director Gary Bennett has made a cheap propaganda piece substituting cardboard figures for human beings and straw arguments for conflicting moral principles. Unfairly caricatures the moral issue of abortion. O (PG-13)

Rainbow, The (1989) British adaptation of the 1915 D. H. Lawrence novel about the sexual and political awakening of an adolescent girl (Sammi Davis) occasioned by her maverick swimming instructor (Amanda Donohoe). Despite writer-director Ken Russell's uncharacteristically restrained treatment of the material, there are several needlessly explicit depictions of heterosexual and lesbian encounters. O (R) 15

Rainbow Brite and the Star Stealer (1985) In her film debut, Rainbow Brite, the creation of toy manufacturers, must save the universe from destruction. Not strong on imagination or substance but lots of color and action designed to sell dolls to the toddler crowd. A-I (G)

Raise the Red Lantern (1992) Exquisitely mounted period piece about a young Chinese bride (Gong Li) who competes daily with her husband's three other wives to win his favor and establish preeminence in the household. Director Zhang Yimou's tragic story of women reduced to treachery to maintain self-esteem is depicted in the context of a closed, tyrannical society. Subtitles. Much sexual innuendo and malicious intrigue. A-III (PG)

Raise the Titanic! (1980) Failed action melodrama starring Jason Robards and Richard Jordan. Story about attempts by American and Russian soldiers of fortune to recover rare minerals from the sunken luxury liner. Director Jerry Jameson's lackluster underwater adventure is unbelievably lethargic and muddleheaded. A-II (PG)

Raisin in the Sun, A (1961) Fine screen version of the Lorraine Hansberry play about a young black man in a Chicago slum (Sidney Poitier) whose ambitions to get ahead in the world come into conflict with the values of his mother (Claudia McNeil in a remarkable performance). What keeps this story about the evils of racial segregation from being dated is that director Daniel Petrie and a very capable cast have focused their energies on depicting human aspirations common to all and transcending limits of plot and period. A-II (br) A

Raising Arizona (1987) Nicolas Cage and Holly Hunter play a simple-minded childless couple who kidnap one of a set of quintuplets to raise as their own in this madcap comedy

from the Coen brothers, Joel and Ethan. Stridently effective parody of socially conscious drama has some vulgar and brutal moments played with deadpan intensity by Cage and a host of crude and profane heavies, perfectly restrained at the borderline of good taste. A-III (PG-13) 15

Raising Cain (1992) An unfaithful wife (Lolita Davidovich) suspects her eccentric husband (John Lithgow) when neighborhood women and their toddlers, including her own, begin disappearing. Writer-director Brian de Palma parodies his own and other horror movies in a clunky mix of comedy and terror that never meshes individual scenes into a cohesive whole. Intermittent violence, a discreet sexual encounter and occasional rough language. A-III (R) 15

Rake's Progress, The (see: "Notorious Gentleman").

Rambling Rose (1991) A kindly Southern family (headed by Robert Duvall and Diane Ladd) in 1935 takes in an abused 19-year-old (Laura Dern) whose promiscuous habits cause continual problems in the community. Directed by Martha Coolidge, the story begins playfully but sensitive performances and the lead character's eventual maturity make this an uncommon and wistful movie. Discreet scene of foreplay by teenagers, numerous references to promiscuity and a flash of nudity. A-IV (R)

Rambo (see: "First Blood").

Rambo: First Blood Part II (1985) Rambo (Sylvester Stallone) is released from prison to undertake a secret mission to free Americans still being held in Vietnam and, after much slaughter, does so only to face the traitor who wanted the mission to fail. Playing shamelessly upon the fears and hopes of the relatives of MIA's, this comic-strip movie features excessive violence. O (R) 18

Rambo III (1988) One-man wrecking crew John Rambo (Sylvester Stallone) returns to the battlefield, this time in Afghanistan, to save his mentor, Col. Trautman (Richard Crenna), from certain death at the hands of his Soviet captors. Directed by Peter MacDonald, the movie's plot is as simplistic as its politics and Stallone's performance is notable only for some self-mocking humor. Excessive violence and rough language. O (R) 18

Rampage (1992) When a particularly perverse serial murderer (Alex McArthur) pleads insanity at his California trial, the young prosecutor (Michael Biehn) argues that society will only be safe from this mad killer if he is given the death penalty. Writer-director William Friedkin's courtroom drama centers on the slow, tortuous processes of the law rather than the gruesome details of the sadistic crimes, though it becomes increasingly clear that the movie is weighted on the side of capital punishment. Restrained depiction of grisly killings, the desecration of a church and the bizarre ravings of a sick mind. A-III (R)

Rampage at Apache Wells (1966) Hokey German-produced western from a Karl May story about the heroics of veteran frontiersman Old Surehand (Stewart Granger) in saving a wagon train from attack by Indians stirred up by an evil oil baron. Harald Philipps directs the melodramatics with a heavy hand and the ludicrous results are not helped by inept dubbing. Stylized violence and silly frontier stereotypes. A-II (br)

Ramparts of Clay (1971) French director Jean-Louis Bertucelli uses scenes of everyday life in a small Tunisian village at the edge of the Sahara to tell the story of a young woman (Leila Schenna) who can no longer accept the old patterns in which she has been raised. This is a beautiful work showing the dignity of a simple way of life, while conscious of the irreversible forces that will transform it. A-II (GP)

Ran (1985) Samurai version of Shakespeare's King Lear by director Akira Kurosawa is, unfortunately, little more than an opulently staged historical pageant, lacking pathos and tragic force. Many battle scenes, but the violence is stylized. A-II (R) 15

Rancho Deluxe (1975) Jeff Bridges and Sam Waterson star as footloose and free-spirited modern rustlers finally apprehended by a bumbling Slim Pickens. Director Frank Perry's unfunny comedy is further undone by nudity and graphic sexuality. O (R) 15

Ransom (1956) Talky, flat-footed suspenser in which a wealthy executive (Glenn Ford) and his hysterical wife (Donna Reed) agonize about the morality as well as practicality of paying kidnappers to return his young son. Director Alex Segal's serious but simple-minded picture suggests that there would be no kidnappings if no one paid ransom, but the concept is lost in the melodramatics of the harrowing situation. Much soul-searching and emotional duress. A-II (br)

Rape of Love (1979) Difficult French drama about an attractive, self-possessed and quite intelligent young nurse (Nathalie Nell) who is abducted by four men and brutally raped. Directed by Yannick Bellon, it is a serious attempt to deal with a detestable crime of violence and its consequences, not only for the victim, her fiance, family and friends, but also for the rapists and society as a whole. Despite its good intentions, however, the rape scene is unnecessarily graphic and extended. O (nr)

Rapid Fire (1992) Having witnessed a mob murder, a college student (Brandon Lee) is betrayed in the federal witness protection program and reluctantly relies on two Chicago cops (Powers Boothe and Kate Hodge) and his own martial arts skills to stay alive. Dwight H. Little directs a graphic action yarn that does a slick job of exploiting murderous violence as exciting entertainment. Excessive violence, a brief sexual encounter, occasional nudity and much rough language. O (R) 18

Rappin' (1985) A young ex-convict adept at rapping (the street art of fast talking) comes to the aid of the urban poor victimized by nasty landlords and the like. The actors, under Joel Silberg's direction, are personable, but the flimsy story is nothing but a frame for a skill that's not likely to enthrall most viewers. A-II (PG)

Rapture, The (1991) Wooden tale of a depressed woman (Mimi Rogers) who tires of trying to fill the emptiness of her life with meaningless sexual encounters, joins a psuedo-Christian cult and becomes a deranged religious fanatic. Writer-director Michael Tolkin's blankly superficial treatment of the subject results in an unpalatable brew of sex, religious rhetoric and irrational psychology. Excessively graphic depictions of sexual encounters, eccentric interpretations of biblical texts and occasional rough language. O (R)

Rascal (1969) A boy (Bill Mumy), a dog and a mischievous racoon spend a summer together in Small Town, USA, in the innocent days just before World War I. Director Norman Tokar keeps the action lively (especially that of Rascal, the racoon) and the sentiment wholesome in this Disney production celebrating the virtues of rural America. A-I (G)

Raspad (1992) Harrowing political drama, set during and just after the Soviet nuclear reactor explosion at Chernobyl in April 1986, follows a skeptical reporter (Sergei Shakurov) around as the official government continues to deny the enormity of the disaster. Director Mikhail Belikov compellingly converts a tragic incident in history into deeply felt personal statement resonating with moral outrage. Subtitles. Somber theme and flashes of nudity. A-II (nr)

Rasputin (1966) Failed British dramatization of a sinister monk (Christopher Lee) in the Czar's court before the Russian Revolution. Directed by Don Sharp, the evil actions depicted are excessive in their visual detail. O (br)

Ratboy (1986) A boy whose facial deformity makes him look like a rodent becomes exploited for monetary gain. Directed by actress Sandra Locke (who also plays a leading role as one of those exploiting the boy), this version of the beauty-and-the-beast fable lacks any convincing insight and relies upon conventional plot devices, including negative stereotyping of blacks and people in the entertainment business. Liberal sprinklings of profanity. A-III (PG-13) 15

Raw Deal (1986) Fueled by pride and a promise, a small-town sheriff (Arnold Schwarzenegger) massacres an entire crime syndicate in a bloody shootout providing a primitive brand of justice on the behalf of the slain son of his former FBI buddy (Darren McGavin). The excessive violence isn't justified by plot or characterization. O (R) 18

Razor in the Flesh (1974) Brazilian drama about a prostitute tormented by her pimp who in turn is taunted by a homosexual until the roles are reversed and attacker becomes victim and the story becomes a parable about the interchangeable roles of oppressor and oppressed. Directed by Braz Chediak, the movie is about characters living at the last extremities of humanity, vividly reacting with the desperation of those who can only hurt others and themselves because they have nothing left to hope for. As a reminder of our common human frailty, it cuts to the bone. A-IV (nr)

Razor's Edge, The (1984) The path to salvation is hard in this ill-conceived and shallow remake of the 1946 version of the W. Somerset Maugham novel. Bill Murray plays a World War I veteran who travels in Europe to find the meaning of life and some measure of inner peace. Under the direction of John Byrum, Murray has difficulty displaying the emotion and sensitivity required by the role. Empty parable with some harsh language. A-III (PG-13) 15

Re-Animator (1985) In this abysmal effort, a zealous young scientist (Jeffrey Combs) develops a serum to raise the dead. Directed by Stuart Gordon, it's an abundantly gory affair made all the more revolting by its attempts at grisly humor. O (R rating surrendered by distributor and no longer applies.)

Regarding Henry (1991) Inspirational drama about a high-rolling Manhattan attorney (Harison Ford) who loses nearly all his memory and motor functions after a brain injury and must reacquaint himself with his very neglected wife and 11-year-old daughter (Annette Bening and Mikki Allen). The positive message in director Mike Nichols well-acted drama is undercut by the snail-like pace of its leaden, overly manipulative script. A brief scene of violence, some adulterous references and an instance of rough language. A-III (PG-13) 12

Real Genius (1985) When a college science whiz (Val Kilmer) and his fellow students discover they have been tricked by their professor (William Atherton) into helping create a laser weapon for the military establishment, they revolt and destroy their work. Director Martha Coolidge is unable to get any laughs from this failed satire on higher education. Some vulgar language and sexual promiscuity A-III (PG)

Real Glory, The (1939) Training Filipino recruits to defend their land against invading Moros, a handful of American soldiers (notably Gary Cooper; David Niven; Broderick Crawford) help their "little brothers" learn to fight a fanatic enemy while also having to contend with a cholera outbreak. Director Henry Hathaway builds plenty of tension in the plight of the remote island outpost and stages some classy battle scenes but the patriotic melodrama seems dated hokum today, not least because of its patronizing attitude toward the Philippine people. Stylized violence, some of it rather grisly. A-I (br) PG

Real Life (1979) Episodic comedy, written and directed by comedian Albert Brooks, in which he plays the role of a moviemaker who wants to capture on film the life of a real American family, a Phoenix veterinarian (Charles Grodin), his wife (Francis Lee McCain) and their two children. While frequently hilarious, with a touch of black humor, many of the jokes are adult in nature but probably not too strong for older teenagers. A-III (PG)

Real McCoy, The (1993) When her little boy is kidnapped by criminals who need her expertise, a paroled bank robber (Kim Basinger) is forced to attempt one more treacherous bank job, with the help of her inept assistant (Val Kilmer). Russell Mulcahy directs a dull and plodding comedy of no originality, completely lacking romantic sparks between the couple. Intermittent violence, an uncritical attitude toward ill-gotten gain and an instance of rough language. A-III (PG-13)

Reap the Wild Wind (1942) In this 19th-century adventure yarn, a sea captain (John Wayne) and a maritime lawyer (Ray Milland) fall for the same damsel (Paulette Goddard) while fighting a pirate wrecker-salvager (Raymond Massey) operating off the Florida Keys. Director Cecil B. DeMille depicts the era of sailing ships in colorful fashion with some rousing action sequences, including Wayne's battle with a giant squid, but the narrative frequently bogs down in fitful romance and soggy soul-searching. Some menace and stylized violence. A-I (br) A

Rear Window (1954) Stylish thriller in which a Manhattan photographer (James Stewart), immobilized by a broken leg, idly passes the time watching his neighbors across the way until witnessing a murder, then uses his girlfriend (Grace Kelly) to catch the killer (Raymond Burr). Director Alfred Hitchcock gradually notches the level of suspense to fever-pitch in the conclusion. Much menace and a stylized act of violence. A-II (br) PG

Rebecca (1940) Daphne du Maurier's classic tale of mystery and romance tells of the remarriage of a wealthy British widower (Laurence Olivier) whose young bride (Joan Fontaine) is intimidated by the great estate of Manderley and its disapproving housekeeper (Judith Anderson) until she discovers the truth about the death of her husband's former wife. Alfred Hitchcock's first movie to be directed in the U.S. is slow and deliberate in turning Manderley into a sinister setting whose empty halls reverberate with the echoes of her brooding husband's deceased wife. Though more romantic than mysterious, its effectiveness as an eerie exercise in suspense might rattle the very young. A-II (br) PG

Rebecca of Sunnybrook Farm (1938) Pedestrian Shirley Temple vehicle gives her the role of a "self-reliant" motherless child whose country aunt (Helen Westley) won't hear of her becoming a radio star until talent wins out. Directed by Allan Dwan, the predictable plot complications keep getting in the way of mild romance (Randolph Scott and Gloria Stuart), pale comedy (Slim Summerville, Jack Haley and William Demarest) and Shirley's singing and hoofing with Bill Robinson. Dated but innocent fun. A-I (br) U

Rebel with a Cause (see: "The Loneliness of the Long Distance Runner").

Rebel Without a Cause (1955) Unconvincing tale of teenage angst portrays troubled Los Angeles youths (James Dean, Natalie Wood and Sal Mineo) whose alienation from affluent parents propels them into dangerous scrapes that eventually end in tragedy. Directed by Nicholas Ray, the picture's intended theme is more substantial than its clumsy execution and self-serving picture of adults as hypocritical and uncaring. Stylized violence. A-II (br) PG

Rebellion in Patagonia (1977) When armed violence broke out in 1921 between the landowners and striking workers of Patagonia, Argentina's southernmost state, the government intervened by sending in troops to help the landowners crush the workers. Large-scale Argentinian re-creation directed by Hector Olivera has much colorful action with hard-riding gaucho bands pitted against columns of soldiers in vintage autos. There are, however, some strong scenes of violence illustrating the inequities of power and class. A-III (nr)

Reckless (1984) Pretentious, slow-moving account of star-crossed teenaged lovers (Aidan Quinn and Daryl Hannah) in a grimy, impoverished steel town treads numbingly familiar ground. It seems that director James Foley has found no way to recharge the old formula nor has writer Chris Columbus discovered anything of significance. Aimed at a teenage audience, the film has an abundance of nudity and graphic sex. O (R)

Reckoning, The (1970) Nicol Williamson gives a brilliant performance as a London businessman who drinks too much, drives too fast, uses and abuses women, ruins business rivals, and even commits murder to avenge his father's death back in the Liverpool slum where he grew up. It is a portrait of a ruthless, amoral fellow, and yet director Jack Gold's fast-moving action melodrama takes a reckoning not only of him but of a society that rewards his brand of cut-throat tactics in life as well as the business world. A disturbing movie not intended as escapist fare. A-IV (R) X

Red and the White, The (1969) Hungarian dramatization about the confused struggles between Communists and anti-Communists that broke out in Eastern Europe after the Russian Revolution. Director Miklos Jancso's picture of a violent era when a man's shirt was worth more than his life is set against the bleak but hauntingly beautiful Volga countryside. A-III (nr)

Red Badge of Courage, The (1951) Powerful though uneven dramatization of Stephen Crane's novel about an Ohio youth (Audie Murphy) coming of age in combat during the Civil War. Brutally truncated by the studio before its release, what remains of director John Huston's effort is a strong, naturalistic re-creation of the period's bloody warfare of attrition and the human cost for those who fought it. The battlefield violence is strong fare for youngsters. A-I (br) U

Red Beard (1969) Japanese character study of a 19th-century doctor (Toshiro Mifune) who must be incredibly tough and unbending in running a clinic for the poor and yet tender and loving in his ministry to those who need his care. Director Akira Kurosawa's movie conveys the complexities of compassion in the person of this hard-headed, single-minded doctor made credible by Mifune's great performance. Realist depictions of the period's crude operating facilities. A-III (nr)

Red Beret, The (see: "Paratrooper").

Red Dawn (1984) Director John Milius presents a preposterous and heavy-handed war movie with the premise that the U.S. has been invaded by Russian and Cuban troops. A group of teenage Rambo's (led by Patrick Swayze; C. Thomas Howell) take up guerrilla warfare to preserve the integrity of America. Because of its violence and its glorification of the macho rather than patriotism, it's not for immature viewers. A-III (PG-13) 15

Red Desert, The (1965) Vague Italian mood piece about a troubled woman (Monica Vitti) living in the industrial city of Ravenna who struggles to find human warmth and hope in a seemingly alienated world. Directed by Michelangelo Antonioni, the unconventional narrative is more concerned with interior feelings than the exposition of events and many may find its images of disorientation irritatingly abstract and meaningless. Subtitles. Needlessly detailed treatment of sexual matters. A-IV (br)

Red Dragon: The Pursuit of Hannibal Lecter (see: "Manhunter").

Red Heat (1988) Action thriller uses the buddy-cop formula, pairing a tight-lipped Soviet cop (Arnold Schwarzenegger) with a loud-mouthed Chicago cop (Jim Belushi) in a manhunt for a Soviet drug smuggler (Ed O'Ross) on the streets of Chicago. Directed by Walter Hill, the movie's international dimension adds nothing to the tired, overly familiar formula plot. Excessive violence and foul language. O (R) 18

Red Mantle, The (see: "Hagbard and Signe")

Red Psalm (1973) Hungarian import uses a 19th-century peasant revolt as a socialist hymn celebrating the collective power of the people in their continuing struggle against oppression. Director Miklos Jancso's lyric flow of images is choreographed to a symphony of folk song and the movie's poetic strength is rooted in its agrarian setting and Eastern European folk traditions. Some may be offended by the work's appropriation of religious symbolism in a revolutionary context. A-IV (nr)

Red Scorpion (1989) Violence-saturated action adventure set in an obscure African country where a deadly Soviet superagent (Dolph Ludgren) is saved from death by kindly bushmen and is transformed into a good guy who sees firsthand how his fellow Russians are cruelly decimating the native rebels. Director Joseph Zito fills his desert landscape with long, tedious chase and battle sequences, grisly violence, gruesome torture scenes and much profanity. O (R)

Red Sky at Morning (1971) Mindless World War II coming-of-age story set in New Mexico where a callow youth (Richard Thomas) lusts after a plump schoolmate (Catherine Burns) while his boozy mother (Claire Bloom) needs help fending off amorous "uncles." Directed by James Goldstone, the plot's serious level is hindered by the melodramatic treatment, with moral insights getting lost in the shuffle. A-III (PG) X

Red Sonja (1985) Plodding, lackluster sword-and-scorcery movie directed by Richard Fleischer and starring muscleman Arnold Schwarzenegger who helps out a woman warrior intent on vengeance. The only bright spots are bits of unintentional humor. Some violence. A-III (PG-13) PG

Red Sun (1972) The gimmick for this bloody European western teams a hard-bitten cowboy (Charles Bronson) with an inscrutable Samurai warrior (Toshiro Mifune) in order to track down an outlaw (Alain Delon) who double-crossed the cowboy and dishonored the Samurai. Along for the ride is a superfluous prostitute (Ursula Andress). Granted the fantasy plot, director Terence Young treats the derring-do with too little whimsical flair and too much prosaic gore. A-III (GP) AA

Red Tent, The (1971) Ambitious Italian-Russian re-creation of the crash of an Italian dirigible over the North Pole in the spring of 1928. Under the command of General Umberto Nobile (Peter Finch), the crew pitches a red tent, hoping to be spotted by rescuers while three of their members go in search of help. Directed by Mikhail K. Kalatozov, the classic adventure of man vs. nature aspires to epic height but blunders with a frame device of Nobile's tortured memories and feelings of failure. Gruelling picture of struggle for survival that has one of the leading characters (Sean Connery) committing suicide. A-III (G) U

Red, White and Blue (1971) Taking as its pretext the 1971 Report of the Commission on Obscenity and Pornography, the exploitation documentary even gives the President's commissioners a minute or two of interview time before getting to explicit illustrations of the report's subject. O (X)

Redhead and the Cowboy, The (1950) Farfetched western adventure directed by Leslie Fenton follows a Confederate courier (Rhonda Fleming) making her way through Union territory with the help of a genial cowpoke (Glenn Ford) and a Yankee undercover agent (Edmond O'Brien) until she reaches the hideout of a rebel guerrilla leader (Alan Reed). Stylized violence and romantic complications. A-II (br)

Reds (1981) Epic-scale re-creation of the turbulent life and times of radical American journalist John Reed (Warren Beatty), best known for his sympathetic coverage of the 1917 Russian Revolution. Also written and directed by Beatty, the production intelligently balances the sheer spectacle of events with Reed's involvement in them and his personal relations with others, especially his wife (Diane Keaton). Benign view of adultery and revolutionary politics. A-III (R/PG appeal) 15

Reed: Insurgent Mexico (1974) John Reed, the American newspaper correspondent who gained fame through his reports on the Russian Revolution, had previously covered Mexico in the revolutionary chaos of 1913-1914. Reconstructing this period is a Mexican movie following Reed's sojourn with various rebel units, his struggle to maintain his objectivity about events in the face of his inclinations to side with the oppressed, and his symbolic act of solidarity with the revolution that ends the movie. The result has the feeling of an historical document as well as a convincing character study of an idealist. A-II (nr)

Reefer Madness (1936) Reissue of a movie antique about the evils of marijuana has appeal today apparently because it is so easy to laugh at but also perhaps because it all seems so familiar. It underscores the point, however, that preachy exaggeration is the worst kind of propaganda. A-III (PG)

Reflection of Fear, A (1973) Failed Gothic horror movie about a disturbed young woman (Sandra Locke) who lives with her mother (Mary Ure) in a sinister mansion where a series of gruesome murders takes place when her estranged father (Robert Shaw) pays a call. Directed by William Fraker, the film has a good cast and moody atmosphere, but the script is muddled, with a ludicrous conclusion. Heavy-handed sexual implications. A-III (PG) 18

Reflections in a Golden Eye (1967) Screen version of the Carson McCullers' novel about the twisted relationships and abnormal inclinations of a homosexual Army officer (Marlon Brando). Directed by John Huston, the movie's treatment of its various characters communicates little insight or compassion. Exploitative nudity. O (br) X

Reincarnate, The (1971) Creepy 8,000-year-old man (Jack Creley) convinces a reluctant young sculptor (Jay Reynolds) to give up his body when he explains that a mind transplant involves the deflowering of a young virgin. Wooden acting and leaden script detailing the intricacies and advantages of reincarnation result in occult balderdash, seasoned with some coy titillation. A-III (R/GP appeal)

Reincarnation of Peter Proud, The (1975) Young man (Michael Sarrazin) dreams of his own murder in a previous life and falls in love with the woman (Jennifer O'Neill) who was his daughter in that life. Director J. Lee Thompson's muddled story has frequent nudity and graphic sex scenes. O (R) X

Reivers, The (1969) Screen version of William Faulkner's last novel about a 12-year-old boy (Mitch Vogel) from a small southern town in 1905 who is introduced to some of the realities of the adult world when taken on a trip to Memphis by a devil-may-care cousin (Steve McQueen). Director Mark Rydell has created a rich bit of Americana that owes as much to Mark Twain as to Faulkner, but its story of growth toward manhood may be perplexing for youngsters, especially a lengthy brothel sequence. A-III (M) AA

Relations (1971) The stale theme of this Danish exploitation import is the infatuation a middle-aged businessman (Bjorn Puggard) has for a scheming teenager (Gertie Jung) who gets his cash for her procurer-boyfriend (Paul Glargard). Director Hans Abramson prolongs the trio's restless relations to the point of senseless boredom. O (R)

Relentless (1989) L.A. serial killer (Judd Nelson) goes on the rampage, slaughtering victims who share his name, while a mismatched detective duo (Leo Rossi and Robert Loggia) bicker their way to a farfetched capture, though not before viewers witness the psycho's sadism up close. Director William Lustig has too many plotlines to deal with and ends up exploiting the violence and the killer's abusive upbringing. Much grisly sadistic violence and profanity. O (R)

Remains of the Day, The (1993) Having utterly sacrificed his personal life in the service of an English lord (James Fox) who ended up as a disgraced Nazi sympathizer, an aging English butler (Anthony Hopkins) journeys to the west of England in 1958, hoping to rehire and possibly risk romance with the spirited housekeeper (Emma Thompson) whose love he dutifully spurned decades earlier. James Ivory meticulously directs a splendid portrait of personal tragedy as a selfless man sadly comes to realize, in his unquestioned devotion to his master, he has missed out on the all the best things in life. A few emotional confrontations. A-II (PG) U

Remarkable Mr. Kipps, The (1941) When a lowly drapper's apprentice (Michael Redgrave) in Edwardian England inherits a fortune, his childhood sweetheart (Phyllis Calvert) saves him from being turned into a snob by a socialite (Diana Wynyard). Director Carol Reed scores with this leisurely paced, finely detailed version of H. G. Wells' gentle comedy of manners about a easygoing commoner's sudden rise in society. A bit of a stretch for youngsters. A-I (br)

Remember My Name (1979) Woman (Geraldine Chaplin), sent to prison for trying to kill her husband's mistress, returns to harass her now ex-husband (Anthony Perkins) and his new wife (Berry Berenson), at first from a distance, but then moves in for closer encounters of various kinds. The melodrama is rather flat and listless, further dragged down by mannered performances and the uninspired direction of Alan Rudolph. Rough language and adult situations. A-III (R) AA

Remember the Night (1940) Wryly sentimental romance has a New York prosecutor (Fred MacMurray) spend the Christmas recess by taking an accused jewelry-store shoplifter (Barbara Stanwyck) to his mother's home in Indiana where they fall in love, then return to face the music in court. Director Mitchell Leisen keeps the romance bright and amusing, yet gives it substance with a warm depiction of the Hoosier homestead (Beulah Bondi, Elizabeth Patterson and Sterling Holloway) and its homespun values. Innocent romantic situations and legal complications. A-II (br) A

Reminiscences of a Journey to Lithuania (1974) Independent filmmaker Jonas Mekas' record of a visit to the land of his birth is as informal as a family album and as filled with warmth and affection. Mekas serves as an always enthusiastic guide to this celebration of his past through the present and his unpretentious pleasure at showing his family bonds will most likely stimulate remembrances of one's own immigrant roots. A-I (nr)

Remo Williams: The Adventure Begins (1985) A N.Y. cop (Fred Ward) who was apparently slain in an encounter with muggers has actually been given a new identity as a member of a secret organization dedicated to seeing that justice is done despite a defective legal system. Though amoral in concept, director Guy Hamilton's movie is so divorced from reality that it is for the most part inoffensive. Aside from a brutal opening scene, the violence is muted. A-III (PG-13) 15

Renaldo & Clara (1978) Singer Bob Dylan makes his debut as a movie director by taking footage from one of his concert tours and interspersing it with some absurd and awkward episodes acted out in improvisational style by himself, his wife and friends (Sam Shepard; Ronee Blakley; Joni Mitchell; Arlo Guthrie; Joan Baez). The result is a tedious, dismal exercise in self-indulgence. Although there is some rough language, like much of the other dialogue, it is almost unintelligible. A-III (R)

Renegades (1989) An undercover cop (Kiefer Sutherland) and a Native American (Lou Diamond Phillips) uneasily join forces to nab some murderous jewel thieves. The two leads are appealing, and the stunts are hair-raising, but the storyline is implausible, and director Jack Sholder does little with a promising subplot. Some profanity, several cold-blooded murders and intense comic-book chases. A-III (R) 18

Replay (1978) When a young woman (Marie-Jose Nat) loses her memory in an auto crash, her loving husband (Victor Lanoux) seems overly solicitous in his efforts to help her regain her past. Director Michel Drach's psychological melodrama provides little more than some modest diversion, adult in theme, with infidelity figuring as a minor element in the plot. A-III (nr)

Report from China (1971) Japanese documentary filmed in 1966-1967 during the flux of the Cultural Revolution shows the total faith of the Chinese leadership in the efficacy of ideology to solve their many economic and social ills as well as their willingness to sacrifice everything for the future. A-I (nr)

Report on the Party and the Guests, A (1968) A friendly outing in the woods is disrupted when some menacing strangers escort the group of picnickers to a lakeside party where they are commanded to enjoy themselves. When one escapes the party, his friends join in the deadly pursuit. Czechoslovakian director Jan Nemec's parable on freedom and force has a threatening atmosphere of restraint and absurdity that makes for some very unsettling viewing, which is the reason it was originally banned by Communist officials. A-III (br)

Report to the Commissioner (1975) Violent urban drama about a young detective (Michael Moriarity) and his baptism of fire as a member of a New York City undercover narcotics squad. Directed by Milton Katselas, the movie is partially successful in conveying its complex vision of a claustrophobic urban hell. Sordid backgrounds and incidents. A-III (PG)

Reprisal! (1956) Buying a small ranch in an area where killing Indians is considered sport, a half-Indian cowboy (Guy Madison) has to choose sides. Directed by George Sherman, the action plot is nothing out of the ordinary but its pro-Indian slant is emotionally engaging, though not fully realized. Stylized violence. A-II (br)

Reptile, The (1966) Minor British horror movie directed by John Gilling unfolds 19th-century tale of an Englishwoman (Jacqueline Pearce) who returns from travels in Borneo cursed with the power of periodically turning into a deadly human cobra. Stylized violence and mild hokey effects. A-II (br) X

Requiem for Dominic (1991) A Romanian expatriate (Felix Mitterer) returns to his homeland during the December 1989 Revolution to help a wounded friend (August Schmolozer) but discovers the man is dying in police custody after being falsely accused as a terrorist. Using actual footage from the Revolution, director Robert Dornhelm's disjointed dramatization personalizes Romania's political oppression through the fact-based story of a committed Christian who shows remarkable compassion on his deathbed. Subtitles. Graphic views of massacred and naked corpses. A-III (R)

Rescue, The (1988) Implausible fantasy about five youngsters whose larkish, bloodless rescue of their Navy fathers from a North Korean prison camp might have been pulled off by the Hardy Boys, but not by these ragtag Navy brats. Director Ferdinand Fairfax jumps from one farfetched turn to another, with little sense of menace or suspense until the improbable climax. Some rough language and comic-book violence. A-II (PG)

Rescuers, The (1977) Two members of the International Rescue Aid Society of mice are selected to save an orphan girl in the clutches of the wicked Madame Medusa, who is ensconced on her Mississippi sternwheeler beached in the dark Louisiana swamps. The action in this Disney animated feature directed by Wolfgang Reitherman is fast and, at times, perhaps too scary for tiny tots. For all others, however, it is consistently entertaining, helped along by an imaginative group of human and animal characters and several pleasant songs. A-I (G) U

Rescuers Down Under, The (1990) Animated tale about a little boy and a beautiful eagle who must be saved from the snares of an evil poacher by Bernard and Miss Bianca, two top mouse agents. Directors Hendel Butoy and Mike Gabriel have created a delightful family fantasy, a captivating eyeful that never flags and is filled with good humor and innocent charm. Several moments of danger and menace. A-I (G).

Reservoir Dogs (1992) Inept low-budget movie about bungling gangsters (Harvey Keitel among them) featuring incessant rough language and gory brutalities that are pretentiously meant to be outrageous but only dull the sensibilities of unfortunate viewers of the aptly titled woofer written and directed by Quentin Tarantino. O (R) 18

Restless Natives (1986) Lighthearted comedy features exquisite scenic backgrounds of the Scottish highlands in an implausible story about two youths (Joe Mullaney and Vincent Friell) who devise an outlandish scam to extort money from tourists in the hope of gaining financial security before they hit the ripe old age of 20. Their only potential problem is a vacationing CIA agent (Ned Beatty). Director Michael Hoffman concentrates on the relationship between the two friends rather than the flimsy plot and its twist ending. A-II (PG)

Resurrection (1980) Engrossing but flawed drama about a woman (Ellen Burstyn) who discovers that she has the power to heal people after barely surviving a tragic accident in which she loses her husband. The screenplay by Lewis John Carlino sets up a fascinating situation, but neither Carlino nor director Daniel Petrie is able to work it out in satisfactory fashion. The spiritual side of faith healing is dealt with in very unimaginative fashion showing the afterlife, for example, as

being, quite literally, the light at the end of the tunnel. Theme and language require a mature perspective. A-III (PG) AA

Return from Witch Mountain (1978) The further adventures of the two castaway space children from "Escape to Witch Mountain" with Tony falling into the villainous hands of Christopher Lee and Bette Davis who are intent on using the boy's powers for personal gain. Tia, with the aid of the lovable kind of street gang that exists nowhere outside of Disney films, rescues him in the nick of time. Directed by John Hough, the sequel, is a movie that younger children will enjoy. A-I (G) U

Return of a Man Called Horse, The (1976) Sequel finds bored English nobleman (Richard Harris) back in South Dakota when his adopted Indian tribe needs a leader. After another gruesome purification ceremony consisting of mind-altering drugs and of having bones inserted into his chest, he leads his tribe to victory over their enemies. Director Irvin Kershner delivers a serious film, entertaining and beautifully photographed but, its emphasis on violence makes this decidedly mature fare. A-III (PG) 15

Return of Count Yorga, The (1971) Though this time the gentlemanly ghoul (Robert Quarry) falls in love (his one weakness), most of his time is spent, however, preying upon a neighboring orphanage. The sequel is properly amusing and frightening, with director Bob Kelljan sprinkling the proceedings with enough blood, however, to warrant caution for young or squeamish viewers. A-II (GP) 18

Return of Martin Guerre, The (1983) Engrossing, fact-based French production about a 16th-century peasant who abandons his wife and disappears from his native village to reappear some eight years later, much improved in every way. Accepted by his wife and most of the villagers, a squabble over property a few years later provokes the accusation that he's an imposter, and a trial with tragic results ensues. Written by Jean-Claude Carriere and directed by Daniel Vigne, the movie is partly a mystery but most of all a love story that most adults will find intriguing entertainment. Brief nudity and sexual references. A-III (nr)

Return of Maxwell Smart, The (1980) TV's secret agent Maxwell Smart (Don Adams) is assigned to thwart a villain (Vittorio Gassman) who has developed a bomb capable of destroying all the clothing in the world. Director Clive Donner's woefully inept and dull comedy relies on sexual innuendo. A-III (PG)

Return of Sabata (1972) Frank Kramer (alias Gianfranco Parolini) directs this third installment in the spaghetti western series spoofing spaghetti westerns. This time the sooty-suited hero with the twitching nostrils (Lee Van Cleef) matches wits and weapons with the Irish boss of a cardboard Texas town whose citizens are being taxed to the tune of a million dollars. Sabata comes to the rescue and sneers at the audience as he rides away from his bordello beauty and a cast full of sloppily dubbed characters. A-III (PG)

Return of Swamp Thing, The (1989) Forgettable sequel in which the crime-busting human plant (Dick Durock), a former scientist who keeps the bayou safe for kids and damsels in distress, falls for the stepdaughter (Heather Locklear) of a gene-tampering scientist (Louis Jourdan). Directed by Jim Wynorski, the cheesy sets and sleepwalking actors negate the good stuff, which includes clever make-up and the heroic antics of the asparagus stalk with a heart of gold. Some sexual innuendo, rough language, and much comic-book violence. A-III (PG-13)

Return of the Gunfighter (1966) Retired gunslinger (Robert Taylor) sets out to find the murderers of a Mexican couple who were his friends, taking along their daughter (Ana Martin) to identify them as well as a wounded cowboy (Chad Everett) he meets along the way. Director James Neilson's formula western has some good action sequences, a respect for the Mexican settlers of the Southwest and a strong performance from Taylor. Frontier violence. A-I (br) U

Return of the Jedi (1983) In the third installment of the Star Wars trilogy, Luke Skywalker (Mark Hamill) has a revealing confrontation with Darth Vader; Princess Leia (Carrie Fisher) and Han Solo (Harrison Ford) finally get somewhere with their romance; Billy Dee Williams saves the day with his air support; and R2D2 and C3PO steal some major scenes. Directed by Richard Marquand, it's fun for action fans, but the violence and tension from some of the nasty characters (Jabba the Hutt is not only scary, but disgusting) may be too intense for the younger crowd. A-II (PG) 15

Return of the Living Dead (1985) Written and directed by Dan O'Bannon, this is yet another tedious variation on the horror movie theme of the dead coming to life and devouring the living. Nudity, violence and bloody gore. O (R) 18

Return of the Pink Panther, The (1975) The Pink Panther—the sacred jewel of the Middle East kingdom of Lugash—has been stolen again and only Inspector Clouseau (Peter Sellers) can get retrieve it. Directed by Blake Edwards, the comedy is relatively innocent and, thanks to Sellers, has more then a few funny moments. Some slapstick violence. A-II (G) U

Return of the Secaucus Seven, The (1980) Nothing much happens except a weekend of talking during a reunion of seven friends who, as college students on a 1960s' protest march, once spent a night together in jail in Secaucus, N.J. Written and directed by John Sayles on a shoestring budget, the movie won't satisfy everyone, but the dialogue is bright and some of the insights are clever. The frankness of the language, especially about sex, would rule out younger viewers. A-III (R)

Return of the Seven (1966) Director Burt Kennedy's shallow, violent sequel to John Sturges' 1960 "The Magnificent Seven," lacks the original's flair and high-powered sense of adventure. Yul Brynner, Robert Fuller and Jordan Christopher are three of the deadly septet, leading a small parade back to a little Mexican town where one of their companions is being held prisoner. A-III (br) A

Return of the Soldier, The (1985) Wealthy middle-aged man (Alan Bates) returns from World War I with a case of selective amnesia. Forgotten are the years with his spoiled, ill-tempered wife (Julie Christie); remembered instead is his first love, a working-class woman (Glenda Jackson) now grown quite dowdy and, like himself, married. Well-acted English production directed by Alan Bridges from the Rebecca West novel, but the period piece is very slight and its neat resolution is unsatisfying. A-II (nr) PG

Return of the Streetfighter, The (1975) Japanese karate action film, with the villain being the American heading the Mafia branch in the Far East. Minimal production values and excessive violence. O (R)

Return of the Tall Blond Man with the One Black Shoe, The (1976) French production in which Pierre Richard again stars as the concert violinist mistaken for a superspy and unaware that he is the object of assassination attempts. This time the action takes place in Rio de Janeiro with the lovely Mireille Darc on hand as decoration, but director Yves Robert's comic touch is not nearly as deft as it was in the original. Restrained violence. A-III (nr)

Return to Macon County (1975) Two young men (Nick Nolte and Don Johnson) bound for California in a souped-up car pick up a chunky girl who constantly smiles when she is not pointing a large pistol at people and sometimes even when she is. Director Richard Compton's thin, aimless youth movie dips into sexual exploitation for want of anything better to do. O (PG) AA

Return to Oz (1985) Grim, joyless sequel to the grand Judy Garland original that attempts to make up for its lack of warmth and imagination by substituting an abundance of special effects. The scariness of some of the latter are inappropriate for pre-teenagers. A-II (PG)

Return to Peyton Place (1961) Imitation sudser with a lifeless script ineptly directed by Jose Ferrer has the illegitimate daughter (Carol Lynley) of an adulteress (Eleanor Parker) write a best-selling novel about the peccadilloes of the folks in her home town. Sexual references. A-III (br) A

Return to the Blue Lagoon (1991) Insipid fantasy in which once again a boy and girl (Brian Krause; Milla Jovovich) come of age while stranded on an uninhabited South Pacific island. Producer-director William A. Graham handles the adolescents' emerging sexuality with a self-performed wedding ceremony and a lamely predictable storyline that languidly repeats the 1980 original. Brief scenes of violence and a few shots of partial nudity. A-III (PG-13) PG

Reuben, Reuben (1983) Alcoholic, womanizing Scottish poet (Tom Conti) sponges his way through the New England campus circuit in director Robert Ellis Miller's uneven social satire that details the slow disintegration of a creative soul. The script is very literate and Conti's performance is exquisite, but his several sexual conquests compound the movie's already muddled moral perspective. A-III (R) 15

Revenge (1990) Intriguing but ultimately muddled tale of a newly retired Navy pilot (Kevin Costner) who is implausibly lured into an affair with the wife (Madeleine Stowe) of his best friend, a ruthless Mexican powerbroker (Anthony Quinn). Directed by Tony Scott, the exotic Mexican locale takes precedence over character development in this story of male friendship, betrayal and retribution. Some brutally graphic violence, several scenes involving adultery and a rape and incidental rough language. A-III (R) 18

Revenge of the Nerds (1984) Misfit college freshmen (Robert Carradine and Anthony Edwards) form a fraternity to protect themselves and fight the persecution of college jocks. The underdog heroes' attitude toward women is as reprehensible as that of their tormentors. Director Jeff Kanew's farce is full of vulgarities, much nudity and the romantic treatment of what is in effect rape. O (R)

Revenge of the Nerds II: Nerds in Paradise (1987) Director Joe Roth's silly sequel has the goofy Tri Lambdas seeking to retrieve their integrity at a fraternity conference in Fort Lauderdale. Though its theme is not to judge others on surface values, it reinforces false stereotypes of women, bad habits and vulgarity via peekaboo nudity, slapstick humor and crude sight gags. A-III (PG-13)

Revenge of the Ninja (1983) Japanese warrior (Sho Kosugi) comes to the United States where he makes short order of an illegal drug operation and battles old enemies. Directed by Sam Firstenberg, the action is mostly of the martial arts variety, but a number of weapons are used in achieving an extremely bloody victory. Excessive violence and gore. O (R)

Revenge of the Pink Panther (1978) Peter Sellers romps again as the bumbling Inspector Clouseau who gains glory, inadvertently as usual, by breaking up an international drug ring headed by Robert Webber, thanks to some timely help from Webber's mistress, Dyan Cannon. Directed by Blake Edwards, the plot is cluttered and noticeably less scintillating than its predecessors. Some sexual innuendo. A-III (PG)

Revengers, The (1972) William Holden stars as a rancher who, after his family is slaughtered by renegade Indians, dedicates his life to avenging them and, with the help of a second-string wild bunch (including Ernest Borgnine and Woody Strode), he kills just about everyone who crosses his path until gentled by an Irish spinster (Susan Hayward). Directed by Daniel Mann, this violent and bloody western has a totally unmotivated ending. A-III (PG)

Reversal of Fortune (1990) Fact-based recreation of the successful appeal by a Harvard law professor (Ron Silver) of the conviction of Claus von Bulow (Jeremy Irons) for the attempted murder of his socialite wife (Glenn Close). Director Barbet Schroeder's wickedly witty film offers several possible scenarios for the victim's two comas and details how the case was won legally without resolving the question of von Bulow's innocence. Adulterous relationships and occasional rough language. A-III (R) 15

Revolution (1968) Jack O'Connell's documentary presents a one-sided view of the hippie counterculture with an emphasis upon sex and nudity. O (br)

Revolution (1986) Director Hugh Hudson's epic treatment of the American Revolution is grand spectacle but lacks a credible human dimension. What it offers, instead, are underdeveloped characters (notably Al Pacino in the central role) and episodic plot contrivances. Violent battle scenes. A-II (PG)

Revolutionary, The (1970) College student (Jon Voight) moves from a radical student movement, to a socialist worker's organization, to a short-lived stint in the army and, finally, to an anarchists' bomb plot. The result is less the story of a young man's political radicalization than it is the meanderings of a social misfit. Paul Williams' low-keyed direction tends to level rather than highlight plot development and leaves too many significant questions unanswered. A-III (GP)

Reward, The (1965) On the arid, sundrenched plains of Mexico, a small band of bounty hunters are destroyed by their greed and moral decay. Director Serge Bourguignon's story of death in the desert makes its point about life by turning the desperate journey of the last survivor (Max Von Sydow) to reach a lake into the quest for a moral oasis. A-II (br)

Rhapsody in August (1991) Three generations of a Japanese family in Nagasaki react quite differently to a surprise visit by a U.S. relative (Richard Gere) who has come to remember the family patriarch who was killed in the American bombing of the city 45 years earlier. Writer-director Akira Kurosawa presents a poignant look at the futility of war through the eyes of the elderly who remember, the middle-aged who prefer to forget, and children who are curious about their past. Subtitles. References to the horror of mass death and destruction caused by the A-bomb. A-II (PG) U

Rhinestone (1984) Embarrassingly bad romantic match-up in which Dolly Parton tries to make a country-western singer out of tough New York cabby Sylvester Stallone. Director Bob Clark's unfunny musical-comedy exploits Parton's physical attributes and musical abilities but merely makes Stallone look silly. Vulgar dialogue and benign view of casual sex. A-III (PG)

Rich and Famous (1981) Screen version of the John Van Druten play about two very different women (Candice Bergen and Jacqueline Bisset), both writers, who preserve a friendship for more than two decades despite the strains caused by emulation and jealousy. Directed by George Cukor, the glossy soap opera pays more attention to its glamorous locations than to the human dimension of its story. The sole redeeming feature is good acting by the principals. General air of vapid amorality and two graphic sexual sequences. O (R) 18

Rich in Love (1993) A southern teenager (Kathryn Erbe) puzzles over life and love after her mother (Jill Clayburgh) deserts her father (Albert Finney) without explanation and her pregnant sister (Suzy Amis) moves back home, unsure whether she wants to stay married to her new husband (Kyle MacLachlan). Director Bruce Beresford unveils richly textured characters caught between the pain of change and the mundane joys of family living. Implied extramarital relationships. A-III (PG-13) PG

Rich Kids (1979) Uneven melodrama about the effect of divorce on two adolescents (Trini Alvarado and Jeremy Levy) whose wealthy and adulterous parents (John Lithgow and Kathryn Walker) seem unconcerned about their offspring. The two teenagers spend a weekend together in an exotically appointed bachelor apartment. The situation leads to an angry, recriminatory adult confrontation, involving spouses current and former, lovers, friends, and one or two relatively innocent bystanders. Directed by Robert Young, the movie raises but doesn't probe too deeply into questions of parental responsibility and glosses over the sexual implications of the young people's weekend together. A-III (PG) AA

Richard (1972) Political spoof with little satirical bite blending newsreel footage with staged segments in order to trace Richard Nixon's journey from whipping cookie batter of an evening in Whittier, Calif. to fireside reminiscences at the White House. Directed by Lorees Yerby and Harry Hurwitz, the resulting lampoon, more than anything else, provides proof that this is a free country. A-III (PG)

Richard Pryor Live on Sunset Strip (1982) Stand-up comic performance, with the usual obscenities and scatological references, though Pryor is in a mellower, more humane mood than in his previous performance movie. Under Joe Layton's direction, Pryor's humor and his perception of human nature are usually on target and often extremely funny, but his sexually oriented jokes and vulgar language may offend those unfamiliar with his style. A-IV (R)

Ricochet (1991) Hard-edged revenge drama pits a hero cop-turned-prosecutor (Denzel Washington) against an escaped psychopath (John Lithgow) who frames him for murder and involvement in kiddie porn. Solid action scenes and chilling performances are outweighed by director Russell Mulcahy's emphasis on killings and sexual violence. Excessive violence, the repeated use of a graphic rape scene and much rough language. O (R) 18

Riddle of the Sands, The (1984) British film about two chaps from Oxford who accidentally uncover German preparations for an invasion of England in 1901. Michael York and Simon MacCorkindale are fine as the stuffy pair who prove their mettle once the going gets tough, but they can't save a languid movie that lacks even a good villain. Director Tony Maylam succeeds best with the period atmosphere, but the intrigue and derring-do are only mildly diverting. A-II (PG) U

Ride a Wild Pony (1976) Colorful Disney adventure, set in the Australian Outback before World War I, in which a poor lad attempts to recover his pony after it has come into the possession of a spoiled cripple, the little daughter of the town's wealthiest family. It is up to the horse, in the satisfying conclusion, to decide for one child or the other. Better than average children's movie directed by Don Chaffey with some good touches of reality and a solid theme of human selflessness. A-I (G) U

Ride Beyond Vengeance (1966) After a long absence, a buffalo hunter (Chuck Connors) returns home with a sizable sum of money and then revenges on the three who steal it from him. Directed by Bernard McEveety, it is a tough, almost cynical story of human greed and brutality. Much violence. A-III (br) X

Ride the High Country (1962) Hired by a bank to escort a gold shipment from a mining camp in the Sierra Mountains, a retired lawman (Joel McCrea) takes along an old friend (Randolph Scott) who has his own plans for the ore. Director Sam Peckinpah's off-beat Western mixes in a farmer's daughter (Mariette Hartley), a novice gunfighter (Ronald Starr) and a brawling brood of brothers, but the focus is on the two veteran cowboys and their differing notions of duty and honor. Some stylized violence, sexual references and ribald humor. A-III (br) A

Ride the Pink Horse (1947) Atmospheric crime story set in a New Mexico town during a fiesta when a war profiteer (Fred Clark) double-crosses and almost kills a cynical Army vet (Robert Montgomery) who's saved by an Indian girl (Wanda Hendrix), a Mexican merry-go-round operator (Thomas Gomez) and a wry FBI agent (Art Smith). Also directed by Montgomery, the plot is full of holes but the colorful characters make the situation of more than usual interest. Stylized violence. A-II (br) A

Rider on the Rain (1970) Intriguing French mystery thriller about a newlywed (Marlene Jobert) who kills her attacker and then is afraid to tell husband, friends, or the police. After she has disposed of the body, a stranger (Charles Bronson) begins to badger her about it and a neatly matched duel of wits ensues. Director Rene Clement has hit the mark with this suspenseful melodrama, with plenty of moody atmosphere and engaging characterizations. The tribulations of the heroine are not for the youngsters. A-III (GP) AA

Riff-Raff (1993) Gritty look at what Britain's double-digit unemployment statistics mean in the life of one out-of-work laborer (Robert Carlyle) who takes a low-paying job on a nonunion construction project, becomes a squatter in a vacant apartment complex and falls for an untalented, unrealistic would-be singer (Emer McCourt). Using a largely nonprofessional cast whose accents require subtitles, director Ken Loach gets a good measure of blue-collar reality in a variation on the old story of greedy employers, exploited workers and the struggle for economic justice. Its treatment of justice themes includes a devas-

tating accident, a premarital relationship, drug use, crude humor and much rough language. A-III (R) 15

Right On! (1971) Documentary of performances by a talented but angry rock group, The Original Last Poets (Gylan Kain; David Nelson; Felipe Luciano), whose songs echo the pain and frustration of ghetto life and insist on racial pride as the means for redeeming the future. By filming the group in N.Y. slums framed by the Manhattan skyline, director Herbert Danska finds the visual equivalent to their music. Some violent and vulgar lyrics, but motivated by a sense of hope rather than hopelessness. A-IV (nr)

Right Stuff, The (1983) Screen version of Tom Wolfe's book about the original seven astronauts is an extraordinary tribute to the pioneers of the U.S. space program, notably Chuck Yeager (Sam Shepard), Alan Shepard (Scott Glenn) and John Glenn (Ed Harris). Director Philip Kaufman captures the gallant endeavor in a style that's at once respectful yet exuberant, lavishly entertaining and very inspiring. Unfortunately, a scene involving masturbation, intended as a bit of comic relief during a sequence of laboratory tests, is mature fare. A-III (R/PG appeal) 15

Rikky and Pete (1988) Australian road picture pairing a brother–sister team (Stephen Kearney; Nina Landis) who leave their wealthy family in Melbourne to start a new life in a mining town in the Australian Outback. Director Nadia Tass gets some offhand humor in scenes featuring Pete's Rube Goldberg inventions, but the focus is on Rikky who is the stronger of the two and protective of her spacey brother. Brief nudity and much rough language. A-III (R)

Rikyu (1991) A 16th-century Japanese warlord (Tsutomu Yamazaki) and his tea master (Rentaro Mikuni) perfect the art of the tea ceremony while clashing over the warlord's burgeoning political ambitions. Exquisite delicacy and simplicity mark director Hiroshi Teshigahara's homage to Japanese culture with powerful performances from the two opposed characters. Subtitles. Suicide within a cultural perspective. A-II (nr)

Ring of Bright Water (1969) London clerk (Bill Travers) leaves his computerized job to move to a small cottage in the Scottish highlands with an otter. Unpretentious British story directed by Jack Couffer proves intelligent, entertaining family fare. A-I (G) U

Rings Around the World (1966) Compilation movie showing famous circus acts from various countries produced and directed by Gilbert Cates and narrated by Don Ameche. A-I (br)

Rio Bravo (1959) Long-winded but pungent western in which a seasoned sheriff

(John Wayne) tries to keep a killer (Claude Aikens) from being busted out of jail by his brother's army of gunslingers with only a drunken deputy (Dean Martin), an elderly cripple (Walter Brennan), a callow cowboy (Ricky Nelson) and a saloon hostess (Angie Dickinson) to back him up. Director Howard Hawks savors the desperate situation and its collection of odd-ball characters as the tension builds to the long-delayed slambang conclusion. Assorted stylized violence and sexual innuendo. A-III (br) PG

Rio Grande (1950) Veteran cavalry officer (John Wayne) commanding a frontier outpost has his hands full when his estranged wife (Maureen O'Hara) arrives with their West Point son (Claude Jarman Jr.) but the untested youth proves his mettle on a raid across the Mexican border to rescue children captured by the Apaches. Director John Ford plays the commander's domestic problems for laughs but turns grimly serious in the climactic border raid. Stylized violence. A-I (br) U

Rio Lobo (1970) Stylish western with John Wayne as a Civil War veteran pursuing two traitors for hijacking an army payroll, and not perturbed in the least by a small army of hired gunslingers nor a final thunderous shootout with an entire town taking part. Under Howard Hawks' deft direction, there is plenty of rough horseplay and tongue-in-cheek references to Wayne's overweight condition and old age in general. Violence, both physical and psychological, and some adult sexual references. A-III (G) PG

Riot (1968) Realistic drama set within the grime and frustration of prison life, in which an inmate (James Brown), unwittingly caught up in fast-moving events, assumes leadership of a full-scale revolt by the entire prison. Director Buzz Kulik's movie is by no means casual entertainment, but it's very knowing about prison life and injustices. Several violent, bloody sequences bolster the dramatic action; the dialog is a bit rough. A-IV (R/GP) X

Rise of Louis XIV, The (1970) French historical drama meticulously traces the gradual assumption of power by the Sun King, from the time he assumed the crown to his undercutting the nobility by enticing them to spend their lives in the frivolous splendors of the court at Versailles. Directed by Roberto Rossellini, the re-creation of the period is beautifully exquisite and painstakingly detailed, but those uninterested in history may find the pace interminably slow. A-I (G)

Rising Sun (1993) Investigating a sex murder in a Japanese-owned building, two Los Angeles police detectives (Sean Connery and Wesley Snipes) run up against a complex cover-up involving a politically sensitive sale of an American company to Japanese businessmen who must avoid scandal at all costs. Director Philip Kaufman's coldly stylish and wholly cynical thriller from Michael Crichton's novel exploits sexual violence against women in a story presenting a disturbing view of Japanese commerce on our shores. Repeated replay of a taped graphic sex killing, some nasty violence, recurring nudity and much rough language. O (R)

Risky Business (1983) Young, enterprising prostitute (Rebecca DeMornay) persuades a high school senior (Tom Cruise) to turn his plush Chicago home into a bordello for his classmates—while his affluent parents are away on vacation. Written and directed by Paul Brickman, it is much slicker than similar exploitation movies aimed at teenagers, but it is appallingly crass in its celebration of promiscuity. Nudity and graphic sexuality as well as a benign view of deceit, manipulation and sexual indulgence. O (R) 18

Rita, Sue and Bob Too (1987) British sex farce posing as ribald social satire about two lower-class teenagers sexually exploited by a married man who in turn ruin his already failing marriage and then exploit him. Director Alan Clarke displays a callous hand in his graphic depiction of sex with minors, nudity and profanity. O (R)

Ritz, The (1976) Film version of a mediocre Broadway comedy about an Italian-American businessman from Cleveland (Jack Weston) hiding out from a murderous brother-in-law (Jerry Stiller) in a homosexual bathhouse where he is pursued by an off-key Puerto Rican singer (Rita Moreno) who thinks he is a Hollywood producer. Directed by Richard Lester, it's an ugly, disagreeable attempt at farce. Ethnic stereotyping and some foul language O (R) 15

Rivals (1972) Clunker about an Oedipal 10-year-old brat (Scott Jacoby) who is so fatally jealous of his widowed mother (Joan Hackett) and her childish second husband (Robert Klein) that he makes a humiliating mess of trying to have sex with his dumb but nubile babysitter. Director Krishna Shah is hopelessly adrift in dealing with the esoteric life-styles of Americans with too much money. Repugnant trash. O (R)

River, The (1984) Ernest but dull effort to dramatize the plight of the American farmer tells the story of a farm family (Mel Gibson and Sissy Spacek) who must battle nature, bill collectors and public indifference in their struggle to hold on to their land and livelihood. The characters simply do not come alive in an unfocused script directed by Mark Rydell. Some violent encounters and a restrained bedroom scene. A-II (PG-13) 15

River Niger, The (1976) Powerful drama about a black American's struggle to forge his own identity out of a tragic history of blacks as the eternally Displaced Persons of our nation. Though director Krishna Shah fails to overcome the stage origins of the work, this does lessen the value of its hopeful message about the choices facing our society, its moving portrait of closely knit family life and the strong performances of James Earl Jones, Cicely Tyson and Glynn Turman. Mature themes. A-III R)

River Runs Through It, A (1992) Meditative reflections on the experiences of a youth (Craig Sheffer) growing up in rural Montana in the first part of the century, chiefly comprising his relationship with his rebellious younger brother (Brad Pitt), minister father (Tom Skerritt) and the great outdoors. Directed by Robert Redford, the tone of the episodic narrative is earnest, the pace leisurely and the result largely dependent upon how one relates to the poetry of nature. Some scenes of inebriation and discreet sexual references, several shots of rear nudity, teens in a life-threatening situation and occasional profanity. A-III (PG)

River's Edge (1987) The callous sex killing of a young high school girl is viewed by her apathetic peers as an occasion for protective support of her psychopathic boyfriend who becomes the equally innocent victim of an adult psychotic (Dennis Hopper). Director Tim Hunter's picture of several troubled youths downplays emotional and spiritual issues in favor of sensationalistic profanity, nudity and permissive teen sex. O (R) 18

Riverrun (1970) When a sea-going father (John McLiam) visits the sheep farm where his daughter (Louise Ober) and her young man (Mark Jenkins) live, he is at first amused by their attempt to get back to nature and escape the dehumanization of city life, but when he learns that she is pregnant and not formally married, he is determined to take her away. Written and directed by John Korty, the contrivances of romantic melodrama are evident, but the generational theme of value systems is handled sensitively and treated with honesty. A-III (R)

Road House (1989) College-educated bouncer (Patrick Swayze) cleans up a nasty nightclub in Missouri only to incur the wrath of the town's sleazy kingpin (Ben Gazzara). In director Rowdy Herrington's modern-day western, women are the resident playthings and men the resident idiots. Interminable fisticuffs, graphic sexual encounters, nudity and endorsement of vigilantism. O (R) 18

Road Movie (1974) Wildly exaggerated melodrama about two truck drivers (Robert Drivas and Barry Bostwick) whose friendship is shattered when they pick up a fuel-stop prostitute (Regina Baff) in a story that ends with the destruction of the truck and the death of one of them. Directed by Joseph Strick, whatever intentions the movie had as social commentary on the dangers of the road is undone by the movie's meanness of characters and their rough language. A-III (nr)

Road to Hong Kong, The (1962) In the 7th and final "Road'" picture, Bing Crosby and Bob Hope play con artists kidnapped in the Orient by an agent (Joan Collins) of a would-be world dictator (Robert Morley) and they wind up on a one-way rocket trip to the moon. Directed by Norman Panama, the low-budget British production doesn't give the veteran duo much to work with, though occasionally the old boys put some new life in the stale proceedings. Stylized violence and a few mild double entendres. A-I (br) U

Road to Morocco (1942) Wacky comic romp in which castaways Bing Crosby and Bob Hope land in a desert kingdom, vie to wed its princess (Dorothy Lamour) and wind up captives of a rebel Arab chieftain (Anthony Quinn). Directed by David Butler, the third Road comedy continues the pair's genial buffoonery as small-time hustlers trying to woo Lamour amidst throwaway gags, one-liners, talking camels and occasional songs. Some mild sexual innuendo. A-II (br) U

Road to Rio (1947) After accidentally torching a carnival, a hapless pair of musicians (Bing Crosby and Bob Hope) stow away on a Brazilian-bound ocean liner where they befriend an heiress (Dorothy Lamour) hypnotized by her wicked aunt (Gale Sondergaard). Directed by Norman Z. McLeod, the 5th "Road" comedy continues the series' tradition of zany plots strewn with wisecracks, sight gags and musical interludes, this time including the Andrew Sisters and the three manic Wiere Brothers. Silly but fun. A-I (br) U

Road to Salina (1971) Dreadfully pretentious European production set in the middle of a baked salt flat where Lana Turner runs a gas station-cafe and mistakes Robert Walker for her runaway son. Her daughter (Mimsy Farmer) goes along with the situation by engaging in a sexual relationship that had originally sent the son packing. As directed by Georges Lautner, the muddled incest theme is conveyed with many arty scenes of graphic love-making. O (R)

Road to Singapore (1940) Romantic comedy about a scandal-ridden playboy (Bing Crosby) who hides out with a dim but trusted chum (Bob Hope) in a Far Eastern backwater where both fall for a local maid (Dorothy Lamour). Directed by Victor Schertzinger, the thin plot wasn't very funny but the Crosby-

Hope byplay sparked enough laughs to engender their own series in the Road comedies that followed. Some sexual innuendo. A-II (br)

Road to Utopia (1945) Bing Crosby and Bob Hope con their way to the Alaskan gold fields where they foil crooks (Douglass Dumbrille; Jack La Rue) trying to steal a rich mine from its rightful owner (Dorothy Lamour). Directed by Hal Walker, the boys are in fine form masquerading as a pair of wanted killers, with Robert Benchley's addled commentary adding to the zany proceedings. Some sexual innuendo. A-II (br) PG

Road Warrior, The (1982) Set in a post-nuclear wasteland, this Australian action thriller pits a surviving outpost of civilization clustered around a still functioning oil refinery against the barbarian horde who need gasoline for their motley assortment of vehicles. Max (Mel Gibson), a wandering loner, is chosen to deliver the gas through hostile lines. Except for director George Miller's stylish use of the setting, there is little in this blood-and-gore epic to occupy the mind. Excessive violence. O (R)

Roadie (1980) Failed spoof of rock music's subculture follows the misadventures of a country bumpkin (rock singer Meatloaf) who is convinced by a whacky groupie to become a "roadie" or general roustabout and handyman for a traveling rock group. Director Alan Rudolph offers few good sight gags and plenty of bad ones, with lots of ear-numbing music. Some jokes about sex and drugs. A-III (PG) A

Roadside Prophets (1992) Shapeless road movie follows a loner (John Doe) as he motorcycles through the Nevada desert meeting assorted oddballs and outcasts along the way, including a would-be friend (Adam Horovitz) who stubbornly trails him. Writer-director Abbe Wool needles the establishment with minimal wit and drab counterculture twaddle. Implied sexual encounter, fleeting violence and nudity, occasional substance abuse and recurring rough language. A-III (R)

Robbery (1967) Fact-based British thriller about the hijacking of the Royal Mail train with 3 millions pounds in cash and the escape of the robbery's mastermind (Stanley Baker) from the police dragnet. Director Peter Yates builds a lot of excitement and suspense, with a refreshingly minimum amount of violence. A-II (br) U

Robert et Robert (1980) Slight French comedy about two hapless and, apparently, hopeless bachelors (Jacques Villeret and Charles Denner) who meet while enlisting aid from a computerized matrimonial service and find themselves banding together against a hostile world. Directed by Claude Lelouch, the two principals are

forced to fall back upon their quirks of character to keep the humor going. Mature theme and treatment. A-III (nr)

Robin Hood (1973) Disney animated feature offers a humorous version of the exploits of the English folk hero who robbed from the undeserving rich to give to the exploited poor. The cast consists of crisply drawn animals who lend themselves to such characterizations as Robin being a crafty fox and King John as an anemic lion. Older viewers will appreciate the classic Disney-style animation under the direction of Wolfgang Reitherman, while younger viewers enjoy the comic derring-do. A-I (G) U

Robin Hood: Men in Tights (1993) Mel Brooks' wacky send-up of the Sherwood Forest legend has the band of singing, prancing Merry Men attempting to rescue the captured Robin Hood (Cary Elwes) while Maid Marian (Amy Yasbeck) reluctantly agrees to marry the dastardly Sheriff of Rottingham (Roger Rees) to save him. As co-written, produced and directed by Brooks, the goofy spoof has moments of refreshing lunacy as well as his trademark brand of tasteless jokes that make this a hit-and miss affair. Much comic violence and some crude humor. A-III (PG-13)

Robin Hood: Prince of Thieves (1991) Returning from the Crusades, Robin Hood (Kevin Costner) and his Moorish protector (Morgan Freeman) join the outlaws of Sherwood Forest in defiance of the cunning Sheriff of Nottingham (Alan Rickman) and his plans to marry Maid Marian (Mary Elizabeth Mastrantonio). Director Kevin Reynolds gives a frenzied, fresh spin to the oft-told tale which, despite many scattered flaws, boasts glorious cinematography and production design in addition to fine performances, especially Rickman's campy villain. Some gory violence and mild sexual innuendo. A-II (PG-13) PG

Robin Hood of El Dorado, The (1936) Creaky Hollywood saga of California's legendary 19th-century Hispanic outlaw, Joaquin Murrieta (Warner Baxter), who becomes a bandit after gringo gold miners kill his wife and drunken Americanos lynch his brother. Director William Wellman romanticizes the bandits and their exploits in a plot muddled by unresolved notions of justice and revenge that ultimately have tragic consequences. Considerable stylized violence and menace in treating the theme of an oppressed minority. A-III (br) A

Robin and Marian (1976) Disappointing British addition to the Robin Hood legend, set some 20 years after his youthful adventures in Sherwood Forest. Robin (Sean Connery) and his now melancholy men rescue Maid Marian (Audrey Hepburn) from a convent and the clutches of the dastardly Sheriff of Nottingham (Robert Shaw). Under Richard Lester's direction the performances are very good but the mood of the piece is confused, halfway between genuine romance and clumsy demythologizing. Some violence, crude humor and a sympathetically viewed suicide. A-III (PG)

Robinson Crusoe and the Tiger (1972) Amateurish Spanish version of the Daniel Defoe classic of shipwreck and survival, with Crusoe played by Hugo Stiglitz who double-takes his way through various episodes of being chased by everything from sharks and panthers to bats and tigers. Directed by Rene Cardona Jr., the stagey camerawork and droning narration may put the small-fry to sleep. A-I (G) PG

Robinson Crusoe on Mars (1964) Engaging sci-fi variation on the Defoe story with an astronaut (Paul Mantee) marooned on Mars with only a monkey as company, then rescuing a human-like slave (Vic Lundin) from an alien spaceship. Directed by Byron Haskin, the story is told in imaginative fashion holding interest to the end which is a new beginning. A-I (br) U

RoboCop (1987) Futuristic urban crime drama about a good Detroit cop (Peter Weller) shot up by hoods and recycled into a robotized part-man, part-machine programmed to rid the streets of crime. Dutch director Paul Verhoeven doesn't spare any blood and gore in his relentlessly graphic depiction of violent law enforcement tactics used against equally violent criminals. Conveys a dangerous ends-justifies-the-means brand of justice. O (R) 18

RoboCop 2 (1990) About to be relegated to the junk heap, RoboCop (Peter Weller) struggles to maintain his identity while searching for Detroit's drug lord (Tom Noonan), whose demonic mind is being used by an evil corporation to create a far worse enemy: RoboCop 2. Directed by Irvin Kershner, the story is overwhelmed by an endless avalanche of explosive special effects and machine gun mayhem, with the particularly objectionable use of a pre-teen portrayed as a hardened criminal. Excessive violence, intense menace and rough language. O (R) 18

RoboCop 3 (1993) Slack but violent sequel in which the part-human cop (Robert John Burke) joins Detroit's citizen rebels who have gone underground to fight the systematic destruction of their homes by the powerful development corporation that runs the beleaguered city. Directed by Fred Dekker, the long, unrelieved formula tale offers little more than wall-to-wall bullets and bloodshed. Much mindless mayhem and gratuitous violence. O (PG-13)

Rock-a-Doodle (1992) In a story combining animation with live-action, a runaway rooster (voice of Glen Campbell) finds fame as an Elvis impersonator but doesn't forget his barnyard pals when they need him. Director Don Bluth turns out a busy musical fairy tale that holds some fun for the kiddies while being tolerable for adults. A-I (G) U

Rock 'n Roll High School Forever (1991) Doltish teen comedy written and directed by Deborah Brock pits student vulgarian Corey Feldman against school disciplinarian Mary Woronos in a battle marked by gross physical hijinks, tasteless sexual situations and crude language. A-III (PG-13)

Rocket Gibraltar (1988) Limply sentimental story of a family gathering to celebrate the 77th birthday of the clan's patriarch (Burt Lancaster) whose grown children are self-absorbed yuppies with mid-career problems but whose young grandchildren (notably, Macaulay Culkin) heed his wish for burial at sea in a Viking's funeral. Director Daniel Petrie's romanticized version of life and death in a wealthy American suburb looks good but is empty of substance, both cerebral and emotional. Soggy human values, maudlin treatment of death and a benign view of promiscuity. A-III (PG)

Rocket Man, The (1954) Low-budget fantasy about an orphan (George Winslow) whose magic rocket gun saves the town orphanage from a crooked politician. Directed by Oscar Rudolph, the juvenile story offers little except veterans Spring Byington and Charles Coburn as small-town types. A-I (br) U

Rocketeer, The (1991) Dumb story set in 1938 Los Angeles where a gangster (Paul Sorvino) and a movie star-turned-Nazi (Timothy Dalton) conspire to recover a stolen rocket-powered backpack from a daredevil pilot (Bill Campbell) by kidnapping his girlfriend (Jennifer Connelly). Director Joe Johnston's lively but cornball adventure features amusing special effects which help offset the hero's colorless personality. Sporadic comic-book violence. A-II (PG)

Rocky (1976) Underdog Philadelphia club fighter Rocky Balboa (Sylvester Stallone) has a shot at the heavyweight championship with the help of a tough old trainer (Burgess Meredith). Director John Avildsen concentrates on the gritty, back-street quality of life in the old neighborhood and the relationship that grows between Rocky and the introverted sister (Talia Shire) of his best friend (Burt Young). The bloody brutality of the prizefight game is abundantly evident. A-III (PG)

Rocky II (1979) Writer-director Sylvester Stallone stars as the prizefighter unable to settle down with a new wife (Talia Shire), house and baby. Low on cash and brains, he accepts a rematch with Apollo Creed (Carl Weathers), the undefeated champ whom he almost beat in the first film. Though the sequel is formula entertainment with its theme of the victorious underdog, the movie clearly celebrates the violence of the ring, assigning value as much to the brutal sport as to its likeable hero's will and determination. A-III (PG)

Rocky III (1982) Apollo Creed (Carl Weathers) trains his former opponent (Sylvester Stallone) so that he can hold on to his title against a snarling and vicious challenger (Mr. T.). Also written and directed by Stallone, it may not be a knockout but it is good, solid entertainment. The carnage in the ring, though of briefer duration than previously, is still very intense. A-III (PG) A

Rocky IV (1985) Sylvester Stallone gets back in the ring for the fight of his life against a Russian Olympic boxing machine (Dolph Lundgren). Stallone directs himself fighting to avenge the death of Apollo Creed (Carl Weathers) while regaining American honor. The sensitive may find the fight scenes too brutal. A-III (PG) A

Rocky V (1990) When brain damage forces Rocky (Sylvester Stallone) to retire from the ring, he tries a new career as a manager but in the process neglects his wife (Talia Shire) and son (Sage Stallone) until a startling blow from his protege (Tommy Morrison) brings him to his senses. As scripted by Stallone and directed by John Avildsen, there's still energy and brutality left in the sequel formula, which this round concentrates on preserving family values despite the loss of material goods. Graphic boxing violence. A-III (PG-13) PG

Rocky Horror Picture Show, The (1975) An engaged couple (Susan Sarandon and Barry Bostwick), stranded on a back road late at night, wander into an eerie mansion where they join in the kinky games of a Transylvanian transvestite (Tim Curry) and his weird band of followers. Directed by Tim Sharman, this clumsy adaptation of a campy British musical spoofs old horror movies while trashing traditional values in a tiresome display of bad taste and moral vacuity. Excessive emphasis on sexual license and some scenes of violence. O (R) 15

Roger & Me (1989) Arresting documentary on the economically depressed city of Flint, Mich., once the prosperous bastion of good old-fashioned capitalism and now a town with 30,000 unemployed auto workers due to General Motors' plant closings. Written, produced and directed by Michael Moore, a Flint native, the work's subjective treatment contains much irony and black humor as it documents the city's decline and pitiful attempts to rejuvenate itself while trying to bring GM chairman Roger Smith face-to-face with the results of these layoffs. Some profanity laced with vulgar ethnic and sexist references and the gratuitous inclusion of a rabbit's slaughter and skinning. A-III (R) 15

Roger Corman's Frankenstein Unbound (1990) Campy sci-fi horror yarn in which a scientist from the future (John Hurt) zooms back to the 19th century for a perilous confrontation with Dr. Frankenstein (Raul Julia) and his gabby monster (Nick Brimble). Director Roger Corman jumbles genres, using gore for comic effect, in this silly but eye-catching update of the monster myth. Stylized grisly violence and a casual attitude toward promiscuity. A-III (R)

Roller Boogie (1980) Spoiled little rich girl (Linda Blair) flees parents and promising career as flutist for the joys of the roller skating rink. Director Mark L. Lester forgets the plot to focus on scenes of nubile youngsters in scanty costumes skating and dancing to disco rhythms. The boring exercise in coed velocity has little to offer its intended teenage audience. A-III (PG)

Rollerball (1975) The title refers to a brutal game invented by the rulers of a future society in order to keep their subjects docile by watching the violence of others. When one of the star players (James Caan) begins attracting his own followers, he is ordered to retire but instead leads a revolt. Directed by Norman Jewison, the movie has little to offer except the lavish violence of the game and then of the revolt, thereby exploiting what supposedly it intended to condemn. O (R) 15

Rollercoaster (1977) Slack thriller about an extortionist (Timothy Bottoms) who plants bombs on rollercoasters and the safety inspector (George Segal) who chases him across the country. Directed by James Goldstone, the movie's sole aim is visceral excitement unhindered by any larger concerns, including the risk entailed by putting such an idea into the public consciousness. Graphically depicted rollercoaster crash. A-III (PG) A

Rolling Thunder (1977) When a returned Vietnam prisoner-of-war (William Devane) finds that his wife and son have been murdered during a robbery, he sets out to exact a bloody vengeance. Written by Paul Schrader and directed by John Flynn, the movie's mayhem and slaughter exploits the serious issue of the problems of returned prisoners-of-war. Its reverence for guns approaches fetishism. O (R)

Rollover (1981) Slick romantic melodrama about a bank president's widow (Jane Fonda) who uncovers fraud in the international monetary system after Arab financiers decide not to redeposit (rollover) their huge sums in her bank, and her boyfriend (Kris Kristofferson) tries to save the day. Directed by Alan J. Pakula, the plot is so contrived that the proceedings are hard to take. Several restrained sex scenes; some rough language. A-III (R) AA

Roman Holiday (1953) Charming romantic comedy in which a young princess (Audrey Hepburn) on an official visit to Rome slips away from her stuffy entourage to see the sights in the company of two American reporters (Gregory Peck and Eddie Albert), one of whom inevitably falls for her. Directed by William Wyler, the plot begins as lighthearted fluff, proceeds with warm camaraderie along the avenues and byways of the Eternal City, then turns serious as romance blossoms until the bittersweet ending. Romantic situations. A-II (nr) U

Roman Scandals (1933) After dreaming that he's a slave in ancient Rome plotting against a corrupt emperor (Edward Arnold), a jobless menial (Eddie Cantor) awakens to save his small town from a corrupt mayor. Directed by Frank Tuttle, the musical comedy has some good gags and funny routines featuring racing chariots, laughing gas and poisoned food, but several outlandish production numbers featuring slave girls fall flat. Questionable blackface routine and sexual innuendo. A-III (br) PG

Romance of a Horsethief (1971) Folk tale set in a Polish village near the German border in 1904 where most of the peasants subsist by selling stolen horses to the Imperial German Cavalry. When the local Cossack commander (Yul Brynner) requisitions all horses and conscripts the young men for the Czar's war against Japan, some of the villagers (Eli Wallach, David Opatoshu and Lainie Kazan) turn the tables on the Russian officer. Director Abraham Polonsky tells the tale in lively farcical fashion, but some indulgent nudity and rough verbal exchanges between wily Wallach and his mistress Kazan spoil what should have a lighthearted adventure. O (GP) U

Romancing the Stone (1984) Sedate novelist (Kathleen Turner) finds herself plunged into wild adventure when she goes to Colombia to ransom her kidnapped sister, but a handsome American adventurer (Michael Douglas) turns up to save her at fairly regular intervals. Directed by Robert Zemeckis, the exotic romance strives hard for, but never achieves, a tongue-in-cheek style to take the realistic edge off the action and allow for laughs. Some graphic violence, rough language and partial nudity in a bedroom scene. A-III (PG)

Romantic Comedy (1983) Mediocre film version of Bernard Slade's play about a successful Broadway playwriting team (Dudley Moore and Mary Steenburgen), whose professionalism takes a decade or so to ripen into romance. As directed by Arthur Hiller, the movie is not very romantic or comic, but the charm of the principals makes it a shade less unbearable. Though adultery figures in the plot, it is not condoned and the whole enterprise is rather innocuous. A-II (PG) 15

Romantic Englishwoman, The (1975) Starts out in a Central European spa and quickly goes from Baden-Baden to worse in a continental triangle involving Michael Caine, Helmut Berger and Glenda Jackson. Very British production directed by Joseph Losey attempts to be civilized and very arch, but aside from an occasional joke that comes off, it is a pretentious nothing. Sexual situations and some nudity. O (R) 15

Romeo and Juliet (1968) Director Franco Zeffirelli's somewhat free interpretation of Shakespeare's tragedy of young love offers much energetic action in a stylish production with teenaged Olivia Hussey and Leonard Whiting in the title roles. Brief nude scene. A-IV (G/PG) A

Romero (1989) Powerful dramatization of the last three years in the life of Archbishop Oscar Romero of San Salvador whose condemnation of human rights abuses led to his assassination in 1980. Director John Duigan gets a brilliant performance from Raul Julia who invests the title role with an intense spiritual dimension that makes credible Romero's courage in condemning the immorality of a ruthless regime. Its graphic scenes of violence are not for the immature, though most adolescents will understand the justice issues involved. A-II (PG-13) 15

Romper Stomper (1993) Sour Australian production follows a group of skinheads who spout white supremacist slogans while brutalizing Asians and others in and around Melbourne. Writer-director Geoffrey Wright's dreary story of society's rejects and dropouts turning into Neo-Nazi thugs leads nowhere and proves as aimless as the mayhem and destruction it spends all its energy depicting. Excessive violence, explicit sex scenes, racist rhetoric and occasional rough language. O (NC-17) 18

Ronja, Robbersdaughter (1986) Swedish import directed by Tage Danielsson features two children reacting to the selfish insensitivity of their feuding families in a medieval forest setting. Exemplary for its insight and understanding about the feelings of children in relation to parental weaknesses, the movie has two brief scenes of nudity, treated innocently and humorously, in an otherwise delightfully entertaining feature for children. A-I (nr)

Rooftops (1989) Fantasy about New York City street kids who use a form of martial arts called combat dancing to defend their turf from crack dealers. Included are a thwarted love affair between a white boy and an Hispanic girl (Jason Gedrick and Troy Beyer), some comic relief by a graffiti artist (Alexis Cruz) and dastardly deeds by a crack dealer (Eddie Velez). Despite its anti-drug message and some energized music and dance, veteran director Robert Wise's urban fairy tale is no "West Side Story." Much profanity, some intense violence and a fleeting, graphic sexual encounter. A-III (R) 15

Rookie, The (1990) Determined to avenge the murder of his partner, a grizzled detective (Clint Eastwood) is hellbent on nailing the auto thieves responsible (Raul Julia and Sonia Braga) with or without the help of the new rookie (Charlie Sheen) assigned to him. Also directed by Eastwood, the inane action movie lacks imagination or interest while portraying cops as deliberate killers. Intermittent violence condoning vigilante justice, a sordid sex encounter and much rough language. O (R)

Rookie of the Year (1993) Lightweight but mostly enjoyable comedy with a 12-year-old youth (Thomas Ian Nicholas) becoming the star pitcher for the Chicago Cubs after his broken arm heals in a fashion enabling him to throw 103-mph fastballs. Director Daniel Stern pins most of the laughs on the incongruity of a youngster competing successfully with big leaguers, though adults may find the predictable results of this boyhood fantasy rather mechanical little league entertainment. Mild sexual innuendo involving adults. A-II (PG)

Room Service (1938) The Marx Brothers romp in a frenetic Broadway comedy set in a hotel where a penniless producer (Groucho) tries to land a financial backer for his new play while fending off an exasperated manager (Donald MacBride) out to evict him and his entire company from their unpaid rooms. Director William A. Seiter parlays the situation into farcical fun with the madcap antics of Chico and Harpo abetted by Lucille Ball, Frank Albertson, Philip Loeb and Ann Miller. Slapstick rowdiness not for all tastes. A-I (br) U

Room with a View (1986) Radiant romance set in Edwardian England depicts a love triangle resolved when the petulant heroine (Helena Bonham-Carter) chooses the good commoner over the wealthy toff. James Ivory directs from an adaptation of the E. M. Forster story of manners and self-determination. Scene of male nudity is a satiric comment on post-Victorian prudishness. A-III (nr) PG

Roommates (1971) Greenwich Village roommates (Dan Mason and Harvey Marks) with girlfriends who come and go, seemingly available to either, spend a good deal of their time on the street, much of it waiting to cross at intersections. Written and directed by Jack Baran, the material is so thin, so shallow, so uninspired and banal that perhaps its deepest insight is realizing how long it takes a New York traffic light to change. Casual sex scenes. A-IV (R)

Roommates, The (1973) Five permissive college girls vacationing at a California resort become romantically involved with various available males (ranging from a timid teenager to an implacable ex-husband), seemingly undeterred by the news of a perverted killer on the loose. Written and directed by Arthur Marks, the relationships are mere contrivances pandering to prurient taste. O (R)

Rooster Cogburn (1975) Two Hollywood institutions—John Wayne and Katharine Hepburn—spoof one another's on-screen and off-screen images in a Western set against some beautifully photographed Oregon locales. Directed by Stuart Millar, it's a self-indulgent exercise but, for all that, many will still find its stars most engaging performers, though youngsters likely will find it pretty tame fare. A-II (PG) U

Rope (1948) Psychotic college students (Farley Granger and John Dall) murder a classmate, place his body in a chest, then hold a party for friends, including an astute professor (James Stewart). Filming the action in a single take without cuts except to change film rolls, director Alfred Hitchcock's failed experiment results in a stagy, unconvincing drama loosely based on the Leopold–Loeb case. Grisly subject and treatment may be inappropriate for younger adolescents. A-II (br) PPG

Rosalie Goes Shopping (1990) The loving Bavarian wife (Marianne Saegebrecht) of an Arkansas cropduster (Brad Davis) is a compulsive shopper who sinks deeper and deeper into debt despite her talent for forgery and credit juggling. Director Percy Adlon's whimsical comedy about American consumerism uses its likeable heroine to poke fun at materialism as the way to economic disaster. A suggestive sexual situation and a theme satirizing the joys of greed and petty theft. A-III (PG) 15

Rosary Murders, The (1987) Resourceful priest (Donald Sutherland) tries to stop the mysterious serial killer of priests and nuns in his Detroit parish while wrestling with his conscience about revealing the clues obtained in the psychopath's confession. Eerie crime melodrama from director Fred Walton illustrates the rigors and dedication of the religious life but has several chilling murder scenes—one involving the nude body of a novice—and brief profanity. A-III (R)

Rose, The (1979) Glossy romantic tragedy

about a flamboyant, whiskey-swilling rock star of the late 1960s (Bette Midler), someone much like Janis Joplin. When she finds a man she really loves (Frederic Forrest), the blow of losing him shatters whatever stability she has left. Fine performance by Midler and the capable direction of Mark Rydell convey with some force how too much success can alienate one from all those values that give significance to life. Sympathetic depiction of illicit sexual relationships, drug and alcohol indulgence and some very rough language. A-IV (R) 15

Rose for Everyone, A (1967) Italian production directed by Franco Rossi whose treatment tends to be complacent about its charitable but promiscuous heroine (Claudia Cardinale). O (br)

Rose Tattoo, The (1955) Overwrought Tennessee Williams' drama set in a Southern port town where an emotive Sicilian widow (Anna Magnani) learns of her late husband's infidelity, takes up with a thick-headed but good-hearted truck driver (Burt Lancaster) and lets her teen daughter (Marisa Pavan) marry a sailor. Directed by Daniel Mann, the adaptation is stagey and overacted but the relationships are validly drawn with some spicy ethnic flavoring. Mature themes. A-III (br) A

Rosebud (1975) Failed, boring thriller about Middle East terrorists and their captives aboard a pleasure yacht. Directed by Otto Preminger, the movie is a plodding succession of seemingly endless sequences where each minor bit of action is talked to death in frequently redundant dialogue. Some violence. A-III (PG) AA

Roseland (1977) Three nostalgic stories set in the venerable ballroom telling of a widow (Teresa Wright) whose dancing partner (Lou Jacobi) helps her forget her dead husband; a charming gigolo (Christopher Walken) who appeals to a dancing instructor (Helen Gallagher) and a recent divorcee (Geraldine Chaplin); and an elderly German woman (Lilia Skala) who dreams of winning a dance contest despite the shortcomings of her partner (David Thomas). Directed by James Ivory, the film provides a lightly diverting, affectionate look at human foibles. A-III (PG) A

Rosemary's Baby (1968) Modern-day horror story about a young husband (John Cassavetes) who turns his wife (Mia Farrow), body and soul, over to the next-door neighbors, a coven of witches (led by Ruth Gordon and Sidney Blackmer) so she can become the mother of Satan Incarnate. Directed by Roman Polanski, the production values are top-notch and performances completely chilling, but the movie's inverted Christian elements denigrate religious beliefs. Brief nudity. O (R) 18

Rosie (1967) Wealthy widow (Rosalind Russell) alarms her heirs with her spending sprees and, to protect their inheritance, they have her committed to a high-security rest home from which she is rescued by the loyal family lawyer (Brian Aherne). Directed by David Lowell Rich, the material may be predictable but the two veteran leads make it work. Some mature treatment. A-III (br) U

Rough Cut (1980) Fluffy, implausible romantic comedy about a Scotland Yard inspector (David Niven) who blackmails a high-society kleptomaniac (Lesley-Anne Down) to set up her jewel-thief lover (Burt Reynolds) so he can be arrested. Directed by Donald Siegal, the film's pervasive amorality and sexual references make it adult fare. A-III (PG)

Round Midnight (1986) Musical tribute to the expatriate black American jazz musicians who went to Paris to perform in the late-1950s. Director Bertrand Tavernier centers the story on the friendship between a tenor saxophonist (Dexter Gordon) and a young Frenchman (Francois Cluzet), deriving much charm and appeal by interweaving original jazz performances with allusions to the art, craft and personalities of the period's jazz scene. Some harsh language. A-II (R) 15

Round-Up, The (1969) Hungarian dramatization of the Austrian repression of those who took part in the Revolution of 1848 and became guerrillas after its failure. Director Miklos Jancso gets haunting black-and-white images of the prisoners' isolation and the pressures to betray others. Some physical but mostly psychological violence and brief nudity. A-IV (nr)

Roxanne (1987) Written and performed by Steve Martin, this contemporary version of Cyrano de Bergerac is an unfunny combination of slapstick, physical comedy and perfunctory sexual tease. Director Fred Schepisi offers only a vanity production for a remarkably untalented Daryl Hannah whose portrayal of young womanhood is caught between 1960s' mindless love-child and a seductive Botticelli Venus. Slapstick violence, dumb jokes and casual acceptance of premarital sex defeat any sense of romantic idealism. A-III (PG)

Royal African Rifles, The (1953) When a shipment of machine guns is stolen enroute to British forces in East Africa at the start of World War I, the naval officer (Louis Hayward) from whom they were taken treks off into the jungle to get them before the Germans do. Directed by Lesley Selander, it's a minor adventure yarn with more talk than action, though an African corporal (Roy Glenn) proves the most interesting character. A-I (br) U

Royal Flash (1975) Disappointing tongue-in-cheek adventure in which the English hero (Malcolm McDowell) incurs the wrath of Otto von Bismarck (Oliver Reed) and gets involved in the 19th-century maneuvering to unite the German states under the Prussian king. Directed by Richard Lester, the action drags and the humor is forced rather than inventive. Romantic situations and restrained violence. A-III (PG) 15

Royal Hunt of the Sun (1969) Disappointing screen version of Peter Shaffer's play about the clash of cultures when 16th-century Spanish adventurers under Pizarro (Robert Shaw) invaded the empire of the Incas ruled by Atahuallpa (Christopher Plummer). Directed by Irving Lerner, the narrative is little more than a series encounters between the two principals who give highly mannered stage performances. A-III (G) U

R.P.M. (1970) When Gary Lockwood and fellow foul-mouthed students take over the campus administration building, college president Anthony Quinn (hopelessly miscast) gets them to stop the agitation, but a million-dollar computer has been damaged and the police intervene with brutal force. Erich Segal's script is a mishmash of easy problems and stereotyped solutions, ploddingly directed by Stanley Kramer. Unconvincing melodrama about student unrest, with much violence and sexual situations. A-IV (R) X

Ruby (1977) Murdered gangster comes back to haunt his killers, all of whom work at a Florida drive-in owned by the dead man's mistress (Piper Laurie). Directed by Curtis Harrington, the absurd and slipshod horror movie tries to shock with excessively violent and crude visual effects. O (R)

Ruby in Paradise (1993) Leaving the confines of rural Tennessee, a reflective young woman (Ashley Judd) becomes a store clerk in a Florida resort town, where she struggles to maintain her independence despite the unwanted attentions of the storeowner's playboy son (Bentley Mitchum) and being romanced by a gentle nurseryman (Todd Field). Writer-director Victor Nunez' modest drama gradually explores the inner life of a solemn young woman, unsure she can survive on her own but unwilling to trust a knight in shining armor to take care of her. A few discreet bedroom scenes, brief shots of topless dancers and a shoplifting incident. A-III (R) 15

Rudy (1993) Earnestly portrayed true story of Daniel Ruettiger, (Sean Astin), a youth so determined to play football for Notre Dame in the 1970s he overcame his slight physical stature, mediocre athletic ability, poor grades and lack of emotional or financial support from his family to gain admission to the university and wear the uniform of the "Fighting Irish." David Anspaugh's narrowly focused direction results in an inspirational but overly sentimental story in which one can admire the young man's bulldog tenacity yet find the movie rather flat and humorless. Numerous football field skirmishes. A-II (PG)

Ruggles of Red Gap (1935) Droll tale of a British butler (Charles Laughton) transplanted to the Wild West after an American cattle baron (Charlie Ruggles) wins his services in a poker game with an English lord (Roland Young). Director Leo McCarey pokes fun at the social pretensions of the newly rich cattleman's wife (Mary Boland) while centering the comedy on Laughton's gradual transformation from straitlaced servant to red-blooded frontier patriot. The comic situation and performances hold up better than the sentimental theme. A-I (br) U

Ruling Class, The (1972) Screen version of Peter Barnes' play satirizing the British upper classes in a story about the demented Earl of Gurney (Peter O'Toole in a madcap virtuoso performance) who, once he is cured of believing he is God, assumes the identity of Jack the Ripper. Directed by Peter Medak, the looney black comedy has some hilarious song-and-dance numbers, but the nonsense goes on much too long and becomes repetitive. Some may take the casebook condition of claiming to be the Deity as irreverent, but religion is not at all under attack here. A-IV (PG)

Rumble Fish (1983) Failed film version of S. E. Hinton's novel with Matt Dillon giving an overwrought Brando imitation as a teenager trying to live up to the bad reputations of his brother (Mickey Rourke) and drunken father (Dennis Hopper). Director Francis Ford Coppola's confusing portrait of a youth struggling to regain self-esteem is marred by gang-war violence, nudity and brief, graphic sex. O (R) 18

Run (1991) A resourceful law student (Patrick Dempsey) flees for his life, pursued by the mob and corrupt cops, after being innocently involved in the death of the son of a mob boss (Ken Pogue). Director Geoff Burrowes delivers a fast track of action and suspense abetted by Dempsey's winning performance and the movie's gallows humor. Considerable violence within a realistic, nongratuitous context and minimal rough language. A-IV (R)

Run After Me—Until I Catch You (1979) Soggy French farce about the owner of a canine beauty parlor (Annie Girardot) and her romance with a tax collector (Jean-Pierre Marielle). Director Robert Pouret makes a feeble attempt to show that middle-aged people can be as romantic, foolish and funny as any other age group. Adult situations. A-III (PG)

Run Before the Wind (1972) N.Y. art director (Jean Yves) races a sailboat from San Francisco to Tokyo in a semi-documentary that captures the breathtaking ocean vistas and challenging duties of the 6,000-mile contest. Written, produced and directed by Brud Talbot, the movie becomes exploitation fare by punctuating the voyage with a series of sexually graphic daydreams. O (R)

Run for Your Wife (1967) Weak comedy about an Italian's search for an American bride highlights promiscuous sex. O (br)

Run the Wild River (1971) Shooting the rapids in huge rubber pontoons is a rugged way to find adventure, the challenge here taking the form of a river in southern Mexico that had never been run before. The thrills are real enough, with boats bouncing off rocks and swirling in the foaming waters, but too much footage is devoted to travelogue excursions into the surrounding countryside to pad out a documentary short into a full-length feature. A-I (nr)

Run of the Arrow (1957) After the Civil War, an unreconstructed rebel (Rod Steiger) moves West, joins a Sioux tribe (whose chief is Charles Bronson) and tries to avert a war with Army troops (led by Ralph Meeker). Written, produced and directed by Samuel Fuller, the ambitious scenario is largely unrealized on the screen, partly because of its disjointed treatment of themes including regional rivalries, Native American tribalism and the foibles of ordinary people. Much stylized violence, some of it quite bloody. A-II (br) U

Run Wild, Run Free (1969) British story in which a mute country child (Mark Lester) is befriended by a retired Army officer (John Mills) who teaches him to train a falcon and tame a wild colt, with predictable but quite satisfying results. Directed by Richard C. Sarafian, the story has appeal for adults as well as children both for its human qualities and the delights of nature. A-I (G) U

Runaway (1984) Silly science-fiction vehicle for Tom Selleck who plays a futuristic cop on the runaway squad, a branch of the police force assigned to corralling robots that have run amok. Directed by Michael Crichton, its unintentionally funny high-tech mayhem provides passable entertainment for action fans. Some violence and brief nudity. A-III (PG-13) 15

Runaway Train (1985) Alaskan train, whose steely-black locomotive is hurtling out of control, carries two escaped convicts (Jon Voight and Eric Roberts) along with a napping railroad worker (Rebecca DeMornay). Directed by Andrei Konchalovsky and based on a screenplay by Akira Kurosawa, something has been lost in the translation. Senseless plot, excessive violence and coarse language. O (R) 18

Runner Stumbles, The (1979) Fact-based story of a gifted but morose pastor (Dick Van Dyke) of a small-town parish in the 1920s who is accused of murdering a young nun (Kathleen Quinlan) to whom he had shown special attention. Director Stanley Kramer delicately tries to avoid the sensational, but the movie's superficial treatment of the Catholic context, sketchy characterizations and a bizarre climax add up to a disappointing muddle. Because it deals with the emotional involvement of a priest and nun under extremely melodramatic circumstances, it is mature viewing fare that some may find distasteful. A-IV (PG) A

Running (1979) Aging marathon runner (Michael Douglas), who has a reputation for choking up in the clutch both in running and in life, resolves to vindicate himself and win back his estranged wife (Susan Anspach) by making it to the Olympics. Directed by Steven Hillard Stern, the grimly determined athlete featured in the foreground proves less compelling than the pageantry of Montreal's Olympics in the background. Some foul language. A-III (PG)

Running on Empty (1988) After injuring a janitor in college bombing as a protest against the Vietnam War, a couple (Judd Hirsch and Christine Lahti) have been on the run from the FBI for 15 years, but problems arise when their 17-year-old son (River Phoenix) wants to go to college and lead a normal life under his own identity. Director Sidney Lumet presents a universal family crisis within the context of an unusual family whose children have been forced to carry the burden of their parents' crime of conscience. Rough language and an implied teenage sexual liaison. A-III (R) 15

Running Scared (1986) Director Peter Hyams' rough-edged action comedy about veteran Chicago undercover cops (Billy Crystal and Gregory Hines) making their last drug bust before early retirement to the good life in Key West is waylaid by violence, harsh language, brief nudity and ethnic stereotyping. O (R) 15

Rush (1991) Two romantically involved cops in a narcotics unit (Jennifer Jason Leigh and Jason Patric) use drugs to protect their cover as junkies, then struggle with addiction and their superiors' illegal demands to frame a suspect (Gregg Allman). Novice director Lili Fini Zanuck presents a gritty, harrowing look at the drug netherworld and the moral ambiguities of the war against drugs. Graphic shots of drug abuse, occasional violence including a suicide, brief bedroom scenes with a flash of nudity and frequent rough language. A-IV (R) 18

Russia House, The (1990) A Russian

woman (Michelle Pfeiffer) sends a politically sensitive manuscript written by her former lover (Klaus Maria Brandauer) to a British publisher (Sean Connery) who falls for her while checking out the document's authenticity for Allied intelligence agencies. Director Fred Schepisi's version of the John le Carre novel lacks a sense of urgency and the romance is flat, leaving only Connery's performance and scenic Russian locations to hold interest. Mild sexual innuendo and occasional rough language. A-III (R) 15

Russian Adventure (1966) Picturesque Russian travelogue showing scenes of cities and countryside, the Bolshoi Ballet and the Moscow State Circus, but anyone hoping to learn more about what life in the Soviet Union is like will be disappointed. A-I (br)

Russian Roulette (1975) Mediocre Canadian melodrama about the attempted assassination of a Soviet leader visiting Vancouver in which a Mountie (George Segal) becomes the unwitting tool of both Russian and Canadian counterintelligence. Directed by Lou Lombardo, the plot is too convoluted for its own good but it's diverting, especially the lovely location photography. Some violence. A-III (PG) A

Russians Are Coming, the Russians Are Coming, The (1966) Inspired farce built around the accidental grounding of a Russian submarine off the coast of Cape Cod. Producer-director Norman Jewison ably handles a fine cast including Alan Arkin, Carl Reiner, Eva Marie Saint and Jonathan Winters. The movie's satire can be appreciated at several levels and will be enjoyed by the whole family. A-I (br) U

Rustler's Rhapsody (1985) Spoof of the singing cowboy movies, written and directed by Hugh Wilson and starring Tom Berenger, starts out promisingly enough but soon goes flat. A-II (PG)

Ruthless People (1986) Corrupt garment industry magnate (Danny DeVito) is delighted when his wife (Bette Midler) is kidnapped by a couple (Helen Slater and Judge Reinhold) he has wronged, but the three become friends and hatch a scheme to ruin the magnate. The hostility and profanity in this movie directed by Jim Abrahams, David Zucker and Jerry Zucker are excessive and the use of nudity in a sight gag in a movie produced by the Disney subsidiary Touchstone virtually defiles the memory of the man whose name is synonymous with family entertainment. O (R) 18

Ryan's Daughter (1970) Robert Mitchum is a rural Irish schoolteacher married to simmering Sarah Miles who develops a mad passion for British officer Christopher Jones. Huge, sweeping drama written by Robert Bolt and directed by David Lean is set along the ruggedly beautiful coast of Dingle during the explosive time of the 1916 Easter Rebellion. Caught in the middle between forces of political upheaval and old-fashioned lust is village pastor Trevor Howard. The performances of both Howard and Mitchum bring depth and breadth to match the sprawling visualization of what is, on balance, a rather confused moral drama on a theme of adultery. Brief nudity. A-III (PG) 15

Ryder P. I. (1986) Inept, humorless parody of a TV detective show starring Bob Nelson relies on silliness and gross humor for a few laughs. Sexually derived vulgarities pervade the sophomoric narrative. A-III (PG-13)

S

Sabata (1970) A sharp-eyed marksman (Lee Van Cleef) wipes out a couple of hundred baddies in record time in this tongue-in-cheek Italian western directed by Frank Kramer. Superficially this is a little above the cartoon level of derring-do. What makes it fun is the skill with which the stunts are conceived and executed and the wry wit with which the film regards its own shaggy story. Stylized violence. A-III (GP)

Saboteur (1942) Accused of sabotage, a war plant worker (Robert Cummings) flees the police to hunt down the real culprit (Norman Lloyd) and, with the help of a spunky blonde (Priscilla Lane), traps him atop the Statue of Liberty. Director Alfred Hitchcock's uneven thriller delivers the usual goose bumps as the cross-country chase leads to a homegrown nest of spies (led by Otto Kruger), though the proceedings are slowed by much wartime flag-waving. More menace than violence. A-II (br) A

Saboteur, Code Name Morituri, The (see: "Morituri").

Sabre and the Arrow, The (see: "Last of the Comanches").

Sacco & Vanzetti (1971) European co-production about two Italian immigrants, cobbler Sacco (Riccardo Cucciolla) and fishmonger Vanzetti (Gian Maria Volonte), who were convicted of murder and, despite protests that this was a miscarriage of justice, executed in 1927 by the State of Massachusetts. Director Giuliano Montaldo centers not on the question of their guilt but on the judicial process in a trial tainted by prejudice and perjury because of the pair's anarchist views. The mostly courtroom dramatization is uneven, but much of it works extremely well. Accessible for most older teenagers. A-III (GP)

Sacrifice, The (1986) Swedish production in which a group of adults and one child pass through a night of confusion and fear, including portents of a nuclear-devastated landscape. Director Andrei Tarkovsky's murky religious allegory of an aging writer's bargaining with God to save others relies upon long silences, ritualized dialog and beautiful but static photography. This is a very personal film about love and compassion. Its effect is strangely cold and distant. A-III (PG) 15

Saddles and Sagebrush (1943) Grade-B western with Russell Hayden as a straight-shooter who sides with homesteaders against a cattle baron's hired guns. Director William Berke paces the formula action plot with the singing of Bob Wills and Dub Taylor's

comic relief. Stylized violence. A-I (br)

Safe Place, A (1971) Tuesday Weld plays a New Yorker who spends most of her time in and around Central Park, remembering her past and fantasizing about the present, though no reason is ever indicated why this young woman is so tied to her childhood. Written and directed by Henry Jaglom, the movie has no substance beyond its self-conscious attempt to reflect the way a disoriented mind copes with the passage of time. A-III (GP)

Saga of Death Valley (1940) Years after his father's murder, a cowboy (Roy Rogers) avenges his death and finds his long-lost kid brother in a low-budget but effective Western directed by Joseph Kane. Unpretentious action fare with frontier violence. A-I (br)

Sahara (1943) Sturdy World War II action melodrama follows an American tank commander (Humphrey Bogart) as he picks up an international cast of survivors (among them, Rex Ingram; J. Carrol Naish; Kurt Kreuger) to make a stand at a waterhole in the desert war against Rommel. Directed by Zoltan Korda, the action is as uncomplicated as the tone is patriotic with good ensemble acting and a big finish. Wartime violence. A-I (br) A

Sailor of the King (1953) Escaping from captivity on a German raider when it anchors at a remote island for repairs, a Canadian sharpshooter (Jeffrey Hunter) wins the Victoria Cross by pinning down its crew with rifle fire until the British Navy arrives. C. S. Forester's intriguing story of naval action and personal courage in World War II suffers from Roy Boulting's pedestrian direction and a romantic subplot involving the lad's parents (Wendy Hiller and Michael Rennie). Wartime violence and discreet treatment of a premarital relationship. A-II (br)

Sailor Who Fell from Grace with the Sea, The (1976) Failed adaptation of Yukio Mishima's novel in which a sailor (Kris Kristofferson) decides to give up the sea and marry a wealthy widow (Sarah Miles), but a gang of schoolboys takes drastic action to prevent him from betraying his manly career. Writer-director Lewis John Carlino has turned this into a glossy, sentimental love story ruined by a bunch of rotten kids. Ludicrous, excessive sex scenes. O (R) X

Saint Jack (1979) Screen version of the Paul Theroux novel about an expatriate American (Ben Gazzara) who makes his way with flare and humor as a procurer in modern-day Singapore but balks at blackmailing a visiting U.S. Senator. Director Peter Bogdanovich's rather thin and slow-paced melodrama shows far too benign an attitude toward the hero's character and profession, and it also has one quite suggestive sequence. O (R) X

Saint Joan (1957) Screen version of George Bernard Shaw's play about the French heroine (Jean Seberg) whose voices led her to take up arms for her king against the English who put her to death as a heretic. Adapted by Graham Greene and directed by Otto Preminger, the result is flat and static, but Shaw's jabs at authority, secular and religious, emerge often enough to make it interesting. A-II (br) U

Saint of Fort Washington, The (1993) Impoverished Vietnam vet (Danny Glover) and the fragile schizophrenic youth (Matt Dillon) he has befriended plan to rent a small apartment by washing car windshields until victimized by a vicious thug (Ving Rhames) who preys on N.Y. City's homeless. Director Tim Hunter's realistic portrait of homeless men trying to reestablish themselves is heartbreaking, but the characters are simplistically portrayed as angels or devils. Brief violence and some rough language. A-II (R)

Salaam Bombay! (1988) After coming to Bombay to earn the 500 rupees needed by his mother to pay a debt, a 10-year-old country lad struggles to keep from being swallowed up in the sordid slums of an overcrowded city. Directed with warm humanity and some humor by Mira Nair, her work manages to avoid both sentimentality and cynicism in relating a sympathetic tale of hope amidst squalor and injustice. Though the subtitled movie affirms the human dignity of India's poor and homeless, there are several restrained scenes in a brothel, a few drug transactions and some violence, including a knifing. A-II (nr) 15

Salesman (1969) Documentary showing the day-to-day life of four door-to-door Bible salesmen who work the Boston area and then start a campaign in Florida. It is not about the commercialization of religion or the tricks of the trade, though viewers will see a little bit of both. It is essentially about the effect of this trade upon these individuals and their relations with others. Directed by Albert and David Maysles, it is a rare picture of people seen through the perspective of their line of work. A-II (G)

Sallah (1965) Israeli comedy about a Jewish immigrant from the Orient (Haym Topol) who outsmarts the bureaucratic system in its attempts to integrate him and his large family into their new community. Writer-director Ephraim Kishon has created a highly amusing satire that succeeds best with its outrageous sight gags and Topol's larger-than-life performance in the title role as the wily alien. Subtitles. A-II (nr)

Salo (1977) Italian sex fantasy directed by Pier Paolo Pasolini set in the Fascist state during the final days of World War II when four officials decide to finish their lives by perversely victimizing a group of boys and girls rounded up by their thuggish guards. O (nr)

Salome's Last Dance (1988) In yet another of his flamboyant films about eccentric artists, writer-director Ken Russell zeroes in on Oscar Wilde (Nicholas Grace) who watches as his friends (Imogene Millais-Scott; Stratford Johns; Glenda Jackson) stage a performance of his banned play "Salome." Wall-to-wall nudity, rough language of a sexual nature and much implied and some exhibited sexual activity. O (R) 18

Salsa (1988) Latino dance movie about a young Puerto Rican-American (Robby Rosa) who dreams of winning a local salsa contest in East Los Angeles but is distracted by the social blossoming of his teenage sister (Magali Alvarado) and by his new partner (Miranda Garrison). Director Boaz Davidson's minimal plot and weak acting are overshadowed by dazzling salsa numbers choreographed by Kenny Ortega. Some sexually suggestive dancing inappropriate for children or younger adolescents. A-II (PG)

Salt and Pepper (1968) Witless British espionage spoof about nightclub owners (Sammy Davis Jr. and Peter Lawford) who get mixed up in a plot against the government. Directed by Richard Donner, the mostly unfunny proceedings depend largely on sexually oriented dialogue and situations. O (G) A

Salut L'Artiste (1976) Charming French trifle directed by Yves Robert about a second-rate actor (Marcello Mastroianni), who thinks his Italian accent robs him of good roles, and his mistress (Francoise Fabian) who knows his frailties only too well. Incidental nudity. A-IV (nr)

Salvador (1987) Out-of-work photojournalist (James Woods) takes his buddy (James Belushi) on a trek to Latin America for fun and games but finds instead the harsh realities of civil war and militarism's reckless disregard for the value of human life. Profuse profanity and extensive depiction of war atrocities make director Oliver Stone's political essay palatable only for the thick-skinned and tough-minded. A-IV (R) 18

Salzburg Connection, The (1972) Fitful film version of a Helen MacInnes novel of international intrigue as various agents (Barry Newman; Karen Jensen; Klaus-Maria Brandauer) vie to find a chest containing the names of World War II Nazi collaborators hidden on the bottom of a sinister Alpine lake. Directed by Lee Katzin, aside from some sparkling but occasionally violent action sequences, the escapist adventure has little but the beautiful setting of Salzburg and the surrounding Austrian Alps to recommend it. A-III (PG)

Sam Whiskey (1969) Angie Dickinson tries to protect the family name by seducing Burt

Reynolds into retrieving some gold bars stolen by her dead husband and returning them to the U.S. Mint before the theft is discovered. Directed by Arnold Laven, the movie's sense of morality displays the same lightheadedness as that of the heroine. Some nudity. O (PG) AA

Sam's Son (1985) Hollywood producer returns to his hometown for a premiere and recalls his loving father, who always had faith in him. Writer-director Michael Landon's first feature is very sentimental, unabashedly uplifting entertainment and succeeds in large part because of some good acting. A-II (PG)

Sambizanga (1973) Effective Angolan-made drama about the colonial injustices that led to their struggle for independence from Portuguese rule, as seen in the story of a wife's search for her husband, taken by the police in a dawn raid on their village. Directed by Sarah Maldoror, it is a sophisticated study of simple people, oppressed but beginning to learn the possibility of alternatives. The enemy is presented as colonialism and not race (whites are among the revolutionaries and blacks among the police). A-II (nr)

Same Time, Next Year (1978) Screen version of Bernard Slade's slick comedy of extramarital bliss in which an accountant from New Jersey (Alan Alda) meets a demure housewife (Ellen Burstyn) at a California seaside resort in 1951, and they begin an affair that continues for the next 26 years, limited to a single weekend each year. Directed by Robert Mulligan, there is a moderate amount of cleverness and amusing lines but, though the fantasy-level of the proceedings makes somewhat less offensive the condoning of this particular brand of adultery, there remains something intrinsically offensive about the premise of the movie. O (PG) 15

Samson and Delilah (1949) Flat-footed biblical epic from producer-director Cecil B. DeMille lumbers along with Victor Mature rarely credible as the Israelite hero, Hedy Lamarr less than subtle as the pagan seductress and a labored spectacle hardly worth the effort. Stylized violence and sexual innuendo. A-II (br) U

Sand Pebbles, The (1966) Steve McQueen stars as a hard-bitten member of the crew of an American gunboat assigned to Chinese waters in 1926 to protect U.S. commercial interests by its presence during a time of social and political unrest. Director Robert Wise manages to sustain interest and suspense almost to the end of this convoluted epic, which is mostly a serious, sometimes grim study of the causes and effects of intervention by one country in the affairs of another. Some rather intense violence. A-III (M) 15

Sandakan 8 (1977) Japanese film about a feminist (Komaki Kurihara) researching the life of an old woman (Kinuyo Tanaka) who as a girl had been sold into prostitution at the beginning of the century. Director Kei Kumai has made a work of some cultural and historical value and gets superb performances, but his feminist message is rather preachy and somewhat sentimental. Mature themes. A-III (R)

Sandlot, The (1993) An adult recalls how baseball influenced his life in the summer of 1962 when, as a newcomer in town, the 11-year-old boy (Tom Guiry) makes friends with a scruffy gang of youngsters who introduce him to the national pastime's craft and lore by playing their heart out every day on a sandlot behind whose left field fence lurks a fearsome canine. Director David Mickey Evans' strained portrayal of the events of that summer rarely measures up to the narrator's supposed fond memories of them and its packaging of sentimentalized nostalgia is too superficial to provide any genuine insights into pre-teen friendships, fears, anxieties and sexual awakenings. Some fantasy menace, occasional coarse language and a few mild sexual references. A-II (PG)

Sands of Iwo Jima (1949) John Wayne gives a standout performance as a tough Marine sergeant leading his men against the Japanese in the Pacific. Director Allan Dwan's film of men in battle is a fairly realistic portrayal of island warfare and the not-so-easy courage of those who fought it. A-II (br) PG

Sands of the Kalahari (1966) British melodrama about the struggle of six survivors of a plane crash in the African desert, among them the usual assortment of good (Harry Andrews) and bad (Nigel Davenport), hard (Stanley Baker) and soft (Theodore Bikel) stereotypes. Directed by Cy Enfield, the lone woman passenger (Susannah York) is almost raped, and the proceedings are grim, thirsty going. A-III (br) A

Santa Claus Conquers the Martians (1964) Silly twaddle directed by Nicholas Webster has jolly old Santa (John Call) and two earthling tots being whisked to Mars in order to bring Christmas cheer to sober-sided Martian youngsters. Low-budget clunker awash in humbug sentimentality. A-I (br)

Santa Claus: The Movie (1985) The story of Santa Claus (David Huddleston) gets off to a good start but slows down to a crawl when a subplot about a disillusioned elf (Dudley Moore) and a wicked 20th-century toy maker (John Lithgow) is introduced. The beautiful cinematography of the North Pole and Santa's workshop is wasted on an ultimately silly and forgettable story. A-II (PG) U

Santa Fe Satan (see: "Catch My Soul").

Santa Fe Trail (1940) West Point graduate Jeb Stuart (Errol Flynn) goes after abolitionist firebrand John Brown (Raymond Massey) while vying with a former classmate, George Armstrong Custer (Ronald Reagan), for the affections of the same woman (Olivia de Havilland). Director Michael Curtiz is hampered by a weak script, though some of the action scenes still hold interest. Stylized violence. A-I (br) U

Sapphire (1959) Engrossing British murder mystery with an unflappable Scotland Yard inspector (Nigel Patrick) on the trail of the murderer of a mulatto music student (Yvonne Mitchell) who made many enemies when she began passing for white. Director Basil Dearden follows the case suspect by suspect, but the real quest is uncovering British class divisions and racial barriers. Implied sexual liaisons and bigoted racial attitudes. A-III (br) A

Sarafina! (1992) Inspired by the arrest of a teacher (Whoopi Goldberg) for encouraging black pride among her students, a teenage girl (Leleti Khumalo) confronts the oppression of South Africa's racist policies in beleaguered Soweto Township in 1986. Directed by Darrell James Roodt, this vibrant musical makes a strong human as well as political statement about racial injustice, though the abrupt cuts from brutal military killings to the schoolchildren's joyous musical numbers are distractingly ineffective. Frequent violence, including beatings, shootings and torture of youngsters, and a murderous act of retaliation by adolescents. A-III (PG-13) 15

Sasquatch (1978) Psuedo-documentary about a motley expedition's venture into the wilds of British Columbia in search of the legendary ape-like creature called Sasquatch by the Indians. The acting is atrocious and the general tone is one of tedium, which some stock footage of wildlife and scenic views does little to alleviate. A-I (G)

Sasuke Against the Wind (1973) Japanese Samurai movie about warring feudal clans whose loyalties shift back and forth while Ninja (Samurai spies) sow dissension and mistrust among their enemies. Director Masahiro Shinoda portrays the Ninja as figures of moral ambiguity, i.e., men in any period of history using violence and corruption for "higher" ends. The visually beautiful black-and-white action film has some strong violence serving to open up the question of moral values in a violent world. A-III (nr)

Satan Met a Lady (1936) Wild and woolly version of Dashiell Hammett's "The Maltese Falcon" changes hard-boiled private eye Sam Spade into wise-cracking, money-hungry Ted Shane (Warren William) snookered by a double-crossing blonde (Bette Davis at her most coquettish) into joining the search for the fabled 8th-century, jewel-laden Horn of Roland. Director William Dieterle plays the crime story as if it were screwball comedy and, though the result has many good moments with its cast of eccentric crooks (notably, Alison Skipworth and Arthur Treacher) and Shane's wacky secretary (Marie Wilson), it never quite jells into a consistent whole. Some stylized violence and sexual innuendo. A-II (br) A

Satan's Brew (1977) German movie directed by Rainer Werner Fassbinder in which an author suffering acute writer's block tries a number of desperate measures to break through, each of them involving cruel exploitation of one sort or another, sexual more often than not. Excess in sexual treatment. O (nr)

Satan's Sadists (1971) Clean-cut ex-marine (Gary Kent) battles in his own merciless manner a gang of motorcycle maniacs (led by Russ Tamblyn) in order to save a mindless coed (Jackie Taylor). Directed by Al Adamson, the crude proceedings are excessively violent. O (R)

Satisfaction (1988) Lightweight teen saga starring TV actress Justine Bateman as the leader of a high school rock band made up of four girls and one boy—all misfits until they play a summer gig at a yuppie beach resort. Director Joan Freeman updates a tired subject with some good music but unappealing characters. Implied sex scene, drug abuse by a principal character and much profanity. A-III (PG-13) 15

Saturday Morning (1971) Dated documentary recording a group-encounter session with 20 southern California teenagers talking, at times quite crudely, among themselves about parents, sex and love. Directed by Kent MacKenzie, what emerges from their statements is general confusion and uncertainty about their identity and social roles. Perhaps useful for group discussion purposes but without some mature guide, it can only further confuse young viewers. A-III (R/GP appeal)

Saturday Night at the Baths (1975) Low-budget film about the initiation into homosexuality of a young pianist hired to play at a mecca for homosexuals in New York City. The quality of its inspiration and characterization is more sad than gay. O (R)

Saturday Night Fever (1978) Brooklyn youth (John Travolta) works hard six days a week and escapes into the magic time of Saturday night at the local discotheque, where he is the king of the dance floor and girls are readily available. The movie's dramatic tension comes from the youth's gradually becoming aware of the emptiness of his life. Directed by John Badham, this vivid portrayal of blue-collar youth at play is filled with coarse language and sexual references, but it comes to grips with some fundamental and extremely painful moral and social problems. A-IV (R/PG) 18

Saturn 3 (1980) Mediocre British sci-fi movie with Kirk Douglas and Farrah Fawcett living in tranquility aboard a deep-space station until psychotic Harvey Keitel drops in with a robot named Hector who kills people who disagree with him. Directed by Stanley Donen, there is a very violent finale and some nudity in a sexual context. O (R) 15

Savage! (1973) American mercenary (James Iglehardt) brings along his carnival girlfriends when he joins rebels in their struggle to overthrow sadistic military leaders in an obscure jungle country. Director Cirio H. Santiago exploits the women for casual sex and steers hundreds of puppet soldiers into bloody massacres. Terrible rubbish. O (R)

Savage, The (1952) Involving western in which an orphaned white youth (Charlton Heston) is raised as the son of a Sioux chief, then faces divided loyalties when the U.S. orders the tribe onto a reservation. Directed by George Marshall, the clash-of-cultures theme is too patly resolved but the Indian lore and South Dakota locales are interesting enough. Some stylized violence. A-I (br) U

Savage Guns, The (1961) Clunky western directed by Michael Carreras follows a worn-out veteran gunfighter (Richard Basehart) who comes to Mexico hoping to hang up his guns for good but instead finds himself in the middle of a land war. Lots of stylized killings and assorted mayhem before the good guys win. A-II (br) U

Savage Is Loose, The (1974) Soggy melodrama about a shipwrecked family stranded on a remote island where their young son grows to adolescence and his sexual longings lead him to taunt his father (George C. Scott) to mortal combat, with winner take all, meaning Mom (Trish Van Devere). Also produced and directed by Scott, the plodding narrative is dramatically unconvincing while its treatment of incest is exploitative and the story's resolution morally unsupportable. The movie could be severely disturbing to youngsters, particularly those wrestling with their own growing awareness of sexuality. O (R)

Savage Island (1985) Director Edward Muller's story of women behind bars in the tropics is filled with violence and graphic sex. O (R)

Savage Messiah (1972) Uneven British screen biography of Henri Gaudier-Brzeska (Scott Anthony), a young French painter who came to London in 1910, began his career in a great burst of energy and died at the age of 23 in the trenches of World War I. Director Ken Russell makes convincing the young artist's brother-sister relationship with an older woman (Dorothy Tutin) who inspires his love and artistic endeavors. In placing the figure in his times, however, Russell strays over the edge of taste in some scenes at the decadent Vortex Club and in depicting at great length the crass vulgarity of a naked society girl. O (R) Z

Savage Seven, The (1968) Deadly motorcycle gang movie directed by Richard Rush makes no pretense that it is anything more than a vehicle for an exhibition of sadistic brutality and casual sex. O (br)

Savage Sisters (1974) Philippine exploitation movie about a trio of women (Gloria Hendry, Cheri Caffaro and Rosanna Ortiz) who team to hunt down the villains who have stolen a million dollars intended to finance a revolution. Directed by Eddie Romero, the low-budget action movie limps along on excessive violence and soft-core sex. O (R)

Savage Streets (1984) Director Danny Steinmann's crude and violent exploitation movie about teenage gangs and vengeance, with one of the ringleaders being Linda Blair. Sexual violence. O (R)

Savage Wild, The (1970) George Eastman wrote, produced, directed and stars in a documentary providing a remarkably vivid portrait of the lives and habits of three Alaskan wolves that he caught as cubs and photographed over a period of two years before releasing them in the wilds. Young audiences will relate to the director's daughter who shares in the raising of the cubs, though they may be slightly alarmed at seeing the grown wolves hunting down and devouring a caribou. A-I (G)

Savages (1972) Failed fable in which a primitive tribe is civilized in one day by the decaying remains of a higher culture and then that night falls back into barbarism. Director James Ivory tries an allegorical form and satiric style clearly foreign to his previous compassionate intercultural studies and the result is a hodgepodge of individual scenes that fail to mesh into a consistent whole. Some bizarre sexual scenes. O (nr) AA

Save the Children (1973) Documentary directed by Stan Lathan records the vibrant performances at the 1972 PUSH (People United to Save Humanity) Expo's celebration of the black musical heritage from basic gospel through classic rhythm and blues to the soul sound and polished nightclub swinging. The final segment is in Rev. Jesse Jackson's church, where he preaches the message of saving children and all sorts of other people in a way that has a compelling effect upon the congregation and, deservedly, the viewer. A-I (G)

Save the Tiger (1973) Harried West Coast clothing executive (Jack Lemmon) goes through a personal and business crisis over a 36-hour period and discovers that there is nothing left to believe in. Directed by John G. Avildsen, the movie is not without interest or rewards, and it is especially good at conveying a sense of the American everyman caught in the pressure-cooker of gritty, everyday life. The problem is that the character has no other values than his material affluence, and his fear of losing it evokes only pity rather than sympathy. A-III (R) AA

Say Anything (1989) Charming teen love story between a misfit jock (John Cusack) and a beautiful brain (Ione Skye) that also addresses the problematic issues of open communication, honesty and trust between parent and child. Written and directed by Cameron Crowe, the film portrays teens sensitively, with minimal profanity, some solid relationships and no blaring filler music. Though the girl ultimately has sex (off-screen) with her boyfriend, she discusses the pressures to do so with her father (John Mahoney) who does not condone the situation. A-III (PG-13) 15

Say Hello to Yesterday (1971) Through the course of a single sunny day, a British suburban matron (Jean Simmons) is encountered, pursued, and seduced by an obnoxious, devil-may-care youth (Leonard Whiting). Directed by Alvin Rakoff, the unwholesome story of a brief encounter offers implausible characters in a shallow plot about a superficial relationship whose inevitable denouement is a slightly ludicrous bedroom scene. O (PG) AA

Say One for Me (1959) Artificial melodrama about a parish priest (Bing Crosby) in an off-Broadway church who sings a little and reforms a few show people (Robert Wagner; Debbie Reynolds; Ray Walston). Directed by Frank Tashlin, the proceedings are contrived and the sentiment is somewhat hollow. A-II (br) U

Sayonara (1957) Well-intentioned but heavy-handed adaptation of the James Michener novel in which a U.S. Air Force major (Marlon Brando) stationed in Japan bucks the military's nonfraternization policy to woo a popular entertainer (Miko Taka). Directed by Joshua Logan, the cultural tour is lovely but the East-meets-West romance is forced, and a tragic subplot with an enlisted man (Red Buttons) and his Japanese bride (Miyoshi Umeki) is unconvincing. Veiled sexual inferences and an off-screen double suicide. A-II (br) PG

Scalawag (1973) Middling pirate adventure based loosely on Robert Louis Stevenson stars peg-legged Kirk Douglas (who also directs) as he sails along the California coast robbing gold-laden merchantmen, as well as hobbling upon the hardscrabble coastal area, where Mark Lester and his pretty sister are trying to maintain a faltering homestead. There's old-fashioned romance, double-crosses and a climactic fight deep inside a cave holding a fortune in gold doubloons. What is not old-fashioned is a clumsy rape attempt played for laughs. A-II (G) A

Scalpel (1978) Plastic surgeon remakes the face of a beaten-up go-go dancer to resemble that of his runaway daughter in order to cash in on a $5 million will left in his daughter's name. Directed by John Grissmer, the movie indulges in some gore, has a casual attitude toward the value of human life and uses nudity and titillating references to incest. O (PG)

Scalphunters, The (1968) Frontier trapper (Burt Lancaster) sets out to retrieve his winter haul of furs stolen by Indians who in return have left him with a runaway slave (Ossie Davis)—a situation further complicated when white scalphunters take the furs from the Indians. Directed by Sidney Pollack, the western narrative is well researched and scores some telling points on racial prejudice, but the result chiefly demonstrates what a fine actor Davis can be. Some violence. A-II (nr) PG

Scandal (1989) Based on the notorious 1963 Profumo Affair that toppled the Macmillan government, this British production sketches in the story of teenage sexual playmate, Christine Keeler (Joanne Whalley-Kilmer), and her platonic mentor, society osteopath Stephen Ward (John Hurt). Directed by Michael Caton-Jones, the movie has not a single character to stir human empathy, nor does it provide any insight into its sordid proceedings. Much nudity, sexual promiscuity, drug abuse and violence. O (R) 18

Scandal at Scourie (1953) Norman Corwin's story about a Protestant couple (Greer Garson; Walter Pidgeon) who adopt a Catholic orphan—an act that scandalizes their Canadian community. Directed by Jean Negulesco, the situation is interesting but the treatment is not very convincing. A-II (br) U

Scandalous (1984) TV journalist (Robert Hays), working on an expose of an uncle-niece team of con artists (John Gielgud; Pamela Stephenson), suddenly finds himself accused of murdering his unloving, rich spouse. Director Rob Cohen's mishmash plot becomes a wasted effort for all concerned. Some adult humor. A-III (PG) 15

Scandalous John (1971) Irascible, unpredictable old man (Brian Keith), who dreams of the old days when he and the West were young and exciting, begins imagining himself as a western Don Quixote, and the man (Alfonso Arua) hired to care for him becomes his jovial Sancho Panza as the two do battle against some land developers. Keith faultlessly treads the narrow line between comic madness and pathos in a thoroughly delightful Disney production directed by Robert Butler. A-I (G) U

Scanners (1981) Repellent Canadian horror movie about the super-intelligent people of the title whose highly developed brains can cause such things as heads to explode when they put their minds to it. Directed by David Cronenberg, the flimsy plot about tracking down some deviant scanners is only an excuse for gory special effects of explicit violence. O (R) 18

Scarecrow (1973) Uneven buddy movie about two drifters (Gene Hackman; Al Pacino) who meet on a western road, throw in together and decide to go back East to open a carwash. What follows is an odyssey of hitch-hiking and hopping freights from one tank town to another, and some of their encounters with American low-lifes are quite gross. Directed by Jerry Schatzberg, the two principals give solid performances of the mismatched characters, but the film is more discouraging than illuminating in its portrayal of the male bond. Tawdry details abound and among the sordid incidents are a brutal rape attempt, a savage prison beating and a brief but graphic encounter with a prostitute. O (R) 18

Scarecrow in a Garden of Cucumbers (1972) Amateurish musical comedy spoof about a star-struck Kansan (female impersonator Holly Woodlawn) who encounters the expected variety of vulgar N.Y. City types in quest of Broadway fame. Film school graduate Robert J. Kaplan gets a failing grade for his purported direction. A-III (nr)

Scarface (1983) Repellent remake of Howard Hawk's 1932 gangster classic is set in present-day Miami, where a Cuban immigrant and hardened criminal (Al Pacino) in no time makes it from the bottom rung to the top of the drug rackets. Director Brian De Palma's ugly, turgid, foul-mouthed and violent movie owes little to the original and is classic only in the sense of its crude self-indulgence. Perversely excessive violence. O (X/R appeal) 18

Scarlet Blade, The (see "The Crimson Blade").

Scars of Dracula (1971) Nearby villagers are unable to help three young people trapped in the castle lair of Dracula (Christopher Lee), but two of them survive after a bolt of lightening finally destroys the monster. British production directed by Roy Ward Baker is one of the less interesting of the Dracula films. Though less frightening than tedious, its visualization of blood-lust makes it inappropriate for youngsters. A-III (R) X

Scavenger Hunt (1980) Uninvolving plot about a rich eccentric (Vincent Price) whose will decrees that his fortune go to the heir that scores the most points in a scavenger hunt. Robert Morley, as his lawyer, manages to give the only dignified performance in this excruciatingly silly movie directed by Michael Schultz. A-II (PG)

Scavengers, The (1970) Demented, racist captain (Jonathan Bliss) spurs his mangy band of Confederates on to rape and murder as they commandeer a Civil War-torn Kentucky town to capture a Union gold shipment. Director R. L. Frost treats the gross killings and sexual abuse with repulsive intensity. O (R)

Scenes from a Mall (1991) The 16th wedding anniversary of a wealthy couple (Bette Midler; Woody Allen) is marked by guiltily shared secrets, recriminations and eventual insight about their honest feelings toward each other. Produced and directed by Paul Mazursky, it's a realistic story of limited wry humor that would work better as a radio play since the visual medium is wasted here. Adulterous references and minimal rough language. A-III (R) 15

Scenes from a Marriage (1974) Episodic Swedish drama about a middle-aged couple (Liv Ullmann, Erland Josephson) who, after ten years of a seemingly ideal marriage, get divorced when the husband falls in love with a younger woman. Seven years later, though married to different partners, they drift into an affair with each other, relatively happy in their newfound discovery of themselves. Written, produced and directed by Ingmar Bergman, the film uses exterior moments in the couple's relationship to tellingly reveal the interior pain and loneliness that constitute the motivation for their actions. Some may object to its depiction of the intimate details of married life but, for many, it will hit the mark for honesty and truth in showing the frail attempts by which one individual reaches out to another. A-IV (PG)

Scenes from the Class Struggle in Beverly Hills (1989) Shamelessly acid satire and sex farce focusing on a weekend with a recently widowed ex-sitcom star (Jacqueline Bisset), her family, neighbors and servants, all of whom are bored and sexually frustrated. Sex partners are swapped and bartered; clothes, sets and music are deliberately lush and peccadilloes are decadently warped. Even though Paul Bartel's direction is sharp, and the production and acting credits are top-notch, the explicit sexual focus and raw language will offend many. Nudity and lewd behavior. O (R) 18

Scent of a Woman, The (1976) Director Dino Risi's tedious, sentimental and often distasteful account of a blinded Italian army officer (Vittorio Gassman) who journeys from Turin to Naples to carry out a suicide pact with a fellow officer but is redeemed by the love of a young woman. Excessive nudity and graphic sex. O (R)

Scent of a Woman (1992) A high school student (Chris O'Donnell), needing to earn some extra money, accompanies a blind, retired military officer (Al Pacino) for Thanksgiving weekend in New York City where the despairing ex-soldier intends to live it up before killing himself. Bo Goldman's literate script and an exceptionally nuanced performance from Pacino allow producer-director Martin Brest to orchestrate an ultimately satisfying drama of human failings transformed by renewed hope. An implied sexual encounter, momentary violence, several coarse sexual references and recurring rough language. A-III (R) 15

Schindler's List (1993) Sobering account of an opportunistic German businesssman (Liam Neeson) who comes to occupied Poland to make his fortune by exploiting Jewish capital and labor but, after witnessing the increasing barbarism of Nazi racial policies and the sadistic perversions of the local concentration camp commandant (Ralph Fiennes), he risks his life by using his talents for manipulation to save the Jews in his employ. Director Steven Spielberg painstakingly restages the appalling history of the Holocaust on an epic scale that gives horrifying dimension to one man's attempt to save some innocent lives, but the narrative provides little insight into the German's moral transformation or the individual lives of his slave laborers. Realistically graphic treatment of an infamous historical period and its crimes against humanity, a few discreet sexual scenes and occasional rough language. A-III (R) 15

Schizoid (see: "A Lizard in a Woman's Skin").

School Daze (1988) Fraternity hijinks and political conflicts divide students during Homecoming weekend at the fictional, all-black Mission College. Writer-producer-director Spike Lee's musical comedy features rousing dance numbers, lackluster music and politicized lyrics highlighting differences between blacks on their own turf but unlikely to appeal to a wide audience. Explicit sex scenes and much street language. O (R)

School Ties (1992) A 1950's working-class high school senior (Brendan Fraser) gets a football scholarship to an exclusive private academy where he finds friendship and acceptance—until a jealous teammate (Matt Damon) reveals the newcomer is Jewish. Director Robert Mandel orchestrates a fine ensemble movie that dramatically explores the harmful effects of anti-Semitism. Minor fisticuffs, a few sexual references and brief rear nudity. A-II (PG-13)

Schoolgirls, The (1972) German exploitation movie directed by Ernst Hoffbauer offers dreary dramatizations of a so-called psychologist's case histories demonstrating the morality of various forms of sexual promiscuity. O (nr)

Schoolgirls Growing Up (1972) In this sequel to the German exploitation piece, director Ernst Hoffbauer offers fuller illustrations of female teenagers' lunchtime confessions, with even more gross graphics. O (nr)

Scorchy (1976) Narcotics agent Connie Stevens is ever eager to give her all in the fight against crime. Much sex, much mayhem, no intelligence. O (R)

Scorpio (1973) Good espionage thriller about a CIA agent (Burt Lancaster) who senses his number is up and tries to disappear with his wife and the money he has made selling classified information. Director Michael Winner fills in the plot, which has enough twists to satisfy spy buffs, with plenty of solid action and fast-paced excitement. The amoral world of espionage stories is very evident here and the cynicism of its characters is not for anyone who might take them seriously. A-III (PG) 15

Scott Joplin (1977) Screen biography of the gifted black ragtime composer (Billy Dee Williams) does not gloss over the less entertaining aspects of his career and grim death. Thanks to some good performances, the colorful backgrounds of the era and, above all, Joplin's music, it's an enjoyable, and at times, affecting movie in spite of the self-conscious direction of Jeremy Paul Kagan. A-II (PG)

Scratch Harry (1969) Although the film's plot had some potential for making valid comments on marriage and social values, it loses dramatic perspective on its amoral characters with the introduction of an extended lesbian sequence, a completely gratuitous love-making episode and sporadic nudity. O (R)

Scream and Scream Again (1970) British horror movie in which Vincent Price plays a mad doctor assembling living organs to create a master race. Director Gordon Hessler's thriller leaves little to the imagination by dwelling at length on violence, blood and gore. O (PG) 18

Scream, Blacula, Scream (1973) Sequel in which Blacula (William Marshall) rises from the dust to put the bite on the brothers and sisters of Los Angeles, but he winds up on the wrong end of a voodoo pin-sticking spree when he tangles with sexy Pam Grier. Director Bob Kelljan's campy B-grade horror film has fanged ghouls coming out of the woodwork at the eerie mansion where much of the action, including a gory climax, takes place. A-III (PG)

Scream of Terror, The (see: "Point of Terror").

Screwballs (1983) Mindless, unfunny comedy about five high school students and their pursuit of the one unattainable girl at their school. Director Rafal Zielinski's focus is totally on sex with excessive reliance upon nudity as a source of humor. O (R) 18

Scrooge (for 1951 version, see: "A Christmas Carol").

Scrooge (1970) This British musical version of Charles Dickens' "A Christmas Carol" concentrates on poor old misanthropic Scrooge (Albert Finney), a thoroughly craven humbug whose disagreeableness is never believable and hence all the more fun to watch. Directed by Ronald Neame, it is a light, intelligent, and very amusing effort that wisely concentrates on the plot, using song and dance sparingly but well. The acting by the ghosts (Alec Guinness; Edith Evans; Kenneth More) is especially imaginative and the mood of the film is closely tied to Ronald Searle's delightful caricatures appearing with the credits. It's a movie for those who still have enough of the child within them to be able to relax and enjoy an old-fashioned bit of make-believe. A-I (G) U

Scrooged (1988) The youngest, nastiest network president in the history of TV (Bill Murray) is forced to live through his own "Christmas Carol" until redeemed in the end from his crass materialistic view of programming and life in general. Director Richard Donner satirizes the TV ratings game and other mindless yuppie aspirations with with savvy technical effects, a large cast of notable comic performers and lots of one-liners. The satiric humor, however, is laced with vulgarities and sexual innuendo, as well as locker-room language and brief nudity. A-IV (PG-13) PG

Scuba (1973) Documentary follows six young diving enthusiasts in the Caribbean as they search the ocean floor for buried treasure, feed fish and visit the decaying hulks of ancient wrecks. Narrated by Lloyd Bridges and directed by Ambrose Gaines, there is some quite engaging underwater photography of sea life that provides an experience of nature's beauty. A-I (G)

Sea Gull, The (1968) Screen version of Anton Chekhov's play about a dacha full of characters (Simone Signoret; Vanessa Redgrave; James Mason; David Warner) quietly destroying themselves and one another through lovelessness and infatuation for the wrong people. Director Sidney Lumet brings a fresh eye to the play's tensions and impending sense of tragedy, but some will find it rather static and overlong. A-III (G)

Sea Gypsies, The (1978) Handsome widower (Robert Logan), his two young daughters, a woman photographer (Mikki Jamison-Olsen), and a little black stowaway set off on a round-the-world sailing trip, but the boat sinks off the Alaskan coast and the film becomes a family-style Robinson Crusoe adventure. Needless to say, everyone cooperates in coping with the forbidding terrain and climate and the incursions of hostile animals. Writer-director Stewart Raffill has made a pleasant and unpretentious entertainment for the whole family. Very young children, however, might be frightened by skillfully done scenes involving unfriendly animals. A-I (G)

Sea Hawk, The (1940) Classic Hollywood swashbuckler about an Elizabethan privateer whose raids on the Spanish Main end when its crew is captured and chained to the oars of an enemy galleon until their dashing captain (Errol Flynn) leads them to take over the ship and sail to London to warn the Queen (Flora Robson) of the impending attack by the Spanish Armada. Action director Michael Curtiz handles the swordplay and sea battles with gusto, abetted by a colorful host of Warner Bros. character actors (Alan Hale, Donald Crisp, Henry Daniell, Una O'Connor, among others) and a sweeping musical score by Erich Wolfgang Korngold. First-class entertainment for action fans, but its romanticized version of history with anti-Spanish stereotypes and sanitized violence needs to be clarified for young viewers. A-I (br)

Sea of Grass (1947) Draggy, episodic western from Conrad Richter's novel about a strong-willed cattle baron (Spencer Tracy) who tries to keep farmers from settling on his range, forces his wife (Katharine Hepburn) to leave when he suspects her of infidelity, then is finally broken when his son (Robert Walker) dies defending his father's honor. Directed by Elia Kazan, the socioeconomic conflict between cattle ranchers and farmers proves more interesting than the personal story of a marriage floundering in misunderstandings and unspoken feelings. Some stylized violence and references to illegitimacy. A-II (br) A

Sea of Love (1989) Nasty crime thriller about a hard-drinking, morose New York City cop (Al Pacino) who, while tracking down a serial sex killer through the personal columns, falls madly in love with his principal suspect (Ellen Barkin). As directed by Harold Becker, the cat-and-mouse situation is so convoluted and dragged out that one loses patience long before the killer is unmasked. Excessive violence, the sexual nature of the murders, several graphic sex scenes and much rough language. O (R) 18

Sea Pirate, The (1967) Mediocre Italian adventure movie about the crew of a corsair who turn to piracy when the French take all the booty, one half of which, according to the unwritten code of the high seas, belongs to the crew. Directed by Roy Rowland, its story of an outlaw hero (Gerald Barray) is leagues away from the Robin Hood legend, but its swashbuckling violence is relatively innocuous. A-II (br)

Sea Wolves, The (1981) Fact-based World War II story about some overage, overweight British civilians in India who steal into the neutral harbor of Goa to destroy a German freighter. Director Andrew V. McLaglen focuses not on the gallantry of the amateur commandos but on the derring-do of two intelligence agents (Gregory Peck and Robert Moore) who prepare the way. Preposterous subplot involves a dalliance between Moore and a beautiful German spy (Barbara Kellerman). Some violence, vulgar language and incidental nudity. A-III (PG) A

Seance on a Wet Afternoon (1964) Intelligent British mystery about a neurotic medium (Kim Stanley), her weak but compassionate husband (Richard Attenborough) and the kidnapping of a small child. Director Bryan Forbes builds a stark, somber atmosphere as riveting as it is disquieting, in a work that has a lot of psychological tension but no cheap thrills. A-II (br) A

Search, The (1948) Stationed in post-war Germany, an American soldier (Montgomery Clift) tries to find the relatives of a street urchin (Ivan Jandl) he has befriended while the boy's mother (Jarmila Novotna) desperately searches for her missing child. Director Fred Zinnemann's picture of World War II's displaced persons is entirely credible in its treatment of their problems and genuinely moving in its respect for the human dignity of all involved. A-I (br)

Search for Signs of Intelligent Life in the Universe, The (1991) In the movie version of her one-woman play, Lily Tomlin tartly interprets a dozen characters who have been affected by the women's movement during the last two decades. Jane Wagner's stageplay looks dated and John Bailey's artsy direction softens its impact, but Miss Tomlin still delivers a performance with considerable wit and some insight into modern relationships. Several sex, drug and suicide references. A-III (PG-13)

Search for Solutions, The (1980) This extremely well-done inquiry into the scientific method of problem solving is designed to stimulate the interest of youngsters. Director Michael Jackson and producer James C. Crimmins lead viewers through an imaginative and thoughtful odyssey that is part dramatization, part newscast; part interview, part straight documentary. Very entertaining as well as informative. A-I (G)

Searchers, The (1956) Returning from the Civil War, a seasoned westerner (John Wayne) stops to visit his brother's family but, after an Indian war party raids the ranch, kills the family and abducts his young niece (Natalie Wood), he sets out to rescue her in a quest that spans many years and a variety of frontier experiences that mellow the aging man of action. Classic western directed by John Ford, its themes of pioneer vs. Indian and civilization vs. the freedom of nature are conveyed through the rich and often surprisingly warm interplay of its diverse characters amid the striking landscapes of Monument Valley. Fairly balanced view of Native Americans and some frontier violence. A-II (br) U

Searching for Bobby Fischer (1993) Fact-based story of the struggle of a 7-year-old (Max Pomeranc) to become a champion chess player without becoming as obsessed by winning as are his sportswriter dad (Joe Mantegna) and single-minded tutor (Ben Kingsley). Director Steve Zaillian nicely captures the conflict between well-meaning adults and the sweet-natured child in a dark-hued, sluggishly paced movie that nonetheless has good points to make about respecting the individuality of a child. Adults in heated conflict over a child's development. A-II (PG)

Sebastian (1967) British satire about the rehumanization of a mathematical genius (Dirk Bogarde) who is so obsessed with his government work that he barely notices that all of his assistants are pretty young women, until the prettiest one of them (Susannah York) ultimately manages to make him look up from his desk and try a little tenderness. Slightly marred by cliche visits to a discotheque and an LSD-type freakout, but it has some genuinely witty dialogue and Bogarde's top-notch acting. A-III (br) A

Second Gun, The (1973) Tedious documentary attempts to prove that Sen. Robert F. Kennedy was assassinated not by Sirhan B. Sirhan, the man convicted of the murder, but by a nearby security guard. Director Gerard Alcan raises some intriguing questions but hardly supplies enough convincing evidence and his argument requires some maturity to sort things out and place them in proper perspective. A-III (PG)

Second Hand Hearts (1981) Barbara Harris plays a widow with three children, and Robert Blake is a self-described bum who marries her in a drunken stupor but awakes to face up to his responsibilities and they try to find happiness as a family. The comedy's heart, second-hand or otherwise, is in the right place, but it suffers from an uncertainty of tone under Hal Ashby's direction. Some vulgarities and a homosexual encounter. A-III (PG)

Second Sight (1989) Dim-bulb comedy about a goofy team of gumshoes (John Larroquette; Stuart Pankin) tracking down the kidnapped Cardinal of Boston with the help of a psychic (Bronson Pinchot) and a feisty nun (Bess Armstrong) who ultimately leaves the convent to tame the duo's male chauvinist (Larroquette). Directed by Joel Zwick, the result is silly and senseless. Some rough language and mild sexual innuendo. A-III (PG)

Seconds (1966) Middle-aged banker, fed up with his deadening routine, pays a mysterious organization to provide him with a new identity, but he finds his new life is not what he expected. As directed by John Frankenheimer, it's an intriguing mystery with a troubling ending. Sexually exploitative sequence. O (br) X

Secret, The (1975) French thriller about a man (Jean-Louis Trintignant) who escapes from a psychiatric ward and is given refuge by a couple (Philippe Noiret and Marlene Jobert) after telling them that he is hiding from government agents ordered to kill him. Directed by Robert Enrico, the suspense and red herrings are handled rather clumsily, but the skillful acting and characterizations keep one's attention to the chilling climax. Some violence and sexual implications. A-III (nr)

Secret Admirer (1985) A girl's anonymous love letters to a boy who is her best friend keep falling into the wrong hands, including those of their respective parents, making for all sorts of complications in this inept teenage comedy from director David Greenwalt. Benign view of teenage drinking and promiscuity, brief nudity and some harsh language. O (R)

Secret Agent Fireball (1966) Mediocre Italian spy melodrama directed by Martin Donan about an American agent (Richard Harrison) assigned to Europe to protect an international scientific project. Stylized violence. A-II (br)

Secret Agent Super Dragon (1966) Routine European-made spy melodrama directed by Calvin J. Padgett about a CIA agent (Ray Danton) who foils the plans of an underground group to control the world through a drug that turns people into human robots. Stylized violence and mild sexual innuendo. A-III (br)

Secret Cave, The (see: "The Black Pearl").

Secret Ceremony (1968) Morbid, disquieting melodrama about the unhealthy relationship between a middle-aged prostitute (Elizabeth Taylor) and a retarded girl (Mia Farrow) who, though they need help, cannot help each other. As directed by Joseph Losey, its story has a heavy touch of madness, incest, suicide and sexual shenanigans introduced by Robert Mitchum's uninvited presence. A-IV (R) X

Secret Friends (1992) Lumbering, stream-of-consciousness fantasies and memories enable a trainbound amnesiac (Alan Bates) to piece together who he is and why he has violent sexual thoughts about his wife (Gina Bellman). Writer-director Dennis Potter's trite conclusions regarding the power of guilt and sexual repression are hardly worth the time spent witnessing Ms. Bellman's hammy acting and one-dimensional characterization. Briefly violent flashbacks, much sexual suggestiveness and minimal rough language. A-III (nr)

Secret Garden, The (1993) Winning dramatization of Frances Hodgson Burnett's children's classic about a little Victorian orphan girl (Kate Maberly) who comes to live in her uncle's remote manor on the English moors, where she uncovers the mystery of a locked garden, transforms her sickly cousin (Heydon Prowse) and wins the friendship of a local country lad (Andrew Knott). Directed by Agnieszka Holland, the appealing tale of three lonely children discovering the wonder and joy of life in tending a long-neglected garden is vividly told through evocative visuals ranging from the forbidding gloom of the manor to the enchanting beauty of the natural world outside. A rich experience for all members of the family. A-I (G)

Secret Life of an American Wife, The (1968) Failed satire in which a bored suburban housewife (Anne Jackson) tries to convince a movie star (Walter Matthau) that she's a high-priced call girl. Directed by George Axelrod, the situation is not only unfunny but its blatant toying with adultery is punctuated by tasteless sight-gags and language. O (R) X

Secret Life of Walter Mitty, The (1947) Disappointing Danny Kaye vehicle from James Thurber's story of a mild-mannered proofreader of pulp magazines whose daydreams of glory turn perilously real when he helps a young woman (Virginia Mayo) save Holland's national treasures from a gang of cutthroats (led by Boris Karloff). Director Norman Z. McLeod turns Thurber's witty whimsy into broad comedy featuring frantic buffoonery, much mugging and a couple of Kaye's distinctive patter songs. Some comic violence and menace. A-I (br) U

Secret of Magic Island (1964) Real (not animated) domestic animals, employed with remarkable skill, are the only performers in this simple fairy tale that will be of special interest to animal lovers and the very young. A-I (br)

Secret of My Success, The (1987) Ambitious college-educated Kansas farmboy (Michael J. Fox) takes the sexual route to the top of the corporate ladder as a mailboy impersonating an executive in a madcap comedy about business ethics and the new American dream of instant achievement. Helen Slater is the love interest and Margaret Whitton plays the amorous woman who gets him to the top. Director Herbert Ross goes the bedroom-humor route dependent upon sexual innuendo, negative stereotypes of women and acceptance of adultery. O (PG-13) A

Secret of NIMH, The (1982) Uneven animated feature about a mother mouse who, anxious to save her family and home from a farmer's plow, seeks help from some rats with human intelligence gained inadvertently when they were subjected to various experiments at the National Institute for Mental Health (NIMH). Though director Don Bluth's graphics have the style and texture of the Walt Disney classics, unfortunately it lacks both a compelling story and a strong central character. It is on balance better than average family entertainment, with some scary moments for the very young. A-I (G) U

Secret of Santa Vittoria, The (1969) Anthony Quinn and Anna Magnani star in an adaptation of Robert Crichton's comic novel about an Italian village hiding its prize wine from the Germans during World War II. Directed by Stanley Kramer, it's broad in style, but its characters are warm and the plot is entertaining. A-II (PG) A

Secret of the Sword, The (1985) Animated feature starring He-Man, a hero who has progressed from toy to movie star. The plot has to do with He-Man's quest for his long-lost twin sister, She-Ra. Too unsubstantial to sustain a feature-length movie and the animation is entirely undistinctive. A-I (G)

Secret Policeman's Other Ball, The (1982) Filmed record of two London revues that the British Monty Python troupe did for Amnesty International. Some of the skits are very funny, but the rock interludes are undistinguished. Only for the most avid Python fans. Some sexually oriented humor and occasional rough language. A-III (R) AA

Secret Rites (1971) Italian psuedo-documentary collection of what it describes as "weird practices" from around the world. Others would call it a bizarre, vulgar and sensationalistic peep show, presented by director Ramiro Arango without pretext of cultural context or sociological significance. O (R)

Secret Service of the Air (1939) Low-budget programmer about a pilot (Ronald Reagan) recruited by the U.S. Secret Service to infiltrate a gang flying aliens across the Mexican border. Directed by Noel Smith, it's standard action fare, chiefly of interest as the first of three 1939 quickies with Reagan as agent Brass Bancroft. Some stylized violence. A-I (br) U

Secret War of Harry Frigg, The (1968) Grinning Paul Newman fills the title role in this off-base Army comedy about a private who's only adept at escaping from the base stockade, a skill that gets him promoted to the rank of brigadier general in order to help spring a covey of fellow generals from an Italian POW camp. Directed by Jack Smight, it's an unfunny clunker in which even Newman looks bad. A-II (br) U

Secret World, The (1969) Treehouse-centered world of an 11-year-old boy is the secret world of the title but that is not the central interest of this French film. Instead, it is the youth's random consideration of the relationships among his uncle, his mistress and his wife. An ambiguous friendship grows between the uncle's mistress and the youngster, which turns out to be a modified mother-son relationship, sought by the boy who has lost his real mother in a car accident. A-III (PG)

Secretary, The (1972) Amateurish melodrama about a broker who encourages his wife's affair with his best friend while he enjoys the charms of his secretary and her pot-smoking friends. Written, produced and directed by William Diehl Jr., it is blatantly sex-oriented entertainment. O (R)

Secrets (1979) Young couple (Jacqueline Bisset and Robert Powell) revitalize their sagging marriage with an afternoon of therapeutic adultery—she with a Swedish businessman, he with a woman executive. Trivial, low-budget movie directed by Philip Saville insults the intelligence while exploiting nudity and condoning adultery. O (R)

Secuestro: The Story of a Kidnapping (1994) Documentary chronicling the three months of financial negotiations between a Columbian father and the kidnappers of his 20-year-old daughter. Director Camila Motta dispassionately presents the drawn-out story of her family's ordeal in a troubled society where kidnapping is a commonplace crime. Momentary menace and an atmosphere of potential deadly violence. Subtitles. A-II (nr)

Seducers, The (1971) Italian exploitation film about a group of unpleasant people on a yachting excursion who spend the entire movie seducing one another in various combinations. Director Ottavio Alessi makes the stultifying action even more unpleasant by filming it in bilious seaweed-green hues. Stay ashore. O (X/R)

Seduction, The (1982) Failed suspense thriller about a mentally disturbed young man (Andrew Stevens) who pursues and terrorizes a beautiful Los Angeles television newswoman (Morgan Fairchild). Directed by David Schmoeller, it's a deadly dull affair that exploits the subject with a great deal of nudity. O (R)

Seduction of Inga, The (1972) Swedish exploitation movie about a rural innocent (Marie Liljedahl) trying to cope with urban males. O (R)

Seduction of Joe Tynan, The (1979) Failed melodrama about the moral disintegration of an ambitious politician (Alan Alda) whose affair with a beautiful civil rights lawyer (Meryl Streep) almost destroys his marriage and career. Directed by Jerry Schatzberg, the story borders on soap opera despite some good acting. Though the adultery is presented as wrong, it is depicted quite vividly in some bedroom scenes and there is also vulgar and profane language. A-III (R) 15

Seduction of Mimi, The (1974) Italian satire about a Sicilian metal-worker (Giancarlo Giannini) who gets fired for voting against the bosses, works hard at a factory in Turin, is promoted back to his home town but, in seeking revenge for his wife's unfaithfulness, gets unwanted help from the Mafia and becomes trapped forever serving those he had originally opposed. Written and directed by Lina Wertmuller, the theme of the poor being exploited by the powerful is entirely serious but the treatment is in hilarious black-comedy style. Some excesses in sexual treatment and language. O (R)

See No Evil (1971) Effective British thriller about a blind woman (Mia Farrow) who awakes to discover that everyone in the household has been slaughtered and panics when she realizes that the killer will return to recover some incriminating evidence. Though director Richard Fleischer doesn't play quite fair in his emotional manipulations, he achieves some high-intensity terror found in the best of Hitchcock. The violence is more implicit than explicit but its aura of psychological horror is not meant for youngsters to handle. A-III (GP)

See No Evil, Hear No Evil (1989) When a deaf newsstand proprietor (Gene Wilder) and his blind employee (Richard Pryor) are mistakenly arrested for a murder they've witnessed, they engage in comic hijinks to prove their innocence and nab the real murderers. Director Arthur Hiller's hilarious buddy movie manages, despite a flimsy plot and Pryor's excessive profanity, to keep the characters lovable and to score some points about physical disabilities. Slapstick violence; sexual innuendo; brief nudity. A-III (R) 15

See You in the Morning (1989) Heavy-handed story of the remarriage of a woman (Alice Krige) whose husband commits suicide and a man (Jeff Bridges) whose wife divorces him and how they deal with the children as well as the psychological baggage from their first marriages. Director Alan J. Pakula tries to get more than a superficial grip on the pain and humor of such blended families, but it's chock-full of precious, pretentious moments that it could well have done without. Adult situations and some rough language. A-III (PG-13) 12

Seems Like Old Times (1980) Offbeat romance about a liberal lawyer (Goldie Hawn) whose ex-husband (Chevy Chase) seeks her help when he becomes a fugitive mistakenly wanted for bank robbery, even though she is married to a stuffy district attorney (Charles Grodin). Predictable comedy, written by Neil Simon and directed by Jay Sandrich, is a guileless, innocent adult entertainment that succeeds in delivering a large number of laughs. Some bedroom pranks and occasional profanities. A-III (PG) A

Seizure (1975) Turgid Canadian chiller about a horror writer-illustrator whose imaginings become real when a group of weekend visitors arrive at his eerie estate and a series of gruesome murders ensues, everything from knifings to head crushings. Directed by Oliver Stone, the ridiculous plot renders the contrived and clumsily handled violence relatively innocuous. A-III (PG)

Semi-Tough (1977) Burt Reynolds and Kris Kristofferson star in a comedy about pro football players and their playmates. Directed by Michael Ritchie, it has some genuinely funny moments, but its satiric focus is unclear, often turning nasty and relying for humor on foul language and nudity. O (R)

Send Me No Flowers (1964) Flimsy romantic comedy sputters along with a hypochondriac (Rock Hudson) mistakenly convinced he has only a few weeks to live and obsessed with finding a second husband for his future widow (Doris Day) who interprets his odd behavior as evidence of an affair. Director Norman Jewison plays the anemic proceedings as broad farce but the only laughs come from the supporting cast (Tony Randall, Paul Lynde and Edward Andrews). Silly romantic misunderstandings. A-II (br) A

Sender, The (1982) Horror clunker about a troubled amnesiac (Zeliko Ivanel) in the care of a pretty psychiatrist (Kathryn Harrold), given to wearing provocative clothing, who discovers that her patient has the deadly power to transmit his nightmares to other people. Directed by Roger Christian, this incoherent and violent movie contains gore, sexual innuendo and flirts with blasphemy. O (R) 18

Sense of Loss, A (1972) In his disturbing documentary about the violent strife in

Northern Ireland, Marcel Ophuls examines the conflict by allowing its inhabitants, from all corners and levels, to speak for themselves. The result is a document that addresses with chilling directness a situation apparently beyond control of political forces and national aims and, indeed, very nearly beyond rational comprehension. A-II (nr)

Senso (1970) Set in the 19th century during the time of Garibaldi, this 1954 Italian melodrama relates the story of a passionately indiscreet countess (Alida Valli) and an unscrupulous lieutenant (Farley Granger). Directed by Luchino Visconti, the movie probes the relationship of personal and class attitudes, love and infidelity, evoking the ambivalences and decadence of a society in transition. A-III (nr) A

Sensual Man, The (1977) Giancarlo Giannini is wasted in this muddled movie about the sexual misadventures of the lustful son of a noble Sicilian family. Writer-director Marco Vicario has taken Vitaliano Brancati's acclaimed novel, one of whose themes was the linking of sexual exploitation with the economic and social, and made a fatuous and tedious movie that itself exploits sex. O (R)

Sensuous Teenager, The (1972) French exploitation movie directed by Max Pecas with Sandra Jullien acting the role of an incontinent nymphomaniac in a soft-core sex fantasy. O (R)

Sentinel, The (1977) Young couple (Christina Raines and Chris Sarandon) experiences terror and unnatural phenomena in a New York brownstone. Although director Michael Winner's horror movie purports to depict a struggle between good and evil, it deals in gross violence and nudity. O (R) 18

Separate Beds (see: "The Wheeler Dealers").

Separate Peace, A (1972) Faithful screen version of the novel by John Knowles, set in a New England prep school just before World War II, in which a shy and studious student (Parker Stevenson) leaves adolescence forever behind after inadvertently causing the death of his gregarious and athletic roommate (John Heyl). Directed by Larry Peerce, the film captures the spirit of the original in its ambiguous statement about the effect of the past in the formation of the mature adult. A-II (PG)

September Affair (1950) Slick tale of a romantic triangle involving a successful engineer (Joseph Cotton) who leaves wife (Jessica Tandy) and son for Italy and a mid-life crisis with a pianist (Joan Fontaine) after both are reported dead in a plane crash. Director William Dieterle pulls out all the emotional stops with romantic music and picturesque sites in Rome, Naples and Florence, but the wistful love story is strictly a formula affair and its reaffirmation of the bonds of marriage rings hollow. Discreet treatment of an unmarried relationship. A-III (br) A

September 30, 1955 (see: "24 Hours of the Rebel").

Serafino (1970) An earthy Italian comedy concerning the misadventures, mainly amorous, of a lustful but dense shepherd (Adriano Celentano) who is almost snared by his beautiful cousin (Ottavia Piccolo) but escapes marriage at the cost of his lean inheritance. Director Pietro Germi departs from his usual sophisticated brand of satire for a gritty, sweaty, extremely loud comedy with only modest results. Bawdy humor and coarse language. A-III (GP)

Serail (1976) Stylish French movie about a novelist who buys a chateau because he is intrigued by the odd behavior of its housekeeper (Leslie Caron), its owner (Marie-France Pisier) and its apparent ghost (Bulle Ogier). Written and directed by Eduardo de Gregorio, the mystery deepens until, at last, the mood shifts from suspense to horror. A sequence employs sexually explicit dialogue as unnecessary as it is offensive. O (R)

Sergeant, The (1968) Outwardly tough but inwardly unstable Army sergeant (Rod Steiger) gets into real trouble when a young recruit (John Phillip Law) challenges his latent-homosexual superior. Director John Flynn helps enhance Steiger's fine performance by carefully creating the bleak post-war Army environment with effective detail in this solid, finely wrought, adult drama. A-III (R) X

Sergeant Rutledge (1960) Good western in which a black trooper (Woody Strode) faces a court martial charged with murder and rape. Director John Ford tells the story in flashbacks as the court examines the evidence, with Strode coming across as a strong figure of considerable integrity. A-II (br)

Sergeant Ryker (1968) Korean War story of a soldier (Lee Marvin) accused of collaborating with the enemy but who insists he was following the orders of an officer now dead. Directed by Buzz Kulik, the courtroom drama raises a number of moral questions about responsibility in wartime. A-II (br)

Sergeant York (1941) In the dark months preceding America's entry into World War II, Gary Cooper had one of his best roles as Alvin C. York, a backwoodsman from the Tennessee hills who wrestled with his religious conviction that killing was immoral to become a battlefield hero in World War I. Director Howard Hawks succeeds best in evoking the honest, homespun virtues of rural America but is less convincing in portraying the moral conflict between pacifism and patriotism. Though its resolution may seem dated today, the issue remains basically unchanged in our nuclear age. Wartime violence. A-I (br) A

Serial (1980) Cynical social satire about the effects of experimenting with hedonistic life-styles and the narcissistic search for cures by a California couple (Martin Mull and Tuesday Weld) and their rebellious teenage daughter (Jennifer McAlister). Directed by Bill Persky, the movie lacks the intelligence and integrity to carry off the satire and settles instead for sexual orgies, nudity, rough language and easy stereotypes. O (R) 18

Serpent, The (see: "Night Flight from Moscow").

Serpent and the Rainbow, The (1988) Failed horror movie about an American anthropologist (Bill Pullman) in Haiti whose quest to learn the voodoo secret of turning people into zombies leads to his being buried alive. Director Wes Craven is anything but subtle in his depiction of occult practices and rituals. Excessively gory visuals and graphic bedroom scene. O (R) 18

Serpent's Egg, The (1978) Director Ingmar Bergman's story of an American Jew (David Carradine) stranded in Berlin in 1923, with the German economy in total collapse and anti-Semitism on the rise is a dramatic muddlement that seems to be aiming at some sort of political commentary but failing badly. The somberness of its atmosphere and its vivid depictions of the squalor of the times make it decidedly mature fare. A-IV (R) X

Serpico (1973) Film version of the life and hard times of Frank Serpico (Al Pacino), the New York City patrolman whose disclosure of deep and insidious corruption within the police force went unheard until he told the press, after which a commission was set up to reform the department. Director Sidney Lumet's movie is gritty and uncompromising, convincingly realistic, yet engrossing in its human drama and tension. Its theme of corruption is unpleasantly graphic and some will find its implications frightening. A-IV (R) 18

Servant and Mistress (1978) French melodrama about a man (Victor Lanoux) who comes to claim his inheritance when his wealthy uncle dies but finds that the entire estate has been left to the maid (Andrea Ferreol). Seeking revenge, she gives him the option of leaving without a penny or staying on as her servant. Director Bruno Gantillon's well-acted but tedious parable on the misuse of power in human relations is seriously offensive in several scenes of sexuality. O (nr)

Set-Up, The (1949) Classic picture of the fight game in which an aging boxer (Robert Ryan) refuses to take a dive in a bout his manager has agreed to fix and suffers the consequences when he scores a KO. Directed by Robert Wise, the brutality inside the ring is reflected in the bloodlust of the spectators and the hard cases who make their living off prizefights. Ryan brings an inner sense of dignity to the role as does Audrey Totter as his caring wife. The violence is brutal but meaningful. A-III (br) A

Seven Alone (1975) Disappointing re-creation of an historical incident that took place in 1843 when seven children, led by their 14-year-old brother (Stewart Peterson), traveled a good portion of the Oregon Trail on their own after losing their parents. Earl Bellamy's uncertain direction lacks the feel of pioneer realities and stereotypes the Indians. Fair viewing for children if there is nothing else to see, but don't expect a great deal. A-I (G)

Seven Beauties (1976) Italian tragicomedy about a petty crook (Giancarlo Giannini) in 1930s' Naples who bungles a murder, gets drafted in World War II, deserts while being shipped to the Russian front, is interned in a concentration camp but survives having learned nothing. Director Lina Wertmuller's vision, though dark and stormy, is also permeated with a love for the beauty and richness of life. Some grisly violence and an earthy treatment of sex. A-IV (R)

Seven Brides for Seven Brothers (1954) Western musical about Oregon pioneers who, when their brother (Howard Keel) brings home a bride (Jane Powell), go out and kidnap some local belles. Directed by Stanley Donen, the zest of the music, dancing and story carry the movie in highly enjoyable fashion. A-II (br) U

Seven Cities of Gold (1955) Plodding melodrama about Spanish conquistadores hunting for Indian gold with the good Padre Junipero Serra (Michael Rennie) trying to avert bloodshed. Directed by Robert D. Webb, it's a well-intentioned but shallow historical adventure. A-I (br) U

Seven Days Leave (1942) Witless comedy directed by Tim Whelan with some music (Ginny Sims, Les Brown's orchestra and others) and a meandering plot about a soldier (Victor Mature) who learns he will inherit a fortune if he marries a Civil War general's descendant (Lucille Ball) before the week is up. Romantic complications and some sexist humor. A-I (br) U

Seven Days in May (1964) When a top American general (Burt Lancaster) plots to take over the government to stop the President (Fredric March) from signing a disarmament agreement with the Russians, a loyal Army colonel (Kirk Douglas) tries to avert the coup. Director John Frankenheimer's suspense thriller is thoroughly involving, credibly done and provides some food for thought. Much tension and some menace. A-II (br) U

Seven Days to Noon (1950) Excellent British thriller about a deranged scientist (Barry Jones) who threatens to destroy London with an atomic bomb unless the world disarms. Directed by Roy and John Boulting, the plot is neatly worked out, the acting is first rate and the suspense has real point. A-II (br) A

Seven Faces of Dr. Lao (1964) Diverting entertainment focusing on a traveling circus owned by the mysterious Dr. Lao (Tony Randall who also plays seven other roles) whose performances work strange effects on his audience in an Old West town. Director George Pal's fantasy has imaginative special effects and its story should intrigue youngsters and amuse adults. A-I (br) U

Seven Golden Men (1969) Routine Italian heist movie about the intricate maneuvers used to get into a bank vault, steal the loot and then lose it in a series of double crosses. Director Marco Vacario's crime movie is not a spoof, though it does have some humor and some personable crooks (Philippe Leroy, Gastone Moschin, Jose Suarez, Rossana Podesta). A-II (G) U

Seven Little Foys, The (1955) Bob Hope plays Eddie Foy, popular turn-of-the-century vaudeville star who, after the death of his forbearing wife (Milly Vitale), creates a stage act featuring his seven young children. Director Melville Shavelson does well with the show-biz setting, including a zesty turn by James Cagney as George M. Cohan, but Foy as an absentee father remains largely unsympathetic until the end when he takes the kids on the road to keep the family together. A-II (br) U

Seven Minutes, The (1971) Numbingly sensationalistic rendering of Irving Wallace's novel about a California pornography trial has all the depth of a Hollywood press release and all the titillation of an arcade peep show. Director Russ Meyer's characters are uniformly stereotypes, the relevant issues are hopelessly obscured and there is some explicit sexual action. O (R/PG) X

Seven Percent Solution, The (1976) Sigmund Freud (Nichol Williamson) meets Sherlock Holmes (Alan Arkin) in a stylish and mostly entertaining mystery directed by Herbert Ross. An incidental brothel scene and some frightening images that occur while Holmes is suffering from narcotic withdrawal symptoms are not for youngsters. A-III (PG) AA

Seven Sinners (1940) Marlene Dietrich stars as a cabaret singer in a South Seas port where her charms provoke a battle royal between a dangerous gangster (Oscar Homolka) and a U.S. naval officer (John Wayne). Action director Tay Garnett expends a lot of energy on goonish brawls but there's plenty of comic relief (Billy Gilbert, Mischa Auer and Broderick Crawford) as well as Dietrich's alluring yet sympathetic performance. Veiled sexual references. A-III (br) A

Seven-Ups, The (1974) Action-packed but hackneyed story of a special police unit, headed by Roy Scheider, that gets in the middle of an elaborate gangland war. Directed by Phil D'Antoni, N.Y. City is well used as the battleground where cop and criminal shoot it out, and where it is hard to tell the hunter from the hunted. Elaborate and intense car chases and an assortment of other special effects violence. A-III (PG) X

Seven Waves Away (see: "Abandon Ship!").

1776 (1972) Entertaining film version of the popular Broadway musical by Sherman Edwards and Peter Stone about the travails of the Continental Congress in forging the Declaration of Independence utilizes most of the original cast from William Daniels' John Adams to Howard Da Silva's Benjamin Franklin. Director Peter Hunt, who also directed the stage musical, relies on the original staging rather than trying for any big-screen effects and it works well in mixing some light, diverting entertainment with some serious asides, such as slavery and marital loneliness. A-II (G)

7th Cavalry (1956) Strictly formula western directed by Joseph H. Lewis in which a cavalry officer (Randolph Scott) returns from leave to learn of his troop's massacre at the Little Big Horn, then to prove he's not a coward volunteers to bring back the bodies of Custer and his officers. Frontier violence. A-I (br) U

Seventh Continent, The (1968) Czech-Yugoslav children's fantasy about a magical island that becomes the refuge for all the youngsters of the world who are ignored and forgotten by their busy parents, leaving the adult world behind in squabbles about how their children can be gotten back. Directed by Dustan Vukotic, it has a number of highly imaginative scenes and good special effects but tends to dwell too long on the tiresome adults. A-I (br)

Seventh Seal (1956) Intense medieval morality tale follows the journey of a disillusioned knight (Max Von Sydow) on his return from the Crusades to a plague-ravaged land where he forestalls Death (Bengt Ekerot) by wagering his life on a game of chess, during the course of which he saves a traveling player named Joseph (Nils Poppe), his wife Mary (Bibi Andersson) and their infant son. Swedish director Ingmar Bergman convincingly re-creates the religious context of the Middle Ages, but the knight's quest to find meaning in a world of physical suffering and spiritual emptiness has less to do with faith than with the contemporary search for the meaning of life in our own age of doubt and uncertainty. Subtitles. Recurring images of death, some stylized violence and instances of religious fanaticism. A-III (br) X

Seventh Sign, The (1988) Although the Apocalypse appears to be near at hand, a pregnant woman (Demi Moore) finds she has the power to stop it. Director Carl Schultz's convoluted thriller makes glossy, ultimately exploitative use of the New Testament's Book of Revelation. Several scenes of intense violence involving the woman and some brief nudity. O (R)

7th Voyage of Sinbad, The (1958) Exciting Arabian Nights adventure with Sinbad (Kerwin Matthews) battling a one-eyed Cyclops, a two-headed Roc, a ferocious dragon and a sword-wielding skeleton in order to rescue a princess (Kathryn Grant) from a wicked magician (Torin Thatcher). Director Nathan Juran teams with special effects artist Ray Harryhausen to create a satisfying action fantasy that will enthrall youngsters without boring their parents. Some scary scenes with menace and stylized violence. A-I (G)

Severed Head, A (1971) Failed British adaptation of Iris Murdoch's novel purports to be a sophisticated comedy of manners about the savagely civilized exercise of mixing and matching mates (Lee Remick, Richard Attenborough, Claire Bloom, Clive Revill). Among all the soap opera forsaking of partners, director Dick Clement forsakes taste with some unnecessarily bare anatomy. A-IV (R) X

Sex Drugs Rock & Roll (1991) Overlong but occasionally incisive one-man show with Eric Bogosian acting out ten characters caught up in their separate minidramas. As written by Bogosian and directed by John McNaughton, this filmed stageplay is well-acted by Bogosian but his insights into his smug, braggardly characters soon repeat themselves. Positive drug references within a satirical framework, allusions to promiscuity and frequent rough language. A-III (R)

Sex, Lies, and Videotape (1989) In this quirky contemporary morality tale, the relationships between an unhappy wife (Andie MacDowell), her philandering husband (Peter Gallagher) and her spiteful sister (Laura San Giacomo) who is having an affair with the husband are thrown up for grabs by the arrival of a visitor (James Spader) who is obsessed with videotaping women talking about their sexual experiences. Written and directed by Steven Soderbergh, the result is more or less morally satisfying as self-deceptions are unmasked and more positive relationships are initiated. Mature themes with some graphic sexual language and several suggestive scenes. A-IV (R) 18

Sex of Angels, The (1969) Italian import in which three affluent female delinquents trick a medical student onto a yachting trip and cause his death with drugs is lurid trash. O (X)

Sex with a Smile (1976) Perhaps the least offensive element in this unfunny, softcore, four-part Italian sex farce about four lusting men is that Marty Feldman, billed as the star, appears in only one segment. O (R)

Sextette (1979) Mae West plays a glamourous movie star whose wedding night with husband number six is interrupted by former husbands and the need to rescue a summit conference near shambles. Director Ken Hughes's farce is insufferably boring and, as might be expected, overflowing with an abundance of double-entendres. A-III (PG)

Sgt. Pepper's Lonely Hearts Club Band (1978) Peter Frampton and the Bee Gees attempt to turn the Beatles' famous music album into a movie in which they play small-town musicians temporarily corrupted by becoming Los Angeles rock stars. When they learn that baddies have despoiled their home town, they return to right all wrongs. Director Michael Schultz gets more the feel of an animated cartoon than a live-action and George Burns does some narration since the movie has no dialogue. Some suggestive gestures and lyrics as well as pot smoking and the use of cocaine. A-III (PG)

Shadow of a Doubt (1943) Young girl (Teresa Wright) begins to suspect that her favorite uncle (Joseph Cotton) is wanted for a series of murders. Director Alfred Hitchcock unfolds his usual dark doings in the commonplace setting of small-town America's solid citizenry with uncommonly suspenseful results. A classic psychological thriller rich in visual understatement rather than shocking graphics. A-II (br)

Shadow of the Hawk, The (1976) Terribly amateurish movie about an Indian medicine man (Chief Dan George) who wants his grandson (Jan-Michael Vincent), an IBM executive, to take over his practice and ward off the evil that threatens the tribe. Canadian production directed by George McCowan, the story is awfully farfetched and not particularly scary. A-II (PG)

Shadow of the Wolf (1993) When an Eskimo hunter (Lou Diamond Phillips) kills a drunken white trader in the Far North of 1935, he and his wife (Jennifer Tilly) flee their village to live in the vast Arctic wilderness on their own, but they cannot escape the curse of his shaman father (Toshiro Mifune) and the inexorable pursuit of white justice. In this beautifully photographed Canadian production based on the novel by Yves Theriault and directed by Jacques Dorfmann, the story of the individual hunter's struggle with the elements gets lost in the larger story of a native people's eroding culture but, dwarfing all, is the awesome splendor of this isolated, inhospitable, frozen world. Some stylized violence, including savage native customs, several sexual situations with fleeting nudity and a few instances of profanity. A-III (PG-13)

Shadowlands (1993) Fact-based story of Anglican writer and Oxford don C. S. Lewis (Anthony Hopkins), whose closely guarded scholarly seclusion is unsettled late in life by one of his readers, a divorced American writer (Debra Winger) who stirs the lifelong bachelor to discover the friendship of a woman, then the emotional fulfillment of marriage and finally the pain of loss when she dies of cancer. Director Richard Attenborough's 1950s' period piece explores the gradual transformation of a withdrawn intellectual by a woman whose death plunges him into dark despair, which challenges the consolation of his Christian faith. The tragic ending to this romantic story raises questions of life's true meaning. A-II (PG) U

Shadows and Fog (1992) Drafted by vigilantes hunting a strangler in a 1920's European town, a timid clerk (Woody Allen) wanders the nighttime streets afraid of his own shadow until befriending a jilted circus performer (Mia Farrow) whose spunk inspires him. Using atmospheric black-and-white photography reminiscent of German silent movies, writer-director Allen creates a spooky story of chance meetings that hits as often as it misses with its forays into wry humor and philosophical musings. Some stylized violence and sexual innuendo. A-III (PG-13) 15

Shaft (1971) Director Gordon Parks adroitly uses N.Y. City as the backdrop for what is really only a routine, if fast-paced and savvy, detective story involving a private-eye (Richard Roundtree) and the police department in a power struggle between a black mobster (Moses Gunn) and the Mafia to control the drug, prostitution and numbers racket in Harlem. Some sharp and vicious violence, brief nudity and realistic street language. A-III (R) 15

Shaft in Africa (1973) John Shaft (Richard Roundtree) is taken out of Harlem by an African diplomat who requires his services to break up a contemporary slave ring being run by a depraved Arab (Frank Finlay). Directed by John Guillermin, the plot is merely a pretext for indulging in graphic violence, explicit nudity and extremely crude dialogue. O (R) X

Shaft's Big Score (1972) When a big-time Harlem numbers operator dies, there is a scramble by black and white mobsters to take over the racket. Director Gordon Parks has turned his sequel into black exploitation,

once again using Richard Roundtree as his hip private detective, but this time smothering him in both easy (and often nude) women and gimmicky situations. Abundance of explicit violence and nudity. O (R) X

Shag: The Movie (1989) Nostalgic, feel-good story, set in 1963, tracks the last weekend fling of four recent high school grads (Page Hannah; Bridget Fonda; Annabeth Gish; Phoebe Cates) at Myrtle Beach, South Carolina, where boys, the annual Sun Fun Festival and a Shag dance contest are attractions. When one loses her virginity and breaks her engagement, the stage is set for an agonizing moral dilemma despite the cartoon plot. Director Zelda Barron respects her young subjects who giggle a lot about sex but have mostly harmless things on their minds. Some locker-room language laced with mild sexual vulgarities. A-III (PG) 15

Shaggy D.A., The (1977) Disney sequel has the now grown-up hero (Dean Jones) a crusading district attorney candidate running against a crooked incumbent (Keenan Wynn) and severely inconvenienced by his sudden transformations. Directed by Robert Stevenson, the humor is very broad and the slapstick heavy-handed even by Disney standards. All but very young children will likely be bored much of the time. A-I (G) U

Shaggy Dog, The (1959) Disney comedy directed by Charles Barton about a teenager whom a magic ring turns into a dog every now and then. The comic premise will appeal to youngsters, if not their parents. A-I (br)

Shake Hands with the Devil (1959) American student (Don Murray) in Ireland in the 1920s gets drawn into the struggle against British rule by a tough rebel leader (James Cagney). Director Michael Anderson is less interested in the issues of the conflict than in the human casualties in this cycle of violence. A-II (br) A

Shakedown (1988) Another buddy crime-buster movie in which a flaky legal aid attorney (Peter Weller) and a vigilante plainclothes detective (Sam Elliot) attempt to snare some crooked N.Y. City cops who live high on the hog by stealing from drug dealers. With little chemistry between the leads, director James Glickenhaus relies on intense chase scenes and graphic violence. Gritty scenes within a posh drug club and a grim 42nd Street sex parlor featuring frontal nudity and much street language. O (R)

Shakespeare Wallah (1966) Director James Ivory's gentle study of the old and the new in modern India centers on an itinerant group of Shakespearean actors who find it difficult to bridge the gap between the old Anglo-Indian past and the changing values of the new India. One of the highlights is its ironic contrast between the romantic notions of a young English actress (Felicity Kendal) and the materialism of an Indian movie star to whom she is attracted. Many adults will find it an utterly disarming picture of a culture in transition. A-III (br) A

Shakes the Clown (1992) A womanizing alcoholic clown (Bobcat Goldthwait) is framed for the drug-related murder of his boss (Paul Dooley) by a rival clown (Tom Kenny). Also written and directed by Goldthwait, the poorly made black comedy wallows in the spiritual emptiness of the characters and is unredeemed by a phony righteous ending. Sporadic nasty violence, incessant rough language, numerous sexual references and recreational drug use. O (R)

Shakiest Gun in the West, The (1968) Western comedy in which Don Knotts stars as a dentist who bungles his way to becoming a hero. As directed by Alan Rafkin, it is a pint-sized version of Bob Hope's "Paleface" but not nearly as amusing. A-I (br) U

Shalako (1968) Unconvincing western about an aristocratic hunting expedition caught poaching on Apache land and rescued by a wily Indian fighter (Sean Connery). Director Edward Dmytryk handles the episodic action quite clumsily and the contrived love interest is ridiculous. Stylized violence. A-III (PG) A

Shame (1969) Bleak Swedish drama about a couple (Liv Ullmann; Max Von Sydow) who escape a civil war by living on an island where they torment one another until the war drives them to a lifeboat drifting to sea. Director Ingmar Bergman's theme is the responsibility, personal and societal, for the kind of self-destruction imaged by civil war. Very intense, introspective movie but powerfully told and worth seeing. Violence. A-III (R) 15

Shame (1988) Woman barrister skilled in the martial arts (Deborra-Lee Furness) motorcycles into a rural Australian town whose menfolk think nothing of molesting and raping women as a group sport. Director Steve Jodrell's heroine uses the time-honored methods of macho screen stars to right these wrongs. Rough language with sexual connotations; a climactic sense of menace and intense grisly climax. A-III (R)

Shameless Old Lady, The (1966) Gently satiric French story of an old lady (Sylvie), widowed in her seventies, who is clear-sighted enough not to let her offspring take charge of her affairs but uses her small estate to enjoy the final months of her life. Directed by Rene Allio, it is an objective yet tender look at old age and the passive role assigned to it by social convention. A-II (br)

Shampoo (1975) Warren Beatty stars as a Beverly Hills hairdresser who becomes involved with his clients, especially Julie Christie, Goldie Hawn and Lee Grant. Directed by Hal Ashby, it is mindless fare as much devoid of humor as of humanity. Verbal obscenities and graphic depiction of sexual misbehavior. O (R) X

Shamus (1973) Tough private-eye from Brooklyn (Burt Reynolds) gets embroiled in a nasty little adventure involving diamond-heisting, gun-running, and double-crossing double-crossers. Directed by Buzz Kulik, the shallow plot's fast-paced action is done with some genial humor that helps diffuse numerous savage beatings and several restrained sex scenes. A-III (PG) X

Shane (1953) Classic western about a former gunfighter (Alan Ladd) who is befriended by a farm family (Van Heflin, Jean Arthur and young Brandon De Wilde) and saves them from being run off their land by a rancher's hired gun (Jack Palance). Directed by George Stevens, it's an epic tale of the conflict over land rights pitting the cattlemen's six-shooters against the homesteaders' moral fortitude and family roots. Stylized frontier violence. A-II (br) U

Shanghai Killers, The (1973) Routine martial arts programmer from Hong Kong in which the warrior swords go snicker-snack and the studio crew throw rubber hands and arms and buckets of blood around with wild abandon, all in service of the usual senseless violence. O (R)

Shanghai Surprise (1986) Sean Penn and Madonna give woefully inadequate performances in a supposedly romantic adventure set in 1930s' China involving a search for a lost shipment of opium intended for wounded soldiers in a mission hospital. Brutal violence, sex scenes and profanity. A-III (PG-13) 15

Shanks (1974) Odd but inept chiller starring French mime Marcel Marceau in the dual role of an ancient scientist and his deaf-mute assistant in a story-within-a-story involving an electronic device that can restore the dead to life. Directed by William Castle, the disjointed segments of the generally aimless and confused plot are introduced by title cards that don't help a bit. Some gruesome and violent visuals. A-III (PG)

Sharks' Treasure (1975) Not very exciting movie about diving for sunken treasure and a boat hijacking by murderous escaped convicts. Directed by Cornel Wilde (who also stars), it's routine adventure fare, save for a homosexual reference in the plot. A-III (PG)

Sharky's Machine (1981) Burt Reynolds (who also directed) plays a tough and aggressive Atlanta detective demoted for overzealousness to the vice squad where he cracks down on prostitutes and drug dealers. Though the crime movie has some good moments (such as burly policeman Bernie Casey being a Zen devotee) and is consistently entertaining until its lackluster conclusion, the action includes a harrowing and farfetched torture scene, some other graphic violence and very crude language. A-III (R) X

Shattered (1991) Convoluted thriller in which a wealthy land developer (Tom Berenger) suffering from amnesia after a near-fatal car crash enlists a cagey gumshoe (Bob Hoskins) to determine if his adulterous wife (Greta Scacchi) set up the accident. Writer-director Wolfgang Petersen spins an intricate tale of treachery and deceit greatly abetted by Hoskins' colorful characterization. Brief but recurring adulterous shots with nudity, momentary violence and some rough language. A-III (R)

She (1965) Slim escapist entertainment from H. Rider Haggard's novel of adventurers (Peter Cushing, Christopher Lee and John Richardson) exploring the African desert in search of a hidden city, a lost civilization and an eternal female (Ursula Andress). Director Robert Day adds nothing new to the old story of derring-do in quest of the fantastic. Stylized violence and romantic situations. A-II (br) U

She-Devil (1989) Plodding comic fantasy about the revenge of a wife (Roseanne Barr) on her philandering husband (Ed Begley Jr.) and his rich mistress (Meryl Streep). Produced and directed by Susan Seidelman, the comic premise is handled so methodically that it quickly loses interest, except for Streep's broadly funny performance as an empty-headed, outrageously pretentious author of romance novels. Some profanity and several sex scenes intended as satire. A-III (PG-13) 15

She Wore a Yellow Ribbon (1949) Superior western about a frontier outpost where a veteran cavalry officer (John Wayne) averts an Indian war on the eve of his mandatory retirement. Director John Ford's tribute to the horse soldiers who pacified the western wilderness makes glorious use of Monument Valley in framing the action and warmly depicts the details of garrison life. Frontier violence. A-I (br) U

She's Gotta Have It (1986) A seriocomic film about a strong-willed, independent black woman (Tracy Camila Johns) who confounds three egocentric males. Director Spike Lee brings imagination and vitality to this low-budget, black-and-white feature that offers some interesting characterizations with an accomplished all-black cast. Explicitly depicted sexual encounters; nudity; one scene of sexual brutality. O (R) 18

She's Having a Baby (1988) Writer-producer-director John Hughes' coming-of-age comedy about a young man (Kevin Bacon) who must learn to face the responsibilities of married life before he and his wife (Elizabeth McGovern) have a baby. Fantasy sequences comically reflect his inner turmoil, but the technique is overused, deterring from the narrative. Sexual situations within marriage; fleeting nudity; some profanity. A-III (PG-13) 15

She's Out of Control (1989) Mindless, one-joke film about an overly protective single father (Tony Danza) who lies and spies on his 15-year-old daughter (Ami Dolenz) when she begins dating. Directed by Stan Dragoti, there are no subtleties in this picture of a distrustful parent-child relationship. Some sexually vulgar innuendos. A-III (PG) 15

Sheba Baby (1975) Avenging black woman (Pam Grier) annihilates an army of hoods of various hues. Directed by William Girdler, it is a tasteless fantasy of sex and violence, though handled with some restraint. A-III (PG)

Sheena (1984) Comic-book jungle drama about a female Tarzan named Sheena (Tanya Roberts) who runs through Africa scantily clad in animal skins, pursued by a romantic TV reporter (Ted Wass). Directed by John Guillermin, it is so bad that it provokes laughter in all the wrong places. Extensive nudity. O (PG)

Shelia Levine Is Dead and Living in New York (1975) Failed screen version of Gail Parent's acerbicly witty novel about a small-town girl (Jeannie Berlin) who escapes to New York in search of meaning and marriage, finds a doctor (Roy Scheider) and convinces him that country virtues are better than urban sophistication. Not only are the principals miscast, but director Sidney Furie is out of his element in working with a script that has the deadly mediocre level of TV situation comedy. A-III (PG)

Sheltering Sky, The (1990) Visiting North Africa in the late 1940s, a troubled married couple (Debra Winger; John Malkovich) and their traveling companion (Campbell Scott) take a trip into the Sahara where they encounter typhoid fever, infidelity and madness. Director Bernardo Bertolucci's bleak journey into the void is a roadmap to despair given some poignancy by the beautifully photographed desert environment that devours the characters in this intense and harrowing film. A number of graphic adulterous liaisons with brief shots of full nudity. O (R) 18

Shenandoah (1965) Civil War story of a Virginia family patriarch (James Stewart) whose opposition to slavery keeps him out of the war until one of his sons is captured and he fights his way through Union lines trying to find him. Director Andrew McLaglen does best with the action scenes showing the futile havoc of war but is less effective in portraying its consequences on the family and its members. Wartime violence. A-I (br)

Sheriff of Fractured Jaw, The (1959) Leaden western spoof directed by Raoul Walsh delivers a mirthless misfire with Kenneth More as an English gun salesman pressed into service to protect a frontier town from warring ranchers (Bruce Cabot and William Campbell), with only Jayne Mansfield and a motley band of Indians for support. Stylized violence and mild sexual innuendo. A-II (br)

Sherlock Holmes and the Secret Code (see: "Dressed to Kill").

Shinbone Alley (1971) Disappointing cartoon version of the Broadway musical based on Don Marquis' classic "Archy and Mehitabel" concerning the cockroach chronicler of the irrepressible alley cat whose spirit has transmigrated from Cleopatra. Directed by John D. Wilson, with the central characters voiced by Eddie Bracken and Carol Channing, the result simply lacks the elemental zest and witty irony of the Marquis original. A-I (G)

Shining, The (1980) Disappointing film version of Stephen King's novel is a haunted-house movie on a grand scale, with Jack Nicholson as a writer who takes on the job of winter caretaker of a hotel resort in the Colorado Rockies, accompanied by wife (Shelley Duvall) and young son (Danny Lloyd). Tormented and manipulated by the evil lurking in the massive hotel (the scene of a brutal axe murder), he is taken to the brink of madness and tries to kill his family. Director Stanley Kubrick's ponderous horror film is predictable and slow-paced in building to its violent climax. Graphic violence, a needlessly extended erotic sequence and some rough language. O (R) X

Shining Through (1992) Blandly romantic World War II espionage tale follows an OSS colonel (Michael Douglas) into Nazi Germany to rescue his spy-girlfriend (Melanie Griffith) who's trying to get crucial war plans from a high-ranking German officer (Liam Neeson). Though the actors try their best, they cannot overcome the plot implausibilities underlying writer-director David Seltzer's slack wartime love story. Brief violence and fleeting bedroom scene. A-III (R) 15

Ship of Fools (1965) Abby Mann's flawed yet powerful adaptation of Katherine Anne Porter's allegorical novel centers on the foibles and self-delusions of some two dozen passengers (including Vivien Leigh, Oskar Werner, Simone Signoret, Jose Ferrer and Lee Marvin) on a German liner sailing from Mexico to its home port in 1933, the year Hitler came to power. Though producer-director Stanley Kramer is not always successful in giving dramatic credibility to the truncated stories of the numerous characters, he does manage to convey the inability of most to comprehend the Nazi menace as well as to suggest through the narrator (Michael Dunn) that viewers may discover something of themselves in this portrayal of human frailty. Some anti-Semitic references and sexual situations. A-III (br) A

Shipwrecked (1991) Young Norwegian lad (Stian Smestad) goes to sea as a cabin boy but his ship is shanghaied by pirates, then wrecked by a tropical storm and the boy washed overboard to wind up on a deserted island where he finds the pirates' treasure and frees his shipmates from their fearsome captor (Gabriel Byrne). Directed by Nils Gaup, the 19th-century adventure of a youth coping in a man's world has the excitement of an ocean voyage under full sail and the inventiveness of a 14-year-old Robinson Crusoe, but the personal level tends to get lost in the narrative's constant action. Much menace and some frightening moments for young children. A-I (PG)

Shirley Valentine (1989) In a British comedy of some wit and intelligence, a 42-year-old Liverpool housewife (Pauline Collins) leaves hubby and grown children for a two-week holiday in Greece where she meets a clay-footed womanizer (Tom Conti) but rediscovers on her own a long-submerged zest for life. Adapted from his own stage play by Willy Russell and directed a bit too literally by Lewis Gilbert, the adult comedy about a spunky middle-aged woman has a lot of heart and a memorable title performance. Some mature themes, fleeting nudity and comic use of a sexual expletive. A-III (R) 15

Shoah (1985) Death camp survivors, former Nazi officials and Poles living in the vicinity of the extermination sites are interviewed by producer-director Claude Lanzmann in this French documentary on the Holocaust. Although it does not show any photographs of Hitler's mass murder of European Jewry, the survivors' oral history of events is powerful and often shocking, all the more so because it personalizes the horror of the camps. Subtitled and more than nine hours in length, the work is a valuable educational resource on the Holocaust. A-II (nr) PG

Shock to the System, A (1990) Mild-mannered Manhattan ad exec (Michael Caine) finds that he can easily murder his demanding wife (Swoosie Kurtz) and yuppie colleague (Peter Riegert), among others who stand in his way. With flat direction by Jan Egleson, the film balances uncomfortably between a satiric black comedy and a serial-murder drama, providing a view of moral corruption that would be utterly distasteful if not for Caine's fine performance. Condones murder as an acceptable means to an end, a jokey on-screen suicide, some rough language and sexual innuendos. O (R) 15

Shock Troops (1968) French-Italian production about a group of French resistance fighters in World War II who raid a German prison to rescue 12 men sentenced to death but find that they have saved one man too many (Michel Piccoli) and suspect he may be a spy. Directed by Costa-Gavras, the story is much like other movies about the French Resistance, though its action scenes are almost documentary-like in effect. Wartime violence and brutality. A-III (R)

Shocker (1989) When a TV repairman (Mitch Pileggi) is electrocuted for murdering entire families, he is sucked into the TV airwaves from which he returns to slash more families until freeze-framed by a telepathic college football hero (Peter Berg). Writer-director Wes Craven mixes black humor and simple-minded satire with much profanity and grisly mass murders. O (R) 18

Shocking Miss Pilgrim, The (1947) Mild musical comedy set in 1874 when Boston's first woman typist (Betty Grable) has a hard time keeping her job with a sexist boss (Dick Haymes) who ultimately proposes marriage. Writer-director George Seaton tries to have some fun playing both sides of the street but neither feminists nor chauvinists are likely to be amused, though some may enjoy the Gershwin music. Bland romantic complications and dated treatment of gender roles. A-I (br) U

Shoes of the Fisherman, The (1968) Uneven screen version of the Morris L. West novel about a Russian bishop (Anthony Quinn) who becomes Pope and decides that the Vatican's wealth be given to the world's poor gets lost in a series of subplots. Directed by Michael Anderson, there is a lot of religious pageantry and international intrigue, but mainly conveyed on a superficial level. A-I (br) U

Shogun Assassin (1980) Samurai swordsman wields his blade tirelessly in dispatching legions of assassins in this campy Americanized version of a Japanese martial arts movie directed by Kenji Jisumi. Narrated by a child, the action is a visual ballet of incessant violence and bloodshed. O (R)

Shoot (1976) Painfully well-intentioned diatribe directed by Harvey Hart against the cult of guns has a preposterous story of two groups of hunters who, because of an accidental shooting death, begin an armed war against each other. Much violence. A-III (R)

Shoot the Moon (1982) Successful Hollywood writer (Albert Finney) walks out on his wife (Diane Keaton) and four young daughters in director Alan Parker's account of sometimes savage martial strife. Though there are some effective touches, the film withholds so much vital information about the principals that it becomes irritating and pretentious. Some intense violence; very rough language. A-III (R) AA

Shoot to Kill (1988) Taut, at times harrowing, thriller about a street-smart FBI agent (Sidney Poitier) and a woods-wise guide (Tom Berenger) who learn to trust one another in the course of tracking down a psychotic killer. Director Roger Spottiswoode handles the action scenes effectively, but the relationship between the two principals is too contrived to be entirely convincing. Some brief but intense violence and considerable menace. A-III (R)

Shooting Party, The (1985) In the fall of 1913, some aristocrats gather at the estate of a nobleman (James Mason) to do a bit of shooting and carry on some romantic intrigues on the eve of the war that would end their world forever. Alan Bridges directs a thoughtful and entertaining film, if a bit slow-moving and predictable at times. Superbly acted, but it does contain a rather explicit bedroom scene. A-IV (nr) 15

Shootist, The (1976) Uneven western directed by Don Siegel in which a legendary gunfighter (John Wayne), told by a doctor (James Stewart) that he is dying of cancer, engages in a final shootout. The movie's glossing over of the hero's various moral failings makes it mature fare. A-III (PG)

Shootout (1971) Familiar revenge plot about a stoic ex-con (Gregory Peck) on his way to settle accounts with a double-crossing partner starts going astray when he is detained by a dependent widow (Pat Quinn) and a homeless waif (Dawn Lyn) who may be his daughter by a prostitute. Director Henry Hathaway leaves family audiences far behind with some sadistic violence, including a gang rape in a brothel and coarse language out of the mouth of a nine-year-old. Grim stuff. O (GP) AA

Shop on Main Street, The (1966) Czechoslovakian tragicomedy of life under a puppet Nazi regime sensitively details the unusual friendship that develops between a simple man (Josef Kroner) and an elderly Jewish widow (Ida Kaminska) over whose button shop he has been appointed "Aryan Controller." Director Jan Kadar draws the situation with a loving sense of human character that helps underscore the movie's condemnation of moral passivity in the face of inhumanity. Subtitles. A-III (br) A

Short Circuit (1986) No. 5 is a lovable robot who acquires human attributes after being struck by lightning and befriended by Ally Sheedy, an ill-tempered snack-wagon operator. Steve Guttenberg plays No. 5's inventor in this routine romance from director John Badham. Some suggestive comments and mild profanity are lost in the context of chase scenes. A-I (PG) U

Short Circuit 2 (1988) Robot No. 5 returns as Johnny Five to help a friend (Fisher Stevens) launch a toy robot company, but gets caught up in all sorts of mayhem, including a jewel heist. Directed by Kenneth Johnson, the lovable erector set steals the show, but some harrowing attacks on the robot may upset very young children. Rough language. A-II (PG)

Short Cuts (1993) Long, sprawling narrative intertwines the troubled lives and eccentric experiences of nine families numbering 21 major characters (among them, Andie MacDowell; Bruce Davison; Jack Lemmon; Matthew Modine; Anne Archer; Tim Robbins; Lily Tomlin) over the course of several days in a Los Angeles suburb. Loosely based on short stories by Raymond Carver and directed by Robert Altman, the result is a messy collage of egocentric lives, arbitrarily thrown together through overlapping storylines, whose flawed characters and dysfunctional behavior turn into a dreary sideshow of human frailties. Extramarital affairs, explicit sexual discussions, nudity, violence, substance abuse and rough language. O (R) 18

Short Eyes (1977) Screen version of Miguel Pinero's play about prison life tells the story of a man (Bruce Davison), accused of molesting a little girl, who is thrust into a volatile environment where the other prisoners subject him to systematic and brutal harassment as someone who is lower than the lowest. Directed by Robert M. Young, the movie's strength is in the almost overpowering realism of its mood and setting and the compelling personalities of its characters. Although the rough language, the violence and the threatening atmosphere are thoroughly justified in content, the movie is not for everyone. A-IV (R)

Short Time (1990) Mildly amusing comedy about a Seattle police officer who, after being mistakenly told he has only a few weeks to live, sets out to be killed in the line of duty so his ex-wife can collect his insurance and send his son to Harvard. Directed by Gregg Champion, the one-joke comedy is an uneasy melange of slapstick humor, melodramatic sentimentality and action stunts, but its chief asset is Coleman who knows how to wring a good laugh from slim material. Mature theme, some hard-edged violence,

a bedroom scene and needless profanity. A-III (PG-13) 12

Shout, The (1979) Intriguing psychological thriller about a mysterious stranger (Alan Bates), who threatens the husband (John Hurt) of a woman he wants to take (Susannah York) with the lethal power of a shout that's capable of killing everything within hearing distance—a mystical technique he learned during a long stay among Australian aborigines. This British production directed by Jerzy Skolimowski is beautifully photographed and performed, but it cannot sustain its fragile premise. Mature treatment. A-III (R) AA

Shout (1991) Lame 1950s youth drama set in a delinquent boys' home where a rebellious teen (James Walters) defies the man in charge (Richard Jordan), pursues his daughter (Heather Graham) and conspires with a music teacher (John Travolta) to form a forbidden rock 'n' roll band. Director Jeffrey Hornaday milks familiar anti-authority and coming-of-age themes for a plastic story lacking dramatic or even musical energy. A brief bedroom scene with adolescents and momentary violence. A-III (PG-13)

Shout at the Devil (1976) Comedy about a boozy buccaneer (Lee Marvin) in World War I Southeast Africa who cons upright Britisher (Roger Moore) into a little elephant-tusk poaching on German territory suddenly turns nasty when Moore's wife is brutalized and his infant daughter burned to death by German forces. Directed by Michael Klinger, the movie has a blood-and-gore conclusion. A-III (PG)

Show Boat (1936) Fine version of the Jerome Kern-Oscar Hammerstein musical about the daughter (Irene Dunne) of a Mississippi riverboat captain (Charles Winninger) and her stormy marriage to an inveterate gambler (Allan Jones) which is counterpointed by a tragic subplot involving a mulatto singer (Helen Morgan). Director James Whale gets some real feeling out of the sentimental melodrama with a talented cast and a convincing turn-of-the-century setting that helps make the nostalgic musical as much a part of Americana as Paul Robeson's deckhand singing "Old Man River." Period depiction of race relations and domestic difficulties. A-II (nr) U

Show of Force, A (1990) Plodding political thriller centers on a San Juan TV reporter (Amy Irving) who puts her life in danger tracking evidence of apparent collusion between U.S. and Puerto Rican officials in the deaths of two men at a communications facility. Brazilian director Bruno Barreto depicts the controversial 1978 slayings as being staged by a repressive government in an effort to discredit the local independence movement, but the murky, disjointed treatment strains credibility, despite good performances by Andy Garcia as the prosecutor and by Lou Diamond Phillips as a double-agent. Several strong scenes of graphic violence, much menace and minimal rough language. A-III (R) 15

Showdown (1973) Saddle-worn tale of two boyhood chums whose trails diverge but intertwine years later when one of them, an outlaw on the run (Dean Martin) seeks refuge from a one-time girlfriend (Susan Clark), now the wife of the other, an upright sheriff (Rock Hudson). George Seaton directs the B-grade western with deadly earnestness, relieved only by some foggy flashbacks of the pair's boyhood escapades and a few good action scenes. A-II (PG) AA

Shuttered Room, The (1967) British suspense thriller directed by David Greene about a couple (Carol Lynley and Gig Young) who journey to a New England island to take possession of the house where the wife grew up but find themselves harassed by the islanders and warned of a dire evil in the house. Excessive violence, a near rape and scenes with seminudity. O (br) X

Shy People (1988) Brash N.Y. writer (Jill Clayburgh) and nymphet daughter (Martha Plimpton) come upon some sinister goings-on in a Louisiana bayou while visiting a distant relative (Barbara Hershey) and her four wild sons. Director Andrei Konchalovsky fills the hothouse drama with American stereotypes. Some intense violence, drug abuse, an explicit striptease sequence and teen sexual promiscuity. O (R) 15

Sibling Rivalry (1990) When a frustrated housewife's (Kirstie Alley) one instance of infidelity kills the guy (Sam Elliott), she makes a hapless salesman (Bill Pullman) think he's responsible, and together they concoct a suicide scene that leads to further complications. Director Carl Reiner's minor screwball comedy wedges a tasteless scene among several madcap moments animated by the leads' flair for physical comedy. Comic treatment of extramarital sex and minimal profanity. A-III (PG-13) 15

Sicilian, The (1987) Failed film version of the Mario Puzo novel focuses on Salvatore Giuliano (Christopher Lambert), a historical figure whose rebellion against Sicily's Mafia, landowners and churchmen ended in 1950 with his murder. Directed by Michael Cimino, the film is muddled and disjointed, with a narrative that is often ludicrous and lacking in a sense of the area's culture and history. Graphic violence, brief nudity and some rough language. A-IV (R) 15

Sicilian Clan, The (1970) Epic French heist tale is a duel of wits and guts between a crime patriarch (Jean Gabin) and an ambitious Parisian hood (Alain Delon) over an impossibly complicated plane hijack of a fortune in jewels, with frustrated but persistent police inspector (Lino Ventura) keeping one step behind all the way. Directed by Henri Verneuil, the briskly paced story of honor among thieves has a number of superior action sequences from an ingenious jail escape at the start to a grandly anti-climactic shootout. A-III (GP) PG

Sid and Nancy (1987) All the sordid details of physical and spiritual disintegration are celebrated in this harsh and excessively explicit portrait of the sadistic, self-destructive lives of British punk rock music star Sid Vicious and his American girlfriend, Nancy. Without care for the reasons behind Sid's tragic self-destruction, the film is masochistically exploitative. O (R) 18

Siddhartha (1973) Screen version of Hermann Hesse's novel about a Brahmin's son, Siddhartha (Shashi Kapoor), who rebels at his father's asceticism, rejects the message of various holymen, is disappointed with the pleasures of sex and the rewards of business, but finally discovers enlightenment in nature and the unity of life. Written, produced and directed by Conrad Rooks, the movie attempts to create a mystic experience, rendering the abstract and sometimes ponderous philosophizing of the text into the sheer beauty of poetic imagery, ably supplied by Sven Nykvist's camera. Some will find it an uplifting experience, while others will see only an album of pretty pictures. Restrained but erotic sex scene. A-III (R)

Sidecar Racers (1975) Young American (Ben Murphy), at loose ends in Australia, becomes involved in the hazardous sport of sidecar motorcycle racing. Directed by Earl Bellamy. Innocuous, mildly diverting action movie; some romantic complications aren't for youngsters. A-III (PG)

Sidekicks (1993) Corny tale of asthmatic teen student of karate (Jonathan Brandis) who daydreams of rescuing damsels in distress alongside karate hero Chuck Norris (playing himself), then finds himself partnered with his idol at a competition. Director Aaron Norris depicts his brother Chuck as an awesome good guy in this dull and predictable vanity production that caters to teen macho fantasies. Stylized martial arts violence and periodic menace. A-III (PG)

Sidewalk Stories (1989) The story of a homeless N.Y. City street artist (Charles Lane) and the two-year-old waif (Nicole Alysia) he shelters is told in a virtually silent, black-and-white movie that depends upon the eloquent body language of the actors and an energetic musical score by Marc Marder. Lane also wrote, produced and directed this Chaplinesque tale of two black outcasts, which presents a poignant if sentimentalized view of the plight of the homeless. Brief frontal nudity in an erotic dream sequence and some comic-book violence. A-III (R)

Sidewinder 1 (1977) Mediocre motorcycle racing movie directed by Earl Bellamy in which engineer Alex Cord develops a new cycle and goes into partnership with driver Michael Parks to refine it. An extramarital relationship makes it adult fare. A-III (PG)

Siege of the Saxons (1963) When King Arthur (Mark Dignam) is slain by a Cornish usurper (Ronald Howard) in league with Saxony, his daughter (Janette Scott) is rescued by a forest outlaw (Ronald Lewis), proclaimed Camelot's queen by Merlin (John Laurie) and routs England's foes. Director Nathan Juran's cut-rate British production muddles through the outlandish proceedings with the help of action scenes lifted straight out of "The Black Knight" (1954). Clunky Arthurian tale with stylized violence. A-I (br)

Sierra Passage (1950) Low-budget western directed by Frank MacDonald tells the tale of an orphan raised by a minstrel troupe (headed by Roland Winters) to be a sharpshooter (Chester Morris), but his sole interest is tracking down the laughing gunman (Alan Hale Jr.) who murdered his father. Stylized violence and vigilante theme. A-III (br)

Sierra Stranger (1957) Formula western about a cowboy (Howard Duff) who rides into the middle of a dispute over a mining claim and winds up on the wrong side. Directed by Lee Sholem, the plot is tired and the action tiresome. Stylized violence and mild romance. A-II (br)

Sign of the Virgin (1969) Failed Czechoslovakian comedy about a lonely soldier whose girlfriend is smuggled onto the base by his comrades so they can spend the evening together in sick bay. Director Zbynek Brynych's attempts at humor are disappointingly clumsy as are several unnecessarily graphic scenes of the young couple. O (nr)

Signs of Life (1989) Sketchy drama about the impending closure of a venerable New England family's boat-building business and the effects on its elderly owner (Arthur Kennedy), assorted employees and hangers-on. Directed by John David Coles, its inconsequential narrative hints at the occult, includes a botched suicide, a near-drowning and a pointless robbery. Some rough language; brief sexual encounter. A-III (PG-13)

Silence of the Lambs, The (1991) An FBI trainee (Jodie Foster) seeks the identity of a psychotic serial killer (Ted Levine) from a brilliantly manipulative psychiatrist (Anthony Hopkins), himself an imprisoned multiple murderer. Jonathan Demme di-rects a riveting thriller eliciting superb performances from Foster and Hopkins while attempting a straightforward treatment of repugnant subject matter by focusing on the novice agent's dedication to her assignment. Some intense violence and graphic shots of mutilated bodies, a flash of nudity and occasional rough language. A-IV (R) 18

Silence of the North, The (1982) Fact-based Canadian story of a spunky 1920s' farm woman (Ellen Burstyn) who, after her husband (Tom Skerritt) perishes trapping in the Northwest Territories, moves to Calgary to raise her three children during the Depression. Director Allan Winton King succeeds in showing the fearsome beauty of Canada's northern wilderness, but the human drama of pioneer folk is smothered in low-key, dull performances. The deadly menace of a hostile environment and a few instances of profanity. A-II (PG)

Silencers, The (1966) Shabby imitation spy spoof of James Bond adventure movies with Dean Martin playing Matt Helm, free-lance superspy who spends much of his time cracking heads and getting his own bent occasionally. When not thus engaged, he chases an assortment of comely female spies around the set. The comic level is uniformly low and so is the moral tone of the action. O (br) A

Silent Movie (1976) Writer-director Mel Brooks stars as a washed-up director who gets the head of his studio (Sid Caesar) to let him make a silent comedy provided he can get Hollywood's biggest stars to participate. The result is sometimes funny, sometimes not. Harmless fun and less vulgar than other Brooks' comedies. Adult humor. A-III (PG) A

Silent Night, Deadly Night (1984) Maniac dressed in a Santa Claus costume uses an axe to kill people. Dreadfully produced exploitative horror suggests that director Charles Sellier Jr. should think about another line of work. Excessive gory violence. O (R)

Silent Night, Evil Night (see: "Black Christmas").

Silent Partner, The (1979) Dull bankteller (Elliott Gould) keeps out a large cache of money for himself during a bank hold-up, but the robber (Christopher Plummer) is a cunning sadist who does not like being made the fool. What follows includes a brutal murder and a savage beating. Directed by Daryl Duke, the film is cleverly done and well acted, but the cheap, corrosive cynicism that permeates it, together with the sex and violence inserted to jolt the audience, is seriously offensive. O (R)

Silent Rage (1982) Small-town sheriff (martial-arts whiz Chuck Norris) confronts a seemingly indestructible superman fashioned by an irresponsible scientist. Directed by Michael Miller, it is an utterly inconsequential effort of deadening predictability. Considerable violence, though stylized, and some fleeting nudity. A-III (R)

Silent Running (1972) Above average tale of ecological disaster in the not-too-distant future where the commander (Bruce Dern) of a space ark refuses the order to destroy its precious cargo of plant life that can no longer grow on earth. Directed by Douglas Trumbull, the sci-fi effects are good and the story's theme of humanity's relationship to the environment is thoughtful. Unfortunately, the weak storyline ends in the confusion of madness and restrained mayhem. A-II (GP/G) U

Silk Stockings (1957) Belabored musical updating the 1939 romantic comedy, "Ninotchka," has a Soviet commissar (Cyd Charisse) arriving in Paris to replace three faltering comrades (Peter Lorre, Jules Munshin and Sam Wanamaker), then falling for a capitalist movie producer (Fred Astaire). Despite spirited Cole Porter songs, director Rouben Mamoulian fails to convey any romantic sparks between the Astaire-Charisse duo and the flashy production numbers fail to pep up the lethargic proceedings. Sexual innuendo. A-III (br) U

Silken Skin (see: "The Soft Skin").

Silkwood (1983) Fact-based story of Karen Silkwood (Meryl Streep), a worker in a plutonium processing factory who died in a 1974 auto accident, on her way to tell a reporter what she knew about unsafe conditions in the plant. The movie does not confront the question of whether this was indeed an accident or a murder committed to prevent her evidence from being revealed. Instead, director Mike Nichols has invested a great deal of labor and care in depicting something of Silkwood's independent life-style on the job and in relations to her roommate (Cher) and boyfriend (Kurt Russell). The result is a nicely crafted disappointment. A-III (R) 15

Silver Bears (1978) Michael Caine stars in this leaden-paced, largely unfunny comedy of international intrigue involving a hoax about a silver mine. Directed by Ivan Passer, it affects a sympathetic attitude toward adultery. O (PG)

Silver Bullet (1985) A small town is terrorized by a maniacal killer, coincidentally enough, only when the moon is full. When most of the members of a posse formed to track down the killer are annihilated, it is left to a 12-year-old handicapped boy to convince the town that the killer is a werewolf. Based on a Stephen King novella, director Daniel Attias takes liberties with Hollywood werewolf conventions that may offend hard-core Lon Chaney fans. Graphic violence with gory murder sequences as well as some vulgar language. O (R) 18

Silver Streak (1976) Gene Wilder and Jill Clayburgh battle a ruthless gang of killers aboard a transcontinental train, aided by Richard Pryor, whose comic talents give the movie a much needed lift when he appears halfway through. Directed by Arthur Hiller, it is moderately entertaining but has some unnecessary profanity and a rather crude love scene. A-III (PG)

Silverado (1985) Big, gaudy western, as artificial as its title, in which four strangers meet on the road to Silverado and unite to fight evil and injustice. One problem, among the many that afflict the movie, is that director Lawrence Kasdan fails to make the bad guys seem very formidable competition. Nor can one find much to cheer about in the four lackluster heroes weighed down by a convoluted and contrived storyline and a tone that wavers between spoof and dead seriousness. Some moderate violence. A-II (PG-13) PG

Simon (1980) Anemic satire about a mischievous group of scientists (headed by Austin Pendleton) who brainwash an eccentric philosophy teacher (Alan Arkin) into believing he is from outer space. Written and directed by Marshall Brickman, the acting is good but the laughs are few and far between. Some sexual innuendo and a feeble thrust at organized religion. A-III (PG) A

Simon of the Desert (1969) Surrealistic Mexican fantasy about a hermit (Claudio Brook), who like his 5th-century namesake, Simeon Stylites, exiles himself to the top of a pillar in the wilderness living in prayer, doing penance, and working miracles, but constantly at war with himself, his followers and the devil (Silvia Pinal). Director Luis Bunuel's satiric foray into the sacred and the profane deals in paradox and the contradictions inherent in human nature. His ironic wit and uncomfortable insights will be appreciated most by those willing to reconcile the movie's ambiguities with their own beliefs. A-IV (nr)

Simon the Swiss (1971) French crime thriller about a petty crook (Jean-Louis Trintignant) who thinks he's pulled off the perfect crime when he kidnaps a bank clerk's small child and gets the bank to pay a fortune in ransom. Director Claude Lelouch's plot has all kinds of intricate turns and twists and the likable hero is anything but a Robin Hood. Intelligent entertainment with much psychological tension and some physical violence. A-III (G)

Simple Men (1992) Disjointed story of an unsuccessful criminal (Robert Burke) and his college-student younger brother (William Sage) who are given a place to stay by a Long Island innkeeper (Karen Sillas) while searching for their outlaw father. Written and directed by Hal Hartley, the situation provides a stage for eccentric characters with throwaway dialogue that is by turns comical and mock philosophic, suggesting insights which never materialize. Some stylized violence, sexual references and occasional rough language. A-III (R) 15

Simple Story, A (1980) Moody French portrait of a divorced woman (Romy Schneider) in middle-age crisis and agonizing over whether to have an abortion or raise her child. Directed by Claude Sautet, the movie avoids sentimental melodramatics in favor of thoughtful, sensitive probing of life's moral priorities. A-III (nr)

Sin of Adam and Eve, The (1973) Writer-producer-director Michael Zachary's literal visualization of Genesis uses an off-screen narrator to add some sensual embellishments to the biblical text while on-screen bare, healthy primates George Rivers and Candy Wilson explore an Eden that seems to have been culled from the Burpee Seed Catalogue. O (R)

Sinbad and the Eye of the Tiger (1977) Slow-paced bit of leaden whimsy follows a voyage of Sinbad (Patrick Wayne) to the polar regions to free a prince from a witch's spell. The acting is undistinguished, Sam Wanamaker's direction is haphazard and only a few special effects merit anything more than passing interest. A-II (G) U

Sinful Davey (1969) Tongue-in-cheek adventure movie about an 18th-century Scottish laddie (John Hurt) who deserts the English army and embarks upon a career as a highwayman. Director John Huston relies upon an abundance of misadventures, escapes and turnabouts in a stylish action story done in fun. Some explicit romantic interludes. A-III (PG) A

Sing (1989) Poorly focused, reality-based fantasy about Brooklyn's annual high school performance competitions uses a cliched story of romance between a good girl (Jessica Steen) and a petty hood (Peter Dobson) who is turned around by a tough-minded new teacher (Lorraine Bracco). Director Richard Baskin depends on music-video flourishes to divert attention from his derivative scenario but gets help from a cast of energized teens, a subplot about community pride and an anti-drug message. Some rough language and sexually suggestive dancing. A-III (PG-13) PG

Singin' in the Rain (1951) Engaging musical spoof of early Hollywood as a silent movie star (Gene Kelly) makes the transition into talking pictures with some help from a loyal pal (Donald O'Connor) and a talented young singer (Debbie Reynolds) who dubs the voice of the star's shrill leading lady (Jean Hagen). Directed by Kelly and Stanley Donen, the period nostalgia is served up as lighthearted fun with the Kelly-Reynolds romance sweetly in the background while the plot rolls along with fine songs, zestful comedy routines and lovely production numbers, from O'Connor's solo "Make 'Em Laugh" to Kelly's memorable title number. Minor sexual innuendo. A-II (br) U

Singing Nun, The (1966) Hollywood's tribute to the joyful spirit of a young Dominican nun is colorful, sentimental and lively. Henry Koster's glossy direction is out of tune with the reality of a basically interior story about the difficulty of secular fame for a member of a religious community. Greer Garson as the mother superior turns in a well-balanced performance while Debbie Reynolds sings prettily and Agnes Moorehead provides comic relief. Some pleasant amusement, a little uplift and the music of "Soeur Sourire" is well worth hearing. A-I (br) U

Single White Female (1992) After tossing out her unfaithful fiance (Steven Weber), a young Manhattanite (Bridget Fonda) takes in a shy roommate (Jennifer Jason Leigh) who quickly turns out to be a cunning murderess. Producer-director Barbet Schroeder's tired slasher movie turns a plausible concept into a mindless exercise in sensational violence. Excessive violence, brief sexual encounters, some nudity and occasional rough language. O (R) 18

Singles (1992) Romantic comedy centers on several romances among the twentysomething tenants (including Bridget Fonda, Scott Campbell, Kyra Sedgwick and Matt Dillon) of a small and homey Seattle apartment building. Writer-director Cameron Crowe takes a genial but superficial look at the emotional rollercoaster of the dating wars with sympathetic, marriage-minded characters. Restrained scene of a sexual encounter, a benign attitude toward premarital affairs and an instance of rough language. A-III (PG-13) 12

Sister Act (1992) Having witnessed a mob rubout, a Reno lounge singer (Whoopi Goldberg) hides out in a cloistered San Francisco convent disguised as a nun and horrifies Mother Superior (Maggie Smith) by turning their choir into a local sensation and getting the nuns involved in their neighborhood. Director Emile Ardolino parlays Goldberg's sassiness into a lively comedy that treats nuns both as comic figures and spirited, caring individuals with a positive life-style. References to an extramarital affair and brief comic violence. A-III (PG)

Sister Act 2: Back in the Habit (1993) Fair comedy sequel in which the Las Vegas singer (Whoopi Goldberg) is back in a nun's habit, hoping to save a Catholic high school from closing by transforming a bunch of unruly students into a vibrant choir in time to win the all-state competition. Though lacking the novel premise of the original and off-kilter in its goofy depiction of several priests, director Bill Duke's moderately amusing comedy stresses positive values for youngsters. Mild sexual innuendo, comic treatment of religious characters and an instance of profanity. A-II (PG)

Sisters (1973) Failed horror thriller about a Staten Island reporter (Jennifer Salt) who happens to observe a bloody murder in a neighboring apartment house occupied by a schizophrenic Siamese twin (Margot Kidder) and her mad doctor-husband (Bill Finley). Assisting her investigation is a bumbling, comic-relief detective (Charles Durning) Directed by Brian De Palma, the movie's mixture of mindless comedy and visceral gore presumes an audience willing to participate in such voyeuristic displays of violence. O (R)

Sitting Bull (1954) Failed western tale of a cavalry officer (Dale Robertson) whose friendship with the Sioux chief (J. Carrol Naish) leads to a court martial after Custer's Last Stand. Directed by Sidney Salkow, the mawkish story mauls American history and frontier stereotypes to no discernable advantage. Frontier violence. A-I (br) U

Sitting Ducks (1980) Two bumbling con men (Michael Emil and Zach Norman) steal some mob gambling receipts and flee to Miami with two women who have been hired to bump them off. Amateurish sex farce directed by Henry Jaglom gets off to a good start but becomes progressively less amusing as it wears on. Demeaning treatment of sex and some rough language. O (R) AA

Sitting Pretty (1948) Period comedy in which busy suburban parents (Robert Young and Maureen O'Hara) engage the services of a live-in babysitter (Clifton Webb), a self-proclaimed genius who proves more than capable of handling not only the children but any crisis along the way. Directed by Walter Lang, the whole show is Webb's imperious performance as the unflappable Mr. Belvedere who is more than superior to any situation, including nosy neighbors. Some muted sexual inferences. A-II (br) A

Sitting Target (1972) Atrocious British crime story about an escaped convict (Oliver Reed), his stashed loot and adulterous wife (Jill St. John). Directed by Douglas Hickox, the movie wallows in cruelty, sadism, gore, betrayal and self-destruction. O (R) X

Situation Hopeless—But Not Serious (1965) Failed black comedy of two downed American fliers (Robert Redford and Michael Connors) taken prisoner in 1944 by a lonely German clerk (Alec Guinness) and held cap-

tive in his cellar until six years after World War II's end. Director Gottfried Reinhardt concentrates on the ludicrous humor of the situation rather than the characters and their relationships, with little to show for it except adding to the Guinness gallery of odd characterizations. Uneasy humor in a desperate situation. A-II (br) A

Six Degrees of Separation (1993) New York art dealer (Donald Sutherland) and wife (Stockard Channing) recount to their amused uppercrust friends how a troubled homosexual youth (Will Smith), by pretending to be Sidney Poitier's son, insinuated himself into their lives hoping to become part of their privileged world. Based on John Guare's play and directed by Fred Schepisi, the deftly acted movie uncomfortably mixes scathing satire about patronizing rich folk with the murky plight of a lost, delusional young man. Fleeting homosexual encounter with a flash of frontal nudity, brief violence including suicide and occasional rough language. A-III (R)

Six in Paris (1969) Light, colorful and entertaining compilation of short vignettes by six French directors (Jean-Luc Godard, Jean-Daniel Pollet, Jean Rouch, Jean Douchet, Claude Chabrol and Eric Rohmer). Despite the assortment of stories and styles, they cohere nicely and leave viewers with a memorable experience of several interesting Parisian characters. Mature themes and treatment. A-III (nr)

Six Pack (1982) Kenny Rodgers plays a fading racecar driver who becomes the surrogate father of six needy orphans. Soon he's back on top with the kids as his pit crew and he even decides to marry Erin Gray whom he favors with his presence every few months. Directed by Daniel Petrie, it's sheer, contrived mediocrity from start to finish. Foul language out of the mouths of babes and a benign attitude toward casual sex. A-III (PG) AA

Six-Pack Annie (1975) Young girl (Lindsay Bloom) becomes a prostitute in order to save her aunt's restaurant from foreclosure. Directed by Graydon F. David, the tedious, flat movie is as consistently vulgar as it is unfunny. O (R)

633 Squadron (1964) Routine World War II story directed by Walter Grauman has an American (Cliff Robertson) heading a squadron of British bombers on a raid to destroy a mountain-sheltered German war factory in Norway. Stylized violence and hokey heroics. A-II (br) A

Six Weeks (1982) Congressional candidate (Dudley Moore) befriends a youngster dying of leukemia (Katherine Healy) who persuades her wealthy mother (Mary Tyler Moore) to back his campaign, but when she succumbs to his charm, he reciprocates and his marriage is in jeopardy. Director Tony Bill's romance is outrageously sentimental, totally detached from both political and human realities and cloyingly smug in its hedonistic values. A-III (PG)

Sixteen Candles (1984) A girl (Molly Ringwald) is devastated when her family, in the throes of preparing for her older sister's marriage, forgets about her 16th birthday. Were that not enough, she is pursued by a skinny freshman (Anthony Michael Hall) while longing for a handsome, unattainable senior (Michael Schoeffling). Director John Hughes' old-fashioned comedy about the anguish of adolescence is updated, alas, by a dose of foul language, pervasive vulgarity, some shower room nudity and a benign view of casual sex. Some other not-so-bright spots include nasty stereotyping of Orientals and Italians and some National Lampoon-style laughs at the expense of a girl in a body brace. O (PG) 15

Skateboard (1978) Down-on-his-luck agent (Allen Garfield) extricates himself from the clutches of a loan shark by becoming a skateboard entrepreneur. Directed by George Gage, it is a very bad little movie hastily and cheaply slapped together to cash in on a fad, it is also offensive in its benign attitude toward teenage promiscuity and drinking. O (PG) A

Skatetown, U.S.A. (1979) Ho-hum homage to the fad of disco roller skating pits a nice young man against a tough dude in competing for the big skating crown. Written, produced and directed by William Levey, the undernourished storyline constantly breaks for unfunny comic sketches (Ruth Buzzey and Flip Wilson), undistinguished songs and skating numbers. Frequently sleazy mood and abundance of marijuana consumption in the background, and sometimes the foreground, make it highly dubious fare for any but mature viewers. A-III (PG)

Skezag (1971) Well-intended but amateurish documentary about drug abuse goes on endlessly with New York addicts using street language describing the scene. In the last sequence, however, filmmakers Joel Freedman and Phil Messina revisit an addict who is now a walking dead man, hollow of soul and poisoned of body, conveying most effectively what had been missing so incessantly in the preceding footage. Those last few minutes say more than anyone needs to know about the white powder that destroys so many young Americans. A-IV (nr)

Ski Bum, The (1970) Failed screen version of a Romain Gary novel about a young drifter (Zalman King) hanging around a Colorado winter resort who becomes embroiled in a crooked business scheme, is roundly double-crossed and left emotionally shattered by the experience. Directed by Bruce Clark, the plot is episodic and underdeveloped, the characters are superficial and their motivations often enigmatic. A confused morality underpins the story. O (R)

Ski Fever (1969) Ski instructor (Martin Milner) at an Austrian ski lodge finds his contract requires him to socialize with the guests and, by the time of the movie's romantic fade-out, he has teamed up with one of them (Claudia Martin). Directed by Curt Siodmak, it's an inept story built around some footage of the Austrian Giant Slalom, but not even ski enthusiasts will find it worth seeing. A-III (M)

Ski Patrol (1990) The schemes of a sleazy land developer (Martin Mull) to take over a trendy ski resort run owned by a popular old-timer (Ray Walston) are thwarted by its dauntless young staff of ski patrollers whose talents also include dancing, singing and partying. Director Richard Correll combines his paint-by-numbers cast with dumb, vulgar hijinks to concoct a basically innocuous sophomoric comedy highlighted by snazzy ski togs and funky daredevil skiing. Minor sexual innuendos, bathroom humor and incidental rough language. A-II (PG)

Skidoo (1969) Retired thug (Jackie Gleason) is ordered by his old boss (Groucho Marx) to rub out a loquacious friend (Mickey Rooney) safely ensconced in prison. As directed by Otto Preminger, it's a mixture of inert comedy and ponderous satire, done in consistently bad taste with some lecherous dialogue and sexual shenanigans. O (M) AA

Skin Deep (1989) Menopausal male saga about a famous writer (John Ritter) suffering simultaneously from alcoholism, writer's block and an obsession to bed every nubile female who crosses his path. Written and directed by Blake Edwards, the movie lacks any moral insight in following the Lothario from one pointless liaison to another while romanticizing his lust for sex and alcohol. Some nudity and much profanity. O (R) 18

Skin Game (1971) In the pre-Civil War border states, a cunning con-artist (James Garner) makes the rounds selling his slave (Lou Gossett) and then waiting with the cash for him to escape and proceed to the next con, until another crook (Susan Clark) adds a new dimension of confusion. Director Paul Bogart blends large doses of improbability with pinches of reality to keep the interracial swindle skimming along its superficial surface, only touching on the serious for comic effect. A-III (GP) U

Skull, The (1965) Weak British horror story about a student of the occult (Peter Cushing) who becomes obsessed by the evil powers of the Marquis de Sade's skull.

Directed by Freddie Francis, the trappings of black magic and witchcraft are as hokey as the action is clunky. Stylized violence and creaky menace. A-II (br) X

Skullduggery (1970) Witless, at times tasteless, comedy about an anthropologist (Susan Clark) whose New Guinea expedition is led by their guide (Burt Reynolds) into uncharted territory where they discover a species of apes that manifest distinctly human qualities. Directed by Gordon Douglas, the question of whether the creatures are indeed human is kicked around in aimless fashion, matched by banal dialogue and half-dimensional characterizations. Reference to bestiality. A-III (PG) AA

Sky Bandits (1986) A British production set in World War I France tells the comic adventures of two bank robbers (Scotty McGinnis; Jeff Osterhage) who join the army to avoid prison and blunder their way through the war in a series of stolen airplanes. Directed by Zoran Perisic, the charm of this elegantly photographed movie derives from high-spirited performances and fanciful sets, props and special effects. Post-bedroom scene and some very stylized wartime violence. A-II (PG)

Sky Riders (1976) Routine melodrama about the rescue of a family kidnapped by terrorists through the intervention of some daring hang-gliding enthusiasts is distinguished only by some spectacular aerial photography. Directed by Douglas Hickox, the movie's violent elements include the terrorists' threatening of a small child. A-III (PG) A

Skyjacked (1972) Effective thriller about an American airliner hijacked to Russia. Capt. Charlton Heston keeps his plane-load of problem characters under control on a flight chock full of dangerous situations, ending in a shootout at Moscow airport. John Guillermin directs with emphasis upon suspense rather than trying to develop characterization or the numerous subplots. Unpretentious escapist entertainment. A-II (PG) A

Slams, The (1973) Super-bad, super-cool Jim Brown is in the penitentiary but has stashed away $1.5 million in Mafia drug money for his planned break-out to escape to the Caribbean with girlfriend Judy Pace. Directed by Jonathan Kaplan, the brutal and sadistic action is as relentless and explicit as the prison language, which consists largely of racial, sexual and just plain mean insults. O (R)

Slap, The (1976) Lightweight comedy-drama—sort of an updated "Father of the Bride"—in which talented actors Lino Ventura, Annie Giradot and Isabelle Adjani struggle gallantly with an aimless script more suited to American TV than a French film. Sexual innuendo. A-III (PG)

Slap Shot (1977) Paul Newman stars as an aging player-coach who rejuvenates an inept bush-league hockey team by introducing the wonders of dirty playing to his charges. Directed by George Roy Hill, the playing is but one of the dirty elements in a crude, foul-mouthed comedy. Some nudity. O (R) X

Slaughter (1972) Black exploitation story of an ex-Green Beret (Jim Brown) who pummels his way into an international conspiracy and becomes the unwilling employee of the U.S. Government. Directed by Jack Starrett, the production values are minimal, with the emphasis on the hero's biceps and his winning ways with knuckles and bullets. Excessively graphic violence and sex. O (R) X

Slaughter Hotel (1973) The hotel referred to in the title is a country rest home where medieval weapons decorate the parlors and become the means by which a prowling psychopath viciously disposes of sexually frustrated women and their nurses. Dreadfully inept Italian production directed by Fernanado Di Leo with gross violence. O (R)

Slaughter's Big Rip-Off (1973) Big, bad Jim Brown mows his way through the Los Angeles branch of the Syndicate (headed by Ed McMahon) and plows through a number of willing female sex objects. Directed by Gordon Douglas, rip-off is the operative word in this cheap sex-and-violence exploitation job. O (R) X

Slaughterhouse Five (1972) Uneven film version of Kurt Vonnegut Jr.'s time-tripping novel about the progress of a soldier (Michael Sacks) from POW chaplain's assistant, to witness at the 1945 firebombing of Dresden, to post-war participant in the American Way of Life and, at last, the captive of a Hollywood starlet (Valerie Perrine), the girl of his erotic dreams. Directed by George Roy Hill, the wildly seriocomic satire on American manners and mores is mostly on target and the acting is first-rate, though its hero's helplessness in dropping in and out of time tends to be confusing and, at times, incoherent. Marred by unnecessary nudity. A-IV (R) X

Slaughterhouse Rock (1988) Even some funny moments cannot save this teen horror film set on Alcatraz Island, which a local student (Nicholas Celozzi) and his friends visit one night to confront the source of his bad dreams—the marauding ghost of a cannibal who once inhabited the island. Directed by Dimitri Logothetis, it is an amateurish production with a nonsensical plot. Much gore and violence, several nude scenes, an attempted rape and some profanity. O (R)

Slave of Love, A (1978) Movie company in the Crimea grinds out melodramatic romances seemingly oblivious to the Bolshevik revolution sweeping across 1917 Russia. In the end, the company's empty-headed but beautiful star (Elena Solovei) joins her cameraman in smuggling out film of czarist atrocities in the area. Gorgeously photographed and engagingly acted, director Nikita Mikhalkov's nostalgic tribute to the silent movies and their age of innocence is an enjoyable experience in spite of perfunctory Soviet propaganda. A-III (nr)

Slaves (1969) Inept melodrama about a hard-working slave (Ossie Davis) who is unjustly sold to a bad master (Stephen Boyd) whose mistreatment drives him to foment a slave uprising. Director Herbert Biberman depends largely upon dialogue rather than visuals to convey the historical reality of the terrible injustices of slavery. It's an important subject and it's unfortunate that it has been done poorly. Several scenes with nudity. A-III (R) X

Slaves of New York (1989) Director James Ivory's unsuccessful satire of the contemporary downtown Manhattan art scene works overtime to reproduce its chaotic glitz but fails to provide more than superficial commentary on the hedonistic, narcissistic denizens of this throwaway subculture. Satiric glamorization of sexual promiscuity and drug abuse, brief nudity and some profanity. O (R) 15

Slayground (1984) The getaway car in a robbery crashes into a limousine, killing the young daughter of a millionaire who retaliates by hiring a professional hitman to track down the gang's leader (Peter Coyote), a sensitive fellow already badly upset by the tragic turn of events. British production directed by Terry Bedford is a run-of-the-mill chase movie with some pretentious literary overtones. Stylized violence. A-III (R) 18

Sleeper (1973) Typically wacky Woody Allen spoof on contemporary society's pop foibles in a plot casting Woody as a chap who goes into the hospital for routine surgery and wakes up 200 years from now in a world gone mad with people dependent upon electronic gadgets (most of which don't work). Without an identity, he becomes tapped to lead a revolution and soon finds that his new friends are often more dangerous than his intended enemies. The humor is rapid-fire, mainly of the one-liner and sight gag variety and his satirical targets include just about every institution or group on the scene. A-III (PG) A

Sleeping Beauty (1959) This classic story of love conquering evil remains the late Walt Disney's last great achievement of storytelling in fully detailed animation. Fine family entertainment. A-I (G) U

Sleeping Car Murders, The (1966) French suspense thriller about a homicidal maniac.

Directed by Costa-Gavras, it affects a benign attitude toward premarital sex and unnecessarily graphic treatment of several erotic sequences. O (br) X

Sleeping with the Enemy (1991) When a psychotically jealous husband (Patrick Bergin) discovers his abused wife (Julia Roberts) has faked her own death to escape him, he tracks her down and finds her in the arms of her new love (Kevin Anderson). Director Joe Ruben's sleek thriller efficiently creates suspense by making full use of Robert's beautifully played vulnerability, but falters with a needless cliche at the end. Some violence, restrained marital encounter and minimal rough language. A-III (R) 15

Sleepless in Seattle (1993) After hearing a Seattle widower (Tom Hanks and his boy (Ross Malinger) on a syndicated radio talk show on Christmas Eve, a young reporter (Meg Ryan) feels irresistibly drawn to the man even though she is engaged and lives in Baltimore. Director Nora Ephron turns in a highly appealing if unabashedly romantic love story about singles and families, liberally sprinkled with comic moments. Some mild sexual references and a live-in relationship. A-III (PG)

Sleepwalkers (see: "Stephen King's Sleepwalkers").

Slender Thread, The (1966) A telephone is the only means by which a psychology student (Sidney Poitier) can hope to save a woman (Anne Bancroft) who has taken an overdose of barbiturates. Director Sydney Pollack's story has an overabundance of contrivances, but the acting of the principals makes it all seem urgent and worth the emotional involvement. A-II (br) A

Sleuth (1972) Stylish screen version of Anthony Shaffer's play about an urbane writer of detectives stories (Laurence Olivier) who invites his wife's lover (Michael Caine) to his mansion and the two engage in a game of wits that becomes progressively more deadly. Directed by Joseph Mankiewicz, the intricately plotted thriller is carried off by the tautly balanced performances of the two principals, but attentive viewers will see through the mystery early on. Some sharp tension and suspense make it mature fare. A-III (PG) AA

Slipper and the Rose, The (1976) Richard Chamberlain and Gemma Craven star in a pleasant and very entertaining British version of the Cinderella story as directed by Bryan Forbes. A-I (G)

Slither (1973) Offbeat comedy adventure concerning a dense ex-con (James Caan) and his equally bumbling partner (Peter Boyle) who wend their way across rural California in search of a hidden stash of embezzled cash. Directed by Howard Zieff, there's plenty of fun along the way as the inept pair try to figure out the secret of the loot's location, but the chuckles trail off badly with a twist ending. Some rough language. A-III (PG) AA

Sliver (1993) Boring potboiler about a book editor (Sharon Stone) moving into a death-plagued Manhattan high-rise where, after becoming sexually involved with the owner (William Baldwin), she learns he is secretly videotaping the private activities of all his tenants and may have murdered some of them. Under Phillip Noyce's lifeless direction, the story lacks suspense, focusing instead on the sexual proclivities of fuzzy, shallow characters of interest only to voyeurs. Several graphic sex scenes, recurring nudity, many sexist references, some violence and intermittent rough language. O (R) 18

Slogan (1970) French story of a love affair between a married middle-aged director of television commercials (Serge Gainsbourg) and a mixed-up adolescent (Jane Birkin) might be taken as a parody of other glamorous but empty screen romances. Directed by Pierre Grimblat, this film's characters serve simply as cardboard contrivances for glossy photographic effects and for sensationalizing what should have been a rather painful moral dilemma. O (GP)

Slow Dancing in the Big City (1978) Tough, streetwise columnist for a New York newspaper (Paul Sorvino) falls in love with a beautiful Canadian dancer (Anne Ditchburn) who is making her debut at Lincoln Center but is afraid it might be her finale. Thanks to an appealing performance by Sorvino, the movie has a few good moments but, as directed by John G. Avildsen, its blatant sentimentality, its contrived plot and its shallow characterizations prevent it from being anything more than mediocre entertainment. A-II (PG) AA

Slugger's Wife, The (1985) Failed Neil Simon comedy about a baseball star (Michael O'Keefe) married to a rock singer (Rebecca DeMornay). Some sexually oriented scenes and a rather benign view of premarital sex. A-III (PG-13)

Small Change (1976) Episodic French serio-comedy about the natural innocence of childhood that protects youngsters from being overwhelmed by the harsher realities of life. Director Francois Truffaut offers older viewers a chance to rediscover their own childhood as well as being more sympathetic to the needs of youngsters who depend upon them. Excellent movie for parents to share with their youngsters. A-II (PG) A

Small Circle of Friends, A (1980) Radcliffe coed (Karen Allen) becomes the mistress of two Harvard students (Brad Davis; Jameson Parker) during the late-1960s' campus anti-war activities. Director Rob Cohen's trio appear less committed to the protest movement than to indulging their selfish egos. Benign view of illicit sex and some graphic visuals of sexual activity. O (R) X

Small Town in Texas, A (1976) Young convict (Timothy Bottoms) gets out of prison and returns home to find himself harassed by the corrupt sheriff who framed him. Director Jack Starrett's mindlessly violent chase movie is of no interest. O (R) A

Smashing the Money Ring (1939) Standard B-budget programmer in which secret service operative Brass Bancroft (Ronald Reagan) masquerades as a convict in order to get the goods on a counterfeiting gang using the prison print shop. Directed by Terry Morse, the threadbare plot paces the forgettable action with occasional comic relief from Eddie Foy Jr. as a gabby federal agent. Stylized violence. A-III (br) A

Smashing Time (1968) English musical satire on London's Mod Scene, which draws two country girls (Rita Tushingham and Lynn Redgrave) who become overnight successes, but disillusioned with fame, they return home. Directed by Desmond Davis, the movie is an uncomfortable mixture of realism and stylization, superficial plot and slapstick treatment. A-III (br) A

Smic Smac Smoc (1972) French romantic comedy about three Marseilles dock workers (Charles Gerard; Jean Collomb; Amidou), one of whom decides to marry the baker's maid (Catherine Allegret) and the other two host a wacky wedding-day celebration that lands all the revelers in the clink. Unpretentious little movie with plenty of charm and smiles, directed by Claude Lelouch with a few of his friends, including composer Francis Lai as a blind accordionist playing lush themes from earlier Lelouch movies. Some earthy dialogue. A-III (GP)

Smile (1975) Facile car salesman (Bruce Dern) is a judge in the American Miss beauty contest who, by its end, begins to realize that his philosophy of life has been as empty as that of the contest. Director Michael Ritchie's satire affects a snickering, superior attitude toward the people it pictures as crass and ludicrous and itself becomes nothing more than a peep show, lacking in a sense of humanity that might have redeemed its dabbling in voyeurism. Sexual situations. O (PG) A

Smile Orange (1976) Comedy directed by Trevor Rhone and set in Jamaica deals with a black waiter and his encounters with American tourists, which result in some satiric but good-natured thrusts at human nature whether black, white or brown. Its paper-thin story, however, grows increasingly silly and some exploitative nudity could easily have been done without. O (PG)

Smilin' Through (1941) Sentimental Victorian sudser in which an Englishman (Brian Aherne) devotes himself to raising an orphaned niece (Jeanette MacDonald), then she falls for the son (Gene Raymond) of the man who had killed her uncle's beloved on their wedding day. Directed by Frank Borzage, the fanciful romantic melodrama counterpoints the young people's courtship with the uncle's tragic love, all sweetly embellished by MacDonald's rendering of period ballads. Heavy sledding for youngsters. A-I (br) A

Smith (1969) Contemporary western about a cattle rancher (Glenn Ford) who champions an Indian accused of murder. Unusually good Disney effort dealing with racial intolerance and the need for people of different cultures to get along together, though director Michael O'Herlihy's sentimental lack of realism mars the central trial sequences. Good family setting with warmly likable characters. A-I (G)

Smokey and the Bandit (1977) Burt Reynolds, Sally Field and Jackie Gleason star in this chase comedy about a daredevil trucker pursued by a state trooper. Director Hal Needham's action comedy has little humor and lots of elaborate but boring car crashes. Some rough language, many vulgarities and suggestion of premarital sex. A-III (PG)

Smokey and the Bandit II (1980) Burt Reynolds, Sally Field and Jackie Gleason do it again in a sequel that, like the original, is essentially a live-action version of a Road Runner cartoon. Directed by Hal Needham, this time the plot involves trucking a pregnant elephant over several state lines, with the usual car chases and crashes, an abundance of crude sexual references and vulgar language. A-III (PG)

Smokey and the Bandit, Part III (1983) Burt Reynolds makes but the briefest of appearances in this sequel about a trucker (Jerry Reed) racing the clock to transport a plastic replica of a shark on time inspite of being pursued by a loud-mouthed sheriff (Jackie Gleason). Director Dick Lowry's chase farce hits new lows in moral as well as entertainment terms. Demeaning sexual humor and foul language. O (PG)

Smoky (1966) Fess Parker stars in a nicely done family-type western based on the Will James novel about a rancher and an outlaw mustang stallion. Directed by George Sherman, it affords plenty of outdoor action for all. A-I (br) U

Smooth Talk (1986) Written and directed by Joyce Chopra, it's the story of a maturing teenage girl (Laura Dern) who places herself in a dangerous situation when a soft-spoken stranger (Treat Williams) talks her into accepting him as her first lover. The movie seems to accept this as a reasonable introduction to womanhood. O (PG-13) 15

Snake Pit, The (1948) Earnest story of a woman (Olivia DeHavilland) who suffers a nervous breakdown and the treatment she receives from a dedicated psychiatrist (Leo Genn) in an overcrowded state mental institution. Directed by Anatole Litvak, the movie's sympathetic treatment of a mental case broke new ground in its day but seems dated now. Stylized depiction of a psychotic condition and the use of shock treatment. A-II (br) A

Snapper, The (1993) Upset Irish parents (Colm Meaney; Ruth McCabe) stand by their pregnant 20-year-old daughter (Tina Kelleher) when she refuses to name the father whom gossipy neighbors suspect is a middle-aged married man (Pat Laffan). Director Stephen Frears' failed comedy presents a boisterous family coping to maintain dignity under fire, but while the parents are sympathetic characters, their immature daughter is not and her predicament tends to be trivialized. Brief bedroom scenes, minor violence, frequent rough language and much heavy drinking. A-III (R) 18

Sneakers (1992) Duped into giving top-secret computer information to the mob, an eccentric team of security experts (including Robert Redford; Sidney Poitier; Dan Aykroyd) risk their lives in attempting to retrieve it for the government. Director Phil Alden Robinson's high-tech comic-flavored caper frequently bogs down in glaring script implausibilities. Lighthearted attitude toward computer crime, brief violence, a sexual reference and minimal rough language. A-III (PG-13) 12

Sniper (1993) Lethargic action thriller teams a Marine sniper (Tom Berenger) with a novice intelligence agent (Billy Zane) in sloughing through the Panamanian jungle on a covert mission to assassinate a rebel leader. Director Luis Llosa fails to build much interest in the personal antagonism between the two assassins, focusing instead on the deadly fantasy of Americans licensed to kill on behalf of some shady U.S. government officials. Sanctions assassins as heroes, some graphic violence and occasional rough language. O (R) 15

Snoopy, Come Home (1972) Disappointing animated feature from the Peanuts gang of Charles M. Schulz uses a lot of aimless skits to pad out a saccharine story of Snoopy's visit to his original owner, a little girl who lies ailing in the hospital. Directed by Bill Melendez, the result lacks author Schulz's characteristic humor and intelligence in dealing with the little joys and anxieties of childhood. A-I (G) U

Snow Job (1972) Failed caper movie involves ex-ski champion Jean-Claude Killy in the robbery of a posh ski resort high in the Italian Alps from which he skies down the impossible slope of an adjacent glacier in a heart-thumping display of skiing skills and thrills, some of which are pretty terrifying. Aside from that, director George Englund can't do much with a silly plot, shallow characterizations and the star's impressive lack of acting talent. A-III (G)

Snow White and the Seven Dwarfs (1937) Walt Disney's first feature-length fairy tale remains an amazingly fresh and inventive landmark in the history of movie animation. Sequences such as Snow White's flight from the terrifying Queen, the antics of the dwarfs and the forest animals racing to the rescue through a frightening storm retain their original vitality and impact. Disney's combination of sentiment, laughter, and excitement makes the movie an especially satisfying entertainment for every age. A-I (G) U

Snowball Express (1972) Big-city accountant (Dean Jones) leaves his boring job to run a tumbledown Colorado ski resort hotel inherited from a distant relative and his enthusiasm is enjoyably infectious as he wins out over avalanches, bank foreclosures, burst water pipes and other impossible odds. Above-average Disney comedy directed by Norman Tokar has some very funny moments, a fine supporting cast and a story that should hold the interest of the entire family. A-I (G) U

Soapdish (1991) The interlocking personal lives of a soap opera cast and crew (Sally Field, Kevin Kline, Whoppi Goldberg, Elisabeth Shue and Robert Downey Jr.) get progressively crazier than their daily TV melodrama. Some good satirical lines and a sharp ensemble cast make director Michael Hoffman's fitfully funny spoof more zany than racy. Frequent bawdy innuendo and minimal rough language. A-III (PG-13) 15

So Big (1953) Edna Ferber's period family saga about an independent woman (Jane Wyman) who, after the death of her husband (Sterling Hayden), builds a successful truck-farming business near Chicago, then tries to save her architect son (Steve Forrest) from getting involved with the wrong society set. Directed by Robert Wise, Wyman's performance is good enough to almost make this manipulative melodrama worth watching. Pre-teens will find the later portions heavy-going. A-I (br) U

So Fine (1981) Meek college professor (Ryan O'Neal) comes out of his shell to save his father's garment business by accidentally inventing jeans with transparent seats but gets into trouble through a reluctant affair with a gangster's wife (Mariangela

Melato). Written and directed by Andrew Bergman, the vulgar and mostly unfunny comedy tries to get laughs from overt sexuality and obscene language. O (R) AA

So I Married an Axe Murderer (1993) Sophomoric comedy in which a young man (Mike Myers) suspects his bride (Nancy Travis) is a notorious murderess who has axed her last three husbands to death. Director Thomas Schlamme lets a slightly amusing situation lurch out of control as it careens toward a contrived and hammy climax. Some comic violence, a live-in relationship, momentary rear nudity and an instance of rough language. A-III (PG-13)

So Proudly We Hail (1943) Maudlin morale booster about Army nurses (Claudette Colbert, Paulette Goddard, Veronica Lake and others) caring for the wounded during the battle of Bataan, then the siege of Corregidor, all the while fearing capture by the Japanese. Directed by Mark Sandrich, the emphasis is on the heroism of the Americans and their Filipino allies against the overwhelming forces of an inhuman enemy, relieved only by some battlefield romances (George Reeves and Sonny Tufts). Wartime violence and patriotic rhetoric. A-II (br) A

S.O.B. (1981) Hollywood producer (Richard Mulligan) attempts to transform his multimillion dollar flop into a box office winner by persuading its star, who's also his wife (Julie Andrews), to forsake her wholesome screen image and bare her breasts on camera. Directed by Blake Edwards, the satiric comedy has some very funny moments, but they do not soften the movie's basically cynical outlook and amoral perspective that exploits its audience in the same way as the moviemakers it criticizes. Some sequences involving nudity. O (R) 15

Socrates (1971) Italian director Roberto Rossellini re-creates the life of the Greek philosopher drawing heavily on the works of Plato and other traditional sources for script and setting. In the title role, Jean Sylvere is quite acceptable and the drama of his trial and subsequent death becomes increasingly involving and poignant. However, so much philosophy reduced to English subtitles for 120 minutes becomes essentially a rapid reading exercise. A-I (nr)

Sofie (1993) Slow but graceful story of a close-knit Jewish family in late-19th-century Copenhagen where their only daughter (Karen-Lise Mynster) falls in love with a gentile artist (Jesper Christensen) but dutifully marries a dull, seemingly prosperous Jewish merchant (Torben Zeller) to please her parents (Erland Josephson and Ghita Norby) and preserve the family's Jewish heritage. Director Liv Ullmann unfolds an episodic tale of family life, treating each character with equal compassion, while focusing on the daughter's struggle to find happiness within the confines of her parents' world. Subtitles. Some sexual innuendo and a traumatic scene with nudity. A-III (nr)

Soft Skin, The (1965) Quiet yet absorbing story examining the relationship of a middle-aged publisher (Jean Desailly) to his wife and to a lovely airline stewardess. In this mature and sensitive work, director Francois Truffaut takes a rather commonplace situation and gives it a moral weight that becomes extremely involving. Subtitles. Theme of marital infidelity. A-III (br)

Sol Madrid (1968) Routine crime melodrama directed by Brian G. Hutton in which an undercover agent (David McCallum) is sent to Mexico to break up a narcotics ring, which he does by using a gangster's girlfriend as bait. Some fairly heavy violence. A-III (br)

Solarbabies (1986) Sci-fi escapist fantasy about a group of rebellious adolescents who escape from a state-run orphanage of the distant future and help save their planet from destruction. Silly plot but imaginative special effects from director Alan Johnson who doesn't help matters by trying to enliven the action with stylized violence. A-II (PG-13)

Soldier Blue (1970) Based on the notorious 1864 Sand Creek Massacre of some 500 Cheyenne braves, women and children by the U.S. Cavalry, the account begins with a tedious romance between a soldier (Peter Strauss) and a former Indian captive (Candice Bergen) who, when she learns of the impending attack on the Indian village, tries to prevent the slaughter. Director Ralph Nelson's well-intentioned attempt to confront a military atrocity becomes itself a brutalizing experience by wallowing in graphic depictions of bloodshed and rape. Excessive, stomach-wrenching violence. O (R) X

Soldier in Skirts (see: "Triple Echo").

Soldier of Orange (1979) Dutch production about a wealthy, aristocratic young student (Rutger Hauer in a superb performance) who is caught up in the catastrophe of the Nazi invasion and becomes a hero of the Resistance. Directed by Paul Verhoeven, it is at its best as an old-fashioned war movie fortified with a credibility and heightened emotions that are above the usual. Too often, however, it indulges in showy stunts that have a jarring effect and its depiction of sexuality is excessively graphic. O (R)

Soldiers Three (1951) Pale imitation-Kipling tale of British privates (Stewart Granger; Robert Newton; Cyril Cusak) in Imperial India where their sophomoric antics help put down a rebellion to the satisfaction of their regimental commander (Walter Pidgeon). Director Tay Garnett's treatment of all these mock-heroics

flounders erratically and the trio's supposed camaraderie is painfully artificial and belabored. Stylized violence. A-II (br) U

Soldier's Story, A (1984) When a black sergeant (Adolph Caesar) is murdered at an Army camp in 1944, the investigating officer (Howard Rollins Jr.) discovers that the victim was a ruthless tyrant who had been well hated by his men. Director Norman Jewison's fine production looks at racial prejudice from a number of perspectives with unusually effective results. Some violence and rough language. A-II (PG) 15

Soleil-O (1973) Young accountant from a former French African colony (Robert Linesol) arrives in Paris looking for work but finds instead racism, ranging from the subtle to the blatant, becomes increasingly bewildered and finally ends on the brink of violent despair. Mauritanian production written and directed by Mel Hondo, the use of ironic humor and lively music keeps the plight of the black emigrant worker from becoming totally depressing. A-III (nr)

Solid Gold Cadillac, The (1956) Delightful comedy about a small shareholder (Judy Holliday) in a large corporation who ejects its corrupt board of directors through the proxies of other small shareholders and the savvy of an honest business executive (Paul Douglas). Directed by Richard Quine, Holliday's eccentric brand of comedy is perfectly suited to this populist tale of ordinary people triumphing over corporate sharks. Mild romantic complications. A-II (br)

Some Call It Loving (1973) Pretentious hothouse fantasy about a musician (Zalman King) who buys a Sleeping Beauty from a sideshow, wakes the sleeper (Tisa Farrow) and has her join him and his strange companions (Carol White; Veroncia Anderson) in perverse games. Directed by James B. Harris, it's a glossy exercise in voyeurism and its leering attitude toward women and sex is degrading. O (R) X

Some Girls Do (1971) Bulldog Drummond (Richard Johnson) returns as an anemic James Bond imitation with a gaggle of gorgeous girls on a secret island hideout from which the baddies plan to rule the world with a super-destructive weapon. Lackluster British movie directed by Ralph Thomas goes one step further in reducing women to objects by making them mechanical dummies activated by a convenient off/on switch behind the ear. A-III (G) A

Some Kind of a Nut (1969) When a bank teller (Dick Van Dyke) grows a beard, his boss takes it as a sign of nonconformity and orders him to shave it off. As fellow employees and associates choose sides in the course of the dispute, the hero rediscovers the sterling qualities of his about-to-be ex-wife (Angie Dickinson). Director Garson Kanin fails in his attempt at a whimsical examination of a man's search for integrity and individuality. A-III (PG) U

Some Kind of Hero (1982) Returned Vietnam prisoner of war (Richard Pryor) finds himself neck-deep in trouble when a high-priced prostitute (Margot Kidder) falls in love with him and he gets involved with organized crime. Ill-assorted mix of comedy and melodrama, which director Michael Pressman is unable to organize into any semblance of unity. Some graphic sex, cheap thrills and low humor. O (R)

Some Kind of Wonderful (1987) A confused teenager struggles against authority figures and shallow advice from parents and schoolmates in overcoming his insecurities while asserting his nonconformist aspirations. Director John Hughes' adolescent soap opera passively accepts teen sex as a natural outcome of rapid physical and underdeveloped emotional maturity as well as subtly undermining trust in the values of the adult world. A-III (PG-13)

Some of My Best Friends Are . . . (1971) Mervyn Nelson's documentary on the patrons of a gay bar borders on exploitation of its subject through demeaning cliche and stereotype that contribute nothing of understanding nor insight into homosexuality and how it affects these men's lives. O (R)

Somebody Killed Her Husband (1978) Innocuous bit of fluff in which a bumbling but charming clerk (Jeff Bridges) in Macy's toy department falls in love with a beautiful customer (Farrah Fawcett) who soon becomes a widow when somebody kills her husband. Directed by Lamont Johnson, it's a fairly entertaining mystery comedy except for its benign view of adultery. A-III (PG) A

Someone Behind the Door (1971) Plodding murder melodrama about a neurologist (Anthony Perkins) who plans to kill his wife's lover by using an escaped lunatic (Charles Bronson) but the plan goes badly awry. Directed by Nicolas Gessner, the dull and static movie contains a rape scene that is ludicrous despite its ferocity. A-III (GP) 15

Someone to Watch Over Me (1987) Failed romantic thriller in which a police detective (Tom Berenger) falls in love with the rich socialite (Mimi Rogers) he is supposed to be protecting from a killer, conveniently forgetting that he is already married to a good woman (Lorraine Bracco). Director Ridley Scott's muddled tearjerker is equally slack as a suspense thriller. Excessive violence, lush treatment of adultery and much rough language. O (R) 15

Something Big (1971) Failed western spoof about an outlaw (Dean Martin) who abducts the wife (Honor Blackman) of a U.S. Cavalry officer (Brian Keith) in order to trade her for a Gatling gun so he can mow down an army of Mexican bandits and take their hoard of stolen treasure. Directed by Andrew V. McLaglen, the comedy consists of overacting and double-entendre and the action is of the tired fantasy variety. A-III (GP) A

Something for Everyone (1970) Bleak comedy about an aspiring footman (Michael York), in the employ of an enchanting countess (Angela Lansbury), who decides that the swiftest path to noble rank is through the bedroom, with a few slayings along the way. Directed by Harold Prince, there are a few pleasant moments in this adult fairy tale, but not nearly enough for most tastes. Stylized sex and violence. A-IV (R) X

Something Short of Paradise (1979) On-again, off-again comedy romance between the manager of a New York art cinema (David Steinberg) and a journalist (Susan Sarandon) develops rather slowly, hampered by a needlessly complex flashback structure. As directed by David Helpern, the result is only moderately entertaining. The nature of the relationship between the two lovers makes it adult fare. A-III (PG)

Something to Sing About (1937) Silly but unpretentious romantic comedy in which a bandleader (James Cagney) returns from his honeymoon to discover he's an overnight Hollywood sensation with a movie contract that forces him to pretend he's not married. Directed by Victor Schertzinger, the Cagney vehicle is entirely predictable but provides a lot of light, fluffy fun, especially the period music. A-I (br) U

Something Wicked This Way Comes (1983) Disney adaptation of the Ray Bradbury story about a strange traveling carnival that disrupts life in a small Illinois town sometime in the 1920s. The evil carnival master (Jonathan Pryce) fulfills peoples's desires, but in a way that costs them dearly. When two adventurous boys (Vidal Peterson and Shawn Carson) tumble to the carnival master's secret, they become the special object of his malevolence. Jack Clayton directs all this with just the right blend of tension and human warmth, but some of the special effects are definitely not for younger viewers. A-II (PG)

Something Wild (1986) Eccentric young woman (Melanie Griffith) seduces a corruptible yuppie (Jeff Daniels) into a kinky romance based on mutual deception but, when her husband (Ray Liotta) gets out of prison, the affair becomes deadly. Although indicating the moral bankruptcy of the central characters, director Jonathan Demme's emphasis on the sexual nature of their relationship results in just another male sex fantasy. Nudity in a sexual context, brutal violence and profanity. O (R) 18

Sometimes a Great Notion (1971) Muddled screen version of the Ken Kesey novel about a family of independent Oregon loggers whose reliance on rugged individualism makes them defy a strike action called by their fellow loggers and this has dire, far-reaching consequences. Directed by Paul Newman, who also stars as the family's leader, the story's action is effectively presented, notably the difficulty and dangers of logging, and is extremely well acted. However, the movie's sympathies about its larger theme of individualism versus society and changing conditions are ambiguous, if not confused, especially in its final, vulgar gesture of defiance. Heavy-going even for adults. A-IV (GP)

Somewhere in Time (1980) Young playwright (Christopher Reeve) wills himself back several generations into the past to meet the famous actress (Jane Seymour) with whose portrait he has fallen in love. Directed by Jeannot Szwarc, the sentimental romance and its lovely images (filmed on Mackinac Island) are for incurable romantics only. A-II (PG) A

Sommersby (1993) An abusive husband (Richard Gere) is so changed for the better after years in a Civil War P.O.W. camp that his wife (Jodie Foster) is sure he is an imposter but plays along until their happiness is shattered when he is tried for murder. Director Jon Amiel's mystery-laden period romance is an engrossing tale of a man's struggle for personal integrity and the positive effects that has on all around him. Mature themes with brief violence and very discreet marital encounters. A-III (PG-13) 12

Son-in-Law (1993) Airhead comedy in which a coed (Carla Gugino) brings a freaky college chum (Pauly Shore) home for the Thanksgiving weekend to her straitlaced farm family, with the two pretending to be engaged to save her from accepting the marriage proposal of a longtime boyfriend. Director Steve Rash fails to sustain the one-joke premise of Shore as a fish out of water in Heartland America, with the humor wholly dependent on anti-authoritarian, often vulgar stabs at humor. Mild sexual innuendo, fleeting nudity, momentary violence and many crude remarks. A-III (PG-13)

Son of Blob (1972) Once again the creeping crimson mass has fun overrunning Small Town USA, sparing no one in its path until a fearless couple (Robert Walker Jr. and Gwynne Gilford) remember the chilling device used by Steve McQueen to stop the blob in the original. Directed by Larry Hagman, the object this time is to glean smiles instead of screams from undemanding viewers who are helped by delightful cameos from the likes of Godfrey Cambridge and Shelley Berman. Fantasy violence. A-II (GP)

Son of Godzilla (1969) Dubbed Japanese production directed by Jun Fukuda has the old monster come to the rescue of a baby Godzilla attacked by gigantic insects on a radioactive Pacific island. Inane plot and cheesy special effects violence. A-II (br)

Son of Paleface (1952) Searching out West for his father's hidden treasure, a Harvard man (Bob Hope) gets mixed up with a lady outlaw (Jane Russell) and a government agent (Roy Rogers). Directed by Frank Tashlin, the "Paleface" sequel has its comic moments but doesn't measure up to the original. Some stylized violence and sexual innuendo. A-III (br) U

Son of the Pink Panther (1993) Unaware he is the illegitimate son of the late great Inspector Clouseau, a bumbling gendarme (Roberto Benigni) assigned to aid the police chief (Herbert Lom) in recovering a kidnapped princess (Debrah Farentino) only further complicates the case with his accident-prone shenanigans. Director Blake Edwards poorly utilizes the comic talents of Benigni by lamely recycling pranks and pratfalls from seven previous *Panther* outings while neglecting to develop a believable or interesting plot. Occasional sexual innuendo and some nasty violence played for laughs. A-III (PG)

Song of Bernadette, The (1943) Durable adaptation of the Franz Werfel novel about Bernadette Soubirous (Jennifer Jones), the French schoolgirl who in 1858 saw apparitions of the Virgin Mary at a grotto near Lourdes, but news of this is initially discredited by her stern pastor (Charles Bickford), the town prosecutor (Vincent Price) and an envious teacher (Gladys Cooper). Directed by Henry King, the story of a young girl's faith withstanding the disbelief of her elders is made dramatically convincing by a fine cast, evocative photography and largely unsentimental treatment. A-I (br) U

Song of Norway (1970) Huge, panoramic biographical portrait of composer Edvard Grieg (Toralv Maurstad), filmed in the natural splendor of his beautiful Norway. Part of the saga involves the two women in his life: the heiress who rejects his love and then tries to buy him back (Christina Schollin) and the patient admirer and singer of his works whom he eventually marries (Florence Henderson). Written and directed by Andrew Stone, the result is a stunning musical postcard, but its personal drama does not measure up to its magnificent location photography. Still, it offers more than enough wholesome entertainment to satisfy most family viewers. A-I (G)

Song of the South (1946) James Baskett gives a winning performance as Uncle Remus, the wise old storyteller who helps a youngster (Bobby Driscoll) understand the ways of the world through folktales about Brer Rabbit and his friends. The Disney version of Joel Chandler Harris' tales from the mythic Old South is a warm and zestful mixture of animation and live action that most parents will enjoy as much as the youngsters. A-I (G) U

Song to Remember, A (1944) Slick Hollywood biography of composer Frederick Chopin (1810-1849) who, after escaping czarist oppression in Warsaw, finds fame and love in Paris with writer George Sand (Merle Oberon), until his death on a concert tour raising money for Polish independence. Directed by Charles Walters, the result focuses on Chopin's nationalism as nurtured by his music teacher (Paul Muni) with little attention to his struggles and achievements as an artist. Discreet depiction of an unmarried relationship. A-II (br) U

Song Without End (1960) Elegant but overblown biography of Hungarian composer Franz Liszt (1811-1886) centers on his unhappy affairs with a French countess (Genevieve Page), then a Russian princess (Capucine), ultimately ending in retirement to a monastery. Directed by Charles Vidor and completed by George Cukor, the result never gets beneath the surface of the characters or the glossy veneer of the Romantic Age, though the music is splendid and Dirk Bogarde's portrayal of Liszt offers an unusual mix of the pious and the profane. Discreet treatment of sexual relationships. A-II (br)

Sons of Katie Elder, The (1965) John Wayne stars as the eldest of four brothers (Dean Martin, Earl Holliman and Michael Anderson Jr.) who reunite at the funeral of their mother, then set out to get the land grabber (James Gregory) who killed their father and stole the family ranch. Directed by Henry Hathaway, the story is overly familiar as well as overlong but there are some rousing action sequences and Wayne is in top form as the mythic western hero who prevails against injustice. Some fairly intense stylized violence. A-I (br) U

Sophie's Choice (1982) Plodding screen version of William Styron's novel about a Polish survivor of Auschwitz (Meryl Streep) who in 1947 has found refuge in a garish pink boarding house in Brooklyn with her lover (Kevin Kline), an American Jew of mercurial temperament. A young, inexperienced southern writer (Peter MacNichol) gets caught up in their lives, their lies and their secrets (including one that gives the story its title). Director Alan J. Pakula gets good performances and tries to keep the sluggish narrative moving, but in the end it seems hardly worth the effort. Suicide figures in the plot and there is some brief nudity and rough language. A-III (R) 15

Sorcerer (1977) Four down-and-outers (Roy Scheider, Bruno Cremer, Francisco Rabal and Amidou) in a South American backwater seize the chance to drive trucks loaded with dynamite over some 200 miles of jungle road in order to put out a burning oil well. Director William Friedkin sketches in the background of each of the four, unlike the original 1953 French movie, "The Wages of Fear," upon which it is based, but in doing so diffuses the impact of the dangerous truck ride. Occasional violence and a scene showing the victims of the oil well explosion. A-III (PG)

Sorrow and the Pity, The (1972) Classic documentary directed by Marcel Ophuls examines France during the German Occupation and replaces the legend of popular resistance with the fact of complicity by large sections of society. Focusing on the town of Clermont-Ferrand, Ophuls uses it as a measure of the nation's collaboration with the Nazis. The object is not to judge the inhabitants of the village but to show how easy it is for people in crisis to accept tyranny and yet believe that they are free. A-II (PG)

Soul Man (1986) Youth from a wealthy family finds a way to pay for his Harvard Law School education by means of a minority student scholarship when he takes pills that blacken the color of his skin. This disappointing youth-oriented comedy fails to deliver any insightful social satire save some foul one-liners. Instead, it affirms the materialistic aspirations of young people, faces issues of racial prejudice only superficially and is accepting of promiscuous sex and false social values. O (PG-13) 15

Soul of Nigger Charley, The (1973) Lame sequel to "The Legend of Nigger Charley" finds the two ex-slaves (Fred Williamson, D'Urville Martin) up against some Confederate aristocrats who are trying to re-create the Old South in Mexico. Director Larry Spangler places the emphasis squarely on the action sequences with lots of special-effects bullet impacts. A-III (R)

Soul Soldier (1972) Low-budget story of the mostly black 10th Cavalry of Fort Davis, Texas, and their heroism against the Indians on the western frontier concentrates on foolishness at the fort rather than fortitude in the field. Directed by John Cardos, the shoddy production wastes a capable cast (Rafer Johnson, Lincoln Kilpatrick, Janee Michelle, Cesar Romero and Robert Dix) in sexual hijinks and violent heroics. O (R/GP)

Soul to Soul (1971) In celebration of its 14th year as an independent African nation,

Ghana sponsored a music festival featuring a number of America's top black rock, jazz, and blues performers, including Wilson Pickett, Roberta Flack, Ike and Tina Turner, Santana and many others. Denis Sanders' fine documentary follows the performers to Ghana, conveys some of their reflections on their participation but mostly encapsulates the festival in a joyous musical entertainment that is universal in its appeal. A-I (G)

Sound of Music, The (1965) Particularly fine screen version of the Rodgers and Hammerstein musical about the formative years of the Trapp Family Singers in Austria between the two world wars. Its interesting story, solid cast (headed by Julie Andrews and Christopher Plummer), lovely music and intelligent lyrics, colorful scenery and pleasant fantasy will entertain the mind and enliven the spirit. Directed by Robert Wise, the movie has held up over the years as thoroughly refreshing family entertainment. A-I (G) U

Sounder (1972) Appealing story about a black family of Louisiana sharecroppers struggling to survive against natural and human odds during the early days of the Depression. When the father (Paul Winfield) is jailed for stealing food, his wife (Cicely Tyson) and three children (Kevin Hooks is the eldest) are left to crop the sugar cane on their own. The boy's subsequent odyssey to find the labor camp where his father is being held provides additional drama. Produced by Robert B. Radnitz and directed by Martin Ritt, it captures the humanity of the characters and a fine, distanced sense of its sleepy Southern locale. The movie earns a deep emotional response from its audience because its story and characters are believable. Not only a valid examination of the black experience in America, it is also a fine family experience. A-I (G) U

Sounder, Part II (see: "Part II, Sounder").

Soup for One (1982) Nice young man (Saul Rubinek) wanders through New York's frenetic singles scene in search of the ideal wife in this sometimes bright but more often erratic and awkward romantic comedy written and directed by Jonathan Kaufer. Some of the jokes are more mean-spirited than genuinely satiric and its rather heavy dependence on nudity for comic relief makes this unsuitable entertainment. O (R)

Soupcon (1980) Celebrating their 25th wedding anniversary, a couple (Jean Carmet and Marie Dubois) declare to their surprised family that they are separating. Both discover in the end, that growing old together is perhaps better than chasing illusions of freedom. French production directed by Jean Charles Tacchella is a Gallic bit of whimsey with some nicely turned characterizations and a frank treatment of sex. A-III (nr)

South Central (1992) While in prison for killing a drug dealer, a member (Glenn Plummer) of a powerful black gang is reformed by a fellow inmate (Carl Lumbly) and emerges to save his young son from being turned into a criminal by the gang's leader (Byron Keith Minns). In depicting the rise of a vicious street gang in a Los Angeles ghetto, writer-director Steve Anderson is a lot more convincing than in showing the moral transformation of a bitter man into a caring father. Much graphic violence, some sexual situations and references, drug abuse and rough language. A-IV (R) 15

Southern Comfort (1981) Louisiana National Guardsmen become lost in the bayous and run afoul of vengeful Cajuns, in this grim, somber, altogether pretentious melodrama directed by Walter Hill. Aside from some spectacular cinematography by Andrew Laszlo, it has little to recommend it, though Powers Boothe makes an effective screen debut as one of the hapless guardsmen. Violence and rough language. A-III (R) 18

Southern Star, The (1969) Fortune-hunter George Segal and girlfriend Ursula Andress trek across Africa's jungles in pursuit of a diamond thief but are themselves pursued by a crook who wants both the prize diamond and the girl. Directed by Sidney Hayers, there's lots of cliched action done in tongue-in-cheek fashion, including Orson Welles as an effeminate outlaw, but there's no reason for its excessive, graphic violence. O (PG) U

Soylent Green (1973) Charlton Heston plays a New York City cop in the year 2022 when lack of food forces people to subsist on a mysterious substance called Soylent Green, the secret of which Heston discovers after the voluntary death of his assistant (Edward G. Robinson). For all its posturing about ecological and moral disaster, it's no more than a routine detective movie with a slick and shallow futuristic setting. A-III (PG) 15

Spaceballs (1987) Space-fantasy parody from writer-director Mel Brooks is a takeoff of "Star Wars" with Rick Moranis and John Candy supplying most of the character spoofs. Brooks plays a dual role in a technically polished but rather self-indulgent farce offering an assortment of movie industry jokes, mild slapstick, sexual innuendo, ethnic stereotypes and vulgar language. A-III (PG)

Spacecamp (1986) Kate Capshaw portrays an astronaut who takes a team of teenagers through training exercises at the National Aeronautics and Space Administration's facility of the same name in Huntsville, Ala. The youngsters are put to the test of courage and determination when they are accidently launched in a space shuttle by an affectionate robot. Director Harry Winer offers a somewhat inspiring and informative promo for the space program that youngsters will find engaging. A-I (PG)

Spaced Invaders (1990) Mildly diverting children's comedy about five bumbling, diminutive Martians who mistakenly invade Earth on Halloween but have trouble convincing people that they're really aliens and not trick-or-treating youngsters. Director Patrick Read Johnson's one-joke movie has so-so special effects and some broad humor, notably from Royal Dano as an old codger who saves the day. Some scenes of menace that may frighten the very young. A-II (PG) U

Spacehunter: Adventures in the Forbidden Zone (1983) Failed sci-fi fantasy about three 21st-century damsels in distress who are rescued from a perverted mutant by the driver of a futuristic junkmobile (Peter Strauss). Directed by Lamont Johnson, this 3-D adventure is only for those who are amused by stupidity and mediocrity. Mild violence. A-II (PG)

Sparkle (1976) Absurdly melodramatic story of a Harlem girl (Irene Cara) who gains success as a singer. In spite of Irene Cara's strong performance, Sam O'Steen's direction cannot make credible the anticlimactic crime elements grafted onto the plot. Restrained depiction of drugs and sex. A-III (PG)

Spartacus (1960) Adventure epic traces the spectacular events that shook the Roman Empire during the great slave revolt of the first century B.C. Kirk Douglas is appropriately brave and sweaty in the title role of the gladiator who leads the revolt with Jean Simmons as the slave girl he loves. Director Stanley Kubrick gets scope and splendor in an historical re-creation that has some sense of history to it. Vivid gladiatorial and battlefield violence and veiled sexual innuendo. A-III (PG-13) PG

Spasmo (1976) Umberto Lenzi directs Suzy Kendall and Robert Hoffman in a murky Italian celebration of sex and bloodshed. O (nr)

Speaking Parts (1990) Chilling, obtuse story of four people (Michael McManus; Arsinee Khanjian; Gabrielle Rose; David Hemblen) who use video to connect with themselves and others. Canadian writer-director Atom Egoyan depicts a world of passive voyeurs so lulled by the use of video technology that their lives are emotional vacuums. Some profanity; much sexual innuendo; graphic masturbatory scene. O (nr) 18

Special Day, A (1977) The day of the title is that of Hitler's state visit to Rome, which is used as the background and counterpoint to an encounter between a down-trodden wife (Sophia Loren) and an harassed homosexual (Marcello Mastroianni) who has been fired from the government radio station and faces even graver measures. Directed by Ettore Scola, the movie focuses not on the moral aspect of the wife's being unfaithful to her brutal husband but upon the human anguish of the two principals. A-IV (nr) AA

Special Delivery (1976) Failed comedy melodrama about a bank robber (Bo Svenson) and a kooky young woman (Cybill Shepherd) teaming up to recover some loot stashed in a mail box. Directed by Paul Wendkos, it is a jumble of many styles and plots, none of them very good. Some sexual innuendo. A-III (PG) 15

Special Section (1975) Story of injustices rendered by a special court instituted by France's Vichy government to satisfy the demands of their Nazi conquerors. Directed by Costa-Gavras, the loosely episodic film is lacking in characterization but excels in its re-creation of the period. As a result one can learn a little bit of history and be fairly entertained but moved hardly at all. A-II (PG)

Specialist, The (1975) Overwrought soap opera about rival lawyers (Adam West and John Anderson) in a small town who get involved in a case of entrapment and blackmail. Directed by Hikmet Avedis, it has a great deal of nudity, probably meant to take one's mind off a talky, determinedly simple-minded script. O (R)

Spectre of Edgar Allan Poe, The (1974) Inept low-budget horror movie about E. A. Poe (Robert Walker Jr.) who delivers his deranged true-love Lenore (Mary Grover) into the hands of the mad Dr. Grimaldi (Cesar Romero) whose asylum is an authentically creepy southern mansion. Written and directed by Mohy Quandour, the silly script is treated so seriously that it becomes unintentionally quite funny. A-II (PG)

Speedway (1968) Routine Elvis Presley musical in which he plays a stock-car racer involved with leading lady Nancy Sinatra and the Internal Revenue Service. Director Norman Taurog keeps the action adventure moving at a pedestrian pace. A-II (G)

Spellbound (1945) Stylish psychological thriller about a psychiatrist (Ingrid Bergman) who falls for an amnesiac (Gregory Peck) accused of murder but whom she's sure can be cleared once she's helped him recover his memory. Director Alfred Hitchcock uses some of Salvador Dali's surrealistic imagery to indicate Bergman's probes of Peck's subconscious but the tightly wound plot takes much too long in its unraveling. A few chills and much unsettling tension. A-II (br) PG

Spetters (1981) Dutch import about three young men with little else on their minds but motorcycle racing, sex and idolizing race champ Rutger Hauer. Directed by Paul Verhoeven, the movie reflects the confused values of a segment of contemporary youth but adds nothing of significance to the subject. Some graphic nudity and sexually explicit scenes. O (R) 18

Sphinx, The (1981) Beautiful Egyptologist (Lesley-Anne Down) with pluck and luck, eludes hordes of Levantine villains and discovers a cache of ancient treasures stolen by grave robbers. The thoroughly muddled thriller, based on a novel by Robin Cook and directed by Franklin J. Schaffner, is so badly done that it will have viewers giggling halfway through and hooting in derision by the end. Some unnecessary violence. A-III (PG) AA

Spices (1989) Indian production set in colonial times tells the story of a feisty married woman (Smita Patil) who refuses to submit to the sexual demands of a visiting tax collector (Naseeruddin Shah) but is pressured by male and female villagers to do so lest the whole village be punished. Directed by Ketan Mehta, this small, technically flawed movie is notable for not only exploring the subservient role of Indian women during this period but also the very essence of oppression and the potential price of bucking the status quo. Some rough language, sexual innuendo and comic-book violence. A-III (nr)

Spider's Stratagem, The (1973) Intriguing Italian mystery about a man (Giulio Brogi) returning to the town where 30 years earlier his father had been murdered by local Fascists and learns more than he wants to know about those responsible. Directed by Bernardo Bertolucci, the well-crafted movie is a satisfying mystery story, yet there is substance in its treatment of corruption in the Mussolini era. Mature theme. A-III (nr)

Spies Like Us (1985) Chevy Chase and Dan Aykroyd sink to the lowest common denominator in a vain attempt to get laughs in this mindless and meandering comedy about two incompetent federal agents who are chosen to be decoys in an international spy ring. Much coarse language and sexual innuendo with brief nudity in a sexual context. O (PG)

Spike of Bensonhurst (1988) A young boxer (Sasha Mitchell) gets into trouble with low-level mob antics in the Italian neighborhood of Bensonhurst, Brooklyn. Director Paul Morrissey's attempt at broad satire fails on all counts save a comic turn by Ernest Borgnine as a mob boss. Ethnic stereotypes, profanity, irresponsible treatment of sex, pregnancy and drug abuse. O (R)

Spikes Gang, The (1974) Formula western about a bank robber (Lee Marvin) who initiates a trio of wide-eyed youngsters (Gary Grimes, Ron Howard, Charlie Martin Smith) into a life of crime and then betrays them. Directed by Richard Fleischer, the B-grade screenplay offers the usual violence; a distasteful scene involving religious articles. A-IV (PG) AA

Spinout (1966) Innocuous Elvis Presley vehicle directed by Norman Taurog in which the singer escapes the clutches of three women who want to marry him. Pre-teens may find it boring but not Presley fans. A-I (br) U

Spirit of the Beehive, The (1976) Spanish movie set in 1940 deals with two children growing up in the aftermath of the Civil War. Directed by Victor Erice, it is one of those rare films that captures something of the secret world of childhood, with its strange notions and innocent rituals, yet also mirrors the adult world and its way of dealing with terrible realities. A-II (nr) AA

Spirit of St. Louis, The (1957) Meticulous but lengthy re-creation follows the thoughts and reflections of Charles Lindbergh (James Stewart) while making aviation history in 1927 as the pilot of the first nonstop flight from New York to Paris. Directed by Billy Wilder, Stewart manages to hold viewer interest on the solo flight across the Atlantic, partly because of the journey's dangers en route but mostly because of the character's courage and determination in accomplishing this feat of early aviation. Some threatening situations. A-I (br) U

Spirits of the Dead (1969) Trilogy of Edgar Allen Poe's short stories, as told by three European directors. Roger Vadim's medieval tale of a decadent heiress (Jane Fonda) who kills her cousin (Peter Fonda) is dull, but Louis Malle's story of a corrupt man (Alain Delon) pursued by his righteous double overdoses on nudity and sadistic violence. In a class by itself is Federico Fellini's "Toby Dammit" about an alcoholic English actor (Terrence Stamp) who comes to Rome to star in a western. It's a small gem, capturing the grotesquely surrealistic, grim and ironic humor of Poe's "Never Bet the Devil Your Head." O (R)

Spite Marriage (1929) Buster Keaton, the great stoic master of silent comedy, plays an actor married out of spite by a jilted actress (Dorothy Sebastian) whose affection he finally wins after overcoming all manner of surrealistic complications. Directed by Edward Sedgwick, Keaton makes the best out of a heavy-handed plot, but his comic efforts seem forced and lack the easy air of spontaneity that marked his best work. A-I (br)

Splash (1984) Mediocre Disney romantic comedy about a mermaid (Daryl Hannah) who falls in love with a human (Tom Hanks). Directed by Ron Howard, the Disney production is modestly successful as escapist entertainment, with slapstick chase scenes and klutzy overacting. Brief nudity and sexual references. A-III (PG) U

Split, The (1968) Inept crime movie directed by Gordon Fleming about a gang's robbery of a box-office during a big sporting event. Gratuitous brutality and graphic sexual treatment. O (R) X

Split Image (1982) Bright young man (Michael O'Keefe) falls in love with a young girl (Karen Allen) and is entrapped by a religious cult (led by Peter Fonda), but his desperate parents hire a seedy deprogrammer (James Woods) to win him back. Director Ted Kotcheff's flashy, melodramatic and highly superficial treatment of a serious social problem may serve some adolescents as a cautionary tale. Some rough language. A-II (R) 15

Split Second (1992) Violent thriller concerns the efforts of an obsessed cop (Rutger Hauer), his murdered partner's widow (Kim Cattrall) and his new partner (Neil Duncan) to kill an inhuman marauding beast that is clawing out the hearts of its victims. A formula macho-action film drenched in buckets of blood amounts to grisly garbage from director Tony Maylan. Excessive violence, brief nudity, many crass sexual references and much rough language. O (R) 18

Spook Who Sat by the Door, The (1973) Black exploitation movie about a token black CIA agent (Lawrence Cook) who returns to his Chicago home where he raises and trains a street army intended first to turn the ghetto into a riot zone and then to take over the city, the state, the nation, the world! Directed by Ivan Dixon, it starts as wry comedy but turns vicious halfway through when it begins taking its message of violent revolution seriously. Dreary abundance of racial cliches and stereotypes. A-III (PG)

Sporting Club, The (1971) Failed version of Thomas McGuane's novel about an exclusive club of Detroit's wealthiest citizens and their alienated offspring and servants who try to wreck it. Directed by Larry Peerce, the movie lacks the wit, imagination and sensitivity needed to suggest, rather than simply depict, the terrible heritage of sex and violence it supposedly is condemning. O (R)

Spot (see: "Dogpound Shuffle").

Spring Fever (1983) Undernourished tale of a Florida tennis tournament for teenage girls stars Susan Anton and Jessica Walters as tennis mothers, with Carling Bassett as the daughter struggling to be a champ. Innocuous little movie directed by Joseph L. Scanlan, a love affair figures in the plot. A-III (PG)

Spy in Your Eye (1966) Routine Italian spy caper directed by Vittorio Sala whose chief gimmick is a mini-camera placed by enemy agents in the glass eye of an American colonel (Dana Andrews) by which they monitor what the Americans are up to. Mild violence and derring-do. A-II (br)

Spy Who Came in from the Cold, The (1966) Sobering screen version of the John Le Carre novel about a shabby British spy (Richard Burton) whose cynicism grows as his assignment in Berlin becomes a maze of betrayals and counter-betrayals. Director Martin Ritt's spy film is not an escapist adventure but one that demonstrates the loss of humanity on the part of those who treat people only as means of achieving their ends. A-III (br) A

Spy Who Loved Me, The (1977) Roger Moore as James Bond and Barbara Bach as a beautiful Russian spy find themselves united against an all-powerful villain, who is bent upon a free enterprise conquest of the world, and his steel-toothed henchman named Jaws (Richard Kiel). Styled sex and violence. A-III (PG)

Spy with a Cold Nose, The (1967) Minor British spy spoof about the bumbling antics of some secret agents (Laurence Harvey and Lionel Jeffries. Directed by Daniel Petrie, the humor is mild and the plot slight. A-III (br) U

S*P*Y*S (1974) Failed comedy with Elliott Gould and Donald Sutherland as two inept CIA agents who, after fouling up a defection by murdering two Russian agents, are on the run as marked men sought by both sides. Blankly directed by Irvin Kershner, the comedy is low, witless and frequently tasteless. A-III (PG) A

Square Dance (1987) Young girl with religious convictions (Winona Ryder) forsakes the custody of her cranky grandpa to live with her tragically flawed mother (Jane Alexander). She overcomes disillusionment with the adult world while expressing the inner strength and grace that propel her with loving enthusiasm toward womanhood. Sexual references and some rough dialogue do not dim the luster of director Dan Petrie's joyous affirmation of the beauty and wisdom of youthful innocence. A-II (PG-13) 15

Squeeze, The (1987) Struggling set designer and compulsive gambler (Michael Keaton) teams up with a process server (Rae Dawn Chong) to confound and foil a scam defrauding the New York lottery with a magnetic box he finds and then loses to corporate thugs. Mild-mannered comedy directed by Roger Young has little else save Keaton's charm, which lessens the casual acceptance of his dangerously amoral behavior. Comic seduction scene and some violence are adult fare. A-III (PG-13) 15

Squeeze Play (1981) Rival community softball teams, with husbands on one side and wives on the other, battle for the play-offs. Amateurish movie directed by Samuel Weil, it contains graphic sex, nudity and unrelieved profanity. O (R)

Squirm (1976) Low-budget horror movie directed by Jeff Lieberman about an invasion of killer worms that almost wipes out a small Southern town. Disgusting scenes of violence. O (R) X

SSSSSSS (1973) Unpretentious thriller about a rather nice but quite mad zoologist (Strother Martin) who is working on a serum to transform people into snakes because reptiles, being cold-blooded, will not be affected when pollution shrouds earth from the sun. Director Bernard Kowalski capitalizes on Martin's fondly dotty performance rather than his experiments with deadly cobras. Viewers with a phobia for snakes should be warned away, but the less squeamish will find it an engaging, at times witty, entertainment. A-III (PG)

St. Elmo's Fire (1985) Seven friends cope with the world after graduating from Georgetown University. Director Joel Schumacher's cast of characters consists almost entirely of shallow, boring, self-absorbed individuals, and their mostly favorable view of sexual promiscuity is in keeping with the amoral atmosphere that pervades the movie. O (R) 15

St. Ives (1976) Formula detective mystery directed by J. Lee Thompson with Charles Bronson as a retired journalist who becomes a go-between in a scheme to recover some stolen papers has too many gaping holes in the plot for even this kind of light entertainment. Some incidental sex and violence. A-III (PG) AA

St. Louis Kid, The (1934) Breezy action melodrama features a truck driver (James Cagney) who has to clear himself of a murder charge during a dairy farmer's strike. Directed by Ray Enright, Cagney is in top form as the cocky, wisecracking charmer who wins the girl (Patricia Ellis), outwits the goons and saves his fists by using his head to knock out opponents. Stylized violence. A-II (br) A

St. Valentine's Day Massacre, The (1967) Bloody re-creation of one of the more lurid episodes in American gangland history when Chicago's Al Capone (Jason Robards) wiped out some of his competitors. Directed by Roger Corman, the acting is overdone but, then, so too is the violence. A-III (br) X

Stage Door Canteen (1943) Patriotic World War II souvenir with a multitude of show business personalities serving meals and entertaining troops on leave in New York City. Directed by Frank Borzage, a lame romance between a soldier and a canteen hostess keeps getting in the way of the bands, singers, walk-ons and star turns notably by Edgar Bergen, Ray Bolger and Gypsy Rose Lee in a mock strip tease. Some sexual situations and innuendo. A-III (br) U

Stage to Thunder Rock (1964) Contrived western directed by William F. Claxton interweaves the story of a struggling pioneer family (Lon Chaney Jr., Anne Seymour and Marilyn Maxwell) with that of a veteran sheriff (Barry Sullivan) forced to arrest the outlaw son of the man who raised him (Keenan Wynn). Stylized violence and muted references to prostitution. A-II (br) U

Stagecoach (1939) In this western classic, a cowboy (John Wayne) wanted by the law on trumped-up charges joins an odd assortment of passengers (Claire Trevor, Thomas Mitchell, Donald Meek, John Carradine and others) on the stage to Lordsburg in the midst of an Apache uprising. Directed by John Ford, the characters are a microcosm of frontier types, each of whom has a different reason for the journey whose dangers are played out against the majestic vistas of Monument Valley, with a brilliantly staged Indian attack and a final showdown on the streets of Lordsburg bringing the story to a rousing finish. Stylized violence. A-II (br) U

Stagecoach (1966) Poor remake of the western classic about an oddly assorted group (Alex Cord, Bing Crosby, Van Heflin, Slim Pickens) crowded into a stagecoach that is under Indian attack. Directed by Gordon Douglas, there are some good action scenes to enliven the ride, but the characterizations are embarrassingly bad. A-II (br) A

Staircase (1969) The terrible loneliness of two homosexuals (Richard Burton and Rex Harrison) is the subject of Charles Dyer's adaptation of his own play told basically in a series of bickering arguments about their fears, vanity and lack of future. Directed by Stanley Donen, the earnest examination of each man's desperate dependence upon the other fails as entertainment and falls short as a truly insightful human document, partly because two expert actors are more intent on portraying homosexuals than creating two believable human beings. A-IV (R) X

Stakeout (1987) Voyeurism turns into romance when a cop on surveillance (Richard Dreyfuss) falls for the target of his perusal, an escaped con's girl (Madeline Stowe). Director John Badham subverts mystery and in-depth characterization to depiction of a simple love affair. Some violence, brief nudity and a sex scene make this mature fare. A-III (R) 15

Stalking Moon, The (1968) Above-average western in which an Apache (Nathaniel Narciso), feared for his cruelty, follows the trail of those who have taken his young son and leaves his own path of dead settlers while a former Army scout (Gregory Peck), who has the boy, waits on his ranch for the inevitable arrival of his menacing pursuer. Directed by Richard Mulligan, the western has some physical violence, but its cat-and-mouse story is plotted almost totally for its suspense potential, which it achieves with some intelligence. A-I (G)

Stand and Deliver (1988) Quietly affecting movie about an extraordinary real-life math teacher (Edward James Olmos) in an East L.A. high school who transforms a rowdy class of Hispanics into calculus whiz-kids. When test administrators question his students' high grades, the teacher fights back with charges of discrimination. Inspiring story, fine acting by the leads and deft direction by Ramon Menendez. Some profanity in a realistic context. A-II (PG) 15

Stand By Me (1986) The power of this drama lies in the simple, profound truths four boys learn about themselves while on a journey through the backwoods of their rural hometown in the late 1950s. Director Rob Reiner's pre-teen coming-of-age picture carefully avoids excess while focusing upon simple tests of patience, courage, caring and the joys of male camaraderie. Some harsh language, uncharacteristic of the times, and brief violence, but it is an experience some parents might wish to share with their youngsters. A-III (R) 15

Stand Up and Be Counted (1972) Journalist Jacqueline Bisset is assigned to cover the Women's Liberation Movement in her home town and finds plenty of fodder within her own family. Idiotic comedy directed by Jackie Cooper not only belittles women in its contrived episodes involving shrill maidens and audacious matrons but also insults the viewer's intelligence by its parade of unsavory situations and its very explicit sexual banter. O (PG)

Stand Up and Cheer (1934) Musical comedy about the Depression blues starts with the President adding a Secretary of Amusement (Warner Baxter) to his Cabinet in order to regenerate the nation's morale. Directed by Hamilton MacFadden, the curious concept sputters along on the enthusiastic energy of various vaudeville acts, but the showstopper is little Shirley Temple's big finale in James Dunn's production number, "Baby, Take a Bow." Dated fun, but Stepin Fetchit's comic turn as a servile black figure is a period movie convention embarrassing today. A-I (br) U

Stanley (1972) The title critter is a very agile rattlesnake used by a very disturbed Seminole Indian (Chris Robinson) to dispose of a lot of people who annoy him. Produced and directed by William Grefe, the script tosses serpents and victims together guilelessly to evoke clumsy guffaws more than sincere shudders. Some sexual insinuations and vulgar language. A-III (PG)

Stanley & Iris (1990) When an illiterate factory worker (Robert De Niro) asks a friendly co-worker (Jane Fonda) to teach him to read, they fall in love, find fulfillment and go on presumably to live happily ever after. Despite credible performances rooted in a working-class environment, director Martin Ritt's socially conscious melodrama goes about achieving its intention to be uplifting in too obvious fashion to be satisfying. Brief but meaningful treatment of a teen pregnancy and a few instances of profanity. A-II (PG-13) 15

Star! (1968) Lovely, lively musical based on the life of British stage star Gertrude Lawrence who is portrayed as a very nice, very talented, very ambitious and very tough lady. In the role is Julie Andrews whose characterization and singing are excellent in director Robert Wise's brilliant re-creation of British life from World War I through World War II, giving the proceedings a perspective both interesting and illuminating. A-II (G) U

Star Chamber, The (1983) When a judge (Michael Douglas), disillusioned by the legal technicalities that force him to free defendants he considers guilty, joins a secret group who execute those who have escaped the penalty of the law, he finally comes to realize they are no better than criminals. Director Peter Hyams' plodding, contrived and muddled story at least raises some questions about crime, law and vigilante justice. Some brutal violence and much profanity. A-III (R) 15

Star 80 (1983) Fact-based story of Dorothy Stratten, Playboy Playmate and budding movie star (Mariel Hemingway), who was murdered by her husband (Eric Roberts). Though director Bob Fosse is rather superficial in the characterizations and lets the playboy philosophy get off much too easily, the movie is grimly moral in its implications about the consequences of promiscuity. The nature of its theme and frequent nudity, though never in a genuinely erotic context, make it very mature fare. A-IV (R) 15

Star Is Born, A (1976) Third version of the durable classic about the incompatibility between career and marriage proves little more than a starring vehicle for Barbra Streisand as a rock music superstar going to the top of the charts as the career of her husband (Kris Kristofferson) is sinking into oblivion. Director Frank Pierson develops little depth to their relationship and the romantic interludes are silly (though they do provide some relief from the din of the Muzak rock score). Coarse language and vulgar characters. A-III (R) 15

Star Spangled Girl (1971) Mediocre adaptation of Neil Simon's Broadway comedy about the ideological clash between a little gal from Way Down South (Sandy Duncan) and a pair of radical Los Angeles underground newspapermen (Todd Susman and Tony Roberts). Directed by Jerry Paris, the only bright thing about the so-so comic romance is Duncan's cute performance. A-II (G) A

Star Spangled Rhythm (1942) Chaotic World War II frolic revolves around a sailor (Eddie Bracken) bringing his buddies to a Hollywood studio which his father (Victor Moore) pretends to run with the help of a telephone operator (Betty Hutton) sweet on his son. Filmed on the Paramount lot by director George Marshall, the picture ends with Bing Crosby, Bob Hope, Dorothy Lamour, Veronica Lake, Alan Ladd and many of the studio's other players putting on a show for the fleet. Dated wartime entertainment laden with double entendres. A-III (br) U

Star Trek: The Motion Picture (1980) The familiar faces of TV's Starship Enterprise crew are back with William Shatner, now an admiral, and Leonard Nimoy as Spock, to do battle with an ominous alien adversary. Directed by Robert Wise, the heart of the movie is its spectacular special effects with the characters in a supporting role. Trekkies, nevertheless, will find it nostalgic entertainment, but youngsters may find it a long sit. A-I (G) U

Star Trek II: The Wrath of Khan (1982) Capt. Kirk (William Shatner), promoted to a desk job, makes it back to the helm of the Enterprise in time to confront a flamboyant villain (Ricardo Montalban). Director Nicholas Meyer's sequel attempts to be droll and lively but is only slightly more entertaining than its dull and ponderous predecessor. Torture sequence involving the insertion of parasites into the ears of victims is rather strong, but the action is otherwise innocuous. A-II (PG) A

Star Trek III: The Search for Spock (1984) Considerably better than its two predecessors, the sequel involves the efforts of Admiral James Kirk (William Shatner) and his crew to return to the planet Genesis, resting place of Capt. Spock (Leonard Nimoy), who gave his life to save the Enterprise in the last outing, on the chance that he might somehow be restored to life. Some heavy breathing Klingon pirates (led by Christopher Lloyd) try to prevent this, but all obstacles are surmounted for the grand climax on Vulcan (presided over by Judith Anderson). Harve Bennett's intelligent script and Nimoy's capable direction prove that it is possible to be both entertaining and civilized. A-II (PG)

Star Trek IV: The Voyage Home (1986) Admiral Kirk (William Shatner) and the Enterprise crew travel back to 1986 San Francisco to retrieve two humpbacked whales that may be the key to saving Earth from alien destruction. Director Leonard Nimoy makes an entertaining mix out of sci-fi fantasy, ecological advocacy and satiric jabs at contemporary pop culture. Documentary footage of whales being slaughtered and a few coarse words bring home some of the realities of environmental waste. A-II (PG)

Star Trek V: The Final Frontier (1989) Messianic Vulcan (Laurence Luckinbill) hogties the Enterprise's crew and other interplanetary hams, setting a course through the Great Barrier for a meeting with God. Directed by William Shatner, the narrative is suspenseless and overwrought with senseless Klingon attacks. Best scenes feature comedic banter between crew members. Minimal rough language, silly comic-book violence. A-II (PG)

Star Trek VI: The Undiscovered Country (1991) A peace conference between the Federation and the treacherous Klingons is threatened when James Kirk and Dr. McCoy (William Shatner and DeForest Kelley) are framed for the assassination of the Klingon negotiator (David Warner), leaving Spock (Leonard Nimoy) to ferret out the traitor in their midst. Superior production values and a peppy pace make director Nicholas Meyer's sci-fi adventure genial entertainment in spite of its aging characters and familiar situations. Some laser shootouts and explosions. A-II (PG)

Star Wars (1977) Set in a galaxy other than our own, a desperate struggle takes place between evil usurpers of empire and a dedicated band of rebels (Carrie Fisher, Mark Hamill, Harrison Ford and Alec Guinness). Written and directed by George Lucas, the outcome never is in doubt because the movie's conventions are as old-fashioned as its story of good triumphing over evil. The special effects are stunning, the characters imaginative and the narrative intriguing. Much stylized violence. A-II (PG) U

Starchaser (1985) Young Orin uses a magic sword to free his people from enslavement by a wicked despot. This animated 3-D movie is passable entertainment for juveniles except for an abundance of cartoon violence. A-II (PG)

Stardust (1975) Sequel to "That'll Be the Day"—a British movie about a would-be rock star (David Essex)—has the rocker forming a Beatles-like group and becoming a superstar. Directed by Michael Apted, the result has a slickness and pace that are engaging, though it is a bit heavy in showing the corrupt consequences brought about by sudden fame and fortune. A-III (R) AA

Stardust Memories (1980) Dry autobiographical parody from director Woody Allen focuses upon a writer-director (Allen) suffering from middle-class, middle-aged neuroses that come with success. The True Confession-style work is only fitfully funny, and its serious flights of fantasy stop far short of anything with depth. Satirical treatment of promiscuous relationships and frequent profanity. A-III (PG)

Starman (1984) Alien from another planet (Jeff Bridges) takes on the human form of the much-mourned husband of a young widow (Karen Allen). Director John Carpenter does fairly well in creating the mood of a sci-fi fantasy, though he resorts to such scenes as the ever-popular car chase for excitement. Some violence and a restrained bedroom scene. A-II (PG)

Starship Invasions (1978) Inept, ludicrous, boring Canadian movie directed by Ed Hunt about good and bad flying saucers locked in a battle upon which the fate of Earth depends. Violence and tasteless depiction of experiments on human beings. A-III (PG)

Starstruck (1983) Australian musical comedy about the staging of a New Year's Eve show by a young woman (Jo Kennedy) and her cousin (Ross O'Donovan) to raise money to save the family's pub. Directed by Gillian Armstrong, it is good light entertainment but, unfortunately, because of its benign view of casual sex and brief nudity, it cannot be recommended for youngsters. A-III (PG)

Start the Revolution Without Me (1970) Fumbled period comedy about two sets of twins (Gene Wilder and Donald Sutherland), one pair aristocratic and the other of peasant stock, who get switched at birth and, years later, get mixed up again during the French Revolution when those raised as noble twins become confused with the cowardly peasant twins who are unwilling members of the revolting mob led by Jack McGowran. Though the situation is promising, Bud Yorkin's direction is remarkably dull, with heavy slapstick routines, inane dialogue and poorly staged attempt at spoofing the old swashbuckler movies. A-III (PG) A

Starting Over (1979) Divorced man (Burt Reynolds) finds himself drawn to a nice, sensible, but rightly wary school teacher (Jill Clayburgh). The problem is that he is still strongly attached to his former wife (Candice Bergen) who now shows up wanting to give it another try. Directed by Alan J. Pakula, the film is often very funny, largely due to Reynolds' engaging performance, but it grows repetitive and its humor doesn't blend easily with its more serious concerns. Occasional foul language; some sexual references. A-III (R) AA

State of Grace (1990) Undercover cop (Sean Penn) is torn between betrayal and duty when assigned to infiltrate a murderous gang headed by two brothers with whom he had grown up and whose sister (Robin Wright) now falls in love with him. Director Phil Joanou focuses on brutality and casual slaughter without regard for plot or characterization in a synthetic, unconvincing crime melodrama. Excessive violence and rough language, positive treatment of macho, antifeminist attitudes and brief nudity. O (R) 18

State of Siege (1973) Fact-based political drama about an American official (Yves Montand) who in 1970 was kidnapped, accused of being a police specialist in torture and murdered by Uruguayan terrorists. Directed by Costa-Gavras, the movie accepts revolutionary change as necessary but demonstrates the futility of political terrorism, both by those who have power and those who want it. Excessively graphic scene of torture. A-IV (nr) X

State of the Union (1948) Campaigning for the Republican presidential nomination, a self-made millionaire (Spencer Tracy) fights for his political principles with his estranged wife (Katherine Hepburn), his campaign advisor (Van Johnson) and his chief backer (Angela Lansbury). Directed by Frank Capra, the political and domestic battlefields are rendered with wit, intelligence and plenty of good humor. A-II (br) A

State Penitentiary (1950) Director Lew Landers' low-budget quickie features Warner Baxter as a wronged convict who escapes from prison to prove his innocence. Stylized violence and a muddled plot about justice. A-II (br)

Station, The (1992) Sluggish Italian drama about a night in a lonely train station where the timid stationmaster (Sergio Rubini) is called on to protect a beautiful young woman (Margherita Buy) from the increasingly violent attempts of her furious fiance (Ennio Fantastichini) to drag her home. Also directed by Rubini, the narrative alternates long static stretches with sudden horror while gradually revealing the engaged couple's essentially gentle natures. Subtitles. Intermittent violence and some rough language. A-III (nr)

Station West (1948) Offbeat western tale in which an undercover military agent (Dick Powell), on the trail of a gold robber who murdered two soldiers, nails the culprit by getting a job with a shady outfit run by a woman (Jane Greer). Directed by Sidney Lanfield, the killer's identity isn't too difficult to figure out but the situation and tough-guy dialogue hold interest along the way. Stylized violence. A-I (br)

Statue, The (1971) Drearily unfunny one-line joke about the relative size of male organs, belonging in this case to a Nobel Prize-winner (David Niven) and the man who modeled for the lower portion of a large nude statue of the prize-winner. British production directed by Rod Amateau is an exercise in high-density witlessness. O (R) X

Stavisky (1975) French production, set in the Depression of the 1930s, presents an emotionally engaging character study of the era's best known swindler, Serge Alexandre Stavisky (Jean-Paul Belmondo), whose destruction mirrors the collapse of capitalism and the rise of fascism. Directed by Alain Resnais, the powerful visuals and flawless narrative flow make it rewarding viewing, whatever the value of its historical insights about a past world. Mature themes. A-III (PG)

Stay As You Are (1980) A married man in his 50s (Marcello Mastroianni) falls in love with a teenage girl (Nastassja Kinski), who he discovers may be his own daughter. Directed by Alberto Lattuada, the story goes nowhere and evaporates into a series of arty sequences that seems to come from a fashion magazine. Exploitation of the incest theme and extravagant nudity. O (nr)

Stay Away, Joe (1968) Poor Elvis Presley vehicle in which he plays a contemporary Indian who rides a lot of bucking broncos, chases a lot of pretty girls and sings a lot of songs. He also gets in a number of fights trying to get a good deal from the government for his southwestern Indian tribe. Directed by Peter Tewksbury. Burgess Meredith, Joan Blondell and Katy Jurado are miscast, and the Indian stereotypes are ludicrous. A-III (PG) U

Stay Hungry (1976) Muddled story in which Jeff Bridges plays a youth hired by some crooks to dicker the owners of a Southern health spa out of their property but instead befriends its muscleman (Arnold Schwarzenegger) and his ex-girlfriend (Sally Field). Directed by Bob Rafelson, the murky plot resorts to an unhealthy mix of sex and violence. O (R) 18

Stay Tuned (1992) Silly satire about a Seattle couple (John Ritter; Pam Dawber) who must survive 24 hours in the netherworld where the devil (Jeffrey Jones) projects them into the deadly programs offered on "Hellvision." Peter Hyams' anything goes direction ends up going haywire as the visual gags flag and the nonsensical plot lurches out of control. Some mindless comic violence and occasional nasty menace. A-III (PG)

Staying Alive (1983) The disco king of "Saturday Night Fever" (John Travolta) goes from chorus boy to star with the help of the two women in his life (Cynthia Rhodes; Finola Hughes). Director Sylvester Stallone's sequel is a loud, vulgar bit of mediocre entertainment, not at all moving and with no semblance of the bothersome demands of reality. Benign attitude toward casual sex. A-III (PG)

Staying Together (1989) Three young men (Tim Quill, Dermot Mulroney and Sean Astin) must decide their future when their father suddenly closes the family restaurant and retires. Directed by Lee Grant, the badly scripted family saga focuses on the brothers' senseless sexual conquests rather than the implications of the family crisis. Several sexually suggestive encounters including nudity and some profanity. O (R) 15

Steagle, The (1971) Uneven comic fantasy set during the 1962 Cuban missile crisis when a professor (Richard Benjamin) throws caution to the winds by flying off to Chicago for a tryst with his former girlfriend's daughter, on to a Las Vegas romp with a couple of frisky stewardesses and a minister and then to Hollywood for a climactic movie shootout. Written and directed by Paul Sylbert, the movie lacks consistency in its attempts at comedy and satire, too often settling for much that is crudely vulgar and sexually exploitative. Some religious implications that are tasteless if not offensive. O (R)

Stealing Home (1988) Flashbacks detail the lifelong infatuation of a washed-up baseball player (Mark Harmon) with an older family friend (Jodie Foster) whose suicide brings him home to bury her ashes and ultimately put the pieces of his life back together. Writer-directors Steve Kampmann and Will Aldis fail to develop the girl's character beyond that of an unattainable fantasy figure in a soapy melodrama. Brief nudity and several scenes of sexual promiscuity, one including a minor and an adult. A-III (PG-13) 15

Steel Lady, The (1953) Stranded while looking for oil in the Sahara Desert, four adventurers (Rod Cameron; John Dehner; Tab Hunter and Anthony Caruso) come upon an abandoned German tank with a fortune in jewels stolen from an Arab tribe that wants them back. Directed by E. A. Dupont, the low-budget production is a routine exercise in stereotyped characters and contrived situations. Some menace and stylized violence. A-I (br)

Steel Magnolias (1989) Some sassy southern belles (Dolly Parton, Shirley MacLaine, Olympia Dukakis, Daryl Hannah) share the joys and sorrows of a friend (Sally Field) and her headstrong, diabetic daughter (Julia Roberts) in comic and supportive banter at the beauty shop and during key events involving marriage, birth and death. Adapted by Robert Harling from his play and directed by Herb Ross, the movie is a rollicking tearjerker with polished performances and a refreshing focus on women friends who are more seasoned than sexy. Some sexual innuendo. A-III (PG)

Steele Justice (1987) Troubled and vengeful Vietnam veteran (Martin Kove) blasts away a good portion of the Vietnamese underworld dealing in drugs and extortion. Director Robert Boris' tabloid depiction of ruthless crime offers little except equally bloody retribution. Lame acting and dialogue coupled with excessive violence and ethnic stereotyping add up to exploitation. O (R)

Steelyard Blues (1973) Donald Sutherland, Jane Fonda, and Peter Boyle romp aimlessly in a lightweight, adolescent fantasy about three losers who dream of flying away in a reconditioned World War II bomber to find a land without jails. Directed by Alan Myerson, there are some occasional laughs to be had among the elaborate gags and frantic comedy conveying sociopolitical banalities about being free in today's restrictive society. Worth seeing for momentary diversion but not worth a moment's thought. A-III (PG) 15

Stella (1990) Third remake of Olive Higgins Prouty's teary novel about the self-sacrifices of an unwed mother (Bette Midler) for her daughter (Trini Alvarado). Though Midler is both touching and raucous in the title role and the period is updated to the present, director John Erman's melodrama is saddled with one-dimensional characters, some farfetched bits of business and a weepy fairy tale ending. Its portrayal of strong, selfless parenting and a teen's refusal to be coerced into a sexual relationship are positive images for older adolescents. Some rough language, sexual vulgarities and brief violence. A-III (PG-13)

Stella Dallas (1937) Sentimental tale of a small-town wife (Barbara Stanwyck) whose husband (John Boles) gets a good job in New York while she stays behind raising their daughter (Anne Shirley) until she realizes the youngster will have a better life with her father and his new wife. Director King Vidor's classic tearjerker about a mother's love and self-sacrifice has a well-plotted script, neatly defined class distinctions and a standout performance by Stanwyck. Some domestic strife. A-II (br) U

Stepfather, The (1987) Chilling portrait of a psychopath (Terry O'Quinn) who slaughters his family, changes his identity and remarries only to be inspired once again to kill. Director Joseph Rubin's suspense thriller touches upon the precarious nature of modern relationships and mutual trust but gets carried away with brutality, bloody murder and some brief nudity. O (R) 18

Stepford Wives, The (1975) Katherine Ross stars in this failed thriller about suburban wives behaving like docile, mindless windup dolls. Directed by Bryan Forbes, the harder it tries to be frightening and sinister, the more laughable it becomes.

Adult hokum because of language and some visuals. A-III (PG) AA

Stephen King's Graveyard Shift (1990) A drifter (David Andrews) joins a night crew hired to clean out a rat-infested factory basement that is also home to a huge bat-like monster that devours trespassers. Director Ralph Singleton's inane horror film is more repelling than frightening, virtually abandoning storyline and characterization in favor of blood, guts and rodents. Excessive gore and violence, with intermittent rough language. O (R)

Stephen King's Sleepwalkers (1992) Lurid horror movie about an incestuous mother (Alice Krige) and son (Brian Krause) who are shape-shifting ghouls intent on sucking the life out of a virginal high school girl (Madchen Amick). Director Mick Garris exploits sexual violence and extracts needless gore from a gruesome and perverse script. Incestuous bedroom scene, excessive violence and some rough language. O (R) 18

Stepmother, The (1972) Pretentious tale about the tenuous friendships and nebulous liaisons that cause much unhappiness for a devout, temperamental architect (Alejandro Rey) and all those around him. Written, produced and directed by Hikmet L. Avedis, the film indulges in the stale techniques of hazy flashbacks and freeze-frames while attempting to keep viewers awake by tossing in some perfunctory nudity and a few murders. O (R)

Steppenwolf (1974) Max Von Sydow stars as Herman Hesse's alienated outsider whose life illustrates industrial society's need to reconcile the spiritual and physical through people's reestablishing contact between the body and the soul. Writer-director Fred Haines fails to establish the character as anything more than a poor social misfit in what proves to be simply a pictorialization of Hesse's text. Questionable sexual sequence. A-IV (R)

Stepping Out (1991) A past-her-prime tapdance teacher (Liza Minnelli) gamely tries to prepare eight fumbling adult students for their professional debut while evaluating a longtime love affair in light of her unexpected pregnancy. Producer-director Lewis Gilbert infuses a very human drama with many charming comic moments for a warm-hearted look at distinctly different individuals affecting each other for the better. A live-in relationship and momentary violence. A-III (PG)

Sterile Cuckoo, The (1969) Offbeat look at college romance in which a coed (Liza Minelli) comes out of her alienated shell to pursue a naive freshman (Wendell Burton) and involves him in obligations and responsibilities beyond his ability or desire to assume. Director Alan J. Pakula has made a little film with small pretensions about young people's growth to self-awareness and responsible relationships. Some restrained sexual scenes. A-IV (R) X

Stevie (1981) British screen biography of English poet Stevie Smith (Glenda Jackson), the tough but sensitive spinster who lived just about all of her life in the same row house in a London suburb with her loving maiden aunt (Mona Washbourne). Based on Hugh Whitemore's play and directed by Robert Enders, the movie's warmly sympathetic portrayal of these two women is unusually intelligent and articulate. It also proves to be highly entertaining fare, thanks largely to their memorable, very human performances. A-II (PG) AA

Stewardesses, The (1970) Stilted staging, slushy sound and indolent editing ground this plotless 3-D film of a flock of mini-dressed airline hostesses who indulge in sexual adventures between flights. Excessive nudity. O (X/R)

Stick (1985) Burt Reynolds, playing an ex-convict, runs into some nasty people in Miami, makes mincemeat of them and lives happily ever after. Director Reynolds' screen version of the Elmore Leonard novel turns the gritty original into a glossy and cartoonish star vehicle. Excessively graphic violence and amoral tone mark this vanity production. O (R) 18

Sticky Fingers (1988) Lightweight comedy about two erstwhile musicians (Helen Slater; Melanie Mayron) sharing both a New York flat and a lot of trouble after spending money left in their keeping by a friend who turns out to be involved in drugs. Directed by Catlin Adams, the bickering, bubble-headed roommates grow increasingly tiresome and their predicament isn't worth the bother. Some crude language and sexual references as well as a benign attitude toward drugs. A-III (PG-13) 15

Stigma (1972) Cheap exploitational melodrama about a doctor (Philip M. Thomas) trying to track down the prime source of an epidemic of venereal disease among an island community in Massachusetts Bay. Written and directed by David E. Durston, relationships and revelations become ridiculously squalid, while dialogue and situations grow increasingly hysterical and explicit. Trash. O (R)

Stiletto (1969) Cynical, fast-paced crime melodrama about a playboy (Alex Cord) who is called upon to repay a mobster for saving his life and finds himself hopelessly involved in the mob's criminal activities. Directed by Bernard Kowalski, the movie's overriding theme of brute force against force presents a pessimistic, unnerving view of life.

Merciless violence and some nudity. O (R) 18

Still of the Night (1982) N.Y. psychiatrist (Roy Scheider) is irresistibly drawn to a mysterious woman (Meryl Streep) who may have murdered one of his patients and may make him her next victim. Director Robert Benton's attempt at Hitchcock-style suspense has no sense of emotion or reality and none of Hitchcock's stylish virtues. Murky plot and stylized violence are not for the youngsters. A-II (PG) 15

Sting, The (1973) Robert Redford and Paul Newman team up as two Chicago con men who concoct an elaborate scheme involving a phony betting parlor to get revenge on New York gangster Robert Shaw while turning a handsome profit. Director George Roy Hill's action comedy is solid entertainment, though some might find it more than a little contrived. The Depression-era setting includes a house of prostitution. A-III (PG) A

Sting II, The (1983) Dreadfully inept sequel written by David S. Ward and directed by Jeremy Paul Kagan has Jackie Gleason and Mac Davis essay the roles originated by Newman and Redford. A movie to be avoided at all cost. Some sexually oriented humor. A-III (PG)

Stingray (1978) Two callow youths buy a car, unaware that it contains a large quantity of heroin and money, and are pursued by a murderous trio, led by a woman disguised as a nun. Richard Taylor directs the movie-long car chase interspersed with brawls and brutal killings of various sorts. Violence and low moral tone. O (PG)

Stir Crazy (1980) Failed comedy about two losers from New York (Gene Wilder and Richard Pryor) who find themselves doing time in a southwestern prison after being framed on a bank robbery charge. Bruce Jay Friedman's script directed by Sidney Poitier relies on vulgar jokes and crude sight gags that quickly wear thin. Lewd scene in a go-go bar and frequent profanity. O (R)

Stolen Kisses (1969) French director Francois Truffaut carries on the story of young Antoine Doinel (Jean-Pierre Leaud) from "The Four Hundred Blows" (1959) who here takes faltering steps toward maturity in a series of jobs, gets involved with an older woman (Delphine Seyrig) but finally squares himself with his girlfriend. His haphazard misadventures are told in a relaxed episodic manner and Truffaut ends with the implication that Antoine has finally grown up. Some sexual situations and brief nudity. A-IV (R) X

Stone Boy, The (1984) Thoughtful study of a rural family tragedy as bereaved parents (Robert Duvall and Glenn Close) try to come to terms with the death of their teenage son, accidentally shot by his younger brother (Jason Preston). The father's decision to let the boy work out his trauma on his own is a bit hard to take, but otherwise, director Chris Cain's fine, quiet movie is well worth seeing. Some relatively mild profanity used by the boy's grandfather in an attempt to jar his grandson out of his sense of isolation. A-II (PG)

Stone Cold (1991) The FBI persuades a suspended Alabama cop (Brian Bosworth) to infiltrate a deadly motorcycle gang whose leader (Lance Henriksen) has been orchestrating religious and political murders throughout Mississippi. Director Craig R. Baxley's macho bloodbath is couched in the tough, sexist credo of the outlaw bikers who wallow in promiscuity, endless explosions and multiple murders. Excessive violence and rough language, women degraded as sex objects and occasional nudity. O (R) 18

Stone Killer, The (1973) Sprawling crime epic about a tough cop (Charles Bronson) on the trail of a Sicilian mobster (Martin Balsam) who plans to use some Vietnam vets to assassinate the non-Sicilian gang that took over the New York underworld. Directed by Michael Winner, the film's core theme is the nearly interchangeable identities of police and criminal as they act out their respective vicious roles within a society pictured on the verge of collapse. Heavy violence. A-IV (R) 18

Stoolie, The (1974) Seedy, small-time hustler (nightclub comic Jackie Mason) is a police informer who takes the funds intended to set up a crook and flees to Miami where he finds true love (Marcia Jean Kurtz) just as the cops catch up with him. Directed by John Avildsen, the old-fashioned melodrama is long on romance and short on logic and credibility but does have good characterizations and gritty, realistic locales. A-III (PG) A

Stop! Or My Mom Will Shoot (1992) Witless comedy has a meddling mom (Estelle Getty) endlessly fussing over her police sergeant son (Sylvester Stallone) and his neglected girlfriend (JoBeth Williams) while becoming his unwanted partner in a homicide investigation. Genial performances can't rescue director Roger Spottiswoode's one-joke sitcom from its flaccid predictability. Occasional violence and mild profanity. A-II (PG-13) PG

Stop the World—I Want to Get Off (1966) British musical about an average man (Tony Tanner) who marries his employer's daughter, has a couple of kids and a few affairs, winds up with a title and the realization that he has never loved anyone but himself. Director Philip Saville photographs the stage production rather than turning it into a movie. A-III (br)

Stormy Monday (1988) Intriguing thriller set in Newcastle, England, tracks the shady tactics used by a crooked American entrepreneur (Tommy Lee Jones) to control the city's waterfront nightclub district. His principal stumbling blocks include a hard-boiled jazz-club owner (Sting), a reformed party girl (Melanie Griffith) and her young Irish boyfriend (Sean Bean). Written, directed and scored by Mike Figgis, the fine acting, gorgeous cinematography and incredible jazz-blues score make this a haunting film. Some brief scenes of violence and a few scenes with fleeting nudity. A-III (R) 15

Stormy Weather (1943) All-black musical centers on a dancer (Bill Robinson) as he recalls 25 years in show business, starting with his entertaining fellow soldiers in World War I and ending with his performing for World War II troops and reunion with the love of his life (Lena Horne). Director Andrew Stone's loosely constructed, disappointingly thin narrative serves mainly to provide the backdrop for a lively revue of performances by the considerable black talent of the day, including Fats Waller, Cab Calloway, the Nicholas Brothers and Katherine Dunham's dance troupe. This record of the period's segregated artists is offset by its use of black stereotypes. A-II (nr) U

Story of a Love Affair (1975) Italian melodrama about a woman (Lucia Bose) who joins her former lover in causing the death of her jealous industrialist husband with tragic consequences. Made in 1950 by director Michelangelo Antonnioni, the work's chief interest is its focus on the social disparity between the luxury-loving wife and her jobless husband making the conclusion inevitable. A-III (nr)

Story of a Teenager, The (1975) A high school football star tries to make a home for his kid brother but their alcoholic father tragically interferes. The film is well intended as a look at the pressures of adolescence, but its script is simply too melodramatic and its treatment woefully inadequate to the task. Some intense violence. A-III (PG)

Story of a Woman (1970) Romantic tripe about a Swedish pianist studying in Rome (Bibi Andersson) who has an affair but when she discovers her lover (James Farentino) is already married returns to Stockholm and marries an American (Robert Stack). Years later back in Rome, she must choose between her husband and child and her passion for her former lover. Directed by Leonardo Bercovici, this dull, boring effort has an excessively graphic bedroom scene. O (R) A

Story of Adele H., The (1976) French romance of a 19th-century woman (Isabelle Adjani), the daughter of Victor Hugo, who exhausted her health in pursuing a worthless cad around the world, was brought back to France and lived under constant care for another 40 years, keeping a journal devoted to her obsessive passion. Director Francois Truffaut's adaptation of the journal is done with a fine blend of detachment, compassion and respect for a woman who wasted her life in one sense and yet, in another, through the journal, turned it into a creative act. A-III (PG) A

Story of Boys and Girls, The (1991) At a sumptuous feast in 1936 Italy celebrating the engagement of a young couple (Lucrezia Lante Della Rovere and Davide Bechini) from different social classes, the intrigues and secret frustrations of the two families surface. By giving equal weight to more than 30 characters, writer-director Pupi Avati turns the sprawling narrative into an unfocused collection of slice-of-life vignettes. Subtitles. Numerous sexual references. A-III (nr)

Story of Christiane F. (1982) German drama about a 13-year-old girl (Natja Brunkhorst) who drifts into drug addiction because of the squalid environment in which she lives. Director Ulrich Edel's coldly clinical yet lurid account of the hell of drug abuse lacks a moral perspective adequate to the horrific events it matter-of-factly chronicles. Innumerable scenes of needles being thrust into arms and its depiction of sexual activity make this extremely mature fare. A-IV (nr)

Story of F, The (1971) Compilation of excerpts from mostly faded stag movies whose fuzzy photography of mechanically performed sex acts will leave viewers disgusted by the commercial shoddiness of Jim Babb's movie and its anti-censorship narration. O (nr)

Story of Qui Jui, The (1993) A pregnant peasant wife (Gong Li) adamantly seeks justice at increasingly distant and higher levels of Red Chinese bureaucracy when her village chief (Lei Lao Sheng) remains unrepentant after having angrily kicked her husband (Lui Peiqi) in the groin. Building tragic irony with exquisite simplicity, director Zhang Yimou captures the humanity and uncompromising spirit of a powerless woman pursuing justice despite the lethargy of officialdom and the scorn of her village. An instance of rough language. A-II (nr)

Story of Sin (1976) Walerian Borowczyk's screen version of Stefan Zeromski's novel about a hopeless love affair beautifully evokes its turn-of-the-century era but wallows in passionate despair and focuses on the erotic elements of the story. O (R)

Story of Vernon and Irene Castle, The (1939) Nostalgic musical biography of a vaudevillian (Fred Astaire) and his bride (Ginger Rogers) who in 1911 team as ballroom dancers and become international favorites before Vernon's tragic death as an aviator in World War I. Director H.C. Potter's warm portrait of a loving couple is paced by elegant dance numbers, period songs and occasional comic relief (Edna May Oliver; Walter Brennan; Lew Fields). Old-fashioned family fare. A-I (br) U

Story of Women (1988) Grim French production about a poor, uneducated but coldly ambitious woman (Isabelle Huppert) who is executed for performing abortions during the German Occupation of World War II. Director Claude Chabrol uses the wartime setting to distance the subject from the controversy of today, treating the narrative in a somber, unemotional fashion that forces the viewer to confront the moral and social dimensions of abortion without the comfort of any easy answers. Subtitles. Challenging, at times unsettling, fare that requires discernment. A-IV (nr)

Storyville (1992) A third-generation New Orleans politician (James Spader) running for Congress is unwittingly drawn into a murder investigation while his uncle (Jason Robards) discourages him from prying further into a lingering family scandal about parish mineral rights that ended in his father's suicide. Director Mark Frost's potboiler is fairly engrossing melodrama though it is awash in southern and political stereotypes. Some violence, an adulterous encounter, occasional nudity and intermittent rough language. A-III (R)

Straight Talk (1992) Reluctantly posing as a professional psychotherapist, a big-hearted Southerner (Dolly Parton) becomes Chicago's leading radio talk-show personality, unaware that her reporter boyfriend (James Woods) is writing an expose about her. Directed by Barnet Kellman, the character's wholesome, down-home philosophy is smothered in a vanity production featuring a music track composed and sung by its star. Implied sexual relationships. A-III (PG)

Straight Time (1978) Dustin Hoffman plays an ex-con who, when pressured by a cynical parole officer (Emmet Walsh), gives up on going straight and re-enters the criminal underworld. Directed by Ulu Grosbard, there is not enough in the script to involve the viewer with the characters, and while the fine acting and austere texture of the movie earn respect, one cannot really care about what happens to anybody in the story. The violence and rough language are part of the context but the gratuitous nudity is not. O (R) 18

Straight to Hell (1987) Madcap spoof of a spaghetti western, this farcical celebrity showcase from director Alex Cox mixes madness and mayhem with touches of sexual seduction and teasing to evoke a sense of the

Theater of the Absurd. Cameo cast including Joe Strummer, Elvis Costello and Courtney Love are all bandits trying to survive in a zany town. Some violence and sexual sight gags are not for youngsters. A-III (R)

Strait-Jacket (1964) Cheap horror show in which an axe-murderer (Joan Crawford) is released after 20 years in an asylum to live with her daughter (Diane Baker) but soon after she arrives, there are some more axe victims. Written by Robert Bloch and directed by William Castle, the result is highly manipulative in creating an eerie atmosphere and sense of dread that is undercut by a contrived, unsatisfying resolution. Much menace and some special effects violence. A-III (br) X

Strange Affair, The (1968) Failed British crime melodrama about corruption in the London police department in connection with a pornography ring. Directed by David Greene, the slow and contrived plot makes sensationalistic use of violence and nudity. O (R) X

Strange Bedfellows (1964) Thin but frantic romantic comedy in which a London-based oil executive (Rock Hudson) reconciles with his flighty estranged wife (Gina Lollobrigida) before she can remarry in order to get a promotion in his staid company, then she insists on playing Lady Godiva in a left-wing protest at the American Embassy. Directed by Melvin Frank, the sour comedy falls flat on all counts except for the scenes with Terry-Thomas as an undertaker. Sexual situations and innuendo. A-III (br) A

Strange Behavior (1981) Offbeat horror movie about the revenge of a mad scientist, set in the kind of small Midwestern town inextricably bound up with this genre. What makes it unusual is that the town was re-created rather well in New Zealand by director Michael Laughlin who got a few American actors (Michael Murphy and Louise Fletcher) to journey there. Unfortunately, the story piles on the gruesome details of violent deaths to a needlessly excessive degree. O (R)

Strange Brew (1983) The comic duo of Doug and Bob McKenzie (Dave Thomas and Rick Moranis who also directed) lampoon Canada mercilessly as a land of rubes and rustics in an intentionally incoherent plot about a brewery run by archvillain Max von Sydow with Paul Dooley as his cowardly lackey. Chiefly serving as a vehicle for the McKenzie pair of spaced-out zanies, whose substance addiction happens to be beer, the comedy is a random collection of stale sight gags and boisterous stupidities that grow increasingly tiresome. Course language and a visual sexual reference. A-III (PG)

Strange Invaders (1983) Some less-than-cuddly E.T.'s descend upon Centreville, Ill.,

one night in the 1950s and stay on in human form for a quarter of a century wearing the same style clothes as when they first arrived, something quickly noted by a professor (Pal LeMat) who arrives there looking for his missing wife. The silly plot is somewhat engaging, but director Michael Laughlin's handling of it is plodding and uninspired. Some messy special effects when the aliens strip off their human exteriors to reveal their true life forms. A-II (PG)

Strange Shadows in an Empty Room (1977) Director Martin Herbert's frantic exercise in mindless violence about a detective trying to find the murderer of his sister. The Italian production was filmed in Montreal with second-string American leads, and there is not another nice thing to say about it. Nudity, brutality and sheer nastiness. O (R)

Strange Triangle (1946) Contrived story of murder told in flashback by a bank examiner (Preston Foster) who fell for an attractive nuisance (Signe Hasso) with larceny in her heart and a bank director (John Shepperd) under her thumb. Directed by Ray McCarey, the results are hardly worth the effort. Off-screen shooting and mild romantic situations. A-II (br)

Strange Vengeance of Rosalie, The (1972) Botched contemporary horror story about a traveling salesman (Ken Howard) who is tricked by a young girl (Bonnie Bedelia) into visiting her dead grandfather's hovel in a deserted western wasteland and then breaks his leg to keep him there. Director Jack Starrett dissipates the terror of the situation with a subplot about a menacing motorcycle hood (Anthony Zerbe) who harasses the girl both for her grandfather's hidden gold and her body. A-III (R/PG)

Stranger, The (1946) Atmospheric thriller set in a small Connecticut town where a government agent (Edward G. Robinson) tries to persuade the bride (Loretta Young) of a prep-school teacher (Orson Welles) that her husband is an escaped Nazi war criminal. Also directed by Welles, the sunny small-town setting heightens the cat-and-mouse tension of the ensuing manhunt, which concludes in the clockworks high aloft a church steeple. Some menace and stylized violence. A-II (br) A

Stranger, The (1968) Italian-French adaptation of the Albert Camus novel about the senseless murder of an Arab tough by a Frenchman (Marcello Mastroianni) and his subsequent trial and conviction of the crime. Directed by Luchino Visconti, it is a painstaking and often beautiful translation of the Nobel Prize winner's object lesson in existential absurdity. A-IV (br) AA

Stranger Among Us, A (1992) Investigating the murder of a diamond cutter in New York

City's Hasidic community, a cynical detective (Melanie Griffin) is drawn to the sect's spirituality—and its leading Hasidic scholar (Eric Thal). Director Sidney Lumet enriches a standard murder mystery-romance with a sensitive and uplifting look at a little-known religious group. Brief scenes of violence and mild sexual references. A-II (PG-13)

Stranger and the Gunfighter, The (1976) Italian production directed by Anthony Dawson about a gunslinger (Lee Van Cleef) and a kung-fu master (Lo Lieh) who team up to find a lost fortune, clues to which are tattooed on four former mistresses of the deceased owner. Intended as a comic mixture of sex and violence, the result is offensive. O (PG)

Stranger in the House (see: "Black Christmas").

Stranger in Town, A (1967) Sadistic Italian western directed by Vance Lewis in which a stranger in Mexico (Tony Anthony) makes a deal with a bandit gang to help steal a shipment of gold, but when they take it all, he follows and picks them off one by one until he has all the loot. Cynical treatment employs brutal, sadistic violence. O (R)

Stranger Is Watching, A (1982) Rapist-murderer (Rip Torn) kidnaps a young girl (Shawn Von Schreiber) and a TV newswoman (Kate Mulgrew) and holds them prisoner beneath New York's Grand Central Station. Director Sean Cunningham's dull, plodding thriller is derived from a novel by Mary Higgins Clark. Because of violence, rough language and the sordid nature of the story, it is not for young viewers. A-III (R) X

Stranger Returns, The (1968) Standard Italian western directed by Vance Lewis in which a lone stranger (Tony Anthony) sees bandits rob a stagecoach and kill all its passengers, then follows them and exterminates the lot. Much cruelty and violence. A-III (R)

Strangers in Good Company (1991) On a day's outing in the Quebec countryside, a group of elderly women find themselves stranded when their bus breaks down and they have to spend the night in an abandoned farmhouse. By placing nonactors in this bare-bones situation, Canadian director Cynthia Scott comes up with a convincing portrait of seven old women—among them, a nun, a lesbian and a Mohawk Indian matriarch—who pass the time while waiting to be rescued by exchanging reminiscences of their past lives and sharing common concerns about their present circumstances. Simple yet compelling evocation of the mixed blessings of old age, though young children may find some of it confusing. A-II (PG)

Strapless (1990) Fortyish American doctor (Blair Brown), living in England and supporting her fun-loving younger sister, lets down her emotional barriers and marries a mysterious stranger who then disappears. Writer-director David Hare has concocted a moodily intriguing film whose gentle pace allows the viewer to take an intimate look at a repressed woman's mid-life crisis and how it affects those whom she loves. Several instances of rough language, momentary flashes of nudity and a glimpse of a casual sexual encounter. A-III (R) 15

Stratton Story, The (1949) Fact-based dramatization of baseball's Monty Stratton (James Stewart), a Texas farm youth who becomes a star pitcher for the Chicago White Sox until losing a leg in a hunting accident, then tries for a comeback pitching with an artificial leg. Directed by Sam Wood, Stewart gives a fine performance on and off the field, with solid assists from wife June Allyson, mother Agnes Moorehead and pitching scout Frank Morgan. Convincing depiction of a successful athlete overcoming the despair of a devastating disability. A-I (br) U

Straw Dogs (1971) Introverted American mathematician (Dustin Hoffman) takes his sabbatical in the small English village where his wife (Susan George) grew up, and in her boredom, she begins to flirt with her former admirers, leading ultimately to a brutalizing double rape. The movie ends in a bloodbath precipitated by the husband's refusal to let a mob invade his home to lynch an injured man who has taken refuge there. Director Sam Peckinpah benefits from some uncommonly good acting, but the characters are contrived stereotypes who would be more at home in a western movie than the English countryside. As with the rape scene, the attack on the house is particularly brutal and vicious, wallowing in an excess of violence that the plot supposedly condemns. O (R) X

Strawberry Statement, The (1970) Phony screen version of James Kunen's novel purports to be about the radicalizing of a college student (Bruce Davison) who, drawn into participating in a campus sit-in by a pretty revolutionary (Kim Darby), winds up being gassed and bludgeoned when the police and national guard brutalize the protestors. Stuart Hagmann's gimmicky direction calls more attention to itself than to the social and political issues that the movie supposedly is addressing. Further clouding matters is the movie's emphasis on sex and the heavy-handed stylized violence of the riot sequence. O (R) X

Streamers (1983) Screen version of David Rabe's play about barracks tension exploding into violence during the early days of the Vietnam War creates sympathy for its characters (Matthew Modine, Michael Wright and Mitchell Lichtenstein), though the presentation itself remains too stagebound. Directed by Robert Altman, the essential problem with the movie, as with the play, is the attempt to load melodrama with heavy philosophical significance. Admirable intentions but disappointing results. Some violence and rough language. A-III (R) 18

Street Fighter, The (1975) Japanese martial-arts movie revolving around a missing oil heiress and a repulsive thug (Sonny Chiba) who undertakes her rescue. Superior special effects, but excessively violent. O (X/R)

Street People (1976) Aimless, shamelessly derivative gangster movie directed by Maurizio Lucidi in which Roger Moore and Stacy Keach take on a cast of dubbed-in Italian heavies. Some nudity, but most offensive is its mindless brutality. O (R)

Street Smart (1987) Magazine reporter (Christopher Reeve) writes a fictitious account of a pimp's daily activities, passes it off as fact and becomes embroiled in a dilemma when his article is subpoenaed as evidence in the murder trial of a real pimp (Morgan Freeman). Director Jerry Schatzberg's few insights on the subject are lost in a plot featuring mindless revenge, instances of brutality, acceptance of fornication, brief nudity and rough language. O (R) 18

Streetcar Named Desire, A (1951) Screen version of Tennessee Williams' play about the tensions that develop when an emotionally unstable widow (Vivien Leigh) arrives in New Orleans and moves in with her younger sister (Kim Hunter), whose coarse husband (Marlon Brando) resents his sister-in-law's aristocratic pretensions, learns of her shady past and destroys her chance to marry his friend (Karl Malden). Director Elia Kazan probes the loneliness as well as the volatile passions that nearly consume the drama's all-too-human characters. Mature themes, with much sexual innuendo. A-III (PG)

Streets of Fire (1984) Listless, boring rock 'n' roll story about a brooding outsider of a hero (Michael Pare) who rescues a rock star (Diane Lane) from a gang of bikers with the help of a straight-shooting female sidekick (Amy Madigan). Written and directed by Walter Hill, it turns out to be another tedious, stylized celebration of the macho mystique. Violence and a homosexual dance sequence. A-III (R/PG) 15

Streets of Gold (1986) A Jewish emigre (Klaus Maria Brandauer) from the Soviet Union where he had once been an Olympic contender gets some measure of satisfaction from teaching two Brooklyn street kids the art of boxing so they can compete with a visiting Soviet boxing team. In a well-intentioned but predictable plot following the underdog formula, the movie weakly affirms believing in oneself and one's talents. Profanity and violence in and out of the ring by the principals provide no positive role models for youngsters. A-III (R) 15

Streetwalkin' (1985) A prostitute tries to escape from her pimp in this sordid little movie exploiting sex and violence while having pretensions as social commentary. O (R)

Strictly Ballroom (1993) Old-fashioned success story of an Australian youth (Paul Mercurio) with his own ideas about dance steps teaming with an ugly-duckling novice (Tara Morice) to compete for the championship in a traditional ballroom dancing contest. Directed by Baz Luhrmann, the outcome of all this is as obvious as the eventual romance between the two principals is inevitable but the movie's pleasure comes along the way in watching the energy and determination of the young dancers and their innocence in confronting unsympathetic parents and manipulative contest organizers. Mild sexual references, domestic difficulties and several instances of profanity. A-II (PG)

Strictly Business (1991) Predictable romantic comedy about young African Americans in which a mailroom clerk (Tommy Davidson) helps an executive (Joseph C. Phillips) win over the clerk's gorgeous friend (Halle Berry) in exchange for a spot in the management training program. Only the lively music in director Kevin Hooks' uninspired movie relieves the flatness of the uniformly one-dimensional characters. A few discreet bedroom scenes, occasional sexual references, racial slurs and momentary violence. A-III (PG-13)

Strike It Rich (1990) British adaptation of the Graham Greene novella, "Loser Takes All," this fairy-tale bonbon charts the romantic ups and downs of a divorced London accountant (Robert Lindsay) and a demure younger woman (Molly Ringwald) he meets on a bus. Writer-director James Scott nicely re-creates the look of a 1950s' comedy of manners as the couple marry in Monte Carlo while he tries to parlay a "perfect system" at the roulette table into millions. Slight but refreshingly refined exploration of values and the role of chance in romance. Minimal sexual innuendo. A-II (PG)

Strike Me Pink (1936) Weak comedy about an amusement park's meek manager (Eddie Cantor) and his problems fending off a gangster (Brian Donlevy) and his crooked slot machines. Directed by Norman Taurog, Cantor's goofy routines fail to score any big laughs in this lackluster vehicle. Some stylized violence and romantic complications. A-II (br) U

Strike Up the Band (1940) Bouncy teen musical in which a high school band leader

(Mickey Rooney), set on winning a network radio competition of new bands, gets the gang (including Judy Garland) to put on a show raising the fare to New York to perform for contest judge Paul Whiteman. Director Busby Berkeley paces the story's youthful enthusiasm and high hopes with refreshing musical numbers and an idealized view of small-town life and values. Pleasant fun from an optimistic past. A-I (br) U

Striking Distance (1993) Former homicide detective (Bruce Willis), demoted to the Pittsburgh police river patrol alongside a duplicitous female partner (Sarah Jessica Parker), continues to pursue the serial killer he believes murdered his father (John Mahoney), much to the chagrin of his uncle (Dennis Farina), the homicide chief. Director Rowdy Herrington steadily builds suspense in this whodunit, then throws in every cliche in the book in an overwrought climax of absurdly melodramatic proportions. Recurring violence, a fleeting bedroom scene and much rough language. A-III (R)

Stripes (1981) After bungling their way though basic military training, Bill Murray and his troop of losers create havoc in Czechoslovakia. Director Ivan Reitman's mediocre hit-or-miss comedy has only scattered laughs and an occasional serious bit at odds with the rest. Extravagant use of nudity, sexual promiscuity and rough language. O (R) 15

Stripper (1986) Pseudo-documentary on a strip-tease competition is an exploitation movie about women who are paid to display their bodies to voyeurs. O (R)

Stroker Ace (1983) Race car driver (Burt Reynolds) wants to break his contract representing a fried chicken franchiser (Ned Beatty) and to seduce a principled young woman (Loni Anderson). Director Hal Needham's action comedy has plenty of racing sequences, including several crashes, and humor with a minimum of subtlety. Occasional strong language and one relatively mild bedroom scene but, all in all, it's fairly good escapist entertainment for mature viewers. A-III (PG)

Strongest Man in the World, The (1974) Two college students (Kurt Russell and Joe Flynn) accidentally concoct a formula that gives people unlimited strength. Plodding, poorly scripted Disney comedy directed by Vincent McEveety. A-I (G) U

Stroszek (1977) Slight German tale of three Berliners (a street musician, a hapless prostitute and their landlord) who go off to join the landlord's son in Wisconsin, but their hope in the American dream proves to be an empty one. Writer-director Werner Herzog seems to just let things happen and the result is often little more than a home movie with artistic pretensions. Mature themes. A-III (nr) AA

Stuck on You (1984) A palimony suit serves as the peg on which to hang a series of vulgar, unfunny skits in this low-budget comedy directed by Michael Herz and Samuel Weil. Much nudity. O (R)

Stud, The (1979) Directed by Quentin Masters and written by Jackie Collins, this embarrassingly sordid British production stars Joan Collins in a story detailing the rise and fall of a working-class youth (Oliver Tobias) whose only salable asset is his body. O (R) X

Student Nurses, The (1970) Exploitation movie about a group of aging apprentice nurses and their sexual exploits: one has a torrid affair with a resident doctor, another gets pregnant and has an amateur abortion and one has sex with a dying teenager. Directed by Stephanie Rothman, its treatment of the sexual goings on is relatively anemic both visually and morally. O (R)

Stunt Man, The (1980) Fugitive from the police (Steve Railsback) is hidden by a manic movie director (Peter O'Toole) on condition that he do some dangerous stunts, but he makes a mistake by falling for its star (Barbara Hershey). Directed by Richard Rush, the movie-within-a-movie plot starts well but soon becomes repetitious and drags considerably thereafter. Graphic depiction of sex with extensive nudity. O (R) X

Subject Was Roses, The (1968) Fine drama about a Bronx Irish family's domestic crisis succeeds far beyond the limitations of its basically one-set story. Starring Patricia Neal and Jack Albertson as the parents, and Martin Sheen as their serviceman son, the movie probes the love and hate that alternately bind the three together and tear them apart. Adapted from Frank Gilroy's Broadway drama, the movie contains intimate touches of family life, its joys and its frustrations, and is masterful in its revelation of human nature, jealousy and love. Mature themes. A-III (G) A

Submarine X-1 (1968) British World War II story directed by William Graham about the training of submarine crews for an experimental mini-sub under a harsh and disliked commander (James Caan). The underwater sequences with the miniature submarines will be enjoyed by youngsters and the only violence is the sinking of a German battleship. A-I (G) U

Suburban Commando (1991) Mindless sci-fi fantasy has an intergalactic warrior (Hulk Hogan) crash-landing on Earth where a downtrodden architect (Christopher Lloyd) helps him right wrongs and outsmart a pair of pursuing interplanetary bounty hunters. Burt Kennedy directs a silly movie pitting a superhero against klutzy villains in a slapstick comedy of no distinction. Much comic violence. A-II (PG)

Suburban Wives (1972) Lurid British sex melodrama-farce about bored housewives supplementing the family income. Its sense of humor is either unintentional or inappropriate. O (R)

Succubus (1969) Trashy German film about a woman (Janine Reynaud) who does a sadosexual nightclub act and finds it difficult to separate her stage fantasies from her private life. Director Jess Franco's effort is short on plot and characterization, and long only on erotic situations. O (R)

Such a Gorgeous Kid Like Me (1973) Lighthearted French farce about a sociologist (Claude Brasseur) whose research brings him to do a prison interview with a beautiful but amoral murderess (Bernadette Lafont). Enamored, he eventually proves her innocence, but she in turn frames him for her latest murder and becomes a media celebrity. Directed by Francois Truffaut, the comedy bubbles brightly, the plot's twists and turns are delightful and, best of all, it has a feeling for humanity that cloaks even the worst of its characters with an elemental dignity. Some strong language and sexual escapades. A-III (R)

Such Good Friends (1971) Director Otto Preminger has transformed Lois Gould's sly, satirical novel about the seamy underside of New York's cocktail party set into a souped-up sexual soap opera. The film is a series of melodramatic tableaux, which become progressively cheaper in their depiction of the harsh discoveries a youngish wife (Dyan Cannon) makes about her dying husband (Lawrence Luckinbill) and her own series of sexual adventures, past and present. O (R) X

Sucker, The (1966) Funny French comedy directed by Gerard Oury in which a smuggler (Louis de Funes) hires a sucker (Bourvil) to drive him from Naples to Bourdeaux, but when the booby learns that the car is loaded with drugs, gold and jewels, he outsmarts the crooks. Some sexual innuendo. A-III (br)

Sudden Death (1985) Female "Death Wish" variant in which a young woman (Denise Coward) buys a gun after being raped and goes hunting without a license. The woefully inept movie dangerously attempts to find an audience by suggesting vigilantism, yet its central interest is an exploitation of sex and violence. O (R)

Sudden Impact (1983) Dirty Harry (Clint Eastwood who also directs) is back, this time in picturesque Santa Cruz, to halt a series of gruesome shootings that proves to be the work of a gang-rape victim (Sondra Locke) exacting vengeance upon those who brutalized her. With the two having so much in common, the outcome is entirely predictable. Excessive violence and the espousal of an end-justifies-the-means outlook. O (R) 18

Sudden Terror (1971) An above-average British thriller about a youngster (Mark Lester) living on a Mediterranean island who happens to see a policeman shoot the visiting president of an African nation. Afraid of going to the police and unable to convince his grandfather (Lionel Jeffries) that he is telling the truth, the boy is left to the mercy of the murderer in a violent chase crisscrossing the island. Director John Hough offers a mixture of suspense and sly British humor, with a decided Hitchcock flair. Series of violent murders and grisly auto smash-ups. A-III (GP)

Sudden Wealth of the Poor People of Kombach, The (1974) Fact-based German dramatization set in the early 19th century when a group of simple peasants rob a tax-collector but are quickly apprehended since they are the only ones buying goods in an area where everyone else is starving. Director Volker Schlondorff's excellent visual re-creation foreshadows the violent struggles for social justice that break out in Europe a few decades later. A-III (nr)

Suddenly (1954) Modest thriller in which a small band of assassins (led by Frank Sinatra) take captive a family (including Nancy Gates and James Gleason) whose house is on the route to be taken by the U.S. President. Director Lewis Allen builds the tension in realistic detail, especially the gunmen's threatening treatment of the family and the suspicions of the local lawman (Sterling Hayden). Much menace and some stylized violence. A-II (br) A

Suddenly, Last Summer (1959) Uneven adaptation of Tennessee Williams' play in which an aging southern heiress (Katharine Hepburn) tries to induce a neurosurgeon (Montgomery Clift) to perform a lobotomy on a niece (Elizabeth Taylor) traumatized by the bizarre death of the aunt's son. Directed by Joseph L. Mankiewicz, the cast is hard put sustaining interest in the slowly unfolding tale of a mother's unnatural love for her son and a young woman's hysterical repression of witnessing death and degradation in 1937 Spain. Veiled references to homosexuality, cannibalism and loss of virginity as well as restrained depictions of a mental asylum. A-IV (br) X

Suez (1938) Stodgy biographical melodrama based on the life of Ferdinand de Lesseps (Tyrone Power), the French builder of the Suez Canal. Directed by Allan Dwan, the result has little to do with history but the Hollywood version is certainly colorful and heroic, developing two platonic romances (aristocratic Loretta Young and plebeian Annabella) while waffling the international issues delaying the canal's completion. A-II (br) U

Sugar Hill (1974) Ludicrous horror film about a black woman (Marki Bey) who uses voodoo to summon a horde of moss-covered, chrome-eyed zombies to hack to pieces the murderers of her husband. The hacking is bloody enough to be sure, but Paul Maslansky's direction, not to mention the dialogue, the make-up and the acting, is so inept that the entire effort comes off as something of a caricature. A-III (PG)

Sugarland Express, The (1974) A young wife (Goldie Hawn) breaks her small-time criminal hubby (William Atherton) out of a Texas jail and helps him steal a state trooper's car, taking the cop (Michael Saks) as hostage. The unlikely trio picks up a mass following of local lawmen, with the news media reporting the caravan's every turn. Public sentiment builds up to make the edgy wife-husband team into the stuff of legends, inevitably ending in tragedy. Director Steven Spielberg's fact-based story has the feel of real people with very real needs and flaws, achieved by unusually fine performances from the principals. Much tension; some heavy violence. A-III (PG)

Suicide Club, The (1988) A bored, depressed Long Island heiress (Mariel Hemingway) becomes involved with some equally bored overage yuppies whose costume parties end with terminal card games, the winner of which must guzzle a fatal dose of sherry. Directed by James Bruce, the story drowns in a sea of angst, artsy cinematography, somber music and meaningless dialogue. Acceptance of suicide and implications of incest. A-III (R)

Sullivans, The (1944) Enlisting in the Navy the day after Pearl Harbor, five brothers insist on being assigned to the same ship and die together when it's torpedoed off Guadalcanal in 1942. Director Lloyd Bacon's fact-based dramatization centers on the youth's close-knit, working-class family in Waterloo, Iowa, and their loyalty to each other and to country. Simply told with considerable emotional impact, despite wartime flag-waving. A-I (br) U

Sullivan's Travels (1942) Wacky comedy about a lightweight Hollywood director (Joel McCrea) who wants to make a serious movie on the struggles of poor people, sets out to research the subject dressed in rags and winds up on a chain gang where he learns the universal value of laughter. While satirically whaling the tar out of Hollywood and its pretensions, writer-director Preston Sturges uses the comic misadventures of the director's sojourn into the real world to demonstrate the refreshing attributes of a good laugh. Some menace and minor romantic complications. A-II (br) A

Summer House, The (1993) The wedding preparations of a listless young Englishwoman (Lena Headey) engaged to a pompous cad (David Threlfall) take unexpected turns when a flamboyant friend (Jeanne Moreau) of the bride's mother (Julie Walters) arrives from Egypt and connives to prevent the couple's marriage. Director Waris Hussein's strained comedy revolves around casual adultery and alcohol abuse as means of solving life's problems. Glamorization of promiscuity and drunkenness. O (nr)

Summer Lovers (1982) Given an Aegean holiday as a graduation present, a callow youth (Peter Gallagher) takes his girlfriend (Daryl Hannah) to a picturesque Greek island where a French archaeologist (Valerie Quennessen) teaches them that threesomes have more fun than couples. Achieving the emotional level of a tourism poster, writer-director Randall Kleiser's movie is an experience in boredom of appeal only to desperate voyeurs. Excessive nudity. O (R)

Summer of '42 (1971) Sticky little romantic melodrama about three foul-mouthed teens who come of age during the first summer of World War II in a lush Cape Cod setting. Of the three, the focus is on the quiet-but-deep dreamer (Gary Grimes) and his interest in the fetching form of the grief-stricken war widow (Jennifer O'Neill) who invites him to share her bed. Director Robert Mulligan tries to balance all the nostalgia with a little honesty in depicting the limbo of loneliness and longing between adolescence and manhood but stumbles at the end. Mature theme. A-IV (R/PG) X

Summer Paradise (1978) Swedish movie about four generations of a family who gather to spend the summer in a comfortable old house in beautiful natural surroundings becomes an intricate study of their relationships, lives, careers and values. Director Gunnel Lindblom uses her family setting to offer a sharp, passionate but nondoctrinaire critique of modern society, not least of its targets being abortion, mercy killing and the pill. Unnecessary use of nudity in a manner quite incidental to the movie's themes and development. A-IV (nr)

Summer Rental (1985) Innocuous little comedy, directed by Carl Reiner, about a family's Florida vacation simply doesn't have enough humorous material to be worth the effort. Some fairly vulgar sequences say little about family ties or vacationing. A-II (PG)

Summer School (1987) A gym teacher (Mark Harmon) becomes a reluctant remedial English instructor whose nonconformist tactics finally produce positive results with a group of impudent teenagers forced to spend their summer in school. The deals that are struck between teacher and student in writer-director Carl Reiner's light comedy address social and sexual issues requiring a mature perspective. A-III (PG-13)

Summer Stock (1950) Pleasant musical comedy in which a farm girl (Judy Garland) reluctantly lets a theatrical troupe (headed by Gene Kelly) use her barn to put on a musical revue, then winds up the show's star. Directed by Charles Walters, there's not much plot but it's got plenty of music, notably Garland singing "Get Happy" and Kelly building a tap dance around a squeaky floor board and some newspaper pages, paced with intermittent comedy from the likes of Eddie Bracken, Phil Silvers and Marjorie Main. Enjoyable family fare. A-I (br)

Summer Wishes, Winter Dreams (1973) Character study of a woman (Joanne Woodward) whose mother's death initiates a mid-life crisis that, despite her understanding husband (Martin Balsam), nearly sweeps her away. Woodward's moving performance reveals the private agony of a lonely, desperate woman who has allowed life to slip past her because of her refusal to deal with its realities but who tries to struggle for a new understanding of self and a renewed need for others. Gilbert Cates's sensitive direction shows an understanding for the subtleties of intimate relationships, their pain and love. A-III (PG) AA

Summerdog (1977) Mild little comedy about a family who fall in love with a dog that attaches itself to them on their summer vacation. The problem, happily overcome of course, is how to bring him home when their landlord does not allow pets. There is some lovely photography, but it is a movie for younger and less demanding viewers. A-I (G)

Summertime (1955) Katharine Hepburn plays a spinster on a vacation in Venice who becomes enchanted with a handsome Italian (Rosanno Brazzi) but, when she learns he is married, cuts her vacation short and returns home, a sadder but wiser person. British production directed by David Lean is a classic romantic melodrama, faultlessly told with charming, bittersweet humor and the eye-filling, Renaissance splendor of the city of canals. A-III (br)

Summertime Killer (1973) Formula revenge tale about a young man (Christopher Mitchum) who kidnaps the daughter (Olivia Hussey) of a member of the gang that killed his father and then falls in love with her while being trailed to Lisbon by a crooked cop (Karl Malden). Director Antonio Isasi makes the most of motorcycle chases in the picturesque Portuguese countryside but has much less success with tracking a largely incoherent plot. Amoral characters and situations. A-III (PG)

Summertree (1971) Hollow melodrama about a talented guitarist (Michael Douglas) who, drafted before he can enroll in music school, disillusioned by the woman he loves (Brenda Vaccaro) and prevented by his parents (Jack Warden and Barbara Bel Geddes) from escaping to Canada, becomes another victim of the Vietnam era. Directed by Anthony Newley, the characters and their experiences don't add up and its unearned sentimentality trivializes a serious subject. Especially soft-headed is a nude love scene with ludicrous superimpositions of luxuriant vegetation. A-III (PG) AA

Sunburn (1979) Insurance investigator (Charles Grodin) hires a model (Farrah Fawcett) to act as his wife while in Acapulco on a murder-suicide case with a $5 million payout. They are joined by a retired sleuth (Art Carney), and the trio pulls off the solution with lots of assistance from scenery, costumes and sneaky tactics. Directed by Richard C. Sarafian, it's simple escapist fare with well-intentioned bunglers bringing more cunning crooks to justice. A-II (PG)

Sunday, Bloody Sunday (1971) British stiff-upper-lip triangle between a successful middle-aged physician (Peter Finch), an attractive divorcee (Glenda Jackson) and a young, pleasant but uncommitted art designer (Murray Head) whose companionship and affections the two older people knowingly if regretfully share. Directed by John Schlesinger, the locale is contemporary London, peopled by middle-class ciphers who live in a world bereft of hope and spiritual freedom. Sensitive, nuanced portrayal of tortured relationships but morally ambiguous in its conclusion. Details of the homosexual relationship are restrained but central to the plot. A-IV (R) X

Sunday in the Country (1976) Dull, predictable Canadian film about a seemingly mild-mannered farmer (Ernest Borgnine) who takes the law into his own hands in brutal fashion. O (R)

Sunday in the Country, A (1985) Warm, insightful French movie about one day in the life of an old painter (Louis Ducreux). In his country home near Paris on a beautiful spring Sunday in 1912, the old man is visited by his dull son and his even duller wife with their three lively children, joined a little later by the artist's unmarried daughter who is his delight. Nothing happens out of the ordinary except that this marvelously discerning film creates a family context that is universal in showing the bafflements and complexities of human love and ambition. A small masterpiece directed by Bertrand Tavernier. A-I (G) PG

Sunday Lovers (1981) Failed omnibus film about the amorous adventures of four middle-aged men in four different countries presented in separate episodes directed by Bryan Forbes, Eduard Molinaro, Dino Risi and Gene Wilder. The segments range from mediocre to dismal, with Wilder's being the worst. Prolonged nude love scene. O (R)

Sundown (1941) Flagwaving colonial adventure in which the commander (Bruce Cabot) of a British outpost in Kenya's interior gets help from an American hunter (Harry Carey) and an Arab trader's daughter (Gene Tierney) in stopping a Nazi plot to arm a native uprising. Director Henry Hathaway conveys the tensions of a remote frontier post more credibly than the bogus heroism displayed in the big action finish. Stylized violence and African stereotypes. A-II (br)

Sundowners, The (1960) Excellent story about the joys and hardships of an itinerant Australian sheepherder (Robert Mitchum) whose passion for the unencumbered life is in direct conflict with the yearnings of his wife (Deborah Kerr) to settle down. Directed by Fred Zinnemann, the movie's characters and its locale are finely evoked in a story that is part outdoors adventure and part domestic drama. A-II (br) U

Sunflower (1970) Italian tearjerker about a newly married couple (Sophia Loren and Marcello Mastroianni) whose life is disrupted when he is sent to the Russian front during World War II. When he does not return, she journeys to Russia and finds him married and with a child. Eventually following her back to Milan, he learns she is now in love with someone else. Directed by Vittorio De Sica, the movie is not essentially concerned with such matters as marital commitment and fidelity, and younger adolescents are likely to misunderstand the moral ambiguities of the story's human complications. A-III (G) A

Sunnyside (1979) A tough street fighter (Joey Travolta) wants to stop gang warfare and start a new life. Haphazardly directed by Timothy Galfas, the movie brutalizes viewers with incessant violence. O (R)

Sunset (1988) Witless, period buddy movie set in 1929 Hollywood where the unlikely sleuthing team of cowboy movie star Tom Mix (Bruce Willis) and marshal Wyatt Earp (James Garner) uncover a bundle of dirty linen in the movie capital. In this bomb directed by Blake Edwards, colorful characters meander through a vapid, humorless plot. Several scenes of violence, some profanity, brief nudity and implied kinky sex in a brothel. A-III (R) 15

Sunshine Boys, The (1975) Good screen version of the Neil Simon comedy about an old vaudeville team (George Burns and Walter Matthau), long separated, who are brought together, despite their antagonism, for one last performance. Director Herbert Ross gets an excellent performance from Burns, and though Matthau overacts, there are enough laughs to provide an evening's entertainment. Some rough language. A-III (PG) A

Super, The (1991) Shrill comedy concerns a convicted slum landlord (Joe Pesci) forced to live in the same rat-infested building with his own tenants. Director Rod Daniel ruins an amusing concept with clanky, heavy-handed humor and trite stick figures throughout. Much rough language and some base sexual references. A-III (R)

Super Cops, The (1974) Fact-based story about two New York City detectives, nicknamed Batman (Ron Liebman) and Robin (David Selby), whose turf is a Brooklyn ghetto and its liver-colored tenements, gaudy pimp-dope dealer hangouts and crime-ridden streets. As directed by Gordon Parks, there is an undeniable vigor in this fast-paced movie and great appeal in its two central figures and solid supporting cast. However, it goes to excess in its graphic violence, coarse street humor and relentlessly foul language. O (R/PG) A

Super Mario Bros. (1993) Frenetic fantasy adventure with two Brooklyn plumbers (Bob Hoskins and John Leguizamo) falling into another dimension where they rescue a princess (Samantha Mathis) from an evil lizard king (Dennis Hopper) descended from dinosaurs who is planning to conquer Earth. Attempting to capitalize on a popular video game, Rocky Morton and Annabel Jankel direct a dopey live-action plot of mirthless mayhem and chase sequences whose jazzy special effects only momentarily lift the level of interest. Some menace and comic violence. A-II (PG)

Super Stooges Versus the Wonder Women (1974) Inept Italian adventure fantasy about a band of Amazons who meet their match in a trio of super heroes. Director Al Bradley's low-grade sword-and-sandals action offers inane buffoonery, poorly staged battles and minor skirmishes, both military and romantic. A-III (PG)

Superargo and the Faceless Giants (1971) Mad doctor (Guy Madison) turns abducted athletes into bank-robbing robots until foiled by Superargo (Ken Wood), retired wrestler and masked mystic, indomitable in crimson bullet-proof costume, together with ray gun and su-percar. Directed by Paul Maxwell, it is a throwback to the simple spills and thrills of the old Saturday matinee serials but lacks their corny charm. A-I (G)

Superbeast (1972) Shoestring Philippine horror movie about ape-like mutants resulting from the botched attempts of a mad doctor (Craig Littler) in reconditioning hardened criminals on his jungle river island outside Manila. Director George Schenck botches a plot derived from any number of older, better movies, with his only innovation being the use of some stock medical footage of a cadaver's dissection. A-III (R)

Superdad (1974) West Coast teenagers have their summer beach party fun interrupted by a dumb but well-meaning father (Bob Crane) who opposes his daughter's (Kathleen Cody) involvement with a directionless youth (Kurt Russell). Though intended as the usual lightweight Disney family fare, director Vincent McEveety's picture of family life and values is a tasteless mixture of middle-class affluence, alienation and artificiality. A-II (G)

Superfly (1972) Black exploitation movie about a tough, cool drug dealer (Ron O'Neal) who is planning one last deal so he can make a killing and get out, but the police (all white) and a New York City commissioner want in. Directed by Gordon Parks Jr., the super antics of affluent criminals glamorize these fantasy characters as viable, attractive figures to be admired. Excessive violence and sex. O (R)

Superfly T.N.T. (1973) Middling sequel takes the ex-drug dealer (Ron O'Neal who also directed) from Harlem to Rome where he pitches in with his special brand of hustling know-how in order to help an emerging West African nation. The role has taken on some fairly human characteristics but, unfortunately, the change gets lost in the context of a static story offering little but glamorous location photography and mildly violent action. A-III (R)

Supergirl (1984) Superman's cousin (Helen Slater) does battle with a wicked witch, the fate of mankind depending upon the outcome. Faye Dunaway and Brenda Vaccaro are among the nasties in a wooden film directed by Jeannot Szwarc. Restrained attempted rape scene and some profanity. A-II (PG)

Superman (1978) The Man of Steel (Christopher Reeve) is brought to Earth from the dying planet Krypton, nurtured by the kind-hearted Kents and becomes a reporter in Metropolis where he meets Lois Lane (Margot Kidder). As Superman, he encounters evil in the person of master criminal Lex Luthor (Gene Hackman) and his cronies (Ned Beatty and Valerie Perrine). Fun-filled comic book fantasy adventure directed by Richard Donner has some pyrotechnics that may be too intense for the very young. A-II (PG)

Superman II (1981) Exciting, romantic and often very funny sequel has three nasty villains from Krypton show up to wreak havoc just as Superman (Christopher Reeve) gives up his powers in order to make love to an ordinary mortal (Margot Kidder). Directed by Richard Lester, the special effects, especially the climatic battle between superhero and supervillains above the streets of New York, are very effective. Unfortunately, some of the violence is rather intense and the sympathetic portrayal of premarital sex between the principals makes it inappropriate for youngsters. A-III (PG)

Superman III (1983) Weak sequel fails to mesh two plots, the first involving the return of Superman (Christopher Reeve) to Smallville for his high school reunion, and the second concerning a ruthless tycoon (Robert Vaughn) disrupting the world economy with the aid of an incompetent dishwasher-turned-computer-wizard (Richard Pryor). Directed by Richard Lester, it's a muddled, unfocused effort that keeps promising to develop into something entertaining but never quite does. Realistic fight sequence and Superman's bad conduct while under the baleful influence of Kryptonite rule out younger viewers. A-II (PG)

Superman IV: The Quest for Peace (1987) The Man of Steel (Christopher Reeve) battles his evil clone created by Lex Luthor (Gene Hackman) in this even-tempered sequel that features an appearance by Mariel Hemingway as a romantic rival to Lois Lane (Margot Kidder). Director Sidney J. Furie stages a violent conflict that may be too intense for the very young. A-II (PG)

Superstar: The Life and Times of Andy Warhol (1991) Impressionistic biography of the late pop artist follows his controversial course through the art wars of the 1960s and 1970s to his enjoyment of being recognized in the 1980s as a star personality in his own right. Written, produced and directed by Chuck Workman, the documentary uses contrasting views of Warhol's family, friends and associates to further Warhol's reputation as an enigma in the midst of the confusions and contradictions of contemporary American culture. Some references to the promiscuous life-styles of the period and several flashes of frontal nudity. A-III (nr)

Support Your Local Gunfighter (1971) James Garner plays an ingenuous con man who tricks a small town divided by rival mine operators into believing that an innocuous rummy (Jack Elam) is a dangerous gunslinger. Under Burt Kennedy's direction, the amiable western comedy meanders its way through predictable but amusing plot twists and cliches before reaching its long-overdue happy ending. A-II (G) U

Support Your Local Sheriff (1969) Gentle, genuinely funny spoof of the Hollywood western and its heroes. When a gold strike transforms a slow-moving pioneer settlement into a raucous, lawless boom town, the local folk hire quiet drifter James Garner as sheriff and he institutes a series of clever and nonlethal maneuvers aimed at ridding the town of crime and violence. Garner is past master at this kind of genial characterization and his performance combines neatly with Burt Kennedy's deft, offbeat direction to make a very solid comedy. Joan Hackett supplies the romantic interest and Walter Brennan, Jack Elam and Bruce Dern are excellent support. A-I (G) PG

Suppose They Gave a War and Nobody Came (1970) Witless, unfunny slapstick comedy about a skirmish that develops between U.S. military units and the paramilitary units of a town near an Army base somewhere in the Southwest. Viewers should receive Purple Hearts and director Hy Averback should be court-martialed. Most of the senseless violence is between machines with nary a drop of spilt blood. A-III (PG) AA

Sure Thing, The (1985) Two college freshmen (John Cusack and Daphne Zuniga) share a ride to California. He's got a date with a "sure thing" and she's going to join her fiance. What results is mildly amusing. Director Rob Reiner's movie is about romance instead of sex, a refreshing concept for a teenage movie, yet it accepts promiscuity as a way of life for most young people. A comically intended scene involving a sex act occurring in the background further lessens its suitability for youngsters. A-III (PG-13) 15

Surrender (1987) Old-fashioned romantic comedy updated for the sexually explicit 1980s with the story of a writer (Michael Caine) who believes all women to be greedy until he finds one (Sally Field) who does not seem interested in whether he has any money. Written and directed by Jerry Belson, it has some sharp satire on contemporary materialism and a few good sight-gags, but its matter-of-fact acceptance of extramarital relationships is objectionable. O (PG)

Survive (1976) Poorly made, badly dubbed Mexican movie about a plane crash in the Andes whose survivors are forced to eat the flesh of those who were killed in order to survive until rescued. Directed by Rene Cardona Jr., the moral issues involved in the situation are beyond the range of this cheap exploitation effort. A-III (R)

Survivors, The (1983) When a young executive (Robin Williams) and the manager of a gas station (Walter Matthau) thwart the holdup of a diner by a robber (Jerry Reed), they spend the rest of the movie trying to survive the crook's relentless pursuit. Director Michael Ritchie's social satire attempts a bit too much, especially in terms of a sagging American economy, but it is nonetheless an often hilarious, consistently entertaining film. Some adult humor. A-III (R)

Susan Slept Here (1954) Tasteless romantic comedy in which a 17-year-old juvenile delinquent (Debbie Reynolds) spends an unchaperoned Christmas with a cynical screenwriter (Dick Powell) doing research on a story of troubled youth, then complicates his life by falling in love with him. Director Frank Tashlin drags out the contrived situation with over-cute, largely unfunny stabs at humor, including the writer's Oscar (voice of Ken Carpenter) serving as narrator. Much sexual innuendo. A-III (br) A

Suspect (1987) Good suspense story of murder and corruption in the nation's capital stars Cher as a public defender who proves her indigent client innocent, with some assistance from a juror (Dennis Quaid) who has a romantic interest in her. Directed by Peter Yates, the center of the movie is the character played extremely well by Cher who conveys the strength, intelligence, dedication and appeal of the role. Some graphic violence and a lot of moody tension and menace. A-III (R) 15

Suspicion (1941) Suspense tale about a shy Englishwoman (Joan Fontaine) swept off her feet by a dashing charmer (Cary Grant) then, learning after their marriage of his debts, comes to fear that he is planning to murder her for the insurance. Director Alfred Hitchcock starts with a sunny love story that grows increasingly dark as the wife's suspicions deepen until a slapdash ending proves a letdown. Much tension and menace. A-II (br) A

Suspiria (1977) Tasteless Italian horror movie directed by Dario Argento about an innocent ballet student who finds herself in an dance academy run by a coven of witches. Excessive blood and gore. O (R) X

Swappers, The (1970) Pseudo-documentary about affluent middle-class marrieds in Britain who trade mates in sexual games supposedly to heal marital problems or at least provide a thrilling diversion from them. Patent sex exploitation. O (R)

Swarm, The (1978) Air Force General Richard Widmark and scientist Michael Caine try to stop the progress of billions of perturbed killer bees and save the lives of the usual collection of aged and aging actors who assemble for such disaster movies. Since Widmark and Caine spend most of the movie trying to outshout each other, the bees, not surprisingly, almost prevail. Director Irwin Allen's effort would be silly if it were not so inane. A-II (PG)

Swashbuckler (1976) Witless pirate film directed by James Goldstone that, in a mistaken attempt to combine tongue-in-cheek action with straight melodrama, is so achingly bad that a competent cast (Robert Shaw, James Earl Jones, Peter Boyle) can do nothing to make it bearable. Some brief nudity. A-III (PG) A

Sweden, Heaven and Hell (1969) Italian pseudo-documentary filmmaker Luigi Scattini journeys to Sweden to show all manner of excesses, sexual and otherwise, most of which are staged to sanctimonious moralization of the narrator. Sheer exploitation. O (X/R)

Swedish Fly Girls (see: "Christa").

Sweet Body of Deborah (1969) Shoddy Italian-French import about a young man (Jean Sorel) who concocts a scheme to murder his new wife (Carroll Baker) for her insurance money but she double-crosses him. Directed by Romolo Guerrieri, the inept melodrama offers generous portions of sex and nudity. O (R)

Sweet Charity (1969) Overblown screen version of the Broadway musical about a dance-hall hostess (Shirley MacLaine) who gets the romantic runaround from a series of guys who try to break her heart-of-gold. But her spirit is buoyant and there is true love around the corner (John McMartin). Directed by Bob Fosse, it tries so hard it gets tiresome. A-II (G) A

Sweet Dreams (1985) Moving, entertaining biography of country-western singer Patsy Cline (Jessica Lange) whose career was cut short in a 1963 plane crash. Director Karel Reisz concentrates on characterization rather than showbiz glitter and there is some fine acting, but the film's episodic structure undercuts its dramatic impact. Some vulgar language and vividly displayed passion, loving as well as violent, mark the relationship between the heroine and her husband. A-III (PG-13) 15

Sweet Hearts Dance (1988) Fairly innocuous slice of romantic Americana set in small-town Vermont tracks the temporary midlife breakdown of a 15-year marriage (Don Johnson and Susan Sarandon) and the efforts of their kids and friends to get them back together. Nice performances, but director Robert Greenwald provides a stronger portrait of male bonding than marriage. Locker-room language, implied infidelity as well as premarital sex and brief flashes of nudity. A-III (R) 15

Sweet Jesus, Preacher Man (1973) Low-budget black exploitation movie about a criminal (Roger E. Mosley) who poses as the new pastor of a small congregation

(after incinerating the real clergyman) in order to double-cross a white racketeer. Director Henning Schellerup has a flair for confusing characters and situations in dimly lit scenes. Excessive violence, some explicit sex and rough language. O (R)

Sweet Liberty (1986) The lighthearted vehicle written and directed by Alan Alda is a disappointingly shallow view of the sexual and professional frustrations of an amiable historian (Alda) whose book is being made into a movie. The comic touches don't override the movie's celebration of permissive casual sex with several partners as an acceptable route to mutual trust and devotion. O (PG)

Sweet Light in a Dark Room (1966) Czechoslovakian drama set in Nazi-occupied Prague where a student makes an attempt to help a Jewish girl hide from the deportations. Director Jiri Weiss maintains a grim wartime atmosphere and his two young principals (Dana Smutna and Ivan Mistrik) are credible in a life-and-death situation. A-II (br)

Sweet Lorraine (1987) Young woman (Trini Alvarado) rediscovers family ties and a sense of belonging while working for her grandmother (Maureen Stapleton) during a summer at a resort hotel. Director Steve Gomer mixes nostalgia with delicate romance in a family story marred only by some harsh language in a kitchen scene. A-II (PG-13) PG

Sweet November (1968) Sappy romance about a woman (Sandy Dennis) who is in the habit of changing male roommates each month and November happens to be Anthony Newley's turn. The reason for living life in joyous monthly installments is because the woman is dying of the standard Hollywood nondisfiguring but incurable disease. Directed by Robert Ellis Miller, there is some gentle humor at work in the script but the basic theme of the movie is unacceptable, even though given mild treatment. O (br) A

Sweet Revenge (1977) Stockard Channing plays a tough teenage car thief and Sam Waterson is the good-natured lawyer who constantly comes to her rescue only to be rewarded with contempt for his efforts. Director Jerry Schatzberg attempts to carry off a kind of conversion of his heroine at the end of this run-of-the-mill comedy melodrama, but its morality (she sets fire to a valuable car bought with stolen money) is highly ambiguous. A-III (PG) AA

Sweet Ride, The (1968) Trashy tangled tale having to do with the wasted lives and energies of a pack of Malibu beach bums (such as Tony Franciosa and Michael Sarrazin) and their assorted girlfriends (most notably, Jacqueline Bisset). Directed by

Harvey Hart, its sexual misadventures aren't redeemed by one character's sudden moral awakening. O (R) X

Sweet Saviour (1971) Exploitation movie featuring Troy Donahue in a sick and revolting movie based transparently on the Charles Manson-Sharon Tate murder sensation. Writtten, produced and directed by Bob Roberts, it's a tawdry attempt to cash in on a notorious tragedy. O (X/R)

Sweet Sugar (1973) Exploitative women's prison-escape movie with Ella Edwards and Phyllis Davis as the black and white ring leaders. Directed by Michel Levesque in Costa Rica, the bargain basement proceedings are soured with the usual violence, lewd characters, nudity and dirty dialogue. O (R)

Sweet Sweetback's Baadasssss Song (1971) Melvin Van Peeples wrote, produced, directed and stars as Sweetback, a name derived from his sexual prowess, who brutally murders two brutal cops and becomes a fugitive from The Man. The result is a largely incoherent chase film, utterly defeated by flashy camera effects, overly graphic sex and violence, extraordinarily rough language and degrading stereotypes, black and white. O (X/R)

Sweetie (1990) Surreal, off-kilter Australian drama about two bizarre sisters—one thin, sour and inhibited (Karen Colston), the other schizophrenic, plump and insatiable for food, sex and attention (Genevieve Lemon). Directed by Jane Campion, it's an uncomfortable, unconventional study of adult female sibling rivalry and the long-standing ties that bind and choke off all that is good and healthy in a family. Scenes of graphic sexuality and psychological breakdown may be disturbing to some, yet the work's unusual artistic and family vision warrants serious attention. Nudity and rough language. A-IV (R) 15

Swept Away (by an Unusual Destiny in the Blue Sea of August) (1975) Italian satire about a spoiled rich woman (Mariangela Melato) marooned on a deserted island with proletarian brute (Giancarlo Giannini). Directed by Lina Wertmuller, the battle of the sexes between classes gets swept away in some extensive depictions of lovemaking. O (R)

Swimmer, The (1968) Adaptation of the John Cheever story about a middle-aged suburbanite (Burt Lancaster) who swims home through the pools of his affluent neighbors, a journey recalling his wasted life. Directed by Frank Perry, the swim is a long one and the recollections, especially of past affairs, lead to only a banal conclusion. A-III (PG) A

Swimming Pool, The (1970) This static French plot revolves around a triangle (Romy Schneider, Alain Delon and Maurice Ronet) with nubile Jane Birkin coolly observing and finally taking part in their sexual games. Placed in a glamorous resort setting, the inner sterility of these social parasites is conveyed with deadening dullness. Moral issues drown in waves of ennui. O (R/GP) X

Swimming to Cambodia (1987) Moderately interesting monologue written and delivered by actor Spalding Gray who sits at a desk talking about his personal relections on life and his profession, mostly centered on what he experienced in Thailand during the filming of "The Killing Fields" (1984). Director Jonathan Demme makes a straightforward record of Gray's stage performance, punctuated by fades, a few film clips and a modest variety of camera positions. Some graphic descriptions of Khmer Rouge atrocities in Cambodia; a few sexual references, including a brief account of prostitution in Bangkok; some rough language. A-III (nr)

Swindle, The (see: "Il Bidone").

Swing Kids (1993) The friendship of two music-loving adolescents (Robert Sean Leonard and Christian Bale) in 1939 Hamburg is savagely torn apart when they reluctantly join the Hitler Youth and one buys into the racist Nazi philosophy. Despite its good intentions, director Thomas Carter's manipulative drama is a thoroughly artificial-looking Hollywood version of anti-Semitism in pre-war Germany. Some stylized violence, racial and ethnic slurs and an instance of rough language. A-II (PG-13) 12

Swing Shift (1984) Young housewife (Goldie Hawn) takes a job in an aircraft factory after her husband (Ed Harris) enlists in the Navy at the start of World War II. Making friends with an independent young woman (Christine Lahti), she eventually falls into an affair with a personable young man exempt from service (Kurt Russell). Directed by Jonathan Demme, the flawed but superbly acted and often quite moving movie recaptures the hopes and fears, the aspirations and idealism of a now vanished era. Though sympathetic in its depiction of adulterous conduct, it clearly shows that adultery is harmful. Occasional rough language. A-III (PG)

Swing Time (1936) Down-on-his-luck hoofer (Fred Astaire) rides the rails to New York City, teams with a comely dance instructor (Ginger Rogers) and they score as the town's top dancing duo in such numbers as "Waltz in Swing Time" and Astaire's solo showstopper, "Bojangles of Harlem." Director George Stevens keeps the pair's romantic misunderstandings light and lively, gets strong comic relief from Victor Moore and Helen Broderick and effortlessly stages such songs as "A Fine Romance" and

"The Way You Look Tonight." Elegant entertainment for all but the very young. A-I (br) U

Swinger, The (1966) A good girl (Ann-Margret) poses as a bad girl in order to sell some of her stories to a sex magazine. Directed by George Sidney, it is a silly exercise in titillation. O (br) X

Swingin' Pussycats, The (1972) German sex comedy about three sexually agile sisters who scamper insatiably about their spacious estate to romp with any visitor, nobleman or commoner. Directed by Alexis Neve, it's totally unamusing exploitation fare. O (R)

Swingin' Stewardesses, The (1972) Director Michael Thomas turns a standard European travelogue into soft-core pornography in a badly dubbed, ridiculously inept, thoroughly tedious exploitation movie. O (R)

Swiss Family Robinson (1960) Good Disney version of the classic adventure about a shipwrecked family (headed by John Mills and Dorothy McGuire) living in a tree house on a deserted island learning to survive offers an engrossing picture of family devotion and solidarity. Nicely directed by Ken Annakin, much of the fun for children will come from the delightful and inventive conveniences the family builds and their relationships with the island's wildlife including an elephant, turtle and ostrich. A-I (G) U

Switch (1991) Murdered by a trio of his enraged ex-lovers, an incorrigible male chauvinist (Perry King) is returned to earth as a female (Ellen Barkin) to mend his ways or it's hell for him. Writer-director Blake Edwards' one-joke comedy does not sustain the humor beyond obvious, vulgar situations and its contrived, last-minute pro-life message is thoroughly unconvincing. Blatant sexist attitudes, barroom brawls played for laughs, recurring rough language, frequent sexual innuendo, some recreational substance abuse and brief nudity. O (R)

Switching Channels (1988) Failed adaptation of "The Front Page," updated to a 1980s' TV newsroom, tracks the love-hate relationship between a star newswoman (Kathleen Turner) and her ex-husband boss (Burt Reynolds), with a foppish lover (Christopher Reeve) in the wings. Weak chemistry between lead actors and clumsy direction by Ted Kotcheff. Some rough language. A-II (PG)

Swoon (1992) Bizarre, arty dramatization of the 1924 Leopold-and-Loeb murder case stars Craig Chester and Daniel Schlachet as college students convicted of the thrill-killing of a young Chicago boy. Looking like an extended music video, writer-director Tom Kalin's low-budget movie is more concerned with playing up the homophobic and anti-Semitic prejudices of the 1920s than in offering a balanced or insightful examination of the crime and its consequences. A few discreet homosexual bedroom shots, two off-camera murders and minimal rough language. A-III (nr) 18

Sword in the Stone, The (1963) Disney cartoon version of the Arthurian legend of a young squire who, with the help of a wizard, becomes the king of England by pulling a sword from a boulder. Directed by Wolfgang Reitherman and featuring the voices of Sebastian Cabot, Karl Swenson and Rickie Sorenson, the film is pleasant viewing for children but offers little for older family members. A-I (br) U

Sylvester (1985) The story of a girl and her horse. Good acting by Melissa Gilbert and Richard Farnsworth as a gruff but lovable trainer, but little else to recommend this cliched tale directed by Tim Hunter. Vulgar language, a graphic near-rape and implied premarital sex propel the narrative out of its romantic framework. A-III (PG)

Symphony for a Massacre (1965) Low-budget but well-executed French crime story of five thieves trying to figure out which among them is responsible for stealing their loot. Director Jacques Deray works out the seriocomic plot neatly with fine performances from Michel Auclair, Claude Dauphin and Charles Vanel. Subtitles. Stylized violence and sexual situations. A-III (br)

Synanon (1965) Edmond O'Brien, Chuck Connors, Eartha Kitt and Richard Conte star in a movie about the work of Synanon House, a haven for the cure of drug addiction near Santa Monica, California. Directed by Richard Quine, the movie's problem lies in exploiting too many side stories to the detriment of making understandable the problems with which it deals. A-III (br)

T

Table for Five (1983) Failed tearjerker in which a divorced husband (Jon Voight) takes his three children on a Mediterranean cruise, during which his ex-wife (Millie Perkins) dies in an accident and the children's stepfather (Richard Crenna) starts showing up at ports of call demanding custody of the still unknowing children. Directed by David Seltzer, the sentimental hokum seems interminable. Shipboard romance with a lovely Frenchwoman (Marie-Christine Barrault) is adult fare. A-III (R) PG

Taipan (1986) Rambling epic soap opera leaves out the history, drama and details of the economic exploitation of China during the 1840s when British traders dominated the opium and tea trades, centering instead on the sexual exploitation of bare-breasted Chinese women. Based on James Clavell's best-seller about a Scotsman (Bryan Brown) who loses, then regains control of a lucrative Hong Kong trading post, the photography of actual Chinese locales is picturesque, but Daryl Duke's direction is ponderous. Much nudity, sexual activity and brutality. O (R)

Take, The (1974) Billie Dee Williams stars as a cop who's tough on the mob but takes money from them on the side in a muddled detective thriller that tries to create a complex environment where cops and crooks are interchangeable and money makes the world go round. Unfortunately, director Robert Hartford-Davis never bothers to explain the two sides of Williams' character or what the action is really all about, especially why the mob is attacking Paloma, New Mexico. A-III (PG)

Take a Girl Like You (1970) British production about an innocent young teacher (Hayley Mills) being pursued by her landlord (John Bird) and fellow teacher (Oliver Reed), both nasty rather than romantic types. Directed by Jonathan Miller, the heavy-handed melodrama deals in the corrupting influence of swingers and their world of casual sex. O (R) X

Take a Hard Ride (1975) Routine western about a wrangler (Jim Brown), entrusted by his dying boss (Dana Andrews) to bring his widow the money from the sale of a herd, who forms an uncertain alliance with a devil-may-care gambler (Fred Williamson) as various villains pop out of the sagebrush on the way home. Directed by Anthony Dawson, it's bland and harmless save for a lot of unimaginative chases and gunfights. A-II (PG) X

Take Down (1979) Small-town teacher (Edward Herrmann) becomes the reluctant coach of the high school's game but inept wrestling team and has to motivate the one youngster (Lorenzo Lamas) who could boost it to the championship. Though the plot is entirely predictable, director Keith Merrill gives it some heart, and his handling of the young cast members makes it fun. Wholesome teen entertainment. A-II (PG)

Take It All (1966) French-Canadian production directed by Claude Jutra about an immoral young man's sexual experiences is offensive in its suggestive treatment in spite of its superficial condemnation of the hero. O (br)

Take the High Ground (1953) Korean War vet (Richard Widmark) proves to be a tough drill sergeant pushing draftees through 16 grueling weeks of basic training at Fort Bliss, Texas. Director Richard Brooks covers the routine chores of boot camp in pedestrian fashion as the sour sergeant mellows, thanks to a good buddy (Karl Malden) and a girlfriend (Elaine Stewart). Manly posturing and romantic complications. A-II (br) A

Take the Money and Run (1969) Woody Allen stars as the world's least dangerous criminal, botching bank jobs and terrorizing no one but himself. Also directed by Allen, it's an entertaining romp through many fields and styles of humor, one-line witticisms, subtle jokes and sight gags galore. Some sexual references and a few profanities. A-III (PG)

Taking Care of Business (1990) Tame comedy about an escaped con (James Belushi) who blithely assumes the identity of a stuffy corporate executive (Charles Grodin) after finding his appointment book, credit cards and keys to an oceanside mansion. Under Arthur Hiller's direction, the two leads work hard at creating characters likeable enough to overcome the predictable mistaken-identity plot. A brief sexual encounter, a flash of nudity, some slapstick violence and minimal rough language. A-III (R)

Taking of Pelham One Two Three, The (1974) N.Y. City transit policeman (Walter Matthau) has to outwit a heavily armed band of desperate men (led by Robert Shaw) who have seized control of a subway train and are holding its passengers hostage for ransom. Director Joseph Sergent's rattling-good action movie keeps the mood claustrophobic, the suspense tightly wound and paced with just the right amount of comic relief. The cast is top-notch, all of whom hit the mark as New York types. The only distraction is its relentlessly crude language that, unlike the subway, never stops. A-III (R) 15

Taking Off (1971) Uneven satire on the generation gap in suburbia follows the frantic search of parents (Buck Henry, Lynn Carlin) for their teenaged daughter who they think has run away when, in fact, she has only gone to the big city for a rock musical audition. As directed by Milos Forman, the parents fare worse than the kids, partly because they're older and should know better. It is mostly a series of outrageous burlesques, some riotously funny, others merely outrageous or excessive, such as a strip-poker scene and one with youngsters singing an Elizabethan-style ballad with obscene lyrics. A-IV (R) X

Talent for the Game (1991) Well-worn baseball story of a big-league scout (Edward James Olmos) discovering a natural fastball pitcher in the Idaho hinterlands, then fighting to save the untried novice's career when he's put on the mound as a publicity stunt. Directed by Robert M. Young, the story's theme contrasts those who love the sport with the new breed who regard baseball as just another business. Mild treatment of a romantic affair and minimal coarse language. A-III (PG)

Tales from the Crypt (1972) Touring a subterranean burial ground, five sightseers find themselves locked in with the crypt-keeper (Sir Ralph Richardson) who reveals to them the horrible fate that awaits each. Solid British horror movie has a good cast (Peter Cushing, Ian Hendry, Patrick Magee, Nigel Patrick and Joan Collins) and five fairly intriguing tales, which Freddie Francis directs with some verve, a lot of polish and even restraint in the visuals. A-III (PG) X

Tales from the Crypt, Part II (see: "The Vault of Horror").

Tales from the Darkside: The Movie (1990) Clunky horror movie in which a boy delays being served up as dinner by diverting the murderous cook (Deborah Harry) with hackneyed stories of death and doom meted out by an avenging mummy, a diabolical black cat and a lonely monster. Director John Harrison's classy production values and camerawork serve only to dress up an abundance of gory dismemberments and eviscerations. Excessive violence, a sexually promiscuous scene and some rough language. O (R) 18

Tales That Witness Madness (1973) Failed British terror movie with Donald Pleasance as a psychiatrist explaining four case histories (involving Kim Novak, Peter McEnery, Suzy Kendall, Georgia Brown and Joan Collins), which in the end boil down to a padded cell for the good doctor. Directed by Freddie Francis, neither the frights nor the occasional nudity are worthy of comment or the viewer's time. A-III (R) X

Talk of the Town, The (1942) Schoolteacher (Jean Arthur) rents her house to a law professor (Ronald Colman), who discovers a suspected radical (Cary Grant) hiding in the attic. Director George Stevens' romantic comedy contrasts civic corruption with social duty as the teacher finds herself emotionally caught between the two men. A-II (br) U

Talk Radio (1988) Fictional story of a radio talk-show host (Eric Bogosian) who makes his living verbally abusing the lonely, livid or just plain loony souls who call in nightly to bait him. Directed by Oliver Stone, it is an intense indictment of the irresponsible individuals who often host this type of shock radio and raises questions about providing a forum for off-the-wall listeners. The language of the radio host is explicitly vulgar, involving sexual, racial and ethnic slurs and is laced with much profanity. There's also a brief but extremely graphic murder scene. A-IV (R) 18

Tall Blond Man with One Black Shoe, The (1973) Entertaining French farce about a violinist (Pierre Richard) who becomes the pawn in a struggle between two counter-espionage factions for no other reason than that he absentmindedly happens to be wearing an unmatched pair of shoes. Richard's droll performance as a man oblivious to all the assassination attempts surrounding his daily routine is neatly abetted by the comic efforts of Bernard Blier, Jean Rochefort and Mireille Darc. Director Yves Robert turns in an amusing, at time hilarious, comedy of errors carried off in high style. Some sexual innuendos. A-III (PG)

Tall Guy, The (1990) Just when a hapless American actor (Jeff Goldblum) becomes the hit of the London stage in a tasteless musical, his budding romance with a starchy English nurse (Emma Thompson) hits the rocks. Director Mel Smith's comedy is an uneven mix of satire and sex farce, sprinkled with amusing moments, thanks in large part to Goldblum's bumbling but sympathetic performance. Comical treatment of promiscuity, occasional brief nudity and minimal rough language. A-III (R) 15

Tall in the Saddle (1944) After the rancher who hired him is bushwacked, a cowboy (John Wayne) hangs around town dodging bullets and the romantic designs of a local cowgirl (Ella Raines) until he unmasks the killer. Directed by Edwin L. Marin, it's a congenial low-budget western with an unpretentious mystery plot, the usual stock characters (Ward Bond and Gabby Hayes among them) and occasional rough humor. Stylized violence. A-I (br) A

Tall T, The (1957) Credible western in which a cowboy (Randolph Scott) foils the plans of ruthless stagecoach bandits (Richard Boone, Henry Silva and Skip Homeier) to ransom a mine owner's daughter (Maureen O'Sullivan). Director Budd Boetticher establishes the murderous nature of the bandits early on, then builds the tension while waiting for the ransom until the cowboy takes on the trio in the final shootout. Stylized violence and menace. A-II (br) U

Tall Target, The (1951) Engrossing thriller set in 1861 aboard a Washington-bound train as N.Y. City detective John Kennedy (Dick Powell) tries to thwart an assassination plot to kill President-elect Lincoln. Director Anthony Mann keeps the suspense tight and the period details add interest, but the ending is a bit of a let-down. Stylized violence. A-I (br) U

Tall Women, The (1967) Spanish western directed by Sidney Pink about a wagon train of women facing hostile Indians on the wild frontier has excessive violence and sexual innuendo. O (br)

Tam Lin (1971) Domineering, aging millionairess (Ava Gardner), living on a sinister Scottish estate with a coven of coed decadents, keeps her current paramour (Ian McShane) in line by showing him a few grisly snapshots of what happened to past lovers whose attentions wandered. Hothouse melodrama is best summed up as a soggy misfire by novice director Roddy McDowall. A-III (GP) X

Tamarind Seed, The (1974) Russian spy (Omar Sharif) falls in love with a secretary in the British Foreign Office (Julie Andrews) and their romance becomes hopelessly entangled in international intrigue. Directed by Blake Edwards, its fine cast and gorgeous location photography are wasted by a script that misses both as love story and as spy thriller. A-III (PG) 15

Taming of the Shrew, The (1967) Sparkling but noisy adaptation of the Shakespeare play, with bravura performances by Elizabeth Taylor as the comely shrew and Richard Burton as the rowdy tamer. Director Franco Zeffirelli's inventive staging preserves the flavor of the original but never seems firmly in control of the action or the actors. Mature treatment. A-III (br) U

Tammy and the Bachelor (1957) Sappy romantic comedy in which the innocent teenager of the title (Debbie Reynolds), raised by her grandfather (Walter Brennan) in a bayou backwater, knocks the socks off the scion (Leslie Nielsen) of a once-wealthy family. Directed by Joseph Pevney, the silly situation and insufferable homespun wisdom of the heroine were stale then and haven't gotten any fresher since. Sugary confection not for all tastes. A-I (br)

Tammy and the Doctor (1963) The third outing of the homespun lass from the Mississippi bayous sees Tammy (Sandra Dee) as a nurse's aide spreading her country wisdom among the staff (Peter Fonda, Macdonald Carey and Margaret Lindsay) and patients (Beulah Bondi and Reginald Owen) of a Los Angeles hospital. Directed by Harry Keller, the hokey script offers bland situations and plenty of bogus sentimentality, though youngsters may be amused by the silly goings-on. A-I (br) U

Tammy Tell Me True (1961) This time around, Tammy (Sandra Dee) hikes across the swamp to enroll in a nearby college where she helps a rich old lady (Beulah Bondi), saves the marriage of a dean (Virginia Grey) and snags a bemused professor (John Gavin). Director Harry Keller's sugary concoction of contrived situations mistakes the virtue of simplicity for the bane of banality. Bland family fare. A-I (br) U

Tampico (1944) Minor World War II espionage melodrama about the captain (Edward G. Robinson) of an oil tanker who marries a survivor (Lynn Bari) of a torpedoed ship, then suspects she's a Nazi agent. Directed by Lothar Mendes, there's little action and the identity of the traitor is wildly implausible. Wartime violence. A-II (br) A

Tampopo (1987) Wry Japanese satire in which a young widow's unsuccessful noodle business is transformed by a burly truck driver is laced with comic asides relating food to passion, commerce and art. Director Juzo Itami's droll, earthy farce has several sexually suggestive scenes, one with partial nudity, that mar the basically innocent appeal of the story. A-III (nr) 18

Tango & Cash (1989) Ultraviolent supercop saga featuring an unlikely pair of L.A. detectives (Sylvester Stallone; Kurt Russell) who dislike each other's style but wind up working together to nail the criminal mastermind (Jack Palance) behind their being framed for murder. Directed by Andrei Konchalovsky, the result is a sophomoric exercise in rock 'em-sock 'em macho violence and bloodletting. Excessive violence, insulting sexual references and rough language. O (R) 18

Tango Bar (1989) Beautifully filmed and choreographed anthology of tango dancing set in Argentina and framed by the personal and political musings of a fictional trio of cabaret performers (Raul Julia; Ruben Juarez; Valeria Lynch). Keeping the love triangle and repressive politics in the background, Puerto Rican director Marcos Zurinaga concentrates on the trio's songs and monologues about the history and evolution of the tango as well as staging some breathtaking tango numbers plus clips of tango dancing from Hollywood and foreign movies. Subtitles. Implied sexual relationships. A-III (nr)

Tank (1984) Career Army sergeant uses a Sherman tank to rescue his unjustly arrested son from a vicious southern sheriff (G. D. Spradlin) and then heads for the state line, stirring the sympathy of the nation. Audience reaction to director Marvin Chomsky's movie is likely to be much less spectacular because after the breakout, the story becomes increasingly silly and unentertaining. Some violence and rough language. A-III (PG) 15

Tap (1989) An entertaining look at the redemption of a talented tap dancer (Gregory Hines) who took a wrong turn and must choose between a potentially low-paying, rewarding career as a dancer and a lucrative life of crime. Writer-director Nick Castle creates a respectful tribute to this American art form and is especially mindful of tap's black roots. A lusty kissing scene, brief heavily shadowed nudity within a fleeting sexual encounter and some locker-room language. A-III (PG-13) PG

Taps (1981) High-minded teenage cadets take control of a military boarding school when they learn the authorities are going to close it. George C. Scott does his usual fine job as the officer who inspires the boys to make their stand and Timothy Hutton is good as the insurgent leader. Directed by Harold Becker, the rather implausible youth-in-revolt drama fails to make its story of courage and leadership very credible. Some violence and coarse language. A-II (PG)

Target (1985) A middle-aged father (Gene Hackman) gains the admiration of his son (Matt Dillon) when his wife (Gayle Hunnicutt) is kidnapped on a European trip, and dull old Dad, who has a secret CIA past, becomes transformed into a superagent as the two attempt to find Mom. Directed by Arthur Penn, although so preposterous that it skirts parody in spots, it is, nonetheless, entertaining fantasy fare, especially for fathers weary of feeling like Rodney Dangerfield. A bit of rough language and some violence. A-II (R) 15

Targets (1968) Modest crime thriller concerning a psychopathic killer (Tim O'Kelly) on the loose with an arsenal of weapons and a retired movie actor (Boris Karloff) who confront each other in a drive-in movie theater. Written and directed by Peter Bogdanovich, the contrast between the horror of reality and that of fantasy don't quite come off, partly because Karloff in his few scenes steals the film. Some stylized violence but no insights. A-III (R/PG) X

Tarzan and the Great River (1967) Tarzan (Mike Henry) journeys to the upper reaches of the Amazon to put a halt to some occult goings-on by a tribe of headhunting terrorists. Directed by Robert Day, it's an exciting enough adventure, if all-too-familiar for older members of the family. A-I (G) U

Tarzan and the Jungle Boy (1968) Newspaperwoman comes looking for a youngster lost years before in the jungle and runs into a slew of obstacles, including some unfriendly natives (led by Rafter Johnson).

Tarzan (Mike Henry) flexes his muscles and puts everything right in director Robert Day's routine adventure. A-I (G) U

Tarzan and the Valley of Gold (1966) Standard jungle adventure directed by Robert Day with Tarzan (Mike Henry) getting involved with some spies. A-I (br) U

Tarzan the Ape Man (1959) Director Joseph M. Newman's flat and unengaging remake of the 1932 original features a lethargic performance by Dennis Miller in the title role and an anemic portrayal of Jane by Johanna Barnes. Stale wildlife adventure. A-I (br) U

Tarzan, the Ape Man (1981) Embarrassingly inept version of the jungle hero's adventures with Miles O'Keeffe in the title role, Bo Derek in various stages of undress and the ape the only character in the cast to emerge with any dignity from a debacle directed by John Derek. O (R)

Tarzan's Deadly Silence (1970) The Ape Man (Ron Ely), despite being temporarily deafened by an explosion, saves a native tribe from the exploitation of a megalomaniac trying to set up a jungle empire. Directed by Robert L. Friend, it's the usual wilderness adventure, though fans may be disappointed that there is no Jane and no blood-curdling jungle call. Directed by Robert L. Friend. A-I (G) U

Tarzan's Jungle Rebellion (1970) Archaeologist (Sam Jaffe) searching for a lost civilization, a native looking for a sacred statue to establish his rule over the jungle and a group simply after gold come up against the lord of the jungle (Ron Ely). Director William Whitney follows the formula without much conviction. A-I (G) U

Taste the Black Earth (1971) Polish dramatization of the 1920 uprising against the Germans occupying the coal mining region of Silesia is shown through the eyes of a young lad who refuses to let his six older brothers go to battle without him. Written and directed by Kazimierz Kutz, the movie is less an historical narrative than a patriotic ballad told with great feeling, much visual poetry and emphasis on the absurdities of civilians pitted against soldiers. A-II (nr)

Taste the Blood of Dracula (1970) Disappointing British horror film wastes its first half on a ridiculous club dabbling in sex and satanism while the remainder is routine-to-inferior vampire lore in which Dracula (Christopher Lee) has only one big scene. Directed by Peter Sasdy, it offers only some slack suspense and almost no psychological terror. A-III (PG) X

Tatie Danielle (1991) Wickedly dark comedy about a sly 82-year-old widow (Tsilla Chelton) who moves in with her nephew's family and proceeds to make their lives miserable while appearing to be frail and helpless. French production directed by Etienne Chatiliez deftly blends wit and satire while questioning preconceptions about the elderly and skewering adults who patronize them. Subtitles. Occasional sexual innuendo, brief bedroom shot of a married couple and a few vulgar expressions. A-III (PG-13)

Tattoo (1981) Bruce Dern plays a man obsessed with the mystique of tattooing who kidnaps model Maud Adams and proceeds to decorate her body with the fervor of a graffiti artist embroidering his own subway car, until the contrived plot suddenly turns perverted hero into expert lover. As directed by Bob Brooks, the dreary, pretentious story lacks any credible sense of logic. Some nudity and graphic sexuality. O (R) X

Tattooed Swordswoman, The (1974) Japanese Yakuza (gangster) film about an imprisoned woman's dream that, after her release, comes back to haunt her. Director Teyuo Ishii's effort has more interest than the usual spectacular swordplay because it vividly incorporates elements of supernatural horror within its traditional revenge plot. A-III (nr)

Taxi Blues (1991) Set in present-day Moscow, an embittered cabdriver (Pyotr Zaichenko) reluctantly befriends a self-destructive Jewish saxophone player (Pyotr Mamonov) whose alcoholism causes continual crises. Writer-director Pavel Longuine's character study of two vastly divergent personalities touches on class conflicts, alienation and anti-Semitism in Russia's troubled society with compassion, rude humor and unaccustomed frankness. Subtitles. Brief scene of fairly graphic sexual relations, partial nudity, minimal violence and vulgar expressions. A-IV (nr)

Taxi Driver (1976) Disturbing portrait of a troubled New York cabby (Robert De Niro), apparently traumatized by service in Vietnam, lost in his macho fantasies and infatuated with a political worker (Cybill Shepherd) whose rejection triggers his suppressed rage into an orgy of killings. Director Martin Scorsese's excursion into urban alienation and irrational violence lacks a distancing objectivity, and its attempts to shock are excessively graphic in scenes of bloodshed. O (R) 18

Taxing Woman, A (1988) A woman tax collector (Nobuko Miyamoto) faces her biggest case in trying to crack the sleazy operation of an adult hotel scion (Tsutomu Yamazaki), which leads to various comical interactions. Director Juzo Itami delivers a sometimes amusing but overlong satire on tax evasion, which in Japan apparently is fast becoming a national pastime. Subtitles. Several graphic sexual encounters with nudity; a brief sequence involving the physical battering of a woman; some rough language. O (nr) 18

Taxing Woman's Return, A (1989) Sequel picks up the career of the feisty Japanese tax inspector (Nobuko Miyamoto) as she investigates a bogus fundamentalist religious sect helmed by a charismatic influence peddler (Rentaro Mikuni). Written and directed by Juzo Itami, the sharp satire of Japanese tax crimes shows the conflicting roles of women in modern Japan and underscores how exploitative bogus "religions" can be. Some rough language, grisly violence and adultery. A-IV (nr)

Tea for Two (1950) Slack, unimaginative backstage musical loosely based on "No, No, Nanette" and directed by David Butler is set in the 1920s with a frantic producer (Billy De Wolfe) after a socialite (Doris Day) to back his new show of which she becomes the star singing duets with its songwriter (Gordon MacRae). Mild sexual innuendo. A-II (br) U

Teachers (1984) Nick Nolte stars as a harassed but effective, idealistic teacher in a zoo-like high school. Directed by Arthur Hiller, the crude, disjointed effort seems just another teenage exploitation film. Rough language, nudity and a sympathetic view of abortion. O (R) 15

Tear in the Ocean, A (1973) The remnant of the Nazi onslaught of a peaceful Hassidic community in Poland joins the local resistance group operating from the country estate of an idealistic nobleman (Armand Abplanalp) but the ultimate result is tragedy, as the Poles themselves turn on their Jewish allies during the count's absence. Written, produced and directed by Henri Glaeser, the complex movie views the Holocaust from a variety of perspectives, challenging viewers with its questions rather than comforting them with facile answers. A-II (nr)

Ted & Venus (1991) Sour comedy about a would-be poet (Bud Cort) whose obsessive pursuit of a wary social worker (Kim Adams) ends in death when his infatuation proves unstoppable. Fledgling director Cort stars in a pathetic vehicle whose sick humor seems pointless except to put casual sex in an appealing light. Positive portrayal of promiscuity with some gratuitous nudity, violence and rough language. O (R)

Teen Witch (1989) Sappy little story about a teen (Robyn Lively) who learns that she is a witch, uses her magic powers to become the most popular girl in school but discovers that what she really wants is to be liked for herself. Directed by Dorian Walker, there is nothing magical about the inane plot or its trite treatment. Sexually suggestive scene; number of sexual references. A-III (PG-13) PG

Teen Wolf (1985) High school lad (Michael J. Fox) becomes a big man on campus when he discovers that he is a werewolf in this moderately funny teenage comedy. Directed by Rod Daniel, the movie is marred by jokes about alcohol and drugs as well as some vulgarity and sexually oriented humor. A-III (PG)

Teen Wolf Too (1987) Mild sequel in which the younger brother (Jason Bateman) of the high school student who in the original "Teen Wolf" became a basketball star when he turned into a werewolf goes to college and becomes a boxing champ when he discovers his brother's condition runs in the family. Directed by Christopher Leitch, it is more tiresome than silly, except for the violence of its boxing scenes and a benign attitude toward casual sex. A-III (PG)

Teenage Mother (1973) Sleazy movie about the social and sexual rivalries of a class of inane high school students and how they are corrupted by a health instructor. Directed by Jerry Gross, the movie's scenes of rape and seduction are restrained but not so some documentary footage showing the ghastly details of a forceps delivery of a baby. O (GP)

Teenage Mutant Ninja Turtles (1990) Live-action feature film debut of the half-human, half-turtle cartoon heroes who do battle with a rogue Japanese Ninja society to win back their kidnapped rat mentor, Splinter. Though music videomaker Steve Barron's direction is amateurish, Jim Henson's turtle costumes expand the frolicking foursome to entertaining life-sized creatures. Much comic-book violence involving bashing and smashing human and turtle bodies and some mild rough language. A-II (PG)

Teenage Mutant Ninja Turtles II: The Secret of the Ooze (1991) This time, rat mentor Splinter and the feisty foursome are out to recapture the last vial of a dangerously toxic ooze from the clutches of the evil Shredder (Francois Chau) and his Ninja thugs. Director Michael Pressman uses nonstop kung fu battles to disguise the amateur hour plot, and Jim Henson's workshop furnishes two new monsters to keep the eyes entertained up to a point. Considerable slapstick martial arts violence. A-II (PG)

Teenage Mutant Ninja Turtles III (1993) Lifeless sequel has the four teen turtles hurtled back in time to feudal Japan to rescue a friend (Paige Turco) and save a wartorn village. Writer-director Stuart Gillard relies on the turtles' established popularity instead of developing something more than a sophomoric story without liveliness, wit and whimsy. Some ethnic stereotyping and several cartoon-like fight scenes. A-II (PG)

Teenage Sex Report (1973) German exploitation movie about the sexual fears of teenage girls narrated by a "doctor" and directed by Ernst Hofbauer. Ugh. O (R)

Telefon (1977) Russian agent (Charles Bronson) is sent to the U.S. to eliminate a fanatical maverick comrade (Donald Pleasence) who is bent upon activating a long-discarded sabotage scheme. Mediocre thriller made more bearable by a lavish production, Don Siegel's smooth direction and Lee Remick's personable performance as an American double agent. Some graphic violence. A-III (PG) A

Telephone Book, The (1971) Squeaky-voiced Alice (Sarah Kennedy) falls in love with surly-voiced John Smith (Norman Rose) during his first obscene phone call to her. The parade of perverts and exhibitionists that follows in writer-director Nelson Lyon's sour enterprise is sheer sexual exploitation. O (X)

Tell Me a Riddle (1980) Melvyn Douglas and Lila Kedrova play an elderly Jewish immigrant couple, at odds for decades, who are reconciled while visiting their granddaughter (Brooke Adams). Although the fine acting is at times quite moving, Lee Grant's direction of a script awkwardly updating the 1961 story by Tillie Olsen is often clumsy. Somber theme and an implied acceptance of abortion. A-III (PG)

Tell Me That You Love Me, Junie Moon (1970) Film version of Marjorie Kellogg's novel about a disfigured woman (Liza Minnelli), an epileptic (Ken Howard) and a paralyzed homosexual (Robert Moore) who band together to live on their own. Director Otto Preminger's treatment dredges up a dozen sicknesses and perversions with consistent shallowness and lack of understanding, winding up with a limp moral of love conquers all. A-IV (R/GP) X

Tell Them Willie Boy Is Here (1969) Reservation Indian (Robert Blake) at the turn-of-the century is caught between tribal tradition and the white man's law when he kills the father of his sweetheart (Katharine Ross). The clash of two cultures, the injustice of the dominant one and the human fallibility on both sides are themes left largely unexplored in director Abraham Polonsky's drama, which spends more time on the abrasive relationship between the fair-minded sheriff (Robert Redford) and the frustrated reservation doctor (Susan Clark). The result is no more than an average western chase movie with an unhappy ending. A-III (PG) AA

Temp, The (1993) All-too-obvious thriller concerns a devious secretarial fill-in (Lara Flynn Boyle) whose ambitions to advance her cookie company boss (Timothy Hutton) and then herself include killing her way to the top. Director Tom Holland lets Hutton stumble around while the murderous leading lady and co-star Faye Dunaway chew the scenery in this unappetizing, cookie-cutter formula entertainment. Some stylized violence, sexual innuendo and rough language. A-III (R)

Tempest (1982) Famous architect (John Cassavetes), beset with faddish mid-life crisis, flees wife (Gena Rowlands) and job to an idyllic Greek isle with his daughter (Molly Ringwald) and mistress (Susan Sarandon). Director Paul Mazursky's updating of Shakespeare's autumnal comedy is sometimes charming, certainly never dull, but fails to overcome the handicap of its boorish, unappealing hero. Some frank references to sexual matters, including adultery, and rough language. A-III (PG)

Tempter, The (1978) Italian version of "The Exorcist" whose theme of demonic possession is crudely handled by director Alberto de Martino with improbable appearances by Mel Ferrer and Arthur Kennedy, nauseating special effects and heavy doses of brutal violence and dumb sex. O (R)

10 (1979) Successful middle-aged composer (Dudley Moore) abandons his mature lover (Julie Andrews) to pursue a young beauty (Bo Derek), even though she happens to be on her honeymoon. Directed by Blake Edwards, the sometimes funny comedy tries to have it both ways by indulging the same male sex fantasies that supposedly it is satirizing. Frequent nudity, shaky morality and rough language. O (R)

Ten Commandments, The (1956) Less an inspirational story based on biblical sources than a dramatic vehicle with a sense of history, director Cecil B. DeMille's epic production offers some spectacular re-creations, excellent technical effects and good acting from a fine cast, including Charlton Heston as Moses, Yul Brynner, Anne Baxter, Edward G. Robinson and many other stars of the era. A-I (G) U

Ten Days' Wonder (1972) Complex French suspense drama based on an Ellery Queen mystery about a man (Anthony Perkins) who suspects that he has committed murder during a recent mental blackout. Director Claude Chabrol is less interested in the fairly simple mystery than in exploring the relationship between the strange characters (including Orson Welles and Marlene Jobert) living on the man's country estate, the decadent atmosphere that pervades his household and the sense of impending disaster that mounts throughout the film (and it is a shocker). Mature theme. A-III (R/PG)

Ten from Your Show of Shows (1973) Top comedy in some choice cuts from the classic Sid Caesar TV show of the early 1950s, when Sid, Imogene Coca, Carl Reiner and Howie Morris had as much fun doing their wacky bits as viewers have had ever since. For those looking for lots of laughs dished up with a heaping spoonful of plain old nostalgia, this is unsurpassed entertainment. A-I (G)

Ten Little Indians (1966) Director George Pollack's routine remake of the classic Agatha Christie movie mystery, "And Then There Were None" (1945) has a good cast (Hugh O'Brian, Wilfrid Hyde-White, Stanley Holloway, Leo Genn and Dennis Price) and a still intriguing plot. Stylized violence. A-III (br)

Ten Little Indians (1975) Stylish version of the Agatha Christie mystery in which ten strangers (including Oliver Reed, Stephane Audran, Elke Sommer and Richard Attenborough) confess to past crimes before falling victim to swift punishment. Director Peter Collinson moves the action from a remote island to a Byzantine hotel in the middle of a desert and introduces a variant ending written by Dudley Nichols. Restrained violence. A-II (PG) A

10 Rillington Place (1971) Superior fact-based drama about a 1952 British murderer of six women (Richard Attenborough in a brilliant performance as a quite ordinary person about whom something is not quite right) who was apprehended only after the husband (John Hurt) of one of the victims had been hanged for his wife's murder. Directed by Richard Fleischer, the emphasis is on the death of an innocent man and the nonentity who was capable of such brutal crimes. In the end it leaves viewers pondering the human inadequacies of the judicial system. A-III (GP)

Ten Tall Men (1951) Burt Lancaster leads a motley group of French Foreign Legionnaires against the Riffs before they can unite to attack an undermanned garrison town. Directed by Willis Goldbeck, the only thing tall here is the tale which shifts back and forth between straight adventure and spoof. Stylized violence and sexual innuendo. A-III (br) U

10:30 P.M. Summer (1966) Director Jules Dassin's depiction of the complete alienation of an individual (Melina Mercouri) presents a degrading view of life, with some grossly indecent visuals. O (br) X

Ten to Midnight (1983) Retrograde thriller about a police sergeant (Charles Bronson) who, discharged for falsifying evidence against the man terrorizing his daughter (Lisa Eilbacher), sets out on his own to stop the handsome psycho (Andrew Stevens) who kills his victims while in the nude. Directed by J. Lee Thompson, the movie's treatment of violence, nudity and graphic sex is thoroughly objectionable. O (R)

Tenant, The (1976) Mediocre French thriller in which a meek clerk (Roman Polanski, who also directed) rents a room in a sinister Paris apartment house, learns that the former occupant threw herself out of the window and, with increasing paranoia, comes to believe his own life is in danger. Some chilling and effective moments lead only to a disappointing anti-climax. Its theme of madness, depicted with some slashing knives and bouncing heads, are adult fare. A-III (R) 15

Tenchu! (1972) During the civil wars of the 1860s', assassin bands of samurai roamed Japan eliminating political opponents and their followers. This film by Hideo Gosha traces the exploits of one such group and the trouble its leader (Tatsuya Nikadai) has in manipulating his most devoted cutthroat (Shintaro Katsu). The result is a lush production that is little more than a routine exercise in the futility of violence. A-III (nr)

Tender Mercies (1983) A down-on-his-luck country-western singer (Robert Duvall), whose drinking broke up his first marriage, meets and weds a young widow (Tess Harper) who runs a ramshackle motel with her young son (Allan Hubbard). Director Bruce Beresford gets feeling performances from his cast, most especially Duvall in one of his best roles, and treats in a refreshingly uncynical, matter-of-fact manner the widow's strong religious convictions and her quiet pride when she sees her son and husband baptized. A rare movie, tough and gentle, inspiring and immensely entertaining, but the serious nature of the story is more appropriate for adults and older adolescents. A-II (PG)

Tender Moment, The (1971) French production is a failed romantic melodrama about a teenager (Renaud Verley) and an older woman (Nathalie Delon) who fall in love, have an affair and separate when the man the woman had been living with returns. Director Michel Boisrond's story is not one of lost innocence (the boy has been sleeping with a housemaid, even "lending" her to classmates) and his older paramour is presented as something of a nymphomaniac so that the result celebrates nothing but the sexual imperative. O (GP)

Tender Trap, The (1955) Soppy romantic comedy about a New York theatrical agent (Frank Sinatra) who enjoys being a bachelor playing the field until he falls for a singer (Debbie Reynolds) who won't settle for anything but marriage. Director Charles Walters tries to keep it bright and breezy but what works best is the bittersweet romance between one of the agent's girlfriends (Celeste Holm) and a married pal (David Wayne). The playboy philosophy flunks out. A-III (br) A

Tender Warrior, The (1972) Filmed in Georgia, this portrait of a modern Huck Finn provides fine matinee fare for the small fry. The boy (Charles Lee) keeps tabs on all the wild animals of his domain, who respond when he calls them by name. Directed by Stewart Raffill, the photography beautifully captures the swamplands teeming with wildlife as background for this simple story. A-I (G)

Tennessee's Partner (1955) Formula western directed by Allan Dwan uneasily links a cowpoke (Ronald Reagan), a gambler (John Payne) and the proprietor of a fancy house (Rhonda Fleming) in a dusty gold-mining town. Stylized violence, romantic complications and sexual innuendo. A-III (br) A

Tension at Table Rock (1956) Forgettable western about a good badman (Richard Egan) who helps a gun-shy sheriff (Cameron Mitchell) clean up a crooked town. Directed by Charles Marquis Warren, the cliched plot is not worth the effort the actors put into it. Stylized violence. A-II (br) U

Tentacles (1977) Poor Italian imitation of the marine menace formula substitutes a giant octopus for rogue shark. John Huston, Shelley Winters and Henry Fonda are outacted by several killer whales in a story that is more tedious than threatening. Director Oliver Hellman's special effects are unconvincing, except for the grisly visuals of a bloody victim. Some needless profanity. A-III (PG) A

Teorema (1969) Paradoxical Italian drama about the isolated world of a comfortable middle-class family that is transformed by sexual intimacy with a mysterious visitor (Terence Stamp). Director Pier Paolo Pasolini's theme is the corruption of material values, but he approaches it in such coldly intellectual style that one is uninvolved in the events. Though the use of sex is symbolic and not graphically depicted, some viewers will reject its appropriateness as a plot premise. A-IV (nr)

Tequila Sunrise (1988) Slickly produced detective yarn about an L.A. cop (Kurt Russell) who uses a restaurant owner (Michelle Pfeiffer) as a pawn to trap an old friend (Mel Gibson) who's attempting to quit the drug smuggling racket and his notorious Latin American dealer (Raul Julia). Writer-director Robert Towne entangles his attractive cast in a confusing plot that reaches incoherence by the time of the movie's improbable ending. Some rough language, a discreetly filmed sex scene and an intense climax. A-III (R) 15

Teresa the Thief (1979) Italian drama about a woman's tragic life (Monica Vitti) after being abandoned to the streets by an abusive father at age 11, made pregnant by a man who marries her just to escape military service and finally left to a life of prisons and mental institutions. Director Carlo Di Palma only partially achieves the intended blend of pathos and comedy, and the movie's graphic, slice-of-life naturalism is mature fare. A-III (nr)

Term of Trial (1963) Middle-aged schoolmaster (Laurence Olivier), happily married (to Simone Signoret), finds himself pursued by a schoolgirl (Sarah Miles) who works out a nasty trap for him, oblivious to its tragic consequences. Solid adult drama directed by Peter Glenville, with fine performances from all three principals. A-III (br) X

Terminal Man, The (1974) George Segal plays a scientist given to violent seizures who has his brain hooked to a computer to control them, but short circuits turn him into a menace for what appears to be most of Southern California. Director Mike Hodges' version of Michael Crichton's novel takes a ridiculous concept to extremes. Much hokey violence. A-III (PG)

Terminator, The (1984) Violent sci-fi film in which a killing machine in the shape of a man (Arnold Schwarzenegger) comes back from the future to assassinate a young waitress destined otherwise to bear a son who will lead the humans to victory over android rule of a post-nuclear world. James Cameron directs the action in taut, suspenseful fashion, but its violence is overdone and a bedroom scene goes much further than necessary. O (R) 18

Terminator 2: Judgement Day (1991) With the fate of the planet depending on the survival of a plucky lad (Edward Furlong), his ferociously strong mother (Linda Hamilton) escapes a psycho ward to protect him while two rival cyborg terminators (Arnold Schwarzenegger and Robert Patrick) arrive from the future to tip the scales. Producer-director James Cameron's flashy sequel to his 1984 sci-fi fantasy has some stunning special effects but the threadbare storyline merely showcases overblown scenes of callous butchery. Excessive violence and some rough language. O (R) 15

Terms of Endearment (1983) Uneven comedy about a mother-daughter relationship, that of a wealthy, imperious Houston widow (Shirley MacLaine) and her only child (Debra Winger) who marries a man her mother detests. The mother herself becomes involved with the wrong sort of man, in the person of a lecherous, dissipated former astronaut (Jack Nicholson), a confrontation of opposites that is sometimes very funny. Though consistently amusing, there is something uncomfortable about the way in which director James L. Brooks invites laughter at his characters for three-quarters of the way and then demands empathy for them in the tearjerker conclusion. Some fairly graphic references to sexual activity and a benign attitude toward sex outside of marriage. A-III (PG) 15

Terror by Night (1946) Fairly intriguing mystery aboard an express train to Scotland with Sherlock Holmes (Basil Rathbone) and Dr. Watson (Nigel Bruce) solving a locked-compartment murder and the theft of a precious jewel, the Star of Rhodesia. Directed by Roy William O'Neill, the combination of mild humor, elementary deductions, eccentric red herrings and modest thrills make it one of the better examples of this 1942-1946 series. Some menace and stylized violence. A-I (br) A

Terror House (see: "The Night Has Eyes").

Terror in the Wax Museum (1973) Dotty John Carradine's wax dummies appear to come to life and re-enact their grisly crimes in turn-of-the-century London. Director Georg Fenady's plot is as creaky as the museum's backstairs, and the suspense is as phony as the dummies, but for undemanding horror fans it provides some lightweight diversion. A-II (PG)

Terror on a Train (1953) Canadian demolitions expert (Glenn Ford) works through the night trying to find and defuse a bomb on a British munitions train, while the police evacuate the area and seek the saboteur. Director Ted Tetzlaff's tight little exercise in suspense is balanced by the stiff-upper-lip demeanor of British officials and civilians. Much tension. A-I (br)

Terrorists, The (1975) A group of political terrorists seizes a British ambassador in Scandinavia and demands the release of its comrades from a British prison, something that the country's head of security (Sean Connery) sets out to thwart. Directed by Caspar Wrede, the suspense and excitement are well maintained, though in a chilly, abstract manner that makes the ironic ending arbitrary and disappointing. Some violence and much threatened violence. A-III (PG)

Terry Whitmore, for Example (1969) Vietnam deserter Whitmore, a 21-year-old black Marine corporal from Memphis who was wounded and awarded the Bronze Star, explains his reasons for deserting the Corps in an oral-history documentary filmed in Sweden by Bill Brodie. Viewers will have to determine how typical were his experiences and motivation, but his account does not seem to have any political axe to grind. Explicit description of a sexual encounter. A-IV (nr)

Tess (1980) British screen version of the Thomas Hardy novel about the young Wessex woman (Nastassja Kinski) whose life is irrevocably changed when her father discovers that the family are the impoverished descendants of a noble line. Directed by Roman Polanski, it is an always beautiful, at times powerful, drama whose somber theme of a woman doomed by class and circumstance is not for younger viewers. A-II (R) PG

Test of Love, A (1985) A courageous teacher (Angela Punch McGregor) takes an institution to court to effect the release of a bright child suffering from cerebral palsy who has been diagnosed as severely retarded. Fine Australian production directed by Gil Brealey offers solid entertainment and is immensely inspiring. A-II (PG)

Testament (1983) A family in a small American community attempts to cope with the aftermath of a nuclear war in this grim but extraordinary movie about a mother (Jane Alexander) who tries to make life go on for her three children after her husband (William Devane) perishes in the nuclear strike. The warmth and compassion she embodies vivifies and makes moving a story that otherwise might be unbearable. Director Lynne Littman spares the audience most of the more horrific results of nuclear disaster, but what it shows and what it implies are unsettling enough. The subject matter and a restrained bedroom scene are more suited for adults and older adolescents. A-II (PG)

Tex (1982) Good Disney version of S. E. Hinton's story about two teenage brothers, one earnest and responsible (Jim Metzler), one amiable but somewhat feckless (Matt Dillon), who attempt to cope with life while living by themselves on a rundown ranch outside Tulsa. Though director Tim Hunter's plot is overloaded with incident and occasionally veers into extravagant melodrama, its virtues outweigh its flaws, making it entertaining and sometimes moving. Restrained scene of teenage sexual discovery and some jocular references to sex and drugs. A-II (PG)

Texas Across the River (1966) Spanish nobleman (Alain Delon) has trouble adjusting to the ways of the Old West, in particular a peculiar cowboy (Dean Martin) and his Indian companion (Joey Bishop). Director Michael Gordon makes no pretense of plot but strings together a series of humorous mishaps spoofing western conventions. Of little interest but mostly innocuous. A-I (br) U

Texas Carnival (1951) Flat romantic comedy about a small-time carnival concessionaire (Red Skelton) being mistaken for an oil millionaire (Keenan Wynn), with predictable results. Directed by Charles Walters, the comic possibilities of the situation wear out quickly and, except for some tacked-on musical numbers, the rest of the cast (Esther Williams, Ann Miller and Howard Keel) has little to do. Mild romantic complications. A-II (br)

Texas Chainsaw Massacre, The (1974) Fiendish butcher out in the Texas bush country carves up four or five (it is difficult to determine the sum from the scattered parts) outdoors adventurers and then goes on a wild rampage of slaughter with chainsaw and other instruments of destruction, including a meat hook. Directed by Tobe Hooper, what is more dehumanizing than all the violence is that the treatment seems to regard it as amusing. O (R) X

Texas Chainsaw Massacre, Part II, The (1986) Grotesque parody of the blood-and-gore genre of horror films features a leather-faced maniac twitching riotously in the air each time he approaches a new victim with his chainsaw. Making it even worse is director Tobe Hooper's vain attempt to distance the viewer from the film's sadistic action through misconceived comic exaggeration. Gory violence, often in a sexual context. O (R) X

Texas Rangers, The (1951) Low-budget oater directed by Phil Karlson with George Montgomery and Noah Berry Jr. tricking an unlikely collection of legendary badmen—Sam Bass, John Wesley Hardin, Butch Cassidy, the Sundance Kid and many others—into robbing a gold train with the Rangers waiting in ambush. Hokey plot with formula frontier action. A-I (br) A

Texasville (1990) When the former high school sweetheart (Cybill Shepherd) of a nearly broke Texas oilman (Jeff Bridges) arrives back in town, she flirts with her old beau but is more successful in winning over the man's unhappy wife (Annie Potts) and unruly children. Director Peter Bogdanovich's sequel to "The Last Picture Show" is less a touching reunion story than a lame putdown of family life and values wrapped up in a rambling soap opera with little structure, less wit and no dramatic tension. O (R) 15

Texican, The (1966) Plodding formula western in which an outlaw (Audie Murphy) leaves his Mexican refuge to avenge his brother's murder by the vicious boss (Broderick Crawford) of a corrupt border town. Directed by Lesley Selander and filmed in Spain, the dubbed dialogue is as clunky as the phony action. Stylized violence. A-II (br)

Thank God, It's Friday (1978) Youth exploitation movie about the problems that develop one Friday night at a disco, set against a blaring background of frenetic music. Directed by Robert Klane, it juggles a dozen or so stereotyped characters and, though the pace is lively, the comedy is tiresome and repetitious. Some failed jokes about sex and drugs. A-III (PG) A

Thank You and Goodnight! (1992) Fact-based account of a young woman (Jan Oxenberg) coming to terms with the terminal illness of her grandmother (Mae Joffe) who looks back on her life as family and friends comfort her. Writer-producer-star-director Oxenberg uses actual family members and precariously balances a humorously philosophical attitude toward life and death with emotionally honest scenes of pain and loss. A skeptical attitude toward the afterlife. A-II (nr)

Thank You All Very Much (1969) British melodrama in which a young woman (Sandy Dennis) living alone in London becomes pregnant as the result of her first and only sexual experience, decides against abortion and becomes an unwed mother. Director Waris Hussein does well in depicting the life of Londoners and is sensitive to the young woman's situation, but the treatment is superficial and makes no attempt to understand the woman and her future. A-III (PG)

Thank You, Jeeves (1936) Diverting fun with P. G. Wodehouse's sterling butler, Jeeves (Arthur Treacher), who here saves his asinine employer (David Niven) from a gang of spies. Directed by Arthur Greville Collins, the comedy is light and breezy escapist fare. Mild comic violence. A-I (br)

That Championship Season (1982) Jason Miller directs his own adaptation of his prize-winning play about four middle-aged men (Bruce Dern, Paul Sorvino, Stacy Keach, and Martin Sheen) who gather with their former coach (Robert Mitchum) to celebrate the 24th anniversary of winning the state high school basketball championship. As the evening of drinking wears on, the guilty secrets of each come out, but before they do, most viewers will have lost interest. Some strong language. A-III (R) 15

That Cold Day in the Park (1969) Failed psychological melodrama in which a lonely spinster (Sandy Dennis) invites a drifter (Michael Burns) in out of the rain for a hot meal and goes to bizarre lengths trying to get him to share her bed. Director Robert Altman juxtaposes two unbelievable characters in a series of impossibly phony situations that leads to no insights about social alienation but only to morbid, sexually explicit sensationalism. O (R) X

That Darn Cat (1966) Disney live-action adventure comedy in which Hayley Mills gets FBI agent Dean Jones to follow the trail of a mischievous cat who is the only clue to the whereabouts of a kidnapped bank-teller. Robert Stevenson directs the antics, but it is the cat who steals the show. Youngsters will love it and it's not too hard on the parents either. A-I (G) U

That Kind of Woman (1959) Contrived sudser begins in June 1944 aboard a Miami-to-New York train where a small-town Army private (Tab Hunter) falls for the glamorous mistress (Sophia Loren) of a rich war contractor (George Sanders), then spends his leave trying to convince her to marry him. Director Sidney Lumet gets an appealing performance from Loren as well as from Barbara Nichols and Jack Warden in a parallel subplot, but Hunter fails to make the grade and the situation never fulfills its promise. Probes the relationship between love and sex. A-III (br) A

That Man Bolt (1973) Fred Williamson stars as the super-smooth courier of valuables for well-heeled international clients, but this trip he's double-crossed by his employers and he works out a nifty cross of his own. Directed by Henry Levin, it has plenty of action, often quite violent but relieved by whimsical staging, and there's some sexual innuendo. A-III (R) X

That Man from Rio (1964) French production with Jean-Paul Belmondo and Francois Dorleac in an hilarious spoof of stereotype characters and stock situations that typify mystery adventure movies. Directed by Philippe de Broca with real Gallic flair, the comedy is first-class entertainment. A-II (br)

That Night (1993) Coming-of-age melodrama seen from the perspective of a starry-eyed 10-year-old (Eliza Dushku) who idolizes her 17-year-old neighbor (Juliette Lewis) and tries to reunite her with her boyfriend (C. Thomas Howell) after the teen is quietly shipped off to a Catholic home for unwed mothers in the early 1960s. Writer-director Craig Bolotin tries to present a sympathetic portrait of teen passion colliding with painful realities, but his formula treatment of cardboard characters is heavy-handed and muddled by the child's simplistic point-of-view toward the lovers. Premarital relationship, many sexual references, fleeting violence and an instance of profanity. A-III (PG-13)

That Obscure Object of Desire (1977) Disappointing French production in which a wealthy middle-aged Parisian (Fernando Rey) falls hopelessly in love with a young Spanish woman (alternately played by Carole Bouquet and Angela Molina) who leads him a merry chase. Director Luis Bunuel's surrealistic treatment of the romantic situation makes shallow attempts at social commentary. Excessive use of nudity. O (R)

That Splendid November (1970) Failed Italian melodrama about the nymphomaniacal aunt (Gina Lollobrigida) and her determinedly incestuous nephew (Paolo Turco), both of whom are but one small part of a large Sicilian clan specializing in sexual pastimes. Directed by Mauro Bolognini, the result is an inept exercise in studied decadence and heavily erotic atmosphere. O (GP)

That Was Then, This Is Now (1985) From the work of novelist S. E. Hinton, the bard of misunderstood youth, comes a story of two boys (Craig Sheffer and Emilio Estevez)

who hang out together wondering about the meaning of it all until one falls in love and gets a job while the other wallows yet deeper in self-pity. Directed by Christopher Cain, the movie is so dull and pretentious that it is painful to watch. Benign view of premarital sex. O (R) 15

That'll Be the Day (1975) British drama, based loosely on the formation of the Beatles rock group, tells the story of an young man (David Essex) who is helped to find some direction in his life by a casual friend (Ringo Starr in a nonmusical role). Director Claude Whatham's movie is raw, often ragged, but full of feeling and compassion, and it will interest both rock fans and those who like unvarnished pictures of unwashed types. A-III (PG) 15

That's Dancing (1985) A film compilation of great moments in dancing from the film musicals of the 1930s to the recent past. Produced by Jack Haley Jr., the movie is very entertaining, but real fans will note some significant omissions and yearn for more extended selections. A-I (G) U

That's Entertainment (1974) Singing, dancing historical survey of the best of the MGM musicals charms the eye and ear with romantic fantasy. Written, produced and directed by Jack Haley Jr., the selection of excerpts from these musicals demonstrates effortlessly why their appeal endures from generation to generation. A-I (G) U

That's Entertainment, Part II (1976) Fred Astaire and Gene Kelly (who also directs) serve as hosts for this anthology from Hollywood's musical past, though there are brief glimpses of such comedians as the Marx Brothers, Jimmy Durante, Laurel and Hardy, and Abbott and Costello as well as a sequence devoted to the films of Spencer Tracy and Katherine Hepburn. Highly enjoyable but not up to the original's consistent quality. A-I (G) U

That's Life (1986) Fumbling, self-centered husband (Jack Lemmon), preoccupied with thoughts of old age and death, is insensitive to the needs of his wife (Julie Andrews) as she awaits the results of a cancer test. Director Blake Edwards uses sexual encounters as a source of comic relief in an exploration of family ties that has few genuine moments. His infidelity is treated as a symptom of an inner insecurity left unresolved and overshadowed by the image of a strong woman and mother who absorbs all family ills. Brief nudity. A-III (PG-13)

Theatre of Blood (1973) Gruesome British chiller has its genuinely amusing moments as a B-grade Shakespearean actor (Vincent Price) takes his revenge on the stuffy circle of London critics who thwarted his career.

Each execution is conducted through a re-enactment of the murder scene from one of the Bard's tragedies in which the critic had lambasted Price's performance. Director Douglas Hickox stages the action with a distinct flair and the cast of British character actors is marvelous. The gore becomes a bit tacky at times, but horror fans will find it has a touch of class. A-III (R) X

Thelma & Louise (1991) Two girlfriends from Arkansas (Susan Sarandon and Geena Davis), intent on a carefree getaway weekend in a '66 Thunderbird, find themselves dodging police all the way to Arizona after one murders an attempted rapist. Director Ridley Scott's flashy road movie makes the two women highly appealing but glamorizes their willing, sometimes gleefully made choices to break the law and escape the consequences. Rationalization of murder and suicide, casual marital infidelity, brief but graphic attempted rape scene and intermittent rough language. O (R) 15

Thelonious Monk: Straight, No Chaser (1989) Straightforward documentary on the eccentric black jazz pianist and composer gives plenty of screen time to his music but not enough to his biography. Director Charlotte Zwerin incorporates much black-and-white footage of Monk shot by cinematographer Christian Blackwood during a 1967–1968 world tour, which will delight jazz buffs but will not enlighten those who want to know more about the musician whose reputation has continued to grow since his death in 1982. Some profanity and sexual innuendo. A-III (PG-13)

There Was a Crooked Man (1970) Offbeat western about a reform-minded warden (Henry Fonda) who rises to the moral challenge of a convict renegade (Kirk Douglas) to practice what he preaches about rehabilitation and trust. The twist ending has to do with a race to the death for a secret pile of Spanish gold. Directed by Joseph L. Mankiewicz, it's corny but effective, if occasionally violent and tasteless, as the two leads ham up a storm. A-III (R) AA

There's a Girl in My Soup (1970) Disappointing screen version of the popular London play about a sex-obsessed TV gourmet (Peter Sellers) whose freewheeling amorous affairs grind to a halt when he tries to introduce an uninhibited hippie (Goldie Hawn) into his more sumptuous world. Director Roy Boulting's farfetched, frequently tasteless humor, coupled with the compromising situations of a belabored script, thwart the comic talents of Sellers and Hawn. O (R) X

Therese (1986) French dramatization of the life of St. Therese de Lisieux from age 15 when she joined a cloistered convent of

Carmelite nuns to her death there nine years later of tuberculosis. Director Alain Cavalier's impressionistic account of the young woman (luminously played by Catherine Mouchet) who found personal joy, spiritual liberation and the sanctity of selfless simplicity within the restrictive traditions of an austere religious community will challenge contemporary viewers and confound some. The young may find its picture of 19th-century religious life more confusing than inspiring. A-III (nr)

Therese and Isabelle (1968) Director Radley Metzger's account of a lesbian love affair is sexually exploitative. O (br)

Thermidor (1971) Italian documentary about 19th-century European nationalism and the competition for Empire that resulted in the bloodbath of the First World War. Director Tinto Brass relies heavily on the narration to make all the wars and internal strife understandable, but it's a complex period and casual viewers may find it a struggle. History teachers, however, might make good use of its dramatic visuals. A-II (nr)

These Three (1936) Pooling their meager resources after college, two friends (Miriam Hopkins and Merle Oberon) open a school but face ruin because of lies about their relations with the local doctor (Joel McCrea) spread by a malicious student (Bonita Granville). Adapted from Lillian Hellman's play and directed by William Wyler, the result offers an absorbing tale of people's willingness to believe the worst about others. Menacing situations. A-II (br)

They All Laughed (1981) Screwball comedy is aggressively unfunny as it follows the antics of four private detectives, some beautiful women and other odd assortments of New Yorkers (among whom are Audrey Hepburn, Ben Gazzara, John Ritter and Dorothy Stratten). Written and directed by Peter Bogdanovich, the plot is thin to the point of transparency. Illicit sexual relationships. A-III (PG)

They Call Her One Eye (1974) Scandinavian exploitation import about a woman (Christina Lindberg) forced into prostitution who finally takes a sadistic revenge on the vice ring who enslaved her as a prostitute. Absurd sex and violence. O (R)

They Call Me Mister Tibbs! (1970) Routine sequel to "In the Heat of the Night" finds homicide specialist (Sidney Poitier) slithering through slimy red herrings to fish out the strangler of an overworked call girl. The bright spots in the plodding crime melodrama are with his wife (Barbara McNair), though he finds his son's growing pains almost as troublesome as the murder case. Director Gordon

Douglas provides plenty of slam-bang action, including the movie's opening sequence depicting a sadistic sex slaughter and clinical police work in more graphic terms than a lay audience might wish. A-IV (GP)

They Call Me Trinity (1971) Italian western spoof stars the grinning Terence Hill as the grimiest, laziest, fastest outlaw gun on the frontier who is drawn into a conflict involving evil rancher Farley Granger and some pacifist Mormon farmers. He and his brother (Bud Spencer), posing as a lawman, radicalize the farmers and teach them a primitive form of martial arts in time for the climactic showdown. Directed by E. B. Clucher, the shooting and mayhem are comically genial rather than the usual cynical violence of the genre. A-III (G)

They Came from Within (1976) Canadian sci-fi movie about parasites that take over the inhabitants of an apartment building. Directed by David Cronenberg, the amateurish effort is disgusting in its exploitation of gory violence, sex and nudity. O (R)

They Came to Rob Las Vegas (1969) Elke Sommer joins Gary Lockwood in pulling off a spectacular plan to hijack an armored car carrying the mob's casino loot as it speeds across the Nevada desert. European co-production directed by Antonio Isasi has an imaginative heist plot that only works sporadically because unsavory subplots with sex and violence keep getting in the way. A-III (R) A

They Don't Wear Black Tie (1983) Fine Brazilian movie about how a wildcat strike disrupts the domestic life of a working-class family in Sao Paulo. Directed by Leon Hirszman, the essential drama is played out on the family level, leading to a tragic clash between the father who supports the strike and his son who believes people should go their own way. Not a very entertaining movie but one that provides some insights into the human reality behind the headlines of Latin American strife. Some nudity and rough language. A-IV (nr)

They Flew Alone (see "Wings and the Woman").

They Live (1988) An alien race disguised as Yuppies lull Americans into submission through subliminal media advertising. Director John Carpenter's biting satire of the fundamentalist right is a bust due to bad casting (wrestler Roddy Piper stars) and a poor script. Mindless violence, much profanity. O (R) 18

They Live by Night (1949) After the seasoned criminals (Howard da Silva and Jay C. Flippen) with whom he's escaped prison are killed, an inexperienced young man (Farley Granger) and the girl (Cathy O'Donnell) he married on the spur of the moment try to escape a police dragnet. Director Nicholas Ray's portrait of a youth caught in the quagmire of crime is realistic enough but the formula plot never strays far from its predictable course. Stylized violence and criminal acts. A-III (br) A

They Made Me a Criminal (1939) Dated melodrama in which a boxing champ (John Garfield), framed for the murder of a reporter, hides out on an Arizona date farm set up to rehabilitate wayward youths (the Dead End Kids) until a hardbitten New York cop (Claude Rains) spots his photograph. Directed by Busby Berkeley, it's an old story of a heel turned into a hero by the love of a good woman (Gloria Dickson) and the expectations of others, but it's done well and still effective. Stylized violence and mild romance. A-II (br) A

They Met in Bombay (1941) Romantic comedy in which rival jewel thieves (Clark Gable and Rosalind Russell) have to flee the police together aboard a tramp steamer (captained by Peter Lorre) and wind up in Hong Kong as Japanese forces close in. Director Clarence Brown's lighthearted crime caper turns serious when Gable, disguised as a British officer, is ordered to head a relief column evacuating foreign nationals from the mainland. Grand larceny redeemed by wartime heroics and mild romance. A-II (br) U

They Might Be Giants (1971) George C. Scott plays a demented New York judge who believes himself to be Sherlock Holmes and Joanne Woodward is a psychiatrist named Watson enlisted to bring him back to his senses. Between the promising opening scenes and the closing shot in front of a Central Park underpass where the principals bravely face the dread Dr. Moriarity, director Anthony Harvey has supplied too many slack spots and unconnected parts to justify the question of whether the judge or society are the more insane. A-III (G) U

They Only Kill Their Masters (1972) James Garner gives a wry performance as a small-time peace officer who's dumb like a fox, involved in a nasty murder case that unpeels some of the respectable veneer on his little coastal town. Displaced divorcee Katharine Ross finds a place not only in bachelor Gardner's bed but on his list of murder suspects as well. Director James Goldstone can't decide whether to play it straight or go for laughs and winds up doing neither well. A-III (PG) AA

They Rode West (1954) Routine western about an Army doctor (Robert Francis) who averts an Indian uprising by treating the sick members of the tribe despite the orders of a superior (Phil Carey). Directed by Phil Karlson, it's well-intentioned but unconvincing, especially in its portrayal of Indian life and lore. Stylized violence. A-I (br) U

They Shall Have Music (1939) Sentimental melodrama features violinist Jascha Heifetz coming to the rescue of a bankrupt music school for the children of New York's slums. Directed by Archie Mayo, there's plenty of classical music and a game cast (Joel McCrea, Andrea Leeds and Walter Brennan), but the manipulative script keeps tripping over its own bathos. High-minded but artificial inspirational fare. A-I (br) A

They Shoot Horses, Don't They? (1969) Marathon dances were a popular form of distraction from the desperate times of the Depression, the period re-created by director Sydney Pollack's movie with Jane Fonda, Michael Sarrazin, Red Buttons and Susannah York all staggering around under the cruel gaiety of Master of Ceremonies Gig Young, urging the exhausted contestants on to win the $1500 pot at the end of the musical rainbow. Sometimes depressing, not at all pleasant movie, but it does have the grimy texture of an agonized era. A-III (PG) AA

Thief (1981) After a long prison term, a skilled safecracker (James Caan) wants to pull a couple of big jobs and retire on the proceeds but, when he deals with a mob leader (Robert Prosky), he discovers too late that there is no way out of mob connections. Written and directed by Michael Mann, the emotional depth in Caan's characterization places it far above the usual standard of crime movie, though the story may be too grim for some tastes. A lot of tension, some violence and rough language. A-III (R) X

Thief of Bagdad, The (1940) Grand adventure fantasy about an Arabian prince (John Justin) who, helped by a little thief (Sabu) and a gigantic genie (Rex Ingram), overcomes a series of obstacles conjured up by a wicked magician (Conrad Veidt) in order to wed the beautiful princess (June Duprez). Produced by Alexander Korda with fanciful Middle Eastern set designs by his brother Vincent, the result is filled with magic spells, wonderful transformations and such marvels as a winged horse and flying carpet. Delightful family fun. A-I (br) U

Thief of Baghdad (1961) Plodding variation on the Arabian Nights story about a good-hearted vagabond (Steve Reeves) who overcomes a host of obstacles to find the blue rose that will free the sultan's daughter (Georgia Moll) from an evil spell. Director Arthur Lubin plays much of this for laughs and the result is only sporadically entertaining. Italian production dubbed in English. Stylized violence. A-I (br)

Thief of Hearts (1984) Slick, chrome-plated little melodrama about a burglar (Steven Bauer) who falls in love with a woman (Barbara Williams) whose intimate diaries were part of the loot he took from her house. Some serious possibilities of the story lose out to a blaring, obtrusive score and director Douglas Day Stewart's fondness for nudity and graphic sex. O (R) 18

Thief of Paris, The (1967) Fair French satire in which its 19th-century anti-hero (Jean-Paul Belmondo) recalls the motives and circumstances that caused his career as a thief. Directed by Louis Malle, the movie's slow pace is offset by some intelligent criticism of middle-class hypocrisy and some appropriate period costuming and sets. A-III (br)

Thief Who Came to Dinner, The (1973) Pretentious heist film about a computer engineer (Ryan O'Neal) who starts a new career robbing the safes of Houston's finest families and leaving behind a chessman as his trademark. On his trail is a dogged insurance investigator (Warren Oates) who knows but can't prove it. Listlessly directed by Bud Yorkin, the movie never catches fire and begins to irritate with its repetitious comments about society's hypocrisy. A-III (PG) A

Thieves (1977) Often affecting and funny story of an upwardly mobile Manhattan couple (Charles Grodin and Marlo Thomas) whose impending divorce gets sidetracked by the heroine's wild-eyed cabby father (Irwin Corey) and other assorted characters, including the police. Directed by John Berry, the comedy is saved from being too-cute and self-conscious by some exceptionally good acting. Infidelity and abortion figure in the plot (though not favorably), and there is frequent use of blasphemous expletives. A-III (PG)

Thieves Like Us (1974) Set in the Deep South of the 1930s, the story concerns a trio of escaped convicts (Keith Carradine, Bert Remsen and John Schuck) who take to small-time bank robbing. Director Robert Altman's backroads ballad with conventional bloody ending is long on sleepy southern atmosphere and earthy humor but short on engaging characterizations (save Shelley Duvall's tender-waif performance) and narrative. A-III (R)

Thin Blue Line, The (1988) The 1976 murder of a Dallas policeman is the basis for this compelling documentary, which uses some dramatized footage to reexamine the crime and explore the fine line between guilt and innocence. Director Errol Morris provides a chilling look at the man unjustly convicted of the murder, the man who fingered him and the legal eagles responsible for a muddled conviction. Some rough language and repeated murder dramatizations. A-III (nr) 15

Thin Ice (1937) The star ice-skater (Sonja Henie) of an Alpine winter resort falls in love with a prince (Tyrone Power) masquerading as a reporter. Directed by Sidney Lanfield, the romantic comedy's paper-thin plot does not deter from the charming performances of the two principals, the beauty of the ice-skating routines and plenty of comic relief by Joan Davis, Raymond Walburn, Arthur Treacher, Alan Hale and Sig Ruman. Innocent romantic misunderstandings. A-I (br) U

Thin Man, The (1934) Classic murder mystery from the Dashiell Hammett story of private detective Nick Charles (William Powell) who announces his retirement after marrying rich socialite Nora (Myrna Loy), then gets involved in trying to help a young woman (Maureen O'Sullivan) find her missing father, the eccentric inventor of the title (Edward Ellis). Director W. S. Van Dyke II paces the suspenseful plot with numerous suspicious characters, witty dialogue and affectionate kidding between happily married Nick and Nora. Menacing atmosphere, some stylized violence, hard-boiled types and heavy drinking. A-II (br) A

Thing, The (1951) Arctic expedition (led by Kenneth Tobey) digs a flying saucer out of the ice but its thawed occupant turns out to be an alien monster (James Arness) that feeds on human blood. Nicely crafted sci-fi thriller produced by Howard Hawks and directed by Christian Nyby, the conflict is not only with the monster from outer space but between the soldiers and the scientists in the frozen outpost. Growing sense of menace and suspense builds to a violent climax and final warning to "watch the skies." A-II (br)

Thing, The (1982) Director John Carpenter's brutal, simple-minded remake of the classic 1951 horror movie in which a research group in Antarctica struggles with a protean monster from outer space features Kurt Russell, A. Wilford Brimley, Richard Dysart and Richard Masur. Excessive violence and appalling lack of respect for mangled human remains. O (R) 18

Thing with Two Heads, The (1972) Racial bigot (Ray Milland) awakens to find his pale head attached to the hulking black frame of a condemned convict (Rosie Grier) who, buying time to prove his innocence, has volunteered his body for the dying Milland. Director Lee Frost forsakes all hope of evoking horror and simply joins the cast in having some dumb fun. A-II (PG) A

Things Are Tough All Over (1982) Inept comedy with Cheech Marin and Thomas Chong driving a money-laden car from Chicago to Las Vegas for two rich Arabs, whose roles they also take. Directed by Tom Avildsen, it has the usual problem of beating jokes into the ground, but happily, the emphasis on narcotics has been dropped this time, though there is still the customary foul language, coarse humor and a brief bit of nudity. O (R)

Things Change (1988) When a Chicago shoeshine man (Don Ameche) agrees to take the murder rap for a look-alike mob boss, his bungling mob babysitter (Joe Mantegna) takes him on a fantasy weekend to Lake Tahoe. Directed by David Mamet, this fictional slice of mob life entertains adults without relying on sex, violence or special effects. Fine acting, spare dialogue, an improbable pair of buddies and an ironic look at honor among thieves. Some rough language and brief violence. A-III (PG)

Things of Life (1970) French production is a slow-moving portrait of a middle-aged engineer (Michel Piccoli) torn between conflicting feelings toward his estranged wife, his mistress, and his own shaky dreams. Director Claude Sautet juggles together a convoluted tangle of flashes forward and backward, but the slickly confected pastry reveals a definite soap opera base. A-III (GP) AA

Think Dirty (1978) Bumbling, good-natured, happily married ad-man (Marty Feldman) is ordered to launch a lewd ad campaign selling porridge. Feldman, directing his own screenplay, is more interested in laughs than in sexual titillation, but the humor is often heavy-handed and there is some nudity thrown in for bad measure. O (R)

Third Animation Celebration, The (1991) Ninety-five minutes of recent animated shorts from the U.S. and eight other countries, using techniques from traditional line-drawings to clay animation and computer graphics. Producer Terry Thoren's selection stresses offbeat humor, clever satire and fast-moving visuals for an entertaining overview of what's happening in animation around the world. Minor cartoon violence and close-ups of an anatomically accurate male figure. A-II (nr)

Third Man, The (1949) Classic mystery thriller about an American writer of pulp westerns (Joseph Cotton) searching the British sector of post-war Vienna for clues in the death of his old school chum, Harry Lime (Orson Welles). Directed by Carol Reed from a script by Graham Greene, the engrossing result offers a fascinating study in contrasts between the unscrupulous Lime and his naive friend, skillfully abetted by a superior supporting cast (Alida Valli, Trevor Howard, Bernard Lee and Wilford Hyde-White), Robert Krasker's moody photography and the distinctive zither music of Anton Karas. A-II (br) PG

13 Ghosts (1960) Silly horror movie about the frights and scares encountered by a meek paleontologist (Charles Herbert), his wife (Rosemary DeCamp) and two offspring

when they inherit a haunted house with a spooky housekeeper (Margaret Hamilton) and a hidden treasure. Director William Castle provides an eerie soundtrack but neither the superimposed ghosts nor the threadbare plot are likely to frighten anyone. Some occult trappings and supernatural menaces. A-I (br) A

13 West Street (1962) Nasty little thriller in which a rocket engineer (Alan Ladd), after recovering from a senselessly brutal beating by five teens, gives up on the L.A. police detective (Rod Steiger) investigating the case and goes after the delinquents himself. Directed by Philip Leacock, the story of a citizen determined to take the law into his own hands gets increasingly muddled until its contrived ending. Much menace and some stylized violence. A-II (br) A

Thirteen Women (1932) Half-baked hokum about a half-caste Oriental (Myrna Loy) bent on murdering the dozen members (notably Irene Dunne) of a school sorority from which she had been excluded years before. Directed by George Archainbaud, the revenge plot mixes in elements of the occult and hypnotism along with the racially motivated murders but what makes the melodrama even more ludicrous is the bad acting from a good cast. Stylized violence and Asian stereotyping. A-III (br)

30-Foot Bride of Candy Rock, The (1959) Woefully inept comedy about a garbage man (Lou Costello) whose girlfriend (Dorothy Provine) suddenly grows giant-sized, panicking town and Pentagon. Director Sidney Miller's loud, unfunny script and cheesy effects make Costello's last movie a sorry exercise. Minimal entertainment. A-I (br)

39 Steps, The (1935) Classic spy thriller about an innocent Canadian (Robert Donat) pursued across Scotland by the police and a sinister gang of foreign agents while handcuffed for a time to a woman (Madeleine Carroll) who believes him to be a murderer. Director Alfred Hitchcock has a lot of fun concocting surprising visual twists to the fast-paced suspense story, relieved by occasional comic turns of plot and a charming romance that begins in mutual antagonism. Some stylized violence, much menace and mild romantic references. A-II (br) U

Thirty-Nine Steps, The (1980) Lackluster British version of John Buchan's classic espionage yarn, made famous by the Hitchcock movie, about the pursuit both by police and nasty spies of an innocent man (Robert Powell) who has seemingly stumbled onto the plans to start World War I. Directed by Don Sharp, the 1914 setting is fine, the acting is excellent, but the brisk action is by now routine. Stylized violence. A-II (PG) 15

36 Fillette (1989) Sullen 14-year-old (Delphine Zentout) on summer holiday with her family plays cat-and-mouse sexual games with a much older man and finally loses her virginity to a peer. French director Catherine Breillat's irresponsible portrait of teenage angst features a depressing protagonist, her explicit sexual encounters with a middle-aged Lothario and sexually vulgar language. Much nudity. O (nr)

36 Hours (1965) Neat suspense thriller about a fantastic plot by German intelligence to get information about the Allied invasion. Directed by George Seaton with Rod Taylor, Eva Marie Saint and James Garner, the gimmicks are entertaining and most viewers will excuse its melodramatic conclusion. A-II (br) A

This Beast Must Die (see: "This Man Must Die").

This Boy's Life (1993) Powerful coming-of-age drama set in 1950s' Pacific Northwest where a young teen (Leonardo DiCaprio) faces daily jeopardy after his mother (Ellen Barkin) marries an emotionally abusive mechanic (Robert De Niro) who rules his backwater roost with an iron fist. Adapted from Tobias Wolff's memoirs and directed by Michael Caton-Jones, the searing performances and an undercurrent of sardonic wit convey both the boy's traumatic adolescence and his determination to survive the stepfather's monstrous mistreatment. Some scenes of intense physical and verbal abuse, a brief bedroom scene and frequent rough language. A-III (R)

This Gun for Hire (1942) Interesting Americanized version of Graham Greene's novel about a professional hit man (Alan Ladd) whose search for a double-crosser (Laird Cregar) leads to a wartime traitor. Directed by Frank Tuttle, the dark doings are brightened by a good woman (Veronica Lake) who shows some kindness to the hard-bitten gunman. Stylized violence. A-II (br) A

This Happy Feeling (1958) Secretary Debbie Reynolds falls for new boss Curt Jurgens, an older actor, while John Saxon also pursues her. Romantic triangle from director Blake Edwards is typical 1950s' fluff in which feelings of love caused all the complications and sex was relegated to being treated with coy allusions. A-III (br) U

This Is Elvis (1981) Complete but somewhat superficial look at superstar Elvis Presley using a documentary format with candid shots, home footage, scenes from television appearances and dramatic action, all pointing to the image of a man being devoured by his fans. Best are the 38 Presley songs presented. Some sexual innuendo make the movie less suitable for youngsters. A-III (PG)

This Is My Life (1992) Two young daughters (Samantha Mathis and Gaby Hoffmann) be-

come resentful when the growing success of their single mom (Julie Kavner) as a stand-up comedienne starts taking her away from home. Director and co-writer Nora Ephron's lighthearted, mildly insightful treatment of a working mother's frustrations and those of her daughters masks a drama common to many single parent families. Brief bedroom scene with a parent's casual acceptance of her adolescent son's sexual activity and several sexual references. A-III (PG-13) 12

This Is Spinal Tap (1984) Mock documentary on the last, inglorious American tour of an aging English heavy-metal group whose fame is long gone makes the grade as a subtle, sometimes very funny satire both on rock groups and on the documentaries made about them. The four principals (Rob Reiner as the director and Michael McKean, Christopher Guest and Harry Shearer as the not overbright leaders of the group) also collaborated on the script. Reiner tripled as director. There is a great deal of crude language and many sexual references in the dialogue and lyrics, but these are essential to the satirical nature of the film. A-II (R) 15

This Is the Army (1943) Patriotic musical using Irving Berlin's songs from his World War I Army show as recycled for a World War II edition. Director Michael Curtiz blends fact and fancy by restaging the 1917 original with a cast headed by George Murphy and then films the new version with the 1943 Army cast headed by Ronald Reagan as Murphy's son. Standout is Berlin singing one of his own numbers but the flagwaving rhetoric keeps getting in the way of the music and comedy. A-I (br) U

This Man Must Die (1970) Superior French suspense drama follows a father (Michel Duchaussoy) in tracking down the hit-and-run driver (Jean Yanne) who killed his son, but he finds that retribution is not so simple. Director Claude Chabrol convincingly portrays the father's cold determination in seeking revenge but is more interested in the wider circle of guilt that this incurs. Some sexual situations. A-III (GP)

This Property Is Condemned (1966) Trashy soap opera about a young woman (Natalie Wood) in a small southern railroad town during the Depression who falls in love with the man (Robert Redford) sent by the railroad company to fire most of its workers. Directed by Sydney Pollack, the movie is excessively suggestive in its treatment of sexual situations. O (br) X

This Savage Land (1968) Pioneer Ohio widower (Barry Sullivan) brings his family to settle in Kansas after the Civil War, but they are harassed by southern vigilantes in Vincent McEveety's rather pedestrian western. Stylized violence. A-II (br)

This Special Friendship (1967) French story of a homosexual attraction between two boys in a strict Catholic boarding school in the 1920s ends in tragedy. Directed by Jean Delannoy in sensitive and thoughtful fashion, it leaves the viewer to judge the nature of the relationship and the way in which the school authorities dealt with it. Mature fare. A-III (br)

This Time I'll Make You Rich (1975) Totally undistinguished formula kung-fu action adventure produced in Hong Kong by Joseph E. Levine. Restrained violence. A-III (PG)

Thomas Crown Affair, The (1968) Steve McQueen plays a wealthy, clever Bostonian who gets away with two perfect bank robberies before meeting his match in insurance investigator Faye Dunaway and the two engage in a totally amoral game of cat-and-mouse that ends in a love match, with the law left holding the bag. In director Norman Jewison's smoothly calculated, slickly executed work, it seems that crime pays quite well. O (R) PG

Thomasine and Bushrod (1974) Vonetta McGee and Max Julien play a black Bonnie and Clyde duo fighting racial oppression and injustice in the West of 1911. Though it has all the now-standard cliches of period cars, a redneck sheriff (George Murdock), bank robberies, news accounts and a bloody finale, director Gordon Parks Jr. fails to make the characters credible or the situations plausible. A-III (PG)

Thoroughly Modern Millie (1967) In a musical spoof of the Roaring Twenties, Julie Andrews and Mary Tyler Moore seek careers and romance in New York City with the help of handsome John Gavin and debonair James Fox. Director George Roy Hill's irreverent lark gets some good support from Bea Lillie and Carol Channing, some songs that characterize the period and a fast-moving script that has something for everybody. A-I (G) U

Those Calloways (1965) Predictable Disney movie in which a backwoods family (Brian Keith, Vera Miles, Brandon De Wilde) tries to keep hunters from shooting the Canadian geese that migrate through their area. Directed by Norman Tokar, the outdoors sequences are fine, especially those of the wild geese. A-I (br) U

Those Daring Young Men in Their Jaunty Jalopies (1969) The Monte Carlo Rally in the early part of the century served as an endurance test for cars, and in many respects this movie about the rally proves to be much the same kind of test for viewers. Director Ken Annakin has a large cast of comedians (best are Peter Cook and Dudley Moore) but the tired formula racing action is unfunny, though it does some tasteless off-color jokes.

Vintage car fanciers might enjoy it. A-II (G)

Those Fantastic Flying Fools (1967) Phineas T. Barnum (Burl Ives), straight from bankruptcy in the U.S., arrives in Victorian England ready to construct the first rocket ship to the moon. Director Don Sharp can't do much with a script riddled with cliches, but the obvious and predictable slapstick difficulties of building the rocket may prove diverting fun for the very young. A-I (br)

Those Lips, Those Eyes (1980) Sentimental look at summer theater in a 1951 Cleveland suburb where a college student (Tom Hulce) takes a job as a prop man and gets so carried away with show business and one of the dancers (Glynnis O'Conner) that he wants to go to New York, much to the anguish of his father (Jerry Stiller). Directed by Michael Pressman, the nostalgia is unfortunately marred by some explicit nudity in a bedroom scene, compounded by the movie's rather benign attitude toward casual sex. O (R)

Those Magnificent Men in Their Flying Machines (1965) Early vintage aircraft are the real stars and source of fun in this colorful comedy spectacular about a 1910 air race from England to France. Good musical score, tongue-in-cheek script and international cast including Alberto Sordi, Gert Frobe, Jean-Pierre Cassell, Terry Thomas and Red Skelton, are some of the reasons for the success of this entertainment package from director Ken Annakin. A-I (G)

Thousand Clowns, A (1966) Screen version of Herb Gardner's Broadway comedy about a cheerful eccentric (Jason Robards) who has withdrawn from society to live as he pleases until a social worker (Barbara Harris) perks his romantic interest and he must decide how to adjust to the demands of responsibility. Producer-director Fred Coe retains the good-natured wit and feeling for people in its humorous digs at social conformity, though the closer it strives for contemporary relevance, the more it loses its shield of fantasy and romantic innocence. Mature treatment. A-III (br) U

Three (1969) Three young people (Robie Porter; Sam Waterston; Charlotte Rampling) spend a summer touring Europe and come to know one another and themselves better. There's not much plot or action, but there's plenty of gorgeous scenery and some shallow characterizations intended to show the subtle development of human relationships and self-awareness. A-III (PG)

Three Amigos (1986) Steve Martin stars in and produces but doesn't dominate this pictorially grand but sometimes brutal western parody about three silent screen actors playing silly caballeros in a Mexican village that mistakes them for hired gunmen. Chevy Chase and Martin Short supply the slapstick and wit for director John Landis whose interest seems rooted in the physical comedy and dangerous stunts. Stylized violence and some rough language. A-II (PG)

Three Brothers (1982) French-Italian drama in which three brothers whose lives have taken divergent paths return to their native village in southern Italy when their mother dies. Director Francesco Rosi's warmly human study of family bonds has fine acting, especially Charles Vanel's awesome presence as their peasant father, and many touching moments, mostly in flashbacks. Despite its many virtues, the story fails to come together as a whole and the result is a disappointment. A-II (PG) A

Three Bullets for a Long Gun (1972) Formula Italian western plods the traditional trail with an unscrubbed hero (Beau Brummell) and his bungling sidekick (Keith G. Wat) who together outwit a horde of rapacious renegade soldiers. Director Peter Henkel has no fresh ideas to dress up the violence in this dreary, low-budget programmer. A-III (PG)

Three Caballeros, The (1945) Walt Disney's colorful celebration of our neighbors to the South follows Donald Duck's tuneful trip to Latin America. Among the animated characters that he meets are Jose Carioca and Panchito who teach him about their customs and culture. Informative as well as good fun. A-I (G)

Three Came Home (1950) Interned by the Japanese after the fall of Borneo, an American writer (Claudette Colbert) looks after her young son (Mark Kuening) while enduring the deprivations and humiliations of a prison camp until reunited with her husband (Patric Knowles) at war's end. Director Jean Negulesco suggests more than he shows of the hardships shared by the women prisoners whose fear of their captors is epitomized in the misunderstandings between the level-headed heroine and the camp's commander (Sessue Hayakawa). Much tension and some stylized violence. A-II (br) A

Three Cases of Murder (1954) Dull trilogy of murder stories opens with Roderick Wilkinson's fantasy about an art museum where people live inside the paintings (director: Wendy Toye); an inane Brett Halliday mystery about the murder of a woman who comes between two lifelong chums (director: David Eady); and concludes with W. Somerset Maugham's tale of a British Foreign Secretary tormented by dreams of killing a political rival (director: George More O'Ferrall). Only this last effort shows any imagination in plot construction or character development as the conflict builds between domineering government official (Orson Welles) and sneering opponent (Alan Badel). Some deadly menace and

minimal stylized violence. A-II (br) A

Three Comrades (1938) Sentimental adaptation of the Erich Maria Remarque novel in which a trio of German front-line veterans (Robert Taylor, Robert Young and Franchot Tone), struggle to make a living after World War I, take a fragile young woman (Margaret Sullavan) under their wing, then learn she is dying of tuberculosis. While director Frank Borzage concentrates on the veterans' camaraderie and tender friendship with the woman, viewers today are likely to be more interested in the movie's depiction of post-war Germany's poverty and despair as the breeding ground of fascism. Stylized violence, including a suicide. A-III (br) A

Three Days of the Condor (1975) CIA agent (Robert Redford), on the run from assassins who may be fellow agents, happens on a woman (Faye Dunaway) who lends him at first reluctant, then enthusiastic assistance. Directed by Sydney Pollack, it's a slickly done but shallow movie whose heroics are implausible and whose idealism is more than a little inconsistent. Some violence, occasional rough language and a love affair between the two principals. A-III (R) AA

Three Faces of Eve, The (1957) Sober fact-based dramatization, introduced by journalist Alistair Cooke, portrays the struggle within a prim Georgia housewife (Joanne Woodward) as she tries, with the help of a psychiatrist (Lee J. Cobb), to resolve the conflict between her multiple personalities. Written, produced and directed by Nunnally Johnson, the case study of a psychiatric condition achieves a credible human dimension, thanks primarily to Woodward's touching tour-de-force performance. Psychological abnormalities and domestic upheavals. A-III (br) A

Three for the Road (1987) Director B. W. L. Norton's teen comedy-romance disguised as rebellious youth road movie features Charlie Sheen as an aspiring politician who delivers a senator's troubled daughter (Kerri Green) to a prison-like school. Falling in love, he helps her to escape into the custody of her estranged mom (Sally Kellerman) who has a change of heart. Shows how idealistic dedication can lead to misplaced trust when duty and conscience conflict. Some rough language and mildly permissive attitude toward teen romance. A-II (PG)

Three Fugitives (1989) Writer-director Francis Veber's English-language version of his 1986 French film about a novice robber (Martin Short) who takes a hostage (Nick Nolte) in a bank heist and then the pair of misfits spend the rest of the time trying to extricate themselves from each other and the cops. Also on the lam is the robber's tiny, troubled daughter (Sarah Rowland Doroff) who adds implausible, sentimentalized heart to this nutty slapstick comedy. Much rough language; intense comic-book violence. A-III (PG-13) 15

Three Godfathers (1948) After robbing a bank, an outlaw trio (John Wayne, Pedro Armendariz and Harry Carey Jr.) pause to help a dying woman (Mildred Natwick) deliver her infant son on Christmas Eve, then take the babe with them as they are pursued across a desert wasteland. Dedicated by director John Ford to western actor Harry Carey Sr., the story may be unabashedly sentimental and the action romanticized, but its lyrical images and religious resonances celebrate the myth of the Old West and its rugged heroes with good hearts. Off-screen suicide of one of the principals. A-II (br) A

Three in the Attic (1969) Grade-B youth sex fantasy in which a three-timing college student (Christopher Jones) is abducted by the wronged trio (Yvette Mimieux, Judy Page and Maggie Thrett) and punished with having to indulge them incessantly in the sorority-house attic. Producer-director Richard Wilson rings the changes on a thoroughly tasteless situation. O (R) X

Three in the Cellar (see: "Up in the Cellar").

Three into Two Won't Go (1969) British drama about a couple (Rod Steiger and Claire Bloom) whose marriage is in serious trouble because of the husband's habit of picking up women on his business trips. Directed by Peter Hall, the movie's dramatic potential in probing the problems of married life is, unfortunately, undermined by focus on the prurient antics of the husband's latest misadventure (Judy Geeson). O (R)

Three Lives (1971) Author Kate Millet's documentary consists of interviews with three women who, in a series of separate monologues, express the message of Women's Liberation and, among other things, the male influences in their lives. Its plain and simple technique adds rather than detracts from credibility of the three who seem to epitomize the personal commitment that Women's Lib requires of those who espouse it. Some strong language. A-III (nr)

Three Men and a Baby (1987) The carefree life of three bachelors (Tom Selleck; Steve Guttenberg; Ted Danson) changes when they become responsible for an infant girl fathered by one of them. Director Leonard Nimoy gets a few genuine laughs out of the situation, but the entertainment level is pretty flat. Benign view of casual sex. A-III (PG)

Three Men and a Cradle (1986) French comedy in which three single, macho males confront their shallow emptiness when an unexpected visitor—a baby— changes their life-style and elicits feelings of tenderness

and devotion. For male audiences, Writer-director Coline Serreau's film is uplifting, even inspirational in its demonstration that tenderness is an important aspect of manliness. A-II (PG-13)

Three Men and a Little Lady (1990) Three bachelors (Tom Selleck; Ted Danson; Steve Guttenberg) take drastic action when Sylvia (Nancy Travis) announces she and little Mary (Robin Weisman) will no longer be living with them as she is marrying and returning to England. Director Emile Ardolino's sprightly sequel tries hard to be a screwball comedy with an old-fashioned romance thrown in, but the likeable performers never quite capture the fun of the baby situation in the original. Very mild sexual innuendo. A-II (PG)

Three Musketeers, The (1974) Satiric British version of the Dumas classic zestfully follows the shambling trail of the raw and foolish D'Artagnan (Michael York) in his quest to become one of the Musketeers (Oliver Reed, Richard Chamberlain and Frank Finlay). Directed by Richard Lester, it is an energetic swashbuckler in the grand style, offering an entertaining mix of romantic adventure and slapstick comedy, even if the frenetic humor sometimes wears a bit thin. Some restrained sexual innuendo. A-II (PG) U

Three Musketeers, The (1993) Trashy comic-book adaptation of the Alexandre Dumas tale of a country lad (Chris O'Donnell) joining a rollicking trio of musketeers (Kiefer Sutherland; Charlie Sheen; Oliver Pratt) to save the throne of France from the wicked Cardinal Richelieu (Tim Curry). Director Stephen Herek's heavy-handed attempts to portray lighthearted heroes trouncing atrocious comic villains turn a durable adventure classic into campy, often mean-spirited comedy. Much stylized violence, sexual references and jokey treatment of religion. A-III (PG)

3 Ninjas (1992) Thoroughly contrived comedy follows the three young sons of a neglectful FBI dad (Alan McRae) as they outsmart an arms dealer (Rand Kingsley), thanks to martial arts training by their grandpa (Victor Wong). Directed by Jon Turtletaub, the manipulative formula movie tries to make the youngsters' brutalizing of adults seem hysterically funny, despite inept plot and poor acting. Frequent comic violence and some toilet humor. A-III (PG)

Three of Hearts (1993) A bizarre triangle develops when a male escort (William Baldwin) falls for a bisexual teacher (Sherilyn Fenn) he has been hired to romance and dump, in hopes she will then return to the lesbian nurse (Kelly Lynch) she left behind. Director Yurek Bogayevicz' uneven movie stresses the humanity, not the sexuality, of its characters, especially the gigolo who gradually gains self-respect and rejects his sleazy life-style. An uncritical treatment of homosexuality, brief bedroom scenes, fleeting nudity, minor violence and recurring rough language. A-IV (R) 18

Three on a Couch (1966) Jerry Lewis directs himself in the story of an inventive fellow using his wits and several disguises (including that of a female) in order to win the heart of his psychiatrist fiancee (Janet Leigh) who keeps postponing the wedding date because she claims her patients need her more. Typical Lewis vehicle though with more than usual sexual innuendo. A-III (br) U

3 Ring Circus (1954) Two Army buddies get menial jobs in a circus and, after much blundering, one (Dean Martin) becomes the manager and the other (Jerry Lewis) its top clown. Directed by Joseph Pevney, the colorful circus acts and a good supporting cast (Joanne Dru, Zsa Zsa Gabor, Wallace Ford and Elsa Lanchester) help make up for Dean's singing and Lewis' mugging. Small children may enjoy it. A-I (br)

Three Sisters, The (1969) Russian adaptation of the Chekhov play about a 19th-century family whose financial reverses keep them in a remote garrison town, each of them overwhelmed by the sense of frustrated desires and the ultimate hopelessness of their fate. Writer-director Sergei Samsonov is faithful to the original by centering the movie on characterization and mood rather than on dramatic plot. A-II (nr) U

Three Smart Girls (1936) In her screen debut, Deanna Durbin plays the youngest of three sisters (Barbara Read and Nan Gray are the others) who hope to reunite their divorced parents by saving their father (Charles Winniger) from marrying a golddigger (Binnie Barnes). Director Henry Koster's sentimental comedy relies on the old wheeze of mistaken identities (Ray Milland and Mischa Auer), the mischievous conniving of the teen sisters and young Durbin's singing talents. Wholesome but dated entertainment. A-I (br)

Three Stooges Follies, The (1974) Entertaining collection of World War II-vintage movie short-subjects, headlining the Stooges' Neanderthal variety of slapstick humor, an acquired taste perhaps best left uncultivated. On the other hand, this package of instant nostalgia includes a Buster Keaton short, a wartime serial with Batman and Robin fighting a Japanese spy ring and a rousing finale with Kate Smith singing a flag-waving medley of patriotic songs. All in glorious black-and-white. A-I (G)

Three Stripes in the Sun (1955) Gentle clash-of-cultures tale concerns a sergeant (Aldo Ray) stationed in 1949 Osaka where he overcomes his hostility to the Japanese in helping the Sisters of Charity rebuild an orphanage, then falls in love with a helpful interpreter (Mitsuko Tamura). Written and directed by Richard Murphy, the fact-based story has its sentimental moments but is mostly clear-eyed in its account of interracial misunderstandings and healings. Youngsters may need some help with the cultural barriers separating the two principals. A-I (br)

Three the Hard Way (1974) Black exploitation movie about three superheroes (Jim Brown, Fred Williamson and Jim Kelly) who join in tracking down a villain plotting to put a serum in America's drinking water that will kill only blacks. Ineptly directed by Gordon Parks Jr., the movie's plot premise borders on the socially irresponsible. Some brutal as well as sadistic violence. O (R)

Three Tough Guys (1974) Hard-hitting priest (Lino Ventura) and a down-at-the-heels detective (Isaac Hayes) join forces in solving a bank robbery that has cost the one a parishioner and the other his job. The plot's trail of corpses is fairly routine, but one can enjoy the fine performances of the two principals. Italian production directed by Duccio Tessari makes intelligent use of Chicago's architecture and lakefront, often making the background more interesting to watch than any of the fantasy violence that clutters the view. A-III (PG)

Three Warriors (1977) Native American (Lois Red Elk) returns to the reservation with her young son who learns about his people's customs and heritage from his grandfather, assisted by a lame horse and a good-natured forest ranger (Randy Quaid) who's chasing rustlers. In the context of credible acting, the beautiful cinematography of Bruce Surtees and the sensitive direction of Keith Merrill, it is a good family movie that parents can enjoy as much as their children. A-I (G)

3 Women (1977) Director Robert Altman explores the friendship between two single women (Shelley Duvall; Sissy Spacek), both unskilled workers in a geriatric facility, and an unhappily married artist (Janice Rule) whose work on a grotesque mural keeps her on the periphery until the movie's bleak, simplistic resolution, which brings the three together in a strong, sexless relationship. Though the film is thoughtful in its character study of the women, promiscuity figures in the plot and the camera's obsession with the exaggerated sexual characteristics of the mural's semi-human figures makes it questionable fare. A-IV (PG)

Threesome (1970) Stale Danish exploitation film about an innocent young woman's (Judy Brown) journey down some of the darker corridors of sexual corruption. Fashion designer setting, with copious and explicit sex scenes. O (nr)

Threshold (1983) Canadian drama about an American heart specialist (Donald Sutherland) and an eccentric but brilliant research biologist (Jeff Goldblum) who join forces to develop an artificial heart. Director Richard Pearce successfully avoids all the melodramatic cliches inherent in the situation and the result is a good, if not especially inspired movie. A-II (PG)

Throw Momma from the Train (1987) After seeing Hitchcock's "Strangers on a Train," a dim-witted student sets out to kill the hated ex-wife of his adult education writing instructor (Billy Crystal), mistakenly expecting his domineering mother to be killed by the teacher in return. Also directed by DeVito, the broad performance of Anne Ramsey as the mother is so outrageous that it cannot be taken seriously but the rest of the humor pales in comparison. Black comedy treatment of a murder plot and a casual attitude toward sex. A-III (PG-13) PG

Thumb Tripping (1972) Two idealistic college students (Meg Foster and Michael Burns) waste their summer (and the viewer's time) hitchhiking East from Big Sur and meet bigots, thugs and perverts along the way. Directed by Quentin Martin, the treatment of the episodes is explicit in both visuals and language, but far more offensive is the movie's smug attitude toward its finally disillusioned youngsters. O (R) X

Thunder Alley (1967) Suspended race car driver (Fabian) takes a job as stunt driver while trying to prove his innocence. Directed by Richard Rush, the routine action film is marred by scenes of casual sex. O (br)

Thunder and Lightning (1977) Mediocre chase thriller in which a hippie moonshiner and his girl (David Carradine and Kate Jackson) race across the Florida Everglades with tough Northeastern bootleggers in hot pursuit. Daring stunts, failed humor and lame dialogue dominate in a movie directed by Corey Allen. Gratuitous use of slapstick violence and nudity. O (PG)

Thunderbirds Are Go (1967) British space fantasy uses animated puppets to tell the story of the Thunderbirds International Rescue unit who are on the job when sabotage wrecks a flight to Mars. Lots of action and noise as well as imaginative puppet work and special effects. Should engage the 7-13 crowd, and parents won't get too bored in the process. A-I (br)

Thunderbolt and Lightfoot (1974) Clint Eastwood and Jeff Bridges play a pair of bungling bank robbers teamed up with former gang members George Kennedy and Geoffrey Lewis. The character study of good and bad criminals is couched in amoral terms, with viewers expected to sympathize with the first two. Instead of settling for a solid, albeit fantasy-prone, action adventure, director Michael Cimino goes for cheap thrills with needless nudity and profanity, bringing it to a close with some downright ugly, savage deaths. O (R) 18

Thunderheart (1992) Murder investigation on a South Dakota reservation in the late-1970s forces a yuppie FBI agent (Val Kilmer) to confront his Native American heritage when he is presented with conflicting evidence by his superior (Sam Shepherd) and a tribal police officer (Graham Greene). Director Michael Apted's intriguing look at Native American spirituality, reservation living conditions and governmental indifference gets trapped inside a stagnant mystery thriller. Recurring rough language, a few grisly shots of dead bodies and several shootouts. A-III (R) 15

Thunder in the City (1937) On a vacation in London, a high-powered American advertising executive (Edward G. Robinson) uses his promotional talents to help a hard-up distant relative sell shares in a questionable mining company. British director Marion Gering pokes some gentle fun at the outspoken U.S. go-getter as well as his stuffy English peers (including Ralph Richardson and Nigel Bruce) but the satiric effect has faded with the years. Tough sledding for small-fry. A-I (br)

Thunder in the East (1953) Stilted political melodrama pits an American gunrunner (Alan Ladd) against the pacifist leader (Charles Boyer) of a small state in northern India who refuses to use force to stop an uprising after the 1947 British withdrawal. Director Charles Vidor gets a credible performance from Boyer but wastes a good cast (notably, a blind Deborah Kerr as the love interest) in an empty exercise undermining the concept of nonviolence. Stylized violence and much menace. A-II (br)

THX 1138 (1971) In a futuristic underground world, a minor technician named THX 1138 (Robert Duvall) rebels against its sterile, dehumanizing conditions and tries to escape through a maze of electronic devices and guard robots to the unknown outside world. Director George Lucas creates a terrifying technological future out of the materials of today, but it is difficult to empathize with the story's dehumanized characters who have been stripped of all sensitivity and emotion. Though the movie is visually extraordinary and its story has substance, a rather explicit love scene and an extended sequence with a nude dancer limit its audience. A-IV (GP) 15

Tick . . . Tick . . . Tick . . . (1970) Using their newly acquired voting privileges, the blacks of a small county in the South elect one of their own (Jim Brown) as sheriff and, after some stereotyped black and white hostilities, a crisis unites both races behind their sheriff and the ending indicates a rosy future of racial harmony. Shallow treatment by director Ralph Nelson of a serious subject. A-III (G) A

Ticket to Heaven (1981) Well-made Canadian movie about the efforts to rescue a young man (Nick Mancuso) who left his Toronto home and turned up in San Francisco, gaunt-cheeked and hollow-eyed, selling flowers on a street corner as a member of a religious cult. Directed by Ralph L. Thomas, the dramatization has unusual credibility and will be of special interest to teenagers and concerned parents. A-II (PG) AA

Tidal Wave (1975) Clumsy Americanized version of a Japanese disaster movie directed by Shiro Mariano is not only episodic and lacking any sense of pace but it is badly dubbed and cluttered with unconvincing inserts of Lorne Greene as a U.N. delegate. Though one gets bored of the same old shot of lava flowing into the sea, several scenes are too graphic for very young viewers. A-III (PG)

Tie Me Up! Tie Me Down! (1990) Released mental patient (Antonio Banderas) binds and gags an actress (Victoria Abril), holding her prisoner in her apartment until she falls in love with him. Writer-director Pedro Almodovar's Spanish production tries to parlay a sick male sexual fantasy into a kinky sex comedy, but there is nothing amusing in seeing a woman's brutal victimization. Perverse theme and extended depictions of sex acts. O (NC-17) 18

Tiger Makes Out, The (1967) Postman Eli Wallach decides one day to revolt against bureaucratic routine, kidnaps suburban housewife Anne Jackson and she undertakes to educate her captor. Directed by Arthur Hiller, the subsequent action tends to be overdone, but what is enjoyable are the excellent performances of the two principals. A-III (br) A

Tight Spot (1955) Potential government witness (Ginger Rogers) against a crime boss (Lorne Greene) holes up in a New York hotel room while the federal prosecutor (Edward G. Robinson) tries to persuade her to testify and a swarm of policemen (led by Brian Keith) try to keep her from being killed by the mob. Director Phil Karlson's classy crime melodrama paces the suspense with some nifty curves and a sassy performance by Rogers as a one-time shady lady with a chance to be a gangbuster. Stylized violence and mild sexual innuendo. A-II (br) A

Tightrope (1984) Clint Eastwood plays a New Orleans police detective searching for a sadistic killer whose aberrant sexual proclivities he fears he might share. Written and directed by Richard Tuggle, the film embodies an interesting theme, but the execution of it falls short, even though Eastwood's performance is one of his best. The sex and violence loom much too large. O (R) 18

Tiko and the Shark (1966) Harmless, sometimes charming story of the romance between a Polynesian boy and girl, the lad's friendship with a shark and their role in the activities of an island fishing village. Directed by Falco Quilici, the movie's simple story and gorgeous photography should appeal to youngsters. A-I (br)

Till Marriage Do Us Part (1979) Italian sex comedy directed by Luigi Comencini deals with the many tribulations endured by a noble Sicilian lady (Laura Antonelli) who discovers on her wedding night that her husband is in fact her brother. Excessive nudity; graphic sexuality. O (R)

Time After Time (1979) H. G. Wells (Malcolm McDowell) uses a time machine to pursue Jack the Ripper (David Warner) to modern-day San Francisco, where the author and a liberated woman executive (Mary Steenburgen) get involved in a duel of wits with the mad killer. Director Nicholas Meyer's romantic thriller is moderately entertaining, especially the satiric asides about modern technology, but it has some rather violent touches involving the Ripper's crimes, some profanity and implied premarital sex. A-III (PG)

Time Bandits (1981) Witty British comedy about a gang of greedy but good-hearted dwarfs who steal a map of creation from the Supreme Being (Ralph Richardson) and use it to bring an adventurous lad into a variety of historical epochs, meeting Napoleon (Ian Holm), Greek warrior Agamemnon (Sean Connery) and Robin Hood (John Cleese). Directed by Terry Gilliam, it is sometimes amusing and always intelligent, but its appeal for youngsters is spoiled by typical Monty Python vulgarities and black humor, some of it violent. A-III (PG) A

Time Bomb (see: "Terror on a Train").

Time for Burning, A (1967) Extraordinary documentary of what happened when a pastor tried to get his all-white congregation to meet with nearby blacks. Produced by the Lutheran Film Associates and directed by William Jersey, it is a moving document of troubled times and the need for human understanding. A-I (br)

Time for Killing, A (see: "The Long Ride Home").

Time Machine, The (1960) Imaginative adaptation of H. G. Wells' fanciful tale of an English inventor (Rod Taylor) who travels from 1900 into the far distant future where he tries to rally an oppressed people against their loathsome overlords, the radiation-damaged Morlocks. Directed by George Pal, the special effects may not be very elaborate but they're effective enough to convey the fantastic nature of the sci-fi scenario and its underlying anti-war theme. Some stylized violence. A-II (br) PG

Time in the Sun, A (1969) Sensitive Swedish drama about a young journalist (Lars Passgard) who pursues and wins the woman (Grynet Molvig) of his dreams, despite the fact that she is fatally afflicted with Hodgkin's Disease. Director Ake Falck invests a good deal of human warmth in an unusual story of married life, human suffering and the healing power of love. Restrained love-making scene. A-III (R)

Time Lost and Time Remembered (1966) Unhappily married woman (Sarah Miles) returns to her home town in the west of Ireland to find the boy she loved now engaged to another. Director Desmond Davis evokes the Irish atmosphere and locale beautifully, but sentimentalizes the story somewhat. Mature themes. A-III (br)

Time of Destiny, A (1988) Old-fashioned romantic melodrama set during World War II in San Diego and Italy traces the catastrophic effects on the family of a wealthy Basque-American rancher when he interferes in the elopement of his favorite daughter (Melissa Leo) with a young penniless soldier (Timothy Hutton). The filmmakers, Gregory Nava and Anna Thomas ("El Norte"), handle the themes of young love, revenge and Old-World values with operatic relish. A few scenes of intense violence and some profanity. A-III (PG-13) 15

Time of Roses (1970) Tangled tale from Finland about a supposedly perfect society in 2012 whose government manipulates the news, unaware of a plot to expose its deceptive methods through a television documentary about a woman who died in 1976. Directed by Rista Jarva, the movie's intriguing and challenging themes are treated with a cerebral aloofness that leaves the viewer uninvolved and unmoved. A-III (nr)

Time of the Gypsies (1990) Yugoslavian import tells of a Gypsy adolescent (Davor Dujmovic) who is lured to his destruction after poverty and his sister's illness force him to seek help from the richest, most corrupt Gypsy in town. Relying on a largely non-professional cast, director Emir Kusturica provides some insight into Gypsy myth, morality and family life. Subtitles. Some violence, sexually suggestive scenes with nudity and the rape of a minor. A-III (R) 16

Time of Their Lives, The (1946) Killed mistakenly as traitors in the Revolutionary War, two ghosts (Lou Costello and Marjorie Reynolds) cause comic havoc for the residents (Bud Abbott; Binnie Barnes; Gale Sondergaard) of a country estate until proof of their loyalty is found. Directed by Charles Barton, this classy Abbott and Costello effort replaces the usual string of gags with a real story that has plenty of charm and engaging humor with simple yet amusing special effects. The spirits and their predicament as well as a spooky seance scene may scare very young children. A-II (br) U

Time of Your Life, The (1948) Static version of William Saroyan's play set in a San Francisco bar whose easygoing owner (William Bendix) enjoys his eccentric clientele, including a philosophical lounger (James Cagney), his dim gofer (Wayne Morris), a lonely woman (Jeanne Cagney), a dancer (Paul Draper) and a woolly teller of tall tales (James Barton). Under H. C. Potter's direction, the scenes sputter unevenly without ever jelling into a whole, though Saroyan's exotic characters certainly hold attention. A scene of stylized violence and some sexual inferences. A-II (br) A

Time to Remember, A (1988) Young boy (Ruben Gomez) regains his voice when he has a vision of the Madonna during Christmas Midnight Mass. Directed by Tom Travers, the well-intended but inept and saccharine melodrama offers some wholesome, if shallow, entertainment for undemanding viewers. A-I (G)

Time to Sing, A (1968) Country musical-comedy about a farm boy (Hank Williams Jr.) who becomes a singing star despite many obstacles in a cliched, sentimental but tuneful picture directed by Arthur Dreifuss. For those who enjoy the country music sound. A-I (br)

Timerider (1983) Motorcycle racer (Fred Ward) finds himself whisked back in time to the late-19th century where he gets mixed up with some low-lifes of various sorts. Directed by William Dear, it is a simple-minded attempt to combine science fiction and the western with little result. Considerable, though restrained, sex and violence. A-III (PG)

Tin Drum, The (1980) German adaptation of Gunter Grass' satiric novel about a boy (David Bennent) who, in protest against the absurd world of adults, decides to stop growing on his third birthday and shows his anguish at events by beating on a tin drum. Directed by Volker Schlondorff, the work is a serious attempt to show the moral and political corruption of the 1930s that led to Germany's defeat in the cataclysm of World War II. Though it has moments of brilliance, it founders on trying to accommodate its vivid, often gross slice-of-life realism to some abrupt and arbitrary excursions into absurdity. Crudely graphic treatment of sex, especially in scenes with the 13-year-old Bennent. O (R)

Tin Men (1987) Danny DeVito and Richard Dreyfuss are 1960s' aluminum siding salesman obsessed with getting even with each other over a car accident. Barbara Hershey plays DeVito's estranged wife who becomes fair game for the vindictive seduction by Dreyfuss in director Barry Levinson's wry and ribald comedy. Profanity and adultery are the sources of humor in this film. O (R) 15

Tin Star, The (1957) Solid western in which a veteran bounty hunter (Henry Fonda) helps a young sheriff (Anthony Perkins) capture a pair of outlaws and stop a lynching. Scripted by Dudley Nichols and directed by Anthony Mann, the laconic hero and his grudging protege are fully developed as likeable individuals in an involving, well-paced and low-keyed story of frontier justice. Some stylized violence. A-I (br) U

Titicut Follies (1967) Emotionally wrenching documentary looks unblinkingly and without commentary at the appalling conditions of life for inmates at Massachusetts' Bridgewater State Hospital for the Criminally Insane. Produced, directed and edited by Frederick Wiseman, its impressionistic picture of this state institution ranges from a musical entertainment put on by staff and inmates to scenes from the ward for the profoundly disturbed (where inmates are housed without clothing) as well as a staff meeting with an inmate who claims to have been wrongly committed. Though some adults may find certain scenes quite distressing, it is important that the public be aware of such conditions and, indeed, an afterward states that Bridgewater has since changed. Scenes of brutalizing conditions, some frontal male nudity and occasional rough language. A-IV (nr)

TNT Jackson (1975) Standard black exploitation film directed by Cirio Santiago with Jeanne Bell as a martial arts addict. Excessive violence and nudity. O (R)

To Be Free (1973) Psychiatrist tries hypnotism as short-cut therapy for a sexually confused young woman, with obviously dire consequences for them both. Director Ned Bosnick's banal plot is treated with gimmicky camera techniques and a softcore approach to sexual anomalies. O (R)

To Be or Not to Be (1942) Classic World War II comedy about a Polish actor (Jack Benny) whose impersonation of a murdered Nazi spy hoodwinks Warsaw's bumbling Gestapo chief (Sig Ruman) and saves his wife (Carole Lombard), his theater company and the Polish underground. Director Ernst Lubitsch, a master of sophisticated comedy, finds much humor and some wit in what is essentially a darkly menacing wartime subject and Benny, teamed with Lombard, was never better or funnier. Restrained violence and a sexual innuendo or two. A-II (br)

To Be or Not to Be (1983) Director Mel Brooks fails in his attempt to remake the 1942 Ernst Lubitsch black comedy about a Warsaw drama troupe who outwit the Nazis and save the Polish underground, with himself and Anne Bancroft in the roles created by Jack Benny and Carole Lombard. Unfortunately, Brooks has neither the sophisticated wit of Lubitsch nor Benny's subtlety and sense of timing. Instead his humor runs from crude slapstick to bad taste, trivializing the Nazis and there is nothing intrinsically amusing about the Gestapo, however klutzy, however roly-poly. A-II (PG) U

To Catch a Thief (1955) Fluffy romantic thriller set on the French Riviera, where a string of jewel robberies have the local gendarmes chasing a one-time cat burglar (Cary Grant) who uses an heiress (Grace Kelly) to catch the real crook. Alfred Hitchcock directs the chic proceedings with his usual flair for the eccentric and off-beat, but there's more romance than suspense. Some stylized violence and veiled sexual references. A-II (br) A

To Commit a Murder (1969) French spy thriller in which an agent (Louis Jordan) either has to prevent a noted scientist from defecting to Red China or kill him and his accomplice (Edmond O'Brien). Directed by Eduard Molinaro, the formula plot is neatly packaged and moderately entertaining. Some violence. A-III (PG)

To Die in Madrid (1966) Excellent French documentary by Nicole Stephane and Frederic Rossif describes the bitter struggle that was the Spanish Civil War. Fine editing and a poetic commentary by Madeleine Chapsal help re-create the anguished emotions of 1936–1939 and derive some significance from the tragic war. A-II (br)

To Die of Love (1972) Fact-based French drama about a teacher (Annie Girardot) who falls in love with a 17-year-old student (Bruno Pradal) and wants to marry him but, harassed by officials, she commits suicide. Directed by Andre Cayatte, the movie is more concerned with the impersonal bureaucratic system responsible for the tragedy than it is with the two main characters. Those viewing it as nothing more than a love story will find it romanticizing a relationship that the film does not even try to make dramatically credible. A-IV (GP)

To Each His Own (1946) Slick tearjerker about a World War I unwed mother (Olivia de Havilland) who gives up her baby boy, then watches from afar as he grows into manhood until they meet by chance during

World War II. Directed by Mitchell Leisen, the flashback form of the narrative is mightily contrived and emotionally manipulative, but de Havilland makes the mother's heartache seem real enough. A-II (br) A

To Find a Man (1972) Self-centered Catholic girl (Pamela Martin) finds herself pregnant and returns home for the Christmas holidays to find an abortionist with some help from the boy next door (Darren O'Connor). The trouble with director Buzz Kulik's mediocre effort is its shallow treatment of adolescent values and acceptance of abortion as natural in a society where everything, including morality, is disposable. O (R/GP) X

To Hell and Back (1955) Audie Murphy plays himself in the Hollywood version of how he came to be the most decorated U.S. soldier in World War II. Directed by Jesse Hibbs, Murphy seems less self-conscious on the battlefield than off in portraying himself as a soft-spoken, patriotic Texas boy who enlists at 16, then proceeds to win medals fighting through North Africa, Sicily, Italy and France. Wartime violence and heroics as well as several muted sexual references. A-II (br) A

To Kill a Mockingbird (1962) When a southern lawyer (Gregory Peck) undertakes the defense of a black man (Brock Peters) accused of rape, he has to help his young children cope with the town's racial hostilities and their own fears of a retarded neighbor (Robert Duvall). In this fine adaptation of the Harper Lee novel, director Robert Mulligan evokes a nostalgic picture of small-town life as seen mostly through the eyes of a youngster whose father is a reassuring figure of integrity in the confusing world of adults. Excellent for discussions of racial prejudice. A-II (nr) PG

To Kill a Priest (1989) Uneven fictionalized drama based on actual events in 1984 Poland when Father Jerzy Popieluszko, a popular pro-Solidarity activist (Christopher Lambert), was murdered by state security police on the orders of a captain (Ed Harris) obsessed by his conviction that the priest is a dangerous subversive. Filmed in France in English by Polish director Agnieszka Holland, the movie contrasts the spiritual power and national appeal of the priest with the wavering Marxist dedication of the psychologically troubled officer. The work succeeds best in its depiction of the historical context, an armed government at war with its own people and their faith. Some hard-edged violence; a bedroom scene; several instances of rough language. A-III (R)

To Live and Die in L.A. (1985) Director William Friedkin attempts to make a southern California version of the "French Connection" in this story of two Treasury agents (William Petersen and John Pankow) pursuing a vicious counterfeiter (Willem Dafoe). The result, however, has no more depth than an extended music video. Brutal and so amoral that it's hard to tell the good guys from the bad. O (R) 18

To Sir with Love (1967) Warm British melodrama about an American (Sidney Poitier) who takes a teaching job in London, where he tries to turn teenage students from a Cockney slum into ladies and gentlemen. Though the story offers some pat solutions for real problems and the student transformations seem overswift, director James Clavell gets winning performances from Poitier and his fine supporting cast to show aspects of life, love and adolescence that American audiences will find familiar, despite the accent. A-II (br) PG

To Sleep with Anger (1990) Tensions within a black middle-class family escalate when a boyhood pal from the Deep South (Danny Glover) shows up on the Los Angeles doorstep of the family patriarch (Paul Butler) and slyly insinuates himself into the family circle. Glover's multilayered performance and a fine ensemble cast help director Charles Burnett meld comedy and drama into a cohesive whole, contrasting the servile ways of the rural South with modern urban life. Mild violence and a few vulgarities. A-II (PG)

To Trap a Spy (1966) Movie version of the TV spy series, "The Man from U.N.C.L.E.," features Robert Vaughn going through his paces as a superagent with little help from the sets, the gimmicks or director Don Medford. Violence and sexual innuendo. A-III (br) A

Tobruk (1967) World War II story about a British commando column (Rock Hudson; George Peppard; Nigel Green) disguised as a German convoy bringing Allied prisoners through the desert into the German base of Tobruk to destroy its oil stockpiles. Directed by Arthur Hiller, the straightforward action narrative alludes to the absurdity of war and has an interesting subplot dealing with anti-Semitism. It brings a measure of intelligence to the usual mindless war formula. Stylized violence. A-II (br) A

Toby Tyler, Or Ten Weeks with a Circus (1960) Sturdy little Disney production about the turn-of-the-century adventures of an orphan (Kevin Corcoran) when he runs away from his aunt and uncle to join a traveling one-ring circus. Directed by Charles Barton, the earnest little fellow makes a lot of friends, the most notable being a mischievous monkey. Pleasant, uncomplicated story, though its main appeal is to youngsters. A-I (br) U

Today We Kill . . . Tomorrow We Die! (1971) Poor Italian western about a rancher (Montgomery Ford) who recruits four gunslingers to wipe out the gang responsible for the rape-murder of his wife. Director Tonino Cervi's production values are laughable but the violence is not. A-III (GP)

Todd Killings, The (1971) Lurid fact-based melodrama about a perverse killer (Robert F. Lyons) who sexually assaulted and mutilated a number of teenage girls in Tucson, Ariz. Directed by Barry Shear, the movie dwells on the sensational aspects of the case and as a result is quite sordid in its details. O (R) X

Together (1971) Pseudo-documentary promotes a summertime romp at the estate of a self-proclaimed pioneer in sexual guidance. Filmmakers Roger Murphy and Sean C. Cunningham encounter uninhibited and unclad couples who explicate and demonstrate their host's theories of tactile therapy. O (R)

Together Brothers (1974) Good action movie, filmed in steamy Galveston, Texas, with a cast largely of unknowns, it involves a black street gang tracking down the killer of a cop who treated them fairly. Director William A. Graham gets some extraordinarily sensitive character portrayals and conveys a feel for the ramshackle black ghettos of Galveston. Though there is a minimum of street language, the sudden, concluding violence is adult fare. A-III (PG)

Tokoloshe (1971) Uneven South African production about a winsome Bantu youngster (Saul Pelle) who escapes the curse of the evil spirit of the title through his mother's intervention and reaches safety in Johannesburg. Directed by Peter Prowse, the sequences in the city unfortunately lack the narrative interest and sense of conviction found in the earlier portions of the movie. A-I (G)

Tokyo Story (1972) Elderly couple on their first visit to the Tokyo homes of their children meet only disguised rejection except, ironically, for the kindness of their dead son's wife. When the mother dies shortly upon returning to their country village, it is only the widowed daughter-in-law who shows any real feeling of loss. Director Yasujiro Ozu's eloquent treatment of old age makes it a uniquely moving hymn to life. A-I (nr) U

Tom and Jerry—The Movie (1993) When their home is demolished, the mischievous cartoon cat-and-mouse duo must take to the mean streets where they rescue a poor little rich girl from the clutches of a greedy aunt who's after her trust fund. Producer-director Phil Roman's adventuresome animated tale of the scrappy twosome will hold the small-fry, while some of the six musical numbers sprinkled throughout this amiable cartoon may entertain grown-ups as well. A-I (G)

Tom, Dick and Harry (1941) Daffy comedy in which a telephone operator (Ginger Rogers) has strange dreams about her persistent suitors—a rich socialite (Alan Marshal), a car salesman (George Murphy) and a genial dreamer (Burgess Meredith)—with her choice coming as no surprise. Director Garson Kanin has a lot of fun with the attitudes of the time, especially in the wacky dream sequences, but the love story's sentimentality wears less well. Romantic complications. A-II (br) U

Tom Horn (1980) Frontier hero at the end of his career (Steve McQueen) is hired by a group of ranchers to stop some rustlers, a job he performs with such murderous zeal that they decide to get rid of him by framing him for murder. Though director William Wiard fails to provide much dramatic steam, McQueen's solid performance raises the material a notch above the standard western. Some graphic violence. A-III (R) 15

Tom Jones (1963) Zestful adaptation of Henry Fielding's classic novel about the misadventures, largely amorous, of a young man (Albert Finney) among the highborn and low of 18th-century England. Director Tony Richardson treats the melodramatic proceedings with a droll combination of mock heroics, antic slapstick, bawdy asides and much social satire. Though the humor is often coarse and the blood-lust of a deer hunt is brutally graphic, it succeeds largely as a period comedy of manners and morals. A-IV (br) PG

Tom Sawyer (1973) Reader's Digest musical adaptation of the Mark Twain classic with Johnny Whitaker as Tom, Jeff East as Huck, Jodie Foster as Becky and Celeste Holm as Aunt Polly. Directed by Don Taylor, the movie is a quite diverting though undistinguished bit of nostalgia that, if it misses the wit and cultural perceptions of the original, succeeds nonetheless in being continually engaging. Young viewers will be delighted. A-I (G) U

Tom Thumb (1958) Amiable retelling of the Brothers Grimm fairy tale about a woodsman and his wife (Bernard Miles and Jessie Matthews) whose thumb-sized son (Russ Tamblyn) thwarts the scheme of a comic pair of villains (Terry-Thomas and Peter Sellers) to rob the village treasury. Director George Pal mixes a variety of animation and special effects with occasional lyrics sung by Peggy Lee to fashion a pleasant fantasy that will amuse children and pacify parents, though of less appeal for more demanding viewers. A-I (br) U

Tombstone (1993) Bloody retelling of the legendary events of 1879 in the Arizona town of the title, where a gang of murderous outlaws (led by Michael Biehn; Powers Boothe) come up against the new sheriff Wyatt Earp (Kurt Russell), his brothers (Sam Elliott; Bill Paxton) and Doc Holliday (Val Kilmer), who have decided to wipe them out. George P. Cosmatos directs a glossy dud filled with shootouts between wooden characters mouthing cliches while attired in western high-fashion. Excessive violence including numerous grisly murders, acceptance of cold-blooded murder, recurring substance abuse and an instance of rough language. O (R) 15

Tommy (1975) British adaptation of Peter Townshend's rock opera about a pinball wizard (Roger Daltrey) who becomes a religious guru and ends as a rejected mystic calling out for a new consciousness. Though the performances of Eric Clapton, Elton John and Tina Turner are excellent, director Ken Russell's treatment is ludicrously out of control, obscuring the sense of the opera by an undue emphasis on visual pyrotechnics that is not dramatic but destructive. Satiric jabs at religion are excessive if taken literally. A-IV (PG) 15

Tomorrow (1972) Winter watchman (Robert Duvall) for a backwoods Mississippi sawmill gives shelter to a pregnant woman (Olga Bellin) abandoned by her husband. As the winter passes, he falls in love with her, but she dies shortly after her child is born. Adapted from a William Faulkner story by Horton Foote and directed by Joseph Anthony, the material is sparse, even tedious, but the characters—the taciturn man of the land and the worn-out woman—convey a genuine sense of the American rural ethic. A-II (PG)

Tonka the Comanche (1958) Director Lewis R. Foster's mildly entertaining Disney movie is set in the Old West where a young Indian (Sal Mineo) captures a wild stallion, loses him and then gets back again. A-I (br) U

Tony Rome (1967) Frank Sinatra stars as a Miami private-eye who displays a nice sense of values and humor as his work takes him deeper and deeper into the corrupt layers of the resort town. Directed by Gordon Douglas, its sporadic gunplay and fist-fights are standard, but some of the subject matter is sordid and some of the language is rough. A-III (br) X

Too Beautiful for You (1990) Wealthy Frenchman (Gerard Depardieu) shocks his beautiful wife (Carole Bouquet) and their friends by falling madly in love with a plain, plump woman (Josiane Balasko). Director Bertrand Blier twists the cliches of marital infidelity and French film convention with this seriocomic farce that mixes fantasy with reality and raises but does not answer philosophical questions about love, infidelity and the nature of sexual attraction. Subtitles. Some sexually explicit dialogue. A-IV (R)

Too Late the Hero (1970) Routine World War II movie set on a small Pacific island in which an Allied patrol (Cliff Robertson and Michael Caine) makes its way to the far end of the island, blows up the Japanese radio transmitter and returns to home base. Director Robert Aldrich offers the usual amount of blood and violence in glossy color, but all except hardened action buffs will find it disappointing. A-III (GP) 15

Too Much Sun (1991) The fortune left in an old man's will galvanizes various money grabbers, including the man's gay son (Eric Idle), his lesbian daughter (Andrea Martin) and his unscrupulous parish priest (Jim Haynie). Director Robert Downey's sex farce mocks gays and religious in a lame attempt at outrageous humor that never gets beyond tasteless twaddle. Promiscuous encounters, heavy homosexual innuendo and much rough language. O (R) 18

Too Outrageous (1987) Low-budget Canadian production about a homosexual (Craig Russell) whose career as a female impersonator leads to a chance at television stardom if he will change his act, but he prefers to remain the way he is. Written and directed by Dick Benner, the movie condones but does not glamorize homosexual relationships. O (R)

Tootsie (1982) Very funny movie about an unemployed actor (Dustin Hoffman) who dresses up as a woman to get a part in a TV soap opera, but his success in the role complicates matters when he falls in love with the show's beautiful co-star (Jessica Lange). Director Sydney Pollack's romantic comedy makes some witty points about being a woman in a man's world. Adult sexual humor. A-III (PG)

Top Gun (1986) The bravado of a Navy hotshot jet pilot (Tom Cruise) wins the grudging admiration of his comrades, the affection of his female flight instructor (Kelly McGillis) and audience commendation for his patriotic hip-shooting heroism. Director Tony Scott's high-flying celebration of peacetime military training is mostly a hollow exercise in macho derring-do. Fairly restrained bedroom scene, brief nudity and incidental profanity. A-III (PG) 15

Top of the Heap (1972) Black policeman in Washington, D.C., (Christopher St. John who also wrote, produced and directed) works with racist, bribe-taking fellow officers and off the job his wife browbeats him, his daughter experiments with sex and drugs and even his boozy mistress mocks him with abandon. He proves as nasty as anyone else in a movie that goes out of its way to alienate viewers with needless, salacious nudity and an endless barrage of gutter epithets. O (R)

Top Secret (1984) Creators of "Airplane" (Jim Abrahams, David Zucker and Jerry

Zucker) have set out to parody movies of international intrigue. But this time they haven't gotten it right and most of the jokes misfire. Some sexually oriented humor. A-III (PG) 15

Topkapi (1964) Entertaining adaptation of Eric Ambler's comic thriller in which a bungling two-bit con man (Peter Ustinov) becomes part of a fantastic plot to steal a priceless jeweled dagger from the Istanbul Museum. Directed with gusto by Jules Dassin, the suspenseful caper is pulled off in sparkling style by a cast including Melina Mercouri, Maximillian Schell and Robert Morley, but they are all upstaged by a little bird. Some stylized violence and mild sexual innuendo. A-III (br) U

Topaz (1969) Alfred Hitchcock's adaptation of the pulpy Leon Uris novel about high-powered espionage and counterspying in a variety of exotic locales. The dialogue is mostly banal and the action largely unconvincing, but there are occasional glimmers of the Hitchcock touch in subtle plot twists here and blind alleys there. Diverting if ultimately disappointing. Some physical and psychological violence and a lot of confusing intrigue. A-III (PG) A

Topo Gigio (1966) Delightful little movie about a small talking mouse who outwits a wicked magician to save his friends. Young children will love it and the puppet characterization is droll enough to please their parents. A-I (br)

Tora! Tora! Tora! (1970) Huge, sprawling and occasionally unfocused wartime epic based on the events leading up to the surprise Japanese attack on Pearl Harbor. Director Richard Fleischer alternates American and Japanese points-of-view as the one side goes about its daily routines unsuspecting the deadly assault that the other side is preparing. The Japanese segments are the more interesting in showing less-known aspects of a strategy that some realized would start an unwinnable war. A-I (G) U

Torch Song Trilogy (1988) Screen version of Harvey Fierstein's play about a homosexual (Fierstein) who works as a female impersonator in a drag revue and his unfulfilling love life and ongoing mother-son conflicts. Directed by Paul Bogart, the movie compassionately and often raucously shows the common threads that connect heterosexual and homosexual family relationships, courtship and love, but its validation of homosexuality and depiction of promiscuity in the 1970s is disturbing, especially in light of the AIDS epidemic. A few fleeting scenes of male kissing and discreet touching, a scene of a brutal beating, much rough language with homosexual innuendos and a few

bawdy musical drag numbers. O (R) 15

Torchlight (1985) The destruction of a successful businessman and loving husband (Steve Railsback) by cocaine is a serious and important theme, but director Tom Wright's treatment is so uninspired and at times ludicrous that the movie fails even as a cautionary tale. Explicit depiction of drug taking. A-III (R)

Torn Apart (1990) Trite romance about an Israeli youth (Adrian Pasdar) and a Palestinian girl (Cecilia Peck) who defy the wishes of their families only to be sacrificed to the political conflict that engulfs them. Director Jack Fisher fails to develop the characters as individuals and the narrative never gets beyond a superficial examination of Mid-East tensions and the human realities behind them. Intermittent scenes of bloodshed and violence and a restrained scene of sexual passion. A-III (R)

Torn Curtain (1966) Slack Alfred Hitchcock suspense thriller about an American physicist (Paul Newman) who pretends to defect to East Germany in order to get some secret information. The predictable plot is further marred by a detailed treatment of a realistically brutal killing. O (br) 18

Torrents of Spring (1990) Visually lovely, emotionally bland version of Ivan Turgenev's novel about a 19th-century Russian nobleman (Timothy Hutton) traveling in Germany who becomes engaged to a sweet Italian immigrant (Valeria Golino) but then falls passionately in love with the wanton wife (Nastassja Kinski) of an old school chum. Director Jerzy Skolimowski fails to delineate clearly the time and place of this oddly cast, multinational movie whose one-dimensional characters undercut its cautionary tale of misdirected love. Lengthy, clothed sexual liaison. A-III (nr) PG

Torrid Zone (1940) Tough-guy romantic comedy set in Latin America where the cynical manager (Pat O'Brien) of a banana export company uses a stranded nightclub entertainer (Ann Sheridan) to keep his top troubleshooter (James Cagney) from taking a job in Chicago. Directed by William Keighley, the shifting Cagney-Sheridan romance takes a backseat to the movie's he-man heroics and adolescent pranks that seem less amusing today than then. Stylized violence, ethnic stereotypes and sexual innuendo. A-III (br)

Torso (1975) Low-budget European co-production is a heavy-breathing, sex-and-brutality melodrama directed by Sergio Martino and dubbed into a language at times reminiscent of idiomatic English. O (R)

Torture Dungeon (1970) Bungled medieval tale about a duke's problems in ensuring an heir for his kingdom, preoccupied as he is in dispatching his peers of both sexes by prolonged torture or sudden death. Played apparently for laughs, the movie is far from funny in its own preoccupation with nudity and acts of swift, bloody violence. O (R)

Torture Garden (1967) Five visitors to a carnival fright show run by Dr. Diablo (Burgess Meredith) are given warning visions of the inner evil within each. Written by Robert Bloch and directed by Freddie Francis, the omnibus is more hokey than scary, though the episode about a collector (Jack Palance) of Edgar Allen Poe memorabilia has at least a suitably sinister atmosphere. Fanciful but unconvincing scenes of violence. A-II (br) X

Total Recall (1990) Ultraviolent sci-fi thriller about a man (Arnold Schwarzenegger) who has to travel to Mars to discover why his wife (Sharon Stone), as well as total strangers, are trying to kill him. Director Paul Verhoeven's intricate plot exposes an ugly futuristic society where human life warrants no respect, women are manipulative sexual playthings and the only solution to injustice is massive bloodshed. Excessive violence, sexual exploitation, including nudity, and rough language. O (R) 18

Toto le Heros (1992) Believing he was switched in the hospital nursery with a neighborhood boy who then led a privileged life, an embittered old man (Michel Bouquet) recalls his lifelong envy and fantasies about killing the man who "stole" his life. Using flashbacks and fantasies, Belgian writer-director Jaco Van Dormael imaginatively captures an entire lifespan going from a child's innocence to a crusty old codger, who finally learns to accept the mixed blessings of the life he has led. Subtitles. An implied affair, brief violence and momentary nudity. A-III (PG-13) 15

Touch, The (1971) Failed English-language production written and directed by Ingmar Bergman, the story is of a love triangle involving a busy, sensitive husband (Max von Sydow), his uncertain wife (Bibi Andersson) and her importunate, apparently unbalanced and unfeeling lover (Elliott Gould). Though it has flashes of Bergman's mastery in handling themes of alienation and searching, Gould is a classic case of miscasting and his performance makes the whole affair seem no more than campy soap opera. Ambiguous attitude toward adultery. A-IV (R)

Touch and Go (1975) French World War II comedy about a French deserter (Michel Picoli), an inept British officer (Michael York) and the wife of the Swiss consul (Marlene Jobart) who find themselves fleeing for their lives from Nazis who are certain they are spies. Director Philippe de Broca's comedy is full of sight-gags,

absurd situations and broad humor that not everyone appreciates. His insistence upon the wartime vulnerability of his characters, however, makes the laughter at their ridiculous adventures somewhat uneasy. A-III (nr)

Touch and Go (1987) Improbable romance of a star pro hockey player (Michael Keaton) and a down-and-out Hispanic single parent (Maria Conchita Alonzo) who meet when the hockey star drags her son, who helped mug him, home. Simplistic, forced characterizations with no understanding of parenthood, some foul language and a semi-nude bedroom scene type this as adult fare. A-III (R)

Touch Me (1971) Four couples debase themselves in a mechanical marathon of hard-core theatrics with the encouragement of a "trained psychologist" who alleges that such explicit enactment of fantasies helps release people's human potential. Pseudo-documentary exploitation directed by Sam Weston. O (nr)

Touch of Class, A (1973) London-based American executive (George Segal) and a British career woman (Glenda Jackson) meet, a love affair ensues and then the man's vacationing wife, kids, and in-laws return unexpectedly bringing all the inevitable and predictable complications that follow. Director Melvin Frank's central problem is that his stars don't seem very comfortable as a romantic couple, a feeling many will share about a comedy whose theme is adultery. Frank tries to keep it light and witty but, after a tasteless bedroom scene, the froth goes flat and only a stale aftertaste remains. Some scatological epithets. A-III (PG)

Touch of Evil (1958) Stylish crime thriller about a Mexican policeman (Charlton Heston) whose American bride (Janet Leigh) becomes a foil in the criminal machinations of a top bordertown cop (Orson Welles). Also directed by Welles, the dark, moody narrative has plenty of menace and occasional nasty violence but succeeds best as a character study of a warped crimebuster who metes out justice by placing himself above the law. A-III (br) A

Touchables, The (1968) Dull British sex fantasy ineptly directed by Robert Freeman in which four teenage girls kidnap a rock star and force him to make love to them. O (R/PG)

Touched by Love (1980) Fact-based story about a young nurse (Deborah Raffin) who takes it upon herself to bring a teenage victim of cerebral palsy (Diane Lane) out of her deep depression, partly through an extraordinary exchange of letters with Elvis Presley. Directed by Gus Trikonis, the acting is very credible and the story is

Good Ones to Rent

The Journey of Natty Ga[nn]

The Apple Dumpling Gang

told with just the right balance of emotion and sentimentality. Rare, immensely enjoyable family movie. A-I (PG) U

Tough (1974) Pre-teen (Dion Gosset) has problems with his parents, teachers and, finally, the police. Nothing unusual about this picture of the generation gap except that the family are middle-class blacks living in the suburbs and suffering the same problems as many of their white neighbors. Written, produced, and directed by Horace Jackson, regrettably the characterizations and plot situations are too thinly drawn for either credibility or insight, and the principals rarely rise above stereotypes. A-I (G)

Tough Guys (1986) Silly and somewhat crude comedy exploiting the seasoned acting talents of Burt Lancaster and Kirk Douglas, who star as thieves released after 30 years in prison into a society neglectful and uncaring about its senior citizens. Bemused by the disordered world that confronts them, the proud old-timers decide to pull off one more caper just to show that they can. Unseemly sexual encounter; much harsh language. A-III (PG) 15

Tous les Matins du Monde (1992) An aged royal court musician (Gerard Depardieu) in 17th-century France ruefully recalls his fiery relationship as a cocky young student (Guillaume Depardieu) with his purist teacher (Jean-Pierre Marielle) who shunned him when he discovered the young man's affair with his daughter (Anne Brochet). In a movie of painstaking pace, sublime baroque soundtrack and graceful performances of restrained passion, director Alain Corneau contrasts the approaches of two musicians to their art—the master who saw music as a source of spiritual consolation and the youth as a means to achieve worldly ambitions. Subtitles. A sexual encounter with brief nudity and a suicide. A-III (nr) 12

Tout Va Bien (1973) Muddled French story of a factory strike, with a great deal of ideological debate from all sides. Director Jean-Luc Godard's return to the narrative form and the use of actors (Jane Fonda; Yves Montand) have little appeal except for those interested in political cinema. A-III (nr) X

Tower of Screaming Virgins (1972) The teasing title delivers only a treacherous trio: an icy French queen and her haughty handmaidens who lure lovers to the castle and slay them in the wake of an evening's ecstasy. Swashbuckling Terry Torday foils their scheme while director Francois Legrand indulges the theme of incest in a bloody-awful French-German co-production. O (R)

Towering Inferno (1974) A 135-story office-residential tower goes up in smoke, trapping hundreds of Hollywood extras and a score of past and present stars. Director John Gillermin's disaster movie is weak in plot and characterization, but stunningly realistic in its special effects of death and destruction. A-III (PG) 15

Town Called Hell, A (1971) Mexico in 1895 is the setting for a series of slaughters between revolutionary guerrillas (led by Robert Shaw) and government soldiers (led by Telly Savalas) who torture and execute various peasants and prisoners. Directed by Robert Parrish, the movie is unrelenting in its emphasis on violence and senseless punishment. O (R)

Town That Dreaded Sundown, The (1977) Tedious, solemn and embarrassingly inept fact-based movie, featuring Ben Johnson and Andrew Prine, about the summer-long rampage of a homicidal maniac in 1940s' Texarkana, Ark. Directed by Charles B. Pierce, the movie's depiction of brutal atrocities is all the more disagreeable when the ending states that the killer was never apprehended. O (R)

Toy, The (1979) French comedy about the spoiled 10-year-old son of a tyrannical tycoon (Michel Bouquet) who, told he can have any toy he wants in a store owned by his father, points to a hapless writer in his father's employ. The writer (Pierre Richard) goes along with the joke, develops a warm relationship with the boy and helps bring about the father's comeuppance. Mild, innocuous entertainment. A-II (PG)

Toy, The (1982) Dreary adaptation of a mediocre French comedy about a poor journalist (Richard Pryor) so desperate for money that he lets a ruthless tycoon (Jackie Gleason) hire him to be the playmate of his spoiled, affection-starved son. Directed by Richard Donner, the talents of everyone in the movie are wasted in an embarrassingly failed comedy. Some comically intended scenes with sexual implications. A-III (PG)

Toy Grabbers, The (1971) Toy company head (Julie Newmar) wants the services of a talented toy maker (Wally Cox) and entrusts the task to her imbecilic son (Victor Buono) who uses a string of seductive beauties to secure a contract. From there writer-producer-director Don Joslyn veers into black comedy, adding crude touches that do little to compensate for all the nudity employed in this odious ode to motherhood. O (R/GP/R)

Toy Soldiers (1991) Led by a Colombian drug czar's son (Andrew Divoff), a dozen heavily armed terrorists take over an elite boys' prep school in New England where the most troublesome student (Sean Astin) covertly organizes a high-risk counterattack. Director Daniel Petrie Jr.'s fast-moving formula action movie features a thoroughly likable young cast plus a good performance from Louis Gossett Jr., but all it adds up to is empty escapist fare. Some gratuitous violence, a flash of nudity, fleeting sexual references and intermittent rough language. A-III (R) 15

Toys (1992) The suspicions of a gentle brother (Robin Williams) and sister (Joan Cusack) are aroused when their career officer uncle (Michael Gambon) inherits their father's toy factory, bringing in his militaristic son (LL Cool J) to begin secretly creating miniature deadly weapons disguised as toys. Director Barry Levinson's madly uneven movie practically cancels itself out by starting with dreamlike visual delights and ending in a morass of mirthless mayhem. Much menace, an off-screen sexual encounter and some suggestive remarks. A-III (PG-13) PG

Toys Are Not for Children (1972) Marcia Forbes sleepwalks through her starring role as a young woman afflicted with an Electra complex, obsessively searching for dear old daddy. Though not quite soft-core pornography, there are enough visuals and coarse language to offend everyone. O (R)

Traces of Red (1992) Womanizing Palm Beach police detective (James Belushi) investigating a series of lurid sex killings himself becomes a prime suspect, as does in turn his wealthy lover (Lorraine Bracco), his cop partner (Tony Goldwyn) and his politically ambitious brother (William Russ). Director Andy Wolk turns in a sleazy potboiler weighted down by obvious plot contrivances and Ms. Bracco's stilted acting. Acceptance of sexual promiscuity, including several depictions of sex encounters, brief nudity, some violence and frequent rough language. O (R) 15

Track 29 (1988) An affluent North Carolina housewife (Therese Russell) spends her days drinking and hallucinating about the son (Gary Oldman) she as a teen had given up for adoption, while her physician husband (Christopher Lloyd) dallies with his nurse (Sandra Bernhard) and dabbles with his computer-operated toy train set. British director Nicolas Roeg concocts an alien view of America in a surreal black comedy that makes little distinction between fantasy and reality. Much vulgar language, explicit sexual encounters of a kinky and incestuous nature, some nudity and a gory fantasy climax. O (R) 18

Trackdown (1976) Vicious vigilante potboiler in which a Montana rancher (Robert Mitchum) comes to Los Angeles to wreak havoc among the scum who have brutalized his young runaway sister (Karen Lamm). Directed by Richard T. Heffron, the brutalization is dwelt upon with sickening detail that would be intolerable even in a movie dealing seriously with the social problems that this one cynically exploits. Excessive violence and sexual perversion, nudity and some racist attitudes. O (R) X

Tracks (1979) Jumpy Army sergeant (Dennis Hopper), escorting home the body of a Vietnam comrade, finds himself drawn to a college girl (Taryn Power), but his problems seem to stem more from an unrequited love for mama than the horrors of Vietnam. Directed by Henry Jaglom, the soppy, self-indulgent movie is less ambiguous than it is pointless. Excessive nudity. O (R) X

Trading Places (1983) Caustic streetwise con man (Eddie Murphy) switches roles with a wealthy snob in a brokerage firm (Dan Aykroyd) in a less than noble experiment concocted by the two billionaire brothers who own the firm. The elaborate game of greed provides some insight into aspects of prejudice, but director John Landis relies too often on nudity, vulgarity and profanity as sources of humor. O (R) 15

Traffic (1972) Fine French comedy from director Jacques Tati, who returns in his comic character of Monsieur Hulot in a story following the series of mishaps that occurs as he shepherds a station-wagon camper from Paris to Amsterdam for an automobile show. There is no need for dialogue (grunts and groans suffice) because the situations are as universal as the visual gags that develop from them. The comedy is relaxed, refreshing and even the habitually grouchy will get a few belly-laughs. A-I (G) 15

Tragedy of a Ridiculous Man (1982) Italian drama about a wealthy factory owner (Ugo Tognazzi) whose son is kidnapped by political terrorists. Directed by Bernardo Bertolucci, the movie's modest premise provided a chance to come to grips with the realities of contemporary terrorism, but instead it tries to make obscurity and ambiguity do duty for profundity. One is never quite sure what's going on, and neither is Bertolucci. Some wholly gratuitous nudity. O (PG) AA

Trail of the Pink Panther (1982) Collection of outtakes and reprises of earlier movies in the series stitched together with some flat and uninspired new material using the gimmick of a TV reporter trying to find out what Inspector Clouseau was really like. It's a poor excuse for a movie, though if writer-director Blake Edwards only intended to show how much the late Peter Sellers is missed, he has succeeded admirably. Brief nudity; some sexually oriented humor. A-III (PG) A

Train, The (1965) Resistance leader (Burt Lancaster) tries to stop a Nazi colonel (Paul Scofield) from taking a train loaded with French art treasures into Germany during the last days of the Occupation. Directed by John Frankenheimer, the overlong story has some exciting action with spectacular train wrecks and a monumental scheme of deception, yet never probes whether works of art are worth more than human lives. Much tension and stylized violence. A-I (br) PG

Train Robbers, The (1973) Good western about a poor widow (Ann-Margret) who gets a tough hombre (John Wayne) and a couple of his pals (Ben Johnson; Rod Taylor) to go to Mexico to retrieve a fortune in stolen gold and bring it back past hordes of outlaws. Along the way there's plenty of entertaining action, slowed only by a few too many reflections on the old days. Director Burt Kennedy's witty dialogue and light touch keep this melodramatic tale moving at a fast and breezy clip. A-II (PG) U

Traitor's Gate (1966) Uneven British thriller directed by Freddie Francis about an attempt to steal the crown jewels from the Tower of London has a complicated plot with some violence and a restrained striptease scene. A-II (br) A

Traitors, The (1974) Argentinian drama parallels corruption of a Peronist union leader who sells out the workers with the growth of a revolutionary group determined to destroy him and the ruling class he has come to represent. Fictional story easily encompasses the realities of the country's social, economic and political history. Viewers may find it a helpful introduction to the complexities of Latin American political developments. A-III (nr) U

Tramplers, The (1966) Leaden-paced Italian western ineptly directed by Albert Band about a family feud that ultimately drives the father (Joseph Cotten) insane. Stylized violence. A-II (br)

Trans-Europ-Express (1968) Convoluted French movie-within-a-movie directed by Alain Robbe-Grillet about a drug smuggler (Jean-Louis Trintignant) and a prostitute (Marie-France Pisier) for whom he entertains sadistic as well as amorous feelings. Excessive in its treatment of sexual themes. O (br)

Transylvania 6-5000 (1985) Two bumbling reporters (Jeff Goldblum and Ed Begley Jr.) for a tabloid magazine get hot on the trail of the Frankenstein monster and some of his friends. Director Rudy DeLuca works hard but there are few laughs, even for viewers in a very silly mood. Some mild sexually oriented jokes. A-II (PG)

Trash (1970) Apt title for director Andy Warhol's listless story of a heroin addict (Joe Dallesandro) whose habit has rendered him listless and impotent while his transvestite lover (Holly Woodlawn) has a passion for scrounging in garbage heaps. Total nudity, graphic drug use and gutter language. O (nr)

Traveling Executioner, The (1970) Clunker about an itinerant with an electric chair (Stacy Keach) who makes the rounds of southern prisons in the 1920s until a beautiful murderess (Mariana Hill) seduces him into helping her escape, the plan misfires and he winds up being strapped into his device. Directed by Jack Smight, the unfunny black comedy suffers from Keach's grotesque performance and an excess of sexual scenes and references. O (R) X

Travels with My Aunt (1972) Primly proper British accountant (Alec McCowen) is suddenly whisked off to Paris by his wildly eccentric aunt (Maggie Smith) and finds himself an accessory to drug smuggling and other illegal activities, which he comes to find exhilarating. Smith is badly miscast, and director George Cukor is given to mounting grandiose but leaden set pieces that turn Graham Greene's light comedy into a heavy fantasy that will strike some as vulgar farce. A-IV (PG) AA

T. R. Baskin (1971) Bright, ambitious woman from a small Ohio town (Candice Bergen) has a hard time adjusting to life in Chicago, especially creepy blind dates and swinging singles places. Among the men who disappoint her is a children's book editor (James Caan). By movie's end, the audience will have lost interest in all the contrived nonsense that director Herbert Ross puts his confused heroine through. A-III (GP)

Treasure Island (1934) The classic Hollywood version of the Robert Louis Stevenson adventure saga, with Wallace Berry outstanding as Long John Silver and Jackie Cooper as the stout-hearted Jim Hawkins. Directed by Victor Fleming, it is still enjoyable family fare, though youngsters may be disappointed by its black-and-white photography. A-I (br) U

Treasure Island (1950) Disney version of Stevenson's classic stars Robert Newton as a scenery-chewing Long John Silver, with little Bobby Driscoll as a suitably serious Jim Hawkins. Directed by Byron Haskin, the adventure gets fairly intense at times but the kids will love it. A-I (G)

Treasure Island (1972) Disappointing British screen version of the R. L. Stevenson classic, with Orson Welles garbling the role of Long John Silver. Director John Hough takes a rather uninspired literal approach to the high adventure of the novel, the characters are but cardboard caricatures and the cast simply read their lines against the pretty Spanish coast. Nonetheless, the little ones will still enjoy this classic tale of buried treasure. A-I (G) U

Treasure of Matecumbe (1976) Routine Walt Disney adventure about two boys (Johnny Doran; Billy Attmore) and some buried treasure in the exotic Florida Keys.

Directed by Vincent McEveety, the search goes on a bit too long, but younger viewers should enjoy the locale and the Huck Finn hijinks. A-I (G) U

Treasure of San Gennaro, The (1968) Italian heist spoof in which two American gangsters (Harry Guardino and Senta Berger) come to Naples to rob its cathedral of a fortune in jewels and enlist the help of a good-hearted, somewhat dim local crook (Nino Manfredi). During the course of the thoroughly wacky, bungled theft, director Dino Risi builds a consistently amusing, often hilarious satiric comedy on Neapolitan manners and mores. A-II (br)

Treasure of the Four Crowns, The (1983) Dreadful Spanish-made 3-D movie about a Mission Impossible attempt, led by Tony Anthony, to recover some crowns having mystical powers from the hands of the villainous head of a cult. Directed by Fernando Baldi with the emphasis upon things whizzing out at the viewer and murkily photographed, it achieves intense boredom and eyestrain. Some violence. A-II (PG)

Treasure of the Sierra Madre, The (1948) A trio of down-on-their-luck Americans in Mexico (Humphrey Bogart; Walter Huston; Tim Holt) pool their stakes to prospect for gold in the mountainous backcountry, stumble upon a rich vein of ore and then face dissension over dividing their sudden wealth and getting it past a local band of murderous cutthroats. Director John Huston's suspenseful adventure tale features standout performances by his father Walter as a happy-go-lucky veteran prospector and Bogart as a penny-ante drifter driven over the edge by greed. Some intense menace. A-II (br) PG

Tree Grows in Brooklyn, A (1945) Solid adaptation of Betty Smith's novel about a young girl (Peggy Ann Garner) growing up in a working-class Brooklyn neighborhood around 1900. Under Elia Kazan's sensitive direction, the movie chronicles her troubled family's hand-to-mouth existence, with father (James Dunn) mostly unemployed and often inebriated, mother (Dorothy McGuire) holding the household together and the kids experiencing the various pains and joys of being young during hard times. Warmly evocative picture of family life, though a bit heavy for youngsters. A-II (br) A

Tree of Wooden Clogs, The (1979) Quiet, richly textured Italian drama about the lives of four peasant families who work as tenant farmers on a Lombardy estate at the end of the last century. Beginning with the fall harvest and ending with the spring planting, the movie depicts the everyday life of rural people who endure with human dignity in spite of the oppressive system that exploits their labor. Written, photographed and directed by Ermanno Olmi, this is a loving portrait of ordinary life in an age of social injustice. Some tense scenes. A-II (nr) A

Tremors (1990) When some huge, reptilian underground monsters suddenly begin gobbling up the locals in and around a desolate Nevada desert town, two losers (Kevin Bacon; Fred Ward) helm a monster-bashing survival team. Director Ron Underwood splatters a lot of comic-book gore in this send-up of 1950s' sci-fi flicks, which might have been innocuous fun if it hadn't also been strewn with locker-room language. A-III (PG-13) 15

Trenchcoat (1983) Poor Disney comedy about a would-be mystery story writer (Margot Kidder) who runs into all sorts of nasty people during a vacation on Malta. The script is matched in ineptness only by the direction of Michael Tuchner, which underscores everything that would have been better passed over as quickly as possible. Some moderate violence and a few mild vulgarities. A-II (PG)

Trespass (1992) Senseless thriller about two white firemen (Bill Paxton and William Sadler) searching for stolen loot in a long-abandoned factory where they are trapped after being discovered witnessing a brutal slaying by a gang of black drug dealers (headed by Ice-T). Directed by Walter Hill, the situation grows increasingly preposterous as the graphic violence escalates until it exhausts itself in a cheap, throwaway ending. Excessive violence and incessant rough language. O (R) 18

Trial, The (1993) Slack British adaptation of the Franz Kafka novel about Josef K. (Kyle MacLachlan), a bank official in Prague making various futile attempts to defend himself from charges of a crime that is never specified. Director David Jones can't blend the surreal aspects of the labyrinthine narrative with the sparkling setting of turn-of-the-century Prague, though some of the minor roles are effective, especially Anthony Hopkins as the austere prison chaplain and Jason Robards as an aged, roguish lawyer. Some fairly restrained sex scenes. A-III (nr) 12

Trial of Billy Jack, The (1974) Using the same mixture of violence and simpleminded idealism that marked the original "Billy Jack," co-writer-director-star Tom Laughlin's sequel offers as an alternative to contemporary injustices only a shallow romanticism that has little relevance to the real world. A-IV (PG)

Trial of Joan of Arc, The (1965) Based on the actual trial transcript, the courtroom conflict between the Maid of Orleans and her judges is presented objectively with impersonal camerawork that builds in stark intensity to the catharsis of the inevitable burning at the stake. Director Robert Bresson's 1962 French production succeeds in making an overly familiar story freshly interesting, partly through the use of nonprofessional actors who give the impression of actually undergoing the trial process and not just playing at it. Subtitles. Heavy-going for children. A-I (br)

Trial of the Catonsville Nine, The (1972) Screen version of Rev. Daniel Berrigan's play about the 1968 trial of nine Vietnam War protestors who readily admitted burning draft records in Catonsville, Md., using the trial as a forum to argue against the war's morality. Handsomely photographed by Haskell Wexler, the movie employs the same cast and director (Gordon Davidson) as the stage version. Producer Gregory Peck deserves credit for preserving on film this particular aspect of the peace movement. A-II (PG)

Tribute (1980) Screen version of the Bernard Slade play about a lecherous, incorrigibly nonserious but lovable press agent (Jack Lemmon) who, knowing he has but a short time to live, tries to make peace with his priggish son (Robby Benson) and remarried ex-wife (Lee Remick). Directed by Bob Clark, it is civilized entertainment but not nearly as moving or funny as it was meant to be. Brief nudity and some rough language. A-III (PG) AA

Tribute to a Bad Man (1956) Dark, brooding western about a pioneer rancher (James Cagney) who rules the range with an iron hand until his hard heart is softened by an eastern tenderfoot (Don Dubbins) and a strong woman (Irene Pappas). Directed by Robert Wise, the flawed plot is of less interest than the character study of a man who comes to realize that people mean more than possessions. Stylized violence and implied live-in relationship. A-II (br) A

Trick Baby (1972) Gritty street movie about two Philadelphia con artists, one of whom is black (Mel Stewart) while the other (Kiel Martin) insists he was born black and only looks white. Together they are truly democratic in hustling everyone, regardless of race. Director Larry Yust makes an entertaining game of watching them keep one step ahead of the cops and the avenging mob, though its genial air of amorality, some nudity and rough language limit its audience considerably. A-IV (R)

Trilogy (1969) Theatrical adaptation of three television plays written by Truman Capote and directed by Frank Perry consists of "Miriam" about a retired nurse (Mildred Natwick); "Among the Paths to Eden" about an aging spinster (Maureen Stapleton); and

"A Christmas Memory" about the elderly relative (Geraldine Page) of an orphaned boy (narrated by Capote). Creatively made and beautifully acted, the work reaffirms the delight to be found in ordinary lives and people when they are observed by a humane sensibility. Some intense scenes. A-II (G)

Trinity Is Still My Name (1972) Terence Hill repeats his role as the vagabond outlaw Trinity, as does Bud Spencer as his ornery, hulking brother. Director E. B. Clucher plays everything for laughs and the hijinks are refreshingly in good-humor. The fun is constant, no one gets killed and there's not even a shot fired. A few risque lines will zoom right over the heads of youngsters. A-II (G)

Trip, The (1967) Director Roger Corman's movie about the psychedelic experiences of LSD presents a one-sided, excitement-ladened view of the drug's effects. The result serves not to enlighten, but to expose impressionable viewers to the temptation of dangerous experimentation. Exploitative use of sexual imagery. O (br)

Trip to Bountiful, The (1986) Geraldine Page gives a memorable performance as a feisty old woman who can't stand living with her daughter-in-law and, when her son refuses to take her, sets off by herself to see her home town of Bountiful, Texas. On this journey to a place that is now a ghost town, the viewer comes to respect the indomitable spirit of a strong personality who refuses to give up in spite of waning physical strength. John Masterson directs Horton Foote's story with dignity and compassion, though some of the old woman's difficulties might be upsetting to the very young. A-II (PG)

Triple Cross (1967) Lengthy, fact-based World War II espionage movie is a vehicle for Christopher Plummer as Eddie Chapman, a safecracker and opportunist who worked both sides of the Channel as double-agent for Germany and England. Director Terence Young's complicated plot tries too hard for effects that seem more often cynical than ironic. Restrained bedroom scenes. A-III (br) A

Triple Echo (1973) Fetid British drama about a woman (Glenda Jackson) whose husband is in a World War II POW camp and an Army deserter (Brian Deacon) whom she dresses up as a woman and passes off as her sister until a lecherous army sergeant (Oliver Reed) discovers the deception. Director Michael Apted's talented cast tries so hard to make this credible but can't overcome an overwhelming sense of disbelief. It all seems a rather pointless exercise in the by-ways of sexual ambivalence and self-identity. O (R) X

Tristana (1970) Spanish film about an innocent young woman (Catherine Deneuve)

who, after being seduced by her guardian (Fernando Rey), runs away with a painter only to return to torment her former guardian in his old age. Surrealist director Luis Bunuel is in top form in this story of ironic role reversal that rests on such themes as middle-class materialism, anti-clericalism, human deformity and the dead hand of convention. Bunuel is a moralist rather than a realist and his sense of evil and dark humor are not for casual viewers. A-III (GP)

Triumph of Hercules, The (1964) Dubbed Italian production directed by Alberto De Martino has the muscle-bound hero (Dan Vadis) save the kingdom of Mycenae from a witch's son and her magic men of gold. Pulp timewaster with comic-book violence. A-III (br)

Triumph of the Spirit (1989) Grim, unrelenting Holocaust drama, set almost entirely within the Auschwitz death camp where it was filmed, re-creates the fact-based story of a Greek Jew and champion boxer, Salamo Arouch (Willem Dafoe), whose survival hinged on his ability to win some 200 fights held to entertain the SS guards. Realistically directed by Robert M. Young, the fine cast includes Wendy Gazelle as Salamo's girlfriend and Edward James Olmos as a gypsy inmate. Some particularly grisly concentration camp scenes of torture, murder and degradation. A-III (R) 15

Trog (1970) Low-budget British monster movie in which the head of a research laboratory (Joan Crawford) subdues, studies, and educates a rather ludicrous apeman that is eventually killed by the local townspeople because of fear and superstition. Director Freddie Francis treats the story as a serious, if heavy-handed, plea for human understanding, but the result is only slow and melodramatic entertainment. A-II (GP) AA

Trojan Women, The (1971) Directed by Michael Cacoyannis, this adaptation of Euripides tragedy about the shattering effect of war on society is faithful to the original and frequently flamboyant. In spite of the stately acting of Katharine Hepburn as Hecuba, the Trojan queen, and Irene Papas as Helen, the cause of the war, the result is of more interest to the student of ancient Greek drama than the casual moviegoer. A-III (GP) U

Troma's War (1988) Sleazy exploitation movie about the perils facing a band of ditzy tourists when their plane crash lands on a Caribbean island infested with terrorists out to overthrow the United States. Directed by Michael Herz and Samuel Weil, this truly awful parody of the "Airport" genre profanes everything from motherhood to religion and AIDS. Wall-to-wall

oozing gore and slice 'n' dice violence as well as sexual and bathroom vulgarities. O (R)

Tron (1982) Disney high-tech sci-fi adventure in which three heroes (Jeff Bridges, Cindy Morgan and Bruce Boxleitner), on the trail of a greedy villain (David Warner), get caught in the workings of a computerized video game. Fortunately, director Steven Lisberger has treated the material with a certain amount of humor, but how much you enjoy it depends upon your enthusiasm for the special effects, which are the movie's reason for being. Some violence and also the clear implication that the heroine has gone to bed with both of her heroic companions. A-III (PG) A

Troop Beverly Hills (1989) Faced with a pending divorce and an empty life of shopping and party-going, a Beverly Hills matron (Shelley Long) decides to dedicate her time to her daughter's floundering Wilderness Girls troop. This lightweight satire of materialism works mainly because of Long's spunky performance and Jeff Kanew's spirited direction. Fleeting rough language and minimal sexual innuendo. A-II (PG)

Tropic of Cancer (1970) Screen version of Henry Miller's long-banned autobiographical novel about an impoverished expatriate writer (Rip Torn) and his chiefly sexual exploits in the Paris of the early 1930s. Directed by Joseph Strick, the movie's most serious failure is not its shallow characterization of the writer, nor its crude images and cruder language, but its overall disregard of women as no more than sex objects. O (X)

Tropical Ecstasy (1970) The theme of the prostitute redeemed by love provides a flimsy excuse for Argentina's Isabel Sarli to spend half the movie stripping and sitting in the shallow surf with a poor fisherman, played by Armando Bo, her real-life husband, who also wrote, produced and directed this paltry exercise in exploitation. O (nr)

Trouble in Mind (1986) Unlikable crime melodrama directed by Alan Rudolph about a cynical ex-cop (Kris Kristofferson) who tries to help a young punk in trouble (Keith Carradine) but gets romantically involved with two women (Genevieve Bujold and Lori Singer). Excessive violence and sex scenes. O (R)

Trouble Man (1972) Slick black action movie about a supertough, supercool dude (Robert Hooks) who is being used by one black gambling ring to wipe out another, but when he catches on they all go down in a series of shootouts. Directed by Ivan Dixon, its violent action and constant rough language, despite coy restraint in several sex scenes, is for undemanding but hardy adults. A-III (R)

Trouble with Angels, The (1966) Episodic screen version of Jane Trahey's comic recollections of life in a Catholic girls' boarding school revolves around the finely balanced battle of wit and will between the girls and the nuns. Rosalind Russell is in top form as the mother superior who squelches the adolescent mischief concocted by Hayley Mills and June Harding. Save for a few mawkish scenes, director Ida Lupino has made the sentimental comedy seem amusingly fresh and enjoyable. A-I (br)

Trouble with Girls, The (1969) The Chautauqua show, a bit of Americana that was part carnival, part educational forum, serves as a the background for an Elvis Presley movie set in the 1920s. Peter Tewksbury has not helped matters much by directing the picture as if it were all high camp, and the plot bogs down in some heavy dramatics about a local murder, but on the whole, it's a relaxed venture into nostalgia. A-III (G) U

Truck Turner (1974) Los Angeles tracker of bail-jumpers (Isaac Hayes) is kept busy looking for pimps, prostitutes, dope dealers and other low types while trying to keep his feisty girlfriend (Annazette Chase) out of prison. Director Jonathan Kaplan's work is so relentlessly awful, in terms of both quality and its view of humanity, that its excessive violence is almost beside the point. O (R)

True Believer (1989) Formerly idealistic lawyer (James Woods) who now makes easy money defending drug dealers takes the case of a young Korean (Yuji Okumoto) unjustly incarcerated for a Chinatown murder, thereby restoring the lawyer's waning self-respect and integrity. An intriguing premise, a flamboyant performance by Woods and classy direction by Joseph Ruben often make this courtroom thriller quite diverting. Some grisly violence, intense menace and rough language. A-III (R)

True Colors (1991) Ambition threatens the friendship of two law students (John Cusack and James Spader) when one steals the other's girlfriend (Imogen Stubbs) to further his political ambitions by working for her father (Richard Widmark), a powerful Senator. Director Herbert Ross gets some sharp performances in an engrossing, if overbaked, tale of greed, betrayal and revenge. Restrained premarital encounters, intermittent rough language and minimal violence. A-III (R)

True Confessions (1981) Uneven screen version of John Gregory Dunne's novel about troubled brothers in late-1940s' Los Angeles, the one (Robert De Niro) being a monsignor adept at political infighting and the other (Robert Duvall) a tough police sergeant intent on solving the murder of a prostitute. Director Ulu Grosbard uses the crime as the core of this interesting but

only moderately effective melodrama intertwining religion, politics and crime. Because of its relentless concentration upon the seamy side of things (brothels, morgues and a pornographic film), some adults may find it unsuitable entertainment. A-IV (R) 15

True Grit (1969) Rousing western adventure based on the Charles Portis novel about a justice-minded little gal with true grit (Kim Darby) who tracks down her father's killer with the aid of a gruff overweight U.S. Marshall (John Wayne) and an overeager Texas Ranger (Glenn Campbell). Directed with gusto by Henry Hathaway, their adventures and scrapes with death are furious and action-packed, though leavened nicely with human touches and good humor. Because of some stylized violence, young children may need the support of older members of the family. A-I (G) U

True Identity (1991) A young black actor (Lenny Henry) disguises himself as a white man to keep from being killed after accidentally learning the secret identity of a mob kingpin (Frank Langella). Director Charles Lane gets some mileage out of this mildly diverting combination of gangland spoof and racial farce but it's more a showcase for Henry with its one-joke premise stretched to the breaking point. Comic violence, implied promiscuity and intermittent rough language. A-III (R) 15

True Love (1989) Low-budget independent comedy charting the rocky road to marital bliss taken by a young, Italian-American Bronx couple (Annabella Sciorra and Ron Eldard) whose well-meaning family and friends as well as their own naivete play havoc with their upcoming nuptials. Directed by Nancy Savoca, the result is true-to-life, consistently fresh and lightly satirical without being judgmental. Much profanity laced with sexual vulgarities and implied premarital sex. A-III (R) 15

True Romance (1993) Brutally violent tale of a call-girl bride (Patricia Arquette) and her reckless groom (Christian Slater) on the run from police and gangsters while trying to peddle a suitcase full of cocaine stolen from the woman's murdered pimp. Director Tony Scott fills the screen with recurring scenes of graphic gore and mayhem in a story conveying the abhorrent message that murder is "cool" and crime pays handsomely. Excessive violence, a bedroom scene with nudity, recreational drug use, many racial slurs and constant rough language. O (R) 18

True Stories (1986) Director David Byrne presents a sociological vision of arcane Americana in this whimsical movie about the style, spirit and substance of small-town life in the Southwest. With Byrne himself serving as a somewhat sardonic on-screen commentator, the movie offers a series of documentary vignettes of more or less ordinary town activities. Driven by an eclectic musical score, the result is a wholesome and innocent post-modern version of "Our Town." A-II (PG)

Truly, Madly, Deeply (1991) An Englishwoman (Juliet Stevenson) is emotionally paralysed long after the sudden death of her lover (Alan Rickman) until his ghost materializes, thereby enabling her to end their relationship and open herself to new possibilities. Anthony Minghella wrote and directed this gentle, rather mawkish romance, enlivened by its eccentric humor and sensitive performances. Discreet treatment of sexual relationships. A-III (PG)

Trust (1991) Mean-spirited attempt at black comedy in which a pregnant teenager considering abortion (Adrienne Shelly) brings home a volatile stranger (Martin Donovan) but her mother (Merritt Nelson) and sister (Edie Falco) react with extreme treachery. Writer-director Hal Hartley presents a vicious vision of middle-class family life with no insights but plenty of nasty role models. Casual attitude toward abortion, poisonous parental figures, minor violence and intermittent rough language. O (R) 15

Truth About Spring, The (1965) Despite different social backgrounds, an adolescent tomboy (Hayley Mills) and a young Harvard graduate (James MacArthur) find romance while searching the Caribbean for sunken pirate treasure. Directed by Richard Thorpe, the comedy adventure is set aboard a sailing ship whose captain (John Mills) and rascally crew (Lionel Jeffries, Harry Andrews and Niall MacGinnis) abet the growing friendship between the charming young couple. Gentle, old-fashioned entertainment. A-I (br) U

Trygon Factor, The (1968) Muddled British mystery directed by Cyril Frankel in which a Scotland Yard inspector (Stewart Granger) traces a series of unsolved robberies to a bogus order of nuns. Violence. A-III (br) 15

Tsar to Lenin (1971) Documentary on the Russian Revolution presents rare footage of the royal family, the Bolshevik leaders, the complicated events of the February and October revolutions and the subsequent terrors of the Civil War. Valuable as this footage is, the movie is relatively unsophisticated in the use it makes of it. A-I (nr)

Tucker: The Man and His Dream (1988) Dramatized portrait of the maverick (Jeff Bridges) whose innovative automobile designs challenged the lackluster product of Detroit's car industry after World War II. Director Francis Coppola has a hard time

blending the documentary and dramatic aspects of his scenario and ends up portraying his subject in mostly one-dimensional terms, with moral issues (good guys vs. bad guys) treated in similar black-and-white fashion as well. Mild rough language. A-II (PG)

Tuff Turf (1985) WASP golden boy finds himself at inner-city high school and makes things even tougher for himself by going after the girlfriend of a gang leader. Mindless youth exploitation movie directed by Fritz Kiersch with a blaring musical score and some scenes of despicable violence. O (R) 18

Tune, The (1992) Fanciful animated story in which a struggling songwriter on his way to the office to meet a deadline gets sidetracked in a surreal world of wacky characters who give him the inspiration for a hit tune. Director Bill Plympton's slyly witty tale boasts a distinctive visual style and 10 whimsical songs, but its helter-skelter procession of events seems padded to accommodate a feature-length running time. Some cartoon violence. A-II (nr)

Tune in Tomorrow . . . (1990) Comedy set in the 1950s about a flamboyant writer of radio soap operas (Peter Falk) who manipulates a romance between a novice news writer (Keanu Reeves) and his 35-year-old aunt by marriage (Barbara Hershey) as grist for his sudsy scripts. Director Jon Amiel orchestrates an offbeat but overproduced comic fantasy that is enlivened by Falk and Hershey's feisty performances, great period costumes and vibrant New Orleans setting. Some make-believe violence, mild sexual innuendo and minimal rough language. A-III (PG-13)

Tunnelvision (1976) Sick satire about television programming of the future features Howard Hesseman, Betty Thomas, Chevy Chase and Larraine Newman. Directed by Neal Israel and Brad Swirnoff, it offers a series of degrading, detestable and altogether unfunny vignettes. O (R)

Turk 182 (1985) In rescuing a little girl from a burning building, an off-duty New York fireman (Robert Urich) is badly injured. When he's refused compensation, his young brother (Timothy Hutton) embarks on a campaign for justice by embarrassing the mayor with graffiti signed "Turk 182," his injured brother's nickname and badge number. A crude, noisy movie directed by Bob Clark with pretensions to folk epic grandeur. Sexual promiscuity. O (PG-13) 15

Turner & Hooch (1989) Diverting man-and-beast comedy about a small-town cop (Tom Hanks) who takes in the nasty, drooling watchdog of a murder victim (John McIntire), becomes fond of the overgrown pet and the mismatched duo end up solving the murder. Scenes pairing the ugly dog with handsome Hanks are amusing and the pooch enables the cop to fall in love with the local veterinarian (Mare Winningham). Director Roger Spottiswoode manages to make the lightweight tale entertaining and somewhat affecting. Brief but intense violence, an implied sexual encounter and minimal locker-room language. A-III (PG)

Turning Point, The (1977) Shirley MacLaine and Anne Bancroft star as one-time rival ballerinas who renew their feud when MacLaine's daughter (Leslie Browne) joins Bancroft's troupe. Directed by Herbert Ross, the old-fashioned sentimental melodrama is set against the glamorous world of ballet, with plenty of grand dance sequences. Brief nudity and a benign attitude toward illicit sex. A-III (PG)

Turtle Diary (1986) Adaptation of playwright Harold Pinter's story of an author (Glenda Jackson) and a bookseller (Ben Kingsley) who are brought together by their mutual aspiration to free three sea turtles from the London aquarium. Director John Irvin's delicate, contemplative narrative is a testament to gentle souls who set simple goals and celebrate small, private victories. Brief but intense scene of violence. A-II (PG)

Twelve Chairs, The (1970) Uneven comedy set in the Soviet Union of 1927 when a deposed nobleman (Ron Moody) learns that the family jewels were hidden in a confiscated dining room chair, but his search is complicated by a suave con artist (Frank Langella) and a greedy priest (Dom DeLuise). Written and directed by Mel Brooks, the comedy depends upon old-fashioned mugging and slapstick spiked with some modern cynicism but by the end the farce turns to bathos and disappointment. A-III (GP/G appeal)

Twelve Chairs, The (1973) Soviet cinema is not known for its levity or wit and yet both are in evidence in this large-scale extravaganza in the picturesque adventures of a grasping ex-aristocrat (A. Gomiashvili) and a conniving proletarian (S. Filippov) who are forced to work together in searching for a fortune hidden in a chair seized during the Revolution. Directed by Leonid Gaidai, it is a good-humored and often hilarious picture of the flaws and strengths that made up life in the Soviet Union of the 1920s and the ending has considerably more bite than the boisterous 1970 Mel Brooks version. A-II (nr) U

25th Hour, The (1967) Well-intentioned European co-production showing how senseless coincidences and petty officials separate a Romanian peasant (Anthony Quinn) from his wife (Virna Lisi) during World War II. Their ultimate reunion as a beaten family of displaced persons demonstrates the devastating effects of war on the innocent. Director Henri Verneuil has a worthy theme, but the plot contrivances are thin and the production is flat and plodding. A-II (br)

24-Hour Lover (1970) Heavy-handed German sex farce about a young wine salesman who dallies on his daily round of kitchens and parlors, until ultimately collapsing from sheer exhaustion. The movie just repeats one long tired joke without wit or style. O (R)

24 Hours of the Rebel (1977) Mediocre story about the effect the news of actor James Dean's death has upon a group of college students in a small Arkansas town who seem to find movies more real than their own lives. Written and directed by James Bridges, the movie fails to build much sympathy for its two principal characters (Richard Thomas and Deborah Benson) or explain why they are drawn so compulsively to Dean's screen persona. Several scenes of youthful sexual explorations and vulgar language. A-III (PG)

29th Street (1991) The fractious relationship between a shiftless but uncommonly lucky young man (Anthony LaPaglia) and his debt-ridden father (Danny Aiello) reaches crisis level when the son becomes a $6 million lottery finalist. Writer-director George Gallo turns in a shrill comedy that affirms family ties with stereotypical characters and sledgehammer humor. Benign depiction of car insurance fraud and much rough language. A-III (R)

Twenty-One (1991) Trashy comedy in which a smugly promiscuous 21-year-old swinger (Patsy Kensit) recounts her meaningless sexual adventures in London before heading to New York for more of the same. Co-writer-director Don Boyd presents only crass, self-involved characters in a tasteless and repelling movie not worth 21 seconds' viewing. Positive attitude toward promiscuity, several bedroom scenes with brief nudity, shots of drug mainlining and much rough language. O (R) 15

20,000 Leagues Under the Sea (1954) Marvelous Disney version of the classic Jules Verne sea yarn about a terrifying, red-eyed monster sinking whalers and other 19th-century vessels, a survivor of which (Kirk Douglas) is taken aboard the submarine "Nautilus" by the nefarious Captain Nemo (James Mason) who wants to rule the high seas. Others aboard are a marine scientist (Paul Lukas) and his droll assistant (Peter Lorre). Directed by Richard Fleischer, the story is great fun for all ages and the special effects are really special. A-I (G) U

Twice in a Lifetime (1985) This is a big, glossy valentine to adultery in which a 50-year old steelworker (Gene Hackman) falls in love with a barmaid (Ann-Margret) and leaves his wife (Ellen Burstyn) and children. Directed by Bud Yorkin, the movie lacks authentic characters and motivation, relying instead upon a dense sentimental smokescreen in its attempts to justify the husband's wholly selfish actions. O (R) 15

Twice-Told Tales (1963) Vincent Price stars in Nathaniel Hawthorne stories of love beyond the grave ("Dr. Heidigger's Experiment"), a father's obsessive protectiveness ("Rappaccini's Daughter") and a Puritan family curse ("The House of the Seven Gables"). Directed by Sidney Salkow, the adaptations are largely flat and unimaginative, though the last evokes something of the eerie atmosphere intended by Hawthorne. Stylized violence and romantic complications. A-II (br)

Twilight People (1972) The title refers to the gruesome results of a mad doctor (Charles Macaulay) in trying to create a new breed of humans but his experiments have yielded only a bat man, a panther woman, a wolf girl and assorted other odd hybrids. Low-budget Philippine production directed by Eddie Romero, the childish story goes from the utterly unbelievable to the ludicrous, but its violent conclusion is not for the youngsters. A-III (PG)

Twilight Zone—The Movie (1983) Anthology movie, inspired by the popular 1960s television series, is made up of five separate episodes by four different directors, and only the one about an airline passenger (John Lithgow) who spots an odd-looking creature sitting on the wing, rises above mediocrity. Some frightening effects here and in three of the other four segments make it inappropriate fare for younger viewers. A-II (PG) 15

Twilight's Last Gleaming (1977) Burt Lancaster plays a cashiered Air Force general who seizes control of a nuclear missile launching site in an attempt to alter government policies. director Robert Aldrich, not known for his subtlety, has made an extremely clumsy, if well-intentioned movie, whose ham-handed approach to a complex moral issue, as well as its extreme, if sporadic, violence and rough language make it questionable fare at best. O (R) AA

Twin Peaks: Fire Walk with Me (1992) The characters from the "Twin Peaks" TV series appear in a big-screen clunker about events leading up to the murder of promiscuous, drug-addicted teenager Laura Palmer (Sheryl Lee). Director David Lynch's sleazy, self-indulgent horror show goes nowhere slowly, spending an endless 134 minutes revealing nothing of interest beyond Ms. Lee's inability to act. Numerous perverse sexual situations, some of them violent, several bloody murders, frequent drug and alcohol abuse, recurring nudity and rough language. O (R) 18

Twinkle, Twinkle, Killer Kane (see: "The Ninth Configuration").

Twins (1988) Often hilarious tale of twin brothers separated at birth but reunited 35 years later after the big guy (Arnold Schwarzenegger) has been raised to be sound of mind and body on a South Pacific island while the little guy (Danny DeVito) grew up in an orphanage where he began his sleazy life of petty crime and womanizing. Though sluggishly directed by Ivan Reitman, the two actors manage to carry this tale of mismatched twins who learn to love and trust one another so that, in the end, goodness, family and marriage triumph over greed, gluttony and sexual promiscuity. Some violent cartoon fisticuffs and graphic rub-outs mostly played for laughs as well as some locker-room language and promiscuous behavior. A-III (PG)

Twins of Evil (1972) British horror movie about a 17th-century witch-hunter (Peter Cushing) whose voluptuous twin nieces catch the eye of a depraved devil worshiper (Damien Thomas). Soon one of them is drawn into his evil sphere, but Cushing is unable to tell which is the witch. Directed by John Hough, it's an exercise in pumped-up suspense with more than usual reliance on graphic gore, nudity and a spot of kinky eroticism. O (R) 18

Twist of Sand, A (1968) Returning to the African coast where years before he had sunk a Nazi sub and massacred its crew, a British sea captain (Richard Johnson) and his partners (Jeremy Kemp; Honor Blackman) retrieve a fortune in diamonds but one of them wants it all. Directed by Don Chaffey, the crime caper has plenty of atmosphere but suffers from a hokey plot and an overly contrived ending. Much menace and some nasty violence. A-II (br) U

Twist and Shout (1986) Danish import about two teenagers experiencing the pains of growing up in the 1960s without any parental guidance to help them cope with their adolescent sexual desires and the tragic consequences that result. Nudity, sexual encounters and graphic depiction of abortion. O (R)

Twisted Nerve (1969) British psychological thriller about an unstable young man (Hywel Bennett) who gradually loses control of his faculties and becomes a homicidal maniac. Directed by Roy Boulting, the plot tries to integrate the effects of heredity and environment upon the youth, but the sexual nature of the problems touched upon in the course of the movie make it adult fare. A-III (PG) X

Twisted Obsession (1990) American screenwriter (Jeff Goldblum) living in Paris is lured into a web of deceit and infidelity by the teenage sister (Liza Walker) of the director (Dexter Fletcher) with whom he is working. Filmed in dark, murky fashion by director Fernando Trueba, the minimal plot serves little purpose but to exploit the innocent appeal of a young actress depicted as an experienced sexual manipulator. Exploitative use of nudity, some restrained scenes of sexual activity and occasional rough language. O (R)

Twitch of the Death Nerve, The (1973) Sadistic Italian terror movie directed by Mario Bava starts with the strangling of a crippled countess and from there goes to nonstop slaughter of her husband, offspring, hirelings and neighbors. The horror is the sickening way in which the murders are perpetrated. Repugnant violence. O (R)

Two (1969) Danish exploitation sequel to "I, a Woman" makes no pretense at being anything but a cold exercise in senseless promiscuity, almost mechanical in its frequent exposure of Gio Petre's body. Director Mac Ahlberg adds insult to injury by tacking on an absurdly insincere moral ending. O (nr)

Two English Girls (1972) Director Francois Truffaut has made the perfect companion movie for his previous "Jules and Jim." The situation this time is neatly reversed, with the man (Jean-Pierre Leaud) in love with two sisters and unable to make a commitment to either. Some viewers will find the situation completely amoral, and often ridiculously romantic. But as a picture of life at the turn-of-the-century, with its very formal etiquette, suppressed emotions and artificial manners, it couldn't be better. A-IV (nr)

Two for the Road (1967) Producer-director Stanley Donen's saga about a modern marriage on wheels that skids dangerously but doesn't quite crack up, teams Audrey Hepburn and Albert Finney as the troubled couple. By following the pair on their various jaunts through Europe, Donen provides both a fluid vehicle for narrative development as well as strikingly scenic backgrounds. A-III (br) PG

Two Gentlemen Sharing (1969) Failed British drama about a white Londoner (Robin Phillips) and an upwardly mobile black from the West Indies (Hal Frederick) who share a London mews apartment, have their separate problems and end with one discovering his homosexuality and the other returning to Jamaica. Director Ted Kotcheff's treatment lacks any subtlety, especially in several love-making scenes. A-III (R) X

200 Motels (1971) Written, produced and directed by Frank Zappa, the title refers to the bleak digs occupied by touring groups such as Zappa's The Mothers of Invention during the course of an average year. It features, however, rough language and a smutty lyric, explained with glee by a pair of semi-nude groupies, as well as a raunchy cartoon sequence depicting the sleazy side of life. O (R) X

Two Jakes, The (1990) Sequel to "Chinatown" (1974) has its L.A. private-eye (Jack Nicholson) haunted by painful memories of a previous case while trying to uncover the real reasons why his client (Harvey Keitel) killed the man having an affair with his wife (Meg Tilly). Also directed by Nicholson, the well-crafted performances and lushly atmospheric setting gets bogged down from the start with too many characters and an overly intricate plot. Sporadic violence, restrained sexual depictions and occasional rough language. A-III (R) 15

Two Men of Karamoja (1974) Documentary account of seven months of conflict and change in Uganda's Kidepo Valley National Park as the British chief warden prepares to turn the preserve over to a native warden. Directed by Natalie and Eugene Jones, the movie examines not only the park's wildlife problems but its native population whose tribal structures are changing with the times. Much of this ethnographic material is best suited for adults and older adolescents. A-III (R/PG appeal)

Two Minute Warning (1976) Gathered in the Los Angeles Coliseum are an assortment of disaster veterans (Charlton Heston, John Cassavetes, Martin Balsam and David Janssen) and 100,000 extras; when a sniper is spotted, the police move in and the arena is turned into a Roman forum of bloodshed and graphic violence. Directed by Larry Peerce the mindless fantasy plays on fears and anxieties of random senseless violence in extreme fashion. O (R)

Two Moon Junction (1988) Slick soap opera about a rich southern belle (Sherilyn Fenn) set upon marrying a rich Yuppie (Martin Hewitt), but not before being lustfully distracted by a carnal worker (Richard Tyson). Although artfully photographed, with gorgeous plantation settings and a solid supporting cast (Louise Fletcher; Burl Ives; Kristy McNichol), writer-director Zalman King comes up with nothing more than glorified soft-porn. A sequence of extreme violence; several scenes with frontal nudity; explicit sexual encounters and much locker-room language. O (R) 18

Two Mules for Sister Sara (1970) Prostitute masquerading as a nun (Shirley MacLaine) in order to help Mexican rebels is joined by cowboy loner (Clint Eastwood) in undertaking the capture of a French garrison and they fall in love. Directed by Don Siegel, there are some good action sequences, but the comic irreverences (a supposed nun smoking, drinking and cursing like a trooper), like the movie, are not to be taken seriously. A-III (PG) 15

Two of a Kind (1983) John Travolta and Olivia Newton-John have the misfortune to star in a dreadful movie about God's sending a quartet of angels to earth to try and reform two nasty people. Written and directed by John Herzfield, it is for the most part innocuous, except for some profanity. A-III (PG)

Two of Us, The (1968) Excellent French story of a little Jewish boy (Alain Cohen) who is hidden from the Nazis on a remote farm in Occupied France by an elderly anti-Semite (Michael Simon). Directed by Claude Berri, the movie is a very touching, gentle sort of comedy, told simply through an accumulation of incidents rather than a tightly knit plot. Everyone can identify with and enjoy the warm, human relationship between the old man and the young lad. A-I (br)

Two or Three Things I Know About Her (1970) Director Jean-Luc Godard's paean to Paris (the "Her" of the title) follows the fragmentary story of a part-time prostitute (Marina Vlady), but Raoul Coutar's camera is focused on the ever-changing face of a modern city. Though the movie is heavily laced with philosophical asides and interruptions, it is often amusing, at times illuminating, and always stunningly beautiful in its picture of a great city. A-III (nr)

Two People (1973) Trivial romantic claptrap about a Vietnam deserter (Peter Fonda) and a jaded divorcee (Lindsay Wagner) who meet in Marrakech, talk their way to Casablanca, make love in Paris and finally fly to New York where he is going to turn himself in. Directed by Robert Wise, the budding romance is totally unmotivated and certainly made no more credible by a ridiculously overextended, semi-nude love scene. A-IV (R)

Two Rode Together (1961) On a mission to rescue women and children taken captive by Comanches, an idealistic cavalry officer (Richard Widmark) bickers along the way with a frontier marshal (James Stewart) who's only interested in the reward offered by the captives' families. Director John Ford uses the conflict between familiar western character types to take a darker, less poetic view of the tragic confrontation between the forces of civilization and the waning powers of a less developed native culture. Some stylized violence. A-II (br) PG

2001: A Space Odyssey (1968) Director Stanley Kubrick's epic work, co-written with Arthur C. Clarke, is both science fiction and metaphysical poetry using an unconventional mixture of visuals and music to bridge humanity's reconstructed past, identifiable present and projected future, all tied together by the recurring image of a monolith as symbol of a superhuman existence. The central narrative follows the struggle of two astronauts (Keir Dullea and Gary Lockwood) to wrest control of their spacecraft from HAL, a talking computer (voice of Douglas Rain), on a half-billion-mile trip to Jupiter and the unknown. For young people and imaginative adults but too long, deep and intense for children. A-II (G) A

2010 (1985) Sequel to "2001: A Space Odyssey" in which Roy Scheider leads a joint American-Soviet probe of Jupiter to discover the fate of the spacecraft sent there in the original. Writer-director Peter Hyams overwhelms the story with spectacular special effects, but young people especially should find it an engaging voyage into space. A-I (PG)

2000 Years Later (1969) Weak satire in which an ancient Roman (John Abbott), sent by the god Mercury, fails to warn society of the consequences of its moral corruption. Bert Tenser's low-budget, amateurish production, lacking any moral focus of its own, merely exaggerates and exploits the more obviously decadent elements of the day. O (R)

Two Weeks in September (1967) Failed French romance directed by Serge Bourguignon in which a model (Brigitte Bardot), living with a man in Paris, accepts an assignment in London where she acquires a new lover and then can't decide which one she really wants. suggestive treatment of illicit sex. O (br)

Two-Lane Blacktop (1971) Introspective young man (folk-rock singer James Taylor) who lives on the road in his 1955 Chevy coupe races the owner of a Pontiac G.T.O. (Warren Oates) in a backroads tour across America. Director Monte Hillman's low-key approach does not romanticize his drifters of the road but along the way shows some of the reasons why they have opted out of the mainstream. Some realistic street language, A-III (R) X

Tycoon (1947) Long but intriguing drama in which an American engineer (John Wayne) is hired by a South American aristocrat (Cedric Hardwicke) to build a railroad tunnel through a mountain, then makes an enemy of his powerful employer by wooing his daughter (Lorraine Day). Director Richard Wallace alternates the hard, dangerous work of construction with the cultural differences dividing engineer and employer, not least of which are differing notions of romance and marriage. Some stylized violence and romantic complications. A-II (br) U

U

Ugly American, The (1963) Muddled Cold-War tale set in a Southeast Asian country where the new U.S. Ambassador (Marlon Brando) learns the hard way that nationalism is not the same as communism. Produced and directed by George Englund, the Asian locales are authentic but the plot is more political lecture than human drama and Brando is disappointing as the know-it-all American humbled by events. Stylized violence and political posturing. A-I (br) U

Ugly Dachshund, The (1966) Disney comedy about a Great Dane puppy who gets mixed in with a litter of dachshunds but wins a place with the family of Dean Jones and Suzanne Pleshette. Directed by Norman Tokar, it is for dog lovers and small children. A-I (br) U

Ugly Ones, The (1968) Sordid Italian-Spanish western directed by Eugenio Martin about a bounty hunter (Richard Wyler) on the trail of a depraved Mexican bandit (Tomas Milian). It revels in protracted scenes of violence and brutality. O (R)

UHF (1989) Pop culture satirist "Weird Al" Yankovic stars as a loser with a vivid imagination who takes over as manager of a family-owned TV station and concocts offbeat shows to save it from bankruptcy. Director Jay Levey's slim storyline relies on silly slapstick parodies, though a tasteless animal kingdom show may encourage kids to mishandle pets. Minimal rough language, vulgar antics and nonmenacing cartoon violence played for laughs. A-II (PG-13) PG

Ulysses (1967) Director Joseph Strick's adaptation of the James Joyce classic makes a static movie, but it may be of interest to those who have studied the Irish author's work. Those unfamiliar with the novel are likely not only to find the movie incomprehensible but its verbal treatment of sexual and religious matters to be offensive. A-IV (br) X

Ulzana's Raid (1972) Tracking a band of marauding Apaches is a hardened scout (Burt Lancaster), his Indian sidekick (Jorge Luke) and a greenhorn officer fresh out of West Point (Bruce Davison), unsure of himself and his religious inhibitions about the brutal methods used to hunt and destroy the Indians. On the action level, director Robert Aldrich's western works fairly well, but it raises moral questions of justice and retribution that require more than well-staged fight scenes and good location photography. The violent visuals of frontier savagery borders on the exploitative. A-IV (R) 18

Umbrellas of Cherbourg (1965) Everybody sings instead of talks in this romantic French musical about a brief, ecstatic love affair and the mature reflections of the lovers when they meet years later. With music by Michel Legrand and lyrics by director Jacques Demy, the bittersweet story of heedless youth and the pragmatic demands of maturity are lovely but fragile and not to everyone's taste. Subtitles. Mature theme. A-III (br)

Un Couer en Hiver (1993) French character study of a man (Daniel Auteuil) who perversely steals the affections of a concert violinist (Emmanuelle Beart) with whom his business partner (Andre Dussollier) is in love, then coldly rejects her because he is unable to love anyone, including himself. Director Claude Sautet's strange portrait of an individual untouched by passion is all the more chilling set in the soulful world of music and the emotional lives of musicians, but the result of all this is itself empty of feeling. Subtitles. Discreet treatment of sexual relationships and passing reference to a mercy killing. A-III (nr)

Unbearable Lightness of Being, The (1988) Adapted from a novel about a womanizing brain surgeon (Daniel Day-Lewis) and his relationship with two women in particular—an artistic free spirit (Lena Olin) and his wife (Juliette Binoche)—before, during and after the Russian invasion of Cechoslavakia in 1968. Directed by Philip Kaufman, it is a moving evocation of the period and its effect on the protagonists. The movie's remarkable performances, however, are marred by numerous scenes of graphic nudity and explicit sex. O (R) 18

Unbelievable Truth, The (1990) A rebellious daughter (Adrienne Shelly) is attracted to an ex-con (Robert Burke) who works in her father's garage and is rumored to be a mass murderer. Writer-director Hal Hartley delivers a clumsy drawn-out tale peopled with minimally interesting characters, save for the laconic ex-con who turns out to have more integrity than the respectable citizens around him. Some rough language and references to teen sex. A-III (R) 15

Uncle, The (1966) Warm British movie about the groping, confused efforts of a 7-year-old lad to cope with the mysteries of birth, death and growing up over the course of a summer. Directed by Desmond Davis, the movie is unusual in its realistic depiction of a wholesome childhood set within the context of happy family life. Though about the world of a child, young children may find some of its aspects perplexing. A-II (br) U

Uncle Buck (1989) Limited laughs in a situation comedy involving a cloddish bachelor looking after his brother's three children for a couple of days. Directed by John Hughes, it is little more than a vehicle for John Candy's comic talents as a screen buffoon with a heart of gold. Some sexual situations, double entendres and vulgar language. A-III (PG) 15

Uncle Joe Shannon (1979) Burt Young stars in his own screenplay about a trumpet player who hits the skids after the tragic death of his wife and young son but regains his self-esteem and starts on the road back when he becomes the unofficial guardian of a young boy. Directed by Joseph C. Hanwright, the result is mawkish melodrama chock-full of embarrassingly bad moments. A-II (PG)

Uncle Tom's Cabin (1977) Sincere but woefully inept retelling of the famous Harriet Beecher Stowe classic, unfortunately contains some crass exploitation scenes. Though the main part of the movie was apparently made abroad, the American distributors seem to have clumsily inserted scenes of sex and brutality utterly at variance with the rest of the narrative. O (R)

Uncle Vanya (1972) Brooding Soviet version of Anton Chekhov's play takes place in the claustrophobic rooms of a dilapidated manor where Vanya (Innokenty Smoktunovsky), the estate's caretaker despairs at his wasted life and the local doctor (Sergei Bondarchuk) is the only character who sees the absurd social injustices of his time. Writer-director Andrei Mikhalkov-Konchalovsky evokes the impoverished spirit of pre-revolutionary Russia by alternating scenes of one-tone sepia with those of muted color and the result will affect all who care about the depths of human feelings. A-II (nr)

Uncommon Valor (1983) Wealthy Texas oilman (Robert Stack), whose son is a Vietnam War MIA, hires a Marine colonel (Gene Hackman) to rescue him and his comrades, among them the colonel's own son. Though Joe Gayton's script is fairly literate, director Ted Kotcheff does not do much to lift it above the level of routine action-adventure. Violence; and heroic depiction of native drug dealer who gives his all for the U.S. cause. A-III (R)

Undefeated, The (1969) Post-Civil War story in which a group of Confederate families (led by Rock Hudson) heading for asylum in Mexico under Emperor Maximillian join forces with a former Union officer (John Wayne) bringing a herd of horses south of the border as they fight off Mexican bandits and get embroiled in the Mexican Civil War. Directed by Andrew V. McLaglen, it's an unpretentious, old-fashioned cowboy movie that can be enjoyed by any who likes western action and adventure. A-I (G) PG

Under Fire (1983) American photojournalist (Nick Nolte) covering the Sandinista revolution in Nicaragua loses his sense of detachment at seeing the brutality of the Somoza regime and agrees to fake a story suggested by his lover and fellow journalist (Joanna Cassidy). Directed by Ron Shelton and Clayton Frohman, the powerful and extremely entertaining film conveys the feel of guerrilla warfare, especially in an urban environment, with uncanny force. Violence and rough language. A-III (R) 15

Under Milk Wood (1973) British dramatization of the Dylan Thomas poem-play, with Richard Burton and Ryan Davies as the two narrators who pass through the little Welsh seacoast town of Llareggub and share the lives of its inhabitants with the viewer much as did the Stage Manager in "Our Town." Directed by Andrew Sinclair, its great compression of incidents involving some 60 actors in a fast-paced, impressionistic scenario does not lend itself to casual viewing. Several scenes of unabashed sensuality and earthiness. A-IV (R/PG) AA

Under Siege (1992) Two traitors (Tommy Lee Jones and Gary Busey) hijack the U.S.S. Missouri planning to sell its nuclear arsenal to the highest bidder, unaware that the ship's cook (Steven Seagal) is an ex-Navy SEAL bent on outsmarting them. While director Andrew Davis' action yarn is fairly engrossing, it is fueled by graphic violence treated as heroic and exciting. Excessive violence, a flash of nudity and occasional rough language. O (R)

Under Suspicion (1992) A private-eye (Liam Neeson) suspected of murdering both his wife (Maggie O'Neill) and a client develops an affair with another suspect—the client's mistress (Laura San Giacomo). Writer-director Simon Moore's amoral but engrossing thriller is done in by its cynical treatment of lurid situations. Adulterous and homosexual encounters with recurring nudity, some violence and minimal rough language. O (R) 15

Under the Cherry Moon (1986) Rock star Prince and his comic sidekick Jerome Benton try to resurrect the age of Valentino's sensual mystique in this shimmering black-and-white male fantasy about black American gigolos trying to strike it rich in the beautiful resort city of Nice, France. The movie's preoccupation with sex distorts the meaning of a loving relationship. A-III (PG-13) 15

Under the Rainbow (1981) Legendary off-screen drunken carousing by the diminutive actors playing Munchkins in "The Wizard of Oz" (1938) becomes the central premise of a dim comedy burdened by slapstick subplots involving a mad assassin and Axis spies, all in service of a predictable romance between a Secret Service agent (Chevy Chase) and a movie studio assistant (Carrie Fisher). Director Steve Rash lavishes his energies on re-creating the Depression era and evoking some measure of nostalgia, but the movie's many sight gags fall embarrassingly flat. Coarse language, double-entendres and bawdy situations as well as tasteless stereotyping of little people. A-III (PG)

Under the Volcano (1984) Screen version of the Malcolm Lowry novel about an alcoholic English diplomat serving in Mexico (Albert Finney) is an impressive work but fails to convey the inner drama that gave such tragic force to the original, despite Finney's powerful performance. Nevertheless, director John Huston's effort is well worth seeing, though its adult treatment includes a vicious, sordid scene in a brothel. A-III (R) 15

Undercover Blues (1993) While vacationing in New Orleans, husband-and-wife espionage agents (Kathleen Turner and Dennis Quaid) reluctantly agree to a dangerous, top-secret assignment, taking along their baby girl as they dodge curious cops, a persistent mugger (Stanley Tucci) and assorted armed goons. Director Herbert Ross imitates the breezy style of the "Thin Man" movies, but his formula comedy is overwhelmed by klutzy, cardboard characters and a wrongheaded assumption that bullets and babies make for a laughfest. Intermittent violence played for laughs and an instance of rough language. A-III (PG-13) 12

Undercovers Hero (1975) Peter Sellers plays six roles, ranging from a British intelligence agent to Adolf Hitler, in a sex farce about how World War II was really won in a Paris bordello run by Lila Kedrova. Directed by Roy Boulting, the thoroughly inane script works on the same low level of wit as the pun of the title. O (R)

Underground (1970) B-grade World War II movie about the abduction of a Nazi general by the French underground (led by Robert Goulet). Little attempt is made to advance sympathy for either side in a weak story with confusing flashbacks, lackluster action photography and elements of sex and torture. A-III (PG)

Underground (1976) Documentary about what happened to some of those who were radicalized by the failure of the protest movements of the 1960s. Directed by Emile de Antonio, Mary Lampson and Haskell Wexler, the film consists essentially of a group interview with five surviving members of the Weather Underground who went into hiding after the explosion of their New York bomb factory in 1970. A tragic part of American history. A-III (nr)

Undertaker and His Pals, The (1972) Sharing the bodies of the young ladies they slay, the pals serve choice cuts to customers in their luncheonette while the mortician dresses up the remains and gives trading stamps to the grieving family. Awful amateurish production coats its tongue-in-cheek gruesomeness with excessively graphic views of the murdered victims. O (R)

Underwater City, The (1962) Pseudo-scientific hokum about an experimental base built on the bottom of the ocean by a would-be space engineer (William Lundigan). Director Frank MacDonald's corny scenario and cheesy model work are a boring waste of time. Mild menace and stylized violence. A-I (br)

Underworld, U.S.A. (1960) Brutal crime melodrama in which an ex-convict (Cliff Robertson) joins a syndicate run by the men who murdered his father in order to take revenge on them. Directed by Samuel Fuller, the plot is hokey but the criminal environment is realistic and the action tough-minded. Much stylized violence and menace. A-III (br) X

Une Femme Douce (1971) French drama about a woman (Dominique Sanda) who commits suicide and her husband (Guy Frangin) who tries to find out why. Director Robert Bresson's investigation is really into the emptiness of middle-class lives in which material objects consume people's entire interest to the detriment of interpersonal relationships. Sparse and demanding, it is a very interior film whose text is the ambiguous surface of reality. A-III (nr)

Unfaithfully Yours (1948) Black comedy in which a symphony orchestra conductor (Rex Harrison) suspects his wife (Linda Darnell) is unfaithful and imagines three scenarios in which he takes his revenge. Directed by Preston Sturges, there are some hilarious moments but the conductor's fumbling attempts at murder are not among them. Fantasy violence. A-II (br) A

Unfaithfully Yours (1984) Symphony conductor (Dudley Moore) wrongly suspects his wife (Nastassja Kinski) of being unfaithful and fantasizes revenge while on the podium. Director Howard Zieff's expensively mounted comedy is not anywhere near as funny as the 1948 Preston Sturges' original. Though otherwise innocuous, it is marred by an ill-conceived shower scene and an excessive bedroom sequence. O (PG)

Unfinished Dance, The (1947) A young girl (Margaret O'Brien) maliciously causes an accident ending the career of a ballerina (Cyd Charisse) but the child's remorse helps rectify the damage done. Directed by Henry Koster, the sugary story has little to offer but its ballet setting and dance numbers. A-I (br) U

Unforgiven, The (1960) Muddled western saga of a pioneer Texas family (widow Lillian Gish and sons Burt Lancaster and Audie Murphy) deserted by their neighbors when their grown daughter (Audrey Hepburn) is accused of being an orphaned Kiowa Indian raised from infancy as one of their own. Directed by John Huston, the theme of frontier racial hostility develops slowly, then grows increasingly ponderous until swept away in the fiery climax of the family's desperate stand against a band of Kiowa attackers. Uneven treatment of a serious theme and stylized violence. A-II (nr) A

Unforgiven (1992) A reformed gunfighter (Clint Eastwood) and his former partner (Morgan Freeman) join a novice bounty hunter (Jaimz Woolvett) to hunt down two cowboys wanted for cutting up a prostitute, but find a despotic sheriff (Gene Hackman) squarely in their way. Also produced and directed by Eastwood, the richly textured movie demythologizes the western hero while portraying the main character's moral downfall as tragic. Intermittent violence motivated by revenge and vigilante justice, fleeting bedroom shots, an uncritical acceptance of prostitution and occasional rough language. A-IV (R) 15

Unholy Rollers, The (1972) The rise of a young roller skater (Claudia Jennings) into the big-time roller derby involves women slugging it out like animals in one small-town rink after another, shown with an excess of breast-bashing, groin-stomping visuals. Directed by Vernon Zimmerman, the movie's off-camera commentary is provided by a pair of ringside announcers using tongue-in-cheek burlesque humor. O (R)

Unidentified Flying Oddball (1979) Good Disney comedy about an American space scientist (Dennis Dugan) and his look-alike robot who land in King Arthur's Court and save the monarch (Kenneth More) from being overthrown by Merlin (Ron Moody) and Sir Mordred (Jim Dale). Russ Mayberry directs the proceedings with proper charm and ingenuous good humor, leaving family audiences happier for the viewing. A-I (G)

Uninhibited, The (1968) Mediocre Spanish drama about a group of dropouts from life trying to rekindle some sense of direction and responsibility. Directed by Juan Antonio Bardem, the movie's theme has merit but its amoral setting and treatment may offend some adult viewers. A-IV (br)

Uninvited, The (1944) An English writer (Ray Milland) and his sister (Ruth Hussey) move into a house apparently haunted by the troubled spirit of the mother of a young woman (Gail Russell) who once lived there. Director Lewis Allen's intriguing ghost story revolves around solving the mystery of the mother's death in a movie buttressed by the whimsical attitude of the skeptical writer and a number of spooky effects. Some mild scares and restless spirits. A-II (br) A

Universal Soldier (1992) Two soldiers (Jean-Claude Van Damme and Dolph Lundgren), who killed each other in Vietnam but were secretly regenerated by the government for use as mindless killing machines, turn on one another with brute force. Director Roland Emmerich makes a repulsive movie out of constant images of degradation, death and phony heroics. Excessive violence, some nudity and much rough language. O (R) 18

Unlawful Entry (1992) Violent thriller centers on a psychotic cop (Ray Liotta) whose obsession with a married woman (Madeleine Stowe) leads him to frame her husband (Kurt Russell) for a drug felony. Jonathan Kaplan directs a transparent plot geared to set up a bloodthirsty ending that justifies murder. Several sexual encounters with nudity, recurring violence and much rough language. O (R) 18

Unman, Wittering and Zigo (1971) Group of British schoolboys murder their teacher and threaten to do likewise to his replacement (David Hemmings) unless he goes along with their plans. Hemmings doesn't believe them at first, and by the time he does, no one else will. This juxtaposition of innocence and corruption is powerful material, but director John MacKenzie loses control of it early on in the film, making several scenes involving sex ludicrous and dramatically implausible. A-III (GP) X

Unmarried Woman, An (1978) Jill Clayburgh stars as a reasonably happy wife who is forced to begin a new life when her husband (Michael Murphy) deserts her and their teenage daughter for a younger woman. Though it supposedly is about the trauma and suffering of a woman struggling to forge a new identity, writer-director Paul Mazursky's work is a bit too slick and sentimental to be very moving or very convincing. Extremely well-acted and relatively sincere effort contains some rough language, nudity and one needlessly graphic love-making scene. O (R) X

Unsinkable Molly Brown, The (1964) Ponderous screen version of Meredith Willson's stage musical about a Colorado backwoods tomboy (Debbie Reynolds) who, after a stint singing in a frontier bar, marries a rich miner (Harve Presnell) but is snubbed by Denver society until she's accepted by European nobility and survives the Titanic. Director Charles Walters tries to keep the narrative bright and lighthearted but Molly's elitist hankerings never square with her free-spirited, egalitarian manner, a central flaw compounded by lackluster songs and flat-footed production numbers. Some romantic complications, sexual innuendo and occasional crude language. A-II (br)

Untamed Heart (1993) Bogus sentiments litter this unlikely tale of romance between a Minneapolis waitress (Marisa Tomei) and a taciturn loner (Christian Slater) who grew up in an orphanage with a serious heart condition. Producer-director Tony Bill gets likeable performances from Tomei and Rosie Perez as her co-worker but the main event with Slater is hopelessly contrived and maudlin to boot. Some sexual situations and references, an attempted rape and occasional rough language. A-III (PG-13) 15

Until September (1984) Young American in Paris (Karen Allen) becomes involved with a suave Frenchman quite capable of juggling a wife, two children and a mistress, but she wants to play for keeps. Director Richard Marquand's limp and uninventive romance falls back upon abundant nudity in a vain attempt to sustain interest. Benign view of adultery. O (R)

Until the End of the World (1991) Vaguely futuristic road movie in which a thrill-seeking woman (Solveig Dommartin) joins a wanted man (William Hurt) on a mysterious mission around the world, one step ahead of her ex-boyfriend (Sam Neill) and assorted bounty hunters. German director Wim Wenders gets the strange, overly long narrative off to a good start, but the incidents along the way fail to sustain emotional involvement or intellectual interest. Momentary violence, brief bedroom shots with fleeting nudity and minimal rough language. A-III (R) 15

Untouchables, The (1987) Brian De Palma, not known for directorial subtleties, provides an almost camp parody of the TV original as federal agent Eliot Ness (Kevin Costner), portrayed as an inept family man, gets the goods on infamous Chicago gang boss Al Capone (Robert De Niro). The violence is dreamlike and distanced in a highly stylized crime-stopper movie that has some harsh language and brutal intensity. A-III (R) 15

Up in Arms (1944) World War II musical features draftee Danny Kaye with pals Dana Andrews, Dinah Shore and Constance Dowling aboard a troop ship bound for the Pacific where he becomes an improbable hero. Directed by Elliott Nugent, Kaye's patter songs in his screen debut were then a welcome novelty but the movie's disjointed narrative and heavy-handed slapstick have not worn well. Romantic complications and brief comic violence. A-II (br) U

Up in Smoke (1978) Utterly mindless comedy about two California pot-heads (counterculture figures Cheech Marin; Tommy Chong) who travel to Tijuana in search of some marijuana and subsequent pursuit by bumbling narcotics cop (Stacey Keach). Director Lou Adler's jokes, when not witless cliches about the pleasures of the drug culture, depend heavily on the titillating and the scatological. O (R)

Up in the Cellar (1970) Deprived of a college scholarship by a discerning computer, a youth (Wes Stern) seeks revenge on the college's pompous president (Larry Hagman) by seducing his wife, daughter, and black mistress-secretary. Though a number of director Ted Flicker's well-deserved jabs sting the college administration scene, the light touch never gets funny enough and the moral tone never gets high enough to save this slipshod attempt at adult entertainment. O (R)

Up the Academy (1980) Tedious, sophomoric romp set in a military academy ruled by a sadistic headmaster (Ron Leibman, who wisely had his name taken off the credits). Though director Robert Downey's visuals are restrained, the movie makes excessive use of sexual innuendo, rough language and all-around vulgarity. O (R)

Up the Creek (1984) Four college losers (Tim Matheson, Jennifer Runyon, Stephen Furst and Dan Monahan) battle military cadets and intense preppies to win a raft race in another exercise in brain-dead humor. Directed by Robert Butler, the movie contains abundant nudity and crude sexual humor. O (R)

Up the Down Staircase (1967) Film version of Bel Kaufman's novel about a dedicated young school teacher (Sandy Dennis) who is overwhelmed by regulations, supply shortages, overcrowding, disciplinary problems and some misguided colleagues, but who manages to do some real teaching in spite of it all. Director Robert Mulligan's realistic drama about the problems of a big city high school is helped by some humor and a fine supporting cast. A-II (br) A

Up the Junction (1968) Peter Collinson directs the British story of a rich woman (Suzy Kendall) seeking to find some sense of purpose in the slums of Battersea. It will impress some viewers as an honest essay in social realism while striking others as patronizing and banal. Casual moviegoers may find its coarse and vulgar language offensive. A-IV (br) 18

Up the MacGregors (1967) Forgettable Italian-Spanish western directed by Dario Sabatello is routine Saturday matinee fare. Mild violence. A-II (br)

Up the Sandbox (1972) Seriocomic story of a somewhat mad Manhattan housewife (Barbra Streisand) who finds herself experiencing an acute identity crisis and creates a soaring fantasy life that enables her to escape a myriad of troubles and even transcend them. Directed by Irvin Kershner, the housewife's struggle for liberation is what makes the film, despite its cinematic flaws in some of the flights of fantasy (including an abortion clinic), engagingly healthy and at times quite wise. A-IV (R) AA

Up Tight (1968) Updated version of "The Informer" (1936) replaces the IRA with a black revolutionary group, one of whom is wanted for murder and is betrayed for the reward by a former member of the group (Julian Mayfield). Directed by Jules Dassin, the movie has raw power and plenty of tension but oversimplifies the issues facing black Americans after Martin Luther King Jr.'s assassination. Mature themes. A-III (PG) X

Up to His Ears (1966) Failed French adventure comedy directed by Philippe De Broca about a bored millionaire who is chased around exotic Oriental locales by hired killers. Sexual innuendo. A-III (br)

Uptown Saturday Night (1974) Sidney Poitier and Bill Cosby play a couple of would-be sharpies who get caught in the middle of a Harlem gang war when they try to enlist the services of gangster Harry Belafonte to get back the money stolen from them. Also directed by Poitier, it's a pleasantly entertaining, good-natured comedy with some good acting. A-III (PG)

Uranus (1991) An innocent barkeep (Gerard Depardieu) is implicated when two compassionate Frenchmen (Philippe Noiret and Jean-Pierre Marielle) hide a Nazi collaborator (Gerard Desarthe) immediately after World War II. Writer-director Claude Berri uncovers many sides of the human condition in this tragicomedy which has Depardieu's over-the-top performance as its centerpiece. Subtitles. Brief violence, discreet references to sexual liaisons and occasional rough language. A-III (nr) 15

Urban Cowboy (1980) John Travolta plays a rural Texan who comes to the big city of Houston to find work and becomes romantically involved with Debra Winger in a honkytonk saloon whose feature attraction is a mechanical bronco. Directed by James Bridges, it's a boring, embarrassingly adolescent movie celebrating the masculine virtues of hard drinking, fighting and wenching. O (PG) 15

Used Cars (1980) Nasty supposed comedy about rival car dealers with Kurt Russell,

Jack Warden, Deborah Harmon and Andrew Duncan. Directed by Robert Zemeckis, there is nothing funny about the totally amoral and tasteless story that also employs nudity and rough language. O (R)

Used People (1992) After secretly admiring her for the past 23 years, an impassioned Italian widower (Marcello Mastroianni) pursues an emotionally repressed, newly bereaved Jewish widow (Shirley MacLaine) in 1969 Queens, encouraging her in the process to embrace life and reconcile with her divorced daughters (Kathy Bates and Marcia Gay Harden). Director Beeban Kidron's genial ethnic comedy features an appealing cast in a heartwarming story but the script works overtime extracting comedy from dysfunctional family relationships. Brief bedroom scene and an instance of rough language. A-III (R) 12

Utamaro and His Five Women (1972) Encapsulating the vision of an 18th-century Japanese artist, known especially for his prints of beautiful women, director Kenji Mizoguchi's movie succeeds admirably is showing an artist's view of his world. It is a paean to a vital classicism, both in subject and technique, idealizing a society in which people worked and lived in a harmony unknown in modern times. A-III (nr)

U2: Rattle and Hum (1988) A feature-length concert documentary on U2, the popular Irish rock band with a conscience. Directed in uninspired fashion by fan Phil Joanou, the film is a montage of U2's record-breaking 1987 American performances, backstage rap and rehearsal, much of which is shot in grainy black and white. Fans will love this, but it won't enlighten those unfamiliar with U2's political concerns. Mild rough language. A-II (PG-13)

Utz (1993) An American art dealer (Peter Riegert) arrives in Prague to purchase a priceless collection of Meissen porcelain and in the process learns about the late owner's (Armin Mueller-Stahl) unconventional life and strange relationship with his devoted housekeeper (Brenda Fricker). Dutch director George Sluizer fashions a multilayered but emotionally alienating story of obsessive and eccentric characters. Subtitles. Some sexual innuendo and a distant shot of nudity. A-III (nr)

V

Vagabond (1986) French director Agnes Varda offers a somber, flawed observation of spiritual and moral decay as a young female drifter's last days are recounted by the people she's met on the road to self-effacement. As a vision of alienated youth, the movie depicts casual sex as symptomatic of spiritual disintegration with much more emotional ground to be explored. Simple yet profound, although a potentially confusing work. A-III (nr)

Valachi Papers, The (1972) Charles Bronson plays the role of Joe Valachi, the late Mafia informer whose revelations formed the book by Peter Maas upon which the movie is based. Director Terence Young has passed up the opportunity to provide a rare glimpse inside the workings of organized crime in order to produce one more straight action movie, filled with brutality and sudden violence. Several scenes of gangland inhumanity require a strong stomach. A-IV (R/PG) X

Valdez Is Coming (1971) Tedious western in which a Mexican American deputy (Burt Lancaster) tries to collect some money for an Indian widow from those who had mistakenly shot her husband and then goes after the rancher responsible. Directed by Edwin Sherin, the heavy-handed plot development contains much violence and smatterings of sex and near-nudity. A-III (GP) AA

Valentino (1977) British screen biography of Rudolph Valentino (Rudolf Nureyev) as directed by Ken Russell is a boring, overdone piece of pretentious trash having only the remotest connection with the famous movie star's life. Nudity and graphic sexuality. O (R)

Valentino Returns (1989) Lackluster 1950s' coming-of-age drama about the frustrations of a young adult male (Barry Tubb) searching for sex on a typical Saturday night in his pink Cadillac. First-time director Peter Hoffman's effort fizzles into small-town vignettes that lack punch. Some rough language laced with sexual vulgarities, implied promiscuity and some nudity. A-III (R) X

Valerie and Her Week of Wonders (1974) Czechoslovakian fantasy in which a 13-year-old girl's daydreaming transforms her ordinary world into one filled with strange adventures, bizarre characters and the first vague stirrings of sexual awareness. Directed by Jaromil Jires, the setting is a picturesque village at the turn-of-the-century, affording lush imagery, striking compositions, colorful costuming and ornamental detail that lend themselves easily to a surrealistic picture of a young adolescent's imagination. Literal-minded viewers may be confused by the movie's lack of narrative guideposts, but the juxtaposition of religious and Freudian symbolism invites deeper psychological probing by those so inclined. A-IV (nr)

Valley Girl (1983) San Fernando Valley girl (Deborah Foreman) throws over her handsome but dumb Valley boyfriend in favor of a punk rocker from Hollywood (Nicolas Cage), much to the consternation of her friends. Directed by Martha Coolige, this Romeo and Juliet variation makes some gestures in the direction of satire, but essentially is another teen exploitation movie, with graphic nudity and rough language. O (R)

Valley of Gwangi, The (1969) A group of riders from a Wild West show (headed by James Franciscus) go in search of a major attraction in a hidden Mexican valley where prehistoric monsters survive protected from the outside world by a band of mysterious gypsies. Director James O'Connolly has done a routine job in directing what is essentially a nonsensical exercise of the special effects department and one's imagination. A-I (G) A

Valley of Mystery (1967) Airliner crash-lands in South American jungle among whose perils are a tribe of headhunters, but the pilot (Richard Egan) manages to keep the survivors alive until rescued by helicopters. Director Josef Leytes turns a routine adventure story into a slack melodrama of little interest. Stylized violence. A-II (br) A

Valley of the Dolls (1967) Trashy melodrama based on a trashy novel about decadence in the world of show business and the deleterious effects of gulping pep and sleeping pills. Directed by Mark Robson, the insight is nil, most of the acting is embarrassingly bad and it elicits only pained disbelief at its amateurishness and a few laughs where none was intended. O (br) X

Valley of the Kings (1954) American archeologist (Robert Taylor) helps an Englishwoman (Eleanor Parker) search for evidence proving the biblical account of Joseph's sojourn in the land of the pharaohs. Director Robert Pirosh muddies matters with murderous conniving by greedy traffickers in antiquities, but the result is worth seeing for its grand vistas of famous sites in ancient Egypt. Some menace and stylized violence. A-II (br) U

Valley of the Sun (1941) Oddball western in which an Army scout (James Craig) averts an Apache uprising by exposing a corrupt Indian agent (Dean Jagger) while wooing the sidewinder's girlfriend (Lucille Ball). Director George Marshall mixes in a lot of rough humor with the low-budget action and flavorsome romancing. Some positive Indian stereotyping and a bit of stylized violence. A-I (br) U

Valmont (1989) Visually lush but emotionally empty adaptation of the 18th-century novel, "Les Liaisons Dangereuses." Story centers on the sexual intrigues among a circle of French aristocrats, notably the title character (Colin Firth) and his one-time paramour (Annette Bening). Though director Milos Forman tries to humanize these upper-class libertines, he seems more interested in re-creating the rich opulence and frivolous style of a world that disappeared with the French Revolution. Restrained treatment of immoral relationships. A-III (R) 15

Vampire Circus (1972) British horror film in which a traveling troupe of gypsy vampires (Adrienne Corri and Anthony Corlan) visits a Serbian village to revive a dead count who had been killed there 15 years before. Director Robert Young tries to make up for the script's lack of wit and suspense with a fair sprinkling of incidental sex, but with little success. A-III (R/PG) 18

Vampire Lovers (1970) Minimal British horror film about a female vampire with lesbian inclinations who ravages the young maidens of a peaceful little hamlet. Directed by Roy Ward Baker, the movie emphasizes blood and sex at the expense of traditional horror elements. O (R) 15

Vampire's Kiss (1989) After picking up a vampire (Jennifer Beals) in a singles' bar, a New York Yuppie (Nicolas Cage) turns into a blood-sucking vampire by night and a manic monster terrorizing his young secretary (Maria Conchita Alonso) by day. Directed by Robert Bierman, the misogynist movie depicts men as sorry victims of women who exist only to lure men to self-destruction. Much profanity and promiscuity, laced with flashes of nudity and bloody sexual encounters. O (R)

Van, The (1977) Gawky youth (Stuart Getz) becomes a Don Juan when he buys a van in this shoddy low-budget sex-exploitation movie directed by Sam Grossman. O (R) X

Van Gogh (1992) Laborious depiction of the final days of the suicidal artist (Jacques Dutronc) living in the suburbs of 1890s' Paris where he distracts himself with an alleged affair with the daughter (Alexandra London) of his benefactor (Gerard Sety). Maurice Pialat's tedious direction and Dutronc's stony performance only reveal surface details of the artist's mundane existence without adequately conveying his mental state or the scores of paintings he feverishly finished in his final days. Implied affairs and some nudity. Subtitles. A-III (R) 12

Vanishing, The (1991) Three years after the disappearance of his wife (Johanna Ter Steege), the husband (Gene Bervoets) is contacted by the abductor (Bernard-Pierre Donnadieu) and eventually learns her fate—as well as meets his own. Directed by George Sluizer, the Dutch-French production is an unsettling and farfetched psychological study in which the good guy is no match for the seemingly normal sociopath he's pitted against. Subtitles. Much menace and occasional restrained violence. A-III (nr) 12

Vanishing, The (1993) Flat Hollywood remake by Dutch director George Sluizer of his own eerie 1991 foreign thriller pitting a methodic maniac (Jeff Bridges) against a young man (Kiefer Sutherland) obsessed with finding his long-missing girlfriend (Sandra Bullock), even if it means losing his new love (Nancy Travis) or his own life. In bowing to alleged American preferences for action over emotional complexity, Sluizer strips the narrative of the suspense and mounting sense of dread that made the original so memorable. Brief but intense climatic violence, a live-in relationship and minimal rough language. A-III (R) 15

Vanishing Point (1971) Speed demon (Barry Newman) attempts to outrun the police of four states aided by a blind disc jockey (Cleavon Little) who monitors police frequencies. Directed by Richard C. Sarafian, the plot is aimless, marked by a number of hair-raising race crack-ups and some gratuitous nudity. O (GP) AA

Vanishing Wilderness (1974) Slow-moving, incoherent parade of unrelated wildlife scenes, directed by Arthur Dubs and Heinz Seilmann, with an obnoxiously cute narration by Rex Allen. It ranks low on the scale of well-made nature documentaries. A-I (G)

Variety Lights (1950) Delightful Italian comedy about a traveling theatrical troupe whose frustrated star (Peppino De Flippo) drops his fiancee (Giulietta Masina) when a novice actress (Carla Del Poggio) joins the troupe. Directed by Federico Fellini and Alberto Lattuada, the world of small-time show people is filled with infectious good humor, much whimsy and some pathos. Subtitles. Romantic complications. A-III (br)

Vault of Horror, The (1973) Unimaginative British horror film offers five tales, interwoven with vampires, voodoo, murder and torture, with a cast including Daniel Massey, Terry Thomas, Glynis Johns and Curt Jurgens. Directed by Roy Ward Baker, there is too much emphasis on mutilation and blood for younger viewers, and not enough psychological terror to chill the hearts and imaginations of horror devotees. A-III (R/PG) 18

Velvet Touch, The (1948) Psychological drama in which a Broadway actress (Rosalind Russell) kills her manipulative producer (Leon Ames), then matches wits with the policeman (Sydney Greenstreet) investigating the murder. Director John Gage does well with a fine cast and dandy backstage settings but stumbles in dragging out a less-than-perfect crime story. An act of deadly violence, much tension and some romantic complications. A-II (br)

Velvet Vampire, The (1971) Low-budget horror about newlyweds (Michael Blodgett and Sherry Miles) who come for a weekend in a desert hotel whose hostess (Celeste Yarnall) is desperate for new blood. Director Stephanie Rothman requires hardly a stitch of clothing for the atrocious acting of all participants in this silly exercise. O (R)

Vengeance of Fu Manchu, The (1967) Master criminal Fu Manchu (Christopher Lee) sets out to murder all the world's chiefs of police and, through plastic surgery, replace them with his own men but is foiled by Scotland Yard's Nayland Smith (Douglas Wilmer). Directed by Jeremy Summers, the British production's weak story makes middling adventure entertainment. Stylized violence. A-II (br)

Vengeance of She, The (1968) Weak British adventure fantasy based on characters created by H. Rider Haggard in which an occult power compels a young woman (Olinka Berova) to journey to a hidden city in North Africa to become the lost queen of its ruler (John Richardson). Directed Cliff Owen, the action is pedestrian and the plot mistakes silliness for imagination. Mild violence. A-II (G) A

Vengeance Valley (1951) Below-par western in which a ranch foreman (Burt Lancaster) protects his shiftless half-brother (Robert Walker) until the nasty lad's treachery leads to a final showdown between them. Directed by Richard Thorpe, the drearily detailed plot of mistaken loyalties is relieved only by occasional scenes of cowboy life on the open range. Stylized violence and an unwed-mother subplot. A-II (br) A

Venice–Venice (1992) Frail, talky story in which a self-consumed director (Henry Jaglom), promoting his movie at the Venice Film Festival, becomes involved with an adoring Parisian journalist (Nelly Allard) who follows him home to Venice, Calif. to pursue their relationship. Also written and directed by Jaglom, the thin plot is given some interest by intercutting remarks from a variety of women who feel betrayed by Hollywood movies that led them to believe life would be filled with glamor and perfect romance. Benign attitude towards unmarried intimacy and some rough language. A-III (nr)

Venom (1982) Deadly snake cavorts about a household taken over by ruthless international terrorists in this mediocre and farfetched melodrama directed by Piers Haggard. A fine cast, including Nicol Williamson, Klaus Kinski, Oliver Reed, Sarah Miles and Sterling Hayden is wasted in a mindless effort that features violence and some restrained sexual activity. A-III (R) AA

Venus in Furs (1970) European co-production about a beautiful woman who, after being raped, mutilated and murdered, returns from the dead seeking vengeance on her killers. Directed by Jess Franco, its below-standard production values complement its ludicrous sex-exploitation plot. O (R)

Verdict, The (1982) When a drunken wreck of a lawyer (Paul Newman) presses a medical malpractice suit against a Boston Catholic hospital represented by a powerful attorney (James Mason), he overcomes his personal problems by relying upon his heart instead of his mind during the extended court battle. Though director Sidney Lumet's script has a faulty perspective on church procedures, Newman's performance outweighs such defects. The sexual aspects of the story are done with the greatest restraint, but it does contain some foul language from one of its characters. A-II (R) 15

Veronico Cruz (1990) This Argentinian film tracks the life of a shepherd boy (Gonzalo Morales) whose isolation in a remote region is lifted by a new schoolteacher (Juan Jose Camero) who ultimately brings the boy to the city to search for his political-dissident father. Director and co-writer Miguel Pereira captures well the indigenous population, the stark landscape and the encroachment of the outside world, including political turmoil from revolving military dictatorships and the Falklands War. English subtitles. Incidental rough language, some brief intense political interrogations. A-II (nr) PG

Veronique (1976) This warm, sensitive French film follows a perceptive 13-year-old girl's not especially eventful summer. Director Claudine Ghuilmain fulfills her modest aims in showing the youngster's experiences and some misunderstandings in what is little more than a string of vignettes best appreciated by adult viewers. A-III (nr)

Vertigo (1958) Fine suspense thriller from Alfred Hitchcock in the tale of a retired detective (James Stewart) called back for a private investigation of a seemingly shady lady (Kim Novak). Naturally, they fall in love and land in high danger. Jimmy gulps and stammers a lot, Kim just smolders and Hitch masterfully pulls the strings. A-II (PG)

Very Curious Girl, A (1970) French social satire about the revenge a young gypsy (Bernadette Lafont) takes on the people of a small village who have exploited her and her mother. Director Claude Makovski has elicited strong and convincing performances from a cast mainly of villagers and peasants in creating a strange atmosphere of a primitive morality based on ignorance, simplicity and superstition. A-IV (R)

Very Happy Alexander (1969) Elegant French comedy about middle-age rebellion in which a brow-beaten husband (Philippe Noiret) scandalizes his neighbors by leading a life of lazy indolence after the death of his finger-snapping wife. He finds a soulmate in a shiftless woman (Marlene Jobert) but when she snaps her fingers, he leaves her at the altar. Directed by Yves Robert, it is essentially a bucolic poem in which Noiret's warm, human performance makes convincing the urge to return to the unregimented life of Eden. A-II (nr)

Very Natural Thing, A (1974) Young man leaves the monastic life, becomes a high school teacher and takes a male lover whose promiscuity eventually results in a break-up. Director Christopher Larkin's film is a sincere and obviously deeply felt effort to present the moral dilemmas of a homosexual relationship, but it is painfully naive about film technique and embarrassingly romantic about its theme. Several nude scenes of male grapplings. O (R)

V. I. Warshawski (1991) Hard-boiled Chicago private-eye (Kathleen Turner, in the title role) gets stuck with a scrappy 13-year-old (Angela Goethals) when her father is killed and the girl becomes the next murder target. Turner's tough, sassy and supremely confident performance is at the center of director Jeff Kanew's standard suspenser that keeps the action going full tilt even when the plot becomes opaque. Mostly stylized violence, recurring sexual references and intermittent rough language. A-III (R) 15

Vibes (1988) Three spirited performers can't save this muddled mess about two psychics (Cyndi Lauper; Jeff Goldblum) lured to Ecuador by a seedy adventurer (Peter Falk) hoping to psyche out hidden Incan treasure. Director Ken Kwapis misuses many comic lines as well as his talented cast. Some sexual innuendo and minimal rough language. A-III (PG)

Vice Squad (1982) A prostitute (Season Hubley) is saved from the clutches of a brutal pimp (Wings Hauser) by a stalwart policeman (Gary Hanson) in a loathsome, unremittingly brutal and squalid movie directed by Gary A. Sherman. O (R)

Victor/Victoria (1982) Unemployed singer (Julie Andrews) dresses up as a man in order to get a job as a female impersonator and soon is the toast of 1934 Paris. Helping her along the way is an aging homosexual (Robert Preston) and complicating her life is a Chicago nightclub owner (James Garner). Directed by Blake Edwards, the humor is fitful, more slapstick than witty, and the situation stretches itself thin long before movie's end. Benign attitude toward homosexuality, though given the farcical context, unlikely to blur the moral outlook of adults. A-IV (PG) 15

Victory (1981) World War II story about a soccer game staged for propaganda purposes between a crack German team and a ragtag group of Allied prisoners-of-war (Michael Caine, Sylvester Stallone and legendary Brazilian soccer star Pele, among others) who use the match to effect an escape from the packed Paris stadium where they are playing. Effectively directed by John Huston, the result is a sports movie with some taut wartime suspense. Solid entertainment for the whole family. A-I (PG)

Videodrome (1983) Seedy operator of a sleazy television station (James Woods) gets hooked on the unrelenting sadomasochism of a program called Videodrome, which is actually a sinister plot against humanity carried out by some villains steeped, like the movie itself, in ill-digested media theories of Marshall McLuhan. Written and directed by David Cronenberg, there are some hints of satire, but no hint of intelligence or perspective, and its imagination is as dull as it is perverse. Sadomasochistic sex and exceedingly gory violence. O (R) 18

Vietnam, Texas (1990) Trashy drama about a Catholic priest (Robert Ginty) battling a gang of Vietnamese emigres in Houston while searching for the daughter he fathered as a soldier during the Vietnam War. Also directed by Ginty, the inept result is an unsatisfying mixture of ambiguous idealism and lethal mayhem. Hard-edged violence, references to prostitution and occasional rough language. A-III (R)

View to a Kill, A (1985) In another 007 adventure for the perpetually adolescent, James Bond (Roger Moore) is pitted against a rather pallid villain (Christopher Walken) who wants to remove all competition for his new computer chip by inducing an earthquake that will obliterate Silicon Valley. Director John Glen's pulp action-adventure fantasy has excessive violence and a benign view of promiscuity. O (PG)

Vigilante (1983) Brutal variation on the theme of the good guys getting fed up and taking the law into their own hands features Robert Forster joining forces with some vigilantes after his family is attacked by degenerate punks. Directed by William Lustig, the proceedings are cynically exploitative and incredibly violent. O (R)

Viking Queen, The (1967) Generally inept, tawdry spear-and-sandal epic set in rustic Britain during the Roman occupation where the haughty overseer (Don Murray) of a defeated-but-proud Viking tribe falls in love with its queen (Carita). British production directed by Don Chaffey, the tale of carnage and intrigue lavishes the budget on bloody action and skimps on the costuming to near-nudity. O (br) A

Vikings, The (1958) Energetic re-creation of the Norse sea raids on England during the Dark Ages pits a Viking leader (Ernest Borgnine) and his son (Kirk Douglas) against an English princess (Janet Leigh) and the escaped slave who becomes her champion (Tony Curtis). Directed by Richard Fleischer, the story is romanticized hokum, but the action is full-blooded and the performances colorful. Much stylized bloodshed and carnage, as well as some sexual references. A-III (br) A

Villa Rides (1968) Buzz Kulik directs a dismissible, violent western, starring Yul Brynner as the menacing Mexican revolutionary and Robert Mitchum as a tough American gunrunner. Kulik ignores the historical complexity of the period and emphasizes its violence, with men being lined up and slaughtered, ad nauseam. O (R) 15

Village of the Giants (1965) Sophomoric sci-fi clunker about some beach party-goers (Beau Bridges, Trisha Sterling, et al.) who take over a town after growing to giant-size, thanks to a juvenile scientist (Ronny Howard). Director Bert I. Gordon's inane story and bargain-basement special effects are embarrassingly bad. Sexual innuendo. A-III (br)

Villain (1971) Nasty excursion into the lower depths of the British underworld in which a small-time homosexual hood (Richard Burton) carves up a stool pigeon, blackmails a lusty Member of Parliament and bungles a payroll heist, while being tracked by a rumpled Scotland Yard detective (Nigel Davenport) who exacts his just desserts, but just barely. Directed by Michael Tuchner, the acting is very good, the action and plot only routine, but the overall tint of moral decay and degradation is suffocating. O (R) 18

Villain, The (1979) Kirk Douglas, Ann-Margret and Arnold Schwarzenegger toil through director Hal Needham's spoof of western outlaws and other heavies to no avail. One is left with the impression of watching a live-action version of a Road-Runner cartoon for no apparent reason. Vulgar language and suggestive gowns. A-III (PG)

Vincent & Theo (1990) Emotionally charged biography chronicles the troubled lives and early deaths of frustrated artist Vincent Van Gogh (Tim Roth) and Theo (Paul Rhys), his singularly devoted younger brother who supported him to the end. Director Robert Altman's handsomely mounted film uses a bright palette of sumptuous colors as a backdrop for the dark side of the brothers' symbiotic relationship, portrayed with convincing passion by Roth and Rhys. Restrained treatment of promiscuous relationships, occasional studio scenes with nude models, some violence and Van Gogh's suicide. A-III (PG-13) 15

Vincent, Francois, Paul and the Others (1976) Disappointing French import deals with the crisis of middle age in a series of loosely strung-together sketches exhibiting little but the Gallic charm of such performers as Yves Montand, Michel Piccoli, Serge Reggiani, and Stephane Audran. Directed by Claude Sautet, it is not much of a movie but, for those interested, the performances are worth observing. A-III (nr)

Violent Four, The (1968) Italian crime melodrama about a gang of ruthless bank-robbers (led by Gian Maria Volonte and Tomas Milian) who are so successful that the police call in troops to hunt them down. Directed by Carlo Lizzani, the clumsy and overlong narrative uses a forced semi-documentary style and suffers from tired images out of American gangster movies. Much violence. A-III (M)

Violent Men, The (1955) Muddled, unconvincing western directed by Rudolph Mate pits law-abiding small rancher (Glenn Ford) against unscrupulous cattle baron (Edward G. Robinson) whose faithless wife (Barbara Stanwyck) is in cahoots with crippled hubby's snarling hired gun (Brian Keith). Pacifism loses out to the usual stylized violence. A-II (br) A

Violets Are Blue (1986) Kevin Kline plays the big fish in a small pond who slips in and out of an extramarital relationship with his former sweetheart (Sissy Spacek) who has returned home on vacation after being away for 13 years. Infidelity is treated as an ego-centricity, not a moral breakdown. The script tends also to celebrate characters without conscience as its anti-hero gets his old flame out of his system without any consequences. Director Jack Fisk's movie romanticizes adultery. O (PG-13) PG

Violette (1978) Fact-based French dramatization of a 1933 case in which a 14-year-old girl (Isabelle Hupert) decided that she would be happier as an orphan and poisoned her parents, but her mother (Stephane Audran) survived to become her most vehement accuser. Whatever political, social or artistic implications this somber event may have remain obscure because director Claude Chabrol centers on the depiction of the heroine's promiscuity as the motivation for her callous crime. A-IV (R) X

Virgin and the Gypsy, The (1970) British adaptation of the D. H. Lawrence story about two sisters who return from a French finishing school to their father's country rectory where one is content to settle down and the other (Joanna Shimkus) falls in love with a gypsy (Franco Nero). Directed by Christopher Miles, the re-creation of the 1925 English countryside is lovely to look at, though the dated romantic story doesn't quite fare as well. Brief nudity and a resolution some may mistake as an endorsement of promiscuity. A-IV (R) 15

Virgin Soldiers (1970) Group of bumbling, ill-suited young British draftees (Hywel Bennett; Nigel Davenport; Jack Sheperd) in a 1951 Malayan transit camp are initiated into the arts of love and war. Directed by John Dexter, the central failure of the movie is its inability to decide whether or not to take itself seriously and the result is a curiously flat, not very amusing string of incidents. Some violence, bloodshed, a sequence with a Singapore prostitute and two sexual encounters. A-III (R) X

Virgin Witch, The (1972) British potboiler about runaway sisters who hitchhike to London, meet the lesbian proprietress of a modeling agency and later become willing initiates in a coven of orgiastic witches. Director Ray Austin exploits everybody concerned, including the audience. O (R)

Virility (1976) One more satire on Sicilian honor, this one about a father's frantic efforts to prove to the rumor mongers that his son is not a homosexual. There is nothing light or subtle about Paola Cavara's direction of the film's offensive material. O (R)

Viscount, The (1967) Failed European spy movie directed by Maurice Cloche features excessive brutality and sexual suggestiveness. O (br)

Vision Quest (1985) Gung-ho high school wrestler (Matthew Modine) is distracted from his goal of a state championship and a scholarship by a sultry young woman (Linda Fiorentino). What happens is, like its young hero, a bore in a movie directed by Harold Becker with a blaring soundtrack and rough language typical of such youth films. Though there is no nudity, characters talk about sex and its desirability constantly, presenting a benign view of fornication. O (R)

Visions of Eight (1973) Eight directors (Arthur Penn; Kon Ichikawa; Milos Forman; Claude Lelouch; John Schlesinger; Mai Zetterling; Michael Pfleghar; Juri Ozerov) offer eight different views of the 1972 Munich Olympics. Despite the inevitable unevenness, it is a rewarding experience affording viewer's a different, more personal perspective of a familiar sports competition. A-I (G)

Visions of Light (1993) Illuminating documentary about the art and the craft of the cinematographer as practiced by its masters since the turn of the century. Using interviews with leading cinematographers of today as well as excerpts from some 125 movies, directors Arnold Glassman, Todd McCarthy and Stuart Samuels illustrate how creative camerawork is not dependent upon the medium's technological changes. Fleeting nude shot and a brutal boxing match. A-II (nr)

Visit to a Chief's Son (1974) American anthropologist (Richard Mulligan) brings his teenage son (Philip Hodgdon) to Kenya on a trip studying and photographing the Masai tribes and their lives become enmeshed in those of the people they have come to visit. Directed by Lamont Johnson, this crosscultural tale of how a father and his son achieve a healthy relationship in the picturesque African veldt is a good family experience, though some parents may not appreciate a brief skinny-dip in the wilds. A-II (G)

Visiting Hours (1982) Minimal Canadian effort at a horror movie with Lee Grant playing a woman terrorized by beefy maniac Michael Ironside. Directed by Jean Claude Lord, the stupid plot is frequently revolting and has not a single redeeming quality. O (R) 18

Visitors, The (1971) Two recent parolees from prison who were convicted of rape and murder committed in Vietnam visit a third vet who testified against them at their trial, now living on a farm with his common-law wife, and after interminable tension, the final, inevitable scenes of rape and violence occur. Directed by Elia Kazan, the story's pessimism is as deep and dark as its moral perspective is shallow and glossy. O (R) X

Vital Signs (1990) Sudsy melodrama about five medical students (most notably, Adrian Pasdar; Jack Gwaltney) trying to make the grade as doctors while dealing with their personal problems, chiefly those of the heart. Directed by Marisa Silver, the film fails to generate anything but surface interest in its youthful characters and the daily round of critical cases in a teaching hospital will be of interest only to inveterate fans of medical programs. Several sexual encounters, one of which is depicted graphically in the shadows of a medical supply room. A-III (R) 15

Viva Italia (1978) Bland anthology film featuring several stories done by directors Mario Monicelli, Dino Risi and Ettore Scola, with such stars as Vittorio Gassman, Alberto Sordi, and Ugo Tognazzi. Most of the incidents are comic, ranging from moderately amusing to boring and tasteless, with the serious vignettes faring not much better. Coarse language and humor. A-III (R)

Viva Knievel (1977) Flamboyant motorcycle stuntman Evel Knievel gets the chance to play himself in a rather innocent and sentimental little melodrama that presents its folk hero as instrumental in reuniting a father and his young son as well as thwarting a gang of narcotics smugglers. Directed by Gordon Douglas, it is for the young and very undemanding. A-II (PG) A

Viva la Muerte (1973) Written and directed by avant-garde playwright Fernando Arrabal, this is an impassioned, surrealistic expression of growing up during the Spanish Civil War. The film's central experience (which is autobiographical) concerns a youngster's growing realization that his mother has betrayed his father into the hands of the local fascists. Some viewers will be repelled by its emotional ferocity and pervasive imagery of seduction, mutilation, degradation and sexual fantasies. O (nr)

Viva Las Vegas (1964) Breezy Elvis Presley vehicle in which he plays a race car driver who falls for a Las Vegas resort employee (Ann-Margret) while trying to line up a car for the big race. Directed by George Sidney, the romantic storyline is less interesting than the colorful Nevada scenery. Sexual innuendo. A-III (br) U

Viva Max (1969) Peter Ustinov plays a bumbling Mexican general who recaptures the Alamo with a hundred equally bumbling soldiers while Jonathan Winters as a National Guard general mainly battles the witless script. Director Jerry Paris simply misses the mark in trying to expand a single gag into a feature comedy. A-I (G) U

Vivacious Lady (1938) Slight romantic comedy about a college prof (James Stewart) who can't bring himself to tell his stuffy father (Charles Coburn) that he's gotten married to a showgirl (Ginger Rogers). Directed by George Stevens, the plot complications stemming from this flimsy premise tax credibility but are often amusing and occasionally hilarious. Some comic brawling and inebriation as a source of humor. A-II (br) U

Vixen (1969) Sex-exploitation movie directed by Russ Meyers alludes to such social issues as racial prejudice, the draft and politics as an excuse to offer graphic displays of adultery, lesbianism, incest and an attempted rape. O (X/R)

Vladimir and Rosa (1971) Low-budget, politically committed French film dealing with the 1969 Chicago Conspiracy Trial as part of the process in changing the capitalistic system. Director Jean-Luc Godard's work possesses a coherence of style and content (and even some humor) but, as political propaganda, it is preaching only to the already converted. A-IV (nr)

Voices (1979) A young singer (Michael Ontkean) and a deaf girl (Amy Irving) who wants to be a dancer fall in love, but the story is slight and the dialogue often ludicrous. A subplot involving the hero's raucous all-male family is so awkwardly handled by director Robert Markowitz that it is at best a distraction. Ambiguous view of premarital sex and a suggestive dance sequence. A-III (PG)

Voices of Sarafina (1989) Documentary focusing on the rehearsal, performance and backstage action surrounding the hit Broadway musical "Sarafina!" in which the troupe of black teenagers from South Africa discuss and enact their struggles growing up under the repression of apartheid. Directed by Nigel Noble, it's an eloquent introduction to the role played by South African youngsters in the struggle for black liberation. Some violently staged numbers may be too intense for young children. A-II (nr)

Volcano (1977) Director Donald Brittain's documentary reconstructs the life of Malcom Lowry, author of "Under the Volcano," who died from an overdose of sleeping pills in 1957, relying upon interviews with family, friends and associates and by visiting places where he had lived in England, the United States, Mexico and Canada. The short passages read by Richard Burton from his novel are too few for one to gain any sense of the work's literary merit, but anyone interested in literature or in people will find it a fascinating experience of life on the edge. A-II (nr)

Volere Volare (1993) Silly Italian sex farce about a bashful cartoon sound technician (Maurizio Nichetti) whose dates with a mysterious woman of the night (Angela Finocchiaro) are complicated by the fact that he is gradually turning into a cartoon character himself. Written and directed by Nichette and Guido Manuli, the irreverent mix of slapstick live action and zany animation eventually substitutes raciness for originality. Subtitles. Much sexual innuendo and fleeting nudity. A-III (R) 15

Volunteers (1985) Supposedly madcap adventures of Peace Corps volunteers (John Candy and Tom Hanks) in the jungles of Thailand range from dull to vapid in a mindless comedy directed by Nicholas Meyer. Some nudity and vulgarity are the sole, albeit offensive, punctuations in a simplistic story about evading a gambling debt. O (R) 15

Von Richthofen and Brown (1971) Director Roger Corman's anti-war extravaganza makes camera fodder out of the air aces of World War I (John Phillip Law and Don Stroud are the opposing aviators of the title). Though director Roger Corman's movie has stilted dialogue and wooden acting, it is saved by the excellence of its biplane footage. The planes dominate the screen, making an interesting contrast to more familiar scenes of modern warfare's carefully programmed annihilation of distant, dehumanized enemies. A-II (PG) A

Von Ryan's Express (1965) Fast-paced World War II action thriller focuses on some prisoners-of-war (with Frank Sinatra as their leader) who escape by train through the Italian Alps into Switzerland. Directed by Mark Robson, the movie has a fine international supporting cast and moments of high excitement, though some scenes are played too heavily for laughs and patriotism. A-I (br) PG

Voyage of Silence (1968) Impressive French drama about the victimization of illegal Portuguese workers who slip across the border seeking work in France. Directed by Christian de Chalogne, it shows the aloofness of society and its institutions in the face of suffering and exploitation. An important work on social justice. A-II (br)

Voyage of the Damned (1977) Fact-based story about a German ship carrying some 900 Jewish refugees on the eve of World War II but were denied entry by Cuba and the United States. Director Stuart Rosenberg has turned the tragedy into sluggish melodrama with a disjointed script and an all-star cast (including Faye Dunaway, Oskar Werner and Max Von Sydow). Frank treatment of a couple's marital problems. A-III (PG)

Voyage to Grand Tartarie (1978) Failed French satire in which a young man (Jean-Luc Bideau), whose wife is the victim of a random killing, drops everything and embarks on a wild, eccentric journey through France beset with all sorts of social, political, spiritual and physical ills. Director Jean-Charles Tacchella's effort lacks both humor and perception as well as makes excessive use of nudity. O (nr)

Voyeur (1991) Bizarre Dutch melodrama involves a 31-year-old recluse (Alex van Warmerdam), his overprotective mother and frustrated father (Olga Zuiderhoek and Henri Garcin) and a nude dancer (Annet Malherbe) who seduces both men. There's little point to the sick behavior of the wildly dysfunctional family in writer-director-star van Warmerdam's self-indulgent and perverse black comedy. Subtitles. Frequent adulterous and promiscuous situations with nudity and some violence. O (nr)

Vulture, The (1966) Low-budget, unimaginative science-fiction movie written and directed by Lawrence Huntington with Akim Tamiroff in the cliched role of mad scientist. For undemanding viewers only. A-I (br) A

W

W (1974) Ridiculous B-grade suspense thriller in which Twiggy plods through her role as the nervous heroine being terrorized by her mad ex-husband (Dirk Benedict) who has escaped from prison after his conviction for her murder. Directed by Richard Quine, the senseless plot is only an excuse for putting a vulnerable young woman at the mercy of a maniacal sadist. Some feeble psychological and physical violence. A-III (PG) AA

Wackiest Ship in the Army, The (1960) Comic drama in which a Navy lieutenant (Jack Lemmon) takes a broken-down sailing ship with an inexperienced crew on a 1943 mission to the South Pacific where they land an Australian observer (Chips Rafferty) on a Japanese-held island just before the Battle of the Bismarck Sea. Director Richard Murphy plays the action for laughs, most of which are good-natured except for some unfunny scenes of hand-to-hand combat. Wartime violence. A-I (br) U

Wacky World of Mother Goose (1968) Animated fantasy in which Mother Goose (voice of Margaret Rutherford) leaves all her nursery rhyme characters to visit her sister on the moon, but they are imprisoned by a wicked count and she has to come to the rescue. Very young children may enjoy all the movie's repetitions, but parents will find it rather dull and unimaginative. A-I (br)

Waco (1966) Routine western directed by R. G. Springsteen in which a gunslinger (Howard Keel) is reformed by his former girlfriend (Jane Russell) and her minister husband (Wendell Corey). Stylized violence. A-II (br) A

Wages of Fear, The (1953) Stranded in Central America, four down-on-their-luck Europeans (Yves Montand; Charles Vanel; Folco Lulli; Peter Van Eyck) jump at the money offered to drive two truckloads of volatile nitroglycerine over primitive roads crossing mountains and jungle to blow out a fire raging in an American-owned oilfield. French director Henri-Georges Clouzot's classic thriller builds the suspense as the dangers of the fearsome journey take their toll on the desperate drivers. Subtitles. Extreme menace, brief stylized violence and sordid situations of life among the impoverished. A-III (br)

Wagons West (1952) Routine oater directed by Ford Beebe with a veteran wagonmaster (Rod Cameron) shepherding a train of pilgrims from Missouri to California while romancing one of the company (Peggy Castle) and stopping a gang selling rifles to Cheyenne renegades. Stylized violence. A-I (br)

Wait Until Dark (1967) Audrey Hepburn stars as a recently blinded housewife who undergoes a harrowing trial when three men (Alan Arkin; Richard Crenna; Jack Weston) invade her apartment in search of a doll containing a cache of heroin. Director Terence Young's adaptation of Frederick Knott's hit play is scripted and edited with such intensity that even its slightly incredible elements pass in a taut suspense melodrama for all but the youngest members of the family. A-II (br) X

Waiting for Caroline (1969) Canadian version of the old story about the girl (Alexandra Stewart) who can't make up her mind which of her two lovers to marry and in the end gets neither. Writer-director Ron Kelly is more interested in social comment than making the characters interesting, let alone credible. Some nudity. O (nr)

Waiting for the Light (1990) A single mother of two (Teri Garr) struggles to make a go of an old diner until an apparition staged by her eccentric aunt (Shirley MacLaine) is mistaken for a miracle and draws crowds to the sight. Lackadaisical direction by Christopher Monger results in a sluggish, too pat comedy enlivened by MacLaine's zesty performance but lacking the wry satire the story calls for. Minor violence and some vulgar expressions. A-II (PG)

Wake Island (1942) Above-average World War II picture of the small Marine garrison on a tiny Pacific island overwhelmed at war's start by a Japanese naval task force. Directed by John Farrow, the script downplays the heroics of the doomed outpost comprising the usual cross-section of American types with a solid cast headed by Brian Donlevy. Wartime violence and Japanese stereotypes. A-I (br) A

Walk, Don't Run (1966) Cary Grant is the main attraction in this genial situation comedy about a rooming shortage during the Tokyo Olympics where he serves as matchmaker for roommates Samantha Eggar and Jim Hutton. Director Charles Walters brings off the sight-gags and zany dialogue in relaxed style. A-III (br) U

Walk in the Shadow (1966) Good British movie of rights in conflict when a father's religious beliefs cause him to refuse a blood transfusion for his daughter and her death results in his being put on trial. Director Basil Dearden builds the situation with precision and fairness to all concerned until, after the verdict, it reveals its own point of view. A-II (br)

Walk in the Spring Rain, A (1970) Happily married professor (Fritz Weaver) takes a sabbatical to write a book in the Great Smoky Mountains where his wife (Ingrid Bergman) finds herself falling in love with the kind, earthy handyman (Anthony Quinn). Directed by Guy Green, it's a slow-moving, old-fashioned sentimental melodrama that romantics will love and others dismiss as a tearjerker. A-III (PG) A

Walk Proud (1979) Sensitive but inarticulate Chicano youth (Robby Benson), trapped in a morass of machismo and gang warfare in Los Angeles, tries to go straight when he falls in love with a dentist's daughter. Under Robert Collins' direction, Benson is just not credible as a Chicano, and he and his gang are a singularly elderly collection of teenagers. Some violence. A-III (PG)

Walk with Love and Death, A (1969) Failed medieval romance about two young lovers (Anjelica Huston; Assaf Dayan) caught in the midst of a peasant's war and doomed to death either by knight's sword or serf's cudgel. Directed by John Huston, the dark atmosphere of feudalism is convincing but little else is, especially the acting of its two young principals. Mature theme and treatment. A-III (PG)

Walkabout (1971) Australian story of a lovely teenager (Jenny Agutter) and her six-year-old brother (Lucien John) who, stranded deep in the wilderness after their father commits suicide, are rescued by a young aborigine (David Gumpilil) who leads them to eventual safety. Nicolas Roeg does better with his stunning location photography than he does with his heavy-handed direction of a movie that practically shouts out its theme of noble savagery. Extended nude swimming scene and the aborigine's suicide are questionable elements. A-IV (R/GP appeal) AA

Walker (1987) Mangled story of William Walker, the American adventurer who overthrew the Nicaraguan government in 1855 and set up his own corrupt regime until deposed two years later. The potential drama of these historical events is ignored by director Alex Cox who treats the events instead in an exaggerated style closer to slapstick than satire or surrealism. Muddled treatment of a past episode of contemporary political significance, much graphic violence and some sexual references. A-IV (R) 18

Walking Hills, The (1949) Contemporary western in which an odd assortment of characters (headed by Randolph Scott; Edgar Buchanan; John Ireland; Arthur Kennedy; Ella Raines) join in searching for a fortune in gold carried by a wagon train lost crossing Death Valley in 1852. Director John Sturges' melodramatic but intriguing tale is fueled by greed, personal rivalries and guilty pasts, with plenty of moody atmosphere from endlessly shifting desert dunes and lonesome ballads performed by Josh White. Some moral muddlement and stylized violence. A-II (br) A

Walking Stick, The (1970) Young girl crippled with polio (Samantha Eggar) is courted and won by a persistent young artist (David Hemmings) who is obviously not as sincere in his affections as he appears. Director Eric Till proceeds with such a heavy hand that any subtleties are lost in a welter of dramatic close-ups and romantic bursts of color photography. A-III (PG) A

Walking Tall (1973) Fact-based story of Tennessee sheriff Buford Pusser (Joe Don Baker) who walks tall and clubs freely in his campaign to close down rural vice in the county where he lives as well as root out the accommodating political corruption that allows the vice to flourish. Nice objectives but the means used to achieve them in director Phil Karlson's dramatization are ignoble, ugly and downright vicious. Super-violent rendering of a noxious vigilante message. O (R) X

Walking Tall, Part II (see: "Part II, Walking Tall").

Walkover (1969) Polish drama directed by Jerzy Skolimowski carries on the story of "Identification Marks: None" whose young hero is now making a meager living as a boxer unable to get a factory job. Scheduled to fight a tough ring opponent, he flees town but returns to face the challenge, and presumably the challenge of life in a socialist state. Its theme of alienation and its episodic presentation serve to disorient the viewer but the work leads to a positive conclusion of self-awareness. A-II (nr)

Wall in Jerusalem, A (1972) Excellent documentary account of the birth of the state of Israel in 1948, and its struggle for survival ever since, limits itself chiefly to political history, detailing various major events and the leaders who participated in them. Director Frederic Rossif's compilation of archival footage makes a fascinating visual chronicle and Richard Burton's narration lets the images communicate the emotion while it understates the facts. A-I (nr)

Wall Street (1987) An earnest young stockbroker (Charlie Sheen) wants to make an honest million but a financial wheeler-dealer (Michael Douglas) teaches him that there are easier ways to make money than working for it. Directed by Oliver Stone, the cautionary tale does a creditable job in showing how part of the financial community has made greed a way of life but is somewhat unconvincing in its dramatization of the corruption of an innocent and his ultimate redemption. Several scenes depicting sexual activity and some very rough language. A-IV (R)

Wanda (1971) Low-budget but impressive portrait of a woman, a nobody wandering through life conditioned to being badly used by others, who meets an insecure petty thief (Michael Higgins) and the two go off together, leaving viewers hoping this relationship will turn out better than her other experiences. Directed by and starring Barbara Loden, the movie succeeds in making an unvarnished plea for understanding the needs of isolated, impoverished human beings. A-III (GP)

Wanda Nevada (1979) Laid-back gambler (Peter Fonda who also directs) wins an orphan (Brooke Shields) in a poker game and then goes hunting for gold with her in the Grand Canyon. Indian ghosts and a couple of flesh-and-blood villains complicate matters, but not enough to make things interesting. Some violence and the unresolved nature of the relationship between the two principals make this aimless movie adult fare. A-III (PG)

Wanderer, The (1969) French screen version of the Alain-Fournier novel about the romantic illusions of youth melting into the realities and responsibilities of adulthood in a story focusing on the one boy in the class who never quite matures and ultimately brings tragedy to those he loves most. Director Jean-Gabriel Albicocco has beautifully filmed the simple narrative, conveying well the glow of nostalgia of the adult narrator remembering the years of growing up. A-II (G) X

Wanderers, The (1979) Screen version of the novel by Richard Price about a group of Italian teenagers growing up in the Bronx in 1963 has a lot of vitality and some good acting (Ken Wahl; John Friedrich; Karen Allen). Philip Kaufman's direction, however, is too pretentious to stir any real emotional response in a movie that lacks a significant context. Violence, sexual references and foul language. O (R)

Wannsee Conference, The (1987) German dramatization of the meeting held on January 20, 1942, at which the final decision was made by the Nazi leadership to exterminate all European Jews. Directed by Heinz Schirk, it's an historical document filled with anti-Semitic statements but the brutish manner of the participants shows them clearly as racists. Mature theme and treatment. A-III (nr)

Wanted Dead or Alive (1987) Bounty hunter (Rutger Hauer) tracks down a ruthless international terrorist (Gene Simmons), but is then set up as bait, loses his best friend and his lover, resulting in his inflicting a terrible vengeance on those responsible. Its rough language, bloodshed and brutality are not redeemed by director Gary Sherman's eye-for-an-eye brand of justice. O (R)

War and Peace (1956) Episodic Hollywood version of Leo Tolstoy's epic novel centers on Russian aristocrats (Mel Ferrer; Audrey Hepburn; Henry Fonda) caught up in the Napoleonic Wars. Directed by King Vidor, the U.S.-Italian co-production muddles through the human dimension of events but excels in its reenactment of military movements and historic battles, especially Napoleon's retreat from Moscow through the devastations of a Russian winter. Stylized violence and muted romance. A-I (br)

War and Peace (1968) Massive Russian version of the Tolstoy novel, originally released in three parts, evokes both the feeling of an era (1805 Russia threatened by Napoleon's march East) and Tolstoy's vision of individuals and destiny. Directed by and starring Sergei Bondarchuk as the contemplative Pierre, the movie in its sweep and detail provides an absorbing visual rendition of a great classic. A-I (GP) A

War Between Men and Women, The (1972) Caustic cartoonist with failing eyesight (Jack Lemmon) hates women, children and dogs, and naturally succumbs to the charms of a divorcee (Barbara Harris) who has three children and a terrier. Losing his sight completely, he is overtaken by a bout of self-pity that cuts him off from wife and children. Written and directed by Melville Shavelson, it tries to wring humor and pathos out of a human tragedy by using casual profanity, misanthropic wit and finally cloying sentimentality. A-III (PG) A

War Between the Planets (1971) Italian sci-fi programmer about the choleric commander (Jack Stuart) of a space expedition whose mission is to destroy a gaseous asteroid that is causing tidal waves and other catastrophic destruction on Earth. Director Anthony Dawson tries to compensate for his undernourished script by using low-budget special effects, but they don't hide the fact that this is a colossal clunker. A-I (G)

War Devils, The (1973) Routine Italian action film with Guy Madison leading a squadron of U.S. paratroopers behind German lines in Tunisia, but he turns the mission into a personal battle between himself and the German commander (Van Tenney). Director Bert Albertini serves up World War II according to the war-is-fun formula with a lot of special effects flourishes. A-III (PG)

War Game, The (1967) British docudrama about the effects of nuclear warfare on a civilian population features nonprofessionals in realistically simulated scenes. Produced, written and directed by Peter Watkins, the film gets considerable shock value from its hypothetical events, but in making the unthinkable appear possible, it raises important questions of public concern. A-III (br)

War Games (see: "Suppose They Gave a War and Nobody Came?").

War Lover, The (1962) Uneven version of the John Hersey novel set in 1943 England where a daredevil American B-24 bomber pilot (Steve McQueen) grows increasingly psychopathic while his conscientious co-pilot (Robert Wagner) finds comfort in an affair with an Englishwoman (Shirley Anne Field). Director Philip Leacock does better with the dangers of daylight bombing raids than with the story of the conflict between a social misfit who enjoys employing his destructive talents in the military and a subordinate who has a normal fear of dying. Wartime violence and discreet depiction of an affair. A-III (br) X

War of the Gargantuas (1970) Below-average Japanese monster movie about a scientist (Russ Tamblyn) whose experiments on a baby ape go awry and it and a companion grow large enough to crush the city of Tokyo. Director Inoshiro Honda relies on nature and the special effects crew to resolve the difficulty, while leaving a few cardboard buildings standing for a sequel. A-I (G)

War of the Roses, The (1989) Black comedy on the battle of the sexes has a divorce lawyer (Danny DeVito) telling the story of a couple (Michael Douglas and Kathleen Turner) who go from happy penury to wealthy discontent and then divorce proceedings that turn into a horror show as they fight over house and possessions. As director, DeVito does a good job satirizing the anger and greed of divorce settlements but has little sensitivity to the problems underlying the breakup. Nasty cartoon-like marital violence, brief but explicit sexual encounters and some rough language. A-IV (R) 15

War of the Worlds, The (1953) First-rate version of H. G. Wells' sci-fi classic about Martians invading Earth with deadly heat rays from whose destructive path through California flee nuclear physicist Gene Barry and companion Ann Robinson until the aliens meet with the unexpected. Produced by George Pal and directed by Byron Haskin, the tale is tautly told with often frightening effect, thanks to its superior model work and astonishing special effects. Some religious dimension, much menace and stylized violence. A-I (G) PG

War Paint (1953) Trekking through the desert with a peace treaty promised to an Indian chief, a cavalry officer (Robert Stack) copes with all manner of problems as his small column of troopers is decimated from without and within. Directed by Lesley Selander, the deadly journey is outlandishly contrived, though gains some interest by being filmed appropriately in Death Valley. Stylized violence, including the attempted rape of a captured Indian woman. A-III (br)

War Room, The (1993) Human interest documentary centers on the political strategies used by George Stephanopoulos and James Carville during the 1992 presidential campaign to get Bill Clinton elected. In low-key but entertaining fashion, directors D. A. Pennebaker and Chris Hegedus capture the very different styles of the two men in deflecting issues of the candidate's personal character to concentrate on a weak national economy as the reason to vote for change. Discreet sexual references and an off-screen instance of rough language. A-II (nr)

War Wagon, The (1967) Familiar western story about a supertough hombre (John Wayne) just out of jail and bent on robbing a gold shipment belonging to the villain (Bruce Cabot) who framed him and now has hired a gunman (Kirk Douglas) to kill him. Director Burt Kennedy mixes some comedy into the rough, he-man action but the result is nothing out of the ordinary. Stylized violence. A-II (br) U

Warehouse (1974) Strange Japanese tale of a blind sculptor who kidnaps a beautiful model and imprisons her in his hidden studio where she becomes as obsessed as he with tactile sensations, leading to tragedy for both. As an allegory on the consequences of enslavement to the senses, director Yasuzo Masumura's treatment will please neither hedonist nor puritan, but its technical virtuosity •.ı creating the intensely physical world of a mad artist does have some interest. A-IV (nr)

WarGames (1983) Good teen suspense thriller about a high school computer-wizard (Matthew Broderick) who breaks into a government nuclear-strategy computer and starts playing a war game, the logical conclusion of which is nuclear Armageddon. Directed by John Badham, the story loses much of its momentum when the program's designer (John Wood) is tracked down and points out the just desserts of human folly just before the slack conclusion. A few vulgar expletives. A-II (PG)

Warlock (1959) Muddled western in which the title town hires a pair of gunmen (Henry Fonda; Anthony Quinn) to enforce the law, then a former outlaw (Richard Widmark) takes the vacant job of sheriff and comes up against both the hired guns and his old gang. Director Edward Dmytryk's variation on law-and-order themes is tangled with complications that add nothing to the basic plot of justice prevailing at the end of a six-shooter. Stylized shootouts and some romantic complications. A-II (br) U

Warlock (1991) A time traveler (Richard E. Grant) from the 17th century enlists the aid of a spunky California girl (Lori Singer) to defeat a male witch (Julian Sands) on the verge of destroying humanity. Strong performances and a steady build-up of suspense help bolster producer-director

Steve Miner's preposterous tale of black magic mumbo-jumbo. Some stylized violence; minimal rough language. A-III (R) 15

Warlords of Atlantis (1978) Innocuous British adventure with two young scientists (Doug McClure; Peter Gilmore) who find themselves in the power of the rulers of an undersea kingdom where they encounter a beautiful and apparently ageless princess (Cyd Charisse). Directed by Kevin Connor, there's plenty of papier-mache monsters, wooden dialogue and leaden comic relief. A-II (PG) A

Warm December, A (1973) Black doctor (Sidney Poitier) is racing motorcycles on a vacation in England when he runs across the gorgeous niece of an African ambassador (Ester Anderson), falls in love but then learns she is dying of sickle cell anemia. Also directed by Poitier, the romantic melodrama is laid on with a sledgehammer to the tune of "Love Story" and its entertainment appeal is limited to devotees of the TV soaps. A-III (PG)

Warning Shot (1966) Story begins interestingly as a social drama about a policeman (David Janssen) who kills a highly regarded public figure. From there the movie turns into a routine detective thriller directed by Buzz Kulik with little suspense but more than a little violence. A-II (br) A

Warning Sign (1985) An accident in a genetic engineering lab where biological warfare experiments are being carried on causes those inside to be transformed into crazed zombies save for a lone security guard (Kathleen Quinlan). Written and directed by Hal Barwood, it is a run-of-the-mill exercise in gory violence. O (R) 15

Warpath (1951) Civil War veteran (Edmond O'Brien) enlists in the 7th Cavalry to track down his girlfriend's killers (Forrest Tucker; Dean Jagger), becomes a heroic Indian-fighter and warns Custer that the Sioux are massing for an attack before riding off with his new love (Polly Bergen). Director Byron Haskin's routine western has an earnest cast and some mildly interesting plot twists. Frontier violence and Indian stereotypes. A-I (br) U

Warrior Empress, The (1960) Dubbed Italian clunker directed by Pietro Francisci is set in ancient Greece where a rebel (Kerwin Matthews) fights an unjust king while wooing his poetic niece, Sappho (Tina Louise). Stylized violence, sexual innuendo and bevies of scantily clad maidens. A-III (br)

Warriors, The (1955) While leading the English forces defending Aquitaine during the Hundred Years War, Edward Prince of Wales (Errol Flynn) takes time out to rescue a lady (Joanne Dru) abducted by a French nobleman (Peter Finch). Directed by Henry Levin, the colorful British production has a good cast and well-mounted action sequences, though it takes itself more seriously than the story warrants. Much derring-do and stylized battle scenes. A-I (br)

Warriors, The (1979) Film version of Sol Yurick's novel about a youth gang trying to make their way back to their own neighborhood through a N.Y. City in which every hand is turned against them. Directed by Walter Hill, the gang's sordid adventures are of even less interest than the one-dimensional characters and stilted dialogue. Constant violence and glorification of vicious behavior. O (R) X

Wash, The (1988) Poignant chronicle of the end of a long-term Japanese-American marriage in which the wife (Nobu McCarthy) is quietly determined to forge a new, happy life for herself after years of being ignored and belittled by her husband (Mako). Director Michael Toshiyuki Uno does a wonderfully restrained job of exploring the fears that plague the couple and their grown children in coming to terms with the marriage's dissolution. Incidental rough language, a fairly explicit sexual encounter within marriage and implications of cohabitation outside marriage. A-III (nr)

Washington Story (1952) Assigned to do a hatchet job on novice congressman Van Johnson, journalist Patricia Neal has a change of heart when he stands up for the national interest. Written and directed by Robert Pirosh, it's less a drama than a patriotic civics lesson, chiefly of interest for its picture of the relatively unsophisticated trappings of yesteryear's federal government. A-I (br) U

Watched! (1974) Interesting independent production about a drug case prosecutor (Stacy Keach) who is set up by his own agents after he begins to have second thoughts about the legality of their surveillance methods. Written and directed by John Parsons, the movie suggests that bugging has become a way of life in America, with some well-executed scenes of extralegal surveillance techniques. A-III (R)

Watcher in the Woods, The (1980) Mediocre Disney suspense-thriller in which an American teenager (Lynn-Holly Johnson) staying in a gloomy English country house tries to solve the mystery of what happened to the teenage girl who disappeared from the house 30 years before. Directed by John Hough, the script and its mystery are rather banal, but the film does have its frightening moments. Too scary for pre-teens, its primary appeal is to younger teenagers. A-II (PG)

Water (1986) This adult comedy is funnier on paper as Michael Caine stars as the frustrated governor of an underdeveloped island nation in the Caribbean, where prosperity and independence are achieved only after diuretic mineral water and oil are discovered at a defunct U.S. drilling rig. Ethnic jokes, TV sitcom-style humor and sexual innuendo predominate as "Water" oozes rather than bubbles. A-III (PG-13) 15

Waterdance, The (1992) Insightful drama of a newly wheelchair-bound writer (Eric Stoltz) in a multiracial rehabilitation center where he must deal with two battling patients (Wesley Snipes; William Forsythe) and a decision regarding his married girlfriend (Helen Hunt). Co-directed by Neal Jimenez and Michael Steinberg and based on Jimenez' experiences, the movie is an emotionally honest and exceptionally well-acted look at four distinct personalities, each at a turning point in their lives. Some discreet bedroom encounters, brief nudity and occasional rough language. A-III (R) 15

Waterhole No. 3 (1967) When the fastest con artist in the West (James Coburn) lifts a thief's wallet containing a map to a cache of stolen gold, he lights out for the loot with the robber in pursuit and the Army pursuing him. Directed by William Graham, the film's tone is coarse, bawdy and frequently just plain crude. O (br) AA

Waterland (1992) A middle-aged history teacher (Jeremy Irons) recounts to his class his own troubled adolescent history and the resulting guilt that weighs so heavily on his rocky marriage to a woman (Sinead Cusack) who is suffering a nervous breakdown. Stephen Gyllenhaal directs a rambling, unwieldy story of dark sexual secrets, madness and murder whose tragic elements are dissipated by the jarring flashbacks. Much discussion of sexual matters, a discreet sexual encounter and some nudity. A-III (R) 15

Waterloo (1971) Stately, grandiose set piece re-creates Napoleon's return from exile on Elba to his final defeat at Waterloo. Director Sergei Bondarchuk reduces the two principal opponents, Napoleon (Rod Steiger) and Wellington (Christopher Plummer), to little more than historical caricatures speaking the famous epigrams attributed to them. Yet the movie comes alive in the broad, colorful sweep of action sequences showing an epic moment in european history. A-II (G) U

Watermelon Man (1970) When a mindlessly bigoted white (Godfrey Cambridge) one night turns black, he undergoes the indignities and injustices of white America. Unfortunately, in dealing with all-too-familiar racial stereotypes (sexual, musical, commercial), director Melvin Van Peebles' satire is crude, embarrassing, and at times consciously offensive. Though terribly uneven, it at least attempts to deal with the festering ulcer of everyday racial prejudice. A-IV (R) X

Watership Down (1978) British animated adaptation of Richard Adams' popular novel about a band of brave rabbits making a dangerous journey in search of a new home has been done with taste and intelligence under Martin Rosen's direction. Some of the voices belong to John Hurt, Ralph Richardson, Denholm Elliot and Harry Andrews, with Zero Mostel providing comic relief as a zany German seagull. Some scenes may be too intense for younger children. A-II (PG) U

Wattstax (1973) Exciting documentary directed by Mel Stuart with rock, jazz, and general all-around soul performers (Issac Hayes; The Staple Singers; Bar-Kays), centering on the black experience and, in particular, the Los Angeles community of Watts. Giving it continuity is a funny but sad and, at times, raunchy commentary by Richard Pryor. A-III (R)

Way, Way Out! (1966) Jerry Lewis movie about a trip to the moon is preoccupied with sex in its dialogue, costuming and situations. O (br) A

Way We Live Now, The (1970) Advertising agency director (Nicholas Pryor), separated from his wife, has long conversations with himself and imaginary famous visitors but his time is mostly given to stalking and bedding women. Written, produced, directed and photographed by Barry Brown, the incessant talk is pretentious and the long string of sexual adventures tedious but exploitative. O (R)

Way We Were, The (1973) Robert Redford and Barbra Streisand as ill-matched lovers in a seriocomic story sweeping from Ivy League idylls in the late-1930s into World War II and on to Hollywood in the postwar era of blacklisting. There is just too much material here for anyone to put into a coherent shape, and director Sydney Pollack succumbs to the temptation of trivializing the periods and their events in favor of the sheer glamour of it all. It's slick and shallow, but romantics may find it diverting. A-III (PG) A

Way West, The (1967) Fairly good pioneer western with Kirk Douglas as a harried wagonmaster trying to get a wagon train of western settlers through the mountains and past Indian perils. Director Andrew V. McLaglen gets rugged acting support from Richard Widmark and Robert Mitchum, with Lola Albright on hand for the boys to fight over. A-III (br) A

Wayne's World (1992) Dopey comedy about two bumblers (Mike Myers; Dana Carvey) whose cable access talk show is threatened by a smarmy producer (Rob Lowe). Director Penelope Spheeris stretches what was originally a "Saturday Night Live" TV skit into 95 mindless minutes of numbing nonsense.

Sexist attitudes, implied premarital encounter, some sexual innuendo and toilet humor. A-III (PG-13) PG

Wayne's World 2 (1993) Inane comedy sequel in which overgrown adolescents Wayne and Garth (Mike Myers; Dana Carvey) juggle trouble with girlfriends (Tia Carrere; Kim Basinger) while throwing a Woodstock-like rock concert without performers or ticket sales. Director Stephen Surjik simply cranks up the sophomoric humor, adding spoofs of other movies to liven up the lads' lame repertoire of airhead asides. Frequent sexual innuendo, recurring rear nudity, minor violence and occasional profanity. A-III (PG-13) PG

W. C. Fields and Me (1976) Directed by Arthur Hiller, this story of the romance between the Hollywood comedian (Rod Steiger) and Carlotta Monti (Valerie Perrine) distorts the people and events of an era shamelessly and has a tone of leering vulgarity that destroys any pretense of serious intent. O (PG) AA

We All Loved Each Other So Much (1977) Warm and moving Italian comedy about three men (Vittorio Gassman; Nino Manfredi; Stefano Satta Flores) who love the same woman (Stefania Sandrelli) at one time or another, with varying degrees of intensity, over the course of three decades. Directed by Ettore Soola, it is a rare, wise and entertaining movie on the theme of love and friendship. A-II (PG)

We Dive at Dawn (1943) Taut World War II picture in which a British submarine tracks a German battleship into the enemy waters of the Baltic, then runs out of fuel after torpedoing it. Director Anthony Asquith turns the action story into a character study of men in war, focusing on the sub's capable captain (John Mills) and two seamen (Eric Portman and Niall MacGinnis) with very different marital problems. Wartime violence and domestic misunderstandings. A-II (br) U

We Live Again (1934) Hollywood version of Leo Tolstoy's novel, "Resurrection," about a Russian prince (Fredric March) who learns years later that he has ruined the life of a peasant girl (Anna Sten) on his aunt's estates by leaving her pregnant, then tries to atone by joining her when she is sent to Siberia for a crime of which she is innocent. Director Rouben Mamoulian evokes both the beauty of the Russian spirit and the injustices of the czarist regime but the characters and their emotions are melodramatically thin. Muddled treatment of an idealistic theme. A-II (br)

We Will All Meet in Paradise (1978) Thin French comedy about the life and times of four overaged, overindulged, middle-class Dead End Kids (Jean Rochfort; Claude Brasseur; Guy Bedos; Victor Lanoux) as they go through a round of sophomoric escapades.

Directed by Yves Robert, the result is a tepid comedy of manners whose sole merit is the considerable charm of the performers. Adultery figures in the plot. A-III (PG)

We're Back! A Dinosaur's Story (1993) Magically transported to present-day N.Y. City, four friendly dinos are saved by a gruff street urchin and a lonely little girl when an evil circus master changes the prehistoric creatures into snarling monsters. Steven Spielberg's animated production of Hudson Talbott's children's story sacrifices much of its charm and character appeal for an overabundance of busy and noisy misadventures that may delight children a lot more than their elders. A-I (G)

We're No Angels (1989) Heavy-handed comic misadventure in which two escaped convicts (Robert De Niro and Sean Penn) hide out in a monastery pretending to be priests while they figure out a way to cross the border into Canada. David Mamet's script has plenty of comic possibilities in contrasting the spiritual impoverishment of the two earthbound clods with the faith and innocence of the unworldly community of monks, but director Neil Jordan plays the piece so broadly that the result may appear to some as an irreverent farce, questionable in taste and treatment of religion. Some sexual references, several scenes of hard-edged violence and a bemused agnostic attitude toward religion. A-IV (PG-13) 15

Weapons of the Spirit (1989) Pierre Sauvage is a Jew who survived the Holocaust only because he happened to be born in 1944 in Le Chambon-sur-Lignon, a French town that provided safe harbor for some 5,000 Jews during the Second World War. Returning to this largely Protestant community to make a documentary about those remaining strong-minded Christian farmers, educators, and clergy who risked their lives as an act of faith against Nazi racism, Sauvage examines how and why they managed to get away with their massive unorganized opposition when other French resistance fighters faced reprisals. The result is a moving tribute to human solidarity and a reminder of the power of Christian teachings. A-II (nr)

Wedding, A (1978) Some 20 major characters, and perhaps twice as many minor ones, assemble for a satiric assault on the extravagance of a wedding in a family recently risen to affluence. With no central plot worth mentioning, director Robert Altman lets the action go in every direction at once, much of it revolving around the many skeletons in the family closet. The actors (among them, Lillian Gish; John Cromwell; Vittorio Gassman; Dina Merrill; Howard

Duff; Carol Burnett; Paul Dooley) are better than the material in this extremely uneven effort that is further marred by sexual goings-on and gratuitous nudity. O (R) 15

Wedding Banquet, The (1993) A homosexual couple in New York decides to help a Chinese friend (May Chin) get a green card by having one of them (Winston Chao) marry her in name only, but wind up living together when the groom's elderly parents (Sihung Lung; Ah-Leh Gua) arrive from Taiwan for a prolonged stay with the newlyweds. Director Ang Lee stresses the human side of the comic complications in a bittersweet comedy of manners. A sympathetic portrayal of a gay live-in relationship, fleeting nudity and occasional rough language. A-IV (R) 15

Wedding in Blood (1974) Disappointing French crime story about a couple (Stephane Audran, Michel Piccoli) who, drawn together by an almost incendiary passion, conspire to murder their spouses. Instead of trying to create a truly chilling horror film out of this story of forbidden desire and desperate murder, director Claude Chabrol uses it to express his moralistic views of the middle class and their loss of values. A-III (PG)

Wedding in White (1973) Hard-edged but compassionate Canadian drama set in a small town during World War II tells the story of a father (Donald Pleasence) who, learning his teenage daughter (Carol Kane) is pregnant after an assault by a drunken soldier, persuades his best friend (Leo Phillips), a bachelor in his mid-50s, to marry the girl, thereby saving the family reputation. Director William Fruet uses the situation to focus on the limited horizons and narrow attitudes of small-town life, which proves just as much a closed society as the nearby prisoner-of-war camp where the father works. A-IV (R)

Wedding Night (1970) Irish movie about a young Catholic woman (Tessa Wyatt) whose fears of sex and pregnancy make her unable to consummate her marriage. Directed by Piers Haggard, the story is told in strong and pointed discussions of the contraceptive pill, morality, the medical profession and an uncomprehending husband. Thoughtful drama about a deeply emotional subject, but offers no posittive solutions. A-IV (PG)

Wedding Party, The (1969) Unsure about marrying his fiance (Jill Clayburgh), a prospective bridegroom (Charles Pfluger) tries a variety of ruses to call off the wedding. Directed by Cynthia Munroe, Brian De Palma and Wilford Leach. the low-budget black-and-white production tries all kinds of camera tricks but can't save its hodgepodge of comedy, satire and fantasy. A-III (nr)

Wednesday's Child (1972) British dramatization of the gradual psychic destruction of a young woman (Sandy Ratcliff) by her repressive working-class parents and by the behaviorist theories practiced on her in a government-run mental hospital. Written by David Mercer and directed by Kenneth Loach, the result is a plea for respect for the individuality of the person that is a powerfully moving, incontrovertible statement. A-III (nr)

Wee Willie Winkie (1937) Unlikely but likeable Shirley Temple vehicle from a Rudyard Kipling story in which she stars as the American granddaughter of the crusty commander (C. Aubrey Smith) of a British Army post in northern India where she has a glorious time playing a soldier of the Queen under the tutelage of a seasoned sergeant (Victor McLaglen), becomes the friend of the local rebel chief (Cesar Romero) and stops a border uprising. Director John Ford gets some lively humor from the ranks of the military post together with a few good battle scenes but does best with Shirley parading around in her kilted uniform and in her childish byplay with the burly McLaglen. Colonial rhetoric doesn't impede the sentimental fun. A-I (br)

Weekend (1968) Apocalyptic French vision of modern civilization's self-destruction is constructed out of a disjointed narrative of motorized mayhem, dehumanized people and mindless revolution. Directed by Jean-Luc Godard, the movie's attempt to shock and its static militant speeches become simplistic attacks on traditional morality and existing social values. O (nr) X

Weekend at Bernie's (1989) Silly, one-joke farce about two witless, low-level executives (Andrew McCarthy; Jonathan Silverman) who hide the fact that their boss (Terry Kiser) has been murdered so they can take advantage of his weekend beach house invitation. Director Ted Kotcheff knocks the conscienceless, self-absorbed hedonists who don't notice that their host is dead, but the main focus is on how easy it is to lie to get whatever you want in the way of materialistic ambitions. Alcohol and drug abuse, sexual innuendos and implied necrophilia. O (PG-13) 15

Weekend at Bernie's II (1993) Moronic sequel set in the Caribbean, where two junior executives (Andrew McCarthy; Jonathan Silverman) pass off the corpse of their boss (Terry Kiser) as alive so they can get the funds he embezzled in order to clear their reputations. Writer-director Robert Klane's witless comedy resorts to a voodoo subplot in which the corpse becomes a dancing zombie, but nothing can save a script that was already dead on arrival. Disrespectful treatment of a dead person, some mild sexual innuendo and tasteless gallows humor. A-III (PG)

Weekend at Dunkirk (1966) French sergeant (Jean-Paul Belmondo), among the mass of troops trapped by the Germans in the Dunkirk pocket in June 1940, has to decide whether to try to escape with the British, desert and return home, or stay and be captured. Directed by Henri Verneuil, the beaches of Dunkirk were a bitter French defeat, and this movie is a grim picture of war without any of the usual movie heroics. A-III (br)

Weekend Murders (1972) Routine Italian mystery movie in which the relatives (among them, Anna Moffo) of a deceased British earl gather at his plush estate to learn of their legacies, fall prey to grisly pranks, sexual dalliances and ultimately five murders. The real villain of the piece is director Michele Lupo, who indulges in acute camera angles, and wears out his zoom lens in a supreme display of technique over talent. A-III (R)

Weekend Pass (1984) Four sailors just out of boot camp hit Los Angeles on a weekend pass in this mediocre effort. Writer-director Lawrence Bassoff has put a variety of Los Angeles backgrounds to good use, but his script is thoroughly pedestrian. Although veering toward romantic wholesomeness, some graphic, utterly gratuitous nudity in an early cabaret sequence is highly offensive. O (R)

Weekend with the Babysitter (1970) Low-budget exploitation movie about a suburban husband's marijuana smoking with the family's teenage sitter while his wife shoots heroin with cutthroat drug smugglers. Sexual activity predominates in a ludicrous script with amateur actors. O (R)

Weird Science (1985) Two high school nerds conjure up their idea of the perfect woman (Kelly LeBrock) on a computer and have all their dreams of popularity and wild adventure fulfilled. Essentially a one-joke affair, written with an excess of rough language and directed with too many sexual inferences by John Hughes, it's a vulgar, mediocre effort that does a hard sell of promiscuity to teenagers. O (PG-13) 15

Welcome Home (1989) Shot down over Cambodia in 1970, an Air Force flyer (Kris Kristofferson) is officially declared dead, but 17 years later, when illness separates him from his new Cambodian family, he returns to the States to renew ties with the American family he left behind. As directed by Franklin J. Schaffner, this weepy melodrama fails to shed light on the very real problems facing Vietnam veterans and their kin. Some profanity and an adulterous sexual encounter. A-III (R)

Welcome Home Roxy Carmichael (1990) A small town anticipates the return of its one Hollywood celebrity, but no one in town awaits the return more eagerly than her former beau (Jeff Daniels), now a family man, and an alienated 15-year-old (Winona Ryder) who suspects Roxy may secretly be her mom. Director Jim Abrahams takes a basically frivolous story and, helped by Ryder's fine performance, develops it with charm, warmth and a small dose of insight about human relationships. References to a premarital relationship, minimal vulgar expressions and a flash of nudity. A-II (PG-13) 12

Welcome Home, Soldier Boys (1972) Four Vietnam vets (Joe Don Baker, Alan Vint, Paul Koslo and Elliott Street) pull into the sleepy hamlet of Hope, New Mexico, gang-rape a girl, kill everyone in town and then burn it to the ground. Directed by Richard Compton, the gruesome and ultimately cynical movie contributes nothing to understanding the problems of Vietnam veterans. O (R) X

Welcome to L.A. (1977) Listless and pretentious account of the amorous adventures of a young songwriter (Keith Carradine) whose charm is such that women jostle and trample one another in a mad rush to enjoy his favor. Writer-director Alan Rudolph's unsurprising message is that sex without love is unrewarding and that Los Angeles has some sort of monopoly on self-deception. Gratuitous nudity. O (R) AA

Welcome to the Club (1971) Generally witless comedy about a naive Quaker morale officer (Brian Foley) who attempts to integrate a postwar Hiroshima officer's club, and comes off more as a fool than as a nice guy going through some sobering disillusionment. Directed by William Shenson, the result is rather depressing and, whatever its good intentions in trying to satirize both the military and bigotry, it contains considerable offensiveness, notably foul language. O (R) X

West Side Story (1961) Rousing Broadway musical, with choreography by Jerome Robbins and music by Leonard Bernstein, is a contemporary, inner-city adaptation of the classic Romeo and Juliet theme, in which Richard Beymer and Natalie Wood play Tony and Maria, the star-crossed lovers set apart ethnically and by their opposing street gang backgrounds. Directed by Robert Wise, the movie captures the grit of life in the city's lower depths, with glimmers of hope and elements of tragedy in a delicate balance. In terms of energy and verve, its songs and dance numbers are outstanding. Some of the social issues, relationships and street language, however, require a fairly mature sensibility on the part of the viewer. A-III (br) A

Westbound (1959) Standard western about a Union officer (Randolph Scott) put in charge of a stagecoach line carrying California gold past Confederate sympathizers (led by Andrew Duggan). Directed by Budd Boetticher, it offers the usual brand of heroics and villainy but little else. Stylized violence. A-I (br) U

Western Union (1941) A reformed outlaw (Randolph Scott) and a rich tenderfoot (Robert Young) help a Western Union engineer (Dean Jagger) fight off Indians and Confederate raiders (headed by Barton MacLane) while stringing the last link in the telegraph line connecting the East and West coasts in 1861. The heroic theme is directed by Fritz Lang, with plenty of western action and colorful characters galore, including Slim Summerville's comically fearful cook. Frontier violence and Indian stereotypes. A-I (br) U

Westerner, The (1940) Cowboy Gary Cooper sides with the homesteaders against the cattlemen led by Roy Bean (Walter Brennan), the hanging judge of Vinegaroon, Texas. Directed by William Wellman, the situation is familiar but flavorsome and wryly fashioned, particularly Brennan's performance as the ornery judge whose ideal is the English singer, Lily Langtry. Periodic stylized violence. A-I (br) U

Westward the Women (1951) Western chronicles the adventures of 140 women (Denise Darcel, Marilyn Erskine, Hope Emerson, et al.) recruited in Chicago as prospective brides for California settlers, making their way crosscountry in a wagon train led by a tough but increasingly bemused wagonmaster (Robert Taylor). Directed by William A. Wellman, there are plenty of dangers and some losses along the trail but the trek's sentimental ending is never in doubt. Stylized frontier violence and mild sexual references. A-II (br) A

Westworld (1973) James Brolin and Richard Benjamin vacation in a futuristic resort where, during the fun and games, a western gunslinger robot (Yul Brynner) malfunctions, turns on the vacationers and starts to stalk them. Unfortunately, after about ten minutes, writer-director Michael Crichton has explored all the subtleties of the one-idea situation. Some ludicrous nonsense about "willing" female robots. A-III (PG) AA

Wetherby 1985) Vanessa Redgrave plays a schoolteacher in a small town who becomes the indirect victim of an act of violence that seems to be wholly unprovoked. But was it? This superbly acted but somewhat thin and contrived murder mystery, written and directed by playwright David Hare, explores the question of suicide in a careful, literate and sometimes compelling fashion. Good entertainment for mature viewers, although there is some violence and a few fairly restrained bedroom scenes. A-III (R) 15

Whales of August, The (1987) Two aged sisters (Bette Davis and Lillian Gish), sharing a cottage on an island off the coast of Maine, rely upon each other since one is blind but wealthy and the other is poor but kind. Director Lindsay Anderson's picture of old age and sibling rivalries is finely told through mood and characterization, and though sentimental, it is full of heart and small truths. Some incidental profanity. A-II (PG)

What? (1973) Innocent young woman (Sydne Rome) wanders into the house of an eccentric millionaire (Hugh Griffith) and is assaulted by various perverted characters, stripped of her identity as well as her clothes and spends the rest of the movie in various stages of undress. Director Roman Polanski apparently intended this bizarre Alice-in-Wonderland story to be amusing, but its gross sexual activity and extensive nudity, as well as some violently scabrous language, make it anything but. O (X/R)

What a Way to Die (see: "Beyond Control").

What about Bob? (1991) Multiphobic kook (Bill Murray) drives his shrink (Richard Dreyfuss) bonkers by tagging along on the doctor's family vacation at a New Hampshire lake. Frank Oz's relaxed direction picks up speed halfway through, providing ample lightweight laughs in predictable predicaments. Some mildly vulgar expressions and cartoonish violence. A-II (PG)

What Am I Bid? (1967) The son of a country music star decides to forgo cattle auctioneering and launch his own singing career is the thin storyline used to showcase some old and new talent in the world of country and western music. Written and directed by Gene Nash, it's pleasant if unimaginative entertainment. A-I (br)

What Became of Jack and Jill? (1972) Paul Nicholas and Vanessa Howard are the title characters who gruesomely plot the death of Jack's 78-year-old grandmother (Mona Washbourne) so they can enjoy London with the old lady's money. The moral of this rather improbable, mediocre little horror is offset by director Bill Blain's sleazy resort to a lot of ogling, pawing and some attic sex. O (GP)

What Did You Do in the War, Daddy? (1966) The combination of bosomy Italian girls and a local wine festival sidetrack a platoon of invading G.I.s (Dick Shawn; Carroll O'Connor; James Coburn; Cameron Mitchell; Aldo Ray) who are supposed to be out after Nazi troops. Directed by Blake Edwards, vulgarity and dumb sight-gags are the order of the day in a movie presumably showing that war isn't hellish at all but just a lot of off-color fun. O (br) A

What Do You Say to a Naked Lady? (1970) Allen Funt employs the familiar hidden-camera techniques of the TV show, except that here he focuses on nudity as a supposed source of humor. Unfortunately, the use of unsuspecting victims confronted with completely naked men and women walking out of office elevators or flagging down taxis shows no more maturity or insight than the silly pranks on the TV show. O (X/R)

What Lola Wants (see: "Damn Yankees").

What Next? (1970) Swedish exploitation movie about a prostitute, her incestuous relationship with her father, her blackmailing of the man who killed him and her purification in a flaming finale, which only adds to the repugnance of the proceedings. O (nr)

What Price Hollywood? (1932) Alcoholic movie director (Lowell Sherman) turns a waitress into a top star (Constance Bennett) who marries a handsome stuffed shirt (Neil Hamilton) with predictable results. Director George Cukor's dated period piece plays the Hollywood scene first for laughs, then tragedy with a good supporting cast including Gregory Ratoff, Eddie Anderson and Louise Beavers. Mild black stereotyping, romantic complications and a suicide. A-III (br)

What's Eating Gilbert Grape (1993) A compassionate stranger (Juliette Lewis) helps a frustrated young man (Johnny Depp) deal with the burden of heading a dysfunctional household consisting of his mom (Darlene Cates), who is a 500-pound recluse, and his mentally disabled younger brother (Leonardo DiCaprio), who is often a danger to himself. Though the narrative sometimes ambles and rambles, director Lasse Hallstrom's offbeat, often downbeat drama features finely honed performances and a poignant script that never insults the emotional, mental or physical frailties of its characters. An implied affair and brief violence. A-III (PG-13)

What's Good for the Goose (1970) Failed British movie in which a glum bank manager (Norman Wisdom) is introduced to the psychedelic world of free love, loud music and general aimlessness by an uninhibited hitchhiker (Sally Geeson) who is always ready to disrobe and jump into bed. Directed by Menahem Golan, the movie's attempt to pass this off as social comment fails to overcome the exploitative elements that predominate. O (R) U

What's Love Got to Do with It (1993) Musical biography of rock singer Tina Turner (played by Angela Bassett) focusing on her rise to fame and troubled marriage to abusive husband Ike (Laurence Fishburne)

until she left him and established a solo career. Director Brian Gibson serves up a spirited but ultimately superficial look at the entertainer, offsetting the ugly hysterics of a violent relationship with glossy musical set-pieces. A discreet bedroom scene, some intense domestic violence, occasional recreational drug use and recurring rough language. A-III (R)

What's New Pussycat? (1965) Wacky plot about a demented psychiatrist (Peter Sellers) whose efforts to sort out his hectic life bring him into contact with an inordinate number of loony types (Peter O'Toole; Capuchine; Woody Allen; Paula Prentiss; Ursula Andress) running free and easy, in and around Paris. Directed by Clive Donner, the laughs in this attempt at screwball comedy are only intermittent and their taste level is abysmally low. O (br) U

What's So Bad About Feeling Good (1968) Colorful tropical bird infects the rude, scowling citizens of New York City with a mysterious happiness virus and within hours everyone is smiling and polite to one another, including a couple of reformed hippies (George Peppard; Mary Tyler Moore). But when New Yorkers also quit gambling, smoking and drinking, the government develops an antidote to protect tax revenues. Producer-director George Seaton has an amusing little satire on urban life that some may find infectious. Romantic complications. A-III (br) A

What's the Matter with Helen? (1971) Two mothers (Debbie Reynolds; Shelley Winters) with a troubled past start a dance school for children in 1930s' Hollywood until poor Shelley goes bonkers and puts her entire rabbit warren to the knife. Director Curtis Harrington has a lot of fun with the gaudy period settings and fashions but mixes in a bit too much blood and gore for younger viewers—but they wouldn't appreciate Reynolds' tap dances and tangos anyway. A-III (GP) X

What's Up, Doc? (1972) Funny, stylish and entertaining comedy loosely strings two plots together, one involving a group of four identical valises, the other following a kooky student (Barbra Streisand) in her zany pursuit of an absent-minded college professor (Ryan O'Neal) who has come to San Francisco with his persistent fiancee (Madeline Kahn) to receive a research grant. Produced and directed by Peter Bogdanovich, this throwback to the Hollywood screwball comedies of the 1930s is great fun for family audiences. A-I (G) U

What's Up Tiger Lily? (1966) Woody Allen's re-editing and dubbing of a Japanese spy movie is at times amusing, often self-conscious but mostly tiresome. Some smutty dialogue and visuals. O (br)

Whatever Happened to Aunt Alice? (1969) Suspense thriller with Geraldine Page as a widow, left without any observable means of income, who combines murder and gardening as profitable pastimes in bilking a series of housekeepers out of their life savings. Routine chiller directed by Lee H. Katzin. A-II (PG) 15

Wheeler Dealers, The (1963) Romantic comedy about a cunning Texas high-roller (James Garner) who falls for a Wall Street broker (Lee Remick), then is indicted for helping her sell stock in a product that went out with high-button shoes. Director Arthur Hiller's comic treatment of financial plungers is no longer as wacky as it once seemed, though the characters still please. Romantic situations. A-II (br)

When a Stranger Calls (1979) Homicidal maniac (Tony Beckley) stalks a babysitter (Carol Kane) in this plodding, mediocre thriller directed by Fred Walton. Some intense violence and the impending threat of violence are adult fare. A-III (R) AA

When Dinosaurs Ruled the Earth (1971) British film directed by Val Guest is a few cuts above the average prehistoric monster movie and, aside from some Hollywood bikinis on the cavewomen, has some authentic-looking overgrown reptiles, birds, and dinosaurs. It's enjoyable for the youngsters, not too scary and colorful enough to hold attention. A-I (G) PG

When Eight Bells Toll (1971) British adaptation of an Alistair MacLean novel about a Bond-type government agent (Anthony Hopkins) and his gentle partner (Corin Redgrave) who are dispatched to the Western Highland lochs to find out what lies behind the disappearance of several gold-carrying ships. Directed by Etienne Perier, the plot employs masterful twists and crosscurrents, but though handled with restraint, it is adult fare both in story and treatment. A-III (GP) 15

When Father Was Away on Business (1985) Yugoslavian production set in the time of Tito's break with the Soviet Union, has a plot following a philandering husband who is denounced by his mistress as a political deviant and ends up in a labor camp. This warm human comedy by director Emir Kusturica ends in the resolution of personal problems and political differences during a madcap wedding feast of family forgiveness. Some coarse language and partial nudity are treated with restraint. A-III (R) 18

When Harry Met Sally . . . (1989) Story of the unlikely ways people connect with suitable marriage partners focuses on the comic and touching travails of one couple (Billy Crystal and Meg Ryan) over a dozen years as they wander in and out of each other's lives. Director Rob Reiner's comedy about love, commitment, sex and friendship intercuts distracting testimonials from elderly couples about how they met. Though there is much graphic talk about sex and love in Yuppieland and an indiscreet spoof of female orgasm, the movie demonstrates that true love and commitment are still here to stay. Implied sexual promiscuity. A-IV (R) 15

When the Daltons Rode (1940) Forced off their land by a crooked developer (George Bancroft), the Dalton Brothers (Broderick Crawford, Brian Donlevy and Stewart Irwin) become feared outlaws, though a steadfast friend (Randolph Scott) tries to clear their name. Directed by George Marshall, the old story is played for all its worth until the final demise of the Dalton Gang in a Kansas City shootout. Stylized violence. A-II (br) A

When the Legends Die (1972) Above-average western in which a sharp rodeo hustler (Richard Widmark) takes in an 18-year-old Ute Indian (Frederic Forrest) and teaches him the tricks of the trade, but the youth does not see the value in taking money from suckers and returns to the reservation, sadder but wiser. Produced and directed by Stuart Millar, the fine character study of the two principals is chiefly what is of interest here, and not its commonplace message. Implied sexual affair. A-III (PG) A

When the Whales Came (1989) Some seventy years after an 1844 legend about a curse befalling England's Scilly Isles for slaughtering a pack of beached whales, a deaf hermit (Paul Scofield) successfully manages to warn neighboring islanders to lay off some newly beached whales. In a tedious adaptation of Michael Morpurgo's children's book, director Clive Rees lets a lovely story with the gentle hermit, two island children and an ecological theme get bogged down in boring extraneous action and predictable period caricatures. Occasional menace involving parental abuse and minimal rough language. A-II (PG)

When Time Ran Out (1980) Paul Newman, Jacqueline Bisset, Burgess Meredith, Ernest Borgnine and other unfortunates are trapped on a Pacific island when the local volcano lets go. Directed by James Goldstone, the disaster epic is so dreadful that it could put an end to the disaster epic once and for all, though it probably won't. A-II (PG)

When Worlds Collide (1951) With Earth doomed to destruction by an onrushing star, scientists build a rocket ship to serve as a new Noah's ark hoping to continue the human race on a new planet. Director Rudolph Mate's doomsday scenario is about as convincing as the wooden romance between Barbara Rush and Richard Derr, though the special effects by producer George Pal hold some interest. Stylized violence. A-II (br)

When You Comin' Back, Red Ryder? (1979) A half-crazed Vietnam vet (Marjoe Gortner) and his hippie girlfriend (Candy Clark) terrorize and humiliate five people (notably, Lee Grant and Pat Hingle) in a roadside diner in a desolate region of New Mexico. Though there are some credible performances in this adaptation of Mark Medoff's play directed by Milton Katselas, its psychological as well as physical violence and frequent sexual crudities destroy whatever social comment may have been intended. O (R)

Where Angels Fear to Tread (1992) Satiric comedy filters through tragedy in E. M. Forster's turn-of-the-century story of a wealthy English widow (Helen Mirren) who impulsively marries a penniless young Italian (Giovanni Guidelli) against the wishes of her in-laws. As directed by Charles Sturridge, the cultural clash between fiery Italian and straightlaced Britons affords several well-observed character studies. Brief violence. A-II (PG)

Where Angels Go . . . Trouble Follows! (1968) Weak sequel to "The Trouble with Angels" in which a liberal young nun (Stella Stevens) tries to update the convent boarding school headed by a traditionalist Mother Superior (Rosalind Russell) by leading a busload of nuns and their students to a peace rally. Directed by James Neilson, the old pros overcome the painfully contrived story and turn it into light, unsophisticated entertainment. A-I (G) U

Where Danger Lives (1950) Dark, muddled tale of a doctor (Robert Mitchum) on the run from the police with the wife (Faith Domergue) of the man (Claude Rains) he believes he killed. Directed by John Farrow, the tension is artificial in a situation that has little interest. Stylized violence and romantic complications. A-II (br) A

Where Does It Hurt? (1972) Failed comedy about a slick California hospital and its administrator (Peter Sellers), who divides his time between fleecing unwitting patients and molesting the pretty females on the staff. Directed by Rod Amateau, the result is not only unfunny, but unrelentingly tasteless and offensive. O (R) X

Where Eagles Dare (1969) A spy-counterspy melodrama set in the Bavarian Alps during World War II pits Richard Burton, Clint Eastwood and Mary Ure against what must be half the German army ensconced in a castle literally inaccessible except by cable car. Brian Hutton directs the Alistair MacLean script, which consists of an interminable, totally implausible series of killings, escapes and pyrotechnic displays. A-III (PG)

Where It's At (1969) Las Vegas casino owner (David Janssen) teaches his disinterested son

(Robert Drivas) the tricks of exploiting the tourist trade, but the lad beats his father at his own game, gains control of the casino and then hands it back, realizing it is his father's whole life but will never be his. Director Garson Kanin tries to gloss over a most implausible script by resorting to some sexual diversions. O (R) X

Where the Boys Are '84 (1984) Four women college students (Lisa Hartman, Lorna Luft, Wendy Schaal and Lynn-Holly Johnson) go to Fort Lauderdale for the spring break and carry on like amateur hookers, but viewers are supposed to believe its very wholesome and therapeutic. Director Hy Averback's updating of a silly 1960 movie contains nudity, sexually oriented humor and an appalling moral outlook. O (R) 15

Where the Buffalo Roam (1980) Bill Murray portrays famed underground journalist Hunter S. Thompson, who seems to have derived much of his inspiration from drugs and alcohol. Director Art Linson tries to blend serious social concern with outrageous comedy but is only intermittently successful. Rough language and use of drugs. A-III (PG)

Where the Heart Is (1990) Pointless, humorless farce about a wealthy demolitions expert (Dabney Coleman) who attempts to teach his three grown but spoiled offspring a lesson in self-sufficiency by leaving them stranded in an abandoned Brooklyn tenement. Director John Boorman shows little sensitivity to family responsibilities and is offensively crass in dealing with minority issues and the reality of homelessness. Some nudity in the context of artwork, rough language and sexual innuendos. A-III (R) A

Where the Lilies Bloom (1974) Four sturdy Appalachian children keep the death of their widowed father a secret so the state won't take them away to an orphan's home and provide for themselves out of the profits of "wildcrafting" (collecting and preparing certain herbs and wild flowers prized for their medicinal qualities). The Robert B. Radnitz production directed by William A. Graham tells its story of youngsters learning to care for themselves in the adult world with warm humor and genuine sensitivity for the conditions of life for the rural poor. A rare and satisfying entertainment for the entire family. A-I (G)

Where the Sidewalk Ends (1950) Quirky crime story of a hardened cop (Dana Andrews) who accidentally kills a suspect, then falls for the dead man's girlfriend (Gene Tierney) while trying to pin the murder on a slippery mobster (Gary Merrill). Director Otto Preminger diverts attention from the improbable plot twists by focusing on the gritty atmosphere and matching characterizations. Stylized violence and troubled relationships. A-II (br)

Where Were You When the Lights Went Out? (1968) Typical Doris Day vehicle revolving around a woman's honor seemingly compromised but untarnished in the final reel. The only novelty here is that the story is placed in the context of the 1965 power failure that darkened New York City and director Hy Averback does get some good comic bits from Robert Morse and Terry Thomas who are caught up in the contrived circumstances of the plot during the Great Blackout. A-III (PG) A

Where's Jack? (1969) British adventure story set in 18th-century London about a locksmith's apprentice (Tommy Steele) turned thief and highwayman by necessity and a popular hero by virtue of his incredible escapes from prison. Director James Clavell carefully ensures that the cruelty and violence of the period do not overpower the human values of loyalty and comradeship that are at its heart. A-II (G) U

Where's Poppa? (1970) New York lawyer (George Segal) tries to cope with his senile mother (Ruth Gordon) by hiring a nurse (Trish Van Devere) to care for her. Directed by Carl Reiner, the situation becomes a black-humored nightmare, with gags involving rape, muggings, nursing homes and other human ills, going beyond the line of tastelessness. O (R) A

Which Way Is Up? (1977) A poor fruit-picker (Richard Pryor), suddenly finds himself the chosen tool of the powerful and in a position to be rewarded amply for his subservience. Directed by Michael Schultz and adapted from Lina Wertmuller's "The Seduction of Mimi," the serious nature of the comedy is fatally undercut by Pryor's too broad performance. Excessive reliance on foul language and sex to get laughs. O (R)

Which Way to the Front? (1970) Jerry Lewis directs and stars as a man who's rejected by the army in World War II, forms his own fighting force composed of similar rejects, defeats the Axis in Europe and proceeds to win the war in the Pacific. Some isolated skits are funny, but on the whole, poor timing and dull material make the comic fantasy seem interminable. Fantasy violence. A-II (G) U

Whiffs (1975) Elliott Gould plays a medically discharged Army private whose use as a chemical warfare guinea pig has, among other ill effects, left him impotent. Gould gets his revenge, and cures his malady, by using stolen Army gas to disable an entire town and clean out its banks. Director Ted Post does nothing to redeem a singularly unfunny and tasteless screenplay, many of whose failed jokes have to do with the hero's sexual incapacity. O (PG) AA

Whirlpool (1970) Danish exploitation import about a wealthy woman (Pia Anderson), her psychopathic nephew (Karl Lanchbury) and a young model (Vivian Neves) lured into a sex triangle that ends with her rape-murder. Director J. R. Larrath, inept at fashioning suspense or terror, suffocates his English-speaking cast in a cesspool of stupefying dialogue, sex and blood. O (X)

Whisperers, The (1967) Dame Edith Evans gives a brilliant performance as an impoverished old woman, beset by loneliness and physical infirmity, victimized and abandoned by an unfeeling husband and son, and finding her only comfort in the world of her imagination. Directed by Bryan Forbes, it is a compassionate examination of the struggles of old age and achieved without false sentimentality. A-II (br) A

Whispering Smith (1948) Offbeat western in which a soft-spoken railroad trouble-shooter (Alan Ladd) has to go after his best friend (Robert Preston) when he teams up with a crook (Donald Crisp). Directed by Leslie Fenton, the railroad setting has some interest as does the soured friendship, though the story's treatment is fairly routine. Frontier violence. A-I (br) A

Whispers in the Dark (1992) Lurid, violent melodrama has a psychiatrist (Annabella Sciorra) seeking help from her mentor (Alan Alda) after one of her patients (Deborah Unger) is murdered and her lover (Jamey Sheridan) and another patient (John Leguizamo) become prime suspects. Writer-director Christopher Crowe exploits sexual violence against women in a manipulative, tawdry potboiler. Recurring violence and nudity, graphic photos of tortured women, sexually explicit dialogue and situations and much rough language. O (R)

Whistle Blower, The (1987) Veteran spy Michael Caine finds a way to avenge the death of his son, a British intelligence agent, without jeopardizing his position in the international club of spy organizations. British director Simon Langton's murder mystery has a plot device concerning infidelity and a far more subtle, pulpy and pernicious political bite that may confuse youngsters and certainly annoy sophisticated adults. A-III (PG)

White Christmas (1954) Cheerful but synthetic musical comedy about two World War II veterans (Bing Crosby and Danny Kaye) who use their popularity as entertainers to make a success out of the winter resort opened by their wartime commander (Dean Jagger). Directed by Michael Curtiz, the postwar feel-good plot is less memorable than Kaye's clowning and Crosby's crooning of the title song among other Irving

Berlin numbers originally written for the earlier, better "Holiday Inn" (1942) pairing Crosby with Fred Astaire. While not a classic, it offers some good family entertainment. A-I (br) U

White Cliffs of Dover, The (1943) Dated patriotic sudser about an American tourist (Irene Dunne) whose whirlwind marriage to an English aristocrat (Alan Marshal) ends with his death in World War I but their child (Roddy McDowell) inherits the title and grows to become a military casualty (Peter Lawford) in World War II. Directed by Clarence Brown, it's an earnest, well-crafted sermon on Anglo-American relations with too little humor and too much bathos to be convincing. Of some interest as a period piece. A-II (br) U

White Comanche (1968) Dubbed european production directed by Gilbert Lee Kay has William Shatner playing twin brothers born of a captive white woman and a Comanche brave—one raised by whites, the other by Indians—until they meet on opposite sides in a range war that the local sheriff (Jospeh Cotton) has been unable to stop. Hokey plot and treatment paced with assorted stylized violence, including an off-screen rape. A-III (br)

White Dawn, The (1974) Challenging fact-based story of three whalers (Warren Oates, Timothy Bottoms and Lou Gossett) marooned in the 1890s on Baffin Island, 700 miles below the North Pole, who are taken in by local Eskimos but their initial warm relationship degenerates into mistrust and finally vengeance as the two alien cultures threaten each other. Directed by Philip Kaufman, the corrupting influence of civilization on the savage innocence of the natives is depicted in realistic, often grisly, detail and Eskimo sexual customs are treated without sensation or exploitation. A-III (R/PG) AA

White Fang (1991) While goldhunting with an older prospector (Klaus Maria Brandauer) on the Alaskan frontier in 1898, a youth (Ethan Hawke) befriends a snarling, attack-trained wolf-dog that helps them fend off marauders. Director Randal Kleiser's film of Jack London's classic novel combines authentic Alaskan settings, untamed wildlife and a mildly suspenseful adventure to make pleasant family fare for all but young children. Much simulated violence to animals and menace to humans. A-II (PG)

White Hunter, Black Heart (1990) Egotistical director (Clint Eastwood) persuades a writer friend (Jeff Fahey) to collaborate on making a movie in Africa, but once there the director's obsession with killing a bull elephant puts the entire project in jeopardy. Eastwood also produced and directed this blandly uninvolving adaptation of a novel about director John Huston's experiences while filming "The African Queen," but the result is best enjoyed for its on-location cinematography. Minimal violence and vulgar expressions. A-II (PG)

White Lightning (1973) Routine country melodrama in which hard-driving Arkansas moonshiner (Burt Reynolds) is paroled from prison in order to get the goods on a county sheriff (Ned Beatty) who is not only taking graft but also murdered Reynolds' kid brother. Crisply directed by Joseph Sargent, the fragmented story of rough backwoods codes and justice is of less interest than the high-powered car chases that keep the dust swirling on those backcountry roads. Some romantic escapades. A-III (PG) X

White Line Fever (1975) Young trucker Jan-Michael Vincent fights corruption in director Jonathan Kaplan's passably entertaining, though needlessly violent action movie. Benign attitude toward vigilantism. A-III (PG)

White Men Can't Jump (1992) While trying to hold onto his hot-tempered girlfriend (Rosie Perez) and elude loan sharks, a white basketball player and small-time con artist (Woody Harrelson) meets his match in a black street hustler (Wesley Snipes) who joins in on his scams. Writer-director Ron Shelton drops the ball early on in this shrill comedy of pointlessly tiresome macho posturing. Continual rough language, brief bedroom shots, much gambling and some nasty menace. A-III (R) 15

White Mischief (1988) Fact-based story of the debauched life-styles of wealthy British colonists living near Nairobi, Kenya, in 1940–1941, and the doomed adulterous affair between a rogue earl (Charles Dance) and the beautiful young wife (Greta Scacchi) of an aged landowner (Joss Ackland). Director Michael Radford depicts an exotic, decadent society whose people exhibit few morals, little political or social conscience and no remorse. Treatment includes graphic sexual scenes, much explicit sexual language and some intense violence. O (R) 18

White Nights (1985) Excellent dance sequences highlight this contrived story of a dissident American tap-dancer (Gregory Hines) and a Russian ballet star (Mikhail Baryshnikov) who join forces in escaping from the Soviet Union. Director Taylor Hackford gets little suspense from a muddled plot clogged with political posturing, but Twyla Tharp's choreography generates some cultural excitement for those interested. Some romantic complications and coarse language. A-II (PG-13) PG

White Palace (1990) A 27-year-old yuppie (James Spader) is embarrassed by his affair with a common and much older waitress (Susan Sarandon) who insists on brutal honesty in their relationship. Luis Mandoki directs a moderately interesting story of a couple who find sex before love and then struggle to overcome age and class differences in hopes of surviving as a couple. Emphasis on an unmarried sexual relationship, some partial nudity and minimal rough language. A-IV (R)

White Sands (1992) Investigating a man's mysterious death by assuming his identity, a persistent New Mexico cop (Willem Dafoe) finds himself up against a slippery arms dealer (Mickey Rourke), a seductive heiress (Mary Elizabeth Mastrantonio) and a quicksilver FBI agent (Samuel L. Jackson). Roger Donaldson directs a well-acted thriller marred by a dense, confusing storyline. Recurring violence, a sexually suggestive scene with momentary nudity and frequent rough language. A-III (R) 15

White Sister (1973) Uneven Italian melodrama about the Mother Superior (Sophia Loren) of a hospital in northern Italy whose confrontations with a male staffer (Adriano Celentano), a lusty malingerer and a communist to boot, leads inevitably to a rather idealized romance, very platonic but serious enough to make both parties come to mature decisions about their lives. Director Alberto Lattuada plays it broadly, offering some pithy comic moments in the best tradition of Italian social comedy, but not enough to overcome the story's underlying sentimentality. A-III (R)

White Tower, The (1950) While vacationing in Switzerland, an American (Glenn Ford) joins a party of climbers (Alida Valli, Claude Rains, Oscar Homolka and Lloyd Bridges) trying to scale an unconquered peak. Directed by Ted Tetzlaff, the Alpine grandeur of the location climbing sequences far surpass the pretentious studio-bound character study of who will make it to the top. Much danger and some stylized violence. A-I (br) U

Who Framed Roger Rabbit? (1988) Down-and-out 1940s' Hollywood gumshoe (Bob Hoskins) attempts to clear the name of murder suspect Roger Rabbit, a cartoon stunt clown. Director Robert Zemeckis and animator Richard Williams achieve a seamless interaction of animated and human characters in this touching, hilarious movie. Some scary threats of violence and humorous sexual references. A-II (PG)

Who Is Harry Kellerman and Why Is He Saying Those Terrible Things About Me? (1971) Wealthy composer-singer of pop hits (Dustin Hoffman) is a 40-year-old schizophrenic whose life is being pulled apart by personal and business problems and to top it all off, some guy named Harry Kellerman is calling all of his girlfriends and saying "terrible things" about him.

Directed by Ulu Grosbard, the confused psychodrama is too introverted, too slick and too specialized to appeal to a wide audience. Adult themes, brief nudity and some rough language. A-III (GP) AA

Who Is Killing the Great Chefs of Europe? (1978) Screen version of the novel by Nan and Ivan Lyons about an epicurean publisher (Robert Morley) of a gourmet magazine whose list of the world's best chefs are being murdered one by one in the manner of the preparation of their specialty. Ted Kotcheff's heavy-handed direction doesn't help a talented cast including Jacqueline Bisset, Jean-Pierre Cassel, Philippe Noiret, Jean Rochefort and George Segal. Some violent visuals and much tasteless humor. A-III (PG)

Who Killed Mary What's 'ername? (1971) No one really much cares, except a rich diabetic, former boxing champ (Red Buttons) who sets out to track down the killer of a Greenwich Village hooker. Director Ernie Pintoff doesn't seem able to cope with the twisted plots and tangled lines of this rather sordid mystery story. A-III (GP) AA

Who Says I Can't Ride a Rainbow? (1971) Fact-based story of Barney Morovitz (Jack Klugman), founder of PONY foundation, a homemade zoo in a rundown section of New York's Greenwich Village, who frantically has to relocate his enterprise after Big Business encroaches upon his cherished patch of ground. Directed by Edward Mann, besides the sincere acting of all involved, its chief merit is that it cares about youngsters, especially kids of different races who grow up together on the cold concrete streets of a big city. A-I (G)

Who Shot Patakango? (1990) Bouncy, nostalgia-drenched look at life in a Brooklyn vocational high school in 1957 borrows freely from "West Side Story," with a working-class youth falling for an affluent, suburban girl while trying to prevent an outside gang from inciting violence at his interracial school. Filmmakers Robert and Halle Brooks convey the vitality and innocence of the era, but their treatment of student life is sophomoric and sugarcoated. Some petty thievery played for laughs, sporadic minor violence and a sexually ambiguous scene. A-III (nr)

Who Slew Auntie Roo? (1972) The best aspect of this garden-variety horror film is its integration of the familiar Hansel and Gretel story with the on-screen tale, set in the turn-of-the-century English countryside, in which orphaned Mark Lester and Chloe Franks have been taken in by Shelley Winters, who in Lester's eyes is trying to fatten them up. Though Ralph Richardson and Lionel Jeffries steal some colorful moments in bit parts, under Curtis Harrington's direction most of the picture is drab and slow-moving. Some scenes may be too intense for younger viewers. A-II (GP)

Who'll Stop the Rain? (1978) Hard-edged screen version of a Robert Stone novel about a Vietnam War correspondent (Michael Moriarty) who sends his wife (Tuesday Weld) two kilos of heroin. But things go awry, and the wife assisted by an old Marine buddy (Nick Nolte) is off on an existential odyssey, trailed by ugly thugs and corrupt policemen. Director Karel Reisz explores an America as full of dope, death and depravity as the Vietnam that had generated the illicit cargo. Adult themes, drug use and strong language. A-III (R)

Who's Afraid of Virginia Woolf? (1966) Director Mike Nichols' adaptation of the Edward Albee play amounts to a high-then-low-level encounter-group session involving two college faculty couples who thrash out their bitterness and frustrations during a semi-drunken evening. The main event features Richard Burton and Elizabeth Taylor who are old veterans of marital bouts, while George Segal and Sandy Dennis are rank amateurs, and as the tension mounts and they begin going for each other's throats, verbally, the air turns rather blue. The very nature of the film, with its rough language and unsavory slice of married life and human relationships needs an adult's perception for full comprehension and understanding. It's definitely not for the casual viewer. A-IV (br) X

Who's Harry Crumb? (1989) Dimwitted detective (John Candy) is enabled by good intentions and dumb luck to find a kidnapped heiress. Candy is dandy, but director Paul Flaherty has a field day with his larkish depiction of adultery. Sexually suggestive encounters and some rough language laced with sexual vulgarities. O (PG-13) PG

Who's Minding the Mint? (1967) Labored comedy about a needy U.S. Mint employee (Jim Hutton) whose scheme to print money after hours relies on one too many harebrained confederates (Jamie Farr). Directed by Howard Morris, the cast of thieves (Walter Brennan, Dorothy Provine, Milton Berle, Jack Gilford, Joey Bishop, Bob Denver and Victor Buono) is better than the material. Comic treatment of crime. A-II (br) U

Who's Minding the Store? (1963) Jerry Lewis comedy in which he makes a shambles of an entire department store, while in the process boosting sales and winning the girl (Jill St. John). Directed by Frank Tashlin, it's the usual slapstick affair with a good supporting cast (Agnes Moorehead, John McGiver and Ray Walston) and plenty of sight-gags, including an exploding golf machine. Strictly for Lewis fans. A-I (br) U

Who's That Girl (1987) Dull and lifeless vanity production showcasing music idol Madonna as an ex-con trying to vindicate herself while ruining the marriage plans of her escort (Griffin Dunne). Director James Foley is unable to tone down the hard edge of the essentially irresponsible role model his star awkwardly creates in this failed action-comedy of interest only to diehard fans. A-III (PG)

Who's That Knocking at My Door? (1969) Potentially interesting but unrealized attempt to show an Italian American youth's reexamination of his emotionally religious upbringing in relation to his sexual hang-ups. Director Martin Scorsese handles the subject with little depth or conviction and goes to extremes with a lengthy erotic montage. O (R)

Who's the Man? (1993) Bumbling Harlem barbers (comics Doctre Dre and Ed Lover) become rookie cops, then set out to solve the murder of their ex-boss (Jim Moody) whose barbershop is firebombed when he refuses to sell to a ruthless developer. Director Ted Demme overloads a goofy, hip-hop comedy by abruptly changing gears, tossing in the social concerns of the inner city without giving them the serious treatment they deserve. Occasional violence, some ethnic stereotyping, a few crude sexual references and minimal rough language. A-III (R)

Whole Truth, The (1992) Boring, long-winded and utterly predictable account of two singles (Dyan Kane; Dan Cohen) who get together, break up and then reunite. Also written and co-directed by Cohen, the shallow vanity production lacks romantic credibility and comic sensibility. Superficial treatment of a serious subject and occasional profanity. A-III (nr)

Wholly Moses (1980) Boring biblical comedy in which the brother-in-law of Moses (Dudley Moore) believes he is the one entrusted with a mission from God. Directed by Gary Weis, its attempts at humor can best be described as tiresome, mirthless, and witless. Occasional vulgar jokes and some incidental irreverence. A-III (PG) AA

Whoopee! (1930) Primitive color version of the Ziegfeld stage musical with Eddie Cantor as a nervous wreck vacationing on a lazy western dude ranch until finding himself pursued by a posse while helping the rancher's daughter reach her outcast boyfriend on an Indian reservation. Directed by Thornton Freeland, the hokey plot provides the comic context for Cantor's goofy clowning and corny one-liners, abetted by Gus Kahn's songs (notably "Making Whoopee") and Busby Berkeley's splashy production numbers. Some sexual innuendo and period comedy conventions that give offense today, including Native American stereotypes and a blackface routine. A-III (br)

Whore (1991) A prostitute (Theresa Russell) provides those interested with a detailed account of the tricks of the trade and its degradations. Directed by Ken Russell, the low-budget production is tedious and unenlightening. Excessively graphic in its descriptions and simulations of sex acts as well as occasional violence and profanity. O (NC-17) 18

Whose Life Is It, Anyway? (1981) Brilliant, witty sculptor (Richard Dreyfuss), paralyzed from an auto accident and dependent upon a dialysis machine and constant medication, retains a lawyer to force the hospital to release him, an action that will result in his speedy death. Directed by John Badham, the movie pits the patient's reasons for being allowed to die against his doctor's (John Cassavetes) determination to keep him alive at all costs. The treatment of the theme as well as a nude sequence make this questionable adult fare. A-IV (R) AA

Why? (1972) Italian morality tale about a family vacation that turns into a nightmare when the father (Alberto Sordi) is arrested for an unspecified crime, shunted from prison to prison, until finally accused of murdering a man he's never even heard of. By the time the mistake is cleared up and he is released, he is a broken man. Director Nanni Loy allows nothing to be overstated, but omits none of the harrowing details that indict a society that permits such bureaucratic indifference and brutal prison conditions to exist. A-III (PG)

Why Anna? (see: "Diary of a Schizophrenic Girl").

Why Does Herr H. Run Amok? (1978) Tedious German melodrama about a hardworking, inoffensive husband who suddenly goes over the edge and murders his wife and children and some other people unfortunate enough to be within reach at the moment. Director Rainer Werner Fassbinder does not answer the question his title poses but simply records the events that end in such violent tragedy. A-III (nr)

Why Not! (1979) Thin French comedy directed by Coline Serreau deals with the lives and domestic habits of a cozy trio (Sami Frey; Mario Gonzales; Christine Murillo) whose sleeping arrangements are quite complicated. Though the focus is not exclusively on sex, and there is an occasional droll sequence, its use of nudity and benign attitude toward moral anarchy are offensive. O (nr)

Why Would I Lie? (1980) Social worker (Treat Williams), who's also a compulsive liar, adopts a young boy (Gabriel Swann) and then tries to reunite him with his ex-con mother (Lisa Eichhorn). Directed by Larry Peerce, the pointless plot contains vulgarity, profanity and a warm endorsement of promiscuity. O (PG)

Wicked Dreams of Paula Schultz, The (1968) Low burlesque about an East German woman decathlon champ (Elke Sommer) who tries to defect to the West rather than be sent to work in a tractor factory. Directed by George Marshall, the feeble attempts at humor resort to some very crudely contrived calendar-art shots and sequences, a lesbian joke and other misguided attempts at humor. O (br)

Wicked Lady (1983) Thoroughly inept remake of a 1945 British Restoration-era film about a bored English noblewoman (Faye Dunaway) who turns to highway robbery for diversion. Under Michael Winner's aimless direction, not only does Dunaway give a poor performance but also cast adrift are Alan Bates, John Gielgud, Denholm Elliott and Prunella Scales. Abundant nudity and crass vulgarity. O (R) 18

Wicked, Wicked (1973) Clumsy thriller about the hunt for a psycho (Randolph Roberts) who murders blondes checking into an old seaside resort whose new singer (Tiffany Bolling) sports a blonde wig. Written, produced and directed by Richard L. Bare, the movie uses an ineffective split screen process. Restrained sex and violence. A-III (PG)

Wicker Man, The (1980) British melodrama in which a police sergeant (Edward Woodward) is called to a small island off the west coast of Scotland to investigate the disappearance of a child whom, he finds, has been made a human sacrifice in a pagan rite. Directed by Robin Hardy, the movie shows signs of intelligence and sophistication, but its tragic ending is unprepared from what has gone before. Excessive nudity. O (R) X

Wide Sargasso Sea (1993) Passions cool between a proper 1840s' English gentleman (Nathaniel Parker) and his sensuous Jamaican bride (Karina Lombard) when he suspects she is using voodoo to bewitch him. Director John Duigan's turgid romance rarely ventures beyond the couple's melodramatic bedroom hysterics, which end unhappily. Some simulated sex and frequent nudity. O (NC-17) 18

Widow Couderc, The (1974) Complex French melodrama set in the 1930s in which a killer (Alain Delon) hides out working on the farm of a widow (Simone Signoret), but life is so peaceful there that he begins thinking of it as home until someone in the small, inbred rural community calls the attention of the police to the outsider. Director Pierre Granier-Deferre's picture of country life contrasts human frailty with the beauty of the natural order, lust with love, and death with life in a way that may discomfort some but evoke a sympathetic response in others. A-IV (nr)

Wifemistress (1979) Italian sex-comedy in which a rich merchant (Marcello Mastroianni), implicated in a crime and forced into hiding in a building across the street from his home, observes the erotic as well as humanitarian activities of his formerly repressed wife (Laura Antonelli) who thinks he is dead. Directed by Marco Vicario, it is little more than a tepid and uninspired period comedy whose simplistic anti-religious views and frequent nudity are offensive. O (R)

Wilby Conspiracy, The (1975) Sidney Poitier and Michael Caine star in a political chase melodrama set against the background of apartheid South Africa, but Nicol Williamson steals the show as a cooly fanatic policeman. Director Ralph Nelson's movie is taut and well acted, but it is marred by some unnecessary sexual hijinks and a violent conclusion that sets up a moral problem beyond its depth. O (PG)

Wild Angels, The (1966) Motorcycle-gang movie with Peter Fonda and directed by Roger Corma is excessively violent and its theme of social protest is bogus. O (br) X

Wild at Heart (1990) Madly in love, a reckless couple (Nicholas Cage; Laura Dern) tear across the Deep South on the run from the law and killers hired by the girl's obsessive mother (Diane Ladd). Writer-director David Lynch captures the lovers' sensual passion, but the movie's sluggish pace is accentuated by a tiresome parade of psychotic characters, revolting images and violent episodes that turn an upbeat ending into self-indulgent sham. Excessive violence, graphic sexual content and much rough language. O (R) 18

Wild Bunch, The (1969) William Holden and Ernest Borgnine star in director Sam Peckinpah's violent and unglamorized account of the end of an outlaw band who had outlived the frontier era. Though its intentions are to show the ugly reality underlying the western movie myth, the general viewer is apt to find the work's brutality and several sexual scenes quite excessive. A-IV (R) X

Wild Child, The (1970) An exceptional French dramatization about a young boy who was found in 1798 living as an animal in a forest and the doctor who, rather than place in an asylum, took him into his own home for more intense care. Director Francois Truffaut (who also plays the doctor) creates an austerity of image, settings and music (Vivaldi) to mirror the child's alienation and gradual response to the doctor's openness. Most of all, the moving drama is an affirmation of the tireless efforts of educators to overcome environmental handicaps and an act of faith that humanity will survive in spite of itself. A-II (PG)

Wild Country, The (1971) Pittsburgh family (Steve Forrest; Vera Miles; Ron Howard; Clint Howard) arrives in the Wyoming territory of the 1880s full of hope and fervor of the early settlers, but their farm is below expectations, their water supply jeopardized by cattlemen and a devastating cyclone nearly destroys their homestead. Above-average Disney production directed by Robert Totten provides a wholesome, quality adventure story for solid family entertainment. A-I (G) U

Wild Duck, The (1977) Pallid German adaptation of the Ibsen classic. Director Hans W. Geissendorfer unwisely "opens up" the play to the extent of showing Hedvig's cherished wild duck, but has made a much more critical mistake in casting a fat and clownish actor (Peter Kern) as the feckless but attractive Hjalmar. A-II (nr) AA

Wild Eye, The (1968) Italian story about a sleazy movie director (Philippe Leroy) who makes exploitation pseudo-documentaries by inventing what he thinks the public wants to believe is real. Director Paolo Cavara proceeds to demonstrate this sort of dishonesty by himself staging a number of sadomasochistic scenes. O (nr)

Wild Geese, The (1978) Richard Burton, assisted by Roger Moore, Richard Harris and Hardy Kruger, lead a mercenary army to Africa to rescue a democratic African leader (Winston Ntshona). Although director Andrew V. McLaglen has a talented cast, a literate script and some well-photographed action sequences, the complexity of its racial and political context is beyond the movie's capability to treat responsibly. The graphic nature of its brutal violence and accompanying rough language are excessive. O (R)

Wild Hearts Can't Be Broken (1991) During the Great Depression, a blind 15-year-old orphan (Gabrielle Anwar) convinces a crusty stunt-show owner (Cliff Robertson) that she can ride a speeding stallion and leap into a pool of water as their new horse diver—from 40 feet above Atlantic City's famed Steel Pier. Director Steve Miner's spunky heroine overcomes various obstacles and a harrowing tragedy in an inspiring, fact-based movie that shimmers in sun-drenched cinematography. Fine family fare. A-I (G)

Wild Horse Stampede (1943) Low-budget cowboy stars Ken Maynard and Hoot Gibson tangle with a band of renegades hired to halt the construction of a railroad. Directed by Alan James, it's strictly formula fare for undemanding western fans. Stylized violence. A-I (br)

Wild in the Sky (1972) Brandon de Wilde and two fellow draft-dodgers escape jail by commandeering a SAC bomber captained by Robert Lansing and try to make it to Cuba as Gen. Keenan Wynn back at SAC headquarters issues insane orders to stop them. Directed by William T. Naud, this low-budget flying Ship of Fools tries to work both the hijack and anti-war angles but is consistent only in its cheap vulgarities and exploitation of serious themes. O (GP) AA

Wild in the Streets (1968) Young pop singer (Chris Jones) mobilizes America's youth, gets himself elected President and puts everyone over 30 into concentration camps. Director Barry Shear tries to satirize the youth culture of the 1960s while exploiting it as well, but it is the kind of free-from-responsibility fantasy that is not good for adolescents. A-III (R/GP) X

Wild Life, The (1984) Dreary sequel to "Fast Times at Ridgemont High" shows what happens to Eric Stoltz after he graduates and moves into a swinging-singles apartment complex. Directed by Art Linson, the proceedings feature the same sort of benignly viewed sexual amorality that permeated the first movie. Nudity and rough language. O (R)

Wild North, The (1952) Rugged outdoor adventure in Canada's frozen backcountry where a Mountie (Wendell Corey) gets his man—a French-Canadian hunter (Stewart Granger) accused of murder—then needs his help to survive a series of disasters on the trail back. Directed by Andrew Marton, the plot is more than a little contrived but the vigorous action is in keeping with the remote setting, and the shifting relationship between captor and captive has a satisfying human dimension. Much menace and some brutal violence, notably an attack by starving wolves. A-II (br) U

Wild One, The (1953) Motorcycle gang (led by Marlon Brando) stops off in a small California town and, after being joined by a rival gang (led by Lee Marvin), the bikers go on a rampage trashing the town and terrorizing its inhabitants. Directed by Laslo Benedek, the work is badly dated in subject and style, especially the romantic subplot with Mary Murphy, but there is still some edge in its early look at the violence in American countercultures. Much menace and stylized violence, including vigilante action. A-III (br) PG

Wild Orchid (1990) Boring voyeuristic exercise in titillation over the sexual awakening of an innocent young woman (Carre Otis) by a sleazy international operator (Mickey Rourke). Director Zalman King's hothouse fantasy about unappealing characters offers unrelieved tedium except for travelogue views of Rio de Janeiro and its environs. Several simulated sex acts. O (R) 18

Wild Orchid 2: Two Shades of Blue (1992) Dreary sex drama about a teenager (Nina Siemaszko) lured into very lucrative prostitution after the death of her addict father (Tom Skeritt). Writer-director Zalman King can't imbue this soft-core peep show with any redeeming qualities. Prostitution glamorized, much nudity, brief violence, drug abuse and some rough language. O (R)

Wild Pack, The (1972) Produced, directed and written by Hall Bartlett from a novel by Jorge Amado, the movie follows the fates of a gang of homeless children in Bahia, Brazil, as they struggle to survive on the fringes and in the slums of an indifferent South American society. It unfortunately clutters its statement of revolutionary protest with a romantic subplot and a graphic rape sequence. O (nr)

Wild Party, The (1975) Part musical, part study of late-1920s' Hollywood decadence and part compassionate character study of a silent film comedian (James Coco) ruined by the coming of sound pictures. Directed by James Ivory, these diverse elements fail to fuse and the result is an aimless, repetitious and more than a little distasteful melodrama. Excessive sexual display. O (R) 18

Wild Racers, The (1968) American race car driver (Fabian) gets a shot at the Grand Prix circuit and leaves behind a trail of compliant women. Director Dan Haller intercuts stock racing footage with numerous suggestive situations in the story of a man who values machines more than human beings. O (br) A

Wild Rovers (1971) William Holden and Ryan O'Neal are quite effective in this flawed but engagingly bittersweet study of ordinary cowpokes who dream of owning a little ranchero down in Mexico, rob a Montana bank and head toward the distant border. Written and directed by Blake Edwards, the characterizations are its strong point, the plot rather shaky and slow-moving and the resolution is a downer. Some brutal violence and a gratuitous bordello scene. A-III (GP)

Wild Season (1968) Belgian film about the life of North Sea fishermen centers on a young boy who tries to prove to his father that he can be just as good a man as was the son lost at sea. Directed by Emil Nofal, the natural elements surpass the labored efforts of the actors, but younger audiences will enjoy the outdoor adventure aspects of the story without much concern about character motivations. A-I (nr)

Wild Seed, The (1965) A drifter (Michael Parks) reluctantly helps a young runaway (Celia Kaye) cross the country to find her father but she gives up the search when they decide to get married. Directed by Brian Hutton, the contrived situation of the journey yields little interior growth in the two young people and the conclusion is not promising. Mature theme. A-III (br) A

Wild Strawberries (1958) During the day on which he is to be awarded an honorary degree from a nearby university, a 78-year-old retired scholar (Victor Sjostrom in a masterful performance) is visited with dreams and reveries about his past life, especially his failures and disappointments in personal relationships. Swedish director Ingmar Bergman brilliantly develops the man's interior journey from pangs of regret and anxiety to a refreshing sense of peace and reconciliation summed up in blissful images of his happy youth. One of the great films about aging; touches universal chords in all viewers. English subtitles. A-III (br) A

Wild Thing (1987) Orphaned child (Rob Knepper) grows up essentially on his own in the bowels of a deserted inner-city hovel and one day avenges his parents' death at the hands of ruthless drug dealers while saving a young social worker (Kathleen Quinlan). Director Mac Reid uses the thematic razor's edge of revenge to mutilate scriptwriter John Sayles' childlike fable. Restrained violence and a scene of implied sex lessen the urban Tarzan yarn's suitability for youngsters. A-III (PG-13)

Wildcats (1986) Goldie Hawn stars in this failed comedy about a woman coach of an inner-city high school football team. Excessive amounts of streetwise profanity, brief nudity and a scene involving simulated fornication make this vanity production by director Michael Ritchie off limits for its intended youthful audience. O (R) 15

Wilder Napalm (1993) Seriocomic misfire about the showdown between two brothers, both born with telekinetic powers to make objects burst into flame, when the older (Arliss Howard) tries to keep the younger (Dennis Quaid) from exploiting this power to gain fame, fortune and his brother's free-spirited wife (Debra Winger). Directed by Glenn Gordon Caron, the movie generates little interest as the conflict between the brothers over whether their unique power is a gift or a curse is slowly dragged out until the climactic fiery confrontation, with only occasional comic diversions to pass the time. Special-effects violence, sexual situations; coarse language. A-III (PG-13)

Wilderness Family, Part II, The (see: "The Further Adventures of the Wilderness Family").

Wilderness Journey (1972) In the Far North, a 12-year-old Eskimo lad (Tony Tucker Williams) embarks on a courageous canoe journey to find his father (Richard

Stitt), a hunting-party guide whose assistance is needed back home. The boy's adventure is made suspenseful and engrossing by Chuck D. Keen's superlative photography of the region and its wildlife and by the reverent narration explaining the tradition of the boy's ancestors. Directed by Ford Beebe, whose career in films dates back to 1914, the movie is splendid family entertainment. A-I (G)

Will Penny (1968) Fine western about an illiterate, aging but still capable cowhand (Charlton Heston) who, after the fall roundup, is sent to tend the cattle wintering in the hills, where he gives shelter to a lost pioneer woman (Joan Hackett) and her son until the spring thaw. Director Tom Gries has achieved a realistic portrait of a cowboy whose code of morality reflects the rigors of frontier life, the shortage of marriageable women and the rudimentary nature of early western justice. A-III (br) A

Will the Real Norman Mailer Please Stand Up? (1970) Low-budget documentary gives a rather interesting and fairly objective account of the life and times of popular author Norman Mailer, centering on his views and activities related to the anti-Vietnam movement. Unfortunately, the result provides little more than a superficial understanding of this enigmatic public figure and the rather amateurish production further detracts from its value. A-III (nr)

Willard (1971) Horror fantasy about a psychotic young man (Bruce Davidson) who, after the death of his mother (Elsa Lanchester), trains an army of rats to exact revenge for the injustices heaped upon him and his family by a businessman (Ernest Borgnine), but alas, he trains the little beasties all too well. Tighter editing and pacing might have given director Daniel Mann a first-class horror movie but, as it is, animal trainer Moe Di Sesso runs away with the prize for his direction of the rats. A-II (GP) X

Willie & Phil (1980) Writer-director Paul Mazursky's tale of a three-sided friendship begins with the 1970 meeting of Willie (Michael Ontkean) and Phil (Ray Sharkey) as they come out of a screening of Truffaut's triangle movie, "Jules and Jim," the inspiration for Mazursky's work. The trio is completed a few days later when they meet free-spirited Jeannette (Margot Kidder) and the film follows their shifting relationships over the entire decade of the 1970s. Mazursky has created three charming characters and places their quest for meaning and fulfillment within the context of the ethnic, moral and religious traditions each represents. However, the nature and treatment of the theme make this strictly mature viewing. A-III (R) X

Willie Dynamite (1974) Big city's most successful pimp (Roscoe Orman) vies with a reformed hooker-turned-social worker (Diana Sands) over the girls he tries to keep on the street while she tries to get them off. Directed by Gilbert Moses, it is a lifeless, aimless and meaningless attempt to blend outright black exploitation material with a sober examination of the psychology of the pimp and his women. The result is largely a waste of time. O (R)

Willow (1988) Fantasy adventure in which the tiny hero of the title (Warwick Davis) attempts at all odds to protect the baby girl prophesied to bring the downfall of the wicked sorceress (Jean Marsh) who rules the land. Directed by Ron Howard from a story by George Lucas, the tale is jam-packed with strangely shaped and oddly sized characters, forbidding medieval sets and a complex plot. Breathtaking chases, dramatic sword fights and fearsome creatures may rattle the small fry. A-II (PG)

Willy Wonka and the Chocolate Factory (1971) Screen version of Roald Dahl's children's story about a candy manufacturer (Gene Wilder) who conducts an electrifying tour of his factory for the five lucky children who learn that greed and selfishness can be their own reward. Even the punishments, occasionally a bit gruesome for younger children, are in good fun. Director Mel Stuart manages to avoid the cloying sentimentality of similar children's movies, though it's never quite as magical as one would have hoped. A-I (G) U

Winchester '73 (1950) After his prize rifle is stolen, a determined cowboy (James Stewart) sets out to find it and the man (Stephen McNally) who took it. Director Anthony Mann's meandering but energetic western follows the trail through chance encounters with homesteaders, Indians and outlaws before the final showdown reveals the personal nature of the cowboy's persistent quest. Stylized violence. A-II (br)

Wind (1992) After losing the America's Cup to Australia, a young sailboat skipper (Matthew Modine) teams with his ex-fiancee (Jennifer Grey) and her boyfriend (Stellan Skarsgard) to build a new boat for the re-match Down Under. Carroll Ballard directs a splendidly photographed but otherwise ordinary root-for-the-underdog picture that works best in the racing sequences. Implied premarital affairs. A-III (PG-13) PG

Wind and the Lion, The (1975) Writer-director John Milius takes some liberties with the 1904 incident in which Teddy Roosevelt (Brian Keith) thundered against a Moroccan brigand (Sean Connery) for kidnapping an American citizen (Candice Bergen). The historical facts are more interesting than this artificial romance; bogus adventure movie that glamorizes weapons and their use. Violence. A-III (PG) A

Wind from the East (1972) French director Jean-Luc Godard's first directly political work, this 1969 effort fails both as a movie and as Maoist propaganda. Basically a film of ideas, its dialectical progress fitfully winds down to a final call for total revolution, but it is unlikely to persuade viewers to accept its convictions. A-IV (nr)

Windows (1980) Failed thriller about a psychotic, homicidal lesbian (Elizabeth Ashley) who cherishes an unholy and, at times, quite noisy passion for a mousy friend (Talia Shire). Director Gordon Willis leaves his actresses to their own devices in the heavy-breathing and crying department while he devotes his energies to getting some exquisite views of the Manhattan skyline and landmarks. A brutal scene involving sexual assault is needlessly graphic. O (R)

Windwalker (1981) A dying Cheyenne patriarch (Trevor Howard) yearns to see once again the son who was kidnapped by hostile Crows when he was an infant. Aside from the miscasting of Howard, director Keith Merrill has created an extremely authentic picture of Indian life told in an unusually absorbing story. Because of the violence and conflict essential to the plot, it is not suited to very young children, but for older ones, the dignity with which it portrays Indians and their culture recommends it highly. A-II (PG)

Windy City (1984) Written and directed by Armyan Bernstein, this story of young men growing up on Chicago's North Side with their dreams unrealized has some good acting (John Shea; Kate Capshaw; Josh Mostel; Jim Borrelli) but can't overcome the handicaps of banal dialogue and sketchy characterizations. Considerable violence and gore. A-III (R)

Wings (1927) Silent screen epic about two young men (Buddy Rogers; Richard Allen), in love with the same girl (Jobyna Ralston), who wind up in the same flying squadron during World War I, where their rivalry turns to friendship until one of them is accidentally killed by the other. Clara Bow is the girl-next-door who follows Rogers to France as a nurse. Directed by William Wellman, it's a classic adventure film with a refreshing sense of innocence unembarrassed by any doubts about the justice of the actions of the principals. A-II (br)

Wings and the Woman (1941) British wartime morale booster about 1930s' record-setting aviatrix Amy Johnson (Anna Neagle) and her aviator husband Jim Mollison (Robert Newton). Produced and directed by Herbert Wilcox, the fact-based story treats the dangers facing the era's pilots in proper stiff-upper-lip fashion, ending in a patriotic flourish lauding the role of women in the war effort. A-II (br)

Wings of Desire (1988) Art-house film follows the lonely work of two angels (Bruno Ganz; Otto Sander) who wander about and above Berlin listening to the joys and travails of people in libraries, a circus and even on an American movie set (starring Peter Falk as himself). One angel chooses to shed his wings for the chance of expressing human emotions and love for a woman. German director Wim Wenders is by turns ponderous, playful, reflective and philosophic. Subtitles. Some sexually suggestive material, fleeting nudity and some profanity. A-IV (PG-13)

Wings of Eagles, The (1957) Uneven but colorful bio of Frank "Spig" Wead (John Wayne), a pioneering naval aviator in the 1920s who became a writer after a spine injury in the 1930s. Director John Ford's sentimental tribute to the Navy has plenty of romanticized action and broad humor, with a solid cast including Maureen O'Hara as Wead's wife, Dan Dailey as his orderly and Ward Bond as a Ford-like movie director. Much drinking and brawling as well as some domestic strife. A-I (br) U

Winners, The (see: "My Way").

Winning (1969) Paul Newman is ruggedly impressive as a race car driver whose obsession with the track leads his neglected wife (Joanne Woodward) to dally with his chief competitor (Robert Wagner). Directed by James Goldstone, the movie is as slick and quick as the race cars that provide its action thrills, and its message boils down to the fact that sometimes winning is really losing. A-III (PG) A

Winter Kills (1979) Failed screen version of Richard Condon's novel about the brother (Jeff Bridges) of an assassinated U.S. President who years later discovers that the actual assassin was not the man accused but another who was the agent of a vast and intricate conspiracy. Directed by William Richert, nothing makes much sense in this ill-conceived and badly executed melodrama that exploits memories of a tragic moment in American history. Some scenes of graphic sex. O (R) X

Winter People (1989) Melodramatic tale of love and revenge unfolds in the snowy hills of North Carolina during the Depression when an honorable city man (Kurt Russell) tries to protect an unfortunate country woman (Kelly McGillis) from the wild mountain man who fathered her illegitimate child. Directed by Ted Kotcheff, its family feud subplot, while key to the suspense, is poorly realized and its lush rural landscapes are wasted in an implau-

sible period plot. Some rough language, a grisly bear hunt and several scenes of sadistic violence. A-III (PG-13) 15

Winter Soldier (1972) During winter 1971, 200 men calling themselves Vietnam Veterans Against the War, sat before members of the press in Detroit and ruefully related their military experiences. The Pentagon refuted none of their testimony, which found its way into the Congressional Record. Eighteen anonymous friends of the veterans preserved the recollections of some of these men in a documentary that eminently deserves to be seen as part of the record of a very troubled time in the history of our nation. A-III (nr)

Winter Wind (1970) Hungarian director Miklos Jancso relates an incident about a Croatian anarchist in the 1930s who is considered a hero by his followers but only after they have destroyed him. The film is not for casual viewers, but those interested in foreign films or european politics will find it worth seeing. A-III (nr)

Winterset (1936) Depression-era drama from Maxwell Anderson's play in which a young drifter (Burgess Meredith) finds the gangster (Eduardo Ciannelli) who years before had committed the crime for which the youth's anarchist father (John Carradine) was executed. Directed by Alfred Santell, the theatrical style of the adaptation fairly creaks, but the justice theme and characterizations of good people in hard times still hold interest. Some stylized violence. A-II (br)

Wired (1989) Muddled movie about the self-destruction of media personality John Belushi (Michael Chiklis), who died of a drug overdose in 1982. Director Larry Peerce fails to mesh diverse and contradictory elements of a narrative told largely in flashbacks, but the film's anti-drug stance is clearly unambiguous. Graphic depictions of substance abuse and much foul language. A-III (R) 18

Wisdom (1986) Ridiculous teenage Bonnie-and-Clyde team (Emilio Estevez; Demi Moore) show their defiance of adult authority and social injustice by destroying mortgage records. The vanity production, written and directed by Estevez, centers on an unhealthy preoccupation with guns and violence along with profanity and casual sex. O (R)

Wise Blood (1980) Screen version of Flannery O'Connor's novel about a God-haunted young man (Brad Dourif) who on his way to Taulkinham, Tenn., to preach a new religion, meets such bizarre characters as a failed preacher pretending he is blind (Harry Dean Stanton), his mildly depraved daughter (Amy Wright) and a jovial evangelist (Ned Beatty). Director John Huston has made a powerful and provocative movie whose spiritual implications are as compelling as its artistic excellence. The incidental violence and moral complexity are more appropriate for adult viewers. A-III (PG) AA

Wise Guys (1986) Brian De Palma's audacious and brash parody of the gangster film relies too heavily upon profanity and violence as source of humor. Although Danny De Vito and Joe Piscopo create frantically likable but bungling small-time hoods, their stereotyped characterizations, along with others in the film, are likely to give offense to some Italian and Jewish viewers. O (R)

Wish You Were Here (1987) British director David Leland's sensitive, bittersweet evocation of a youngster's coming-of-age in a 1950s' English coastal town focuses upon her sexual initiation, disappointments with her father and encounters with the male-dominated working-class society of the period. The sexually explicit but emotionally accurate portrait of a young woman's discovery of self-worth and meaning has brief nudity and some vulgar language. A-III (R) 15

Wishing Machine, The (1970) Czechoslovakian children's story about two boys whose visit to an industrial fair leads them to imagine they can make a trip to the moon. Written and directed by Josef Pinkava, the movie (dubbed into English) has imaginative visuals and a pleasant story that small children will enjoy because it is, from beginning to end, entirely made for them. A-I (G)

Witchboard (1987) Bloody consequences of using a Ouija board alone are demonstrated in this horror tale of a young woman (Tawny Kitaen) whose jousts with an evil spirit manage to get her former boyfriend killed and her current lover nearly dismembered. Writer-director Kevin Tenney's story of the supernatural presents all its gory excesses and vulgarities in broad daylight. O (R)

Witchcraft '70 (1970) Self-described as a serious documentary study of contemporary witchcraft throughout the world, it's anything but, though it flits from place to place, seeking out what, apparently, is the main ingredient for any occult ceremony, namely, that the participants be as naked as possible. Few will be bewitched, many will be bothered, and almost all will be bewildered. O (X/R)

Witches, The (1990) Uneven adaptation of Roald Dahl's contemporary fairy tale in which a grandmother (Mai Zetterling) aids her 9-year-old grandson (Jasen Fisher) in thwarting the plans of the Grand High Witch (Anjelica Huston) to turn all of Britain's children into mice. Produced by Jim Henson and directed by Nicolas Roeg, the fantasy starts well and has some cute mice puppetry but bogs down in the frenetic flamboyance of a witches' convention in a posh British spa. Some intense menace, several discreet sexual references and an instance of profanity. A-II (PG)

Witches of Eastwick, The (1987) Jack Nicholson plays a devil summoned via the wishful thinking of three lonely, frustrated women (Cher; Susan Sarandon; Michelle Pfeiffer) who allow themselves to be seduced and impregnated while living a life of reckless abandon at the demon's mansion. In director George Miller's version of John Updike's sardonic, allegorical novel about the battle of the sexes, the action is entirely on the sexual level obscuring other dimensions of its theme while trying to find humor in vulgar excesses, promiscuous behavior and sexually derived profanity. O (R) 18

Witchmaker, The (1971) Psychology professor (Alvy Moore) stupidly leads his students into the Louisiana swamplands to investigate a series of occult-oriented murders, where they succumb to spells cast by a maniacal fiend (John Lodge) who drains his victims' blood for use in satanic orgies. Written, produced and directed by William O. Brown, the feeble horror concoction keeps the camera at a distance from the mayhem. A-III (M/R)

With Six You Get Egg Roll (1968) Doris Day plays a widow in coveralls with three sons and Brian Keith is a widower with one daughter. They try to keep their courtship a secret from the children and then get them to all act in harmony as part of the new family. Director Howard Morris is not only stuck with a contrived and saccharine situation with four overcute children, but the movie gags on attempts at slapstick humor. The result is the kind of entertainment film that gives family pictures a bad name. A-II (G) U

Withnail and I (1987) British drama about two struggling young actors (Richard E. Grant; Paul McGann) who, at the end of the 1960s' hippie era, spend a weekend on the country estate of the wealthy uncle of one of them. Their friendship dissolves in remorseful recognition of the hurt they cause their host (Richard Griffiths) by preying upon his homosexual tendencies. Director Bruce Robinson's movie is spotted with harsh language and some drug and sexual references but manages to convey a kind of elegiac farewell to the excesses of the times. A-III (R) 15

Without a Clue (1988) This bit of British comic fluff reverses the roles of Sherlock Holmes and Dr. Watson by having Watson (Ben Kingsley) be secretly the supersleuth who writes stories about the fictional Holmes. To cover his tracks, Watson hires a third-rate actor (Michael Caine) to impersonate Holmes, but the actor's ineptitude and liberties with wine, women and song drive Watson to distraction. As directed by Thom Eberhardt, their comic relationship wears thin, but there are some hilarious moments. Fleeting violence with humorous undertones and mild sexual innuendo. A-II (PG)

Without a Stitch (1970) To cure the frigidity of a young girl who is introduced to a life of sex and perversion, she is taught that anything is permissible as long as it doesn't hurt anybody. What's particularly insidious about this exploitation film is that it not only portrays and exploits nudity and immorality, but it makes a clear effort to win its viewers to accept a similar mode of thinking and living. O (R)

Without a Trace (1983) Fact-based story of a six-year-old boy who is kidnapped on the way to school in New York City and his mother (Kate Nelligan) who convinces a police detective (Judd Hirsch) to stay on the case even when it looks as if there is no hope. Thanks largely to the performances of Hirsh and Nelligan, there are some good moments, but for the rest director Stanley Jaffe's effort remains a flat and uninspired story, sorely lacking any real dramatic development and with a ludicrous sentimental ending. Some strong language. A-II (PG) 15

Without Apparent Motive (1972) Tough, ruthless detective (Jean-Louis Trintignant) must flush out a madman who's been going about the picturesque city of Nice popping off one victim after another with his sniper's rifle. Nearly every encounter in director Philippe Labro's movie has sex simmering just below the surface and, as the story builds toward climax and resolution; twisted sexual relations not surprisingly provide all the keys. A-III (PG)

Without You I'm Nothing (1990) Loosely structured film version of Sandra Bernhard's one-woman show allows the comedienne to bad-mouth current pop idols, the political scene, commercial products and anything resembling conventional behavior. Directed by John Boskovich, the result is emotionally uninvolving with drawn-out musical numbers and sketches whose barbed humor and cold delivery accomplish little more than alienating the audience. Scenes of sexual exploitation with nudity; much rough language; a positive portrayal of drug use. O (R) 18

Witness (1985) Tough Philadelphia police detective (Harrison Ford) hides out among the Amish to protect his life and that of a young boy who witnessed a murder committed by a corrupt fellow detective. He and the boy's widowed mother (Kelly McGillis) are drawn to each other despite their different worlds. Director Peter Weir gets excellent performances in a good romantic melodrama that also offers some relatively thoughtful reflections on violence and non-violence. Some graphic violence and brief nudity are handled as restrained but essential plot devices. A-IV (R) 15

Witness for the Prosecution (1957) Twisty Agatha Christie courtroom puzzler in which British barrister Charles Laughton defends accused lady killer Tyrone Power in a murder trial complicated by mysterious title character Marlene Dietrich and a double surprise ending. Director Billy Wilder plays the case's red herrings for all they're worth, helped by solid comic relief from ailing lawyer Laughton's feud with dictatorial nurse Elsa Lanchester. Implications of marital infidelity and stylized violence. A-II (br) U

Wives and Lovers (1963) Flat satire of marital woes caused by the sudden success of a struggling writer (Van Johnson) whose wife (Janet Leigh) has a fling with an actor (Jeremy Slate) when she suspects her husband of having an affair with his agent (Martha Hyer). Director John Rich wrings little humor out of a contrived situation that grows tiresome as the bogus misunderstandings escalate until the counterfeit sentimental ending. Sexual situations. A-III (br) X

Wiz, The (1978) Diana Ross stars as Dorothy, the girl who flies over the rainbow in a black musical version of "The Wizard of Oz." Chasing Toto into a snowstorm in Harlem, she winds up on the yellow brick road with the Scarecrow (Michael Jackson), the Tin Man (Nipsey Russell) and the Cowardly Lion (Ted Ross) on their way to meet the Wiz (Richard Pryor). Directed by Sidney Lumet, it has lavishly staged musical numbers, opulent costumes and colorful settings, but it's overlong and its humor seems addressed more to adults and teenagers than younger viewers. A-II (G) U

Wizard, The (1989) Small-fry version of "Rain Man" tracks the exploits of a 13-year-old (Fred Savage) who kidnaps his emotionally disturbed 9-year-old brother (Luke Edwards) from an institution to enter him in a video game championship for a crass feel-good ending. Directed by Todd Holland, the far-fetched, sentimental plot plugs everything from Nintendo games to the Universal City Studios tour. Some rough language and an unfortunate gag about child molestation. A-II (PG)

Wizard of Loneliness, The (1988) Bitter, precocious 12-year-old (Lukas Haas), who's forced to live with his grandparents in Vermont after his mother's death while his father's off fighting World War II, finally overcomes his resentment and accepts the unconditional love offered by an uncritical grandfather (John Randolph), gently seductive aunt (Lea Thompson) and tiny cousin (Jeremiah Warner). Director Jenny Bowen gets some fine acting in a richly detailed family drama based on a semi-autobiographical novel by John Nichols. Much rough language from the youthful protagonist, a clothed but intense sexual encounter, an assault on a child and a graphic murder scene. A-III (PG-13)

Wizard of Oz, The (1939) Dorothy rides her tornado to the magic land over the rainbow in director Victor Fleming's classic that skyrocketed Judy Garland's career and has given generations of families prime entertainment again and again. The 50th anniversary edition has 17 minutes of material not included in the original release. A-I (G) U

Wizard of Speed and Time, The (1990) A special-effects artist (Mike Jittlov) tries to crack the big-time in Hollywood only to come up against some sleazy TV producers who take advantage of him. Also written and directed by Jittlov, this amateurish bit of self-promotion is badly written and acted, though youngsters may enjoy the zany special effects. Some sexual innuendos. A-II (PG)

Wizards (1977) Animated feature starts with a thermonuclear destruction of human life on earth, then jumps to the far distant future in which mutants inhabit radioactive lands and elves and fairies live in the uncontaminated area where are born twin wizards who battle for the future of the planet. It is animator Ralph Bakshi's most polished effort with bold, imaginative graphics and effective integration of live action footage. A number of violent visuals. A-III (PG)

Wolf Man, The (1941) Creaky monster classic in which the son (Lon Chaney Jr.) of an English lord (Claude Rains) is bitten by a werewolf (Bela Lugosi) but only realizes his fate when transformed into a human beast at the next full moon. Director George Waggner excels in creating a fearful atmosphere out of nighttime shadows and misty moors, with Chaney winning sympathy as the man who loathes what he becomes and the venerable Maria Ouspenskaya adding some dignity to the proceedings as the wise Gypsy matriarch who tries to help the tormented victim. Menacing situation and stylized violence. A-II (br) A

Wolfen (1981) Murky thriller in which a hard-boiled, nearly burnt-out detective (Albert Finney) investigating three brutal murders links them to some menacing wolf-like creatures seen roaming the New York City streets. Directed by Michael Wadleigh, with some spectacular camera effects, the story suggests that these preternatural creatures are punishment for the sins of a rapacious society, but its sense of moral indig-

nation doesn't justify the violence and graphic depiction of blood and gore. A-III (R) X

Woman at Her Window, A (1978) Slack French 1930s' political drama in which an Austrian woman (Romy Schneider) tries to help a Communist fugitive (Victor Lanoux) escape the secret police in Athens by involving her husband (Umberto Orsini) and a wealthy friend (Philippe Noiret). Director Pierre Granier-Deferre's narrative is needlessly complex and muddled, though it has compelling acting and some philosophical depth. Several scenes of police brutality. A-III (nr)

Woman in Green, The (1945) Convoluted mystery with Sherlock Holmes (Basil Rathbone) and Dr. Watson (Nigel Bruce) on the trail of the nefarious master criminal, Dr. Moriarity (Henry Daniell), who this time heads a blackmail scheme employing hypnosis and murder. Under Roy William O'Neill's direction, Holmes faces death by auto fumes, an assassin's bullet and a walk off a ledge high above the street before the case is closed. Some fairly effective menace and minimal stylized violence. A-I (br) A

Woman in Red, The (1984) Gene Wilder directs and also stars as a philandering advertising manager who pursues a beautiful model (Kelly Le Brock) while keeping his wife (Judith Ivy) in the dark. It is an ill-conceived and clumsily executed attempt to recast a French farce about adultery ("Pardon Mon Affaire") in an American mold. Nudity and a benign attitude toward illicit sex. O (PG-13) 15

Woman Next Door, The (1981) Weak French romantic melodrama about a happily married couple who move next door to another happily married couple but, as it happens, the wife who has just moved in (Fanny Ardant) and the husband next door (Gerard Depardieu) had a stormy love affair seven years before and soon the two are off and running again. Director Francois Truffaut handles this material with his usual adroitness, but to little purpose in a story that proves banal and unmoving, with some questionable amorous sequences. A-IV (R) AA

Woman Obsessed (1959) Turgid sudser from the Canadian northwest where a farmer's widow (Susan Hayward) marries her brawny, inarticulate hired man (Stephen Boyd) but comes to regret it. Directed by Henry Hathaway, the picturesque locales of the setting are a lot easier to watch than the cliched story of a woman's soured romance. Domestic misunderstandings and natural catastrophes. A-II (br) A

Woman of the Ganges (1974) French writer Marguerite Duras' story of a man at a resort during its winter off-season where he meets, or perhaps imagines that he meets, the woman of the title whom he had loved in India long ago. Also directed by Duras, the highly verbal movie takes place not on the screen, but in the mind of the beholder willing to plumb its blend of time, memory and illusion. A-III (nr)

Woman Times Seven (1967) Italian potpourri of comedy, farce and pathos is directed by Vittorio De Sica with Shirley MacLaine as the heroine of each episode. It is needlessly marred by one tasteless and provocative sequence. O (br) X

Woman Under the Influence, A (1974) The woman of the title (Gena Rowlands) is a mother of three small children in the middle of a nervous breakdown while her husband (Peter Falk), a rough, callous but loving man is totally unable to cope with the situation. Directed by John Cassavetes in his characteristic improvisational style, the result is full of the small realities and individual details that make up ordinary human experience, but it is short on the sort of heightened drama one expects from a conventional movie narrative. A-III (R) AA

Woman's Decision, A (1977) Sensitive, extremely well-acted Polish triangle story whose heroine (Maya Komorowska) is married to a wonderful husband (Piotr Franczewski), has an affectionate son and a modern apartment in Warsaw but finds herself wanting to give it all up for the company of a footloose man (Marek Piwowski). Directed by Krzystof Zanussi, it is a perceptive study of the interior struggle each of the characters undergoes during the course of the narrative. A-III (nr)

Woman's Tale, A (1992) Somber drama about an elderly, cancer-ridden woman (Sheila Florance) who, with her devoted young nurse (Gosia Dobrowolska) at her side, grittily determines to extract all the enjoyment she can from her final days. Though director Paul Cox elicits moving performances from both women, the life-affirming theme is delivered with belabored heavy-handedness. Uncritical attitude toward the nurse's extramarital affair and brief nudity. A-III (PG-13)

Women (1978) Sensitive Hungarian character study of an unlikely and slowly developing friendship between the wife of a successful engineer (Marina Vlady) and a factory worker (Lili Monori) whose husband is an alcoholic. The melodramatic plot and its soap opera problems simply provide the background against which director Marta Meszaros explores the human needs that draw these two women together despite their differences in character, education and social position. Mature themes. A-III (nr)

Women in Cages (1971) Philippine exploitation movie directed by Gerry De Leon about a group of women prisoners who use their sadistic lesbian matron as a hostage to escape into the jungle where they fall prey to bounty hunters and flesh-peddlers. Heavy-duty debasement. O (R)

Women in Cellblock 7 (1977) Inanely plotted, badly acted and atrociously dubbed Italian exploitation movie about a woman who goes to prison to get evidence to save her father. Abundant nudity. O (R)

Women in Love (1970) British adaptation of D. H. Lawrence's novel about the gradual involvement of two couples, one (Alan Bates; Glenda Jackson) having a rather healthy though incomplete relationship while the other (Oliver Reed; Jennie Linden) tragically ends in suicide. Directed by Ken Russell, the acting is first-rate, the photography almost too beautiful, and the treatment of the convoluted relationships remains on the superficial level of the physical. A lengthy naked wrestling match between the men is more symbolic than erotic. O (R) X

Women in Revolt (1972) Three women from different social levels (female impersonators Candy Darling; Holly Woodlawn; Jackie Curtis) get caught up in the Women's Liberation Movement. Typical of the poor film quality and sexual explicitness of Andy Warhol's efforts in the past, it makes men, women and sex look ridiculous, ugly and perverted. O (nr)

Women on the Verge of a Nervous Breakdown (1988) After an actress (Carmen Maura) is deserted by her live-in lover (Fernando Guillen), she attempts to face down the coward before he leaves town with another woman. Written and directed by Pedro Almodovar, this Spanish farce explores without exploitation the comic vicissitudes of male-female relationships. Subtitles. Some rough language and a benign attitude toward sex and pregnancy outside of marriage. A-IV (R) 15

Won Ton Ton, the Dog Who Saved Hollywood (1976) Director Michael Winner's wretchedly thrown-together slapstick comedy about a wonder dog of the old silent movie era is made all the more tasteless by seeing performers one once admired in a series of painfully inane cameos. It is definitely not for young viewers. O (PG) A

Wonder Man (1945) Sappy Danny Kaye vehicle in which he doubles as a murdered nightclub comic whose spirit inhabits the body of his scholarly twin brother, thereby confounding police, gangsters and the brothers' girlfriends (Virginia Mayo; Vera-Ellen). Directed by Bruce Humberstone, there are a couple of good song-and-dance numbers and some funny routines but the phantom-brother gimmick wears thin. Minimal stylized violence. A-II (br)

Wonders of Aladdin, The (1961) Embarrassingly inept comic adventure with Donald O'Connor as an overaged Aladdin and Vittorio de Sica as a cut-rate genie all mixed up in the old story of a magic lamp. Directed by Mario Bava and Henry Levin, this dubbed Italian misfire suffers from an impoverished script and threadbare fantasy effects. Much sexual innuendo and comic violence, including a sadistic torture scene. A-III (br)

Wonderful Crook, The (1977) Offbeat French comedy about a good-natured, but inept young man (Gerard Depardieu) who, in order to pay the employees' wages of his family's furniture business, undertakes a series of holdups and falls in love with one of his victims (Marlene Jobert). Neither his wife (Dominique Labourier) nor his employees suspect his double life until the police arrive to arrest him. Directed by Claude Goretta, the film details in a warmly humorous manner the complications that can arise from a simplistic notion of "doing good." Brief nudity and vulgar language. A-III (nr)

Wonderful World of the Brothers Grimm, The (1962) Lavish but plodding Cinerama production interweaving the story of the 19th-century German brothers (Laurence Harvey; Karl Boehm) with dramatizations of three of the many folk tales they popularized despite personal adversities. Co-directed by George Pal and Henry Levin, the Rhineland locales and period settings are better realized than either the biographical material or the special effects used in the fairy tales. Intermittently diverting for youngsters, though a long sit for their elders. A-I (G) U

Wooden Soldiers (see: "March of the Wooden Soldiers").

Woodstock (1970) Documentary about the landmark musical event that brought together a half-million young people to hear a parade of such talented performers as Richie Havens; Joan Baez; Country Joe and the Fish; The Who; Sha-Na-Na; Arlo Guthrie; Crosby, Stills and Nash; Joe Cocker, and so on. Directed by Michael Wadleigh, it is dazzling in image and sound but as a record of this particular music festival, it concentrates on the positive themes of love and peace, giving scant attention to the drugs and commercialism that for many marred the event. Brief nudity and some rough language and lyrics. A-IV (R)

Work Is a Four-Letter Word (1968) British comedy about a man (David Warner) who grows halucinogenic mushrooms. Directed by Peter Hall, its premise is better than the results. A-III (br)

Working Girl (1988) A 30-year-old secretary (Melanie Griffith) with the training and dreams to make it big as a Wall Street stockbroker is held back by sexist male bosses and a treacherous female boss (Sigourney Weaver), but when she transforms herself into a polished professional, her appealing vulnerability attracts the right boss (Philip Bosco) and suitor (Harrison Ford). Directed by Mike Nichols, the upbeat story balances its women-in-the-workplace concerns with a delightful Cinderella story that will entertain and enlighten even diehard anti-feminists. Rough language laced with sexual innuendo; some frontal nudity within brief graphic sexual situations. A-IV (R) 15

World According to Garp, The (1982) Uneven screen version of John Irving's novel about a fragile writer (Robin Williams) overwhelmed by catastrophes, bizarre events and his indomitable mother (Glenn Close). Under George Roy Hill's direction, Williams by going all out to turn the character into a lovable schnook makes his problems seem even crueler and more arbitrary than they might have been. Some nudity and graphic sexual references. A-III (R) 15

World Apart, A (1988) Fact-based drama set in 1963 South Africa concerns an anti-apartheid white journalist (Barbara Hershey) and her inability to give her three young daughters the same love and devotion she channels into the political arena. Director Chris Menges skirts over the political and social issues to focus on the mother-daughter conflict. Some emotional and physical political violence, an off-camera suicide attempt and the suffering caused one of the daughters because of her parents' political activities. A-II (PG)

World in His Arms, The (1952) Romantic adventure with a Yankee ship captain (Gregory Peck) who's grown so rich poaching seals in Russian-owned Alaska that he decides to buy it from the Czar, but along the way he falls for a Russian countess (Ann Blythe), battles a Portuguese freeboater (Anthony Quinn) and is captured by a Russian gunboat. Director Raoul Walsh submerges the 19th-century romance in high-seas derring-do and imperial despotism with the action sputtering to a bogus ending. Stylized violence and romantic complications. A-I (br) U

World of Buckminster Fuller, The (1974) Educational documentary directed by Robert Snyder provides a coherent outline of Fuller's basic concepts as well as a personal portrait of a humanist who put his scientific knowledge to the task of considering the present under the aspects of the future rather than from the conventional wisdom of the past. A-I (nr)

World of Hans Christian Andersen, The (1971) Feature-length cartoon about the childhood of young Hans and where he got some of the ideas for his highly imaginative fairy tales. The animation is colorful and creative, though stylistically comparable to Saturday morning TV shows. It provides a wonderful world of fantasy to absorb the small fry. A-I (G)

World of Henry Orient, The (1964) Peter Sellers stars in a wacky comedy about a fair-to-middling concert pianist whose pursuit of extra-curricular love (Paula Prentiss) is foiled by the unwitting but persistent efforts of two teenage girls who just may be his only fans in all the world. Directed by George Roy Hill, the acting is very good; the comedy nicely paced; background romantic element. A-II (br) U

World of Susie Wong, The (1961) Exotic but unappetizing tale of the rough life and times of a Hong Kong lady-of-the-night, toned down from Paul Osborn's play in the Hollywood version starring Nancy Kwan as Susie and William Holden as her American love interest. Directed by Richard Quine, its plush production of a sentimental romance may have some interest for hardy adults, but not for youngsters or those with reservations about a drama that unfolds, for the most part, in a seamy brothel. O (br) A

World Without Sun (1964) Documentary made by oceanaut Jacques-Yves Cousteau details the human conquest of underwater space. It is an opportunity to see and experience an incredibly beautiful part of creation, till now hidden from human eyes. A-I (br)

World's Greatest Athlete, The (1973) Frustrated coach (John Amos) vacationing in Africa discovers a Tarzan-like jungle youth (Jan-Michael Vincent) and brings him to his California campus, where he starts making a shambles of the record books. Directed by Robert Scheerer, it's the Disney Studio's special-effects men who save the day for sports as well as for parents who, with their children, will have to take the yawns along with the laughs. A-I (G) U

World's Greatest Lover, The (1977) Failed comedy by writer-director Gene Wilder who also stars as a hapless oaf who goes to Hollywood in the 1920s hoping to win a studio-sponsored World's Greatest Lover contest. The direction is inept; the writing shows no wit or originality; Wilder's performance is loud, vulgar and supremely unfunny. Boring; but its low-level humor isn't for young viewers. A-III (PG) A

Worth Winning (1989) Adolescent male fantasy about a shallow Philadelphia TV weatherman (Mark Harmon) who bets a friend (Mark Blum) that he can propose marriage to three women (chosen by the friend) in three months and be accepted by each. The heel gets his comeuppance, but

director Will MacKenzie treats him more sympathetically than the three female guinea pigs (Maria Holvoe; Madeleine Stowe; Lesley Ann Warren) in a sexist exercise demeaning to women. Sexual promiscuity including adultery and some profanity laced with sexual vulgarities. O (PG-13)

Woyzeck (1979) Stark German adaptation of Georg Buchner's 19-century play about a much-abused soldier (Klaus Kinski) in a small garrison town who goes mad and brutally murders the woman (Eva Mattes) he has been too poor to marry. Directed by Werner Herzog, the story of a man's alienation and descent into irrationality is powerfully acted and its dark mood unrelieved. A-III (nr) AA

WR—Mysteries of the Organism (see: "Mysteries of the Organism").

Wraith, The (1986) A brutally murdered teenager (Charlie Sheen) returns as an avenging angel to race to their deaths the depraved auto gang that had killed him. A deadly supernatural demolition derby filmed on the picturesque highways of Arizona sells violence, vengeance and a few sexual inferences with foul language to a youth market already overburdened with negative role models. A-III (PG-13)

Wrath of God, The (1972) Hard-drinking, gun-toting renegade priest (Robert Mitchum) joins forces with two other fugitive misfits to erase a fanatical madman-rancher in Central America during the revolutionary 1920s. As directed by Ralph Nelson, the result is just downright painful in some sections, embarrassing and simply ludicrous in others. Some heavy violence. A-IV (PG) X

Wrecking Crew, The (1968) The only funny aspect of this limp spy spoof is watching Dean Martin lumber through it as superagent Matt Helm entrusted to guard a gold shipment from Denmark to London, giving rise to jokes about Danish pastries (one of whom is Elke Sommer). Directed by Phil Karlson, the level of crude sexual humor is beneath adolescent interest. O (PG)

Wrestling Ernest Hemingway (1993) Slow-moving, sentimental portrait of the unlikely friendship that developes between two lonely old men—a foul-mouthed, lecherous former sea captain (Richard Harris) and an introverted retired barber from Cuba (Robert Duvall). Directed by Randa Haines, it's an actors' feast with Harris chewing up whatever scenery he can find while Duvall concentrates on being slow and deliberate in everything, including his Hispanic accent, though Sandra Bullock's performance as a friendly waitress is brightly refreshing. Some lengthy discussions of love and sex, flashes of rear nudity and occasional rough language. A-III (PG-13) A-I (br)

Written on the Wind (1956) Soapy sudser about the troubled life and death of a weak-willed Texas oil tycoon (Robert Stack), the strong wife (Lauren Bacall) who tries to reform him and his best friend (Rock Hudson) who secretly loves her while disdaining the love offered him by the oil man's dissolute sister (Dorothy Malone). Director Douglas Sirk's trashy exercise in sentimental melodrama is slickly contrived and mindlessly boring. Much alcohol abuse, some stylized violence and veiled sexual references. A-II (br) A

Wrong Box, The (1966) British black comedy revolves around the bumbling attempts of someone to kill off members of a family in order to obtain a large inheritance. Directed by Bryan Forbes, the script is not very sharp, but the acting of John Mills, Ralph Richardson, Michael Caine and Peter Sellers is first-rate. The most hilarious performance, a classic of its kind, belongs to Wilfred Lawson as the old family retainer. A-II (br) U

Wrong Guys, The (1988) Often entertaining story about a wilderness reunion of a pack of one-time Cub Scouts who are threatened by bullies from the old neighborhood and an escaped con who wields a mighty range of weaponry. Director Danny Bilson is aided by a cast of young, stand-up comics (Louie Anderson; Richard Lewis; Richard Belzer; Franklyn Ajay; Tim Thomerson) who have their own particular shticks. Mild profanity. A-II (PG)

Wrong Is Right (1982) Failed black comedy in which Sean Connery plays a TV news commentator who finds himself in the middle of a struggle between a U.S. President (George Grizzard), his political rival (Leslie Nielsen), Arab terrorists and assorted villains to gain possession of two suitcases containing nuclear bombs. Writer-director Richard Brooks tries to satirize amorality in high places, but the humor is flat and the story terribly jumbled. Graphic violence. A-III (R)

Wrong Move, The (1978) Tedious, empty German drama in which a moody would-be writer (Rudiger Vogler), who doesn't like people and has no interest in politics, takes a rambling journey through West Germany. Written by Peter Hanke and directed by Wim Wenders, the random incidents and various characters met along the way occasion little interest for the young man and less for the viewer. Mature themes. A-III (nr)

WUSA (1970) Confused political melodrama about the right-wing owner (Pat Hingle) of a New Orleans radio station, its liberal disc jockey (Paul Newman), his waitress girlfriend (Joanne Woodward) and a manic social worker (Tony Perkins). Director Stuart Rosenberg toys with ill-formed notions of political polarization and reduces them to cliches in a nearly incoherent plot. A-III (PG)

Wuthering Heights (1970) Good British version of the Emily Bronte romantic classic of tragic love on the moors stars Anna Calder-Marshall as Cathy and Timothy Dalton as Heathcliff. Director Robert Fuest has made a conscious effort to enable young viewers to identify with the doomed pair but in doing so, he has softened the rough edges of the characters and the malevolent nature of their relationship. Good cast and fine creation of mood and period. A-II (G) A

W. W. and the Dixie Dancekings (1975) Burt Reynolds plays a professional con man who takes in hand a hapless group of country musicians. Director John G. Avildsen's comedy is often hilarious and is marked by fine acting. One scene at a drive-in is adult fare. A-III (PG) A

Wyoming Renegades (1955) Murky tale of an ex-outlaw (Phil Carey) who tries to go straight but has to shoot it out with Butch Cassidy's Wild Bunch before his reformation is accepted by his neighbors. Directed by Fred F. Sears, it's a tired exercise in overly familiar territory. Stylized violence. A-I (br)

X

X, Y & Zee (1972) Shrill British sex melodrama involving a self-destructive, affluent, childless couple (Elizabeth Taylor and Michael Caine) and an attractive widow (Susannah York) with whom the husband falls in love and the wife tries to seduce in order to thwart the interest of her errant spouse. Directed by Brian G. Hutton, the perverse triangle is a vulgar, one-dimensional affair with brief nudity and considerable abusive language. O (R/PG)

Xala (1975) Black African satire, filmed in Senegal, about a prosperous businessman who takes a third wife but, unable to consummate the marriage, is convinced someone has cursed him with a spell of impotence and spends all his money seeking the help of witch doctors. Director Ousmane Sembene's metaphor of impotence is vividly applied to the neocolonialist values of the African middle class that is the movie's main target. A-III (nr) AA

Xanadu (1980) Olivia Newton-John sings her way through her role as a materialized Greek muse who inspires a middle-aged musician (Gene Kelly) and a young artist (Michael Beck) to become partners in a nightclub. Directed by Robert Greenwald, the movie offers little but special effects, optical devices and a few vulgar dance numbers in what is essentially an illustrated sound-track album. A-II (PG) A

Y

Yaaba (1989) Two youngsters befriend an old woman who lives as an outcast on the outskirts of their tiny village in the African country of Burkina Faso. Director Idrissa Ouedraogo's beautifully photographed movie shows the virtues as well as the foibles of the villagers in warmly human terms evoking a certain sense of kinship on the part of interested viewers, though those looking for casual entertainment are likely to be disappointed. English subtitles. Some youngsters may be confused or perplexed by aspects of this very different culture. A-II (nr) PG

Yakuza, The (1975) Robert Mitchum plays an American back in Japan, where he had served in the Occupation, to help rescue a friend's kidnapped daughter (Keiko Kishi) by having a top gangster (Ken Takadura) repay the favor he owes the American. Though Mitchum is able to rise above the inane story with some dignity, director Sydney Pollack's Japanese gangster movie (which is what the title means) proves silly as well as repugnant in its exotic brutality and simple-minded concept of manhood. A-III (R) AA

Yankee Doodle Dandy (1942) Born on the Fourth of July, George M. Cohan melded patriotism with Irish charm in his rise from song-and-dance vaudevillian to leading Broadway songwriter and producer in a career celebrated by this nostalgic, flag-waving musical starring James Cagney as the feisty entertainer. Directed by Michael Curtiz, it features a grand collection of Cohan's best-remembered songs as well as Cagney at the top of his form singing and dancing his way to an Academy Award for the year's best performance. Fine family fare. A-I (br) U

Yanks (1979) Overlong but beautifully photographed re-creation of a worn and ravaged England during World War II offers the thin story of two English women (Vanessa Redgrave; Lisa Eichhorn) and two American soldiers (William Devane; Richard Gere) told in terms of parallel romances. Directed by John Schlesinger, the story suffers from a slow-moving pace and lack of focus that leave it without much dramatic force. Adultery figures in the plot, with some profane language and bedroom scenes. A-III (R) 15

Year My Voice Broke, The (1988) Coming-of-age drama set in Australia in 1962 tells of a 15-year-old's (Noah Taylor) infatuation with his 16-year-old childhood friend (Loene Carmen) who has set her eyes on a wilder lad (Ben Mendelsohn) for her first sexual involvement, forcing the younger boy to stand by and watch her ruin her life. Writer-director John Duigan's sensitive, nonexploitative handling of puberty results in a touching portrayal of boy-girl friendship and first love. Some rough language and the implications of sex and pregnancy outside marriage. A-III (PG-13)

Year of Living Dangerously, The (1983) Murky story set in 1965 Indonesia where a newly arrived Australian correspondent (Mel Gibson) comes to depend upon an Asian news photographer (Linda Hunt in a male role) for information about an impending revolution, but along the way the Aussie's attention is distracted by a torrid love affair with a British intelligence agent (Sigourney Weaver). Director Peter Weir re-creates the place and chaotic period very effectively but characterizations are sketchy and the action lacks coherence. Though it has compassion for the poor and oppressed, the sexual relationship makes it mature fare. A-III (PG)

Year of the Comet (1992) Contrived chase story of a mismatched couple (Penelope Ann Miller and Tim Daly) on the run from assorted villains (led by Louis Jourdan) while trying to deliver a priceless bottle of Napoleonic wine to an auction. Producer-director Peter Yates' sprightly and visually delightful caper is all but ruined by its self-consciously precious tone. Occasional stylized violence and discreet sexual innuendo with a flash of nudity. A-III (PG-13)

Year of the Dragon (1985) A police captain and Vietnam veteran (Mickey Rourke) wages war against a dapper but ruthlessly deadly Chinatown gang lord (John Lone). Directed by Michael Cimino, and written by Oliver Stone, the film is muddled almost to the point of incoherence by extreme amounts of profanity and violence while being pointedly racist and sexist. O (R) 18

Year of the Gun (1991) Standard political thriller set in 1978 terrorist-ravaged Rome where a naive American reporter (Andrew McCarthy) becomes involved with an Italian divorcee (Valeria Golino), a university professor (John Pankow) and an aggressive photojournalist (Sharon Stone) who is convinced the reporter is her ticket inside the Red Brigades terrorist organization. Routine performances dilute director John Frankenheimer's shadowy story of personal ambition and surprise betrayals, interestingly set against the political backdrop of President Aldo Moro's kidnapping and murder. A few bedroom scenes with nudity, sporadic brutal violence and some rough language. A-III (R) 15

Year of the Quiet Sun, A (1985) A U.S. soldier (Scott Wilson) and a Polish widow (Maja Komorowska) fall in love despite their lack of a common language in Russian-occupied Poland in the grim days following World War II. Under Krzysztof Zanussi's masterful direction, the Polish production probes the tragic complications arising from a relationship foundering over cultural differences. Sensitive treatment of serious matters. A-II (PG)

Year of the Woman (1973) Pretentious documentary on the politicization of women's rights adds, unfortunately, little enlightenment about the subject. It suffers not only from missed opportunities to demonstrate systematic injustice, but from the misuse of interviews with articulate individuals, edited mainly to serve the needs of filmmaker Sandra Hochman. A-IV (nr)

Yearling, The (1946) A young boy's attachment to an orphaned fawn relieves the loneliness of life in the Florida wilderness but brings grief as the deer grows to threaten the family's crops in this classic version of Marjorie Kinnon Rawlings' story. With credible performances by Gregory Peck and Jane Wyman as the parents and Claude Jarman Jr. as the youth, director Clarence Brown has fashioned a genuine portrait of rural American life as well as a sincere celebration of family values. A-I (G) U

Years of Lightning, Day of Drums (1966) Celebratory documentary about the promise of President Kennedy's years in office as seen from the perspective of his tragic assassination and burial. It recalls vividly the feeling of personal loss experienced by people around the world during that terrible November in 1963. A-I (br)

Yellow Rolls-Royce, The (1965) Slickly elegant romantic melodrama in which the automobile of the title passes from an English aristocrat (Rex Harrison) in Ascot to an American gangster (George C. Scott) in Florence and a Scandinavian heiress (Ingrid Bergman) in Yugoslavia. Directed by Anthony Asquith, the love interests are Jeanne Moreau, Shirley MacLaine and Omar Sharif, respectively, but only the third tale has any weight and that scarcely memorable. Sexual situations and some stylized violence. A-IV (br) A

Yellow Submarine (1968) Wonderful animated feature for young and old, with music from the Beatles' Sergeant Pepper album, follows the adventures of John, George, Paul and Ringo to the never-never world of Pepperland, where they find that the Blue Meanies are overrunning its lovely terrain. Director George Dunning's animation is a wonder, the music a delight and, of course, Sgt. Pepper and his Lonelyhearts Club Marching Band get their peaceful land back at the end, and those Blue Meanies are not all that mean. A-I (G) U

Yellowbeard (1983) Several of the Monty Python troupe join forces with Cheech and Chong, Susannah York, James Mason, Peter Boyle, Madeline Kahn, and Marty Feldman in this leaden, stultifyingly unfunny pirate spoof directed by Mel Damski. Brief nudity and an abundance of coarse jokes. A-III (PG)

Yentl (1983) Barbra Streisand musical in which she stars in the title role as an intelligent Jewish woman living in Eastern Europe at the turn-of-the-century who dresses as a man in order to study in a yeshiva (male religious school) and finds herself attracted to a student (Mandy Patinkin) already engaged to be married. When the engagement is called off, Yentl is persuaded to become the bridegroom instead, but all is resolved when she leaves handsome student and his beloved by emigrating to America and less restrictive educational prerequisites. Streisand, who also produced, directed and coauthored the script, is on center stage for almost the entire length of the movie, a bit much for all but her most avid fans. Yentl's mock marriage to another woman makes the movie inappropriate for young viewers. A-III (PG)

Yes, Giorgio (1982) Operatic tenor Luciano Pavarotti makes his film debut as a great opera star who, despite his wife in Italy, has a love affair with a beautiful American doctor (Kathryn Harrold) during a U.S. tour. Pavarotti's singing would be enough to recommend it, except that director Franklin J. Schaffner's supremely silly movie takes a benign attitude toward the adulterous affair, which is not just incidental, but the main focus of the plot throughout. O (PG)

Yesterday's Enemy (1959) While sloughing through the Burmese jungle in 1942, a squad of British soldiers (led by Stanley Baker) execute some villagers to get information about the Japanese invaders, then ironically face the same treatment when captured by the Japanese. Directed by Val Guest, the tough-minded World War II drama effectively raises moral questions of military expediency and basic human rights. Much tension amid wartime violence. A-III (br) A

Yo Yo (1967) French comedy about a millionaire's son (Pierre Etaix) who, after his father is ruined in the Depression, becomes a renowned clown, makes a fortune in the novelty business but ultimately rejects the grand yet lonely style of life in which he had been raised. Also directed by Etaix, the episodic tale is told mainly through sight-gags and visual humor that bear comparison with the antics of Keaton, Chaplin and Lloyd. A-II (br)

Yog—Monster from Space (1971) Japanese monster-movie maker Ishiro Honda has picked the farthest recesses of his brain to create an elephantine octopus with a mitre-shaped head. The sight of this super squid might thrill moppets, but older kids may yawn and yearn for more imaginative stuff, and they are right. A-I (G)

You Are What You Eat (1968) Pseudo-documentary about the youth counter-culture of the 1960s presents a montage of disjointed scenes of the so-called love generation engaged in various sexual activities, pot smoking, rock-song gatherings and street happenings, sprinkled with scenes of cult heroes of the period. Directed by Barry Feinstein, it tries to be outrageous but is mostly tasteless and vulgar. Some exploitative nudity. O (br)

You Can't Beat Love (1937) Dated situation comedy about a wealthy playboy (Preston Foster) who runs for mayor on a bet, then falls for his opponent's daughter (Joan Fontaine). Directed by Christy Cabanne, the comedy gets heavy-handed on the issue of municipal corruption, but Paul Hurst scores as a tough union leader aiming to become chief of police. A-I (br)

You Can't Run Away from It (1956) Dim musical version of "It Happened One Night" with exasperated reporter Jack Lemmon helping spoiled heiress June Allyson elude domineering father Charles Bickford. Producer-director Dick Powell's mirthless remake of a classic romantic comedy has all the appeal of a flat tire. Sexual situations and innuendo. A-III (br)

You Can't Take It with You (1938) Good adaptation of the George Kaufman-Moss Hart screwball comedy about an impoverished family of eccentrics whose daughter (Jean Arthur) falls for a rich man's son (James Stewart). Directed by Frank Capra, the zany guests of the wacky household come and go as the family's head (Lionel Barrymore) tries to convince the rich man (Edward Arnold) that happiness has nothing to do with money. That sentiment may seem less convincing today than in the Depression, but the cheerfully uninhibited antics of this house of fools are still very funny indeed. A-I (br) U

You Can't Steal Love (see: "Live a Little, Steal a Lot").

You Can't Win 'Em All (1970) Tony Curtis and Charles Bronson cavort through post-World War I Turkey as a pair of roguish mercenaries, periodically betraying each other for the least whiff of beauty or booty. Director Peter Collison's tired, formula adventure features Turkey's matinee idol, Fikret Hakan, but the real star of this turkey is a beautiful old steam-engine, lovingly photographed against picturesque Turkish locations. A-II (PG) 12

You Light Up My Life (1977) Young singer-composer (Didi Conn) breaks away from the smothering influence of her comedian father and comes to N.Y. determined to rely on no one but herself. Director Joseph Brooks neatly packaged bit of nothing fails to hold its thin storyline together despite Conn's good performance. An incident of premarital sex is presented as a moral lapse, which the heroine immediately regrets. A-II (PG)

You Only Live Twice (1967) Sean Connery in his fifth appearance as James Bond goes through the motions of tracking down some mission space capsules amidst oriental intrigue in Japan and finally bests his arch foe Blofeld (Donald Pleasence). The Agent 007 formula of impersonal sex and violence has worn thin with the result that director Lewis Gilbert's Bond movie is just another mediocre spy thriller. A-III (GP) PG

You Only Love Once (1969) Unpretentious French romance depicting the loving relationship of a couple (Karen Blanguernon and Frederic de Pasquale) from first fancy to marriage, parenthood, estrangement and reconciliation. Directed by Dirk Sanders, it is a gay, moody, colorful expression of the simple things in real life, often having the effect of a lilting visual ballet, and is well worth seeing for its vision of the constancy of love. A-II (G)

You Talkin' to Me? (1987) By dyeing his hair blonde, struggling New York actor (Jim Youngs) meets tanned California girl (Faith Ford) whose Disney-like daddy (James Noble) casts him as the evangelical host of a family TV show. Director Charles Winkler uncovers some further inbred elements of the Hollywood scene but doesn't explore them. Racial violence and some profanity. A-III (R)

You'll Find Out (1940) Creaky vehicle for radio personality Kay Kyser who takes his orchestra, including comic Ish Kabibble and vocalist Ginny Simms, to a debutante's isolated mansion where they spend a stormy night amidst sinister goings-on with ominous visitors (Boris Karloff; Peter Lorre; Bela Lugosi). Director David Butler's spooky comedy mixes silly period humor with tepid menace and hokey suspense. Unmemorable save for the period music. A-I (br) A

You'll Like My Mother (1972) When her husband is killed in Vietnam, the pregnant widow (Patty Duke) visits her mother-in-law but is met with unaccountable hostility, troubled by a menacing man lurking in the shadows and gradually realizes she is being kept a prisoner in the creaky old mansion. Directed by Lamont Johnson, the twisting plot of this tight little mystery thriller offers a goodly number of chills and shocks. A-III (PG) AA

You're a Big Boy Now (1967) Wacky comedy about a young man (Peter Kaster), trying to make the transition from adolescence to independence from overbearing father (Rip Torn) and clinging mother (Geraldine Page), gets his own apartment and becomes infatuated with an actress (Elizabeth Hartman). Directed by Francis Ford Coppola, its exaggerated comic style does not always succeed, especially with some of the erotic elements. A-IV (br) X

You're Lying (1973) Powerful Swedish semi-documentary indictment of the inadequacies and outright injustices existing in a penal system that prides itself on being the best in the world. Directed by Vilgot Sjoman, it demonstrates the contradictions between official policy and the actual practice of using prisons to effect social rehabilitation as well as society's indifference to how its prisons actually operate. Excessively explicit treatment of sexual matters. O (nr)

You're My Everything (1949) Boston socialite (Anne Baxter) and vaudeville song-and-dance man (Dan Dailey) marry, make it big in early movies, then argue about whether to let their daughter (Shari Robinson) become a Shirley Temple-like child star. Director Walter Lang gets some brisk fun with old Hollywood nostalgia but the characters are superficial and the domestic situations syrupy. Few bright spots for youngsters. A-I (br) U

You're Only Young Once (1938) Judge Hardy (Lewis Stone) and family vacation at the seashore with romantic complications furnished by son Andy (Mickey Rooney) and daughter Marian (Cecilia Parker). Director George B. Seitz's pleasant but lightweight entry in the Hardy series is notable chiefly for its period picture of fun at a family resort. A-I (br)

You're Telling Me! (1934) W. C. Fields comedy in which he plays a hard-drinking small-town inventor whose bad luck is changed by a chance encounter with a foreign princess (Adrienne Ames). Directed by Erle C. Kenton, the plot's not much but Fields makes what's there hilarious, especially a classic comic routine on the golf links. Intemperance and malicious gossip as sources of humor. A-II (br)

You've Got to Walk It Like You Talk It or You'll Lose That Beat (1971) Director Peter Locke's low-budget story of a confused young man in search of himself (Zalman King) is a witless attempt to satirize the Establishment, but all that emerges is a stupefying amount of visual and verbal crudity. O (nr)

Young Americans (1967) Semi-documentary on a national tour of teenage singers presenting a program of show tunes, spirituals, folk songs and traditional melodies. Written and directed by Alex Grasshoff, the material is blended into a pleasant story of personal interaction among the talented young musicians and the reaction of audiences to the troupe's humor and enthusiasm. A-I (br)

Young Animals, The (1968) Crudely contrived story of Mexican American teenagers trying to win acceptance and equal rights in a California small-town high school. Exploitative treatment of violence and teenage sexual relations. O (PG)

Young Billy Young (1969) Standard western about the new marshal (Robert Mitchum) of a lawless town who takes the job in order to avenge the killing of his son while befriending a wild youth (Robert Walker) who reminds him of his dead boy. Directed by Burt Kennedy, the story is entirely predictable and the relationship between the older man and the youth is never explored with any depth. Some rather bloody shootouts. A-II (G) AA

Young Cassidy (1965) Somewhat fictionalized biography of young Sean O'Casey (Rod Taylor) explores the background of poverty, ignorance, injustice and rebellion in Ireland that was to shape the playwright's dramatic vision. Directed by Jack Cardiff and John Ford, the British production is rich in period detail and attains some human dimension but is rather romanticized in its picture of Irish life. Some stylized violence and sexual references. A-III (br) A

Young Couple, A (1971) Familiar French tale of a young couple (Anna Gael and Alain Libolt) who marry, enjoy a rich party-going life but separate when the self-centered wife and the husband cannot reconcile their different visions of life. Directed by Rene Gainville, it is a well-made but somewhat fleeting portrait of early married life and the consequences of infidelity. A-III (nr)

Young Doctors in Love (1982) Stupid spoof of doctor movies and soap operas intermixes sketches and sight-gags with a narrative line about the adventures of first-year interns. Directed by Gary Marshall, there are a few good laughs along the way, but excessive vulgarity sours the humor. Some nudity. O (R) AA

Young Einstein (1989) Wacky Australian comedy links the physicist who gave us the Theory of Relativity to the origins of rock music. Writer-director-editor-co-producer-star Yahoo Serious pratfalls his way through an eccentric interpretation of Einstein's youth, taking Monty Pythonesque liberties and introducing a comedy persona rivaling that of Pee-wee Herman. Shower scene with rear male nudity; minimal sexual innuendo. A-II (PG)

Young Frankenstein (1974) Director Mel Brooks' spoof of the venerable horror classic stars Gene Wilder as an American doctor who inherits the family's Transylvanian estate, with Peter Boyle as the monster whose prodigious sexual appetite provides the one-liner for the movie. Bright spots are Cloris Leachman as the housekeeper whose name causes horses to whinny and Marty Feldman whose pop-eyes are upstaged by his shifting hump. Though generally amusing, with some clever bits and occasionally hilarious moments, it features much vulgarity, verbal and otherwise. A-IV (PG) 15

Young Girls of Rochefort, The (1967) French musical romance in which false values are nicely ribbed, star-crossed lovers are united and everyday dreams come true when a fair comes to town and two local girls (Catherine Deneuve; Francoise Dorleac) join in the fun. Directed by Jacques Demy, the production has some simple charm but suffers from a static setting, lack of continuity and a surfeit of nonprofessional singing. A-II (br) U

Young Guns (1988) Young Billy the Kid (Emilio Estevez) teams up with a group known as the Regulators to avenge the murder of his mentor, a good-guy cattle rancher (Terence Stamp). Director Christopher Cain depicts Billy and his buddies (Kiefer Sutherland; Lou Diamond Phillips; Charlie Sheen) cavorting like Robin Hood's merry band as they destroy a corrupt rancher and his murderous gang. Some intense violence and bloodshed, much profanity, a sequence glorifying drug use and implications of sexual impropriety. A-III (R) 18

Young Guns II (1990) Claiming to be Billy the Kid, a grizzled old cowboy (Emilio Estevez) recounts in flashback what really happened after his one-time friend, Pat Garrett (William Petersen), put on a sheriff's badge and set out to kill the Kid and his gang. Director Geoff Murphy's spirited sequel has some good performances and eye-catching scenery but tends to idealize the outlaws as hip and funny true-blue buddies—especially troubling as they introduce a young teen to their lusty, lawless way of life. Some gory violence, implied sexual liaisons, several shots of rear nudity and occasional profanity. A-III (PG-13) 12

Young Mr. Lincoln (1939) Henry Fonda gives a warm, ingratiating performance as the young country lawyer whose self-deprecating wit and common-sense intelligence are put to the test in defending an innocent youth charged with murder. Director John Ford is at his best in this leisurely slice of Americana that gains stature in credibly foreshadowing the homespun virtues which would soon propel young Abe into Illinois politics and the White House. Durable family fare that is as meaningful as it is entertaining. A-I (br) A

Young People (1940) Tired Shirley Temple vehicle in which the moppet actress plays an orphan whose vaudevillian foster parents (Jack Oakie and Charlotte Greenwood) retire to an unfriendly town. Despite some lively song-and-dance numbers, director Allan Dwan fails to find any fresh angles on the formula plot and stereotyped characters. Best for the young and undemanding. A-I (br) U

Young Runaways, The (1968) Contrived story of three teenagers who flee abusive home situations and find their fate on their own even worse. Director Arthur Dreifuss treats a significant social subject in a superficial manner, leaving viewers with no clear insight into the reasons or solutions of the problem. Mature themes. A-III (R)

Young Sherlock Holmes (1985) A series of fatal accidents in Victorian London baffles the police but not the student Sherlock Holmes (Nicolas Rowe) and his school chum John Watson (Alan Cox). Directed by Barry Levinson, Chris Columbus' script gives a convincing account of Holmes' early school days that is entirely in keeping with the character of the master sleuth found in the pages of Arthur Conan Doyle's classic stories. The special-effects are spectacular, but never gory or overdone, though some nightmare sequences may frighten young children. A-II (PG-13) PG

Young Tom Edison (1940) Hollywood version of the inventor's youth in a small Midwestern town features Mickey Rooney whose curiosity about how things work and why constantly gets him in trouble until his ingenuity saves his mother's life and stops a train wreck. Directed by Norman Taurog, it's manipulative and obvious but goes down easily enough thanks to a good cast and credible period production. While inspirational fare for youngsters, their elders may find it only a sentimental exercise. A-I (br)

Young Winston (1972) British dramatization of Churchill's memoir, "My Early Life," retells uncritically his own version of his formative years from war correspondent in the Boer War to Parliament, with Simon Ward in the title role. Directed by Richard Attenborough, it excels as a panorama of life in the Empire before World War I, through a succession of tableaux of balls and battles, of parliamentary debates and family discourses. Although not a perfect film, it is a film of idealism and very enjoyable on a number of levels. A-II (PG)

Young World (1966) This French film about sexual excesses of contemporary youth indulges in needlessly detailed erotic treatment. O (br)

Youngblood (1978) Black youth (Bryan O'Dell) joins a street gang for self-protection and, when the gang takes on the local drug organization, finds himself on a collision course with his older brother. An excessively violent movie whose morality is as muddled as its storyline. O (R) 15

Youngblood (1986) Rob Lowe stars as the young and talented amateur hockey player who must come to terms with the violence of his sport and his determination to be a winner. When turning the other cheek doesn't work, he learns how to be tough but still proves he can outclass the brutes. Nevertheless, he can't resist a final display of macho combat to satisfy his critics. Brutality, an explicit nude sex scene and ambivalent values ruin a simple tale about sports ethics for youngsters. O (R)

Younger Brothers, The (1949) Routine western in which paroled outlaw Cole Younger (Wayne Morris) and his three brothers try to go straight, despite an old friend (Janis Page) who wants them to join her gang and an ex-lawman (Fred Clark) who wants them dead. Director Edwin L. Marin's weak shoot-'em-up is filled with cliches, though the double-take bank robbery in the finale is one for the books. Stylized gunplay and fisticuffs. A-II (br) U

Your Three Minutes Are Up (1973) Unemployed swinger (Ron Liebman) initiates his younger, hard-working buddy (Beau Bridges) into a series of con games that at first seem easy and fun but then threaten the young man's approaching marriage (to Janet Margolin), and in the end events take an ugly turn. Director Douglas Schwartz introduces some heavyhanded and explicit sex scenes that only compound the problem of its murky underlying morality. O (R)

Your Turn, My Turn (1979) Unpleasant French comedy romance starring Marlene Jobert as the mother of an 8-year-old boy who meets Philip Leotard, the father of a 9-year-old girl, and though encumbered by their perceptive children, they begin an adulterous affair. As directed by Francoise Leterrier, the movie's Gallic view of life is not especially amusing, despite its frothy treatment. Benign attitude toward adultery. O (nr)

Yours, Mine and Ours (1968) Fact-based story of a Navy widower (Henry Fonda) and a Navy widow (Lucille Ball) who fall in love, get married and merge their 18 children into one big, happy family. Director Melville Shavelson's comedy has predictable but genuinely funny complications such as interrupted honeymoon, identity crises, bathroom lineups, troop-movement planning and buying, but it also keeps in touch with human reality. Underneath it all is a gently moving story of love the way it is. Admittedly directed toward popular appeal, it is humorous enough for sophisticated tastes as well. Truly a family picture. A-I (br)

Z

Z (1969) When a leftist minister (Yves Montand) in the Greek government is assassinated, the investigating magistrate (Jean-Louis Trintignant) tries to untangle the shadowy affair in order to find those responsible. The French dramatization directed by Costa-Gavras is a taut political thriller that goes beyond Greek politics and party labels because it is interested in justice and critical of any system of government that justifies criminal acts and violence in attaining its objectives. A-II (PG) A

Zabriskie Point (1970) Taking its title from a promontory that overlooks Death Valley, director Michelangelo Antonioni's first movie about America is critical of its ill-treatment of youth and its self-cannibalism through violence and material excess, topped off in an explosive finale. Yet, because the message is expressed largely via cliches, all that it underscores is that perhaps middle-aged filmmakers should avoid making youth-oriented movies about other cultures. Some excessive sexual scenes. O (R) 15

Zachariah (1971) Director George Englund updates the western with rock music, hippie garb, the search for identity and a plea for peace, all laced together with self-parody and an incurable romanticism. The two heroes (Don Johnson and John Rubenstein) show the audience that peace, love and friendship are possible in a world of violence, hate and mistrust. Hokey as it sounds, the movie works if given a chance, and its overriding values and goals cannot be dismissed too lightly. A-III (GP)

Zandy's Bride (1974) Gene Hackman plays a rough and tough western rancher circa 1870 who is finally mellowed by Liv Ullmann, his mail order bride from Minnesota. Though the narrative is disappointingly little more than a disorganized series of scenes between two extreme character types, director Jan Troell re-creates the frontier era with authority, gets excellent performances from his principals and conveys some insights into human relations. Adult material, including a rape. A-III (PG) AA

Zardoz (1974) British sci-fi fantasy set in 2293 when technology has given the power of eternal life to a single enclave of humans whose paradise is penetrated and ultimately destroyed by a barbarian (Sean Connery) from the Outlands. Director John Boorman's vision of the shapelessness of things to come needs a road map simply to follow the plot and sort out its intended parables. Some violence, confused religious references and brief nudity. A-III (R) 18

Zatoichi Meets Yojimbo (1972) Japanese movie hero Zatoichi (Shintaro Katsu) is a blind masseur whose skill with a stick sword makes him invulnerable to the gangs of cut-throats and Samurai bands that inhabit the medieval milieu of his films. Director Kihachi Okamoto pits Zatoichi against Toshiro Mifune's classical characterization of the samurai professional-turned-free-agent in an action fantasy about a violent world where death is only as real as the special-effects man can make it. A-III (nr)

Zatoichi: The Blind Swordsman (see: "Zatoichi's Conspiracy").

Zatoichi's Conspiracy (1974) Director Kimiyoshi Yasuda is back with another adventure of Zatoichi (Shintaro Katsu), the blind, flabby, masseur whose exploits with a cane-sword make him the terror of criminals and equal to a samurai squad. Zatoichi is visiting his home town just as it is taken over by a vicious crook in league with the corrupt bailiff of the district. There is the final showdown in a crescendo of special effects. A-III (PG)

Zebra in the Kitchen (1965) A lot of silliness occurs when a town is overrun by wild animals freed from the local zoo by a young lad (Jay North) opposed to caging animals. But no harm is done, thanks to the zoo's dedicated director (Martin Milner) and head keeper (Andy Devine). Director Ivan Tors mixes in some mild-mannered slapstick along with the message of treating animals humanely, but its contrived cuteness is not for all tastes. A-I (G) U

Zebrahead (1992) Violence flares when a white senior (Michael Rapaport) in a predominantly black Detroit high school engages in an interracial romance with the cousin (N'Bushe Wright) of his best friend (DeShonn Castle). Writer-director Anthony Drazan's sobering look at teenage and adult racial prejudice dramatizes in a low-keyed manner the tragic effects of senseless casual violence. Implied sexual encounters, brief violence, a few crude sexual references and occasional rough language. A-III (R)

Zelig (1983) Director Woody Allen spoofs the American obsession with celebrity in this comedy about an obscure clerk (also Allen) in the 1920s who wants so desperately to fit in that he develops a malady transforming him physically and mentally into a person quite like whomever he happens to be with. A mildly amusing comedy in which the camerawork of Gordon Willis weaves the Zelig saga into actual historical footage, making for some good sight-gags. A-II (PG)

Zelly and Me (1988) Sensitive film set in 1950s' Virginia relates the story of a wealthy, orphaned 11-year-old (Alexandra Johnes) who is emotionally abused by her grandmother (Glynis Johns) and loved unconditionally by her governess (Isabella Rossellini). Writer-director Tina Rathborne explores the gentle child's heartbreaking attempts to cope with her grandmother's volatile and irrational demands. Some intense scenes of emotional abuse and humiliation may be disturbing to very young children. A-II (PG)

Zentropa (1992) Absorbing story of a naive American (Jean-Marc Barr) working in postwar Germany who becomes ensnared between an alluring seductress (Barbara Sukowa) and a manipulative colonel (Eddie Constantine) with the American Occupation. Impressive technique and style surpass the substance of Danish director Lars Von Trier's surreal tale of multiple deceptions. Some subtitles. A discreet sexual encounter, brief violence and an instance of rough language. A-III (nr)

Zeppelin (1971) While the Kaiser's dirigibles bomb London from heights out of range of early World War I biplanes, British intelligence decides to slip a spy into the Zeppelin works, where he learns of a secret mission to destroy British morale. Director Etienne Perier's old-fashioned tale of wartime adventure features a good cast (Michael York; Marius Goring; Elke Sommer; Alexandra Stewart) and action laced with humor, suspense and some quite good special-effects work. Wartime violence. A-I (G) U

Zero Population Growth (1972) In some brave new world of the future, joy has gone out of life because childbirth has been made punishable by death, though Oliver Reed and Geraldine Chaplin risk all to procreate. Directed by Michael Campus, the film pretends to be an indictment of 20th-century decadence but is simply a rather plodding exercise, with a ridiculously anticlimactic outcome. Adult theme. A-III (PG) X

Zig Zag (1970) George Kennedy plays a man dying of a brain tumor who sets himself up to be convicted of an unsolved crime and arranges through a lawyer (Eli Wallach) that his wife (Anne Jackson) receive the reward offered by the insurance company. Directed by Richard Colla, the plot complications become a jumble of events, and the incredibly contrived ending makes it not worth the effort. A-II (GP)

Zig Zag (1976) Catherine Deneuve and Bernadette Lafont play slightly talented showgirls eager to get ahead, in an erratic French movie directed by Laszlo Szabo that attempts to tell a tragicomic story against the background of a seedy entertainment world. Graphic sexual depiction. O (R)

Zita (1968) Evocative but flawed French movie of a young girl (Joanna Shimkus) trying to accept the trauma of her beloved aunt's impending death. Though beautifully directed by Robert Enrico, the story is susceptible to the interpretation that maturity is achieved through casual sex. O (M)

Zorba the Greek (1965) Anthony Quinn embodies the zestful, warmly human title character who helps his withdrawn English employer (Alan Bates) learn to enjoy life in spite of its imperfections, including sad encounters along the way with a lonely widow (Irene Papas) and an elderly courtesan (Lila Kedrova). Directed by Michael Cacoyannis, the realistic depiction of harsh living conditions on the island of Crete is transformed by the movie's joyful affirmation of life. Some brutish coarseness and sexual references. A-IV (br) PG

Zorro, The Gay Blade (1981) George Hamilton plays the son of Zorro, the legendary righter of wrongs and champion of oppressed peasants in Old California, with a twin brother (Hamilton again) who is a foppish homosexual. Directed by Peter Medak, the one-joke comedy has a lackluster plot, slow pacing and the smiles are few and far between. Occasional mild vulgarity and the homosexual aspect is amiably farcical. A-II (PG)

Z.P.G. (see: "Zero Population Growth").

APPENDIX

A Choice Collection of Family Movies

Something for Everybody

ADVENTURE

Buccaneer, The
Damn the Defiant!
Drums
Elephant Boy
55 Days at Peking
Flame Over India
Four Feathers, The
Kidnapped
Mysterious Island
Prisoner of Zenda, The
Shipwrecked

ANIMALS

American Tail: Fievel Goes West, An
Challenge to Lassie
Clarence the Cross-eyed Lion
Courage of Lassie
Flipper
Homeward Bound: The Incredible Journey
Lad: A Dog
My Friend Flicka
Palomino, The

FANTASY

Babes in Toyland
Beast of Hollow Mountain, The

Captain January
Captains Courageous
Cheaper by the Dozen
Chump at Oxford, A
Come to the Stable
David Copperfield
Destination Tokyo
Edison, the Man
Family Affair, A
Father of the Bride
Fort Apache
Four Men and a Prayer
Go for Broke
Happy Years, The
Hondo
Huckleberry Finn
I Remember Mama
Inn of the Sixth Happiness
Intruder in the Dust
It Happens Every Spring
Little Nuns, The
Little Princess, The
Murder Ahoy
My Father's Glory
One of Our Aircraft Is Missing
Our Hearts Were Young and Gay
Our Town
Overlanders, The
Pastime
Pride of the Yankees, The
Prisoner of Shark Island, The
Proud Rebel, The
Rebecca of Sunnybrook Farm
Remarkable Mr. Kipps, The
Rio Grande

DRAMA (cont'd.)

She Wore a Yellow Ribbon
So Big
Stratton Story, The
Sullivans, The
Tall Target, The
Three Smart Girls
Three Stripes in the Sun
Tom Sawyer
Truth about Spring, The
Unfinished Dance, The
Wee Willie Winkie
Wild Hearts Can't Be Broken
Young Mr. Lincoln
Young Tom Edison

COMEDY

Abbott and Costello Meet Dr. Jekyll and Mr. Hyde
Court Jester, The
Ghost Breakers, The
Gold Rush, The
Help!
Mouse That Roared, The
Ruggles of Red Gap
Thank You, Jeeves

MUSICALS

Easter Parade
Strike Up the Band

RELIGIOUS

Keys of the Kingdom, The
Miracle of Our Lady of Fatima, The
Song of Bernadette, The
Trial of Joan of Arc, The

For Teens and Grown-ups Too

ADVENTURE

Adventures of Huck Finn, The
Adventures of Marco Polo, The
Against All Flags
At Sword's Point
Far Off Place, A
If I Were King
Mutiny on the Bounty
Quentin Durward
Robin Hood: Prince of Thieves
White Fang

FANTASY

Blob, The (1958)
Cat People
Crack in the World
Dead of Night
Devil and Daniel Webster
Dr. Cyclops
Forbidden Planet
Harvey
Haunting, The
Hocus Pocus
Honey, I Blew Up the Kid
Hook
Invasion of the Body Snatchers (1956)
Jurassic Park
King Kong
Man Who Could Work Miracles, The
Matinee

FANTASY (cont'd.)

Miracle on 34th Street
Mummy, The
Phantom of the Opera, The
Rookie of the Year
Star Trek VI: The Undiscovered Country
Thing, The (1951)
Time Machine, The
Uninvited, The
When Worlds Collide

MUSICALS

American in Paris, An
Band Wagon, The
Carousel
Forty-Second Street
Singin' in the Rain
Unsinkable Molly Brown, The

HUMOR

Adam's Rib
Addams Family, The
Arsenic and Old Lace
Ball of Fire
Bebe's Kids
Beethoven
Bride Came C.O.D., The
Cat Ballou
Coneheads
Curly Sue
Dennis the Menace
Ernest Scared Stupid
Egg and I, The
Encino Man
Great McGinty, The
Groundhog Day

Horn Blows at Midnight, The
It Happened One Night
King Ralph
Ladybugs
Late for Dinner
Man Who Came to Dinner, The
Mom and Dad Save the World
Mr. Blandings Builds His Dream House
Murder, He Says
My Favorite Spy
Please Don't Eat the Daisies
Sitting Pretty
Solid Gold Cadillac, The
Sullivan's Travels
Time of Their Lives, The
Tom, Dick and Harry
What about Bob?
Who's Minding the Mint?

DRAMA

Affair to Remember, An
Alias Nick Beal
Bell for Adano, A
Big Parade, The
Big Steal, The
Citizen Kane
City of Joy
City Slickers
Cross My Heart
Crowd, The
Daughters of the Dust
David and Lisa
Detective Story
Doctor, The

Efficiency Expert, The
Enchanted April
Free Willy
Fried Green Tomatoes
Glass Key, The
Golden Boy
Great Imposter, The
Great Man, The
High Noon
How Green Was My Valley
Howards End
I'll Cry Tomorrow
Informer, The
Johnny Belinda
Journey of Hope
League of Their Own, A
Lighthorsemen, The
Little Foxes, The
Little Man Tate
Lonely Are the Brave
Long Voyage Home, The
Lorenzo's Oil
Man Hunt
Man in the Gray Flannel Suit, The
Marked Woman
Marty
Member of the Wedding, The
My Girl
My Mother's Castle
Naked Jungle, The
Princes in Exile
Pure Country
Quiet Man, The
Rear Window